A TEXTUAL
CONCORDANCE
of the
HOLY SCRIPTURES

"The words that I have spoken to
you, are spirit and life."
—John 6:64

A TEXTUAL
CONCORDANCE
of the
HOLY SCRIPTURES

By

Father Thomas David Williams

ARRANGED BY TOPIC
AND GIVING THE ACTUAL PASSAGES

*"For the word of God is living and
effectual, and more piercing than any
two edged sword; and reaching unto
the division of the soul and the spirit,
of the joints also and the marrow, and
is a discerner of the thoughts and intents of the heart."*

—Hebrews 4:12

TAN BOOKS AND PUBLISHERS, INC.
Rockford, Illinois 61105

Nibil Obstat.

REMY LAFORT,
Censor Librorum.

Imprimatur.

✠ JOHN M. FARLEY,
Archbishop of New York

NEW YORK, June 19, 1908.

TAN BOOKS AND PUBLISHERS, INC.
P.O. Box 424
Rockford, Illinois 61105

1985

PUBLISHER'S PREFACE

We are very pleased to present to contemporary readers this new printing of *A Textual Concordance of the Holy Scriptures* by Father Thomas David Williams. A brief examination will convince the reader that this is a monumental work of careful compilation and arrangement of various texts of the Bible according to topic. The concept of this concordance is simple in the extreme—but brilliant. Especially will this become evident as one steeps himself in the reading. In the first place, there is a tone of holiness and an air of authority permeating Holy Scripture that is quite unlike any other writing. But combining the various verses of the Old and the New Testaments on the same subject and presenting them together at one time, on one page, deliver an impact that is truly awesome, especially so when joined with that distinctive, holy and authoritative tone of the Bible.

The reader will find himself impelled, as it were, from topic to topic, moved by a sort of holy curiosity. And from this point of view, *A Textual Concordance* is perhaps the best introduction to Bible reading imaginable, for it truly whets a person's interest and quickly imparts the flavor of Scripture.

As a teaching tool, it is unparalleled. Here one has over 1,900 topics and over 18,000 actual verses from the Bible on these various topics, all arranged in alphabetical order for easy reference, making this book a quick way to learn just what the Bible says on a host of subjects. And in this sense it is better than any Bible-study course imaginable. One would be hard-pressed to find a more comprehensive presentation by a teacher than he can receive independently just by reading this book. As such, therefore, it is ideal for home reading, for Bible study classes, as a religion teacher's aid, and for the priest in preparing his sermons.

For those who are troubled and searching for consolation, *A Textual Concordance of the Holy Scriptures* is an excellent companion to help them find just those key passages that will bring the comfort which they seek. For there is nothing like Scripture to give a person that spiritual uplift in time of personal need. This book will provide a lifetime of spiritual inspiration and insight, and is one book we predict the reader will refer to again and again.

In no way can it be said that it is exhaustive; the author clearly admits as much in his "Author's Preface." But certainly it goes a very long way toward presenting what the Bible teaches on a host of topics. Nor can this book possibly replace reading the Bible itself. Rather, it should, and predictably will, lead directly into a more regular and intensive reading of Scripture on the part of the person who uses it.

Originally compiled to assist parish priests in preparing their sermons, this book, like all greatly conceived and greatly executed works, has a far wider range of appeal than its intended purpose. With the tremendous increase in higher education today—in contrast to the time in which the book was assembled—there exists a far larger potential readership than its author could have ever dreamed possible. The author would indeed be gratified to learn that his work—conceived as it was for a specific purpose—has reached a universal audience, especially of lay people, as this book is now achieving.

A Textual Concordance will also help the reader to see the integral unity of the Bible—in language, in symbol, in history, in topic, in prophecy, and in overall intent. It conveys profoundly the impression that the Bible is indeed one book, with one essential Author, Almighty God, and that, despite its various books being written at different times in history and by different authors, it nonetheless retains an amazing unity—a factor recognized by every serious student of Holy Writ, and attributable, it is universally admitted, to only one possible source, divine inspiration.

Further, a reading of this book will profoundly impress upon the reader that the Bible is a Catholic book, for here are to be found the many scriptural passages that support one tenet after another of the Catholic Faith. In this respect, it is destined to accomplish a great deal of good. For Catholics today are abandoning their faith at an incredible rate, due primarily to their lack of knowledge of that Faith. Many are being attracted to Fundamentalist-type denominations because of the emphasis there on Scripture, for Scripture "breathes" Authority and that indefinable "Spirit of God." But in this book, they will see that "Authority" and "Spirit of God" presented in defense of the teachings of the "Mother of all the Churches."

Perhaps this book (since it will undoubtedly also be used by our non-Catholic Christian brethren) will be instrumental in opening the door for many a profound Bible-reading Christian to see that it is in fact within the Catholic Church that they are to find that unity of faith Our Lord calls for in His prayer: "That they all may be one, as thou, Father, in me, and I in thee; that they also may be one in us; that the world may believe that thou hast sent me. And the glory which thou hast given me, I have given to them; that they may be one, as we also are one." (*Jn.* 17:21-22). All believing Christians know that we must be one with Christ in His Mystical Body in order to find salvation. As St. Paul says in *Ephesians* 4:1-6, "I, therefore, a prisoner in the Lord, beseech you that you walk worthy of the vocation in which you are called, with all humility and mildness, with patience, supporting one another in charity. Careful to keep the *unity* of the Spirit in the bond of peace. *One* body and *one* Spirit; as you are called in *one* hope of your calling. *One* Lord, *one* faith, *one* baptism. *One* God and *Father of all*, who is above all, and through all, and in us all." Clearly, Our Lord expects of us unity in faith, for He said in *John* 10:16, "And other sheep I have who are not of this fold: them also I must bring, and they shall hear my voice, and there shall be *one* fold and *one* shepherd." (Emphasis mine).

Finally a word needs to be said about the version of Sacred Scripture used in *A Textual Concordance of the Holy Scriptures*. At the time this book was compiled, there was only one English Catholic Bible in universal use, and that was the Douay-Rheims version, which this concordance uses. Those who have been reading the modern Catholic Bibles in English or one of the several Protestant versions will discover in this translation a power, clarity and succinctness—yes, an authority—not to be found in other versions.

The reason for this is simple. The Douay-Rheims Bible is an exact, literal, word-for-word (slavishly faithful, if you will) translation of St. Jerome's Latin Vulgate Bible (translated approximately 375-415 A.D.). In turn, the Vulgate was a faithful, word-for-word, literal translation of the Bible from its original texts. The Vulgate quickly became the only Bible universally used in the Western or Latin Rite Church, the largest rite by far of the Roman Catholic Church—and this during a period of some 1500 years. (To illustrate its importance, the first book printed by Johann Gutenberg and his associates was St. Jerome's Latin Vulgate Bible.)

The ancient translators of the Bible were extremely careful to render their translations in a faithful, word-for-word manner, as were the translators of the Douay-Rheims version. The result is that, to the extent possible in any translation, the true and literal meaning of the Bible comes through in this one. Modern translators, on the other hand, in the interest of making the Bible more intelligible to contemporary readers, quite often have made rather loose translations—translations wherein they, the translators, would try to determine the meaning which the inspired writers were trying to convey in the original tongues and then translate into English *that* meaning which they understand the Scriptures to have. This may appear to be a valid method, but in my opinion, it errs in two respects: The first is that if they mistake the meaning intended by the inspired writers, then the English reader is deprived of the *true* meaning. And the second is that the Bible often has multidimensional meanings, even though expressed in simple words; by translating "meanings" rather than the literal words, the modern translators often render only one of the meanings contained in the original.

For these reasons, therefore, the Douay-Rheims possesses a clarity and a power which are often missing in other versions. In fact, this version is so packed with meaning that often a single phrase can yield profound spiritual insight, and thus the solemnity, profundity and penetrating truth of the Word of God really come through in this translation.

Much more could be said along this line, though space does not permit a full exposition here. Nonetheless, it should be realized that the Douay-Rheims version is a completely faithful translation of the Latin Vulgate Bible of St. Jerome (347-420) and that St. Jerome spoke Greek and Latin as you and I speak English, that he had made nearly a lifetime study of Hebrew, that he had manuscripts of the various books of the Bible which were ancient even then and which have been lost to history, that he was a transcendent linguistic genius and far and away *the* greatest man in the history of biblical translation, that our early manuscripts of his Vulgate are older and more reliable than either the Greek manuscripts of the New Testament or the Septuagint (Old Testament), on the one hand, or, on the other, of the original Hebrew manuscripts. Thus, one might safely conclude, in my opinion, that, as the Holy Spirit has inspired Sacred Scripture, He must perforce also watch over it and protect it if mankind is to enjoy it intact; and that insofar as the Vulgate was the only bible in universal use throughout Christendom for over a thousand years (415 to 1444, when printing was invented and modern language translations began to appear), then the Vulgate *is* the Bible in its essential accuracy—if the Church during those thousand years can be said to have had the Bible.

In fact, the Sacred Council of Trent (1545-1564) proclaimed as much: "Moreover, the same Holy Council . . . ordains and declares that the old Latin Vulgate Edition, which, in use for so many hundreds of years, has been approved by the Church, be in public lectures, disputations, sermons and expositions held as authentic, and that no one dare or presume under any pretext whatsoever to reject it." (Fourth Session, April 8, 1546). As Pope Pius XII stated in his 1943 encyclical letter *On the Promotion of Biblical Studies*, this means that the Vulgate is "free from any error whatsoever in matters of faith and morals." (Paragraph 21). To repeat, the Douay-Rheims Bible is a completely faithful translation of the Vulgate, which is the official Bible of the Roman Catholic Church. Therefore, this concordance employs the very best English translation of the Bible.

A Textual Concordance of the Holy Scriptures, finally, demonstrates again and again, topic after topic, how God filled the Old Testament with prefigurements and foreshadowings of the Christian mysteries and doctrines. And for this reason, it provides a built-in Catholic guide to the reading of the Bible.

It is important for all to study Scripture, for, as St. Jerome has said, "Ignorance of Scripture is ignorance of Christ." May this book, therefore, provide its readers with a lifetime of inspiring, informative and formational reading, and through it may they grow in the knowledge and love of Sacred Scripture and thereby in the knowledge and love of God Himself.

Thomas A. Nelson
October 15, 1985

AUTHOR'S PREFACE

Leo XIII, in his encyclical, *Providentissimus Deus* (Nov. 18, 1893), on the study of Holy Scripture, speaking of the life and power that the frequent use of the Sacred Text gives to the utterances of the preacher of the Divine Word, adds: "And it is this peculiar and singular power of Holy Scripture, arising from the inspiration of the Holy Ghost, which gives authority to the sacred orator, fills him with apostolic liberty of speech, and communicates force and power to his eloquence. For those who infuse into their efforts the spirit and strength of the Word of God speak not in word only, but in power also, and in the Holy Ghost, and in much fullness. Hence, those preachers are foolish and improvident who, in speaking of religion and proclaiming the things of God, use no words but those of human science and human prudence, trusting to their own reasonings rather than to those of God. Their discourses may be brilliant and fine, but they must be feeble and they must be cold, for they are without the fire of the utterance of God, and they must fall far short of that mighty power which the speech of God possesses."

To give this power, and to place at more ready disposal the treasures of this sacred mine, the present work has been compiled, and is now offered. This work is a textual concordance of Holy Scripture, arranged especially for use in preaching. It follows simply the alphabetical order of subjects; and is divided into two parts or books, moral and dogmatic; to which is added an appendix containing principally the miracles, prophecies, and parables of Christ.

In accordance with the purpose of this work, it has been the aim of the compiler to choose only such subjects, or headings, as would be of practical use in preaching; and under them to place only such texts as clearly and strongly bear upon the subjects to which they refer.

This concordance necessarily is far from exhaustive; but it is hoped that each topic is sufficiently enriched with the Scripture texts pertaining to it to furnish meat and substance for many discourses.

This work differs largely from that masterpiece of Scripture compilation, *The Divine Armoury*, by Father Vaughan, both in arrangement and in choice of subjects or headings. A glance at the index of both works will show this sufficiently. It differs also from the *Thesaurus Biblicus* of Father Lambert, being more restricted in choice of subjects and of texts. The first part, which constitutes the bulk of the work, is simply the result of frequent perusals of the Sacred Text, and was compiled, in the course of some seven years, neither by reference to, nor by the aid of, any other work of this or a similar nature.

In the second part, which contains the scriptural proofs in the course of dogma, I have followed in great measure that clear and excellent work, *Synopsis Theologiae Dogmaticae*, by Father Tanquerey.

In the appendix, on the miracles and prophecies of Christ, I have followed, in part, the *Manuel Biblique* of Bacuez and Vigouroux, and *The Christ the Son of God*, by the Abbe Constant Fouard.

It is earnestly hoped that this work, in spite of its many imperfections, may be of some slight aid, to enable the preacher of the Divine Word to follow the desire and instruction of our late Holy Father, expressed in the same encyclical:

"Let all, therefore, especially the novices of the ecclesiastical army, understand how deeply the sacred books should be esteemed, and with what eagerness and reverence they should approach this great arsenal of heavenly arms. For those whose duty it is to handle Catholic doctrine before the learned or unlearned will nowhere find more ample matter or more abundant exhortation ... 'Let the speech of the priest be ever seasoned with scriptural reading.'"

Thomas David Williams

PART I

MORAL

ABANDON US, GOD DOES NOT

Now it came to pass after the death of Moses the servant of the Lord, that the Lord spoke to Josue the son of Nun, the minister of Moses, and said to him: . . . No man shall be able to resist you all the days of thy life: as I have been with Moses, so will I be with thee: I will not leave thee nor forsake thee.—*Jos.* i. 1, 5.

And David said to Solomon his son: Act like a man and take courage, and do: fear not, and be not dismayed: for the Lord thy God will be with thee, and will not leave thee nor forsake thee, till thou hast finished all the work for the service of the house of the Lord.—1 *Paral.* xxviii. 20.

And let them trust in thee who know thy name: for thou hast not forsaken them that seek thee, O Lord.—*Ps.* ix. 11.

For my father and my mother have left me: but the Lord hath taken me up.—*Ps.* xxvi. 10.

But I said in the excess of my mind: I am cast away from before thy eyes.

Therefore thou hast heard the voice of my prayer, when I cried to thee.—*Ps.* xxx. 23.

For the Lord loveth judgment, and will not forsake his saints: they shall be preserved for ever.—*Ps.* xxxvi. 28.

For the Lord will not cast off his people: neither will he forsake his own inheritance.—*Ps.* xciii. 14.

My children, behold the generations of men: and know ye that no one hath hoped in the Lord, and hath been confounded.

For who hath continued in his commandment, and hath been forsaken? or who hath called upon him, and he despised him?—*Ecclus.* ii. 11, 12.

And Sion said: The Lord hath forsaken me, and the Lord hath forgotten me.

Can a woman forget her infant, so as not to have pity on the son of her womb? And if she should forget, yet will I not forget thee.

Behold I have graven thee in my hands: thy walls are always before my eyes.—*Is.* xlix. 14-17.

And Daniel said: Thou hast remembered me, O God, and thou hast not forsaken them that love thee.—*Dan.* xiv. 37.

And therefore he (God) never withdraweth his mercy from us: but though he chastise his people with adversity, he forsaketh them not.—2 *Mach.* vi. 16.

Let your manners be without covetousness, contented with such things as you have: for he hath said: I will not leave thee, neither will I forsake thee.

So that we may confidently say: The Lord is my helper: I will not fear what man shall do to me.—*Heb.* xiii. 5, 6.

ABANDON US, EVEN IN OUR GREATEST DISTRESS, GOD DOES NOT

And she (Agar) departed, and wandered in the wilderness of Bersabee.

And when the water in the bottle was spent, she cast the boy under one of the trees that were there.

And she went her way, and sat over against him a great way off, as far as a bow can carry, for she said: I will not see the boy die: and sitting over against, she lifted up her voice, and wept.

And God heard the voice of the boy: and an angel of God called to Agar from heaven, saying: What art thou doing, Agar? fear not: for God hath heard the voice of the boy, from the place wherein he is. . . .

And God opened her eyes: and she saw a well of water, and went and filled the bottle, and gave the boy to drink.—*Gen.* xxi. 14-18, 19.

Do manfully and be of good heart: fear not, nor be ye dismayed at their sight: for the Lord thy God, he himself is thy leader, and will not leave thee nor forsake thee.—*Deut.* xxxi. 6.

The sorrows of death surrounded me and the torrents of iniquity troubled me.

The sorrows of hell encompassed me: and the snares of death prevented me.

In my affliction I called upon the Lord, and I cried to my God.

And he heard my voice from his holy temple: and my cry before him came into his ears.—*Ps.* xvii. 5-8.

For though I should walk in the midst of the shadow of death, I will fear no evils, for thou art with me.— *Ps.* xxii. 4.

Because he hoped in me, I will deliver him: I will protect him, because he hath known my name.

He shall cry to me, and I will hear him: I am with him in tribulation, I will deliver him, and I will glorify him. —*Ps.* xc. 14, 15.

And their heart was humbled with labors: they were weakened, and there was none to help them.

Then they cried to the Lord in their affliction: and he delivered them out of their distresses.

And he brought them out of darkness, and the shadow of death; and broke their bonds in sunder.—*Ps.* cvi. 12-15.

They that go down to the sea in ships, doing business in the great waters:

These have seen the works of the Lord, and his wonders in the deep.

He said the word, and there arose a storm of wind: and the waves thereof were lifted up.

They mount up to the heavens, and they go down to the depths: their soul pined away with evils.

They were troubled, and reeled like a drunken man: and all their wisdom was swallowed up.

And they cried to the Lord in their affliction: and he brought them out of their distresses.

And he turned the storm into a breeze: and its waves were still.

And they rejoiced because they were still: and he brought them to the haven which they wished for.—*Ps.* cvi. 23-31.

If I shall walk in the midst of tribulation, thou wilt quicken me: and thou hast stretched forth thy hand against the wrath of my enemies: and thy right hand hath saved me.—*Ps.* cxxxvii. 7.

O Lord, Lord, the strength of my salvation: thou hast overshadowed my head in the day of battle.—*Ps.* cxxxix. 8.

But to the penitent he hath given the way of justice, and he hath strengthened them that were fainting in patience, and he hath appointed to them the lot of truth.—*Ecclus.* xvii. 20.

Who is there among you that feareth the Lord, that heareth the voice of his servant, that hath walked in darkness, and hath no light? let him hope in the name of the Lord, and lean upon his God.—*Is.* l. 10.

O poor little one, tossed with tempest, without all comfort, behold I will lay thy stones in order, and will lay thy foundations with sapphires. . . . All thy children shall be taught of the Lord: and great shall be the peace of thy children.

And thou shalt be founded in justice: depart far from oppression, for thou shalt not fear; and from terror, for it shall not come near thee.—*Is.* liv. 11, 13, 14.

The Lord is good and giveth strength in the day of trouble: and knoweth them that hope in him.—*Nahum* i. 7.

In all things we suffer tribulation. but are not distressed; we are straitened, but are not destitute;

We suffer persecution, but are not forsaken; we are cast down, but we perish not.—*2 Cor.* iv. 8, 9.

At my first answer, no man stood with me, but all forsook me: may it not be laid to their charge.

But the Lord stood by me, and strengthened me, that by me the preaching may be accomplished, and that all the Gentiles may hear: and I was delivered out of the mouth of the lion.—*2 Tim.* iv. 16, 17.

ABANDON US, PRAYER TO GOD NOT TO

The Lord our God be with us, as he was with our fathers, and not leave us, nor cast us off.—*3 Kings* viii. 57.

I was cast upon thee from the womb. From my mother's womb thou art my God, depart not from me. For tribulation is very near; for there is none to help me.—*Ps.* xxi. 11, 12.

Turn not away thy face from me; decline not in thy wrath from thy servant.

Be thou my helper, forsake me not; do not thou despise me, O God my Saviour.—*Ps.* xxvi. 9.

Forsake me not, O Lord my God: do not thou depart from me.

Attend unto my help, O Lord, the God of my salvation.—*Ps.* xxxvii. 22, 23.

For thou art God my strength: why hast thou cast me off? and why do I go sorrowful whilst the enemy afflicteth me?—*Ps.* xlii. 2.

Arise, why sleepest thou, O Lord? arise, and cast us not off to the end.

Why turnest thou thy face away? and forgettest our want and our trouble?—*Ps.* xliii. 23, 24.

Cast me not away from thy face; and take not thy holy spirit from me.—*Ps.* l. 13.

And turn not away thy face from thy servant: for I am in trouble, hear me speedily.—*Ps.* lxviii. 18.

Cast me not off in the time of old age: when my strength shall fail, do not thou forsake me. . . .

O God, be not thou far from me: O my God, make haste to my help. . . .

And unto old age and grey hairs: O God, forsake me not.—*Ps.* lxx. 9, 12, 18.

O God, why hast thou cast us off unto the end: why is thy wrath enkindled against the sheep of thy pasture?

Remember thy congregation, which thou hast possessed from the beginning.

The sceptre of thy inheritance which thou hast redeemed: mount Sion in which thou hast dwelt.—*Ps.* lxxiii. 1, 2.

I will keep thy justifications: O! do not thou utterly forsake me.—*Ps.* cxviii. 8.

Give me not up, O Lord, from my desire to the wicked: they have plotted against me; do not thou forsake me, lest they should triumph.—*Ps.* cxxxix. 9.

Hear me speedily, O Lord: my spirit hath fainted away.

Turn not away thy face from me, lest I be like unto them that go down into the pit.—*Ps.* cxlii. 7.

I called upon the Lord, the father of my Lord, that he would not leave me in the day of my trouble, and in the time

of the proud without help.—*Ecclus.* li. 14.

O expectation of Israel, the Saviour thereof in time of trouble: why wilt thou be as a stranger in the land, and as a wayfaring man turning in to lodge?

Why wilt thou be as a wandering man, as a mighty man that cannot save? but thou, O Lord, art among us, and thy name is called upon us, forsake us not.—*Jer.* xiv. 8, 9.

But thou, O Lord, shalt remain for ever, thy throne from generation to generation.

Why wilt thou forget us for ever? why wilt thou forsake us for a long time?—*Lam.* v. 19, 20.

May he (God) hear your prayers, and be reconciled unto you, and never forsake you in the evil time.—2 *Mach.* i. 5.

But [1]they constrained him; saying: Stay with us, because it is towards evening, and the day is now far spent. And he went in with them.—*Luke* xxiv. 29.

ABANDONMENT OF ONESELF TO GOD

Into thy hands I commend my spirit: thou hast redeemed me, O Lord, the God of truth.—*Ps.* xxx. 6.

Commit thy way to the Lord, and trust in him, and he will do it.

And he will bring forth thy justice as the light, and thy judgment as the noonday.—*Ps.* xxxvi. 5, 6.

Cast thy care upon the Lord, and he shall sustain thee: he shall not suffer the just to waver for ever.—*Ps.* liv. 23.

My heart is ready, O God, my heart is ready.—*Ps.* cvii. 2.

I am ready, and am not troubled: that I may keep thy commandments.

The cords of the wicked have encompassed me: but I have not forgotten thy law.—*Ps.* cxviii. 60, 61.

Whatsoever shall befall the just man, it shall not make him sad: but the wicked shall be filled with mischief.—*Prov.* xii. 21.

Be not solicitous, therefore, saying, What shall we eat; or what shall we drink, or wherewith shall we be clothed?

[1]The disciples meeting Christ, on the **road to** Emmaus.

For after all these things do the heathens seek. For your Father knoweth that you have need of all these things.

Seek ye therefore first the kingdom of God, and his justice, and all these things shall be added unto you.

Be not therefore solicitous for tomorrow; for the morrow will be solicitous for itself. Sufficient for the day is the evil thereof.—*Matt.* vi. 31-34.

For which cause I also suffer these things: but I am not ashamed. For I know whom I have believed, and I am certain that he is able to keep that which I have committed unto him, against that day.—2 *Tim.* i. 12.

Be you humbled therefore under the mighty hand of God, that he may exalt you in the time of visitation:

Casting all your care upon him, for he hath care of you.—1 *Peter* v. 6, 7.

ABIDING IN GOD

See: Near to God, we should keep— page 342.

ABIDING IN US, GOD

See: Dwelling in us, God—page 119.

ABSTINENCE FROM WINE

The Lord also said to Aaron:

You shall not drink wine nor any thing that may make drunk, thou nor thy sons, when you enter into the tabernacle of the testimony, lest you die: because it is an everlasting precept through your generations:

And that you may have knowledge to discern between holy and unholy, between unclean and clean.—*Lev.* x. 8-11.

And the Lord spoke to Moses, saying:

Speak to the children of Israel, and thou shalt say to them: When a man, or woman, shall make a vow to be sanctified, and will consecrate themselves to the Lord:

They shall abstain from wine, and from every thing that may make a man drunk. They shall not drink vinegar of wine, or of any other drink, nor any thing that is pressed out of the grape: nor shall they eat grapes either fresh or dried.

All the days that they are consecrated to the Lord by vow: they shall eat nothing that cometh of the vineyard, from the raisin even to the kernel.—*Num.* vi. 1-5.

Now there was a certain man of Saraa, and of the race of Dan, whose name was Manue, and his wife was barren.

And an angel of the Lord appeared to her, and said: Thou art barren and without children: but thou shalt conceive and bear a son.

Now therefore beware and drink no wine nor strong drink, and eat not any unclean thing.

Because thou shalt conceive and bear a son, and no razor shall touch his head: for he shall be a Nazarite of God from his infancy, and from his mother's womb, and [1]he shall begin to deliver Israel from the hands of the Philistines. . . .

And the angel of the Lord said to Manue: From all the things I have spoken of to thy wife, let her refrain herself:

And let her eat nothing that cometh of the vine, neither let her drink wine or strong drink, nor eat any unclean thing: and whatsoever I have commanded her, let her fulfil and observe. —*Judges* xiii. 2-6, 13, 14.

Look not upon the wine when it is yellow, when the color thereof shineth in the glass: it goeth in pleasantly,

But in the end, it will bite like a snake, and will spread abroad poison like a basilisk.—*Prov.* xxiii. 31, 32.

And I set before the sons of the house of the Rechabites pots full of wine, and cups: and I said to them: Drink ye wine.

And they answered: We will not drink wine: because Jonadab the son of Rechab, our father, commanded us, saying: You shall drink no wine, neither you, nor your children, for ever. . . .

Therefore we have obeyed the voice of Jonadab the son of Rechab, our father, in all things that he commanded us: so as to drink no wine all our days: neither we, nor our wives, nor our sons, nor our daughters. . . .

And Jeremias said to the house of

[1]Samson.

the Rechabites: Thus saith the Lord of hosts, the God of Israel: Because you have obeyed the commandment of Jonadab your father, and have kept all his precepts, and have done all that he commanded you:

Therefore thus saith the Lord of hosts, the God of Israel: There shall not be wanting a man of the race of Jonadab, the son of Rechab, standing before me for ever.—*Jer.* xxxv. 5, 6, 8, 18, 19.

And no priest shall drink wine when he is to go into the inner court.—*Ezech.* xliv. 21.

But the angel said to him: Fear not, Zachary, for thy prayer is heard; and thy wife Elisabeth shall bear thee a son, and thou shalt call his name John. . . . For he shall be great before the Lord; and shall drink no wine nor strong drink: and he shall be filled with the Holy Ghost, even from his mother's womb.—*Luke* i. 13, 15.

It is good not to eat flesh, and not to drink wine, nor any thing whereby thy brother is offended, or scandalized, or made weak.—*Rom.* xiv. 21.

ACCESSORY TO THE SINS OF OTHERS

Who can understand sins? from my secret ones cleanse me, O Lord:

And from those of others spare thy servant. If they shall have no dominion over me, then shall I be without spot: and I shall be cleansed from the greatest sin.—*Ps.* xviii. 13, 14.

The messenger of the wicked shall fall into mischief.—*Prov.* xiii. 17.

He that is partaker with a thief, hateth his own soul: he heareth one putting him to his oath, and discovereth not.—*Prov.* xxix. 24.

For he that did prevail hath failed, the scorner is consumed, and they are all cut off that watched for iniquity:

That made men sin by word, and supplanted him that reproved them in the gate, and declined in vain from the just.—*Is.* xxix. 20, 21.

Who, having known the justice of God, did not understand that they who do such things, are worthy of death; and not only they that do them, but

they also that consent to them that do them.—*Rom.* i. 32.

Impose not hands lightly upon any man, neither be partaker of other men's sins.—1 *Tim.* v. 22.

ACKNOWLEDGMENT OF MAN'S WEAKNESS AND MISERY

Have mercy on me, O Lord, for I am weak: heal me, O Lord, for my bones are troubled.—*Ps.* vi. 3.

Look thou upon me, and have mercy on me; for I am alone and poor.

The troubles of my heart are multiplied: deliver me from my necessities.

See my abjection and my labor; and forgive me all my sins.—*Ps.* xxiv. 16-19.

But I am a beggar and poor: the Lord is careful for me.—*Ps.* xxxix. 18.

But I am poor and sorrowful: thy salvation, O God, hath set me up.— *Ps.* lxviii. 30.

But I am needy and poor; O God, help me.—*Ps.* lxix. 6.

. . . Do thou deliver me,

For I am poor and needy, and my heart is troubled within me.—*Ps.* cviii. 21, 22.

ACKNOWLEDGMENT THAT WE DESERVE PUNISHMENT

And [1]they talked one to another: We deserve to suffer these things, because we have sinned against our brother, seeing the anguish of his soul, when he besought us, and we would not hear: therefore is this affliction come upon us. —*Gen.* xlii. 21.

And thou (God) art just in all things that have come upon us: because thou hast done truth, but we have done wickedly.—2 *Esd.* ix. 33.

But esteeming these very punishments to be less than our sins deserve, let us believe that these scourges of the Lord, with which, like servants, we are chastised, have happened for our amendment, and not for our destruction.—*Judith* viii. 27.

[2]He shall look upon men, and shall

[1]Joseph's brethren.
[2]One suffering tribulation from the hands of God.

say: I have sinned, and indeed I have offended, and I have not received what I have deserved.—*Job* xxxiii. 27.

We have sinned in thy sight, and therefore thou hast delivered us into the hands of our enemies:

For we have worshipped their gods. Thou art just, O Lord.—*Esther* xiv. 6, 7.

For I am ready for scourges: and my sorrow is continually before me.

For I will declare my iniquity: and I will think for my sin.—*Ps.* xxxvii. 18, 19.

He hath not dealt with us according to our sins: nor rewarded us according to our iniquities.—*Ps.* cii. 10.

The Lord is just, for I have provoked his mouth to wrath: hear, I pray you, all ye people, and see my sorrow: my virgins, and my young men are gone into captivity.—*Lam.* i. 18.

For we have sinned, and committed iniquity, departing from thee: and we have trespassed in all things:

And we have not hearkened to thy commandments, nor have we observed nor done as thou hadst commanded us, that it might go well with us. Wherefore all that thou hast brought upon us, and every thing that thou hast done to us, thou hast done in true judgment.—*Dan.* iii. 29-32.

O Lord, to us belongeth confusion of face, to our princes, and to our fathers, that have sinned. But to thee, the Lord our God, mercy and forgiveness, for we have departed from thee:

And we have not hearkened to the voice of the Lord our God, to walk in his law, which he set before us by his servants, the prophets.—*Dan.* ix. 8-11.

I will bear the wrath of the Lord, because I have sinned against him; until he judge my cause and execute judgment for me.—*Mich.* vii. 9.

For if in the green wood they do ¹these things, what shall be done in the dry?—*Luke* xxiii. 31.

And one of those robbers who were hanged, blasphemed him, saying: If thou be Christ, save thyself and us. But the other, answering, rebuked him, saying: Neither dost thou fear God,

¹The sufferings of Christ in His passion.

seeing thou art under the same condemnation?

And we, indeed, justly, for we receive the due reward of our deeds; but this man hath done no evil.—*Luke* xxiii. 39-42.

ACKNOWLEDGMENT OF SIN

My God I am confounded and ashamed to lift up my face to thee: for our iniquities are multiplied over our heads, and our sins are grown up even unto heaven,

From the days of our fathers: and we ourselves also have sinned grievously unto this day.—1 *Esd.* ix. 6, 7.

O Lord God of Israel, thou art just: for we remain yet to be saved as at this day.

Behold we are before thee in our sin, for there can be no standing before thee in this matter.—1 *Esd.* ix. 15.

Let thy ears be attentive, and thy eyes open, to hear the prayer of thy servant, which I pray before thee now, night and day, for the children of Israel, thy servants: and I confess the sins of the children of Israel, by which they have sinned against thee: I and my father's house have sinned.

We have been seduced by vanity, and have not kept thy commandments, and ceremonies and judgments, which thou hast commanded thy servant Moses.—2 *Esd.* i. 6, 7.

And now, O Lord, great are thy judgments, because we have not done according to thy precepts, and have not walked sincerely before thee.—*Tob.* iii. 5.

We have sinned with our fathers, we have done unjustly, we have committed iniquity:

Have thou mercy on us, because thou art good, or punish our iniquities by chastising us thyself, and deliver not them that trust in thee to a people that knoweth not thee.—*Judith* vii. 19, 20.

We have sinned in thy sight, and therefore thou hast delivered us into the hands of our enemies:

For we have worshipped their gods. Thou art just, O Lord.—*Esther* xiv. 6, 7.

I have sinned: what shall I do to thee, O keeper of men? why hast thou set me opposite to thee, and I am become burdensome to myself?

Why dost thou not remove my sin, and why dost thou not take away my iniquity?—*Job* vii. 20, 21.

'He shall look upon men, and shall say: I have sinned, and indeed I have offended, and I have not received what I have deserved.—*Job* xxxiii. 27.

For thy name's sake, O Lord, thou wilt pardon my sin: for it is great.—*Ps.* xxiv. 11.

For I am ready for scourges: and my sorrow is continually before me.

For I will declare my iniquity: and I will think for my sin.—*Ps.* xxxvii. 18, 19.

I said: O Lord, be thou merciful to me: heal my soul, for I have sinned against thee.—*Ps.* xl. 5.

Wash me yet more from my iniquity, and cleanse me from my sin.

For I know my iniquity, and my sin is always before me.

To thee only have I sinned, and have done evil before thee: that thou mayst be justified in thy words, and mayst overcome when thou art judged.—*Ps.* l. 4-7.

All we like sheep have gone astray, every one hath turned aside into his own way: and the Lord hath laid on him the iniquity of us all.—*Is.* liii. 6.

For our iniquities are multiplied before thee, and our sins have testified against us: for our wicked doings are with us, and we have known our iniquities:

In sinning and lying against the Lord: and we have turned away so that we went not after our God, but spoke calumny and transgression: we have conceived, and uttered from the heart, words of falsehood.—*Is.* lix. 12, 13.

We shall sleep in our confusion, and our shame shall cover us, because we have sinned against the Lord our God, we and our fathers from our youth, even to this day, and we have not hearkened to the voice of the Lord our God.—*Jer.* iii. 25.

If our iniquities have testified against us, O Lord, do thou it for thy name's sake, for our rebellions are

¹One in tribulation and suffering.

many, we have sinned against thee.—*Jer.* xiv. 7.

We acknowledge, O Lord, our wickedness, the iniquities of our fathers, because we have sinned against thee.—*Jer.* xiv. 20.

We have sinned before the Lord our God, and have not believed him, nor put our trust in him:

And we were not obedient to him, and we have not hearkened to the voice of the Lord our God, to walk in his commandments, which he hath given us. . . .

And we have gone away every man after the inclinations of his own wicked heart, to serve strange gods, and to do evil in the sight of the Lord our God.—*Bar.* i. 17, 18, 22.

We have sinned, we have done wickedly, we have acted unjustly, O Lord our God, against all thy justices.—*Bar.* ii. 12.

For we have sinned, and committed iniquity, departing from thee: and we have trespassed in all things:

And we have not hearkened to thy commandments, nor have we observed nor done as thou hadst commanded us, that it might go well with us.—*Dan.* iii. 29, 30.

And I prayed to the Lord my God, and I made my confession, and said: I beseech thee, O Lord God, great and terrible, who keepest the covenant, and mercy to them that love thee and keep thy commandments.

We have sinned, we have committed iniquity, we have done wickedly, and have revolted: and we have gone aside from thy commandments, and thy judgments.—*Dan.* ix. 4, 5.

I will bear the wrath of the Lord, because I have sinned against him; until he judge my cause and execute judgment for me.—*Mich.* vii. 9.

Then went out to 'him Jerusalem and all Judea, and all the country about Jordan:

And were baptized by him in the Jordan, confessing their sins.—*Matt.* iii. 5, 6.

²Which when Simon Peter saw, he

¹John, the Baptist.

²The miraculous draught of fishes.

fell down at Jesus' knees, saying: Depart from me, for I am a sinful man, O Lord.—*Luke* v. 8.

For all have sinned, and do need the glory of God.—*Rom.* iii. 23.

For in many things we all offend. If any man offend not in word, the same is a perfect man.—*James* iii. 2.

ACKNOWLEDGMENT OF SIN NECESSARY

You shall perish among the Gentiles, and an enemy's land shall consume you.

And if of them also some remain, they shall pine away in their iniquities, in the land of their enemies, and they shall be afflicted for the sins of their fathers, and their own:

Until they confess their iniquities and the iniquities of their ancestors, whereby they have transgressed against me, and walked contrary unto me.— *Lev.* xxvi. 38-41.

And the Lord spoke to Moses, saying: Say to the children of Israel: When a man or woman shall have committed any of all the sins that men are wont to commit, and by negligence shall have transgressed the commandment of the Lord, and offended,

They shall confess their sin, and restore the principal itself, and the fifth part over and above, to him against whom they have sinned.—*Num.* v. 5-8.

For what shall I do when God shall rise to judge? and when he shall examine, what shall I answer him? . . .

If as a man I have hid my sin, and have concealed my iniquity in my bosom.—*Job* xxxi. 14, 33.

He that hideth his sins, shall not prosper: but he that shall confess, and forsake them, shall obtain mercy.— *Prov.* xxviii. 13.

For thy soul be not ashamed to say the truth.

For there is a shame that bringeth sin, and there is a shame that bringeth glory and grace. . . . Be not ashamed to confess thy sins, but submit not thyself to every man for sin.—*Ecclus.* iv. 24, 25, 31.

And thou hast said: I am without sin and am innocent: and therefore let thy anger be turned away from me. Behold, I will contend with thee in judgment, because thou hast said: I have not sinned.—*Jer.* ii. 35.

Return, O rebellious Israel, saith the Lord, and I will not turn away my face from you: for I am holy, saith the Lord, and I will not be angry for ever.

But yet acknowledge thy iniquity, that thou hast transgressed against the Lord thy God: and thou hast scattered thy ways to strangers under every green tree, and hast not heard my voice, saith the Lord.—*Jer.* iii. 12, 13.

If we say that we have no sin, we deceive ourselves, and the truth is not in us.

If we confess our sins, he is faithful and just, to forgive us our sins, and to cleanse us from all iniquity.

If we say that we have not sinned, we make him a liar, and his word is not in us.—1 *John* i. 8, 9, 10.

ACKNOWLEDGMENT OF SIN REWARDED

And David said to Nathan: I have sinned against the Lord. And Nathan said to David: The Lord also hath taken away thy sin: thou shalt not die. —2 *Kings* xii. 13.

But if they sin against thee (for there is no man who sinneth not) and thou being angry deliver them up to their enemies, so that they be led away captives into the land of their enemies far or near;

Then if they do penance in their heart in the place of captivity, and being converted make supplication to thee in their captivity, saying: We have sinned, we have done unjustly, we have committed wickedness:

And return to thee with all their heart, and all their soul, in the land of their enemies, to which they had been led captives: . . .

Then hear thou in heaven, in the firmament of thy throne, their prayers and their supplications, and do judgment for them:

And forgive thy people that have sinned against thee, and all their iniquities, by which they have transgressed against thee.—3 *Kings* viii. 46-51.

I have acknowledged my sin to thee, and my injustice I have not concealed.

I said, I will confess against myself my injustice to the Lord: and thou hast forgiven the wickedness of my sin.—*Ps.* xxxi. 5.

I will arise, and will go to my father, and say to him: Father, I have sinned against heaven, and before thee:

I am not worthy to be called thy son: make me as one of thy hired servants.

And rising up, he came to his father. And when he was yet a great way off, his father saw him, and was moved with compassion, and running to him, fell upon his neck, and kissed him.—*Luke* xv. 18-21.

And the publican standing afar off, would not so much as lift up his eyes towards heaven; but struck his breast, saying: O God, be merciful to me, a sinner.

I say to you, this man went down into his house justified, rather than the other: because every one that exalteth himself, shall be humbled: and he that humbleth himself, shall be exalted.—*Luke* xviii. 13, 14.

ADMONITION, GIVING

Rebuke not a scorner, lest he hate thee. Rebuke a wise man, and he will love thee.—*Prov.* ix. 8.

Speak not in the ears of fools: because they will despise the instruction of thy speech.—*Prov.* xxiii. 9.

He that rebuketh a man, shall afterward find favor with him, more than he that by a flattering tongue deceiveth him.—*Prov.* xxviii. 23.

How much better is it to reprove, than to be angry, and not to hinder him that confesseth in prayer.—*Ecclus.* xx. 1.

And why seest thou the mote that is in thy brother's eye; and seest not the beam that is in thy own eye?

Or, how sayest thou to thy brother: Let me cast the mote out of thy eye; and behold a beam is in thy own eye?

Thou hypocrite, cast out first the beam out of thy own eye, and then shalt thou see to cast out the mote out of thy brother's eye.—*Matt.* vii. 3-6.

But the servant of God must not wrangle; but be mild towards all men, apt to teach, patient, with modesty admonishing them that resist the truth: if peradventure, God may give them repentance to know the truth,

And they may recover themselves from the snares of the devil, by whom they are held captive at his will.—2 *Tim.* ii. 24, 25, 26.

My brethren, if any of you err from the truth, and one convert him:

He must know that he who causeth a sinner to be converted from the error of his way, shall save his soul from death, and shall cover a multitude of sins.—*James* v. 19, 20.

ADMONITION GIVING, COMMANDED

Thou shalt not hate thy brother in thy heart, but reprove him openly, lest thou incur sin through him.—*Lev.* xix. 17.

But if thy brother shall offend against thee, go, and rebuke him between thee and him alone. If he shall hear thee, thou shalt gain thy brother.

And if he will not hear thee, take with thee one or two more: that in the mouth of two or three witnesses every word may stand.—*Matt.* xviii. 15, 16.

If thy brother sin against thee, reprove him: and if he do penance, forgive him.—*Luke* xvii. 3.

ADMONITION GIVING, EXHORTED

Reverence not thy neighbor in his fall:

And refrain not to speak in the time of salvation.—*Ecclus.* iv. 27, 28.

Reprove a friend, lest he may not have understood, and say: I did it not: or if he did it, that he may do it no more.

Reprove thy neighbor, for it may be he hath not said it: and if he hath said it, that he may not say it again.

Admonish thy friend: for there is often a fault committed. . . .

Admonish thy neighbor, before thou threaten him.—*Ecclus.* xix. 13-16, 17.

Brethren, and if a man be overtaken in any fault, you, who are spiritual, instruct such a one in the spirit of meekness, considering thyself, lest thou also be tempted.—*Gal.* vi. 1.

And we beseech you, brethren, rebuke the unquiet, comfort the feeble minded, support the weak, be patient towards all men.—1 *Thess.* v. 14.

And if any man obey not our word by this epistle, note that man, and do not keep company with him, that he may be ashamed:

Yet do not esteem him as an enemy, but admonish him as a brother.— 2 *Thess.* iii. 14, 15.

Them that sin reprove before all: that the rest also may have fear.— 1 *Tim.* v. 20.

ADMONITION OR CORRECTION, RECEIVING

The just man shall correct me in mercy, and shall reprove me: but let not the ¹oil of the sinner fatten my head.—*Ps.* cxl. 5.

Because the commandment is a lamp, and the law a light, and reproofs of instruction are the way of life.—*Prov.* vi. 23.

The way of life to him that observeth correction: but he that forsaketh reproofs goeth astray.—*Prov.* x. 17.

He that loveth correction, loveth knowledge: but he that hateth reproof is foolish.—*Prov.* xii. 1.

Poverty and shame to him that refuseth instruction: but he that yieldeth to reproof, shall be glorified.—*Prov.* xiii. 18.

A fool laugheth at the instruction of his father: but he that regardeth reproofs shall become prudent.—*Prov.* xv. 5.

The ear that heareth the reproofs of life, shall abide in the midst of the wise.—*Prov.* xv. 31.

He that rejecteth instruction, despiseth his own soul: but he that yieldeth to reproof, possesseth understanding.— *Prov.* xv. 32.

A reproof availeth more with a wise man, than a hundred stripes with a fool.—*Prov.* xvii. 10.

The wicked man impudently hard-

¹That is, the flattery, or deceitful praise.

eneth his face: but he that is righteous, correcteth his way.—*Prov.* xxi. 29.

Open rebuke is better than hidden love.

Better are the wounds of a friend, than the deceitful kisses of an enemy. —*Prov.* xxvii. 5, 6.

It is better to be rebuked by a wise man, than to be deceived by the flattery of fools.—*Eccles.* vii. 6.

A man that is prudent and well instructed, will not murmur when he is reproved.—*Ecclus.* x. 28.

ADMONITION OR CORRECTION, REFUSING

Then shall they call upon me, and I will not hear: they shall rise in the morning, and shall not find me:

Because they have hated instruction, and received not the fear of the Lord,

Nor consented to my counsel, but despised all my reproof.

Therefore they shall eat the fruit of their own way, and shall be filled with their own devices.—*Prov.* i. 28-32.

And thou mourn at the last, when thou shalt have spent thy flesh and thy body, and say:

Why have I hated instruction, and my heart consented not to reproofs,

And have not heard the voice of them that taught me, and have not inclined my ear to masters? . . .

He shall die, because he hath not received instruction, and in the multitude of his folly he shall be deceived.— *Prov.* v. 11-14, 23.

The way of life to him that observeth correction: but he that forsaketh reproofs goeth astray.—*Prov.* x. 17.

He that loveth correction, loveth knowledge: but he that hateth reproof is foolish.—*Prov.* xii. 1.

Poverty and shame to him that refuseth instruction: but he that yieldeth to reproof shall be glorified.—*Prov.* xiii. 18.

A fool laugheth at the instruction of his father: but he that regardeth reproofs shall become prudent.—*Prov.* xv. 5.

Instruction is grievous to him that forsaketh the way of life: he that hateth reproof shall die.—*Prov.* xv. 10.

A corrupt man loveth not one that reproveth him: nor will he go to the wise. —*Prov.* xv. 12.

He that rejecteth instruction, despiseth his own soul: but he that yieldeth to reproof possesseth understanding.— *Prov.* xv. 32.

He that maketh his house high, seeketh a downfall: and he that refuseth to learn, shall fall into evils.—*Prov.* xvii. 16.

A fool receiveth not the words of prudence: unless thou say those things which are in his heart.—*Prov.* xviii. 2.

The man that with a stiff neck despiseth him that reproveth him, shall suddenly be destroyed: and health shall not follow him.—*Prov.* xxix. 1.

For he that rejecteth wisdom, and discipline, is unhappy: and their hope is vain, and their labors without fruit, and their works unprofitable.—*Wis.* iii. 11.

He that hateth to be reproved, walketh in the trace of a sinner: and he that feareth God, will turn to his own heart. —*Ecclus.* xxi. 7.

He that is not wise in good, will not be taught.—*Ecclus.* xxi. 14.

A sinful man will flee reproof, and will find an excuse according to his will.—*Ecclus.* xxxii. 21.

ADORING GOD

Let all the earth adore thee, and sing to thee: let it sing a psalm to thy name. —*Ps.* lxv. 4.

Come, let us adore and fall down: and weep before the Lord that made us.

For he is the Lord our God: and we are the people of his pasture and the sheep of his hand.—*Ps.* xciv. 6, 7.

Adore ye the Lord in his holy court. Let all the earth be moved at his presence.—*Ps.* xcv. 9.

Let them be all confounded that adore graven things, and that glory in their idols.

Adore him, all you his angels.—*Ps.* xcvi. 7.

Exalt ye the Lord our God, and adore at his holy mountain: for the Lord our God is holy.—*Ps.* xcviii. 9.

For [1]that which could not be de-

[1]The manna in the desert.

stroyed by fire, being warmed with a little sunbeam presently melted away:

That it might be known to all, that we ought to prevent the sun to bless thee, and adore thee at the dawning of the light.—*Wis.* xvi. 27, 28.

He that adoreth God with joy, shall be accepted, and his prayer shall approach even to the clouds.—*Ecclus.* xxxv. 20.

In that day man shall bow down himself to his Maker, and his eyes shall look to the Holy One of Israel.—*Is.* xvii. 7.

When Jesus therefore was born in Bethlehem of Juda, in the days of king Herod, behold, there came wise men from the east to Jerusalem,

Saying, Where is he that is born king of the Jews? For we have seen his star in the east, and are come to adore him. . . .

And entering into the house, they found the child with Mary his mother, and falling down they adored him; and opening their treasures, they offered him gifts; gold, frankincense, and myrrh.—*Matt.* ii. 1, 2, 11.

Then Jesus saith to him: Begone, Satan: for it is written, The Lord thy God shalt thou adore, and him only shalt thou serve.—*Matt.* iv. 10.

Jesus saith to her: Woman, believe me, that the hour cometh, when you shall neither on this mountain, nor in Jerusalem, adore the Father.

You adore that which you know not: we adore that which we know; for salvation is of the Jews.

But the hour cometh, and now is, when the true adorers shall adore the Father in spirit and in truth. For the Father also seeketh such to adore him.

God is a spirit; and they that adore him, must adore him in spirit and in truth.—*John* iv. 21-25.

And I saw another angel flying through the midst of heaven, having the eternal gospel, to preach unto them that sit upon the earth, and over every nation, and tribe, and tongue, and people:

Saying with a loud voice: Fear the Lord, and give him honor, because the hour of his judgment is come; and adore ye him, that made heaven and earth, the sea, and the fountains of waters.—*Apoc.* xiv. 6, 7.

ADULTERY

Thou shalt not commit adultery.— *Ex.* xx. 14.

The eye of the adulterer observeth darkness, saying: No eye shall see me: and he will cover his face.

He diggeth through houses in the dark, as in the day they had appointed for themselves, and they have not known the light.

If the morning suddenly appear, it is to them the shadow of death: and they walk in darkness as if it were in light.—*Job* xxiv. 15-18.

If my heart hath been deceived upon a woman, and if I have laid wait at my friend's door: . . . For this is a heinous crime, and a most grievous iniquity.

It is a fire that devoureth even to destruction, and rooteth up all things that spring.—*Job.* xxxi. 9, 11, 12.

Counsel shall keep thee, and prudence shall preserve thee.

. . . That thou mayst be delivered from the strange woman, and from the stranger, who softeneth her words:

And forsaketh the guide of her youth,

And hath forgotten the covenant of her God: for her house inclineth unto death, and her paths to hell.—*Prov.* ii. 11, 16-19.

Mind not the deceit of a woman.

For the lips of a harlot are like a honeycomb dropping, and her throat is smoother than oil.

But her end is bitter as wormwood, and sharp as a two-edged sword.

Her feet go down into death, and her steps go in as far as hell.

They walk not by the path of life, her steps are wandering, and unaccountable.

Now therefore, my son, hear me, and depart not from the words of my mouth.

Remove thy way far from her, and come not nigh the doors of her house.

Give not thy honor to strangers, and thy years to the cruel.

Lest strangers be filled with thy strength, and thy labors be in another man's house,

And thou mourn at the last, when thou shalt have spent thy flesh and thy body, and say:

Why have I hated instruction, and my heart consented not to reproof,

And have not heard the voice of them that taught me, and have not inclined my ear to masters? . . .

Drink water out of thy own cistern, and the streams of thy own well.

Let thy vein be blessed, and rejoice with the wife of thy youth. . . .

Why art thou seduced, my son, by a strange woman, and art cherished in the bosom of another?—*Prov.* v. 2-14, 15, 18, 20.

Let not thy heart covet her beauty, be not caught with her winks:

For the price of a harlot is scarce one loaf: but the woman catcheth the precious soul of a man.

Can a man hide fire in his bosom, and his garments not burn?

Or can he walk upon hot coals, and his feet not be burnt?

So he that goeth in to his neighbor's wife, shall not be clean when he shall touch her.

The fault is not so great when a man hath stolen: for he stealeth to fill his hungry soul:

But he that is an adulterer, for the folly of his heart shall destroy his own soul.—*Prov.* vi. 25-31, 32.

Say to wisdom: Thou art my sister: and call prudence thy friend,

That she may keep thee from the woman that is not thine, and from the stranger who sweeteneth her words.— *Prov.* vii. 4, 5.

For I look out of the window of my house through the lattice,

And I see little ones, I behold a foolish young man,

Who passeth through the street by the corner, and goeth nigh the way of her house;

In the dark, when it grows late, in the darkness and obscurity of the night,

And behold, a woman meeteth him in harlot's attire, prepared to deceive souls; talkative and wandering; . . .

And catching the young man, she

kisseth him, and with an impudent face, flattereth, saying: . . .

For my husband is not at home, he is gone a very long journey.

She entangled him with many words, and drew him away with the flattery of her lips.

Immediately he followeth her as an ox led to be a victim, and as a lamb playing the wanton, and not knowing that he is drawn like a fool to bonds,

Till the arrow pierce his liver: as if a bird should make haste to the snare, and knoweth not that his life is in danger.

Now therefore, my son, hear me, and attend to the words of my mouth.

Let not thy mind be drawn away in her ways: neither be thou deceived with her paths.

For she hath cast down many wounded, and the strongest have been slain by her.

Her house is the way to hell, reaching even to the inner chambers of death.—*Prov.* vii. 6-11, 13, 19, 21-27.

'Such also is the way of an adulterous woman, who eateth and wipeth her mouth, and saith: I have done no evil. —*Prov.* xxx. 20.

For the children that are born of unlawful beds, are witnesses of wickedness against their parents in their trial. —*Wis.* iv. 6.

Give not thy soul to harlots in any point: lest thou destroy thyself and thy inheritance.—*Ecclus.* ix. 6.

Many by admiring the beauty of another man's wife, have become reprobate, for her conversation burneth as fire.

Sit not at all with another man's wife, nor repose upon the bed with her:

And strive not with her over wine, lest thy heart decline towards her, and by thy blood thou fall into destruction. —*Ecclus.* ix. 11-13.

Every man that passeth beyond his own bed, despising his own soul, and saying: Who seeth me?

Darkness compasseth me about, and the walls cover me, and no man seeth me: whom do I fear? the most High will not remember my sins.

And he understandeth not that his

[1] Uncertain, and hard to follow.

eye seeth all things, for such a man's fear driveth from him the fear of God, and the eyes of men fearing him.— *Ecclus.* xxiii. 25-27.

Every one that putteth away his wife, and marrieth another, committeth adultery: and he that marrieth her that is put away from her husband, committeth adultery.—*Luke* xvi. 18.

ADULTERY, PUNISHMENT OF

Thou shalt not lie with thy neighbor's wife, nor be defiled with mingling of seed: . . .

Every soul that shall commit any of the abominations, shall perish from the midst of his people.—*Lev.* xviii. 20, 29.

If any man commit adultery with the wife of another, and defile his neighbor's wife, let them be put to death, both the adulterer and the adulteress.— *Lev.* xx. 10.

The eye of the adulterer observeth darkness, saying: No eye shall see me: and he will cover his face. . . .

Cursed be his portion on the earth, let him not walk by the way of the vineyards.

Let him pass from the snow waters to excessive heat, and his sin even to hell.

Let mercy forget him: may worms be his sweetness: let him be remembered no more, but be broken in pieces as an unfruitful tree.

For he hath fed the barren that beareth not, and to the widow he hath done no good.

He hath pulled down the strong by his might: and when he standeth up, he shall not trust to his life.

God hath given him place for penance, and he abuseth it unto pride: but his eyes are upon his ways.

They are lifted up for a little while and shall not stand, and shall be brought down as all things, and shall be taken away, and as the tops of the ears of corn they shall be broken.— *Job* xxiv. 15, 18-24.

For 'her house inclineth unto death, and her paths to hell.

None that go in unto her shall return again, neither shall they take hold of the paths of life.—*Prov.* ii. 18, 19.

[1] The house of the prostitute.

But he that is an adulterer, for the folly of his heart, shall destroy his own soul:

He gathereth to himself shame and dishonor, and his reproach shall not be blotted out.—*Prov.* vi. 32, 33.

Wine and women make wise men fall off, and shall rebuke the prudent:

And he that joineth himself to harlots, will be wicked. Rottenness and worms shall inherit him, and he shall be lifted up for a greater example, and his soul shall be taken away out of the number.—*Ecclus.* xix. 2, 3.

Every man that passeth beyond his own bed, despising his own soul, and saying: Who seeth me? . . .

This man shall be punished in the streets of the city, and he shall be chased as a colt: and where he suspected not, he shall be taken.

And he shall be in disgrace with all men, because he understood not the fear of the Lord.

So every woman also that leaveth her husband, and bringeth in an heir by another:

For first, she hath been unfaithful to the law of the most High: and secondly, she hath offended against her husband: thirdly, she hath fornicated in adultery, and hath gotten her children of another man. . . .

She shall leave her memory to be cursed, and her infamy shall not be blotted out.—*Ecclus.* xxiii. 25, 30-33, 36.

And I will come to you in judgment, and will be a speedy witness against sorcerers, and adulterers, and false swearers, and them that oppress the hireling in his wages.—*Malach.* iii. 5.

Know you not that the unjust shall not possess the kingdom of God? Do not err: neither fornicators, nor idolaters, nor adulterers . . . shall possess the kingdom of God.—1 *Cor.* vi. 9, 10.

Marriage honorable in all, and the bed undefiled. For fornicators and adulterers God will judge.—*Heb.* xiii. 4.

AFFLICTED WITH BODILY INFIRMITIES, THE

So going in ¹he saluted him, and said: Joy be to thee always.

¹The angel Raphael, under the guise of a young man.

And Tobias said: What manner of joy shall be to me, who sit in darkness, and see not the light of heaven?

And the young man said to him: Be of good courage, thy cure from God is at hand.—*Tob.* v. 11-13.

The Lord enlighteneth the blind.—*Ps.* cxlv. 8.

And in that day the deaf shall hear the words of the book, and out of darkness and obscurity the eyes of the blind shall see.—*Is.* xxix. 18.

Then shall the eyes of the blind be opened, and the ears of the deaf shall be unstopped.

Then shall the lame man leap as a hart, and the tongue of the dumb shall be free: for waters are broken out in the desert, and streams in the wilderness.—*Is.* xxxv. 5, 6.

And I will lead the blind into the way which they know not: and in the paths which they were ignorant of, I will make them walk: I will make darkness light before them, and crooked things straight: these things have I done to them, and have not forsaken them.—*Is.* xlii. 16.

And we beseech you, brethren, rebuke the unquiet, comfort the feeble-minded, support the weak, be patient towards all men.—1 *Thess.* v. 14.

AGED, THE

See: Old age—page 351.

ALL, GOD OUR

The Lord is the portion of my inheritance and of my cup: it is thou that wilt restore my inheritance to me.

The lines are fallen unto me in goodly places: for my inheritance is goodly to me.—*Ps.* xv. 5, 6.

For what have I in heaven? and besides thee, what do I desire upon earth?

For thee my flesh and my heart have fainted away: thou art the God of my heart, and the God that is my portion for ever.—*Ps.* lxxii. 25, 26.

We shall say much, and yet shall want words: but the sum of our words is, He is all.—*Ecclus.* xliii. 29.

He that loveth father or mother more than me, is not worthy of me; and he that loveth son or daughter more than me, is not worthy of me.—*Matt.* x. 37.

For in him we live, and move, and are.—*Acts* xvii. 28.

For in 'him dwelleth all the fulness of the Godhead corporeally;

And you are filled in him, who is the head of all principality and power.—*Col.* ii. 9, 10.

Where there is neither Gentile nor Jew, circumcision nor uncircumcision, Barbarian nor Scythian, bond nor free. But Christ is all, and in all.—*Col.* iii. 11.

ALMSGIVING

He that oppresseth the poor, upbraideth his Maker: but he that hath pity on the poor, honoreth him.—*Prov.* xiv. 31.

He that is just will give, and will not cease.—*Prov.* xxi. 26.

²She hath opened her hand to the needy, and stretched out her hands to the poor.—*Prov.* xxxi. 20.

The alms of a man is as a signet with him, and shall preserve the grace of a man as the apple of the eye.—*Ecclus.* xvii. 18.

The lips of many shall bless him that is liberal of his bread, and the testimony of his truth is faithful.—*Ecclus.* xxxi. 28.

Then shall the king say to them that shall be on his right hand: Come, ye blessed of my Father, possess you the kingdom prepared for you from the foundation of the world.

For I was hungry, and you gave me to eat; I was thirsty, and you gave me to drink; I was a stranger, and you took me in:

Naked, and you covered me; sick, and you visited me: I was in prison, and you came to me.

Then shall the just answer him, saying: Lord, when did we see thee hungry, and fed thee: thirsty, and gave thee drink?

And when did we see thee a stranger, and took thee in? or naked, and covered thee?

Or when did we see thee sick or in prison, and came to thee?

And the king answering, shall say to them:

Amen I say to you, as long as you

¹Christ.
²The wise woman.

did it to one of these my least brethren, you did it to me.—*Matt.* xxv. 34-40.

And looking on, he saw the rich men cast their gifts into the treasury.

And he saw also a certain poor widow casting in two brass mites.

And he said: Verily I say to you, that this poor widow hath cast in more than they all:

For all these have of their abundance cast into the offerings of God: but she of her want, hath cast in all the living that she had.—*Luke* xxi. 1-4.

I have showed you all things, how that so laboring you ought to support the weak, and to remember the word of the Lord Jesus, how he said: It is a more blessed thing to give, rather than to receive.—*Acts* xx. 35.

ALMSGIVING BRINGS DOWN THE BLESSING OF GOD

If any of thy brethren that dwelleth within the gates of thy city in the land which the Lord thy God will give thee, come to poverty: thou shalt not harden thy heart, nor close thy hand. . . . But thou shalt give to him: neither shalt thou do anything craftily in relieving his necessities: that the Lord thy God may bless thee at all times, and in all things to which thou shalt put thy hand. —*Deut.* xv. 7, 10.

When thou hast reaped the corn in thy field, and hast forgot and left a sheaf, thou shalt not return to take it away: but thou shalt suffer the stranger, and the fatherless and the widow to take it away: that the Lord thy God may bless thee in all the works of thy hands.—*Deut.* xxiv. 19.

Give alms out of thy substance, and turn not away thy face from any poor person: so that it shall come to pass that the face of the Lord shall not be turned from thee.—*Tob.* iv. 7.

He that despiseth his neighbor, sinneth: but he that showeth mercy to the poor, shall be blessed.—*Prov.* xiv. 21.

He that is inclined to mercy shall be blessed: for of his bread he hath given to the poor.—*Prov.* xxii. 9.

And stretch out thy hand to the poor, that thy expiation and thy blessing may be perfected.—*Ecclus.* vii. 36.

And do not forget to do good, and to

impart; for by such sacrifices God's favor is obtained.—*Heb.* xiii. 16.

ALMSGIVING, REWARDED BY GOD

If thou have much, give abundantly: if thou have little, take care even so to bestow willingly a little.

For thus thou storest up to thyself a good reward for the day of necessity.

For alms deliver from all sin, and from death, and will not suffer the soul to go into darkness. Alms shall be a great confidence before the most high God, to all them that give it.—*Tob.* iv. 9-12.

Prayer is good with fasting and alms, more than to lay up treasures of gold:

For alms delivereth from death, and the same is that which purgeth away sins, and maketh to find mercy and life everlasting.—*Tob.* xii. 8, 9.

Blessed is he that understandeth concerning the needy and the poor: the Lord will deliver him in the evil day.

The Lord preserve him and give him life, and make him blessed upon the earth: and deliver him not up to the will of his enemies.

The Lord help him on his bed of sorrow.—*Ps.* xl. 2-4.

Acceptable is the man that showeth mercy and lendeth: he shall order his words with judgment: because he shall not be moved for ever. . . . He hath distributed, he hath given to the poor: his justice remaineth for ever and ever: his horn shall be exalted in glory.—*Ps.* cxi. 5, 6, 9.

Some distribute their own goods, and grow richer: others take away what is not their own, and are always in want. —*Prov.* xi. 24.

He that hath mercy on the poor, lendeth to the Lord: and he will repay him. —*Prov.* xix. 17.

He that giveth to the poor, shall not want: he that despiseth his entreaty, shall suffer indigence.—*Prov.* xxviii. 27.

Cast thy bread upon the running waters: for after a long time thou shalt find it again.—*Eccles.* xi. 1.

Water quencheth a flaming fire, and alms resisteth sins:

And God provideth for him that showeth favor: he remembereth him afterwards, and in the time of his fall he shall find a sure stay.—*Ecclus.* iii. 33, 34.

Shut up alms in the heart of the poor, and it shall obtain help for thee against all evil.

Better than the shield of the mighty, and better than the spear:

It shall fight for thee against thy enemy.—*Ecclus.* xxix. 15-17.

Deal thy bread to the hungry, and bring the needy and the harborless into thy house: when thou shalt see one naked, cover him, and despise not thy own flesh.

Then shall thy light break forth as the morning, and thy health shall speedily arise, and thy justice shall go before thy face, and the glory of the Lord shall gather thee up.

Then shalt thou call, and the Lord shall hear: thou shalt cry, and he shall say, Here I am.

When thou shalt pour out thy soul to the hungry, and shalt satisfy the afflicted soul, then shall thy light rise up in darkness, and thy darkness shall be as the noonday.

And the Lord will give thee rest continually, and will fill thy soul with brightness, and deliver thy bones, and thou shalt be like a watered garden, and like a fountain of water, whose waters shall not fail.—*Is.* lviii. 7-11.

Wherefore, O king, let my counsel be acceptable to thee, and redeem thou thy sins with alms, and thy iniquities with works of mercy to the poor: perhaps he will forgive thy offences.—*Dan.* iv. 24.

And whosoever shall give to drink to one of these little ones a cup of cold water only in the name of a disciple, amen I say to you, he shall not lose his reward.—*Matt.* x. 42.

Jesus saith to him: If thou wilt be perfect, go, sell what thou hast, and give to the poor, and thou shalt have treasure in heaven: and come, follow me.—*Matt.* xix. 21.

Then shall the king say to them that shall be on his right hand: Come, ye blessed of my Father, possess you the kingdom prepared for you from the foundation of the world.

For I was hungry, and you gave me to eat; I was thirsty, and you gave me to drink; I was a stranger, and you took me in:

Naked, and you covered me: sick, and you visited me: I was in prison, and you came to me.

Then shall the just answer him, saying: Lord, when did we see thee hungry, and fed thee; thirsty, and gave thee drink?

And when did we see thee a stranger, and took thee in? or naked, and covered thee?

Or when did we see thee sick or in prison, and came to thee?

And the king answering, shall say to them: Amen I say to you, as long as you did it to one of these my least brethren, you did it to me.—*Matt.* xxv. 34-40.

Give, and it shall be given to you: good measure and pressed down and shaken together and running over shall they give into your bosom. For with the same measure that you shall mete withal, it shall be measured to you again.—*Luke* vi. 38.

Sell what you possess and give alms. Make to yourselves bags which grow not old, a treasure in heaven which faileth not: where no thief approacheth, nor moth corrupteth.—*Luke* xii. 33.

But when thou makest a feast, call the poor, the maimed, the lame, and the blind;

And thou shalt be blessed, because they have not wherewith to make thee recompense: for recompense shall be made thee at the resurrection of the just.—*Luke* xiv. 13, 14.

And in Joppe there was a certain disciple named Tabitha, which by interpretation is called Dorcas. This woman was full of good works and almsdeeds which she did.

And it came to pass in those days that she was sick, and died. Whom when they had washed, they laid her in an upper chamber. . . .

And Peter rising up went with them. And when he was come they brought him into the upper chamber. And all the widows stood about him weeping, and showing him the coats and garments which Dorcas made them.

And they all being put forth, Peter kneeling down prayed, and turning to the body, he said: Tabitha, arise. And she opened her eyes; and seeing Peter, she sat up.—*Acts* ix. 36, 37, 39, 40.

And there was a certain man in Cæsarea, named Cornelius, a centurion of that which is called the Italian band;

A religious man, and fearing God with all his house, giving much alms to the people, and always praying to God.

This man saw in a vision manifestly, about the ninth hour of the day, an angel of God coming in unto him, and saying to him: Cornelius.

And he, beholding him, being seized with fear, said: What is it, Lord? And he said to him: Thy prayers and thy alms are ascended for a memorial in the sight of God.—*Acts* x. 1-4.

Now this I say: He who soweth sparingly, shall also reap sparingly: and he who soweth in blessings, shall also reap blessings. . . .

And he that ministereth seed to the sower, will both give you bread to eat, and will multiply your seed, and increase the growth of the fruits of your justice.—*2 Cor.* ix. 6, 10.

ALMSGIVING, COMMANDED BY GOD

When thou reapest the corn of thy land, thou shalt not cut down all that is on the face of the earth to the very ground: nor shalt thou gather the ears that remain.

Neither shalt thou gather the bunches and grapes that fall down in thy vineyard, but shalt leave them to the poor and the strangers to take.—*Lev.* xix. 9, 10.

If one of thy brethren that dwelleth within the gates of thy city in the land which the Lord thy God will give thee, come to poverty: thou shalt not harden thy heart, nor close thy hand,

But shalt open it to the poor man, thou shalt lend him that which thou perceivest he hath need of.

Beware lest perhaps a wicked thought steal in upon thee, and thou say in thy heart: The seventh year of remission draweth nigh; and thou turn away thy eyes from thy poor brother, denying to lend him that which he asketh: lest he cry against thee to the Lord, and it become a sin unto thee.

But thou shalt give to him: neither shalt thou do anything craftily in relieving his necessities: that the Lord thy God may bless thee at all times, and in all things to which thou shalt put thy hand.

There will not be wanting poor in the land of thy habitation: therefore I command thee to open thy hand to thy needy and poor brother that liveth in the land.—*Deut.* xv. 7-11.

When thou hast reaped the corn in thy field, and hast forgot and left a sheaf, thou shalt not return to take it away: but thou shalt suffer the stranger, and the fatherless and the widow to take it away: that the Lord thy God may bless thee in all the works of thy hands.

If thou have gathered the fruit of thy olive trees, thou shalt not return to gather whatsoever remaineth on the trees: but shalt leave it for the stranger, for the fatherless, and the widow.

If thou make the vintage of thy vineyard, thou shalt not gather the clusters that remain, but they shall be for the stranger, the fatherless, and the widow.

Remember that thou also wast a bondman in Egypt, and therefore I command thee to do this thing.—*Deut.* xxiv. 19-22.

Help the poor because of the commandment: and send him not away empty handed because of his poverty.—*Ecclus.* xxix. 12.

And the Lord said to 'him:

But yet that which remaineth, give alms; and behold, all things are clean unto you.—*Luke* xi. 41.

ALMSGIVING, EXHORTATION TO

Give alms out of thy substance, and turn not away thy face from any poor person: for so it shall come to pass that the face of the Lord shall not be turned from thee.

According to thy ability be merciful. If thou have much give abundantly: if thou have little, take care even so to bestow willingly a little. . . .

Eat thy bread with the hungry and

¹The Pharisee who invited Him to dinner.

the needy, and with thy garments cover the naked.—*Tob.* iv. 7-9, 17.

Cast thy bread upon the running waters: for after a long time thou shalt find it again.—*Eccles.* xi. 1.

Son, defraud not the poor of alms, and turn not away thy eyes from the poor.

Despise not the hungry soul: and provoke not the poor in his want.

Afflict not the heart of the needy, and defer not to give to him that is in distress.

Reject not the petition of the afflicted: and turn not away thy face from the needy.

Turn not away thy eyes from the poor for fear of anger: and leave not to them that ask of thee to curse thee behind thy back.

For the prayer of him that curseth thee in the bitterness of his soul, shall be heard, for he that made him will hear him.—*Ecclus.* iv. 1-6.

Neglect not to pray, and to give alms: . . .

And stretch out thy hand to the poor, that thy expiation and thy blessing may be perfected.—*Ecclus.* vii. 10, 36.

Do good to thy friend before thou die, and according to thy ability, stretching out thy hand, give to the poor.—*Ecclus.* xiv. 13.

Remember poverty in the time of abundance, and the necessities of poverty in the day of riches.—*Ecclus.* xviii. 25.

But yet towards the poor be thou more hearty, and delay not to show him mercy.

Help the poor because of the commandment: and send him not away empty handed because of his poverty.

Lose thy money for thy brother and thy friend: and hide it not under a stone to be lost.—*Ecclus.* xxix. 11-13.

Deal thy bread to the hungry, and bring the needy and the harborless into thy house: when thou shalt see one naked, cover him, and despise not thy own flesh.—*Is.* lviii. 7.

Wherefore, O king, let my counsel be acceptable to thee, and redeem thou thy sins with alms, and thy iniquities with works of mercy to the poor: perhaps he will forgive thy offences.—*Dan.* iv. 24.

And the people asked ¹him, saying: What then shall we do?

And he answering, said to them: He that hath two coats, let him give to him that hath none; and he that hath meat, let him do in like manner.—*Luke* iii. 10, 11.

Give to every one that asketh thee, and of him that taketh away thy goods, ask them not again.—*Luke* vi. 30.

Sell what you possess and give alms. Make to yourselves bags which grow not old, a treasure in heaven which faileth not: where no thief approacheth, nor moth corrupteth.—*Luke* xii. 33.

Charge the rich of this world . . . to do good, to be rich in good works, to give easily, to communicate to others,

To lay up in store for themselves a good foundation against the time to come, that they may lay hold on the true life.—1 *Tim.* vi. 18, 19.

And do not forget to do good, and to impart; for by such sacrifices God's favor is obtained.—*Heb.* xiii. 16.

ALMSGIVING, THE PROPER MANNER OF

According to thy ability be merciful.

If thou have much, give abundantly; if thou have little, take care even so to bestow willingly a little.—*Tob.* iv. 8, 9.

Say not to thy friend: Go, and come again: and tomorrow I will give to thee: when thou canst give at present. —*Prov.* iii. 28.

My son, in thy good deeds, make no complaint, and when thou givest any thing, add not grief by an evil word.

Shall not the dew assuage the heat? so also the good word is better than the gift.

Lo, is not a word better than a gift? but both are with a justified man.

A fool will upbraid bitterly: and a gift of one ill taught consumeth the eyes.—*Ecclus.* xviii. 15-18.

In every gift show a cheerful countenance, and sanctify thy tithes with joy. —*Ecclus.* xxxv. 11.

Be ashamed of upbraiding speeches before friends: and after thou hast given, upbraid not.—*Ecclus.* xli. 28.

Take heed that you do not your jus-
¹John the Baptist.

tice before men, to be seen by them: otherwise you shall not have a reward of your Father who is in heaven.

Therefore when thou dost an almsdeed, sound not a trumpet before thee, as the hypocrites do in the synagogues and in the streets, that they may be honored by men. Amen, I say to you, they have received their reward.

But when thou dost alms, let not thy left hand know what thy right hand doth.

That thy alms may be in secret, and thy Father who seeth in secret will repay thee.—*Matt.* vi. 1-4.

Now this I say: He who soweth sparingly, shall also reap sparingly: and he who soweth in blessings, shall also reap blessings.

Every one as he hath determined in his heart, not with sadness, or of necessity: for God loveth a cheerful giver.— 2 *Cor.* ix. 6, 7.

And if a brother or sister be naked, and want daily food:

And one of you say to them: Go in peace, be ye warmed and filled; yet give them not those things that are necessary for the body, what shall it profit? —*James* ii. 15, 16.

My little children, let us not love in word, nor in tongue, but in deed, and in truth.— 1 *John* iii. 18.

AMENDMENT OF LIFE

See also: Turning away from sin— page 527.

If thou wilt put away from thee the iniquity that is in thy hand, and let not injustice remain in thy tabernacle:

Then mayst thou lift up thy face without spot, and thou shalt be steadfast, and shalt not fear.

Thou shalt also forget misery, and remember it only as waters that are passed away.

And brightness like that of the noonday, shall arise to thee at evening: and when thou shalt think thyself consumed, thou shalt rise as the day star.

And thou shalt have confidence, hope being set before thee, and being buried, thou shalt sleep secure.

Thou shalt rest, and there shall be none to make thee afraid: and many shall entreat thy face.—*Job* xi. 14-19.

And I said, Now I have begun: this is the change of the right hand of the most High.—*Ps.* lxxvi. 11.

By what doth a young man correct his way? by observing thy words.—*Ps.* cxviii. 9.

He that loveth God, shall obtain pardon for his sins by prayer, and shall refrain himself from them, and shall be heard in the prayer of days.—*Ecclus.* iii. 4.

And thou shalt say to them: Thus saith the Lord: Shall not he that falleth, rise again? and he that is turned away, shall he not turn again?—*Jer.* viii. 4.

But if the wicked do penance for all his sins which he hath committed, and keep all my commandments, and do judgment, and justice, living he shall live, and shall not die.

I will not remember all his iniquities that he hath done: in his justice which he hath wrought, he shall live.—*Ezech.* xviii. 21, 22.

What shall we say then? shall we continue in sin, that grace may abound?

God forbid. For we that are dead to sin, how shall we live any longer therein? . . .

For we are buried together with him by baptism into death; that as Christ is risen from the dead by the glory of the Father, so we also may walk in newness of life. . . .

Knowing this, that our old man is crucified with him, that the body of sin may be destroyed, to the end that we may serve sin no longer.—*Rom.* vi. 1, 2, 4, 6.

AMENDMENT OF LIFE, EXHORTATION TO

Turn to the Lord, and forsake thy sins:

Make thy prayer before the face of the Lord, and offend less.

Return to the Lord, and turn away from thy injustice, and greatly hate abomination.

And know the justices and judgments of God, and stand firm in the lot set before thee, and in prayer to the most high God.—*Ecclus.* xvii. 21-24.

My son, hast thou sinned? do so no more: but for thy former sins also pray that they may be forgiven thee.—*Ecclus.* xxi. 1.

Wash yourselves, be clean, take away the evil of your devices from my eyes: cease to do perversely,

Learn to do well: seek judgment, relieve the oppressed, judge for the fatherless, defend the widow.

And then come, and accuse me, saith the Lord: if your sins be as scarlet, they shall be made as white as snow: and if they be red as crimson, they shall be white as wool.—*Is.* i. 16-18.

Let the wicked forsake his way, and the unjust man his thoughts, and let him return to the Lord, and he will have mercy on him, and to our God: for he is bountiful to forgive.—*Is.* lv. 7.

For thus saith the Lord to the men of Juda and Jerusalem: Break up anew your fallow ground, and sow not upon thorns. . . .

Wash thy heart from wickedness, O Jerusalem, that thou mayst be saved: how long shall hurtful thoughts abide in thee?—*Jer.* iv. 3, 14.

Now therefore, tell the men of Juda, and the inhabitants of Jerusalem, saying: Thus saith the Lord: Behold I frame evil against you, and devise a device against you: let every man of you return from his evil way, and make ye your ways and your doings good.—*Jer.* xviii. 11.

Now therefore amend your ways, and your doings, and hearken to the voice of the Lord your God: and the Lord will repent him of the evil that he hath spoken against you.—*Jer.* xxvi. 13.

Cast away from you all your transgressions, by which you have transgressed, and make to yourselves a new heart, and a new spirit: and why will you die, O house of Israel?—*Ezech.* xviii. 31.

But now put you also all away: anger, indignation, malice, blasphemy, filthy speech out of your mouth.

Lie not one to another: stripping yourselves of the old man with his deeds,

And putting on the new, him who is renewed unto knowledge, according to the image of him that created him.—*Col.* iii. 8-10.

Draw nigh to God, and he will draw nigh to you. Cleanse your hands, ye sinners: and purify your hearts, ye double minded.—*James* iv. 8.

ANGER

Anger indeed killeth the foolish one, and envy slayeth the little one.—*Job* v. 2.

Be ye angry, and sin not: the things that you say in your hearts, be sorry for them upon your beds.—*Ps.* iv. 5.

A mild answer breaketh wrath: but a harsh word stirreth up fury. . . .

A passionate man stirreth up strifes: he that is patient appeaseth those that are stirred up.—*Prov.* xv. 1, 18.

The spirit of a man upholdeth his infirmity: but a spirit that is easily angered, who can bear?—*Prov.* xviii. 14.

As coals are to burning coals, and wood to fire, so an angry man stirreth up strife.—*Prov.* xxvi. 21.

A stone is heavy, and sand weighty: but the anger of a fool is heavier than them both.

Anger hath no mercy, nor fury when it breaketh forth: and who can bear the violence of one provoked?—*Prov.* xxvii. 3, 4.

A passionate man provoketh quarrels: and he that is easily stirred up to wrath, shall be more prone to sin.—*Prov.* xxix. 22.

There is a lying rebuke in the anger of an injurious man.—*Ecclus.* xix. 28.

How much better is it to reprove, than to be angry, and not to hinder him that confesseth in prayer.—*Ecclus.* xx.1.

There is no head worse than the head of a serpent:

And there is no anger above the anger of a woman. It will be more agreeable to abide with a lion and a dragon, than to dwell with a wicked woman.—*Ecclus.* xxv. 22, 23.

For a passionate man kindleth strife, and a sinful man will trouble his friends, and bring in debate in the midst of them that are at peace.

For as the wood of the forest is, so the fire burneth: and as a man's strength is, so shall his anger be, and according to his riches he shall increase his anger.—*Ecclus.* xxviii. 11, 12.

And let every man be swift to hear, but slow to speak, and slow to anger.

For the anger of man worketh not the justice of God.—*James* i. 19, 20.

ANGER, FOLLY AND SINFULNESS OF

A fool immediately showeth his anger: but he that dissembleth injuries is wise.—*Prov.* xii. 16.

Be not quickly angry: for anger resteth in the bosom of a fool.—*Eccles.* vii. 10.

Anger and fury are both of them abominable, and the sinful man shall be subject to them.—*Ecclus.* xxvii. 33.

Envy and anger shorten a man's days, and pensiveness will bring old age before the time.—*Ecclus.* xxx. 26.

Thus saith the Lord: For three crimes of Edom, and for four, I will not convert him: because he hath pursued his brother with the sword, and hath cast off all pity, and hath carried on his fury, and hath kept his wrath to the end.—*Amos* i. 11.

But I say to you, that whosoever is angry with his brother, shall be in danger of the judgment. And whosoever shall say to his brother, Raca, shall be in danger of the council. And whosoever shall say, Thou fool, shall be in danger of hell fire.—*Matt.* v. 22.

ANGER, EXHORTATION AGAINST

Therefore let not anger overcome thee to oppress any man.—*Job* xxxvi.18.

Cease from anger, and leave rage; have no emulation to do evil.—*Ps.* xxxvi. 8.

Be not quickly angry: for anger resteth in the bosom of a fool.—*Eccles.* vii. 10.

Remove anger from thy heart, and put away evil from thy flesh. For youth and pleasure are vain.—*Eccles.* xi. 10.

Be not as a lion in thy house, terrifying them of thy household, and oppressing them that are under thee.—*Ecclus.* iv. 35.

Remember the fear of God, and be not angry with thy neighbor.—*Ecclus.* xxviii. 8.

Be angry, and sin not. Let not the sun go down upon your anger. . . .

Let all bitterness, and anger, and indignation, and clamor, and blasphemy, be put away from you, with all malice. —*Eph.* iv. 26, 31.

And let every man be swift to hear, but slow to speak, and slow to anger. —*James* i. 19.

ANGER OF GOD, THE

The kings of the earth stood up, and the princes met together, against the Lord, and against his Christ. . . . He that dwelleth in heaven shall laugh at them: and the Lord shall deride them. Then shall he speak to them in his anger, and trouble them in his rage.— *Ps.* ii. 2, 4, 5.

Embrace discipline, lest at any time the Lord be angry, and you perish from the just way.

When his wrath shall be kindled in a short time, blessed are all they that trust in him.—*Ps.* ii. 12, 13.

For wrath is in his indignation; and life in his good will.—*Ps.* xxix. 6.

Thy wrath hath come upon me: and thy terrors have troubled me.

They have come round about me like water all the day: they have compassed me about together.—*Ps.* lxxxvii. 17, 18.

Forty years long was I offended with that generation, and I said: These always err in heart.

And these men have not known my ways: so I swore in my wrath that they shall not enter into my rest.—*Ps.* xciv. 10, 11.

And he will sharpen his severe wrath for a spear, and the whole world shall fight with him against the unwise.— *Wis.* v. 21.

Delay not to be converted to the Lord, and defer it not from day to day. For his wrath shall come on a sudden, and in the time of vengeance he will destroy thee.—*Ecclus.* v. 8, 9.

Remember wrath, for it will not tarry long.—*Ecclus.* vii. 18.

For mercy and wrath are with him. He is mighty to forgive, and to pour out indignation.—*Ecclus.* xvi. 12.

The Lord is a jealous God, and a revenger: the Lord is a revenger, and hath wrath: the Lord taketh vengeance on his adversaries, and he is angry with his enemies.—*Nahum* i. 2.

And the angel that spoke in me, said to me: Cry thou, saying: Thus saith the Lord of hosts: I am zealous for Jerusalem, and Sion with a great zeal.

And I am angry with a great anger with the wealthy nations: for I was angry a little, but they helped forward the evil.—*Zach.* i. 14, 15.

And seeing many of the Pharisees and Sadducees, coming to his baptism, [1]he said to them: Ye brood of vipers, who hath showed you to flee from the wrath to come?

Bring forth therefore fruit worthy of penance.—*Matt.* iii. 7, 8.

For the wrath of God is revealed from heaven against all ungodliness and injustice of those men that detain the truth of God in injustice.—*Rom.* i. 18.

Or despisest thou the riches of his goodness, and patience, and longsuffering? Knowest thou not, that the benignity of God leadeth thee to penance?

But according to thy hardness and impenitent heart, thou treasurest up to thyself wrath, against the day of wrath, and revelation of the just judgment of God.—*Rom.* ii. 4, 5.

But to them that are contentious, and who obey not the truth, but give credit to iniquity, wrath and indignation.—*Rom.* ii. 8.

And one of the four living creatures gave to the seven angels seven golden vials, full of the wrath of God, who liveth for ever and ever. . . .

And I heard a great voice out of the temple, saying to the seven angels: Go, and pour out the seven vials of the wrath of God upon the earth.—*Apoc.* xv. 7; xvi. 1.

ANGER OF GOD, POWER OF THE

And in the multitude of thy glory thou hast put down thy adversaries: thou hast sent thy wrath, which hath devoured them like stubble.

And with the blast of thy anger the waters were gathered together: the flowing water stood, the depths were gathered together in the midst of the sea. . . . Thy wind blew and the sea

[1]John the Baptist.

ANGER

31

covered them: they sunk as lead in the mighty waters.—*Ex.* xv. 7, 8, 10.

On the contrary I have seen those who work iniquity, and sow sorrows, and reap them,

Perishing by the blast of God, and consumed by the spirit of his wrath.—*Job* iv. 8, 9.

God, whose wrath no man can resist, and under whom they stoop that bear up the world.—*Job* ix. 13.

Rebuke me not, O Lord, in thy indignation; nor chastise me in thy wrath. . . .

There is no health in my flesh, because of thy wrath: there is no peace for my bones, because of my sins.—*Ps.* xxxvii. 2, 4.

Thou art terrible, and who shall resist thee? [1]from that time thy wrath.—*Ps.* lxxv. 8.

Who knoweth the power of thy anger, and for thy fear can number thy wrath? —*Ps.* lxxxix. 11, 12.

Because of thy anger and indignation: for having lifted me up, thou hast thrown me down.—*Ps.* ci. 11.

The Lord at thy right hand hath broken kings in the day of his wrath.

He shall judge among nations, he shall fill ruins: he shall crush the heads in the land of many.—*Ps.* cix. 5, 6.

By the wrath of the Lord of hosts the land is troubled, and the people shall be as fuel for the fire.—*Is.* ix. 19.

Behold the name of the Lord cometh from afar, his wrath burneth, and is heavy to bear: his lips are filled with indignation, and his tongue as a devouring fire.

His breath as a torrent overflowing even to the midst of the neck, to destroy the nations unto nothing, and the bridle of error that was in the jaws of the people.—*Is.* xxx. 27, 28.

Behold the whirlwind of the Lord's indignation shall come forth, and a tempest shall break out and come upon the head of the wicked. The wrath of the Lord shall not return till he execute it, and till he accomplish the thought of his heart: in the latter days you shall understand his counsel.—*Jer.* xxiii. 19, 20.

[1]That is, from the time that thy wrath shall break out.

Who can stand before the face of his indignation? and who shall resist in the fierceness of his anger? his indignation is poured out like fire: and the rocks are melted by him.—*Nahum* i. 6.

ANGER OF GOD, TERROR OF THE

A fire is kindled in my wrath, and shall burn even to the lowest hell: and shall devour the earth with her increase, and shall burn the foundations of the mountains.—*Deut.* xxxii. 22.

For the arrows of the Lord are in me, the rage whereof drinketh up my spirit, and the terrors of the Lord war against me.—*Job* vi. 4.

The earth shook and trembled: the foundations of the mountains were troubled and were moved, because he was angry with them.

There went up a smoke in his wrath: and a fire flamed from his face: coals were kindled by it. . . .

Then the fountains of water appeared, and the foundations of the earth were discovered:

At thy rebuke, O Lord, at the blast of the spirit of thy wrath.—*Ps.* xvii. 8, 9, 16.

For in thy wrath we have fainted away: and are troubled in thy indignation.

Thou hast set our iniquities before thy eyes: our life in the light of thy countenance.

For all our days are spent; and in thy wrath we have fainted away.—*Ps.* lxxxix. 7-9.

Behold the day of the Lord shall come, a cruel day, and full of indignation, and of wrath, and fury, to lay the land desolate, and to destroy the sinners thereof out of it. . . .

For this I will trouble the heaven: and the earth shall be moved out of her place, for the indignation of the Lord of hosts, and for the day of his fierce wrath.—*Is.* xiii. 9, 13.

But the Lord is the true God: he is the living God, and the everlasting king: at his wrath the earth shall tremble, and the nations shall not be able to abide his threatening.—*Jer.* x. 10.

In thy anger thou wilt tread the earth,

under foot: in thy wrath thou wilt astonish the nations.—*Hab.* iii. 12.

And the kings of the earth, and the princes, and tribunes, and the rich, and the strong, and every bondman, and every freeman, hid themselves in the dens and in the rocks of mountains:

And they say to the mountains and the rocks: Fall upon us, and hide us from the face of him that sitteth upon the throne, and from the wrath of the Lamb:

For the great day of their wrath is come, and who shall be able to stand?—*Apoc.* vi. 15, 16, 17.

And the angel thrust in his sharp sickle into the earth, and gathered the vineyard of the earth, and cast it into the great press of the wrath of God:

And the press was trodden without the city, and blood came out of the press, up to the horses' bridles, for a thousand and six hundred furlongs.—*Apoc.* xiv. 19, 20.

ANGER OF GOD, A PRAYER TO AVERT THE

O Lord, rebuke me not in thy indignation, nor chastise me in thy wrath.—*Ps.* vi. 2.

How long, O Lord, wilt thou be angry for ever: shall thy zeal be kindled like a fire?—*Ps.* lxxviii. 5.

Convert us, O God our saviour: and turn off thy anger from us.

Wilt thou be angry with us for ever: or wilt thou extend thy wrath from generation to generation?—*Ps.* lxxxiv. 5, 6.

How long, O Lord, turnest thou away unto the end? shall thy anger burn like fire?

Remember what my substance is: for hast thou made all the children of men in vain?—*Ps.* lxxxviii. 47, 48.

Be not very angry, O Lord, and remember no longer our iniquity: behold, see we are all thy people.—*Is.* lxiv. 9.

We have sinned, we have done wickedly, we have acted unjustly, O Lord our God, against all thy justices.

Let thy wrath be turned away from us: for we are left a few among the nations where thou hast scattered us.—*Bar.* ii. 12, 13.

And now, O Lord our God, . . . we have sinned, we have committed iniquity,

O Lord, against all thy justice: let thy wrath and thy indignation be turned away, I beseech thee, from thy city Jerusalem, and from thy holy mountain. For by reason of our sins, and the iniquities of our fathers, Jerusalem, and thy people are a reproach to all that are round about us.—*Dan.* ix. 15, 16.

APOSTATES

A man that is an apostate, an unprofitable man, walketh with a perverse mouth. . . .

To such a one his destruction shall presently come, and he shall suddenly be destroyed, and shall no longer have any remedy.—*Prov.* vi. 12, 15.

Woe to you, apostate children, saith the Lord, that you would take counsel, and not of me: and would begin a web, and not by my spirit, that you might add sin upon sin.—*Is.* xxx. 1.

Thy own wickedness shall reprove thee, and thy apostasy shall rebuke thee. Know thou, and see that it is an evil and a bitter thing for thee, to have left the Lord thy God, and that my fear is not with thee, saith the Lord the God of hosts.—*Jer.* ii. 19.

For you have forgotten God, who brought you up, and you have grieved Jerusalem that nursed you.—*Bar.* iv. 8.

But he that shall deny me before men, I will also deny him before my Father who is in heaven.—*Matt.* x. 33.

APPROVE OF EVIL-DOERS AND THEIR WORK, WE MUST NOT

See: Wicked; we must not uphold the—page 597.

ASCENSION OF CHRIST INTO HEAVEN

Lift up your gates, O ye princes, and be ye lifted up, O eternal gates: and the King of Glory shall enter in.

Who is this King of Glory? the Lord who is strong and mighty: the Lord mighty in battle.

Lift up your gates, O ye princes, and be ye lifted up, O eternal gates: and the King of Glory shall enter in.

Who is this King of Glory? the Lord of hosts, he is the King of Glory.—*Ps.* xxiii. 7-10.

God is ascended with jubilee, and the Lord with the sound of trumpet.—*Ps.* xlvi. 6.

Sing ye to God, sing a psalm to his name, make a way for him who ascendeth upon the west: the Lord is his name.—*Ps.* lxvii. 5.

The chariot of God is attended by ten thousands; thousands of them that rejoice: the Lord is among them in Sina, in the holy place.

Thou hast ascended on high, thou hast led captivity captive; thou hast received gifts in men.—*Ps.* lxvii. 18, 19.

Sing to God, ye kingdoms of the earth: sing ye to the Lord. Sing ye to God, who mounteth above the heaven of heavens, to the east.—*Ps.* lxvii. 33, 34.

And the Lord Jesus, after he had spoken to them, was taken up into heaven, and sitteth on the right hand of God.—*Mark* xvi. 19.

And he led them out as far as Bethania: and lifting up his hands, he blessed them.

And it came to pass, whilst he blessed them, he departed from them, and was carried up to heaven.—*Luke* xxiv. 50, 51.

And no man hath ascended into heaven, but he that descended from heaven, the Son of man who is in heaven.—*John* iii. 13.

But Jesus, knowing in himself, that his disciples murmured at this, said to them: Doth this scandalize you?

If then you shall see the Son of man ascend up where he was before?—*John* vi. 62, 63.

I came forth from the Father, and am come into the world: again I leave the world, and I go to the Father.—*John* xvi. 28.

Jesus saith to her: Do not touch me, for I am not yet ascended to my Father. But go to my brethren, and say to them: I ascend to my Father and to your Father, to my God and your God.—*John* xx. 17.

And when he had said these things, while they looked on, he was raised up: and a cloud received him out of their sight.

And while they were beholding him going up to heaven, behold two men stood by them in white garments.

Who also said: Ye men of Galilee, why stand you looking up to heaven? This Jesus who is taken up from you into heaven, shall so come, as you have seen him going into heaven.—*Acts* i. 9-11.

Wherefore he saith: Ascending on high, he led captivity captive; he gave gifts to men.

Now that he ascended, what is it, but because he also descended first into the lower parts of the earth?

He that descended is the same also that ascended above all the heavens, that he might fill all things.—*Eph.* iv. 8-10.

For Jesus is not entered into the holies made with hands, the patterns of the true: but into heaven itself, that he may appear now in the presence of God for us.—*Heb.* ix. 24.

ATHEISTS

After these things Moses and Aaron went in, and said to Pharao: Thus saith the Lord God of Israel: Let my people go that they may sacrifice to me in the desert.

But he answered: Who is the Lord, that I should hear his voice, and let Israel go? I know not the Lord, neither will I let Israel go.—*Ex.* v. 1, 2.

The fool hath said in his heart: There is no God.—*Ps.* xiii. 1.

For thou showest thy power, when men will not believe thee to be absolute in power, and thou convincest the boldest of them that know thee not.—*Wis.* xii. 17.

But all men are vain, in whom there is not the knowledge of God: and who by these good things that are seen, could not understand him that is, neither by attending to the works have acknowledged who was the workman. . . .

But yet as to these they are less to be blamed. For they perhaps err, seeking God, and desirous to find him.

For being conversant among his works, they search: and they are persuaded that the things are good which are seen.

But then again they are not to be pardoned.

For if they were able to know so much as to make a judgment of the world: how did they not more easily find out the Lord thereof?—*Wis.* xiii. 1, 6-9.

For his heart is ashes, and his hope vain earth, and his life more base than clay:

Forasmuch as he knew not his maker and him that inspired into him the soul that worketh, and that breathed into him a living spirit.

Yea, and they have counted our life a pastime, and the business of life to be gain, and that we must be getting every way, even out of evil.—*Wis.* xv. 10-12.

But it is impossible to escape thy hand.

For the wicked that denied to know thee, were scourged by the strength of thy arm, being persecuted by strange waters, and hail, and rain, and consumed by fire.—*Wis.* xvi. 15, 16.

And to you who are troubled, rest with us when the Lord Jesus shall be revealed from heaven, with the angels of his power:

In a flame of fire, giving vengeance to them who know not God, and who obey not the gospel of our Lord Jesus Christ.

Who shall suffer eternal punishment in destruction, from the face of the Lord, and from the glory of his power. —2 *Thess.* i. 7-9.

ATONEMENT FOR SIN

See: Penance—page 375.

AUTHORITY OR POWER IS FROM GOD, ALL

By [1]me kings reign, and lawgivers decree just things,

By me princes rule, and the mighty decree justice.—*Prov.* viii. 15, 16.

Hear therefore, ye kings, and understand: learn, ye that are judges of the ends of the earth.

Give ear, you that rule the people,

[1]The wisdom of God.

and that please yourselves in multitudes of nations:

For power is given to you by the Lord, and strength by the most High, who will examine your works, and search out your thoughts.—*Wis.* vi. 2-4.

The power of the earth is in the hand of God, and in his time he will raise up a profitable ruler over it.—*Ecclus.* x. 4.

This is the decree by the sentence of the watchers, and the word and demand of the holy ones; till the living know that the most High ruleth in the kingdom of men; and he will give it to whomsoever it shall please him, and he will appoint the basest man over it. . . .

This is the interpretation of the sentence of the most High, which is come upon my lord the [1]king.

They shall cast thee out from among men, and thy dwelling shall be with cattle and with wild beasts, and thou shalt eat grass as an ox, and shalt be wet with the dew of heaven: and seven times shall pass over thee, till thou know that the most High ruleth over the kingdom of men, and giveth it to whomsoever he will.

But whereas he commanded, that the stump of the roots thereof, that is, of the tree, should be left: thy kingdom shall remain to thee after thou shalt have known that power is from heaven. —*Dan.* iv. 14, 21-23.

Let every soul be subject to higher powers: for there is no power but from God: and those that are, are ordained of God.

Therefore he that resisteth the power, resisteth the ordinance of God. And they that resist purchase to themselves damnation. . . .

For he is God's minister to thee, for good. But if thou do that which is evil, fear: for he beareth not the sword in vain. For he is God's minister: an avenger to execute wrath upon him that doth evil.

Wherefore be subject of necessity, not only for wrath, but also for conscience' sake.

For therefore also you pay tribute. For they are the ministers of God, serv-

[1]Nabuchodonosor.

ing unto this purpose.—*Rom.* xiii. 1, 2, 4-6.

Be ye subject therefore to every human creature for God's sake: whether it be to the king as excelling;

Or to governors as sent by him for the punishment of evil-doers, and for the praise of the good:

For so is the will of God, that by doing well you may put to silence the ignorance of foolish men.—1 *Peter* ii. 13-15.

AVARICE

See: Covetousness—page 86, and Riches, love of—page 492.

BACKBITING

See: Detraction—page 110.

BEAUTY OF BODY IS VAIN AND OF LITTLE VALUE

And the Lord said to Samuel: Look not on his countenance, nor on the height of his stature: because I have rejected him, nor do I judge according to the look of man: for man seeth those things that appear, but the Lord beholdeth the heart.—1 *Kings* xvi. 7.

Favor is deceitful, and beauty is vain: the woman that feareth the Lord, she shall be praised.—*Prov.* xxxi. 30.

Praise not a man for his beauty, neither despise a man for his look.—*Ecclus.* xi. 2.

Look not upon a woman's beauty, and desire not a woman for beauty.—*Ecclus.* xxv. 28.

BISHOPS OF THE CHURCH, CHARACTER AND DUTIES REQUIRED OF THE

Take heed to yourselves, and to the whole flock, wherein the Holy Ghost hath placed you bishops, to rule the church of God, which he hath purchased with his own blood.—*Acts* xx. 28.

A faithful saying: if a man desire the office of a bishop, he desireth a good work.

It behoveth therefore a bishop to be blameless, the husband of one wife, sober, prudent, of good behavior, chaste, given to hospitality, a teacher,

Not given to wine, no striker, but modest, not quarrelsome, not covetous, but

One that ruleth well his own house, having his children in subjection with all chastity.

But if a man know not how to rule his own house, how shall he take care of the church of God?

Not a neophyte: lest being puffed up with pride, he fall into the judgment of the devil.

Moreover he must have a good testimony of them who are without: lest he fall into reproach and the snare of the devil.—1 *Tim.* iii. 1-7.

Impose not hands lightly upon any man, neither be partaker of other men's sins. Keep thyself chaste.—1 *Tim.* v. 22.

For a bishop must be without crime, as the steward of God: not proud, not subject to anger, not given to wine, no striker, not greedy of filthy lucre:

But given to hospitality, gentle, sober, just, holy, continent:

Embracing that faithful word which is according to doctrine, that he may be able to exhort in sound doctrine, and to convince the gainsayers.—*Titus* i. 7-10.

For every high priest taken from among men, is ordained for men in the things that appertain to God, that he may offer up gifts and sacrifices for sins:

Who can have compassion on them that are ignorant and that err: because he himself also is compassed with infirmity.

And therefore he ought, as for the people, so also for himself, to offer for sins.

Neither doth any man take the honor to himself, but he that is called by God, as Aaron was.—*Heb.* v. 1-4.

The ancients therefore that are among you, I beseech, who am myself also an ancient, and a witness of the sufferings of Christ: as also a partaker of that glory which is to be revealed in time to come:

Feed the flock of God which is among you, taking care of it, not by constraint, but willingly, according to God: not for filthy lucre's sake, but voluntarily:

Neither as lording it over the clergy, but being made a pattern of the flock from the heart.

And when the prince of pastors shall appear, you shall receive a never-fading crown of glory.—1 *Peter* v. 1-4.

BLASPHEMY

And thou shalt speak to the children of Israel: the man that curseth his God, shall bear his sin:

And he that blasphemeth the name of the Lord, dying let him die: all the multitude shall stone him, whether he be a native or a stranger. He that blasphemeth the name of the Lord, dying let him die.—*Lev.* xxiv. 15, 16.

Whom hast thou reproached, and whom hast thou blasphemed? against whom hast thou exalted thy voice, and lifted up thy eyes on high? against the holy one of Israel.—4 *Kings* xix. 22.

For such as bless ¹him shall inherit the land: but such as curse him shall perish.—*Ps.* xxxvi. 22.

Then was offered to him one possessed with a devil, blind and dumb: and he healed him, so that he spoke and saw.

And all the multitudes were amazed, and said: Is not this the son of David?

But the Pharisees hearing it, said: This man casteth not out devils but by Beelzebub, the prince of the devils.—*Matt.* xii. 22-24.

And whosoever speaketh a word against the Son of man, it shall be forgiven him: but to him that shall blaspheme against the Holy Ghost, it shall not be forgiven.—*Luke* xii. 10.

The Jews therefore answered, and said to him: Do not we say well that thou art a Samaritan, and hast a devil?

Jesus answered: I have not a devil: but I honor my Father, and you have dishonored me.—*John* viii. 48, 49.

But now, put you also all away: anger, indignation, malice, blasphemy, filthy speech out of your mouth.—*Col.* iii. 8.

In like manner these men also defile the flesh, and despise dominion, and blaspheme majesty.

When Michael the archangel, disputing with the devil, contended about the

¹The Lord.

body of Moses, he durst not bring against him the judgment of railing speech, but said: The Lord command thee.

But these men blaspheme whatever things they know not. . . .

Now of these Enoch also, the seventh from Adam, prophesied, saying: Behold, the Lord cometh with thousands of his saints,

To execute judgment upon all, and to reprove all the ungodly for all the works of their ungodliness, whereby they have done ungodly, and of all the hard things which ungodly sinners have spoken against God.—*Jude* i. 8-10, 14, 15.

BLESS GOD, EXHORTATION TO

Blessed be the Lord the God of Israel from eternity to eternity: and let all the people say Amen, and a hymn to God.—1 *Paral.* xvi. 36.

Bless God at all times: and desire of him to direct thy ways.—*Tob.* iv. 20.

Then ¹he said to them secretly: Bless ye the God of heaven, give glory to him in the sight of all that live, because he hath shown his mercy to you.—*Tob.* xii. 6.

Bless ye the Lord, all his elect, keep days of joy, and give glory to him.—*Tob.* xiii. 10.

My soul, bless thou the Lord, because the Lord our God hath delivered Jerusalem his city from all her troubles.—*Tob.* xiii. 19.

Sing ye to the Lord, and bless his name: show forth his salvation from day to day.—*Ps.* xcv. 2.

Bless the Lord, O my soul: and let all that is within me bless his holy name.

Bless the Lord, O my soul, and never forget all that he hath done for thee.—*Ps.* cii. 1, 2.

Bless the Lord, all ye his angels: you that are mighty in strength, and execute his word, hearkening to the voice of his orders.

Bless the Lord, all ye his hosts: you ministers of his that do his will.

Bless the Lord, all his works: in every place of his dominion, O my soul, bless thou the Lord.—*Ps.* cii. 20, 21, 22.

¹The angel Raphael to Tobias and his son.

Behold now bless ye the Lord, all ye servants of the Lord:

Who stand in the house of the Lord, in the courts of the house of our God.

In the nights lift up your hands to the holy places, and bless ye the Lord.— *Ps.* cxxxiii. 1, 2.

Bless the Lord, O house of Israel: bless the Lord, O house of Aaron.

Bless the Lord, O house of Levi: you that fear the Lord, bless the Lord.—*Ps.* cxxxiv. 19, 20.

For ¹that which could not be destroyed by fire, being warmed with a little sunbeam presently melted away:

That it might be known to all that we ought to prevent the sun to bless thee, and adore thee at the dawning of the light.—*Wis.* xvi. 27, 28.

And for all these things bless the Lord, that made thee, and that replenisheth thee with all his good things.— *Ecclus.* xxxii. 17.

Now therefore with the whole heart and mouth praise ye him, and bless the name of the Lord.—*Ecclus.* xxxix. 41.

Look upon the rainbow, and bless him that made it: it is very beautiful in its brightness.—*Ecclus.* xliii. 12.

Blessing the Lord, exalt him as much as you can: for he is above all praise.

When you exalt him, put forth all your strength, and be not weary, for you can never go far enough.—*Ecclus.* xliii. 33, 34.

All ye works of the Lord, bless the Lord: praise and exalt him above all for ever.

O ye angels of the Lord, bless the Lord: praise and exalt him above all for ever. . . .

O ye sons of men, bless the Lord: praise and exalt him above all for ever.

O let Israel bless the Lord: let them praise and exalt him above all for ever.

O ye priests of the Lord, bless the Lord: praise and exalt him above all for ever.

O ye servants of the Lord, bless the Lord: praise and exalt him above all for ever.

O ye spirits and souls of the just, bless the Lord: praise and exalt him above all for ever.

O ye holy and humble of heart, bless

¹The manna in the desert.

the Lord: praise and exalt him above all for ever. . . .

O all ye religious, bless the Lord the God of gods: praise him and give him thanks, because his mercy endureth for ever and ever.—*Dan.* iii. 57, 58, 82-87, 90.

BLESSING OF GOD, THE

And ¹they shall invoke my name upon the children of Israel, and I will bless them.—*Num.* vi. 27.

And thou hast begun to bless the house of thy ²servant, that it may be always before thee: for seeing thou blessest it, O Lord, it shall be blessed for ever.—1 *Paral.* xvii. 27.

Salvation is of the Lord: and thy blessing is upon thy people.—*Ps.* iii. 9.

The Lord hath been mindful of us, and hath blessed us.

He hath blessed the house of Israel: he hath blessed the house of Aaron.

He hath blessed all that fear the Lord, both little and great.—*Ps.* cxiii. (*Heb.* cxv.) 12, 13.

The blessing of the Lord is upon the head of the just.—*Prov.* x. 6.

The blessing of the Lord maketh men rich: neither shall affliction be joined to them.—*Prov.* x. 22.

The blessing of God maketh haste to reward the just, and in a swift hour his blessing beareth fruit.—*Ecclus.* xi. 24.

In the blessing of God I also have hoped: and as one that gathereth grapes, have I filled the winepress.— *Ecclus.* xxxiii. 17.

His blessing hath overflowed like a river.

And as a flood hath watered the earth.—*Ecclus.* xxxix. 27, 28.

Blessed be the God and Father of our Lord Jesus Christ, who hath blessed us with spiritual blessings in heavenly ³places, in Christ.—*Eph.* i. 3.

BLESSING OF GOD, A PRAYER FOR THE

The Lord bless thee, and keep thee.

The Lord show his face to thee, and have mercy on thee.

The Lord turn his countenance to

¹Aaron and his sons in their priestly functions.
²David.
³Or, in heavenly things.

thee, and give thee peace.—*Num.* vi. 24-26.

Look from thy sanctuary, and thy high habitation of heaven, and bless thy people Israel, and the land which thou hast given us, as thou didst swear to our fathers, a land flowing with milk and honey.—*Deut.* xxvi. 15.

Save, O Lord, thy people, and bless thy inheritance: and rule them and exalt them for ever.—*Ps.* xxvii. 9.

May God, our God, bless us, may God bless us: and all the ends of the earth fear him.—*Ps.* lxvi. 7, 8.

May the Lord add blessings upon you: upon you, and upon your children. Blessed be you of the Lord, who made heaven and earth.—*Ps.* cxiii. (*Heb.* cxv.) 14, 15.

May the Lord out of Sion bless thee, he that made heaven and earth.—*Ps.* cxxxiii. 3.

BLESSINGS, THE VALUE OF

And the Lord spoke to Moses, saying: Say to Aaron and his sons: Thus shall you bless the children of Israel, and you shall say to them:

The Lord bless thee, and keep thee.

The Lord show his face to thee, and have mercy on thee.

The Lord turn his countenance to thee, and give thee peace.

And they shall invoke my name upon the children of Israel, and I will bless them.—*Num.* vi. 22-27.

And the priests and the Levites rose up and blessed the people: and their voice was heard: and their prayer came to the holy dwelling place of heaven.— 2 *Paral.* xxx. 27.

For every creature of God is good, and nothing to be rejected that is received with thanksgiving:

For it is sanctified by the word of God and prayer.—1 *Tim.* iv. 4, 5.

BLIND, THE

See: Afflicted with bodily infirmities, the—page 22.

BLINDNESS OF HEART A PUNISHMENT FROM GOD

They shall meet with darkness in the day, and grope at noon-day as in the night.—*Job* v. 14.

He changeth the heart of the princes of the people of the earth, and deceiveth them that they walk in vain where there is no way.

They shall grope as in the dark, and not in the light, and he shall make them stagger like men that are drunk. —*Job* xii. 24, 25.

Therefore we have erred from the way of truth, and the light of justice hath not shined unto us, and the sun of understanding hath not risen upon us.

We wearied ourselves in the way of iniquity and destruction, and have walked through hard ways, but the way of the Lord we have not known.—*Wis.* v. 6, 7.

And he (God) said: Go, and thou shalt say to this people: Hearing, hear, and understand not: and see the vision, and know it not.

Blind the heart of this people, and make their ears heavy, and shut their eyes: lest they see with their eyes, and hear with their ears, and understand with their heart, and be converted and I heal them.—*Is.* vi. 9, 10.

Many shall be chosen, and made white, and shall be tried as fire: and the wicked shall deal wickedly, and none of the wicked shall understand, but the learned shall understand.— *Dan.* xii. 10.

And he (Christ) said to them: To you it is given to know the mystery of the kingdom of God: but to them that are without, all things are done in parables:

That seeing they may see, and not perceive; and hearing they may hear, and not understand: lest at any time they should be converted, and their sins should be forgiven them.—*Mark* iv. 11, 12.

And whereas he (Christ) had done so many miracles before them, they believed not in him:

That the saying of Isaias the prophet might be fulfilled, which he said: Lord, who hath believed our hearing? and to whom hath the arm of the Lord been revealed?

Therefore they could not believe, because Isaias said again:

He hath blinded their eyes, and hardened their heart, that they should not see with their eyes, nor understand with their heart, and be converted, and I should heal them.—*John* xii. 37-40.

And not as Moses put a veil upon his face, that the children of Israel might not steadfastly look on the face of that which is made void.

But their senses were made dull. For, until this present day, the self-same veil, in the reading of the old testament, remaineth not taken away (because in Christ it is made void).

But even until this day, when Moses is read, the veil is upon their heart.

But when they shall be converted to the Lord, the veil shall be taken away. —2 *Cor.* iii. 13-16.

And if our gospel be also hid, it is hid to them that are lost,

In whom the god of this world hath blinded the minds of unbelievers, that the light of the gospel of the glory of Christ, who is the image of God, should not shine unto them.—2 *Cor.* iv. 3, 4.

BLINDNESS OF HEART, WILFUL

They have been rebellious to the light, they have not known his ways, neither have they returned by his paths. —*Job* xxiv. 13.

The words of his mouth are iniquity and guile: he would not understand that he might do well.—*Ps.* xxxv. 4.

And man when he was in honor did not understand; he is compared to senseless beasts, and is become like to them.—*Ps.* xlviii. 13.

The wicked are alienated from the womb; they have gone astray from the womb: they have spoken false things.

Their madness is according to the likeness of a serpent: like the deaf asp that stoppeth her ears:

Which will not hear the voice of the charmers; nor of the wizard that charmeth wisely.—*Ps.* lvii. 4-6.

And ¹he hath poured out upon him the indignation of his fury, and a strong battle, and hath burnt him round about, and he knew not: and set him on fire, and he understood not.—*Is.* xlii. 25.

Bring forth the people that are blind,

¹God punishing the sinner.

and have eyes: that are deaf, and have ears.—*Is.* xliii. 8.

O Lord, thy eyes are upon truth: thou hast struck them, and they have not grieved: thou hast bruised them, and they have refused to receive correction: they have made their faces harder than the rock, and they have refused to return.—*Jer.* v. 3.

And looking round about on them with anger, being grieved for the blindness of their hearts, he (Christ) sayeth to the man: Stretch forth thy hand. And he stretched it forth: and his hand was restored unto him.—*Mark* iii. 5.

In him was life, and the life was the light of men.

And the light shineth in darkness, and the darkness did not comprehend it. . . .

He was in the world, and the world was made by him, and the world knew him not.—*John* i. 4, 5, 10.

And this is the judgment: because the light is come into the world, and men loved darkness rather than the light: for their works were evil.

For every one that doth evil hateth the light, and cometh not to the light, that his works may not be reproved.— *John* iii. 19, 20.

If I had not come, and spoken to them, they would not have sin; but now they have no excuse for their sin. . . .

If I had not done among them the works that no other man hath done, they would not have sin; but now they have both seen and hated both me and my Father.—*John* xv. 22, 24.

For they that inhabited Jerusalem, and the rulers thereof, not knowing ¹him, nor the voice of the prophets, which are read every Sabbath, judging him, have fulfilled them.—*Acts* xiii. 27.

And some believed the things that were said; but some believed not.

And when they agreed not among themselves, they departed, Paul speaking this one word: Well did the Holy Ghost speak to our fathers by Isaias the prophet,

Saying: Go to this people, and say to them: With the ear you shall hear,

¹Christ, the Saviour.

and shall not understand; and seeing you shall see, and shall not perceive.

For the heart of this people is grown gross, and with their ears have they heard heavily, and their eyes have they shut; lest perhaps they should see with their eyes, and hear with their ears, and understand with their heart, and should be converted, and I should heal them.—*Acts* xxviii. 24-27.

This then I say and testify in the Lord: That henceforward you walk not as also the Gentiles walk in the vanity of their mind,

Having their understanding darkened, being alienated from the life of God through the ignorance that is in them, because of the blindness of their hearts,

Who despairing, have given themselves up to lasciviousness, unto the working of all uncleanness, unto covetousness.—*Eph.* iv. 17-19.

Now as Jannes and Mambres resisted Moses, so these also resist the truth, men corrupted in mind, reprobate concerning the faith.—2 *Tim.* iii. 8.

Knowing this first, that in the last days there shall come deceitful scoffers, walking after their own lusts,

Saying: Where is his promise, or his coming? for since the time that the fathers slept, all things continue as they were from the beginning of the creation.

For this they are wilfully ignorant of, that the heavens were before, and the earth, out of water, and through water, consisting by the word of God.— 2 *Peter* iii. 3-5.

BLINDNESS OF HEART, COMPLAINT OF GOD AGAINST THOSE GUILTY OF WILFUL

And the Lord said to Moses: How long will this people detract me? how long will they not believe me for all the signs that I have wrought before them?—*Num.* xiv. 11.

Woe to you that call evil good, and good evil: that put darkness for light, and light for darkness: that put bitter for sweet, and sweet for bitter.—*Is.* v. 20.

For it is a people that provoketh to wrath, and lying children, children that will not hear the law of God.

Who say to the seers: See not: and to them that behold: Behold not for us those things that are right: speak unto us pleasant things, see errors for us.

Take away from me the way, turn away the path from me, let the Holy One of Israel cease from before us.— *Is.* xxx. 9-11.

Hear, ye deaf, and, ye blind, behold that you may see.

Who is blind, but my servant? or deaf, but he to whom I have sent my messengers? Who is blind, but he that is sold? or who is blind, but the servant of the Lord?

Thou that seest many things, wilt thou not observe them? thou that hast ears open, wilt thou not hear?—*Is.* xlii. 18-20.

Why will you contend with me in judgment? you have all forsaken me saith the Lord.

In vain have I struck your children they have not received correction.—*Jer* ii. 29, 30.

Thy habitation is in the midst of deceit: through deceit they have refused to know me, saith the Lord.—*Jer.* ix. 6

But they did not hear, nor incline their ear: but hardened their neck that they might not hear me, and might not receive instruction.—*Jer.* xvii. 23.

And I was like a foster father to Ephraim, I carried them in my arms: and they knew not that I healed them. —*Osee* xi. 3.

BLINDNESS OF HEART, PUNISHMENT OF WILFUL

From morning till evening they shall be cut down: and because no one understandeth, they shall perish for ever. —*Job* iv. 20.

He hath struck them, as being wicked, in open sight.

Who as it were on purpose have revolted from him, and would not understand all his ways.—*Job* xxxiv. 26, 27.

Because they have not understood the works of the Lord, and the operations of his hands: thou shalt destroy them, and shalt not build them up.—*Ps.* xxvii. 5.

The kite in the air hath known her

time: the turtle, and the swallow, and the stork have observed the time of their coming: but my people have not known the judgment of the Lord.

How do you say: We are wise, and the law of the Lord is with us? Indeed the lying pen of the scribes hath wrought falsehood.

The wise men are confounded, they are dismayed and taken: for they have cast away the word of the Lord, and there is no wisdom in them.—*Jer.* viii. 7-9.

Jesus saith to them: Amen, I say to you, that the publicans and the harlots shall go into the kingdom of God before you.

For John came to you in the way of justice, and you did not believe him. But the publicans and the harlots believed him: but you, seeing it, did not even afterwards repent, that you might believe him.—*Matt.* xxi. 31, 32.

And when he drew near, seeing the city, he wept over it, saying:

If thou also hadst known, and that in this thy day, the things that are to thy peace; but now they are hidden from thy eyes.

For the days shall come upon thee: and thy enemies shall cast a trench about thee, and compass thee round, and straiten thee on every side,

And beat thee flat to the ground, and thy children who are in thee: and they shall not leave in thee a stone upon a stone: because thou hast not known the time of thy visitation.—*Luke* xix. 41-44.

And as they liked not to have God in their knowledge, God delivered them up to a reprobate sense, to do those things which are not convenient. . . .

Who, having known the justice of God, did not understand that they who do such things, are worthy of death; and not only they that do them, but they also that consent to them that do them.—*Rom.* i. 28, 32.

And then that wicked one shall be revealed, whom the Lord Jesus shall kill with the spirit of his mouth; and shall destroy with the brightness of his coming, him,

Whose coming is according to the working of Satan, in all power, and signs, and lying wonders,

And in all seduction of iniquity to them that perish; because they receive not the love of the truth, that they might be saved. Therefore God shall send them the operation of error, to believe lying:

That all may be judged who have not believed the truth, but have consented to iniquity.—*2 Thess.* ii. 8-11.

BOASTING

As clouds, and wind, when no rain, followeth, so is the man that boasteth, and doth not fulfil his promises.—*Prov.* xxv. 14.

Boast not for to-morrow, for thou knowest not what the day to come may bring forth.—*Prov.* xxvii. 1.

Let another praise thee, and not thy own mouth: a stranger, and not thy own lips.—*Prov.* xxvii. 2.

He that boasteth, and puffeth up himself, stirreth up quarrels: but he that trusteth in the Lord shall be healed.—*Prov.* xxviii. 25.

Be not hasty in thy tongue: and slack and remiss in thy works.—*Ecclus.* iv. 34.

Extol not thyself in doing thy work, and linger not in the time of distress.—*Ecclus.* x. 29.

Better is he that laboreth, and aboundeth in all things, than he that boasteth himself, and wanteth bread.—*Ecclus.* x. 30.

Two men went up into the temple to pray: the one a Pharisee, and the other a publican.

The Pharisee standing, prayed thus with himself: O God, I give thee thanks that I am not as the rest of men, extortioners, unjust, adulterers, as also is this publican.

I fast twice in a week: I give tithes of all that I possess.

And the publican, standing afar off, would not so much as lift up his eyes towards heaven; but struck his breast, saying: O God, be merciful to me a sinner.

I say to you, this man went down into his house justified rather than the other: because every one that exalteth himself, shall be humbled: and he that humbleth himself, shall be exalted.—*Luke* xviii. 10-14.

And if some of the branches be broken, and thou, being a wild olive, art ingrafted in them, and art made partaker of the root, and of the fatness of the olive tree,

Boast not against the branches. But if thou boast, thou bearest not the root, but the root thee.

Thou wilt say then: The branches were broken off that I might be grafted in.

Well: because of unbelief they were broken off. But thou standest by faith: be not high-minded, but fear.

For if God hath not spared the natural branches, fear lest perhaps he also spare not thee.—*Rom.* xi. 17-21.

But he that glorieth, let him glory in the Lord.

For not he who commendeth himself, is approved, but he whom God commendeth.—*2 Cor.* x. 17, 18.

BODY, SANCTITY OF OUR

I beseech you, therefore, brethren, by the mercy of God, that you present your bodies a living sacrifice, holy, pleasing unto God, your reasonable service.—*Rom.* xii. 1.

Know you not, that you are the temple of God, and that the spirit of God dwelleth in you?

But if any man violate the temple of God, him shall God destroy. For the temple of God is holy, which you are.—1 *Cor.* iii. 16, 17.

But the body is not for fornication, but for the Lord, and the Lord for the body. . . .

Know you not that your bodies are the members of Christ? Shall I then take the members of Christ, and make them the members of an harlot? God forbid. . . .

Or know you not that your members are the temple of the Holy Ghost, who is in you, whom you have from God; and you are not your own?

For you are bought with a great price. Glorify and bear God in your body.—1 *Cor.* vi. 13, 15, 19, 20.

For you are the temple of the living God; as God saith: I will dwell in them, and walk among them; and I will be their God, and they shall be my people.—2 *Cor.* vi. 16.

For this is the will of God, your sanctification; that you should abstain from fornication;

That every one of you should know how to possess his vessel in sanctification and honor:

Not in the passion of lust, like the Gentiles that know not God . . .

For God hath not called us unto uncleanness, but unto sanctification.

Therefore, he that despiseth these things, despiseth not man but God, who also hath given his holy Spirit in us. —1 *Thess.* iv. 3-5, 7, 8.

BODY A PRISON FOR THE SOUL, THE

Wherefore I will not spare my mouth, I will speak in the affliction of my spirit: I will talk with the bitterness of my soul.

Am I a sea, or a whale, that thou hast enclosed me in a prison?—*Job* vii. 11, 12.

For the corruptible body is a load upon the soul, and the earthly habitation presseth down the mind that museth upon many things.—*Wis.* ix. 15.

Unhappy man that I am, who shall deliver me from the body of this death? —*Rom.* vii. 24.

BOND FOR ANOTHER, DANGER OF GIVING

My son, if thou be surety for thy friend, thou hast engaged fast thy hand to a stranger.

Thou art ensnared with the words of thy mouth, and caught with thy own words.

Do therefore, my son, what I say, and deliver thyself: because thou art fallen into the hand of thy neighbor. Run about, make haste, stir up thy friend:

Give not sleep to thy eyes, neither let thy eyelids slumber.

Deliver thyself as a doe from the hand, and as a bird from the hand of the fowler.—*Prov.* vi. 1-5.

He shall be afflicted with evil, that is surety for a stranger: but he that is aware of the snares, shall be secure.— *Prov.* xi. 15.

A foolish man will clap hands, when

he is surety for his friend.—*Prov.* xvii. 18.

Be not with them that fasten down their hands, and that offer themselves sureties for debts:

For if thou have not wherewith to restore, what cause is there, that he should take the covering from thy bed? —*Prov.* xxii. 26, 27.

Be not surety above thy power: and if thou be surety, think as if thou wert to pay it.—*Ecclus.* viii. 16.

Evil suretyship hath undone many of good estate, and hath tossed them as a wave of the sea.

It hath made powerful men to go from place to place round about, and they have wandered in strange countries.—*Ecclus.* xxix. 23, 24.

BORROWING, AGAINST

The rich ruleth over the poor: and the borrower is servant to him that lendeth.—*Prov.* xxii. 7.

Make not thyself poor by borrowing to contribute to feasts when thou hast nothing in thy purse; for thou shalt be an enemy to thy own life.—*Ecclus.* xviii. 33.

Owe no man anything, but to love one another.—*Rom.* xiii. 8.

BRIBERY

Neither shalt thou take bribes, which even blind the wise, and pervert the words of the just.—*Ex.* xxiii. 8.

For the congregation of the hypocrite is barren, and fire shall devour their tabernacles, who love to take bribes.— *Job* xv. 34.

Therefore let not anger overcome thee to oppress any man: neither let multitude of gifts turn thee aside.—*Job* xxxvi. 18.

Lord, who shall dwell in thy tabernacle? or who shall rest in thy holy hill? . . .

He that hath not put out his money to usury, nor taken bribes against the innocent.—*Ps.* xiv. 1, 5.

He that is greedy of gain troubleth his own house: but he that hateth bribes shall live.—*Prov.* xv. 27.

The wicked man taketh gifts out of the bosom, that he may pervert the paths of judgment.—*Prov.* xvii. 23.

Presents and gifts blind the eyes of judges, and make them dumb in the mouth, so that they cannot correct.— *Ecclus.* xx. 31.

All bribery, and injustice shall be blotted out, and fidelity shall stand for ever.—*Ecclus.* xl. 12.

Her princes have judged for bribes, and her priests have taught for hire, and her prophets divined for money: and they leaned upon the Lord, saying: Is not the Lord in the midst of us? no evil shall come upon us.

Therefore, because of you, Sion shall be plowed as a field, and Jerusalem shall be as a heap of stones, and the mountain of the temple as the high places of the forests.—*Mich.* iii. 11, 12.

BROTHERHOOD OF MAN

See also: Equal in the sight of God, all men are—page 125.

If I have despised to abide judgment with my man-servant, or my maid-servant, when they had any controversy against me:

For what shall I do when God shall rise to judge? and when he shall examine, what shall I answer him?

Did not he that made me in the womb make him also: and did not one and the same form me in the womb?— *Job* xxxi. 13-15.

Behold God hath made me as well as thee, and of the same clay I also was formed.—*Job* xxxiii. 6.

All flesh shall perish together, and man shall return into ashes.—*Job* xxxiv. 15.

Have we not all one father? hath not one God created us? why then doth every one of us despise his brother, violating the covenant of our fathers? —*Malach.* ii. 10.

Thus therefore shall you pray: Our Father who art in heaven, hallowed be thy name.—*Matt.* vi. 9.

But be not you called Rabbi. For one is your master; and all you are brethren.—*Matt.* xxiii. 8.

Is he the God of the Jews only? Is he not also of the Gentiles? Yes, of the Gentiles also.—*Rom.* iii. 29.

For you have not received the spirit of bondage again in fear; but you have received the spirit of adoption of sons, whereby we cry: Abba (Father).

For the Spirit himself giveth testimony to our spirit, that we are the sons of God.

And if sons, heirs also; heirs indeed of God, and joint heirs with Christ.—*Rom.* viii. 15-17.

For as in one body we have many members, but all the members have not the same office:

So we being many, are one body in Christ, and every one members one of another.—*Rom.* xii. 4, 5.

Loving one another with the charity of brotherhood, with honor preventing one another.—*Rom.* xii. 10.

But thou, why judgest thou thy brother? or thou, why dost thou despise thy brother? For we shall all stand before the judgment seat of Christ.—*Rom.* xiv. 10.

For in one Spirit were we all baptized into one body, whether Jews or Gentiles, whether bond or free; and in one Spirit we have all been made to drink.—1 *Cor.* xii. 13.

Now you are the body of Christ, and members of member.—1 *Cor.* xii. 27.

For you are all the children of God by faith, in Christ Jesus. . . .

There is neither Jew nor Greek: there is neither bond nor free: there is neither male nor female. For you are all one in Christ Jesus.

And if you be Christ's, then are you the seed of Abraham, heirs according to the promise.—*Gal.* iii. 26, 28, 29.

For by him we have access both in one Spirit to the Father.

Now therefore you are no more strangers and foreigners; but you are fellow citizens with the saints, and the domestics of God.—*Eph.* ii. 18, 19.

Wherefore putting away lying, speak ye the truth every man with his neighbor; for we are members one of another.—*Eph.* iv. 25.

But if we walk in the light, as he also is in the light, we have fellowship one with another, and the blood of Jesus Christ his Son, cleanseth us from all sin.—1 *John* i. 7.

BROTHERLY LOVE

[1]She answered: Be not against me, to desire that I should leave thee and depart; for whithersoever thou shalt go, I will go; and where thou shalt dwell, I also will dwell. Thy people shall be my people, and thy God my God.

The land that shall receive thee dying, in the same will I die: and there will I be buried. The Lord do so and so to me, and add more also, if aught but death part me and thee.—*Ruth* j. 16, 17.

And it came to pass, when he had made an end of speaking to Saul, the soul of Jonathan was knit with the soul of David, and Jonathan loved him as his own soul.—1 *Kings* xviii. 1.

I grieve for thee, my brother Jonathan: exceeding beautiful, and amiable to me above the love of women. As the mother loveth her only son, so did I love thee.—2 *Kings* i. 26.

Behold how good and how pleasant it is for brethren to dwell together in unity.—*Ps.* cxxxii. 1.

A brother that is helped by his brother, is like a strong city.—*Prov.* xviii. 19.

Every one shall help his neighbor, and shall say to his brother: Be of good courage.—*Is.* xli. 6.

And the multitude of believers had but one heart and one soul: neither did any one say that aught of the things which he possessed, was his own; but all things were common unto them. . . . For neither was there any one needy among them. For as many as were owners of lands or houses sold them, and brought the price of the things they sold,

And laid it down before the feet of the Apostles. And distribution was made to every one, according as he had need.—*Acts* iv. 32, 34, 35.

But as touching the charity of brotherhood, we have no need to write to you: for yourselves have learned of God to love one another.—1 *Thess.* iv. 9.

Let the charity of the brotherhood abide in you.—*Heb.* xiii. 1.

Purifying your souls in the obedience

[1]Ruth, the Moabitess, speaking to Noemi, her mother-in-law.

of charity, with a brotherly love, from a sincere heart love one another earnestly.—1 *Peter* i. 22.

Honor all men. Love the brotherhood.—1 *Peter* ii. 17.

And in fine, be ye all of one mind, having compassion one of another, being lovers of the brotherhood, merciful, modest, humble:

Not rendering evil for evil, nor railing for railing, but contrariwise, blessing: for unto this are you called, that you may inherit a blessing.—1 *Peter* iii. 8, 9.

CALUMNY

See: Detraction—page 110.

CARELESSNESS

He that is loose and slack in his work, is the brother of him that wasteth his own works.—*Prov.* xviii. 9.

Be not hasty in thy tongue: and slack and remiss in thy works.—*Ecclus.* iv. 34.

Cursed be he that doth the work of the Lord 'deceitfully.—*Jer.* xlviii. 10.

CARNAL MINDED, THE

For they that are according to the flesh, mind the things that are of the flesh; but they that are according to the spirit, mind the things that are of the spirit.

For the wisdom of the flesh is death; but the wisdom of the spirit is life and peace.

Because the wisdom of the flesh is an enemy to God; for it is not subject to the law of God, neither can it be.

And they who are in the flesh, cannot please God. . . . For if you live according to the flesh, you shall die; but if by the Spirit, you mortify the deeds of the flesh, you shall live.—*Rom.* viii. 5-8, 13.

But the sensual man perceiveth not these things that are of the Spirit of God; for it is foolishness to him, and he cannot understand, because it is spiritually examined.—1 *Cor.* ii. 14.

Now this I say, brethren, that flesh and blood cannot possess the kingdom of God; neither shall corruption possess incorruption.—1 *Cor.* xv. 50.

¹In the Greek, negligently.

For the flesh lusteth against the spirit: and the spirit against the flesh; for these are contrary one to another: so that you do not the things that you would. . . .

Now the works of the flesh are manifest, which are fornication, uncleanness, immodesty, luxury.—*Gal.* v. 17,19.

Dearly beloved, I beseech you as strangers and pilgrims, to refrain yourselves from carnal desires which war against the soul.—1 *Peter* ii. 11.

But others save, pulling them out of the fire. And on others have mercy, in fear, hating also the spotted garment which is carnal.—*Jude* i. 23.

CAUSE OR REASON FOR EVERYTHING, THERE IS A

Nothing upon earth is done without a cause, and sorrow doth not spring out of the ground.—*Job* v. 6.

For thus saith the Lord that created the heavens, God himself that formed the earth, and made it, the very maker thereof: he did not create it in vain: he formed it to be inhabited.—*Is.* xlv. 18.

For thus saith the Lord: Although I shall send in upon Jerusalem, my four grievous judgments, the sword, and the famine, and the mischievous beasts, and the pestilence, to destroy out of it man and beast,

Yet there shall be left in it some that shall be saved, who shall bring away their sons and daughters: behold they shall come among you, and you shall see their way and their doings: and you shall be comforted concerning the evil that I have brought upon Jerusalem, in all things that I have brought upon it.

And they shall comfort you, when you shall see their ways and their doings: and you shall know that I have not done without cause all that I have done in it, saith the Lord God.—*Ezech.* xiv. 21, 22, 23.

CHARITABLE MAN, THE

Behold thou hast taught many, and thou hast strengthened the weary hands:

Thy words have confirmed them that were staggering, and thou hast strengthened the trembling knees.—*Job* iv. 3, 4.

The ear that heard me blessed me, and the eye that saw me gave witness to me:

Because I had delivered the poor man that cried out; and the fatherless, that had no helper. The blessing of him that was ready to perish came upon me, and I comforted the heart of the widow: . . .

I was an eye to the blind, and a foot to the lame.

I was the father of the poor: and the cause which I knew not, I searched out most diligently.—*Job* xxix. 11-13,15,16.

Blessed is he that understandeth concerning the needy and the poor: the Lord will deliver him in the evil day.

The Lord preserve him and give him life, and make him blessed upon the earth: and deliver him not up to the will of his enemies.—*Ps.* xl. 2, 3.

She hath opened her hand to the needy, and stretched out her hands to the poor.—*Prov.* xxxi. 20.

The lips of many shall bless him that is liberal of his bread, and the testimony of his truth is faithful.—*Ecclus.* xxxi. 28.

And in Joppe there was a certain disciple named Tabitha, which by interpretation is called Dorcas. This woman was full of good works and almsdeeds which she did.

And it came to pass in those days that she was sick, and died. Whom when they had washed, they laid her in an upper chamber. . . .

And Peter rising up went with them. And when he was come, they brought him into the upper chamber. And all the widows stood about him weeping, and showing him the coats and garments which Dorcas made them.

And they all being put forth, Peter kneeling down, prayed, and turning to the body, he said: Tabitha, arise. And she opened her eyes; and seeing Peter, she sat up.—*Acts* ix. 36, 37, 39, 40.

CHARITY

1st. Referring Both to the Love of God and of Our Neighbor

If I speak with the tongues of men, and of angels, and have not charity, I am become as sounding brass, or a tinkling cymbal.

And if I should have prophecy and should know all mysteries, and all knowledge, and if I should have all faith, so that I could remove mountains, and have not charity, I am nothing.

And if I should distribute all my goods to feed the poor, and if I should deliver my body to be burned, and have not charity, it profiteth me nothing.

Charity is patient, is kind: charity envieth not, dealeth not perversely; is not puffed up;

Is not ambitious, seeketh not her own, is not provoked to anger, thinketh no evil;

Rejoiceth not in iniquity, but rejoiceth with the truth;

Beareth all things, believeth all things, hopeth all things, endureth all things.

Charity never falleth away: whether prophecies shall be made void, or tongues shall cease, or knowledge shall be destroyed. . . .

And now there remain faith, hope, and charity, these three: but the greatest of these is charity.—1 *Cor.* xiii. 1-8, 13.

But the fruit of the Spirit is charity, joy, peace, patience, benignity, goodness, longanimity.—*Gal.* v. 22.

Now the end of the commandment is charity, from a pure heart, and a good conscience, and an unfeigned faith.— 1 *Tim.* i. 5.

2d. Referring Principally to Love for God

For in Christ Jesus neither circumcision availeth anything, nor uncircumcision; but faith that worketh by charity.—*Gal.* v. 6.

As he chose us in him (Christ) before the foundation of the world, that we should be holy and unspotted in his sight in charity.—*Eph.* i. 4.

That Christ may dwell by faith in

your hearts; that being rooted and founded in charity,

You may be able to comprehend, with all the saints, what is the breadth, and length, and height and depth:

To know also the charity of Christ, which surpasseth all knowledge, that you may be filled unto all the fulness of God.—*Eph.* iii. 17-19.

But let us, who are of the day, be sober, having on the breastplate of faith and charity, and for a helmet the hope of salvation.—1 *Thess.* v. 8.

He who saith that he knoweth him (Christ), and keepeth not his commandments, is a liar, and the truth is not in him.

But he that keepeth his word, in him in very deed the charity of God is perfected; and by this we know that we are in him.—1 *John* ii. 4, 5.

God is charity: and he that abideth in charity, abideth in God, and God in him. . . .

Fear is not in charity: but perfect charity casteth out fear, because fear hath pain. And he that feareth, is not perfected in charity.—1 *John* iv. 16, 18.

For this is the charity of God, that we keep his commandments.—1 *John* v. 3.

And this is charity, that we walk according to his commandments.—2 *John* i. 6.

3d. Referring Principally to the Love of Our Neighbor

Hatred stirreth up strifes: and charity covereth all sins.—*Prov.* x. 12.

Many waters cannot quench charity, neither can the floods drown it: if a man should give all the substance of his house for love, he shall despise it as nothing.—*Cant.* viii. 7.

And because iniquity hath abounded, the charity of many shall grow cold.—*Matt.* xxiv. 12.

Knowledge puffeth up; but charity edifieth.—1 *Cor.* viii. 1.

Let all your things be done in charity.—1 *Cor.* xvi. 14.

But doing the truth in charity, we may in all things grow up in him who is the head, even Christ.—*Eph.* iv. 15.

And this I pray, that your charity may more and more abound in knowl-edge and in all understanding.—*Philipp.* i. 9.

Fulfil ye my joy, that you be of one mind, having the same charity, being of one accord, agreeing in sentiment.—*Philipp.* ii. 2.

But above all these things have charity, which is the bond of perfection.—*Col.* iii. 14.

And may the Lord multiply you, and make you abound in charity towards one another, and towards all men.—1 *Thess.* iii. 12.

But thou, O man of God, fly these things: and pursue justice, godliness, faith, charity, patience, mildness.—1 *Tim.* vi. 11.

And let us consider one another, to provoke unto charity, and to good works.—*Heb.* x. 24.

Let the charity of the brotherhood abide in you.—*Heb.* xiii. 1.

But before all things, have a constant mutual charity among yourselves: for charity covereth a multitude of sins.—1 *Peter* iv. 8.

Dearly beloved, let us love one another, for charity is of God. And every one that loveth is born of God, and knoweth God.

He that loveth not, knoweth not God: for God is charity.—1 *John* iv. 7, 8.

CHASTITY

Thou knowest, O Lord, that I never coveted a husband, and have kept my soul clean from all lust. . . .

But a husband I consented to take, with thy fear, not with my lust.—*Tob.* iii. 16, 18.

For thou hast done manfully, and thy heart has been strengthened, because thou hast loved chastity, and after thy husband, hast not known any other: therefore also the hand of the Lord hath strengthened thee, and therefore thou shalt be blessed for ever.—*Judith* xv. 11.

And Judith was made great in Bethulia. . . .

And chastity was joined to her virtue, so that she knew no man all the days of her life, after the death of Manasses her husband.—*Judith* xvi. 25, 26.

I made a covenant with my eyes, that I would not so much as think upon a virgin.—*Job* xxxi. 1.

Who shall ascend into the mountain of the Lord: or who shall stand in his holy place?

The innocent in hands, and clean of heart.

He shall receive a blessing from the Lord, and mercy from God his Saviour.—*Ps.* xxiii. 3-5.

For happy is the barren: and the undefiled, that hath not known bed in sin: she shall have fruit in the visitation of holy souls.

And the eunuch that hath not wrought iniquity with his hands, nor thought wicked things against God: for the precious gift of faith shall be given to him, and a most acceptable lot in the temple of God.—*Wis.* iii. 13, 14.

O how beautiful is the chaste generation with glory: for the memory thereof is immortal: because it is known both with God and with men.

When it is present, they imitate it: and they desire it when it hath withdrawn itself, and it triumpheth crowned for ever, winning the reward of undefiled conflicts.—*Wis.* iv. 1, 2.

And the keeping of 'her laws is the firm foundation of incorruption:

And incorruption bringeth near to God.—*Wis.* vi. 19, 20.

And as I knew that I could not otherwise be continent, except God gave it, and this also was a point of wisdom, to know whose gift it was: I went to the Lord, and besought him.—*Wis.* viii. 21.

A holy and shamefaced woman is grace upon grace.

And no price is worthy of a continent soul.—*Ecclus.* xxvi. 19, 20.

Blessed are the clean of heart, for they shall see God.—*Matt.* v. 8.

And as he (Paul) treated of justice, and chastity, and of the judgment to come, Felix, being terrified, answered: For this time, go thy way: but when I have a convenient time, I will send for thee.—*Acts* xxiv. 25.

But the fruit of the spirit is . . . Mildness, faith, modesty, continency, chastity.—*Gal.* v. 22, 23.

¹The laws of wisdom.

CHASTITY, EXHORTATION TO THE PRACTICE OF

Take heed to keep thyself, my son, from all fornication, and beside thy wife, never endure to know a crime.—*Tob.* iv. 13.

I beseech you, therefore, brethren, by the mercy of God, that you present your bodies a living sacrifice, holy, pleasing unto God, your reasonable service.—*Rom.* xii. 1.

For this is the will of God, your sanctification; that you should abstain from fornication;

That every one of you should know how to possess his vessel in sanctification and honor:

Not in the passion of lust, like the Gentiles that know not God. . . .

For God hath not called us unto uncleanness, but unto sanctification.

Therefore he that despiseth these things, despiseth not man, but God, who also hath given his holy Spirit in us.—*1 Thess.* iv. 3-5, 7, 8.

Keep thyself chaste.—*1 Tim.* v. 22.

Dearly beloved, I beseech you as strangers and pilgrims, to refrain yourselves from carnal desires which war against the soul.—*1 Peter* ii. 11.

CHEATING

See: Fraud—page 161.

CHEERFULNESS

A glad heart maketh a cheerful countenance: but by grief of mind the spirit is cast down.—*Prov.* xv. 13.

A joyful mind maketh age flourishing: a sorrowful spirit drieth up the bones.—*Prov.* xvii. 22.

Rich or poor, if his heart is good, his countenance shall be cheerful at all times.—*Ecclus.* xxvi. 4.

The joyfulness of the heart is the life of a man, and a never failing treasure of holiness: and the joy of a man is length of life.

Have pity on thy own soul, pleasing God, and contain thyself: gather up thy heart in his holiness: and drive away sadness far from thee.—*Ecclus.* xxx. 23, 24.

In every gift show a cheerful counte-

nance, and sanctify thy tithes with joy.
—*Ecclus.* xxxv. 11.

Every one as he hath determined in his heart, not with sadness, or of necessity: for God loveth a cheerful giver.— 2 *Cor.* ix. 7.

Is any of you sad? Let him pray. Is he cheerful in mind? Let him sing. —*James* v. 13.

CHILDREN

And the ¹priests put on haircloths, and they caused the little children to lie prostrate before the temple of the Lord, and the altar of the Lord they covered with haircloth.—*Judith* iv. 8.

Out of the mouths of infants and of sucklings thou hast perfected praise, because of thy enemies, that thou mayst destroy the enemy and the avenger. —*Ps.* viii. 3.

The law of the Lord is unspotted, converting souls: the testimony of the Lord is faithful, giving wisdom to little ones.—*Ps.* xviii. 8.

Who shall ascend into the mountain of the Lord: or who shall stand in his holy place?

The innocent in hands, and clean of heart, who hath not taken his soul in vain, nor sworn deceitfully to his neighbor.

He shall receive a blessing from the Lord, and mercy from God his Saviour. —*Ps.* xxiii. 3-5.

Praise the Lord, ye children: praise ye the name of the Lord.—*Ps.* cxii. 1.

The declaration of thy words giveth light: and giveth understanding to little ones.—*Ps.* cxviii. 130.

By his inclinations a child is known, if his works be clean and right.—*Prov.* xx. 11.

Folly is bound up in the heart of a child, and the rod of correction shall drive it away.—*Prov.* xxii. 15.

The rod and reproof give wisdom: but the child that is left to his own will bringeth his mother to shame.— *Prov.* xxix. 15.

For wisdom opened the mouth of the dumb, and made the tongues of infants eloquent.—*Wis.* x. 21.

Rejoice not in ungodly children, if they be multiplied: neither be delighted

¹During the invasion of Holofernes.

in them, if the fear of God be not with them. . . .

For better is one that feareth God, than a thousand ungodly children.

And it is better to die without children, than to leave ungodly children.— *Ecclus.* xvi. 1, 3, 4.

A horse not broken becometh stubborn, and a child left to himself will become headstrong.—*Ecclus.* xxx. 8.

At that time Jesus answered and said: I confess to thee, O Father, Lord of heaven and earth, because thou hast hid these things from the wise and prudent, and hast revealed them to little ones.

Yea, Father; for so hath it seemed good in thy sight.—*Matt.* xi. 25, 26.

And the chief priests and scribes, seeing the wonderful things that he did, and the children crying in the temple, and saying: Hosanna to the son of David; were moved with indignation,

And said to him: Hearest thou what these say? And Jesus said to them: Yea, have you never read: Out of the mouth of infants and of sucklings thou hast perfected praise?—*Matt.* xxi. 15, 16.

CHILDREN, GOD'S LOVE FOR

The Lord is the keeper of little ones. —*Ps.* cxiv. 6.

Blessed are the clean of heart: for they shall see God.—*Matt.* v. 8.

And Jesus calling unto him a little child, set him in the midst of them,

And said: Amen I say to you, unless you be converted, and become as little children, you shall not enter into the kingdom of heaven.

Whosoever therefore shall humble himself as this little child, he is the greater in the kingdom of heaven.

And he that shall receive one such little child in my name, receiveth me.

But he that shall scandalize one of these little ones that believe in me, it were better for him that a millstone should be hanged about his neck, and that he should be drowned in the depth of the sea.—*Matt.* xviii. 2-6.

See that you despise not one of these little ones: for I say to you, that their angels in heaven always see the face of my Father who is in heaven.—*Matt.* xviii. 10.

Even so it is not the will of your Father, who is in heaven, that one of these little ones should perish.—*Matt.* xviii. 14.

And taking a child, he (Jesus) set him in the midst of them. Whom when he had embraced, he saith to them:

Whosoever shall receive one such child as this in my name, receiveth me. And whosoever shall receive me, receiveth not me, but him that sent me.—*Mark* ix. 35, 36.

And they brought to him young children, that he might touch them. And the disciples rebuked them that brought them.

Whom when Jesus saw, he was much displeased, and saith to them: Suffer the little children to come unto me, and forbid them not; for of such is the kingdom of God.

Amen I say to you, whosoever shall not receive the kingdom of God as a little child, shall not enter into it.

And embracing them, and laying his hands upon them, he blessed them.—*Mark* x. 13-16.

CHILDREN, WE MUST BECOME AS

The Lord is the keeper of little ones: I was humbled, and he delivered me.—*Ps.* cxiv. 6.

At that hour the disciples came to Jesus, saying: Who thinkest thou is the greater in the kingdom of heaven?

And Jesus calling unto him a little child, set him in the midst of them,

And said: Amen I say to you, unless you be converted, and become as little children you shall not enter into the kingdom of heaven.

Whosoever therefore shall humble himself as this little child, he is the greater in the kingdom of heaven.—*Matt.* xviii. 1-4.

But Jesus said to them: Suffer the little children, and forbid them not to come to me: for the kingdom of heaven is for such.—*Matt.* xix. 14.

Amen I say to you: Whosoever shall not receive the kingdom of God as a child, shall not enter into it.—*Luke* xviii. 17.

Brethren, do not become children in sense: but in malice be children, and in sense be perfect.—1 *Cor.* xiv. 20.

CHILDREN OF GOD BY ADOPTION, WE BECOME

See also: Father; God, our—page 140.

And it shall be in the place where it shall be said to them: You are not my people: it shall be said to them: Ye are the sons of the living God.—*Osee* i. 10.

Blessed are the peacemakers: for they shall be called the children of God.—*Matt.* v. 9.

But I say to you, Love your enemies: do good to them that hate you: and pray for them that persecute and calumniate you:

That you may be the children of your Father who is in heaven, who maketh his sun to rise upon the good and bad, and raineth upon the just and the unjust.—*Matt.* v. 44, 45.

But they that shall be accounted worthy of that world, and of the resurrection from the dead, shall neither be married, nor take wives.

Neither can they die any more: for they are equal to the angels, and are the children of God, being the children of the resurrection.—*Luke* xx. 35, 36.

But as many as received him (Christ), he gave them power to be made the sons of God, to them that believe in his name.

Who are born, not of blood, nor of the will of the flesh, nor of the will of man, but of God.—*John* i. 12, 13.

For whosoever are led by the Spirit of God, they are the sons of God.

For you have not received the spirit of bondage again in fear; but you have received the spirit of adoption of sons, whereby we cry: Abba (Father).

For the Spirit himself giveth testimony to our spirit, that we are the sons of God.—*Rom.* viii. 14-16.

For we know that every creature groaneth and travaileth in pain, even till now.

And not only it, but ourselves also, who have the first fruits of the Spirit, even we ourselves groan within ourselves, waiting for the adoption of the sons of God, the redemption of our body.—*Rom.* viii. 22, 23.

For you are all the children of God by faith, in Christ Jesus.—*Gal.* iii. 26.

But when the fulness of the time was come, God sent his Son, made of a woman, made under the law:

That he might redeem them who were under the law: that we might receive the adoption of sons.

And because you are sons, God hath sent the Spirit of his Son into your hearts, crying: Abba, Father.

Therefore now he is not a servant, but a son.

And if a son, an heir also through God.—*Gal.* iv. 4-7.

Who hath predestinated us unto the adoption of children through Jesus Christ unto himself: according to the purpose of his will.—*Eph.* i. 5.

And do ye all things without murmurings and hesitations;

That you may be blameless, and sincere children of God, without reproof, in the midst of a crooked and perverse generation; among whom you shine as lights in the world.—*Philipp.* ii. 14, 15.

Behold what manner of charity the Father hath bestowed upon us, that we should be called, and should be the sons of God.—1 *John* iii. 1.

Dearly beloved, we are now the sons of God; and it hath not yet appeared what we shall be. We know that when he shall appear, we shall be like to him: because we shall see him as he is.—1 *John* iii. 2.

He that shall overcome shall possess these things, and I will be his God; and he shall be my son.—*Apoc.* xxi. 7.

CHOOSING BETWEEN GOD AND HIS ENEMY

But if it seem evil to you to serve the Lord, you have your choice: choose this day that which pleaseth you, whom you would rather serve, whether the gods which your fathers served in Mesopotamia, or the gods of the Amorrhites, in whose land you dwell: but as for me and my house, we will serve the Lord.—*Jos.* xxiv. 15.

And Elias coming to all the people, said: How long do you halt between two sides? if the Lord be God, follow him: but if Baal, then follow him.—3 *Kings* xviii. 21.

Again the devil took him up into a very high mountain, and showed him all the kingdoms of the world, and the glory of them,

And said to him: All these will I give thee, if falling down thou wilt adore me.

Then Jesus saith to him: Begone, Satan; for it is written, The Lord thy God shalt thou adore, and him only shalt thou serve.—*Matt.* iv. 8-10.

No man can serve two masters. For either he will hate the one, and love the other: or he will sustain the one, and despise the other. You cannot serve God and mammon.—*Matt.* vi. 24.

And Pilate gave sentence that it should be as they required.

And he released unto them him who for murder and sedition, had been cast into prison, whom they had desired; but Jesus he delivered up to their will. —*Luke* xxiii. 24, 25.

But you have a custom that I should release one unto you at the pasch: will you, therefore, that I release unto you the king of the Jews?

Then cried they all again, saying: Not this man, but Barabbas. Now Barabbas was a robber.—*John* xviii. 39, 40.

But you denied the Holy One and the Just, and desired a murderer to be granted unto you.

But the author of life you killed, whom God hath raised from the dead, of which we are witnesses.—*Acts* iii. 14, 15.

But Peter and John answering, said to 'them: If it be just in the sight of God, to hear you rather than God, judge ye.—*Acts* iv. 19.

CHOOSING BETWEEN GOOD AND EVIL

Behold I set forth in your sight this day a blessing and a curse:

A blessing, if you obey the commandments of the Lord your God, which I command you this day:

A curse, if you obey not the commandments of the Lord your God, but

¹The council of the Jews which forbade them to preach Christ.

revolt from the way which now I show you, and walk after strange gods which you know not.—*Deut.* xi. 26-28.

Consider that I have set before thee this day life and good, and on the other hand, death and evil.—*Deut.* xxx. 15.

I call heaven and earth to witness this day, that I have set before you life and death, blessing and cursing. Choose therefore life, that both thou and thy seed may live.—*Deut.* xxx. 19.

God made man from the beginning, and left him in the hand of his own counsel. . . .

He hath set fire and water before thee: stretch forth thy hand to which thou wilt.

Before man is life and death, good and evil, that which he shall choose, shall be given him.—*Ecclus.* xv. 14, 17, 18.

Good is set against evil, and life against death: so also is the sinner against the just man. And so look upon all the works of the most High. Two and two, and one against another. —*Ecclus.* xxxiii. 15.

And to this people thou shalt say: Thus saith the Lord: Behold I set before you the way of life, and the way of death.—*Jer.* xxi. 8.

Seek ye good, and not evil, that you may live: and the Lord the God of hosts will be with you, as you have said.

Hate evil, and love good, and establish judgment in the gate: it may be the Lord the God of hosts may have mercy on the remnant of Joseph.— *Amos* v. 14, 15.

For where thy treasure is, there is thy heart also.—*Matt.* vi. 21.

Know you not, that to whom you yield yourselves servants to obey, his servants you are whom you obey, whether it be of sin unto death, or of obedience unto justice.—*Rom.* vi. 16.

What will you? Shall I come to you with a rod; or in charity, and in the spirit of meekness?—1 *Cor.* iv. 21.

CHOOSING GOD, AND HIS LAW

Thou hast chosen the Lord this day to be thy God, and to walk in his ways and keep his ceremonies, and precepts, and judgments, and obey his command.

And the Lord hath chosen thee this day, to be his peculiar people, as he hath spoken to thee, and to keep all his commandments:

And to make thee higher than all nations which he hath created, to his own praise, and name, and glory: that thou mayst be a holy people of the Lord thy God, as he hath spoken.—*Deut.* xxvi. 17, 18, 19.

I call heaven and earth to witness this day, that I have set before you life and death, blessing and cursing. Choose therefore life, that both thou and thy seed may live:

And that thou mayst love the Lord thy God, and obey his voice, and adhere to him (for he is thy life, and the length of thy days) that thou mayst dwell in the land, for which the Lord swore to thy fathers Abraham, Isaac, and Jacob that he would give it to them.—*Deut.* xxx. 19, 20.

And Josue said to the people: You are witnesses, that you yourselves have chosen you the Lord to serve him. And they answered: We are witnesses.—*Jos.* xxiv. 22.

[1]She answered: Be not against me to desire that I should leave thee and depart: for whithersoever thou shalt go, I will go: and where thou shalt dwell, I also will dwell. Thy people shall be my people, and thy God my God. . . .

The Lord render unto thee for thy work, and mayst thou receive a full reward of the Lord the God of Israel, to whom thou art come, and under whose wings thou art fled.—*Ruth* i. 16; ii. 12.

The Lord is the portion of my inheritance and of my cup: it is thou that wilt restore my inheritance to me.

The lines are fallen unto me in goodly places: for my inheritance is goodly to me.—*Ps.* xv. 5, 6.

Hearken, O daughter, and see, and incline thy ear: and forget thy people and thy father's house.

And the king shall greatly desire thy beauty; for he is the Lord thy God, and him they shall adore.—*Ps.* xliv. 11, 12.

[1]Ruth refusing to leave Noemi, her mother-in-law.

For what have I in heaven? and besides thee, what do I desire upon earth?

For thee my flesh and my heart hath fainted away: thou art the God of my heart, and the God that is my portion for ever.—*Ps.* lxxii. 25, 26.

I have chosen the way of truth: thy judgments I have not forgotten.

I have stuck to thy testimonies, O Lord: put me not to shame.

I have run the way of thy commandments, when thou didst enlarge my heart.

. . . Let thy hand be with me to save me; for I have chosen thy precepts. —*Ps.* cxviii. 30-32, 173.

My son, give me thy heart: and let thy eyes keep my ways.—*Prov.* xxiii. 26.

The Lord is my portion, said my soul: therefore will I wait for him.— *Lam.* iii. 24.

But Peter and the apostles answering, said: We ought to obey God, rather than men.—*Acts* v. 29.

By faith, Moses, when he was grown up, denied himself to be the son of Pharao's daughter;

Rather choosing to be afflicted with the people of God, than to have the pleasure of sin for a time.

Esteeming the reproach of Christ greater riches than the treasure of the Egyptians. For he looked unto the reward.—*Heb.* xi. 24-26.

CHRIST, OUR BROTHER

And as he (Christ) was yet speaking to the multitudes, behold his mother and his brethren stood without, seeking to speak to him.

And one said unto him: Behold thy mother and thy brethren stand without, seeking thee.

But he answering him that told him, said: Who is my mother, and who are my brethren?

And stretching forth his hand towards his disciples, he said: Behold my mother and my brethren.

For whosoever shall do the will of my Father, that is in heaven, he is my brother, and sister, and mother.—*Matt.* xii. 46-50.

Jesus saith to her (Mary Magdalen): Do not touch me, for I am not yet ascended to my Father. But go to my brethren, and say to them: I ascend to my Father and to your Father, to my God and your God.—*John* xx. 17.

For both he that sanctifieth, and they who are sanctified, are all of one. For which cause he is not ashamed to call them brethren, saying:

I will declare thy name to my brethren; in the midst of the church will I praise thee.—*Heb.* ii. 11, 12.

For no where doth he take hold of the angels: but of the seed of Abraham he taketh hold.

Wherefore it behooved him in all things to be made like unto his brethren, that he might become a merciful and faithful high-priest before God, that he might be a propitiation for the sins of the people.—*Heb.* ii. 16, 17.

CHURCH, HUMBLE BEGINNING OF THE

Another parable he proposed unto them, saying: The kingdom of heaven is like to a grain of mustard-seed, which a man took and sowed in his field.

Which is the least indeed of all seeds; but when it is grown up, it is greater than all herbs, and becometh a tree, so that the birds of the air come, and dwell in the branches thereof.

Another parable he spoke to them: The kingdom of heaven is like to leaven, which a woman took and hid in three measures of meal, until the whole was leavened.—*Matt.* xiii. 31-34.

[1]All these were persevering with one mind in prayer with the women, and Mary the mother of Jesus, and with his brethren.

In those days Peter rising up in the midst of the brethren, said: (now the number of persons together was about one hundred and twenty:)—*Acts* i. 14, 15.

For see your vocation, brethren, that there are not many wise according to the flesh, not many mighty, not many noble:

But the foolish things of the world hath God chosen, that he may confound the wise; and the weak things of the world hath God chosen, that he may confound the strong.

And the base things of the world, and

[1]The eleven Apostles, after the Ascension of Christ.

the things that are contemptible, hath God chosen, and things that are not, that he might bring to nought things that are:

That no flesh should glory in his sight.—1 *Cor.* i. 26-29.

CHURCH, GOD IS THE PROTECTOR OF THE

In that day there shall be singing to the vineyard of pure wine.

I am the Lord that keep it, [1] I will suddenly give it drink: lest any hurt come to it, I keep it night and day.— *Is.* xxvii. 2, 3.

And I say to thee: That thou art Peter; and upon this rock I will build my church, and the gates of hell shall not prevail against it.—*Matt.* xvi. 18.

Going therefore, teach ye all nations; baptizing them in the name of the Father, and of the Son, and of the Holy Ghost.

Teaching them to observe all things whatsoever I have commanded you: and behold I am with you all days, even to the consummation of the world.—*Matt.* xxviii. 19, 20.

CHURCH, LOVE FOR THE

If I forget thee, O Jerusalem, let my right hand be forgotten.

Let my tongue cleave to my jaws, if I do not remember thee:

If I make not Jerusalem the beginning of my joy.—*Ps.* cxxxvi. 5, 6.

Rejoice with Jerusalem, and be glad with her, all you that love her: rejoice for joy with her, all you that mourn for her.

That you may suck, and be filled with the breasts of her consolations: that you may milk out, and flow with delights, from the abundance of her glory. —*Is.* lxvi. 10, 11.

CHURCH, PRAYER FOR THE

Turn again, O God of hosts, look down from heaven, and see, and visit this vineyard:

And perfect the same which thy right hand hath planted.—*Ps.* lxxix. 15, 16.

And now I am not in the world, and these are in the world, and I come

to thee. Holy Father, keep them in thy name whom thou hast given me; that they may be one, as we also are. . . .

I pray not that thou shouldst take them out of the world, but that thou shouldst keep them from evil.

They are not of the world, as I also am not of the world.

Sanctify them in truth. Thy word is truth.

. . . And not for them only do I pray, but for them also who through their word shall believe in me;

That they all may be one, as thou, Father, in me, and I in thee; that they also may be one in us; that the world may believe that thou hast sent me.— *John* xvii. 11, 15-17, 20, 21.

[1] Who having heard it, with one accord lifted up their voice to God, and said: Lord, thou art he that didst make heaven and earth, the sea, and all things that are in them.

Who, by the Holy Ghost, by the mouth of our father David, thy servant, hath said: Why did the Gentiles rage, and the people meditate vain things?

The kings of the earth stood up, and the princes assembled together against the Lord and against his Christ.

For of a truth there assembled together in this city against thy holy child Jesus, whom thou hast anointed, Herod, and Pontius Pilate, with the Gentiles and the people of Israel,

To do what thy hand and thy counsel decreed to be done.

And now, Lord, behold their threatenings, and grant unto thy servants, that with all confidence they may speak thy word,

By stretching forth thy hand to cures, and signs, and wonders to be done by the name of thy holy Son Jesus.—*Acts* iv. 24-30.

CHURCH, PERSECUTION OF THE

Why have the Gentiles raged, and the people devised vain things?

The kings of the earth stood up, and the princes met together against the Lord and against his Christ. Let us

---

[1]Or, as the Hebrew may also be rendered: I will continually water it.

[1]The disciples, after the release of Peter and John by the council of the Jews.

break their bonds asunder: and let us cast away their yoke from us.

He that dwelleth in heaven shall laugh at them: and the Lord shall deride them.

Then shall he speak to them in his anger, and trouble them in his rage.—*Ps.* ii. 1-5.

They have set fire to thy sanctuary: they have defiled the dwelling place of thy name on the earth.

They said in their heart, the whole kindred of them together: Let us abolish all the festival days of God from the land.—*Ps.* lxxiii. 7, 8.

For lo, thy enemies have made a noise: and they that hate thee have lifted up the head.

They have taken a malicious counsel against thy people, and have consulted against thy saints.

They have said: Come and let us destroy them, so that they be not a nation: and let the name of Israel be remembered no more.

For they have contrived with one consent: they have made a covenant together against thee.—*Ps.* lxxxii. 3-6.

But beware of men. For they will deliver you up in councils, and they will scourge you in their synagogues.

And you shall be brought before governors, and before kings for my sake, for a testimony to them and to the Gentiles. . . .

The brother also shall deliver up the brother to death, and the father, the son: and the children shall rise up against their parents, and shall put them to death.

And you shall be hated by all men for my name's sake: but he that shall persevere unto the end, he shall be saved.

And when they shall persecute you in this city, flee into another. Amen I say to you, you shall not finish all the cities of Israel, till the Son of man come.—*Matt.* x. 17, 18, 21-23.

Then shall they deliver you up to be afflicted, and shall put you to death: and you shall be hated by all nations for my name's sake.—*Matt.* xxiv. 9.

Remember my word that I said to you: The servant is not greater than his master. If they have persecuted

me, they will also persecute you.—*John* xv. 20.

They will put you out of the synagogues: yea, the hour cometh, that whosoever killeth you, will think that he doth a service to God.

And these things will they do to you; because they have not known the Father, nor me.

But these things I have told you: that when the hour shall come, you may remember that I told you of them.—*John* xvi. 2-4.

I have given them thy word, and the world hath hated them, because they are not of the world; as I also am not of the world.—*John* xvii. 14.

¹Who having heard it, with one accord lifted up their voice to God, and said: Lord, thou art he that didst make heaven and earth, the sea, and all things that are in them.

Who by the Holy Ghost, by the mouth of our father David, thy servant, hast said: Why did the Gentiles rage, and the people meditate vain things:

The kings of the earth stood up, and the princes assembled together against the Lord and against his Christ:

For of a truth there assembled together in this city against thy holy child Jesus, whom thou hast anointed, Herod, and Pontius Pilate, with the Gentiles and the people of Israel,

To do what thy hand and thy counsel decreed to be done.

And now, Lord, behold their threatenings, and grant unto thy servants, that with all confidence they may speak thy word.—*Acts* iv. 24-29.

And at that time there was raised a great persecution against the church which was at Jerusalem; and they were all dispersed through the countries of Judea, and Samaria, except the Apostles.—*Acts* viii. 1.

And at the same time Herod the king stretched forth his hands, to afflict some of the church.

And he killed James, the brother of John, with the sword.

And seeing that it pleased the Jews, he proceeded to take up Peter also.—*Acts* xii. 1-3.

Take heed to yourselves, and to the

¹The disciples.

whole flock, wherein the Holy Ghost hath placed you bishops, to rule the church of God, which he hath purchased with his own blood.

I know that, after my departure, ravening wolves will enter in among you, not sparing the flock.—*Acts* xx. 28, 29.

But [1]we desire to hear of thee what thou thinkest; for as concerning this sect, we know that it is everywhere contradicted.—*Acts* xxviii. 22.

Now we, brethren, as Isaac was, are the children of promise.

But as then [2]he that was born according to the flesh, persecuted him that was after the spirit; so also it is now.—*Gal.* iv. 29.

CHURCH, ESTABLISHED AND WORKING, THE

See: Church, Part II—page 679.

CHURCH IS THE HOUSE OF GOD, THE

See: House of God—page 214.

COME TO THE LORD, AN INVITATION TO

Come ye to him, and be enlightened: and your faces shall not be confounded.—*Ps.* xxxiii. 6.

Come over to me, all ye that desire me, and be filled with my fruits.

For my spirit is sweet above honey, and my inheritance above honey and the honeycomb.

My memory is unto everlasting generations.

They that eat me, shall yet hunger: and they that drink me, shall yet thirst.

He that hearkeneth to me, shall not be confounded: and they that work by me, shall not sin.—*Ecclus.* xxiv. 26-30.

All you that thirst, come to the waters: and you that have no money make haste, buy, and eat: come ye, buy wine and milk without money, and without any price.

Why do you spend money for that which is not bread, and your labor for that which doth not satisfy you? Hearken diligently to me, and eat that

which is good, and your soul shall be delighted in fatness.

Incline your ear and come to me: hear, and your soul shall live, and I will make an everlasting covenant with you, the faithful mercies of David.—*Is.* lv. 1-3.

Come to me, all you that labor, and are burdened, and I will refresh you.—*Matt.* xi. 28.

And Jesus said to them: I am the bread of life: he that cometh to me, shall not hunger: and he that believeth in me, shall never thirst.—*John* vi. 35.

And on the last, and great day of the festivity, Jesus stood and cried, saying: If any man thirst, let him come to me, and drink.—*John* vii. 37.

And when she (Martha) had said these things, she went and called her sister Mary secretly, saying: The master is come, and calleth for thee.—*John* xi. 28.

COMFORT THE AFFLICTED AND THE SORROWING, WE SHOULD

Have pity on me, have pity on me, at least you my friends, because the hand of the Lord hath touched me.—*Job* xix. 21.

I wept heretofore for him that was afflicted, and my soul had compassion on the poor.—*Job* xxx. 25.

Grief in the heart of a man shall bring him low, but with a good word he shall be made glad.—*Prov.* xii. 25.

Be not wanting in comforting them that weep, and walk with them that mourn.

Be not slow to visit the sick: for by these things thou shalt be confirmed in love.—*Ecclus.* vii. 38, 39.

Rejoice with them that rejoice; weep with them that weep.—*Rom.* xii. 15.

Blessed be the God and Father of our Lord Jesus Christ, the Father of mercies, and the God of all comfort.

Who comforteth us in all our tribulation; that we also may be able to comfort them who are in all distress, by the exhortation wherewith we also are exhorted by God.—*2 Cor.* i. 3, 4.

Bear ye one another's burdens; and so you shall fulfil the law of Christ.—*Gal.* vi. 2.

[1]The Jews at Rome speaking to Paul.
[2]As Esau persecuted Isaac.

And we beseech you, brethren, rebuke the unquiet, comfort the feeble-minded, support the weak, be patient towards all men.—1 *Thess.* v. 14.

COMFORTER, GOD OUR

Wherefore I will pray to the Lord, and address my speech to God:
. . . Who setteth up the humble on high, and comforteth with health those that mourn.—*Job* v. 8, 11.

Show me a token for good: that they who hate me may see, and be confounded, because thou, O Lord, hast helped me and hast comforted me.—*Ps.* lxxxv. 17.

According to the multitude of my sorrows in my heart, thy comforts have given joy to my soul.—*Ps.* xciii. 19.

My eyes have failed for thy word, saying: When wilt thou comfort me?—*Ps.* cxviii. 82.

Be comforted, be comforted, my people, saith your God.

Speak ye to the heart of Jerusalem, and call to her: for her evil is come to an end, her iniquity is forgiven.—*Is.* xl. 1, 2.

Give praise, O ye heavens, and rejoice, O earth, ye mountains, give praise with jubilation: because the Lord hath comforted his people, and will have mercy on his poor ones.—*Is.* xlix. 13.

I, I myself will comfort you: who art thou, that thou shouldst be afraid of a mortal man, and of the son of man, who shall wither away like grass?—*Is.* li. 12.

The spirit of the Lord is upon me, because the Lord hath anointed me: he hath sent me to preach to the meek, to heal the contrite of heart, and to preach a release to the captives, and deliverance to them that are shut up.

To proclaim the acceptable year of the Lord, and the day of vengeance of our God: to comfort all that mourn:

To appoint to the mourners of Sion, and to give them a crown for ashes, the oil of joy for mourning, a garment of praise for the spirit of grief.—*Is.* lxi. 1-3.

As one whom the mother caresseth, so will I comfort you, and you shall be comforted in Jerusalem.—*Is.* lxvi. 13.

Blessed are they that mourn: for they shall be comforted.—*Matt.* v. 5.

Blessed be the God and Father of our Lord Jesus Christ, the Father of mercies, and the God of all comfort.

Who comforteth us in all our tribulation: that we also may be able to comfort them who are in all distress, by the exhortation wherewith we also are exhorted by God.

For as the sufferings of Christ abound in us: so also by Christ doth our comfort abound.—2 *Cor.* i. 3-5.

Now our Lord Jesus Christ himself, and God and our Father, who hath loved us, and hath given us everlasting consolation, and good hope in grace,

Exhort your hearts, and confirm you in every good work and word.—2 *Thess.* ii. 15, 16.

And you have forgotten the consolation, which speaketh to you, as unto children, saying: My son, neglect not the discipline of the Lord; neither be thou wearied whilst thou art rebuked by him.

For whom the Lord loveth, he chastiseth; and he scourgeth every son whom he receiveth.—*Heb.* xii. 5, 6.

COMMANDMENTS OF GOD, THE

Let not the book of this law depart from thy mouth: but thou shalt meditate on it day and night, that thou mayst observe and do all things that are written in it: then shalt thou direct thy way, and understand it.—*Jos.* i. 8.

The law of the Lord is unspotted, converting souls: the testimony of the Lord is faithful, giving wisdom to little ones.

The justices of the Lord are right, rejoicing hearts: the commandment of the Lord is lightsome, enlightening the eyes.—*Ps.* xviii. 8, 9.

All his commandments are faithful: confirmed for ever and ever, made in truth and equity.—*Ps.* cx. 8.

I meditated also on thy commandments, which I loved.

And I lifted up my hands to thy commandments, which I loved: and I was exercised in thy justifications.—*Ps.* cxviii. 47, 48.

Unless thy law had been my meditation, I had then perhaps perished in my abjection.

Thy justifications I will never forget: for by them thou hast given me life.—*Ps.* cxviii. 92, 93.

O how have I loved thy law, O Lord! it is my meditation all the day.

Through thy commandment, thou hast made me wiser than my enemies: for it is ever with me. . . .

By thy commandments I have had understanding: therefore have I hated every way of iniquity.—*Ps.* cxviii. 97, 98, 104.

Because the commandment is a lamp, and the law a light, and reproofs of instruction are the way of life.—*Prov.* vi. 23.

God created man of the earth, and made him after his own image. . . .

He created of him a helpmate like to himself: he gave them counsel, and a tongue, and eyes, and ears, and a heart to devise: and he filled them with the knowledge of understanding. . . .

Moreover he gave them instructions, and the law of life for an inheritance. —*Ecclus.* xvii. 1, 5, 9.

A wise man hateth not the commandments and justices, and he shall not be dashed in pieces as a ship in a storm.

A man of understanding is faithful to the law of God, and the law is faithful to him.—*Ecclus.* xxxiii. 2, 3.

Hear, O Israel, the commandments of life: give ear, that thou mayst learn wisdom.—*Bar.* iii. 9.

Do not think that I am come to destroy the law, or the prophets. I am not come to destroy, but to fulfil.

For amen I say unto you, till heaven and earth pass, one jot, or one tittle shall not pass of the law, till all be fulfilled.—*Matt.* v. 17, 18.

And it is easier for heaven and earth to pass, than one tittle of the law to fall.—*Luke* xvi. 17.

For I have not spoken of myself; but the Father who sent me, he gave me commandment what I should say, and what I should speak.

And I know that his commandment is life everlasting.—*John* xii. 49, 50.

Wherefore the law indeed is holy, and the commandment holy, and just, and good.—*Rom.* vii. 12.

COMMANDMENTS OF GOD ARE NOT ABOVE OUR STRENGTH, THE

This commandment, that I command thee this day, is not above thee, nor far off from thee:

Nor is it in heaven, that thou shouldst say: Which of us can go up to heaven to bring it unto us, and we may hear, and fulfil it in work?

Nor is it beyond the sea: that thou mayst excuse thyself, and say: Which of us can cross the sea, and bring it unto us: that we may hear, and do that which is commanded?

But the word is very nigh unto thee, in thy mouth and in thy heart, that thou mayst do it.—*Deut.* xxx. 11-14.

I have not spoken in secret, in a dark place of the earth: I have not said to the seed of Jacob: Seek me in vain. I am the Lord that speak justice, that declare right things.—*Is.* xlv. 19.

Take up my yoke upon you, and learn of me, because I am meek, and humble of heart: and you shall find rest to your souls.

For my yoke is sweet and my burden light.—*Matt.* xi. 29, 30.

For this is the charity of God, that we keep his commandments: and his commandments are not heavy.—*1 John* v. 3.

COMMANDMENTS, KEEPING GOD'S

And now, Israel, what doth the Lord thy God require of thee, but that thou fear the Lord thy God, and walk in his ways, and love him, and serve the Lord thy God, with all thy heart and with all thy soul:

And keep the commandments of the Lord, and his ceremonies, which I command thee this day, that it may be well with thee?—*Deut.* x. 12, 13.

I have not departed from the commandments of his lips, and the words of his mouth, I have hid in my bosom. —*Job* xxiii. 12.

Blessed is the man who hath not walked in the counsel of the ungodly.

nor stood in the way of sinners, nor sat in the chair of pestilence.

But his will is in the law of the Lord, and on his law he shall meditate day and night.—*Ps.* i. 1, 2.

Thou hast commanded thy commandments to be kept most diligently.

O! that my ways may be directed to keep thy justifications.

Then shall I not be confounded, when I shall look into all thy commandments. . . .

So shall I always keep thy law for ever and ever.—*Ps.* cxviii. 4-6, 44.

Much peace have they that love thy law, and to them there is no stumbling block.—*Ps.* cxviii. 165.

Put thy feet into 'her fetters, and thy neck into her chains:

Bow down thy shoulder, and bear her, and be not grieved with her bands. . . .

Search for her, and she shall be made known to thee, and when thou hast gotten her, let her not go:

For in the latter end, thou shalt find rest in her, and she shall be turned to thy joy.

Then shall her fetters be a strong defence for thee, and a firm foundation, and her chain a robe of glory:

For in her is the beauty of life, and her bands are a healthful binding.—*Ecclus.* vi. 25, 26, 28-31.

As everlasting foundations upon a solid rock, so the commandments of God in the heart of a holy woman.—*Ecclus.* xxvi. 24.

He that keepeth the law, multiplieth offerings.

It is a wholesome sacrifice to take heed to the commandments, and to depart from all iniquity.—*Ecclus.* xxxv. 1, 2.

Blessed is he that is conversant in these good things: and he that layeth them up in his heart, shall be wise always.

For if he do them, he shall be strong to do all things: because the light of God guideth his steps.—*Ecclus.* l. 30, 31.

And I gave them my statutes, and I showed them my judgments, which if a man do, he shall live in them.—*Ezech.* xx. 11.

¹The wisdom of doctrine.

Then Mathathias answered, and said with a loud voice: Although all nations obey king Antiochus, so as to depart every man from the service of the law of his fathers, and consent to his commandments:

I and my sons and my brethren will obey the law of our fathers.

God be merciful unto us: it is not profitable for us to forsake the law, and the justices of God:

We will not hearken to the words of king Antiochus, neither will we sacrifice, and transgress the commandments of our law, to go another way.—1 *Mach.* ii. 19-22.

For I am delighted with the law of God, according to the inward man.—*Rom.* vii. 22.

Circumcision is nothing, and uncircumcision is nothing: but the observance of the commandments of God.—1 *Cor.* vii. 19.

COMMANDMENTS, KEEPING GOD'S, IS TRUE WISDOM

You know that I have taught you statutes and justices, as the Lord my God hath commanded me: so shall you do them in the land which you shall possess:

And you shall observe and fulfil them in practice. For this is your wisdom, and understanding in the sight of nations, that hearing all these precepts, they may say: Behold a wise and understanding people, a great nation.—*Deut.* iv. 5, 6.

Who is wise, and will keep these things; and will understand the mercies of the Lord?—*Ps.* cvi. 43.

I have had understanding above ancients: because I have sought thy commandments.—*Ps.* cxviii. 100.

He that keepeth the law is a wise son.—*Prov.* xxviii. 7.

And they that remain shall know, that there is nothing better than the fear of God: and that there is nothing sweeter than to have regard to the commandments of the Lord.—*Ecclus.* xxiii. 37.

A man of understanding is faithful to the law of God, and the law is faithful to him.—*Ecclus.* xxxiii. 3.

COMMANDMENTS, KEEPING GOD'S, A PROOF OF OUR FAITH AND LOVE

They that fear the Lord will not be incredulous to his word: and they that love him, will keep his way. . . .

They that fear the Lord, keep his commandments, and will have patience even until his visitation.—*Ecclus.* ii. 18, 21.

In every work of thine, regard thy soul in faith: for this is the keeping of the commandments.

He that believeth God, taketh heed to the commandments.—*Ecclus.* xxxii. 27, 28.

If you love me, keep my commandments.—*John* xiv. 15.

He that hath my commandments and keepeth them; he it is that loveth me. . . .

Jesus answered and said to him: (Judas, not the Iscariot): If any man love me, he will keep my word, and my Father will love him, and we will come to him, and will make our abode with him.—*John* xiv. 21, 23.

And by this we know that we have known him, if we keep his commandments.

He who saith that he knoweth him, and keepeth not his commandments, is a liar, and the truth is not in him.

But he that keepeth his word, in him in very deed the charity of God is perfected; and by this we know that we are in him.—*1 John* ii. 3-5.

And this is charity, that we walk according to his commandments.—*2 John* i. 6.

COMMANDMENTS, KEEPING GOD'S, GAINS FOR US HIS MERCY AND BLESSING

I am the Lord thy God, mighty, jealous, visiting the iniquity of the fathers upon the children, unto the third and fourth generation of them that hate me:

And showing mercy unto thousands to them that love me, and keep my commandments.—*Ex.* xx. 5, 6.

And he will be merciful to us, if we keep and do all his precepts before the Lord our God, as he hath commanded us.—*Deut.* vi. 25.

But the mercy of the Lord is from eternity and unto eternity upon them that fear him:

And his justice unto children's children, to such as keep his covenant,

And are mindful of his commandments to do them.—*Ps.* cii. 17, 18.

When prophecy shall fail, the people shall be scattered abroad: but he that keepeth the law is blessed.—*Prov.* xxix. 18.

For who hath continued in his commandment, and hath been forsaken? or who hath called upon him, and he despised him?—*Ecclus.* ii. 12.

Thus saith the Lord: Keep ye judgment, and do justice: for my salvation is near to come, and my justice to be revealed.

Blessed is the man that doth this, and the son of man that shall lay hold on this: that keepeth the sabbath from profaning it, that keepeth his hands from doing any evil.—*Is.* lvi. 1, 2.

And I prayed to the Lord my God, and I made my confession, and said: I beseech thee, O Lord God, great and terrible, who keepest the covenant, and mercy to them that love thee, and keep thy commandments.—*Dan.* ix. 4.

If you know these things, you shall be blessed, if you do them.—*John* xiii. 17.

COMMANDMENTS, REWARD OF KEEPING GOD'S, IN THIS LIFE

Do my precepts, and keep my judgments, and fulfil them: that you may dwell in the land without any fear,

And the ground may yield you its fruits, of which you may eat your fill, fearing no man's invasion.—*Lev.* xxv. 18, 19.

If you walk in my precepts, and keep my commandments, and do them, I will give you rain in due seasons,

And the ground shall bring forth its increase, and the trees shall be filled with fruit: . . .

And you shall eat your bread to the full, and dwell in your land without fear.

I will give peace in your coasts: you shall sleep, and there shall be none to make you afraid.

. . . I will set my tabernacle in the midst of you, and my soul shall not cast you off.

I will walk among you, and will be your God, and you shall be my people.—*Lev.* xxvi. 3-6, 11, 12.

Keep his precepts and commandments, which I command thee: that it may be well with thee, and thy children after thee, and thou mayst remain a long time upon the land, which the Lord thy God will give thee.—*Deut.* iv. 40.

For then thou shalt be able to prosper, if thou keep the commandments, and judgments, which the Lord commanded Moses to teach Israel: take courage, and act manfully, fear not, nor be dismayed.—1 *Paral.* xxii. 13.

My son, forget not my law, and let thy heart keep my commandments.

For they shall add to thee length of days, and years of life and peace.—*Prov.* iii. 1, 2.

My son, let not these things depart from thy eyes: keep the law and counsel:

And there shall be life to thy soul, and grace to thy mouth.

Then shalt thou walk confidently in thy way, and thy foot shall not stumble:

If thou sleep, thou shalt not fear: thou shalt rest, and thy sleep shall be sweet.

Be not afraid of sudden fear, nor of the power of the wicked falling upon thee.

For the Lord will be at thy side, and will keep thy foot, that thou be not taken.—*Prov.* iii. 21-26.

He that keepeth the commandment, shall find no evil.—*Eccles.* viii. 5.

If thou wilt keep the commandments and perform acceptable fidelity for ever, they shall preserve thee.—*Ecclus.* xv. 16.

As a fearful heart in the thought of a fool at all times will not fear, so neither shall he that continueth always in the commandments of God.—*Ecclus.* xxii. 23.

O that thou hadst hearkened to my commandments: thy peace had been as a river, and thy justice as the waves of the sea.—*Is.* xlviii. 18.

Jesus answered, and said to him: If any man love me, he will keep my word, and my Father will love him, and we will come to him, and will make our abode with him.—*John* xiv. 23.

If you keep my commandments, you shall abide in my love; as I also have kept my Father's commandments, and do abide in his love.

. . . You are my friends, if you do the things that I command you.—*John* xv. 10, 14.

And whatsoever we shall ask, we shall receive of him: because we keep his commandments, and do those things which are pleasing in his sight. . . .

And he that keepeth his commandments, abideth in him, and he in him.—1 *John* iii. 22, 24.

COMMANDMENTS, REWARD, IN THE NEXT LIFE, OF KEEPING GOD'S

If you walk in my precepts, and keep my commandments, and do them, . . .

I will set my tabernacle in the midst of you, and my soul shall not cast you off.

I will walk among you, and will be your God, and you shall be my people —*Lev.* xxvi. 3, 11, 12.

The justices of the Lord are right, rejoicing hearts: the commandment of the Lord is lightsome, enlightening the eyes. . . .

For thy servant keepeth them, and in keeping them there is a great reward.—*Ps.* xviii. 9, 12.

Expect the Lord, and keep his way: and he will exalt thee to inherit the land: when the sinners shall perish thou shalt see.—*Ps.* xxxvi. 34.

He that keepeth the commandment, keepeth his own soul: but he that neglecteth his own way, shall die.—*Prov.* xix. 16.

Place thy treasure in the commandments of the most High, and it shall bring thee more profit than gold.—*Ecclus.* xxix. 14.

For thus saith the Lord to the eunuchs, They that shall keep my sabbaths, and shall choose the things that please me, and shall hold fast to my covenant:

I will give to them in my house, and within my walls, a place, and a name, better than sons and daughters: I will give them an everlasting name which shall never perish.—*Is.* lvi. 4, 5.

This is the book of the commandments of God, and the law, that is for ever: all they that keep it, shall come to life: but they that have forsaken it, to death.—*Bar.* iv. 1.

He therefore that shall break one of these least commandments, and shall so teach men, shall be called the least in the kingdom of heaven. But he that shall do and teach, he shall be called great in the kingdom of heaven.—*Matt.* v. 19.

And behold one came and said to him: Good master, what good shall I do that I may have life everlasting?

Who said to him: Why askest thou me concerning good? One is good, God. But if thou wilt enter into life, keep the commandments.—*Matt.* xix. 16, 17.

And behold, a certain lawyer stood up, tempting him, and saying, Master, what must I do to possess eternal life?

But he said to him: What is written in the law? how readest thou?

He answering, said: Thou shalt love the Lord thy God with thy whole heart, and with thy whole soul, and with all thy strength, and with all thy mind: and thy neighbor as thyself.

And he said to him: Thou hast answered right: this do, and thou shalt live.—*Luke* x. 25-28.

COMMANDMENTS OF GOD, EXHORTATION TO KEEP THE

Keep my laws and my judgments, which if a man do, he shall live in them. —*Lev.* xviii. 5.

Keep his precepts and commandments, which I command thee: that it may be well with thee and thy children after thee, and thou mayst remain a long time upon the land, which the Lord thy God will give thee.—*Deut.* iv. 40.

Receive the law of his mouth, and lay up his words in thy heart.—*Job* xxii. 22.

Expect the Lord, and keep his way: and he will exalt thee to inherit the land: when the sinners shall perish, thou shalt see.—*Ps.* xxxvi. 34.

My son, forget not my law, and let thy heart keep my commandments.—*Prov.* iii. 1.

My son, let not these things depart from thy eyes: keep the law and counsel.—*Prov.* iii. 21.

My son, keep my words, and lay up my precepts with thee. Son,

Keep my commandments, and thou shalt live: and my law as the apple of thy eye:

Bind it upon thy fingers, write it upon the tablets of thy heart.—*Prov.* vii. 1-3.

Let us all hear together the conclusion of the discourse. Fear God, and keep his commandments: for this is all man.—*Eccles.* xii. 13.

Give ear, my son, and take wise counsel, and cast not away my advice.

Put thy feet into her fetters, and thy neck into her chains:

Bow down thy shoulder, and bear her, and be not grieved with her bands.

Come to her with all thy mind, and keep her ways with all thy power.—*Ecclus.* vi. 24-27.

Place thy treasure in the commandments of the most High, and it shall bring thee more profit than gold.—*Ecclus.* xxix. 14.

This is the book of the commandments of God, and the law, that is for ever. . . .

Return, O Jacob, and take hold of it, walk in the way by its brightness, in the presence of the light thereof.—*Bar.* iv. 1, 2.

I charge thee before God, who quickeneth all things, and before Christ Jesus, who gave testimony under Pontius Pilate, a good confession,

That thou keep the commandment without spot, blameless, unto the coming of our Lord Jesus Christ.—1 *Tim.* vi. 13, 14.

COMMANDMENTS, TRANSGRESSING GOD'S

But if you will not hear me, nor do all my commandments,

If you despise my laws, and contemn

my judgments, so as not to do those things which are appointed by me, and to make void my covenant; . . .

I will set my face against you, and you shall fall down before your enemies, and shall be made subject to them that hate you, you shall flee when no man pursueth you. . . .

And I will break the pride of your stubbornness, and I will make to you the heaven above as iron, and the earth as brass. . . .

I also will walk contrary to you, and will strike you seven times for your sins.—*Lev.* xxvi. 14, 15, 17, 19, 24.

Thus saith the Lord God: Why transgress you the commandment of the Lord, which will not be for your good, and have forsaken the Lord, to make him forsake you?—*2 Paral.* xxiv. 20.

Thou hast rebuked the proud: they are cursed who decline from thy commandments.—*Ps.* cxviii. 21.

That seed of men shall be honored, which feareth God: but that seed shall be dishonored which transgresseth the commandments of the Lord.—*Ecclus.* x. 23.

Better is a man that hath less wisdom, and wanteth understanding, with the fear of God, than he that aboundeth in understanding, and transgresseth the law of the most High.—*Ecclus.* xix. 21.

This is the book of the commandments of God, and the law, that is for ever: all they that keep it, shall come to life: but they that have forsaken it, to death.—*Bar.* iv. 1.

God be merciful unto us: it is not profitable for us to forsake the law, and the justices of God.—*1 Mach.* ii. 21.

He therefore that shall break one of these least commandments, and shall so teach men, shall be called the least in the kingdom of heaven.—*Matt.* v. 19.

And I lived some time without the law. But when the commandment came, sin revived,

And I died. And the commandment that was ordained to life, the same was found to be unto death to me.

For sin, taking occasion by the commandment, seduced me, and by it killed me.—*Rom.* vii. 9-11.

COMMANDMENTS, WE MUST OBEY ALL THE

Better is wisdom than weapons of war: and he that shall offend in one, shall lose many good things.—*Eccles.* ix. 18.

He therefore that shall break one of these least commandments, and shall so teach men, shall be called the least in the kingdom of heaven.—*Matt.* v. 19.

And whosoever shall keep the whole law, but offend in one point, is become guilty of all.—*James* ii. 10.

COMMUNING WITH GOD

See: Speaking to us, God—page 542.

COMMUNION, HOLY

I will hear what the Lord God will speak in me: for he will speak peace unto his people:

And unto his saints: and unto them that are converted to the heart.—*Ps.* lxxxiv. 9.

Let the mercies of the Lord give glory to him: and his wonderful works to the children of men.

For he hath satisfied the empty soul, and hath filled the hungry soul with good things.—*Ps.* cvi. 8, 9.

He hath made a remembrance of his wonderful works, being a merciful and gracious Lord:

He hath given food to them that fear him.—*Ps.* cx. 4, 5.

In me is all grace of the way, and of the truth, in me is all hope of life and of virtue.

Come over to me, all ye that desire me, and be filled with my fruits.

For my spirit is sweet above honey, and my inheritance above honey and the honeycomb.

My memory is unto everlasting generations.—*Ecclus.* xxiv. 25-28.

All you that thirst, come to the waters: and you that have no money, make haste, buy, and eat: come ye, buy wine and milk without money, and without any price.

Why do you spend money for that which is not bread, and your labor for that which doth not satisfy you?

Hearken diligently to me, and eat that which is good, and your soul shall be delighted in fatness.—*Is.* lv. 1, 2.

For I have inebriated the weary soul: and I have filled every hungry soul.—*Jer.* xxxi. 25.

Then came to him the disciples of John, saying: Why do we, and the Pharisees, fast often, but thy disciples do not fast?

And Jesus said to them: Can the children of the bridegroom mourn, as long as the bridegroom is with them? But the days will come, when the bridegroom shall be taken away from them, and then they shall fast.—*Matt.* ix. 14, 15.

And when Jesus was come to the place, looking up, he saw him, and said to him: Zacheus, make haste and come down; for this day I must abide in thy house.

And he made haste and came down; and received him with joy.—*Luke* xix. 5, 6.

And Jesus said to them: I am the bread of life: he that cometh to me shall not hunger; and he that believeth in me shall never thirst.

. . . I am the bread of life.

Your fathers did eat manna in the desert, and are dead.

This is the bread which cometh down from heaven; that if any man eat of it, he may not die.

I am the living bread which came down from heaven.

If any man eat of this bread, he shall live for ever; and the bread that I will give, is my flesh, for the life of the world. . . .

Then Jesus said to them: Amen, amen I say unto you: Except you eat the flesh of the Son of man, and drink his blood, you shall not have life in you.

He that eateth my flesh, and drinketh my blood, hath everlasting life: and I will raise him up in the last day.

For my flesh is meat indeed: and my blood is drink indeed.

He that eateth my flesh and drinketh my blood, abideth in me, and I in him.

As the living Father hath sent me, and I live by the Father; so he that eateth me, the same also shall live by me.

This is the bread that came down from heaven. Not as your fathers did eat manna, and are dead. He that eateth this bread, shall live for ever.—*John* vi. 35, 48-52, 54-59.

I will not leave you orphans, I will come to you.—*John* xiv. 18.

The chalice of benediction, which we bless, is it not the communion of the blood of Christ? And the bread, which we break, is it not the partaking of the body of the Lord?—1 *Cor.* x. 16.

For as often as you shall eat this bread, and drink the chalice, you shall show the death of the Lord, until he come.—1 *Cor.* xi. 26.

COMMUNION, HOLY, PREFIGURED

And when the children of Israel saw it, they said one to another: Manhu! which signifieth: What is this! for they knew not what it was. And Moses said to them: This is the bread, which the Lord hath given you to eat. . . .

And the house of Israel called the name thereof Manna: and it was like coriander seed, white, and the taste thereof like to flour with honey.—*Ex.* xvi. 15, 31.

And the angel of the Lord came again the second time, and touched him (Elias), and said to him: Arise, eat: for thou hast yet a great way to go.

And he arose, and ate, and drank, and walked in the strength of that food, forty days and forty nights, unto the mount of God, Horeb.—3 *Kings* xix. 7, 8.

And he had commanded the clouds from above, and had opened the doors of heaven.

And had rained down manna upon them, to eat, and had given them the bread of heaven.

Man ate the bread of angels.—*Ps.* lxxvii. 23-25.

Instead of which things, thou didst feed thy people with the food of angels, and gavest them bread from heaven, prepared without labor; having in it all that is delicious, and the sweetness of every taste.—*Wis.* xvi. 20.

COMMUNION, HAPPINESS OF HOLY

O how great is the multitude of thy sweetness, O Lord, which thou hast hidden for them that fear thee!

Which thou hast wrought for them that hope in thee, in the sight of the sons of men.—*Ps.* xxx. 20.

O taste, and see that the Lord is sweet.—*Ps.* xxxiii. 9.

My beloved to me, and I to him who feedeth among the lilies.—*Cant.* ii. 16.

From the beginning of the world, they have not heard, nor perceived with the ears: the eye hath not seen, O God, besides thee, what things thou hast prepared for them that wait for thee.—*Is.* lxiv. 4.

Come to me, all you that labor, and are burdened, and I will refresh you.—*Matt.* xi. 28.

If so be you have tasted that the Lord is sweet.—1 *Peter* ii. 3.

And he (the angel) said to me: Write: Blessed are they that are called to the marriage supper of the Lamb.—*Apoc.* xix. 9.

COMMUNION, DESIRE FOR HOLY

As the hart panteth after the fountains of water, so my soul panteth after thee, O God.

My soul hath thirsted after the strong, living God; when shall I come and appear before the face of God?—*Ps.* xli. 2, 3.

O God, my God, to thee do I watch at break of day.

For thee my soul hath thirsted; for thee my flesh, O how many ways!

In a desert land, and where there is no way, and no water: so in the sanctuary have I come before thee, to see thy power and thy glory.—*Ps.* lxii. 2, 3.

For what have I in heaven? and besides thee, what do I desire upon earth?

For thee my flesh and my heart hath fainted away: thou art the God of my heart, and the God that is my portion for ever.—*Ps.* lxxii. 25, 26.

How lovely are thy tabernacles, O Lord of hosts! my soul longeth and fainteth for the courts of the Lord.

My heart and my flesh have rejoiced in the living God.—*Ps.* lxxxiii. 2, 3.

Lord, bow down thy heavens, and descend.—*Ps.* cxliii. 5.

When I had a little passed by them, I found him whom my soul loveth; I held him; and I will not let him go, till I bring him into my mother's house, and into the chamber of her that bore me.—*Cant.* iii. 4.

Come over to me, all ye that desire me, and be filled with my fruits. . . .

They that eat me, shall yet hunger: and they that drink me, shall yet thirst.—*Ecclus.* xxiv. 26, 29.

Give us this day our supersubstantial bread.—*Matt.* vi. 11.

But [1]they constrained him; saying: Stay with us, because it is towards evening, and the day is now far spent. And he went in with them.—*Luke* xxiv. 29.

COMMUNION, PREPARATION FOR HOLY

If any one that is defiled, shall eat of the flesh of the sacrifice of peace offerings, which is offered to the Lord, he shall be cut off from his people.—*Lev.* vii. 20.

And the Lord spoke to Moses, saying:

Say to them and to their posterity: Every man of your race, that approacheth to those things that are consecrated, and which the children of Israel have offered to the Lord, in whom there is uncleanness, shall perish before the Lord. I am the Lord.—*Lev.* xxii. 1, 3.

And the priest answered David, saying: I have no common bread at hand, but only holy bread, if the young men be clean, especially from women.—1 *Kings* xxi. 4.

And king David said to all the assembly: Solomon my son, whom alone God hath chosen, is as yet young and tender: and the work is great, for a house is prepared not for man, but for God.—1 *Paral.* xxix. 1.

Who then can be worthy to build him a worthy house? If heaven, and the heavens of heavens cannot contain

[1]The disciples on the way to Emmaus, meeting Christ after the resurrection.

him: who am I that I should be able to build him a house?—2 *Paral.* ii. 6.

The voice of one crying in the desert: Prepare ye the way of the Lord, make straight in the wilderness the paths of our God.

Every valley shall be exalted, and every mountain and hill shall be made low, and the crooked shall become straight, and the rough ways plain.—*Is.* xl. 3, 4.

Give not that which is holy to dogs; neither cast ye your pearls before swine. —*Matt.* vii. 6.

And the centurion making answer, said: Lord, I am not worthy that thou shouldst enter under my roof: but only say the word, and my servant shall be healed.—*Matt.* viii. 8.

And the king went in to see the guests: and he saw there a man who had not on a wedding garment.

And he saith to him: Friend, how camest thou in hither, not having on a wedding garment? But he was silent.

Then the king said to the waiters: Bind his hands and feet, and cast him into the exterior darkness: there shall be weeping and gnashing of teeth.—*Matt.* xxii. 11-13.

You cannot drink the chalice of the Lord, and the chalice of devils: you cannot be partakers of the table of the Lord, and of the table of devils.—1 *Cor.* x. 21.

Therefore, whosoever shall eat this bread, or drink the chalice of the Lord unworthily, shall be guilty of the body and of the blood of the Lord.

But let a man prove himself: and so let him eat of that bread, and drink of the chalice.

For he that eateth and drinketh unworthily, eateth and drinketh judgment to himself, not discerning the body of the Lord.—1 *Cor.* xi. 27-29.

COMPANY, KEEPING GOOD

My eyes were upon the faithful of the earth, to sit with me: the man that walked in the perfect way, he served me.—*Ps.* c. 6.

I am a partaker with all them that fear thee, and that keep thy commandments.—*Ps.* cxviii. 63.

He that walketh with the wise, will be wise.—*Prov.* xiii. 20.

He that feareth God, shall likewise have good friendship: because according to him, shall his friend be.—*Ecclus.* vi. 17.

Stand in the multitude of ancients that are wise, and join thyself from thy heart to their wisdom, that thou mayst hear every discourse of God, and the sayings of praise may not escape thee.

And if thou see a man of understanding, go to him early in the morning, and let thy foot wear the steps of his doors.—*Ecclus.* vi. 35, 36.

According to thy power beware of thy neighbor, and treat with the wise and prudent.

Let just men be thy guests, and let thy glory be in the fear of God.—*Ecclus.* ix. 21, 22.

Go to the side of the holy age, with them that live and give praise to God. —*Ecclus.* xvii. 25.

In the midst of the unwise, keep in the word till its time: but be continually among men that think.—*Ecclus.* xxvii. 13.

But be continually with a holy man, whomsoever thou shalt know to observe the fear of God,

Whose soul is according to thy own soul: and who, when thou shalt stumble in the dark, will be sorry for thee.—*Ecclus.* xxxvii. 15, 16.

COMPANY, KEEPING BAD

And Jehu, the son of Hanani the seer, met him (Josaphat), and said to him: Thou helpest the ungodly, and thou art joined in friendship with them that hate the Lord, and therefore thou didst deserve indeed the wrath of the Lord.—2 *Paral.* xix. 2.

If thou didst see a thief thou didst run with him: and with adulterers thou hast been a partaker.—*Ps.* xlix. 18.

Who will pity an enchanter struck by a serpent, or any one that come near wild beasts? so is it with him that keepeth company with a wicked man, and is involved in his sins.—*Ecclus.* xii. 13.

If the wolf shall at any time have fellowship with the lamb, so the sinner with the just.

What fellowship hath a holy man with a dog, or what part hath the rich with the poor?—*Ecclus*. xiii. 21, 22.

COMPANY, DANGER OF KEEPING BAD

Thou shalt not enter into league with [1]them, nor with their gods.

Let them not dwell in thy land, lest perhaps they make thee sin against me, if thou serve their gods: which undoubtedly will be a scandal to thee.—*Ex*. xxiii. 32, 33.

Beware thou never join in friendship with the inhabitants of that land, which may be thy ruin.

. . . Make no covenant with the men of those countries, lest, when they have committed fornication with their gods, and have adored their idols, some one call thee to eat of the things sacrificed.—*Ex*. xxxiv. 12, 15.

But if you will embrace the errors of these nations that dwell among you, and make marriages with them, and join friendships:

Know ye for a certainty that the Lord your God will not destroy them before your face, but they shall be a pit and a snare in your way, and a stumbling-block at your side, and stakes in your eyes, till he take you away, and destroy you from off this excellent land, which he hath given you.—*Jos*. xxiii. 12, 13.

He that walketh with the wise, shall be wise: a friend of fools, shall become like to them.—*Prov*. xiii. 20.

Be not a friend to an angry man, and do not walk with a furious man:

Lest perhaps thou learn his ways, and take scandal to thy soul.—*Prov*. xxii. 24, 25.

Go not on the way with a bold man, lest he burden thee with his evils: for he goeth according to his own will, and thou shalt perish together with his folly.—*Ecclus*. viii. 18.

Use not much the company of her that is a dancer, and hearken not to her, lest thou perish by the force of her charms.—*Ecclus*. ix. 4.

He that toucheth pitch, shall be de-

[1]The idolatrous tribes or people of Palestine.

filed with it: and he that hath fellowship with the proud, shall put on pride. —*Ecclus*. xiii. 1.

The discourse of sinners is hateful, and their laughter is at the pleasures of sin.—*Ecclus*. xxvii. 14.

Know you not that a little leaven corrupteth the whole lump?—1 *Cor*. v. 6.

Be not seduced: Evil communications corrupt good manners.—1 *Cor*. xv. 33.

And I heard another voice from heaven, saying: Go out from [1]her, my people; that you be not partakers of her sins, and that you receive not of her plagues.—*Apoc*. xviii. 4.

COMPANY, AVOIDING BAD

I have not sat with the council of vanity: neither will I go in with the doers of unjust things.

I have hated the assembly of the malignant; and with the wicked I will not sit.—*Ps*. xxv. 4, 5.

The perverse heart did not cleave to me: and the malignant, that turned aside from me, I would not know.

The man that in private detracted his neighbor, him did I persecute. . . .

He that worketh pride shall not dwell in the midst of my house: he that speaketh unjust things did not prosper before my eyes.—*Ps*. c. 4, 5, 7.

Incline not my heart to evil words; to make excuses in sins.

With men that work iniquity: and I will not communicate with the choicest of them.—*Ps*. cxl. 4.

COMPANY, EXHORTATION TO AVOID BAD

Lay out thy bread, and thy wine upon the burial of a just man, and do not eat and drink thereof with the wicked. —*Tob*. iv. 18.

My son, if sinners shall entice thee, consent not to them.

If they shall say: Come with us, let us lie in wait for blood, let us hide snares for the innocent without cause. . . .

Cast in thy lot with us, let us all have one purse.

[1]The wicked and fallen Babylon.

My son, walk not thou with them, restrain thy foot from their paths.—*Prov.* i. 10, 11, 14, 15.

Be not delighted in the paths of the wicked, neither let the way of evil men please thee.

Flee from it, pass not by it: go aside, and forsake it.—*Prov.* iv. 14, 15.

Be not in the feasts of great drinkers, nor in their revellings, who contribute flesh to eat:

Because they that give themselves to drinking, and that club together shall be consumed; and drowsiness shall be clothed with rags.—*Prov.* xxiii. 20, 21.

Seek not to be like evil men, neither desire to be with them.—*Prov.* xxiv. 1.

My son, fear the Lord and the king: and have nothing to do with detracters.—*Prov.* xxiv. 21.

Winnow not with every wind, and go not into every way: for so is every sinner proved by a double tongue.—*Ecclus.* v. 11.

Depart from the unjust, and evils shall depart from thee.—*Ecclus.* vii. 2.

Number not thyself among the multitude of the disorderly.—*Ecclus.* vii. 17.

Take no pleasure in riotous assemblies, be they ever so small: for their concertation is continual.—*Ecclus.* xviii. 32.

Talk not much with a fool, and go not with him that hath no sense.

Keep thyself from him, that thou mayst not have trouble, and thou shalt not be defiled with his sin.

Turn away from him, and thou shalt find rest, and shalt not be wearied out with his folly.—*Ecclus.* xxii. 14-16.

Now I beseech you, brethren, to mark them who make dissensions and offences contrary to the doctrine which you have learned, and avoid them.—*Rom.* xvi. 17.

I wrote to you in an epistle, not to keep company with fornicators. . . .

But now I have written to you, not to keep company, if any man that is named a brother, be a fornicator, or covetous, or a server of idols, or a railer, or a drunkard, or an extortioner: with such a one, not so much as to eat. . . .

Put away the evil one from among yourselves.—1 *Cor.* v. 9, 11, 13.

Bear not the yoke with unbelievers. For what participation hath justice with injustice? Or what fellowship hath light with darkness?

And what concord hath Christ with Belial? Or what part hath the faithful with the unbeliever?

And what agreement hath the temple of God with idols? For you are the temple of the living God. . . .

Wherefore, Go out from among them, and be ye separate, saith the Lord, and touch not the unclean thing. —2 *Cor.* vi. 14-17.

And we charge you, brethren, in the name of our Lord Jesus Christ, that you withdraw yourselves from every brother walking disorderly, and not according to the tradition which they have received of us.—2 *Thess.* iii. 6.

And if any man obey not our word by this epistle, note that man, and do not keep company with him, that he may be ashamed:

Yet do not esteem him as an enemy, but admonish him as a brother.— 2 *Thess.* iii. 14, 15.

Know also this, that in the last days, shall come dangerous times.

Men shall be lovers of themselves, covetous, haughty, proud, blasphemers, disobedient to parents, ungrateful, wicked,

Without affection, without peace, slanderers, incontinent, unmerciful, without kindness,

Traitors, stubborn, puffed up, and lovers of pleasure more than of God:

Having an appearance indeed of godliness, but denying the power thereof. Now these avoid.—2 *Tim.* iii. 1-5.

COMPASSION FOR THE DISTRESSED

See: Comfort the afflicted, we should —page 56.

COMPASSION FOR THE SORROWING AND THE AFFLICTED, GOD'S

See also: Mercy of God to those in sorrow and distress—page 318.

O God, I have declared to thee my

life: thou hast set my tears in thy sight.—*Ps.* lv. 9.

And thou, O Lord, art a God of compassion, and merciful, patient, and of much mercy, and true.—*Ps.* lxxxv. 15.

Because he hath looked forth from his high sanctuary: from heaven the Lord hath looked upon the earth.

That he might hear the groans of them that are in fetters: that he might release the children of the slain.—*Ps.* ci. 20, 21.

Who is as the Lord our God, who dwelleth on high: and looketh down on the low things in heaven and in earth?

Raising up the needy from the earth, and lifting up the poor out of the dunghill:

That he may place him with princes, with the princes of his people.

Who maketh a barren woman to dwell in a house, the joyful mother of children.—*Ps.* cxii. 5-9.

He will not despise the prayers of the fatherless; nor the widow, when she poureth out her complaint.

Do not the widow's tears run down the cheek, and her cry against him that causeth them to fall?

For from the cheek they go up even to heaven, and the Lord that heareth will not be delighted with them.—*Ecclus.* xxxv. 17-19.

The bruised reed he shall not break, and smoking flax he shall not quench.—*Is.* xlii. 3.

COMPASSION FOR THE AFFLICTED, CHRIST'S

And Jesus went about all Galilee, teaching in their synagogues, and preaching the gospel of the kingdom: and healing all manner of sickness and every infirmity, among the people.

And his fame went throughout all Syria, and they presented to him all sick people that were taken with divers diseases and torments, and such as were possessed by devils, and lunatics, and those that had the palsy, and he cured them.—*Matt.* iv. 23, 24.

And when he had entered into Capharnaum, there came to him a centurion, beseeching him,

And saying: Lord, my servant lieth at home sick of the palsy, and is grievously tormented.

And Jesus saith to him: I will come and heal him.—*Matt.* viii. 5-7.

And when evening was come, they brought to him many that were possessed with devils: and he cast out the spirits with his word: and all that were sick he healed:

That it might be fulfilled, which was spoken by the prophet, Isaias, saying: He took our infirmities, and bore our diseases.—*Matt.* viii. 16, 17.

And seeing the multitudes, he had compassion on them: because they were distressed, and lying like sheep that have no shepherd.—*Matt.* ix. 36.

Come to me, all you that labor, and are burdened, and I will refresh you.—*Matt.* xi. 28.

And he coming forth saw a great multitude, and had compassion on them, and healed their sick.—*Matt.* xiv. 14.

And Jesus called together his disciples, and said: I have compassion on the multitudes, because they continue with me now three days, and have not what to eat, and I will not send them away fasting, lest they faint in the way. —*Matt.* xv. 32.

And behold two blind men sitting by the wayside, heard that Jesus passed by, and they cried out, saying: O Lord, thou son of David, have mercy on us. . . . .

And Jesus stood, and called them, and said: What will ye, that I do to you?

They say to him: Lord, that our eyes be opened.

And Jesus, having compassion on them, touched their eyes. And immediately they saw, and followed him.—*Matt.* xx. 30, 32, 33, 34.

And there came a leper to him, beseeching him, and kneeling down, said to him: If thou wilt, thou canst make me clean.

And Jesus having compassion on him, stretched forth his hand; and touching him, saith to him: I will. Be thou made clean.

And when he had spoken, immediately the leprosy departed from him, and he was made clean.—*Mark* i. 40-42.

A d it came to pass afterwards, that he went into a city that is called Naim; and there went with him his disciples and a great multitude.

And when he came nigh to the gate of the city, behold a dead man was carried out, the only son of his mother; and she was a widow; and a great multitude of the city was with her.

Whom when the Lord had seen, being moved with mercy towards her, he said to her: Weep not.

And he came near, and touched the bier. And they that carried it, stood still. And he said: Young man, I say to thee, arise.

And he that was dead, sat up, and began to speak. And he gave him to his mother.—*Luke* vii. 11-15.

And behold there was a woman, who had a spirit of infirmity eighteen years, and she was bowed together, neither could she look upwards at all.

Whom when Jesus saw, he called her unto him, and said to her: Woman, thou art delivered from thy infirmity.

And he laid his hands upon her, and immediately she was made straight, and glorified God.—*Luke* xiii. 11-13.

When Mary therefore was come where Jesus was, seeing him, she fell down at his feet, and saith to him: Lord, if thou hadst been here, my brother had not died.

Jesus therefore, when he saw her weeping, and the Jews that were come with her, weeping, groaned in the spirit, and troubled himself,

And said: Where have you laid him? They say to him: Lord, come and see.

And Jesus wept.

The Jews therefore said: Behold how he loved him.—*John* xi. 32-36.

For we have not a high-priest, who cannot have compassion on our infirmities: but one tempted in all things like as we are, without sin.—*Heb.* iv. 15.

COMPLAINING

See: Murmuring—page 330.

CONCEIT

Be not wise in thy own conceit: fear God, and depart from evil.—*Prov.* iii. 7.

Hast thou seen a man wise in his own conceit? there shall be more hope of a fool than of him.—*Prov.* xxvi. 12.

Woe to you that are wise in your own eyes, and prudent in your own conceits.—*Is.* v. 21.

Being of one mind one towards another. Not minding high things, but consenting to the humble. Be not wise in your own conceits.—*Rom.* xii. 16.

CONCORD, LIVING IN

Abram therefore said to Lot: Let there be no quarrel, I beseech thee, between me and thee, and between my herdsmen and thy herdsmen: for we are brethren.

Behold the whole land is before thee: depart from me, I pray thee: if thou wilt go to the left hand, I will take the right: if thou choose the right hand, I will pass to the left.—*Gen.* xiii. 8, 9.

God who maketh men of one manner to dwell in a house.—*Ps.* lxvii. 7.

Behold how good and how pleasant it is for brethren to dwell together in unity.—*Ps.* cxxxii. 1.

Better is a dry morsel with joy, than a house full of victims with strife.—*Prov.* xvii. 1.

With three things my spirit is pleased, which are approved before God and men:

The concord of brethren, and the love of neighbors, and man and wife that agree well together.—*Ecclus.* xxv. 1, 2.

Now the God of patience and of comfort grant you to be of one mind one towards another, according to Jesus Christ:

That with one mind, and with one mouth, you may glorify God and the Father of our Lord Jesus Christ.—*Rom.* xv. 5, 6.

Now I beseech you, brethren, by the name of our Lord Jesus Christ, that you all speak the same thing, and that there be no schisms among you; but that you be perfect in the same mind, and in the same judgment.—1 *Cor.* i.10.

Only let your conversation be worthy of the gospel of Christ: that, whether I come and see you, or, being absent, may hear of you, that you stand fast in one spirit, with one mind laboring together

for the faith of the gospel.—*Philipp.*
i. 27.

Fulfil ye my joy, that you be of one
mind, having the same charity, being
of one accord, agreeing in sentiment.

Let nothing be done through contention, neither by vain glory; but in humility, let each esteem others better
than themselves:

Each one not considering the things
that are his own, but those that are
other men's.—*Philipp.* ii. 2-4.

And in fine, be ye all of one mind,
having compassion one of another, being lovers of the brotherhood, merciful,
modest, humble:

Not rendering evil for evil, nor railing for railing, but contrariwise, blessing: for unto this are you called, that
you may inherit a blessing.—1 *Peter* iii.
8, 9.

CONDESCENSION TO US, GOD'S

See: Unworthiness of God and His
favors, man's—page 573.

CONFIDENCE IN GOD

Although he should kill me, I will
trust in him.—*Job* xiii. 15.

In the Lord I put my trust: how then
do you say to my soul: Get thee away
from hence to the mountain like a
sparrow?—*Ps.* x. 2.

Judge me, O Lord, for I have walked
in my innocence: and I have put my
trust in the Lord, and shall not be weakened.—*Ps.* xxv. 1.

But I have put my trust in thee, O
Lord: I said:

Thou art my God. My lots are in thy
hands.—*Ps.* xxx. 15, 16.

The Lord will redeem the souls of
his servants: and none of them that
trust in him shall offend.—*Ps.* xxxiii. 23.

O, how hast thou multiplied thy
mercy, O God! But the children of
men shall put their trust under the
covert of thy wings.—*Ps.* xxxv. 8.

Blessed is the man whose trust is in
the name of the Lord; and who hath
not had regard to vanities, and lying
follies.—*Ps.* xxxix. 5.

From the height of the day I shall
fear: but I will trust in thee. . . .

In what day soever I shall call upon
thee, behold, I know thou art my God.
—*Ps.* lv. 4, 10.

He will not deprive of good things
them that walk in innocence: O Lord
of hosts, blessed is the man that trusteth in thee.—*Ps.* lxxxiii. 13.

It is good to confide in the Lord,
rather than to have confidence in man.

It is good to trust in the Lord, rather
than to trust in princes.—*Ps.* cxvii.
8, 9.

So shall I answer them that reproach
me in any thing; that I have trusted in
thy words.—*Ps.* cxviii. 42.

They that trust in the Lord, shall be
as mount Sion: he shall not be moved
for ever that dwelleth in Jerusalem.—
Ps. cxxiv. 1.

They that trust in him, shall understand the truth: and they that are
faithful in love, shall rest in him: for
grace and peace is to his elect.—*Wis.*
iii. 9.

Behold, God is my saviour, I will
deal confidently, and will not fear: because the Lord is my strength, and my
praise, and he is become my salvation.
—*Is.* xii. 2.

Blessed is the man that trusteth in
the Lord, and the Lord shall be his
confidence.

And he shall be as a tree that is
planted by the waters, that spreadeth
out its roots towards moisture: and it
shall not fear when the heat cometh.
And the leaf thereof shall be green, and
in the time of drought, it shall not be
solicitous, neither shall it cease at any
time to bring forth fruit.—*Jer.* xvii.
7, 8.

And I am not troubled, following
thee for my pastor.—*Jer.* xvii. 16.

For, said he (Judas Machabeus),
they trust in their weapons, and in
their boldness: but we trust in the Almighty Lord, who at a beck can utterly
destroy both them that come against us,
and the whole world.—2 *Mach.* viii. 18.

And Simon answering, said to him:
Master, we have labored all the night,
and have taken nothing: but at thy
word, I will let down the net.—*Luke*
v. 5.

In whom we have boldness and access

with confidence by the faith of him (Christ).—*Eph.* iii. 12.

And this is the confidence which we have towards him: That, whatsoever we shall ask according to his will, he heareth us.—1 *John* v. 14.

CONFIDENCE IN GOD, EXHORTATION TO

Offer up the sacrifice of justice, and trust in the Lord: many say, Who showeth us good things?—*Ps.* iv. 6.

And let them trust in thee who know thy name: for thou hast not forsaken them that seek thee, O Lord.—*Ps.* ix. 11.

Trust in him, all ye congregation of people: pour out your hearts before him. God is our helper for ever.—*Ps.* lxi. 9.

Have confidence in the Lord with all thy heart, and lean not upon thy own prudence.—*Prov.* iii. 5.

Believe God, and he will recover thee: and direct thy way, and trust in him.—*Ecclus.* ii. 6.

Say to the faint-hearted: Take courage, and fear not: behold, your God will bring the revenge of recompense: God himself will come and will save you.—*Is.* xxxv. 4.

Let not your heart be troubled. You believe in God, believe also in me.—*John* xiv. 1.

Let us go, therefore, with confidence to the throne of grace: that we may obtain mercy, and find grace in seasonable aid.—*Heb.* iv. 16.

Casting all your care upon him, for he hath care of you.—1 *Peter* v. 7.

CONFIDENCE IN GOD, VARIOUS MOTIVES FOR

I. God Provides for Our Wants

See: Providence of God—page 450.

II. God is Always Faithful to His Promises

See: Fidelity of God—page 150.

III. God is with Us in Danger and Distress, Ready to Protect and Help Us

See also: Abandon us, God does not —page 9.

Fearlessness engendered by confidence in God—page 149.

Near us, when we need Him most, God is—page 340.

His master (Putiphar) hearing these things, and giving too much credit to his wife's words, was very angry.

And cast Joseph into the prison, where the king's prisoners were kept, and he was there shut up.

But the Lord was with Joseph, and having mercy upon him, gave him favor in the sight of the chief keeper of the prison.—*Gen.* xxxix. 19-21.

Moses said: I beseech thee, Lord, I am not eloquent from yesterday and the day before: and since thou hast spoken to thy servant, I have more impediment and slowness of tongue.

The Lord said to him: Who made man's mouth? or who made the dumb and the deaf, the seeing and the blind? did not I?

Go therefore, and I will be in thy mouth: and I will teach thee what thou shalt speak.—*Ex.* iv. 10-12.

And in the wilderness (as thou hast seen) the Lord thy God hath carried thee, as a man is wont to carry his little son, all the way that you have come, until you came to this place.—*Deut.* i. 31.

Hear, O Israel, you join battle this day against your enemies, let not your heart be dismayed, be not afraid, do not give back, fear ye them not:

Because the Lord your God is in the midst of you, and will fight for you against your enemies, to deliver you from danger.—*Deut.* xx. 3, 4.

Behold, I command thee, take courage and be strong. Fear not, and be not dismayed: because the Lord thy God is with thee in all things whatsoever thou shalt go to.—*Jos.* i. 9.

It shall not be you that shall fight, but only stand with confidence, and you shall see the help of the Lord over you, O Juda and Jerusalem; fear ye not, nor be you dismayed: to-morrow you shall go out against them, and the Lord will be with you.—2 *Paral.* xx. 17.

He will overshadow thee with his shoulders: and under his wings thou shalt trust.

His truth shall compass thee with a

shield: thou shalt not be afraid of the terror of the night.

. . . For he hath given his angels charge over thee; to keep thee in all thy ways.

In their hands they shall bear thee up: lest thou dash thy foot against a stone.—*Ps.* xc. 4, 5, 11, 12.

If I said: My foot is moved: thy mercy, O Lord, assisted me.—*Ps.* xciii. 18.

For thy name's sake, O Lord, thou wilt quicken me in thy justice.

Thou wilt bring my soul out of trouble.—*Ps.* cxlii. 11.

And now, thus saith the Lord that created thee, O Jacob, and formed thee, O Israel: Fear not, for I have redeemed thee, and called thee by thy name: thou art mine.

When thou shalt pass through the waters, I will be with thee, and the rivers shall not cover thee: when thou shalt walk in the fire, thou shalt not be burnt, and the flames shall not burn in thee.—*Is.* xliii. 1, 2.

Be not afraid at their presence: for I am with thee, to deliver thee, saith the Lord.—*Jer.* i. 8.

I have called upon thy name, O Lord, from the lowest pit.

Thou hast heard my voice: turn not away thy ear from my sighs, and cries.

Thou drewest near in the day, when I called upon thee, thou saidst: Fear not.—*Lam.* iii. 55-57.

For behold, our God, whom we worship, is able to save us from the furnace of burning fire, and to deliver us out of thy hands, O king.—*Dan.* iii. 17.

And immediately Jesus spoke to them, saying: Be of good heart: it is I, fear ye not.—*Matt.* xiv. 27.

And the Lord said to Paul in the night, by a vision: Do not fear, but speak; and hold not thy peace,

Because I am with thee: and no man shall set upon thee, to hurt thee.—*Acts* xviii. 9, 10.

What shall we then say to these things? If God be for us, who is against us?—*Rom.* viii. 31.

But we had in ourselves the answer of death, that we should not trust in ourselves, but in God who raiseth the dead.

Who hath delivered, and doth deliver us out of so great dangers: in whom we trust that he will yet also deliver us.—*2 Cor.* i. 9, 10.

IV. God Rewards Our Confidence in Him

God, his way is immaculate, the word of the Lord is tried by fire: he is the shield of all that trust in him.—*2 Kings* xxii. 31.

For the eyes of the Lord behold all the earth, and give strength to those who with a perfect heart trust in him. —*2 Paral.* xvi. 9.

Josaphat, standing in the midst of them, said: Hear me, ye men of Juda, and all the inhabitants of Jerusalem: believe in the Lord your God, and you shall be secure: believe his prophets, and all things shall succeed well.— *2 Paral.* xx. 20.

Show forth thy wonderful mercies; thou who savest them that trust in thee.—*Ps.* xvi. 7.

Some trust in chariots, and some in horses: but we will call upon the name of the Lord our God.

They are bound, and have fallen; but we are risen, and are set upright.—*Ps.* xix. 8, 9.

In thee have our fathers hoped: they have hoped, and thou hast delivered them.

They cried to thee, and they were saved: they trusted in thee, and were not confounded.—*Ps.* xxi. 5, 6.

Trust in the Lord, and do good, and dwell in the land, and thou shalt be fed with its riches.

. . . Commit thy way to the Lord, and trust in him, and he will do it.

And he will bring forth thy justice as the light, and thy judgment as the noon-day.—*Ps.* xxxvi. 3, 5, 6.

Cast thy care upon the Lord, and he shall sustain thee: he shall not suffer the just to waver for ever.—*Ps.* liv. 23.

He that boasteth, and puffeth up himself, stirreth up quarrels: but he that trusteth in the Lord, shall be healed.— *Prov.* xxviii. 25.

He that feareth man, shall quickly fall: he that trusteth in the Lord, shall be set on high.—*Prov.* xxix. 25.

He that believeth God, taketh heed

to the commandments: and he that trusteth in him, shall fare never the worse.—*Ecclus.* xxxii. 28.

When thou shalt cry, let thy companies deliver thee, but the wind shall carry them all off, a breeze shall take them away, but he that putteth his trust in me, shall inherit the land, and shall possess my holy mount.—*Is.* lvii. 13.

For there is no confusion to them that trust in thee.—*Dan.* iii. 40.

And thus consider through all generations: that none that trust in him shall fail in strength.—1 *Mach.* ii. 61.

Do not therefore lose your confidence, which hath a great reward.—*Heb.* x. 35.

V. Confidence in God, a Claim to His Mercy

And he (Asa) called upon the Lord God, and said: Lord, there is no difference with thee, whether thou help with few, or with many: help us, O Lord our God: for with confidence in thee, and in thy name, we are come against this multitude.—2 *Paral.* xiv. 11.

O Lord my God, in thee have I put my trust: save me from all them that persecute me, and deliver me.—*Ps.* vii. 2.

Preserve me, O Lord, for I have put my trust in thee.—*Ps.* xv. 1.

To thee, O Lord, have I lifted up my soul.

In thee, O my God, I put my trust; let me not be ashamed.

Neither let my enemies laugh at me: for none of them that wait on thee shall be confounded.—*Ps.* xxiv. 1-3.

But I have put my trust in thee, O Lord; I said: Thou art my God.

My lots are in thy hands.

Deliver me out of the hands of my enemies; and from them that persecute me.—*Ps.* xxx. 15, 16.

Let thy mercy, O Lord, be upon us, as we have hoped in thee.—*Ps.* xxxii. 22.

Have mercy on me, O God, have mercy on me: for my soul trusteth in thee.

And in the shadow of thy wings will I hope, until iniquity pass away.—*Ps.* lvi. 2.

Deliver me from my enemies, O Lord, to thee have I fled.—*Ps.* cxlii. 9.

CONFIDENCE IN GOD CREATES FEARLESSNESS

See: Fearlessness—page 148.

CONFIDENCE OF A FRIEND, WE SHOULD NOT BETRAY THE

Practice not evil against thy friend, when he hath confidence in thee.—*Prov.* iii. 29.

He that walketh deceitfully, revealeth secrets: but he that is faithful, concealeth the thing committed to him by his friend.—*Prov.* xi. 13.

Meddle not with him that revealeth secrets, and walketh deceitfully, and openeth wide his lips.—*Prov.* xx. 19.

To a friend, if thou hast opened a sad mouth, fear not, for there may be a reconciliation: except upbraiding, and reproach, and pride, and disclosing of secrets, or a treacherous wound: for in all these cases, a friend will flee away.—*Ecclus.* xxii. 27.

He that discloseth the secret of a friend loseth his credit, and shall never find a friend to his mind.

Love thy neighbor, and be joined to him with fidelity.

But if thou discover his secrets, follow no more after him. . . .

Thou canst no more bind him up. And of a curse there is reconciliation

But to disclose the secrets of a friend, leaveth no hope to an unhappy soul.—*Ecclus.* xxvii. 17-19, 23, 24.

Repeat not the word which thou hast heard, and disclose not the thing that is secret; so shalt thou be truly without confusion, and shalt find favor before all men.—*Ecclus.* xlii. 1.

CONFORMITY TO THE WILL OF GOD

See: Will of God—page 602.

CONSCIENCE, THE VOICE OF

But do not apply thy heart to all words that are spoken: lest perhaps thou hear thy servant reviling thee.

For thy conscience knoweth that thou also hast often spoken evil of others.—*Eccles.* vii. 22, 23.

For when the Gentiles, who have not the law, do by nature those things that are of the law; these having not the law, are a law to themselves;

Who show the work of the law written in their hearts, their conscience bearing witness to them, and their thoughts between themselves accusing, or also defending one another,

In the day when God shall judge the secrets of men by Jesus Christ, according to my gospel.—*Rom.* ii. 14-16.

CONSCIENCE, A GOOD

For behold my witness is in heaven, and he that knoweth my conscience is on high.—*Job* xvi. 20.

Prove me, O God, and know my heart: examine me, and know my paths. And see if there be in me the way of iniquity.—*Ps.* cxxxviii. 23, 24.

But he that doth truth, cometh to the light, that his works may be made manifest, because they are done in God. —*John* iii. 21.

And herein do I endeavor to have always a conscience without offence towards God, and towards men.—*Acts* xxiv. 16.

Now the end of the commandment is charity, from a pure heart, and a good conscience, and an unfeigned faith.— 1 *Tim.* i. 5.

This precept I commend to thee, O son Timothy; according to the prophecies going on before thee, that thou war in them a good warfare,

Having faith and a good conscience, which some rejecting, have made shipwreck concerning the faith.—1 *Tim.* i. 18, 19.

Deacons in like manner chaste, not double-tongued, not given to much wine, not greedy of filthy lucre:

Holding the mystery of faith in a pure conscience.—1 *Tim.* iii. 8, 9.

Let us draw near with a true heart, in fulness of faith, having our hearts sprinkled from an evil conscience, and our bodies washed with clean water.— *Heb.* x. 22.

For we trust we have a good conscience, being willing to behave ourselves well in all things.—*Heb.* xiii. 18.

But sanctify the Lord Christ in your hearts, being ready always to satisfy every one that asketh you a reason of that hope which is in you.

But with modesty and fear, having a good conscience; that whereas they speak evil of you, they may be ashamed, who falsely accuse your good conversation in Christ.—1 *Peter* iii. 15, 16.

CONSCIENCE, THE TESTIMONY OF A GOOD

My justification, which I have begun to hold, I will not forsake: for my heart doth not reprehend me in all my life.—*Job* xxvii. 6.

I have glorified thee on the earth; I have finished the work which thou gavest me to do.—*John* xvii. 4.

For I am not conscious to myself of anything, yet am I not hereby justified; for he that judgeth me, is the Lord.— 1 *Cor.* iv. 4.

For our glory is this, the testimony of our conscience, that in simplicity of heart and sincerity of God, and not in carnal wisdom, but in the grace of God, we have conversed in this world: and more abundantly towards you.— 2 *Cor.* i. 12.

CONSCIENCE, THE FRUIT OF A GOOD

But if thou wilt put away from thee the iniquity that is in thy hand, and let not injustice remain in thy tabernacle:

Then mayst thou lift up thy face without spot, and thou shalt be steadfast, and shalt not fear.—*Job* xi. 14, 15.

The just shall be in everlasting remembrance: he shall not fear the evil hearing.

His heart is ready to hope in the Lord: his heart is strengthened.—*Ps.* cxi. 7, 8.

But he that shall hear me, shall rest without terror, and shall enjoy abundance, without fear of evils.—*Prov.* i. 33.

My son, let not these things depart from thy eyes: keep the law and counsel. . . .

Then shalt thou walk confidently in thy way, and thy foot shall not stumble:

If thou sleep, thou shalt not fear: thou shalt rest, and thy sleep shall be sweet.

Be not afraid of sudden fear, nor of the power of the wicked falling upon thee.

For the Lord will be at thy side, and will keep thy foot that thou be not taken.—*Prov.* iii. 21, 23-26.

He that walketh sincerely, walketh confidently.—*Prov.* x. 9.

A secure mind is like a continual feast.—*Prov.* xv. 15.

The wicked man fleeth, when no man pursueth: but the just, bold as a lion, shall be without dread.—*Prov.* xxviii. 1.

As a fearful heart in the thought of a fool at all times will not fear, so neither shall he that continueth always in the commandments of God.—*Ecclus.* xxii. 23.

Rich or poor, if his heart is good, his countenance shall be cheerful at all times.—*Ecclus.* xxvi. 4.

He that feareth the Lord shall tremble at nothing, and shall not be afraid: for he is his hope.—*Ecclus.* xxxiv. 16.

Dearly beloved, if our heart do not reprehend us, we have confidence towards God.—1 *John* iii. 21.

CONSCIENCE, AN EVIL

And when they heard the voice of the Lord God walking in paradise at the afternoon air, Adam and his wife hid themselves from the face of the Lord God, amidst the trees of paradise.

And the Lord God called Adam, and said to him: Where art thou?

And he said: I heard thy voice in paradise; and I was afraid, because I was naked, and I hid myself.—*Gen.* iii. 8-10.

For the Lord will give thee a fearful heart, and languishing eyes, and a soul consumed with pensiveness:

And thy life shall be as it were hanging before thee. Thou shalt fear night and day, neither shalt thou trust thy life.

In the morning thou shalt say: Who will grant me evening? and at evening: Who will grant me morning? for the fearfulness of thy heart, wherewith thou shalt be terrified, and for those things which thou shalt see with thy eyes.—*Deut.* xxviii. 65-67.

The wicked man is proud all his days, and the number of the years of his tyranny is uncertain.

The sound of dread is always in his ears: and when there is peace, he always suspecteth treason.

He believeth not that he may return from darkness to light, looking round about for the sword on every side.

When he moveth himself to seek bread, he knoweth that the day of darkness is ready at his hand.

Tribulation shall terrify him, and distress shall surround him, as a king that is prepared for the battle.

For he hath stretched out his hand against God, and hath strengthened himself against the Almighty.—*Job* xv. 20-25.

They have not called upon God: there have they trembled for fear, where there was no fear.—*Ps.* lii. 6.

The wicked man fleeth, when no man pursueth.—*Prov.* xxviii. 1.

For they who promised to drive away fears and troubles from a sick soul, were sick themselves of a fear worthy to be laughed at. . . .

For whereas wickedness is fearful, it beareth witness of its condemnation: for a troubled conscience always forecasteth grievous things.

For fear is nothing else but a yielding up of the succors from thought.— *Wis.* xvii. 8, 10, 11.

He is troubled in the vision of his heart, as if he had escaped in the day of battle. In the time of his safety, he rose up, and wondered that there is no fear:

Such things happen to all flesh, from man even to beast, and upon sinners are seven-fold more.—*Ecclus.* xl. 7, 8.

Enter thou into the rock, and hide thee in the pit from the face of the fear of the Lord, and from the glory of his majesty.—*Is.* ii. 10.

There is no peace to the wicked, saith the Lord.—*Is.* xlviii. 22.

Then shall they begin to say to the mountains: Fall upon us; and to the hills: Cover us.—*Luke* xxiii. 30.

For every one that doth evil, hateth the light, and cometh not to the light, that his works may not be reproved.—*John* iii. 20.

And as he (Paul) treated of justice, and chastity, and of the judgment to come, Felix being terrified, answered: For this time, go thy way: but when I have a convenient time, I will send for thee.—*Acts* xxiv. 25.

Tribulation and anguish upon every soul of man that worketh evil, of the Jew first, and also of the Greek.—*Rom.* ii. 9.

CONSCIENTIOUSNESS

In every work of thine regard thy soul in ¹faith: for this is the keeping of the commandments.—*Ecclus.* xxxii. 27.

For one judgeth between day and day: and another judgeth every day: let every man abound in his own sense.—*Rom.* xiv. 5.

If any of them that believe not, invite you, and you be willing to go; eat of anything that is set before you, asking no questions for conscience' sake.

But if any man say: This has been sacrificed to idols, do not eat of it for his sake that told it, and for conscience' sake.—1 *Cor.* x. 27, 28.

All things are clean to the clean: but to them that are defiled, and to unbelievers, nothing is clean: but both their mind and their conscience are defiled.—*Titus* i. 15.

CONSIDERATION FOR OTHERS

Remember the covenant of the most High, and overlook the ignorance of thy neighbor.—*Ecclus.* xxviii. 9.

Now him that is weak in faith, take unto you: not in disputes about thoughts.

For one believeth that he may eat all things: but he that is weak, let him eat herbs.

Let not him that eateth, despise him that eateth not: and he that eateth not, let him not judge him that eateth. For God hath taken him to him.—*Rom.* xiv. 1-3.

Now we that are stronger, ought to bear the infirmities of the weak, and not to please ourselves.

Let every one of you please his

¹In faith, that is, follow sincerely thy soul in her faith and conscience.

neighbor unto good, to edification.—*Rom.* xv. 1, 2.

But take heed lest perhaps this your liberty become a stumbling-block to the weak.

For if a man see him that hath knowledge sit at meat in the idol's temple, shall not his conscience, being weak, be emboldened to eat those things which are sacrificed to idols?

And through thy knowledge shall the weak brother perish, for whom Christ hath died?

Now when you sin thus against the brethren, and wound their weak conscience, you sin against Christ.

Wherefore if meat scandalize my brother, I will never eat flesh, lest I should scandalize my brother.—1 *Cor.* viii. 9-13.

Let no man seek his own, but that which is another's.—1 *Cor.* x. 24.

If any of them that believe not, invite you, and you be willing to go; eat of anything that is set before you, asking no question for conscience' sake.

But if any man say: This has been sacrificed to idols, do not eat of it, for his sake that told it, and for conscience' sake.

Conscience, I say, not thy own, but the other's.—1 *Cor.* x. 27-29.

As I also in all things please all men, not seeking that which is profitable to myself, but to many, that they may be saved.—1 *Cor.* x. 33.

Let nothing be done through contention, neither by vainglory: but in humility, let each esteem others better than themselves:

Each one not considering the things that are his own, but those that are other men's.—*Philipp.* ii. 3, 4.

CONSOLE THE AFFLICTED, WE SHOULD

See: Comfort the afflicted—page 56.

CONSOLES US IN SORROW AND AFFLICTION, GOD

See: Tribulations, God comforts us in our—page 566.

CONSTANCY

See: Fortitude—page 161.

CONTEMPT FOR OUR NEIGHBOR

See also: Poor, despising the—page 387.

He (the Lord) shall scorn the scorners, and to the meek, he will give grace.—*Prov.* iii. 34.

Consider the works of God, that no man can correct whom he hath despised.—*Eccles.* vii. 14.

Laugh no man to scorn in the bitterness of his soul: for there is one that humbleth and exalteth, God who seeth all.—*Ecclus.* vii. 12.

Despise not a man that turneth away from sin, nor reproach him therewith: remember that we are all worthy of reproof.

Despise not a man in his old age; for we also shall become old.—*Ecclus.* viii. 6, 7.

Praise not a man for his beauty, neither despise a man for his look.—*Ecclus.* xi. 2.

Woe to thee that spoilest, shalt not thou thyself also be spoiled? and thou that despisest, shalt not thyself also be despised? when thou shalt have made an end of spoiling, thou shalt be spoiled: when being wearied, thou shalt cease to despise, thou shalt be despised.—*Is.* xxxiii. 1.

Have we not all one father? hath not one God created us? why then doth every one of us despise his brother, violating the covenant of our fathers?—*Malach.* ii. 10.

But I say to you, that whosoever is angry with his brother, shall be in danger of the judgment. And whosoever shall say to his brother, Raca, shall be in danger of the council. And whosoever shall say, Thou fool, shall be in danger of hell fire.—*Matt.* v. 22.

And the voice spoke to him (Peter) again the second time: That which God hath cleansed, do not thou call common.

. . . And he (Peter) said to them, You know how abominable it is for a man that is a Jew, to keep company or to come unto one of another nation: but God hath showed to me, to call no man common or unclean.—*Acts* x. 15, 28.

But thou, why judgest thou thy brother? or thou, why dost thou despise thy brother? For we shall all stand before the judgment seat of Christ.—*Rom.* xiv. 10.

CONTENTMENT

Better is a little to the just, than the great riches of the wicked.—*Ps.* xxxvi. 16.

Better is a little with the fear of the Lord, than great treasures without content.—*Prov.* xv. 16.

Better is a little with justice, than great revenues with iniquity.—*Prov.* xvi. 8.

Two things I have asked of thee, deny them not to me before I die.

Remove far from me vanity, and lying words. Give me neither beggary, nor riches: give me only the necessaries of life:

Lest perhaps, being filled, I should be tempted to deny, and say: Who is the Lord? or being compelled by poverty, I should steal, and forswear the name of my God.—*Prov.* xxx. 7-9.

This therefore hath seemed good to me, that a man should eat and drink, and enjoy the fruit of his labor, wherewith he hath labored under the sun, all the days of his life, which God hath given him: and this is his portion.—*Eccles.* v. 17.

The chief thing for man's life is water and bread, and clothing, and a house to cover shame.

Better is the poor man's fare under a roof of boards, than sumptuous cheer abroad in another man's house.

Be contented with little instead of much, and thou shalt not hear the reproach of going abroad.—*Ecclus.* xxix. 27-29.

The life of a laborer that is content with what he hath, shall be sweet, and in it thou shalt find a treasure.—*Ecclus.* xl. 18.

And the soldiers also asked him (the Baptist) saying: And what shall we do? And he said to them: Do violence to no man; neither calumniate any man; and be content with your pay.—*Luke* iii. 14.

I speak not as it were for want. For

I have learned, in whatsoever state I am, to be content therewith.

I know both how to be brought low, and I know how to abound: (everywhere, and in all things I am instructed) both to be full, and to be hungry; both to abound, and to suffer need.—*Philipp.* iv. 11, 12.

But godliness with contentment is great gain.

For we brought nothing into this world: and certainly we can carry nothing out.

But having food, and wherewith to be covered, with these we are content. —1 *Tim.* vi. 6-8.

Let your manners be without covetousness, contented with such things as you have; for he hath said: I will not leave thee, neither will I forsake thee. —*Heb.* xiii. 5.

CONTRITE OF HEART, THE

The Lord is nigh unto them that are of a contrite heart: and he will save the humble of spirit.—*Ps.* xxxiii. 19.

A sacrifice to God is an afflicted spirit: a contrite and humbled heart, O God, thou wilt not despise.—*Ps.* l. 19.

For thus saith the High and the Eminent that inhabiteth eternity: and his name is Holy, who dwelleth in the high and holy place, and with a contrite and humble spirit, to revive the spirit of the humble, and to revive the heart of the contrite.—*Is.* lvii. 15.

The spirit of the Lord is upon me, because the Lord hath anointed me: he hath sent me to preach to the meek, to heal the contrite of heart, and to preach a release to the captives, and deliverance to them that are shut up.— *Is.* lxi. 1.

But to whom shall I have respect, but to him that is poor, and little, and of a contrite heart, and that trembleth at my words?—*Is.* lxvi. 2.

But the soul that is sorrowful for the greatness of evil she hath done, and goeth bowed down, and feeble, and the eyes that fail, and the hungry soul, giveth glory and justice to thee, the Lord.—*Bar.* ii. 18.

Neither is there at this time prince, or leader, or prophet, or holocaust, or sacrifice, or oblation, or incense, or place of first-fruits before thee,

That we may find thy mercy: nevertheless in a contrite heart and humble spirit, let us be accepted.—*Dan.* iii. 38, 39.

CONTRITION

See: Sin, sorrow for—page 527.

CONVERSATIONS, IDLE

See: Idle words—page 226.

CONVERSATIONS, EVIL

See also: Tongue, bad use of the— page 558.

Who is the man that desireth life: who loveth to see good days?

Keep thy tongue from evil, and thy lips from speaking guile.—*Ps.* xxxiii. 13, 14.

But the king shall rejoice in God, all they shall be praised that swear by him: because the mouth is stopped of them that speak wicked things.—*Ps.* lxii. 12.

The lips of the just consider what is acceptable: and the mouth of the wicked uttereth perverse things.—*Prov.* x. 32.

The mouth of a fool is his destruction: and his lips are the ruin of his soul.—*Prov.* xviii. 7.

Death and life are in the power of the tongue: they that love it, shall eat the fruits thereof.—*Prov.* xviii. 21.

For the spirit of wisdom is benevolent, and will not acquit the evil speaker from his lips: for God is witness of his reins, and he is a true searcher of his heart, and a hearer of his tongue.—*Wis.* i. 6.

The discourse of sinners is hateful, and their laughter is at the pleasures of sin.—*Ecclus.* xxvii. 14.

Hedge in thy ears with thorns, hear not a wicked tongue, and make doors and bars to thy mouth.—*Ecclus.* xxviii. 28.

Let no evil speech proceed from your mouth.—*Eph.* iv. 29.

But fornication, and all uncleanness, or covetousness, let it not so much as be named among you, as becometh saints:

Or obscenity, or foolish talking, or

scurrility, which is to no purpose; but rather giving of thanks.—*Eph.* v. 3, 4.

But now, put you also all away: anger, indignation, malice, blasphemy, filthy speech out of your mouth.—*Col.* iii. 8.

CONVERSATIONS, GOOD

See also: Tongue, proper use of the —page 559.

And the words of my mouth shall be such as may please: and the meditation of my heart always in thy sight. O Lord my helper and my redeemer.—*Ps.* xviii. 15.

And my tongue shall meditate thy justice, thy praise all the day long.—*Ps.* xxxiv. 28.

The mouth of the just shall bring forth wisdom: the tongue of the perverse shall perish.

The lips of the just consider what is acceptable.—*Prov.* x. 31, 32.

And let the thought of God be in thy mind, and all thy discourse on the commandments of the Highest.—*Ecclus.* ix. 23.

The flute and the psaltery make a sweet melody, but a pleasant tongue is above them both.—*Ecclus.* xl. 21.

Let no evil speech proceed from thy mouth; but that which is good, to the edification of faith, that it may administer grace to the hearers.—*Eph.* iv. 29.

Only let your conversation be worthy of the gospel of Christ.—*Philipp.* i. 27.

But our conversation is in heaven; from whence also we look for the Saviour, our Lord Jesus Christ.—*Philipp.* iii. 20.

Let no man despise thy youth: but be thou an example of the faithful in word, in conversation, in charity, in faith, in chastity.—1 *Tim.* iv. 12.

Who is a wise man, and endued with knowledge among you? Let him show, by a good conversation, his work in the meekness of wisdom.—*James* iii. 13.

But according to him that hath called you, who is holy, be you also, in all manner of conversation, holy:

Because it is written: you shall be holy, for I am holy.—1 *Peter* i. 15, 16.

Dearly beloved, I beseech you as strangers and pilgrims, to **refrain** yourselves from carnal desires, which war against the soul,

Having your conversation good among the Gentiles: that whereas they speak against you as evildoers, they may, by the good works which they shall behold in you, glorify God in the day of visitation.—1 *Peter* ii. 11, 12.

CONVERSION OF HEART

See: Returning to God—page 478.

CONVERSION, DELAY OF

See: Delay—page 105.

CONVERTED TO THE LORD, EXHORTATION TO BE

See also: Return to God, exhortation to—page 479.

Be converted, therefore, ye sinners, and do justice before God, believing that he will show his mercy to you.—*Tob.* xiii. 8.

And thou hast said: Be converted, O ye sons of men.—*Ps.* lxxxix. 3.

Turn to the Lord, and forsake thy sins. . . .

How great is the mercy of the Lord, and his forgiveness to them that turn to him!—*Ecclus.* xvii. 21, 28.

I have blotted out thy iniquities as a cloud, and thy sins as a mist: return to me, for I have redeemed thee.—*Is.* xliv. 22.

Be converted to me, and you shall be saved, all ye ends of the earth: for I am God, and there is no other.—*Is.* xlv. 22.

Let the wicked forsake his way, and the unjust man his thoughts, and let him return to the Lord, and he will have mercy on him, and to our God: for he is bountiful to forgive.—*Is.* lv. 7.

Therefore will I judge every man according to his way, O house of Israel, saith the Lord God. Be converted, and do penance for all your iniquities: and iniquity shall not be your ruin. . . .

For I desire not the death of him that dieth, saith the Lord God, return ye and live.—*Ezech.* xviii. 30, 32.

Therefore turn thou to thy God: keep mercy and judgment, and hope in thy God always.—*Osee* xii. 6.

Return, O Israel, to the Lord thy God: for thou hast fallen down by thy iniquity.—*Osee* xiv. 2.

Now therefore saith the Lord: Be converted to me with all your heart, in fasting, and in weeping, and in mourning.

And rend your hearts, and not your garments, and turn to the Lord your God: for he is gracious and merciful, patient and rich in mercy, and ready to repent of the evil.

Who knoweth but he will return, and forgive, and leave a blessing behind him, sacrifice and libation to the Lord your God?—*Joel* ii. 12-14.

Turn ye to me, saith the Lord of hosts: and I will turn to you, saith the Lord of hosts.

Be not as your fathers, to whom the former prophets have cried, saying: Thus saith the Lord of hosts: Turn ye from your evil ways, and from your wicked thoughts: but they did not give ear, neither did they hearken to me, saith the Lord.—*Zach.* i. 3, 4.

Be penitent, therefore, and be converted, that your sins may be blotted out.—*Acts* iii. 19.

CORRECTION FROM GOD

And thou hast given me the protection of thy salvation: and thy right hand hath held me up:

And thy discipline hath corrected me unto the end: and thy discipline, the same shall teach me.—*Ps.* xvii. 36.

The days of our years in them are three-score and ten years.

But if in the strong they be four-score years: and what is more of them is labor and sorrow. For mildness is come upon us; and we shall be corrected.—*Ps.* lxxxix. 10.

O how good and sweet is thy spirit, O Lord, in all things!

And therefore thou chastisest them that err, by little and little: and admonishest them, and speakest to them, concerning the things wherein they offend: that leaving their wickedness, they may believe in thee, O Lord.—*Wis.* xii. 1, 2.

According as his mercy is, so his correction judgeth a man according to his works.—*Ecclus.* xvi. 13.

And thou, my servant Jacob, fear not, saith the Lord: because I am with thee, for I will consume all the nations to which I have cast thee out: but thee I will not consume, but I will correct thee in judgment, neither will I spare thee as if thou wert innocent.—*Jer.* xlvi. 28.

And when the high priest was praying, the same young men in the same clothing stood by Heliodorus, and said to him: Give thanks to Onias the priest: because for his sake the Lord hath granted thee life.

And thou having been scourged by God, declare unto all men the great works and the power of God.—2 *Mach.* iii. 33, 34.

For it is a token of great goodness when sinners are not suffered to go on in their ways for a long time, but are presently punished.

For, not as with other nations (whom the Lord patiently expected, that when the day of judgment shall come, he may punish them in the fulness of their sins):

Doth he also deal with us, so as to suffer our sins to come to their height, and then take vengeance on us.

And therefore he never withdraweth his mercy from us: but though he chastise his people with adversity, he forsaketh them not.—2 *Mach.* vi. 13-16.

CORRECTION FROM GOD, RECEIVING

Blessed is the man whom God correcteth: refuse not therefore the chastising of the Lord:

For he woundeth and cureth: he striketh, and his hands shall heal.—*Job* v. 17, 18.

My son, reject not the correction of the Lord: and do not faint when thou art chastised by him:

For whom the Lord loveth, he chastiseth: and as a father in the son he pleaseth himself.—*Prov.* iii. 11, 12.

He hath mercy, and teacheth, and correcteth, as a shepherd doth his flock.

He hath mercy on him that receiveth the discipline of mercy.—*Ecclus.* xviii. 13, 14.

Correct me, O Lord, but yet with

judgment: and not in thy fury, lest thou bring me to nothing.—*Jer.* x. 24.

And you have forgotten the consolation, which speaketh to you, as unto children, saying: My son, neglect not the discipline of the Lord; neither be thou wearied whilst thou art rebuked by him.

For whom the Lord loveth he chastiseth; and he scourgeth every son whom he receiveth.

Persevere under discipline. God dealeth with you as with his sons; for what son is there, whom the father doth not correct?

But if you be without chastisement, whereof all are made partakers, then are you bastards, and not sons.—*Heb.* xii. 5-8.

CORRECTION FROM GOD, REFUSING

He that rejoiceth in iniquity, shall be censured, and he that hateth chastisement, shall have less life.—*Ecclus.* xix. 5.

In vain have I struck your children, they have not received correction: your sword hath devoured your prophets, your generation is like a ravaging lion. —*Jer.* ii. 30.

O Lord, thy eyes are upon truth: thou hast struck them, and they have not grieved: thou hast bruised them, and they have refused to receive correction: they have made their faces harder than the rock, and they have refused to return.—*Jer.* v. 3.

She hath not hearkened to the voice, neither hath she received discipline: she hath not trusted in the Lord, she drew not near to her God.—*Soph.* iii. 2.

I said: Surely thou wilt fear me, thou wilt receive correction: and her dwelling shall not perish, for all things, wherein I have visited her: but they rose early, and corrupted all their thoughts.—*Soph.* iii. 7.

CORRUPTION OF THE WORLD, BEFORE THE REDEMPTION

And God seeing that the wickedness of men was great on the earth, and that all the thought of their heart was bent upon evil at all times.

It repented him that he had made man on the earth.—*Gen.* vi. 5, 6.

And the earth was corrupted before God, and was filled with iniquity.

And when God had seen that the earth was corrupted (for all flesh had corrupted its way upon the earth,)

He said to Noe: The end of all flesh is come before me, the earth is filled with iniquity through them, and I will destroy them with the earth.—*Gen.* vi. 11-13.

Save me, O Lord, for there is now no saint: truths are decayed from among the children of men.

They have spoken vain things, every one to his neighbor: with deceitful lips, and with a double heart have they spoken.—*Ps.* xi. 2, 3.

The fool hath said in his heart, there is no God.

They are corrupt, and are become abominable in their ways: there is none that doth good, no not one.

The Lord hath looked down from heaven upon the children of men, to see if there be any that understand and seek God.

They are all gone aside, they are become unprofitable together: there is none that doth good, no not one.

Their throat is an open sepulchre: with their tongues they acted deceitfully; the poison of asps is under their lips.

Their mouth is full of cursing and bitterness; their feet are swift to shed blood.

Destruction and unhappiness are in their ways: and the way of peace they have not known: there is no fear of God before their eyes.—*Ps.* xiii. 1-3.

And it was not enough for them (idolaters) to err about the knowledge of God, but whereas they lived in a great war of ignorance, they call so many and so great evils peace.

For either they sacrifice their own children, or use hidden sacrifices, or keep watches full of madness,

So that now they neither keep life, nor marriage undefiled, but one killeth another through envy, or grieveth him by adultery:

And all things are mingled together, blood, murder, theft, and dissimulation, corruption and unfaithfulness, tumults and perjury, disquieting of the good,

Forgetfulness of God, defiling of souls, changing of nature, disorder in marriage, and the irregularity of adultery and uncleanness.

For the worship of abominable idols is the cause, and the beginning and end of all evil.

For either they are mad when they are merry: or they prophesy lies, or they live unjustly, or easily forswear themselves.

For whilst they trust in idols, which are without life, though they swear amiss, they look not to be hurt.—*Wis.* xiv. 22-29.

Hear the word of the Lord, ye children of Israel, for the Lord shall enter into judgment with the inhabitants of the land: for there is no truth, and there is no mercy, and there is no knowledge of God in the land.

Cursing, and lying, and killing, and theft, and adultery have overflowed, and blood hath touched blood.—*Osee* iv. 1, 2.

The holy man is perished out of the earth, and there is none upright among men: they all lie in wait for blood, every one hunteth his brother to death.

The evil of their hands they call good: the prince requireth, and the judge is for giving: and the great man hath uttered the desire of his soul, and they have troubled it.

He that is best among them, is as a brier: and he that is righteous, as the thorn of the hedge. The day of thy inspection, thy visitation cometh: now shall be their destruction.

Believe not a friend, and trust not in a prince: keep the doors of thy mouth from her that sleepeth in thy bosom.

For the son dishonoreth the father, and the daughter riseth up against her mother, the daughter-in-law against her mother-in-law: and a man's enemies are they of his own household.—*Mich.* vii. 2-6.

And they changed the glory of the incorruptible God into the likeness of the image of a corruptible man, and of birds, and of four-footed beasts, and of creeping things.

Wherefore God gave them up to the desires of their heart, unto uncleanness, to dishonor their own bodies among themselves.

Who changed the truth of God into a lie; and worshipped and served the creature rather than the Creator, who is blessed for ever. Amen.

For this cause God delivered them up to shameful affections. For their women have changed the natural use into that use which is against nature.

And in like manner, the men also, leaving the natural use of a woman, have burned in their lusts one towards another, men with men working that which is filthy, and receiving in themselves the recompense which was due to their error.

And as they liked not to have God in their knowledge, God delivered them up to a reprobate sense, to do those things which are not convenient;

Being filled with all iniquity, malice, fornication, avarice, wickedness, full of envy, murder, contention, deceit, malignity, whisperers,

Detractors, hateful to God, contumelious, proud, haughty, inventors of evil things, disobedient to parents,

Foolish, dissolute, without affection, without fidelity, without mercy.

Who, having known the justice of God, did not understand that they who do such things, are worthy of death; and not only they that do them, but they also that consent to them that do them.—*Rom.* i. 23-32.

COURAGE

See: Fortitude—page 161.

COVENANT OF THE OLD LAW

And Moses went up to God: and the Lord called unto him from the mountain, and said: Thus shalt thou say to the house of Jacob, and tell the children of Israel:

You have seen what I have done to the Egyptians, how I have carried you upon the wings of eagles, and have taken you to myself.

If therefore you will hear my voice, and keep my covenant, you shall be my peculiar possession above all peoples: for all the earth is mine.

And you shall be to me a priestly kingdom, and a holy nation. These are the words thou shalt speak to the children of Israel.—*Ex.* xix. 3-6.

Keep my sabbaths, and reverence my sanctuary: I am the Lord.

If you walk in my precepts, and keep my commandments, and do them, . . .

I will set my tabernacle in the midst of you, and my soul shall not cast you off.

I will walk among you, and will be your God, and you shall be my people. —*Lev.* xxvi. 2, 3, 11, 12.

Because thou art a holy people to the Lord thy God. The Lord thy God hath chosen thee, to be his peculiar people of all peoples that are upon the earth.

Not because you surpass all nations in number, is the Lord joined unto you, and hath chosen you, for you are the fewest of any people:

But because the Lord hath loved you, and hath kept his oath, which he swore to your fathers: and hath brought you out with a strong hand, and redeemed you from the house of bondage, out of the hand of Pharao, the king of Egypt. . . . Keep therefore the precepts, and ceremonies, and judgments which I command thee this day to do.

If after thou hast heard these judgments, thou keep and do them, the Lord thy God will also keep his covenant to thee, and the mercy which he swore to thy fathers.—*Deut.* vii. 6-8, 11, 12.

Thou hast chosen the Lord this day to be thy God, and to walk in his ways, and keep his ceremonies, and precepts, and judgments, and obey his command.

And the Lord hath chosen thee this day, to be his peculiar people, as he hath spoken to thee, and to keep all his commandments:

And to make thee higher than all nations which he hath created, to his own praise, and name, and glory: that thou mayst be a holy people of the Lord thy God, as he hath spoken.—*Deut.* xxvi. 17, 18, 19.

For the law was given by Moses; grace and truth came by Jesus Christ. —*John* i. 17.

There is indeed a setting aside of the former commandment, because of the weakness and unprofitableness thereof:

(For the law brought nothing to perfection,) but a bringing in of a better hope, by which we draw nigh to God.— *Heb.* vii. 18, 19.

COVENANT OF THE OLD LAW, ABROGATION OF THE

Behold the days shall come, saith the Lord, and I will make a new covenant with the house of Israel, and with the house of Juda:

Not according to the covenant which I made with their fathers, in the day that I took them by the hand, to bring them out of the land of Egypt: the covenant which they made void, and I had dominion over them, saith the Lord. —*Jer.* xxxi. 31, 32.

The law and the prophets were until John; from that time the kingdom of God is preached, and every one useth violence towards it.—*Luke* xvi. 16.

Now if the ministration of death, engraven with letters upon stones, was glorious; so that the children of Israel could not steadfastly behold the face of Moses, for the glory of his countenance, which is made void:

How shall not the ministration of the spirit be rather in glory? . . .

For if that which is done away was glorious, much more that which remaineth is in glory.—*2 Cor.* iii. 7, 8, 11.

If then perfection was by the Levitical priesthood, (for under it the people received the law,) what further need was there that another priest should rise according to the order of Melchisedech, and not be called according to the order of Aaron?

For the priesthood being translated, it is necessary that a translation also be made of the law.—*Heb.* vii. 11, 12.

There is indeed a setting aside of the former commandment, because of the weakness and unprofitableness thereof:

(For the law brought nothing to perfection,) but a bringing in of a better hope, by which we draw nigh to God.— *Heb.* vii. 18, 19.

By so much is Jesus made a surety of a better testament.—*Heb.* vii. 22.

But now he hath obtained a better ministry, by how much also he is a mediator of a better testament, which is established on better promises.

For if that former had been faultless, there should not indeed a place have been sought for a second.

For finding fault with them, he saith: Behold, the days shall come, saith the Lord: and I will perfect unto the house of Israel, and unto the house of Juda, a new testament. . . .

Now in saying a new, he hath made the former old. And that which decayeth and groweth old, is near its end.—*Heb.* viii. 6-8, 13.

Wherefore, when he cometh into the world, he saith: Sacrifice and oblation thou wouldst not: but a body thou hast fitted to me:

Holocausts for sin did not please thee.

Then said I: Behold, I come: in the head of the book it is written of me: that I should do thy will, O God.

In saying before, Sacrifices, and oblations, and holocausts for sin thou wouldst not, neither are they pleasing to thee, which are offered according to the law.

Then said I: Behold, I come to do thy will, O God: he taketh away the first, that he may establish that which followeth.—*Heb.* x. 5-9.

COVENANT OF THE NEW LAW

Mercy and truth have met each other: justice and peace have kissed.—*Ps.* lxxxiv. 11.

The law and the prophets were until John; from that time the kingdom of God is preached, and every one useth violence towards it.—*Luke* xvi. 16.

For the law was given by Moses; grace and truth came by Jesus Christ.—*John* i. 17.

Be it known therefore to you, men, brethren, that through him forgiveness of sins is preached to you: and from all the things from which you could not be justified by the law of Moses.—*Acts* xiii. 38.

For you have not received the spirit of bondage again in fear; but you have received the spirit of adoption of sons, whereby we cry: Abba (Father).—*Rom.* viii. 15.

For God hath not given us the spirit of fear: but of power, and of love, and of sobriety.—2 *Tim.* i. 7.

But now he hath obtained a better ministry, by how much also he is a mediator of a better testament, which is established on better promises.

For if that former had been faultless, there should not indeed a place have been sought for a second.

For finding fault with them, he saith: Behold, the days shall come, saith the Lord; and I will perfect unto the house of Israel, and unto the house of Juda, a new testament:

Not according to the testament which I made to their fathers, on the day when I took them by the hand to lead them out of the land of Egypt: because they continued not in my testament: and I regarded them not, saith the Lord.

For this is the testament which I will make to the house of Israel after those days, saith the Lord: I will give my laws into their mind, and in their heart will I write them: and I will be their God, and they shall be my people.

And they shall not teach every man his neighbor and every man his brother, saying, Know the Lord: for all shall know me, from the least to the greatest of them.

Because I will be merciful to their iniquities, and their sins I will remember no more.—*Heb.* viii. 6-12.

And therefore he is the mediator of the new testament: that by means of his death, for the redemption of those transgressions, which were under the former testament, they that are called may receive the promise of eternal inheritance.—*Heb.* ix. 15.

COVENANT OF THE NEW LAW IS THE FULFILMENT AND PERFECTION OF THE OLD LAW

Do not think that I am come to destroy the law, or the prophets. I am not come to destroy, but to fulfil.

For amen I say unto you, till heaven and earth pass, one jot, or one tittle shall not pass of the law, till all be fulfilled.—*Matt.* v. 17, 18.

And it is easier for heaven and earth

to pass, than one tittle of the law to fall.—*Luke* xvi. 17.

Do we, then, destroy the law through faith? God forbid: but we establish the law.—*Rom.* iii. 31.

Now if the ministration of death, engraven with letters upon stones, was glorious; so that the children of Israel could not steadfastly behold the face of Moses, for the glory of his countenance, which is made void:

How shall not the ministration of the spirit be rather in glory?

For if the ministration of condemnation be glory, much more the ministration of justice aboundeth in glory.

For even that which was glorious in this part was not glorified, by reason of the glory that excelleth.

For if that which is done away was glorious, much more that which remaineth is in glory.—2 *Cor.* iii. 7-11.

COVETOUSNESS

Thou shalt not covet thy neighbor's house: neither shalt thou desire his wife, nor his servant, nor his handmaid, nor his ox, nor his ass, nor any thing that is his.—*Ex.* xx. 17.

He that is greedy of gain, troubleth his own house: but he that hateth bribes shall live.—*Prov.* xv. 27.

He that hateth covetousness shall prolong his days.—*Prov.* xxviii. 16.

A covetous man shall not be satisfied with money: and he that loveth riches, shall reap no fruit from them: so this also is vanity.—*Eccles.* v. 9.

Yea and they have counted our life a pastime, and the business of life to be gain, and that we must be getting every way, even out of evil.—*Wis.* xv. 12.

But nothing is more wicked than the covetous man.—*Ecclus.* x. 9.

Riches are not comely for a covetous man and a niggard, and what should an envious man do with gold?—*Ecclus.* xiv. 3.

For the iniquity of his covetousness I was angry, and I struck him: I hid my face from thee, and was angry: and he went away wandering in his own heart.—*Is.* lvii. 17.

Do not err: neither fornicators, nor idolaters, nor adulterers,

. . . Nor covetous, nor drunkards, nor railers, nor extortioners, shall possess the kingdom of God.—1 *Cor.* vi. 9, 10.

COVETOUSNESS, DANGER OF

So the ways of every covetous man destroy the souls of the possessors.—*Prov.* i. 19.

A faithful man shall be much praised: but he that maketh haste to be rich, shall not be innocent.—*Prov.* xxviii. 20.

The eye of the covetous man is insatiable in his portion of iniquity: he will not be satisfied till he consume his own soul, drying it up.—*Ecclus.* xiv. 9.

For the desire of money is the root of all evils; which some coveting, have erred from the faith, and have entangled themselves in many sorrows.—1 *Tim.* vi. 10.

COVETOUSNESS, EXHORTATION AGAINST

Labor not to be rich: but set bounds to thy prudence.

Lift not up thy eyes to riches which thou canst not have: because they shall make themselves wings like those of an eagle, and shall fly towards heaven.—*Prov.* xxiii. 4, 5.

And he (Christ) said to them: Take heed, and beware of all covetousness; for a man's life doth not consist in the abundance of things which he possesseth.—*Luke* xii. 15.

But fornication, and all uncleanness, or covetousness, let it not be so much as named among you, as becometh saints.—*Eph.* v. 3.

Let your manners be without covetousness, contented with such things as you have; for he hath said: I will not leave thee, neither will I forsake thee.—*Heb.* xiii. 5.

COWARDICE

And as to them that shall remain of you, I will send fear in their hearts in the countries of their enemies, the sound of a flying leaf shall terrify them, and they shall flee as it were from the sword: they shall fall, when no man pursueth them,

And they shall every one fall upon their brethren as fleeing from wars, none of you shall dare to resist your enemies.—*Lev.* xxvi. 36, 37.

There have they trembled for fear, where there was no fear.—*Ps.* xiii. 5.

I waited for him that hath saved me from pusillanimity of spirit, and a storm.—*Ps.* liv. 9.

The wicked man fleeth, when no man pursueth: but the just, bold as a lion, shall be without dread.—*Prov.* xxviii. 1.

For they who promised to drive away fears and troubles from a sick soul, were sick themselves of a fear worthy to be laughed at.

. . . For whereas wickedness is fearful, it beareth witness of its condemnation: for a troubled conscience always forecasteth grievous things.

For fear is nothing else but a yielding up of the succors from thought.—*Wis.* xvii. 8, 10, 11.

He is troubled in the vision of his heart, as if he had escaped in the day of battle. In the time of his safety he rose up, and wondereth that there is no fear.—*Ecclus.* xl. 7.

Then the disciples all, leaving him, fled.—*Matt.* xxvi. 56.

But Peter sat without in the court: and there came to him a servant maid, saying: Thou also wast with Jesus the Galilean.

But he denied before them all, saying: I know not what thou sayest.

And as he went out of the gate another maid saw him, and she saith to them that were there: This man also was with Jesus of Nazareth.

And again he denied with an oath: I know not the man.

And after a little while they came that stood by, and said to Peter: Surely thou also art one of them; for even thy speech doth discover thee.

Then he began to curse and to swear that he knew not the man. And immediately the cock crew.—*Matt.* xxvi. 69-74.

CREATION OBEYS GOD, THE LOWER

See: Obedience to God—page 344.

CREATION PRAISES GOD, THE LOWER

And Tobias said: Lord God of our fathers, may the heavens and the earth, and the sea, and the fountains, and the rivers, and all thy creatures that are in them, bless thee.—*Tob.* viii. 7.

When the morning stars praised me together, and all the sons of God made a joyful melody.—*Job* xxxviii. 7.

The floods have lifted up, O Lord: the floods have lifted up their voice.

The floods have lifted up their waves, with the noise of many waters.

Wonderful are the surges of the sea: wonderful is the Lord on high.—*Ps.* xcii. 3, 4.

Praise ye him, O sun and moon: praise him, all ye stars and light.

Praise him, ye heavens of heavens: and let all the waters that are above the heavens praise the name of the Lord. . . .

Praise the Lord from the earth, ye dragons, and all ye deeps:

Fire, hail, snow, ice, stormy winds which fulfil his word:

Mountains and all hills, fruitful trees and all cedars:

Beasts and all cattle: serpents and feathered fowls. . . .—*Ps.* cxlviii. 3-5, 7-10.

All ye works of the Lord, bless the Lord: praise and exalt him above all for ever. . . .

O ye sun and moon, bless the Lord: praise and exalt him above all for ever.

O ye stars of heaven, bless the Lord: praise and exalt him above all for ever.

O every shower and dew, bless ye the Lord: praise and exalt him above all for ever. . . .

O ye ice and snow, bless the Lord: praise and exalt him above all for ever.

O ye nights and days, bless the Lord: praise and exalt him above all for ever.

O ye light and darkness, bless the Lord: praise and exalt him above all for ever.

O ye lightnings and clouds, bless the Lord: praise and exalt him above all for ever.

O let the earth bless the Lord: let it praise and exalt him above all for ever.

O ye mountains and hills, bless the Lord: praise and exalt him above all for ever.

O all ye things that spring up in the earth, bless the Lord: praise and exalt him above all for ever. . . .

O ye seas and rivers, bless the Lord: praise and exalt him above all for ever.

O ye whales, and all that move in the waters, bless the Lord: praise and exalt him above all for ever.

O all ye fowls of the air, bless the Lord: praise and exalt him above all for ever.

O all ye beasts and cattle, bless the Lord: praise and exalt him above all for ever.—*Dan.* iii. 57, 62-64, 70-76, 78-81.

CREATION SEEMS TO FEAR GOD, INANIMATE

O Lord, when thou wentest out of Seir, and passedst by the regions of Edom, the earth trembled, and the heavens dropped water.

The mountains melted before the face of the Lord, and Sinai before the face of the Lord the God of Israel.—*Judges* v. 4, 5.

The pillars of heaven tremble, and dread at his beck.—*Job* xxvi. 11.

The earth shook and trembled: the foundations of the mountains were troubled and were moved, because he was angry with them.—*Ps.* xvii. 8.

Nations were troubled, and kingdoms were bowed down: he uttered his voice, the earth trembled.—*Ps.* xlv. 7.

The waters saw thee, O God, the waters saw thee: and they were afraid, and the depths were troubled. . . .

Thy lightnings enlightened the world: the earth shook and trembled.—*Ps.* lxxvi. 17, 19.

His lightnings have shone forth to the world: the earth saw and trembled.

The mountains melted like wax, at the presence of the Lord: at the presence of the Lord of all the earth.—*Ps.* xcvi. 4, 5.

The deep like a garment is its clothing: above the mountains shall the waters stand.

At thy rebuke they shall flee: at the voice of thy thunder they shall fear.—*Ps.* ciii. 6, 7.

He looketh upon the earth, and maketh it tremble: he toucheth the mountains, and they smoke.—*Ps.* ciii. 32.

Behold the heaven, and the heavens of heavens, the deep, and all the earth, and the things that are in them, shall be moved in his sight,

The mountains also, and the hills, and the foundations of the earth: when God shall look upon them they shall be shaken with trembling.—*Ecclus.* xvi. 18, 19.

The mountains tremble at him, and the hills are made desolate: and the earth hath quaked at his presence, and the world, and all that dwell therein.

Who can stand before the face of his indignation? and who shall resist in the fierceness of his anger? his indignation is poured out like fire: and the rocks are melted by him.—*Nahum* i. 5, 6.

The mountains saw thee, and were grieved: the great body of waters passed away.

The deep put forth its voice: the deep lifted up its hands.

The sun and the moon stood still in their habitation, in the light of thy arrows, they shall go in the brightness of thy glittering spear.—*Hab.* iii. 10, 11.

CREATION TELLS US OF GOD

But ask now the beasts, and they shall teach thee: and the birds of the air, and they shall tell thee.

Speak to the earth, and it shall answer thee: and the fishes of the sea shall tell.

Who is ignorant that the hand of the Lord hath made all these things?

In whose hand is the soul of every living thing, and the spirit of all flesh of man.—*Job* xii. 7-10.

The heavens show forth the glory of God, and the firmament declareth the work of his hands.

Day to day uttereth speech, and night to night showeth knowledge.

There are no speeches nor languages, where their voices are not heard.

Their sound hath gone forth into all the earth: and their words unto the ends of the world.—*Ps.* xviii. 2-5.

The heavens shall confess thy wonders, O Lord: and thy truth in the church of the saints.—*Ps.* lxxxviii. 6.

The heavens declared his justice: and all people saw his glory.—*Ps.* xcvi. 6.

Let all thy works, O Lord, praise thee: and let thy saints bless thee.

They shall speak of the glory of thy kingdom: and shall tell of thy power:

To make thy might known to the sons of men: and the glory of the magnificence of thy kingdom.—*Ps.* cxliv. 10-12.

But all men are vain, in whom there is not the knowledge of God: and who by these good things that are seen could not understand him that is, neither by attending to the works have acknowledged who was the workman.

. . . With whose beauty, if they, being delighted, took them to be gods: let them know how much the Lord of them is more beautiful than they: for the first author of beauty made all those things.

Or, if they admired their power and their effects, let them understand by them, that he that made them is mightier than they:

For by the greatness of the beauty, and of the creature, the creator of them may be seen, so as to be known thereby. —*Wis.* xiii. 1, 3-5.

The firmament on high is his beauty, the beauty of heaven with its glorious show.

The sun when he appeareth showing forth at his rising, an admirable instrument, the work of the most High. . . .

The glory of the stars is the beauty of heaven; the Lord enlighteneth the world on high. . . .

Look upon the rainbow, and bless him that made it: it is very beautiful in its brightness.

It encompasseth the heaven about with the circle of its glory, the hands of the most High have displayed it.— *Ecclus.* xliii. 1, 2, 10, 12, 13.

Because that which is known of God is manifest in them. For God hath manifested it unto them.

For the invisible things of him, from the creation of the world, are clearly seen, being understood by the things that are made; his eternal power also, and divinity: so that they are inexcusable.—*Rom.* i. 19, 20.

CREATOR, GOD OUR

And he said: Let us make man to our image and likeness: and let him have dominion over the fishes of the sea, and the fowls of the air, and the beasts, and the whole earth, and every creeping creature that moveth upon the earth.

And God created man to his own image: to the image of God he created him: male and female he created them. —*Gen.* i. 26, 27.

And the Lord God formed man of the slime of the earth: and breathed into his face the breath of life, and man became a living soul.—*Gen.* ii. 7.

Then the Lord God cast a deep sleep upon Adam: and when he was fast asleep, he took one of his ribs, and filled up flesh for it.

And the Lord God built the rib which he took from Adam into a woman: and brought her to Adam.—*Gen.* ii. 21, 22.

Come let us adore and fall down: and weep before the Lord that made us.— *Ps.* xciv. 6.

Let Israel rejoice in him that made him: and let the children of Sion be joyful in their king.—*Ps.* cxlix. 2.

With all thy strength love him that made thee.—*Ecclus.* vii. 32.

God created man of the earth, and made him after his own image.

And he turned him into it again, and clothed him with strength according to himself. . . .

He created of him a helpmate like to himself: he gave them counsel, and a tongue, and eyes, and ears, and a heart to devise: and he filled them with the knowledge of understanding.— *Ecclus.* xvii. 1, 2, 5.

And now, thus saith the Lord that created thee, O Jacob, and formed thee, O Israel: Fear not, for I have redeemed thee, and called thee by thy name: thou art mine.—*Is.* xliii. 1.

Thus saith the Lord, the Holy One of Israel, his maker: Ask me of things to come, concerning my children, and concerning the work of my hands give ye charge to me.

I made the earth: and I created man upon it.—*Is.* xlv. 11, 12.

CREATOR, ACKNOWLEDGMENT THAT GOD IS OUR

Thy hands have made me, and fashioned me wholly round about, and dost thou thus cast me down headlong on a sudden?

Remember, I beseech thee, that thou hast made me as the clay, and thou wilt bring me into dust again. . . .

Thou hast clothed me with skin and flesh: thou hast put me together with bones and sinews:

Thou hast granted me life and mercy, and thy visitation hath preserved my spirit.—*Job* x. 8, 9, 11, 12.

The spirit of God made me, and the breath of the Almighty gave me life.—*Job* xxxiii. 4.

Know ye that the Lord he is God: he made us, and not we ourselves.—*Ps.* xcix. 3.

Thy hands have made me and formed me: give me understanding, and I will learn thy commandments.—*Ps.* cxviii. 73.

And now, O Lord, thou art our father, and we are clay: and thou art our maker, and we all are the works of thy hands.—*Is.* lxiv. 8.

Have we not all one father? hath not one God created us? why then doth every one of us despise his brother, violating the covenant of our fathers?—*Malach.* ii. 10.

For we are his workmanship, created in Christ Jesus in good works, which God hath prepared that we should walk in them.—*Eph.* ii. 10.

CREATOR OF ALL THINGS, GOD THE

In the beginning God created heaven, and earth.

And the earth was void and empty, and darkness was upon the face of the deep; and the spirit of God moved over the waters.—*Gen.* i. 1, 2.

But ask now the beasts, and they shall teach thee: and the birds of the air, and they shall tell thee.

Speak to the earth, and it shall answer thee: and the fishes of the sea shall tell.

Who is ignorant that the hand of the Lord hath made all these things?—*Job* xii. 7-9.

By the word of the Lord the heavens were established; and all the power of them by the spirit of his mouth:

Gathering together the waters of the sea, as in a vessel; laying up the depths in storehouses.

Let all the earth fear the Lord, and let all the inhabitants of the world be in awe of him.

For he spoke and they were made: he commanded and they were created.—*Ps.* xxxii. 6-9.

Blessed is he who hath the God of Jacob for his helper, whose hope is in the Lord his God:

Who made heaven and earth, the sea, and all things that are in them.—*Ps.* cxlv. 5, 6.

He that liveth for ever created all things together.—*Ecclus.* xviii. 1.

And to whom have ye likened me, or made me equal, saith the Holy One?

Lift up your eyes on high, and see who hath created these things: who bringeth out their host by number, and calleth them all by their names: by the greatness of his might, and strength, and power, not one of them was missing.—*Is.* xl. 25, 26.

Thus saith the Lord God that created the heavens, and stretched them out: that established the earth, and the things that spring out of it: that giveth breath to the people upon it, and spirit to them that tread thereon.—*Is.* xlii. 5.

Thus saith the Lord thy redeemer, and thy maker, from the womb: I am the Lord that make all things, that alone stretch out the heavens, that establish the earth, and there is none with me.—*Is.* xliv. 24.

Thus saith the Lord, the Holy One of Israel, his maker: Ask me of things to come, concerning my children, and concerning the work of my hands, give ye charge to me.

I made the earth: and I created man upon it: my hand stretched forth the heavens, and I have commanded all their host.—*Is.* xlv. 11, 12.

Hearken to me, O Jacob, and thou Israel whom I call: I am he, I am the first, and I am the last.

My hand also hath founded the earth,

and my right hand hath measured the heavens: I shall call them, and they shall stand together.—*Is.* xlviii. 12, 13.

I made the earth, and the men, and the beasts that are upon the face of the earth, by my great power, and by my stretched out arm: and I have given it to whom it seemed good in my eyes.—*Jer.* xxvii. 5.

Thus saith the Lord, who stretcheth forth the heavens, and layeth the foundations of the earth, and formeth the spirit of man in him.—*Zach.* xii. 1.

I beseech thee, my son, look upon heaven and earth, and all that is in them: and consider that God made them out of nothing, and mankind also.—*2 Mach.* vii. 28.

In the beginning was the Word, and the Word was with God, and the Word was God.

. . . All things were made by him; and without him was made nothing that was made.

. . . He was in the world, and the world was made by him, and the world knew him not.—*John* i. 1, 3, 10.

For in 'him were all things created in heaven and on earth, visible and invisible, whether thrones, or dominations, or principalities, or powers; all things were created by him and in him. And he is before all, and by him all things consist.—*Col.* i. 16, 17.

By faith we understand that the world was framed by the word of God; that from invisible things visible things might be made.—*Heb.* xi. 3.

For this they are wilfully ignorant of, that the heavens were before, and the earth out of water, and through water, consisting by the word of God.—*2 Peter* iii. 5.

CREATOR OF ALL THINGS, ACKNOWLEDGMENT THAT GOD IS THE

Thou thyself, O Lord alone, thou hast made heaven, and the heaven of heavens, and all the host thereof: the earth and all things that are in it: the seas and all that are therein: and thou givest life to all these things, and the host of heaven adoreth thee.—*2 Esd.* ix. 6.

'Christ.

Let all creatures serve thee: because thou hast spoken, and they were made: thou didst send forth thy spirit, and they were created, and there is no one that can resist thy voice.—*Judith* xvi. 17.

Thou hast made heaven and earth, and all things that are under the cope of heaven.—*Esther* xiii. 10.

For I will behold thy heavens, the works of thy fingers: the moon and the stars which thou hast founded.—*Ps.* viii. 4.

The earth is the Lord's, and the fulness thereof: the world, and all they that dwell therein.

For he hath founded it upon the seas; and hath prepared it upon the rivers.—*Ps.* xxiii. 1, 2.

Thine is the day, and thine is the night: thou hast made the morning light and the sun.

Thou hast made all the borders of the earth: the summer and the spring were formed by thee.—*Ps.* lxxiii. 16, 17.

Thine are the heavens, and thine is the earth: the world and the fulness thereof thou hast founded:

The north and the sea thou hast created.—*Ps.* lxxxviii. 12, 13.

For in his hand are all the ends of the earth: and the heights of the mountains are his.

For the sea is his, and he made it: and his hands formed the dry land.—*Ps.* xciv. 4, 5.

In the beginning, O Lord, thou foundedst the earth: and the heavens are the works of thy hands.—*Ps.* ci. 26.

Praise ye him, O sun and moon: praise him, all ye stars and light.

Praise him, ye heavens of heavens: and let all the waters that are above the heavens praise the name of the Lord.

For he spoke, and they were made: he commanded, and they were created.

He hath established them for ever, and for ages of ages: he hath made a decree, and it shall not pass away.—*Ps.* cxlviii. 3-6.

For thy almighty hand, which made the world of matter without form, was not unable to send upon 'them a multitude of bears, or fierce lions.—*Wis.* xi. 18.

But the Lord hath made all things,

'The Egyptians who persecuted the Israelites.

and to the godly he hath given wisdom. —*Ecclus.* xliii. 37.

For behold he that formeth the mountains, and createth the wind, and declareth his word to man, he that maketh the morning mist, and walketh upon the high places of the earth: the Lord the God of hosts is his name.—*Amos* iv. 13.

[1]Who having heard it, with one accord lifted up their voice to God, and said: Lord, thou art he that didst make heaven and earth, the sea, and all things that are in them.—*Acts* iv. 24.

Thou art worthy, O Lord our God, to receive glory, and honor, and power: because thou hast created all things; and for thy will they were, and have been created.—*Apoc.* iv. 11.

CRUEL, GOD IS NOT

See also: Mercy of God—page 311.

For God made not death, neither hath he pleasure in the destruction of the living.

For he created all things that they might be: and he made the nations of the earth for health: and there is no poison of destruction in them, nor kingdom of hell upon the earth.—*Wis.* i. 13, 14.

For thou lovest all things that are, and hatest none of the things which thou hast made: for thou didst not appoint, or make anything, hating it.— *Wis.* xi. 25.

As I live, saith the Lord God, I desire not the death of the wicked, but that the wicked turn from his way, and live. Turn ye, turn ye from your evil ways: and why will you die, O house of Israel?—*Ezech.* xxxiii. 11.

CRUELTY

A merciful man doth good to his own soul: but he that is cruel casteth off even his own kindred.—*Prov.* xi. 17.

The just regardeth the lives of his beasts: but the bowels of the wicked are cruel.—*Prov.* xii. 10.

Thus saith the Lord: For three crimes of Edom, and for four, I will

[1]The disciples in Jerusalem, at the release of Peter and John.

not convert him: because he hath pursued his brother with the sword, and hath cast off all pity, and hath carried on his fury, and hath kept his wrath to the end.—*Amos* i. 11.

And as they liked not to have God in their knowledge, God delivered them up to a reprobate sense, to do those things which are not convenient.

Being filled with all iniquity, . . .

Foolish, dissolute, without affection, without fidelity, without mercy.—*Rom.* i. 28, 29, 31.

CRY OF ONE IN SORROW AND DISTRESS, A

Have pity on me, have pity on me, at least you my friends, because the hand of the Lord hath touched me.—*Job* xix. 21.

I expected good things, and evils are come upon me: I waited for light, and darkness broke out.—*Job* xxx. 26.

The sorrows of death surrounded me: and the torrents of iniquity troubled me.

The sorrows of hell encompassed me: and the snares of death prevented me.

In my affliction I called upon the Lord, and I cried to my God.—*Ps.* xvii. 5-7.

O God, my God, look upon me: why hast thou forsaken me?

Far from my salvation are the words of my sins.

O my God, I shall cry by day, and thou wilt not hear: and by night, and it shall not be reputed as folly in me. . . .

I am poured out like water; and all my bones are scattered.

My heart is become like wax melting in the midst of my bowels.

My strength is dried up like a potsherd, and my tongue hath cleaved to my jaws: and thou hast brought me down into the dust of death.—*Ps.* xxi. 2, 3, 15, 16.

Because I was silent, my bones grew old; whilst I cried out all the day long.

For day and night thy hand was heavy upon me: I am turned in my anguish, whilst the thorn is fastened.— *Ps.* xxxi. 3, 4.

All thy heights and thy billows have passed over me. . . .

I will say to God: Thou art my support.

Why hast thou forgotten me? and why go I mourning, whilst my enemy afflicteth me? . . .

Whilst they say to me day by day: Where is thy God?

Why art thou cast down, O my soul? and why dost thou disquiet me?—*Ps.* xli. 8, 10, 11, 12.

My heart is troubled within me: and the fear of death is fallen upon me.

Fear and trembling are come upon me: and darkness hath covered me.—*Ps.* liv. 5, 6.

O Lord God of hosts, how long wilt thou be angry against the prayer of thy servant?

How long wilt thou feed us with the bread of tears: and give us for drink tears in measure?—*Ps.* lxxix. 5, 6.

O Lord, the God of my salvation: I have cried in the day, and in the night before thee. . . .

For my soul is filled with evils: and my life hath drawn nigh to hell.

I am counted among them that go down to the pit: I am become as a man without help, free among the dead.

Like the slain sleeping in the sepulchres, whom thou rememberest no more: and they are cast off from thy hand. . . .

Thy wrath is strong over me: and all thy waves thou hast brought in upon me. . . .

All the day I cried to thee, O Lord; I stretched out my hands to thee.—*Ps.* lxxxvii. 2, 4-6, 8, 10.

But I, O Lord, have cried to thee: and in the morning my prayer shall prevent thee.

Lord, why castest thou off my prayer: why turnest thou away thy face from me?

I am poor, and in labors from my youth: and being exalted, have been humbled and troubled.

Thy wrath hath come upon me: and thy terrors have troubled me.

They have come round about me like water all the day: they have compassed me about together.—*Ps.* lxxxvii. 14-18.

I cried with my whole heart, hear me, O Lord: I will seek thy justifications.

I cried unto thee, save me: that I may keep thy commandments.

I prevented the dawning of the day, and cried: because in thy words I very much hoped.—*Ps.* cxviii. 145-147.

Thus saith the Lord, the God of Israel, to thee, Baruch:

Thou hast said: Woe is me, wretch that I am, for the Lord hath added sorrow to my sorrow: I am wearied with my groans, and I find no rest.—*Jer.* xlv. 2, 3.

Behold, O Lord, for I am in distress, my bowels are troubled: my heart is turned within me, for I am full of bitterness: abroad the sword destroyeth, and at home there is death alike:

. . . For my sighs are many, and my heart is sorrowful.—*Lam.* i. 20, 22.

And Jonas prayed to the Lord his God out of the belly of the fish.

And he said: I cried out of my affliction to the Lord, and he heard me: I cried out of the belly of hell, and thou hast heard my voice.

And thou hast cast me forth into the deep, in the heart of the sea, and a flood hath compassed me: all thy billows, and thy waves have passed over me.

And I said: I am cast away out of the sight of thy eyes: but yet I shall see thy holy temple again.

The waters compassed me about even to the soul: the deep hath closed me round about, the sea hath covered my head.

I went down to the lowest parts of the mountains: the bars of the earth have shut me up for ever: and thou wilt bring up my life from corruption, O Lord my God.—*Jonas* ii. 2-7.

How long, O Lord, shall I cry, and thou wilt not hear? shall I cry out to thee, suffering violence, and thou wilt not save?

Why hast thou shown me iniquity and grievance, to see rapine and injustice before me? and there is a judgment, but opposition is more powerful.

Therefore the law is torn in pieces, and judgment cometh not to the end: because the wicked prevaileth against the just, therefore wrong judgment goeth forth.—*Hab.* i. 2-4.

CRY OF THOSE IN SORROW AND DISTRESS REACHES GOD, THE

Now after a long time the king of Egypt died: and the children of Israel groaning, cried out because of the works: and their cry went up unto God from the works.

And he heard their groaning, and remembered the covenant which he made with Abraham, Isaac, and Jacob. —*Ex.* ii. 23, 24.

In my affliction I called upon the Lord, and I cried to my God:

And he heard my voice from his holy temple; and my cry before him came into his ears.—*Ps.* xvii. 7.

In thee have our fathers hoped: they have hoped, and thou hast delivered them.

They cried to thee, and they were saved: they trusted in thee, and were not confounded.—*Ps.* xxi. 5, 6.

O Lord my God, I have cried to thee, and thou hast healed me.—*Ps.* xxix. 3.

But I have cried to God, and the Lord will save me.—*Ps.* liv. 17.

O God, I have declared to thee my life: thou hast set my tears in thy sight.—*Ps.* lv. 9.

He shall cry to me, and I will hear him: I am with him in tribulation, I will deliver him, and I will glorify him. —*Ps.* xc. 15.

Because he hath looked forth from his high sanctuary: from heaven the Lord hath looked upon the earth.

That he might hear the groans of them that are in fetters: that he might release the children of the slain.—*Ps.* ci. 20, 21.

They were hungry and thirsty: their soul fainted in them.

And they cried to the Lord in their tribulation: and he delivered them out of their distresses.—*Ps.* cvi. 5, 6.

They that go down to the sea in ships, doing business in the great waters:

These have seen the works of the Lord, and his wonders in the deep.

He said the word, and there arose a storm of wind: and the waves thereof were lifted up.

They mount up to the heavens, and they go down to the depths: their soul pined away with evils.

They were troubled, and reeled like a drunken man; and all their wisdom was swallowed up.

And they cried to the Lord in their affliction: and he brought them out of their distresses.

And he turned the storm into a breeze: and its waves were still.

And they rejoiced because they were still: and he brought them to the haven which they wished for.—*Ps.* cvi. 23-30.

In my trouble I cried to the Lord; and he heard me.—*Ps.* cxix. 1.

For the people of Sion shall dwell in Jerusalem: weeping, thou shalt not weep, he will surely have pity on thee: at the voice of thy cry, as soon as he shall hear, he will answer thee.—*Is.* xxx. 19.

I have called upon thy name, O Lord, from the lowest pit.

Thou hast heard my voice: turn not away thy ear from my sighs and cries.

Thou drewest near in the day when I called upon thee, thou saidst: Fear not.—*Lam.* iii. 55-57.

CRY OF THE WRONGED REACHES GOD, THE

You shall not hurt a widow or an orphan.

If you hurt them, they will cry out to me, and I will hear their cry:

And my rage shall be enkindled, and I will strike you with the sword, and your wives shall be widows, and your children, fatherless.—*Ex.* xxii. 22-24.

If thou lend money to any of my people that is poor, that dwelleth with thee, thou shalt not be hard upon them as an extortioner, nor oppress them with usuries.

If thou take of thy neighbor a garment in pledge, thou shalt give it him again before sunset.

For that same is the only thing wherewith he is covered, the clothing of his body, neither hath he any other to sleep in: if he cry to me, I will hear him, because I am compassionate.—*Ex.* xxii. 25-27.

Out of the cities they have made men to groan, and the soul of the wounded hath cried out, and God doth not suffer it to pass unrevenged.—*Job* xxiv. 12.

He hath struck them, as being wicked, in open sight.

Who as it were on purpose have revolted from him, and would not understand all his ways:

So that they caused the cry of the needy to come to him, and he heard the voice of the poor.—*Job* xxxiv. 26-28.

The Lord will not accept any person against a poor man, and he will hear the prayer of him that is wronged.

He will not despise the prayers of the fatherless; nor the widow, when she poureth out her complaint.

Do not the widow's tears run down the cheek, and her cry against him that causeth them to fall?

For from the cheek they go up even to heaven, and the Lord that heareth will not be delighted with them.—*Ecclus.* xxxv. 16-19.

And will not God revenge his elect who cry to him day and night: and will he have patience in their regard?

I say to you, that he will quickly revenge them.—*Luke* xviii. 7, 8.

Behold the hire of the laborers, who have reaped down your fields, which by fraud has been kept back by you, crieth: and the cry of them hath entered into the ears of the Lord of sabaoth.—*James* v. 4.

CURIOSITY

And they brought him (Lot) forth, and set him without the city: and there they spoke to him, saying: Save thy life: look not back, neither stay thou in all the country about: but save thyself in the mountain, lest thou be also consumed. . . .

And his wife looking behind her, was turned into a statue of salt.—*Gen.* xix. 17, 26.

Let not others by any curiosity see the things that are in the sanctuary before they be wrapped up, otherwise they shall die.—*Num.* iv. 20.

Seek not the things that are too high for thee, and search not into things above thy ability: but the things that

God hath commanded thee, think on them always, and in many of his works be not curious.

For it is not necessary for thee to see with thy eyes those things that are hid.

In unnecessary matters be not over curious, and in many of his works, thou shalt not be inquisitive.—*Ecclus.* iii. 22-24.

And Herod seeing Jesus, was very glad; for he was desirous of a long time to see him, because he had heard many things of him; and he hoped to see some sign wrought by him.

And he questioned him in many words. But he answered him nothing.—*Luke* xxiii. 8, 9.

As I desired thee to remain at Ephesus when I went into Macedonia, that thou mightest charge some not to teach otherwise,

Not to give heed to fables and endless genealogies: which furnish questions rather than the edification of God, which is in faith.—1 *Tim.* i. 3, 4.

And withal, being idle, they learn to go about from house to house: and are not only idle, but tattlers also, and busybodies, speaking things which thev ought not.—1 *Tim.* v. 13.

CURSING

For I have not given my mouth to sin, by wishing a curse to 'his soul.—*Job* xxxi. 30.

And he loved cursing, and it shall come unto him: and he would not have blessing, and it shall be far from him.

And he put on cursing like a garment: and it went in like water into his entrails, and like oil in his bones.

May it be unto him like a garment which covereth him; and like a girdle with which he is girded continually.—*Ps.* cviii. 18, 19.

As a bird flying to other places, and a sparrow going here or there: so a curse uttered without cause shall come upon a man.—*Prov.* xxvi. 2.

There is a generation that curseth their father, and doth not bless their mother.

A generation that are pure in their

¹Job speaking of his enemy.

own eyes, and yet are not washed from their filthiness.—*Prov.* xxx. 11, 12.

While the ungodly curseth the devil, he curseth his own soul.—*Ecclus.* xxi. 30.

In the quarrels of the proud is the shedding of blood: and their cursing is a grievous hearing.—*Ecclus.* xxvii. 16.

When one prayeth, and another curseth: whose voice will God hear?—*Ecclus.* xxxiv. 29.

For by thy words thou shalt be justified, and by thy words thou shalt be condemned.—*Matt.* xii. 37.

DANCING

All things have their season, and in their times all things pass under heaven. . . .

A time to weep, and a time to laugh. A time to mourn, and a time to dance. —*Eccles.* iii. 1, 4.

DANCING, OFTEN THE OCCASION OF EVIL

Use not much the company of her that is a dancer, and hearken not to her, lest thou perish by the force of her charms.—*Ecclus.* ix. 4.

And when the daughter of the same Herodias had come in, and had danced, and pleased Herod, and them that were at table with him, the king said to the damsel: Ask of me what thou wilt, and I will give it thee.

. . . Who when she was gone out, said to her mother, What shall I ask? But she said: The head of John the Baptist.

And when she was come in immediately with haste to the king, she asked, saying: I will that forthwith thou give me in a dish the head of John the Baptist.—*Mark* vi. 22, 24, 25.

DEAD, THE

Shall any one in the sepulchre declare thy mercy: and thy truth in destruction?—*Ps.* lxxxvii. 12.

The dead shall not praise thee, O Lord: nor any of them that go down to hell.—*Ps.* cxiii. (*Heb.* cxv.) 17.

For the living know that they shall die, but the dead [1]know nothing more,

[1]Viz., as to the transactions of this world, in which they have now no part, unless it be

neither have they a reward any more: for the memory of them is forgotten.

Their love also, and their hatred, and their envy are all perished, neither have they any part in this world, and in the work that is done under the sun.— *Eccles.* ix. 5, 6.

For among the dead, there is no accusing of life.—*Ecclus.* xli. 7.

Open thy eyes, and behold: for the dead that are in hell, whose spirit is taken away from their bowels, shall not give glory and justice to the Lord.— *Bar.* ii. 17.

DEAD, GRIEVING FOR THE

Weep for the dead, for his light hath failed: and weep for the fool, for his understanding faileth.

Weep but a little for the dead, for he is at rest.—*Ecclus.* xxii. 10, 11.

My son, shed tears over the dead, and begin to lament as if thou hadst suffered some great harm, and according to judgment cover his body, and neglect not his burial.

And for fear of being ill spoken of weep bitterly for a day, and then comfort thyself in thy sadness.

And make mourning for him according to his merit for a day or two, for fear of detraction.—*Ecclus.* xxxviii. 16-18.

When the dead is at rest, let his remembrance rest, and comfort him in the departing of his spirit.—*Ecclus.* xxxviii. 24.

And we will not have you ignorant, brethren, concerning them that are asleep, that you be not sorrowful, even as others who have no hope.

For if we believe that Jesus died, and rose again; even so them who have slept through Jesus, will God bring with him. . . .

Wherefore, comfort ye one another with these words.—1 *Thess.* iv. 12, 13, 17.

DEATH

And the Lord God took man, and put him into the paradise of pleasure, to dress it, and to keep it.

revealed to them; neither have they any knowledge or power now of doing anything to secure their eternal state, nor can they now procure themselves any good, as the living always may do, by the grace of God.

And he commanded him, saying: Of every tree of paradise thou shalt eat: But of the tree of knowledge of good and evil, thou shalt not eat. For in what day soever thou shalt eat of it, thou shalt die the death.—*Gen.* ii. 15-17.

And to Adam he said: Because thou hast hearkened to the voice of thy wife, and hast eaten of the tree, whereof I commanded thee that thou shouldst not eat, cursed is the earth in thy work; with labor and toil shalt thou eat thereof all the days of thy life. . . .

In the sweat of thy face shalt thou eat bread till thou return to the earth, out of which thou wast taken: for dust thou art, and into dust thou shalt return.—*Gen.* iii. 17, 19.

And all the time that Adam lived came to nine hundred and thirty years, and he died. . . .

And all the days of Mathusala were nine hundred and sixty-nine years, and he died.—*Gen.* v. 5, 27.

As a cloud is consumed, and passeth away: so he that shall go down to hell shall not come up.

Nor shall he return any more into his house, neither shall his place know him any more.—*Job* vii. 9, 10.

A tree hath hope: if it be cut, it groweth green again, and the boughs thereof sprout.

If its root be old in the earth, and its stock be dead in the dust:

At the scent of water, it shall spring, and bring forth leaves, as when it was first planted.

But man when he shall be dead, and stripped, and consumed, I pray you, where is he?

As if the waters should depart out of the sea, and an emptied river should be dried up:

So man when he is fallen asleep shall not rise again; till the heavens be broken, he shall not awake, nor rise up out of his sleep.—*Job* xiv. 7-12.

Shall man that is dead, thinkest thou, live again? All the days in which I am now in warfare, I expect until my change come.

Thou shalt call me, and I will answer thee: to the work of thy hands thou shalt reach out thy right hand.—*Job* xiv. 14, 15.

I have said to rottenness: Thou art my father; to worms, my mother and my sister.—*Job* xvii. 14.

All that I have shall go down into the deepest pit: thinkest thou that there at least I shall have rest?—*Job* xvii. 16.

Because man shall go into the house of his eternity, and the mourners shall go round about in the street.

Before the silver cord be broken, and the golden fillet shrink back, and the pitcher be crushed at the fountain and the wheel be broken upon the cistern,

And the dust return into its earth, from whence it was, and the spirit return to God, who gave it.—*Eccles.* xii. 5-7.

For when a man shall die, he shall inherit serpents, and beasts, and worms. —*Ecclus.* x. 13.

O death, thy sentence is welcome to the man that is in need, and to him whose strength faileth:

Who is in a decrepit age, and that is in care about all things, and to the distrustful that loseth patience!— *Ecclus.* xli. 3, 4.

I said: In the midst of my days, I shall go to the gates of hell: I sought for the residue of my years.

I said: I shall not see the Lord God in the land of the living. I shall behold man no more, nor the inhabitant of rest.

My generation is at an end, and it is rolled away from me, as a shepherd's tent. My life is cut off, as by a weaver: whilst I was yet but beginning, he cut me off: from morning even to night, thou wilt make an end of me.— *Is.* xxxviii. 10-12.

I will deliver them out of the hand of death. I will redeem them from death: O death, I will be thy death; O hell, I will be thy bite.—*Osee* xiii. 14.

I must work the works of him that sent me, whilst it is day: the night cometh, when no man can work.— *John* ix. 4.

And when this mortal hath put on immortality, then shall come to pass the saying that is written: Death is swallowed up in victory.

O death, where is thy victory? O death, where is thy sting?

Now the sting of death is sin.—*1 Cor.* xv. 54-56.

For we know, if our earthly house of this habitation be dissolved, that we have a building of God, a house not made with hands, eternal in heaven.—*2 Cor.* v. 1.

But the end of all is at hand. Be prudent, therefore, and watch in prayers.—*1 Peter* iv. 7.

DEATH, CERTAINTY OF

In the sweat of thy face shalt thou eat bread till thou return to the earth, out of which thou wast taken: for dust thou art, and into dust thou shalt return.—*Gen.* iii. 19.

Remember, I beseech thee, that thou hast made me as the clay, and thou wilt bring me into dust again.—*Job* x. 9.

The days of man are short, and the number of his months is with thee: thou hast appointed his bounds, which cannot be passed.—*Job* xiv. 5.

Who is the man that shall live, and not see death: that shall deliver his soul from the hand of hell?—*Ps.* lxxxviii. 49.

Man's days are as grass, as the flower of the field, so shall he flourish.

For the spirit shall pass in him, and he shall not be: and he shall know his place no more.—*Ps.* cii. 15, 16.

His spirit shall go forth, and he shall return into his earth: in that day all their thoughts shall perish.—*Ps.* cxlv. 4.

It is not in man's power to stop the spirit, neither hath he power in the day of death.—*Eccles.* viii. 8.

There is no man that liveth always, or that hopeth for this.—*Eccles.* ix. 4.

And of the same clay, by a vain labor, he maketh a god: he who a little before was made of earth himself, and a little after, returneth to the same out of which he was taken, when his life, which was lent him, shall be called for again.—*Wis.* xv. 8.

Remember that death is not slow, and that the ¹covenant of hell hath been shown to thee: for the covenant of this world shall surely die.—*Ecclus.* xiv. 12.

Remember my judgment: for thine

¹i.e. The decree by which all are to go down to the regions of death.

also shall be so: yesterday for me, and to-day for thee.—*Ecclus.* xxxviii. 23.

And as it is appointed unto men once to die, and after this the judgment:

So also Christ was offered once to exhaust the sins of many.—*Heb.* ix. 27, 28.

DEATH, FOR ALL FLESH, CERTAINTY OF

Behold this day I am going into the way of all the earth.—*Jos.* xxiii. 14.

We all die, and like waters that return no more, we fall down into the earth: neither will God have a soul to perish, but recalleth, meaning that he that is cast off, should not altogether perish.—*2 Kings* xiv. 14.

And the days of David drew nigh that he should die, and he charged his son Solomon, saying:

I am going the way of all flesh: take thou courage, and show thyself a man.—*3 Kings* ii. 1, 2.

I know that thou wilt deliver me to death, where a house is appointed for every one that liveth.—*Job* xxx. 23.

All flesh shall perish together, and man shall return into ashes.—*Job* xxxiv. 15.

For all men have one entrance into life, and the like going out.—*Wis.* vii. 6.

Rejoice not at the death of thy enemy; knowing that we all die, and are not willing that others should rejoice at our death.—*Ecclus.* viii. 8.

And after this God looked upon the earth, and filled it with his goods.

The soul of every living thing hath shown forth before the face thereof, and into it they return again.—*Ecclus.* xvi. 30, 31.

All things that are of the earth, shall return to the earth again, and all waters shall return to the sea.—*Ecclus.* xl. 11.

This sentence is from the Lord upon all flesh.—*Ecclus.* xli. 5.

DEATH, UNCERTAINTY OF THE TIME OF

See also: Life, uncertainty of this— page 281.

Man knoweth not his own end: but as fishes are taken with the hook, and as birds are caught with the snare, so men are taken in the evil time, when it shall suddenly come upon them.—*Eccles.* ix. 12.

I said: In the midst of my days I shall go to the gates of hell: I sought for the residue of my years. . . .

My generation is at an end, and it is rolled away from me, as a shepherd's tent. My life is cut off, as by a weaver: whilst I was yet but beginning, he cut me off: from morning even to night thou wilt make an end of me.—*Is.* xxxviii. 10, 12.

Then shall the kingdom of heaven be like to ten virgins, who taking their lamps went out to meet the bridegroom and the bride. . . .

And the bridegroom tarrying, they all slumbered and slept.

And at midnight there was a cry made: Behold, the bridegroom cometh, go ye forth to meet him.

. . . Watch ye therefore, because you know not the day nor the hour.—*Matt.* xxv. 1, 5, 6, 13.

Watch ye therefore, (for you know not when the lord of the house cometh: at even, or at midnight, or at the cockcrowing, or in the morning,)

Lest coming on a sudden, he find you sleeping.

And what I say to you, I say to all: Watch.—*Mark* xiii. 35, 36, 37.

And he spoke a similitude to them, saying:

The land of a certain rich man brought forth plenty of fruits.

And he thought within himself, saying: What shall I do, because I have no room where to bestow my fruits?

And he said: This will I do: I will pull down my barns, and will build greater; and into them will I gather all things that are grown to me, and my goods.

And I will say to my soul: Soul, thou hast much goods laid up for many years, take thy rest; eat, drink, make good cheer.

But God said to him: Thou fool, this night do they require thy soul of thee: and whose shall those things be which thou hast provided?—*Luke* xii. 16-20.

Be you then also ready: for at what hour you think not, the Son of man will come.—*Luke* xii. 40.

For yourselves know perfectly, that the day of the Lord shall so come, as a thief in the night.

For when they shall say, peace and security; then shall sudden destruction come upon them, as the pains upon her that is with child, and they shall not escape.—1 *Thess.* v. 2, 3.

If then thou shalt not watch, I will come to thee as a thief, and thou shalt not know at what hour I will come to thee.—*Apoc.* iii. 3.

DEATH LEVELS ALL DISTINCTION

The small and great are there, and the servant is free from his master.—*Job* iii. 19.

One man dieth strong, and hale, rich and happy.

. . . But another dieth in bitterness of soul, without any riches:

And yet they shall sleep together in the dust, and worms shall cover them.—*Job* xxi. 23, 25, 26.

The poor man and the creditor have met one another: the Lord is the enlightener of them both.—*Prov.* xxix. 13.

DEATH, BITTERNESS OF

And Samuel said: Bring hither to me Agag, the king of Amalec. And Agag was presented to him, very fat, and trembling. And Agag said: Doth bitter death separate in this manner?—1 *Kings* xv. 32.

Shall not the fewness of my days be ended shortly? suffer me, therefore, that I may lament my sorrow a little:

Before I go, and return no more, to a land that is dark and covered with the mist of death:

A land of misery and darkness, where the shadow of death, and no order, but everlasting horror dwelleth.—*Job* x. 20, 21, 22.

O death, how bitter is the remembrance of thee to a man that hath peace in his possessions!

To a man that is at rest, and whose ways are prosperous in all things, and that is yet able to take meat!—*Ecclus.* xli. 1, 2.

O death, where is thy victory? O death, where is thy sting?

Now the sting of death is sin.—1 *Cor.* xv. 55, 56.

DEATH, REMEMBRANCE OF

It is better to go to the house of mourning, than to the house of feasting: for in that, we are put in mind of the end of all, and the living thinketh what is to come.—*Eccles.* vii. 3.

If a man live many years, and have rejoiced in them all, he must remember the darksome time, and the many days: which when they shall come, the things past shall be accused of vanity.—*Eccles.* xi. 8.

In all thy works, remember thy last end, and thou shalt never sin.—*Ecclus.* vii. 40.

Remember that death is not slow, and that the covenant of hell hath been shown to thee: for the covenant of this world shall surely die.—*Ecclus.* xiv. 12.

Remember thy last things, and let enmity cease.—*Ecclus.* xxviii. 6.

Give not up thy heart to sadness, but drive it from thee: and remember the latter end.

Forget it not: for there is no returning.

. . . Remember my judgment: for thine also shall be so: yesterday for me, and to-day for thee.—*Ecclus.* xxxviii. 21-23.

DEATH, PREPARATION FOR

Shall man that is dead, thinkest thou, live again? all the days in which I am now in warfare, I expect until my change come.—*Job* xiv. 14.

Into thy hands I commend my spirit: thou hast redeemed me, O Lord, the God of truth.—*Ps.* xxx. 6.

But he that had received the one talent, came and said: Lord, I know that thou art a hard man; thou reapest where thou hast not sown, and gatherest where thou hast not strewed.

And being afraid, I went and hid thy talent in the earth: behold, here thou hast that which is thine.

And his lord, answering, said to him: Wicked and slothful servant, thou knewest that I reap where I sow not, and gather where I have not strewed:

Thou oughtest therefore to have committed my money to the bankers, and at my coming I should have received my own with usury.

Take ye away, therefore, the talent from him, and give it him that hath ten talents.—*Matt.* xxv. 24-28.

And the Lord said: Who, (thinkest thou,) is the faithful and wise steward, whom his lord setteth over his family, to give them their measure of wheat in due season?

Blessed is that servant, whom when his lord shall come, he shall find so doing.

Verily I say to you, he will set him over all that he possesseth.

But if that servant shall say in his heart: My lord is long a coming; and shall begin to strike the men-servants and maid-servants, and to eat, and to drink, and be drunk:

The lord of that servant will come in the day that he hopeth not, and at the hour that he knoweth not, and shall separate him, and shall appoint him his portion with unbelievers.—*Luke* xii. 42-46.

I die daily, I protest by your glory, brethren, which I have in Christ Jesus our Lord.—1 *Cor.* xv. 31.

Seeing then that all these things are to be dissolved, what manner of people ought you to be in holy conversation and godliness?—2 *Peter* iii. 11.

Behold I come as a thief. Blessed is he that watcheth, and keepeth his garments, lest he walk naked, and they see his shame.—*Apoc.* xvi. 15.

DEATH, EXHORTATION TO PREPARE FOR

O that they would be wise and would understand, and would provide for their last end.—*Deut.* xxxii. 29.

In those days Ezechias was sick unto death: and Isaias, the son of Amos, the prophet, came and said to him: Thus saith the Lord God: Give charge concerning thy house, for thou shalt die, and not live.—4 *Kings* xx. 1.

Do good to thy friend before thou die, and according to thy ability, stretching out thy hand, give to the poor.—*Ecclus.* xiv. 13.

Thou shalt not appear empty in the sight of the Lord.—*Ecclus.* xxxv. 6.

Watch ye therefore, because you know not what hour your Lord will come.

But this know ye, that if the goodman of the house knew at what hour the thief would come, he would certainly watch, and would not suffer his house to be broken open.

Wherefore, be you also ready, because at what hour you know not the Son of man will come.—*Matt.* xxiv. 42-44.

Watch ye, therefore, because you know not the day nor the hour.—*Matt.* xxv. 13.

Take ye heed, watch and pray. For ye know not when the time is.—*Mark* xiii. 33.

Watch ye, therefore, (for you know not when the lord of the house cometh: at even, or at midnight, or at the cockcrowing, or in the morning,)

Lest coming on a sudden, he find you sleeping.

And what I say to you, I say to all: Watch.—*Mark* xiii. 35, 36, 37.

Let your loins be girt, and lamps burning in your hands.

And you yourselves like to men who wait for their lord, when he shall return from the wedding; that when he cometh and knocketh, they may open to him immediately.

Blessed are those servants, whom the Lord when he cometh, shall find watching. Amen I say to you, that he will gird himself, and make them sit down to meat, and passing will minister unto them.—*Luke* xii. 35-37.

Watch ye, therefore, praying at all times, that you may be accounted worthy to escape all these things that are to come, and to stand before the Son of man.—*Luke* xxi. 36.

This therefore I say, brethren; the time is short; it remaineth, that they also who have wives, be as if they had none;

And they that weep, as though they wept not; and they that rejoice, as if they rejoiced not; and they that buy, as though they possessed not;

And they that use this world, as if they used it not: for the fashion of this world passeth away.—1 *Cor.* vii. 29-31.

For yourselves know perfectly, that the day of the Lord shall so come, as a thief in the night. . . .

But you, brethren, are not in darkness, that that day should overtake you as a thief.

For all you are the children of light, and children of the day: we are not of the night, nor of darkness.

Therefore, let us not sleep, as others do; but let us watch, and be sober.— 1 *Thess.* v. 2, 4-6.

Let us hold fast the confession of our hope without wavering (for he is faithful that hath promised),

And let us consider one another, to provoke unto charity and to good works:

Not forsaking our assembly, as some are accustomed; but comforting one another, and so much the more as you see the day approaching.—*Heb.* x. 23-25.

But the end of all is at hand. Be prudent, therefore, and watch in prayers.—1 *Peter* iv. 7.

Have in mind, therefore, in what manner thou hast received and heard: and observe, and do penance. If then thou shalt not watch, I will come to thee as a thief, and thou shalt not know at what hour I will come to thee.— *Apoc.* iii. 3.

DEATH OF THE SINNER

This I know from the beginning, since man was placed upon the earth,

That the praise of the wicked is short, and the joy of the hypocrite but for a moment.

If his pride mount up even to heaven, and his head touch the clouds:

In the end he shall be destroyed like a dunghill, and they that had seen him, shall say: Where is he?

As a dream that fleeth away, he shall not be found, he shall pass as a vision of the night:

The eyes that had seen him shall see him no more, neither shall his place any more behold him. . . .

His bones shall be filled with the vices of his youth, and they shall sleep with him in the dust.—*Job* xx. 4-9, 11.

The death of the wicked is very evil: and they that hate the just shall be guilty.—*Ps.* xxxiii. 22.

Because the wicked shall perish.

And the enemies of the Lord, presently after they shall be honored and exal ed, shall come to nothing, and vanish like smoke.—*Ps.* xxxvi. 20.

When the wicked man is dead, there shall be no hope any more: and the expectation of the solicitous shall perish.—*Prov.* xi. 7.

And if they die quickly, they shall have no hope, nor speech of comfort in the day of trial.

For dreadful are the ends of a wicked race.—*Wis.* iii. 18, 19.

And they (the wicked) shall fall after this without honor, and be a reproach among the dead for ever: for he shall burst them puffed up and speechless, and shall shake them from the foundations, and they shall be utterly laid waste: they shall be in sorrow, and their memory shall perish.

They shall come with fear at the thought of their sins, and their iniquities shall stand against them to convict them.—*Wis.* iv. 19, 20.

The congregation of sinners is like tow heaped together, and the end of them is a flame of fire.

The way of sinners is made plain with stones, and in their end is hell, and darkness, and pains.—*Ecclus.* xxi. 10, 11.

Woe to you, ungodly men, who have forsaken the law of the most high Lord.

And if you be born, you shall be born in malediction: and if you die, in malediction shall be your portion.

All things that are of the earth, shall return into the earth: so the ungodly shall from malediction to destruction.—*Ecclus.* xli. 11-13.

But if that evil servant shall say in his heart: My lord is long a coming:

And shall begin to strike his fellow-servants, and shall eat and drink with drunkards:

The lord of that servant shall come in a day that he hopeth not, and at an hour that he knoweth not:

And shall separate him, and appoint his portion with the hypocrites. There shall be weeping and gnashing of teeth.—*Matt.* xxiv. 48-51.

For we know him that hath said: Vengeance belongeth to me, and I will repay. And again: The Lord shall judge his people.

It is a fearful thing to fall into the hands of the living God.—*Heb.* x. 30, 31.

DEATH OF THE JUST

Blessed is he whom thou hast chosen and taken to thee: he shall dwell in thy courts.

We shall be filled with the good things of thy house.—*Ps.* lxiv. 5.

They that are planted in the house of the Lord, shall flourish in the courts of the house of our God.—*Ps.* xci. 14.

Precious in the sight of the Lord is the death of his saints.—*Ps.* cxv. 15.

The wicked man shall be driven out in his wickedness; but the just hath hope in his death.—*Prov.* xiv. 32.

But the souls of the just are in the hand of God, and the torment of death shall not touch them.

In the sight of the unwise they seemed to die; and their departure was taken for misery:

And their going away from us, for utter destruction: but they are in peace.

And though in the sight of men they suffered torments, their hope is full of immortality.

Afflicted in few things, in many they shall be well rewarded: because God hath tried them, and found them worthy of himself.

As gold in the furnace, he hath proved them, and as a victim of a holocaust, he hath received them, and in time there shall be respect had to them.—*Wis.* iii. 1-6.

But the just man, if he be prevented with death, shall be in rest.—*Wis.* iv. 7.

He pleased God and was beloved, and living among sinners, he was translated.

He was taken away lest wickedness should alter his understanding, or deceit beguile his soul. . . .

For his soul pleased God: therefore he hastened to bring him out of the midst of iniquities: but the people see this, and understand not, nor lay up such things in their hearts. . . .—*Wis.* iv. 10, 11, 14.

With him that feareth the Lord, it shall go well in the latter end, and in the day of his death, he shall be blessed.—*Ecclus.* i. 13.

And they shall say in that day: Lo, this is our God, we have waited for him, and he will save us: this is the Lord, we have patiently waited for him, we shall rejoice and be joyful in his salvation.—*Is.* xxv. 9.

The just perisheth, and no man layeth it to heart, and men of mercy are taken away, because there is none that understandeth; for the just man is taken away from before the face of evil.

Let peace come, let him rest in his bed, that hath walked in his uprightness.—*Is.* lvii. 1, 2.

I will deliver them out of the hand of death. I will redeem them from death: O death, I will be thy death; O hell, I will be thy bite.—*Osee* xiii. 14.

But when these things begin to come to pass, look up, and lift up your heads, because your redemption is at hand.—*Luke* xxi. 28.

And he said to Jesus: Lord, remember me, when thou shalt come into thy kingdom.

And Jesus said to him: Amen I say to thee, this day thou shalt be with me in paradise.—*Luke* xxiii. 42, 43.

In a moment, in the twinkling of an eye, at the last trumpet: for the trumpet shall sound, and the dead shall rise again incorruptible: and we shall be changed.

For this corruptible must put on incorruption; and this mortal must put on immortality.

And when this mortal hath put on immortality, then shall come to pass the saying that is written: Death is swallowed up in victory.

O death, where is thy victory? O death, where is thy sting?—1 *Cor.* xv. 52-55.

Wherefore he saith: Rise, thou that sleepest, and arise from the dead: and Christ shall enlighten thee.—*Eph.* v. 14.

But I am straitened between two: having a desire to be dissolved and to be with Christ, a thing by far the better.—*Philipp.* i. 23.

And we will not have you ignorant, brethren, concerning them that are asleep, that you be not sorrowful, even as others who have no hope.

For if we believe that Jesus died, and rose again; even so them who have slept through Jesus, will God bring with him. . . .

Then we who are alive, who are left, shall be taken up together with them in the clouds, to meet Christ, into the air, and so shall we be always with the Lord.—1 *Thess.* iv. 12, 13, 16.

I have fought a good fight, I have finished my course, I have kept the faith.

As to the rest, there is laid up for me a crown of justice, which the Lord, the just judge, will render to me in that day: and not only to me, but to them also that love his coming.—2 *Tim.* iv. 7, 8.

And I heard a voice from heaven, saying to me: Write: Blessed are the dead, who die in the Lord. From henceforth now, saith the Spirit, that they may rest from their labors; for their works follow them.—*Apoc.* xiv. 13.

Blessed and holy is he that hath part in the first resurrection. In these the second death hath no power; but they shall be priests of God and of Christ; and shall reign with him a thousand years.—*Apoc.* xx. 6.

DEATH OF THE YOUNG

For venerable old age is not that of long time, not counted by the number of years: but the understanding of a man is grey hairs,

And a spotless life is old age.

He pleased God and was beloved, and living among sinners he was translated.

He was taken away lest wickedness should alter his understanding, or deceit beguile his soul.

For the bewitching of vanity obscureth good things, and the wandering of concupiscence overturneth the innocent mind.

Being made perfect in a short space, he fulfilled a long time:

For his soul pleased God: therefore he hastened to bring him out of the midst of iniquities: but the people see this, and understand not, nor lay up such things in their hearts. . . .

But the just that is dead condemneth the wicked that are living, and youth soon ended, the long life of the unjust. —*Wis.* iv. 8-14, 16.

DEATH, PRAYER FOR A GOOD

Let my soul die the death of the just, and my last end be like to them.—*Num.* xxiii. 10.

O forgive me, that I may be refreshed, before I go hence, and be no more.—*Ps.* xxxviii. 14.

DEBTS, WE SHOULD PAY OUR JUST

See also: Justice in our dealings with one another—page 268.

If any man hath done any work for thee, immediately pay him his hire, and let not the wages of thy hired servant stay with thee at all.—*Tob.* iv. 15.

The sinner shall borrow, and not pay again; but the just showeth mercy, and shall give.—*Ps.* xxxvi. 21.

Lend to thy neighbor in the time of need, and pay thou thy neighbor again in due time.

Keep thy word, and deal faithfully with him: and thou shalt always find that which is necessary for thee.

Many have looked upon a thing lent as a thing found, and have given trouble to them that helped them.

Till they receive, they kiss the hands of the lender, and in promises they humble their voice:

But when they should repay, they will ask time, and will return tedious and murmuring words, and will complain of the time:

And if he be able to pay, he will stand off, he will scarce pay one half, and will count it as if he had found it:

But if not, he will defraud him of his money, and he shall get him for an enemy without cause:

And he will pay him with reproaches and curses, and instead of honor and good turn will repay him injuries.

Many have refused to lend, not out of wickedness, but they were afraid to be defrauded without cause.—*Ecclus.* xxix. 2-10.

Woe to him that buildeth up his house by injustice, and his chambers not in judgment: that will oppress his friend without cause, and will not pay him his wages.—*Jer.* xxii. 13.

DECEITFULNESS

You shall not steal. You shall not lie, neither shall any man deceive his neighbor.—*Lev.* xix. 11.

Draw me not away together with the wicked; and with the workers of iniquity destroy me not:

Who speak peace with their neighbor, but evils are in their hearts.—*Ps.* xxvii. 3.

O Lord, deliver my soul from wicked lips, and a deceitful tongue.

What shall be given to thee, or what shall be added to thee, to a deceitful tongue?—*Ps.* cxix. 2, 3.

The dissembler with his mouth deceiveth his friend: but the just shall be delivered by knowledge.—*Prov.* xi. 9.

The deceitful man shall not find gain: but the substance of a just man shall be precious gold.—*Prov.* xii. 27.

Deceitful souls go astray in sins: the just are merciful and show mercy.—*Prov.* xiii. 13.

Be not witness without cause against thy neighbor: and deceive not any man with thy lips.—*Prov.* xxiv. 28.

As he is guilty that shooteth arrows and lances unto death:

So is the man that hurteth his friend deceitfully: and when he is taken, saith: I did it in jest.—*Prov.* xxvi. 18, 19.

He that covereth hatred deceitfully, his malice shall be laid open in the public assembly.—*Prov.* xxvi. 26.

A deceitful tongue loveth not truth: and a slippery mouth worketh ruin.—*Prov.* xxvi. 28.

Better are the wounds of a friend, than the deceitful kisses of an enemy.—*Prov.* xxvii. 6.

Of one spark cometh a great fire, and of one deceitful man much blood.—*Ecclus.* xi. 34.

If one cast a stone on high, it will fall upon his own head: and the deceitful stroke will wound the deceitful.—*Ecclus.* xxvii. 28.

He that seeketh the law, shall be filled with it: and he that dealeth deceitfully, shall meet with a stumbling-block therein.—*Ecclus.* xxxii. 19.

Wherefore have a shame of these

things I am now going to speak of. . . .

Of leaning with thy elbow over meat, and of deceit in giving and taking.—*Ecclus.* xli. 19, 24.

The vessels of the deceitful are most wicked: for he hath framed devices to destroy the meek, with lying words, when the poor man speaketh judgment.—*Is.* xxxii. 7.

Wherefore, laying away all malice, and all guile, and dissimulations, and envies, and all detractions,

As new-born babes, desire the rational milk without guile, that thereby you may grow unto salvation.—1 *Peter* ii. 1, 2.

DECEITFULNESS, HATEFUL TO GOD

Thou hatest all the workers of iniquity: thou wilt destroy all that speak a lie.

The bloody and the deceitful man the Lord will abhor.—*Ps.* v. 7.

The fear of the Lord hateth evil: I hate arrogance, and pride, and every wicked way, and a mouth with a double tongue.—*Prov.* viii. 13.

DECEITFULNESS, PUNISHED BY GOD

May the Lord destroy all deceitful lips, and the tongue that speaketh proud things.—*Ps.* xi. 4.

Let deceitful lips be made dumb

Which speak iniquity against the just, with pride and abuse.—*Ps.* xxx. 19.

But thou, O God, shalt bring them down into the pit of destruction.

Bloody and deceitful men shall not live out half their days.—*Ps.* liv. 24.

No good shall come to the deceitful son: but the wise servant shall prosper in his dealings, and his way shall be made straight.—*Prov.* xiv. 15.

He that deceiveth the just in a wicked way, shall fall in his own destruction; and the upright shall possess his goods.—*Prov.* xxviii. 10.

Their tongue is a piercing arrow, it hath spoken deceit: with his mouth, one speaketh peace with his friend, and secretly he lieth in wait for him.

Shall I not visit them for these things saith the Lord? or shall not my soul be revenged on such a nation?—*Jer.* ix. 8, 9.

DECEIVE GOD, WE CANNOT

See also: Searcher of hearts, God the—page 507.

With him is strength and wisdom: he knoweth both the deceiver, and him that is deceived.—*Job* xii. 16.

Or shall it please him, from whom nothing can be concealed? or shall he be deceived as a man, with your deceitful dealings?—*Job* xiii. 9.

If thou say: I have not strength enough: he that seeth into the heart, he understandeth, and nothing deceiveth the keeper of thy soul, and he shall render to a man according to his works.—*Prov.* xxiv. 12.

Woe to you scribes and Pharisees, hypocrites; because you make clean the outside of the cup and of the dish, but within you are full of rapine and uncleanness.

Thou blind Pharisee, first make clean the inside of the cup and of the dish, that the outside may become clean.

Woe to you scribes and Pharisees, hypocrites; because you are like to whited sepulchres, which outwardly appear to men beautiful, but within are full of dead men's bones, and of all filthiness.

So you also outwardly indeed appear to men just; but inwardly you are full of hypocrisy and iniquity.—*Matt.* xxiii. 25-28.

Now the Pharisees, who were covetous, heard all these things: and they derided him (Christ).

And he said to them: You are they who justify yourselves before men, but God knoweth your hearts; for that which is high to men, is an abomination before God.—*Luke* xvi. 14, 15.

DELAY OF CONVERSION

Delay not to be converted to the Lord, and defer it not from day to day.

For his wrath shall come on a sudden, and in the time of vengeance he will destroy thee.—*Ecclus.* v. 8, 9.

Seek ye the Lord while he may be found: call upon him while he is near.—*Is.* lv. 6.

But he said to another: Follow me. And he said: Lord, suffer me first to go, and to bury my father.

And Jesus said to him: Let the dead bury their dead: but go thou, and preach the kingdom of God.

And another said: I will follow thee, Lord; but let me first take my leave of them that are at my house.

Jesus said to him: No man putting his hand to the plough, and looking back, is fit for the kingdom of God.—*Luke* ix. 59-62.

But when the master of the house shall be gone in, and shall shut the door, you shall begin to stand without, and knock at the door, saying: Lord, open to us. And he answering, shall say to you: I know you not whence you are.—*Luke* xiii. 25.

DEPENDENCE UPON GOD, MAN'S

See also: Hands of God, we are in the—page 192.

Also: Help, our need of God's—page 202.

The tabernacles of robbers abound, and they provoke God boldly; whereas it is he that hath given all into their hands.—*Job* xii. 6.

Look thou upon me, and have mercy on me; for I am alone and poor.—*Ps.* xxiv. 16.

Behold as the eyes of servants are on the hands of their masters,

As the eyes of the handmaid are on the hands of her mistress: so are our eyes unto the Lord our God, until he have mercy on us.—*Ps.* cxxii. 2.

I turned me to another thing, and I saw that under the sun, the race is not to the swift, nor the battle to the strong, nor bread to the wise, nor riches to the learned, nor favor to the skilful: but time and chance in all.—*Eccles.* ix. 11.

And how could any thing endure, if thou wouldst not? or be preserved, if not called by thee?—*Wis.* xi. 26.

Shall the axe boast itself against him that cutteth with it? or shall the saw exalt itself against him by whom it is drawn? as if a rod should lift itself up against him that lifteth it up, and a staff exalt itself, which is but wood.—*Is.* x. 15.

Woe to you, apostate children, saith the Lord, that you would take counsel, and not of me; and would begin a web, and not by my spirit, that you might add sin upon sin:

Who walk to go down into Egypt, and have not asked at my mouth, hoping for help in the strength of Pharao, and trusting in the shadow of Egypt.

And the strength of Pharao shall be to your confusion, and the confidence of the shadow of Egypt to your shame. —*Is.* xxx. 1-3.

Thus saith the Lord: Let not the wise man glory in his wisdom, and let not the strong man glory in his strength, and let not the rich man glory in his riches:

But let him that glorieth, glory in this, that he understandeth and knoweth me, for I am the Lord that exercise mercy, and judgment, and justice in the earth: for these things please me, saith the Lord.—*Jer.* ix. 23, 24.

But he answering, said: Every plant which my heavenly Father hath not planted, shall be rooted up.—*Matt.* xv. 13.

For in him we live, and move, and are; as some also of your own poets said: For we are also his offspring.— *Acts* xvii. 28.

Yet to us there is but one God, the Father, of whom are all things, and we unto him; and one Lord Jesus Christ, by whom are all things, and we by him. —1 *Cor.* viii. 6.

Not that we are sufficient to think any thing of ourselves, as of ourselves: but our sufficiency is from God.— 2 *Cor.* iii. 5.

Behold, now you that say: To-day or to-morrow we will go into such a city, and there we will spend a year, and will traffic, and make our gain.

Whereas you know not what shall be on the morrow.

For what is your life? It is a vapor which appeareth for a little while, and afterwards shall vanish away. For that you should say: If the Lord will, and if we shall live, we will do this or that. —*James* iv. 13-15.

DESIGNS OF GOD ARE WONDER-FUL, THE

See: Ways of God are unsearchable —page 584.

DESIRE FOR GOD

I shall see him, but not now: I shall behold him, but not near. A star shall rise out of Jacob, and a sceptre shall spring up from Israel.—*Num.* xxiv. 17.

As the hart panteth after the fountains of water; so my soul panteth after thee, O God.

My soul hath thirsted after the strong, living God; when shall I come and appear before the face of God?—*Ps.* xli. 2, 3.

O God, my God, to thee do I watch at break of day.

For thee my soul hath thirsted; for thee my flesh, O how many ways! —*Ps.* lxii. 2.

For what have I in heaven? and besides thee, what do I desire upon earth?

For thee my flesh and my heart hath fainted away: thou art the God of my heart, and the God that is my portion for ever.—*Ps.* lxxii. 25, 26.

How lovely are thy tabernacles, O Lord of hosts!

My soul longeth and fainteth for the courts of the Lord.

My heart and my flesh have rejoiced in the living God.—*Ps.* lxxxiii. 2, 3.

My soul hath fainted after thy salvation: and in thy word I have very much hoped. . . .

I have longed for thy salvation, O Lord; and thy law is my meditation.—*Ps.* cxviii. 81, 174.

My beloved to me, and I to him who feedeth among the lilies.—*Cant.* ii. 16.

And in the way of thy judgments, O Lord, we have patiently waited for thee: thy name, and thy remembrance are the desire of the soul.

My soul hath desired thee in the night; yea, and with my spirit within me, in the morning early I will watch to thee.—*Is.* xxvi. 8, 9.

Drop down dew, ye heavens, from above, and let the clouds rain the just: let the earth be opened, and bud forth a saviour.—*Is.* xlv. 8.

Thy kingdom come.—*Matt.* vi. 10.

And it came to pass, that while ¹they talked and reasoned with themselves, Jesus himself also drawing near, went with them. . . .

And they drew nigh to the town, whither they were going: and he made as though he would go farther.

But they constrained him, saying: Stay with us, because it is towards evening, and the day is now far spent. And he went in with them.—*Luke* xxiv. 15, 28, 29.

But I am straitened between two: having a desire to be dissolved, and to be with Christ, a thing by far the better.—*Philipp.* i. 23.

DESIRES, EVIL

The desire of the just is all good: the expectation of the wicked is indignation.—*Prov.* xi. 23.

Well doth he rise early who seeketh good things; but he that seeketh after evil things shall be oppressed by them. —*Prov.* xi. 27.

Follow not in thy strength the desires of thy heart:

And say not: How mighty am I? and who shall bring me under for my deeds? for God will surely take revenge.— *Ecclus.* v. 2, 3.

An evil eye is towards evil things: and he shall not have his fill of bread, but shall be needy and pensive at his own table.—*Ecclus.* xiv. 10.

Go not after thy lusts, but turn away from thy own will.

If thou give thy soul her desires, she will make thee a joy to thy enemies.— *Ecclus.* xviii. 30, 31.

And if he be hindered from sinning for want of power, if he shall find opportunity to do evil, he will do it.— *Ecclus.* xix. 25.

There is that is hindered from sinning through want, and in his rest he shall be pricked.—*Ecclus.* xx. 23.

You have heard that it was said to them of old: Thou shalt not commit adultery.

But I say to you, that whosoever shall look on a woman to lust after her, hath already committed adultery in his heart.—*Matt.* v. 27, 28.

¹The two disciples on the way to Emmaus.

For of these sort are they who creep into houses, and lead captive silly women laden with sins, who are led away with divers desires.—2 *Tim.* iii. 6.

For the grace of God our Saviour hath appeared to all men;

Instructing us, that denying ungodliness and worldly desires, we should live soberly, and justly, and godly in this world.—*Titus* ii. 11, 12.

From whence are wars and contentions among you? Are they not hence, from your concupiscences, which war in your members?

You covet, and have not: you kill, and envy, and cannot obtain.—*James* iv. 1, 2.

Dearly beloved, I beseech you as strangers and pilgrims, to refrain yourselves from carnal desires, which war against the soul.—1 *Peter* ii. 11.

DESIRES, GOOD

The desire of the just is all good: the expectation of the wicked is indignation.—*Prov.* xi. 23.

And he (the angel Gabriel) instructed me, and spoke to me, and said: O Daniel, I am now come forth to teach thee, and that thou mightest understand.

From the beginning of thy prayers the word came forth: and I am come to show it to thee, because thou art a man of desires: therefore do thou mark the word, and understand the vision.—*Dan.* ix. 22, 23.

Blessed are they that hunger and thirst after justice: for they shall have their fill.—*Matt.* v. 6.

Follow after charity, be zealous for spiritual gifts.—1 *Cor.* xiv. 1.

DESOLATION OF SPIRIT

See also: Withdraw from us; God seems to—page 616.

So going in he (Raphael) saluted him and said: Joy be to thee always.

And Tobias said: What manner of joy shall be to me, who sit in darkness, and see not the light of heaven?

And the young man said to him: Be of good courage, thy cure from God is at hand.—*Tob.* v. 11-13.

Why is light given to him that is in misery, and life to them that are in bitterness of soul? . . .

To a man whose way is hidden, and God hath surrounded him with darkness?—*Job* iii. 20, 23.

In his hands he hideth the light, and commandeth it to come again.—*Job* xxxvi. 32.

But I said in the excess of my mind: I am cast away from before thy eyes.

Therefore thou hast heard the voice of my prayer, when I cried to thee.—*Ps.* xxx. 23.

For thou art God my strength: why hast thou cast me off? and why do I go sorrowful, whilst the enemy afflicteth me?—*Ps.* xlii. 2.

Save me, O God: for the waters are come in even unto my soul.

I stick fast in the mire of the deep: and there is no sure standing.

I am come into the depth of the sea: and a tempest hath overwhelmed me.

I have labored with crying; my jaws are become hoarse: my eyes have failed, whilst I hope in my God.—*Ps.* lxviii. 2-4.

My soul hath slumbered through heaviness: strengthen thou me in thy words.—*Ps.* cxviii. 28.

My soul hath fainted after thy salvation: and in thy word I have very much hoped.

My eyes have failed for thy word, saying: When wilt thou comfort me?—*Ps.* cxviii. 81, 82.

I stretched forth my hands to thee: my soul is as earth without water unto thee.

Hear me speedily, O Lord, my soul hath fainted away.

Turn not away thy face from me, lest I be like unto them that go down into the pit.—*Ps.* cxlii. 6, 7.

Who is there among you that feareth the Lord, that heareth the voice of his servant, that hath walked in darkness, and hath no light? let him hope in the name of the Lord, and lean upon his God.—*Is.* l. 10.

O poor little one, tossed with tempest, without all comfort, behold I will lay thy stones in order, and will lay thy foundations with sapphires.

. . . All thy children shall be taught of the Lord; and great shall be the peace of thy children.—*Is.* liv. 11, 13.

Therefore do I weep, and my eyes run down with water: because the comforter, the relief of my soul, is far from me.—*Lam.* i. 16.

And about the ninth hour Jesus cried with a loud voice, saying: Eli, Eli, lamma sabacthani? that is, My God, my God, why hast thou forsaken me?—*Matt.* xxvii. 46.

DESPAIR

And Cain said to the Lord: My iniquity is greater than that I may deserve pardon.—*Gen.* iv. 13.

He shall not believe, being vainly deceived by error, that he may be redeemed with any price.—*Job* xv. 31.

Happy is he that hath had no sadness of his mind, and who is not fallen from his hope.—*Ecclus.* xiv. 2.

Keep thy foot from being bare, and thy throat from thirst. But thou saidst: I have lost all hope, I will not do it: for I have loved strangers, and I will walk after them.—*Jer.* ii. 25.

Thus saith the Lord: Let every man of you return from his evil way, and make ye your ways and your doings good.

And they said: We have no hopes: for we will go after our own thoughts, and we will do every one according to the perverseness of his evil heart.—*Jer.* xviii. 11, 12.

Then Judas, who betrayed him, seeing that he was condemned, repenting himself, brought back the thirty pieces of silver to the chief priests and ancients,

Saying: I have sinned in betraying innocent blood. But they said: What is that to us? look thou to it.

And casting down the pieces of silver in the temple, he departed: and went and hanged himself with a halter.—*Matt.* xxvii. 3-5.

This then I say and testify in the Lord: That henceforward you walk not as also the Gentiles walk in the vanity of their mind: . . .

Who despairing, have given themselves up to lasciviousness, unto the working of all uncleanness, unto covetousness.—*Eph.* iv. 17, 19.

DESPAIR, TEMPTATION TO

Many say to my soul: There is no salvation for him in his God.—*Ps.* iii. 3.

DESPISING OUR NEIGHBOR

See: Contempt of our neighbor—page 78.

DETACHMENT FROM THINGS OF EARTH

And (Job) said: Naked came I out of my mother's womb, and naked shall I return thither: the Lord gave, and the Lord hath taken away: as it has pleased the Lord, so it is done: blessed be the name of the Lord.—*Job* i. 21.

Blessed are the poor in spirit: for theirs is the kingdom of heaven.—*Matt.* v. 3.

Lay not up to yourselves treasures on earth: where the rust, and moth consume, and where thieves break through and steal.

But lay up to yourselves treasures in heaven: where neither the rust nor moth doth consume, and where thieves do not break through, nor steal.

For where thy treasure is, there is thy heart also.—*Matt.* vi. 19-21.

This therefore I say, brethren; the time is short; it remaineth, that they also who have wives, be as if they had none;

And they that weep, as though they wept not; and they that rejoice, as if they rejoiced not; and they that buy, as though they possessed not;

And they that use this world, as if they used it not: for the fashion of this world passeth away.—*1 Cor.* vii. 29-31.

But God forbid that I should glory, save in the cross of our Lord Jesus Christ; by whom the world is crucified to me, and I to the world.—*Gal.* vi. 14.

But the things that were gain to me, the same I have counted loss for Christ.

Furthermore, I count all things to be but loss for the excellent knowledge of Jesus Christ my Lord; for whom I have suffered the loss of all things, and count them but as dung, that I may gain Christ.—*Philipp.* iii. 7, 8.

Therefore, if you be risen with

Christ, seek the things that are above; where Christ is sitting at the right hand of God:

Mind the things that are above, not the things that are upon the earth.—*Col.* iii. 1, 2.

DETACHMENT FROM THINGS OF EARTH, MOTIVES OR REASONS FOR

See also: Riches, vanity of—page 490.

All that I have shall go down into the deepest pit: thinkest thou that there at least I shall have rest?—*Job* xvii. 16.

O death, how bitter is the remembrance of thee to a man that hath peace in his possessions!

To a man that is at rest, and whose ways are prosperous in all things, and that is yet able to take meat!—*Ecclus.* xli. 1, 2.

For we brought nothing into this world: and certainly we can carry nothing out.—1 *Tim.* vi. 7.

DETRACTION

Thou shalt not calumniate thy neighbor, nor oppress him by violence.—*Lev.* xix. 13.

Thou shalt not be a detractor, nor a whisperer among the people. Thou shalt not stand against the blood of thy neighbor. I am the Lord.—*Lev.* xix. 16.

Sitting, thou didst speak against thy brother, and didst lay a scandal against thy mother's son: these things hast thou done, and I was silent.

Thou thoughtest unjustly that I should be like to thee: but I will reprove thee, and set before thy face.—*Ps.* xlix. 20, 21.

For they have whetted their tongues like a sword; they have bent their bow, a bitter thing, to shoot in secret the undefiled.—*Ps.* lxiii. 4, 5.

The man that in private detracted his neighbor, him did I persecute.—*Ps.* c. 5.

Let them that detract me be clothed with shame: and let them be covered with their confusion as with a double cloak.—*Ps.* cviii. 29.

The thought of a fool is sin: and the detractor is the abomination of men.—*Prov.* xxiv. 9.

My son, fear the Lord and the king: and have nothing to do with detractors.

For their destruction shall rise suddenly: and who knoweth the ruin of both?—*Prov.* xxiv. 21, 22.

For thy conscience knoweth that thou also hast often spoken evil of others.—*Eccles.* vii. 23.

If a serpent bite in silence, he is nothing better that backbiteth secretly.—*Eccles.* x. 11.

Therefore he that speaketh unjust things, cannot be hid, neither shall the chastising judgment pass him by.—*Wis.* i. 8.

The whisperer and the double-tongued is accursed: for he hath troubled many that were at peace.

The tongue of a third person hath disquieted many, and scattered them from nation to nation.—*Ecclus.* xxviii. 15, 16.

Admonish them . . . to speak evil of no man, not to be litigious, but gentle: showing all mildness towards all men.—*Titus* iii. 1, 2.

DETRACTION, EXHORTATION TO AVOID

Remove from thee a froward mouth, and let detracting lips be far from thee.—*Prov.* iv. 24.

Keep yourselves, therefore, from murmuring, which profiteth nothing, and refrain your tongue from detraction, for an obscure speech shall not go for nought: and the mouth that belieth, killeth the soul.—*Wis.* i. 11.

Be not called a whisperer, and be not taken in thy tongue, and confounded.

For confusion and repentance is upon a thief, and an evil mark of disgrace upon the double-tongued, but to the whisperer, hatred, and enmity, and reproach.—*Ecclus.* v. 16, 17.

Devise not a lie against thy brother: neither do the like against thy friend.—*Ecclus.* vii. 13.

Hast thou heard a word against thy neighbor? let it die within thee, trusting that it will not burst thee.—*Ecclus.* xix. 10.

And the soldiers also asked him, saying: And what shall we do? And he (the Baptist) said to them: Do violence to no man; neither calumniate any man; and be content with your pay.—*Luke* iii. 14.

Detract not one another, my brethren. He that detracteth his brother, or he that judgeth his brother, detracteth the law, and judgeth the law. But if thou judge the law, thou art not a doer of the law, but a judge.—*James* iv. 11.

Wherefore laying aside all malice, and all guile, and dissimulations, and envies, and all detractions,

As new-born babes, desire the rational milk without guile, that thereby you may grow unto salvation.—1 *Peter* ii. 1, 2.

DEVIL AND HIS ANGELS, THE

Behold they that serve him are not steadfast, and in his angels he found wickedness.—*Job* iv. 18.

And he sent upon them (the Egyptians) the wrath of his indignation: indignation and wrath and trouble, which he sent by evil angels.—*Ps.* lxxvii. 49.

How art thou fallen from heaven, O Lucifer, who didst rise in the morning? how art thou fallen to the earth, that didst wound the nations?

And thou saidst in thy heart: I will ascend into heaven, I will exalt my throne above the stars of God, I will sit in the mountain of the covenant, in the sides of the north.

I will ascend above the height of the clouds, I will be like the most High.

But yet thou shalt be brought down to hell, into the depth of the pit.—*Is.* xiv. 12-15.

And he said to them: I saw Satan like lightning falling from heaven.—*Luke* x. 18.

You are of your father the devil, and the desires of your father you will do. He was a murderer from the beginning, and he stood not in the truth; because truth is not in him. When he speaketh a lie, he speaketh of his own: for he is a liar, and the father thereof.—*John* viii. 44.

Know you not that we shall judge angels? how much more things of this world?—1 *Cor.* vi. 3.

And you, when you were dead in your offences and sins,

Wherein in time past you walked according to the course of this world, according to the prince of the power of this air, of the spirit that now worketh on the children of unbelief.—*Eph.* ii. 1, 2.

Thou believest that there is one God. Thou dost well: the devils also believe and tremble.—*James* ii. 19.

For if God spared not the angels that sinned, but delivered them, drawn down by infernal ropes to the lower hell, unto torments, to be reserved unto judgment.—2 *Peter* ii. 4.

He that committeth sin is of the devil: for the devil sinneth from the beginning. For this purpose the Son of God appeared, that he might destroy the works of the devil.—1 *John* iii. 8.

And the angels who kept not their principality, but forsook their own habitation, he hath reserved unto darkness in everlasting chains, unto the judgment of the great day.—*Jude* i. 6.

And there was seen another sign in heaven: and behold, a great red dragon, having seven heads and ten horns: and on his heads, seven diadems:

And his tail drew the third part of the stars of heaven, and cast them to the earth: and the dragon stood before the woman who was ready to be delivered; that, when she should be delivered, he might devour her son.—*Apoc.* xii. 3, 4.

And there was a great battle in heaven, Michael and his angels fought with the dragon, and the dragon fought, and his angels:

And they prevailed not, neither was their place found any more in heaven.

And that great dragon was cast out, that old serpent, who is called the devil and Satan, who seduceth the whole world; and he was cast unto the earth, and his angels were thrown down with him.—*Apoc.* xii. 7-9.

DEVIL SEEKS THE RUIN OF MAN, THE

And it came to pass, when on a certain day the sons of God came, and stood before the Lord, and Satan came among them, and stood in his sight,

That the Lord said to Satan: Whence comest thou? And he answered and said: I have gone round about the earth, and walked through it.—*Job* ii. 1, 2.

For God created man incorruptible, and to the image of his own likeness he made him.

But by the envy of the devil, death came into the world:

And they follow him that are of his side.—*Wis.* ii. 23-25.

The sower went out to sow his seed. And as he sowed, some fell by the wayside, and it was trodden down, and the fowls of the air devoured it.

. . . Now the parable is this: The seed is the word of God.

And they by the wayside are they that hear; then the devil cometh, and taketh the word out of their heart, lest believing they should be saved.—*Luke* viii. 5, 11, 12.

For what I have pardoned, if I have pardoned anything, for your sakes have I done it in the person of Christ.

That we be not over-reached by Satan. For we are not ignorant of his devices.—*2 Cor.* ii. 10, 11.

For Satan himself transformeth himself into an angel of light.—*2 Cor.* xi. 14.

Be sober and watch: because your adversary the devil, as a roaring lion, goeth about seeking whom he may devour. —*1 Peter* v. 8.

Woe to the earth, and to the sea, because the devil is come down unto you, having great wrath, knowing that he hath but a short time.—*Apoc.* xii. 12.

DEVIL AND HIS TEMPTATIONS, GAINING THE MASTERY OVER THE

And Jesus rebuked him, and the devil went out of him, and the child was cured from that hour.

Then came the disciples to Jesus secretly, and said: Why could not we cast him out?

Jesus said to them: Because of your unbelief.

. . . But this kind is not cast out but by prayer and fasting.—*Matt.* xvii. 17-20.

For though we walk in the flesh, we do not war according to the flesh.

For the weapons of our warfare are not carnal, but mighty to God, unto the pulling down of fortifications, destroying counsels,

And every height that exalteth itself against the knowledge of God, and bringing into captivity every understanding unto the obedience of Christ. —*2 Cor.* x. 3-5.

And they that are Christ's, have crucified their flesh, with the vices and concupiscences.—*Gal.* v. 24.

Give not place to the devil.—*Eph.* iv. 27.

Put you on the armor of God, that you may be able to stand against the deceits of the devil.

For our wrestling is not against flesh and blood; but against principalities and powers, against the rulers of the world of this darkness, against the spirits of wickedness in the high places.

Therefore take unto you the armor of God, that you may be able to resist in the evil day, and to stand in all things perfect. . . .

In all things taking the shield of faith, wherewith you may be able to extinguish all the fiery darts of the most wicked one.—*Eph.* vi. 11-13, 16.

Be subject therefore to God, but resist the devil, and he will fly from you. —*James* iv. 7.

Be sober, and watch: because your adversary the devil, as a roaring lion, goeth about, seeking whom he may devour.

Whom resist ye, strong in faith: knowing that the same affliction befalls your brethren who are in the world.— 1 *Peter* v. 8, 9.

DEVIL AND HIS TEMPTATIONS, REWARD PROMISED TO THOSE WHO OVER- COME THE

He that hath an ear, let him hear what the Spirit saith to the churches: To him that overcometh, I will give to eat of the tree of life, which is in the paradise of my God.—*Apoc.* ii. 7.

He that shall overcome, shall not be hurt by the second death.—*Apoc.* ii. 11.

To him that overcometh, I will give the hidden manna, and will give him a white counter, and in the counter a new name written, which no man knoweth, but he that receiveth it.—*Apoc.* ii. 17.

And he that shall overcome, and keep my works unto the end, I will give him power over the nations.—*Apoc.* ii. 26.

He that shall overcome, shall thus be clothed in white garments, and I will not blot his name out of the book of life, and I will confess his name before my Father, and before his angels. —*Apoc.* iii. 5.

He that shall overcome, I will make him a pillar in the temple of my God; and he shall go out no more; and I will write upon him the name of my God, and the name of the city of my God, the new Jerusalem, which cometh down out of heaven from my God, and my new name.—*Apoc.* iii. 12.

To him that shall overcome, I will give to sit with me in my throne: as I also have overcome, and am set down with my Father in his throne.—*Apoc.* iii. 21.

To him that thirsteth, I will give of the fountain of the water of life freely.

He that shall overcome, shall possess these things, and I will be his God; and he shall be my son.—*Apoc.* xxi. 6, 7.

DIFFIDENCE

See: Distrust of self—page 117.

DILIGENCE OR INDUSTRY

The slothful hand hath wrought poverty: but the hand of the industrious getteth riches. . . .

He that gathered in the harvest, is a wise son: but he that snoreth in the summer, is the son of confusion.— *Prov.* x. 4, 5.

A diligent woman is a crown to her husband.—*Prov.* xii. 4.

Better is the poor man that provideth for himself, than he that is glorious, and wanteth bread.—*Prov.* xii. 9.

Substance got in haste, shall be diminished: but that which by little and little is gathered with the hand shall increase.—*Prov.* xiii. 11.

In much work there shall be abundance: but where there are many words, there is oftentimes want.—*Prov.* xiv. 23.

The thoughts of the industrious always bring forth abundance: but every sluggard is always in want.—*Prov.* xxi. 5.

Prepare thy work without, and diligently till thy ground: that afterward thou mayst build thy house.—*Prov.* xxiv. 27.

Who shall find a valiant woman? far and from the uttermost coasts is the price of her. . . .

She hath sought wool and flax, and hath wrought by the counsel of her hands. . . .

She hath put out her hand to strong things, and her fingers have taken hold of the spindle. . . .

She shall not fear for her house in the cold of snow: for all her domestics are clothed with double garments.

She hath made for herself clothing of tapestry: fine linen, and purple is her covering. . . .

She hath looked well to the paths of her house, and hath not eaten her bread idle.—*Prov.* xxxi. 10, 13, 19, 21, 22, 27.

In the morning sow thy seed, and in the evening let not thy hand cease: for thou knowest not which may rather spring up, this or that: and if both together, it shall be the better.—*Eccles.* xi. 6.

DILIGENCE, OR INDUSTRY, REWARD OF

But if thou be diligent, thy harvest shall come as a fountain, and want shall flee far from thee.—*Prov.* vi. 11.

The sluggard willeth and willeth not: but the soul of them that work, shall be made fat.—*Prov.* xiii. 4.

Hast thou seen a man swift in his work? he shall stand before kings, and shall not be before those that are obscure.—*Prov.* xxii. 29.

He that tilleth his ground, shall be filled with bread: but he that followeth idleness shall be filled with poverty.— *Prov.* xxviii. 19.

In all thy works be quick, and no infirmity shall come to thee.—*Ecclus.* xxxi. 27.

DISCIPLE, OR FOLLOWER OF CHRIST, WHAT IT MEANS TO BE A

The disciple is not above the master, nor the servant above his lord.

It is enough for the disciple that he be as his master, and the servant as his lord. If they have called the goodman of the house Beelzebub, how much more them of his household?—*Matt.* x. 24, 25.

He that loveth father or mother more than me, is not worthy of me; and he that loveth son or daughter more than me, is not worthy of me.

And he that taketh not up his cross, and followeth me, is not worthy of me.—*Matt.* x. 37, 38.

Then Jesus said to his disciples: If any man will come after me, let him deny himself, and take up his cross, and follow me.

For he that will save his life, shall lose it: and he that shall lose his life for my sake, shall find it.—*Matt.* xvi. 24, 25.

And Jesus answering, said: You know not what you ask. Can you drink the chalice that I shall drink? They say to him: We can.

He saith to them: My chalice indeed you shall drink.—*Matt.* xx. 22, 23.

The disciple is not above his master: but every one shall be perfect, if he be as his master.—*Luke* vi. 40.

If any man come to me, and hate not his father, and mother, and wife, and children, and brethren, and sisters, yea, and his own life also, he cannot be my disciple.

And whosoever doth not carry his cross, and come after me, cannot be my disciple. . . .

So likewise every one of you that doth not renounce all that he possesseth, cannot be my disciple.—*Luke* xiv. 26, 27, 33.

By this shall all men know that you are my disciples, if you have love one for another.—*John* xiii. 35.

Remember my word that I said to you: The servant is not greater than his master. If they have persecuted me, they will also persecute you: if they have kept my word, they will keep yours also.

But all these things they will do to you for my name's sake: because they know not him that sent me.—*John* xv. 20, 21.

Know you not that all we who are baptized in Christ Jesus, are baptized in his death?

For we are buried together with him by baptism into death; that as Christ is risen from the dead by the glory of the Father, so we also may walk in newness of life.

For if we have been planted together in the likeness of his death, we shall be also in the likeness of his resurrection.—*Rom.* vi. 3-5.

And they that are Christ's, have crucified their flesh, with the vices and concupiscences.—*Gal.* v. 24.

But God forbid that I should glory, save in the cross of our Lord Jesus Christ; by whom the world is crucified to me, and I to the world.—*Gal.* vi. 14.

And all that will live godly in Christ Jesus, shall suffer persecution.—2 *Tim.* iii. 12.

Wherefore Jesus also, that he might sanctify the people by his own blood, suffered without the gate.

Let us go forth therefore to him without the camp, bearing his reproach.—*Heb.* xiii. 12, 13.

DISCIPLINE, NEED OF

Embrace discipline, lest at any time the Lord be angry, and you perish from the just way.—*Ps.* ii. 12.

But to the sinner God hath said: Why dost thou declare my justices, and take my covenant in thy mouth?

Seeing thou hast hated discipline: and hast cast my words behind thee.—*Ps.* xlix. 16, 17.

Teach me goodness, and discipline, and knowledge: for I have believed thy commandments.—*Ps.* cxviii. 66.

For he that rejecteth wisdom and discipline is unhappy: and their hope is vain, and their labors without fruit, and their works unprofitable.—*Wis.* iii. 11.

There is success in evil things to a man without discipline, and there is a finding that turneth to loss.—*Ecclus.* xx. 9.

Draw near to me, ye unlearned, and gather yourselves together into the house of discipline.

. . . I have opened my mouth, and have spoken: buy her for yourselves without silver,

And submit your neck to the yoke, and let your soul receive discipline: for she is near at hand to be found. . . .

Receive ye discipline as a great sum of money, and possess abundance of gold by her.—*Ecclus.* li. 31, 33, 34, 36.

DISCONTENT

See: Murmuring—page 330.

DISCORD

See: Dissensions—page 116.

DISCOURAGEMENT, AGAINST

See also: Faint-hearted, the—page 131.

If thou lose hope, being weary in the day of distress, thy strength shall be diminished.—*Prov.* xxiv. 10.

If thou say: I have not strength enough: he that seeth into the heart, he understandeth, and nothing deceiveth the keeper of thy soul, and he shall render to a man according to his works.—*Prov.* xxiv. 12.

In the day of good things, be not unmindful of evils: and in the day of evils, be not unmindful of good things. —*Ecclus.* xi. 27.

Happy is he that hath had no sadness of his mind, and who is not fallen from his hope.—*Ecclus.* xiv. 2.

But to the penitent he hath given the way of justice, and he hath strengthened them that were fainting in patience, and hath appointed to them the lot of truth.—*Ecclus.* xvii. 20.

Now when he had ceased to speak, he said to Simon: Launch out into the deep, and let down your nets for a draught.

And Simon answering, said to him: Master, we have labored all the night, and have taken nothing: but at thy word I will let down the net.—*Luke* v. 4, 5.

These things have I spoken to you that you may not be scandalized.

They will put you out of the synagogues: yea, the hour cometh, that whosoever killeth you, will think that he doth a service to God.

And these things will they do to you; because they have not known the Father, nor me.

But these things I have told you, that when the hour shall come, you may remember that I told you of them.

But I told you not these things from the beginning, because I was with you.

And now I go to him that sent me, and none of you asketh me: Whither goest thou?

But because I have spoken these things to you, sorrow hath filled your heart.

But I tell you the truth: it is expedient for you that I go: for if I go not, the Paraclete will not come to you; but if I go, I will send him to you.—*John* xvi. 1-7.

For think diligently upon him that endureth such opposition from sinners against himself; that you be not wearied, fainting in your minds.

For you have not yet resisted unto blood, striving against sin:

And you have forgotten the consolation, which speaketh to you, as unto children, saying: My son, neglect not the discipline of the Lord; neither be thou wearied, whilst thou art rebuked by him.

For whom the Lord loveth, he chastiseth; and he scourgeth every son whom he receiveth.—*Heb.* xii. 3-6.

DISCRETION IN ACTION

See: Prudence in conduct—page 454.

DISCRETION IN SPEECH

See: Prudence in words—page 455.

DISINTERESTEDNESS

See also: Forgetfulness of self—page 155.

And if you love them that love you, what thanks are to you? for sinners also love those that love them.

And if you do good to them who do good to you, what thanks are to you? for sinners also do this.

And if you lend to them of whom you hope to receive, what thanks are to you? for sinners also lend to sinners, for to receive as much.

But love ye your enemies: do good, and lend, hoping for nothing thereby: and your reward shall be great, and you shall be the sons of the Highest; for he is kind to the unthankful and to the evil.—*Luke* vi. 32-35.

And he said to him also that had invited him: When thou makest a dinner or a supper, call not thy friends, nor thy brethren, nor thy kinsmen, nor thy neighbors who are rich; lest perhaps they also invite thee again, and a recompense be made to thee.

But when thou makest a feast, call the poor, the maimed, the lame, and the blind;

And thou shalt be blessed, because they have not wherewith to make thee recompense: for recompense shall be made thee at the resurrection of the just.—*Luke* xiv. 12-14.

For I seek not the things that are yours, but you. For neither ought the children to lay up for the parents, but the parents for the children.

But I most gladly will spend, and be spent myself for your souls; although loving you more, I be loved less.—2 *Cor.* xii. 14, 15.

DISOBEDIENCE TO GOD

See: Rebellion against God—page 458.

DISOBEDIENCE TO GOD, PUNISHMENT OF

See: Sin, punishment of—page 529.

DISSENSIONS

And Jesus knowing their thoughts, said to them: Every kingdom divided against itself shall be made desolate: and every city or house divided against itself shall not stand.—*Matt.* xii. 25.

Now I beseech you, brethren, to mark them who make dissensions and offences contrary to the doctrine which you have learned, and avoid them.

For they that are such, serve not Christ our Lord, but their own belly; and by pleasing speeches and good words, seduce the hearts of the innocent.—*Rom.* xvi. 17, 18.

For whereas there is among you envying and contention, are you not carnal, and walk according to man?—1 *Cor.* iii. 3.

For I fear lest perhaps when I come, I shall not find you such as I would, and that I shall be found by you such as you would not. Lest perhaps contentions, envyings, animosities, dissensions, detractions, whisperings, swellings, seditions, be among you.—2 *Cor.* xii. 20.

Now the works of the flesh are manifest, which are, . . . idolatry, witchcrafts, enmities, contentions, emulations, wraths, quarrels, dissensions, sects. . . .

Of the which I foretell you, as I have foretold to you, that they who do such things shall not obtain the kingdom of God.—*Gal.* v. 19-21.

But if you have bitter zeal, and there be contentions in your hearts; glory not, and be not liars against the truth.

For this is not wisdom, descending from above: but earthly, sensual, devilish.

For where envying and contention is, there is inconstancy, and every evil work.—*James* iii. 14-16.

DISTRESS, WE SHOULD COMFORT THOSE IN

See: Comfort the afflicted—page 56.

DISTRESS, PRAYER OF ONE IN

See: Prayer—page 398.

DISTRUST OF GOD

And all the congregation of the children of Israel murmured against Moses and Aaron in the wilderness.

And the children of Israel said to them: Would to God we had died by the hand of the Lord in the land of Egypt, when we sat over the flesh pots, and ate bread to the full. Why have you brought us into this desert, that you might destroy all the multitude with famine?—*Ex.* xvi. 2, 3.

And he (Moses) called the name of that place Temptation, because of the chiding of the children of Israel, and for that they tempted the Lord, saying: Is the Lord amongst us or not?—*Ex.* xvii. 7.

And they spoke ill of God: they said: Can God furnish a table in the wilderness?

Because he struck the rock, and the waters gushed out, and the streams overflowed.

Can he also give bread, or provide a table for his people?

Therefore the Lord heard, and was angry: and a fire was kindled against Jacob, and wrath came up against Israel.

Because they believed not in God: and trusted not in his salvation.—*Ps.* lxxvii. 19-22.

Woe to them that are faint-hearted, who believe not God: and therefore they shall not be protected by him.—*Ecclus.* ii. 15.

They that fear the Lord, will not be incredulous to his word: and they that love him, will keep his way.—*Ecclus.* ii. 18.

Be not thou incredulous to his word. —*Ecclus.* xvi. 29.

DISTRUST OF SELF

See also: Presuming upon ourselves, against—page 415.

Have confidence in the Lord with all thy heart, and lean not upon thy own prudence.—*Prov.* iii. 5.

The steps of man are guided by the Lord: but who is the man that can understand his own way?—*Prov.* xx. 24.

He that trusteth in his own heart is a fool: but he that walketh wisely, he shall be saved.—*Prov.* xxviii. 26.

But we had in ourselves the answer of death, that we should not trust in ourselves, but in God who raiseth the dead.—*2 Cor.* i. 9.

DO TO OTHERS AS WE WOULD BE DONE BY, WE SHOULD

See thou never do to another what thou wouldst hate to have done to thee by another.—*Tob.* iv. 16.

Rejoice not at the death of thy enemy; knowing that we all die, and are not willing that others should rejoice at our death.—*Ecclus.* viii. 8.

All things, therefore, whatsoever you would that men should do to you, do you also to them. For this is the law and the prophets.—*Matt.* vii. 12.

And as you would that men should do to you, do you also to them in like manner.—*Luke* vi. 31.

DO TO OTHERS, SO SHALL BE DONE TO US, AS WE

For the day of the Lord is at hand upon all nations: as thou hast done, so shall it be done to thee: he will turn thy reward upon thy own head.—*Ab.* i. 15.

For with what judgment you judge, you shall be judged: and with what measure you mete, it shall be measured to you again.—*Matt.* vii. 2.

And he said to them: Take heed what you hear. In what measure you shall mete, it shall be measured to you again, and more shall be given to you.—*Mark* iv. 24.

Judge not, and you shall not be judged. Condemn not, and you shall not be condemned. Forgive, and you shall be forgiven.

Give, and it shall be given to you: good measure and pressed down and shaken together and running over shall they give into your bosom. For with the same measure that you shall mete withal, it shall be measured to you again.—*Luke* vi. 37, 38.

Now this I say: He who soweth sparingly, shall also reap sparingly: and he who soweth in blessings, shall also reap blessings.—*2 Cor.* ix. 6.

DOMINION OF GOD OVER US

See: Master, God our—page 305.

DOMINION OF GOD OVER ALL THINGS

See: Master of all things, God the— page 306.

DREAMS

And when Joseph was come in to ¹them in the morning, and saw them sad,

¹Pharao's chief butler and baker.

He asked them, saying: Why is your countenance sadder to-day than usual? They answered: We have dreamed a dream, and there is nobody to interpret it to us. And Joseph said to them: Doth not interpretation belong to God? Tell me what you have dreamed.—*Gen.* xl. 6-8.

You shall not divine nor observe dreams.—*Lev.* xix. 26.

Neither let there be found among you any one that shall expiate his son or daughter, making them to pass through the fire: or that consulteth soothsayers, or observeth dreams and omens, neither let there be any wizard.—*Deut.* xviii. 10.

Then thou spokest in a vision to thy saints, and saidst: I have laid help upon one that is mighty, and have exalted one chosen out of my people.—*Ps.* lxxxviii. 20.

Where there are many dreams, there are many vanities, and words without number: but do thou fear God.—*Eccles.* v. 6.

The man that giveth heed to lying visions, is like to him that catcheth at a shadow, and followeth after the wind. —*Ecclus.* xxxiv. 2.

The vision of dreams is the resemblance of one thing to another: as when a man's likeness is before the face of a man. . . .

Except it be a vision sent forth from the most High, set not thy heart upon them.

For dreams have deceived many, and they have failed that put their trust in them.—*Ecclus.* xxxiv. 3, 6, 7.

DRUNKENNESS

He that is delighted in passing his time over wine, leaveth a reproach in his strongholds.—*Prov.* xii. 11.

Wine is a luxurious thing, and drunkenness riotous: whosoever is delighted therewith shall not be wise.— *Prov.* xx. 1.

A drunken woman is a great wrath: and her reproach and shame shall not be hid.—*Ecclus.* xxvi. 11.

Fire trieth hard iron: so wine drunk to excess, shall rebuke the hearts of the proud.—*Ecclus.* xxxi. 31.

Wine was created from the beginning to make men joyful, and not to make them drunk.—*Ecclus.* xxxi. 35.

Woe to you that rise up early in the morning to follow drunkenness, and to drink till the evening, to be inflamed with wine. . . .

Woe to you that are mighty to drink wine, and stout men at drunkenness.— *Is.* v. 11, 22.

Woe to the crown of pride, to the drunkards of Ephraim, and to the fading flower, the glory of his joy, who were on the head of the fat valley, staggering with wine. . . .

The crown of pride of the drunkards of Ephraim shall be trodden under feet. —*Is.* xxviii. 1, 3.

His watchmen are all blind, they are all ignorant: dumb dogs not able to bark, seeing vain things, sleeping and loving dreams. . . .

Come, let us take wine, and be filled with drunkenness: and it shall be as to-day, so also to-morrow, and much more.—*Is.* lvi. 10, 12.

Awake, ye that are drunk, and weep, and mourn all ye that take delight in drinking sweet wine: for it is cut off from your mouth.—*Joel* i. 5.

Do not err: neither fornicators, nor idolaters, nor adulterers . . . nor drunkards . . . shall possess the kingdom of God.—1 *Cor.* vi. 9, 10.

Now the works of the flesh are manifest, which are fornication, uncleanness, immodesty, luxury,

. . . Envies, murders, drunkenness, revellings, and such like. Of the which I foretell you, as I have foretold to you, that they who do such things shall not obtain the kingdom of God.—*Gal.* v. 19, 21.

DRUNKENNESS, EVIL EFFECTS OF

Who hath woe? whose father hath woe? who hath contentions? who falls into pits? who hath wounds without cause? who hath redness of eyes?

Surely they that pass their time in wine, and study to drink off their cups. . . .

Thy eyes shall behold strange women, and thy heart shall utter perverse things.

And thou shalt be as one sleeping in the midst of the sea, and as a pilot fast asleep, when the stern is lost.

And thou shalt say: They have beaten me, but I was not sensible of pain: they drew me, and I felt not: when shall I awake, and find wine again?—*Prov.* xxiii. 29, 30, 33-35.

A workman that is a drunkard shall not be rich.

. . . Wine and women make wise men fall off, and shall rebuke the prudent.—*Ecclus.* xix. 1, 2.

Watching, and choler, and gripes are with an intemperate man.—*Ecclus.* xxxi. 23.

What is his life, who is diminished with wine?. . . Wine drunken with excess raiseth quarrels, and wrath, and many ruins.

Wine drunken with excess is bitterness of the soul.

The heat of drunkenness is the stumbling-block of the fool, lessening strength, and causing wounds.—*Ecclus.* xxxi. 33, 38-40.

But these also have been ignorant through wine, and through drunkenness have erred: the priest and the prophet have been ignorant through drunkenness, they are swallowed up with wine, they have gone astray in drunkenness, they have not known him that seeth, they have been ignorant of judgment.—*Is.* xxviii. 7.

Fornication, and wine, and drunkenness take away the understanding.—*Osee* iv. 11.

DRUNKENNESS, EXHORTATION AGAINST

Be not in the feasts of great drinkers, nor in their revellings, who contribute flesh to eat:

Because they that give themselves to drinking, and that club together, shall be consumed; and drowsiness shall be clothed with rags.—*Prov.* xxiii. 20, 21.

Look not upon the wine when it is yellow, when the color thereof shineth in the glass: it goeth in pleasantly,

But in the end, it will bite like a snake, and will spread abroad poison like a basilisk.—*Prov.* xxiii. 31, 32.

Give not to kings, O Lamuel, give not wine to kings: because there is no secret where drunkenness reigneth:

And lest they drink, and forget judgments, and pervert the cause of the children of the poor.—*Prov.* xxxi. 4, 5.

Challenge not them that love wine: for wine hath destroyed very many.—*Ecclus.* xxxi. 30.

And take heed to yourselves, lest perhaps your hearts be overcharged with surfeiting and drunkenness, and the cares of this life, and that day come upon you suddenly.—*Luke* xxi. 34.

Let us walk honestly, as in the day: not in rioting and drunkenness, not in chambering and impurities, not in contention and envy.—*Rom.* xiii. 13.

And be not drunk with wine, wherein is luxury; but be ye filled with the holy Spirit.—*Eph.* v. 18.

DRYNESS, SPIRITUAL

See: Desolation of spirit—page 108.

DUTY WE OWE TO ONE ANOTHER

See: Good to one another, we must do—page 169.

DUTY, FIDELITY TO

See: Practical in our religion, we must be—page 392.

DUTIES OF HUSBAND AND WIFE, MUTUAL

See: Marriage—page 301.

DWELLING IN US, GOD

But let all them be glad that hope in thee: they shall rejoice for ever, and thou shalt dwell in them.—*Ps.* v. 12.

And I will ask the Father, and he shall give you another Paraclete, that he may abide with you for ever.

The spirit of truth, whom the world cannot receive, because it seeth him not, nor knoweth him: but you shall know him; because he shall abide with you, and shall be in you.—*John* xiv. 16, 17.

If any one love me, he will keep my word, and my Father will love him, and we will come to him, and will make our abode with him.—*John* xiv. 23.

I am the vine; you the branches: he that abideth in me, and I in him, the same beareth much fruit: for without me you can do nothing.—*John* xv. 5.

And the glory which thou hast given me, I have given to them; that they may be one, as we also are one:

I in them, and thou in me; that they may be made perfect in one.—*John* xvii. 22, 23.

That they should seek God, if happily they may feel after him or find him, although he be not far from every one of us.—*Acts* xvii. 27.

Know you not, that you are the temple of God, and that the Spirit of God dwelleth in you?—1 *Cor.* iii. 16.

Or know you not, that your members are the temple of the Holy Ghost, who is in you, whom you have from God; and you are not your own?—1 *Cor.* vi. 19.

For you are the temple of the living God; as God saith: I will dwell in them, and walk among them; and I will be their God, and they shall be my people.—2 *Cor.* vi. 16.

Try your own selves, if you be in the faith; prove ye yourselves. Know you not your own selves, that Christ Jesus is in you, unless perhaps you be reprobates?—2 *Cor.* xiii. 5.

For this cause I bow my knees to the Father of our Lord Jesus Christ, . . .

That he would grant you, according to the riches of his glory, to be strengthened by his Spirit with might, unto the inward man,

That Christ may dwell by faith in your hearts.—*Eph.* iii. 14, 16, 17.

One God and Father of all, who is above all, and through all, and in us all.—*Eph.* iv. 6.

Therefore, he that despiseth these things, despiseth not man, but God, who also hath given his holy Spirit in us.—1 *Thess.* iv. 8.

In this we know that we abide in him, and he in us: because he hath given us of his spirit.—1 *John* iv. 13.

DYING, THE

O forgive me, that I may be refreshed, before I go hence, and be no more.—*Ps.* xxxviii. 14.

When the dead is at rest, let his remembrance rest, and comfort him in the departing of his spirit.—*Ecclus.* xxxviii. 24.

EARNESTNESS

I will give praise to thee, O Lord, with my whole heart: I will relate all thy wonders.—*Ps.* ix. 2.

Blessed are they that search his testimonies: that seek him with their whole heart.—*Ps.* cxviii. 2.

With my whole heart have I sought after thee: let me not stray from thy commandments.—*Ps.* cxviii. 10.

Whatsoever thy hand is able to do, do it earnestly: for neither work, nor reason, nor wisdom, nor knowledge shall be in hell, whither thou art hastening. —*Eccles.* ix. 10.

With all thy soul fear the Lord, and reverence his priests.

With all thy strength love him that made thee.

. . . Honor God with all thy soul.— *Ecclus.* vii. 31-33.

Now therefore with the whole heart and mouth praise ye him, and bless the name of the Lord.—*Ecclus.* xxxix. 41.

Glorify the Lord as much as ever you can, for he will yet far exceed, and his magnificence is wonderful.

Blessing the Lord, exalt him as much as you can: for he is above all praise.

When you exalt him, put forth all your strength, and be not weary: for you can never go far enough.—*Ecclus.* xliii. 32-34.

You shall seek me, and shall find me: when you shall seek me with all your heart.—*Jer.* xxix. 13.

Now, therefore, saith the Lord: Be converted to me with all your heart, in fasting, and in weeping, and in mourning.—*Joel* ii. 12.

And so much the more did they wonder, saying: He hath done all things well.—*Mark* vii. 37.

Whatsoever you do, do it from the heart, as to the Lord, and not to men:

Knowing that you shall receive of the Lord the reward of inheritance.—*Col.* iii. 23, 24.

Take heed to thyself and to doctrine: be earnest in them. For in doing this, thou shalt both save thyself and them that hear thee.—1 *Tim.* iv. 16.

EARNESTNESS IN THE SERVICE OF GOD

See: Service of God, earnestness in the—page 513.

EAVESDROPPING

A fool will peep through the window into the house: but he that is well taught, will stand without.

It is the folly of a man to hearken at the door: and a wise man will be grieved with the disgrace.—*Ecclus.* xxi. 26, 27.

END DOES NOT JUSTIFY THE MEANS, THE

Hath God any need of your lie, that you should speak deceitfully for him?— *Job* xiii. 7.

For if the truth of God hath more abounded through my lie, unto his glory, why am I also yet judged as a sinner?

And not rather (as we are slandered, and as some affirm that we say) let us do evil, that there may come good? whose damnation is just.—*Rom.* iii. 7, 8.

END OF MAN, THE

Let us all hear together the conclusion of the discourse. Fear God, and keep his commandments: for this is all man.—*Eccles.* xii. 13.

God created man of the earth, and made him after his own image. . . .

He created of him a helpmate like to himself: he gave them counsel and a tongue, and eyes, and ears, and a heart to devise: and he filled them with the knowledge of understanding. . . .

That they might praise the name which he hath sanctified: and glory in his wondrous acts, that they might declare the glorious things of his works. —*Ecclus.* xvii. 1, 5, 8.

And every one that calleth upon my name, I have created him for my glory, I have formed him, and made him.— *Is.* xliii. 7.

This people have I formed for my-self, they shall show forth my praise. —*Is.* xliii. 21.

For we know, that if our earthly house of this habitation be dissolved, that we have a building of God, a house not made with hands, eternal in heaven. . . .

Now he that maketh us for this very thing is God, who hath given us the pledge of the Spirit.—2 *Cor.* v. 1, 5.

END, OR PURPOSE, OF THE MATERIAL CREATION

And God blessed Noe and his sons. And he said to them: Increase and multiply, and fill the earth.

And let the fear and dread of you be upon all the beasts of the earth, and upon all the fowls of the air, and all that move upon the earth: all the fishes of the sea are delivered into your hand.

And everything that moveth and liveth shall be meat for you: even as the green herbs, have I delivered them all to you.—*Gen.* ix. 1-3.

Lest perhaps lifting up thy eyes to heaven, thou see the sun and the moon, and all the stars of heaven, and being deceived by error, thou adore and serve them, which the Lord thy God created for the service of all the nations, that are under heaven.—*Deut.* iv. 19.

The Lord hath made all things for himself.—*Prov.* xvi. 4.

Hath not the Lord made the saints to declare all his wonderful works, which the Lord Almighty hath firmly settled to be established for his glory?— *Ecclus.* xlii. 17.

For thus saith the Lord that created the heavens, God himself that formed the earth and made it, the very maker thereof: he did not create it in vain: he formed it to be inhabited.—*Is.* xlv. 18.

END OF THE WORLD

In the beginning, O Lord, thou foundedst the earth: and the heavens are the works of thy hands. They shall perish, but thou remainest: and all of them shall grow old like a garment:

And as a vesture, thou shalt change them, and they shall be changed.—*Ps.* ci. 26, 27.

Behold the day of the Lord shall come, a cruel day, and full of indignation, and of wrath, and fury, to lay the land desolate, and to destroy the sinners thereof out of it.

For the stars of heaven, and their brightness, shall not display their light: the sun shall be darkened in his rising, and the moon shall not shine with her light.—*Is.* xiii. 9, 10.

With desolation shall the earth be laid waste, and it shall be utterly spoiled: for the Lord hath spoken this word.

The earth mourned and faded away, and is weakened: the world faded away, and the height of the people of the earth is weakened.—*Is.* xxiv. 3, 4.

And all the host of the heavens shall pine away, and the heavens shall be folded together as a book: and all their host shall fall down as the leaf falleth from the vine, and from the fig-tree.—*Is.* xxxiv. 4.

Lift up your eyes to heaven, and look down to the earth beneath: for the heavens shall vanish like smoke, and the earth shall be worn away like a garment, and the inhabitants thereof shall perish in like manner: but my salvation shall be for ever, and my justice shall not fail.—*Is.* li. 6.

For behold, I create new heavens, and a new earth: and the former things shall not be in remembrance, and they shall not come upon the heart.—*Is.* lxv. 17.

For as the new heavens, and the new earth, which I will make to stand before me, saith the Lord: so shall your seed stand, and your name.—*Is.* lxvi. 22.

Even as cockle, therefore, is gathered up, and burnt with fire: so shall it be at the end of the world.

The Son of man shall send his angels, and they shall gather out of his kingdom all scandals, and them that work iniquity.

And shall cast them into the furnace of fire: there shall be weeping and gnashing of teeth.—*Matt.* xiii. 40-42.

And this gospel of the kingdom shall be preached in the whole world, for a testimony to all nations, and then shall the consummation come. . . .

For there shall be then great tribulation, such as hath not been from the beginning of the world until now, neither shall be. . . .

For as lightning cometh out of the east, and appeareth even into the west: so shall also the coming of the Son of man be. . . .

And immediately after the tribulation of those days, the sun shall be darkened, and the moon shall not give her light, and the stars shall fall from heaven, and the powers of heaven shall be moved:

And then shall appear the sign of the Son of man in heaven: and then shall all tribes of the earth mourn: and they shall see the Son of man coming in the clouds of heaven, with much power and majesty.

And he shall send his angels with a trumpet, and a great voice: and they shall gather together his elect from the four winds, from the farthest parts of the heavens to the utmost bounds of them.

. . . Heaven and earth shall pass, but my words shall not pass.

But of that day and hour no one knoweth, no, not the angels of heaven, but the Father alone.—*Matt.* xxiv. 14, 21, 27, 29-32, 35, 36.

And there shall be signs in the sun, and in the moon, and in the stars; and upon the earth distress of nations, by reason of the confusion of the roaring of the sea and of the waves;

Men withering away for fear, and expectation of what shall come upon the whole world. For the powers of heaven shall be moved. . . .

But when these things begin to come to pass, look up, and lift up your heads, because your redemption is at hand.— *Luke* xxi. 25, 26, 28.

But the heavens and the earth which are now, by the same word are kept in store, reserved unto fire, against the day of judgment and perdition of the ungodly men.—*2 Peter* iii. 7.

But the day of the Lord shall come as a thief, in which the heavens shall pass away with great violence, and the elements shall be melted with heat, and the earth and the works which are in it, shall be burnt up.

Seeing then that all these things are

to be dissolved, what manner of people ought you to be in holy conversation and godliness?

Looking for and hasting unto the coming of the day of the Lord, by which the heavens, being on fire, shall be dissolved, and the elements shall melt with the burning heat?

But we look for new heavens and a new earth according to his promises, in which justice dwelleth.—2 *Peter* iii. 10-13.

And I saw, when he (the angel) had opened the sixth seal, and behold there was a great earthquake, and the sun became black as sackcloth of hair: and the whole moon became as blood:

And the stars from heaven fell upon the earth, as the fig-tree casteth its green figs when it is shaken by a great wind;

And the heaven departed as a book folded up: and every mountain, and the islands were moved out of their places.

And the kings of the earth, and the princes, and tribunes, and the rich, and the strong, and every bondman, and every free man, hid themselves in the dens and in the rocks of mountains:

And they say to the mountains and the rocks: Fall upon us, and hide us from the face of him that sitteth upon the throne, and from the wrath of the Lamb:

For the great day of their wrath is come, and who shall be able to stand?—*Apoc.* vi. 12-17.

And the angel whom I saw standing upon the sea and upon the earth, lifted up his hand to heaven,

And he swore by him that liveth for ever and ever, who created heaven and the things which are therein; and the earth and the things which are in it; and the sea and the things which are therein: That time shall be no longer.—*Apoc.* x. 5, 6.

And I saw a new heaven and a new earth. For the first heaven and the first earth was gone, and the sea is now no more.—*Apoc.* xxi. 1.

ENEMIES, WE SHOULD DO GOOD TO OUR

See: Forgiving injuries—page 158.

ENEMIES OF GOD, THE

So let all thy enemies perish, O Lord; but let them that love thee shine, as the sun shineth in his rising.—*Judges* v. 31.

The adversaries of the Lord shall fear him: and upon them shall he thunder in the heavens.—1 *Kings* ii. 10.

Let God arise, and let his enemies be scattered: and let them that hate him flee from before his face.

As smoke vanisheth, so let them vanish away: as wax melteth before the fire, so let the wicked perish at the presence of God.—*Ps.* lxvii. 2, 3.

Lift up thy hands against their pride unto the end; see what things the enemy hath done wickedly in the sanctuary.

And they that hate thee have made their boasts, in the midst of thy solemnity. . . .

They have set fire to thy sanctuary: they have defiled the dwelling place of thy name on the earth.

They said in their heart, the whole kindred of them together: Let us abolish all the festival days of God from the land. . . .

How long, O God, shall the enemy reproach: is the adversary to provoke thy name for ever?—*Ps.* lxxiii. 3, 4, 7, 8, 10.

Arise, O God, judge thy own cause: remember thy reproaches with which the foolish man hath reproached thee all the day.

Forget not the voices of thy enemies: the pride of them that hate thee ascendeth continually.—*Ps.* lxxiii. 22, 23.

The enemies of the Lord have lied to him: and their time shall be for ever. —*Ps.* lxxx. 16.

For lo, thy enemies have made a noise: and they that hate thee have lifted up the head.

They have taken a malicious counsel against thy people, and have consulted against thy saints.—*Ps.* lxxxii. 3, 4.

Have I not hated them, O Lord, that hated thee: and pined away because of thy enemies?

I have hated them with a perfect hatred; and they are become enemies to me.—*Ps.* cxxxviii. 21, 22.

But he that shall sin against me, shall

hurt his own soul. All that hate me, love death.—*Prov.* viii. 36.

ENEMIES OF GOD DEFEATED AND PUNISHED, THE

And in the multitude of thy glory, thou hast put down thy adversaries: thou hast sent thy wrath, which hath devoured them like stubble.—*Ex.* xv. 7.

And thou shalt know that the Lord thy God, he is a strong and faithful God. . . .

And repaying forthwith them that hate him, so as to destroy them, without further delay immediately rendering to them what they deserve.—*Deut.* vii. 9, 10.

If I shall whet my sword as the lightning, and my hand take hold on judgment: I will render vengeance to my enemies, and repay them that hate me.—*Deut.* xxxii. 41.

Let thy hand be found by all thy enemies: let thy right hand find out all them that hate thee.

Thou shalt make them as an oven of fire, in the time of thy anger: the Lord shall devour them in his wrath, and fire shall devour them.—*Ps.* xx. 9, 10.

And the enemies of the Lord, presently after they shall be honored and exalted, shall come to nothing, and vanish like smoke.—*Ps.* xxxvi. 20.

Thou hast humbled the proud one, as one that is slain: with the arm of thy strength thou hast scattered thy enemies.—*Ps.* lxxxviii. 11.

For behold thy enemies, O Lord, for behold thy enemies shall perish: and all the workers of iniquity shall be scattered.—*Ps.* xci. 10.

The Lord is a jealous God, and a revenger: the Lord is a revenger, and hath wrath: the Lord taketh vengeance on his adversaries, and he is angry with his enemies.—*Nahum* i. 2.

He said therefore: A certain nobleman went into a far country, to receive for himself a kingdom, and to return. . . .

But his citizens hated him: and they sent an embassage after him, saying: We will not have this man to reign over us. . . .

But as for those my enemies, who would not have me reign over them,

bring them hither, and kill them before me.—*Luke* xix. 12, 14, 27.

ENVY

And it came to pass after many days that Cain offered, of the fruits of the earth, gifts to the Lord.

Abel also offered of the firstlings of his flock, and of their fat: and the Lord had respect to Abel, and to his offerings.

But to Cain and his offerings he had no respect: and Cain was exceedingly angry, and his countenance fell.—*Gen.* iv. 3-5.

Now Israel loved Joseph above all his sons, because he had him in his old age: and he made him a coat of divers colors.

And his brethren, seeing that he was loved by his father more than all his sons, hated him, and could not speak peaceably to him.—*Gen.* xxxvii. 3, 4.

And the women sung as they played, and they said: Saul slew his thousands, and David his ten thousands.

And Saul was exceeding angry, and this word was displeasing in his eyes, and he said: They have given David ten thousands, and to me they have given but a thousand; what can he have more but the kingdom?

And Saul did not look on David with a good eye from that day and forward. —1 *Kings* xviii. 7-9.

Anger indeed killeth the foolish, and envy slayeth the little one.—*Job* v. 2.

Soundness of heart is the life of the flesh: but envy is the rottenness of the bones.—*Prov.* xiv. 30.

A man that maketh haste to be rich, and envieth others, is ignorant that poverty shall come upon him.—*Prov.* xxviii. 22.

For God created man incorruptible, and to the image of his own likeness he made him.

But by the envy of the devil, death came into the world:

And they follow him that are of his side.—*Wis.* ii. 23, 24, 25.

Neither will I go with consuming envy: for such a man shall not be partaker of wisdom.—*Wis.* vi. 25.

There is none worse than he that

envieth himself, and this is the reward of his wickedness.—*Ecclus.* xiv. 6.

The eye of the envious is wicked: and he turneth away his face, and despiseth his own soul.—*Ecclus.* xiv. 8.

Envy and anger shorten a man's days, and pensiveness will bring old age before the time.—*Ecclus.* xxx. 26.

And Pilate answered them, and said: Will you that I release to you the king of the Jews?

For he knew that the chief priests had delivered him up out of envy.—*Mark* xv. 9, 10.

For whereas there is among you envying and contention, are you not carnal, and walk according to man?—1 *Cor.* iii. 3.

Now the works of the flesh are manifest, which are fornication, uncleanness, immodesty, luxury.

. . . Envies, murders, drunkenness, revellings, and such like. Of the which I foretell you, as I have foretold to you, that they who do such things shall not obtain the kingdom of God.—*Gal.* v. 19, 21.

For where envying and contention is, there is inconstancy, and every evil work.—*James* iii. 16.

ENVY, EXHORTATION AGAINST

Be not emulous of evil doers; nor envy them that work iniquity.

For they shall shortly wither away as grass, and as the green herbs shall quickly fall.—*Ps.* xxxvi. 1, 2.

Envy not the man who prospereth in his way; the man who doth unjust things.—*Ps.* xxxvi. 7.

Envy not the unjust man, and do not follow his ways.—*Prov.* iii. 31.

Let not thy heart envy sinners: but be thou in the fear of the Lord all the day long.—*Prov.* xxiii. 17.

Envy not the glory and riches of a sinner: for thou knowest not what his ruin shall be.—*Ecclus.* ix. 16.

Let us walk honestly, as in the day; . . . not in contention and envy.—*Rom.* xiii. 13.

Let us not be made desirous of vain glory, provoking one another, envying one another.—*Gal.* v. 26.

Wherefore, laying aside all malice,

and all guile, and dissimulations, and envies, and all detractions,

As new born babes, desire the rational milk without guile, that thereby you may grow unto salvation.—1 *Peter* ii. 1, 2.

EQUAL IN THE SIGHT OF GOD, ALL MEN ARE

See also: Brotherhood of man—page 43.

The rich and poor have met one another: the Lord is the maker of them both.—*Prov.* xxii. 2.

The poor man and the creditor have met one another: the Lord is the enlightener of them both.—*Prov.* xxix. 13.

For God will not except any man's person, neither will he stand in awe of any man's greatness: for he made the little and the great, and he hath equally care of all.—*Wis.* vi. 8.

And Peter opening his mouth, said: In very deed I perceive that God is not a respecter of persons.

But in every nation, he that feareth him, and worketh justice, is acceptable to him.—*Acts* x. 34, 35.

And God, who knoweth the hearts, gave testimony, giving unto them (the Gentiles) the Holy Ghost, as well as to us;

And put no difference between us and them, purifying their hearts by faith.—*Acts* xv. 8, 9.

For there is no distinction of the Jew and the Greek: for the same is Lord over all, rich unto all that call upon him.—*Rom.* x. 12.

Knowing that whatsoever good thing any man shall do, the same shall he receive from the Lord, whether he be bond or free.

And you masters, do the same things to them, forbearing threatenings, knowing that the Lord both of them and you is in heaven; and there is no respect of persons with him.—*Eph.* vi. 8, 9.

Where there is neither Gentile nor Jew, circumcision nor uncircumcision, Barbarian nor Scythian, bond nor free. But Christ is all, and in all.—*Col.* iii. 11.

For perhaps he therefore departed for a season from thee, that thou mightest receive him again for ever;

Not now as a servant, but instead of a servant, a most dear brother, especially to me: but how much more to thee, both in the flesh and in the Lord? —*Phil.* i. 15, 16.

EQUANIMITY, OR MODERATION OF SPIRIT

In the day of good things, be not unmindful of evils; and in the day of evils, be not unmindful of good things.—*Ecclus.* xi. 27.

Remember poverty in the time of abundance, and the necessities of poverty in the day of riches.—*Ecclus.* xviii. 25.

ESCAPE FROM GOD, WE CANNOT

See also: Hidden from God, we cannot be—page 206.

Whither shall I go from thy spirit? or whither shall I flee from thy face? If I ascend into heaven, thou art there: if I descend into hell, thou art present.

If I take my wings early in the morning, and dwell in the uttermost parts of the sea:

Even there also shall thy hand lead me: and thy right hand shall hold me.— *Ps.* cxxxviii. 7-10.

But it is impossible to escape thy hand.

For the wicked that denied to know thee, were scourged by the strength of thy arm.—*Wis.* xvi. 15, 16.

The sinner shall not escape in his rapines, and the patience of him that showeth mercy shall not be put off.— *Ecclus.* xvi. 14.

Though they go down even to hell, thence shall my hand bring them out: and though they climb up to heaven, thence will I bring them down.

And though they be hid in the top of Carmel, I will search and take them away from thence: and though they hide themselves from my eyes in the depth of the sea, there will I command the serpent, and he shall bite them.— *Amos* ix. 2, 3.

Woe to him that gathereth together an evil covetousness to his house, that

his nest may be on high, and thinketh he may be delivered out of the hand of evil.—*Hab.* ii. 9.

Be not deceived, God is not mocked. --*Gal.* vi. 7.

ETERNAL LIFE

He asked life of thee: and thou hast given him length of days for ever and ever.—*Ps.* xx. 5.

These things Jesus spoke, and lifting up his eyes to heaven, he said: Father, the hour is come, glorify thy Son, that thy Son may glorify thee.

As thou hast given him power over all flesh, that he may give eternal life to all whom thou hast given him.

Now this is eternal life: That they may know thee, the only true God, and Jesus Christ, whom thou hast sent.— *John* xvii. 1-3.

For this corruptible must put on incorruption; and this mortal must put on immortality.

And when this mortal hath put on immortality, then shall come to pass the saying that is written: Death is swallowed up in victory.—1 *Cor.* xv. 53, 54.

And this is the testimony, that God hath given to us eternal life. And this life is in his Son.

He that hath the Son, hath life. He that hath not the Son, hath not life.

These things I write to you, that you may know that you have eternal life, you who believe in the name of the Son of God.—1 *John* v. 11-13.

And we know that the Son of God is come: and he hath given us understanding that we may know the true God, and may be in his true Son. This is the true God and life eternal.—1 *John* v. 20.

ETERNITY

I thought upon the days of old: and I had in my mind the eternal years.—*Ps.* lxxvi. 6.

If the tree fall to the south, or to the north, in what place soever it shall fall, there shall it be.—*Eccles.* xi. 3.

Because man shall go into the house of his eternity, and the mourners shall go round about in the street.—*Eccles.* xii. 5.

The number of the days of men at

the most are a hundred years: as a drop of water. of the sea are they esteemed: and as a pebble of the sand, so are a few years compared to eternity.—*Ecclus.* xviii. 8.

And many of those that sleep in the dust of the earth, shall awake: some unto life everlasting, and others unto reproach, to see it always.—*Dan.* xii. 2.

And the angel whom I saw standing upon the sea and upon the earth, lifted up his hand to heaven,

And he swore by him that liveth for ever and ever. . . . That time shall be no longer.—*Apoc.* x. 5, 6.

ETERNITY OF GOD

And God said to him (Abraham): I am, and my covenant is with thee, and thou shalt be a father of many nations. —*Gen.* xvii. 4.

But Abraham planted a grove in Bersabee, and there called upon the name of the Lord God eternal.—*Gen.* xxi. 33.

Moses said to God: Lo, I shall go to the children of Israel, and say to them: The God of your fathers hath sent me to you. If they should say to me: What is his name? what shall I say to them?

God said to Moses: I am who am. He said: Thus shalt thou say to the children of Israel: He who is, hath sent me to you.—*Ex.* iii. 13, 14.

See ye that I alone am, and there is no other God besides me. . . .

I will lift up my hand to heaven, and I will say: I live for ever.—*Deut.* xxxii. 39, 40.

Behold, God is great, exceeding our knowledge: the number of his years is inestimable.—*Job* xxxvi. 26.

But the Lord remaineth for ever.— *Ps.* ix. 8.

The Lord shall reign to eternity, yea, for ever and ever.—*Ps.* ix. (*Heb.* x.) 16.

For this is God, our God, unto eternity, and for ever and ever: he shall rule us for evermore.—*Ps.* xlvii. 15.

He that liveth for ever created all things together. God only shall be justified, and he remaineth an invincible king for ever.—*Ecclus.* xviii. 1.

He hath beautified the glorious works of his wisdom: and he is from eternity to eternity, and to him nothing may be added.—*Ecclus.* xlii. 21.

Who hath wrought and done these things, calling the generations from the beginning? I the Lord, I am the first and the last.—*Is.* xli. 4.

Being born again, not of corruptible seed, but incorruptible, by the word of God who liveth and remaineth for ever. —1 *Peter* i. 23.

But of this one thing be not ignorant, my beloved, that one day with the Lord is as a thousand years, and a thousand years as one day.—2 *Peter* iii. 8.

John to the seven churches which are in Asia. Grace be unto you, and peace from him that is, and that was, and that is to come, and from the seven spirits which are before his throne.— *Apoc.* i. 4.

I am Alpha and Omega, the beginning and the end, saith the Lord God, who is, and who was, and who is to come, the Almighty.—*Apoc.* i. 8.

I am Alpha and Omega, the first and the last, the beginning and the end.— *Apoc.* xxii. 13.

ETERNITY OF GOD, ACKNOWLEDGMENT OF THE

I will say to God: Do not condemn me: tell me why thou judgest me so. . . .

Are thy days as the days of man, and are thy years as the times of men?— *Job* x. 2, 5.

Thy throne, O God, is for ever and ever: the sceptre of thy kingdom is a sceptre of uprightness.—*Ps.* xliv. 7.

Before the mountains were made, or the earth and the world was formed; from eternity and to eternity thou art God. . . .

For a thousand years in thy sight are as yesterday, which is past.

And as a watch in the night, things that are counted nothing, shall their years be.—*Ps.* lxxxix. 2, 4, 5.

But thou, O Lord, art most high for evermore.—*Ps.* xci. 9.

Thy throne is prepared from of old: thou art from everlasting.—*Ps.* xcii. 2.

But thou, O Lord, endurest for ever:

and thy memorial to all generations.—*Ps.* ci. 13.

Call me not away in the midst of my days: thy years are unto generation and generation.

In the beginning, O Lord, thou foundedst the earth: and the heavens are the works of thy hands.

They shall perish, but thou remainest: and all of them shall grow old like a garment:

And as a vesture thou shalt change them, and they shall be changed. But thou art always the selfsame, and thy years shall not fail.—*Ps.* ci. 25-28.

Thy kingdom is a kingdom of all ages: and thy dominion endureth throughout all generations.—*Ps.* cxliv. 13.

But thou, O Lord, shalt remain for ever, thy throne from generation to generation.—*Lam.* v. 19.

Wast thou not from the beginning, O Lord my God, my holy one?—*Hab.* i. 12.

O Lord God, Creator of all things, dreadful and strong, just and merciful, who alone art the good king,

Who alone art gracious, who alone art just, and almighty, and eternal.— 2 *Mach.* i. 24, 25.

Now to the king of ages, immortal, invisible, the only God, be honor and glory for ever and ever. Amen.— 1 *Tim.* i. 17.

Who only hath immortality, and inhabiteth light inaccessible, whom no man hath seen, nor can see: to whom be honor and empire everlasting. Amen. —1 *Tim.* vi. 16.

ETERNITY OF CHRIST

The Lord said to my Lord: Sit thou at my right hand:

Until I make thy enemies thy footstool. . . .

With thee is the principality in the day of thy strength: in the brightness of the saints: from the womb before the day-star I begot thee.—*Ps.* cix. 1, 3.

In the beginning was the Word, and the Word was with God, and the Word was God.

The same was in the beginning with God.—*John* i. 1, 2.

They said therefore to him: Who art thou? Jesus said to them: The beginning, who also speak unto you.—*John* viii. 25.

The Jews therefore said to him: Thou art not yet fifty years old, and hast thou seen Abraham?

Jesus said to them: Amen, amen I say to you, before Abraham was made, I am.—*John* viii. 58.

Jesus Christ, yesterday, and to-day; and the same for ever.—*Heb.* xiii. 8.

And I turned to see the voice that spoke with me. And being turned, I saw seven golden candlesticks:

And in the midst of the seven golden candlesticks, one like to the Son of man, clothed with a garment down to the feet, and girt about the paps with a golden girdle. . . .

And when I had seen him, I fell at his feet as dead. And he laid his right hand upon me, saying: Fear not. I am the First and the Last,

And alive, and was dead, and behold I am living for ever and ever, and have the keys of death and of hell.—*Apoc.* i. 12, 13, 17, 18.

ETERNITY OF HELL

See: Part II—page 705.

EUCHARIST, THE REAL PRESENCE IN THE HOLY

See also: Communion, Holy—page 63.

I will set my tabernacle in the midst of you, and my soul shall not cast you off.

I will walk among you, and will be your God, and you shall be my people. —*Lev.* xxvi. 11, 12.

Is it credible then that God should dwell with men on the earth? If heaven, and the heavens of heavens do not contain thee, how much less this house which I have built?—2 *Paral.* vi. 18.

For the sparrow hath found herself a house, and the turtle a nest for herself, where she may lay her young ones: Thy altars, O Lord of hosts, my king and my God.—*Ps.* lxxxiii. 4.

Then the creator of all things commanded, and said to me: and he that made me, rested in my tabernacle.— *Ecclus.* xxiv. 12.

EXAMPLE 129

Rejoice, and praise, O thou habitation of Sion: for great is he that is in the midst of thee, the Holy One of Israel.—*Is.* xii. 6.

Verily thou art a hidden God, the God of Israel, the saviour.—*Is.* xlv. 15.

O that thou wouldst rend the heavens, and wouldst come down: the mountains would melt away at thy presence.—*Is.* lxiv. 1.

And I will make a covenant of peace with them, it shall be an everlasting covenant with them: and I will establish them, and will multiply them, and will set my sanctuary in the midst of them for ever:

And my tabernacle shall be with them: and I will be their God, and they shall be my people.—*Ezech.* xxxvii. 26, 27.

But the Lord is in his holy temple: let all the earth keep silence before him. *Hab.* ii. 20.

Sing praise, and rejoice, O daughter of Sion: for behold I come, and I will dwell in the midst of thee: saith the Lord.—*Zach.* ii. 10.

Let all flesh be silent at the presence of the Lord: for he is risen up out of his holy habitation.—*Zach.* ii. 13.

For what is the good thing of him, and what is his beautiful thing, but the corn of the elect, and wine springing forth virgins?—*Zach.* ix. 17.

Behold a virgin shall be with child, and bring forth a son, and they shall call his name Emmanuel, which being interpreted is, God with us.—*Matt.* i. 23.

Thanks be to God for his unspeakable gift.—*2 Cor.* ix. 15.

EUCHARIST, CHRIST'S LOVE FOR US IN INSTITUTING THE HOLY

And my delights were to be with the children of men.—*Prov.* viii. 31.

And he said to them: With desire I have desired to eat this pasch with you, before I suffer.—*Luke* xxii. 15.

Before the festival day of the pasch, Jesus knowing that his hour was come, that he should pass out of this world to the Father: having loved his own who were in the world, he loved them unto the end.—*John* xiii. 1.

EUCHARIST NOT APPRECIATED BY UNGRATEFUL CHRISTIANS, THE HOLY

For a mixt multitude of people, that came up with them, burned with desire, sitting and weeping, the children of Israel also being joined with them, and said: Who shall give us flesh to eat? . . .

Our soul is dry, our eyes behold nothing else but manna.—*Num.* xi. 4, 6.

And speaking against God and Moses, they said: Why didst thou bring us out of Egypt, to die in the wilderness? There is no bread, nor have we any waters: our soul now loatheth this very light food.—*Num.* xxi. 5.

EUCHARIST, INSTITUTION OF THE HOLY

See: Part II—page 694.

EXAMINATION OF CONSCIENCE

I have thought on my ways: and turned my feet unto thy testimonies.— *Ps.* cxviii. 59.

Before sickness, take a medicine, and before judgment, examine thyself, and thou shalt find mercy in the sight of God.—*Ecclus.* xviii. 20.

Let us search our ways, and seek, and return to the Lord.—*Lam.* iii. 40.

And now thus saith the Lord of hosts: Set your hearts to consider your ways.—*Ag.* i. 5.

EXAMPLE, GOOD

But the path of the just, as a shining light, goeth forwards, and increaseth even to perfect day.—*Prov.* iv. 18.

But they that are learned shall shine as the brightness of the firmament: and they that instruct many to justice, as stars for all eternity.—*Dan.* xii. 3.

For it doth not become our age, said he, to dissemble: whereby many young persons might think that Eleazar, at the age of fourscore and ten years, was gone over to the life of the heathens. . . . Wherefore by departing manfully out of this life, I shall show myself worthy of my old age:

And I shall leave an example of fortitude to young men, if with a ready mind and constancy I suffer an honorable death, for the most venerable and most holy laws. And having spoken thus, he was forthwith carried to execution.—2 *Mach.* vi. 24, 27, 28.

Wherefore I beseech you, be ye followers of me, as I also am of Christ.— 1 *Cor.* iv. 16.

For we are the good odor of Christ unto God, in them that are saved, and in them that perish.—2 *Cor.* ii. 15.

But we renounce the hidden things of dishonesty, not walking in craftiness, nor adulterating the word of God; but by manifestation of the truth commending ourselves to every man's conscience, in the sight of God.—2 *Cor.* iv. 2.

For we forecast what may be good not only before God, but also before men.—2 *Cor.* viii. 21.

And do ye all things without murmurings and hesitations;

That you may be blameless, and sincere children of God, without reproof, in the midst of a crooked and perverse generation; among whom you shine as lights in the world.—*Philipp.* ii. 14, 15.

It behooveth therefore a bishop to be blameless, the husband of one wife, sober, prudent, of good behavior, chaste, given to hospitality, a teacher: . . .

Moreover, he must have a good testimony of them who are without: lest he fall into reproach and the snare of the devil.—1 *Tim.* iii. 2, 7.

But with modesty and fear, having a good conscience: that whereas they speak evil of you, they may be ashamed who falsely accuse your good conversation in Christ.—1 *Peter* iii. 16.

EXAMPLE, EXHORTATION TO GIVE GOOD

So let your light shine before men, that they may see your good works, and glorify your Father who is in heaven.— *Matt.* v. 16.

Providing good things, not only in the sight of God, but also in the sight of all men.—*Rom.* xii. 17.

Therefore let us follow after the things that are of peace; and keep the things that are of edification one towards another.—*Rom.* xiv. 19.

Let your modesty be known to all men.—*Philipp.* iv. 5.

Walk with wisdom towards them that are without, redeeming the time.—*Col.* iv. 5.

For which cause, comfort one another; and edify one another, as you also do.—1 *Thess.* v. 11.

Let no man despise thy youth: but be thou an example of the faithful in word, in conversation, in charity, in faith, in chastity.—1 *Tim.* iv. 12.

In all things show thyself an example of good works, in doctrine, in integrity, in gravity,

The sound word that cannot be blamed: that he who is on the contrary part, may be afraid, having no evil to say of us.—*Titus* ii. 7, 8.

Dearly beloved, I beseech you as strangers and pilgrims, to refrain yourselves from carnal desires which war against the soul,

Having your conversation good among the Gentiles: that whereas they speak against you as evil-doers, they may, by the good works which they shall behold in you, glorify God in the day of visitation.—1 *Peter* ii. 11, 12.

In like manner also let wives be subject to their husbands: that if any believe not the word, they may be won without the word, by the conversation of the wives.—1 *Peter* iii. 1.

EXAMPLE, BAD

See: Scandal—page 504.

EXAMPLE OF CHRIST, WE SHOULD FOLLOW THE

Therefore whereas thou chastisest us, thou scourgest our enemies very many ways, to the end that when we judge, we may think on thy goodness: and when we are judged, we may hope for thy mercy.—*Wis.* xii. 22.

Take up my yoke upon you, and learn of me, because I am meek, and humble of heart: and you shall find rest to your souls.—*Matt.* xi. 29.

The disciple is not above his master: but every one shall be perfect, if he be as his master.—*Luke* vi. 40.

For I have given you an example, that as I have done to you, so you do also.—*John* xiii. 15.

Jesus saith to him: I am the way,

and the truth, and the life. No man cometh to the Father, but by me.—*John* xiv. 6.

Be ye therefore followers of God, as most dear children;

And walk in love, as Christ also hath loved us, and hath delivered himself for us, an oblation and a sacrifice to God for an odor of sweetness.—*Eph.* v. 1, 2.

For think diligently upon him that endured such opposition from sinners against himself; that you be not wearied, fainting in your minds.—*Heb.* xii. 3.

Wherefore Jesus also, that he might sanctify the people by his own blood, suffered without the gate.

Let us go forth, therefore, to him, without the camp, bearing his reproach. —*Heb.* xiii. 12, 13.

For what glory is it, if committing sin, and being buffeted for it, you endure? But if doing well, you suffer patiently; this is thankworthy before God.

For unto this are you called: because Christ also suffered for us, leaving you an example, that you should follow his steps.

Who did no sin, neither was guile found in his mouth.

Who, when he was reviled, did not revile: when he suffered, he threatened not: but delivered himself to him that judged him unjustly.—1 *Peter* ii. 20-23.

He that saith he abideth in him, ought himself also to walk, even as he walked.—1 *John* ii. 6.

EXAMPLE OF THE WICKED, WE MUST NOT FOLLOW THE

Be not emulous of evil-doers; nor envy them that work iniquity. . . .
. . . Have no emulation to do evil.
For evil-doers shall be cut off: but they that wait upon the Lord, they shall inherit the land.—*Ps.* xxxvi. 1, 8, 9.

Envy not the unjust man, and do not follow his ways.—*Prov.* iii. 31.

Be not delighted in the paths of the wicked, neither let the way of evil men please thee.

Flee from it, pass not by it: go aside, and forsake it.—*Prov.* iv. 14, 15.

Seek not to be like evil men, neither desire to be with them.—*Prov.* xxiv. 1.

Contend not with the wicked, nor seek to be like the ungodly:

For evil men have no hope of things to come, and the lamp of the wicked shall be put out.—*Prov.* xxiv. 19, 20.

Abide not in the works of sinners. But trust in God, and stay in thy place. —*Ecclus.* xi. 22.

EXPERIENCE, VALUE OF

Much experience is the crown of old men, and the fear of God is their glory. —*Ecclus.* xxv. 8.

What doth he know, that hath not been tried? A man that hath much experience, shall think of many things: and he that hath learned many things, shall show forth understanding.

He that hath no experience, knoweth little: and he that hath been experienced in many things, multiplieth prudence.

He that hath not been tried, what manner of things doth he know? he that hath been surprised, shall abound with subtlety.—*Ecclus.* xxxiv. 9-11.

EXTORTION

See: Usury—page 573.

FAINT-HEARTED, THE

See also: Cowardice—page 86.

Woe to them that are faint-hearted, who believe not God: and therefore they shall not be protected by him.

Woe to them that have lost patience, and that have forsaken the right ways, and have gone aside into crooked ways. —*Ecclus.* ii. 15, 16.

Deliver him that suffereth wrong out of the hand of the proud: and be not faint-hearted in thy soul.—*Ecclus.* iv. 9.

Be not faint-hearted in thy mind.— *Ecclus.* vii. 9.

Strengthen ye the feeble hands, and confirm the weak knees.

Say to the faint-hearted: Take courage, and fear not: behold your God will bring the revenge of recompense: God himself will come and will save you.— *Is.* xxxv. 3, 4.

Wherefore lift up the hands which hang down, and the feeble knees,

And make straight steps with your feet: that no one, halting, may go out of the way; but rather be healed.—*Heb.* xii. 12, 13.

FAITH

For she is an infinite treasure to men! which they that use, become the friends of God, being commended for the gift of discipline.—*Wis.* vii. 14.

For in her is the spirit of understanding: holy, one, manifold, subtile, eloquent, active, undefiled, sure, sweet, loving that which is good, quick, which nothing hindereth, beneficent,

Gentle, kind, steadfast, assured, secure, having all power, overseeing all things, and containing all spirits, intelligible, pure, subtile.—*Wis.* vii. 22, 23.

For it is she that teacheth the knowledge of God, and is the chooser of his works.—*Wis.* viii. 4.

For, to know thee is perfect justice: and to know thy justice, and thy power, is the root of immortality.—*Wis.* xv. 3.

They that fear the Lord, will not be incredulous to his word.—*Ecclus.* ii. 18.

Thus saith the Lord: Let not the wise man glory in his wisdom, and let not the strong man glory in his strength, and let not the rich man glory in his riches:

But let him that glorieth, glory in this, that he understandeth and knoweth me.—*Jer.* ix. 23, 24.

And I will espouse thee to me in faith: and thou shalt know that I am the Lord.—*Osee* ii. 20.

Now this is eternal life: That they may know thee, the only true God, and Jesus Christ, whom thou hast sent.—*John* xvii. 3.

Jesus saith to him: Because thou hast seen me, Thomas, thou hast believed: blessed are they that have not seen, and have believed.—*John* xx. 29.

For the justice of God is revealed therein (*i.e.* in the gospel), from faith unto faith, as it is written: The just man liveth by faith.—*Rom.* i. 17.

But as it is written: That eye hath not seen, nor ear heard, neither hath it entered into the heart of man, what things God hath prepared for them that love him.

But to us God hath revealed them, by his Spirit.—1 *Cor.* ii. 9, 10.

I therefore so run, not as at an uncertainty: I so fight, not as one beating the air.—1 *Cor.* ix. 26.

We see now through a glass, in a dark manner; but then face to face. Now I know in part; but then I shall know, even as I am known.

And now there remain faith, hope and charity, these three: but the greatest of these is charity.—1 *Cor.* xiii. 12, 13.

For we walk by faith, and not by sight.—2 *Cor.* v. 7.

For the weapons of our warfare are not carnal, but mighty to God, unto the pulling down of fortifications, destroying counsels,

And every height that exalteth itself against the knowledge of God, and bringing into captivity every understanding unto the obedience of Christ. —2 *Cor.* x. 4, 5.

Now faith is the substance of things to be hoped for, the evidence of things that appear not. . . .

By faith we understand that the world was framed by the word of God; that from invisible things visible things might be made.—*Heb.* xi. 1, 3.

Thou believest that there is one God. Thou dost well: the devils also believe and tremble.—*James* ii. 19.

FAITH, THE FOUNDATION OF OTHER VIRTUES

He that believeth in the Lord, loveth mercy.—*Prov.* xiv. 21.

The fear of God is the beginning of his love: and the beginning of faith is to be fast joined unto it.—*Ecclus.* xxv. 16.

He that believeth God, taketh heed to his commandments.—*Ecclus.* xxxii. 28.

Behold, he that is unbelieving, his soul shall not be right in himself: but the just shall live in his faith.—*Hab.* ii. 4.

And God, who knoweth the hearts, gave testimony, giving unto them (the Gentiles) the Holy Ghost, as well as to us;

And put no difference between us and them, purifying their hearts by faith.—*Acts* xv. 8, 9.

Now the God of hope fill you with all joy and peace in believing; that you may abound in hope, and in the power of the Holy Ghost.—*Rom.* xv. 13.

I give thanks to my God, always making a remembrance of thee in my prayers. . . .

That the communication of thy faith may be made evident in the acknowledgment of every good work, that is in you in Christ Jesus.—*Phil.* i. 4, 6.

Grace to you and peace be accomplished in the knowledge of God and of Christ Jesus our Lord:

As all things of his divine power which appertain to life and godliness, are given us through the knowledge of him, who hath called us by his own proper glory and virtue.— 2 *Peter* i. 2, 3.

FAITH, THE POWER OF

By mercy and faith sins are purged away.—*Prov.* xv. 27.

And being but one, she can do all things: and remaining in herself the same, she reneweth all things, and through nations, conveyeth herself into holy souls, she maketh the friends of God and prophets.—*Wis.* vii. 27.

For, amen I say to you, if you have faith as a grain of mustard seed, you shall say to this mountain, Remove from hence hither, and it shall remove; and nothing shall be impossible to you.—*Matt.* xvii. 19.

And Jesus answering said to them: Amen I say to you, if you shall have faith, and stagger not, not only this of the fig-tree shall you do, but also if you shall say to this mountain, Take up, and cast thyself into the sea, it shall be done.

And all things whatsoever you shall ask in prayer, believing, you shall receive.—*Matt.* xxi. 21, 22.

And Jesus saith to him: If thou canst believe, all things are possible to him that believeth.—*Mark* ix. 22.

And the Lord said: If you had faith like to a grain of mustard seed, you might say to this mulberry-tree, Be thou rooted up, and be thou transplanted into the sea: and it would obey you.—*Luke* xvii. 6.

But as many as received him, he gave them power to be made the sons of God, to them that believe in his name.—*John* i. 12.

Then Jesus said to those Jews who believed him: If you continue in my word, you shall be my disciples indeed.

And you shall know the truth, and the truth shall make you free.—*John* viii. 31, 32.

I am come a light into the world; that whosoever believeth in me, may not remain in darkness.—*John* xii. 46.

Amen, amen I say to you, he that believeth in me, the works that I do, he also shall do; and greater than these shall he do.—*John* xiv. 12.

And in the faith of his (Jesus') name, this man, whom you have seen and known, hath his name strengthened; and the faith which is by him, hath given this perfect soundness in the sight of you all.—*Acts* iii. 16.

In all things taking the shield of faith, wherewith you may be able to extinguish all the fiery darts of the most wicked one.—*Eph.* vi. 16.

But what shall I yet say? For the time would fail me to tell of Gedeon, Barac, Samson, Jephthe, David, Samuel and the prophets:

Who by faith conquered kingdoms, wrought justice, obtained promises, stopped the mouths of lions,

Quenched the violence of fire, escaped the edge of the sword, recovered strength from weakness, became valiant in battle, put to flight the armies of foreigners:

Women received their dead raised to life again. But others were racked, not accepting deliverance, that they might find a better resurrection.

And others had trial of mockeries and stripes, moreover also of bands and prisons.

They were stoned, they were cut asunder, they were tempted, they were put to death by the sword, they wandered about in sheepskins, in goatskins, being in want, distressed, afflicted:

Of whom the world was not worthy; wandering in deserts, in mountains, and in dens, and in caves of the earth.—*Heb.* xi. 32-38.

Be sober and watch: because your adversary the devil, as a roaring lion, goet ι about seeking whom he may devour.

Whom resist ye, strong in faith.—*1 Peter* v. 8, 9.

For whatsoever is born of God, overcometh the world: and this is the victory which overcometh the world, our faith.

Who is he that overcometh the world, but he that believeth that Jesus is the Son of God?—*1 John* v. 4, 5.

FAITH, THE GIFT OF GOD

I will bless the Lord, who hath given me understanding.—*Ps.* xv. 7.

Thou hast made known to me the ways of life, thou shalt fill me with joy with thy countenance.—*Ps.* xv. 11.

For behold, thou hast loved truth: the uncertain and hidden things of thy wisdom thou hast made manifest to me. —*Ps.* l. 8.

He hath not done in like manner to every nation: and his judgments he hath not made manifest to them.—*Ps.* cxlvii. 20.

And the eunuch that hath not wrought iniquity with his hands, nor thought wicked things against God: for the precious gift of faith shall be given to him, and a most acceptable lot in the temple of God.—*Wis.* iii. 14.

And who shall know thy thought, except thou give wisdom, and send thy Holy Spirit from above:

And so the ways of them that are upon earth may be corrected, and men may learn the things that please thee? —*Wis.* ix. 17, 18.

At that time Jesus answered and said: I confess to thee, O Father, Lord of heaven and earth, because thou hast hid these things from the wise and prudent, and hast revealed them to little ones.

Yea, Father; for so hath it seemed good in thy sight.

All things are delivered to me by my Father. And no one knoweth the Son, but the Father: neither doth any one know the Father, but the Son, and he to whom it shall please the Son to reveal him.—*Matt.* xi. 25-27.

But blessed are your eyes, because they see, and your ears, because they hear.

For, amen I say to you, many prophets and just men have desired to see the things that you see, and have not seen them, and to hear the things that you hear, and have not heard them. —*Matt.* xiii. 16, 17.

Jesus saith to them: But whom do you say that I am?

Simon Peter answered and said: Thou art Christ, the Son of the living God.

And Jesus, answering, said to him: Blessed art thou, Simon Bar-Jona: because flesh and blood hath not revealed it to thee, but my Father who is in heaven.—*Matt.* xvi. 15-17.

Now we have received not the spirit of this world, but the Spirit that is of God; that we may know the things that are given us from God.—*1 Cor.* ii. 12.

But the fruit of the Spirit is charity, joy, peace, patience . . . faith.—*Gal.* v. 22, 23.

Wherefore I also . . . cease not to give thanks for you, making commemoration of you in my prayers,

That the God of our Lord Jesus Christ, the Father of glory, may give unto you the spirit of wisdom and of revelation, in the knowledge of him:

The eyes of your heart enlightened, that you may know what the hope is of his calling, and what are the riches of the glory of his inheritance in the saints.—*Eph.* i. 16-18.

Wherefore, having the loins of your mind girt up, being sober, trust perfectly in the grace which is offered you in the revelation of Jesus Christ.— *1 Peter* i. 13.

FAITH, PLEASING TO GOD

Abram believed God, and it was reputed to him unto justice.—*Gen.* xv. 6.

For she is an infinite treasure to men! which they that use, become the friends of God, being commended for the gift of discipline.—*Wis.* vii. 14.

And being but one, she can do all things: and remaining in herself the same, she reneweth all things, and through nations conveyeth herself into holy souls, she maketh the friends of God and prophets.

For God loveth none but him that dwelleth with wisdom.—*Wis.* vii. 27, 28.

For the fear of the Lord is wisdom and discipline: and that which is agreeable to him,

Is faith and meekness: and he will fill up his treasures.—*Ecclus.* i. 34, 35.

And blessed art thou that hast believed, because those things shall be accomplished that were spoken to thee by the Lord.—*Luke* i. 45.

For the Father himself loveth you, because you have loved me, and have believed that I came out from God.—*John* xvi. 27.

In the promise also of God he (Abraham) staggered not by distrust; but was strengthened in faith, giving glory to God:

Most fully knowing that whatsoever he has promised, he is able also to perform.

And therefore it was reputed to him unto justice.

Now it is not written only for him, that it was reputed to him unto justice,

But also for us, to whom it shall be reputed, if we believe in him that raised up Jesus Christ, our Lord, from the dead.—*Rom.* iv. 20-24.

For in Christ Jesus neither circumcision availeth anything, nor uncircumcision: but faith that worketh by charity.—*Gal.* v. 6.

But my just man liveth by faith; but if he withdraw himself, he shall not please my soul.—*Heb.* x. 38.

FAITH COMMANDED BY GOD

But Jesus having heard the word that was spoken, saith to the ruler of the synagogue: Fear not, only believe.—*Mark* v. 36.

And Jesus answering, saith to them: Have the faith of God.—*Mark* xi. 22.

Therefore I say unto you, all things whatsoever you ask when you pray, believe that you shall receive; and they shall come unto you.—*Mark* xi. 24.

They said therefore unto him: What shall we do, that we may work the works of God?

Jesus answered, and said to them: This is the work of God, that you believe in him whom he hath sent.—*John* vi. 28, 29.

Whilst you have the light, believe in the light, that you may be the children of light.—*John* xii. 36.

Let not your heart be troubled. You believe in God, believe also in me.—*John* xiv. 1.

And this is his commandment, that we should believe in the name of his Son, Jesus Christ: and love one another, as he hath given commandment unto us.—1 *John* iii. 23.

FAITH, THE REWARD OF

I. In the World to Come

Ye that fear the Lord, believe him: and your reward shall not be made void. —*Ecclus.* ii. 8.

And as Moses lifted up the serpent in the desert, so must the Son of man be lifted up:

That whosoever believeth in him, may not perish; but may have life everlasting.

For God so loved the world, as to give his only begotten Son; that whosoever believeth in him, may not perish, but may have life everlasting.—*John* iii. 14-16.

He that believeth in the Son, hath life everlasting; but he that believeth not the Son, shall not see life; but the wrath of God abideth on him.—*John* iii. 36.

Amen, amen, I say unto you, that he who heareth my word, and believeth him that sent me, hath life everlasting; and cometh not into judgment, but is passed from death to life.—*John* v. 24.

And Jesus said to them: I am the bread of life: he that cometh to me shall not hunger; and he that believeth in me shall never thirst.—*John* vi. 35.

And this is the will of my Father that sent me: that every one who seeth the Son, and believeth in him, may have life everlasting, and I will raise him up in the last day.—*John* vi. 40.

Amen, amen I say unto you: He that believeth in me, hath everlasting life.—*John* vi. 47.

Jesus said to her: I am the resurrection and the life: he that believeth in me, although he be dead, shall live:

And every one that liveth, and believeth in me, shall not die for ever.—*John* xi. 25, 26.

Jesus saith to her: Did not I say to thee, that if thou believe, thou shalt see the glory of God?—*John* xi. 40.

But these are written, that you may believe that Jesus is the Christ, the Son of God: and that believing, you may have life in his name.—*John* xx. 31.

For if thou confess with thy mouth the Lord Jesus, and believe in thy heart that God hath raised him up from the dead, thou shalt be saved.

For, with the heart, we believe unto justice; but, with the mouth, confession is made unto salvation.

For the Scripture saith: Whosoever believeth in him, shall not be confounded.—*Rom.* x. 9-11.

Whom, having not seen, you love: in whom also now, though you see him not, you believe: and believing, shall rejoice with joy unspeakable and glorified;

Receiving the end of your faith, even the salvation of your souls.—1 *Peter* i. 8, 9.

FAITH, THE REWARD OF

II. In this Life

That thy children, O Lord, whom thou lovedst, might know that it is not the growing of fruits that nourisheth men, but thy word preserveth them that believe in thee.—*Wis.* xvi. 26.

Believe God, and he will recover thee: and direct thy way, and trust in him.—*Ecclus.* ii. 6.

And behold a leper came and adored him, saying: Lord, if thou wilt, thou canst make me clean.

And Jesus stretching forth his hand, touched him, saying: I will, be thou made clean. And forthwith his leprosy was cleansed.—*Matt.* viii. 2, 3.

And the centurion making answer, said: Lord, I am not worthy that thou shouldst enter under my roof: but only say the word, and my servant shall be healed.

. . . And Jesus said to the centurion: Go, and as thou hast believed, so be it done to thee. And the servant was healed at the same hour.—*Matt.* viii. 8, 13.

And behold they brought to him one sick of the palsy, lying in a bed. And Jesus, seeing their faith, said to the man sick of the palsy: Be of good heart, son, thy sins are forgiven thee.—*Matt.* ix. 2.

And as he was speaking these things unto them, behold a certain ruler came up, and adored him, saying: Lord, my daughter is even now dead; but come, lay thy hand upon her, and she shall live. . . .

And when the multitude was put forth, he went in, and took her by the hand. And the maid arose.—*Matt.* ix. 18, 25.

And behold a woman who was troubled with an issue of blood twelve years, came behind him, and touched the hem of his garment.

For she said within herself: If I shall touch only his garment, I shall be healed.

But Jesus, turning, and seeing her, said: Be of good heart, daughter, thy faith hath made thee whole. And the woman was made whole from that hour.—*Matt.* ix. 20-22.

And as Jesus passed from thence, there followed him two blind men crying out and saying, Have mercy on us, O son of David.

And when he was come to the house, the blind men came to him. And Jesus saith to them: Do you believe that I can do this unto you? They say to him, Yea, Lord.

Then he touched their eyes, saying, According to your faith, be it done unto you.

And their eyes were opened.—*Matt.* ix. 27-30.

And behold, a woman of Canaan, who came out of those coasts, crying out, said to him: Have mercy on me, O Lord, thou son of David: my daughter is grievously troubled by a devil.

Who answered her not a word. . . .

But she came and adored him, saying: Lord, help me. . . .

Then Jesus answering, said to her: O woman, great is thy faith: be it done to thee as thou wilt: and her daughter was cured from that hour.—*Matt.* xv. 22, 23, 25, 28.

And they come to Jericho: and as he

went out of Jericho, with his disciples and a very great multitude, Bartimeus the blind man, the son of Timeus, sat by the wayside, begging.

Who, when he had heard that it was Jesus of Nazareth, began to cry out, and to say: Jesus, son of David, have mercy on me. . . .

And Jesus answering, said to him: What wilt thou that I should do to thee? And the blind man said to him: Rabboni, that I may see.

And Jesus saith to him: Go thy way, thy faith hath made thee whole. And immediately he saw, and followed him in the way.—*Mark* x. 46, 47, 51, 52.

And behold, a woman that was in the city, a sinner, when she knew that he sat at meat in the Pharisee's house, brought an alabaster box of ointment;

And standing behind at his feet, she began to wash his feet with tears, and wiped them with the hairs of her head, and kissed his feet, and anointed them with the ointment.

. . . And he said to the woman: Thy faith hath made thee safe, go in peace.—*Luke* vii. 37, 38, 50.

The ruler saith to him: Lord, come down before that my son die.

Jesus saith to him: Go thy way; thy son liveth. The man believed the word which Jesus said to him, and went his way.

And as he was going down, his servants met him; and they brought word, saying, that his son lived.

He asked therefore of them the hour wherein he grew better. And they said to him: yesterday, at the seventh hour, the fever left him.

The father therefore knew, that it was at the same hour that Jesus said to him, Thy son liveth; and himself believed, and his whole house.—*John* iv. 49-53.

He that believeth in me, as the scripture saith, Out of his belly shall flow rivers of living water.

Now this he said of the Spirit which they should receive, who believed in him: for as yet the Spirit was not given, because Jesus was not yet glorified.—*John* vii. 38, 39.

And there sat a certain man at Lystra, impotent in his feet, a cripple from his mother's womb, who never had walked.

This same heard Paul speaking. Who, looking upon him, and seeing that he had faith to be healed,

Said with a loud voice: Stand upright, on thy feet. And he leaped up, and walked.—*Acts* xiv. 7-9.

FAITH, EXHORTATION TO PRACTISE THE VIRTUE OF

Believe God, and he will recover thee: and direct thy way, and trust in him.

. . . Ye that fear the Lord, believe him: and your reward shall not be made void.—*Ecclus.* ii. 6, 8.

But let us, who are of the day, be sober, having on the breastplate of faith and charity, and for a helmet, the hope of salvation.—1 *Thess.* v. 8.

This precept I commend to thee, O son Timothy; according to the prophecies going before on thee, that thou war in them a good warfare,

Having faith and a good conscience, which some rejecting, have made shipwreck concerning the faith.—1 *Tim.* i. 18, 19.

But thou, O man of God, fly these things; and pursue justice, godliness, faith, charity, patience, mildness.

Fight the good fight of faith: lay hold on eternal life, whereunto thou art called, and hast confessed a good confession before many witnesses.— 1 *Tim.* vi. 11, 12.

Let us draw near with a true heart in fulness of faith, having our hearts sprinkled from an evil conscience, and our bodies washed with clean water.— *Heb.* x. 22.

But you, my beloved, building yourselves upon your most holy faith, praying in the Holy Ghost,

Keep yourselves in the love of God, waiting for the mercy of our Lord Jesus Christ, unto life everlasting.— *Jude* i. 20, 21.

FAITH, NECESSARY FOR SALVATION

See: Part II—page 696.

FAITH, A PRAYER FOR

And Jesus saith to him: If thou canst believe, all things are possible to him that believeth.

And immediately the father of the boy crying out, with tears said: I do believe, Lord: help my unbelief.—*Mark* ix. 22, 23.

And the apostles said to the Lord: Increase our faith.—*Luke* xvii. 5.

For this cause I bow my knees to the Father of our Lord Jesus Christ, . . .

That he would grant you, according to the riches of his glory, to be strengthened by his Spirit, with might unto the inward man,

That Christ may dwell by faith in your hearts.—*Eph.* iii. 14, 16, 17.

FAITH, ACKNOWLEDGING OUR

Every one, therefore, that shall confess me before men, I will also confess him before my Father who is in heaven. —*Matt.* x. 32.

And I say to you, Whosoever shall confess me before men, him shall the Son of man also confess before the angels of God.—*Luke* xii. 8.

For if thou confess with thy mouth the Lord Jesus, and believe in thy heart that God hath raised him up from the dead, thou shalt be saved.

For, with the heart, we believe unto justice; but, with the mouth, confession is made unto salvation.—*Rom.* x. 9, 10.

Fight the good fight of faith: lay hold on eternal life, whereunto thou art called, and hast confessed a good confession before many witnesses.—1 *Tim.* vi. 12.

FAITH, DENYING OUR

But he that shall deny me before men, I will also deny him before my Father who is in heaven.—*Matt.* x. 33.

But Peter sat without in the court: and there came to him a servant maid, saying: Thou also wast with Jesus the Galilean.

But he denied before them all, saying: I know not what thou sayest.

And as he went out of the gate, another maid saw him, and she saith to them that were there: This man also was with Jesus of Nazareth.

And again he denied with an oath: I know not the man.

And after a little while, they came that stood by, and said to Peter: Surely thou also art one of them; for even thy speech doth discover thee.

Then he began to curse and to swear that he knew not the man. And immediately the cock crew.—*Matt.* xxvi. 69-74.

But he that shall deny me before men, shall be denied before the angels of God.—*Luke* xii. 9.

If we deny him, he will also deny us. —2 *Tim.* ii. 12.

FAITH, WEAKNESS IN OUR

Moses therefore took the rod, which was before the Lord, as he had commanded him.

And having gathered together the multitude before the rock, he said to them: Hear, ye rebellious and incredulous: Can we bring you forth water out of this rock?

And when Moses had lifted up his hand, and struck the rock twice with the rod, there came forth water in great abundance, so that the people and their cattle drank.

And the Lord said to Moses and Aaron: Because you have not believed me, to sanctify me before the children of Israel, you shall not bring these people into the land which I will give them.—*Num.* xx. 9-12.

But the boat in the midst of the sea was tossed with the waves: for the wind was contrary.

And in the fourth watch of the night, he came to them, walking upon the sea.

And they seeing him walking upon the sea, were troubled, saying: It is an apparition. And they cried out for fear.

And immediately Jesus spoke to them, saying: Be of good heart: it is I, fear ye not.

And Peter making answer, said: Lord, if it be thou, bid me come to thee upon the waters.

And he said: Come. And Peter going down out of the boat, walked upon the water, to come to Jesus.

But seeing the wind strong, he was afraid: and when he began to sink, he cried out, saying: Lord, save me.

And immediately Jesus stretching forth his hand, took hold of him, and said to him: O thou of little faith, why didst thou doubt?—*Matt.* xiv. 24-31.

And Jesus rebuked him, and the devil went out of him, and the child was cured from that hour.

Then came the disciples to Jesus secretly, and said: Why could not we cast him out?

Jesus said to them: Because of your unbelief.—*Matt.* xvii. 17-19.

The sower went out to sow his seed. And as he sowed, some fell by the wayside, and it was trodden down, and the fowls of the air devoured it.

And other some fell upon a rock: and as soon as it was sprung up, it withered away, because it had no moisture. . . .

Now they upon the rock, are they who, when they hear, receive the word with joy: and these have no roots; for they believe for a while, and in time of temptation, they fall away.—*Luke* viii. 5, 6, 13.

And when they were sailing, he slept; and there came down a storm of wind upon the lake, and they were filled, and were in danger.

And they came, and awaked him, saying: Master, we perish. But he arising, rebuked the wind and the rage of the water; and it ceased, and there was a calm.

And he said to them: Where is your faith? Who being afraid, wondered, saying one to another: Who is this (think you) that he commandeth both the winds and the sea, and they obey him?—*Luke* viii. 23-25.

FAITH, WE MUST NOT BE ASHAMED OF OUR

See also: Human respect—page 217.

And I spoke of thy testimonies before kings: and I was not ashamed.—*Ps.* cxviii. 46.

Be not ashamed of any of these things, and accept no person to sin thereby:

Of the law of the most High, and of his covenant, and of judgment to justify the ungodly.—*Ecclus.* xlii. 1, 2.

Who art thou, that thou shouldst be afraid of a mortal man, and of the son of man, who shall wither away like grass?

And thou hast forgotten the Lord thy maker, who stretched out the heavens, and founded the earth.—*Is.* li. 12, 13.

For he that shall be ashamed of me and of my words, of him the Son of man shall be ashamed, when he shall come in his majesty, and that of his Father, and of the holy angels.—*Luke* ix. 26.

For I am not ashamed of the gospel. For it is the power of God unto salvation to every one that believeth, to the Jew first, and to the Greek.—*Rom.* i. 16.

Be not thou therefore ashamed of the testimony of our Lord, nor of me, his prisoner: but labor with the gospel, according to the power of God.—*2 Tim.* i. 8.

For which cause, I also suffer these things: but I am not ashamed. For I know whom I have believed, and I am certain that he is able to keep that which I have committed unto him, against that day.—*2 Tim.* i. 12.

If you be reproached for the name of Christ, you shall be blessed: for that which is of the honor, glory, and power of God, and that which is his Spirit, resteth upon you.

But let none of you suffer as a murderer, or a thief, or a railer, or a coveter of other men's things.

But if as a Christian, let him not be ashamed, but let him glorify God in that name.—*1 Peter* iv. 14-16.

FAITH, WE SHOULD BE ABLE TO GIVE A REASON FOR OUR

See: Reason—page 458.

FAITH, WE MUST BE PRACTICAL IN OUR

See: Practical in our religion—page 392.

FAITHFUL, PRAYER FOR THE

See also: Church, prayer for the—page 54.

O God, why hast thou cast us off unto the end: why is thy wrath enkindled against the sheep of thy pasture?

Remember thy congregation, which thou hast possessed from the beginning.

The sceptre of thy inheritance which thou hast redeemed: mount Sion in which thou hast dwelt.—*Ps.* lxxiii. 1, 2.

Have mercy on thy people, upon whom thy name is invoked: and upon Israel, whom thou hast raised up to be thy first-born.

Have mercy on Jerusalem, the city which thou hast sanctified, the city of thy rest.

Fill Sion with thy unspeakable words, and thy people with thy glory.

Give testimony to them that are thy creatures from the beginning, and raise up the prophecies which the former prophets spoke in thy name.

Reward them that patiently wait for thee, that thy prophets may be found faithful: and hear the prayers of thy servants,

According to the blessing of Aaron over thy people, and direct us into the way of justice, and let all know that dwell upon the earth, that thou art God, the beholder of all ages. —*Ecclus.* xxxvi. 14-19.

FASTING

See: Part II—page 697.

FATHER, GOD OUR

See also: Children of God by adoption, we become—page 50.

And thou shalt say to him (Pharao): Thus saith the Lord: Israel is my son, my first-born.

I have said to thee: Let my son go, that he my serve me, and thou wouldst not let him go: behold, I will kill thy son, thy first-born. —*Ex.* iv. 22, 23.

In judging, be merciful to the fatherless as a father, and as a husband to their mother.

And thou shalt be as the obedient son of the most High, and he will have mercy on thee more than a mother.— *Ecclus.* iv. 10, 11.

But I said: How shall I put thee among the children, and give thee a lovely land, the goodly inheritance of the armies of the Gentiles? And I said: Thou shalt call me father, and shalt not cease to walk after me.—*Jer.* iii. 19.

Because Israel was a child, and I loved him: and I called my son out of Egypt.—*Osee* xi. 1.

The son honoreth the father, and the servant his master: if then I be a father, where is my honor? and if I be a master, where is my fear? saith the Lord of hosts.—*Malach.* i. 6.

Be you therefore perfect, as also your heavenly Father is perfect.—*Matt.* v. 48.

Thus therefore shall you pray: Our Father, who art in heaven, hallowed be thy name.—*Matt.* vi. 9.

And call none your father upon earth; for one is your father, who is in heaven.—*Matt.* xxiii. 9.

For you have not received the spirit of bondage again in fear; but you have received the spirit of adoption of sons, whereby we cry: Abba (Father).— *Rom.* viii. 15.

And I will receive you; and I will be a Father to you; and you shall be my sons and daughters, saith the Lord Almighty.—*2 Cor.* vi. 18.

And because you are sons, God hath sent the Spirit of his Son into your hearts, crying: Abba, Father.—*Gal.* iv. 6.

For this cause I bow my knees to the Father of our Lord Jesus Christ,

Of whom all paternity in heaven and earth is named.—*Eph.* iii. 14, 15.

One God and Father of all, who is above all, and through all, and in us all.—*Eph.* iv. 6.

And if you invoke as Father him who, without respect of persons, judgeth according to every one's work: converse in fear during the time of your sojourning here.—*1 Peter* i. 17.

FATHER, ACKNOWLEDGMENT THAT GOD IS OUR

Is this the return thou makest to the Lord, O foolish and senseless people? Is not he thy father, that hath possessed thee, and made thee, and created thee?—*Deut.* xxxii. 6.

And he (David) blessed the Lord before all the multitude, and he said: Blessed art thou, O Lord, the God of Israel, our father from eternity to eternity.—*1 Paral.* xxix. 10.

I have found David my servant: with my holy oil I have anointed him. . . .

He shall cry out to me: Thou art my father: my God, and the support of my salvation.—*Ps.* lxxxviii. 21, 27.

He boasteth that he hath the knowledge of God, and calleth himself the son of God.

... We are esteemed by him as triflers, and he abstaineth from our ways as from filthiness, and he preferreth the latter end of the just, and glorieth that he hath God for his father.—*Wis.* ii. 13, 16.

For thou art our father, and Abraham hath not known us, and Israel hath been ignorant of us: thou, O Lord, art our father, our redeemer, from everlasting is thy name.—*Is.* lxiii. 16.

And now, O Lord, thou art our father, and we are clay: and thou art our maker, and we are all the works of thy hands.—*Is.* lxiv. 8.

Therefore at the least, from this time, call to me: Thou art my father, the guide of my virginity.—*Jer.* iii. 4.

Have we not all one father? hath not one God created us? why then doth every one of us despise his brother, violating the covenant of our fathers?—*Malach.* ii. 10.

FATHER FOR US, GOD HAS THE LOVE OF A

I will be to him a father, and he shall be to me a son: and if he commit any iniquity, I will correct him with the rod of men, and with the stripes of the children of men.—2 *Kings* vii. 14.

For whom the Lord loveth, he chastiseth: and as a father in the son he pleaseth himself.—*Prov.* iii. 12.

For when they (*i.e.* the children of Israel) were tried, and chastised with mercy, they knew how the wicked were judged with wrath and tormented.

For thou didst admonish and try them as a father: but the others, as a severe king, thou didst examine and condemn.—*Wis.* xi. 10, 11.

Surely Ephraim is an honorable son to me, surely he is a tender child: for since I spoke of him, I will still remember him. Therefore are my bowels troubled for him: pitying, I will pity him, saith the Lord.—*Jer.* xxxi. 20.

And I was like a foster-father to Ephraim, I carried them in my arms: and they knew not that I healed them. I will draw them with the cords of Adam, with the bands of love: and I will be to them as one that taketh off the yoke on their jaws: and I put his meat to him that he might eat.—*Osee* xi. 3, 4.

FAVOR TO US, GOD'S SPECIAL

Because thou art a holy people to the Lord thy God. The Lord thy God hath chosen thee, to be his peculiar people of all peoples that are upon the earth.

Not because you surpass all nations in number, is the Lord joined unto you, and hath chosen you, for you are the fewest of any people:

But because the Lord hath loved you, and hath kept his oath, which he swore to your fathers: and hath brought you out with a strong hand, and redeemed you from the house of bondage, out of the hand of Pharao, the king of Egypt.—*Deut.* vii. 6-8.

Behold, heaven is the Lord's thy God, and the heaven of heaven, the earth and all things that are therein.

And yet the Lord hath been closely joined to thy fathers, and loved them, and chose their seed after them, that is to say, you, out of all nations, as this day it is proved.—*Deut.* x. 14, 15.

And the Lord hath chosen thee this day, to be his peculiar people, as he hath spoken to thee, and to keep all his commandments:

And to make thee higher than all nations which he hath created, to his own praise, and name, and glory: that thou mayst be a holy people of the Lord thy God, as he hath spoken.—*Deut.* xxvi. 18, 19.

But thou, Israel, art my servant, Jacob, whom I have chosen, the seed of Abraham my friend:

In whom I have taken thee from the ends of the earth, and from the remote parts thereof have called thee, and said to thee: Thou art my servant, I have chosen thee, and have not cast thee away.—*Is.* xli. 8, 9.

Thus saith the Lord thy redeemer, the Holy One of Israel: I am the Lord thy God that teach thee profitable things, that govern thee in the way that thou walkest.—*Is.* xlviii. 17.

For, not as with other nations (whom the Lord patiently expecteth, that when the day of judgment shall come, he may punish them in the fulness of their sins):

Doth he also deal with us, so as to suffer our sins to come to their height, and then take vengeance on us.

And therefore he never withdraweth his mercy from us: but though he chastise his people with adversity, he forsaketh them not.—2 *Mach.* vi. 14-16.

And his disciples came and said to him: Why speakest thou to them in parables?

Who answered, and said to them: Because to you it is given to know the mysteries of the kingdom of heaven: but to them it is not given.—*Matt.* xiii. 10, 11.

But blessed are your eyes because they see, and your ears because they hear.

For, amen, I say to you, many prophets and just men have desired to see the things that you see, and have not seen them, and to hear the things that you hear, and have not heard them. —*Matt.* xiii. 16, 17.

Fear not, little flock, for it hath pleased your Father to give you a kingdom.—*Luke* xii. 32.

Abraham, your father, rejoiced that he might see my day: he saw it, and was glad.—*John* viii. 56.

I will not now call you servants: for the servant knoweth not what his lord doth. But I have called you friends: because all things whatsoever I have heard of my Father, I have made known to you.—*John* xv. 15.

For the promise is to you, and to your children, and to all that are far off, whomsoever the Lord our God shall call.—*Acts* ii. 39.

Blessed be the God and Father of our Lord Jesus Christ, who hath blessed us with spiritual blessings in heavenly places, in Christ:

As he chose us in him before the foundation of the world, that we should be holy and unspotted in his sight in charity.

Who hath predestinated us unto the adoption of children through Jesus Christ unto himself: according to the purpose of his will.—*Eph.* i. 3-5.

Now therefore you are no more strangers and foreigners; but you are fellow-citizens with the saints, and the domestics of God,

Built upon the foundation of the apostles and prophets, Jesus Christ himself being the chief corner stone.— *Eph.* ii. 19, 20.

Giving thanks to God the Father, who hath made us worthy to be partakers of the lot of the saints in light:

Who hath delivered us from the power of darkness, and hath translated us into the kingdom of the Son of his love,

In whom we have redemption through his blood, the remission of sins.—*Col.* i. 12-14.

Whereof (*i.e.* the Church) I am made a minister according to the dispensation of God, which is given me towards you, that I may fulfil the word of God:

The mystery which hath been hidden from ages and generations, but now is manifested to his saints,

To whom God would make known the riches of the glory of this mystery among the Gentiles, which is Christ, in you the hope of glory.—*Col.* i. 25-27.

But when the goodness and kindness of God our Saviour appeared:

Not by the works of justice, which we have done, but according to his mercy he saved us, by the laver of regeneration, and renovation of the Holy Ghost;

Whom he hath poured forth upon us abundantly, through Jesus Christ our Saviour:

That, being justified by his grace, we may be heirs, according to hope of life everlasting.—*Titus* iii. 4-7.

All these died according to faith, not having received the promises, but beholding them afar off, and saluting them, and confessing that they are pilgrims and strangers on the earth.

. . . And all these, being approved by the testimony of faith, received not the promise;

God providing some better thing for us, that they should not be perfected without us.—*Heb.* xi. 13, 39, 40.

Of which salvation the prophets have inquired and diligently searched, who prophesied of the grace to come in you. . . .

To whom it was revealed that not to

themselves, but to you they ministered those things which are now declared to you by them that have preached the gospel to you, the Holy Ghost being sent down from heaven, on whom the angels desire to look.—1 *Peter* i. 10, 12.

But you are a chosen generation, a kingly priesthood, a holy nation, a purchased people: that you may declare his virtues, who hath called you out of darkness into his marvellous light: Who in time past were not a people: but are now the people of God. Who had not obtained mercy; but now have obtained mercy.—1 *Peter* ii. 9, 10.

As all things of his divine power which appertain to life and godliness, are given us, through the knowledge of him who hath called us by his own proper glory and virtue.

By whom he hath given us most great and precious promises: that by these you may be made partakers of the divine nature: flying the corruption of that concupiscence which is in the world.—2 *Peter* i. 3, 4.

FAVOR TO US, ACKNOWLEDGMENT OF GOD'S SPECIAL

O Lord, thou hast crowned us, as with a shield of thy good will.—*Ps.* v. 13.

The Lord ruleth me: and I shall want nothing.

He hath set me in a place of pasture.

He hath brought me up on the water of refreshment:

He hath converted my soul.

He hath led me on the paths of justice, for his own name's sake.—*Ps.* xxii. 1-3.

For behold thou hast loved truth: the uncertain and hidden things of thy wisdom thou hast made manifest to me.—*Ps.* l. 8.

The Lord hath been mindful of us, and hath blessed us.

He hath blessed the house of Israel: he hath blessed the house of Aaron.—*Ps.* cxiii. (*Heb.* cxv.) 12.

The Lord hath done great things for us: we are become joyful.—*Ps.* cxxv. 3.

He hath not done in like manner to every nation: and his judgments he hath not made manifest to them.—*Ps.* cxlvii. 20.

For if thou didst punish the enemies of thy servants, and that deserved to die, with so great deliberation, giving them time and place whereby they might be changed from their wickedness:

With what circumspection hast thou judged thy own children, to whose parents thou hast sworn, and made covenants of good promises?

Therefore, whereas thou chastisest us, thou scourgest our enemies very many ways, to the end that when we judge, we may think on thy goodness: and when we are judged, we may hope for thy mercy.—*Wis.* xii. 20-22.

We are happy, O Israel; because the things that are pleasing to God, are made known to us.—*Bar.* iv. 4.

FAVOR TO US, OBLIGATIONS RESULTING FROM GOD'S SPECIAL

And you, O children of Sion, rejoice, and be joyful in the Lord your God: because he hath given you a teacher of justice, and he will make the early and the latter rain to come down to you as in the beginning.—*Joel* ii. 23.

And that servant who knew the will of his lord, and prepared not himself, and did not according to his will, shall be beaten with many stripes.

But he that knew not, and did things worthy of stripes, shall be beaten with few stripes. And unto whomsoever much is given, of him much shall be required: and to whom they have committed much, of him they will demand the more.—*Luke* xii. 47, 48.

See then the goodness and the severity of God: towards them indeed that are fallen, the severity: but towards thee, the goodness of God, if thou abide in goodness, otherwise thou also shalt be cut off.—*Rom.* xi. 22.

As you know in what manner, entreating and comforting you, (as a father doth his children,)

We testified to every one of you, that you would walk worthy of God, who hath called you unto his kingdom and glory.—1 *Thess.* ii. 11, 12.

Therefore ought we more diligently to observe the things which we have heard, lest perhaps we should let them slip.

For if the word, spoken by angels, became steadfast, and every transgression and disobedience received a just recompense of reward:

How shall we escape if we neglect so great salvation? which having begun to be declared by the Lord, was confirmed unto us by them that heard him.—*Heb.* ii. 1-3.

FEAR OF GOD, THE

And therefore I am troubled at his presence, and when I consider him, I am made pensive with fear.—*Job* xxiii. 15.

For I have always feared God as waves swelling over me, and his weight I was not able to bear.—*Job* xxxi. 23.

But as for me, in the multitude of thy mercy, I will come into thy house; I will worship towards thy holy temple, in thy fear.—*Ps.* v. 8.

The fear of the Lord is holy, enduring for ever and ever.—*Ps.* xviii. 10.

Come, children, hearken to me: I will teach you the fear of the Lord.—*Ps.* xxxiii. 12.

Pierce thou my flesh with thy fear: for I am afraid of thy judgments.—*Ps.* cxviii. 120.

Blessed is the man that is always fearful: but he that is hardened in mind, shall fall into evil.—*Prov.* xxviii. 14.

Favor is deceitful, and beauty is vain: the woman that feareth the Lord, she shall be praised.—*Prov.* xxxi. 30.

The fear of the Lord is honor, and glory, and gladness, and a crown of joy. The fear of the Lord shall delight the heart, and shall give joy, and gladness, and length of days.—*Ecclus.* i. 11, 12.

The fear of God is the glory of the rich, and of the honorable, and of the poor. . . .

The great man, and the judge, and the mighty is in honor: and there is none greater than he that feareth God. *Ecclus.* x. 25, 27.

And they that remain shall know, that there is nothing better than the fear of God: and that there is nothing sweeter than to have regard to the commandments of the Lord.—*Ecclus.* xxiii. 37.

Much experience is the crown of old men, and the fear of God is their glory. —*Ecclus.* xxv. 8.

How great is he that findeth wisdom and knowledge! but there is none above him that feareth the Lord.

The fear of God hath set itself above all things:

Blessed is the man to whom it is given to have the fear of God: he that holdeth it, to whom shall he be likened? —*Ecclus.* xxv. 13-15.

Riches and strength lift up the heart: but above these is the fear of the Lord.

There is no want in the fear of the Lord, and it needeth not to seek for help.

The fear of the Lord is like a paradise of blessing, and they have covered it above all glory.—*Ecclus.* xl. 26-28.

There is none like to thee, O Lord: thou art great, and great is thy name in might.

Who shall not fear thee, O king of nations? for thine is the glory: among all the wise men of the nations, and in all their kingdoms, there is none like unto thee.—*Jer.* x. 6, 7.

My covenant was with [1]him of life and peace: and I gave him fear: and he feared me, and he was afraid before my name.—*Malach.* ii. 5.

Who shall not fear thee, O Lord, and magnify thy name? For thou only art holy: for all nations shall come, and shall adore in thy sight, because thy judgments are manifest.—*Apoc.* xv. 4.

FEAR OF GOD IS TRUE WISDOM, THE

And he said to man: Behold the fear of the Lord, that is wisdom: and to depart from evil, is understanding.—*Job* xxviii. 28.

The fear of the Lord is the beginning of wisdom.—*Ps.* cx. 10.

The fear of the Lord is the lesson of wisdom: and humility goeth before glory.—*Prov.* xv. 33.

The fear of the Lord is the beginning of wisdom, and was created with the faithful in the womb, it walketh with chosen women, and is known with the just and faithful.

[1]Levi.

The fear of the Lord is the religiousness of knowledge.—*Ecclus.* i. 16, 17.

To fear God is the fulness of wisdom, and fulness is from the fruits thereof. . . .

The fear of the Lord is a crown of wisdom, filling up peace and the fruit of salvation. . . .

The root of wisdom is to fear the Lord: and the branches thereof are long-lived.—*Ecclus.* i. 20, 22, 25.

And give place to the fear of the most High: for the fear of God is all wisdom, and therein is to fear God, and the disposition of the law is in all wisdom.—*Ecclus.* xix. 18.

Better is a man that hath less wisdom, and wanteth understanding, with the fear of God, than he that aboundeth in understanding, and transgresseth the law of the most High.—*Ecclus.* xix. 21.

The perfection of the fear of God is wisdom and understanding.—*Ecclus.* xxi. 13.

FEAR OF GOD THE SOURCE OF OTHER VIRTUES, THE

Blessed is the man that feareth the Lord: he shall delight exceedingly in his commandments.—*Ps.* cxi. 1.

They that fear the Lord, have hoped in the Lord: he is their helper and their protector.—*Ps.* cxiii. (*Heb.* cxv.) 11.

In the fear of the Lord is confidence of strength, and there shall be hope for his children.—*Prov.* xiv. 26.

It is good that thou shouldst hold up the just, yea, and from him withdraw not thy hand: for he that feareth God, neglecteth nothing.—*Eccles.* vii. 19.

They that fear the Lord, will not be incredulous to his word. . . .

They that fear the Lord, will seek after the things that are well pleasing to him. . . .

They that fear the Lord, will prepare their hearts, and in his sight, will sanctify their souls.

They that fear the Lord, keep his commandments, and will have patience even until his visitation,

Saying: If we do not penance, we shall fall into the hands of the Lord, and not into the hands of men.—*Ecclus.* ii. 18-22.

He that feareth the Lord, honoreth his parents, and will serve them as his masters, that brought him into the world.—*Ecclus.* iii. 8.

He that feareth God, shall likewise have good friendship: because according to him, shall his friend be.—*Ecclus.* vi. 17.

He that feareth God, will do good.— *Ecclus.* xv. 1.

He that hateth to be reproved, walketh in the trace of a sinner; and he that feareth God, will turn to his own heart.—*Ecclus.* xxi. 7.

The fear of God is the beginning of his love: and the beginning of faith is to be fast joined unto it.—*Ecclus.* xxv. 16.

He that feareth the Lord, will receive his discipline.—*Ecclus.* xxxii. 18.

They that fear the Lord, shall find just judgment, and shall kindle justice as a light.—*Ecclus.* xxxii. 20.

Because for this end thou hast put thy fear in our hearts, to the intent that we should call upon thy name, and praise thee in our captivity, for we are converted from the iniquity of our fathers, who sinned before thee.—*Bar.* iii. 7.

Having therefore these promises, dearly beloved, let us cleanse ourselves from all defilement of the flesh and of the spirit, perfecting sanctification in the fear of God.—2 *Cor.* vii. 1.

FEAR OF GOD KEEPS US FROM SIN, THE

And Moses said to the people: Fear not: for God is come to prove you, and that the dread of him might be in you, and you should not sin.—*Ex.* xx. 20.

The fear of the Lord hateth evil: I hate arrogance, and pride, and every wicked way, and a mouth with a double tongue.—*Prov.* viii. 13.

The fear of the Lord is a fountain of life, to decline from the ruin of death.—*Prov.* xiv. 27.

By mercy and truth, iniquity is redeemed: and by the fear of the Lord, men depart from evil.—*Prov.* xvi. 6.

The fear of the Lord driveth out sin. —*Ecclus.* i. 27.

The Lord hateth all abomination of

error, and they that fear him, shall not love it.—*Ecclus.* xv. 13.

Unless thou hold thyself diligently in the fear of the Lord, thy house shall quickly be overthrown.—*Ecclus.* xxvii. 4.

FEAR OF GOD IMPOSES CERTAIN OBLIGATIONS UPON US, THE

Ye that fear the Lord, praise him: all ye, the seed of Jacob, glorify him.—*Ps.* xxi. 24.

Who is the man that feareth the Lord? He hath appointed him a law, in the way he hath chosen.—*Ps.* xxiv. 12.

Ye that fear the Lord, wait for his mercy: and go not aside from him, lest ye fall.

Ye that fear the Lord, believe him: and your reward shall not be made void.

Ye that fear the Lord, hope in him: and mercy shall come to you, for your delight.

Ye that fear the Lord, love him, and your hearts shall be enlightened.—*Ecclus.* ii. 7-10.

Remember the fear of God, and be not angry with thy neighbor.—*Ecclus.* xxviii. 8.

FEAR OF GOD PLEASING TO THE ALMIGHTY, THE

But they that fear thee, shall be great with thee in all things.—*Judith* xvi. 19.

The Lord taketh pleasure in them that fear him: and in them that hope in his mercy.—*Ps.* cxlvi. 11.

That seed of men shall be honored, which feareth God: but that seed shall be dishonored, which transgresseth the commandments of the Lord.

In the midst of brethren, their chief is honorable: so shall they that fear the Lord, be in his eyes.—*Ecclus.* x. 23, 24.

The eyes of the Lord are towards them that fear him, and he knoweth all the work of man.—*Ecclus.* xv. 20.

But to whom shall I have respect, but to him that is poor and little, and of a contrite heart, and that trembleth at my words?—*Is.* lxvi. 2.

But in every nation, he that feareth him (God), and worketh justice, is acceptable to him.—*Acts* x. 35.

FEAR OF GOD REWARDED IN THIS LIFE

The angel of the Lord shall encamp round about them that fear him: and shall deliver them.—*Ps.* xxxiii. 8.

Fear the Lord, all ye his saints: for there is no want to them that fear him.—*Ps.* xxxiii. 10.

He hath given food to them that fear him.—*Ps.* cx. 5.

They that fear the Lord, have hoped in the Lord: he is their helper and their protector.

. . . He hath blessed all that fear the Lord, both little and great.—*Ps.* cxiii. (*Heb.* cxv.) 11, 13.

Let them that fear the Lord, now say, that his mercy endureth for ever.—*Ps.* cxvii. 4.

Blessed are all they that fear the Lord: that walk in his ways.

For thou shalt eat the labors of thy hands: blessed art thou, and it shall be well with thee.

Thy wife, as a fruitful vine, on the side of thy house.

Thy children, as olive plants, round about thy table.

Behold, thus shall the man be blessed that feareth the Lord.—*Ps.* cxxvii. 1-4.

He will do the will of them that fear him: and he will hear their prayer, and save them.—*Ps.* cxliv. 19.

The fear of the Lord shall prolong days: and the years of the wicked shall be shortened.—*Prov.* x. 27.

No evils shall happen to him that feareth the Lord, but in temptation God will keep him, and deliver him from evils.—*Ecclus.* xxxiii. 1.

He that feareth the Lord, shall tremble at nothing, and shall not be afraid: for he is his hope.

The soul of him that feareth the Lord, is blessed.

To whom doth he look, and who is his strength?

The eyes of the Lord are upon them that fear him, he is their powerful protector, and strong stay, a defence from the heat, and a cover from the sun at noon,

A preservation from stumbling, and a help from falling; he raiseth up the soul, and enlighteneth the eyes, and

giveth health, and life, and blessing.—
Ecclus. xxxiv. 16-20.

FEAR OF GOD REWARDED HEREAFTER, THE

In his sight the malignant is brought to nothing: but he glorifieth them that fear the Lord.—*Ps.* xiv. 4.

Who is the man that feareth the Lord? . . . His soul shall dwell in good things: and his seed shall inherit the land.

The Lord is a firmament to them that fear him: and his covenant shall be made manifest to them.—*Ps.* xxiv. 12-14.

O how great is the multitude of thy sweetness, O Lord, which thou hast hidden for them that fear thee!

Which thou hast wrought for them that hope in thee, in the sight of the sons of men.—*Ps.* xxx. 20.

Behold, the eyes of the Lord are on them that fear him: and on them that hope in his mercy.

To deliver their souls from death; and feed them in famine.—*Ps.* xxxii. 18, 19.

Surely his salvation is near to them that fear him.—*Ps.* lxxxiv. 10.

For according to the height of the heaven above the earth: he hath strengthened his mercy towards them that fear him. . . .

As a father hath compassion on his children, so hath the Lord compassion on them that fear him; for he knoweth our frame.

He remembereth that we are dust.— *Ps.* cii. 11, 13, 14.

But the mercy of the Lord is from eternity and unto eternity upon them that fear him.—*Ps.* cii. 17.

The fear of the Lord is unto life: and he shall abide in fulness, without being visited with evil.—*Prov.* xix. 23.

Let not thy heart envy sinners: but be thou in the fear of the Lord all the day long:

Because thou shalt have hope in the latter end, and thy expectation shall not be taken away.—*Prov.* xxiii. 17, 18.

But though a sinner do evil a hundred times, and by patience be borne withal, I know from thence that it shall be well with them that fear God, who dread his face.—*Eccles.* viii. 12.

With him that feareth the Lord, it shall go well in the latter end, and in the day of his death he shall be blessed. —*Ecclus.* i. 13.

Then they that feared the Lord spoke every one with his neighbor: and the Lord gave ear, and heard it: and a book of remembrance was written before him for them that fear the Lord and think on his name.

And they shall be my special possession, saith the Lord of hosts, in the day that I do judgment: and I will spare them, as a man spareth his son that serveth him.—*Malach.* iii. 16, 17.

But unto you that fear my name, the Sun of justice shall arise, and health in his wings: and you shall go forth, and shall leap like calves of the herd. —*Malach.* iv. 2.

And his mercy is from generation unto generations, to them that fear him.—*Luke* i. 50.

FEAR OF GOD COMMANDED BY THE ALMIGHTY

From the day in which thou didst stand before the Lord thy God in Horeb, when the Lord spoke to me, saying: Call together the people unto me, that they may hear my words, and may learn to fear me all the time that they live on the earth, and may teach their children.—*Deut.* iv. 10.

And now, Israel, what doth the Lord thy God require of thee, but that thou fear the Lord thy God, and walk in his ways, and love him, and serve the Lord thy God, with all thy heart, and with all thy soul?—*Deut.* x. 12.

And I say to you, my friends: Be not afraid of them who kill the body, and after that, have no more that they can do.

But I will show you whom you shall fear: fear ye him, who after he hath killed, hath power to cast into hell. Yea, I say to you, fear him.—*Luke* xii. 4, 5.

FEAR GOD, EXHORTATION TO

Serve ye the Lord with fear: and rejoice unto him with trembling.—*Ps.* ii. 11.

Let all the seed of Israel fear him: because he hath not slighted nor despised the supplication of the poor man.—*Ps.* xxi. 25.

Let all the earth fear the Lord, and let all the inhabitants of the world be in awe of him.—*Ps.* xxxii. 8.

Fear the Lord, all ye his saints: for there is no want to them that fear him. —*Ps.* xxxiii. 10.

Be not wise in thy own conceit: fear God, and depart from evil.—*Prov.* iii. 7.

Let not thy heart envy sinners: but be thou in the fear of the Lord all the day long.—*Prov.* xxiii. 17.

Let us all hear together the conclusion of the discourse. Fear God, and keep his commandments: for this is all man.—*Eccles.* xii. 13.

Be not incredulous to the fear of the Lord: and come not to him with a double heart.—*Ecclus.* i. 36.

Believe God, and he will recover thee: and direct thy way, and trust in him. Keep his fear, and grow old therein.—*Ecclus.* ii. 6.

With all thy soul fear the Lord, and reverence his priests.—*Ecclus.* vii. 31.

Let just men be thy quests, and let thy glory be in the fear of God.—*Ecclus.* ix. 22.

And give place to the fear of the most High: for the fear of God is all wisdom.—*Ecclus.* xix. 18.

Sanctify the Lord of hosts himself: and let him be your fear, and let him be your dread.

And he shall be a sanctification to you.—*Is.* viii. 13, 14.

Having therefore these promises, dearly beloved, let us cleanse ourselves from all defilement of the flesh and of the spirit, perfecting sanctification in the fear of God.—*2 Cor.* vii. 1.

Therefore receiving an immovable kingdom, we have grace; whereby let us serve, pleasing God, with fear and reverence.

For our God is a consuming fire.—*Heb.* xii. 28, 29.

And I saw another angel flying through the midst of heaven, having the eternal gospel, to preach unto them that sit upon the earth, and over every nation, and tribe, and tongue, and people:

Saying with a loud voice: Fear the Lord, and give him honor, because the hour of his judgment is come; and adore ye him, that made heaven and earth, the sea, and the fountains of water.—*Apoc.* xiv. 6, 7.

FEARLESSNESS THAT RESULTS FROM A GOOD CONSCIENCE, THE

See Conscience, the fruit of a good —page 75.

FEARLESSNESS THAT RESULTS FROM CONFIDENCE IN GOD, THE

I have slept and have taken my rest: and I have risen up, because the Lord hath protected me.

I will not fear thousands of the people, surrounding me: arise, O Lord; save me, O my God.—*Ps.* iii. 6, 7.

For though I should walk in the midst of the shadow of death, I will fear no evils, for thou art with me. Thy rod and thy staff, they have comforted me.—*Ps.* xxii. 4.

The Lord is my light and my salvation, whom shall I fear?

The Lord is the protector of my life: of whom shall I be afraid? . . .

If armies in camp should stand together against me, my heart shall not fear.

If a battle should rise up against me, in this will I be confident.—*Ps.* xxvi. 1, 3.

Our God is our refuge and strength: a helper in troubles, which have found us exceedingly.

Therefore we will not fear, when the earth shall be troubled; and the mountains shall be removed into the heart of the sea.—*Ps.* xlv. 2, 3.

In God I will praise my words, in God I have put my trust: I will not fear what flesh can do against me.—*Ps.* lv. 5.

His truth shall compass thee with a shield: thou shalt not be afraid of the terror of the night.

Of the arrow that flieth in the day, of the business that walketh about in the dark: of invasion, or of the noonday devil.

A thousand shall fall at thy side, and ten thousand at thy right hand: but it shall not come nigh thee.—*Ps.* xc. 5-7.

The Lord is my helper: I will not fear what man can do unto me.—*Ps.* cxvii. 6.

I am ready, and am not troubled: that I may keep thy commandments.—*Ps.* cxviii. 60.

He that feareth the Lord, shall tremble at nothing, and shall not be afraid: for he is his hope.—*Ecclus.* xxxiv. 16.

Behold, God is my saviour, I will deal confidently, and will not fear: because the Lord is my strength, and my praise, and he is become my salvation.—*Is.* xii. 2.

The Lord God is my helper, therefore am I not confounded: therefore have I set my face as a most hard rock, and I know that I shall not be confounded.

He is near that justifieth me, who will contend with me? let us stand together, who is my adversary? let him come near to me.

Behold the Lord God is my helper: who is he that shall condemn me? Lo, they shall all be destroyed as a garment, the moth shall eat them up.—*Is.* l. 7-9.

That being delivered from the hand of our enemies, we may serve him without fear,

In holiness and justice before him, all our days.—*Luke* i. 74, 75.

For you have not received the spirit of bondage again in fear; but you have received the spirit of adoption of sons, whereby we cry: Abba (Father).—*Rom.* viii. 15.

What shall we then say to these things? If God be for us, who is against us?—*Rom.* viii. 31.

FEARLESSNESS THAT RESULTS FROM CONFIDENCE IN GOD, EXHORTATION TO HAVE THE

Hear, O Israel, you join battle this day against your enemies, let not your heart be dismayed, be not afraid, do not give back, fear ye them not:

Because the Lord your God is in the midst of you, and will fight for you against your enemies, to deliver you from danger.—*Deut.* xx. 3, 4.

Behold, I command thee, take courage, and be strong. Fear not and be not dismayed: because the Lord thy God is with thee in all things whatsoever thou shalt go to.—*Jos.* i. 9.

If thou sleep, thou shalt not fear: thou shalt rest, and thy sleep shall be sweet.

Be not afraid of sudden fear, nor of the power of the wicked falling upon thee.

For the Lord will be at thy side, and will keep thy foot that thou be not taken.—*Prov.* iii. 24-26.

Fear not, for I am with thee: turn not aside, for I am thy God: I have strengthened thee, and have helped thee, and the right hand of my just one hath upheld thee. . . .

For I am the Lord thy God who take thee by the hand, and say to thee: Fear not, I have helped thee.—*Is.* xli. 10, 13.

Hearken to me, you that know what is just, my people who have my law in your heart: fear ye not the reproach of men, and be not afraid of their blasphemies. . . .

I, I myself will comfort you: who art thou, that thou shouldst be afraid of a mortal man, and of the son of man, who shall wither away like grass?

And thou hast forgotten the Lord thy maker, who stretched out the heavens, and founded the earth.—*Is.* li. 7, 12, 13.

But Jesus, having heard the word that was spoken, saith to the ruler of the synagogue: Fear not, only believe. —*Mark* v. 36.

But they seeing him walking upon the sea, thought it was an apparition, and they cried out.

For they all saw him, and were troubled. And immediately he spoke with them, and said to them: Have a good heart, it is I, fear ye not.—*Mark* vi. 49, 50.

Fear not, little flock, for it hath pleased your Father to give you a kingdom.—*Luke* xii. 32.

Peace I leave with you, my peace I give unto you: not as the world giveth, do I give unto you. Let not your heart be troubled, nor let it be afraid.—*John* xiv. 27.

But who is he that can hurt you, if you be zealous of good?

But if also you suffer any thing for justice' sake, blessed are ye. And be not afraid of their fear, and be not troubled.—1 *Peter* iii. 13, 14.

FEAST DAYS AND THEIR OBSERVANCE

And this day (the Phase) shall be for a memorial to you: and you shall keep it a feast to the Lord in your generations, with an everlasting observance. . . .

The first day shall be holy and solemn, and the seventh day shall be kept with the like solemnity: you shall do no work in them, except those things that belong to eating.—*Ex.* xii. 14, 16.

Three times every year you shall celebrate feasts to me.

Thou shalt keep the feast of unleavened bread. Seven days shalt thou eat unleavened bread, as I commanded thee, in the time of the month of new corn, when thou didst come forth out of Egypt: thou shalt not appear empty before me.

And the feast of the harvest of the first-fruits of thy work, whatsoever thou hast sown in the field. The feast also in the end of the year, when thou hast gathered in all thy corn out of the field.

Thrice a year shall all thy males appear before the Lord thy God.—*Ex.* xxiii. 14-17.

Three times in a year shall all thy males appear before the Lord thy God, in the place which he shall choose: in the feast of unleavened bread, in the feast of weeks, and in the feast of tabernacles. No one shall appear with his hands empty before the Lord:

But every one shall offer according to what he hath, according to the blessing of the Lord his God, which he shall give him.—*Deut.* xvi. 16, 17.

And Nehemias (he is Athersatha), and Esdras the priest and scribe, and the Levites who interpreted to all the people, said: This is a holy day to the Lord our God: do not mourn nor weep: for all the people wept, when they heard the words of the law.

And he said to them: Go, eat fat meats, and drink sweet wine, and send portions to them that have not prepared for themselves: because it is the holy day of the Lord, and be not sad: for the joy of the Lord is our strength.— 2 *Esd.* viii. 9, 10.

[1]They said in their heart, the whole kindred of them together: Let us abolish all the festival days of God from the land.—*Ps.* lxxiii. 8.

This is the day which the Lord hath made: let us be glad, and rejoice therein.—*Ps.* cxvii. 24.

Why doth one day excel another, and one light another, and one year another year, when all come of the sun?

By the knowledge of the Lord they were distinguished, the sun being made, and keeping his commandment.

And he ordered the seasons, and holidays of them, and in them they celebrate festivals at an hour.

Some of them God made high and great days, and some of them he put in the number of ordinary days.— *Ecclus.* xxxiii. 7-10.

What will you do in the solemn day, in the day of the feast of the Lord?— *Osee* ix. 5.

And Judas, and his brethren, and all the church of Israel decreed, that the day of the dedication of the altar should be kept in its season from year to year for eight days, from the five and twentieth day of the month of Casleu, with joy and gladness.— 1 *Mach.* iv. 59.

FIDELITY OF GOD, THE

See also: Truth of God, the—page 568.

God is not a man, that he should lie, nor as the son of man, that he should be changed. Hath he said, then, and will he not do? hath he spoken, and will he not fulfil?—*Num.* xxiii. 19.

And thou shalt know that the Lord thy God, he is a strong and faithful God, keeping his covenant and mercy to them that love him, and to them that keep his commandments, unto a thousand generations.—*Deut.* vii. 9.

[1]The enemies of God and of His people.

The works of God are perfect, and all his ways are judgments: God is faithful, and without any iniquity, he is just and right.—*Deut.* xxxii. 4.

And (Solomon) said: Lord God of Israel, there is no God like thee, in heaven above, or on earth beneath: who keepest covenant and mercy with thy servants that have walked before thee with all their heart.

Who hast kept with thy servant David, my father, what thou hast promised him: with thy mouth, thou didst speak, and with thy hands, thou hast performed, as this day proveth.— 3 *Kings* viii. 23, 24.

For the word of the Lord is right, and all his works are done with faithfulness.—*Ps.* xxxii. 4.

He hath given food to them that fear him. He will be mindful for ever of his covenant.—*Ps.* cx. 5.

The Lord is faithful in all his words; and holy in all his works.—*Ps.* cxliv. 13.

Every word of God is fire tried: he is a buckler to them that hope in him. —*Prov.* xxx. 5.

The Lord of hosts hath sworn, saying: Surely, as I have thought, so shall it be: and as I have purposed, So shall it fall out.—*Is.* xiv. 24, 25.

They (the mercies of the Lord) are new every morning, great is thy faithfulness.—*Lam.* iii. 23.

In the promise also of God, he (Abraham) staggered not by distrust; but was strengthened in faith, giving glory to God,

Most fully knowing, that whatsoever he has promised, he is able also to perform.—*Rom.* iv. 20, 21.

God is faithful: by whom you are called unto the fellowship of his Son, Jesus Christ our Lord.—1 *Cor.* i. 9.

And may the God of peace himself sanctify you in all things; that your whole spirit, and soul, and body, may be preserved blameless in the coming of our Lord Jesus Christ.

He is faithful, who hath called you, who also will do it.—1 *Thess.* v. 23, 24.

But God is faithful, who will strengthen and keep you from evil.— 2 *Thess.* iii. 3.

For which cause I also suffer these things: but I am not ashamed. For I know whom I have believed, and I am certain that he is able to keep that which I have committed unto him, against that day.—2 *Tim.* i. 12.

If we believe not, he continueth faithful, he cannot deny himself.— 2 *Tim.* ii. 13.

For God making promise to Abraham, because he had no one greater by whom he might swear, swore by himself. . . .

Wherein God, meaning more abundantly to show to the heirs of the promise, the immutability of his counsel, interposed an oath:

That by two immutable things, in which it is impossible for God to lie, we may have the strongest comfort, who have fled for refuge, to hold fast the hope set before us.

Which we have as an anchor of the soul, sure and firm, and which entereth in even within the veil.—*Heb.* vi. 13, 17-19.

Let us hold fast the confession of our hope without wavering (for he is faithful that hath promised.)—*Heb.* x. 23.

FIDELITY TO ONE ANOTHER

Lying lips are an abomination to the Lord: but they that deal faithfully, please him.—*Prov.* xii. 22.

Many men are called merciful: but who shall find a faithful man?—*Prov.* xx. 6.

To trust to an unfaithful man in the time of trouble, is like a rotten tooth, and weary foot,

And one that looseth his garment in cold weather.—*Prov.* xxv. 19, 20.

A faithful man shall be much praised.—*Prov.* xxviii. 20.

All bribery and injustice shall be blotted out, and fidelity shall stand for ever.—*Ecclus.* xl. 12.

FLATTERY

As silver is tried in the fining-pot, and gold in the furnace: so a man is tried by the mouth of him that praiseth.—*Prov.* xxvii. 21.

He that rebuketh a man, shall afterward find favor with him, more than he that by a flattering tongue, deceiveth him.—*Prov.* xxviii. 23.

A man that speaketh to his friend with flattering and dissembling words, spreadeth a net for his feet.—*Prov.* xxix. 5.

A prince that gladly heareth lying words, hath all his servants wicked.—*Prov.* xxix. 12.

It is better to be rebuked by a wise man, than to be deceived by the flattery of fools.—*Eccles.* vii. 6.

Praise not any man before death, for a man is known by his children.—*Ecclus.* xi. 30.

When a rich man hath been deceived, he hath many helpers: he hath spoken proud things, and they have justified him.

. . . The rich man spoke, and all held their peace, and what he said, they extol even to the clouds.—*Ecclus.* xiii. 26, 28.

For neither have we used, at any time, the speech of flattery, as you know; nor taken an occasion of covetousness, God is witness.—1 *Thess.* ii. 5.

FOLLOWING GOD

Follow the Lord your God, and fear him, and keep his commandments, and hear his voice: him you shall serve, and to him you shall cleave.—*Deut.* xiii. 4.

It is great glory to follow the Lord: for length of days shall be received from him.—*Ecclus.* xxiii. 38.

And now, we follow thee with all our heart, and we fear thee, and seek thy face.—*Dan.* iii. 41.

FOLLOWING CHRIST

See also: Disciple of Christ—page 114.

And Jesus walking by the sea of Galilee, saw two brethren, Simon, who is called Peter, and Andrew, his brother, casting a net into the sea (for they were fishers).

And he saith to them: Come ye after me, and I will make you to be fishers of men.

And they immediately leaving their nets, followed him.

And going on from thence, he saw other two brethren, James, the son of Zebedee, and John, his brother, in a ship with Zebedee their father, mending their nets: and he called them.

And they forthwith left their nets and father, and followed him.—*Matt.* iv. 18-22.

And a certain scribe came, and said to him: Master, I will follow thee, whithersoever thou shalt go.

And Jesus saith to him: The foxes have holes, and the birds of the air, nests: but the Son of man hath not where to lay his head.

And another of his disciples said to him: Lord, suffer me first to go and bury my father.

But Jesus said to him: Follow me, and let the dead bury their dead.—*Matt.* viii. 19-22.

And when Jesus passed on from thence, he saw a man sitting in the custom house, named Matthew; and he saith to him: Follow me. And he arose up, and followed him.—*Matt.* ix. 9.

Jesus saith to him: If thou wilt be perfect, go, sell what thou hast, and give to the poor, and thou shalt have treasure in heaven; and come, follow me.—*Matt.* xix. 21.

Then Peter answering, said to him: Behold, we have left all things, and have followed thee: what therefore shall we have?

And Jesus said to them: Amen, I say to you, that you who have followed me, in the regeneration, when the Son of man shall sit on the seat of his majesty, you also shall sit on twelve seats, judging the twelve tribes of Israel.—*Matt.* xix. 27, 28.

Again therefore Jesus spoke to them, saying: I am the light of the world: he that followeth me, walketh not in darkness, but shall have the light of life.—*John* viii. 12.

If any man minister to me, let him follow me; and where I am, there also shall my minister be. If any man minister to me, him will my Father honor.—*John* xii. 26.

FOOLISH, THE

O Lord, how great are thy works! thy thoughts are exceeding deep.

The senseless man shall not know:

nor will the fool understand these things.—*Ps.* xci. 6, 7.

A golden ring in a swine's snout, a woman fair and foolish.—*Prov.* xi. 22.

The way of a fool is right in his own eyes: but he that is wise hearkeneth unto counsels.—*Prov.* xii. 15.

A fool will laugh at sin, but among the just, grace shall abide.—*Prov.* xiv. 9.

A wise man feareth and declineth from evil: the fool leapeth over, and is confident.—*Prov.* xiv. 16.

It is better to meet a bear robbed of her whelps, than a fool trusting in his own folly.—*Prov.* xvii. 12.

What doth it avail a fool to have riches, seeing he cannot buy wisdom? —*Prov.* xvii. 16.

A foolish son is the anger of the father: and the sorrow of the mother that bore him.—*Prov.* xvii. 25.

The perverse are hard to be corrected, and the number of fools is infinite.—*Eccles.* i. 15.

Yea, and the fool when he walketh in the way, whereas he himself is a fool, esteemeth all men fools.—*Eccles.* x. 3.

Honor and glory is in the word of the wise, but the tongue of the fool is his ruin.—*Ecclus.* v. 15.

Advise not with fools, for they cannot love but such things as please them.—*Ecclus.* viii. 20.

He that wanteth understanding thinketh vain things: and the foolish, and erring man, thinketh foolish things.—*Ecclus.* xvi. 23.

A fool shall have no friend, and there shall be no thanks for his good deeds.

For they that eat his bread, are of a false tongue. How often, and how many will laugh him to scorn!

For he doth not distribute with right understanding that which was to be had: in like manner also that which was not to be had.—*Ecclus.* xx. 17-19.

A fool lifteth up his voice in laughter: but a wise man will scarce laugh low to himself.—*Ecclus.* xxi. 23.

The lips of the unwise will be telling foolish things: but the words of the wise shall be weighed in a balance. The heart of fools is in their mouth:

and the mouth of wise men is in their heart.—*Ecclus.* xxi. 28, 29.

For my foolish people have not known me: they are foolish and senseless children: they are wise to do evil, but to do good, they have no knowledge. —*Jer.* iv. 22.

FOOLISH DESPISE WISDOM, THE

The fear of the Lord is the beginning of wisdom. Fools despise wisdom and instruction.—*Prov.* i. 7.

O children, how long will you love childishness, and fools covet those things which are hurtful to themselves, and the unwise hate knowledge?—*Prov.* i. 22.

Folly is joy to the fool: and the wise man maketh straight his steps.—*Prov.* xv. 21.

Wisdom shineth in the face of the wise: the eyes of fools are in the ends of the earth.—*Prov.* xvii. 24.

A fool receiveth not the words of prudence: unless you say those things which are in his heart.—*Prov.* xviii. 2.

How very unpleasant is wisdom to the unlearned, and the unwise will not continue with her.

She shall be to them as a mighty stone of trial, and they will cast her from them before it be long.—*Ecclus.* vi. 21, 22.

Doctrine to a fool is as fetters on the feet, and like manacles on the right hand.—*Ecclus.* xxi. 22.

FORGETFULNESS OF GOD

See also: Ingratitude to God— page 239.

Thou hast forsaken the God that begot thee, and hast forgotten the Lord that created thee.—*Deut.* xxxii. 18.

Can the rush be green without moisture? or a sedge-bush grow without water?

When it is yet in flower, and is not plucked up with the hand, it withereth before all herbs.

Even so are the ways of all that forget God, and the hope of the hypocrite shall perish.—*Job* viii. 11-13.

The wicked shall be turned into hell, all the nations that forget God.—*Ps.* ix. 18.

Thy mouth hath abounded with evil, and thy tongue framed deceits.

Sitting, thou didst speak against thy brother, and didst lay a scandal against thy mother's son: these things hast thou done, and I was silent.

Thou thoughtest unjustly that I should be like to thee: but I will reprove thee, and set before thy face.

Understand these things, you that forget God; lest he snatch you away, and there be none to deliver you.—*Ps.* xlix. 19-22.

And they believed his words: and they sang his praises.

They had quickly done, they forgot his works: and they waited not for his counsel. . . .

They forgot God, who saved them, who had done great things in Egypt.—*Ps.* cv. 12, 13, 21.

If I forget thee, O Jerusalem, let my right hand be forgotten.

Let my tongue cleave to my jaws, if I do not remember thee:

If I make not Jerusalem the beginning of my joy.—*Ps.* cxxxvi. 5, 6.

Because thou hast forgotten God thy saviour, and hast not remembered thy strong helper: therefore shalt thou plant good plants, and shalt sow strange seed.—*Is.* xvii. 10.

For whom hast thou been solicitous and afraid, that thou hast lied, and hast not been mindful of me, nor thought on me in thy heart? for I am silent, and as one that seeth not, and thou hast forgotten me.—*Is.* lvii. 11.

Will a virgin forget her ornament, or a bride her stomacher? but my people have forgotten me days without number.—*Jer.* ii. 32.

A voice was heard in the highways, weeping and howling of the children of Israel: because they have made their way wicked, they have forgotten the Lord their God.—*Jer.* iii. 21.

For you have forgotten God, who brought you up, and you have grieved Jerusalem, that nursed you.—*Bar.* iv. 8.

Therefore thus saith the Lord God: Because thou hast forgotten me, and hast cast me off behind thy back, bear thou also thy wickedness, and thy fornications.—*Ezech.* xxiii. 35.

According to their pastures they were filled, and were made full: and they lifted up their heart, and have forgotten me.—*Osee* xiii. 6.

FORGETFULNESS OF GOD, EXHORTATION AGAINST

And when the Lord thy God shall have brought thee into the land, for which he swore to thy fathers, Abraham, Isaac and Jacob: and shall have given thee great and goodly cities, which thou didst not build,

Houses full of riches, which thou didst not set up, cisterns which thou didst not dig, vineyards and oliveyards, which thou didst not plant,

And thou shalt have eaten and be full:

Take heed diligently lest thou forget the Lord, who brought thee out of the land of Egypt, out of the house of bondage.—*Deut.* vi. 10-13.

Take heed, and beware lest at any time thou forget the Lord thy God, and neglect his commandments and judgments and ceremonies, which I command thee this day:

Lest after thou hast eaten and art filled, hast built goodly houses, and dwelt in them,

And shalt have herds of oxen and flocks of sheep, and plenty of gold and of silver, and of all things,

Thy heart be lifted up, and thou remember not the Lord thy God, who brought thee out of the land of Egypt, out of the house of bondage:

And was thy leader in the great and terrible wilderness, wherein there was the serpent burning with his breath, and the scorpion and the dipsas, and no waters at all: who brought forth streams out of the hardest rock,

And fed thee in the wilderness with manna which thy fathers knew not. And after he had afflicted and proved thee, at the last he had mercy on thee,

Lest thou shouldst say in thy heart: My own might, and the strength of my own hand have achieved all these things for me.—*Deut.* viii. 11-17.

Remember these things, O Jacob, and Israel, for thou art my servant. I have formed thee, thou art my servant, O Israel, forget me not.—*Is.* xliv. 21.

FORGETFULNESS OF SELF

See also: Disinterestedness—page 115.

And when they prophesied in the camp, there ran a young man, and told Moses, saying: Eldad and Medad prophesy in the camp.

Forthwith Josue the son of Nun, the minister of Moses, and chosen out of many, said: My lord Moses, forbid them.

But he said: Why hast thou emulation for me? O that all the people might prophesy, and that the Lord would give them his spirit!—*Num.* xi. 27-29.

I speak the truth in Christ, I lie not, my conscience bearing me witness in the Holy Ghost; . . .

For I wished myself to be an anathema from Christ, for my brethren, who are my kinsmen according to the flesh.—*Rom.* ix. 1, 3.

Now this I say, that every one of you saith: I indeed am of Paul; and I am of Apollo; and I of Cephas; and I of Christ.

Is Christ divided? Was Paul then crucified for you? or were you baptized in the name of Paul?

I give God thanks, that I baptized none of you but Crispus and Caius;

Lest any should say that you were baptized in my name.—1 *Cor.* i. 12-15.

For while one saith, I indeed am of Paul; and another, I am of Apollo; are you not men? What then is Apollo, and what is Paul? . . .

I have planted, Apollo watered, but God gave the increase.

Therefore, neither he that planteth is anything, nor he that watereth; but God that giveth the increase.—1 *Cor.* iii. 4, 6, 7.

You are now full: you are now become rich; you reign without us; and I would to God you did reign, that we also might reign with you.—1 *Cor.* iv. 8.

FORGIVENESS OF SINS

The Lord is patient and full of mercy, taking away iniquity and wickedness.—*Num.* xiv. 18.

Who can make him clean that is conceived of unclean seed? is it not thou who only art?—*Job* xiv. 4.

Blessed are they whose iniquities are forgiven, and whose sins are covered.—*Ps.* xxxi. 1.

As far as the east is from the west, so far hath he removed our iniquities from us.

As a father hath compassion on his children, so hath the Lord compassion on them that fear him: for he knoweth our frame.

He remembereth that we are dust.—*Ps.* cii. 12-14.

For God is compassionate and merciful, and will forgive sins in the day of tribulation.—*Ecclus.* ii. 13.

For mercy and wrath are with him. He is mighty to forgive, and to pour out indignation.—*Ecclus.* xvi. 12.

Be comforted, be comforted, my people, saith your God.

Speak ye to the heart of Jerusalem, and call to her: for her evil is come to an end, her iniquity is forgiven.—*Is.* xl. 1, 2.

I am, I am he that blot out thy iniquities for my own sake, and I will not remember thy sins.—*Is.* xliii. 25.

I have blotted out thy iniquities as a cloud, and thy sins as a mist: return to me, for I have redeemed thee.—*Is.* xliv. 22.

He will turn again, and have mercy on us: he will put away our iniquities: and he will cast all our sins into the bottom of the sea.—*Mich.* vii. 19.

And behold they brought to him one sick of the palsy, lying in a bed. And Jesus, seeing their faith, said to the man sick of the palsy: Be of good heart, son, thy sins are forgiven thee.

And behold some of the scribes said within themselves: He blasphemeth.

And Jesus seeing their thoughts, said: Why do you think evil in your hearts?

Whether is easier, to say, Thy sins are forgiven thee: or to say, Arise and walk?

But that you may know that the Son of man hath power on earth to forgive sins, then said he to the man sick of the palsy, Arise, take up thy bed, and go into thy house.

And he arose, and went into his house.—*Matt.* ix. 2-7.

And there came a leper to him, beseeching him, and kneeling down, said to him: If thou wilt, thou canst make me clean.

And Jesus having compassion on him, stretched forth his hand; and touching him, saith to him: I will. Be thou made clean.

And when he had spoken, immediately the leprosy departed from him, and he was made clean.—*Mark* i. 40-42.

Wherefore I say to thee: Many sins are forgiven her, because she hath loved much. But to whom less is forgiven, he loveth less.

And he said to her: Thy sins are forgiven thee.—*Luke* vii. 47, 48.

And when they were come to the place which is called Calvary, they crucified him there; and the robbers, one on the right hand, and the other on the left.

And Jesus said: Father, forgive them, for they know not what they do. —*Luke* xxiii. 33, 34.

Peter saith to him: Thou shalt never wash my feet. Jesus answered him: If I wash thee not, thou shalt have no part with me.—*John* xiii. 8.

But God (who is rich in mercy) for his exceeding charity wherewith he loved us,

Even when we were dead in sins, hath quickened us together in Christ, (by whose grace you are saved,)

And hath raised us up together, and hath made us sit together in the heavenly places, through Christ Jesus.— *Eph.* ii. 4-6.

And you, when you were dead in your sins, and the uncircumcision of your heart; he hath quickened together with him, forgiving you all offences:

Blotting out the handwriting of the decree that was against us, which was contrary to us. And he hath taken the same out of the way, fastening it to the cross.—*Col.* ii. 13, 14.

I write unto you, little children, because your sins are forgiven you for his name's sake.—1 *John* ii. 12.

FORGIVENESS OF SINS, ACKNOWLEDGMENT OF

Thou hast sealed up my offences as it were in a bag, but hast cured my iniquity.—*Job* xiv. 17.

I have acknowledged my sin to thee, and my injustice I have not concealed.

I said, I will confess against myself my injustice to the Lord: and thou hast forgiven the wickedness of my sin.— *Ps.* xxxi. 5.

Thou shalt sprinkle me with hyssop, and I shall be cleansed: thou shalt wash me, and I shall be made whiter than snow.—*Ps.* l. 9.

Thou hast forgiven the iniquity of thy people: thou hast covered all their sins.—*Ps.* lxxxiv. 3.

If thou, O Lord, wilt mark iniquities: Lord, who shall stand it?

For with thee there is merciful forgiveness. . . .

Because with the Lord there is mercy: and with him plentiful redemption.

And he shall redeem Israel from all his iniquities.—*Ps.* cxxix. 3, 4, 7, 8.

But thou hast mercy upon all, because thou canst do all things, and overlookest the sins of men for the sake of repentance.—*Wis.* xi. 24.

How great is the mercy of the Lord, and his forgiveness to them that turn to him!—*Ecclus.* xvii. 28.

But thou hast delivered my soul that it should not perish, thou hast cast all my sins behind thy back.—*Is.* xxxviii. 17.

For I know that thou art a gracious and merciful God, patient and of much compassion, and easy to forgive evil.— *Jonas* iv. 2.

FORGIVENESS OF SINS, PROMISE OF

If I shut up heaven, and there fall no rain, or if I give orders, and command the locust to devour the land, or if I send pestilence among my people:

And my people, upon whom my name is called, being converted, shall make supplication to me, and seek out my face, and do penance for their most wicked ways: then will I hear from heaven, and will forgive their sins and will heal their land.—2 *Paral.* vii. 13, 14.

And they shall teach no more every man his neighbor, and every man his brother, saying: Know the Lord: for all shall know me from the least of them even to the greatest, saith the

Lord: for I will forgive their iniquity, and I will remember their sin no more. —*Jer.* xxxi. 34.

And I will cleanse them from all their iniquity, whereby they have sinned against me: and I will forgive all their iniquities, whereby they have sinned against me, and despised me.— *Jer.* xxxiii. 8.

And if I shall say to the wicked: Thou shalt surely die: and he do penance for his sin, and do judgment and justice,

And if that wicked man restore the pledge, and render what he had robbed, and walk in the commandments of life, and do no unjust thing: he shall surely live, and shall not die.

None of his sins which he hath committed, shall be imputed to him: he hath done judgment and justice, he shall surely live.—*Ezech.* xxxiii. 14-16.

I will heal their breaches, I will love them freely: for my wrath is turned away from them.—*Osee* xiv. 5.

FORGIVENESS OF SINS, GRATITUDE FOR

Blessed is thy name, O God of our fathers: who when thou hast been angry, wilt show mercy, and in the time of tribulation, forgivest the sins of them that call upon thee.—*Tob.* iii. 13.

Bless the Lord, O my soul, and never forget all he hath done for thee.

Who forgiveth all thy iniquities: who healeth all thy diseases.—*Ps.* cii. 2, 3.

And thou shalt say in that day: I will give thanks to thee, O Lord, for thou wast angry with me: thy wrath is turned away, and thou hast comforted me.—*Is.* xii. 1.

FORGIVENESS OF SINS, HOW TO OBTAIN

By mercy and faith, sins are purged away.—*Prov.* xv. 27.

He that loveth God, shall obtain pardon for his sins by prayer, and shall refrain himself from them, and shall be heard in the prayer of days.—*Ecclus.* iii. 4.

My son, hast thou sinned? do so no more: but for thy former sins also pray

that they may be forgiven thee.— *Ecclus.* xxi. 1.

Wash yourselves, be clean, take away the evil of your devices from my eyes: cease to do perversely,

Learn to do well: seek judgment, relieve the oppressed, judge for the fatherless, defend the widow.

And then come, and accuse me, saith the Lord: if your sins be as scarlet, they shall be made as white as snow: and if they be red as crimson, they shall be white as wool.—*Is.* i. 16-18.

Let the wicked forsake his way, and the unjust man his thoughts, and let him return to the Lord, and he will have mercy on him, and to our God: for he is bountiful to forgive.—*Is.*lv. 7.

But if the wicked do penance for all his sins which he hath committed, and keep all my commandments, and do judgment and justice, living he shall live, and shall not die.

I will not remember all his iniquities that he hath done: in his justice which he hath wrought, he shall live.—*Ezech.* xviii. 21, 22.

Now therefore saith the Lord: Be converted to me with all your heart, in fasting, and in weeping, and in mourning.

And rend your hearts, and not your garments, and turn to the Lord your God: for he is gracious and merciful, patient and rich in mercy, and ready to repent of the evil.

Who knoweth but he will return, and forgive, and leave a blessing behind him, sacrifice and libation to the Lord your God?—*Joel* ii. 12-14.

If we confess our sins, he is faithful and just, to forgive us our sins, and to cleanse us from all iniquity.—1 *John* i. 9.

FORGIVENESS OF SINS, PRAYER FOR

Forgive, I beseech thee, the sins of this people, according to the greatness of thy mercy, as thou hast been merciful to them from their going out of Egypt unto this place.—*Num.* xiv. 19.

But if they sin against thee (for there is no man who sinneth not), and thou being angry, deliver them up to their enemies, so that they be led away captives into the land of their enemies far or near;

Then if they do penance in their heart in the place of captivity, and being converted, make supplication to thee in their captivity, saying: We have sinned, we have done unjustly, we have committed wickedness:

And return to thee with all their heart, and all their soul, in the land of their enemies, to which they had been led captives: . . .

Then hear thou in heaven, in the firmament of thy throne, their prayers, and their supplications, and do judgment for them:

And forgive thy people that have sinned against thee, and all their iniquities, by which they have transgressed against thee.—*3 Kings* viii. 46-50.

And now, O Lord, think of me, and take not revenge of my sins, neither remember my offences; nor those of my parents.—*Tob.* iii. 3.

I have sinned: what shall I do to thee, O keeper of men? why hast thou set me opposite to thee, and I am become burdensome to myself?

Why dost thou not remove my sin, and why dost thou not take away my iniquity?—*Job* vii. 20, 21.

If I have sinned, and thou hast spared me for an hour: why dost thou not suffer me to be clean from my iniquity?—*Job* x. 14.

Thou indeed hast numbered my steps, but spare my sins.—*Job* xiv. 16.

The sins of my youth and my ignorances, do not remember. . . .

For thy name's sake, O Lord, thou wilt pardon my sin: for it is great. . . .

See my abjection and my labor; and forgive me all my sins.—*Ps.* xxiv. 7, 11, 18.

O forgive me, that I may be refreshed, before I go hence, and be no more.—*Ps.* xxxviii. 14.

O Lord, be thou merciful to me: heal my soul, for I have sinned against thee.—*Ps.* xl. 5.

Have mercy on me, O God, according to thy great mercy.

And according to the multitude of thy tender mercies, blot out my iniquity.

Wash me yet more from my iniquity, and cleanse me from my sin.

For I know my iniquity, and my sin is always before me. . . .

Turn away thy face from my sins, and blot out all my iniquities.—*Ps.* l. 3-5, 11.

Remember not our former iniquities: let thy mercies speedily prevent us, for we are become exceeding poor.

Help us, O God, our saviour: and for the glory of thy name, O Lord, deliver us: and forgive us our sins for thy name's sake.—*Ps.* lxxviii. 8, 9.

Be not very angry, O Lord, and remember no longer our iniquity: behold, see, we are all thy people.—*Is.* lxiv. 9.

Lord, if thou wilt, thou canst make me clean.—*Matt.* viii. 2.

And forgive us our sins, for we also forgive every one that is indebted to us.—*Luke* xi. 4.

FORGIVING INJURIES

See also: Love of our enemies—
page 298.

The learning of a man is known by patience: and his glory is to pass over wrongs.—*Prov.* xix. 11.

And forgive us our debts, as we also forgive our debtors.—*Matt.* vi. 12.

For if you will forgive men their offences, your heavenly Father will forgive you also your offences.

But if you will not forgive men, neither will your Father forgive you your offences.—*Matt.* vi. 14, 15.

Then his lord called him; and said to him: Thou wicked servant, I forgave thee all the debt, because thou besoughtest me:

Shouldst not thou then have had compassion also on thy fellow-servant, even as I had compassion on thee?

And his lord being angry, delivered him to the torturers, until he paid all the debt.

So also shall my heavenly Father do to you, if you forgive not every one his brother from your hearts.—*Matt.* xviii. 32-35.

And when they were come to the place which is called Calvary, they crucified him there; and the robbers, one on the right hand, and the other on the left.

And Jesus said: Father, forgive them, for they know not what they do. —*Luke* xxiii. 33, 34.

And they stoned Stephen, invoking, and saying: Lord Jesus, receive my spirit.

And falling on his knees, he cried with a loud voice, saying: Lord, lay not this sin to their charge.—*Acts* vii. 58, 59.

FORGIVING INJURIES COMMANDED BY CHRIST

If therefore thou offer thy gift at the altar, and there thou remember that thy brother hath any thing against thee;

Leave there thy offering before the altar, and go first to be reconciled to thy brother: and then coming, thou shalt offer thy gift.—*Matt.* v. 23, 24.

Then came Peter unto him, and said: Lord, how often shall my brother offend against me, and I forgive him? till seven times?

Jesus saith to him: I say not to thee, till seven times; but till seventy times seven times.—*Matt.* xviii. 21, 22.

And when you shall stand to pray, forgive, if you have aught against any man; that your Father also who is in heaven, may forgive you your sins.

But if you will not forgive, neither will your Father that is in heaven, forgive you your sins.—*Mark* xi. 25, 26.

Judge not, and you shall not be judged. Condemn not, and you shall not be condemned. Forgive, and you shall be forgiven.—*Luke* vi. 37.

Take heed to yourselves. If thy brother sin against thee, reprove him: and if he do penance, forgive him.

And if he sin against thee seven times in a day, and seven times in a day be converted unto thee, saying, I repent; forgive him.—*Luke* xvii. 3, 4.

FORGIVE INJURIES, EXHORTATION TO

Remember not any injury done thee by thy neighbor, and do thou nothing by deeds of injury.—*Ecclus.* x. 6.

Forgive thy neighbor, if he hath hurt thee: and then shall thy sins be forgiven to thee when thou prayest.

Man to man reserveth anger, and doth he seek remedy of God?

He hath no mercy on a man like himself, and doth he entreat for his own sins?

He that is but flesh, nourisheth anger, and doth he ask forgiveness of God? who shall obtain pardon for his sins?

Remember thy last things, and let enmity cease.—*Ecclus.* xxviii. 2-6.

Bless them that persecute you: bless, and curse not.—*Rom.* xii. 14.

And be ye kind one to another; merciful, forgiving one another, even as God hath forgiven you in Christ.— *Eph.* iv. 32.

Bearing with one another, and forgiving one another, if any have a complaint against another: even as the Lord hath forgiven you, so do you also. —*Col.* iii. 13.

FORNICATION

See: Unchastity—page 569.

FORSAKING GOD

See also: Turning away from God— page 569.

The beloved grew fat and kicked: he grew fat, and thick and gross, he forsook God who made him, and departed from God his saviour.—*Deut.* xxxii. 15.

Thou hast forsaken the God that begot thee, and hast forgotten the Lord that created thee.—*Deut.* xxxii. 18.

Thus saith the Lord God: Why transgress you the commandment of the Lord, which will not be for your good, and have forsaken the Lord, to make him forsake you?—2 *Paral.* xxiv. 20.

Our fathers have sinned and done evil in the sight of the Lord God, forsaking him: they have turned away their faces from the tabernacle of the Lord, and turned their backs.—2 *Paral.* xxix. 6.

Woe to the sinful nation, a people laden with iniquity, a wicked seed, ungracious children: they have forsaken the Lord, they have blasphemed the Holy One of Israel, they are gone away backwards.—*Is.* i. 4.

Be astonished, O ye heavens, at this, and ye gates thereof, be very desolate, saith the Lord.

For my people have done two evils. They have forsaken me, the fountain of living water, and have digged to themselves cisterns, broken cisterns, that can hold no water.—*Jer.* ii. 12, 13.

Thy own wickedness shall reprove thee, and thy apostasy shall rebuke thee. Know thou, and see that it is an evil and a bitter thing for thee, to have left the Lord thy God, and that my fear is not with thee, saith the Lord, the God of hosts.—*Jer.* ii. 19.

Why will you contend with me in judgment? you have all forsaken me, saith the Lord.—*Jer.* ii. 29.

FORSAKING GOD, PUNISHMENT FOR

If thou seek him (God), thou shalt find him: but if thou forsake him, he will cast thee off for ever.—1 *Paral.* xxviii. 9.

The Lord is with you, because you have been with him. If you seek him, you shall find: but if you forsake him, he will forsake you.—2 *Paral.* xv. 2.

The hand of our God is upon all them that seek him in goodness: and his power and strength, and wrath upon all them that forsake him.—1 *Esd.* viii. 22.

Blessed is he that is defended from a wicked tongue, that hath not passed into the wrath thereof, and that hath not drawn the yoke thereof, and hath not been bound in its bands. . . .

They that forsake God shall fall into it, and it shall burn in them, and shall not be quenched, and it shall be sent upon them as a lion, and as a leopard it shall tear them.—*Ecclus.* xxviii. 23, 27.

And he shall destroy the wicked and the sinners together: and they that have forsaken the Lord, shall be consumed. —*Is.* i. 28.

Is Israel a bondman, or a homeborn slave? why then is he become a prey? . . .

Hath not this been done to thee, because thou hast forsaken the Lord thy God at that time, when he led thee by the way?—*Jer.* ii. 14, 17.

And if you shall say: Why hath the Lord our God done all these things to us? thou shalt say to them: As you have forsaken me, and served a strange god in your own land, so shall you serve strangers in a land that is not your own.—*Jer.* v. 19.

Thou hast forsaken me, saith the Lord, thou art gone backward: and I will stretch out my hand against thee, and I will destroy thee: I am weary of entreating thee.—*Jer.* xv. 6.

For thus saith the Lord of hosts, the God of Israel: Behold, I will take away out of this place in your sight, and in your days, the voice of mirth, and the voice of gladness, the voice of the bridegroom, and the voice of the bride.

And when thou shalt tell this people all these words, and they shall say to thee: Wherefore hath the Lord pronounced against us all this great evil? what is our iniquity? and what is our sin, that we have sinned against the Lord our God?

Thou shalt say to them: Because your fathers forsook me, saith the Lord: and went after strange gods, and served them, and adored them: and they forsook me, and kept not my law.

And you also have done worse than your fathers: for behold every one of you walketh after the perverseness of his evil heart, so as not to hearken to me.

So I will cast you forth out of this land, into a land which you know not, nor your fathers: and there you shall serve strange gods day and night, which shall not give you any rest.—*Jer.* xvi. 9-13.

O Lord, the hope of Israel: all that forsake thee shall be confounded: they that depart from thee, shall be written in the earth: because they have forsaken the Lord, the vein of living waters.—*Jer.* xvii. 13.

FORSAKING THE LAW OF GOD

Thou hast rebuked the proud: they are cursed who decline from thy commandments.

. . . Thou hast despised all them that fall off from thy judgments: for

their thought is unjust.—*Ps.* cxviii.
21, 118.

Woe to them that have lost patience,
and that have forsaken the right ways,
and have gone aside into crooked ways.
And what will they do, when the
Lord shall begin to examine?—*Ecclus.*
ii. 16, 17.

Woe to you, ungodly men, who have
forsaken the law of the most high Lord.
And if you be born, you shall be born
in malediction: and if you die, in
malediction shall be your portion.—
Ecclus. xli. 11, 12.

And the Lord said: Because they
have forsaken my law, which I gave
them, and have not heard my voice,
and have not walked in it.

But they have gone after the perverseness of their own heart, and after
Baalim, which their fathers taught
them.

Therefore thus saith the Lord of
hosts, the God of Israel: Behold I will
feed this people with wormwood, and
give them water of gall to drink.

And I will scatter them among the
nations, which they and their fathers
have not known: and I will send the
sword after them till they be consumed.—*Jer.* ix. 13-16.

This is the book of the commandments of God, and the law, that is for
ever: all they that keep it, shall come
to life: but they that have forsaken it,
to death.—*Bar.* iv. 1.

God be merciful unto us: it is not
profitable for us to forsake the law and
the justices of God.—1 *Mach.* ii. 21.

FORTITUDE

See also: Martyrs, the—page 304.

But now the scourge is come upon
thee, and thou faintest: it hath touched
thee, and thou art troubled.

Where is thy fear, thy fortitude, thy
patience, and the perfection of thy
ways?—*Job* iv. 5, 6.

Do ye manfully, and let your heart
be strengthened, all ye that hope in the
Lord.—*Ps.* xxx. 25.

You therefore, my sons, take courage, and behave manfully in the law:
for by it you shall be glorious.—
1 *Mach.* ii. 64.

And fear ye not them that kill the
body, and are not able to kill the soul:
but rather fear him that can destroy
both soul and body in hell.—*Matt.* x. 28.

And Jesus answering, said: You
know not what you ask. Can you
drink the chalice that I shall drink?
They say to him: We can.—*Matt.* xx. 22.

Thomas therefore, who is called
Didymus, said to his fellow-disciples:
Let us also go, that we may die with
him.—*John* xi. 16.

For which cause we faint not; but
though our outward man is corrupted,
yet the inward man is renewed day by
day.—2 *Cor.* iv. 16.

And (pray) for me, that speech may
be given me, that I may open my mouth
with confidence, to make known the
mystery of the gospel.

For which I am an ambassador in a
chain, so that therein I may be bold to
speak according as I ought.—*Eph.* vi.
19, 20.

FRAUD

The Lord spoke to Moses, saying:

Whosoever shall sin, and despising
the Lord, shall deny to his neighbor the
thing delivered to his keeping, which
was committed to his trust; or shall by
force extort any thing, or commit oppression;

Or shall find a thing lost, and denying it, shall also swear falsely, or shall
do any other of the many things, wherein men are wont to sin:

Being convicted of the offence, he
shall restore

All that he would have gotten by
fraud, in the principal, and the fifth
part besides to the owner, whom he
wronged.—*Lev.* vi. 1-5.

A deceitful balance is an abomination before the Lord: and a just weight
is his will.—*Prov.* xi. 1.

Diverse weights and diverse measures, both are abominable before God.—
Prov. xx. 10.

The bread of lying is sweet to a man:
but afterwards his mouth shall be filled
with gravel.—*Prov.* xx. 17.

Diverse weights are an abomination
before the Lord: a deceitful balance is
not good.—*Prov.* xx. 23.

He that gathereth treasures by a lying tongue, is vain and foolish, and shall stumble upon the snares of death. —*Prov.* xxi. 6.

For among my people are found wicked men, that lie in wait as fowlers, setting snares and traps to catch men.

As a net is full of birds, so their houses are full of deceit: therefore are they become great and enriched. . . .

Shall I not visit for these things, saith the Lord? or shall not my soul take revenge on such a nation?—*Jer.* v. 26, 27, 29.

Woe to him that buildeth up his house by injustice, and his chambers not in judgment: that will oppress his friend without cause, and will not pay him his wages.—*Jer.* xxii. 13.

Hear this, you that crush the poor, and make the needy of the land to fail,

Saying: When will the month be over, and we shall sell our wares: and the sabbath, and we shall open the corn: that we may lessen the measure, and increase the sicle, and may convey in deceitful balances,

That we may possess the needy for money, and the poor, for a pair of shoes, and may sell the refuse of the corn?

The Lord hath sworn against the pride of Jacob: Surely I will never forget all their works.

Shall not the land tremble for this, and every one mourn that dwelleth therein: and rise up altogether as a river, and be cast out, and run down as the river of Egypt?—*Amos* viii. 4-8.

Shall I justify wicked balances, and the deceitful weights of the bag?

By which her rich men were filled with iniquity, and the inhabitants thereof have spoken lies, and their tongue was deceitful in their mouth.

And I therefore began to strike thee with desolation for thy sins.—*Mich.* vi. 11-13.

FRAUD FORBIDDEN BY GOD

Do not any unjust thing in judgment, in rule, in weight, or in measure.

Let the balance be just, and the weights equal, the bushel just, and the sextary equal. I am the Lord your God, that brought you out of the land of Egypt.—*Lev.* xix. 35, 36.

Thou shalt not take nor remove thy neighbor's landmark, which thy predecessors have set in thy possession, which the Lord thy God will give thee in the land that thou shalt receive to possess.—*Deut.* xix. 14.

Thou shalt not have diverse weights in thy bag, a greater and a less:

Neither shall there be in thy house a greater bushel and a less.

Thou shalt have a just and a true weight, and thy bushel shall be equal and true: that thou mayst live a long time upon the land which the Lord thy God shall give thee.

For the Lord thy God abhorreth him that doth these things, and he hateth all injustice.—*Deut.* xxv. 13-16.

For this is the will of God, your sanctification; that you should abstain from fornication; . . .

And that no man overreach, nor circumvent his brother in business: because the Lord is the avenger of all these things, as we have told you before, and have testified.—1 *Thess.* iv. 3, 6.

FREEDOM, TRUE

See: Liberty—page 277.

FRIENDS AND FRIENDSHIP

Have pity on me, have pity on me, at least you my friends, because the hand of the Lord hath touched me.—*Job* xix. 21.

Grace and friendship deliver a man: keep these for thyself, lest thou fall under reproach.—*Prov.* xxv. 10.

Ointment and perfumes rejoice the heart: and the good counsels of a friend are sweet to the soul.—*Prov.* xxvii. 9.

It is better therefore that two should be together, than one: for they have the advantage of their society:

If one fall, he shall be supported by the other: woe to him that is alone, for when he falleth, he hath none to lift him up.—*Eccles.* iv. 9, 10.

A friend, if he continue steadfast, shall be to thee as thyself, and shall act with confidence among them of thy household.—*Ecclus.* vi. 11.

A faithful friend is a strong defence: and he that hath found him, hath found a treasure.

Nothing can be compared to a faithful friend, and no weight of gold and silver is able to countervail the goodness of his fidelity.

A faithful friend is the medicine of life and immortality: and they that fear the Lord, shall find him.

He that feareth God, shall likewise have good friendship: because according to him shall his friend be.—*Ecclus.* vi. 14-17.

A new friend is as new wine: it shall grow old, and thou shalt drink it with pleasure.—*Ecclus.* ix. 15.

A friend shall not be known in prosperity, and an enemy shall not be hidden in adversity.

In the prosperity of a man, his enemies are grieved: and a friend is known in his adversity.—*Ecclus.* xii. 8, 9.

Blessed is he that findeth a true friend, and that declareth justice to an ear that heareth.—*Ecclus.* xxv. 12.

FRIENDS, FIDELITY TO OUR

He that taketh away mercy from his friend, forsaketh the fear of the Lord. —*Job* vi. 14.

He that despiseth his friend, is mean of heart: but the wise man will hold his peace.—*Prov.* xi. 12.

He that is a friend loveth at all times: and a brother is proved in distress.—*Prov.* xvii. 17.

Thy own friend, and thy father's friend forsake not: and go not into thy brother's house in the day of thy affliction.—*Prov.* xxvii. 10.

Do not transgress against thy friend deferring money, nor despise thy dear brother for the sake of gold.—*Ecclus.* vii. 20.

Forsake not an old friend, for the new will not be like to him.—*Ecclus.* ix. 14.

He that flingeth a stone at birds, shall drive them away: so he that upbraideth his friend, breaketh friendship.— *Ecclus.* xxii. 25.

Keep fidelity with a friend in his poverty, that in his prosperity also thou mayst rejoice.

In the time of his trouble, continue faithful to him, that thou mayst also be heir with him in his inheritance. . . .

I will not be ashamed to salute a friend, neither will I hide myself from his face: and if any evil happen to me by him, I will bear it.—*Ecclus.* xxii. 28, 29, 31.

Forget not thy friend in thy mind, and be not unmindful of him in thy riches.—*Ecclus.* xxxvii. 6.

FRIENDS, CAUTION IN THE CHOICE OF

Be in peace with many, but let one of a thousand be thy counsellor.

If thou wouldst get a friend, try him before thou takest him, and do not credit him easily.—*Ecclus.* vi. 6, 7.

Bring not every man into thy house: for many are the snares of the deceitful.—*Ecclus.* xi. 31.

FRIENDS, FALSE

For there is a friend for his own occasion, and he will not abide in the day of thy trouble.

And there is a friend that turneth to enmity; and there is a friend that will disclose hatred and strife and reproaches.

And there is a friend a companion at the table, and he will not abide in the day of distress.—*Ecclus.* vi. 8-10.

If thou give, he will make use of thee: and if thou have nothing, he will forsake thee.

If thou have any thing, he will live with thee, and will make thee bare, and he will not be sorry for thee.

If he have need of thee, he will deceive thee, and smiling upon thee, will put thee in hope: he will speak thee fair, and will say: What wantest thou?

And he will shame thee by his meats, till he have drawn thee dry twice or thrice, and at last he will laugh at thee: and afterward, when he seeth thee, he will forsake thee, and shake his head at thee.—*Ecclus.* xiii. 5-8.

To-day a man lendeth, and to-morrow he asketh it again: such a man as this is hateful.—*Ecclus.* xx. 16.

Every friend will say: I also am his friend: but there is a friend, that is only a friend in name. Is not this a grief even to death?—*Ecclus.* xxxvii. 1.

There is a companion who rejoiceth

with his friend in his joys, but in the time of trouble, he will be against him.

There is a companion who condoleth with his friend for his belly's sake, and he will take up a shield against the enemy.—*Ecclus.* xxxvii. 4, 5.

FRIENDS, WE SHOULD NOT BETRAY THE CONFIDENCE OF OUR

See: Confidence of a friend—page 74.

FRIENDSHIP, OR FAVOR, OF GOD

For wrath is in his indignation; and life in his good will.—*Ps.* xxix. 6.

His throat most sweet, and he is all lovely: such is my beloved, and he is my friend, O ye daughters of Jerusalem.—*Cant.* v. 16.

For she (wisdom) is an infinite treasure to men! which they that use, become the friends of God, being commended for the gift of discipline.—*Wis.* vii. 14.

But thou, Israel, art my servant, Jacob, whom I have chosen, the seed of Abraham my friend.—*Is.* xli. 8.

His sisters therefore sent to him, saying: Lord, behold, he whom thou lovest is sick. . . .

Now Jesus loved Martha, and her sister Mary, and Lazarus.—*John* xi. 3, 5.

You are my friends, if you do the things that I command you.

I will not now call you servants: for the servant knoweth not what his lord doth. But I have called you friends: because all things whatsoever I have heard of my Father, I have made known to you.—*John* xv. 14, 15.

FRUGALITY OR MODERATION IN EATING AND DRINKING

The meadows are open, and the green herbs have appeared, and the hay is gathered out of the mountains.

Lambs are for thy clothing: and kids for the price of the field.

Let the milk of the goats be enough for thy food, and for the necessities of thy house, and for maintenance for thy handmaids.—*Prov.* xxvii. 25, 26, 27.

Use as a frugal man the things that are set before thee: lest, if thou eatest much, thou be hated.—*Ecclus.* xxxi. 19.

How sufficient is a little wine for a man well taught, and in sleeping, thou shalt not be uneasy with it, and thou shalt feel no pain. . . .

Sound and wholesome sleep with a moderate man: he shall sleep till morning, and his soul shall be delighted with him.—*Ecclus.* xxxi. 22, 24.

Wine taken with sobriety is equal life to men: if thou drink it moderately, thou shalt be sober. . . .

Wine was created from the beginning to make men joyful, and not to make them drunk.

Wine drunken with moderation is the joy of the soul and the heart.

Sober drinking is health to soul and body.—*Ecclus.* xxxi. 32, 35-37.

By surfeiting, many have perished: but he that is temperate, shall prolong life.—*Ecclus.* xxxvii. 34.

For every creature of God is good, and nothing to be rejected that is received with thanksgiving.—1 *Tim.* iv. 4.

Do not still drink water, but use a little wine for thy stomach's sake, and thy frequent infirmities.—1 *Tim.* v. 23.

GENEROSITY TOWARD GOD

And the people rejoiced when they promised their offerings willingly: because they offered them to the Lord with all their heart: and David the king rejoiced also with a great joy.

And he blessed the Lord before all the multitude, and he said: . . .

I know, my God, that thou provest hearts, and lovest simplicity, wherefore I also in the simplicity of my heart, have joyfully offered all these things: and I have seen with great joy thy people which are here present, offer thee their offerings.—1 *Paral.* xxix. 9, 10, 17.

Honor the Lord with thy substance, and give him of the first of all thy fruits:

And thy barns shall be filled with abundance, and thy presses shall run over with wine.—*Prov.* iii. 9, 10.

My son, if thou have anything, do good to thyself, and offer to God worthy offerings.—*Ecclus.* xiv. 11.

Give glory to God with a good heart: and diminish not the first fruits of thy hands.

In every gift show a cheerful countenance, and sanctify thy tithes with joy.

Give to the most High according to what he hath given to thee, and with a good eye do according to the ability of thy hands:

For the Lord maketh recompense, and will give thee seven times as much.— *Ecclus.* xxxv. 10-13.

And entering into the house, they found the child with Mary his mother, and falling down, they adored him; and opening their treasures, they offered him gifts; gold, frankincense and myrrh.—*Matt.* ii. 11.

And Jesus sitting over against the treasury, beheld how the people cast money into the treasury, and many that were rich cast in much.

And there came a certain poor widow, and she cast in two mites, which make a farthing.

And calling his disciples together, he saith to them: Amen I say to you, this poor widow hath cast in more than all they who have cast into the treasury.

For all they did cast in of their abundance; but she, of her want, cast in all she had, even her whole living.—*Mark* xii. 41-44.

GENEROSITY TOWARD ONE ANOTHER

According to thy ability, be merciful.

If thou have much, give abundantly: if thou have little, take care even so to bestow willingly a little.

For thus thou storest up to thyself a good reward for the day of necessity.— *Tob.* iv. 8-10.

The lips of many shall bless him that is liberal of his bread, and the testimony of his truth is faithful.—*Ecclus.* xxxi. 28.

Give to him that asketh of thee, and from him that would borrow of thee turn not away.—*Matt.* v. 42.

Heal the sick, raise the dead, cleanse the lepers, cast out devils: freely have you received, freely give.—*Matt.* x. 8.

Now this I say: He who soweth sparingly, shall also reap sparingly: and he who soweth in blessings, shall also reap blessings.

Every one as he hath determined in his heart, not with sadness, or of necessity: for God loveth a cheerful giver.— *2 Cor.* ix. 6, 7.

GIFT, GOD THE AUTHOR OF EVERY GOOD

[1]And take the blessing, which I have brought thee, and which God hath given me, who giveth all things.—*Gen.* xxxiii. 11.

The tabernacles of robbers abound, and they provoke God boldly; whereas it is he that hath given all into their hands.—*Job* xii. 6.

My heart shall rejoice in thy salvation: I will sing to the Lord, who giveth me good things: yea, I will sing to the name of the Lord, the most high.— *Ps.* xii. 6.

And for all these things bless the Lord, that made thee, and that replenisheth thee with all his good things.— *Ecclus.* xxxii. 17.

If you then, being evil, know how to give good gifts to your children: how much more will your Father who is in heaven, give good things to them that ask him?—*Matt.* vii. 11.

Neither is he served with men's hands, as though he needed any thing; seeing it is he who giveth to all life, and breath, and all things.—*Acts* xvii. 25.

He that spared not even his own Son, but delivered him up for us all, how hath he not also, with him, given us all things?—*Rom.* viii. 32.

But to every one of us is given grace, according to the measure of the giving of Christ.

Wherefore he saith: Ascending on high, he led captivity captive; he gave gifts to men.—*Eph.* iv. 7, 8.

Charge the rich of this world not to be high-minded, nor to trust in the uncertainty of riches, but in the living God (who giveth us abundantly all things to enjoy).—1 *Tim.* vi. 17.

Every best gift, and every perfect gift, is from above, coming down from the Father of lights, with whom there

[1]Jacob, on his return from Laban, speaking to Esau.

is n(change, nor shadow of alteration. —*James* i. 17.

GIVE TO GOD OF OUR GOODS, WE SHOULD

See: Generosity toward God— page 164.

GIVE OURSELVES TO GOD, WE SHOULD

My son, give me thy heart: and let thy eyes keep my ways.—*Prov.* xxiii. 26.

My beloved to me, and I to him, who feedeth among the lilies.—*Cant.* ii. 16.

Have pity on thy own soul, pleasing God, and contain thyself: gather up thy heart in his holiness: and drive away sadness far from thee.—*Ecclus.* xxx. 24.

GIVING UP ALL FOR GOD'S SAKE

Hearken, O daughter, and see, and incline thy ear: and forget thy people and thy father's house.

And the king shall greatly desire thy beauty; for he is the Lord thy God, and him they shall adore.—*Ps.* xliv. 11, 12.

He that loveth father or mother more than me, is not worthy of me; and he that loveth son or daughter more than me, is not worthy of me.

And he that taketh not up his cross, and followeth me, is not worthy of me.

He that findeth his life, shall lose it: and he that shall lose his life for me, shall find it.—*Matt.* x. 37-39.

The kingdom of heaven is like unto a treasure hidden in a field. Which a man, having found, hid it, and for joy thereof, goeth and selleth all that he hath, and buyeth that field.

Again the kingdom of heaven is like to a merchant seeking good pearls.

Who, when he had found one pearl of great price, went his way, and sold all that he had, and bought it.—*Matt.* xiii. 44-46.

Then Peter answering, said to him: Behold we have left all things, and have followed thee: what therefore shall we have?

And Jesus said to them: Amen, I say to you, that you, who have followed me, in the regeneration, when the Son of man shall sit on the seat of his majesty, you also shall sit on twelve seats judging the twelve tribes of Israel.

And every one that hath left house, or brethren, or sisters, or father, or mother, or wife, or children, or lands, for my name's sake, shall receive an hundred fold and shall possess life everlasting.—*Matt.* xix. 27-29.

And Jesus looking on him, loved him, and said to him: One thing is wanting unto thee: go, sell whatsoever thou hast, and give to the poor, and thou shalt have treasure in heaven; and come, follow me.—*Mark* x. 21.

So likewise every one of you that doth not renounce all that he possesseth, cannot be my disciple.—*Luke* xiv. 33.

Amen, amen, I say to you, unless the grain of wheat, falling into the ground, die,

Itself remaineth alone. But if it die, it bringeth forth much fruit. He that loveth his life, shall lose it; and he that hateth his life in this world, keepeth it unto life eternal.—*John* xii. 24, 25.

But the things that were gain to me, the same I have counted loss for Christ.

Furthermore I count all things to be but loss for the excellent knowledge of Jesus Christ my Lord; for whom I have suffered the loss of all things, and count them but as dung, that I may gain Christ.—*Philipp.* iii. 7, 8.

By faith, Moses, when he was grown up, denied himself to be the son of Pharao's daughter;

Rather choosing to be afflicted with the people of God, than to have the pleasure of sin for a time,

Esteeming the reproach of Christ, greater riches than the treasure of the Egyptians. For he looked unto the reward.—*Heb.* xi. 24-26.

GLORIFYING GOD

See also: Praising God—page 396.

The Lord is my strength and my praise, and he is become salvation to me: he is my God, and I will glorify him: the God of my father, and I will exalt him.—*Ex.* xv. 2.

But now saith the Lord: Far be this from me: but whosoever shall glorify me, him will I glorify: but they that despise me, shall be despised.—1 *Kings* ii. 30.

I will give glory to the Lord according to his justice: and will sing to the name of the Lord, the most high.—*Ps.* vii. 18.

Therefore will I give glory to thee, O Lord, among the nations, and I will sing a psalm to thy name.—*Ps.* xvii. 50.

In God shall we glory all the day long: and in thy name we will give praise for ever.—*Ps.* xliii. 9.

The sacrifice of praise shall glorify me: and there is the way by which I will show him the salvation of God.— *Ps.* xlix. 23.

I will give glory to thee because thou hast heard me: and art become my salvation.—*Ps.* cxvii. 21.

What shall we be able to do to glorify him? for the Almighty himself is above all his works.

The Lord is terrible, and exceeding great, and his power is admirable. . . .

Who shall see him, and declare him? and who shall magnify him, as he is from the beginning?—*Ecclus.* xliii. 30, 31, 35.

I will give glory to thee, O Lord, O King, and I will praise thee, O God my Saviour.

I will give glory to thy name: for thou hast been a helper and protector to me.—*Ecclus.* li. 1, 2.

Glory to God in the highest; and on earth, peace to men of good will.—*Luke* ii. 14.

And the shepherds returned, glorifying and praising God, for all the things they had heard and seen, as it was told unto them.—*Luke* ii. 20.

In this is my Father glorified; that you bring forth very much fruit, and become my disciples.—*John* xv. 8.

Now to God and our Father be glory, world without end. Amen.—*Philipp.* iv. 20.

Now to the king of ages, immortal, invisible, the only God, be honor and glory for ever and ever. Amen.— 1 *Tim.* i. 17.

GLORIFY GOD, EXHORTA-TION TO

Give ye glory to the Lord, for he is good: for his mercy endureth for ever. —1 *Paral.* xvi. 34.

Bless ye the God of heaven, give glory to him in the sight of all that live, because he hath shown his mercy to you. —*Tob.* xii. 6.

Give glory to the Lord, ye children of Israel, and praise him in the sight of the Gentiles.

. . . See then what he hath done with us, and with fear and trembling give ye glory to him: and extol the eternal King of worlds in your works.— *Tob.* xiii. 3, 6.

Ye that fear the Lord, praise him: all ye, the seed of Jacob, glorify him. —*Ps.* xxi. 24.

Bring to the Lord glory and honor: bring to the Lord glory to his name: adore ye the Lord in his holy court.— *Ps.* xxviii. 2.

Give glory to the Lord, and call upon his name: declare his deeds among the Gentiles.—*Ps.* civ. 1.

Give glory to the God of heaven: for his mercy endureth for ever.

Give glory to the Lord of lords: for his mercy endureth for ever.—*Ps.* cxxxv. 26, 27.

May all the kings of the earth give glory to thee: for they have heard all the words of thy mouth.— *Ps.* cxxxvii. 4.

Give glory to God with a good heart: and diminish not the first-fruits of thy hands.—*Ecclus.* xxxv. 10.

Magnify his name, and give glory to him with the voice of your lips, and with the canticles of your mouths, and with harps, and in praising him, you shall say in this manner:

All the works of the Lord are exceeding good.—*Ecclus.* xxxix. 20, 21.

Glorify the Lord as much as ever you can, for he will yet far exceed, and his magnificence is wonderful. . . .

When you exalt him, put forth all your strength, and be not weary: for you can never go far enough.—*Ecclus.* xliii. 32, 34.

Therefore glorify ye the Lord in instruction: the name of the Lord God of Israel in the islands of the sea.—*Is.* xxiv. 15.

Give ye glory to the Lord your God, before it be dark, and before your feet stumble upon the dark mountains: you shall look for light, and he will turn it into the shadow of death, and into darkness.—*Jer.* xiii. 16.

Now the God of patience and of comfort, grant you to be of one mind, one towards another, according to Jesus Christ:

That with one mind, and with one mouth, you may glorify God and the Father of our Lord Jesus Christ.— *Rom.* xv. 5, 6.

And I heard as it were the voice of a great multitude, and as the voice of many waters, and as the voice of great thunders, saying, Alleluia: for the Lord our God, the Almighty hath reigned.

Let us be glad and rejoice, and give glory to him; for the marriage of the Lamb is come, and his wife hath prepared herself.—*Apoc.* xix. 6, 7.

GLORY OF GOD, THE

And the Lord said: I have forgiven, according to thy word.

As I live: and the whole earth shall be filled with the glory of the Lord.— *Num.* xiv. 20, 21.

But as for me, I will appear before thy sight in justice: I shall be satisfied, when thy glory shall appear.— *Ps.* xvi. 15.

Be thou exalted, O God, above the heavens, and thy glory above all the earth.—*Ps.* lvi. 6.

The heavens declared his justice: and all people saw his glory.—*Ps.* xcvi. 6.

And the Gentiles shall fear thy name, O Lord, and all the kings of the earth, thy glory.

For the Lord hath built up Sion: and he shall be seen in his glory.—*Ps.* ci. 16, 17.

May the glory of the Lord endure for ever: the Lord shall rejoice in his works.—*Ps.* ciii. 31.

The Lord is high above all nations; and his glory above the heavens.—*Ps.* cxii. 4.

And let them sing in the ways of the Lord: for great is the glory of the Lord.—*Ps.* cxxxvii. 5.

He hath established the good things of every one. And who shall be filled with beholding his glory?—*Ecclus.* xlii. 26.

The Lord hath wrought great glory through his magnificence from the beginning.—*Ecclus.* xliv. 2.

And they (the Seraphim) cried one to another, and said: Holy, holy, holy, the Lord God of hosts, all the earth is full of his glory.—*Is.* vi. 3.

I, the Lord, this is my name: I will not give my glory to another, nor my praise to graven things.—*Is.* xlii. 8.

GLORY AND CREDIT TO GOD, WE SHOULD GIVE ALL THE

Not to us, O Lord, not to us; but to thy name give glory.—*Ps.* cxiii. (*Heb.* cxv.) 1.

But of him (God) are you in Christ Jesus, who of God is made unto us wisdom, and justice, and sanctification, and redemption:

That, as it is written: He that glorieth, may glory in the Lord.—1 *Cor.* i. 30, 31.

I have planted, Apollo watered, but God gave the increase.

Therefore, neither he that planteth is anything, nor he that watereth; but God that giveth the increase.—1 *Cor.* iii. 6, 7.

For who distinguisheth thee? Or what hast thou that thou hast not received? And if thou hast received, why dost thou glory, as if thou hadst not received it?—1 *Cor.* iv. 7.

But we have this treasure in earthen vessels, that the excellency may be of the power of God, and not of us.—2 *Cor.* iv. 7.

For by grace you are saved through faith, and that not of yourselves, for it is the gift of God;

Not of works, that no man may glory.—*Eph.* ii. 8, 9.

GLORY OF GOD, DO ALL FOR THE

Therefore, whether you eat or drink, or whatsoever else you do, do all to the glory of God.—1 *Cor.* x. 31.

All whatsoever you do in word or in work, do all in the name of the Lord Jesus Christ, giving thanks to God and the Father by him.—*Col.* iii. 17.

GLUTTONY

He that loveth good cheer, shall be in want: he that loveth wine and fat things, shall not be rich.—*Prov.* xxi. 17.

Thou hast found honey, eat what is sufficient for thee, lest being glutted therewith, thou vomit it up.—*Prov.* xxv. 16.

Art thou set at a great table? be not the first to open thy mouth upon it.

Say not: There are many things which are upon it. . . .

Stretch not out thy hand first, lest being disgraced with envy, thou be put to confusion.

Be not hasty in a feast. . . .

Use as a frugal man the things that are set before thee: lest if thou eatest much, thou be hated.

Leave off first, for manners' sake: and exceed not, lest thou offend.

And if thou sittest among many, reach not thy hand out first of all: and be not the first to ask for drink.—*Ecclus.* xxxi. 12, 13, 16, 17, 19-21.

Watching, and choler, and gripes are with an intemperate man.—*Ecclus.* xxxi. 23.

Be not greedy in any feasting, and pour not out thyself upon any meat:

For in many meats there will be sickness, and greediness will turn to choler.

By surfeiting many have perished: but he that is temperate, shall prolong life.—*Ecclus.* xxxvii. 32-34.

Wherefore have a shame of these things that I am now going to speak of . . .

Of leaning with thy elbow over meat.—*Ecclus.* xli. 19, 24.

And take heed to yourselves, lest perhaps your hearts be overcharged with surfeiting and drunkenness and the cares of this life, and that day come upon you suddenly.—*Luke* xxi. 34.

GOOD TO ONE ANOTHER, WE MUST DO

See also: Help and protect one another—page 201.

And the Lord said to Cain: Where is thy brother Abel? And he answered, I know not: am I my brother's keeper?—*Gen.* iv. 9.

Thou shalt not pass by if thou seest thy brother's ox, or his sheep go astray: but thou shalt bring them back to thy brother.

And if thy brother be not nigh, or thou know him not: thou shalt bring them to thy house, and they shall be with thee, until thy brother seek them, and receive them.

Thou shalt do in like manner with his ass, and with his raiment, and with every thing that is thy brother's, which is lost: if thou find it, neglect it not as pertaining to another.

If thou see thy brother's ass or his ox to be fallen down in the way, thou shalt not slight it, but shalt lift it up with him.—*Deut.* xxii. 1-4.

The soul which blesseth, shall be made fat: and he that inebriateth, shall be inebriated also himself.—*Prov.* xi. 25.

Is not this rather the fast that I have chosen? loose the bands of wickedness, undo the bundles that oppress, let them that are broken go free, and break asunder every burden.

Deal thy bread to the hungry, and bring the needy and the harborless into thy house: when thou shalt see one naked, cover him, and despise not thy own flesh.

Then shall thy light break forth as the morning, and thy health shall speedily arise, and thy justice shall go before thy face, and the glory of the Lord shall gather thee up.

Then shalt thou call, and the Lord shall hear: thou shalt cry, and he shall say, Here I am . . .

When thou shalt pour out thy soul to the hungry, and shalt satisfy the afflicted soul, then shall thy light rise up in darkness, and thy darkness shall be as the noonday.

And the Lord will give thee rest continually, and will fill thy soul with brightness, and will deliver thy bones, and thou shalt be like a watered garden, and like a fountain of water, whose waters shall not fail.—*Is.* lviii. 6-11.

Then shall the king say to them that shall be on his right hand: Come, ye blessed of my Father, possess you the kingdom prepared for you from the foundation of the world.

For I was hungry, and you gave me

to eat; I was thirsty, and you gave me to drink; I was a stranger, and you took me in:

Naked, and you covered me: sick, and you visited me: I was in prison, and you came to me.

Then shall the just answer him, saying: Lord, when did we see thee hungry, and fed thee; thirsty, and gave thee drink?

And when did we see thee a stranger, and took thee in? or naked, and covered thee?

Or when did we see thee sick or in prison, and came to thee?

And the king answering, shall say to them: Amen, I say to you, as long as you did it to one of these my least brethren, you did it to me.—*Matt.* xxv. 34-40.

My brethren, if any of you err from the truth, and one convert him:

He must know that he who causeth a sinner to be converted from the error of his way, shall save his soul from death, and shall cover a multitude of sins.—*James* v. 19, 20.

GOOD TO ONE ANOTHER, EXHORTATION TO DO

See thou never do to another what thou wouldst hate to have done to thee by another.—*Tob.* iv. 16.

Do not withhold him from doing good, who is able: if thou art able, do good thyself also.—*Prov.* iii. 27.

Do good to the just, and thou shalt find great recompense; and if not of him, assuredly of the Lord.—*Ecclus.* xii. 2.

Do good to thy friend, before thou die, and according to thy ability, stretching out thy hand, give to the poor.—*Ecclus.* xiv. 13.

Learn to do well: seek judgment, relieve the oppressed, judge for the fatherless, defend the widow.

And then come, and accuse me, saith the Lord: if your sins be as scarlet, they shall be made as white as snow: and if they be red as crimson, they shall be white as wool.—*Is.* i. 17, 18.

To no man rendering evil for evil. Providing good things, not only in the sight of God, but also in the sight of all men.--*Rom.* xii. 17.

For you, brethren, have been called unto liberty: only make not liberty an occasion to the flesh, but by charity of the spirit serve one another.

For all the law is fulfilled in one word: Thou shalt love thy neighbor as thyself.—*Gal.* v. 13, 14.

And in doing good, let us not fail. For in due time, we shall reap, not failing.

Therefore, whilst we have time, let us work good to all men, but especially to those who are of the household of the faith.—*Gal.* vi. 9, 10.

And do not forget to do good, and to impart; for by such sacrifices God's favor is obtained.—*Heb.* xiii. 16.

GOODNESS OF GOD TOWARD US, THE

See also: Mercy of God—page 311.

I will cry to God the most High; to God who hath done good to me.—*Ps.* lvi. 3.

How good is God to Israel, to them that are of a right heart!—*Ps.* lxxii. 1.

For the Lord will give goodness: and our earth shall yield her fruit.—*Ps.* lxxxiv. 13.

Turn, O my soul, into thy rest: for the Lord hath been bountiful to thee —*Ps.* cxiv. 7.

Give praise to the Lord, for he is good: for his mercy endureth for ever.

Let Israel now say that he is good that his mercy endureth for ever.—*Ps* cxvii. 1, 2.

Thou art good; and in thy goodness, teach me thy justifications.—*Ps.* cxviii. 68.

Praise ye the Lord, for the Lord is good: sing ye to his name, for it is sweet.—*Ps.* cxxxiv. 3.

They shall publish the memory of the abundance of thy sweetness: and shall rejoice in thy justice.

. . . The Lord is sweet to all: and his tender mercies are over all his works.—*Ps.* cxliv. 7, 9.

O how good and sweet is thy spirit, O Lord, in all things!—*Wis.* xii. 1.

For thy power is the beginning of justice: and because thou art Lord of all, thou makest thyself gracious to all. —*Wis.* xii. 16.

And I will make an everlasting covenant with them, and will not cease to do them good. . . .

And I will rejoice over them, when I shall do them good: and I will plant them in this land in truth, with my whole heart, and with all my soul.—*Jer.* xxxii. 40, 41.

The Lord is good and giveth strength in the day of trouble: and knoweth them that hope in him.—*Nahum* i. 7.

GOODS, ILL-GOTTEN

Treasures of wickedness shall profit nothing: but justice shall deliver from death.—*Prov.* x. 2.

Some distribute their own goods, and grow richer: others take away what is not their own, and are always in want. —*Prov.* xi. 24.

He that gathereth treasures by a lying tongue, is vain and foolish, and shall stumble upon the snares of death. —*Prov.* xxi. 6.

He that oppresseth the poor, to increase his own riches, shall himself give to one that is richer, and shall be in need.—*Prov.* xxii. 16.

He that heapeth together riches by usury and loan, gathereth them for him that will be bountiful to the poor.— *Prov.* xxviii. 8.

He that is partaker with a thief, hateth his own soul: he heareth one putting him to his oath, and discovereth not.—*Prov.* xxix. 24.

Set not thy heart upon unjust possessions, and say not: I have enough to live on: for it shall be of no service in the time of vengeance and darkness.— *Ecclus.* v. 1.

Be not anxious for goods unjustly gotten: for they shall not profit thee in the day of calamity and revenge.— *Ecclus.* v. 10.

He that gathereth together by wronging his own soul, gathereth for others, and another will squander away his goods in rioting.—*Ecclus.* xiv. 4.

The offering of him that sacrificeth of a thing wrongfully gotten is stained, and the mockeries of the unjust are not acceptable.—*Ecclus.* xxxiv. 21.

As the partridge hath hatched eggs which she did not lay: so is he that hath gathered riches, and not by right: in the midst of his days, he shall leave them, and in his latter end he shall be a fool.—*Jer.* xvii. 11.

Shall not all these take up a parable against him, and a dark speech concerning him: and it shall be said: Woe to him that heapeth together that which is not his own? how long also doth he load himself with thick clay?—*Hab.* ii. 6.

GOODS, GOD NEEDS NOT OUR

See also: Service, God needs not our —page 515.

I have said to the Lord, thou art my God, for thou hast no need of my goods.—*Ps.* xv. 2.

If I should be hungry, I would not tell thee: for the world is mine, and the fulness thereof.—*Ps.* xlix. 12.

Say not: God will have respect to the multitude of my gifts, and when I offer to the most high God, he will accept my offerings.—*Ecclus.* vii. 11.

What shall I offer to the Lord that is worthy? wherewith shall I kneel before the high God? shall I offer holocausts unto him, and calves of a year old?

May the Lord be appeased with thousands of rams, or with many thousands of fat he goats? shall I give my firstborn for my wickedness, the fruit of my body for the sin of my soul?— *Mich.* vi. 6, 7.

God, who made the world, and all things therein; he, being Lord of heaven and earth, dwelleth not in temples made with hands;

Neither is he served with men's hands, as though he needed anything; seeing it is he who giveth to all life, and breath, and all things.—*Acts* xvii. 24, 25.

Or who hath first given to him, and recompense shall be made him?—*Rom.* xi. 35.

GOSPEL OF CHRIST FOOLISH TO THE WORLD

For the word of the cross, to them indeed that perish, is foolishness; but to them that are saved, that is, to us, it is the power of God.

. . . For seeing that in the wisdom of God, the world, by wisdom, knew not God, it pleased God, by the foolishness of our preaching, to save them that believe.

For both the Jews require signs, and the Greeks seek after wisdom:

But we preach Christ crucified, unto the Jews indeed a stumbling block, and unto the Gentiles foolishness.—1 *Cor.* i. 18, 21-23.

But the sensual man perceiveth not these things that are of the Spirit of God; for it is foolishness to him, and he cannot understand, because it is spiritually examined.—1 *Cor.* ii. 14.

For I give you to understand, brethren, that the gospel which was preached by me, is not according to man.

For neither did I receive it of man, nor did I learn it; but by the revelation of Jesus Christ.—*Gal.* i. 11, 12.

GOSPEL OF CHRIST OUR SALVATION, THE

And he said to them: Go ye into the whole world, and preach the gospel to every creature.

He that believeth and is baptized, shall be saved: but he that believeth not, shall be condemned.—*Mark* xvi. 15, 16.

For I am not ashamed of the gospel. For it is the power of God unto salvation to every one that believeth, to the Jew first, and to the Greek.

For the justice of God is revealed therein, from faith unto faith, as it is written: The just man liveth by faith. —*Rom.* i. 16, 17.

But we preach Christ crucified, unto the Jews indeed a stumbling block, and unto the Gentiles foolishness:

But unto them that are called, both Jews and Greeks, the power of God, and the wisdom of God.—1 *Cor.* i. 23, 24.

Now I make known unto you, brethren, the gospel which I preached to you, which also you have received, and wherein you stand;

By which also you are saved, if you hold fast, after what manner I preached unto you, unless you have believed in vain.—1 *Cor.* xv. 1, 2.

GOSPEL OF CHRIST WITHIN OUR REACH, THE

But what saith the Scripture? The word is nigh thee, even in thy mouth, and in thy heart. This is the word of faith, which we preach.—*Rom.* x. 8.

Faith then cometh by hearing; and hearing by the word of Christ.

But I say: Have they not heard? Yes, verily, their sound hath gone forth into all the earth, and their words unto the ends of the whole world.—*Rom.* x. 17, 18.

And if our gospel be also hid, it is hid to them that are lost.

In whom the god of this world hath blinded the minds of unbelievers, that the light of the gospel of the glory of Christ, who is the image of God, should not shine unto them.

. . . For God, who commanded the light to shine out of darkness, hath shined in our hearts, to give the light of the knowledge of the glory of God, in the face of Christ Jesus.—2 *Cor.* iv. 3, 4, 6.

GRACE OF GOD, THE

O Lord, thou wilt open my lips: and my mouth shall declare thy praise.—*Ps.* l. 17.

Thou hast visited the earth, and hast plentifully watered it; thou hast many ways enriched it. The river of God is filled with water, thou hast prepared their food: for so is its preparation.—*Ps.* lxiv. 10.

He shall come down like rain upon the fleece; and as showers falling gently upon the earth.—*Ps.* lxxi. 6.

Convert us, O God; and show us thy face, and we shall be saved. . . .

Thou shalt quicken us: and we will call upon thy name.—*Ps.* lxxix. 4, 19.

Therefore even then [1]it was transformed into all things, and was obedient to thy grace that nourisheth all, according to the will of them that desired it of thee.—*Wis.* xvi. 25.

In me is all grace of the way and of the truth, in me is all hope of life and of virtue.

Come over to me, all ye that desire me, and be filled with my fruits.

[1]The elements that served for the punishment of the Egyptians.

For my spirit is sweet above honey, and my inheritance above honey and the honeycomb.—*Ecclus.* xxiv. 25-27.

Grace is like a paradise in blessings, and mercy remaineth for ever.—*Ecclus.* xl. 17.

You shall draw waters with joy out of the Saviour's fountains.—Is. xii. 3.

I am come to cast fire on the earth: and what will I, but that it be kindled? —*Luke* xii. 49.

And of his fulness we all have received, and grace for grace.

For the law was given by Moses; grace and truth came by Jesus Christ. —*John* i. 16, 17.

For the wages of sin is death. But the grace of God, life everlasting, in Christ Jesus our Lord.—*Rom.* vi. 23.

I give thanks to my God always for you, for the grace of God that is given you in Christ Jesus.—1 *Cor.* i. 4.

Now there are diversities of graces, but the same Spirit.—1 *Cor.* xii. 4.

But by the grace of God I am what I am; and his grace in me hath not been void, but I have labored more abundantly than all they: yet not I, but the grace of God with me.—1 *Cor.* xv. 10.

Blessed be the God and Father of our Lord Jesus Christ, who hath blessed us with spiritual blessings in heavenly places, in Christ: . . . Unto the praise of the glory of his grace, in which he hath graced us in his beloved son.—*Eph.* i. 3, 6.

Now the grace of our Lord hath abounded exceedingly with faith and love, which is in Christ Jesus.—1 *Tim.* i. 14.

Wherefore having the loins of your mind girt up, being sober, trust perfectly in the grace which is offered you in the revelation of Jesus Christ.— 1 *Peter* i. 13.

Behold, I stand at the gate, and knock. If any man shall hear my voice, and open to me the door, I will come in to him, and will sup with him, and he with me.—*Apoc.* iii. 20.

GRACE OF GOD DRAWING US TO HIM, THE

If he turn his heart to him, he shall draw his spirit and breath unto himself.—*Job* xxxiv. 14.

The Lord hath appeared from afar to me. Yea, I have loved thee with an everlasting love, therefore have I drawn thee, taking pity on thee.—*Jer.* xxxi. 3.

And when she had said these things, she went, and called her sister Mary secretly, saying: The master is come, and calleth for thee.—*John* xi. 28.

And I, if I be lifted up from the earth, will draw all things to myself.— *John* xii. 32.

GRACE OF GOD IMPELLING US TO LOVE AND SERVE HIM, THE

And when the Lord had heard this, he said to me: I have heard the voice of the words of this people, which they spoke to thee: they have spoken all things well.

Who shall give them to have such a mind, to fear me, and to keep all my commandments at all times, that it may be well with them and with their children for ever?—*Deut.* v. 28, 29.

The Lord thy God will circumcise thy heart, and the heart of thy seed: that thou mayst love the Lord thy God with all thy heart, and with all thy soul, that thou mayst live.—*Deut.* xxx. 6.

And I will give them a heart to know me, that I am the Lord: and they shall be my people, and I will be their God: because they shall return to me with their whole heart.—*Jer.* xxiv. 7.

And I will give them one heart and one way, that they may fear me all days: and that it may be well with them, and with their children after them.

And I will make an everlasting covenant with them, and will not cease to do them good: and I will give my fear in their heart, that they may not revolt from me.—*Jer.* xxxii. 39, 40.

And I will give them one heart, and will put a new spirit in their bowels: and I will take away the stony heart out of their flesh, and will give them a heart of flesh:

That they may walk in my commandments, and keep my judgments, and do them: and that they may be my people, and I may be their God.—*Ezech.* xi. 19, 20.

For it is God who worketh in you, both to will and to accomplish, according to his good will.—*Philipp.* ii. 13.

GRACE OF GOD WARNING US AGAINST SIN, THE

Thou hast given a warning to them that fear thee: that they may flee from before the bow:
That thy beloved may be delivered.—*Ps.* lix. 6.
Turn ye at my reproof: behold I will utter my spirit to you, and will show you my words.—*Prov.* i. 23.
O how good and sweet is thy spirit, O Lord, in all things!
And therefore thou chastisest them that err, by little and little: and admonishest them, and speakest to them, concerning the things wherein they offend: that leaving their wickedness, they may believe in thee, O Lord.—*Wis.* xii. 1, 2.

GRACE OF GOD LEADING US IN THE RIGHT WAY, THE

He hath converted my soul.
He hath led me on the paths of justice, for his own name's sake.—*Ps.* xxii. 3.
Send forth thy light and thy truth: they have conducted me, and brought me unto thy holy hill, and into thy tabernacles.—*Ps.* xlii. 3.
I will show thee the way of wisdom, I will lead thee by the paths of equity.—*Prov.* iv. 11.
Blessed is he that is conversant in these good things: and he that layeth them up in his heart, shall be wise always.
For if he do them, he shall be strong to do all things: because the light of God guideth his steps.—*Ecclus.* l. 30, 31.

GRACE, POWER OF GOD'S

She reacheth therefore from end to end mightily, and ordereth all things sweetly.—*Wis.* viii. 1.
He that hearkeneth to me, shall not be confounded: and they that work by me, shall not sin.—*Ecclus.* xxiv. 30.
And the Lord turning, looked on Peter. And Peter remembered the word of the Lord, as he had said: Be-fore the cock crow, thou shalt deny me thrice.
And Peter going out, wept bitterly.—*Luke* xxii. 61, 62.
Unhappy man that I am, who shall deliver me from the body of this death? The grace of God, by Jesus Christ our Lord.—*Rom.* vii. 24, 25.
And God is able to make all grace abound in you; that ye always, having all sufficiency in all things, may abound to every good work.—2 *Cor.* ix. 8.
And he said to me: My grace is sufficient for thee: for power is made perfect in infirmity. Gladly therefore will I glory in my infirmities, that the power of Christ may dwell in me.
For which cause I please myself in my infirmities, in reproaches, in necessities, in persecutions, in distresses, for Christ. For when I am weak, then am I powerful.—2 *Cor.* xii. 9, 10.
For by grace you are saved, through faith, and that not of yourselves, for it is the gift of God.—*Eph.* ii. 8.
I can do all things in him who strengtheneth me.—*Philipp.* iv. 13.
By whom he hath given us most great and precious promises: that by these you may be made partakers of the divine nature: flying the corruption of that concupiscence which is in the world.—2 *Peter* i. 4.
Now to him who is able to preserve you without sin, and to present you spotless before the presence of his glory with exceeding joy, in the coming of our Lord Jesus Christ,
To the only God our Saviour through Jesus Christ our Lord, be glory and magnificence, empire and power, before all ages, and now, and for all ages of ages. Amen.—*Jude* i. 24, 25.

GRACE THE GIFT OF GOD'S MERCY

He (God) answered: I will show thee all good, and I will proclaim in the name of the Lord before thee: and I will have mercy on whom I will, and I will be merciful to whom it shall please me.—*Ex.* xxxiii. 19.
I will greatly rejoice in the Lord, and my soul shall be joyful in my God: for he hath clothed me with the garments

of salvation: and with the robe of justice, he hath covered me, as a bridegroom decked with a crown, and as a bride adorned with her jewels.—*Is.* lxi. 10.

And I will pour out upon the house of David, and upon the inhabitants of Jerusalem, the spirit of grace, and of prayers.—*Zach.* xii. 10.

The Spirit breatheth where he will; and thou hearest his voice, but thou knowest not whence he cometh, and whither he goeth: so is every one that is born of the Spirit.—*John* iii. 8.

For he saith to Moses: I will have mercy on whom I will have mercy; and I will show mercy to whom I will show mercy.

So then it is not of him that willeth, nor of him that runneth, but of God that showeth mercy.—*Rom.* ix. 15, 16.

For by grace you are saved through faith, and that not of yourselves, for it is the gift of God.—*Eph.* ii. 8.

But to every one of us is given grace, according to the measure of the giving of Christ.—*Eph.* iv. 7.

GRACE, OUR NEED OF GOD'S

See also: Need of God, our—page 342.

For what is my strength, that I can hold out? or what is my end, that I should keep patience?—*Job* vi. 11.

Who can make him clean that is conceived of unclean seed? is it not thou who only art?—*Job* xiv. 4.

I know, O Lord, that the way of a man is not his: neither is it in a man to walk, and to direct his steps.—*Jer.* x. 23.

Ephraim shall say, What have I to do any more with idols? I will hear him, and I will make him flourish like a green fir-tree: from me is thy fruit found.—*Osee* xiv. 9.

But he answering, said: Every plant which my heavenly Father hath not planted, shall be rooted up.—*Matt.* xv. 13.

All things are delivered to me by my Father; and no one knoweth who the Son is, but the Father; and who the Father is, but the Son, and to whom the Son will reveal him.—*Luke* x. 22.

Jesus answered, and said to her: If thou didst know the gift of God, and who he is that saith to thee, Give me to drink; thou perhaps wouldst have asked of him, and he would have given thee living water.—*John* iv. 10.

No man can come to me, except the Father, who hath sent me, draw him; and I will raise him up in the last day. —*John* vi. 44.

And he said: Therefore did I say to you, that no man can come to me, unless it be given him by my Father.— *John* vi. 66.

For all have sinned, and do need the glory of God.

Being justified freely by his grace, through the redemption that is in Christ Jesus.—*Rom.* iii. 23, 24.

So then it is not of him that willeth, nor of him that runneth, but of God that showeth mercy.—*Rom.* ix. 16.

I have planted, Apollo watered, but God gave the increase.

Therefore, neither he that planteth is anything, nor he that watereth; but God that giveth the increase.—1 *Cor.* iii. 6, 7.

Wherefore I give you to understand, that no man, speaking by the Spirit of God, saith Anathema to Jesus. And no man can say the Lord Jesus, but by the Holy Ghost.—1 *Cor.* xii. 3.

GRACE, NOW IS THE TIME OF GOD'S

Seek ye the Lord, while he may be found: call upon him, while he is near. —*Is.* lv. 6.

Jesus therefore said to them: Yet a little while I am with you: and then I go to him that sent me.

You shall seek me, and shall not find me: and where I am, thither you cannot come.—*John* vii. 33, 34.

Jesus therefore said to them: Yet a little while, the light is among you. Walk whilst you have the light, that the darkness overtake you not. And he that walketh in darkness, knoweth not whither he goeth.—*John* xii. 35.

And we helping do exhort you, that you receive not the grace of God in vain.

For he saith: In an accepted time have I heard thee; and in the day of salvation have I helped thee. Behold, now is the acceptable time; behold, now is the day of salvation.—2 *Cor.* vi. 1, 2.

But exhort one another every day, whilst it is called to-day, that none of you be hardened through the deceitfulness of sin.

For we are made partakers of Christ: yet so, if we hold the beginning of his substance firm unto the end.

While it is said, To-day if you shall hear his voice, harden not your hearts, as in that provocation.—*Heb.* iii. 13-15.

GRACE OF GOD WITHDRAWN IN PUNISHMENT OF SIN, THE

For wisdom will not enter into a malicious soul, nor dwell in a body subject to sins.

For the Holy Spirit of discipline will flee from the deceitful, and will withdraw himself from thoughts that are without understanding, and he shall not abide, when iniquity cometh in.—*Wis.* i. 4, 5.

And he said: Go, and thou shalt say to this people: Hearing, hear, and understand not: and see the vision, and know it not.

Blind the heart of this people, and make their ears heavy, and shut their eyes: lest they see with their eyes, and hear with their ears, and understand with their heart, and be converted, and I heal them.—*Is.* vi. 9, 10.

For the Lord hath mingled for you the spirit of a deep sleep, he will shut up your eyes, he will cover your prophets and princes that see visions.

And the vision of all shall be unto you as the words of a book that is sealed, which when they shall deliver to one that is learned, they shall say: Read this: and he shall answer: I cannot, for it is sealed.—*Is.* xxix. 10, 11.

For the iniquity of his covetousness I was angry, and I struck him: I hid my face from thee, and was angry: and he went away wandering in his own heart.—*Is.* lvii. 17.

And the pride of Israel shall answer in his face: and Israel and Ephraim shall fall in their iniquity, Juda also shall fall with them.

With their flocks, and with their herds, they shall go to seek the Lord, and shall not find him: he is withdrawn from them.—*Osee* v. 5, 6.

They have sinned deeply as in the days of Gabaa: he will remember their iniquity, and will visit their sin.

. . . Yea, and woe to them, when I shall depart from them.—*Osee* ix. 9, 12.

The Lord hath sworn against the pride of Jacob: surely I will never forget all their works. . . .

Behold the days come, saith the Lord, and I will send a famine into the land: not a famine of bread, nor a thirst of water, but of hearing the word of the Lord.

And they shall move from sea to sea, and from the north to the east: they shall go about seeking the word of the Lord, and shall not find it.—*Amos* viii. 7, 11, 12.

And he said to them: To you it is given, to know the mystery of the kingdom of God: but to them that are without, all things are done in parables:

That seeing they may see, and not perceive; and hearing they may hear, and not understand: lest at any time they should be converted, and their sins should be forgiven them.—*Mark* iv. 11, 12.

GRACE OF GOD, CO-OPERATING WITH THE

And the Lord came and stood: and he called, as he had called the other times: Samuel, Samuel. And Samuel said: Speak, Lord, for thy servant heareth.—1 *Kings* iii. 10.

I sleep, and my heart watcheth: the voice of my beloved knocking: Open to me, my sister, my love, my dove, my undefiled: for my head is full of dew, and my locks of the drops of the nights.—*Cant.* v. 2.

The Lord God hath opened my ear, and I do not resist: I have not gone back.—*Is.* l. 5.

For after thou didst convert me, I did penance: and after thou didst show unto me, I struck my thigh: I am confounded and ashamed, because I have borne the reproach of my youth.—*Jer.* xxxi. 19.

When Jesus therefore was born in Bethlehem of Juda, in the days of king Herod, behold, there came wise men from the east to Jerusalem,

Saying, Where is he that is born king of the Jews? For we have seen his star in the east, and are come to adore him.—*Matt.* ii. 1, 2.

And falling on the ground, he heard a voice saying to him: Saul, Saul, why persecutest thou me?

. . . And he trembling and astonished, said: Lord, what wilt thou have me to do?—*Acts* ix. 4, 6.

But by the grace of God, I am what I am; and his grace in me hath not been void, but I have labored more abundantly than all they: yet not I, but the grace of God with me.—*1 Cor.* xv. 10.

I cast not away the grace of God. For if justice be by the law, then Christ died in vain.—*Gal.* ii. 21.

GRACE OF GOD, REWARD OF CO-OPERATING WITH THE

He (God) shall show them their works, and their wicked deeds, because they have been violent.

He also shall open their ear, to correct them: and shall speak, that they may return from iniquity.

If they shall hear and observe, they shall accomplish their days in good, and their years in glory.—*Job* xxxvi. 9-11.

But he that shall hear me, shall rest without terror, and shall enjoy abundance, without fear of evils.—*Prov.* i. 33.

He that hearkeneth to me, shall not be confounded: and they that work by me, shall not sin.—*Ecclus.* xxiv. 30.

For whosoever are led by the Spirit of God, they are the sons of God.—*Rom.* viii. 14.

Behold, I stand at the gate, and knock. If any man shall hear my voice, and open to me the door, I will come in to him, and will sup with him, and he with me.—*Apoc.* iii. 20.

GRACE OF GOD, EXHORTATION TO CO-OPERATE WITH THE

To-day if you shall hear his voice, harden not your hearts:

As in the provocation, according to the day of temptation in the wilderness: where your fathers tempted me, they proved me, and saw my works.—*Ps.* xciv. 8, 9.

Incline your ear, and come to me: hear, and your soul shall live, and I will make an everlasting covenant with you, the faithful mercies of David.—*Is.* lv. 3.

And we helping, do exhort you, that you receive not the grace of God in vain.

For he saith: In an accepted time have I heard thee; and in the day of salvation, have I helped thee. Behold, now is the acceptable time; behold, now is the day of salvation.—*2 Cor.* vi. 1, 2.

Extinguish not the spirit.—*1 Thess.* v. 19.

For which cause I admonish thee, that thou stir up the grace of God which is in thee, by the imposition of my hands.—*2 Tim.* i. 6.

Thou therefore, my son, be strong in the grace which is in Christ Jesus.—*2 Tim.* ii. 1.

Looking diligently, lest any man be wanting to the grace of God; lest any root of bitterness springing up, do hinder, and by it many be defiled.—*Heb.* xii. 15.

But grow in grace, and in the knowledge of our Lord and Saviour Jesus Christ. To him be glory both now and unto the day of eternity. Amen.—*2 Peter* iii. 18.

GRACE, PROMPTNESS IN ANSWERING THE CALL OF

To-day if you shall hear his voice, harden not your hearts.—*Ps.* xciv. 8.

And Jesus walking by the sea of Galilee, saw two brethren, Simon, who is called Peter, and Andrew his brother, casting a net into the sea (for they were fishers).

And he saith to them: Come ye after me, and I will make you to be fishers of men.

And they immediately leaving their nets, followed him.

And going on from thence, he saw other two brethren, James, the son of Zebedee, and John his brother, in a ship with Zebedee their father, mending their nets: and he called them.

And they forthwith left their nets and father, and followed him.—*Matt.* iv. 18-22.

And when Jesus passed on from thence, he saw a man sitting in the custom house, named Matthew; and he saith to him: Follow me. And he arose up, and followed him.—*Matt.* ix. 9.

Let your loins be girt, and lamps burning in your hands.

And you yourselves like to men who wait for their lord, when he shall return from the wedding; that when he cometh and knocketh, they may open to him immediately.—*Luke* xii. 35, 36.

But when it pleased him, who separated me from my mother's womb, and called me by his grace,

To reveal his Son in me, that I might preach him among the Gentiles, immediately I condescended not to flesh and blood.—*Gal.* i. 15, 16.

GRACE, ABUSE OF GOD'S

They have been rebellious to the light, they have not known his ways, neither have they returned by his paths. —*Job* xxiv. 13.

What is there that I ought to do more to my vineyard, that I have not done to it? was it that I looked, that it should bring forth grapes, and it hath brought forth wild grapes?—*Is.* v. 4.

For with the speech of lips, and with another tongue, he will speak to this people.

To whom he said: This is my rest, refresh the weary, and this is my refreshing: and they would not hear.— *Is.* xxviii. 11, 12.

For it is a people that provoketh to wrath, and lying children, children that will not hear the law of God.

Who say to the seers: See not: and to them that behold: Behold not for us those things that are right: speak unto us pleasant things, see errors for us.

Take away from me the way, turn away the path from me, let the Holy One of Israel cease from before us.— *Is.* xxx. 9-11.

I have spread forth my hands all the day to an unbelieving people, who walk in a way that is not good, after their own thoughts.—*Is.* lxv. 2.

O Lord, thy eyes are upon truth: thou hast struck them, and they have not grieved: thou hast bruised them, and they have refused to receive correction: they have made their faces harder than the rock, and they have refused to return.

But I said: Perhaps these are poor and foolish, that know not the way of the Lord, the judgment of their God.

I will go therefore to the great men, and will speak to them: for they have known the way of the Lord, the judgment of their God: and behold these have altogether broken the yoke more, and have burst the bonds.—*Jer.* v. 3-5.

I spoke to thee in thy prosperity: and thou saidst: I will not hear: this hath been thy way from thy youth, because thou hast not heard my voice.— *Jer.* xxii. 21.

And the Lord hath sent to you all his servants the prophets, rising early, and sending, and you have not hearkened, nor inclined your ears to hear. . . .

And you have not heard me, saith the Lord, that you might provoke me to anger ith the works of your hands, to your own hurt.—*Jer.* xxv. 4, 7.

I destroyed some of you, as God destroyed Sodom and Gomorrha, and you were as a firebrand plucked out of the burning: yet you returned not to me, saith the Lord.—*Amos* iv. 11.

Woe to the provoking and redeemed city, the dove.

She hath not hearkened to the voice, neither hath she received discipline: she hath not trusted in the Lord, she drew not near to her God. . . .

I said: Surely thou wilt fear me, thou wilt receive correction: and her dwelling shall not perish, for all things wherein I have visited her: but they rose early, and corrupted all their thoughts.—*Soph.* iii. 1, 2, 7.

Be not as your fathers, to whom the former prophets have cried, saying: Thus saith the Lord of hosts: Turn ye from your evil ways, and from your wicked thoughts: but they did not give ear, neither did they hearken to me, saith the Lord.—*Zach.* i. 4.

The men of Ninive shall rise in judgment with this generation, and shall condemn it: because they did penance at the preaching of Jonas. And behold a greater than Jonas here.

The queen of the south shall rise in judgment with this generation, and shall condemn it: because she came from the ends of the earth to hear the wisdom of Solomon, and behold a greater than Solomon here.—*Matt.* xii. 41, 42.

He came unto his own, and his own received him not.—*John* i. 11.

And you will not come to me, that you may have life. . . .

I am come in the name of my Father, and you receive me not: if another shall come in his own name, him you will receive.—*John* v. 40, 43.

Jesus said to them: If you were blind, you should not have sin: but now you say: We see. Your sin remaineth.—*John* ix. 41.

But they cried out: Away with him; away with him; crucify him. Pilate saith to them: Shall I crucify your king? The chief priests answered: We have no king but Cæsar.—*John* xix. 15.

You stiffnecked and uncircumcised in heart and ears, you always resist the Holy Ghost: as your fathers did, so do you also. . . .

Who have received the law by the disposition of angels, and have not kept it.—*Acts* vii. 51, 53.

But I have against thee a few things: because thou sufferest the woman Jezabel, who calleth herself a prophetess, to teach, and to seduce my servants, to commit fornication, and to eat of things sacrificed to idols.

And I gave her a time that she might do penance, and she will not repent of her fornication.—*Apoc.* ii. 20, 21.

GRACE, PUNISHMENT OF THE ABUSE OF GOD'S

God hath given him place for penance, and he abuseth it unto pride: but his eyes are upon his ways.

They are lifted up for a little while, and shall not stand, and shall be brought down as all things, and shall be taken away, and as the tops of the ears of corn they shall be broken.—*Job* xxiv. 23, 24.

He shall show them their works and their wicked deeds, because they have been violent.

He also shall open their ear, to correct them: and shall speak, that they may return from iniquity. . . .

But if they hear not, they shall pass by the sword, and shall be consumed in folly.—*Job* xxxvi. 9, 10, 12.

To-day if you shall hear his voice, harden not your hearts:

As in the provocation, according to the day of temptation in the wilderness: where your fathers tempted me, they proved me, and saw my works.

Forty years long was I offended with that generation, and I said: These always err in heart.

And these men have not known my ways: so I swore in my wrath that they shall not enter into my rest.—*Ps.* xciv. 8-11.

Because I called, and you refused: I stretched out my hand, and there was none that regarded.

You have despised all my counsel, and have neglected my reprehensions.

I also will laugh in your destruction, and will mock when that shall come to you which you feared.

When sudden calamity shall fall on you, and destruction, as a tempest, shall be at hand: when tribulation and distress shall come upon you:

Then shall they call upon me, and I will not hear: they shall rise in the morning, and shall not find me:

Because they have hated instruction, and received not the fear of the Lord,

Nor consented to my counsel, but despised all my reproof.—*Prov.* i. 24-30.

Therefore thou hast sent a judgment upon them as senseless children to mock them.

But they that were not amended by mockeries and reprehensions, experienced the worthy judgment of God.—*Wis.* xii. 25, 26.

Wherefore I also will choose their mockeries, and will bring upon them the things they feared: because I called, and there was none that would answer; I have spoken, and they heard not;

and they have done evil in my eyes, and have chosen the things that displease me.—*Is.* lxvi. 4.

Hear, O earth: Behold I will bring evils upon this people, the fruits of their own thoughts: because they have not heard my words, and they have cast away my law.—*Jer.* vi. 19.

And now, because you have done all these works, saith the Lord: and I have spoken to you, rising up early, and speaking, and you have not heard: and I have called you, and you have not answered. . . .

And I will cast you away from before my face, as I have cast away all your brethren, the whole seed of Ephraim.—*Jer.* vii. 13, 15.

Thou hast forsaken me, saith the Lord, thou art gone backward: and I will stretch out my hand against thee, and I will destroy thee: I am weary of entreating thee.—*Jer.* xv. 6.

My God will cast them away, because they hearkened not to him: and they shall be wanderers among the nations.—*Osee* ix. 17.

But they would not hearken, and they turned away the shoulder to depart: and they stopped their ears, not to hear.

And they made their heart as the adamant stone, lest they should hear the law, and the words which the Lord of hosts sent in his spirit, by the hand of the former prophets: so a great indignation came from the Lord of hosts.

And it came to pass that as he spoke, and they heard not: so shall they cry, and I will not hear, saith the Lord of hosts.—*Zach.* vii. 11-13.

And whosoever shall not receive you, nor hear your words: going forth out of that house or city, shake off the dust from your feet.

Amen I say to you, it shall be more tolerable for the land of Sodom and Gomorrha in the day of judgment, than for that city.—*Matt.* x. 14, 15.

Then began he to upbraid the cities wherein were done the most of his miracles, for that they had not done penance.

Woe to thee, Corozain, woe to thee, Bethsaida: for if in Tyre and Sidon had been wrought the miracles that have been wrought in you, they had long ago done penance in sackcloth and ashes.

But I say unto you, It shall be more tolerable for Tyre and Sidon in the day of judgment, than for you.

And thou, Capharnaum, shalt thou be exalted up to heaven? thou shalt go down even unto hell. For if in Sodom had been wrought the miracles that have been wrought in thee, perhaps it had remained unto this day.

But I say unto you, that it shall be more tolerable for the land of Sodom in the day of judgment, than for thee.—*Matt.* xi. 20-24.

Jesus saith to them: Amen I say to you, that the publicans and the harlots shall go into the kingdom of God before you.

For John came to you in the way of justice, and you did not believe him. But the publicans and the harlots believed him: but you, seeing it, did not even afterwards repent, that you might believe him.—*Matt.* xxi. 31, 32.

Jerusalem, Jerusalem, thou that killest the prophets, and stonest them that are sent unto thee, how often would I have gathered together thy children, as the hen doth gather her chickens under her wings, and thou wouldst not?

Behold, your house shall be left to you, desolate.—*Matt.* xxiii. 37, 38.

But I say unto you, that none of those men that were invited, shall taste of my supper.—*Luke* xiv. 24.

If thou also hadst known, and that in this thy day, the things that are to thy peace; but now they are hidden from thy eyes.

For the days shall come upon thee: and thy enemies shall cast a trench about thee, and compass thee round, and straiten thee on every side,

And beat thee flat to the ground, and thy children who are in thee: and they shall not leave in thee a stone upon a stone: because thou hast not known the time of thy visitation.—*Luke* xix. 42-44.

Again therefore Jesus said to them: I go, and you shall seek me, and you shall die in your sin. Whither I go, you cannot come.

. . . Therefore I said to you, that

you shall die in your sins. For if you believe not that I am he, you shall die in your sin.—*John* viii. 21, 24.

For Moses said: A prophet shall the Lord your God raise up unto you of your brethren, like unto me: him you shall hear according to all things whatsoever he shall speak to you.

And it shall be, that every soul which will not hear that prophet, shall be destroyed from among the people. . . .

To you first, God, raising up his Son, hath sent him to bless you; that every one may convert himself from his wickedness.—*Acts* iii. 22, 23, 26.

Beware, therefore, lest that come upon you which is spoken in the prophets:

Behold, ye despisers, and wonder, and perish: for I work a work in your days, a work which you will not believe, if any man shall tell it you.—*Acts* xiii. 40, 41.

Or despisest thou the riches of his goodness, and patience, and longsuffering? Knowest thou not that the benignity of God leadeth thee to penance?

But according to thy hardness and impenitent heart, thou treasurest up to thyself wrath, against the day of wrath, and revelation of the just judgment of God.—*Rom.* ii. 4, 5.

For if the word spoken by angels became steadfast, and every transgression and disobedience received a just recompense of reward:

How shall we escape if we neglect so great salvation? which having begun to be declared by the Lord, was confirmed unto us by them that heard him.—*Heb.* ii. 2, 3.

See that you refuse him not that speaketh. For if they escaped not, who refused him that spoke upon earth, much more shall not we, that turn away from him that speaketh to us from heaven.—*Heb.* xii. 25.

GRACE, ABUSE OF, PUNISHED BY ITS WITHDRAWAL

But my people heard not my voice: and Israel hearkened not to me.

So I let them go according to the desires of their heart: they shall walk in their own inventions.—*Ps.* lxxx. 12, 13.

What is there that I ought to do more to my vineyard, that I have not done to it? was it that I looked that it should bring forth grapes, and it hath brought forth wild grapes?

And now I will show you what I will do to my vineyard. I will take away the hedge thereof, and it shall be wasted: I will break down the wall thereof, and it shall be trodden down.

And I will make it desolate: it shall not be pruned, and it shall not be digged: but briars and thorns shall come up: and I will command the clouds to rain no rain upon it.—*Is.* v. 4-6.

And thou shalt say to them: This is a nation which hath not hearkened to the voice of the Lord their God, nor received instruction: faith is lost, and is taken away out of their mouth.—*Jer.* vii. 28.

Jesus saith to them: Have you never read in the Scriptures: The stone which the builders rejected, the same is become the head of the corner? By the Lord this has been done; and it is wonderful in our eyes.

Therefore I say to you, that the kingdom of God shall be taken from you, and shall be given to a nation yielding the fruits thereof.—*Matt.* xxi. 42, 43.

Jesus therefore said to them: Yet a little while I am with you: and then I go to him that sent me.

You shall seek me, and shall not find me: and where I am, thither you cannot come.—*John* vii. 33, 34.

Then Paul and Barnabas said boldly: To you it behooved us first to speak the word of God: but because you reject it, and judge yourselves unworthy of eternal life, behold we turn to the Gentiles.—*Acts* xiii. 46.

Having faith and a good conscience, which some rejecting, have made shipwreck concerning the faith.—1 *Tim.* i. 19.

Looking diligently, lest any man be wanting to the grace of God; lest any root of bitterness springing up, do hinder, and by it many be defiled.

Lest there be any fornicator, or profane person, as Esau; who for **one** mess, sold his first birthright.

For know ye that afterwards, when he desired to inherit the benediction, he was rejected; for he found no place of repentance, although with tears he had sought it.—*Heb.* xii. 15-17.

GRACE OF GOD, A PRAYER FOR THE

The Lord our God be with us, as he was with our fathers, and not leave us, nor cast us off:

But may he incline our hearts to himself, that we may walk in all his ways, and keep his commandments, and his ceremonies, and all his judgments which he commanded our fathers.— 3 *Kings* viii. 57, 58.

Perfect thou my goings in thy paths: that my footsteps be not moved.—*Ps.* xvi. 5.

Create a clean heart in me, O God; and renew a right spirit within my bowels. . . .

Restore unto me the joy of thy salvation, and strengthen me with a perfect spirit.—*Ps.* l. 12, 14.

Command thy strength, O God: confirm, O God, what thou hast wrought in us.—*Ps.* lxvii. 29.

Convert us, O God; and show us thy face, and we shall be saved. . . .

Turn again, O God of hosts, look down from heaven, and see, and visit this vineyard:

And perfect the same which thy right hand hath planted: and upon the Son of man whom thou hast confirmed for thyself.—*Ps.* lxxix. 4, 15, 16.

With my whole heart have I sought after thee: let me not stray from thy commandments.—*Ps.* cxviii. 10.

Lead me into the path of thy commandments; for this same I have desired.

Incline my heart unto thy testimonies, and not to covetousness.

Turn away my eyes, that they may not behold vanity: quicken me in thy way. . . .

And take not thou the word of truth utterly out of my mouth: for in thy words I have hoped exceedingly.—*Ps.* cxviii. 35-37, 43.

Quicken thou me according to thy mercy: and I shall keep the testimonies of thy mouth.—*Ps.* cxviii. 88.

Teach me to do thy will, for thou art my God.

Thy good spirit shall lead me into the right land.—*Ps.* cxlii. 10.

O Lord, father, and God of my life, leave me not to their devices.

Give me not haughtiness of my eyes, and turn away from me all coveting.

Take from me the greediness of the belly, and let not the lusts of the flesh take hold of me, and give me not over to a shameless and foolish mind.— *Ecclus.* xxiii. 4-6.

Convert us, O Lord, to thee, and we shall be converted: renew our days, as from the beginning.—*Lam.* v. 21.

May God be gracious to you, and remember his covenant that he made with Abraham, and Isaac, and Jacob, his faithful servants:

And give you all a heart to worship him, and to do his will with a great heart, and a willing mind.

May he open your heart in his law, and in his commandments, and send you peace.—2 *Mach.* i. 2-4.

The grace of our Lord Jesus Christ be with you.—1 *Cor.* xvi. 23.

For this cause I bow my knees to the Father of our Lord Jesus Christ. . . .

That he would grant you, according to the riches of his glory, to be strengthened by his Spirit with might unto the inward man.—*Eph.* iii. 14, 16.

And may the Lord multiply you, and make you abound in charity towards one another, and towards all men; as we do also towards you,

To confirm your hearts without blame, in holiness, before God and our Father, at the coming of our Lord Jesus Christ, with all his saints. Amen.—1 *Thess.* iii. 12, 13.

And may the God of peace himself sanctify you in all things; that your whole spirit, and soul, and body, may be preserved blameless in the coming of our Lord Jesus Christ.—1 *Thess.* v. 23.

Now our Lord Jesus Christ himself, and God and our Father, who hath loved us, and hath given us everlasting consolation, and good hope in grace,

Exhort your hearts, and confirm you in every good work and word.—2 *Thess.* ii. 15, 16.

And may the God of peace, who brought again from the dead the great pastor of the sheep, our Lord Jesus Christ, in the blood of the everlasting testament,

Fit you in all goodness, that you may do his will; doing in you that which is well pleasing in his sight, through Jesus Christ, to whom is glory for ever and ever. Amen.—*Heb.* xiii. 20, 21.

GRATITUDE TO GOD

Therefore will I give thanks to thee, O Lord, among the Gentiles, and will sing to thy name.—*2 Kings* xxii. 50.

I will give thanks to thee in a great church; I will praise thee in a strong people.—*Ps.* xxxiv. 18.

In me, O God, are vows to thee, which I will pay, praises to thee.

Because thou hast delivered my soul from death, my feet from falling: that I may please in the sight of God, in the light of the living.—*Ps.* lv. 12, 13.

Come and hear, all ye that fear God, and I will tell you what great things he hath done for my soul.—*Ps.* lxv. 16.

But we thy people, and the sheep of thy pasture, will give thanks to thee for ever.

We will show forth thy praise, unto generation and generation.—*Ps.* lxxviii. 13.

I will give great thanks to the Lord with my mouth: and in the midst of many, I will praise him.

Because he hath stood at the right hand of the poor, to save my soul from persecutors.—*Ps.* cviii. 30, 31.

What shall I render to the Lord, for all the things that he hath rendered to me?—*Ps.* cxv. 12.

I will give glory to thee, because thou hast heard me: and art become my salvation.—*Ps.* cxvii. 21.

He hath not done in like manner to every nation: and his judgments he hath not made manifest to them.—*Ps.* cxlvii. 20.

In all his works he (David) gave thanks to the holy one, and to the most High, with words of glory.—*Ecclus.* xlvii. 9.

I will praise thy name continually, and will praise it with thanksgiving, and my prayer was heard.

And thou hast saved me from destruction, and hast delivered me from the evil time.

Therefore I will give thanks, and praise thee, and bless the name of the Lord.—*Ecclus.* li. 15-17.

And thou shalt say in that day: I will give thanks to thee, O Lord, for thou wast angry with me: thy wrath is turned away, and thou hast comforted me.—*Is.* xii. 1.

I will remember the tender mercies of the Lord, the praise of the Lord, for all the things that the Lord hath bestowed upon us, and for the multitude of his good things to the house of Israel, which he hath given them according to his kindness, and according to the multitude of his mercies.—*Is.* lxiii. 7.

And when he went up into the ship, he that had been troubled with the devil, began to beseech him that he might be with him.

And he admitted him not, but saith to him: Go into thy house, to thy friends, and tell them how great things the Lord hath done for thee, and hath had mercy on thee.

And he went his way, and began to publish in Decapolis how great things Jesus had done for him: and all men wondered.—*Mark* v. 18-20.

And as he entered into a certain town, there met him ten men that were lepers, who stood afar off;

And lifted up their voice, saying: Jesus, master, have mercy on us.

Whom when he saw, he said: Go, show yourselves to the priests. And it came to pass, as they went, they were made clean.

And one of them, when he saw that he was made clean, went back, with a loud voice glorifying God.

And he fell on his face before his feet, giving thanks; and this was a Samaritan.—*Luke* xvii. 12-16.

I give him thanks who hath strengthened me, even to Christ Jesus our Lord, for that he hath counted me faithful, putting me in the ministry.—*1 Tim.* i. 12.

GRATITUDE TO GOD, EXHORTATION TO

Give glory to the Lord, for he is good: for his mercy endureth for ever.

Let them say so that have been redeemed by the Lord, whom he hath redeemed from the hand of the enemy: and gathered out of the countries.—*Ps.* cvi. 1, 2.

Give thanks whilst thou art living, whilst thou art alive and in health thou shalt give thanks, and shalt praise God, and shalt glory in his mercies.—*Ecclus.* xvii. 27.

Forget not the kindness of thy surety: for he hath given his life for thee.—*Ecclus.* xxix. 19.

And for all these things, bless the Lord that made thee, and that replenisheth thee with all his good things.—*Ecclus.* xxxii. 17.

O give thanks to the Lord, because he is good: because his mercy endureth for ever and ever.—*Dan.* iii. 89.

Giving thanks always for all things, in the name of our Lord Jesus Christ, to God and the Father.—*Eph.* v. 20.

Giving thanks to God the Father, who hath made us worthy to be partakers of the lot of the saints in light:

Who hath delivered us from the power of darkness, and hath translated us into the kingdom of the Son of his love.—*Col.* i. 12, 13.

And let the peace of Christ rejoice in your hearts, wherein also you are called in one body: and be ye thankful.—*Col.* iii. 15.

All whatsoever you do in word or in work, do all in the name of the Lord Jesus Christ, giving thanks to God and the Father by him.—*Col.* iii. 17.

Be instant in prayer; watching in it with thanksgiving.—*Col.* iv. 2.

In all things give thanks; for this is the will of God in Christ Jesus concerning you all.—1 *Thess.* v. 18.

GRATITUDE TO GOD, A PRAYER OF

Now therefore, our God, we give thanks to thee, and we praise thy glorious name.—1 *Paral.* xxix. 13.

Blessed be the Lord, for he hath heard the voice of my supplication.—*Ps.* xxvii. 6.

I will extol thee, O Lord, for thou hast upheld me: and hast not made my enemies to rejoice over me.

O Lord my God, I have cried to thee, and thou hast healed me.

Thou hast brought forth, O Lord, my soul from hell: thou hast saved me from them that go down into the pit.

Sing to the Lord, O ye his saints: and give praise to the memory of his holiness.—*Ps.* xxix. 2-5.

Blessed be the Lord, for he hath shown his wonderful mercy to me in a fortified city.—*Ps.* xxx. 22.

Blessed be God, who hath not turned away my prayer, nor his mercy from me.—*Ps.* lxv. 20.

Bless the Lord, O my soul: and let all that is within me bless his holy name.

Bless the Lord, O my soul, and never forget all he hath done for thee.

Who forgiveth all thy iniquities: who healeth all thy diseases.

Who redeemeth thy life from destruction: who crowneth thee with mercy and compassion.—*Ps.* cii. 1-4.

And when this mortal hath put on immortality, then shall come to pass the saying that is written: Death is swallowed up in victory.

O death, where is thy victory? O death, where is thy sting? . . .

But thanks be to God, who hath given us the victory, through our Lord Jesus Christ.—1 *Cor.* xv. 54, 55, 57.

Blessed be the God and Father of our Lord Jesus Christ, the Father of mercies, and the God of all comfort.

Who comforteth us in all our tribulations.—2 *Cor.* i. 3, 4.

Thanks to God for his unspeakable gift.—2 *Cor.* ix. 15.

Blessed be the God and Father of our Lord Jesus Christ, who hath blessed us with spiritual blessings in heavenly places, in Christ:

As he chose us in him before the foundation of the world, that we should be holy and unspotted in his sight in charity.—*Eph.* i. 3, 4.

GREATNESS OF GOD, THE

Because the Lord your God, he is the God of gods, and the Lord of lords, a great God, and mighty and terrible, who accepteth no person nor taketh bribes.—*Deut.* x. 17.

Is it then to be thought that God should indeed dwell upon earth? for if heaven, and the heavens of heavens cannot contain thee, how much less this house which I have built?— 3 *Kings* viii. 27.

Peradventure thou wilt comprehend the steps of God, and wilt find out the Almighty perfectly?

He is higher than heaven, and what wilt thou do? he is deeper than hell, and how wilt thou know?

The measure of him is longer than the earth, and broader than the sea.

If he shall overturn all things, or shall press them together, who shall contradict him?—*Job* xi. 7-10.

Dost thou not think that God is higher than heaven, and is elevated above the height of the stars?—*Job* xxii. 12.

Behold, God is great, exceeding our knowledge: the number of his years is inestimable.—*Job* xxxvi. 26.

We cannot find him worthily: he is great in strength and in judgment, and in justice, and he is ineffable.

Therefore men shall fear him, and all that seem to themselves to be wise, shall not dare to behold him.—*Job* xxxvii. 23, 24.

For the Lord is high, terrible: a great king over all the earth.—*Ps.* xlvi. 3.

For the Lord is a great God, and a great King above all gods.

For in his hand are all the ends of the earth: and the heights of the mountains are his.

For the sea is his, and he made it: and his hands formed the dry land.— *Ps.* xciv. 3-5.

For the Lord is great, and exceedingly to be praised: he is to be feared above all gods.—*Ps.* xcv. 4.

The Lord is high above all nations; and his glory above the heavens.

Who is as the Lord our God, who dwelleth on high:

And looketh down on the low things in heaven and in earth?—*Ps.* cxii. 4-6.

Great is the Lord, and greatly to be praised: and of his greatness there is no end.—*Ps.* cxliv. 3.

Great is our Lord, and great is his power: and of his wisdom there is no number.—*Ps.* cxlvi. 5.

There is one most high Creator Almighty, and a powerful king, and greatly to be feared, who sitteth upon his throne, and is the God of dominion. —*Ecclus.* i. 8.

What shall we be able to do to glorify him? for the Almighty himself is above all his works.

The Lord is terrible and exceeding great, and his power is admirable.

Glorify the Lord as much as ever you can, for he will yet far exceed, and his magnificence is wonderful.

Blessing the Lord, exalt him as much as you can: for he is above all praise.

When you exalt him, put forth all your strength, and be not weary: for you can never go far enough.

Who shall see him, and declare him? and who shall magnify him as he is from the beginning?—*Ecclus.* xliii. 30-35.

Who hath measured the waters in the hollow of his hand, and weighed the heavens with his palm? who hath poised with three fingers the bulk of the earth, and weighed the mountains in scales, and the hills in a balance? . . .

Behold the Gentiles are as a drop of a bucket, and are counted as the smallest grain of a balance: behold the islands are as a little dust.

. . . All nations are before him as if they had no being at all, and are counted to him as nothing, and vanity. —*Is.* xl. 12, 15, 17.

Thus saith the Lord, the king of Israel, and his redeemer, the Lord of hosts: I am the first, and I am the last, and besides me, there is no God.

Who is like to me? let him call and declare: and let him set before me the order, since I appointed the ancient people: and the things to come, and that shall be hereafter, let them show unto them.—*Is.* xliv. 6, 7.

To whom have you likened me, and made me equal, and compared me, and made me like?

. . . Remember the former age, for I am God, and there is no God beside, neither is there the like to me:

Who show from the beginning the things that shall be at last, and from ancient times the things that as yet are not done, saying: My counsel shall stand, and all my will shall be done.—*Is.* xlvi. 5, 9, 10.

He stood and measured the earth.

He beheld, and melted the nations: and the ancient mountains were crushed to pieces.

The hills of the world were bowed down by the journeys of his eternity.—*Hab.* iii. 6.

God, who made the world and all things therein; he, being Lord of heaven and earth, dwelleth not in temples made with hands;

Neither is he served with men's hands, as though he needed any thing; seeing it is he who giveth to all life, and breath, and all things.—*Acts* xvii. 24, 25.

I charge thee: . . . That thou keep the commandment without spot, blameless, unto the coming of our Lord Jesus Christ,

Which in his times he shall show who is the Blessed and only Mighty, the King of kings, and Lord of lords;

Who only hath immortality, and inhabiteth light inaccessible, whom no man hath seen nor can see: to whom be honor and empire everlasting. Amen.—1 *Tim.* vi. 14-16.

GREATNESS OF GOD, ACKNOWL-EDGMENT OF THE

Who is like to thee, among the strong, O Lord? who is like to thee, glorious in holiness, terrible and praiseworthy, doing wonders?—*Ex.* xv. 11.

Thine, O Lord, is magnificence, and power, and glory, and victory: and to thee is praise: for all that is in heaven and in earth is thine: thine is the kingdom, O Lord, and thou art above all princes.

Thine are riches, and thine is glory, thou hast dominion over all, in thy hand is power and might: in thy hand, greatness, and the empire of all things. 1 *Paral.* xxix. 11, 12.

O Adonai, Lord, great art thou, and glorious in thy power, and no one can overcome thee.—*Judith* xvi. 16.

O Lord, our Lord, how admirable is thy name in the whole earth!

For thy magnificence is elevated above the heavens.—*Ps.* viii. 2.

Great is the Lord, and exceedingly to be praised in the city of our God, in his holy mountain.—*Ps.* xlvii. 2.

All the nations thou hast made shall come and adore before thee, O Lord: and they shall glorify thy name.

For thou art great, and dost wonderful things: thou art God alone.—*Ps.* lxxxv. 9, 10.

For who in the clouds can be compared to the Lord: or who among the sons of God shall be like to God?

God, who is glorified in the assembly of the saints: great and terrible above all them that are about him.

O Lord God of hosts, who is like to thee? thou art mighty, O Lord, and thy truth is round about thee.—*Ps.* lxxxviii. 7-9.

For thou art the most high Lord over all the earth: thou art exalted exceedingly above all gods.—*Ps.* xcvi. 9.

Bless the Lord, O my soul: O Lord, my God, thou art exceedingly great.—*Ps.* ciii. 1.

For the whole world before thee is as the least grain of the balance, and as a drop of the morning dew, that falleth down upon the earth.—*Wis.* xi. 23.

There is none like to thee, O Lord; thou art great, and great is thy name in might.

Who shall not fear thee, O king of nations? for thine is the glory: among all the wise men of the nations, and in all their kingdoms there is none like unto thee. . . .

But the Lord is the true God: he is the living God, and the everlasting king: at his wrath, the earth shall tremble, and the nations shall not be able to abide his threatenings.—*Jer.* x. 6, 7, 10.

GREATNESS AND POWER OF GOD SHOWN BY HIS WORKS, THE

Lord God, thou hast begun to show unto thy servant thy greatness and most mighty hand, for there is no other God, either in heaven or earth, that is able to do thy works, or to be compared to thy strength.—*Deut.* iii. 24.

Thou thyself, O Lord, alone, thou hast made heaven, and the heaven of heavens, and all the host thereof: the earth, and all things that are in it: the seas, and all that are therein: and thou givest life to all these things, and the host of heaven adoreth thee.— 2 *Esd.* ix. 6.

He stretcheth out the north over the empty space, and hangeth the earth upon nothing.

He bindeth up the waters in his clouds, so that they break not out and fall down together.

He withholdeth the face of his throne, and spreadeth his cloud over it.

He hath set bounds about the waters, till light and darkness come to an end.

The pillars of heaven tremble, and dread at his beck.

By his power the seas are suddenly gathered together, and his wisdom hath struck the proud one.

His spirit hath adorned the heavens, and his obstetric hand brought forth the winding serpent.

Lo, these things are said in part of his ways: and seeing we have heard scarce a little drop of his word, who shall be able to behold the thunder of his greatness?—*Job* xxvi. 7-14.

Behold, God is great, exceeding our knowledge: the number of his years is inestimable.

He lifteth up the drops of rain, and poureth out showers like floods:

Which flow from the clouds that cover all above.

If he will spread out clouds as his tent,

And lighten with his light from above, he shall cover also the ends of the sea.

For by these he judgeth people, and giveth food to many mortals.

In his hand he hideth the light, and commandeth it to come again.—*Job* xxxvi. 26-32.

He commandeth the snow to go down upon the earth, and the winter rain, and the shower of his strength.— *Job* xxxvii. 6.

Where wast thou when I laid the foundations of the earth? tell me if thou hast understanding.

Who hath laid the measures thereof, if thou knowest? or who hath stretched the line upon it?

Upon what are its bases grounded? or who laid the cornerstone thereof? . . .

Who shut up the sea with doors, when it broke forth as issuing out of the womb?

. . . I set my bounds around it, and made it bars and doors:

And I said: Hitherto thou shalt come, and shalt go no further, and here thou shalt break thy swelling waves.— *Job* xxxviii. 4-6, 8, 10, 11.

The heavens show forth the glory of God, and the firmament declareth the work of his hands.

Day to day uttereth speech, and night to night showeth knowledge.— *Ps.* xviii. 2, 3.

By the word of the Lord the heavens were established; and all the power of them by the spirit of his mouth:

Gathering together the waters of the sea, as in a vessel; laying up the depths in storehouses.

Let all the earth fear the Lord, and let all the inhabitants of the world be in awe of him.

For he spoke, and they were made: he commanded, and they were created. —*Ps.* xxxii. 6-9.

Come and behold ye the works of the Lord: what wonders he hath done upon earth.—*Ps.* xlv. 9.

The heavens shall confess thy wonders, O Lord: and thy truth, in the church of the saints. . . .

Thou rulest the power of the sea: and appeasest the motion of the waves thereof.

Thou hast humbled the proud one, as one that is slain: with the arm of thy strength thou hast scattered thy enemies.—*Ps.* lxxxviii. 6, 10, 11.

Bless the Lord, O my soul: O Lord my God, thou art exceeding great. . . .

Who stretchest out the heaven like a pavilion:

Who coverest the higher rooms thereof with water.

Who makest the clouds thy chariot: who walkest upon the wings of the winds. . . .

Who hast founded the earth upon its own base: it shall not be moved for ever and ever.

The deep, like a garment, is its clothing: above the mountains shall the waters stand.

. . . The mountains ascend, and the plains descend into the place which thou hast founded for them.

Thou hast set a bound which they shall not pass over; neither shall they return to cover the earth.

Thou sendest forth springs in the vales: between the midst of the hills the waters shall pass.—*Ps.* ciii. 1-3, 5, 6, 8-10.

They that go down to the sea in ships, doing business in the great waters:

These have seen the works of the Lord, and his wonders in the deep.

He said the word, and there arose a storm of wind: and the waves thereof were lifted up.

They mount up to the heavens, and they go down to the depths: their soul pined away with evils.

They were troubled, and reeled like a drunken man; and all their wisdom was swallowed up.

And they cried to the Lord in their affliction: and he brought them out of their distresses.

And he turned the storm into a breeze; and its waves were still.—*Ps.* cvi. 23-29.

For I have known that the Lord is great, and our God is above all gods.

Whatsoever the Lord pleased he hath done, in heaven, in earth, in the sea, and in all the deeps.

He bringeth up clouds from the end of the earth: he hath made lightnings for the rain.

He bringeth forth winds out of his stores.—*Ps.* cxxxiv. 5-7.

Praise ye the Lord of lords: for his mercy endureth for ever.

Who alone doth great wonders. . . .

Who made the heavens in understanding. . . .

Who established the earth above the waters. . . .

Who made the great lights. . . .

The sun to rule the day. . . .

The moon and the stars to rule the night.—*Ps.* cxxxv. 3-9.

Generation and generation shall praise thy works: and they shall declare thy power. . . .

And they shall speak of the might of thy terrible acts: and shall declare thy greatness.—*Ps.* cxliv. 4, 6.

But all men are vain, in whom there is not the knowledge of God: and who by these good things that are seen, could not understand him that is, neither by attending to the works have acknowledged who was the workman. . . .

With whose beauty, if they, being delighted, took them to be gods: let them know how much the Lord of them is more beautiful than they: for the first author of beauty made all those things.

Or if they admired their power and their effects, let them understand by them, that he that made them, is mightier than they:

For by the greatness of the beauty, and of the creature, the creator of them may be seen, so as to be known thereby.—*Wis.* xiii. 1, 3-5.

The firmament on high is his beauty, the beauty of heaven with its glorious show.

The sun when he appeareth showing forth at his rising, an admirable instrument, the work of the most High. . . .

Great is the Lord that made him, and at his words he hath hastened his course.

And the moon in all in her season, for a declaration of times and a sign of the world.

. . . The glory of the stars is the beauty of heaven: the Lord enlighteneth the world on high. . . .

Look upon the rainbow, and bless

him that made it: it is very beautiful in its brightness.

It encompasseth the heaven about with the circle of its glory, the hands of the most High have displayed it.

By his commandment he maketh the snow to fall apace, and sendeth forth swiftly the lightnings of his judgment. . . .

By his greatness, he hath fixed the clouds, and the hailstones are broken.

At his sight shall the mountains be shaken, and at his will the south wind shall blow.

The noise of his thunder shall strike the earth, so doth the northern storm, and the whirlwind:

And as the birds lighting upon the earth, he scattereth snow, and the falling thereof is as the coming down of locusts.

The eye admireth at the beauty of the whiteness thereof, and the heart is astonished at the shower thereof.

He shall pour frost as salt upon the earth: and when it freezeth, it shall become like the tops of thistles.

The cold north wind bloweth, and the water is congealed into crystal; upon every gathering together of waters it shall rest, and shall clothe the waters as a breastplate. . . .

At his word the wind is still, and with his thought he appeaseth the deep, and the Lord hath planted islands therein.

Let them that sail on the sea, tell the dangers thereof: and when we hear with our ears, we shall admire.

There are great and wonderful works: a variety of beasts, and of all living things, and the monstrous creatures of whales. . . .

We shall say much, and yet shall want words; but the sum of our words is, He is all. . . .

There are many things hidden from us that are greater than these: for we have seen but a few of his works.—*Ecclus.* xliii. *passim.*

It is he that sitteth upon the globe of the earth, and the inhabitants thereof are as locusts: he that stretcheth out the heavens as nothing, and spreadeth them out as a tent to dwell in. . . .

Lift up your eyes on high, and see who hath created these things: who bringeth out their host by number, and calleth them all by their names: by the greatness of his might and strength and power, not one of them was missing. . . .

Knowest thou not, or hast thou not heard? the Lord is the everlasting God, who hath created the ends of the earth: he shall not faint nor labor, neither is there any searching out of his wisdom. —*Is.* xl. 22, 26, 28.

He that maketh the earth by his power, that prepareth the world by his wisdom, and stretcheth out the heavens by his knowledge.

At his voice, he giveth a multitude of waters in the heaven, and lifteth up the clouds from the ends of the earth: he maketh lightnings for rain, and bringeth forth the wind out of his treasures.—*Jer.* x. 12, 13.

Seek him that maketh Arcturus and Orion, and that turneth darkness into morning, and that changeth day into night: that calleth the waters of the sea, and poureth them out upon the face of the earth: The Lord is his name.

He that with a smile bringeth destruction upon the strong, and waste upon the mighty.—*Amos* v. 8, 9.

GRIEF OF CHRIST OVER THE BLINDNESS OF THE JEWS

Jerusalem, Jerusalem, thou that killest the prophets, and stonest them that are sent unto thee, how often would I have gathered together thy children, as the hen doth gather her chickens under her wings, and thou wouldest not?—*Matt.* xxiii. 37.

And the Pharisees came forth, and began to question with him, asking him a sign from heaven, tempting him.

And sighing deeply in spirit, he saith: Why doth this generation seek a sign? Amen, I say to you, a sign shall not be given to this generation. —*Mark* viii. 11, 12.

And when he drew near, seeing the city, he wept over it, saying:

If thou also hadst known, and that in this thy day, the things that are to thy peace; but now they are hidden from thy eyes.

For the days shall come upon thee: and thy enemies shall cast a trench about thee, and compass thee round, and straiten thee on every side,

And beat thee flat to the ground, and thy children who are in thee: and they shall not leave in thee a stone upon a stone: because thou hast not known the time of thy visitation.—*Luke* xix. 41-44.

GUIDE, OR COUNSELLOR, NEED OF A

Seek counsel always of a wise man. —*Tob.* iv. 19.

Where there is no governor, the people shall fall: but there is safety where there is much counsel.—*Prov.* xi. 14.

The way of a fool is right in his own eyes: but he that is wise hearkeneth unto counsels.—*Prov.* xii. 15.

Among the proud there are always contentions: but they that do all things with counsel, are ruled by wisdom.—*Prov.* xiii. 10.

The prudent man doth all things with counsel: but he that is a fool, layeth open his folly.—*Prov.* xiii. 16.

Designs are brought to nothing where there is no counsel: but where there are many counsellors, they are established.—*Prov.* xv. 22.

Designs are strengthened by counsels: and wars are to be managed by governments.—*Prov.* xx. 18.

The steps of man are guided by the Lord: but who is the man that can understand his own way?—*Prov.* xx. 24.

He that trusteth in his own heart, is a fool: but he that walketh wisely, he shall be saved.—*Prov.* xxviii. 26.

Let not the discourse of the ancients escape thee, for they have learned of their fathers:

For of them thou shalt learn understanding, and to give an answer in time of need.—*Ecclus.* viii. 11, 12.

A frame of wood bound together in the foundation of a building, shall not be loosed: so neither shall the heart that is established by advised counsel. —*Ecclus.* xxii. 19.

My son, do thou nothing without counsel, and thou shalt not repent when thou hast done.—*Ecclus.* xxxii. 24.

In all thy works, let the true word go before thee, and steady counsel before every action.—*Ecclus.* xxxvii. 20.

Gold and silver make the feet stand sure: but wise counsel is above them both.—*Ecclus.* xl. 25.

GUIDE, GOD OUR

And the Lord went before them to show the way by day in a pillar of a cloud, and by night in a pillar of fire: that he might be the guide of their journey at both times.

There never failed the pillar of the cloud by day, nor the pillar of fire by night, before the people.—*Ex.* xiii. 21, 22.

The wickedness of sinners shall be brought to nought: and thou shalt direct the just.—*Ps.* vii. 10.

He will guide the mild in judgment: he will teach the meek his ways.—*Ps.* xxiv. 9.

Thou hast held me by my right hand; and by thy will thou hast conducted me, and with thy glory thou hast received me.—*Ps.* lxxii. 24.

And he took away his own people as sheep: and guided them in the wilderness like a flock.—*Ps.* lxxvii. 52.

The heart of man disposeth his way: but the Lord must direct his steps.— *Prov.* xvi. 9.

The steps of man are guided by the Lord: but who is the man that can understand his own way?—*Prov.* xx. 24.

Blessed is he that is conversant in these good things: and he that layeth them up in his heart, shall be wise always.

For if he do them, he shall be strong to do all things: because the light of God guideth his steps.—*Ecclus.* l. 30, 31.

And I will lead the blind into the way which they know not: and in the paths which they were ignorant of I will make them walk: I will make darkness light before them, and crooked things straight: these things have I done to them, and have not forsaken them.— *Is.* xlii. 16.

Thus saith the Lord thy redeemer, the Holy One of Israel: I am the Lord thy God, that teach thee profitable things, that govern thee in the way that thou walkest.—*Is.* xlviii. 17.

GUIDE, CHRIST OUR

Through the bowels of the mercy of our God, in which the Orient from on high hath visited us:

To enlighten them that sit in darkness, and in the shadow of death: to direct our feet into the way of peace.—*Luke* i. 78, 79.

Thomas saith to him: Lord, we know not whither thou goest; and how can we know the way?

Jesus saith to him: I am the way, and the truth, and the life. No man cometh to the Father, but by me.—*John* xiv. 5, 6.

GUIDANCE FROM GOD, WE SHOULD PRAY FOR

Bless God at all times: and desire of him to direct thy ways, and that all thy counsels may abide in him.—*Tob.* iv. 20.

Have confidence in the Lord with all thy heart, and lean not upon thy own prudence.

In all thy ways think on him, and he will direct thy steps.—*Prov.* iii. 5, 6.

But above all these things, pray to the most High, that he may direct thy way in truth.—*Ecclus.* xxxvii. 19.

I know, O Lord, that the way of a man is not his: neither is it in a man to walk, and to direct his steps.—*Jer.* x. 23.

GUIDANCE, A PRAYER FOR

Then hear thou them in heaven, and forgive the sins of thy servants, and of the people Israel: and show them the good way wherein they should walk.—3 *Kings* viii. 36.

Conduct me, O Lord, in thy justice: because of my enemies, direct my way in thy sight.—*Ps.* v. 9.

Show, O Lord, thy ways to me, and teach me thy paths.

Direct me in thy truth, and teach me; for thou art God my Saviour; and on thee have I waited all the day long. —*Ps.* xxiv. 4, 5.

Set me, O Lord, a law in thy way, and guide me in the right path, because of my enemies.—*Ps.* xxvi. 11.

Conduct me, O Lord, in thy way, and I will walk in thy truth: let my heart rejoice that it may fear thy name. —*Ps.* lxxxv. 11.

Look upon thy servants, and upon their works: and direct their children.

And let the brightness of the Lord our God be upon us: and direct thou the works of our hands over us; yea, the work of our hands do thou direct. —*Ps.* lxxxix. 16, 17.

Lead me into the path of thy commandments; for this same I have desired.—*Ps.* cxviii. 35.

Direct my steps according to thy word: and let no iniquity have dominion over me.—*Ps.* cxviii. 133.

Prove me, O God, and know my heart: examine me, and know my paths.

And see if there be in me the way of iniquity: and lead me in the eternal way.—*Ps.* cxxxviii. 23, 24.

Reward them that patiently wait for thee, that thy prophets may be found faithful: and hear the prayers of thy servants,

According to the blessing of Aaron over thy people, and direct us into the way of justice.—*Ecclus.* xxxvi. 18, 19.

And let the Lord thy God show us the way by which we may walk, and the thing that we must do.—*Jer.* xlii. 3.

And the Lord direct your hearts, in the charity of God, and the patience of Christ.—2 *Thess.* iii. 5.

HABIT OF SIN, THE

For my iniquities are gone over my head: and as a heavy burden are become heavy upon me.—*Ps.* xxxvii. 5.

For evils without number have surrounded me; my iniquities have overtaken me, and I was not able to see. They are multiplied above the hairs of my head: and my heart hath forsaken me.—*Ps.* xxxix. 13.

For they sleep not except they have done evil: and their sleep is taken away, unless they have made some to fall.

They eat the bread of wickedness.

and drink the wine of iniquity.—*Prov.* iv. 16, 17.

It is a proverb: A young man according to his way, even when he is old he will not depart from it.—*Prov.* xxii. 6.

If the Ethiopian can change his skin, or the leopard, his spots: you also may do well, when you have learned evil.—*Jer.* xiii. 23.

Let not sin therefore reign in your mortal body, so as to obey the lusts thereof.—*Rom.* vi. 12.

HANDS OF GOD, WE ARE IN THE

The Lord killeth and maketh alive, he bringeth down to hell, and bringeth back again.

The Lord maketh poor and maketh rich, he humbleth and he exalteth.

He raiseth up the needy from the dust, and lifteth up the poor from the dunghill: that he may sit with princes, and hold the throne of glory. For the poles of the earth are the Lord's, and upon them he hath set the world.

He will keep the feet of his saints, and the wicked shall be silent in darkness, because no man shall prevail by his own strength.—1 *Kings* ii. 6-9.

For thou scourgest, and thou savest: thou leadest down to hell, and bringest up again: and there is none that can escape thy hand.—*Tob.* xiii. 2.

I have sinned: what shall I do to thee, O keeper of men? why hast thou set me opposite to thee, and I am become burdensome to myself?—*Job* vii. 20.

But I have put my trust in thee, O Lord: I said: Thou art my God. My lots are in thy hands.—*Ps.* xxx. 15, 16.

As the divisions of waters, so the heart of the king is in the hand of the Lord: whithersoever he will he shall turn it.—*Prov.* xxi. 1.

If thou say: I have not strength enough: he that seeth into the heart, he understandeth, and nothing deceiveth the keeper of thy soul, and he shall render to a man according to his works. —*Prov.* xxiv. 12.

For in his hand are both we, and our words, and all wisdom, and the knowledge and skill of works.—*Wis.* vii. 16.

As the potter's clay is in his hand, to fashion and order it:

All his ways are according to his ordering: so man is in the hand of him that made him, and he will render to him according to his judgment.— *Ecclus.* xxxiii. 13, 14.

Cannot I do with you, as this potter, O house of Israel, saith the Lord? behold as clay is in the hand of the potter, so are you in my hand, O house of Israel.—*Jer.* xviii. 6.

But (thou) hast lifted thyself up against the Lord of heaven; . . . but the God who hath thy breath in his hand, and all thy ways, thou hast not glorified.—*Dan.* v. 23.

Are not two sparrows sold for a farthing? and not one of them shall fall on the ground without your Father.

But the very hairs of your head are all numbered.

Fear not therefore: better are you than many sparrows.—*Matt.* x. 29-31.

HANDS OF GOD, ALL THINGS ARE IN THE

Who is ignorant that the hand of the Lord hath made all these things?

In whose hand is the soul of every living thing, and the spirit of all flesh of man.—*Job* xii. 9, 10.

Our God is the God of salvation: and of the Lord, of the Lord are the issues from death.—*Ps.* lxvii. 21.

The power of the earth is in the hand of God, and in his time he will raise up a profitable ruler over it.

The prosperity of man is in the hand of God, and upon the person of the scribe he shall lay his honor.—*Ecclus.* x. 4, 5.

Good things and evil, life and death, poverty and riches, are from God.— *Ecclus.* xi. 14.

For it is easy in the eyes of God, on a sudden to make the poor man rich.— *Ecclus.* xi. 23.

And he (God) changeth times and ages: taketh away kingdoms, and establisheth them, giveth wisdom to the wise, and knowledge to them that have understanding.—*Dan.* ii. 21.

Neither is he (God) served with

men's hands, as though he needed any thing; seeing it is he who giveth to all life, and breath, and all things:

And hath made of one, all mankind, to dwell upon the whole face of the earth, determining appointed times, and the limits of their habitation.—*Acts* xvii. 25, 26.

For of him, and by him, and in him, are all things: to him be glory for ever. Amen.—*Rom.* xi. 36.

HANDS OF GOD, WE SHOULD PUT OURSELVES IN THE

See: Abandonment of oneself to God—page 11.

HAPPINESS IS FROM GOD, ALL TRUE

See: Joy, spiritual—page 240.

HAPPINESS IN SERVING GOD

O how great is the multitude of thy sweetness, O Lord, which thou hast hidden for them that fear thee!

Which thou hast wrought for them that hope in thee, in the sight of the sons of men.—*Ps.* xxx. 20.

O taste, and see that the Lord is sweet: blessed is the man that hopeth in him.—*Ps.* xxxiii. 9.

Delight in the Lord, and he will give thee the requests of thy heart.—*Ps.* xxxvi. 4.

For thou hast given me, O Lord, a delight in thy doings: and in the works of thy hands, I shall rejoice.—*Ps.* xci. 5.

Sing joyfully to God, all the earth: serve ye the Lord with gladness.

Come in before his presence with exceeding great joy.—*Ps.* xcix. 2.

Let my speech be acceptable to him: but I will take delight in the Lord.—*Ps.* ciii. 34.

I have been delighted in the way of thy testimonies, as in all riches. . . .

I have purchased thy testimonies for an inheritance for ever: because they are the joy of my heart.—*Ps.* cxviii. 14, 111.

They have called the people happy, that hath these things: but happy is that people whose God is the Lord.—*Ps.* cxliii. 15.

It is joy to the just to do judgment: and dread to them that work iniquity.—*Prov.* xxi. 15.

The fear of the Lord is honor, and glory, and gladness, and a crown of joy.

The fear of the Lord shall delight the heart, and shall give joy, and gladness, and length of days. . . .

Religiousness shall keep and justify the heart, it shall give joy and gladness.—*Ecclus.* i. 11, 12, 18.

If so be you have tasted that the Lord is sweet.—1 *Peter* ii. 3.

HAPPINESS OF THE JUST MAN

See: Just man, happiness of the—page 262.

HATRED

Thou shalt not hate thy brother in thy heart, but reprove him openly, lest thou incur sin through him.—*Lev.* xix. 17.

Hatred stirreth up strifes: and charity covereth all sins.—*Prov.* x. 12.

He that despiseth the poor, reproacheth his Maker; and he that rejoiceth at another man's ruin, shall not be unpunished.—*Prov.* xvii. 5.

When thy enemy shall fall, be not glad, and in his ruin, let not thy heart rejoice:

Lest the Lord see, and it displease him, and he turn away his wrath from him.—*Prov.* xxiv. 17, 18.

Rejoice not at the death of thy enemy; knowing that we all die, and are not willing that others should rejoice at our death.—*Ecclus.* viii. 8.

Let all bitterness, and anger, and indignation, and clamor, and blasphemy, be put away from you, with all malice. —*Eph.* iv. 31.

He that saith he is in the light, and hateth his brother, is in darkness even until now. . . .

But he that hateth his brother is in darkness, and walketh in darkness, and knoweth not whither he goeth; because the darkness hath blinded his eyes.— 1 *John* ii. 9, 11.

Whosoever hateth his brother, is a murderer. And you know that no murderer hath eternal life abiding in himself.—1 *John* iii. 15.

If any man say, I love God, and hateth his brother; he is a liar. For he that loveth not his brother, whom he seeth, how can he love God, whom he seeth not?—*1 John* iv. 20.

HEALING IS FROM GOD, ALL

See: Physician, God our—page 381.

HEALTH OF BODY, A BLESSING

Better is a poor man who is sound, and strong of constitution, than a rich man, who is weak and afflicted with evils.

Health of the soul in holiness of justice, is better than all gold and silver: and a sound body, than immense revenues.

There is no riches above the riches of the health of the body: and there is no pleasure above the joy of the heart.

Better is death, than a bitter life: and everlasting rest, than continual sickness.—*Ecclus.* xxx. 14-17.

HEART, PERVERSITY OF

See also: Inclinations of man, evil —page 234.

A perverse heart is abominable to the Lord: and his will is in them that walk sincerely.—*Prov.* xi. 20.

He that is of a perverse heart, shall not find good: and he that perverteth his tongue, shall fall into evil.—*Prov.* xvii. 20.

The perverse are hard to be corrected, and the number of fools is infinite.—*Eccles.* i. 15.

An evil eye is towards evil things: and he shall not have his fill of bread, but shall be needy and pensive at his own table.—*Ecclus.* xiv. 10.

A perverse heart will cause grief, and a man of experience will resist it. —*Ecclus.* xxxvi. 22.

The heart is perverse above all things, and unsearchable, who can know it?—*Jer.* xvii. 9.

O generation of vipers, how can you speak good things, whereas you are evil? for out of the abundance of the heart the mouth speaketh.

A good man out of a good treasure bringeth forth good things: and an evil man out of an evil treasure bringeth forth evil things.—*Matt.* xii. 34, 35.

But the things which proceed out of the mouth, come forth from the heart, and those things defile a man.

For from the heart come forth evil thoughts, murders, adulteries, fornications, thefts, false testimonies, blasphemies.

These are the things that defile a man.—*Matt.* xv. 18-20.

All things are clean to the clean: but to them that are defiled, and to unbelievers, nothing is clean: but both their mind and their conscience are defiled.—*Titus* i. 15.

HEART, PURITY OF

See also: Innocence—page 244.

Who shall ascend into the mountain of the Lord: or who shall stand in his holy place?

The innocent in hands, and clean of heart, who hath not taken his soul in vain, nor sworn deceitfully to his neighbor.

He shall receive a blessing from the Lord, and mercy from God his Saviour. —*Ps.* xxiii. 3-5.

Create a clean heart in me, O God: and renew a right spirit within my bowels.—*Ps.* l. 12.

Let my heart be undefiled in thy justifications, that I may not be confounded.—*Ps.* cxviii. 80.

With all watchfulness keep thy heart, because life issueth out from it. —*Prov.* iv. 23.

The perverse way of a man is strange: but as for him that is pure, his work is right.—*Prov.* xxi. 8.

He that loveth cleanness of heart, for the grace of his lips, shall have the king for his friend.—*Prov.* xxii. 11.

Blessed are the clean of heart: for they shall see God.—*Matt.* v. 8.

And we know that to them that love God, all things work together unto good, to such as, according to his purpose, are called to be saints.—*Rom.* viii. 28.

Grace be with all them that love our Lord Jesus Christ in incorruption. Amen.—*Eph.* vi. 24.

Now the end of the commandment is charity, from a pure heart, and a good conscience, and an unfeigned faith.— 1 Tim. i. 5.

All things are clean to the clean.— Titus i. 15.

Let us draw near with a true heart in fulness of faith, having our hearts sprinkled from an evil conscience, and our bodies washed with clean water.— Heb. x. 22.

HEART TO GOD, WE SHOULD GIVE ALL OUR

My heart is ready, O God, my heart is ready: I will sing, and will give praise, with my glory.—Ps. cvii. 2.

My son, give me thy heart: and let thy eyes keep my ways.—Prov. xxiii. 26.

'For the bed is straitened, so that one must fall out, and a short covering cannot cover both.—Is. xxviii. 20.

No man can serve two masters. For either he will hate the one, and love the other: or he will sustain the one, and despise the other. You cannot serve God and mammon.—Matt. vi. 24.

HEAVEN

Lift up your gates, O ye princes, and be ye lifted up, O eternal gates: and the King of Glory shall enter in.

Who is this King of Glory? The Lord who is strong and mighty: the Lord mighty in battle.

Lift up your gates, O ye princes, and be ye lifted up, O eternal gates: and the King of Glory shall enter in.

Who is this King of Glory? The Lord of hosts, he is the King of Glory. —Ps. xxiii. 7-10.

Blessed is he whom thou hast chosen and taken to thee: he shall dwell in thy courts.

We shall be filled with the good things of thy house.—Ps. lxiv. 5.

Bless the Lord, O my soul: and let all that is within me bless his holy name. . . .

Who satisfieth thy desire with good things: thy youth shall be renewed like the eagle's.—Ps. cii. 1, 5.

The heaven of heaven is the Lord's:

'It is too narrow to hold two : God will have the bed of our heart all to himself.

but the earth he has given to the children of men.—Ps. cxiii. (Heb. cxv.) 16.

Open ye the gates, and let the just nation, that keepeth the truth, enter in. —Is. xxvi. 2.

They shall not hunger, nor thirst, neither shall the heat nor the sun strike them: for he that is merciful to them, shall be their shepherd, and at the fountains of waters he shall give them drink. —Is. xlix. 10.

Thou shalt no more have the sun for thy light by day, neither shall the brightness of the moon enlighten thee: but the Lord shall be unto thee for an everlasting light, and thy God for thy glory.

Thy sun shall go down no more, and thy moon shall not decrease: for the Lord shall be unto thee for an everlasting light, and the days of thy mourning shall be ended.

And thy people shall be all just, they shall inherit the land for ever, the branch of my planting, the work of my hand to glorify me.—Is. lx. 19-21.

O Israel, how great is the house of God, and how vast is the place of his possession!

It is great, and hath no end: it is high and immense.—Bar. iii. 24, 25.

Then shall the king say to them that shall be on his right hand: Come, ye blessed of my Father, possess you the kingdom prepared for you from the foundation of the world.—Matt. xxv. 34.

In my Father's house there are many mansions. If not, I would have told you: because I go to prepare a place for you.—John xiv. 2.

But, as it is written: That eye hath not seen, nor ear heard, neither hath it entered into the heart of man, what things God hath prepared for them that love him.—1 Cor. ii. 9.

One is the glory of the sun, another the glory of the moon, and another the glory of the stars. For star differeth from star in glory.

So also is the resurrection of the dead. It is sown in corruption, it shall rise in incorruption.

It is sown in dishonor, it shall rise in glory. It is sown in weakness, it shall rise in power.

It is sown a natural body, it shall rise a spiritual body.—1 *Cor.* xv. 41-44.

If I must glory (it is not expedient indeed): but I will come to visions and revelations of the Lord. . . .

And I know such a man (whether in the body, or out of the body, I know not: God knoweth):

That he was caught up into paradise, and heard secret words, which it is not granted to man to utter.—2 *Cor.* xii. 1, 3, 4.

And he gave some apostles and some prophets: . . .

For the perfecting of the saints, for the work of the ministry, for the edifying of the body of Christ:

Until we all meet into the unity of faith, and of the knowledge of the Son of God, unto a perfect man, unto the measure of the age of the fulness of Christ.—*Eph.* iv. 11-13.

But our conversation is in heaven; from whence also we look for the Saviour, our Lord Jesus Christ,

Who will reform the body of our lowness, made like to the body of his glory, according to the operation whereby also he is able to subdue all things unto himself.—*Philipp.* iii. 20, 21.

Therefore they are before the throne of God, and they serve him day and night in his temple: and he that sitteth on the throne shall dwell over them.

They shall no more hunger nor thirst, neither shall the sun fall on them, nor any heat.

For the Lamb, which is in the midst of the throne, shall rule them, and shall lead them to the fountains of the waters of life, and God shall wipe away all tears from their eyes.—*Apoc.* vii. 15, 16, 17.

And I saw no temple therein. For the Lord God Almighty is the temple thereof, and the Lamb.

And the city had no need of the sun, nor of the moon, to shine in it. For the glory of God hath enlightened it, and the Lamb is the lamp thereof. . . .

And the gates thereof shall not be shut by day: for there shall be no night there. . . .

There shall not enter into it any thing defiled, or that worketh abomination or maketh a lie, but they that are written in the book of life of the Lamb.—*Apoc.* xxi. 22, 23, 25, 27.

HEAVEN, A PLACE OF HAPPINESS

Thou hast made known to me the ways of life, thou shalt fill me with joy with thy countenance: at thy right hand are delights even to the end.— *Ps.* xv. 11.

They shall be inebriated with the plenty of thy house; and thou shalt make them drink of the torrent of thy pleasure.

For with thee is the fountain of life; and in thy light, we shall see light.— *Ps.* xxxv. 9, 10.

Glorious things are said of thee, O city of God. . . .

The dwelling in thee is, as it were, of all rejoicing.—*Ps.* lxxxvi. 3, 7.

He shall cast death down headlong for ever: and the Lord God shall wipe away tears from every face, and the reproach of his people he shall take away from off the whole earth: for the Lord hath spoken it.

And they shall say in that day: Lo, this is our God, we have waited for him, and he will save us: this is the Lord, we have patiently waited for him, we shall rejoice and be joyful in his salvation.—*Is.* xxv. 8, 9.

And in that day the deaf shall hear the words of the book, and out of darkness and obscurity the eyes of the blind shall see.

And the meek shall increase their joy in the Lord, and the poor men shall rejoice in the Holy One of Israel.—*Is.* xxix. 18, 19.

Then shall the eyes of the blind be opened, and the ears of the deaf shall be unstopped.

Then shall the lame man leap as a hart, and the tongue of the dumb shall be free: for waters are broken out in the desert, and streams in the wilderness. . . .

And a path and a way shall be there, and it shall be called the holy way: the unclean shall not pass over it, and this shall be unto you a straight way, so that fools shall not err therein.

No lion shall be there, nor shall any

mischievous beast go up by it, nor be found there: but they shall walk there that shall be delivered.

And the redeemed of the Lord shall return, and shall come into Sion with praise, and everlasting joy shall be upon their heads: they shall obtain joy and gladness, and sorrow and mourning shall flee away.—*Is.* xxxv. 5, 6, 8-10.

For behold I create new heavens, and a new earth: and the former things shall not be in remembrance, and they shall not come upon the heart.

But you shall be glad and rejoice for ever in these things which I create: for behold I create Jerusalem a rejoicing, and the people thereof joy.

And I will rejoice in Jerusalem, and joy in my people, and the voice of weeping shall no more be heard in her, nor the voice of crying.—*Is.* lxv. 17-19.

And I heard a great voice from the throne, saying: Behold the tabernacle of God with men, and he will dwell with them. And they shall be his people; and God himself with them shall be their God.

And God shall wipe away all tears from their eyes: and death shall be no more, nor mourning, nor crying, nor sorrow shall be any more, for the former things are passed away.—*Apoc.* xxi. 3, 4.

HEAVEN A PLACE OF REST

There the wicked cease from tumult, and there the wearied in strength are at rest.

And they sometime bound together without disquiet, have not heard the voice of the oppressor.

The small and great are there, and the servant is free from his master.— *Job* iii. 17-19.

Seeing it is a just thing with God to repay tribulation to them that trouble you:

And to you who are troubled, rest with us, when the Lord Jesus shall be revealed from heaven, with the angels of his power.—2 *Thess.* i. 6, 7.

HEAVEN, THE BEATIFIC VISION OF

But as for the just, they shall give glory to thy name: and the upright shall dwell with thy countenance.—*Ps.* cxxxix. 14.

For we know in part, and we prophesy in part.

But when that which is perfect is come, that which is in part, shall be done away. . . .

We see now through a glass in a dark manner; but then face to face. Now I know in part; but then I shall know even as I am known.—1 *Cor.* xiii. 9, 10, 12.

But we all beholding the glory of the Lord with open face, are transformed into the same image, from glory to glory, as by the Spirit of the Lord.— 2 *Cor.* iii. 18.

Dearly beloved, we are now the sons of God; and it hath not yet appeared what we shall be. We know, that, when he shall appear, we shall be like to him: because we shall see him as he is.— 1 *John* iii. 2.

After this, I saw a great multitude, which no man could number, of all nations, and tribes, and peoples, and tongues, standing before the throne, and in sight of the Lamb, clothed with white robes, and palms in their hands. . . .

Therefore they are before the throne of God, and they serve him day and night in his temple: and he that sitteth on the throne, shall dwell over them.—*Apoc.* vii. 9, 15.

And there shall be no curse any more; but the throne of God and of the Lamb shall be in it, and his servants shall serve him.

And they shall see his face: and his name shall be on their foreheads.— *Apoc.* xxii. 3, 4.

HEAVEN, ETERNITY OF

Let nothing hinder thee from praying always, and be not afraid to be justified even to death: for the reward of God continueth for ever.—*Ecclus.* xviii. 22.

God will clothe thee with the double garment of justice, and will set a crown on thy head of everlasting honor.—*Bar.* v. 2.

And these shall go into everlasting punishment: but the just into life everlasting.--*Matt.* xxv. 46.

While we look not at the things which are seen, but at the things which are not seen. For the things which are seen, are temporal; but the things which are not seen, are eternal.—*2 Cor.* iv. 18.

For we know, if our earthly house of this habitation be dissolved, that we have a building of God, a house not made with hands, eternal in heaven.—*2 Cor.* v. 1.

Blessed be the God and Father of our Lord Jesus Christ, who according to his great mercy, hath regenerated us unto a lively hope, by the resurrection of Jesus Christ from the dead,

Unto an inheritance incorruptible and undefiled, and that cannot fade, reserved in heaven for you.—*1 Peter* i. 3, 4.

And night shall be no more: and they shall not need the light of the lamp, nor the light of the sun, because the Lord God shall enlighten them, and they shall reign for ever and ever.—*Apoc.* xxii. 5.

HEAVEN, OUR TRUE HOME

See also: Life, a pilgrimage upon earth—page 282.

All these died according to faith, not having received the promises, but beholding them afar off, and saluting them, and confessing that they are pilgrims and strangers on the earth.

For they that say these things, do signify that they seek a country. . . .

But now they desire a better, that is to say, a heavenly country. Therefore God is not ashamed to be called their God; for he hath prepared for them a city.—*Heb.* xi. 13, 14, 16.

For we have not here a lasting city, but we seek one that is to come.—*Heb.* xiii. 14.

HEAVEN, DESIRE OF

As the hart panteth after the fountains of water; so my soul panteth after thee, O God.

My soul hath thirsted after the strong living God; when shall I come and appear before the face of God?—*Ps.* xli. 2, 3.

Thy kingdom come.—*Matt.* vi. 10.

For we know, if our earthly house of this habitation be dissolved, that we have a building of God, a house not made with hands, eternal in heaven.

For in this also we groan, desiring to be clothed upon with our habitation that is from heaven.

Yet so that we be found clothed, not naked.

For we also, who are in this tabernacle, do groan, being burthened; because we would not be unclothed, but clothed upon, that that which is mortal may be swallowed up by life.—*2 Cor.* v. 1-4.

But we are confident, and have a good will to be absent rather from the body, and to be present with the Lord.

And therefore we labor, whether absent or present, to please him.—*2 Cor.* v. 8, 9.

For to me, to live is Christ: and to die is gain. . . .

But I am straitened between two: having a desire to be dissolved and to be with Christ, a thing by far the better.—*Philipp.* i. 21, 23.

Therefore, if you be risen with Christ, seek the things that are above; where Christ is sitting at the right hand of God:

Mind the things that are above, not the things that are upon the earth.—*Col.* iii. 1, 2.

For they that say these things, do signify that they seek a country. . . .

But now they desire a better, that is to say, a heavenly country.—*Heb.* xi. 14, 16.

For we have not here a lasting city, but we seek one that is to come.—*Heb.* xiii. 14.

And the spirit and the bride say: Come. And he that heareth, let him say: Come. And he that thirsteth, let him come: and he that will, let him take the water of life, freely.—*Apoc.* xxii. 17.

HEAVEN, HOPE OF

For I know that my Redeemer liveth, and in the last day I shall rise out of the earth.

And I shall be clothed again with my skin, and in my flesh I shall see my God.

Whom I myself shall see, and my

eyes shall behold, and not another: this my hope is laid up in my bosom.—*Job* xix. 25-27.

I believe to see the good things of the Lord in the land of the living.—*Ps.* xxvi. 13.

If (according to man) I fought with beasts at Ephesus, what doth it profit me, if the dead rise not again? Let us eat and drink, for to-morrow we shall die.—1 *Cor.* xv. 32.

But let us, who are of the day, be sober, having on the breastplate of faith and charity, and for a helmet, the hope of salvation.—1 *Thess.* v. 8.

Dearly beloved, we are now the sons of God; and it hath not yet appeared what we shall be. We know, that, when he shall appear, we shall be like to him: because we shall see him as he is.

And every one that hath this hope in him, sanctifieth himself, as he also is holy.—1 *John* iii. 2, 3.

HEAVEN, GOD HAS MADE US HEIRS OF

For the Spirit himself giveth testimony to our spirit, that we are the sons of God.

And if sons, heirs also; heirs indeed of God, and joint heirs with Christ: yet so, if we suffer with him, that we may be also glorified with him.—*Rom.* viii. 16, 17.

And because you are sons, God hath sent the Spirit of his Son into your hearts, crying: Abba, Father.

Therefore now he is not a servant, but a son. And if a son, an heir also, through God.—*Gal.* iv. 6, 7.

In whom (Christ) also believing, you were signed with the holy Spirit of promise,

Who is the pledge of our inheritance, unto the redemption of acquisition, unto the praise of his glory.—*Eph.* i. 13, 14.

But when the goodness and kindness of God our Saviour appeared:

Not by the works of justice, which we have done, but according to his mercy, he saved us, by the laver of regeneration, and renovation of the Holy Ghost: . . .

That, being justified by his grace, we may be heirs, according to hope of life everlasting.—*Titus* iii. 4, 5, 7.

Blessed be the God and Father of our Lord Jesus Christ, who according to his great mercy, hath regenerated us unto a lively hope, by the resurrection of Jesus Christ from the dead,

Unto an inheritance incorruptible and undefiled, and that cannot fade, reserved in heaven for you.—1 *Peter* i. 3, 4.

Who (Christ) is on the right hand of God, swallowing down death, that we might be made heirs of life everlasting. —1 *Peter* iii. 22.

HEAVEN, WE MUST WORK AND FIGHT TO GAIN

The life of man upon earth is a warfare, and his days are like the days of a hireling.—*Job* vii. 1.

And from the days of John the Baptist until now, the kingdom of heaven suffereth violence, and the violent bear it away.—*Matt.* xi. 12.

And behold a certain lawyer stood up, tempting him, and saying: Master, what must I do to possess eternal life?

But he said to him: What is written in the law? how readest thou?

He answering, said: Thou shalt love the Lord thy God with thy whole heart, and with thy whole soul, and with all thy strength, and with all thy mind: and thy neighbor as thyself.

And he said to him: Thou hast answered right: this do, and thou shalt live.—*Luke* x. 25-28.

The law and the prophets were until John; from that time, the kingdom of God is preached, and every one useth violence towards it.—*Luke* xvi. 16.

Labor not for the meat which perisheth, but for that which endureth unto life everlasting, which the Son of man will give you. For him hath God, the Father, sealed.—*John* vi. 27.

Know you not that they that run in the race, all run indeed, but one receiveth the prize? So run that you may obtain.

And every one that striveth for the mastery, refraineth himself from all things: and they indeed that they may receive a corruptible crown; but we, an incorruptible one.—1 *Cor.* ix. 24, 25.

This precept I commend to thee, O son Timothy; according to the prophecies going on before thee, that thou war in them a good warfare,

Having faith and a good conscience, which some rejecting, have made shipwreck concerning the faith.—*1 Tim.* i. 18, 19.

Fight the good fight of faith: lay hold on eternal life, whereunto thou art called, and hast confessed a good confession before many witnesses.—*1 Tim.* vi. 12.

Labor as a good soldier of Christ Jesus. . . .

For he also that striveth for the mastery, is not crowned, except he strive lawfully.—*2 Tim.* ii. 3, 5.

I have fought a good fight, I have finished my course, I have kept the faith.

As to the rest, there is laid up for me a crown of justice, which the Lord, the just judge, will render to me in that day: and not only to me, but to them also that love his coming.—*2 Tim.* iv. 7, 8.

And therefore we also, having so great a cloud of witnesses over our head, laying aside every weight and sin which surrounds us, let us run by patience to the fight proposed to us.—*Heb.* xii. 1.

HELL

He shall be punished for all that he did, and yet shall not be consumed: according to the multitude of his devices, so also shall he suffer.—*Job* xx. 18.

The sinners in Sion are afraid, trembling hath seized upon the hypocrites. Which of you can dwell with devouring fire? which of you shall dwell with everlasting burnings?—*Is.* xxxiii. 14.

And if thy hand scandalize thee, cut it off: it is better for thee to enter into life, maimed, than, having two hands, to go into hell, into unquenchable fire:

Where their worm dieth not, and the fire is not extinguished.

And if thy foot scandalize thee, cut it off. It is better for thee to enter lame into life everlasting, than having two feet, to be cast into the hell of unquenchable fire:

Where their worm dieth not, and the fire is not extinguished.

And if thy eye scandalize thee, pluck it out. It is better for thee with one eye to enter into the kingdom of God, than having two eyes, to be cast into the hell of fire:

Where their worm dieth not, and the fire is not extinguished.—*Mark* ix. 42-47.

And it came to pass that the beggar died, and was carried by the angels into Abraham's bosom. And the rich man also died; and he was buried in hell.

And lifting up his eyes, when he was in torments, he saw Abraham afar off, and Lazarus in his bosom:

And he cried, and said: Father Abraham, have mercy on me, and send Lazarus, that he may dip the tip of his finger in water, to cool my tongue: for I am tormented in this flame.

And Abraham said to him: Son, remember that thou didst receive good things in thy lifetime, and likewise Lazarus, evil things, but now he is comforted; and thou art tormented.

And besides all this, between us and you, there is fixed a great chaos: so that they who would pass from hence to you, cannot, nor from thence, come hither.—*Luke* xvi. 22-26.

And to you who are troubled, rest with us, when the Lord Jesus shall be revealed from heaven, with the angels of his power:

In a flame of fire, giving vengeance to them who know not God, and who obey not the gospel of our Lord Jesus Christ.

Who shall suffer eternal punishment in destruction, from the face of the Lord, and from the glory of his power. —*2 Thess.* i. 7-9.

And he (the angel) opened the bottomless pit: and the smoke of the pit arose, as the smoke of a great furnace; and the sun and the air were darkened with the smoke of the pit.—*Apoc.* ix. 2.

HELL A PLACE OF DARKNESS AND HORROR

Suffer me therefore that I may lament my sorrow a little:

Before I go, and return no more, to

a land that is dark, and covered with the mist of death:

A land of misery and darkness, where the shadow of death, and no order, but everlasting horror dwelleth.—*Job* x. 20, 21, 22.

And the unprofitable servant cast ye out into the exterior darkness. There shall be weeping and gnashing of teeth. —*Matt.* xxv. 30.

And the angels who kept not their principality, but forsook their own habitation, he hath reserved under darkness in everlasting chains, unto the judgment of the great day.—*Jude* i. 6.

Raging waves of the sea, foaming out their own confusion; wandering stars, to whom the storm of darkness is reserved for ever.—*Jude* i. 13.

HELL A PLACE OF SUFFERING

For he will give fire, and worms into their flesh, that they may burn, and may feel for ever.—*Judith* xvi. 21.

All darkness is hid in his secret places: a fire that is not kindled shall devour him, he shall be afflicted, when left in his tabernacle.—*Job* xx. 26.

Thou shalt make them as an oven of fire, in the time of thy anger: the Lord shall trouble them in his wrath, and fire shall devour them.—*Ps.* xx. 10.

Humble thy spirit very much: for the vengeance on the flesh of the ungodly is fire and worms.—*Ecclus.* vii. 19.

And they shall go out, and see the carcasses of the men that have transgressed against me: their worm shall not die, and their fire shall not be quenched: and they shall be a loathsome sight to all flesh.—*Is.* lxvi. 24.

Then shall he say to them also that shall be on his left hand: Depart from me, you cursed, into everlasting fire, which was prepared for the devil and his angels. . . .

And thee shall go into everlasting punishment.—*Matt.* xxv. 41, 46.

And the third angel followed them, saying with a loud voice: If any man shall adore the beast and his image, and receive his character in his forehead, or in his hand;

He also shall drink of the wine of the wrath of God, which is mingled with pure wine in the cup of his wrath, and shall be tormented with fire and brimstone in the sight of the holy angels, and in the sight of the Lamb.

And the smoke of their torments shall ascend up for ever and ever: neither have they rest day nor night, who have adored the beast and his image, and whoever receiveth the character of his name.—*Apoc.* xiv. 9-11.

And the beast was taken, and with him the false prophet, who wrought signs before him, wherewith he seduced them who received the character of the beast, and who adored his image. These two were cast alive into the pool of fire, burning with brimstone.—*Apoc.* xix. 20.

And there came down fire from God out of heaven, and devoured them; and the devil, who seduced them, was cast into the pool of fire and brimstone, where both the beast,

And the false prophet shall be tormented day and night for ever and ever. —*Apoc.* xx. 9, 10.

But the fearful, and unbelieving, and the abominable, and murderers, and whoremongers, and sorcerers, and idolaters, and all liars, they shall have their portion in the pool burning with fire and brimstone, which is the second death.—*Apoc.* xxi. 8.

HELL, ETERNITY OF

See: Part II—page 705.

HELP AND PROTECT ONE ANOTHER, WE SHOULD

Deliver him that suffereth wrong out of the hand of the proud: and be not faint-hearted in thy soul.—*Ecclus.* iv. 9.

Every one shall help his neighbor, and shall say to his brother: Be of good courage.—*Is.* xli. 6.

I have showed you all things, how that so laboring, you ought to support the weak, and to remember the word of the Lord Jesus, how he said: It is a more blessed thing to give, rather than to receive.—*Acts* xx. 35.

Bear ye one another's burdens; and so you shall fulfil the law of Christ.— *Gal.* vi. 2.

I therefore, a prisoner in the Lord,

beseech you that you walk worthy of the vocation in which you are called,

With all humility and mildness, with patience, supporting one another in charity.—*Eph.* iv. 1, 2.

And we beseech you, brethren, rebuke the unquiet, comfort the feebleminded, support the weak, be patient towards all men.

See that none render evil for evil to any man; but ever follow that which is good towards each other, and towards all men.—1 *Thess.* v. 14, 15.

Religion clean and undefiled before God and the Father, is this: to visit the fatherless and widows in their tribulation: and to keep one's self unspotted from this world.—*James* i. 27.

HELP ONE ANOTHER IN DOING GOOD, WE SHOULD

Do not withhold him from doing good, who is able: if thou art able, do good thyself also.—*Prov.* iii. 27.

The fruit of the just man is a tree of life: and he that gaineth souls, is wise.—*Prov.* xi. 30.

It is good that thou shouldst hold up the just, yea, and from him withdraw not thy hand: for he that feareth God, neglecteth nothing.—*Eccles.* vii. 19.

Despise not a man that turneth away from sin, nor reproach him therewith: remember that we are all worthy of reproof.—*Ecclus.* viii. 6.

How much better is it to reprove, than to be angry, and not to hinder him that confesseth in prayer.—*Ecclus.* xx. 1.

But they that are learned shall shine as the brightness of the firmament: and they that instruct many to justice, as stars for all eternity.—*Dan.* xii. 3.

Now him that is weak in faith, take unto you: not in dispute about thoughts.—*Rom.* xiv. 1.

And let us consider one another, to provoke unto charity and to good works. —*Heb.* x. 24.

As every man hath received grace, ministering the same one to another: as good stewards of the manifold grace of God.—1 *Peter* iv. 10.

HELP, OUR NEED OF GOD'S

See also: Grace, our need of God's— page 175.

O our God, wilt thou not then judge them? as for us, we have not strength enough, to be able to resist this multitude, which cometh violently upon us. But as we know not what to do, we can only turn our eyes to thee.—2 *Paral.* xx. 12.

And if thou think that battles consist in the strength of the army, God will make thee to be overcome by the enemies: for it belongeth to God both to keep, and to put to flight.—2 *Paral.* xxv. 8.

Behold there is no help for me in myself, and my familiar friends also are departed from me.—*Job* vi. 13.

Depart not from me.

For tribulation is very near: for there is none to help me.—*Ps.* xxi. 12.

Who shall rise up for me against the evil doers? or who shall stand with me against the workers of iniquity?

Unless the Lord had been my helper, my soul had almost dwelt in hell.— *Ps.* xciii. 16, 17.

If it had not been that the Lord was with us, let Israel now say:

If it had not been that the Lord was with us,

When men rose up against us,

Perhaps they had swallowed us up alive.

When their fury was enkindled against us, perhaps the water had swallowed us up.

Our soul hath passed through a torrent: perhaps our soul had passed through a water insupportable.

Blessed be the Lord, who hath not given us to be a prey to their teeth.— *Ps.* cxxiii. 1-6.

Unless the Lord build the house, they labor in vain that build it.

Unless the Lord keep the city, he watcheth in vain, that keepeth it.—*Ps.* cxxvi. 1.

I looked on my right hand, and beheld, and there was no one that would know me.

Flight hath failed me: and there is no one that hath regard to my soul.

I cried to thee, O Lord: I said: Thou art my hope, my portion in the land of the living.

Attend to my supplication: for I am brought very low.

Deliver me from my persecutors; for they are stronger than I.—*Ps.* cxli. 5-7.

How shall we be able to stand before their face, unless thou, O God, help us? —1 *Mach.* iii. 53.

Now when he (Jesus) had ceased to speak, he said to Simon: Launch out into the deep, and let down your nets for a draught.

And Simon answering, said to him: Master, we have labored all the night, and have taken nothing: but at thy word, I will let down the net.—*Luke* v. 4, 5.

HELP, A PRAYER FOR GOD'S

Lord, there is no difference with thee, whether thou help with few, or with many: help us, O Lord our God: for with confidence in thee, and in thy name, we are come against this multitude. O Lord, thou art our God, let not man prevail against thee.—2 *Paral.* xiv. 11.

And she (Esther) prayed to the Lord, the God of Israel, saying: O my Lord, who alone art our king, help me a desolate woman, and who have no other helper but thee.

My danger is in my hands.—*Esther* xiv. 3, 4.

May he send thee help from the sanctuary: and defend thee out of Sion. —*Ps.* xix. 3.

But thou, O Lord, remove not thy help to a distance from me; look towards my defence.—*Ps.* xxi. 20.

Take hold of arms and shield: and rise up to help me.

Bring out the sword, and shut up the way against them that persecute me: say to my soul: I am thy salvation.— *Ps.* xxxiv. 2, 3.

Attend unto my help, O Lord, the God of my salvation.—*Ps.* xxxvii. 23.

O God, come to my assistance; O Lord, make haste to help me.—*Ps.* lxix. 2.

O grant us help from trouble: for vain is the help of man.—*Ps.* cvii. 13.

Help me, O Lord my God; save me according to thy mercy.

And let them know that this is thy hand: and that thou, O Lord, hast done it.—*Ps.* cviii. 26, 27.

Uphold me according to thy word,

and I shall live: and let me not be confounded in my expectation.

Help me, and I shall be saved: and I will meditate always on thy justifications.—*Ps.* cxviii. 116, 117.

HELPER, GOD OUR

Behave like men, and take courage: be not afraid, nor dismayed for the king of the Assyrians, nor for all the multitude that is with him: for there are many more with us than with him.

For with him is an arm of flesh; but with us the Lord our God, who is our helper, and fighteth for us.—2 *Paral.* xxxii. 7, 8.

And the Lord is become a refuge for the poor: a helper in due time in tribulation.—*Ps.* ix. 10.

This poor man cried, and the Lord heard him: and saved him out of all his troubles.

The angel of the Lord shall encamp round about them that fear him: and shall deliver them.—*Ps.* xxxiii. 7, 8.

Blessed is the man whose help is from thee.—*Ps.* lxxxiii. 6.

I have lifted up my eyes to the mountains, from whence help shall come to me.

My help is from the Lord, who made heaven and earth.—*Ps.* cxx. 1, 2.

Blessed is he who hath the God of Jacob for his helper, whose hope is in the Lord his God.—*Ps.* cxlv. 5.

For I am the Lord thy God, who take thee by the hand, and say to thee: Fear not, I have helped thee.—*Is.* xli. 13.

And now hear, O Jacob, my servant, and Israel, whom I have chosen.

Thus saith the Lord, that made and formed thee, thy helper from the womb: Fear not, O my servant Jacob, and thou most righteous whom I have chosen.— *Is.* xliv. 1, 2.

Even to your old age I am the same, and to your grey hairs I will carry you: I have made you, and I will bear: I will carry and will save.—*Is.* xlvi. 4.

Thus saith the Lord: In an acceptable time I have heard thee, and in the day of salvation I have helped thee.— *Is.* xlix. 8.

The Lord God is my helper, therefore am I not confounded: therefore have I set my face as a most hard rock, and I

know that I shall not be confounded.—
Is. l. 7.

The Lord saith to me: Assuredly it
shall be well with thy remnant, assuredly I shall help thee in the time of
affliction, and in the time of tribulation
against the enemy.—*Jer.* xv. 11.

HELPER IN TEMPTATIONS,
GOD OUR

See: Temptation, God our help in—
page 553.

HELPER, ACKNOWLEDGMENT
THAT GOD IS OUR

But deliver us by thy hand, and help
me, who have no other helper but thee,
O Lord, who hast the knowledge of all
things.—*Esther* xiv. 14.

The Lord is my firmament, my
refuge, and my deliverer.

My God is my helper, and in him will
I put my trust.

My protector, and the horn of my salvation, and my support.—*Ps.* xvii. 3.

The Lord is my helper and my protector: in him hath my heart confided, and
I have been helped.—*Ps.* xxvii. 7.

Our soul waiteth for the Lord: for he
is our helper and protector.—*Ps.*
xxxii. 20.

I will say to God: Thou art my support. Why hast thou forgotten me?
and why go I mourning, whilst my
enemy afflicteth me?—*Ps.* xli. 10.

Our God is our refuge and strength:
a helper in troubles, which have found
us exceedingly.—*Ps.* xlv. 2.

For he is my God and my Saviour: he
is my helper, I shall not be moved.

In God is my salvation and my glory:
he is the God of my help, and my hope
is in God.

Trust in him, all ye congregation of
people: pour out your hearts before
him. God is our helper for ever.—*Ps.*
lxi. 7-9.

I am become unto many as a wonder,
but thou art a strong helper.—*Ps.* lxx. 7.

The Lord is my helper: I will not
fear what man can do unto me.

The Lord is my helper: and I will
look over my enemies.—*Ps.* cxvii. 6, 7.

I will give glory to thee, O Lord, O

King, and I will praise thee, O God my
Saviour.

I will give glory to thy name: for
thou hast been a helper and protector to
me.

And hast preserved my body from
destruction, from the snare of an unjust
tongue, and from the lips of them that
forge lies, and in the sight of them that
stood by, thou hast been my helper.—
Ecclus. li. 1-3.

HELPLESSNESS BEFORE GOD,
MAN'S

See: Powerlessness, man's—page 389.

HERESY AND HERETICS

A man that shall wander out of the
way of doctrine, shall abide in the company of the giants.—*Prov.* xxi. 16.

Let them alone: they are blind, and
leaders of the blind. And if the blind
lead the blind, both fall into the pit.
—*Matt.* xv. 14.

For we are not as many, adulterating the word of God; but with sincerity, but as from God, before God, in
Christ we speak.—2 *Cor.* ii. 17.

That henceforth we be no more children tossed to and fro, and carried
about with every wind of doctrine, by
the wickedness of men, by cunning
craftiness, by which they lie in wait to
deceive.—*Eph.* iv. 14.

Now the end of the commandment is
charity, from a pure heart, and a good
conscience, and an unfeigned faith.

From which things some, going
astray, are turned aside unto vain
babbling:

Desiring to be teachers of the law,
understanding neither the things they
say, nor whereof they affirm.—1 *Tim.* i.
5-7.

If any man teach otherwise, and consent not to the sound words of our
Lord Jesus Christ, and to that doctrine
which is according to godliness,

He is proud, knowing nothing, but
sick about questions and strifes of
words; from which arise envies, contentions, blasphemies, evil suspicions,

Conflicts of men corrupted in mind,
and who are destitute of the truth, supposing gain to be godliness.—1 *Tim.*
vi. 3-5.

They went out from us, but they were not of us. For if they had been of us, they would no doubt have remained with us; but that they may be manifest, that they are not all of us.—*1 John* ii. 19.

HERESY AND HERETICS, WE MUST NOT LISTEN TO

But though we, or an angel from heaven, preach a gospel to you besides that which we have preached to you, let him be anathema.

As we said before, so now I say again: If any one preach to you a gospel, besides that which you have received, let him be anathema.—*Gal.* i. 8, 9.

Beware lest any man cheat you by philosophy and vain deceit; according to the tradition of men, according to the elements of the world, and not according to Christ.—*Col.* ii. 8.

Let no man seduce you, willing in humility, and religion of angels, walking in the things which he hath not seen, in vain puffed up by the sense of his flesh,

And not holding the head, from which the whole body, by joints and bands, being supplied with nourishment, and compacted, groweth unto the increase of God.—*Col.* ii. 18, 19.

O Timothy, keep that which is committed to thy trust, avoiding the profane novelties of words, and oppositions of knowledge falsely so called.

Which some promising, have erred concerning the faith.—*1 Tim.* vi. 20, 21.

A man that is a heretic, after the first and second admonition, avoid.

Knowing that he, that is such a one, is subverted, and sinneth, being condemned by his own judgment.—*Titus* iii. 10, 11.

Be not led away with various and strange doctrines.—*Heb.* xiii. 9.

Whosoever revolteth, and continueth not in the doctrine of Christ, hath not God. He that continueth in the doctrine, the same hath both the Father and the Son.

If any man come to you, and bring not this doctrine, receive him not into the house, nor say to him, God speed you.

For he that saith unto him, God speed you, communicateth with his wicked works.—*2 John* i. 9-11.

HERESIES PROPHESIED IN THE CHURCH

Take heed to yourselves, and to the whole flock, wherein the Holy Ghost hath placed you bishops, to rule the church of God, which he hath purchased with his own blood.

I know that, after my departure, ravening wolves will enter in among you, not sparing the flock.

And of your own selves shall arise men speaking perverse things, to draw away disciples after them.—*Acts* xx. 28-30.

For there must be also heresies: that they also, who are approved, may be made manifest among you.—*1 Cor.* xi. 19.

Now the Spirit manifestly saith, that in the last times some shall depart from the faith, giving heed to spirits of error, and doctrines of devils,

Speaking lies in hypocrisy, and having their conscience seared,

Forbidding to marry, to abstain from meats, which God hath created to be received with thanksgiving by the faithful, and by them that have known the truth.—*1 Tim.* iv. 1-3.

For there shall be a time, when they will not endure sound doctrine; but, according to their own desires, they will heap to themselves teachers, having itching ears:

And will indeed turn away their hearing from the truth, but will be turned unto fables.—*2 Tim.* iv. 3, 4.

But there were also false prophets among the people, even as there shall be among you lying teachers, who shall bring in sects of perdition, and deny the Lord who bought them: bringing upon themselves swift destruction.

And many shall follow their riotousness, through whom the way of truth shall be evil spoken of.

And through covetousness, shall they with feigned words make merchandise of you. Whose judgment now of a long time lingereth not, and their perdition slumbereth not.—*2 Peter* ii. 1-3.

HIDDEN FROM GOD, WE CANNOT BE

See also: Omniscience of God— page 356.

'The Lord behold and judge between us when we shall be gone one from the other.

If thou afflict my daughters, and if thou bring in other wives over them: none is witness of our speech but God, who is present and beholdeth.—*Gen.* xxxi. 49, 50.

For his eyes are upon the ways of men, and he considereth all their steps.

There is no darkness, and there is no shadow of death, where they may be hid who work iniquity.—*Job* xxxiv. 21, 22.

I have kept thy commandments and thy testimonies: because all my ways are in thy sight.—*Ps.* cxviii. 168.

And I said: Perhaps darkness shall cover me: and night shall be my light in my pleasures.

But darkness shall not be dark to thee, and night shall be light as the day: the darkness thereof, and the light thereof are alike to thee.—*Ps.* cxxxviii. 11, 12.

For the spirit of the Lord hath filled the whole world: and that which containeth all things, hath knowledge of the voice.

Therefore he that speaketh unjust things cannot be hid, neither shall the chastising judgment pass him by.

For inquisition shall be made into the thoughts of the ungodly: and the hearing of his words shall come to God, to the chastising of his iniquities.—*Wis.* i. 7-9.

Say not: I shall be hidden from God, and who shall remember me from on high?

In such a multitude I shall not be known: for what is my soul in such an immense creation?—*Ecclus.* xvi. 16, 17.

Every man that passeth beyond his own bed, despising his own soul, and saying: Who seeth me?

Darkness compasseth me about, and the walls cover me, and no man seeth me: whom do I fear? the most High will not remember my sins.

And he understandeth not that his eye seeth all things, for such a man's

¹Laban speaking to Jacob.

fear driveth from him the fear of God, and the eyes of men fearing him:

And he knoweth not that the eyes of the Lord are far brighter than the sun, beholding round about all the ways of men, and the bottom of the deep, and looking into the hearts of men, into the most hidden parts.—*Ecclus.* xxiii. 25-28.

The works of all flesh are before him, and there is nothing hid from his eyes. —*Ecclus.* xxxix. 24.

Woe to you that are deep of heart, to hide your counsel from the Lord: and their works are in the dark, and they say: Who seeth us, and who knoweth us?

This thought of yours is perverse: as if the clay should think against the potter, and the work should say to the maker thereof: Thou madest me not: or the thing framed should say to him that fashioned it: Thou understandest not. —*Is.* xxix. 15, 16.

Why sayest thou, O Jacob, and speakest, O Israel: My way is hid from the Lord, and my judgment is passed over from my God?—*Is.* xl. 27.

And I, think ye, a God at hand, saith the Lord, and not a God afar off?

Shall a man be hid in secret places, and I not see him, saith the Lord? Do not I fill heaven and earth, saith the Lord?—*Jer.* xxiii. 23, 24.

And though they be hid in the top of Carmel, I will search, and take them away from thence: and though they hide themselves from my eyes in the depth of the sea, there will I command the serpent, and he shall bite them.— *Amos* ix. 3.

Neither is there any creature invisible in his sight: but all things are naked and open to his eyes, to whom our speech is.—*Heb.* iv. 13.

HOLINESS OF GOD

See: Sanctity of God—page 500.

HOLY GHOST, THE

See: Part II—page 707.

HOLY GHOST, THE GIFTS OF THE

And the spirit of the Lord shall rest upon him: the spirit of wisdom, and of understanding, the spirit of counsel,

and of fortitude, the spirit of knowledge, and of godliness.
And he shall be filled with the spirit of the fear of the Lord.—*Is.* xi. 2, 3.

HOLY GHOST, FRUIT OF THE

But the fruit of the Spirit is, charity, joy, peace, patience, benignity, goodness, longanimity,
Mildness, faith, modesty, continency, chastity.—*Gal.* v. 22, 23.

HOLY GHOST, SINS AGAINST THE

Therefore I say to you: Every sin and blasphemy shall be forgiven men, but the blasphemy of the Spirit shall not be forgiven.
And whosoever shall speak a word against the Son of man, it shall be forgiven him: but he that shall speak against the Holy Ghost, it shall not be forgiven him, neither in this world, nor in the world to come.—*Matt.* xii. 31, 32.
And grieve not the holy Spirit of God: whereby you are sealed unto the day of redemption.—*Eph.* iv. 30.

HOLY GHOST DWELLING IN US, THE

And hope confoundeth not: because the charity of God is poured forth in our hearts, by the Holy Ghost, who is given to us.—*Rom.* v. 5.
But you are not in the flesh, but in the spirit, if so be that the Spirit of God dwell in you. Now if any man have not the Spirit of Christ, he is none of his. . . .
And if the Spirit of him that raised up Jesus from the dead, dwell in you; he that raised up Jesus Christ from the dead, shall quicken also your mortal bodies, because of his Spirit that dwelleth in you.—*Rom.* viii. 9, 11.
Know you not, that you are the temple of God, and that the Spirit of God dwelleth in you?—1 *Cor.* iii. 16.
Or know you not, that your members are the temple of the Holy Ghost, who is in you, whom you have from God; and you are not your own?
For you are bought with a great price. Glorify and bear God in your body.—1 *Cor.* vi. 19, 20.
Now he that confirmeth us with you in Christ, and that hath anointed us, is God:
Who also hath sealed us, and given the pledge of the Spirit in our hearts.—2 *Cor.* i. 21, 22.
And because you are sons, God hath sent the Spirit of his Son into your hearts, crying: Abba, Father.—*Gal.* iv. 6.
Therefore, he that despiseth these things, despiseth not man, but God, who also hath given his holy Spirit in us.—1 *Thess.* iv. 8.
Keep the good things committed to thy trust by the Holy Ghost, who dwelleth in us.—2 *Tim.* i. 14.
But when the goodness and kindness of God our Saviour appeared:
Not by the works of justice which we have done, but according to his mercy, he saved us, by the laver of regeneration, and renovation of the Holy Ghost;
Whom he hath poured forth upon us abundantly, through Jesus Christ our Lord.—*Titus* iii. 4-6.

HOLY GHOST, HIS WORK IN THE WORLD AND IN THE CHURCH

And the earth was void and empty, and darkness was upon the face of the deep; and the spirit of God moved over the waters.—*Gen.* i. 2.
Thou shalt send forth thy spirit, and they shall be created: and thou shalt renew the face of the earth.—*Ps.* ciii. 30.
To whom hath the discipline of wisdom been revealed, and made manifest? and who hath understood the multiplicity of her steps?
There is one most high Creator Almighty, and a powerful king, and greatly to be feared, who sitteth upon his throne, and is the God of dominion.
He created her in the Holy Ghost, and saw her, and numbered her, and measured her.
And he poured her out upon all his works, and upon all flesh according to his gift, and hath given her to them that love him.—*Ecclus.* i. 7-10.
The spirit of the Lord is upon me,

208   *HOLY*

because the Lord hath anointed me: he hath sent me to preach to the meek, to heal the contrite of heart, and to preach a release to the captives, and deliverance to them that are shut up.

To proclaim the acceptable year of the Lord, and the day of vengeance of our God: to comfort all that mourn.— *Is.* lxi. 1, 2.

And it shall come to pass after this, that I will pour out my spirit upon all flesh: and your sons and your daughters shall prophesy: your old men shall dream dreams, and your young men shall see visions.

Moreover upon my servants and handmaids in those days I will pour forth my spirit.—*Joel* ii. 28, 29.

Now the generation of Christ was in this wise: When as his mother Mary was espoused to Joseph, before they came together, she was found with child, of the Holy Ghost.

Whereupon Joseph her husband, being a just man, and not willing publicly to expose her, was minded to put her away privately.

But while he thought on these things, behold the angel of the Lord appeared to him in his sleep, saying: Joseph, son of David, fear not to take unto thee Mary thy wife, for that which is conceived in her, is of the Holy Ghost.—*Matt.* i. 18-20.

I indeed baptize you in water unto penance, but he that shall come after me, is mightier than I, whose shoes I am not worthy to bear; he shall baptize you in the Holy Ghost and fire.—*Matt.* iii. 11.

And Mary said to the angel: How shall this be done, because I know not man?

And the angel answering, said to her: The Holy Ghost shall come upon thee, and the power of the most High shall overshadow thee. And therefore also the Holy which shall be born of thee shall be called the Son of God.—*Luke* i. 34, 35.

And when the days of Pentecost were accomplished, they were all together in one place:

And suddenly there came a sound from heaven, as of a mighty wind coming, and it filled the whole house where they were sitting.

And there appeared to them parted tongues as it were of fire, and it sat upon every one of them:

And they were all filled with the Holy Ghost, and they began to speak with divers tongues, according as the Holy Ghost gave them to speak.—*Acts* ii. 1-4.

While Peter was yet speaking these words, the Holy Ghost fell on all [1]them that heard the word.

And the faithful of the circumcision, who came with Peter, were astonished, for that the grace of the Holy Ghost was poured out upon the Gentiles also.

For they heard them speaking with tongues, and magnifying God.

Then Peter answered: Can any man forbid water, that these should not be baptized, who have received the Holy Ghost as well as we?—*Acts* x. 44-47.

And as they were ministering to the Lord, and fasting, the Holy Ghost said to them: Separate me Saul and Barnabas, for the work whereunto I have taken them. . . .

So they, being sent by the Holy Ghost, went to Seleucia: and from thence they sailed to Cyprus.—*Acts* xiii. 2, 4.

And when [2]they had passed through Phrygia, and the country of Galatia, they were forbidden by the Holy Ghost to preach the word in Asia.

And when they were come into Mysia, they attempted to go into Bithynia, and the Spirit of Jesus suffered them not.—*Acts* xvi. 6, 7.

Having heard these things [3]they were baptized in the name of the Lord Jesus.

And when Paul had imposed his hands on them, the Holy Ghost came upon them, and they spoke with tongues, and prophesied.—*Acts* xix 5, 6.

Take heed to yourselves, and to the whole flock, wherein the Holy Ghost hath placed you bishops, to rule the church of God, which he hath purchased with his own blood.—*Acts* xx. 28.

But, as it is written: That eye hath not seen, nor ear heard, neither hath it

[1]Cornelius and the Gentiles who were with him.
[2]Paul and Silas.
[3]The disciples at Ephesus.

entered into the heart of man, what things God hath prepared for them that love him.

But to us God hath revealed them by his Spirit. For the Spirit searcheth all things, yea, the deep things of God.—1 *Cor.* ii. 9, 10.

Now there are diversities of graces, but the same Spirit. . . .

And the manifestation of the Spirit is given to every man unto profit.

To one indeed, by the Spirit, is given the word of wisdom: and to another, the word of knowledge, according to the same Spirit. . . .

But all these things one and the same Spirit worketh, dividing to every one, according as he will.—1 *Cor.* xii. 4, 7, 8, 11.

For prophecy came not by the will of man at any time: but the holy men of God spoke, inspired by the Holy Ghost.—2 *Peter* i. 21.

HOLY GHOST, HIS WORK IN THE HEARTS OF MEN

And who shall know thy thought, except thou give wisdom, and send thy Holy Spirit from above:

And so the ways of them that are upon earth may be corrected, and men may learn the things that please thee? —*Wis.* ix. 17, 18.

And hope confoundeth not: because the charity of God is poured forth in our hearts, by the Holy Ghost, who is given to us.—*Rom.* v. 5.

Likewise the Spirit also helpeth our infirmity. For we know not what we should pray for as we ought; but the Spirit himself asketh for us with unspeakable groanings.—*Rom.* viii. 26.

Wherefore I give you to understand, that no man, speaking by the Spirit of God, saith Anathema to Jesus. And no man can say the Lord Jesus, but by the Holy Ghost.—1 *Cor.* xii. 3.

But you have the unction from the Holy One, and know all things.— 1 *John* ii. 20.

HOME, HOW WE SHOULD BEHAVE AT, AND TOWARD ONE'S FAMILY

And the parents taking their daughter, kissed her, and let her go:

Admonishing her to honor her father and mother-in-law, to love her husband, to take care of the family, to govern the house, and to behave herself irreprehensibly.—*Tob.* x. 12, 13.

He that troubleth his own house, shall inherit the winds: and the fool shall serve the wise.—*Prov.* xi. 29.

Be not as a lion in thy house, terrifying them of thy household, and oppressing them that are under thee.—*Ecclus.* iv. 35.

Bring not every man into thy house: for many are the snares of the deceitful. —*Ecclus.* xi. 31.

Give not to son or wife, brother or friend, power over thee while thou livest; and give not thy estate to another, lest thou repent, and thou entreat for the same.

As long as thou livest, and hast breath in thee, let no man change thee.

For it is better that thy children should ask of thee, than that thou look towards the hands of thy children.

In all thy works keep the pre-eminence.

Let no stain sully thy glory. In the time when thou shalt end the days of thy life, and in the time of thy decease, distribute thy inheritance.—*Ecclus.* xxxiii. 20-24.

It behooveth therefore a bishop to be blameless. . . .

One that ruleth well his own house, having his children in subjection with all chastity.

But if a man know not how to rule his own house, how shall he take care of the church of God?—1 *Tim.* iii. 2, 4, 5.

But if any widow have children or grandchildren, let her learn first to govern her own house, and to make a return of duty to her parents: for this is acceptable before God.—1 *Tim.* v. 4.

But if any man have not care of his own, and especially of those of his house, he hath denied the faith, and is worse than an infidel.—1 *Tim.* v. 8.

That they (the aged women) may teach the young women to be wise, to love their husbands, to love their children,

To be discreet, chaste, sober, having a care of the house, gentle, obedient to their husbands, that the word of God be not blasphemed.—*Titus* ii. 4, 5.

HONESTY IN OUR DEALINGS WITH ONE ANOTHER

See: Justice—page 268.

HOPE

If thou wilt put away from thee the iniquity that is in thy hand, and let not injustice remain in thy tabernacle:

Then mayst thou lift up thy face without spot, and thou shalt be steadfast, and shalt not fear. . . .

And thou shalt have confidence, hope being set before thee, and being buried, thou shalt sleep secure.—*Job* xi. 14, 15, 18.

My days have passed away, my thoughts are dissipated, tormenting my heart.

They have turned night into day, and after darkness, I hope for light again.—*Job* xvii. 11, 12.

In peace, in the selfsame I will sleep, and I will rest:

For thou, O Lord, singularly hast settled me in hope.—*Ps.* iv. 9, 10.

Therefore my heart hath been glad, and my tongue hath rejoiced: moreover my flesh also shall rest in hope.

Because thou wilt not leave my soul in hell; nor wilt thou give thy holy one to see corruption.—*Ps.* xv. 9, 10.

If thou lose hope, being weary in the day of distress, thy strength shall be diminished.—*Prov.* xxiv. 10.

But the souls of the just are in the hand of God, and the torment of death shall not touch them. . . .

And though in the sight of men, they suffered torments, their hope is full of immortality.—*Wis.* iii. 1, 4.

Thus saith the Lord: Let thy voice cease from weeping, and thy eyes from tears: for there is a reward for thy work, saith the Lord: and they shall return out of the land of the enemy.

And there is hope for thy last end, saith the Lord.—*Jer.* xxxi. 16, 17.

But we glory also in tribulations, knowing that tribulation worketh patience;

And patience, trial; and trial, hope;

And hope confoundeth not: because the charity of God is poured forth in our hearts, by the Holy Ghost, who is given to us.—*Rom.* v. 3-5.

For we are saved by hope. But hope that is seen, is not hope. For what a man seeth, why doth he hope for?

But if we hope for that which we see not, we wait for it with patience.—*Rom.* viii. 24, 25.

Now the God of hope fill you with all joy and peace in believing; that you may abound in hope, and in the power of the Holy Ghost.—*Rom.* xv. 13.

Now our Lord Jesus Christ himself, and God and our Father, who hath loved us, and hath given us everlasting consolation, and good hope in grace,

Exhort your hearts, and confirm you in every good work and word.—*2 Thess.* ii. 15, 16.

And Moses indeed was faithful in all his house as a servant, for a testimony of those things which were to be said:

But Christ as the Son in his own house: which house are we, if we hold fast the confidence and glory of hope unto the end.—*Heb.* iii. 5, 6.

HOPE OF HEAVEN

See: Heaven, hope of—page 198.

HOPE IN GOD

In thee, O Lord, have I hoped, let me never be confounded: deliver me in thy justice.—*Ps.* xxx. 2.

Do ye manfully, and let your heart be strengthened, all ye that hope in the Lord.—*Ps.* xxx. 25.

O taste, and see that the Lord is sweet: blessed is the man that hopeth in him.—*Ps.* xxxiii. 9.

But I, as a fruitful olive tree in the house of God, have hoped in the mercy of God for ever, yea, for ever and ever.—*Ps.* li. 10.

Have mercy on me, O God, have mercy on me: for my soul trusteth in thee.

And in the shadow of thy wings will I hope, until iniquity pass away.—*Ps.* lvi. 2.

In God is my salvation and my glory: he is the God of my help, and my hope is in God.—*Ps.* lxi. 8.

But I will always hope: and will add to all thy praise.—*Ps.* lxx. 14.

But it is good for me to adhere to my God, to put my hope in the Lord God:

That I may declare all thy praises, in the gates of the daughter of Sion.—*Ps.* lxxii. 28.

And take not thou the word of truth utterly out of my mouth: for in thy words I have hoped exceedingly. . . .

Be thou mindful of thy word to thy servant, in which thou hast given me hope.—*Ps.* cxviii. 43, 49.

For with thee there is merciful forgiveness: and by reason of thy law, I have waited for thee, O Lord.

My soul hath relied on his word: my soul hath hoped in the Lord.—*Ps.* cxxix. 4, 5.

The eyes of all hope in thee, O Lord; and thou givest them meat in due season.

Thou openest thy hand, and fillest with blessing every living creature.—*Ps.* cxliv. 15, 16.

Blessed is he who hath the God of Jacob for his helper, whose hope is in the Lord his God.—*Ps.* cxlv. 5.

The Lord taketh pleasure in them that fear him: and in them that hope in his mercy.—*Ps.* cxlvi. 11.

The spirit of those that fear God, is sought after, and by his regard shall be blessed.

For their hope is on him that saveth them.—*Ecclus.* xxxiv. 14, 15.

But they that hope in the Lord shall renew their strength, they shall take wings as eagles, they shall run, and not be weary, they shall walk, and not faint.—*Is.* xl. 31.

Be of good comfort, my children, cry to the Lord, and he will deliver you out of the hand of the princes your enemies.

For my hope is in the Eternal, that he will save you: and joy is come upon me from the Holy One, because of the mercy which shall come to you from our everlasting Saviour.—*Bar.* iv. 21, 22.

But I will look towards the Lord, I will wait for God my Saviour: my God will hear me.

Rejoice not thou, my enemy, over me, because I am fallen: I shall arise, when I sit in darkness, the Lord is my light.

I will bear the wrath of the Lord, because I have sinned against him; until he judge my cause, and execute judgment for me: he will bring me forth into the light, I shall behold his justice.—*Mich.* vii. 7-9.

If in this life only we have hope in Christ, we are of all men most miserable.—1 *Cor.* xv. 19.

For therefore we labor and are reviled, because we hope in the living God, who is the Saviour of all men, especially of the faithful.—1 *Tim.* iv. 10.

Wherein God, meaning more abundantly to show to the heirs of the promise, the immutability of his counsel, interposed an oath:

That by two immutable things, in which it is impossible for God to lie, we may have the strongest comfort, who have fled for refuge to hold fast the hope set before us.

Which we have as an anchor of the soul, sure and firm, and which entereth in even within the veil.—*Heb.* vi. 17-19.

HOPE IN GOD, EXHORTATION TO

Be converted therefore, ye sinners, and do justice before God, believing that he will show his mercy to you.—*Tob.* xiii. 8.

Why art thou sad, O my soul? and why dost thou trouble me?

Hope in God, for I will still give praise to him: the salvation of my countenance, and my God.—*Ps.* xli. 6.

From the morning watch even until night, let Israel hope in the Lord.

Because with the Lord there is mercy; and with him plentiful redemption.

And he shall redeem Israel from all his iniquities.—*Ps.* cxxix. 6-8.

Let Israel hope in the Lord, from henceforth, now and forever.—*Ps.* cxxx. 3.

Who is there among you that feareth the Lord, that heareth the voice of his servant, that hath walked in darkness, and hath no light? let him hope in the name of the Lord, and lean upon his God.—*Is.* l. 10.

Therefore turn thou to thy God: keep mercy and judgment, and hope in thy God always.—*Osee* xii. 6.

Rejoicing in hope. Patient in tribulation. Instant in prayer.—*Rom.* xii. 12.

Let us hold fast the confession of our hope without wavering (for he is faithful that hath promised).—*Heb.* x. 23.

HOPE IN GOD REWARDED BY THE ALMIGHTY

Praise ye the Lord our God, who hath not forsaken them that hope in him.—*Judith* xiii. 17.

But let all them be glad that hope in thee: they shall rejoice for ever, and thou shalt dwell in them.—*Ps.* v. 12.

In thee have our fathers hoped: they have hoped, and thou hast delivered them.—*Ps.* xxi. 5.

O how great is the multitude of thy sweetness, O Lord, which thou hast hidden for them that fear thee!

Which thou hast wrought for them that hope in thee, in the sight of the sons of men.—*Ps.* xxx. 20.

Many are the scourges of the sinner, but mercy shall encompass him that hopeth in the Lord.—*Ps.* xxxi. 10.

Behold the eyes of the Lord are on them that fear him: and on them that hope in his mercy.

To deliver their souls from death; and feed them in famine.—*Ps.* xxxii. 18, 19.

But the salvation of the just is from the Lord, and he is their protector in the time of trouble.

And the Lord will help them and deliver them: and he will rescue them from the wicked, and save them, because they have hoped in him.—*Ps.* xxxvi. 39, 40.

Because he hoped in me, I will deliver him: I will protect him, because he hath known my name.—*Ps.* xc. 14.

The house of Israel hath hoped in the Lord: he is their helper and their protector.

The house of Aaron hath hoped in the Lord: he is their helper and their protector.

They that fear the Lord, have hoped in the Lord: he is their helper and their protector.—*Ps.* cxiii. (*Heb.* cxv.) 9-11.

Every word of God is fire tried: he is a buckler to them that hope in him.—*Prov.* xxx. 5.

Ye that fear the Lord, hope in him: and mercy shall come to you for your delight.—*Ecclus.* ii. 9.

My children, behold the generations of men: and know ye that no one hath hoped in the Lord, and hath been confounded.—*Ecclus.* ii. 11.

I (wisdom) will penetrate to all the lower parts of the earth, and will behold all that sleep, and will enlighten all that hope in the Lord.—*Ecclus.* xxiv. 45.

The old error is passed away: thou wilt keep peace: peace, because we have hoped in thee.

You have hoped in the Lord forevermore, in the Lord God mighty for ever.—*Is.* xxvi. 3, 4.

The Lord is good to them that hope in him, to the soul that seeketh him.

It is good to wait with silence for the salvation of God.—*Lam.* iii. 25, 26.

The Lord is good, and giveth strength in the day of trouble: and knoweth them that hope in him.—*Nahum* i. 7.

Return to the stronghold, ye prisoners of hope, I will render thee double, as I declare to-day.—*Zach.* ix. 12.

HOPE, GOD OUR

And now, what is my hope? is it not the Lord? and my substance is with thee.—*Ps.* xxxviii. 8.

To thee have I cried from the ends of the earth: when my heart was in anguish, thou hast exalted me on a rock.

Thou hast conducted me; for thou hast been my hope; a tower of strength against the enemy.—*Ps.* lx. 3, 4.

Hear us, O God our Saviour, who art the hope of all the ends of the earth, and in the sea afar off.—*Ps.* lxiv. 6.

For thou art my patience, O Lord: my hope, O Lord, from my youth.—*Ps.* lxx. 5.

Because thou, O Lord, art my hope: thou hast made the most High thy refuge.—*Ps.* xc. 9.

I cried to thee, O Lord: I said: Thou art my hope, my portion in the land of the living.—*Ps.* cxli. 6.

He that feareth the Lord, shall tremble at nothing, and shall not be afraid: for he is his hope.—*Ecclus.* xxxiv. 16.

Be not thou a terror unto me, thou art my hope in the day of affliction.—*Jer.* xvii. 17.

And the Lord shall be the hope of his people, and the strength of the children of Israel.—*Joel* iii. 16.

Paul, an apostle of Jesus Christ, according to the commandment of God our Saviour, and of Christ Jesus our hope.—1 *Tim.* i. 1.

HOPE, GOD OUR ONLY

O our God, wilt thou not then judge them? as for us, we have not strength enough, to be able to resist this multitude, which cometh violently upon us. But as we know not what to do, we can only turn our eyes to thee.—2 *Paral.* xx. 12.

O my Lord, who alone art our king, help me a desolate woman, and who have no other helper but thee. . . .

O God, who art mighty above all, hear the voice of them that have no other hope, and deliver us from the hand of the wicked, and deliver me from my fear.—*Esther* xiv. 3, 19.

O grant us help from trouble: for vain is the help of man.—*Ps.* cvii. 13.

Put not your trust in princes:
In the children of men, in whom there is no salvation.—*Ps.* cxlv. 2, 3.

And my life was drawing near to hell beneath.

They compassed me on every side, and there was no one that would help me. I looked for the succor of men, and there was none.

I remembered thy mercy, O Lord, and thy works, which are from the beginning of the world.

How thou deliverest them that wait for thee, O Lord, and savest them out of the hands of the nations.—*Ecclus.* li. 9-12.

Destruction is thy own, O Israel; thy help is only in me.—*Osee* xiii. 9.

HOSPITALITY

And the Lord appeared to him (Abraham) in the vale of Mambre, as he was sitting at the door of his tent, in the very heat of the day.

And when he had lifted up his eyes, there appeared to him three men standing near him: and as soon as he saw them, he ran to meet them from the door of his tent, and adored down to the ground.

And he said: Lord, if I have found favor in thy sight, pass not away from thy servant:

But I will fetch a little water, and wash ye your feet, and rest ye under the tree.

And I will set a morsel of bread, and strengthen ye your heart, afterwards you shall pass on: for therefore are you come aside to your servant. And they said: Do as thou hast spoken.—*Gen.* xviii. 1-5.

And the two angels came to Sodom in the evening, and Lot was sitting in the gate of the city. And seeing them, he rose up and went to meet them: and worshipped prostrate to the ground,

And said: I beseech you, my lords, turn in to the house of your servant, and lodge there: wash your feet, and in the morning you shall go on your way. And they said: No, but we will abide in the street.

He pressed them very much to turn in unto him: and when they were come in to his house, he made them a feast, and baked unleavened bread, and they ate.—*Gen.* xix. 1-3.

The stranger did not stay without, my door was open to the traveller.—*Job* xxxi. 32.

Communicating to the necessities of the saints. Pursuing hospitality.—*Rom.* xii. 13.

It behooveth therefore a bishop to be blameless, the husband of one wife, sober . . . given to hospitality.—1 *Tim.* iii. 2.

Let a widow be chosen of no less than three-score years of age, who hath been the wife of one husband.

Having testimony for her good works, if she have brought up children, if she have received to harbor, if she have washed the saints' feet, if she have ministered to them that suffer tribulation, if she have diligently followed every good work.—1 *Tim.* v. 9, 10.

And hospitality do not forget; for by this, some, being not aware of it, have entertained angels.—*Heb.* xiii. 2.

Using hospitality one towards another, without murmuring.—1 *Peter* iv. 9.

Dearly beloved, thou dost faithfully whatever thou dost for the brethren, and that for strangers,

Who have given testimony to thy charity in the sight of the church: whom thou shalt do well to bring forward on their way, in a manner worthy of God. . . .

We therefore ought to receive such, that we may be fellow-helpers of the truth.—3 *John* i. 5, 6, 8.

HOUSE OF GOD, SANCTITY OF THE

And when Jacob awaked out of sleep, he said: Indeed the Lord is in this place, and I knew it not.

And trembling he said: How terrible is this place! this is no other but the house of God, and the gate of heaven.—*Gen.* xxviii. 16, 17.

And the Lord appeared to him in a flame of fire, out of the midst of a bush; and he saw that the bush was on fire and was not burnt.

And Moses said: I will go and see this great sight, why the bush is not burnt.

And when the Lord saw that he went forward to see, he called to him out of the midst of the bush, and said: Moses, Moses. And he answered: Here I am.

And he said: Come not nigh hither, put off the shoes from thy feet: for the place whereon thou standest is holy ground.—*Ex.* iii. 2-5.

How beautiful are thy tabernacles, O Jacob, and thy tents, O Israel!—*Num.* xxiv. 5.

But thou dwellest in the holy place, the praise of Israel.—*Ps.* xxi. 4.

The stream of the river maketh the city of God joyful: the most High hath sanctified his own tabernacle.

God is in the midst thereof, it shall not be moved: God will help it in the morning early.—*Ps.* xlv. 5, 6.

Blessed is he whom thou hast chosen and taken to thee: he shall dwell in thy courts. We shall be filled with the good things of thy house; holy is thy temple.—*Ps.* lxiv. 5.

Why suspect, ye curdled mountains?

A mountain in which God is well pleased to dwell: for there the Lord shall dwell unto the end.—*Ps.* lxvii. 17.

How lovely are thy tabernacles, O Lord of hosts!

My soul longeth and fainteth for the courts of the Lord.

My heart and my flesh have rejoiced in the living God.

For the sparrow hath found herself a house, and the turtle a nest for herself, where she may lay her young ones:

Thy altars, O Lord of hosts, my king and my God.

Blessed are they that dwell in thy house, O Lord: they shall praise thee for ever and ever.—*Ps.* lxxxiii. 2-5.

The Lord loveth the gates of Sion above all the tabernacles of Jacob.

Glorious things are said of thee, O city of God. . . .

The dwelling in thee is as it were of all rejoicing.—*Ps.* lxxxvi. 2, 3, 7.

Holiness becometh thy house, O Lord, unto length of days.—*Ps.* xcii. 5.

Praise and beauty are before him: holiness and majesty in his sanctuary. . . .

Adore ye the Lord in his holy court. Let all the earth be moved at his presence.—*Ps.* xcv. 6, 9.

Exalt ye the Lord our God, and adore his footstool, for it is holy.—*Ps.* xcviii. 5.

We will go into his tabernacle: we will adore in the place where his feet stood.

Arise, O Lord, into thy resting place: thou and the ark which thou hast sanctified.—*Ps.* cxxxi. 7, 8.

For the Lord hath chosen Sion: he hath chosen it for his dwelling.

This is my rest for ever and ever: here will I dwell, for I have chosen it.—*Ps.* cxxxi. 13, 14.

O Israel, how great is the house of God, and how vast is the place of his possession!—*Bar.* iii. 24.

And you shall know that I am the Lord your God, dwelling in Sion my holy mountain: and Jerusalem shall be holy, and strangers shall pass through it no more.—*Joel* iii. 17.

Thus saith the Lord of hosts: I am returned to Sion, and I will dwell in the midst of Jerusalem: and Jerusalem shall be called, the City of Truth, and the Mountain of the Lord of hosts, the sanctified Mountain.—*Zach.* viii. 3.

And I heard a great voice from the throne, saying: Behold the tabernacle of God with men, and he will dwell with them. And they shall be his people: and God himself with them shall be their God.—*Apoc.* xxi. 3.

HOUSE OF GOD IS A HOUSE OF PRAYER, THE

My eyes also shall be open, and my ears attentive to the prayer of him that shall pray in this place.—2 *Paral.* vii. 15.

If evils fall upon us, the sword of judgment, or pestilence, or famine, we will stand in thy presence before this house, in which thy name is called upon: and we will cry to thee in our afflictions, and thou wilt hear, and save us.—2 *Paral.* xx. 9.

These things I remembered, and poured out my soul in me: for I shall go over into the place of the wonderful tabernacle, even to the house of God:

With the voice of joy and praise; the noise of one feasting.—*Ps.* xli. 5.

I will bring them into my holy mount, and will make them joyful in my house of prayer: their holocausts, and their victims shall please me upon my altar: for my house shall be called the house of prayer, for all nations.—*Is.* lvi. 7.

Thou, O Lord, hast chosen this house, for thy name to be called upon therein, that it might be a house of prayer and supplication for thy people.—1 *Mach.* vii. 37.

And he (Jesus) taught, saying to them: Is it not written, My house shall be called the house of prayer to all nations? But you have made it a den of thieves.—*Mark* xi. 17.

HOUSE OF GOD, REVERENCE AND LOVE FOR THE

And let them be ready against the third day: for on the third day the Lord will come down in the sight of all the people upon mount Sinai.

And thou shalt appoint certain limits to the people round about, and thou shalt say to them: Take heed you go not up into the mount, and that ye touch not the borders thereof: every one that toucheth the mount, dying he shall die.—*Ex.* xix. 11, 12.

Keep ye my sabbaths, and reverence my sanctuary. I am the Lord.—*Lev.* xix. 30.

And when Josue was in the field of the city of Jericho, he lifted up his eyes, and saw a man standing over against him, holding a drawn sword, and he went to him, and said: Art thou one of ours, or of our adversaries?

And he answered: No; but I am prince of the host of the Lord, and now I am come. . . .

Loose, saith he, thy shoes from off thy feet: for the place whereon thou standest is holy. And Josue did as was commanded him.—*Jos.* v. 13, 14, 16.

But as for me, in the multitude of thy mercy, I will come into thy house; I will worship towards thy holy temple, in thy fear.—*Ps.* v. 8.

I have loved, O Lord, the beauty of thy house; and the place where thy glory dwelleth.—*Ps.* xxv. 8.

One thing I have asked of the Lord, this will I seek after; that I may dwell in the house of the Lord all the days of my life. That I may see the delight of the Lord, and may visit his temple.—*Ps.* xxvi. 4.

We have received thy mercy, O God, in the midst of thy temple.—*Ps.* xlvii. 10.

But the Lord is in his holy temple: let all the earth keep silence before him.—*Hab.* ii. 20.

Let all flesh be silent at the presence of the Lord: for he is risen up out of his holy habitation.—*Zach.* ii. 13.

And he (Jesus) suffered not that any man should carry a vessel through the temple.—*Mark* xi. 16.

These things I write to thee, hoping that I shall come to thee shortly.

But if I tarry long, that thou mayst know how thou oughtst to behave thyself in the house of God, which is the church of the living God, the pillar and ground of the truth.—1 *Tim.* iii. 14, 15.

HOUSE, GOD PUNISHES ANY IR-REVERENCE TO HIS

And when they came to the floor of Nachon, Oza put forth his hand to the ark of God, and took hold of it: because the oxen kicked, and made it lean aside.

And the indignation of the Lord was enkindled against Oza, and he struck him for his rashness: and he died there before the ark of God.—*2 Kings* vi. 6, 7.

They have set fire to thy sanctuary: they have defiled the dwelling place of thy name on the earth. . . .

Arise, O God, judge thy own cause: remember thy reproaches with which the foolish man hath reproached thee all the day.—*Ps.* lxxiii. 7, 22.

Is this house, then, in which my name hath been called upon, in your eyes become a den of robbers? I, I am he: I have seen it, saith the Lord.—*Jer.* vii. 11.

And he (Jesus) found in the temple them that sold oxen and sheep and doves, and the changers of money sitting.

And when he had made, as it were, a scourge of little cords, he drove them all out of the temple, the sheep also, and the oxen, and the money of the changers he poured out, and the tables he overthrew.

And to them that sold doves, he said: Take these things hence, and make not the house of my Father a house of traffic.—*John* ii. 14-16.

HOUSE OF GOD IN THE OLD LAW, THE SANCTITY OF THE

And he (God) commanded him (Moses), saying: Speak to Aaron, thy brother, that he enter not at all into the sanctuary, which is within the veil before the propitiatory, with which the ark is covered, lest he die (for I will appear in a cloud over the oracle),

Unless he first do these things: He shall offer a calf for sin, and a ram for a holocaust.

He shall be vested with a linen tunic, he shall cover his nakedness with linen breeches: he shall be girded with a linen girdle, and he shall put a linen mitre upon his head: for these are holy vestments: all which he shall put on, after he is washed.—*Lev.* xvi. 2-4.

Thou shalt not offer the hire of a strumpet, nor the price of a dog, in the house of the Lord thy God, whatsoever it be that thou hast vowed: because both these are an abomination to the Lord thy God.—*Deut.* xxiii. 18.

And king David said to all the assembly: Solomon my son, whom alone God hath chosen, is as yet young and tender: and the work is great, for a house is prepared not for man, but for God.—*1 Paral.* xxix. 1.

For the house which I desire to build is great: for our God is great above all gods.

Who then can be able to build him a worthy house? if heaven, and the heavens of heavens cannot contain him: who am I that I should be able to build him a house? but to this end only, that incense may be burnt before him.—*2 Paral.* ii. 5, 6.

Is it credible then that God should dwell with men on the earth? If heaven, and the heavens of heavens do not contain thee, how much less this house which I have built?

But to this end only it is made, that thou mayst regard the prayer of thy servant and his supplication, O Lord my God; and mayst hear the prayers which thy servant poureth out before thee.

That thou mayst open thy eyes upon this house day and night, upon the place wherein thou hast promised that thy name should be called upon,

And that thou wouldst hear the prayer which thy servant prayeth in it: hearken then to the prayers of thy servant, and of thy people Israel. Whosoever shall pray in this place, hear thou from thy dwelling place, that is, from heaven, and show mercy.—*2 Paral.* vi. 18-21.

And the Lord appeared to him (Solomon) by night, and said: I have heard thy prayer, and I have chosen this place to myself for a house of sacrifice. . . .

My eyes also shall be open, and my ears attentive to the prayer of him that shall pray in this place.

For I have chosen, and have sanctified this place, that my name may be there for ever, and my eyes and my heart may remain there perpetually.—*2 Paral.* vii. 12, 15, 16.

Who is left among you, that saw this house in its first glory? and how do you see it now? is it not in comparison to that, as nothing in your eyes? . . .

And I will move all nations: and the desired of all nations shall come: and I will fill this house with glory: saith the Lord of hosts. . . .

Great shall be the glory of this last house, more than of the first, saith the Lord of hosts: and in this place I will give peace, saith the Lord of hosts.—*Aggeus* ii. 4, 8, 10.

Now these things being thus ordered, into the first tabernacle the priests indeed always entered, accomplishing the offices of sacrifices.

But into the second, the high priest alone, once a year: not without blood, which he offereth for his own, and the people's ignorance.—*Heb.* ix. 6, 7.

HUMAN RESPECT

If I have been afraid at a very great multitude, and the contempt of kinsmen hath terrified me: and I have not rather held my peace, and not gone out of the door.

Who would grant me a hearer, that the Almighty may hear my desire; and that he himself that judgeth would write a book?—*Job* xxxi. 34, 35.

For God hath scattered the bones of them that please men: they have been confounded, because God hath despised them.—*Ps.* lii. 6.

It is not good to accept the person of the wicked, to decline from the truth of judgment.—*Prov.* xviii. 5.

It is not good to have respect to persons in judgment.

They that say to the wicked man: Thou art just: shall be cursed by the people, and the tribes shall abhor them. —*Prov.* xxiv. 23, 24.

He that hath respect to a person in judgment, doth not well: such a man even for a morsel of bread forsaketh the truth.—*Prov.* xxviii. 21.

When a rich man is shaken, he is kept up by his friends: but when a poor man is fallen down, he is thrust away even by his acquaintance.

When a rich man hath been deceived, he hath many helpers: he hath spoken proud things, and they have justified him.

The poor man was deceived, and he is rebuked also: he hath spoken wisely, and could have no place.

The rich man spoke, and all held their peace, and what he said they extol even to the clouds.

The poor man spoke, and they say: Who is this? and if he stumble, they will overthrow him.—*Ecclus.* xiii. 25-29.

For it is not good to keep all shamefacedness: and all things do not please all men in opinion.—*Ecclus.* xli. 20.

For whom hast thou been solicitous and afraid, that thou hast lied, and hast not been mindful of me, nor thought on me in thy heart? for I am silent, and as one that seeth not, and thou hast forgotten me.—*Is.* lvii. 11.

For do I now persuade men, or God? Or do I seek to please men? If I yet pleased men, I should not be the servant of Christ.—*Gal.* i. 10.

My brethren, have not the faith of our Lord Jesus Christ of glory with respect of persons.

For if there shall come into your assembly, a man having a golden ring, in fine apparel, and there shall come in also a poor man in mean attire,

And you have respect to him that is clothed with the fine apparel, and shall say to him: Sit thou here well; but say to the poor man: Stand thou there, or sit under my footstool:

Do you not judge within yourselves, and are become judges of unjust thoughts?—*James* ii. 1-4.

HUMAN RESPECT OFTEN LEADS INTO SIN

And Saul said to Samuel: I have sinned because I have transgressed the commandment of the Lord, and thy words, fearing the people, and obeying their voice.—*1 Kings* xv. 24.

He that feareth man, shall quickly fall: he that trusteth in the Lord, shall be set on high.—*Prov.* xxix. 25.

There is that will destroy his own soul through shamefacedness, and by occasion of an unwise person he will destroy it: and by respect of person he will destroy himself.—*Ecclus.* xx. 24.

However, many of the chief men also believed in him (Jesus); but because of the Pharisees they did not confess him, that they might not be cast out of the synagogue.

For they loved the glory of men more than the glory of God.—*John* xii. 42, 43.

But if you have respect to persons, you commit sin, being reproved by the law as transgressors.—*James* ii. 9.

HUMAN RESPECT, OVERCOMING

And when the ark of the Lord was come into the city of David, Michol, the daughter of Saul, looking out through a window, saw king David leaping and dancing before the Lord: and she despised him in her heart. . . .

And David said to Michol: Before the Lord, who chose me rather than thy father, and than all his house, and commanded me to be ruler over the people of the Lord in Israel,

I will both play and make myself meaner than I have done: and I will be little in my own eyes: and with the handmaids of whom thou speakest, I shall appear more glorious.—*2 Kings* vi. 16, 21, 22.

And calling them, they charged them not to speak at all, nor teach in the name of Jesus.

But Peter and John answering, said to them: If it be just in the sight of God, to hear you rather than God, judge ye.

For we cannot but speak the things which we have seen and heard.—*Acts* iv. 18-20.

But to me, it is a very small thing to be judged by you, or by man's day; but neither do I judge my own self.— 1 *Cor.* iv. 3.

But as we were approved by God that the gospel should be committed to us: even so we speak, not as pleasing men, but God, who proveth our hearts.

For neither have we used, at any time, the speech of flattery, as you know; nor taken an occasion of covetousness, God is witness:

Nor sought we glory of men, neither of you, nor of others.—1 *Thess.* ii. 4-6.

HUMAN RESPECT, EXHORTATION AGAINST

Thou shalt not follow the multitude to do evil: neither shalt thou yield in judgment, to the opinion of the most part, to stray from the truth.—*Ex.* xxiii. 2.

Thou shalt not do that which is unjust, nor judge unjustly. Respect not the person of the poor, nor honor the countenance of the mighty. But judge thy neighbor according to justice.— *Lev.* xix. 15.

For thy soul, be not ashamed to say the truth.

For there is a shame that bringeth sin, and there is a shame that bringeth glory and grace.—*Ecclus.* iv. 24, 25.

Be not ashamed of any of these things, and accept no person to sin thereby:

Of the law of the most High, and of his covenant, and of judgment to justify the ungodly.—*Ecclus.* xlii. 1, 2.

And I say to you, my friends: Be not afraid of them who kill the body, and after that, have no more that they can do.

But I will show you whom you shall fear: fear ye him, who after he hath killed, hath power to cast into hell. Yea, I say to you, fear him.—*Luke* xii. 4, 5.

And who is he that can hurt you, if you be zealous of good?

But if also you suffer any thing for justice' sake, blessed are ye. And be not afraid of their fear, and be not troubled.—1 *Peter* iii. 13, 14.

HUMAN SACRIFICES, GOD'S ABHORRENCE OF

Thou shalt not do in like manner to the Lord thy God. For they have done to their gods all the abominations which the Lord abhorreth, offering their sons and daughters, and burning them with fire.—*Deut.* xii. 31.

And they sacrificed their sons and their daughters to devils.

And they shed innocent blood: the blood of their sons and of their daughters which they sacrificed to the idols of Chanaan.

And the land was polluted with blood, and was defiled with their works: and they went aside after their own inventions.

And the Lord was exceedingly angry with his people: and he abhorred his inheritance.—*Ps.* cv. 37-40.

For those ancient inhabitants of thy holy land, whom thou didst abhor,

Because they did works hateful to thee by their sorceries, and wicked sacrifices,

And those merciless murderers of their own children, and eaters of men's bowels, and devourers of blood from the midst of thy consecration,

And those parents sacrificing with their own hands helpless souls, it was thy will to destroy by the hands of our parents.—*Wis.* xii. 3-6.

HUMBLE ACCEPTABLE TO GOD, PRAYERS OF THE

For thy power, O Lord, is not in a multitude, nor is thy pleasure in the strength of horses, nor from the beginning, have the proud been acceptable to thee: but the prayer of the humble and the meek hath always pleased thee. —*Judith* ix. 16.

He hath had regard to the prayer of the humble: and he hath not despised their petition.—*Ps.* ci. 18.

The prayer of him that humbleth himself, shall pierce the clouds: and till it come nigh he will not be comforted: and he will not depart till the most High behold.—*Ecclus.* xxxv. 21.

HUMILIATIONS, ENDURING

For he that hath been humbled shall be in glory: and he that shall bow down his eyes, he shall be saved.—*Job* xxii.29.

For thou hast humbled us in the place of affliction: and the shadow of death hath covered us.—*Ps.* xliii. 20.

I am poor, and in labors from my youth: and being exalted, have been humbled and troubled.—*Ps.* lxxxvii. 16.

We have rejoiced for the days in which thou hast humbled us: for the years in which we have seen evils.—*Ps.* lxxxix. 15.

The Lord is the keeper of little ones: I was humbled, and he delivered me.— *Ps.* cxiv. 6.

Be thou mindful of thy word to thy servant, in which thou hast given me hope.

This hath comforted me in my humiliation: because thy word hath enlivened me.—*Ps.* cxviii. 49, 50.

Before I was humbled, I offended; therefore have I kept thy word.—*Ps.* cxviii. 67.

It is good for me that thou hast humbled me, that I may learn thy justifications.—*Ps.* cxviii. 71.

I know, O Lord, that thy judgments are equity: and in thy truth thou hast humbled me.—*Ps.* cxviii. 75.

I have been humbled, O Lord, exceedingly: quicken thou me, according to thy word.—*Ps.* cxviii. 107.

I am very young and despised; but I forget not thy justifications.—*Ps.* cxviii. 141.

See my humiliation and deliver me: for I have not forgotten thy law.—*Ps.* cxviii. 153.

It is better to be humbled with the meek, than to divide spoils with the proud.—*Prov.* xvi. 19.

Before destruction, the heart of a man is exalted: and before he be glorified, it is humbled.—*Prov.* xviii.12.

Take all that shall be brought upon thee: and in thy sorrow, endure, and in thy humiliation keep patience.

For gold and silver are tried in the fire, but acceptable men in the furnace of humiliation.—*Ecclus.* ii. 4, 5.

Be you humbled, therefore, under the mighty hand of God, that he may exalt you in the time of visitation.— 1 *Peter* v. 6.

HUMILITY

It is good for me that thou hast humbled me, that I may learn thy justifications.—*Ps.* cxviii. 71.

Lord, my heart is not exalted: nor are my eyes lofty.

Neither have I walked in great matters, nor in wonderful things above me. —*Ps.* cxxx. 1.

Where pride is, there also shall be

reproach: but where humility is, there also is wisdom.—*Prov.* xi. 2.

The fear of the Lord is the lesson of wisdom: and humility goeth before glory.—*Prov.* xv. 33.

It is better to be humbled with the meek, than to divide spoils with the proud.—*Prov.* xvi. 19.

Before destruction, the heart of a man is exalted: and before he be glorified, it is humbled.—*Prov.* xviii. 12.

And (Jesus) said to them: For he that is the lesser among you all, he is the greater.—*Luke* ix. 48.

But God, who comforteth the humble, comforted us by the coming of Titus.—*2 Cor.* vii. 6.

HUMILITY PLEASING TO GOD

A sacrifice to God is an afflicted spirit: a contrite and humbled heart, O God, thou wilt not despise.—*Ps.* l. 19.

The Lord is the keeper of little ones: I was humbled, and he delivered me.—*Ps.* cxiv. 6.

The greater thou art, the more humble thyself in all things, and thou shalt find grace before God:

For great is the power of God alone, and he is honored by the humble.—*Ecclus.* iii. 20, 21.

But to whom shall I have respect, but to him that is poor and little, and of a contrite heart, and that trembleth at my words?—*Is.* lxvi. 2.

At that time Jesus answered and said: I confess to thee, O Father, Lord of heaven and earth, because thou hast hid these things from the wise and prudent, and hast revealed them to little ones.

Yea, Father; for so hath it seemed good in thy sight.—*Matt.* xi. 25, 26.

But the foolish things of the world hath God chosen, that he may confound the wise; and the weak things of the world hath God chosen, that he may confound the strong.

And the base things of the world, and the things that are contemptible, hath God chosen, and things that are not, that he might bring to nought things that are:

That no flesh should glory in his sight.—*1 Cor.* i. 27-29.

HUMILITY, NECESSITY OF

At that hour the disciples came to Jesus, saying: Who thinkest thou is the greater in the kingdom of heaven?

And Jesus calling unto him a little child, set him in the midst of them,

And said: Amen, I say to you, unless you be converted, and become as little children, you shall not enter into the kingdom of heaven.

Whosoever therefore shall humble himself as this little child, he is the greater in the kingdom of heaven.—*Matt.* xviii. 1-4.

Amen, I say to you, whosoever shall not receive the kingdom of God as a little child, shall not enter into it.—*Mark* x. 15.

For if any man think himself to be something, whereas he is nothing, he deceiveth himself.—*Gal.* vi. 3.

HUMILITY, REWARD OF

Wherefore I will pray to the Lord, and address my speech to God; . . .

Who setteth up the humble on high, and comforteth with health those that mourn.—*Job* v. 8, 11.

For he that hath been humbled, shall be in glory: and he that shall bow down his eyes, he shall be saved.—*Job* xxii. 29.

I will be glad, and rejoice in thy mercy. For thou hast regarded my humility, thou hast saved my soul out of distresses.—*Ps.* xxx. 8.

The Lord is nigh unto them that are of a contrite heart: and he will save the humble of spirit.—*Ps.* xxxiii. 19.

The fruit of humility is the fear of the Lord, riches, and glory and life.—*Prov.* xxii. 4.

Humiliation followeth the proud: and glory shall uphold the humble of spirit.—*Prov.* xxix. 23.

God hath made the roots of proud nations to wither, and hath planted the humble of these nations. . . .

God hath abolished the memory of the proud, and hath preserved the memory of them that are humble in mind.—*Ecclus.* x. 18, 21.

For thus saith the High and the Eminent that inhabiteth eternity: and his name is Holy, who dwelleth in the high and holy place, and with a contrite and humble spirit, to revive the spirit of the humble, and to revive the heart of the contrite.—*Is.* lvii. 15.

And many that are first, shall be last: and the last shall be first.—*Matt.* xix. 30.

And whosoever shall exalt himself, shall be humbled: and he that shall humble himself shall be exalted.—*Matt.* xxiii. 12.

And my spirit hath rejoiced in God my Saviour.

Because he hath regarded the humility of his handmaid; for behold from henceforth all generations shall call me blessed.—*Luke* i. 47, 48.

He hath put down the mighty from their seat, and hath exalted the humble.—*Luke* i. 52.

And the publican standing afar off, would not so much as lift up his eyes towards heaven; but struck his breast, saying: O God, be merciful to me a sinner.

I say to you, this man went down into his house, justified rather than the other: because every one that exalteth himself, shall be humbled: and he that humbleth himself, shall be exalted.—*Luke* xviii. 13, 14.

Wherefore he saith: God resisteth the proud, and giveth grace to the humble.—*James* iv. 6.

Be humbled in the sight of the Lord, and he will exalt you.—*James* iv. 10.

HUMILITY, MOTIVES OR REASONS FOR

Behold they that serve him are not steadfast, and in his angels he found wickedness:

How much more shall they that dwell in houses of clay, who have an earthly foundation, be consumed as with the moth?—*Job* iv. 18, 19.

What is a man that thou shouldst magnify him? or why dost thou set thy heart upon him?—*Job* vii. 17.

Behold among his saints none is unchangeable, and the heavens are not pure in his sight.

How much more is man abominable, and unprofitable, who drinketh iniquity like water?—*Job* xv. 15, 16.

I have said to rottenness: Thou art my father; to worms, my mother and my sister.—*Job* xvii. 14.

Can man be justified compared with God, or he that is born of a woman appear clean?

Behold even the moon doth not shine, and the stars are not pure in his sight.

How much less man that is rottenness, and the son of man who is a worm?—*Job* xxv. 4, 5, 6.

Where wast thou when I laid the foundations of the earth? tell me if thou hast understanding.—*Job* xxxviii. 4.

Lord, what is man, that thou art made known to him? or the son of man, that thou makest account of him?—*Ps.* cxliii. 3.

Who can say: My heart is clean, I am pure from sin?—*Prov.* xx. 9.

All these things have I considered in my heart, that I might carefully understand them: there are just men and wise men, and their works are in the hand of God: and yet man knoweth not whether he be worthy of love, or hatred.—*Eccles.* ix. 1.

HUMILITY, EXHORTATION TO

And therefore let us humble our souls before him, and continuing in an humble spirit, in his service:

Let us ask the Lord with tears, that, according to his will, so he would show his mercy to us: that, as our heart is troubled by their pride, so also we may glorify in our humility.—*Judith* viii. 16, 17.

Appear not glorious before the king, and stand not in the place of great men.

For it is better that it should be said to thee: Come up hither; than that thou shouldst be humbled before the prince.—*Prov.* xxv. 6, 7.

Take all that shall be brought upon thee: and in thy sorrow endure, and in thy humiliation keep patience.

For gold and silver are tried in the fire, but acceptable men in the furnace of humiliation.—*Ecclus.* ii. 4, 5.

The greater thou art, the more humble thyself in all things, and thou shalt find grace before God.—*Ecclus.* iii. 20.

Be not without fear about sin for-

given, and add not sin upon sin.—
Ecclus. v. 5.

Humble thy spirit very much: for the
vengeance on the flesh of the ungodly
is fire and worms.—*Ecclus.* vii. 19.

Take up my yoke upon you, and learn
of me, because I am meek, and humble
of heart: and you shall find rest to your
souls.—*Matt.* xi. 29.

But Jesus called them to him, and
said: You know that the princes of the
Gentiles lord it over them; and they
that are the greater, exercise power
upon them.

It shall not be so among you: but
whosoever will be the greater among
you, let him be your minister:

And he that will be first among you,
shall be your servant.—*Matt.* xx. 25-27.

And sitting down, he called the
twelve, and saith to them: If any man
desire to be first, he shall be the last
of all, and the minister of all.—*Mark*
ix. 34.

So you also, when you shall have
done all these things that are commanded you, say: We are unprofitable
servants; we have done that which we
ought to do.—*Luke* xvii. 10.

But thou standest by faith: be not
high-minded, but fear.

For if God hath not spared the natural branches, fear lest perhaps he also
spare not thee.—*Rom.* xi. 20, 21.

I therefore, a prisoner in the Lord,
beseech you, that you walk worthy of
the vocation in which you are called,

With all humility and mildness, with
patience, supporting one another in
charity.—*Eph.* iv. 1, 2.

Let nothing be done through contention, neither by vain glory: but in humility, let each esteem others better
than themselves.—*Philipp.* ii. 3.

Put ye on therefore, as the elect of
God, holy, and beloved, the bowels of
mercy, benignity, humility, modesty,
patience.—*Col.* iii. 12.

But let the brother of low condition,
glory in his exaltation:

And the rich, in his being low; because as the flower of the grass shall he
pass away.—*James* i. 9, 10.

Be humbled in the sight of the Lord,
and he will exalt you.—*James* iv. 10.

And in fine, be ye all of one mind,
having compassion one of another, being lovers of the brotherhood, merciful,
modest, humble.—1 *Peter* iii. 8.

In like manner, ye young men, be
subject to the ancients. And do you
all insinuate humility one to another,
for God resisteth the proud, but to the
humble he giveth grace.

Be you humbled therefore under the
mighty hand of God, that he may exalt
you in the time of visitation.—1 *Peter*
v. 5, 6.

HUMILITY OF CHRIST, THE

Then cometh Jesus from Galilee to
the Jordan, unto John, to be baptized
by him.

But John stayed him, saying: I
ought to be baptized by thee, and comest thou to me?

And Jesus answering, said to him:
Suffer it to be so now. For so it becometh us to fulfil all justice. Then
he suffered him.—*Matt.* iii. 13-15.

Take up my yoke upon you, and
learn of me, because I am meek, and
humble of heart: and you shall find rest
to your souls.—*Matt.* xi. 29.

But whosoever will be the greater
among you, let him be your minister:

And he that will be first among you,
shall be your servant.

Even as the Son of man is not come
to be ministered unto, but to minister,
and to give his life a redemption for
many.—*Matt.* xx. 26-28.

Tell ye the daughter of Sion: Behold thy king cometh to thee, meek, and
sitting upon an ass, and a colt the foal
of her that is used to the yoke.—*Matt.*
xxi. 5.

And he went down with them, and
came to Nazareth, and was subject to
them.—*Luke* ii. 51.

For which is greater, he that sitteth
at table, or he that serveth? Is not
he that sitteth at table? But I am in
the midst of you, as he that serveth.—
Luke xxii. 27.

But I seek not my own glory: there
is one that seeketh and judgeth.—*John*
viii. 50.

Knowing that the Father had given
him all things into his hands, and that
he came from God, and goeth to God;

He riseth from supper, and layeth aside his garments, and having taken a towel, girded himself.

After that, he putteth water into a basin, and began to wash the feet of the disciples, and to wipe them with the towel wherewith he was girded. . . .

Then after he had washed their feet, and taken his garments, being set down again, he said to them: Know you what I have done to you?

You call me Master, and Lord; and you say well, for so I am.

If then I, being *your* Lord and Master, have washed your feet; you also ought to wash one another's feet.

For I have given you an example, that as I have done to you, so you do also.—*John* xiii. 3-5, 12-15.

For let this mind be in you, which was also in Christ Jesus:

Who, being in the form of God, thought it not robbery to be equal with God:

But emptied himself, taking the form of a servant, being made in the likeness of men, and in habit found as a man.

He humbled himself, becoming obedient unto death, even to the death of the cross.—*Philipp.* ii. 5-8.

HUMILITY, EXAMPLES OF

And Abraham answered, and said: Seeing I have once begun, I will speak to my Lord, whereas I am dust and ashes.—*Gen.* xviii. 27.

And Moses said: In the evening the Lord will give you flesh to eat, and in the morning, bread to the full: for he hath heard your murmurings, with which you have murmured against him, for what are we? your murmuring is not against us, but against the Lord.—*Ex.* xvi. 8.

And the Lord looked upon him (Gedeon), and said: Go in this thy strength, and thou shalt deliver Israel out of the hand of Madian: know that I have sent thee.

He answered and said: I beseech thee, my lord, wherewith shall I deliver Israel?

Behold, my family is the meanest in Manasses, and 1 am the least in my father's house.—*Judges* vi. 14, 15.

And the men of Ephraim said to him (Gedeon): What is this that thou meanest to do, that thou wouldst not call us when thou wentest to fight against Madian? and they chid him sharply, and almost offered violence.

And he answered them: What could I have done, like to that which you have done? Is not one bunch of grapes of Ephraim better than the vintages of Abiezer?

The Lord hath delivered into your hands the princes of Madian, Oreb and Zeb: what could I have done like to what you have done? And when he had said this, their spirit was appeased, with which they swelled against him.—*Judges* viii. 1-3.

And Saul answering, said: Am not I a son of Jemini, of the least tribe of Israel, and my kindred the last among all the families of the tribe of Benjamin? Why then hast thou spoken this word to me?—1 *Kings* ix. 21.

And David said to Michol: Before the Lord, who chose me rather than thy father, and than all his house, and commanded me to be ruler over the people of the Lord in Israel,

I will both play and make myself meaner than I have done: and I will be little in my own eyes: and with the handmaids of whom thou speakest, I shall appear more glorious.—2 *Kings* vi. 21, 22.

And Daniel made answer before the king, and said: The secret that the king desireth to know, none of the wise men, or the philosophers, or the diviners, or the soothsayers can declare to the king. . . .

To me also this secret is revealed, not by any wisdom that I have more than all men alive: but that the interpretation might be made manifest to the king, and thou mightest know the thoughts of thy mind.—*Dan.* ii. 27, 30.

And Jesus saith to him: I will come and heal him.

And the centurion making answer, said: Lord, I am not worthy that thou shouldst enter under my roof: but only say the word, and my servant shall be healed.—*Matt.* viii. 7, 8.

But she came and adored him, saying: Lord, help me.

Who answering, said: It is not good to take the bread of the children, and to cast it to the dogs.

But she said: Yea, Lord; for the whelps also eat of the crumbs, that fall from the table of their masters.—*Matt.* xv. 25-27.

And he (John) preached, saying: There cometh after me, one mightier than I, the latchet of whose shoes I am not worthy to stoop down and loose.—*Mark* i. 7.

And Mary said: Behold the handmaid of the Lord; be it done to me according to thy word.—*Luke* i. 38.

And she (Elizabeth) cried out with a loud voice, and said: Blessed art thou among women, and blessed is the fruit of thy womb.

And whence is this to me, that the mother of my Lord should come to me? —*Luke* i. 42, 43.

'Which when Simon Peter saw, he fell down at Jesus' knees, saying: Depart from me, for I am a sinful man, O Lord.—*Luke* v. 8.

And Jesus went with them. And when he was now not far from the house, the centurion sent his friends to him, saying: Lord, trouble not thyself; for I am not worthy that thou shouldst enter under my roof.

For which cause, neither did I think myself worthy to come to thee; but say the word, and my servant shall be healed.—*Luke* vii. 6, 7.

And the publican standing afar off, would not so much as lift up his eyes towards heaven; but struck his breast, saying: O God, be merciful to me a sinner.—*Luke* xviii. 13.

He that hath the bride, is the bridegroom: but the friend of the bridegroom, who standeth and heareth him, rejoiceth with joy, because of the bridegroom's voice. This my joy therefore is fulfilled.

He must increase, but I must decrease.—*John* iii. 29, 30.

For I am the least of the apostles, who am not worthy to be called an apostle, because I persecuted the church of God.—1 *Cor.* xv. 9.

¹The miraculous draught.

A faithful saying, and worthy of all acceptation, that Christ Jesus came into this world to save sinners, of whom I am the chief.—1 *Tim.* i. 15.

HUMILITY, A PRAYER OF

O God of the heavens, creator of the waters, and Lord of the whole creation, hear me a poor wretch, making supplication to thee, and presuming of thy mercy.—*Judith* ix. 17.

Have mercy on me, O Lord, for I am weak: heal me, O Lord, for my bones are troubled.—*Ps.* vi. 3.

What is man, that thou art mindful of him? or the Son of man that thou visitest him?—*Ps.* viii. 5.

Look thou upon me, and have mercy on me; for I am alone and poor. . . .

See my abjection and my labor; and forgive me all my sins.—*Ps.* xxiv. 16, 18.

O Lord, be thou merciful to me: heal my soul, for I have sinned against thee. —*Ps.* xl. 5.

For we, O Lord, are diminished more than any nation, and are brought low in all the earth this day, for our sins. . . .

Nevertheless in a contrite heart and humble spirit, let us be accepted.—*Dan.* iii. 37, 39.

Lord, I am not worthy that thou shouldst enter under my roof: but only say the word, and my servant shall be healed.—*Matt.* viii. 8.

Father, I have sinned against heaven, and before thee:

I am not worthy to be called thy son: make me as one of thy hired servants. —*Luke* xv. 18, 19.

O God, be merciful to me, a sinner. —*Luke* xviii. 13.

HUSBAND AND WIFE, MUTUAL DUTIES OF

See: Marriage, duties in—page 302.

HYPOCRISY

This I know from the beginning, since man was placed upon the earth,

That the praise of the wicked is short, and the joy of the hypocrite but for a moment.—*Job* xx. 4, 5.

For what is the hope of the hypocrite, if through covetousness he take by violence, and God deliver not his soul?

Will God hear his cry, when distress shall come upon him?

Or can he delight himself in the Almighty, and call upon God at all times?—*Job* xxvii. 8-10.

And they loved him with their mouth: and with their tongue they lied unto him:

But their heart was not right with him: nor were they counted faithful in his covenant.—*Ps.* lxxvii. 36, 37.

I saw the wicked buried: who also when they were yet living were in the holy place, and were praised in the city as men of just works: but this also is vanity.—*Eccles.* viii. 10.

Be not incredulous to the fear of the Lord: and come not to him with a double heart.

Be not a hypocrite in the sight of men, and let not thy lips be a stumbling-block to thee. . . .

And God discover thy secrets, and cast thee down in the midst of the congregation.

Because thou camest to the Lord wickedly, and thy heart is full of guile and deceit.—*Ecclus.* i. 36, 37, 39, 40.

An enemy hath tears in his eyes, and while he pretendeth to help thee, will undermine thy feet.

He will shake his head, and clap his hands, and whisper much, and change his countenance.—*Ecclus.* xii. 18, 19.

There is one that humbleth himself wickedly, and his interior is full of deceit.—*Ecclus.* xix. 23.

Hypocrites, well hath Isaias prophesied of you, saying:

This people honoreth me with their lips: but their heart is far from me.—*Matt.* xv. 7, 8.

And all their works they do for to be seen of men. For they make their phylacteries broad, and enlarge their fringes. . . .

Blind guides, who strain out a gnat, and swallow a camel.—*Matt.* xxiii. 5, 24.

Woe to you, scribes and Pharisees, hypocrites; because you make clean the outside of the cup and of the dish, but within, you are full of rapine and uncleanness.

Thou blind Pharisee, first make clean the inside of the cup and of the dish, that the outside may become clean.

Woe to you, scribes and Pharisees, hypocrites; because you are like to whited sepulchres, which outwardly appear to men beautiful, but within, are full of dead men's bones, and of all filthiness.

So you also outwardly indeed appear to men just; but inwardly you are full of hypocrisy and iniquity.—*Matt.* xxiii. 25-28.

Know also this, that, in the last days, shall come dangerous times.

Men shall be lovers of themselves, covetous, haughty, proud, blasphemers, disobedient to parents, ungrateful, wicked: . . .

Having an appearance indeed of godliness, but denying the power thereof. —*2 Tim.* iii. 1, 2, 5.

HYPOCRISY PUNISHED BY GOD

Can the rush be green without moisture? or a sedge bush grow without water?

When it is yet in flower, and is not plucked up with the hand, it withereth before all herbs.

Even so are the ways of all that forget God, and the hope of the hypocrite shall perish:

His folly shall not please him, and his trust shall be like the spider's web.

He shall lean upon his house, and it shall not stand: he shall prop it up, and it shall not rise:

He seemeth to have moisture before the sun cometh, and at his rising, his blossom shall shoot forth.—*Job* viii. 11-16.

And he shall be my saviour: for no hypocrite shall come before his presence.—*Job* xiii. 16.

For the congregation of the hypocrite is barren, and fire shall devour their tabernacles, who love to take bribes.—*Job* xv. 34.

Woe to them that are of a double heart, and to wicked lips, and to the hands that do evil, and to the sinner that goeth on the earth two ways.— *Ecclus.* ii. 14.

A heart that goeth two ways shall not have success, and the perverse of heart shall be scandalized therein.—*Ecclus.* iii. 28.

For I tell you, that unless your justice abound more than that of the scribes and Pharisees, you shall not enter into the kingdom of heaven.—*Matt.* v. 20.

IDLE WORDS

See also: Tongue, control of the—page 560.

A man full of tongue shall not be established in the earth.—*Ps.* cxxxix. 12.

In the multitude of words, there shall not want sin: but he that refraineth his lips is most wise.—*Prov.* x. 19.

The tongue of the wise adorneth knowledge: but the mouth of fools bubbleth out folly.—*Prov.* xv. 2.

Speak not anything rashly, and let not thy heart be hasty to utter a word before God. For God is in heaven, and thou upon earth: therefore let thy words be few.

Dreams follow many cares: and in many words shall be found folly.—*Eccles.* v. 1, 2.

A man full of tongue is terrible in his city, and he that is rash in his word shall be hateful.—*Ecclus.* ix. 25.

He that useth many words, shall hurt his own soul.—*Ecclus.* xx. 8.

For I say unto you, that every idle word that men shall speak, they shall render an account for it in the day of judgment.—*Matt.* xii. 36.

But shun profane and vain babblings: for they grow much towards ungodliness.—2 *Tim.* ii. 16.

And avoid foolish and unlearned questions, knowing that they beget strifes.—2 *Tim.* ii. 23.

For in many things we all offend. If any man offend not in word, the same is a perfect man. He is able also with a bridle to lead about the whole body.—*James* iii. 2.

IDLENESS

See also: Laziness—page 275.

He that tilleth his land shall be satisfied with bread: but he that pursueth idleness is very foolish.

He that is delighted in passing his time over wine, leaveth a reproach in his strongholds.—*Prov.* xii. 11.

Slothfulness casteth into a deep sleep, and an idle soul shall suffer hunger.—*Prov.* xix. 15.

He that tilleth his ground shall be filled with bread: but he that followeth idleness, shall be filled with poverty.—*Prov.* xxviii. 19.

For idleness hath taught much evil.—*Ecclus.* xxxiii. 29.

Behold this was the iniquity of Sodom thy sister, pride, fulness of bread, and abundance, and the idleness of her, and of her daughters: and they did not put forth their hand to the needy, and to the poor.—*Ezech.* xvi. 49.

But about the eleventh hour, he went out and found others standing, and he saith to them: Why stand you here all the day idle?—*Matt.* xx. 6.

For also when we were with you, this we declared to you: that if any man will not work, neither let him eat.

For we have heard there are some among you who walk disorderly, working not at all, but curiously meddling.

Now we charge them that are such, and beseech them by the Lord Jesus Christ, that working with silence, they would eat their own bread.—2 *Thess.* iii. 10-12.

And withal being idle, they learn to go about from house to house: and are not only idle, but tattlers also, and busybodies, speaking things which they ought not.—1 *Tim.* v. 13.

IDOLATRY

Let them be all confounded that adore graven things, and that glory in their idols.—*Ps.* xcvi. 7.

For the beginning of fornication is the devising of idols: and the invention of them is the corruption of life.

For neither were they from the beginning, neither shall they be for ever.

For by the vanity of men they came into the world: and therefore they shall be found to come shortly to an end.

For a father being afflicted with bitter grief, made to himself the image of his son who was quickly taken away: and him who then had died as a man, he began now to worship as a god, and appointed him rites and sacrifices among his servants.

Then in process of time, wicked custom prevailing, this error was kept as a law, and statues were worshipped by the commandment of tyrants.

And those whom men could not honor in presence, because they dwelt far off, they brought their resemblance from afar, and made an express image of the king whom they had a mind to honor: that by this their diligence, they might honor as present, him that was absent.

And to the worshipping of these, the singular diligence also of the artificer helped to set forward the ignorant.

For he being willing to please him that employed him, labored with all his art to make the resemblance in the best manner.

And the multitude of men, carried away by the beauty of the work, took him now for a god, that a little before was but honored as a man.

And this was the occasion of deceiving human life: for men, serving either their affection, or their kings, gave the incommunicable name to stones and wood.

And it was not enough for them to err about the knowledge of God, but whereas they lived in a great war of ignorance, they call so many and so great evils peace.

For either they sacrifice their own children, or use hidden sacrifices, or keep watches full of madness,

So that now they neither keep life, nor marriage undefiled, but one killeth another through envy, or grieveth him by adultery.

And all things are mingled together, blood, murder, theft, dissimulation, corruption and unfaithfulness, tumults and perjury, disquieting of the good,

Forgetfulness of God, defiling of souls, changing of nature, disorder in marriage, and the irregularity of adultery and uncleanness.

For the worship of abominable idols is the cause, and the beginning and end of all evil.—*Wis.* xiv. 12-27.

And they changed the glory of the incorruptible God into the likeness of the image of a corruptible man, and of birds, and of four-footed beasts, and of creeping things.

Wherefore God gave them up to the desires of their heart, unto uncleanness, to dishonor their own bodies among themselves.

Who changed the truth of God into a lie; and worshipped and served the creature rather than the Creator, who is blessed for ever. Amen.—*Rom.* i. 23-25.

IDOLATRY, THE FOLLY OF

The idols of the Gentiles are silver and gold, the works of the hands of men.

They have mouths, and speak not: they have eyes, and see not.

They have ears, and hear not: they have noses, and smell not.

They have hands, and feel not: they have feet, and walk not: neither shall they cry out through their throat.

Let them that make them, become like unto them: and all such as trust in them.—*Ps.* cxiii. (*Heb.* cxv.) 4-8.

Wherefore thou hast also greatly tormented them who in their life have lived foolishly and unjustly, by the same things which they worshipped.

For they went astray for a long time in the ways of error, holding those things for gods which are the most worthless among beasts, living after the manner of children without understanding.

Therefore thou hast sent a judgment upon them as senseless children to mock them.—*Wis.* xii. 23-25.

But unhappy are they, and their hope is among the dead, who have called gods the works of the hands of men, gold and silver, the inventions of art, and the resemblances of beasts, or an unprofitable stone, the work of an ancient hand.

Or if an artist, a carpenter, hath cut down a tree proper for his use in the wood, and skilfully taken off all the bark thereof, and with his art, diligently formeth a vessel profitable for the common uses of life,

And useth the chips of his work to dress his meat:

And taking what was left thereof, which is good for nothing, being a crooked piece of wood, and full of knots, carveth it diligently, when he hath nothing else to do, and by the skill of his art, fashioneth it, and maketh it like the image of a man:

Or the resemblance of some beast, laying it over with vermilion, and painting it red, and covering every spot that is in it:

And maketh a convenient dwelling place for it, and setting it in a wall, and fastening it with iron,

Providing for it, lest it should fall, knowing that it is unable to help itself: for it is an image, and hath need of help.

And then maketh prayer to it, inquiring concerning his substance, and his children, or his marriage. And he is not ashamed to speak to that which hath no life:

And for health, he maketh supplication to the weak, and for life prayeth to that which is dead, and for help calleth upon that which is unprofitable:

And for a good journey, he petitioneth him that cannot walk: and for getting, and for working, and for the event of all things, he asketh him that is unable to do any thing.—*Wis.* xiii. 10-19.

For they have esteemed all the idols of the heathens for gods, which neither have the use of eyes to see, nor noses to draw breath, nor ears to hear, nor fingers of hands to handle, and as for their feet, they are slow to walk.

For man made them: and he that borroweth his own breath, fashioned them. For no man can make a god like to himself.

For being mortal himself, he formeth a dead thing with his wicked hands. For he is better than they whom he worshippeth, because he indeed hath lived, though he were mortal, but they never.—*Wis.* xv. 15-17.

The smith hath wrought with his file, with coals, and with hammers he hath formed it, and hath wrought with the strength of his arm: he shall hunger and faint, he shall drink no water, and shall be weary.

The carpenter hath stretched out his rule, he hath formed it with a plane: he hath made it with corners, and hath fashioned it round with the compass: and he hath made the image of a man, as it were a beautiful man dwelling in a house.

He hath cut down cedars, taken the holm, and the oak that stood among the trees of the forest: he hath planted the pine-tree, which the rain hath nourished.

And it hath served men for fuel: he took thereof, and warmed himself: and he kindled it, and baked bread: but of the rest, he made a god, and adored it: he made a graven thing, and bowed down before it.

Part of it he burnt with fire, and with part of it he dressed his meat: he boiled pottage, and was filled, and was warmed, and said: Aha, I am warm, I have seen the fire.

But the residue thereof he made a god, and a graven thing for himself: he boweth down before it, and adoreth it, and prayeth unto it, saying: Deliver me, for thou art my God.

They have not known, nor understood: for their eyes are covered, that they may not see, and that they may not understand with their heart.

They do not consider in their mind, nor know, nor have the thought to say: I have burnt part of it in the fire, and I have baked bread upon the coals thereof: I have broiled flesh, and have eaten, and of the residue thereof shall I make an idol? shall I fall down before the stock of a tree?

Part thereof is ashes: his foolish heart adoreth it, and he will not save his soul, nor say: Perhaps there is a lie in my right hand.—*Is.* xliv. 12-20.

To whom have you likened me, and made me equal, and compared me, and made me like?

You that contribute gold out of the bag, and weigh out silver in the scales: and hire a goldsmith to make a god: and they fall down and worship.

They bear him on their shoulders, and carry him, and set him in his place, and he shall stand, and shall not stir out of his place. Yea, when they shall cry also unto him, he shall not hear: he shall not save them from tribulation.—*Is.* xlvi. 5-7.

For the laws of the people are vain: for the works of the hand of the workman hath cut a tree out of the forest with an axe.

He hath decked it with silver and gold: he hath put it together with nails and hammers, that it may not fall asunder.

They are framed after the likeness of a palm-tree, and shall not speak: they must be carried to be removed, because they cannot go.

Therefore fear them not, for they can neither do evil nor good.—*Jer.* x. 3-5.

For their tongue that is polished by the craftsman, and themselves laid over with gold and silver, are false things, and they cannot speak. . . .

And these gods cannot defend themselves from the rust, and the moth.

But when they have covered them with a purple garment, they wipe their face, because of the dust of the house, which is very much among them.

This holdeth a sceptre as a man, as a judge of the country, but cannot put to death one that offendeth him.

And this hath in his hand a sword, or an ax, but cannot save himself from war, or from robbers, whereby be it known to you, that they are not gods.

Therefore fear them not. For as a vessel that a man uses, when it is broken, becometh useless, even so are their gods:

When they are placed in the house, their eyes are full of dust by the feet of them that go in.

And as the gates are made sure on every side upon one that hath offended the king, or like a dead man carried to the grave, so do the priests secure the doors with bars and locks, lest they be stripped by thieves.

They light candles to them, and in great number, of which they cannot see one: but they are like beams in the house.

And they say that the creeping things which are of the earth, gnaw their hearts, while they eat them and their garments, and they feel it not.

Their faces are black with the smoke that is made in the house.

Owls, and swallows, and other birds fly upon their bodies, and upon their heads, and cats in like manner.

Whereby you may know that they are no gods. Therefore fear them not.

The gold also which they have, is for show, but except a man wipe off the rust, they will not shine: for neither when they were molten, did they feel it.

Men buy them at a high price, whereas there is no breath in them.

And having not the use of feet, they are carried upon shoulders, declaring to men how vile they are. Be they confounded also that worship them.

Therefore if they fall to the ground, they rise not up again of themselves, nor if a man set them upright, will they stand by themselves, but their gifts shall be set before them, as to the dead. . . .

And whether it be evil that one doth unto them, or good, they are not able to recompense it: neither can they set up a king, nor put him down.

In like manner, they can neither give riches, nor requite evil. If a man make a vow to them, and perform it not, they cannot require it.

They cannot deliver a man from death, nor save the weak from the mighty.

They cannot restore the blind man to his sight: nor deliver a man from distress.

They shall not pity the widow, nor do good to the fatherless.

Their gods, of wood and of stone, and of gold and of silver, are like the stones that are hewn out of the mountains: and they that worship them shall be confounded.

How then is it to be supposed, or to be said, that they are gods? . . .

And they are made by workmen and by goldsmiths. They shall be nothing else but what the priests will have them to be.

For the artificers themselves that make them, are of no long continuance. Can those things then that are made by them, be gods? . . .

They cannot set up a king over the land, nor give rain to men.

T¹ ey determine no causes, nor deliver countries from oppression; because they can do nothing, and are as daws between heaven and earth.

For when fire shall fall upon the house of these gods of wood, and of silver, and of gold, their priests indeed will flee away, and be saved: but they themselves shall be burnt in the midst like beams. . . .

Neither are these gods of wood and of stone, and laid over with gold and with silver, able to deliver themselves from thieves or robbers: they that are stronger than them

Shall take from them the gold and silver, and the raiment wherewith they are clothed, and shall go their way, neither shall they help themselves. . . .

For neither can they curse kings, nor bless them.

Neither do they show signs in the heaven to the nations, nor shine as the sun, nor give light as the moon.

Beasts are better than they, which can fly under a covert, and help themselves.

Therefore there is no manner of appearance that they are gods: so fear them not.

For as a scarecrow in a garden of cucumbers keepeth nothing, so are their gods of wood and of silver, and laid over with gold.

They are no better than a white thorn in a garden, upon which every bird sitteth. . . .

By the purple also and the scarlet which are moth-eaten upon them, you shall know that they are not gods. And they themselves at last are consumed, and shall be a reproach in the country. —*Bar.* vi. *passim.*

IDOLATRY FORBIDDEN

And the Lord spoke all these words: I am the Lord thy God, who brought thee out of the land of Egypt, out of the house of bondage.

Thou shalt not have strange gods before me.

Thou shalt not make to thyself a graven thing, nor the likeness of anything that is in heaven above, or in the earth beneath, nor of those things that are in the waters under the earth.

Thou shalt not adore them, nor serve them.—*Ex.* xx. 1-5.

Adore not any strange god. The Lord his name is Jealous, he is a jealous God.—*Ex.* xxxiv. 14.

Turn ye not to idols, nor make to yourselves molten gods. I am the Lord your God.—*Lev.* xix. 4.

I am the Lord your God: you shall not make to yourselves any idol or graven thing, neither shall you erect pillars, nor set up a remarkable stone in your land, to adore it: for I am the Lord your God.—*Lev.* xxvi. 1.

IDOLATRY, PUNISHMENT OF

He that sacrificeth to gods, shall be put to death, save only to the Lord.—*Ex.* xxii. 20.

But the idol that is made by hands, is cursed, as well it, as he that made it: he, because he made it; and it, because being frail, it is called a god. . . .

For that which is made, together with him that made it, shall suffer torments.—*Wis.* xiv. 8, 10.

Who hath formed a god, and made a graven thing that is profitable for nothing?

Behold, all the partakers thereof shall be confounded: for the makers are men: they shall all assemble together, they shall stand and fear, and shall be confounded together.—*Is.* xliv. 10, 11.

Know you not that the unjust shall not possess the kingdom of God? Do not err: neither fornicators, nor idolaters, nor adulterers . . . shall possess the kingdom of God.—1 *Cor.* vi. 9, 10.

Now the works of the flesh are manifest, which are fornication, uncleanness, immodesty, luxury,

Idolatry, witchcrafts. . . .

Of the which I foretell you, as I have foretold to you, that they who do such things, shall not obtain the kingdom of God.—*Gal.* v. 19-21.

But the fearful and unbelieving, and the abominable, and murderers, and whoremongers, and sorcerers, and idolaters, and all liars, they shall have their portion in the pool burning with fire and brimstone, which is the second death.—*Apoc.* xxi. 8.

Blessed are they that wash their robes in the blood of the Lamb: that they may have a right to the tree of life, and may enter in by the gates into the city.

Without are dogs and sorcerers, and unchaste, and murderers, and servers of idols, and every one that loveth and maketh a lie.—*Apoc.* xxii. 14, 15.

IGNORANCE OF THE DOCTRINE AND LAW OF GOD, EXCUSABLE

And that servant who knew the will of his lord, and prepared not himself, and did not according to his will, shall be beaten with many stripes.

But he that knew not, and did things worthy of stripes, shall be beaten with few stripes.—*Luke* xii. 47, 48.

Jesus said to them: If you were blind, you should not have sin: but now you say: We see. Your sin remaineth. —*John* ix. 41.

I give him thanks who hath strengthened me, even to Christ Jesus our Lord, for that he hath counted me faithful, putting me in the ministry;

Who before was a blasphemer, and a persecutor, and contumelious. But I obtained the mercy of God, because I did it ignorantly in unbelief.—1 *Tim.* i. 12, 13.

IGNORANCE, INEXCUSABLE

See: Blindness, wilful—page 39.

IMITATION OF CHRIST

See: Example of Christ—page 130.

IMMUTABILITY OF GOD

God is not a man that he should lie, nor as the son of man, that he should be changed. Hath he said then, and will he not do? hath he spoken, and will he not fulfil?—*Num.* xxiii. 19.

In the beginning, O Lord, thou foundedst the earth: and the heavens are the works of thy hands.

They shall perish, but thou remainest: and all of them shall grow old like a garment:

And as a vesture thou shalt change them, and they shall be changed.

But thou art always the selfsame, and thy years shall not fail.—*Ps.* ci. 26-28.

He hath beautified the glorious works of his wisdom: and he is from eternity to eternity, and to him nothing may be added,

Nor can he be diminished, and he hath no need of any counsellor.— *Ecclus.* xlii. 21, 22.

I am, I am the Lord: and there is no Saviour besides me. . . .

And from the beginning, I am the same, and there is none that can deliver out of my hand: I will work, and who shall turn it away?—*Is.* xliii. 11, 13.

For I am the Lord, and I change not. —*Malach.* iii. 6.

Jesus Christ, yesterday, and to-day; and the same for ever.—*Heb.* xiii. 8.

Every best gift, and every perfect gift, is from above, coming down from the Father of lights, with whom there is no change, nor shadow of alteration. —*James* i. 17.

IMPARTIALITY

Thou shalt not follow the multitude to do evil: neither shalt thou yield in judgment, to the opinion of the most part, to stray from the truth. . . .

Thou shalt not go aside in the poor man's judgment.—*Ex.* xxiii. 2, 6.

Thou shalt not do that which is unjust, nor judge unjustly. Respect not the person of the poor, nor honor the countenance of the mighty. But judge thy neighbor according to justice.—*Lev.* xix. 15.

Hear them, and judge that which is just: whether he be one of your country, or a stranger.

There shall be no difference of persons, you shall hear the little as well as the great: neither shall you respect any man's person, because it is the judgment of God.—*Deut.* i. 16, 17.

These things also to the wise: It is not good to have respect to persons in judgment.—*Prov.* xxiv. 23.

Justify alike the small and the great. —*Ecclus.* v. 18.

But if you have respect to persons, you commit sin, being reproved by the law as transgressors.—*James* ii. 9.

IMPARTIALITY OF GOD

Because the Lord your God, he is the God of gods and the Lord of lords, a great God and mighty and terrible, who accepteth no person, nor taketh bribes.—*Deut.* x. 17.

Let the fear of the Lord be with you, and do all things with diligence: for there is no iniquity with the Lord our God, nor respect of persons, nor desire of gifts.—2 *Paral.* xix. 7.

For in very deed God will not condemn without cause, neither will the Almighty pervert judgment. . . .

Who accepteth not the persons of princes: nor hath regarded the tyrant, when he contended against the poor man: for all are the work of his hands. —*Job* xxxiv. 12, 19.

For God will not except any man's person, neither will he stand in awe of any man's greatness: for he made the little and the great, and he hath equally care of all.—*Wis.* vi. 8.

And look not upon an unjust sacrifice, for the Lord is judge, and there is not with him respect of person.

The Lord will not accept any person against a poor man, and he will hear the prayer of him that is wronged.—*Ecclus.* xxxv. 15, 16.

And Peter opening his mouth, said: In very deed I perceive that God is not a respecter of persons.

But in every nation, he that feareth him, and worketh justice, is acceptable to him.—*Acts* x. 34, 35.

For he that doth wrong, shall receive for that which he hath done wrongfully: and there is no respect of persons with God.—*Col.* iii. 25.

And if you invoke as Father him who, without respect of persons, judgeth according to every one's work: converse in fear during the time of your sojourning here.—1 *Peter* i. 17.

IMPATIENCE

But now the scourge is come upon thee, and thou faintest: it hath touched thee, and thou art troubled.

Where is thy fear, thy fortitude, thy patience, and the perfection of thy ways?—*Job* iv. 5, 6.

The impatient man shall work folly:

and the crafty man is hateful.—*Prov.* xiv. 17.

He that is patient, is governed with much wisdom: but he that is impatient, exalteth his folly.—*Prov.* xiv. 29.

He that is impatient, shall suffer damage: and when he shall take away, he shall add another thing.—*Prov.* xix. 19.

Woe to them that have lost patience, and that have forsaken the right ways, and have gone aside into crooked ways.

And what will they do, when the Lord shall begin to examine?—*Ecclus.* ii. 16, 17.

IMPENITENCE

See also: Obstinacy in sin—page 349.

And the people are not returned to him who hath struck them, and have not sought after the Lord of hosts.— *Is.* ix. 13.

O Lord, thy eyes are upon truth: thou hast struck them, and they have not grieved: thou hast bruised them, and they have refused to receive correction: they have made their faces harder than the rock, and they have refused to return. . . .

Will you not then fear me, saith the Lord: and will you not repent at my presence? . . .

But the heart of this people is become hard of belief and provoking, they are revolted and gone away.

And they have not said in their heart: Let us fear the Lord our God, who giveth us the early and the latter rain in due season: who preserveth for us the fulness of the yearly harvest.— *Jer.* v. 3, 22-24.

Why then is this people in Jerusalem turned away with a stubborn revolting? they have laid hold on lying, and have refused to return.

I attended, and hearkened; no man speaketh what is good, there is none that doth penance for his sin, saying: What have I done? They are all turned to their own course, as a horse rushing to the battle.—*Jer.* viii. 5, 6.

Thy calf, O Samaria, is cast off, my wrath is kindled against them. How long will they be incapable of being cleansed?—*Osee* viii. 5.

For from the days of your fathers

INCARNATION

you have departed from my ordinances, and have not kept them. Return to me, and I will return to you, saith the Lord of hosts. And you have said: Wherein shall we return?

Shall a man afflict God? for you afflict me? And you have said: Wherein do we afflict thee? in tithes and in firstfruits.—*Malach.* iii. 7, 8.

For I fear. . . . Lest again, when I come, God humble me among you: and I mourn many of them that sinned before, and have not done penance for the uncleanness, and fornication, and lasciviousness, that they have committed. —*2 Cor.* xii. 21.

And the fourth angel poured out his vial upon the sun, and it was given unto him to afflict men with heat and fire:

And men were scorched with great heat, and they blasphemed the name of God, who hath power over these plagues, neither did they penance, to give him glory. . . .

And they blasphemed the God of heaven, because of their pains and wounds, and did not penance for their works.—*Apoc.* xvi. 8, 9, 11.

IMPENITENCE, PUNISHMENT OF

But [1]they that were not amended by mockeries and reprehensions, experienced the worthy judgment of God.— *Wis.* xii. 26.

If we do not penance, we shall fall into the hands of the Lord, and not into the hands of men.—*Ecclus.* ii. 22.

Delay not, to be converted to the Lord, and defer it not from day to day.

For his wrath shall come on a sudden, and in the time of vengeance, he will destroy thee.—*Ecclus.* v. 8, 9.

I have spread forth my hands all the day to an unbelieving people, who walk in a way that is not good after their own thoughts.

A people that continually provoke me to anger before my face. . . .

That say: Depart from me, come not near me, because thou art unclean: these shall be smoke in my anger, a fire burning all the day.

Behold it is written before me: I will

[1]The Chanaanites.

not be silent, but I will render and repay into their bosom. . . .

I will number you in the sword, and you shall all fall by slaughter: because I called, and you did not answer: I spoke, and you did not hear: and you did evil in my eyes, and you have chosen the things that displease me.— *Is.* lxv. 2, 3, 5, 6, 12.

We would have cured Babylon, but she is not healed: let us forsake her, and let us go every man to his own land: because her judgment hath reached even to the heavens, and is lifted up to the clouds.—*Jer.* li. 9.

Thy uncleanness is execrable: because I desired to cleanse thee, and thou art not cleansed from thy filthiness: neither shalt thou be cleansed, before I cause my indignation to rest in thee.—*Ezech.* xxiv. 13.

Or despisest thou the riches of his goodness, and patience, and longsuffering? Knowest thou not that the benignity of God leadeth thee to penance?

But according to thy hardness and impenitent heart, thou treasurest up to thyself wrath, against the day of wrath, and revelation of the just judgment of God.—*Rom.* ii. 4, 5.

IMPOSSIBLE, GOD DOES NOT DEMAND OF US THE

See: Commandments of God are not above our strength, the—page 58.

IMPURITY

See: Unchastity—page 569.

INCARNATION, THE

See also: Redeemer, the coming of the—page 462.

He bowed the heavens, and came down: and darkness was under his feet. —*Ps.* xvii. 10.

Sacrifice and oblation thou didst not desire; but thou hast pierced ears for me.

Burnt offering and sin offering thou didst not require: then said I, Behold, I come.

In the head of the book it is written of me that I should do thy will: O my

God, I have desired it, and thy law in the midst of my heart.—*Ps.* xxxix. 7-9.

For while all things were in quiet silence, and the night was in the midst of her course, Thy almighty word leapt down from heaven from thy royal throne.—*Wis.* xviii. 14, 15.

This is our God, and there shall no other be accounted of in comparison of him. . . .

Afterwards he was seen upon earth, and conversed with men.—*Bar.* iii. 36, 38.

Now the generation of Christ was in this wise. When as his mother Mary was espoused to Joseph, before they came together, she was found with child, of the Holy Ghost.

Whereupon, Joseph her husband, being a just man, and not willing publicly to expose her, was minded to put her away privately.

But while he thought on these things, behold the angel of the Lord appeared to him in his sleep, saying: Joseph, son of David, fear not to take unto thee Mary thy wife, for that which is conceived in her, is of the Holy Ghost.

And she shall bring forth a son: and thou shalt call his name Jesus. For he shall save his people from their sins.

Now all this was done, that it might be fulfilled, which the Lord spoke by the prophet, saying:

Behold a virgin shall be with child, and bring forth a son, and they shall call his name, Emmanuel, which being interpreted is, God with us.

And Joseph rising up from sleep, did as the angel of the Lord had commanded him, and took unto him his wife.

And he knew her not till she brought forth her first-born son: and he called his name Jesus.—*Matt.* i. 18-25.

When Jesus therefore was born in Bethlehem of Juda, in the days of king Herod, behold there came wise men from the east to Jerusalem,

Saying, Where is he that is born king of the Jews? For we have seen his star in the east, and are come to adore him. —*Matt.* ii. 1, 2.

And Joseph also went up from Gali-lee, out of the city of Nazareth, into Judea, to the city of David, which is called Bethlehem: because he was of the house and family of David,

To be enrolled with Mary his espoused wife, who was with child.

And it came to pass that when they were there, her days were accomplished, that she should be delivered.

And she brought forth her first-born son, and wrapped him up in swaddling clothes, and laid him in a manger; because there was no room for them in the inn.

And there were in the same country shepherds watching, and keeping the night watches over their flock. . . .

And the angel said to them: Fear not; for behold, I bring you good tidings of great joy, that shall be to all the people:

For, this day, is born to you a Saviour, who is Christ the Lord, in the city of David.—*Luke* ii. 4-8, 10, 11.

And the Word was made flesh, and dwelt among us, (and we saw his glory, the glory, as it were, of the only begotten of the Father,) full of grace and truth.—*John* i. 14.

For no where doth he take hold of the angels: but of the seed of Abraham he taketh hold.

Wherefore it behooved him in all things to be made like unto his brethren, that he might become a merciful and faithful high priest before God, that he might be a propitiation for the sins of the people.

For in that, wherein he himself hath suffered and been tempted, he is able to succor them also that are tempted.— *Heb.* ii. 16, 17, 18.

INCLINATIONS OF MAN, EVIL

If thou do well, shalt thou not receive? but if ill, shall not sin forthwith be present at the door? but the lust thereof shall be under thee, and thou shalt have dominion over it.—*Gen.* iv. 7.

And the Lord smelled a sweet savor, and said: I will no more curse the earth for the sake of man: for the imagination and thought of man's heart are prone to evil from his youth:

therefore I will no more destroy every living soul, as I have done.—*Gen.* viii. 21.

For she is become weak unto good that dwelleth in bitterness: for evil is come down from the Lord into the gate of Jerusalem.—*Mich.* i. 12.

For when we were in the flesh, the passions of sin, which were by the law, did work in our members, to bring forth fruit unto death. . . .

For I do not that good which I will; but the evil which I hate, that I do. . . .

For I know that there dwelleth not in me, that is to say, in my flesh, that which is good.

For, to will, is present with me; but to accomplish that which is good, I find not.

For the good which I will, I do not; but the evil which I will not, that I do.

Now if I do that which I will not, it is no more I that do it, but sin that dwelleth in me. I find then a law, that when I have a will to do good, evil is present with me.

For I am delighted with the law of God, according to the inward man:

But I see another law in my members, fighting against the law of my mind, and captivating me in the law of sin, that is in my members. . . .

Therefore I myself, with the mind, serve the law of God; but with the flesh, the law of sin.—*Rom.* vii. 5, 15, 18-23, 25.

I say then, walk in the spirit, and you shall not fulfil the lusts of the flesh.

For the flesh lusteth against the spirit: and the spirit against the flesh; for these are contrary one to another: so that you do not the things that you would.—*Gal.* v. 16, 17.

From whence are wars and contentions among you? Are they not hence, from your concupiscences, which war in your members?

You covet, and have not: you kill, and envy, and cannot obtain.—*James* iv. 1, 2.

INCOMPREHENSIBILITY OF GOD

See: Understanding, God is above our—page 572.

INCREDULITY

See also: Infidels—page 237.

In all these things [1]they sinned still; and they believed not for his wondrous works.—*Ps.* lxxvii. 32.

They that fear the Lord, will not be incredulous to his word.—*Ecclus.* ii. 18.

Be not thou incredulous to his word. —*Ecclus.* xvi. 29.

Woe to you that draw iniquity with cords of vanity, and sin, as the rope of a cart.

That say: Let him make haste, and let his work come quickly, that we may see it: and let the counsel of the Holy One of Israel come, that we may know it.—*Is.* v. 18, 19.

And when Jesus was come into the house of the ruler, and saw the minstrels and the multitude making a rout,

He said: Give place, for the girl is not dead, but sleepeth. And they laughed him to scorn.—*Matt.* ix. 23, 24.

And Abraham said to [2]him: They have Moses and the prophets; let them hear them.

But he said: No, father Abraham: but if one went to them from the dead, they will do penance.

And he said to him: If they hear not Moses and the prophets, neither will they believe, if one rise again from the dead.—*Luke* xvi. 29, 30, 31.

And it was Mary Magdalen, and Joanna, and Mary of James, and the other women that were with them, who told [3]these things to the apostles.

And these words seemed to them as idle tales; and they did not believe them.—*Luke* xxiv. 10, 11.

If I have spoken to you earthly things, and you believe not; how will you believe, if I shall speak to you heavenly things?—*John* iii. 12.

Many therefore of his disciples, hearing it, said: This saying is hard, and who can hear it?—*John* vi. 61.

For neither did his brethren believe in him.—*John* vii. 5.

Take heed, brethren, lest perhaps there be in any of you an evil heart of unbelief, to depart from the living God.—*Heb.* iii. 12.

[1]The Israelites in the wilderness.
[2]The rich man in hell.
[3]The resurrection of Christ.

INCREDULITY OF HIS PEOPLE, GOD REBUKES THE

And the Lord said to Moses: How long will this people detract me? how long will they not believe me, for all the signs that I have wrought before them?—*Num.* xiv. 11.

And when the sabbath was come, he began to teach in the synagogue: and many hearing him, were in admiration at his doctrine, saying: How came this man by all these things? and what wisdom is this that is given to him, and such mighty works as are wrought by his hands?

Is not this the carpenter, the son of Mary, the brother of James, and Joseph, and Jude, and Simon? are not also his sisters here with us? And they were scandalized in regard of him.

And Jesus said to them: A prophet is not without honor, but in his own country, and in his own house, and among his own kindred.

And he could not do any miracles there, only that he cured a few that were sick, laying his hands upon them. And he wondered, because of their unbelief.—*Mark* vi. 2-6.

Who (Jesus) answering them, said: O incredulous generation, how long shall I be with you? how long shall I suffer you?—*Mark* ix. 18.

But he rising early the first day of the week, appeared first to Mary Magdalen, out of whom he had cast seven devils.

She went and told them that had been with him, who were mourning and weeping.

And they hearing that he was alive, and had been seen by her, did not believe.

And after that, he appeared in another shape to two of them walking, as they were going into the country.

And they going, told it to the rest: neither did they believe them.

At length he appeared to the eleven as they were at table; and he upbraided them with their incredulity and hardness of heart, because they did not believe them who had seen him after he was risen again.—*Mark* xvi. 9-14.

Then he (Jesus) said to them: O foolish, and slow of heart to believe in all things which the prophets have spoken.—*Luke* xxiv. 25.

Now Thomas, one of the twelve, who is called Didymus, was not with them when Jesus came.

The other disciples therefore said to him: We have seen the Lord. But he said to them: Except I shall see in his hands the print of the nails, and put my finger into the place of the nails, and put my hand into his side, I will not believe.

And after eight days again his disciples were within, and Thomas with them. Jesus cometh, the doors being shut, and stood in the midst, and said: Peace be to you.

Then he saith to Thomas: Put in thy finger hither, and see my hands; and bring hither thy hand, and put it into my side; and be not faithless, but believing.

Thomas answered, and said to him: My Lord, and my God.

Jesus saith to him: Because thou hast seen me, Thomas, thou hast believed: blessed are they that have not seen, and have believed.—*John* xx. 24-29.

INCREDULITY, PUNISHMENT OF

And they spoke ill of God: they said: Can God furnish a table in the wilderness?

Because he struck the rock, and the waters gushed out, and the streams overflowed.

Can he also give bread, or provide a table for his people?

Therefore the Lord heard, and was angry: and a fire was kindled against Jacob, and wrath came up against Israel.

Because they believed not in God: and trusted not in his salvation.—*Ps.* lxxvii. 19-22.

Woe to them that are faint-hearted, who believe not God: and therefore they shall not be protected by him.—*Ecclus.* ii. 15.

Thou wilt say then: The branches were broken off, that I might be grafted in.

Well: because of unbelief they were broken off.—*Rom.* xi. 19, 20.

And to whom did he swear, that they should not enter into his rest: but to them that were incredulous?

And we see that they could not enter in, because of unbelief.—*Heb.* iii. 18, 19.

INDIFFERENCE TO OUR SPIRITUAL INTERESTS

See also: Lukewarmness—page 298.

The triflers that were departed from the law, I will gather together, because they were of thee: that thou mayst no more suffer reproach for them.—*Soph.* iii. 18.

And the lord commended the unjust steward, forasmuch as he had done wisely: for the children of this world are wiser in their generation, than the children of light.—*Luke* xvi. 8.

And we desire that every one of you show forth the same carefulness to the accomplishing of hope unto the end:

That you become not slothful, but followers of them, who through faith and patience shall inherit the promises. —*Heb.* vi. 11, 12.

INDUSTRY

See: Diligence—page 113.

INFIDELS

Dost not thou think that God is higher than heaven, and is elevated above the height of the stars?

And thou sayst: What doth God know? and he judgeth as it were through a mist.

The clouds are his covert, and he doth not consider our things, and he walketh about the poles of heaven. . . .

Who said to God: Depart from us: and looked upon the Almighty as if he could do nothing:

Whereas he had filled their houses with good things: whose way of thinking be far from me.—*Job* xxii. 12-14, 17, 18.

For they have said, reasoning with themselves, but not right: The time of our life is short and tedious, and in the end of a man there is no remedy, and no man hath been known to have returned from hell:

For we are born of nothing, and after this, we shall be as if we had not been: for the breath in our nostrils is smoke: and speech, a spark to move our heart,

Which being put out, our body shall be ashes, and our spirit shall be poured abroad as soft air, and our life shall pass away as the trace of a cloud, and shall be dispersed as a mist, which is driven away by the beams of the sun, and overpowered with the heat thereof. . . .

Come therefore, and let us enjoy the good things that are present, and let us speedily use the creatures as in youth. —*Wis.* ii. 1-3, 6.

Behold, he that is unbelieving, his soul shall not be right in himself: but the just shall live in his faith.—*Hab.* ii. 4.

He that believeth in him is not judged. But he that doth not believe, is already judged: because he believeth not in the name of the only begotten Son of God.

And this is the judgment: because the light is come into the world, and men loved darkness rather than the light: for their works were evil.— *John* iii. 18, 19.

And the Father himself who hath sent me, hath given testimony of me: neither have you heard his voice at any time, nor seen his shape.

And you have not his word abiding in you: for whom he hath sent, him you believe not.—*John* v. 37, 38.

And when he (the Paraclete) is come, he will convince the world of sin, and of justice, and of judgment.

Of sin: because they believed not in me.—*John* xvi. 8, 9.

For the wrath of God is revealed from heaven against all ungodliness and injustice of those men that detain the truth of God in injustice:

Because that which is known of God is manifest in them. For God hath manifested it unto them.

For the invisible things of him, from the creation of the world, are clearly seen, being understood by the things that are made; his eternal power also, and divinity: so that they are inexcusable.

Because that, when they knew God, they have not glorified him as God, or given thanks; but became vain in their thoughts, and their foolish heart was darkened.

For professing themselves to be wise, they became fools.—*Rom.* i. 18-22.

For what if some of them have not believed? Shall their unbelief make the faith of God without effect? God forbid.

But God is true; and every man a liar, as it is written, That thou mayst be justified in thy words, and mayst overcome, when thou art judged.—*Rom.* iii. 3, 4.

Bear not the yoke with unbelievers. For what participation hath justice with injustice? Or what fellowship hath light with darkness?

And what concord hath Christ with Belial? Or what part hath the faithful with the unbeliever?—2 *Cor.* vi. 14, 15.

If we believe not, he continueth faithful, he cannot deny himself.—2 *Tim.* ii. 13.

Wherefore it is said in the scripture: Behold I lay in Sion a chief cornerstone, elect, precious. And he that shall believe in him, shall not be confounded.

To you therefore that believe, he is honor: but to them that believe not, the stone which the builders rejected, the same is made the head of the corner:

And a stone of stumbling, and a rock of scandal to them who stumble at the word, neither do believe, whereunto also they are set.—1 *Peter* ii. 6-8.

Knowing this first, that in the last days there shall come deceitful scoffers, walking after their own lusts,

Saying: Where is his promise, or his coming? for since the time that the fathers slept, all things continue as they were from the beginning of the creation.—2 *Peter* iii. 3, 4.

INFIDELS, PUNISHMENT OF

They spent their days in wealth, and in a moment they go down to hell.

Who have said to God: Depart from us, we desire not the knowledge of thy ways.

Who is the Almighty, that we should serve him? and what doth it profit us, if we pray to him?—*Job* xxi. 13-15.

Give not thy mouth to cause thy flesh to sin: and say not before the angel: There is no providence: lest God be angry at thy words, and destroy all the works of thy hands.—*Eccles.* v. 5.

Therefore thou hast sent a judgment upon them as senseless children, to mock them. . . .

For seeing with indignation that they suffered by those very things which they took for gods, when they were destroyed by the same, they acknowledged him the true God, whom in time past they denied that they knew: for which cause the end also of their condemnation came upon them.— *Wis.* xii. 25, 27.

In the congregation of sinners, a fire shall be kindled, and in an unbelieving nation, wrath shall flame out.—*Ecclus.* xvi. 7.

And I will visit the evils of the world. and against the wicked for their iniquity: and I will make the pride of infidels to cease, and will bring down the arrogancy of the mighty.—*Is.* xiii. 11.

He that believeth in the Son, hath life everlasting; but he that believeth not the Son, shall not see life; but the wrath of God abideth on him.—*John* iii. 36.

Therefore I said to you, that you shall die in your sins. For if you believe not that I am he, you shall die in your sin.—*John* viii. 24.

And as they liked not to have God in their knowledge, God delivered them up to a reprobate sense, to do those things which are not convenient.— *Rom.* i. 28.

Seeing it is a just thing with God to repay tribulation to them that trouble you:

And to you who are troubled, rest with us, when the Lord Jesus shall be revealed from heaven, with the angels of his power:

In a flame of fire, giving vengeance to them who know not God, and who obey not the gospel of our Lord Jesus Christ.

Who shall suffer eternal punishment in destruction, from the face of the Lord, and from the glory of his power.—*2 Thess.* i. 6-9.

And when that wicked one shall be revealed, whom the Lord Jesus shall kill with the spirit of his mouth; and shall destroy with the brightness of his coming, him,

Whose coming is according to the working of Satan, in all power, and signs, and lying wonders,

And in all seduction of iniquity to them that perish; because they receive not the love of the truth, that they might be saved. Therefore God shall send them the operation of error, to believe lying:

That all may be judged, who have not believed the truth, but have consented to iniquity.—*2 Thess.* ii. 8-11.

For the time is that judgment should begin at the house of God. And if first at us, what shall be the end of them that believe not the gospel of God?—*1 Peter* iv. 17.

But the fearful, and unbelieving, and the abominable, and murderers . . . they shall have their portion in the pool burning with fire and brimstone, which is the second death.—*Apoc.* xxi. 8.

INFIDELS, A PRAYER FOR

See: Unbelievers, a prayer for—page 569.

INGRATITUDE TO GOD

See also: Forgetfulness of God—page 153.

The beloved grew fat, and kicked: he grew fat, and thick and gross, he forsook God who made him, and departed from God his saviour.—*Deut.* xxxii. 15.

Dost thou desire to keep the path of ages, which wicked men have trodden? . . .

Who said to God: Depart from us: and looked upon the Almighty as if he could do nothing:

Whereas he had filled their houses with good things: whose way of thinking be far from me.—*Job* xxii. 15,17,18.

For you have forgotten God, who brought you up, and you have grieved Jerusalem that nursed you.—*Bar.* iv. 8.

Hear ye another parable. There was a man, a householder, who planted a vineyard, and made a hedge round about it, and dug in it a press, and built a tower, and let it out to husbandmen; and went into a strange country.

And when the time of the fruits drew nigh, he sent his servants to the husbandmen, that they might receive the fruits thereof.

And the husbandmen laying hands on his servants, beat one, and killed another, and stoned another.

Again he sent other servants, more than the former; and they did to them in like manner.

And last of all, he sent to them his son, saying: They will reverence my son.

But the husbandmen seeing the son, said among themselves: This is the heir: Come, let us kill him, and we shall have his inheritance.

And taking him, they cast him forth out of the vineyard, and killed him.—*Matt.* xxi. 33-39.

He came unto his own, and his own received him not.—*John* i. 11.

INGRATITUDE OF HIS PEOPLE, COMPLAINT OF GOD AGAINST THE

Is this the return thou makest to the Lord, O foolish and senseless people? Is not he thy father, that hath possessed thee, and made thee, and created thee?—*Deut.* xxxii. 6.

For even the man of my peace, in whom I trusted, who ate my bread, hath greatly supplanted me.—*Ps.* xl. 10.

For if my enemy had reviled me, I would verily have borne with it.

And if he that hated me, had spoken great things against me, I would perhaps have hidden myself from him.

But thou, a man of one mind, my guide, and my familiar,

Who didst take sweetmeats together with me: in the house of God we walked with consent.—*Ps.* liv. 13-15.

My heart hath expected reproach and misery. And I looked for one that would grieve together with me, but there was none: and for one that would comfort me, and I found none.

And they gave me gall for my food, and in my thirst they gave me vinegar to drink.—*Ps.* lxviii. 21, 22.

They have spoken against me with deceitful tongues; and they have compassed me about with words of hatred; and have fought against me without cause.

Instead of making me a return of love, they detracted me: but I gave myself to prayer.

And they repaid me evil for good: and hatred for my love.—*Ps.* cviii. 3-5.

Hear, O ye heavens, and give ear, O earth, for the Lord hath spoken. I have brought up children, and exalted them: but they have despised me.

The ox knoweth his owner, and the ass his master's crib: but Israel hath not known me, and my people hath not understood.—*Is.* i. 2, 3.

What is there that I ought to do more to my vineyard, that I have not done to it? was it that I looked that it should bring forth grapes, and it hath brought forth wild grapes? . . .

For the vineyard of the Lord of hosts is the house of Israel: and the man of Juda, his pleasant plant: and I looked that he should do judgment, and behold iniquity: and do justice, and behold a cry.—*Is.* v. 4, 7.

This people have I formed for myself, they shall show forth my praise.

But thou hast not called upon me, O Jacob, neither hast thou labored about me, O Israel.

Thou hast not offered me the ram of thy holocaust, nor hast thou glorified me with thy victims: I have not caused thee to serve with oblations, nor wearied thee with incense.

Thou hast bought me no sweet cane with money, neither hast thou filled me with the fat of thy victims. But thou hast made me to serve with thy sins, thou hast wearied me with thy iniquities.—*Is.* xliii. 21-24.

I am the Lord, and there is none else: there is no God besides me: I girded thee, and thou hast not known me.—*Is.* xlv. 5.

Thus saith the Lord: What iniquity have your fathers found in me, that

they are gone far from me, and have walked after vanity, and are become vain? . . .

Be astonished, O ye heavens, at this, and ye gates thereof, be very desolate, saith the Lord.

For my people have done two evils. They have forsaken me, the fountain of living water, and have digged to themselves cisterns, broken cisterns, that can hold no water.—*Jer.* ii. 5, 12, 13.

How can I be merciful to thee? thy children have forsaken me, and swear by them that are not gods: I fed them to the full, and they committed adultery, and rioted in the harlot's house.— *Jer.* v. 7.

For as the girdle sticketh close to the loins of a man, so have I brought close to me all the house of Israel, and all the house of Juda, saith the Lord: that they might be my people, and for a name, and for a praise, and for a glory: but they would not hear.—*Jer.* xiii. 11.

And when thou wast born, in the day of thy nativity, thy navel was not cut, neither wast thou washed with water for thy health, nor salted with salt, nor swaddled with clouts.

No eye had pity on thee, to do any of these things for thee, out of compassion to thee: but thou wast cast out upon the face of the earth in the abjection of thy soul, in the day that thou wast born.

And passing by thee, I saw that thou wast trodden under foot in thy own blood: and I said to thee when thou wast in thy blood: Live: I have said to thee: Live in thy blood. . . .

And I washed thee with water, and cleansed away thy blood from thee: and I anointed thee with oil.

And I clothed thee with embroidery, and shod thee with violet-colored shoes: and I girded thee about with fine linen, and clothed thee with fine garments.

I decked thee also with ornaments, and put bracelets on thy hands, and a chain about thy neck.

And I put a jewel upon thy forehead, and earrings in thy ears, and a beautiful crown upon thy head.

And thou wast adorned with gold, and silver, and wast clothed with fine linen, and embroidered work, and many colors: thou didst eat fine flour and honey and oil, and wast made exceeding beautiful: and wast advanced to be a queen.

And thy renown went forth among the nations for thy beauty: for thou wast perfect through my beauty, which I had put upon thee, saith the Lord God.

But trusting in thy beauty, thou playedst the harlot, because of thy renown, and thou hast prostituted thyself to every passenger, to be his. . . . And thou hast taken thy sons and thy daughters, whom thou hast borne to me: and hast sacrificed the same to them to be devoured. Is thy fornication small? . . . And after all thy abominations and fornications, thou hast not remembered the days of thy youth, when thou wast naked, and full of confusion, trodden under foot in thy own blood.—*Ezech.* xvi. 4-6, 9-15, 20, 22.

Was it not enough for you to feed upon good pastures? but you must also tread down with your feet the residue of your pastures: and when you drank the clearest water, you troubled the rest with your feet.

And my sheep were fed with that which you had trodden with your feet: and they drank what your feet had troubled.—*Ezech.* xxxiv. 18, 19.

Woe to them, for they have departed from me: they shall be wasted because they have transgressed against me: and I redeemed them: and they have spoken lies against me.—*Osee* vii. 13.

But I am the Lord thy God from the land of Egypt: and thou shalt know no God but me, and there is no Saviour beside me.

I knew thee in the desert, in the land of the wilderness.

According to their pastures they were filled, and were made full: and they lifted up their heart, and have forgotten me.—*Osee* xiii. 4-6.

Let the mountains hear the judgment of the Lord, and the strong foundations of the earth: for the Lord will enter into judgment with his people, and he will plead against Israel.

O my people, what have I done to thee, or in what have I molested thee? answer thou me.

For I brought thee up out of the land of Egypt, and delivered thee out of the house of slaves: and I sent before thy face Moses, and Aaron, and Mary.—*Mich.* vi. 2-4.

And they shall say to him: What are these wounds in the midst of thy hands? And he shall say: With these I was wounded in the house of them that loved me.—*Zach.* xiii. 6.

I have loved you, saith the Lord: and you have said: Wherein hast thou loved us?—*Malach.* i. 2.

Jerusalem, Jerusalem, thou that killest the prophets, and stonest them that are sent unto thee, how often would I have gathered together thy children, as the hen doth gather her chickens under her wings, and thou wouldst not?—*Matt.* xxiii. 37.

And Jesus answering, said, Were not ten made clean? and where are the nine?

There is no one found to return and give glory to God, but this stranger.—*Luke* xvii. 17, 18.

INGRATITUDE TO GOD, EXAMPLES OF

And the people seeing that Moses delayed to come down from the mount, gathering together against Aaron, said: Arise, make us gods, that may go before us: for as to this Moses, the man that brought us out of the land of Egypt, we know not what has befallen him.

And Aaron said to them: Take the golden earrings from the ears of your wives, and your sons and daughters, and bring them to me. . . .

And when he had received them, he fashioned them by founders' work, and made of them a molten calf. And they said: These are thy gods, O Israel, that have brought thee out of the land of Egypt.—*Ex.* xxxii. 1, 2, 4.

And speaking against God and Moses, they said: Why didst thou bring us out of Egypt, to die in the wilderness? There is no bread, nor have we any waters: our soul now loatheth this very light food.—*Num.* xxi. 5.

They kept not the covenant of God: and in his law they would not walk.

And they forgot his benefits, and his wonders that he had shown them. . . .

They remembered not his hand, in the day that he redeemed them from the hand of him that afflicted them.—*Ps.* lxxvii. 10, 11, 42.

Our fathers understood not thy wonders in Egypt: they remembered not the multitude of thy mercies:

And they provoked to wrath, going up to the sea, even the Red Sea.

And he saved them for his own name's sake: that he might make his power known.

. . . And he saved them from the hand of them that hated them: and he redeemed them from the hand of the enemy. . . .

And they believed his words: and they sang his praises.

They had quickly done, they forgot his works: and they waited not for his counsel.—*Ps.* cv. 7, 8, 10, 12, 13.

And he said: Surely they are my people, children that will not deny: so he became their saviour.

In all their affliction, he was not troubled, and the angel of his presence saved them: in his love, and in his mercy, he redeemed them, and he carried them, and lifted them up all the days of old.

But they provoked to wrath, and afflicted the spirit of his holy one: and he was turned to be their enemy, and he fought against them.—*Is.* lxiii. 8-10.

Then went one of the twelve, who was called Judas Iscariot, to the chief priests,

And said to them: What will you give me, and I will deliver him unto you? But they appointed him thirty pieces of silver.

And from thenceforth he sought opportunity to betray him. . . .

And he that betrayed him, gave them a sign, saying: Whomsoever I shall kiss, that is he, hold him fast.

And forthwith coming to Jesus, he said: Hail, Rabbi. And he kissed him. —*Matt.* xxvi. 14-16, 48, 49.

But you have a custom, that I should release one unto you at the pasch: will you, therefore, that I release unto you the king of the Jews?

Then cried they all again, saying: Not this man, but Barabbas. Now Barabbas was a robber.—*John* xviii. 39, 40.

But you denied the Holy One and the Just, and desired a murderer to be granted unto you.

But the author of life you killed, whom God hath raised from the dead, of which we are witnesses.—*Acts* iii. 14, 15.

INGRATITUDE TO GOD, PUNISHMENT OF

The Lord saw, and was moved to wrath: because his own sons and daughters provoked him.

And he said: I will hide my face from them, and will consider what their last end shall be: for it is a perverse generation, and unfaithful children.— *Deut.* xxxii. 19, 20.

For the hope of the unthankful shall melt away as the winter's ice, and shall run off as unprofitable water.—*Wis.* xvi. 29.

Because thou hast forgotten God thy saviour, and hast not remembered thy strong helper: therefore shalt thou plant good plants, and shalt sow strange seed.

In the day of thy planting, shall be the wild grape, and in the morning thy seed shall flourish: the harvest is taken away in the day of inheritance, and shall grieve thee much.—*Is.* xvii. 10, 11.

INGRATITUDE TO OUR FELLOW MEN

Joseph answered: This is the interpretation of the dream: The three branches are yet three days:

After which Pharao will remember thy service, and will restore thee to thy former place: and thou shalt present him the cup according to thy office, as before thou wast wont to do.

Only remember me when it shall be well with thee, and do me this kindness: to put Pharao in mind to take me out of this prison. . . .

But the chief butler, when things prospered with him, forgot his interpreter.—*Gen.* xl. 12-14, 23.

And they said to Moses: Perhaps there were no graves in Egypt, therefore thou hast brought us to die in the wilderness: why wouldst thou do this, to lead us out of Egypt?

Is not this the word that we spoke to thee in Egypt, saying: Depart from us that we may serve the Egyptians? for it is much better to serve them, than to die in the wilderness.—*Ex.* xiv. 11, 12.

So the people were thirsty there for want of water, and murmured against Moses, saying: Why didst thou make us go forth out of Egypt, to kill us, and our children, and our beasts with thirst?

And Moses cried to the Lord, saying: What shall I do to this people? Yet a little more, and they will stone me.—*Ex.* xvii. 3, 4.

He that rendereth evil for good, evil shall not depart from his house.—*Prov.* xvii. 13.

Many have looked upon a thing lent as a thing found, and have given trouble to them that helped them.

Till they receive, they kiss the hands of the lender, and in promises they humble their voice:

But when they should repay, they will ask time, and will return tedious and murmuring words, and will complain of the time:

And if he be able to pay, he will stand off, he will scarce pay one half, and will count it as if he had found it:

But if not, he will defraud him of his money, and he shall get him for an enemy without cause:

And he will pay him with reproaches and curses, and instead of honor and good turn, will repay him injuries.—*Ecclus.* xxix. 4-9.

A sinner attributeth to himself the goods of his surety: and he that is of an unthankful mind, will leave him that delivered him.—*Ecclus.* xxix. 21.

INJURE OTHERS, WE MUST NOT

Thou shalt not speak evil of the deaf, nor put a stumbling-block before the blind: but thou shalt fear the Lord thy God, because I am the Lord.—*Lev.* xix. 14.

As he is guilty that shooteth arrows and lances unto death:

So is the man that hurteth his friend deceitfully: and when he is taken, saith: I did it in jest.—*Prov.* xxvi. 18, 19.

Remember not any injury done thee by thy neighbor, and do thou nothing by deeds of injury.—*Ecclus.* x. 6.

If one cast a stone on high, it will fall upon his own head: and the deceitful stroke will wound the deceitful.

He that diggeth a pit, shall fall into it: and he that setteth a stone for his neighbor, shall stumble upon it: and he that layeth a snare for another, shall perish in it.

A mischievous counsel shall be rolled back upon the author, and he shall not know from whence it cometh to him.—*Ecclus.* xxvii. 28-30.

Thus saith the Lord of hosts, saying: Judge ye true judgment, and show ye mercy and compassion every man to his brother.

And oppress not the widow, and the fatherless, and the stranger, and the poor: and let not a man devise evil in his heart against his brother.—*Zach.* vii. 9, 10.

And let none of you imagine evil in your hearts, against his friend: and love not a false oath: for all these are the things that I hate, saith the Lord.—*Zach.* viii. 17.

And the soldiers also asked him (the Baptist), saying: And what shall we do? And he said to them: Do violence to no man; neither calumniate any man; and be content with your pay.—*Luke* iii. 14.

INJUSTICE

See also: Fraud—page 161.

All bribery and injustice shall be blotted out, and fidelity shall stand for ever.—*Ecclus.* xl. 12.

Wherefore have a shame of these things that I am now going to speak of. . . .

Of injustice before a companion and friend.—*Ecclus.* xli. 19, 23.

Woe to him that buildeth up his house by injustice, and his chambers not in judgment: that will oppress his friend without cause, and will not pay him his wages.—*Jer.* xxii. 13.

Know you not that the unjust shall not possess the kingdom of God?—1 *Cor.* vi. 9.

INNOCENCE, THE EXCELLENCE OF

See also: Heart, purity of—page 194.

Blessed is the man to whom the Lord hath not imputed sin, and in whose spirit there is no guile.—*Ps.* xxxi. 2.

Blessed are the undefiled in the way, who walk in the law of the Lord.—*Ps.* cxviii. 1.

Justice keepeth the way of the innocent: but wickedness overthroweth the sinner.

One is as it were rich, when he hath nothing: and another is as it were poor, when he hath great riches.—*Prov.* xiii. 6, 7.

For venerable old age is not that of long time, nor counted by the number of years: but the understanding of a man is grey hairs.

And a spotless life is old age.—*Wis.* iv. 8, 9.

And incorruption bringeth near to God.—*Wis.* vi. 20.

Religion clean and undefiled before God and the Father is this: to visit the fatherless and widows in their tribulation: and to keep one's self unspotted from this world.—*James* i. 27.

INNOCENCE, THE GIFT OF GOD

And may the God of peace himself sanctify you in all things; that your whole spirit, and soul, and body, may be preserved blameless in the coming of our Lord Jesus Christ.

He is faithful who hath called you, who also will do it.—1 *Thess.* v. 23, 24.

Now to him who is able to preserve you without sin, and to present you spotless before the presence of his glory with exceeding joy, in the coming of our Lord Jesus Christ,

To the only God our Saviour, through Jesus Christ our Lord, be glory and magnificence, empire and power, before all ages, and now, and for all ages of ages. Amen.—*Jude* i. 24, 25.

INNOCENCE, GOD'S LOVE OF

With the holy, thou wilt be holy; and with the innocent man, thou wilt be innocent.—*Ps.* xvii. 26.

And they brought to him young children, that he might touch them. And

the disciples rebuked them that brought them.

Whom when Jesus saw, he was much displeased, and saith to them: Suffer the little children to come unto me, and forbid them not; for of such is the kingdom of God.

Amen I say to you, whosoever shall not receive the kingdom of God as a little child, shall not enter into it.—*Mark* x. 13-15.

Jesus saw Nathanael coming to him: and he saith of him: Behold an Israelite indeed, in whom there is no guile.—*John* i. 47.

Now there was leaning on Jesus' bosom one of his disciples, whom Jesus loved.—*John* xiii. 23.

INNOCENCE, EXHORTATION TO

Keep innocence, and behold justice: for there are remnants for the peaceable man.—*Ps.* xxxvi. 37.

At all times let thy garments be white, and let not oil depart from thy head.—*Eccles.* ix. 8.

Brethren, do not become children in sense: but in malice be children, and in sense be perfect.—1 *Cor.* xiv. 20.

I will therefore that men pray in every place, lifting up pure hands, without anger and contention.—1 *Tim.* ii. 8.

INNOCENCE, THE REWARD OF

The innocent shall be saved, and he shall be saved by the cleanness of his hands.—*Job* xxii. 30.

Lord, who shall dwell in thy tabernacle? or who shall rest in thy holy hill?

He that walketh without blemish, and worketh justice:

He that speaketh truth in his heart, who hath not used deceit in his tongue:

Nor hath done evil to his neighbor: nor taken up a reproach against his neighbors. . . . He that hath not put out his money to usury, nor taken bribes against the innocent:

He that doth these things shall not be moved for ever.—*Ps.* xiv. 1-3, 5.

The Lord knoweth the days of the undefiled; and their inheritance shall be for ever.

They shall not be confounded in the

evil time; and in the days of famine, they shall be filled.—*Ps.* xxxvi. 18, 19.

But thou hast upheld me by reason of my innocence: and hast established me in thy sight for ever.—*Ps.* xl. 13.

He will not deprive of good things them that walk in innocence.—*Ps.* lxxxiii. 13.

For if we sin, we are thine, knowing thy greatness: and if we sin not, we know that we are counted with thee.—*Wis.* xv. 2.

But thou hast a few names in Sardis, which have not defiled their garments: and they shall walk with me in white, because they are worthy.—*Apoc.* iii. 4.

INNOCENCE, PROFESSION OF

O Lord my God, if I have done this thing, if there be iniquity in my hands:

If I have rendered to them that repaid me evils, let me deservedly fall empty before my enemies.

Let the enemy pursue my soul, and take it, and tread down my life on the earth, and bring down my glory to the dust. . . .

Judge me, O Lord, according to my justice, and according to my innocence in me.—*Ps.* vii. 4-6, 9.

And the Lord will reward me according to my justice; and will repay me according to the cleanness of my hands:

Because I have kept the ways of the Lord: and have not done wickedly against my God.

For all his judgments are in my sight: and his justices I have not put away from me.

And I shall be spotless with him: and shall keep myself from my iniquity.

And the Lord will reward me, according to my justice; and according to the cleanness of my hands before his eyes. —*Ps.* xvii. 21-25.

Judge me, O Lord, for I have walked in my innocence: and I have put my trust in the Lord, and shall not be weakened.

Prove me, O Lord, and try me; burn my reins and my heart.

For thy mercy is before my eyes; and I am well pleased with thy truth.

I have not sat with the council of vanity: neither will I go in with the doers of unjust things.

I have hated the assembly of the malignant; and with the wicked I will not sit.

I will wash my hands among the innocent; and will compass thy altar, O Lord.—*Ps.* xxv. 1-6.

For behold they have caught my soul: the mighty have rushed in upon me:

Neither is it my iniquity, nor my sin, O Lord: without iniquity have I run, and directed my steps.—*Ps.* lviii. 4, 5.

Preserve my soul, for I am holy: save thy servant, O my God, that trusteth in thee.—*Ps.* lxxxv. 2.

I walked in the innocence of my heart, in the midst of my house.

I did not set before my eyes any unjust thing: I hated the workers of iniquities.—*Ps.* c. 2, 3.

I have restrained my feet from every evil way: that I may keep thy words.

I have not declined from thy judgments, because thou hast set me a law.—*Ps.* cxviii. 101, 102.

INNOCENCE, REGRET FOR LOST

Who will grant me, that I might be according to the months past, according to the days in which God kept me?

When his lamp shined over my head, and I walked by his light in darkness?

As I was in the days of my youth, when God was secretly in my tabernacle?

When the Almighty was with me?— *Job* xxix. 2-5.

INSTRUCTING OTHERS IN THE WAY OF GOD

I will teach the unjust thy ways: and the wicked shall be converted to thee.—*Ps.* l. 15.

The lips of the just teach many: but they that are ignorant, shall die in the want of understanding.—*Prov.* x. 21.

They that explain me (wisdom), shall have life everlasting.—*Ecclus.* xxiv. 31.

But they that are learned, shall shine as the brightness of the firmament: and they that instruct many to justice, as stars for all eternity.—*Dan.* xii. 3.

He therefore that shall break one of these least commandments, and shall so teach men, shall be called the least in the kingdom of heaven. But he that shall do and teach, he shall be called great in the kingdom of heaven.—*Matt.* v. 19.

INSTRUCTION, RECEIVING

A wise man shall hear, and shall be wiser: and he that understandeth, shall possess governments.—*Prov.* i. 5.

Because the commandment is a lamp, and the law, a light, and reproofs of instruction are the way of life. —*Prov.* vi. 23.

The wise of heart receiveth precepts. —*Prov.* x. 8.

A wise son heareth the doctrine of his father: but he that is a scorner, heareth not when he is reproved.—*Prov.* xiii. 1.

Good instruction shall give grace: in the way of scorners is a deep pit.—*Prov.* xiii. 15.

The heart of the wise seeketh instruction: and the mouth of fools feedeth on foolishness.—*Prov.* xv. 14.

A wise heart shall acquire knowledge: and the ear of the wise seeketh instruction.—*Prov.* xviii. 15.

Such is a wise and silent woman, and there is nothing so much worth as a well instructed soul.—*Ecclus.* xxvi. 18.

INSTRUCTION, EXHORTATION TO RECEIVE

And now, O ye kings, understand: receive instruction, you that judge the earth.—*Ps.* ii. 10.

Come, children, hearken to me: I will teach you the fear of the Lord.—*Ps.* xxxiii. 12.

Hear, ye children, the instruction of a father, and attend, that you may know prudence. . . .

Take hold on instruction, leave it not: keep it, because it is thy life.— *Prov.* iv. 1, 13.

Receive my instruction, and not money: choose knowledge, rather than gold. . . .

Hear instruction and be wise, and refuse it not.—*Prov.* viii. 10, 33.

Hear counsel, and receive instruction, that thou mayst be wise in thy latter end. . . .

Cease not, O my son, to hear instruction, and be not ignorant of the words of knowledge.—*Prov.* xix. 20, 27.

Incline thy ear, and hear the words of the wise: and apply thy heart to my doctrine.—*Prov.* xxii. 17.

Let thy heart apply itself to instruction: and thy ears to words of knowledge.—*Prov.* xxiii. 12.

Receive therefore instruction by my words, and it shall be profitable to you. —*Wis.* vi. 27.

My son, from thy youth up, receive instruction: and even to thy gray hairs, thou shalt find wisdom. . . .

Give ear, my son, and take wise counsel, and cast not away my advice. —*Ecclus.* vi. 18, 24.

Despise not the discourse of them that are ancient and wise, but acquaint thyself with their proverbs.

For of them thou shalt learn wisdom, and instruction of understanding, and to serve great men without blame.

Let not the discourse of the ancients escape thee, for they have learned of their fathers:

For of them thou shalt learn understanding, and to give an answer in time of need.—*Ecclus.* viii. 9-12.

Be thou instructed, O Jerusalem, lest my soul depart from thee, lest I make thee desolate, a land uninhabited.—*Jer.* vi. 8.

Hear, O Israel, the commandments of life: give ear, that thou mayst learn wisdom.—*Bar.* iii. 9.

INTENTION, PURITY OF

Take heed that you do not your justice before men, to be seen by them: otherwise you shall not have a reward of your Father who is in heaven.— *Matt.* vi. 1.

The light of thy body is thy eye. If thy eye be single, thy whole body will be lightsome: but if it be evil, thy body also will be darksome.

Take heed therefore that the light which is in thee, be not darkness.

If then thy whole body be lightsome, having no part of darkness; the whole shall be lightsome; and as a bright lamp, shall enlighten thee.—*Luke* xi. 34-36.

All things indeed are clean: but it is evil for that man who eateth with offence.

. . . Hast thou faith? Have it to thyself before God. Blessed is he that condemneth not himself in that which he alloweth.

But he that discerneth, if he eat is condemned; because not of faith. For all that is not of faith, is sin.—*Rom.* xiv. 20, 22, 23.

Whatsoever you do, do it from the heart, as to the Lord, and not to men: Knowing that you shall receive of the Lord the reward of inheritance.— *Col.* iii. 23, 24.

For every creature of God is good, and nothing to be rejected that is received with thanksgiving:

For it is sanctified by the word of God and prayer.—1 *Tim.* iv. 4, 5.

INVITATION TO COME TO THE LORD

See: Come to the Lord—page 56.

JEALOUS, GOD IS

I am the Lord thy God, mighty, jealous, visiting the iniquity of the fathers upon the children, unto the third and fourth generation of them that hate me.—*Ex.* xx. 5.

Adore not any strange god. The Lord his name is Jealous, he is a jealous God.—*Ex.* xxxiv. 14.

Because the Lord thy God is a consuming fire, a jealous God.—*Deut.* iv. 24.

You shall not go after the strange gods of all the nations that are round about you:

Because the Lord thy God is a jealous God in the midst of thee: lest at any time the wrath of the Lord thy God be kindled against thee, and take thee away from the face of the earth.—*Deut.* vi. 14, 15.

They provoked him (God) to anger on their hills: and moved him to jealousy with their graven things.—*Ps.* lxxvii. 58.

Therefore thus saith the Lord God: Now will I bring back the captivity of Jacob, and will have mercy on all the house of Israel: and I will be jealous for my holy name.—*Ezech.* xxxix. 25.

The Lord is a jealous God, and a revenger: the Lord is a revenger, and hath wrath: the Lord taketh vengeance on his adversaries, and he is angry with his enemies.—*Nahum* i. 2.

Neither shall their silver and their gold be able to deliver them in the day of the wrath of the Lord: all the land shall be devoured by the fire of his jealousy, for he shall make even a speedy destruction of all them that dwell in the land.—*Soph.* i. 18.

Thus saith the Lord of hosts: I have been jealous for Sion with a great jealousy, and with a great indignation have I been jealous for her.—*Zach.* viii. 2.

JEALOUSY

Now Israel loved Joseph above all his sons, because he had him in his old age: and he made him a coat of divers colors.

And his brethren, seeing that he was loved by his father more than all his sons, hated him, and could not speak peaceably to him.—*Gen.* xxxvii. 3, 4.

Now when David returned, after he slew the Philistine, the women came out of all the cities of Israel, singing and dancing, to meet king Saul, with timbrels of joy, and cornets.

And the women sung as they played, and they said: Saul slew his thousands, and David his ten thousands.

And Saul was exceeding angry, and this word was displeasing in his eyes, and he said: They have given David ten thousands, and to me they have given but a thousand; what can he have more but the kingdom?

And Saul did not look on David with a good eye from that day and forward. —1 *Kings* xviii. 6-9.

Be not jealous over the wife of thy bosom, lest she show in thy regard the malice of a wicked lesson.—*Ecclus.* ix.1.

A jealous woman is the grief and mourning of the heart.

With a jealous woman is a scourge of the tongue which communicateth with all.—*Ecclus.* xxvi. 8, 9.

Not as Cain, who was of the wicked one, and killed his brother. And wherefore did he kill him? Because his own works were wicked: and his brother's just.—1 *John* iii. 12.

JOSEPH, SAINT

And when there (in Egypt) also they began to be famished, the people cried to Pharao for food. And he said to them: Go to Joseph: and do all that he shall say to you.—*Gen.* xli. 55.

He that keepeth the fig-tree, shall eat the fruit thereof: and he that is the keeper of his master, shall be glorified. —*Prov.* xxvii. 18.

A faithful man shall be much praised.—*Prov.* xxviii. 20.

And Jacob begot Joseph the husband of Mary, of whom was born Jesus, who is called Christ.—*Matt.* i. 16.

Now the generation of Christ was in this wise.

When as his mother Mary was espoused to Joseph, before they came together, she was found with child, of the Holy Ghost.

Whereupon Joseph, her husband, being a just man, and not willing publicly to expose her, was minded to put her away privately.

But while he thought on these things, behold the angel of the Lord appeared to him in his sleep, saying: Joseph, son of David, fear not to take unto thee Mary thy wife, for that which is conceived in her, is of the Holy Ghost.

And she shall bring forth a son: and thou shalt call his name Jesus. For he shall save his people from their sins. . . .

And Joseph rising up from sleep, did as the angel of the Lord had commanded him, and took unto him his wife.

And he knew her not till she brought forth her first-born son: and he called his name Jesus.—*Matt.* i. 18-21, 24, 25.

And after they (the wise men) were departed, behold an angel of the Lord appeared in sleep to Joseph, saying: Arise, and take the child and his mother, and fly into Egypt: and be there until I shall tell thee. For it will come to pass that Herod will seek the child, to destroy him.

Who arose, and took the child and his mother by night, and retired into Egypt: and he was there until the death of Herod.—*Matt.* ii. 13, 14.

And when Herod was dead, behold an angel of the Lord appeared in sleep to Joseph in Egypt,

Saying: Arise, and take the child and his mother, and go into the land of Israel. For they are dead that sought the life of the child.

Who arose, and took the child and his mother, and came into the land of Israel.

But hearing that Archelaus reigned in Judea in the room of Herod his father, he was afraid to go thither: and being warned in sleep, retired into the quarters of Galilee.

And coming, he dwelt in a city called Nazareth.—*Matt.* ii. 19-23.

And in the sixth month, the angel Gabriel was sent from God into a city of Galilee, called Nazareth,

To a virgin espoused to a man whose name was Joseph, of the house of David; and the virgin's name was Mary.—*Luke* i. 26, 27.

And Joseph also went up from Galilee, out of the city of Nazareth into Judea, to the city of David, which is called Bethlehem: because he was of the house and family of David,

To be enrolled with Mary his espoused wife, who was with child.—*Luke* ii. 4, 5.

And they (the shepherds) came with haste; and they found Mary and Joseph, and the infant lying in the manger.—*Luke* ii. 16.

And his father and mother were wondering at those things which were spoken concerning him.—*Luke* ii. 33.

And his parents went every year to Jerusalem, at the solemn day of the pasch. . . .

And having fulfilled the days, when they returned, the child Jesus remained in Jerusalem; and his parents knew it not.—*Luke* ii. 41, 43.

And seeing him, they wondered. And his mother said to him: Son, why hast thou done so to us? behold, thy father and I have sought thee sorrowing.—*Luke* ii. 48.

And he went down with them, and came to Nazareth, and was subject to them.—*Luke* ii. 51.

And Jesus himself was beginning about the age of thirty years; being (as it was supposed) the son of Joseph.—*Luke* iii. 23.

And all gave testimony to him: and they wondered at the words of grace that proceeded from his mouth, and they said: Is not this the son of Joseph?—*Luke* iv. 22.

The Jews therefore murmured at him, because he had said: I am the living bread which came down from heaven.

And they said: Is not this Jesus, the son of Joseph, whose father and mother we know? How then saith he, I came down from heaven?—*John* vi. 41, 42.

JOY, SPIRITUAL

My heart hath rejoiced in the Lord, and my horn is exalted in my God: my mouth is enlarged over my enemies: because I have joyed in thy salvation.—1 *Kings* ii. 1.

And I and my soul will rejoice in him.—*Tob.* xiii. 9.

I will be glad and rejoice in thee: I will sing to thy name, O thou most high. . . .

I will rejoice in thy salvation.—*Ps.* ix. 3, 16.

We will rejoice in thy salvation; and in the name of our God we shall be exalted.—*Ps.* xix. 6.

I will be glad and rejoice in thy mercy.

For thou hast regarded my humility, thou hast saved my soul out of distresses.—*Ps.* xxx. 8.

For in him our heart shall rejoice: and in his holy name we have trusted.—*Ps.* xxxii. 21.

But my soul shall rejoice in the Lord; and shall be delighted in his salvation.—*Ps.* xxxiv. 9.

My lips shall greatly rejoice, when I shall sing to thee; and my soul, which thou hast redeemed.—*Ps.* lxx. 23.

Blessed is the people that knoweth jubilation.

They shall walk, O Lord, in the light of thy countenance: and in thy name, they shall rejoice all the day, and in thy justice, they shall be exalted.—*Ps.* lxxxviii. 16, 17.

We are filled in the morning with thy mercy: and we have rejoiced, and are delighted all our days.

We have rejoiced for the days in which thou hast humbled us: for the years in which we have seen evils.—*Ps.* lxxxix. 14, 15.

Sion heard, and was glad.

And the daughters of Juda rejoiced, because of thy judgments, O Lord.—*Ps.* xcvi. 8.

Light is risen to the just, and joy to the right of heart.—*Ps.* xcvi. 11.

I rejoiced at the things that were said to me: We shall go into the house of the Lord.—*Ps.* cxxi. 1.

He that adoreth God with joy, shall be accepted, and his prayer shall approach even to the clouds.—*Ecclus.* xxxv. 20.

I will greatly rejoice in the Lord, and my soul shall be joyful in my God: for he hath clothed me with the garments of salvation: and with the robe of justice he hath covered me, as a bridegroom decked with a crown, and as a bride adorned with her jewels.—*Is.* lxi. 10.

But I will rejoice in the Lord: and I will joy in God my Jesus.—*Hab.* iii. 18.

And seeing the star, they (the wise men) rejoiced with exceeding great joy.—*Matt.* ii. 10.

And Mary said: My soul doth magnify the Lord.

And my spirit hath rejoiced in God my Saviour.—*Luke* i. 46, 47.

He that hath the bride is the bridegroom: but the friend of the bridegroom, who standeth and heareth him, rejoiceth with joy because of the bridegroom's voice. This my joy therefore is fulfilled.—*John* iii. 29.

And continuing daily with one accord in the temple, and breaking bread from house to house, they took their meat with gladness and simplicity of heart.—*Acts* ii. 46.

And the disciples were filled with joy and with the Holy Ghost.—*Acts* xiii. 52.

Great is my confidence for you, great is my glorying for you. I am filled with comfort: I exceedingly abound with joy in all our tribulation.—2 *Cor.* vii. 4.

And these things we write to you, that you may rejoice, and your joy may be full.—*1 John* i. 4.

JOY IS FROM GOD, ALL TRUE

The light of thy countenance, O Lord, is signed upon us: thou hast given gladness in my heart.—*Ps.* iv. 7.

Restore unto me the joy of thy salvation, and strengthen me with a perfect spirit.—*Ps.* l. 14.

According to the multitude of my sorrows in my heart, thy comforts have given joy to my soul.—*Ps.* xciii. 19.

May he grant us joyfulness of heart, and that there be peace in our days in Israel for ever.—*Ecclus.* l. 25.

You shall draw waters with joy out of the Saviour's fountains.—*Is.* xii. 3.

And the angel said to them: Fear not; for behold, I bring you good tidings of great joy, that shall be to all the people.—*Luke* ii. 10.

These things I have spoken to you, that my joy may be in you, and your joy may be filled.—*John* xv. 11.

Hitherto you have not asked any thing in my name. Ask, and you shall receive; that your joy may be full.—*John* xvi. 24.

And now I come to thee; and these things I speak in the world, that they may have my joy filled in themselves.—*John* xvii. 13.

Now the God of hope fill you with all joy and peace in believing; that you may abound in hope, and in the power of the Holy Ghost.—*Rom.* xv. 13.

But the fruit of the Spirit is charity, joy, peace, patience, benignity, goodness, longanimity.—*Gal.* v. 22.

JOY, GOD OUR

Thou art my refuge from the trouble which hath encompassed me: my joy, deliver me from them that surround me.—*Ps.* xxxi. 7.

Delight in the Lord, and he will give thee the requests of thy heart.—*Ps.* xxxvi. 4.

Let my speech be acceptable to him: but I will take delight in the Lord.—*Ps.* ciii. 34.

In that day the Lord of hosts shall be a crown of glory, and a garland of joy to the residue of his people.—*Is.* xxviii. 5.

JOY, EXHORTATION TO SPIRITUAL

Bless ye the Lord, all his elect, keep days of joy, and give glory to him.—*Tob.* xiii. 10.

Serve ye the Lord with fear: and rejoice unto him with trembling.—*Ps.* ii. 11.

But let all them be glad that hope in thee: they shall rejoice for ever, and thou shalt dwell them.—*Ps.* v. 12.

Be glad in the Lord, and rejoice, ye just, and glory, all ye right of heart.—*Ps.* xxxi. 11.

Rejoice in the Lord, O ye just: praise becometh the upright.—*Ps.* xxxii. 1.

Let all that seek thee, rejoice and be glad in thee: and let such as love thy salvation, say always: The Lord be magnified.—*Ps.* xxxix. 17.

Shout with joy to God, all the earth, sing ye a psalm to his name; give glory to his praise.—*Ps.* lxv. 1, 2.

And let the just feast, and rejoice before God: and be delighted with gladness.—*Ps.* lxvii. 4.

Rejoice to God, our helper: sing aloud to the God of Jacob.

Take a psalm, and bring hither the timbrel: the pleasant psaltery with the harp.—*Ps.* lxxx. 2, 3.

Come, let us praise the Lord with joy: let us joyfully sing to God our Saviour.

Let us come before his presence with thanksgiving; and make a joyful noise to him with psalms.—*Ps.* xciv. 1, 2.

Let the heavens rejoice, and let the earth be glad, let the sea be moved, and the fulness thereof:

The fields and all things that are in them shall be joyful.

Then shall all the trees of the woods rejoice before the face of the Lord, because he cometh: because he cometh to judge the earth.—*Ps.* xcv. 11-13.

The Lord hath reigned, let the earth rejoice: let many islands be glad.—*Ps.* xcvi. 1.

Rejoice, ye just, in the Lord: and give praise to the remembrance of his holiness.—*Ps.* xcvi. 12.

Sing joyfully to God, all the earth; make melody, rejoice and sing. . . .

Make a joyful noise before the Lord our king.—*Ps.* xcvii. 4, 6.

Sing joyfully to God, all the earth: serve ye the Lord with gladness.

Come in before his presence with exceeding great joy.—*Ps.* xcix. 2.

Glory ye in his holy name: let the heart of them rejoice that seek the Lord.—*Ps.* civ. 3.

This is the day which the Lord hath made: let us be glad and rejoice therein. —*Ps.* cxvii. 24.

Let Israel rejoice in him that made him: and let the children of Sion be joyful in their king.—*Ps.* cxlix. 2.

Let your soul rejoice in his mercy, and you shall not be confounded in his praise.—*Ecclus.* li. 37.

Rejoice and praise, O thou habitation of Sion: for great is he that is in the midst of thee, the Holy One of Israel.—*Is.* xii. 6.

Give praise, O ye heavens, and rejoice, O earth, ye mountains, give praise with jubilation: because the Lord hath comforted his people, and will have mercy on his poor ones.—*Is.* xlix. 13.

And you, O children of Sion, rejoice, and be joyful in the Lord your God: because he hath given you a teacher of justice, and he will make the early and the latter rain to come down to you as in the beginning.—*Joel* ii. 23.

Give praise, O daughter of Sion; shout, O Israel: be glad and rejoice with all thy heart, O daughter of Jerusalem.—*Soph.* iii. 14.

Blessed are ye when they shall revile you, and persecute you, and speak all that is evil against you, untruly, for my sake:

Be glad, and rejoice, for your reward is very great in heaven.—*Matt.* v. 11, 12.

But yet rejoice not in this, that spirits are subject unto you; but rejoice in this, that your names are written in heaven.—*Luke* x. 20.

Rejoicing in hope. Patient in tribulation. Instant in prayer.—*Rom.* xii. 12.

Rejoice in the Lord always; again, I say, rejoice.—*Philipp.* iv. 4.

Let us be glad and rejoice, and give glory to him; for the marriage of the Lamb is come, and his wife hath prepared herself.—*Apoc.* xix. 7.

JUDGE, GOD OUR

God therefore will not hear in vain, and the Almighty will look into the causes of every one.

Yea, when thou shalt say: He considereth not: be judged before him, and expect him.—*Job* xxxv. 13, 14.

And the heavens shall declare his justice: for God is judge.—*Ps.* xlix. 6.

And man shall say: If indeed there be fruit to the just: there is indeed a God that judgeth them on the earth.— *Ps.* lvii. 12.

Many seek the face of the prince: but the judgment of every one cometh forth from the Lord.—*Prov.* xxix. 26.

For the Lord is our judge, the Lord is our lawgiver, the Lord is our king: he will save us.—*Is.* xxxiii. 22.

I am the judge and the witness, saith the Lord.—*Jer.* xxix. 23.

But you are come to mount Sion, and to the city of the living God, the heavenly Jerusalem, and to the company of many thousands of angels,

And to the church of the first-born, who are written in the heavens, and to God, the judge of all, and to the spirits of the just made perfect.—*Heb.* xii. 22, 23.

There is one lawgiver, and judge, that is able to destroy and to deliver.— *James* iv. 12.

Grudge not, brethren, one against another, that you may not be judged. Behold the judge standeth before the door.—*James* v. 9.

JUDGE, GOD A JUST

See also: Justice of God—page 266.

God is a just judge, strong and patient: is he angry every day?—*Ps.* vii. 12.

But the Lord remaineth for ever. He hath prepared his throne in judgment: and he shall judge the world in equity, he shall judge the people in justice.—*Ps.* ix. 8, 9.

Let the nations be glad and rejoice: for thou judgest the people with justice, and directest the nations upon earth.—*Ps.* lxvi. 5.

Then shall all the trees of the woods rejoice before the face of the Lord, because he cometh: because he cometh to judge the earth.

He shall judge the world with justice, and the people with his truth.—*Ps.* xcv. 12, 13.

For there is no other God but thou, who hast care of all, that thou shouldst show that thou dost not give judgment unjustly.—*Wis.* xii. 13.

He shall not judge according to the sight of the eyes, nor reprove according to the hearing of the ears.

But he shall judge the poor with justice, and shall reprove with equity for the meek of the earth.—*Is.* xi. 3, 4.

And a throne shall be prepared in mercy, and one shall sit upon it in truth, in the tabernacle of David, judging and seeking judgment, and quickly rendering that which is just.—*Is.* xvi. 5.

Therefore will I judge every man according to his ways, O house of Israel, saith the Lord God.—*Ezech.* xviii. 30.

I cannot of myself do any thing. As I hear, so I judge: and my judgment is just; because I seek not my own will, but the will of him that sent me.—*John* v. 30.

JUDGE ONE ANOTHER, WE MUST NOT

Do you accept his person, and do you endeavor to judge for God?—*Job* xiii. 8.

Despise not a man that turneth away from sin, nor reproach him therewith: remember that we are all worthy of reproof.—*Ecclus.* viii. 6.

Judge not, that you may not be judged.

For with what judgment you judge, you shall be judged: and with what measure you mete, it shall be measured to you again.

And why seest thou the mote that is in thy brother's eye; and seest not the beam that is in thy own eye?

Or how sayst thou to thy brother: Let me cast the mote out of thy eye; and behold a beam is in thy own eye?

Thou hypocrite, cast out first the beam out of thy own eye, and then shalt thou see to cast out the mote out of thy brother's eye.—*Matt.* vii. 1-5.

Wherefore thou art inexcusable, O man, whosoever thou art that judgest. For wherein thou judgest another, thou condemnest thyself. For thou dost the same things which thou judgest.

. . . And thinkest thou this, O man, that judgest them who do such things, and dost the same, that thou shalt escape the judgment of God?—*Rom.* ii. 1, 3.

Who art thou that judgest another man's servant? To his own lord he standeth or falleth. And he shall stand: for God is able to make him stand.—*Rom.* xiv. 4.

But thou, why judgest thou thy brother? or thou, why dost thou despise thy brother? For we shall all stand before the judgment seat of Christ. . . .

Therefore every one of us shall render account to God for himself.

Let us not therefore judge one another any more. But judge this rather, that you put not a stumbling-block or a scandal in your brother's way.—*Rom.* xiv. 10, 12, 13.

Therefore judge not before the time; until the Lord come, who both will bring to light the hidden things of darkness, and will make manifest the counsels of the hearts; and then shall every man have praise from God.—1 *Cor.* iv. 5.

Detract not one another, my brethren. He that detracteth his brother, or he that judgeth his brother, detracteth the law, and judgeth the law. But if thou judge the law, thou art not a doer of the law, but a judge.

There is one lawgiver and judge, that is able to destroy and to deliver.

But who art thou that judgest thy neighbor?—*James* iv. 11-13.

JUDGES SHOULD BE JUST IN THEIR JUDGMENTS

Thou shalt not follow the multitude to do evil: neither shalt thou yield in judgment to the opinion of the most part, to stray from the truth. . . .

Thou shalt not go aside in the poor man's judgment.—*Ex.* xxiii. 2, 6.

Thou shalt not do that which is unjust, nor judge unjustly. Respect not the person of the poor, nor honor the countenance of the mighty. But judge thy neighbor according to justice.—*Lev.* xix. 15.

Hear them, and judge that which is just: whether he be one of your country, or a stranger.

There shall be no difference of persons, you shall hear the little as well as the great: neither shall you respect any man's person, because it is the judgment of God.—*Deut.* i. 16, 17.

Take heed what you do: for you exercise not the judgment of man, but of the Lord: and whatsoever you judge, it shall redound to you.—2 *Paral.* xix. 6.

Give to the king thy judgment, O God: and to the king's son thy justice:

To judge thy people with justice, and thy poor with judgment.—*Ps.* lxxi. 2.

How long will you judge unjustly: and accept the persons of the wicked?

Judge for the needy and fatherless: do justice to the humble and the poor.

Rescue the poor; and deliver the needy out of the hand of the sinner.—*Ps.* lxxxi. 2-4.

Open thy mouth for the dumb, and for the causes of all the children that pass.

Open thy mouth, decree that which is just, and do justice to the needy and poor.—*Prov.* xxxi. 8, 9.

Love justice, you that are the judges of the earth.—*Wis.* i. 1.

Hear, therefore, ye kings, and understand: learn, ye that are judges of the ends of the earth.

Give ear, you that rule the people, and that please yourselves in multitudes of nations:

For power is given you by the Lord, and strength by the most High, who will examine your works, and search out your thoughts:

Because being ministers of his kingdom, you have not judged rightly, nor kept the law of justice, nor walked according to the will of God.

Horribly and speedily will he appear to you: for a most severe judgment shall be for them that bear rule.—*Wis.* vi. 2-6.

God of my fathers, and Lord of mercy, who hast made all things with thy word,

And by thy wisdom hast appointed man, that he should have dominion over the creature that was made by thee,

That he should order the world according to equity and justice, and execute justice with an upright heart.—*Wis.* ix. 1-3.

Seek not to be made a judge, unless thou have strength enough to extirpate iniquities: lest thou fear the person of the powerful, and lay a stumbling-block for thy integrity.—*Ecclus.* vii. 6.

Thus saith the Lord: Go down to the house of the king of Juda, and there thou shalt speak this word. . . .

Thus saith the Lord: Execute judgment and justice, and deliver him that is oppressed out of the hand of the oppressor: and afflict not the stranger, the fatherless and the widow, nor oppress them unjustly: and shed not innocent blood in this place.—*Jer.* xxii. 1, 3.

These then are the things which you shall do: Speak ye truth, every one to his neighbor: judge ye truth and judgment of peace in your gates.—*Zach.* viii. 16.

Judge not according to the appearance, but judge just judgment.—*John* vii. 24.

JUDGES SHOULD BE MERCIFUL IN THEIR JUDGMENTS

Therefore, whereas thou chastisest us, thou scourgest our enemies very many ways, to the end that when we judge, we may think on thy goodness: and when we are judged, we may hope for thy mercy.—*Wis.* xii. 22.

In judging, be merciful to the fatherless as a father, and as a husband to their mother.

And thou shalt be as the obedient son of the most High, and he will have mercy on thee more than a mother.—*Ecclus.* iv. 10, 11.

JUDGMENT, DAY OF

The God of gods, the Lord hath spoken: and he hath called the earth.

From the rising of the sun, to the going down thereof. . . .

God shall come manifestly: our God shall come, and shall not keep silence.

A fire shall burn before him: and a mighty tempest shall be round about him,

He shall call heaven from above, and the earth, to judge his people.—*Ps.* xlix. 1, 3, 4.

The heavens declared his justice: and all people saw his glory.—*Ps.* xcvi. 6.

I saw under the sun, in the place of judgment, wickedness, and in the place of justice, iniquity.

And I said in my heart: God shall judge both the just and the wicked, and then shall be the time of every thing.—*Eccles.* iii. 16, 17.

But I know their works and their thoughts: I come that I may gather them together with all nations and tongues: and they shall come, and shall see my glory.—*Is.* lxvi. 18.

But at that time shall Michael rise up, the great prince, who standeth for the children of thy people: and a time shall come, such as never was from the time that nations began, even until that time. And at that time shall thy people be saved, every one that shall be found written in the book.

And many of those that sleep in the dust of the earth, shall awake: some unto life everlasting, and others unto reproach, to see it always.—*Dan.* xii. 1, 2.

Let them arise, and let the nations come up into the valley of Josaphat: for there I will sit, to judge all nations round about.—*Joel* iii. 12.

He that is best among them is as a brier: and he that is righteous, as the thorn of the hedge. The day of thy inspection, thy visitation cometh: now shall be their destruction.—*Mich.* vii. 4.

The just Lord is in the midst thereof, he will not do iniquity: in the morning, in the morning he will bring his judgment to light, and it shall not be hid: but the wicked man hath not known shame. . . .

Wherefore expect me, saith the Lord, in the day of my resurrection that is to come, for my judgment is to assemble the Gentiles, and to gather the kingdoms: and to pour upon them my indignation, all my fierce anger: for with the fire of my jealousy shall all the earth be devoured.—*Soph.* iii. 5, 8.

Behold I will send you Elias the prophet, before the coming of the great and dreadful day of the Lord.—*Malach.* iv. 5.

Whose fan is in his hand, and he will thoroughly cleanse his floor, and gather his wheat into the barn; but the chaff he will burn with unquenchable fire.—*Matt.* iii. 12.

And the servants of the goodman of the house coming, said to him: Sir, didst thou not sow good seed in thy field? whence then hath it cockle?

And he said to them: An enemy hath done this. And the servants said to him: Wilt thou that we go and gather it up?

And he said: No, lest perhaps gathering up the cockle, you root up the wheat also together with it.

Suffer both to grow until the harvest, and in the time of the harvest I will say to the reapers: Gather up first the cockle, and bind it into bundles to burn, but the wheat gather ye into my barn. . . .

So shall it be at the end of the world. The angels shall go out, and shall separate the wicked from among the just.

And shall cast them into the furnace of fire: there shall be weeping and gnashing of teeth.—*Matt.* xiii. 27-30, 49, 50.

For as lightning cometh out of the east, and appeareth even into the west: so shall also the coming of the Son of man be. . . .

And then shall appear the sign of the Son of man in heaven: and then shall all tribes of the earth mourn: and they shall see the Son of man coming in the clouds of heaven with much power and majesty.

And he shall send his angels with a trumpet, and a great voice: and they shall gather together his elect from the four winds, from the farthest parts of the heavens, to the utmost bounds of them.—*Matt.* xxiv. 27, 30, 31.

And when the Son of man shall come in his majesty, and all the angels with him, then shall he sit upon the seat of his majesty:

And all nations shall be gathered together before him, and he shall separate them one from another, as the shepherd separateth the sheep from the goats:

And he shall set the sheep on his right hand, but the goats on his left.

Then shall the king say to them that shall be on his right hand: Come, ye blessed of my Father, possess you the kingdom prepared for you from the foundation of the world.

For I was hungry, and you gave me to eat; I was thirsty, and you gave me to drink; I was a stranger, and you took me in:

Naked, and you covered me: sick, and you visited me: I was in prison, and you came to me.

Then shall the just answer him, saying: Lord, when did we see thee hungry, and fed thee; thirsty, and gave thee drink?

And when did we see thee a stranger, and took thee in? or naked, and covered thee?

Or when did we see thee sick or in prison, and came to thee?

And the king answering, shall say to them:

Amen, I say to you, as long as you did it to one of these my least brethren, you did it to me.

Then shall he say to them also that shall be on his left hand: Depart from me, you cursed, into everlasting fire, which was prepared for the devil and his angels.

For I was hungry, and you gave me not to eat: I was thirsty, and you gave me not to drink. I was a stranger, and you took me not in: naked, and you covered me not: sick and in prison, and you did not visit me.

Then they also shall answer him, saying: Lord, when did we see thee hungry, or thirsty, or a stranger, or naked, or sick, or in prison, and did not minister to thee?

Then he shall answer them, saying: Amen I say to you, as long as you did it not to one of these least, neither did you do it to me.

And these shall go into everlasting punishment: but the just, into life everlasting.—*Matt.* xxv. 31-46.

Wonder not at this; for the hour cometh, wherein all that are in the graves, shall hear the voice of the Son of God.

And they that have done good things, shall come forth unto the resurrection of life; but they that have done evil, unto the resurrection of judgment.— *John* v. 28, 29.

He that despiseth me, and receiveth not my words, hath one that judgeth him; the word that I have spoken, the same shall judge him in the last day. —*John* xii. 48.

Now of these Enoch also, the seventh from Adam, prophesied, saying: Behold, the Lord cometh with thousands of his saints,

To execute judgment upon all, and to reprove all the ungodly for all the works of their ungodliness, whereby they have done ungodly, and of all the hard things which ungodly sinners have spoken against God.—*Jude* i. 14, 15.

Behold, he cometh with the clouds, and every eye shall see him, and they also that pierced him. And all the tribes of the earth shall bewail themselves because of him. Even so. Amen. —*Apoc.* i. 7.

And the seventh angel sounded the trumpet: and there were great voices in heaven, saying: The kingdom of this world is become our Lord's, and his Christ's, and he shall reign for ever and ever. Amen. . . .

We give thee thanks, O Lord, God Almighty, who art, and who wast, and who art to come: because thou hast taken to thee thy great power, and thou hast reigned.

And the nations were angry, and thy wrath is come, and the time of the dead, that they should be judged, and that thou shouldst render reward to thy servants the prophets and the saints, and to them that fear thy name, little and great, and shouldst destroy them who have corrupted the earth.—*Apoc.* xi. 15, 17, 18.

And I saw a great white throne, and one sitting upon it, from whose face the earth and heaven fled away, and there was no place found for them.

And I saw the dead, great and small, standing in the presence of the throne, and the books were opened; and another book was opened, which is the book of life; and the dead were judged by those things which were written in the books, according to their works.

And the sea gave up the dead that were in it, and death and hell gave up their dead that were in them; and they were judged, every one according to their works. . . .

And whosoever was not found written in the book of life, was cast into the pool of fire.—*Apoc.* xx. 11-13, 15.

JUDGMENT, CERTAINTY OF THE DAY OF

Flee then from the face of the sword, for the sword is the revenger of iniquities: and know ye that there is a judgment.—*Job* xix. 29.

But thou, why judgest thou thy brother? or thou, why dost thou despise thy brother? For we shall all stand before the judgment seat of Christ. . . . Therefore every one of us shall render account to God for himself.—*Rom.* xiv. 10, 12.

For we must all be manifested before the judgment seat of Christ, that every one may receive the proper things of the body, according as he hath done, whether it be good or evil.—2 *Cor.* v. 10.

The Lord knoweth how to deliver the godly from temptation, but to reserve the unjust unto the day of judgment, to be tormented.—2 *Peter* ii. 9.

But the heavens and the earth which are now, by the same word are kept in store, reserved unto fire against the day of judgment and perdition of the ungodly men.

But of this one thing be not ignorant, my beloved, that one day with the Lord is as a thousand years, and a thousand years as one day.

The Lord delayeth not his promise, as some imagine, but dealeth patiently for your sake, not willing that any should perish, but that all should return to penance.—2 *Peter* iii. 7-9.

JUDGMENT DAY, A DAY OF FEAR AND OF TERROR, THE

If he examine on a sudden, who shall answer him? or who can say: Why dost thou so?

God, whose wrath no man can resist, and under whom they stoop that bear up the world.—*Job* ix. 12, 13.

Thou hast caused judgment to be heard from heaven: the earth trembled and was still,

When God arose in judgment, to save all the meek of the earth.—*Ps.* lxxv. 9, 10.

They shall come with fear at the thought of their sins, and their iniquities shall stand against them, to convict them.—*Wis.* iv. 20.

The lofty eyes of man are humbled, and the haughtiness of men shall be made to stoop: and the Lord alone shall be exalted in that day.

Because the day of the Lord of hosts shall be upon every one that is proud and high-minded, and upon every one that is arrogant, and he shall be humbled. . . .

And they shall go into the holes of rocks, and into the caves of the earth, from the face of the fear of the Lord, and from the glory of his majesty, when he shall rise up to strike the earth. —*Is.* ii. 11, 12, 19.

Howl ye, for the day of the Lord is near: it shall come as a destruction from the Lord.

Therefore shall all hands be faint, and every heart of man shall melt. . . .

Behold, the day of the Lord shall come, a cruel day, and full of indignation, and of wrath, and fury, to lay the land desolate, and to destroy the sinners thereof out of it. . . .

And I will visit the evils of the world, and against the wicked for their iniquity: and I will make the pride of infidels to cease, and will bring down the arrogancy of the mighty.—*Is.* xiii. 6, 7, 9, 11.

For behold the Lord will come with fire, and his chariots are like a whirlwind, to render his wrath in indignation, and his rebuke with flames of fire.

For the Lord shall judge by fire, and by his sword unto all flesh, and the slain of the Lord shall be many.—*Is.* lxvi. 15, 16.

And the word of the Lord came to me, saying:

Son of man, prophesy, and say: Thus saith the Lord God: Howl ye, Woe, woe to the day:

For the day is near, yea, the day of the Lord is near: a cloudy day, it shall be the time of the nations.—*Ezech.* xxx. 1-3.

And the high places of the idol, the sin of Israel shall be destroyed: the bur and the thistle shall grow up over their altars: and they shall say to the mountains: Cover us; and to the hills: Fall upon us.—*Osee* x. 8.

Blow ye the trumpet in Sion, sound an alarm in my holy mountain, let all the inhabitants of the land tremble: because the day of the Lord cometh, because it is nigh at hand.

A day of darkness, and of gloominess, a day of clouds and whirlwinds: a numerous and strong people as the morning spread upon the mountains: the like to it hath not been from the beginning, nor shall be after it, even to the years of generation and generation.

Before the face thereof a devouring fire, and behind it a burning flame: the land is like a garden of pleasure before it, and behind it a desolate wilderness, neither is there any one that can escape it. . . .

And the Lord hath uttered his voice before the face of his army: for his armies are exceeding great, for they are strong, and execute his word: for the day of the Lord is great and very terrible: and who can stand it?—*Joel* ii. 1-3, 11.

Woe to them that desire the day of the Lord: to what end is it for you? the day of the Lord is darkness, and not light.

As if a man should flee from the face of a lion, and a bear should meet him: or enter into the house, and lean with his hand upon the wall, and a serpent should bite him.

Shall not the day of the Lord be darkness, and not light: and obscurity, and no brightness in it?—*Amos* v. 18-20.

The great day of the Lord is near, it is near, and exceeding swift: the voice of the day of the Lord is bitter, the mighty man shall there meet with tribulation.

That day is a day of wrath, a day of tribulation and distress, a day of calamity and misery, a day of darkness and obscurity, a day of clouds and whirlwinds. . . .

And I will distress men, and they shall walk like blind men, because they have sinned against the Lord: and their blood shall be poured out as earth, and their bodies as dung.

Neither shall their silver and their gold be able to deliver them in the day of the wrath of the Lord: all the land shall be devoured by the fire of his jealousy, for he shall make even a speedy destruction of all them that dwell in the land.—*Soph.* i. 14, 15, 17, 18.

But according to thy hardness and impenitent heart, thou treasurest up to thyself wrath, against the day of wrath, and revelation of the just judgment of God.—*Rom.* ii. 5.

For we know him that hath said: Vengeance belongeth to me, and I will repay. And again: The Lord shall judge his people.

It is a fearful thing to fall into the hands of the living God.—*Heb.* x. 30, 31.

And the kings of the earth, and the princes, and tribunes, and the rich, and the strong, and every bondman, and every freeman, hid themselves in the dens and in the rocks of mountains:

And they say to the mountains and the rocks: Fall upon us, and hide us from the face of him that sitteth upon the throne, and from the wrath of the Lamb:

For the great day of their wrath is come, and who shall be able to stand?—*Apoc.* vi. 15, 16, 17.

JUDGMENT DAY A TIME OF JUSTICE AND NOT OF MERCY, THE

But the Lord remaineth for ever. He hath prepared his throne in judgment: and he shall judge the world in equity, he shall judge the people in justice.—*Ps.* ix. 8, 9.

Then shall all the trees of the woods rejoice before the face of the Lord, because he cometh: because he cometh to judge the earth.

He shall judge the world with justice, and the people with his truth.—*Ps.* xcv. 12, 13.

Remember the wrath that shall be at the last day, and the time of repay-

ing, when he shall turn away his face.
—*Ecclus.* xviii. 24.

An end is come, the end is come, it hath awaked against thee: behold it is come. . . .

Now very shortly I will pour out my wrath upon thee, and I will accomplish my anger in thee: and I will judge thee according to thy ways, and I will lay upon thee all thy crimes.

And my eye shall not spare, neither will I show mercy: but I will lay thy ways upon thee, and thy abominations shall be in the midst of thee: and you shall know that I am the Lord that strike.—*Ezech.* vii. 6, 8, 9.

For the day of the Lord is at hand upon all nations: as thou hast done, so shall it be done to thee: he will turn thy reward upon thy own head.—*Ab.* i. 15.

For the Son of man shall come in the glory of his Father with his angels: and then will he render to every man according to his works.—*Matt.* xvi. 27.

And God indeed having winked at the times of this ignorance, now declareth unto men, that all should everywhere do penance.

Because he hath appointed a day wherein he will judge the world in equity, by the man whom he hath appointed; giving faith to all, by raising him up from the dead.—*Acts* xvii. 30, 31.

For we must all be manifested before the judgment seat of Christ, that every one may receive the proper things of the body, according as he hath done, whether it be good or evil.—*2 Cor.* v. 10.

As to the rest, there is laid up for me a crown of justice, which the Lord, the just judge, will render to me in that day: and not only to me, but to them also that love his coming.—*2 Tim.* iv. 8.

For the time is, that judgment should begin at the house of God. And if first at us, what shall be the end of them that believe not the gospel of God?

And if the just man shall scarcely be saved, where shall the ungodly and the sinner appear?—*1 Peter* iv. 17, 18.

Behold, I come quickly; and my reward is with me, to render to every man according to his works.—*Apoc.* xxii. 12.

JUDGMENT DAY, ALL THINGS SHALL BE DISCLOSED AND JUDGED AT THE

The heavens shall reveal his iniquity, and the earth shall rise up against him. —*Job* xx. 27.

Thy eyes did see my imperfect being, and in thy book all shall be written.—*Ps.* cxxxviii. 16.

Rejoice therefore, O young man, in thy youth, and let thy heart be in that which is good in the days of thy youth, and walk in the ways of thy heart, and in the sight of thy eyes: and know that for all these, God will bring thee into judgment.—*Eccles.* xi. 9.

And all things that are done, God will bring into judgment for every [1]error, whether it be good or evil.—*Eccles.* xii. 14.

But I say unto you, that every idle word that men shall speak, they shall render an account for it in the day of judgment.—*Matt.* xii. 36.

For there is nothing covered that shall not be revealed: nor hidden, that shall not be known.

For whatsoever things you have spoken in darkness, shall be published in the light; and that which you have spoken in the ear in the chambers, shall be preached on the housetops.—*Luke* xii. 2, 3.

Who show the work of the law written in their hearts, their conscience bearing witness to them, and their thoughts between themselves accusing, or also defending one another,

In the day when God shall judge the secrets of men, by Jesus Christ, according to my gospel.—*Rom.* ii. 15, 16.

Every man's work shall be manifest; for the day of the Lord shall declare it, because it shall be revealed in fire; and the fire shall try every man's work, of what sort it is.—*1 Cor.* iii. 13.

Therefore judge not before the time; until the Lord come, who both will bring to light the hidden things of darkness, and will make manifest the counsels of the hearts; and then shall every man have praise from God.—*1 Cor.* iv. 5.

Some men's sins are manifest, going

[1]Error, or hidden and secret thing.

JUDGMENT

259

before to judgment: and some men they follow after.

In like manner also good deeds are manifest: and they that are otherwise, cannot be hid.—1 *Tim.* v. 24, 25.

JUDGMENT DAY, WE MUST PREPARE FOR THE

If he examine on a sudden, who shall answer him? or who can say: Why dost thou so?—*Job* ix. 12.

For what shall I do when God shall rise to judge? and when he shall examine, what shall I answer him?—*Job* xxxi. 14.

Before sickness, take a medicine, and before judgment, examine thyself, and thou shalt find mercy in the sight of God.—*Ecclus.* xviii. 20.

Remember the wrath that shall be at the last day, and the time of repaying, when he shall turn away his face.—*Ecclus.* xviii. 24.

What will you do in the day of visitation, and of the calamity which cometh from afar? to whom will ye flee for help? and where will ye leave your glory?—*Is.* x. 3.

Therefore I will do these things to thee, O Israel; and after I shall have done these things to thee, be prepared to meet thy God, O Israel.—*Amos* iv. 12.

Assemble yourselves together, be gathered together, O nation not worthy to be loved:

Before the decree bring forth the day as dust passing away, before the fierce anger of the Lord come upon you, before the day of the Lord's indignation come upon you.

Seek the Lord, all ye meek of the earth, you that have wrought his judgment: seek the just, seek the meek: if by any means you may be hid in the day of the Lord's indignation.—*Soph.* ii. 1-3.

And take heed to yourselves, lest perhaps your hearts be overcharged with surfeiting and drunkenness, and the cares of this life, and that day come upon you suddenly.

For as a snare shall it come upon all that sit upon the face of the whole earth.

Watch ye, therefore, praying at all times, that you may be accounted worthy to escape all these things that are to come, and to stand before the Son of man.—*Luke* xxi. 34-36.

And God indeed having winked at the times of this ignorance, now declareth unto men, that all should everywhere do penance.

Because he hath appointed a day, wherein he will judge the world in equity, by the man whom he hath appointed; giving faith to all, by raising him up from the dead.—*Acts* xvii. 30, 31.

But if we would judge ourselves, we should not be judged.—1 *Cor.* xi. 31.

So speak ye, and so do, as being to be judged by the law of liberty.—*James* ii. 12.

But the end of all is at hand. Be prudent therefore, and watch in prayers.—1 *Peter* iv. 7.

But the day of the Lord shall come as a thief, in which the heavens shall pass away with great violence, and the elements shall be melted with heat, and the earth and the works which are in it, shall be burnt up.

Seeing then that all these things are to be dissolved, what manner of people ought you to be in holy conversation and godliness?

Looking for and hasting unto the coming of the day of the Lord, by which the heavens being on fire, shall be dissolved, and the elements shall melt with the burning heat?

. . . Wherefore, dearly beloved, waiting for these things, be diligent, that you may be found before him unspotted and blameless in peace.—2 *Peter* iii. 10-12, 14.

And now, little children, abide in him, that when he shall appear, we may have confidence, and not be confounded by him at his coming.—1 *John* ii. 28.

Because thou hast kept the word of my patience, I will also keep thee from the hour of temptation, which shall come upon the whole world to try them that dwell upon the earth.—*Apoc.* iii. 10.

JUDGMENT AFTER DEATH, THE

Thou hast set our iniquities before thy eyes: our life, in the light of thy countenance.—*Ps.* lxxxix. 8.

If thou, O Lord, wilt mark iniquities: Lord, who shall stand it?—*Ps.* cxxix. 3.

Woe to them that have lost patience, and that have forsaken the right ways, and have gone aside into crooked ways.

And what will they do, when the Lord shall begin to examine?—*Ecclus.* ii. 16, 17.

For it is easy before God in the day of death to reward every one according to his ways.—*Ecclus.* xi. 28.

Remember my judgment: for thine also shall be so: yesterday for me, and to-day for thee.—*Ecclus.* xxxviii. 23.

And he said also to his disciples: There was a certain rich man who had a steward: and the same was accused unto him, that he had wasted his goods. And he called him, and said to him: How is it that I hear this of thee? give an account of thy stewardship: for now thou canst be steward no longer.—*Luke* xvi. 1, 2.

And as it is appointed unto men once to die, and after this, the judgment.—*Heb.* ix. 27.

JUDGMENTS OF GOD, THE

Thou art just, O Lord, and all thy judgments are just, and all thy ways mercy, and truth, and judgment. . . .

And now, O Lord, great are thy judgments, because we have not done according to thy precepts, and have not walked sincerely before thee.—*Tob.* iii. 2, 5.

The Lord shall be known when he executeth judgments: the sinner hath been caught in the works of his own hands.—*Ps.* ix. 17.

The judgments of the Lord are true, justified in themselves.—*Ps.* xviii. 10.

Thy justice is as the mountains of God, thy judgments are a great deep.—*Ps.* xxxv. 7.

Let mount Sion rejoice, and the daughters of Juda be glad; because of thy judgments, O Lord.—*Ps.* xlvii. 12.

He is the Lord our God: his judgments are in all the earth.—*Ps.* civ. 7.

I remembered, O Lord, thy judgments of old: and I was comforted.—*Ps.* cxviii. 52.

I know, O Lord, that thy judgments are equity: and in thy truth, thou hast humbled me.—*Ps.* cxviii. 75.

When thou shalt do thy judgments on the earth, the inhabitants of the world shall learn justice.—*Is.* xxvi. 9.

For thou art just in all that thou hast done to us, and all thy works are true, and thy ways right, and all thy judgments true.

For thou hast executed true judgments in all the things that thou hast brought upon us, and upon Jerusalem the holy city of our fathers: for according to truth and judgment, thou hast brought all these things upon us for our sins.—*Dan.* iii. 27, 28.

I cannot of myself do any thing. As I hear, so I judge: and my judgment is just; because I seek not my own will, but the will of him that sent me.—*John* v. 30.

For we know that the judgment of God is, according to truth, against them that do such things.

And thinkest thou this, O man, that judgest them who do such things, and dost the same, that thou shalt escape the judgment of God?—*Rom.* ii. 2, 3.

O the depth of the riches of the wisdom and of the knowledge of God! How incomprehensible are his judgments, and how unsearchable his ways!—*Rom.* xi. 33.

And I heard the angel of the waters saying: Thou art just, O Lord, who art, and who wast, the Holy One, because thou hast judged these things. . . .

And I heard another, from the altar, saying: Yea, O Lord God Almighty, true and just are thy judgments.—*Apoc.* xvi. 5, 7.

JUDGMENT, RASH

Before thou inquire, blame no man: and when thou hast inquired, reprove justly.—*Ecclus.* xi. 7.

Judge not according to the appearance, but judge just judgment.—*John* vii. 24.

JUST, THE

Thou hast proved my heart, and visited it by night, thou hast tried me by fire; and iniquity hath not been found in me.

That my mouth may not speak the works of men: for the sake of the words of thy lips, I have kept hard ways.—*Ps.* xvi. 3, 4.

Better is a little to the just, than the great riches of the wicked.—*Ps.* xxxvi. 16.

The mouth of the just shall meditate wisdom: and his tongue shall speak judgment.

The law of his God is in his heart, and his steps shall not be supplanted.—*Ps.* xxxvi. 30, 31.

All the glory of the king's daughter is within, in golden borders.—*Ps.* xliv. 14.

The just shall rejoice in the Lord, and shall hope in him: and all the upright in heart shall be praised.—*Ps.* lxiii. 11.

Blessed are they that keep judgment, and do justice at all times.—*Ps.* cv. 3.

But the path of the just, as a shining light, goeth forwards and increaseth even to perfect day.—*Prov.* iv. 18.

The memory of the just is with praises: and the name of the wicked shall rot.—*Prov.* x. 7.

The work of the just is unto life: but the fruit of the wicked, unto sin.—*Prov.* x. 16.

The expectation of the just is joy; but the hope of the wicked shall perish. —*Prov.* x. 28.

Whatsoever shall befall the just man, it shall not make him sad: but the wicked shall be filled with mischief.—*Prov.* xii. 21.

Justice keepeth the way of the innocent: but wickedness overthroweth the sinner.

One is as it were rich, when he hath nothing: and another is as it were poor, when he hath great riches.—*Prov.* xiii. 6, 7.

The just is first accuser of himself: his friend cometh, and shall search him.—*Prov.* xviii. 17.

For a just man shall fall seven times, and shall rise again: but the wicked shall fall down into evil.—*Prov.* xxiv. 16.

The wicked man fleeth, when no man pursueth: but the just, bold as a lion, shall be without dread.—*Prov.* xxviii. 1.

The just taketh notice of the cause of the poor: the wicked is void of knowledge.—*Prov.* xxix. 7.

Blessed is the rich man that is found without blemish: and that hath not gone after gold, nor put his trust in money nor in treasures.

Who is he, and we will praise him? for he hath done wonderful things in his life.

Who hath been tried thereby, and made perfect, he shall have glory everlasting. He that could have transgressed, and hath not transgressed; and could do evil things, and hath not done them:

Therefore are his goods established in the Lord, and all the church of the saints shall declare his alms.—*Ecclus.* xxxi. 8-11.

Say to the just man that it is well, for he shall eat the fruit of his doings. —*Is.* iii. 10.

My elect shall not labor in vain, nor bring forth in trouble; for they are the seed of the blessed of the Lord, and their posterity with them.—*Is.* lxv. 23.

O ye spirits and souls of the just, bless the Lord: praise and exalt him above all for ever.—*Dan.* iii. 86.

Then shall the king say to them that shall be on his right hand: Come, ye blessed of my Father, possess you the kingdom prepared for you from the foundation of the world.

For I was hungry, and you gave me to eat; I was thirsty, and you gave me to drink; I was a stranger, and you took me in:

Naked, and you covered me: sick, and you visited me: I was in prison, and you came to me.

Then shall the just answer him, saying: Lord, when did we see thee hungry, and fed thee; thirsty, and gave thee drink?

And when did we see thee a stranger, and took thee in? or naked, and covered thee?

Or when did we see thee sick or in prison, and came to thee?

And the king answering, shall say to them: Amen I say to you, as long as you did it to one of these my least brethren, you did it to me.—*Matt.* xxv. 34-40.

But he that doth truth, cometh to

the light, that his works may be made manifest, because they are done in God. —*John* iii. 21.

Whosoever is born of God, committeth not sin: for his seed abideth in him, and he cannot sin, because he is born of God.

In this the children of God are manifest, and the children of the devil. Whosoever is not just, is not of God, nor he that loveth not his brother.— 1 *John* iii. 9, 10.

Dearly beloved, follow not that which is evil, but that which is good. He that doth good, is of God; he that doth evil, hath not seen God.—3 *John* i. 11.

And he said to me: Write: Blessed are they that are called to the marriage supper of the Lamb. And he saith to me: These words of God are true.— *Apoc.* xix. 9.

JUST, GOD'S SPECIAL FAVOR AND LOVE FOR THE

How good is God to Israel, to them that are of a right heart!—*Ps.* lxxii. 1.

Acceptable is the man that showeth mercy and lendeth: he shall order his words with judgment:

Because he shall not be moved for ever.—*Ps.* cxi. 5, 6.

The Lord loveth the just.—*Ps.*cxlv.8.

The blessing of the Lord is upon the head of the just: but iniquity covereth the mouth of the wicked.—*Prov.* x. 6.

He that is good, shall draw grace from the Lord.—*Prov.* xii. 2.

The way of the wicked is an abomination to the Lord: but he that followeth justice is beloved by him.—*Prov.*xv.9.

JUST, HAPPINESS OF THE

See also: Joy, spiritual—page 249.

But let all them be glad that hope in thee: they shall rejoice for ever, and thou shalt dwell in them.

And all they that love thy name shall glory in thee:

For thou wilt bless the just.

O Lord, thou hast crowned us, as with a shield of thy good will.—*Ps.* v. 12, 13.

I set the Lord always in my sight: for he is at my right hand, that I be not moved.

Therefore my heart hath been glad, and my tongue hath rejoiced: moreover my flesh also shall rest in hope.

Because thou wilt not leave my soul in hell; nor wilt thou give thy holy one to see corruption.

Thou hast made known to me the ways of life, thou shalt fill me with joy, with thy countenance: at thy right hand are delights even to the end.— *Ps.* xv. 8-11.

They shall be inebriated with the plenty of thy house; and thou shalt make them drink of the torrent of thy pleasure.—*Ps.* xxxv. 9.

Light is risen to the just, and joy to the right of heart.—*Ps.* xcvi. 11.

The voice of rejoicing and of salvation is in the tabernacles of the just.— *Ps.* cxvii. 15.

Much peace have they that love thy law, and to them there is no stumbling-block.—*Ps.* cxviii. 165.

But he that feareth the commandment, shall dwell in peace.—*Prov.* xiii. 13.

It is joy to the just to do judgment: and dread to them that work iniquity. —*Prov.* xxi. 15.

In the joy of the just, there is great glory.—*Prov.* xxviii. 12.

The fear of the Lord is honor, and glory, and gladness, and a crown of joy.

The fear of the Lord shall delight the heart, and shall give joy and gladness, and length of days.—*Ecclus.* i. 11, 12.

But yet, rejoice not in this, that spirits are subject unto you; but rejoice in this, that your names are written in heaven.—*Luke* x. 20.

JUST, REWARD OF THE

See: Reward God gives to those who serve Him, the—page 480.

JUST, PROTECTED AND ASSISTED BY GOD, THE

Remember, I pray thee, who ever perished being innocent? or when were the just destroyed?—*Job* iv. 7.

He will not take away his eyes from the just.—*Job* xxxvi. 7.

The wickedness of sinners shall be brought to nought: and thou shalt direct the just: the searcher of hearts and reins is God.

Just is my help from the Lord: who saveth the upright of heart.—*Ps.* vii. 10, 11.

Thou shalt hide them (the just) in the secret of thy face, from the disturbance of men.

Thou shalt protect them in thy tabernacle from the contradiction of tongues.—*Ps.* xxx. 21.

Many are the afflictions of the just; but out of them all will the Lord deliver them.

The Lord keepeth all their bones, not one of them shall be broken.—*Ps.* xxxiii. 20, 21.

Extend thy mercy to them that know thee, and thy justice to them that are right in heart.—*Ps.* xxxv. 11.

For the arms of the wicked shall be broken in pieces; but the Lord strengtheneth the just.—*Ps.* xxxvi. 17.

I have been young, and now am old; and I have not seen the just forsaken nor his seed seeking bread.— *Ps.* xxxvi. 25.

The wicked watcheth the just man, and seeketh to put him to death.

But the Lord will not leave him in his hands; nor condemn him, when he shall be judged.—*Ps.* xxxvi. 32, 33.

But the salvation of the just is from the Lord, and he is their protector in the time of trouble.

And the Lord will help them, and deliver them: and he will rescue them from the wicked, and save them, because they have hoped in him.—*Ps.* xxxvi. 39, 40.

Cast thy care upon the Lord, and he shall sustain thee: he shall not suffer the just to waver for ever.—*Ps.* liv. 23.

You that love the Lord, hate evil: the Lord preserveth the souls of his saints, he will deliver them out of the hand of the sinner.—*Ps.* xcvi. 10.

He hath made a remembrance of his wonderful works, being a merciful and gracious Lord: he hath given food to them that fear him.

He will be mindful for ever of his covenant.—*Ps.* cx. 4, 5.

For the Lord will not leave the rod of sinners upon the lot of the just: that the just may not stretch forth their hands to iniquity.

Do good, O Lord, to those that are good, and to the upright of heart.— *Ps.* cxxiv. 3, 4.

The Lord keepeth all them that love him; but all the wicked he will destroy. —*Ps.* cxliv. 20.

He will keep the salvation of the righteous, and protect them that walk in simplicity,

Keeping the paths of justice, and guarding the ways of saints.—*Prov.* ii. 7, 8.

The just is delivered out of distress: and the wicked shall be given up for him.—*Prov.* xi. 8.

But the just shall live for evermore: and their reward is with the Lord, and the care of them with the most High.

Therefore shall they receive a kingdom of glory, and a crown of beauty at the hand of the Lord: for with his right hand, he will cover them, and with his holy arm he will defend them.—*Wis.* v. 16, 17.

And the Lord will not be slack, but will judge for the just, and will do judgment.—*Ecclus.* xxxv. 22.

And who is he that can hurt you, if you be zealous of good?

But if also you suffer any thing for justice' sake, blessed are ye. And be not afraid of their fear, and be not troubled.—1 *Peter* iii. 13, 14.

JUST, GOD HEARS THE PRAYERS OF THE

Now therefore restore the man (Abraham) his wife, for he is a prophet: and he shall pray for thee, and thou shalt live.

. . . And when Abraham prayed, God healed Abimelech and his wife, and his handmaids, and they bore children.—*Gen.* xx. 7, 17.

And again the Lord said to Moses: See that this people is stiffnecked:

Let me alone, that my wrath may be kindled against them, and that I may destroy them, and I will make of thee a great nation.

And Moses besought the Lord his God, saying: Why, O Lord, is thy indignation enkindled against thy people, whom thou hast brought out of the land of Egypt, with great power, and with a mighty hand? . . .

Let thy anger cease, and be appeased upon the wickedness of thy people. . . .

And the Lord was appeased from doing the evil which he had spoken against his people.—*Ex.* xxxi. 9-12, 14.

The eyes of the Lord are upon the just: and his ears unto their prayers. . . .

The just cried, and the Lord heard them: and delivered them out of all their troubles.—*Ps.* xxxiii. 16, 18.

He will do the will of them that fear him: and he will hear their prayer, and save them.—*Ps.* cxliv. 19.

The Lord is far from the wicked: and he will hear the prayers of the just.— *Prov.* xv. 29.

The sacrifice of the just is acceptable, and the Lord will not forget the memorial thereof.—*Ecclus.* xxxv. 9.

Is not this rather the fast that I have chosen? loose the bands of wickedness, undo the bundles that oppress, let them that are broken go free, and break asunder every burden.

Deal thy bread to the hungry, and bring the needy and the harborless into thy house: when thou shalt see one naked, cover him, and despise not thy own flesh.

. . . Then shalt thou call, and the Lord shall hear: thou shalt cry, and he shall say, Here I am.—*Is.* lviii. 6, 7, 9.

My elect shall not labor in vain, nor bring forth in trouble; for they are the seed of the blessed of the Lord, and their posterity with them.

And it shall come to pass, that before they call, I will hear; as they are yet speaking, I will hear.—*Is.* lxv. 23, 24.

Now we know that God doth not hear sinners: but if a man be a server of God, and doth his will, him he heareth. —*John* ix. 31.

And there was a certain man in Cæsarea, named Cornelius, a centurion of that which is called the Italian band;

A religious man, and fearing God, with all his house, giving much alms to the people, and always praying to God.

This man saw in a vision manifestly, about the ninth hour of the day, an

angel of God coming in unto him, and saying to him: Cornelius.

And he, beholding him, being seized with fear, said: What is it, Lord? And he said to him: Thy prayers and thy alms are ascended for a memorial in the sight of God.—*Acts* x. 1-4.

Confess therefore your sins one to another: and pray one for another, that you may be saved. For the continual prayer of a just man availeth much.— *James* v. 16.

JUST, GOD OFTEN AFFLICTS THE

I that was formerly so wealthy, am all on a sudden broken to pieces: he hath taken me by my neck, he hath broken me, and hath set me up to be his mark. . . .

He hath torn me with wound upon wound, he hath rushed in upon me like a giant. . . .

My face is swollen with weeping, and my eyelids are dim.

These things have I suffered without the iniquity of my hand, when I offered pure prayers to God.

O earth, cover not thou my blood, neither let my cry find a hiding place in thee.

For behold my witness is in heaven, and he that knoweth my conscience is on high.—*Job* xvi. 13, 15, 17-20.

Now also my words are in bitterness, and the hand of my scourge is more grievous than my mourning. . . .

But he knoweth my way, and has tried me as gold that passeth through the fire:

My foot hath followed his steps, I have kept his way, and have not declined from it.

I have not departed from the commandments of his lips, and the words of his mouth I have hid in my bosom.— *Job* xxiii. 2, 10-12.

Many are the afflictions of the just; but out of them all will the Lord deliver them.—*Ps.* xxxiii. 20.

Thou hast shown thy people hard things: thou hast made us drink the wine of sorrow.—*Ps.* lix. 5.

There is also another vanity, which is done upon the earth. There are just men to whom evils happen, as though they had done the works of the wicked: and there are wicked men, who are as secure, as though they had the deeds of the just: but this also I judge most vain.—*Eccles.* viii. 14.

And though in the sight of men they suffered torments, their hope is full of immortality.

Afflicted in few things, in many they shall be well rewarded: because God hath tried them, and found them worthy of himself.

As gold in the furnace he hath proved them, and as a victim of a holocaust he hath received them, and in time there shall be respect had to them. —*Wis.* iii. 4-6.

For gold and silver are tried in the fire, but acceptable men in the furnace of humiliation.—*Ecclus.* ii. 5.

JUST DESPISED AND HATED BY THE WORLD AND THE WICKED, THE

He that is mocked by his friends, as I, shall call upon God, and he will hear him: for the simplicity of the just man is laughed to scorn.

The lamp despised in the thoughts of the rich, is ready for the time appointed.—*Job* xii. 4, 5.

The sinner shall watch the just man: and shall gnash upon him with his teeth.

But the Lord shall laugh at him: for he foreseeth that his day shall come.— *Ps.* xxxvi. 12, 13.

Fools hate them that flee from evil things.—*Prov.* xiii. 19.

He that walketh in the right way, and feareth God, is despised by him that goeth by an infamous way.—*Prov.* xiv. 2.

Bloodthirsty men hate the upright: but just men seek his soul.—*Prov.* xxix. 10.

The just abhor the wicked man: and the wicked loathe them that are in the right way.—*Prov.* xxix. 27.

Let us therefore lie in wait for the just, because he is not for our turn, and he is contrary to our doings, and upbraideth us with transgressions of the law, and divulgeth against us the sins of our way of life.

. . . He is become a censurer of our thoughts.

He is grievous unto us, even to behold: for his life is not like other men's, and his ways are very different.

We are esteemed by him as triflers, and he abstaineth from our ways as from filthiness, and he preferreth the latter end of the just, and glorieth that he hath God for his father.—*Wis.* ii. 12, 14-16.

For they shall see the end of the wise man, and shall not understand what God hath designed for him, and why the Lord hath set him in safety.

They shall see him, and shall despise him: but the Lord shall laugh them to scorn.—*Wis.* iv. 17, 18.

Then shall the just stand with great constancy against those that have afflicted them, and taken away their labors.

These seeing it, shall be troubled with terrible fear, and shall be amazed at the suddenness of their unexpected salvation.

Saying within themselves, repenting. and groaning for anguish of spirit: These are they, whom we had some time in derision, and for a parable of reproach.

We fools esteemed their life madness, and their end without honor.

Behold how they are numbered among the children of God, and their lot is among the saints.—*Wis.* v. 1-5.

And you shall be hated by all men, for my name's sake. . . .

The disciple is not above the master, nor the servant above his lord.

It is enough for the disciple that he be as his master, and the servant as his lord. If they have called the goodman of the house, Beelzebub, how much more them of his household?—*Matt.* x. 22, 24, 25.

If the world hate you, know ye, that it hath hated me before you.

If you had been of the world, the world would love its own: but because you are not of the world, but I have chosen you out of the world, therefore the world hateth you.

Remember my word that I said to you: The servant is not greater than his master. If they have persecuted me, they will also persecute you: if they have kept my word, they will keep yours also.

But all these things they will do to you for my name's sake: because they know not him that sent me.—*John* xv. 18-21.

I have given them (the disciples) thy word, and the world hath hated them, because they are not of the world; as I also am not of the world.—*John* xvii. 14.

And all that will live godly in Christ Jesus, shall suffer persecution.— 2 *Tim.* iii. 12.

Wonder not, brethren, if the world hate you.—1 *John* iii. 13.

JUST, AGAINST HATING OR DESPISING THE

The death of the wicked is very evil: and they that hate the just, shall be guilty.—*Ps.* xxxiii. 22.

He that justifieth the wicked, and he that condemneth the just, both are abominable before God.—*Prov.* xvii. 15.

They shall perish in a snare that are delighted with the fall of the just: and sorrow shall consume them before they die.—*Ecclus.* xxvii. 32.

Woe to you . . . that justify the wicked for gifts, and take away the justice of the just from him.—*Is.* v. 23.

JUST MEN, EXAMPLES OF

See: Appendix—page 755.

JUSTICE OF GOD, THE

See also: Judge, God a just— page 251.

Doth God pervert judgment, or doth the Almighty overthrow that which is just?—*Job* viii. 3.

For he will render to a man his work, and according to the ways of every one, he will reward them.

For in very deed God will not condemn without cause, neither will the Almighty pervert judgment.—*Job* xxxiv. 11, 12.

And the heavens shall show forth his justice to a people that shall be born, which the Lord hath made.—*Ps.* xxi. 32.

And my tongue shall meditate thy justice, thy praise all the day long.—*Ps.* xxxiv. 28.

Thy justice is as the mountains of God, thy judgments are a great deep.— *Ps.* xxxv. 7.

Extend thy mercy to them that know thee, and thy justice to them that are right in heart.—*Ps.* xxxv. 11.

And the heavens shall declare his justice: for God is judge.—*Ps.* xlix. 6.

The Lord hath made known his salvation: he hath revealed his justice in the sight of the Gentiles.—*Ps.* xcvii. 2.

He will put on justice as a breastplate, and will take true judgment instead of a helmet.

He will take equity for an invincible shield.—*Wis.* v. 19, 20.

For so much then as thou art just, thou orderest all things justly: thinking it not agreeable to thy power, to condemn him who deserveth not to be punished.—*Wis.* xii. 15.

And the Lord of hosts shall be exalted in judgment, and the holy God shall be sanctified in justice.—*Is.* v. 16.

And justice shall be the girdle of his loins: and faith, the girdle of his reins. —*Is.* xi. 5.

Lift up your eyes to heaven, and look down to the earth beneath: for the heavens shall vanish like smoke, and the earth shall be worn away like a garment, and the inhabitants thereof shall perish in like manner: but my salvation shall be for ever, and my justice shall not fail.—*Is.* li. 6.

But let him that glorieth, glory in this, that he understandeth and knoweth me, for I am the Lord that exercise mercy, and judgment, and justice in the earth: for these things please me, saith the Lord.—*Jer.* ix. 24.

To destroy a man wrongfully in his judgment, the Lord hath not approved. —*Lam.* iii. 36.

What shall we say then? Is there injustice with God? God forbid.—*Rom.* ix. 14.

JUSTICE OF GOD IN REWARDING GOOD, THE

And the Lord will reward me according to my justice; and will repay me according to the cleanness of my hands. —*Ps.* xvii. 21.

But the mercy of the Lord is from eternity and unto eternity upon them that fear him: And his justice unto children's children, to such as keep his covenant,

And are mindful of his commandments to do them.—*Ps.* cii. 17, 18.

With a good will serving, as to the Lord, and not to men.

Knowing that whatsoever good thing any man shall do, the same shall he receive from the Lord, whether he be bond or free.—*Eph.* vi. 7, 8.

For God is not unjust, that he should forget your work, and the love which you have shown in his name, you who have ministered, and do minister to the saints.—*Heb.* vi. 10.

JUSTICE OF GOD IN PUNISHING EVIL, THE

For he doth not now bring on his fury, neither doth he revenge wickedness exceedingly.—*Job* xxxv. 15.

For thus saith the Lord: Although I shall send in upon Jerusalem my four grievous judgments, the sword and the famine, and the mischievous beasts, and the pestilence, to destroy out of it man and beast; . . .

You shall know that I have not done without cause all that I have done in it, saith the Lord God.—*Ezech.* xiv. 21, 23.

Then shall they begin to say to the mountains: Fall upon us; and to the hills: Cover us.

For if in the green wood they do these things, what shall be done in the dry?—*Luke* xxiii. 30, 31.

But if our injustice commend the justice of God, what shall we say? Is God unjust, who executeth wrath?

(I speak according to man.) God forbid: otherwise, how shall God judge this world?—*Rom.* iii. 5, 6.

For he that doth wrong, shall receive for that which he hath done wrongfully: and there is no respect of persons with God.—*Col.* iii. 25.

And if the just man shall scarcely be saved, where shall the ungodly and the sinner appear?—1 *Peter* iv. 18.

JUSTICE OF GOD, ACKNOWLEDGMENT OF THE

The works of God are perfect, and all his ways are judgments: God is faithful, and without any iniquity, he is just and right.—*Deut.* xxxii. 4.

And thou art just in all things that have come upon us: because thou hast done truth, but we have done wickedly.—2 *Esd.* ix. 33.

For the Lord is just, and hath loved justice: his countenance hath beheld righteousness.—*Ps.* x. 8.

According to thy name, O God, so also is thy praise unto the ends of the earth: thy right hand is full of justice.—*Ps.* xlvii. 11.

Justice and judgment are the preparation of thy throne.

Mercy and truth shall go before thy face.—*Ps.* lxxxviii. 15.

His work is praise and magnificence: and his justice continueth for ever and ever. . . .

All his commandments are faithful: confirmed for ever and ever, made in truth and equity.—*Ps.* cx. 3, 8.

I know, O Lord, that thy judgments are equity: and in thy truth, thou hast humbled me. . . .

Thy justice is justice for ever: and thy law is the truth.—*Ps.* cxviii. 75,142.

The Lord is just in all his ways: and holy in all his works.—*Ps.* cxliv. 17.

And you shall say: To the Lord our God belongeth justice, but to us confusion of our face: as it is come to pass at this day to all Juda, and to the inhabitants of Jerusalem.—*Bar.* i. 15.

For thou art just in all that thou hast done to us, and all thy works are true, and thy ways right, and all thy judgments true.—*Dan.* iii. 27.

O Lord God, Creator of all things, dreadful and strong, just and merciful, who alone art the good king,

Who alone art gracious, who alone art just, and almighty, and eternal.—2 *Mach.* i. 24, 25.

And I heard the angel of the waters saying: Thou art just, O Lord, who art, and who wast, the Holy One, because thou hast judged these things. . . .

And I heard another, from the altar, saying: Yea, O Lord God Almighty, true and just are thy judgments.—*Apoc.* xvi. 5, 7.

JUSTICE OF GOD, WE CANNOT ESCAPE THE

See also: Deceive God, we cannot—page 105.

Neither are they content not to return thanks for benefits received, and to violate in themselves the laws of humanity, but they think they can also escape the justice of God who seeth all things.—*Esther* xvi. 4.

According as his mercy is, so his correction judgeth a man according to his works.

The sinner shall not escape in his rapines, and the patience of him that showeth mercy shall not be put off.—*Ecclus.* xvi. 13, 14.

[1]For though for the present time, I should be delivered from the punishments of men, yet should I not escape the hand of the Almighty, neither alive nor dead.—*2 Mach.* vi. 26.

But do not think that thou shalt escape unpunished, for that thou hast attempted to fight against God.—*2 Mach.* vii. 19.

But [2]thou, O wicked, and of all men most flagitious, be not lifted up without cause with vain hopes, whilst thou art raging against his servants.

For thou hast not yet escaped the judgment of the almighty God, who beholdeth all things.—*2 Mach.* vii. 34, 35.

Be not deceived, God is not mocked.

For what things a man shall sow, those also shall he reap. For he that soweth in his flesh, of the flesh also shall reap corruption. But he that soweth in the spirit, of the spirit shall reap life everlasting.—*Gal.* vi. 7, 8.

JUSTICE IN OUR DEALINGS WITH ONE ANOTHER

See also: Debts, we should pay our just—page 104.

If I have despised to abide judgment with my manservant, or my maidservant, when they had any controversy against me:

For what shall I do when God shall rise to judge? and when he shall examine, what shall I answer him?

Did not he that made me in the womb, make him also: and did not one and the same form me in the womb?—*Job* xxxi. 13-15.

Blessed are they that keep judgment, and do justice at all times.—*Ps.* cv. 3.

[1]Eleazar refusing to eat swine's flesh at Antiochus' command.
[2]King Antiochus.

The beginning of a good way is to do justice; and this is more acceptable with God, than to offer sacrifices.—*Prov.* xvi. 5.

To do mercy and judgment, pleaseth the Lord more than victims.—*Prov.* xxi. 3.

He that followeth justice and mercy, shall find life, justice, and glory.—*Prov.* xxi. 21.

The offering of him that sacrificeth of a thing wrongfully gotten, is stained, and the mockeries of the unjust are not acceptable.

The Lord is only for them that wait upon him in the way of truth and justice.—*Ecclus.* xxxiv. 21, 22.

All bribery and injustice shall be blotted out, and fidelity shall stand for ever.—*Ecclus.* xl. 12.

If you know that he is just, know ye, that every one also who doth justice, is born of him.—*1 John* ii. 29.

JUSTICE IN OUR DEALINGS WITH ONE ANOTHER, EXHORTATION TO

Thou shalt not do that which is unjust, nor judge unjustly. Respect not the person of the poor, nor honor the countenance of the mighty. But judge thy neighbor according to justice. . . .

Do not any unjust thing in judgment, in rule, in weight, or in measure.

Let the balance be just and the weights equal, the bushel just, and the sextary equal.—*Lev.* xix. 15, 35, 36.

Thou shalt follow justly after that which is just: that thou mayst live and possess the land, which the Lord thy God shall give thee.—*Deut.* xvi. 20.

If in very deed you speak justice: judge right things, ye sons of men.

For in your heart you work iniquity: your hands forge injustice in the earth.—*Ps.* lvii. 2, 3.

Masters, do to your servants that which is just and equal: knowing that you also have a master in heaven.—*Col.* iv. 1.

And that no man overreach, nor circumvent his brother in business: because the Lord is the avenger of all these things, as we have told you before, and have testified; . . .

And that you walk honestly towards them that are without; and that you want nothing of any man's.—1 *Thess.* iv. 6, 11.

For they that will become rich, fall into temptation, and into the snare of the devil, and into many unprofitable and hurtful desires, which drown men into destruction and perdition. . . .

But thou, O man of God, fly these things: and pursue justice, godliness, faith, charity, patience, mildness.— 1 *Tim.* vi. 9, 11.

KIND WORDS

Behold thou hast taught many, and thou hast strengthened the weary hands:

Thy words have confirmed them that were staggering, and thou hast strengthened the trembling knees.—*Job* iv. 3, 4.

Grief in the heart of a man shall bring him low, but with a good word, he shall be made glad.—*Prov.* xii. 25.

My son, in thy good deeds, make no complaint, and when thou givest any thing, add not grief by an evil word.

Shall not the dew assuage the heat? so also the good word is better than the gift.

Lo, is not a word better than a gift? but both are with a justified man.— *Ecclus.* xviii. 15-17.

For by thy words thou shalt be justified, and by thy words thou shalt be condemned.—*Matt.* xii. 37.

KINDNESS

Clemency prepareth life: and the pursuing of evil things, death.—*Prov.* xi. 19.

And whosoever shall give to drink to one of these little ones a cup of cold water only, in the name of a disciple, amen I say to you, he shall not lose his reward.—*Matt.* x. 42.

But the fruit of the Spirit is charity, joy, peace, patience, benignity, goodness, longanimity.—*Gal.* v. 22.

And be ye kind one to another; merciful, forgiving one another, even as God hath forgiven you in Christ.— *Eph.* iv. 32.

Put ye on, therefore, as the elect of God, holy and beloved, the bowels of mercy, benignity, humility, modesty, patience.—*Col.* iii. 12.

KING, GOD OUR

For the kingdom is the Lord's; and he shall have dominion over the nations.—*Ps.* xxi. 29.

The Lord maketh the flood to dwell: and the Lord shall sit king for ever.— *Ps.* xxviii. 10.

O clap your hands, all ye nations: shout unto God with the voice of joy,

For the Lord is high, terrible: a great king over all the earth. . . .

Sing praises to our God, sing ye: sing praises to our king, sing ye.

For God is the king of all the earth: sing ye wisely.—*Ps.* xlvi. 2, 3, 7, 8.

For the sparrow hath found herself a house, and the turtle a nest for herself, where she may lay her young ones: Thy altars, O Lord of hosts, my king and my God.—*Ps.* lxxxiii. 4.

Sing praise to the Lord on the harp, on the harp, and with the voice of a psalm: with long trumpets, and sound of cornet.

Make a joyful noise before the Lord our king.—*Ps.* xcvii. 5, 6.

I will extol thee, O God my king: and I will bless thy name for ever; yea, for ever and ever.—*Ps.* cxliv. 1.

Let Israel rejoice in him that made him: and let the children of Sion be joyful in their king.—*Ps.* cxlix. 2.

There is one most high Creator Almighty, and a powerful king, and greatly to be feared, who sitteth upon his throne, and he is the God of dominion.—*Ecclus.* i. 8.

He that liveth for ever, created all things together. God only shall be justified, and he remaineth an invincible king for ever.—*Ecclus.* xviii. 1.

I will give glory to thee, O Lord, O King, and I will praise thee, O God my Saviour.—*Ecclus.* li. 1.

And the Lord shall be king over all the earth: in that day there shall be one Lord, and his name shall be one. —*Zach.* xiv. 9.

Cursed is the deceitful man that hath in his flock a male, and making a vow, offereth in sacrifice that which is feeble to the Lord: for I am a great King, saith the Lord of hosts, and my name is dreadful among the Gentiles. —*Malach.* i. 14.

Now to the king of ages, immortal, invisible, the only God, be honor and glory for ever and ever. Amen.—1 *Tim.* i. 17.

I charge thee: . . . That thou keep the commandment without spot, blameless, unto the coming of our Lord Jesus Christ,

Which in his times he shall show, who is the Blessed and only Mighty, the King of kings, and Lord of lords.—1 *Tim.* vi. 14, 15.

KING, ACKNOWLEDGMENT THAT GOD IS OUR

O Lord God of our fathers, thou art God in heaven, and rulest over all the kingdoms and nations, in thy hand is strength and power, and no one can resist thee.—2 *Paral.* xx. 6.

Thou art thyself my king and my God, who commandest the saving of Jacob.—*Ps.* xliii. 5.

But God is our king before ages: he hath wrought salvation in the midst of the earth.—*Ps.* lxxiii. 12.

For the Lord is our judge, the Lord is our lawgiver, the Lord is our king: he will save us.—*Is.* xxxiii. 22.

But the Lord is the true God: he is the living God, and the everlasting king.—*Jer.* x. 10.

O Lord God, Creator of all things, dreadful and strong, just and merciful, who alone art the good king.—2 *Mach.* i. 24.

KING, CHRIST OUR

When Jesus therefore was born in Bethlehem of Juda, in the days of king Herod, behold, there came wise men from the east to Jerusalem,

Saying, Where is he that is born king of the Jews? For we have seen his star in the east, and are come to adore him.

. . . But they said to him: In Bethlehem of Juda. For so it is written by the prophet:

And thou Bethlehem the land of Juda art not the least among the princes of Juda: for out of thee shall come forth the captain that shall rule my people Israel.—*Matt.* ii. 1, 2, 5, 6.

And Pilate asked him, saying: Art thou the king of the Jews? But he answering, said: Thou sayest it.—*Luke* xxiii. 3.

And on the next day a great multitude that was come to the festival day, when they had heard that Jesus was coming to Jerusalem,

Took branches of palm-trees, and went forth to meet him, and cried: Hosanna, blessed is he that cometh in the name of the Lord, the king of Israel.

And Jesus found a young ass, and sat upon it, as it is written:

Fear not, daughter of Sion: behold, thy king cometh, sitting on an ass's colt.—*John* xii. 12-15.

Then therefore Pilate took Jesus, and scourged him.

And the soldiers platting a crown of thorns, put it upon his head; and they put on him a purple garment.

And they came to him, and said: Hail, king of the Jews; and they gave him blows.

Pilate therefore went forth again, and saith to them: Behold, I bring him forth unto you, that you may know that I find no cause in him.

(Jesus therefore came forth, bearing the crown of thorns and the purple garment.) And he saith to them: Behold the Man.—*John* xix. 1-5.

And it was the parasceve of the pasch, about the sixth hour, and he saith to the Jews: Behold your king.

But they cried out: Away with him; away with him; crucify him. Pilate saith to them: Shall I crucify your king? The chief priests answered: We have no king but Cæsar.—*John* xix. 14, 15.

And Pilate wrote a title also, and he put it upon the cross. And the writing was: Jesus of Nazareth, the King of the Jews.—*John* xix. 19.

KINGDOM OF GOD IN HEAVEN, THE

Thou art great, O Lord, for ever, and thy kingdom is unto all ages.—*Tob.* xiii. 1.

Thy throne, O God, is for ever and ever: the sceptre of thy kingdom is a sceptre of uprightness.—*Ps.* xliv. 7.

The Lord hath prepared his throne in

heaven: and his kingdom shall rule over all.—*Ps.* cii. 19.

They shall speak of the glory of thy kingdom: and shall tell of thy power:

To make thy might known to the sons of men: and the glory of the magnificence of thy kingdom.

Thy kingdom is a kingdom of all ages: and thy dominion endureth throughout all generations.—*Ps.* cxliv. 11-13.

The Lord shall reign for ever: thy God, O Sion, unto generation and generation.—*Ps.* cxlv. 10.

Fear not, little flock, for it hath pleased your Father to give you a kingdom.—*Luke* xii. 32.

There shall be weeping and gnashing of teeth, when you shall see Abraham and Isaac and Jacob, and all the prophets, in the kingdom of God, and you yourselves thrust out.

And there shall come from the east and the west, and the north and the south; and shall sit down in the kingdom of God.—*Luke* xiii. 28, 29.

So you also, when you shall see these things come to pass, know that the kingdom of God is at hand.—*Luke* xxi. 31.

Jesus answered: My kingdom is not of this world. If my kingdom were of this world, my servants would certainly strive that I should not be delivered to the Jews: but now my kingdom is not from hence.—*John* xviii. 36.

Now this I say, brethren, that flesh and blood cannot possess the kingdom of God: neither shall corruption possess incorruption.—1 *Cor.* xv. 50.

For know you this, and understand, that no fornicator, or unclean, or covetous person (which is a serving of idols), hath inheritance in the kingdom of Christ and of God.—*Eph.* v. 5.

But you are come to mount Sion, and to the city of the living God, the heavenly Jerusalem, and to the company of many thousands of angels,

And to the church of the first-born, who are written in the heavens, and to God, the judge of all, and to the spirits of the just made perfect.—*Heb.* xii. 22, 23.

And I heard as it were the voice of a great multitude, and as the voice of many waters, and as the voice of great thunders, saying, Alleluia: for the Lord our God the Almighty hath reigned.—*Apoc.* xix. 6.

KINGDOM OF GOD ON EARTH, THE

Let the heavens rejoice, and the earth be glad: and let them say among the nations: The Lord hath reigned.

Let the sea roar, and the fulness thereof: let the fields rejoice, and all things that are in them.

Then shall the trees of the wood give praise before the Lord: because he is come to judge the earth.—1 *Paral.* xvi. 31-33.

Sing praises to our God, sing ye: sing praises to our king, sing ye.

For God is the king of all the earth: sing ye wisely.

God shall reign over the nations: God sitteth on his holy throne.—*Ps.* xlvi. 7-9.

And he shall rule from sea to sea, and from the river unto the ends of the earth. . . .

And all kings of the earth shall adore him: all nations shall serve him.—*Ps.* lxxi. 8, 11.

For a child is born to us, and a son is given to us, and the government is upon his shoulder: and his name shall be called, Wonderful, Counsellor, God the Mighty, the Father of the world to come, the Prince of Peace.

His empire shall be multiplied, and there shall be no end of peace: he shall sit upon the throne of David, and upon his kingdom; to establish it and strengthen it with judgment and with justice, from henceforth and for ever: the zeal of the Lord of hosts will perform this.—*Is.* ix. 6, 7.

The wolf shall dwell with the lamb: and the leopard shall lie down with the kid: the calf, and the lion, and the sheep shall abide together, and a little child shall lead them.

The calf and the bear shall feed: their young ones shall rest together: and the lion shall eat straw like the ox.

And the sucking child shall play on the hole of the asp: and the weaned child shall thrust his hand into the den of the basilisk.

They shall not hurt, nor shall they kill in all my holy mountain, for the earth is filled with the knowledge of the Lord, as the covering waters of the sea. —*Is.* xi. 6-9.

For he that made thee shall rule over thee, the Lord of hosts is his name: and thy Redeemer, the Holy One of Israel, shall be called the God of all the earth. —*Is.* liv. 5.

And the Lord shall be king over all the earth: in that day there shall be one Lord, and his name shall be one.— *Zach.* xiv. 9.

Thy kingdom come.—*Matt.* vi. 10.

The kingdom of heaven is like to a householder, who went out early in the morning to hire laborers into his vineyard.—*Matt.* xx. 1.

He said therefore: To what is the kingdom of God like, and whereunto shall I resemble it?

It is like to a grain of mustard seed, which a man took, and cast into his garden, and it grew, and became a great tree, and the birds of the air lodged in the branches thereof.

And again he said: Whereunto shall I esteem the kingdom of God to be like?

It is like to leaven, which a woman took and hid in three measures of meal, till the whole was leavened.—*Luke* xiii. 18-21.

And the seventh angel sounded the trumpet: and there were great voices in heaven, saying: The kingdom of this world is become our Lord's and his Christ's, and he shall reign for ever and ever. Amen.—*Apoc.* xi. 15.

KINGDOM OF GOD WITHIN US, THE

All the glory of the king's daughter is within in golden borders.—*Ps.* xliv. 14.

Another parable he spoke to them: The kingdom of heaven is like to leaven, which a woman took and hid in three measures of meal, until the whole was leavened.—*Matt.* xiii. 33.

The kingdom of heaven is like unto a treasure hidden in a field. Which a man, having found, hid it, and for joy thereof goeth, and selleth all that he hath, and buyeth that field.—*Matt.* xiii. 44.

And being asked by the Pharisees, when the kingdom of God should come? he answered them, and said: The kingdom of God cometh not with observation:

Neither shall they say: Behold here, or behold there. For lo, the kingdom of God is within you.—*Luke* xvii. 20, 21.

God is a spirit; and they that adore him, must adore him in spirit and in truth.—*John* iv. 24.

For the kingdom of God is not meat and drink; but justice, and peace, and joy in the Holy Ghost.—*Rom.* xiv. 17.

KNOWLEDGE

See also: Wisdom—page 607.

Teach me goodness, and discipline and knowledge; for I have believed thy commandments.—*Ps.* cxviii. 66.

Receive my instruction, and not money: choose knowledge rather than gold.—*Prov.* viii. 10.

A man shall be known by his learning: but he that is vain and foolish, shall be exposed to contempt.—*Prov.* xii. 8.

Knowledge is a fountain of life to him that possesseth it: the instruction of fools is foolishness.—*Prov.* xvi. 22.

A wise heart shall acquire knowledge: and the ear of the wise seeketh instruction.—*Prov.* xviii. 15.

The fear of the Lord is the religiousness of knowledge.—*Ecclus.* i. 17.

I (wisdom) am the mother of fair love, and of fear, and of knowledge, and of holy hope.—*Ecclus.* xxiv. 24.

I directed my soul to her (*i. e.* wisdom), and in knowledge I found her.— *Ecclus.* li. 27.

Therefore is my people led away captive, because they had not knowledge, and their nobles have perished with famine, and their multitude were dried up with thirst.—*Is.* v. 13.

KNOWLEDGE, LITTLENESS OF MAN'S

Dost thou know when God commanded the rains, to show his light of his clouds?

Knowest thou the great paths of the clouds, and the perfect knowledges?— *Job* xxxvii. 15, 16.

Where wast thou when I laid the

foundations of the earth? tell me if thou hast understanding.

Who hath laid the measures thereof, if thou knowest? or who hath stretched the line upon it?

Upon what are its bases grounded? or who laid the cornerstone thereof? . . .

Hast thou entered into the depths of the sea, and walked in the lowest parts of the deep?

Have the gates of death been opened to thee, and hast thou seen the darksome doors?

Hast thou considered the breadth of the earth? tell me, if thou knowest all things?

Where is the way where light dwelleth, and where is the place of darkness:

That thou mayst bring every thing to its own bounds, and understand the paths of the house thereof.

Didst thou know then that thou shouldst be born? and didst thou know the number of thy days?

Hast thou entered into the storehouses of the snow, or hast thou beheld the treasures of the hail:

Which I have prepared for the time of the enemy, against the day of battle and war?

By what way is the light spread, and heat divided upon the earth?

Who gave a course to violent showers, or a way for noisy thunder:

That it should rain on the earth without man in the wilderness, where no mortal dwelleth:

That it should fill the desert and desolate land, and should bring forth green grass?

Who is the father of rain? or who begot the drops of dew?

Out of whose womb came the ice; and the frost from heaven, who hath gendered it? . . .

Dost thou know the order of heaven, and canst thou set down the reason thereof on the earth? . . .

Who hath put wisdom in the heart of man? or who gave the cock understanding? . . .

When was the dust poured on the earth, and the clods fastened together?—*Job* xxxviii. 4-6, 16-29, 33, 36, 38.

The Lord knoweth the thoughts of men, that they are vain.—*Ps.* xciii. 11.

As it is not good for a man to eat much honey, so he that is a searcher of majesty, shall be overwhelmed by glory. —*Prov.* xxv. 27.

All things are hard: man cannot explain them by word. The eye is not filled with seeing, neither is the ear filled with hearing.—*Eccles.* i. 8.

He hath made all things good in their time, and hath delivered the world to their consideration, so that man cannot find out the work which God hath made from the beginning to the end.—*Eccles.* iii. 11.

Only this I have found, that God made man right, and he hath entangled himself with an infinity of questions. Who is as the wise man? and who hath known the resolution of the word?—*Eccles.* vii. 30.

And I understood that man can find no reason of all those works of God that are done under the sun: and the more he shall labor to seek, so much the less shall he find: yea, though the wise man shall say, that he knoweth it, he shall not be able to find it.—*Eccles.* viii. 17.

A fool multiplieth words. A man cannot tell what hath been before him: and what shall be after him, who can tell him?—*Eccles.* x. 14.

As thou knowest not what is the way of the spirit, nor how the bones are joined together in the womb of her that is with child: so thou knowest not the works of God, who is the maker of all.—*Eccles.* xi. 5.

For who among men is he that can know the counsel of God? or who can think what the will of God is?

For the thoughts of mortal men are fearful, and our counsels uncertain.

For the corruptible body is a load upon the soul, and the earthly habitation presseth down the mind that museth upon many things.

And hardly do we guess aright at things that are upon the earth: and with labor do we find the things that are before us. But the things that are in heaven, who shall search out?

And who shall know thy thought, except thou give wisdom, and send thy Holy Spirit from above?—*Wis.* ix. 13-17.

Who hath numbered the sand of the sea, and the drops of rain, and the days of the world? Who hath measured the height of heaven, and the breadth of the earth, and the depth of the abyss? Who hath searched out the wisdom of God that goeth before all things?—*Ecclus.* i. 2, 3.

Seek not the things that are too high for thee, and search not into things above thy ability: but the things that God hath commanded thee, think on them always, and in many of his works, be not curious.

For it is not necessary for thee to see with thy eyes those things that are hid.

In unnecessary matters be not over curious, and in many of his works, thou shalt not be inquisitive.

For many things are shown to thee above the understanding of men.

And the suspicion of them hath deceived many, and hath detained their minds in vanity.—*Ecclus.* iii. 22-26.

O, how desirable are all his works, and what we can know is but as a spark!—*Ecclus.* xlii. 23.

What shall we be able to do to glorify him? for the Almighty himself is above all his works. . . .

There are many things hidden from us, that are greater than these: for we have seen but a few of his works.—*Ecclus.* xliii. 30, 36.

But if any man think that he knoweth any thing, he hath not yet known as he ought to know.—1 *Cor.* viii. 2.

For we know in part, and we prophesy in part.

But when that which is perfect is come, that which is in part shall be done away. . . .

We see now through a glass in a dark manner; but then face to face. Now I know in part; but then I shall know even as I am known.—1 *Cor.* xiii. 9, 10, 12.

KNOWLEDGE OF GOD, THE

See: Wisdom of God—page 607; and Omniscience of God—page 356.

KNOWS HIS OWN, GOD

I am the good shepherd; and I know mine, and mine know me.—*John* x. 14.

But if any man love God, the same is known by him.—1 *Cor.* viii. 3.

But the sure foundation of God standeth firm, having this seal: the Lord knoweth who are his; and let every one depart from iniquity who nameth the name of the Lord.—2 *Tim.* ii. 19.

LABOR

The life of a laborer that is content with what he hath, shall be sweet, and in it thou shalt find a treasure.—*Ecclus.* xl. 18.

Behold with your eyes how I have labored a little, and have found much rest to myself. . . .

Work your work before the time, and he will give you your reward in his time.—*Ecclus.* li. 35, 38.

He that stole, let him now steal no more; but rather let him labor, working with his hand the thing which is good, that he may have something to give to him that suffereth need.—*Eph.* iv. 28.

Neither did we eat any man's bread for nothing, but in labor and in toil we worked night and day, lest we should be chargeable to any of you. . . .

For also when we were with you, this we declared to you: that, if any man will not work, neither let him eat.

For we have heard that there are some among you who walk disorderly, working not at all, but curiously meddling.

Now we charge them that are such, and beseech them by the Lord Jesus Christ, that working with silence, they would eat their own bread.—2 *Thess.* iii. 8, 10-12.

LABOR A LAW OF GOD

And to Adam, he said: Because thou hast hearkened to the voice of thy wife, and hast eaten of the tree, whereof I commanded thee that thou shouldst not eat, cursed is the earth in thy work; with labor and toil shalt thou eat thereof all the days of thy life.

Thorns and thistles shall it bring forth to thee; and thou shalt eat the herbs of the earth.

In the sweat of thy face shalt thou eat bread till thou return to the earth, out of which thou wast taken: for dust thou art, and into dust thou shalt return.—*Gen.* iii. 17-19.

Man is born to labor, and the bird to fly.—*Job* v. 7.

Man shall go forth to his work, and to his labor until the evening.—*Ps.* ciii. 23.

This therefore hath seemed good to me, that a man should eat and drink, and enjoy the fruit of his labor, wherewith he hath labored under the sun, all the days of his life which God hath given him: and this is his portion.—*Eccles.* v. 17.

Hate not laborious works, nor husbandry ordained by the most High.—*Ecclus.* vii. 16.

Great labor is created for all men, and a heavy yoke is upon the children of Adam, from the day of their coming out of their mother's womb, until the day of their burial into the mother of all.—*Ecclus.* xl. 1.

LAW OF GOD, THE

See: Commandments of God— page 57.

LAW OF GOD, OBEDIENCE AND SUBMISSION TO THE

See: Commandments of God, keeping the—page 58.

LAW, THE OLD AND NEW

See: Covenant—page 83.

LAZY, THE

He that gathereth in the harvest, is a wise son: but he that snoreth in the summer, is the son of confusion.—*Prov.* x. 5.

As vinegar to the teeth, and smoke to the eyes, so is the sluggard to them that sent him.—*Prov.* x. 26.

The sluggard willeth and willeth not: but the soul of them that work, shall be made fat.—*Prov.* xiii. 4.

The way of the slothful is as a hedge of thorns; the way of the just is without offence.—*Prov.* xv. 19.

Fear casteth down the slothful: and the souls of the effeminate shall be hungry.—*Prov.* xviii. 8.

The slothful hideth his hand under his armpit, and will not so much as bring it to his mouth.—*Prov.* xix. 24.

Desires kill the slothful: for his hands have refused to work at all.

He longeth and desireth all the day: but he that is just will give, and will not cease.—*Prov.* xxi. 25. 26.

The slothful man saith: There is a lion without, I shall be slain in the midst of the streets.—*Prov.* xxii. 13.

The slothful man saith: There is a lion in the way, and a lioness in the roads.

As the door turneth upon its hinges, so doth the slothful upon his bed.

The slothful hideth his hand under his armpit, and it grieveth him to turn it to his mouth.

The sluggard is wiser in his own conceit, than seven men that speak sentences.—*Prov.* xxvi. 13-16.

The sluggard is pelted with a dirty stone and all men will speak of his disgrace.

The sluggard is pelted with the dung of oxen: and every one that toucheth him will shake his hands.—*Ecclus.* xxii. 1, 2.

LAZINESS, CONSEQUENCES OF

How long wilt thou sleep, O sluggard? when wilt thou rise out of thy sleep?

Thou wilt sleep a little, thou wilt slumber a little, thou wilt fold thy hands a little to sleep:

And want shall come upon thee, as a traveller, and poverty as a man armed. But if thou be diligent, thy harvest shall come as a fountain, and want shall flee far from thee.—*Prov.* vi. 9-11.

The slothful hand hath wrought poverty: but the hand of the industrious getteth riches.—*Prov.* x. 4.

The hand of the valiant shall bear rule: but that which is slothful, shall be under tribute.—*Prov.* xii. 24.

Slothfulness casteth into a deep sleep, and an idle soul shall suffer hunger.—*Prov.* xix. 15.

Because of the cold the sluggard would not plough: he shall beg therefore in the summer, and it shall not be given him.—*Prov.* xx. 4.

The thoughts of the industrious always bring forth abundance: but every sluggard is always in want.—*Prov.* xxi. 5.

I passed by the field of the slothful

man, and by the vineyard of the foolish man:

And behold it was all filled with nettles, and thorns had covered the face thereof, and the stone wall was broken down.

Which when I had seen, I laid it up in my heart, and by the example, I received instruction.

Thou wilt sleep a little, said I, thou wilt slumber a little, thou wilt fold thy hands a little to rest:

And poverty shall come to thee as a runner, and beggary as an armed man.—*Prov.* xxiv. 30-34.

By slothfulness a building shall be brought down, and through the weakness of hands, the house shall drop through.—*Eccles.* x. 18.

He that observeth the wind, shall not sow: and he that considereth the clouds, shall never reap.—*Eccles.* xi. 4.

LAZINESS, EXHORTATION AGAINST

Go to the ant, O sluggard, and consider her ways, and learn wisdom.—*Prov.* vi. 6.

Love not sleep, lest poverty oppress thee: open thy eyes, and be filled with bread.—*Prov.* xx. 13.

A wise man will fear in every thing, and in the days of sins, will beware of sloth.—*Ecclus.* xviii. 27.

In carefulness not slothful. In spirit fervent. Serving the Lord.—*Rom.* xii. 11.

And we desire that every one of you show forth the same carefulness to the accomplishing of hope unto the end:

That you become not slothful, but followers of them, who through faith and patience, shall inherit the promises.—*Heb.* vi. 11, 12.

LEADER, GOD OUR

In thy mercy, thou hast been a leader to the people which thou hast redeemed: and in thy strength, thou hast carried them to thy holy habitation.—*Ex.* xv. 13.

Do manfully, and be of good heart: fear not, nor be ye dismayed at their sight: for the Lord thy God, he himself is thy leader, and will not leave thee nor forsake thee. . . .

And the Lord who is your leader, he himself will be with thee: he will not leave thee nor forsake thee: fear not, neither be dismayed.—*Deut.* xxxi. 6, 8.

The Lord alone was his (the Israelite's) leader: and there was no strange god with him.—*Deut.* xxxii. 12.

Thou hast conducted thy people like sheep, by the hand of Moses and Aaron.—*Ps.* lxxvi. 21.

They wandered in a wilderness, in a place without water: they found not the way of a city for their habitation.

They were hungry and thirsty: their soul fainted in them.

And they cried to the Lord in their tribulation: and he delivered them out of their distresses.

And he led them into the right way, that they might go to a city of habitation.—*Ps.* cvi. 4-7.

Lead me into the path of thy commandments; for this same I have desired.—*Ps.* cxviii. 35.

Teach me to do thy will, for thou art my God.

Thy good spirit shall lead me into the right hand.—*Ps.* cxlii. 10.

LEADING OTHERS INTO EVIL

See also: Scandal—page 504.

For they sleep not except they have done evil: and their sleep is taken away unless they have made some to fall.—*Prov.* iv. 16.

An unjust man allureth his friend: and leadeth him into a way that is not good.—*Prov.* xvi. 29.

As vinegar upon nitre, so is he that singeth songs to a very evil heart.—*Prov.* xxv. 20.

He that diggeth a pit, shall fall into it: and he that rolleth a stone, it shall return to him.—*Prov.* xxvi. 27.

A little leaven corrupteth the whole lump.—*Gal.* v. 9.

For, speaking proud words of vanity, they allure by the desires of fleshly riotousness, those who for a little while escape, such as converse in error:

Promising them liberty, whereas they themselves are the slaves of corruption.—*2 Peter* ii. 18, 19.

LEGISLATORS, UNJUST

Woe to them that make wicked laws: and when they write, write injustice:

To oppress the poor in judgment, and do violence to the cause of the humble of my people: that widows might be their prey, and that they might rob the fatherless.

What will you do in the day of visitation, and of the calamity which cometh from afar? to whom will ye flee for help? and where will ye leave your glory?—*Is.* x. 1-3.

LIBERTY, TRUE

O Lord, for I am thy servant: I am thy servant, and the son of thy handmaid. Thou hast broken my bonds.—*Ps.* cxv. 16.

The spirit of the Lord is upon me, because the Lord hath anointed me: he hath sent me to preach to the meek, to heal the contrite of heart, and to preach a release to the captives, and deliverance to them that are shut up.—*Is.* lxi. 1.

Blessed be the Lord God of Israel; because he hath visited, and wrought the redemption of his people. . . .

That being delivered from the hand of our enemies, we may serve him without fear,

In holiness and justice before him, all our days.—*Luke* i. 68, 74, 75.

Then Jesus said to those Jews who believed him: If you continue in my word, you shall be my disciples indeed.

And you shall know the truth, and the truth shall make you free.

They answered him: We are the seed of Abraham, and we have never been slaves to any man: how sayest thou: You shall be free?

Jesus answered them: Amen, amen I say unto you: that whosoever committeth sin, is the servant of sin.

Now the servant abideth not in the house for ever; but the son abideth for ever.

If therefore the son shall make you free, you shall be free indeed.—*John* viii. 31-36.

For you have not received the spirit of bondage again in fear; but you have received the spirit of adoption of sons, whereby we cry: Abba (Father).—*Rom.* viii. 15.

Because the creature also itself shall be delivered from the servitude of cor-ruption, into the liberty of the glory of the children of God.—*Rom.* viii. 21.

For he that is called in the Lord, being a bondman, is the freeman of the Lord. Likewise, he that is called, being free, is the bondman of Christ.—1 *Cor.* vii. 22.

Now the Lord is a Spirit. And where the Spirit of the Lord is, there is liberty.—2 *Cor.* iii. 17.

So then, brethren, we are not the children of the bondwoman, but of the free: by the freedom wherewith Christ has made us free.—*Gal.* iv. 31.

But he that hath looked into the perfect law of liberty, and hath continued therein, not becoming a forgetful hearer, but a doer of the work; this man shall be blessed in his deed.—*James* i. 25.

LIBERTY, FALSE; OR LICENSE

A vain man is lifted up into pride. and thinketh himself born free like a wild ass's colt.—*Job* xi. 12.

For you, brethren, have been called unto liberty: only make not liberty an occasion to the flesh, but by charity of the spirit, serve one another.—*Gal.* v. 13.

Be ye subject, therefore, to every human creature for God's sake: whether it be to the king as excelling;

Or to governors, as sent by him for the punishment of evil doers, and for the praise of the good:

For so is the will of God, that by doing well, you may put to silence the ignorance of foolish men:

As free, and not as making liberty a cloak for malice, but as the servants of God.—1 *Peter* ii. 13-16.

For, speaking proud words of vanity, they allure by the desires of fleshly riotousness, those who for a little while escape, such as converse in error:

Promising them liberty, whereas they themselves are the slaves of corruption. For by whom a man is overcome, of the same also he is the slave.—2 *Peter* ii. 18, 19.

LIES

O ye sons of men, how long will you be dull of heart? why do you love vanity, and seek after lying?—*Ps.* iv. 3.

He that trusteth to lies, feedeth the winds: and the same runneth after birds that fly away.—*Prov.* x. 4.

Lying lips hide hatred.—*Prov.* x. 18.

The just shall hate a lying word: but the wicked confoundeth, and shall be confounded.—*Prov.* xiii. 5.

A needy man is merciful: and better is the poor than the lying man.—*Prov.* xix. 22.

The bread of lying is sweet to a man: but afterwards his mouth shall be filled with gravel.—*Prov.* xx. 17.

A man that beareth false witness against his neighbor, is like a dart and a sword and a sharp arrow.—*Prov.* xxv. 18.

Lying men shall not be mindful of her (*i.e.* wisdom): but men that speak truth, shall be found with her, and shall advance, even till they come to the sight of God.—*Ecclus.* xv. 8.

A lie is a foul blot in a man, and yet it will be continually in the mouth of men without discipline.

A thief is better than a man that is always lying: but both of them shall inherit destruction.

The manners of lying men are without honor: and their confusion is with them without ceasing.—*Ecclus.* xx. 26-28.

Three sorts my soul hateth, and I am greatly grieved at their life:

A poor man that is proud: a rich man that is a liar: an old man that is a fool, and doting.—*Ecclus.* xxv. 3, 4.

And a man shall mock his brother, and they will not speak the truth: for they have taught their tongue to speak lies: they have labored to commit iniquity.—*Jer.* ix. 5.

You are of your father, the devil, and the desires of your father you will do. He was a murderer from the beginning, and he stood not in the truth; because truth is not in him. When he speaketh a lie, he speaketh of his own: for he is a liar, and the father thereof. —*John* viii. 44.

LIES FORBIDDEN BY GOD

Thou shalt not bear false witness against thy neighbor.—*Ex.* xx. 16.

Thou shalt not receive the voice of a lie: neither shalt thou join thy hand to bear false witness for a wicked person. . . .

Thou shalt fly lying.—*Ex.* xxiii. 1, 7.

You shall not steal. You shall not lie, neither shall any man deceive his neighbor.—*Lev.* xix. 11.

LIES DISPLEASING TO GOD

Six things there are which the Lord hateth, and the seventh, his soul detesteth:

Haughty eyes, a lying tongue, hands that shed innocent blood, . . .

A deceitful witness that uttereth lies, and him that soweth discord among brethren.—*Prov.* vi. 16, 17, 19.

Lying lips are an abomination to the Lord: but they that deal faithfully please him.—*Prov.* xii. 22.

LIES, PUNISHMENT OF

Thou hatest all the workers of iniquity: thou wilt destroy all that speak a lie.—*Ps.* v. 7.

A false witness shall not be unpunished: and he that speaketh lies, shall perish.—*Prov.* xix. 9

A lying witness shall perish.—*Prov.* xxi. 28.

But Peter said: Ananias, why hath Satan tempted thy heart, that thou shouldst lie to the Holy Ghost, and by fraud keep part of the price of the land? . . .

Thou hast not lied to men, but to God.

And Ananias hearing these words, fell down, and gave up the ghost. And there came great fear upon all that heard it.—*Acts* v. 3-5.

But the fearful and unbelieving, and the abominable, and murderers, and whoremongers, and sorcerers, and idolaters, and all liars, they shall have their portion in the pool burning with fire and brimstone, which is the second death.—*Apoc.* xxi. 8.

There shall not enter into it (the new Jerusalem) any thing defiled, or that worketh abomination, or maketh a lie, but they that are written in the book of life of the Lamb.—*Apoc.* xxi. 27.

Blessed are they that wash their robes in the blood of the Lamb: that they may have a right to the tree of life, and may enter in by the gates into the city.

Without are dogs and sorcerers, and unchaste, and murderers, and servers of idols, and every one that loveth and maketh a lie.—*Apoc.* xxii. 14, 15.

LIES, EXHORTATION AGAINST

In nowise speak against the truth, but be ashamed of the lie of thy ignorance.—*Ecclus.* iv. 30.

Devise not a lie against thy brother: neither do the like against thy friend.

Be not willing to make any manner of lie: for the custom thereof is not good.—*Ecclus.* vii. 13, 14.

Wherefore putting away lying, speak ye the truth, every man with his neighbor; for we are members one of another.—*Eph.* iv. 25.

Lie not, one to another: stripping yourselves of the old man with his deeds.—*Col.* iii. 9.

But if you have bitter zeal, and there be contentions in your hearts; glory not, and be not liars against the truth.—*James* iii. 14.

LIFE, EMPTINESS OF THIS

The life of man upon earth is a warfare, and his days are like the days of a hireling.

As a servant longeth for the shade, as the hireling looketh for the end of his work;

So I also have had empty months, and have numbered to myself wearisome nights.

If I lie down to sleep, I shall say: When shall I arise? and again I shall look for the evening, and shall be filled with sorrows even till darkness.

My flesh is clothed with rottenness and the filth of dust, my skin is withered and drawn together.—*Job* vii. 1-5.

Man, born of a woman, living for a short time, is filled with many miseries.—*Job* xiv. 1.

But yet his flesh, while he shall live, shall have pain, and his soul shall mourn over him.—*Job* xiv. 22.

Surely man passeth as an image: yea, and he is disquieted in vain.

He storeth up: and he knoweth not for whom he shall gather these things. —*Ps.* xxxviii. 7.

The days of our years in them are threescore and ten years.

But if in the strong they be fourscore years: and what is more of them is labor and sorrow.—*Ps.* lxxxix. 10.

Laughter shall be mingled with sorrow, and mourning taketh hold of the end of joy.—*Prov.* xiv. 13.

Vanity of vanities, said Ecclesiastes: vanity of vanities, and all is vanity.

What hath a man more of all his labor, that he taketh under the sun? . . .

I have seen all things that are done under the sun, and behold, all is vanity, and vexation of spirit.—*Eccles.* i. 2, 3, 14.

I said in my heart: I will go, and abound with delights, and enjoy good things. And I saw that this also was vanity. . . .

And whatsoever my eyes desired, I refused them not: and I withheld not my heart from enjoying every pleasure, and delighting itself in the things which I had prepared: and esteemed this my portion, to make use of my own labor.

And when I turned myself to all the works which my hands had wrought, and to the labors wherein I had labored in vain, I saw in all things vanity, and vexation of mind, and that nothing was lasting under the sun. . . .

For what profit shall a man have of all his labor, and vexation of spirit, with which he hath been tormented under the sun?

All his days are full of sorrows and miseries, even in the night, he doth not rest in mind: and is not this vanity?— *Eccles.* ii. 1, 10, 11, 22, 23.

As he came forth naked from his mother's womb, so shall he return, and shall take nothing away with him of his labor.

A most deplorable evil: as he came, so shall he return. What then doth it profit him that he hath labored for the wind?

All the days of his life he eateth in darkness, and in many cares, and in misery and sorrow.—*Eccles.* v. 14-16.

Great labor is created for all men, and a heavy yoke is upon the children of Adam, from the day of their coming out of their mother's womb, until the day of their burial into the mother of all.

Their thoughts, and fears of the heart, their imagination of things to come, and the day of their end:

From him that sitteth on a glorious throne, unto him that is humbled in earth and ashes:

From him that weareth purple, and beareth the crown, even to him that is covered with rough linen: wrath, envy, trouble, unquietness, and the fear of death, continual anger, and strife. . . .

Such things happen to all flesh, from man even to beast, and upon sinners are sevenfold more. . . .

All things that are of the earth, shall return to the earth again, and all waters shall return to the sea.—*Ecclus.* xl. 1-4, 8, 11.

And there are some, of whom there is no memorial: who are perished, as if they had never been: and are become, as if they had never been born, and their children with them.—*Ecclus.* xliv. 9.

O Lord, if man's life be such, and the life of my spirit be in such things as these, thou shalt correct me, and make me to live.

Behold in peace is my bitterness most bitter.—*Is.* xxxviii. 16, 17.

The voice of one, saying: Cry. And I said: What shall I cry? All flesh is grass, and all the glory thereof as the flower of the field.

The grass is withered, and the flower is fallen, because the spirit of the Lord hath blown upon it. Indeed the people is grass:

The grass is withered, and the flower is fallen: but the word of our Lord endureth for ever.—*Is.* xl. 6-8.

LIFE, SHORTNESS OF THIS

After this, Joseph brought in his father to the king, and presented him before him: and he blessed him.

And being asked by him: How many are the days of the years of thy life?

He answered: The days of my pilgrimage are a hundred and thirty years, few and evil, and they are not come up to the days of the pilgrimage of my fathers.—*Gen.* xlvii. 7-9.

For we are sojourners before thee,

and strangers, as were all our fathers. Our days upon earth are as a shadow, and there is no stay.—1 *Paral.* xxix. 15.

My days have passed more swiftly than the web is cut by the weaver, and are consumed without any hope.—*Job* vii. 6.

For we are but of yesterday, and are ignorant that our days upon earth are but a shadow.—*Job* viii. 9.

My days have been swifter than a post: they have fled away, and have not seen good.

They have passed by as ships carrying fruits, as an eagle flying to the prey.—*Job* ix. 25, 26.

Shall not the fewness of my days be ended shortly? suffer me, therefore, that I may lament my sorrow a little:

Before I go, and return no more, to a land that is dark, and covered with the mist of death.—*Job* x. 20, 21.

Man, born of a woman, living for a short time, is filled with many miseries.

Who cometh forth like a flower, and is destroyed, and fleeth as a shadow, and never continueth in the same state. . . .

The days of man are short, and the number of his months is with thee: thou hast appointed his bounds which cannot be passed. . . .

Thou hast strengthened him for a little while, that he may pass away for ever: thou shalt change his face, and shalt send him away.—*Job* xiv. 1, 2, 5, 20.

For behold, short years pass by, and I am walking in a path by which I shall not return.—*Job* xvi. 23.

I spoke with my tongue: O Lord, make me know my end.

And what is the number of my days: that I may know what is wanting to me.

Behold, thou hast made my days measurable: and my substance is as nothing before thee. . . .

Surely man passeth as an image: yea, and he is disquieted in vain.—*Ps.* xxxviii. 5-7.

In the morning, man shall grow up like grass; in the morning, he shall flourish and pass away: in the evening he shall fall, grow dry, and wither. . . .

Our years shall be considered as a

spider: the days of our years in them are threescore and ten years.

But if in the strong, they be fourscore years: and what is more of them is labor and sorrow.—*Ps.* lxxxix. 6, 9, 10.

Man's days are as grass, as the flower of the field, so shall he flourish.

For the spirit shall pass in him, and he shall not be: and he shall know his place no more.—*Ps.* cii. 15, 16.

Man is like to vanity: his days pass away like a shadow.—*Ps.* cxliii. 4.

For our time is as the passing of a shadow, and there is no going back of our end: for it is fast sealed, and no man returneth.—*Wis.* ii. 5.

What hath pride profited us? or what advantage hath the boasting of riches brought us?

All those things are passed away like a shadow, and like a post that runneth on,

And as a ship that passeth through the waves: whereof when it is gone by, the trace cannot be found, nor the path of its keel in the waters:

Or as when a bird flieth through the air, of the passage of which no mark can be found, but only the sound of the wings beating the light air, and parting it by the force of her flight; she moved her wings, and hath flown through, and there is no mark found afterwards of her way:

Or as when an arrow is shot at a mark, the divided air presently cometh together again, so that the passage thereof is not known:

So we also being born, forthwith ceased to be: and have been able to show no mark of virtue: but are consumed in our wickedness.

Such things as these the sinners said in hell.—*Wis.* v. 8-14.

And of the same clay, by a vain labor, he maketh a god: he who a little before was made of earth himself, and a little after, returneth to the same out of which he was taken, when his life, which was lent him, shall be called for again.—*Wis.* xv. 8.

All flesh shall fade as grass, and as the leaf that springeth out on a green tree.

Some grow, and some fall off: so is the generation of flesh and blood, one cometh to an end, and another is born.—*Ecclus.* xiv. 18, 19.

The number of the days of men at the most are a hundred years: as a drop of water of the sea are they esteemed: and as a pebble of the sand, so are a few years compared to eternity.—*Ecclus.* xviii. 8.

From the morning until the evening, the time shall be changed, and all these are swift in the eyes of God.—*Ecclus.* xviii. 26.

I said: In the midst of my days I shall go to the gates of hell: I sought for the residue of my years. . . .

My generation is at an end, and it is rolled away from me, as a shepherd's tent. My life is cut off, as by a weaver: whilst I was yet but beginning, he cut me off: from morning even to night, thou wilt make an end of me.—*Is.* xxxviii. 10, 12.

This therefore I say, brethren: The time is short; it remaineth that they also who have wives, be as if they had none;

And they that weep, as though they wept not; and they that rejoice, as if they rejoiced not; and they that buy, as though they possessed not;

And they that use this world, as if they used it not: for the fashion of this world passeth away.—*1 Cor.* vii. 29-31.

But let the brother of low condition glory in his exaltation:

And the rich, in his being low; because as the flower of the grass shall he pass away.

For the sun rose with a burning heat, and parched the grass, and the flower thereof fell off, and the beauty of the shape thereof perished: so also shall the rich man fade away in his ways.—*James* i. 9-11.

For what is your life? It is a vapor, which appeareth for a little while, and afterwards shall vanish away.—*James* iv. 15.

For all flesh is as grass; and all the glory thereof as the flower of grass. The grass is withered, and the flower thereof is fallen away.—*1 Peter* i. 24.

LIFE, UNCERTAINTY OF THIS

See also: Death, uncertainty of the time of—page 98.

If I lie down to sleep, I shall say: When shall I arise? and again I shall look for the evening, and shall be filled with sorrows even till darkness.—*Job* vii. 4.

For I know not how long I shall continue, and whether, after a while, my Maker may take me away.—*Job* xxxii. 22.

I spoke with my tongue: O Lord, make me know my end.

And what is the number of my days: that I may know what is wanting to me.—*Ps.* xxxviii. 5.

Boast not for to-morrow, for thou knowest not what the day to come may bring forth.—*Prov.* xxvii. 1.

Behold now, you that say: To-day or to-morrow we will go into such a city, and there we will spend a year, and will traffic, and make our gain.

Whereas you know not what shall be on the morrow.

For what is your life? It is a vapor which appeareth for a little while, and afterwards shall vanish away. For that you should say: If the Lord will, and if we shall live, we will do this or that. —*James* iv. 13-15.

LIFE A WARFARE, THIS

See: Heaven, we must fight and work to gain—page 199.

LIFE A PILGRIMAGE ON EARTH

And (Jacob) being asked by him (Pharao): How many are the days of the years of thy life?

He answered: The days of my pilgrimage are a hundred and thirty years, few and evil, and they are not come up to the days of the pilgrimage of my fathers.—*Gen.* xlvii. 8, 9.

For we are sojourners before thee, and strangers, as were all our fathers. Our days upon earth are as a shadow, and there is no stay.—1 *Paral.* xxix. 15.

Hear my prayer, O Lord, and my supplication: give ear to my tears.

Be not silent: for I am a stranger with thee, and a sojourner, as all my fathers were.—*Ps.* xxxviii. 13.

I am a sojourner on the earth: hide not thy commandments from me.—*Ps.* cxviii. 19.

Woe is me, that my sojourning is prolonged! I have dwelt with the inhabitants of Cedar: my soul hath been long a sojourner.—*Ps.* cxix. 5.

What needeth a man to seek things that are above him, whereas he knoweth not what is profitable for him in his life, in all the days of his pilgrimage, and the time that passeth like a shadow?—*Eccles.* vii. 1.

Arise ye, and depart, for there is no rest here for you.—*Mich.* ii. 10.

All these died according to faith, not having received the promises, but beholding them afar off, and saluting them, and confessing that they are pilgrims and strangers on the earth.

For they that say these things, do signify that they seek a country.—*Heb.* xi. 13, 14.

For we have not here a lasting city, but we seek one that is to come.—*Heb.* xiii. 14.

Dearly beloved, I beseech you as strangers and pilgrims, to refrain yourselves from carnal desires, which war against the soul.—1 *Peter* ii. 11.

LIFE OF SUFFERING, A

So going in, he (the angel) saluted him, and said: Joy be to thee always.

And Tobias said: What manner of joy shall be to me, who sit in darkness, and see not the light of heaven?

And the young man said to him: Be of good courage, thy cure from God is at hand.—*Tob.* v. 11-13.

Why is light given to him that is in misery, and life to them that are in bitterness of soul?

That look for death, and it cometh not, as they that dig for a treasure:

And they rejoice exceedingly, when they have found the grave.

To a man whose way is hidden, and God hath surrounded him with darkness?—*Job* iii. 20-23.

LIFE THE TIME FOR GAINING MERIT AND WORKING FOR HEAVEN

For there is no one in death that is mindful of thee: and who shall confess to thee in hell?—*Ps.* vi. 6.

I will sing to the Lord, as long as I

live: I will sing praise to my God while I have my being.—*Ps.* ciii. 33.

The dead shall not praise thee, O Lord; nor any of them that go down to hell.

But we that live bless the Lord: from this time now and for ever.—*Ps.* cxiii. (*Heb.* cxv.) 17, 18.

I will please the Lord in the land of the living.—*Ps.* cxiv. 9.

If the tree fall to the south or to the north, in what place soever it shall fall, there shall it be.—*Eccles.* xi. 3.

For hell shall not confess to thee, neither shall death praise thee: nor shall they that go down into the pit, look for thy truth.

The living, the living, he shall give praise to thee, as I do this day.—*Is.* xxxviii. 18, 19.

Look down upon us, O Lord, from thy holy house, and incline thy ear, and hear us.

Open thy eyes, and behold: for the dead that are in hell, whose spirit is taken away from their bowels, shall not give glory and justice to the Lord:

But the soul that is sorrowful for the greatness of evil she hath done, and goeth bowed down, and feeble, and the eyes that fail, and the hungry soul giveth glory and justice to thee, the Lord.—*Bar.* ii. 16-18.

I must work the works of him that sent me, whilst it is day: the night cometh when no man can work.—*John* ix. 4.

Jesus answered: Are there not twelve hours of the day? If a man walk in the day, he stumbleth not, because he seeth the light of this world:

But if he walk in the night, he stumbleth, because the light is not in him.—*John* xi. 9, 10.

And we helping, do exhort you, that you receive not the grace of God in vain.

For he saith: In an accepted time have I heard thee; and in the day of salvation have I helped thee. Behold, now is the acceptable time; behold, now is the day of salvation.—*2 Cor.* vi. 1, 2.

And I heard a voice from heaven, saying to me: Write: Blessed are the dead, who die in the Lord. From henceforth, now, saith the Spirit, that they may rest from their labors; for their works follow them.—*Apoc.* xiv. 13.

LIFE, EXHORTATION TO DO GOOD IN THIS

Do good to thy friend before thou die, and according to thy ability, stretching out thy hand, give to the poor.

Defraud not thyself of the good day, and let not the part of a good gift overpass thee. . . .

Before thy death, work justice: for in hell there is no finding food.—*Ecclus.* xiv. 13, 14, 17.

Tarry not in the error of the ungodly, give glory before death. Praise perisheth from the dead as nothing.

Give thanks whilst thou art living, whilst thou art alive and in health thou shalt give thanks, and shalt praise God, and shalt glory in his mercies.—*Ecclus.* xvii. 26, 27.

Work your work before the time, and he will give you your reward in his time.—*Ecclus.* li. 38.

Seek ye the Lord while he may be found: call upon him while he is near.—*Is.* lv. 6.

Give ye glory to the Lord your God, before it be dark, and before your feet stumble upon the dark mountains: you shall look for light, and he will turn it into the shadow of death, and into darkness.—*Jer.* xiii. 16.

Sow for yourselves in justice, and reap in the mouth of mercy, break up your fallow ground: but the time to seek the Lord is, when he shall come that shall teach you justice.—*Osee* x. 12.

Seek the Lord, all ye meek of the earth, you that have wrought his judgment: seek the just, seek the meek: if by any means, you may be hid in the day of the Lord's indignation.—*Soph.* ii. 3.

Jesus therefore said to them: Yet a little while the light is among you. Walk whilst you have the light, that the darkness overtake you not. And he that walketh in darkness, knoweth not whither he goeth.

Whilst you have the light, believe in the light, that you may be the children of light.—*John* xii. 35, 36.

And that knowing the season; that it is now the hour for us to rise from sleep. For now our salvation is nearer than when we believed.

The night is passed, and the day is at hand. Let us therefore cast off the works of darkness, and put on the armor of light.—*Rom.* xiii. 11, 12.

And in doing good, let us not fail. For in due time, we shall reap, not failing.

Therefore, whilst we have time, let us work good to all men, but especially to those who are of the household of the faith.—*Gal.* vi. 9, 10.

Charge the rich of this world. . . . To do good, to be rich in good works, to give easily, to communicate to others,

To lay up in store for themselves a good foundation against the time to come, that they may lay hold on the true life.—1 *Tim.* vi. 18, 19.

But exhort one another every day, whilst it is called to-day, that none of you be hardened through the deceitfulness of sin.—*Heb.* iii. 13.

LIFE USELESS AND VOID OF GOOD, A

See also: Omission, sins of—page 352.

All the foolish of the earth were troubled. They have slept their sleep; and all the men of riches have found nothing in their hands.—*Ps.* lxxv. 6.

And their days were consumed in vanity, and their years in haste.—*Ps.* lxxvii. 33.

So we also being born, forthwith ceased to be: and have been able to show no mark of virtue: but are consumed in our wickedness.

Such things as these the sinners said in hell.—*Wis.* v. 13, 14.

Thou shalt not appear empty in the sight of the Lord.—*Ecclus.* xxxv. 6.

We have conceived, and been, as it were, in labor, and have brought forth wind: we have not wrought salvation on the earth.—*Is.* xxvi. 18.

And this is the writing that is written: Mane, Thecel, Phares. . . .

Thecel: thou art weighed in the balance, and art found wanting.—*Dan.* v. 25, 27.

Every tree that bringeth not forth good fruit, shall be cut down, and shall be cast into the fire.—*Matt.* vii. 19.

And in the morning, returning into the city, he was hungry.

And seeing a certain fig-tree by the wayside, he came to it, and found nothing on it but leaves only, and he saith to it: May no fruit grow on thee henceforward for ever. And immediately the fig-tree withered away.—*Matt.* xxi. 18, 19.

For even as a man going into a far country, called his servants, and delivered to them his goods:

And to one he gave five talents, and to another, two, and to another, one, to every one according to his proper ability: and immediately he took his journey. . . .

But he that had received the one, going his way, digged into the earth, and hid his lord's money. . . .

And his lord answering, said to him: Wicked and slothful servant, thou knewest that I reap where I sow not, and gather where I have not strewed:

Thou oughtest therefore to have committed my money to the bankers, and at my coming, I should have received my own with usury.

Take ye away therefore the talent from him, and give it to him that hath ten talents.

For to every one that hath, shall be given, and he shall abound: but from him that hath not, that also which he seemeth to have shall be taken away.

And the unprofitable servant cast ye out into the exterior darkness. There shall be weeping and gnashing of teeth. —*Matt.* xxv. 14, 15, 18, 26-30.

And to the angel of the church of Sardis write: These things saith he, that hath the seven spirits of God, and the seven stars: I know thy works, that thou hast the name of being alive: and thou art dead.

Be watchful, and strengthen the things that remain, which are ready to die. For I find not thy works full before my God.—*Apoc.* iii. 1, 2.

LIFE OF A CHRISTIAN, THE

I have glorified thee on the earth; I have finished the work which thou gavest me to do.—*John* xvii. 4.

Now if we be dead with Christ, we believe that we shall live also together with Christ. . . .

So do you also reckon, that you are dead to sin, but alive unto God, in Christ Jesus our Lord.—*Rom.* vi. 8, 11.

There is now therefore no condemnation to them that are in Christ Jesus, who walk not according to the flesh. . . .

For they that are according to the flesh, mind the things that are of the flesh; but they that are according to the spirit, mind the things that are of the spirit.—*Rom.* viii. 1, 5.

Therefore, my beloved brethren, be ye steadfast and unmovable; always abounding in the work of the Lord, knowing that your labor is not in vain in the Lord.—1 *Cor.* xv. 58.

For I, through the law, am dead to the law, that I may live to God: with Christ I am nailed to the cross.

And I live, now not I; but Christ liveth in me. And that I live now in the flesh: I live in the faith of the Son of God, who loved me, and delivered himself for me.—*Gal.* ii. 19, 20.

Therefore we also, from the day that we heard it, cease not to pray for you, and to beg that you may be filled with the knowledge of his will, in all wisdom, and spiritual understanding:

That you may walk worthy of God, in all things pleasing; being fruitful in every good work, and increasing in the knowledge of God:

Strengthened with all might, according to the power of his glory, in all patience and longsuffering with joy,

Giving thanks to God the Father, who hath made us worthy to be partakers of the lot of the saints in light. —*Col.* i. 9-12.

For you are dead; and your life is hid with Christ in God.

When Christ shall appear, who is your life, then you also shall appear with him in glory.—*Col.* iii. 3, 4.

I have fought a good fight, I have finished my course, I have kept the faith.

As to the rest, there is laid up for me a crown of justice, which the Lord, the just judge, will render to me in that day: and not only to me, but to them also that love his coming.—2 *Tim.* iv. 7, 8.

For the grace of God our Saviour hath appeared to all men;

Instructing us, that, denying ungodliness and worldly desires, we should live soberly, and justly, and godly in this world,

Looking for the blessed hope and coming of the glory of the great God and our Saviour Jesus Christ,

Who gave himself for us, that he might redeem us from all iniquity, and might cleanse to himself a people acceptable, a pursuer of good works.— *Titus* ii. 11-14.

Dearly beloved, I beseech you as strangers and pilgrims, to refrain yourselves from carnal desires which war against the soul,

Having your conversation good among the Gentiles: that whereas they speak against you as evil-doers, they may, by the good works, which they shall behold in you, glorify God in the day of visitation.—1 *Peter* ii. 11, 12.

And you, employing all care, minister in your faith, virtue; and in virtue, knowledge;

And in knowledge, abstinence; and in abstinence, patience; and in patience, godliness;

And in godliness, love of brotherhood; and in love of brotherhood, charity.

For if these things be with you, and abound, they will make you to be neither empty nor unfruitful in the knowledge of our Lord Jesus Christ.— 2 *Peter* i. 5-8.

LIFE, WE CANNOT BE NEUTRAL IN THE BATTLE OF

See: Neutral in the battle of life—page 343.

LIFE, GOD OUR

And that thou mayst love the Lord thy God, and obey his voice, and adhere to him (for he is thy life, and the length of thy days).—*Deut.* xxx. 20.

For with thee is the fountain of life; and in thy light we shall see light.— *Ps.* xxxv. 10.

For he is not the God of the dead,

but of the living: for all live to him.—
Luke xx. 38.

Neither is he served with men's hands, as though he needed anything; seeing it is he who giveth to all life, and breath, and all things. . . .

For in him we live and move, and are. —*Acts* xvii. 25, 28.

LIFE, CHRIST OUR

In him was life, and the life was the light of men.—*John* i. 4.

The thief cometh not, but for to steal, and to kill, and to destroy. I am come that they may have life, and may have it more abundantly.—*John* x. 10.

Jesus said to her (Martha): I am the resurrection and the life: he that believeth in me, although he be dead, shall live.—*John* xi. 25.

Jesus saith to him (Thomas): I am the way, and the truth, and the life.—*John* xiv. 6.

But the author of life you killed, whom God hath raised from the dead, of which we are witnesses.—*Acts* iii. 15.

And I live, now not I; but Christ liveth in me.—*Gal.* ii. 20.

When Christ shall appear, who is your life, then you also shall appear with him in glory.—*Col.* iii. 4.

For the life was manifested; and we have seen, and do bear witness, and declare unto you the life eternal, which was with the Father, and hath appeared to us.—*1 John* i. 2.

And this is the testimony, that God hath given to us eternal life. And this life is in his Son.

He that hath the Son, hath life. He that hath not the Son, hath not life. —*1 John* v. 11, 12.

LIGHT, GOD OUR

For thou art my lamp, O Lord; and thou, O Lord, wilt enlighten my darkness.—*2 Kings* xxii. 29.

The light of thy countenance, O Lord, is signed upon us: thou hast given gladness in my heart.—*Ps.* iv. 7.

The Lord is my light and my salvation, whom shall I fear?—*Ps.* xxvi. 1.

Come ye to him, and be enlightened: and your faces shall not be confounded. —*Ps.* xxxiii. 6.

Blessed is the people that knoweth jubilation.

They shall walk, O Lord, in the light of thy countenance.—*Ps.* lxxxviii. 16.

Blessed is he that is conversant in these good things: and he that layeth them up in his heart, shall be wise always.

For if he do them, he shall be strong to do all things: because the light of God guideth his steps.—*Ecclus.* l. 30, 31.

Rejoice not, thou, my enemy, over me, because I am fallen: I shall arise, when I sit in darkness, the Lord is my light.—*Mich.* vii. 8.

LIGHT OF THE WORLD, GOD THE

For with thee is the fountain of life; and in thy light, we shall see light.— *Ps.* xxxv. 10.

Thou enlightenest wonderfully from the everlasting hills.—*Ps.* lxxv. 5.

The Lord enlighteneth the blind.— *Ps.* cxlv. 8.

And he (Samuel) was known to be faithful in his words, because he saw the God of light.—*Ecclus.* xlvi. 18.

For God, who commanded the light to shine out of darkness, hath shined in our hearts, to give the light of the knowledge of the glory of God, in the face of Christ Jesus.—*2 Cor.* iv. 6.

And this is the declaration which we have heard from him, and declare unto you: That God is light, and in him there is no darkness.—*1 John* i. 5.

LIGHT OF THE WORLD, CHRIST THE

And I have given thee for a covenant of the people, for a light of the Gentiles:

That thou mightest open the eyes of the blind, and bring forth the prisoner out of prison, and them that sit in darkness out of the prison house.—*Is.* xlii. 6, 7.

Arise, be enlightened, O Jerusalem: for thy light is come, and the glory of the Lord is risen upon thee.

For behold darkness shall cover the earth, and a mist the people: but the Lord shall arise upon thee, and his glory shall be seen upon thee.

And the Gentiles shall walk in thy light, and kings in the brightness of thy rising.—*Is.* lx. 1-3.

For Sion's sake I will not hold my peace, and for the sake of Jerusalem, I will not rest till her just one come forth as brightness, and her saviour be lighted as a lamp.—*Is.* lxii. 1.

And leaving the city Nazareth, he came and dwelt in Capharnaum on the sea coast, in the borders of Zabulon and of Nephthalim;

That it might be fulfilled which was said by Isaias the prophet:

Land of Zabulon and land of Nephthalim, the way of the sea beyond the Jordan, Galilee of the Gentiles:

The people that sat in darkness, hath seen great light: and to them that sat in the region of the shadow of death, light is sprung up.—*Matt.* iv. 13-16.

Through the bowels of the mercy of our God, in which the Orient from on high hath visited us:

To enlighten them that sit in darkness, and in the shadow of death: to direct our feet into the way of peace.— *Luke* i. 78, 79.

Now thou dost dismiss thy servant, O Lord, according to thy word in peace;

Because my eyes have seen thy salvation,

Which thou hast prepared before the face of all peoples:

A light to the revelation of the Gentiles, and the glory of thy people Israel.—*Luke* ii. 29-32.

In him was life, and the life was the light of men.

And the light shineth in darkness, and the darkness did not comprehend it. . . .

That was the true light, which enlighteneth every man that cometh into this world.—*John* i. 4, 5, 9.

And this is the judgment: because the light is come into the world, and men loved darkness rather than the light: for their works were evil.—*John* iii. 19.

Again therefore Jesus spoke to them, saying: I am the light of the world: he that followeth me, walketh not in darkness, but shall have the light of life.—*John* viii. 12.

As long as I am in the world, I am the light of the world.—*John* ix. 5.

Jesus therefore said to them: Yet a little while, the light is among you. Walk whilst you have the light, that the darkness overtake you not. And he that walketh in darkness, knoweth not whither he goeth.

Whilst you have the light, believe in the light, that you may be the children of light. . . .

I am come a light into the world; that whosoever believeth in me, may not remain in darkness.—*John* xii. 35, 36, 46.

Wherefore he saith: Rise, thou that sleepest, and arise from the dead; and Christ shall enlighten thee.—*Eph.* v. 14.

LIGHT, WE ARE CHILDREN OF THE

Whilst you have the light, believe in the light, that you may be the children of light.—*John* xii. 36.

For you were heretofore darkness, but now light in the Lord. Walk then as children of the light.

For the fruit of the light is in all goodness, and justice, and truth.—*Eph.* v. 8, 9.

But you, brethren, are not in darkness, that that day should overtake you as a thief.

For all you are the children of light, and children of the day: we are not of the night, nor of darkness.

Therefore let us not sleep, as others do; but let us watch, and be sober.— 1 *Thess.* v. 4-6.

LIGHT, WE MUST WALK IN THE

O house of Jacob, come ye, and let us walk in the light of the Lord.—*Is.* ii. 5.

For you were heretofore darkness, but now light in the Lord. Walk then as children of the light.

For the fruit of the light is in all goodness, and justice, and truth;

Proving what is well pleasing to God; And have no fellowship with the unfruitful works of darkness, but rather reprove them.—*Eph.* v. 8-11.

And this is the declaration which we have heard from him, and declare unto you: That God is light, and in him there is no darkness.

If we say that we have fellowship with him, and walk in darkness, we lie, and do not the truth.

But if we walk in the light, as he also is in the light, we have fellowship one with another, and the blood of Jesus Christ, his Son cleanseth us from all sin.—1 *John* i. 5-7.

LIGHT OF FAITH, THE

In his hands he hideth the light, and commandeth it to come again.

He showeth his friend concerning it, that it is his possession, and that he may come up to it.—*Job* xxxvi. 32, 33.

Send forth thy light and thy truth: they have conducted me, and brought me unto thy holy hill, and into thy tabernacles.—*Ps.* xlii. 3.

For behold thou hast loved truth: the uncertain and hidden things of thy wisdom thou hast made manifest to me.—*Ps.* l. 8.

Thy word is a lamp to my feet, and a light to my paths.—*Ps.* cxviii. 105.

I made that in the heavens there should rise light that never faileth. . . .

I am the mother of fair love, and of fear, and of knowledge, and of holy hope.

In me is all grace of the way and of the truth, in me is all hope of life and of virtue.

Come over to me, all ye that desire me, and be filled with my fruits. . . .

He that hearkeneth to me, shall not be confounded: and they that work by me, shall not sin. . . .

For her thoughts are more vast than the sea, and her counsels more deep than the great ocean. . . .

For I make doctrine to shine forth to all as the morning light, and I will declare it afar off.

I will penetrate to all the lower parts of the earth, and will behold all that sleep, and will enlighten all that hope in the Lord.

I will yet pour out doctrine as prophecy, and will leave it to them that seek wisdom, and will not cease to instruct their offspring even to the holy age.—*Ecclus.* xxiv. 6, 24-26, 30, 39, 44-46.

Delivering thee from the people, and from the nations, unto which now I send thee:

To open their eyes, that they may be converted from darkness to light, and from the power of Satan to God, that they may receive forgiveness of sins, and a lot among the saints, by the faith that is in me.—*Acts* xxvi. 17, 18.

For God, who commanded the light to shine out of darkness, hath shined in our hearts, to give the light of the knowledge of the glory of God, in the face of Christ Jesus.—2 *Cor.* iv. 6.

And we have the more firm prophetical word: whereunto you do well to attend, as to a light that shineth in a dark place, until the day dawn, and the day star arise in your hearts.—2 *Peter* i. 19.

Again a new commandment I write unto you, which thing is true both in him and in you; because the darkness is passed, and the true light now shineth.—1 *John* ii. 8.

LIGHT, SINNING AGAINST THE

See: Blindness, wilful—page 39.

LIGHT, A PRAYER FOR

Consider, and hear me, O Lord my God.

Enlighten my eyes, that I never sleep in death: lest at any time my enemy say: I have prevailed against him.—*Ps.* xii. 4, 5.

For thou lightest my lamp, O Lord: O my God, enlighten my darkness.—*Ps.* xvii. 29.

Show, O Lord, thy ways to me, and teach me thy paths.

Direct me in thy truth, and teach me; for thou art God, my Saviour; and on thee have I waited all the day long.—*Ps.* xxiv. 4, 5.

Send forth thy light and thy truth: they have conducted me, and brought me unto thy holy hill, and into thy tabernacles.—*Ps.* xlii. 3.

May God have mercy on us, and bless us: may he cause the light of his countenance to shine upon us, and may he have mercy on us.

That we may know thy way upon earth: thy salvation in all nations.—*Ps.* lxvi. 2, 3.

Blessed art thou, O Lord: teach me thy justifications. . . .

Open thou my eyes: and I will consider the wondrous things of thy law. . . .

Make me to understand the way of thy justifications: and I shall be exercised in thy wondrous works. . . .

Give me understanding, and I will search thy law; and I will keep it with my whole heart. . . . .

Make thy face to shine upon thy servant: and teach me thy justifications. . . .

Thy testimonies are justice for ever: give me understanding, and I shall live. —*Ps.* cxviii. 12, 18, 27, 34, 135, 144.

Make the way known to me wherein I should walk: for I have lifted up my soul to thee. . . .

Teach me to do thy will, for thou art my God.—*Ps.* cxlii. 8, 10.

And Jesus stood and called ¹them, and said: What will ye that I do to you?

They say to him: Lord, that our eyes be opened.—*Matt.* xx. 32, 33.

And Jesus standing, commanded ²him to be brought unto him. And when he was come near, he asked him,

Saying: What wilt thou that I do to thee? But he said: Lord, that I may see.—*Luke* xviii. 40, 41.

LIGHT TO KNOW OUR SINS, A PRAYER FOR

How many are my iniquities and sins? make me know my crimes and offences.—*Job* xiii. 23.

LISTEN TO US, A PRAYER THAT GOD WILL

See: Prayer—page 398.

LISTENING TO THE VOICE OF GOD

And the Lord came and stood: and he called, as he had called the other times: Samuel, Samuel. And Samuel said: Speak, Lord, for thy servant heareth.—1 *Kings* iii. 10.

Hear, O my people, and I will speak:

¹The two blind men of Jericho.
²The blind man of Jericho.

O Israel, and I will testify to thee: I am God, thy God.—*Ps.* xlix. 7.

I will hear what the Lord God will speak in me: for he will speak peace unto his people:

And unto his saints: and unto them that are converted to the heart.—*Ps.* lxxxiv. 9.

To-day, if you shall hear his voice, harden not your hearts:

As in the provocation, according to the day of temptation in the wilderness: where your fathers tempted me, they proved me, and saw my works.—*Ps.* xciv. 8, 9.

Behold, I stand at the gate, and knock. If any man shall hear my voice, and open to me the door, I will come in to him, and will sup with him, and he with me.—*Apoc.* iii. 20.

LITTLE THINGS, FIDELITY IN

He that contemneth small things, shall fall by little and little.—*Ecclus.* xix. 1.

For amen, I say unto you, till heaven and earth pass, one jot, or one tittle shall not pass of the law, till all be fulfilled.

He therefore that shall break one of these least commandments, and shall so teach men, shall be called the least in the kingdom of heaven. But he that shall do and teach, he shall be called great in the kingdom of heaven.— *Matt.* v. 18, 19.

His lord said to him: Well done, good and faithful servant, because thou hast been faithful over a few things, I will place thee over many things: enter thou into the joy of thy lord. —*Matt.* xxv. 21.

He that is faithful in that which is least, is faithful also in that which is greater: and he that is unjust in that which is little, is unjust also in that which is greater.—*Luke* xvi. 10.

And he said to him: Well done, thou good servant, because thou hast been faithful in a little, thou shalt have power over ten cities.—*Luke* xix. 17.

LITTLENESS OF MAN'S KNOWLEDGE

See: Knowledge—page 272.

LIVE FOR GOD, WE SHOULD

And to him my soul shall live: and my seed shall serve him.—*Ps.* xxi. 31.

And Christ died for all; that they also who live, may not now live to themselves, but unto him who died for them, and rose again.—*2 Cor.* v. 15.

LIVING IN US, CHRIST

See: Life, Christ our—page 286.

LIVING IN US, GOD

See: Dwelling in us, God—page 119.

LONGSUFFERING OF GOD, THE

See: Patience of God, the—page 370.

LOOK TO GOD IN ALL OUR NEEDS, WE SHOULD

My eyes are ever towards the Lord: for he shall pluck my feet out of the snare.—*Ps.* xxiv. 15.

Cast thy care upon the Lord, and he shall sustain thee: he shall not suffer the just to waver for ever.—*Ps.* liv. 23.

In all thy ways, think on him, and he will direct thy steps.—*Prov.* iii. 6.

Lay open thy works to the Lord: and thy thoughts shall be directed.—*Prov.* xvi. 3.

The soul of him that feareth the Lord, is blessed.

To whom doth he look, and who is his strength?—*Ecclus.* xxxiv. 17, 18.

In that day man shall bow down himself to his Maker, and his eyes shall look to the Holy One of Israel.—*Is.* xvii. 7.

LOOK DOWN UPON US IN PITY, A PRAYER THAT GOD WILL

See: Prayer—page 411.

LORD'S DAY, KEEPING HOLY THE

And on the seventh day God ended his work which he had made: and he rested on the seventh day from all his work which he had done.

And he blessed the seventh day, and sanctified it: because in it he had rested from all his work which God created and made.—*Gen.* ii. 2, 3.

Remember that thou keep holy the sabbath day.

Six days shalt thou labor, and shalt do all thy works.

But on the seventh day is the sabbath of the Lord thy God: thou shalt do no work on it, thou nor thy son, nor thy daughter, nor thy man-servant, nor thy maid-servant, nor thy beast, nor the stranger that is within thy gates.

For in six days the Lord made heaven and earth, and the sea, and all things that are in them, and rested on the seventh day: therefore the Lord blessed the seventh day, and sanctified it.—*Ex.* xx. 8-11.

Speak to the children of Israel, and thou shalt say to them: See that thou keep my sabbath: because it is a sign between me and you in your generations: that you may know that I am the Lord, who sanctify you.

Keep you my sabbath: for it is holy unto you: he that shall profane it, shall be put to death: he that shall do any work in it, his soul shall perish out of the midst of his people.

Six days shall you do work: in the seventh day is the sabbath, the rest holy to the Lord. Every one that shall do any work on this day, shall die.

Let the children of Israel keep the sabbath, and celebrate it in their generations. It is an everlasting covenant Between me and the children of Israel, and a perpetual sign. For in six days the Lord made heaven and earth, and in the seventh, he ceased from work.—*Ex.* xxxi. 13-17.

Six days shall ye do work: the seventh day, because it is the rest of the sabbath, shall be called holy. You shall do no work on that day: it is the sabbath of the Lord in all your habitations. —*Lev.* xxiii. 3.

Observe the day of the sabbath, to sanctify it, as the Lord thy God hath commanded thee.

Six days shalt thou labor, and shalt do all thy works.

The seventh is the day of the sabbath, that is, the rest of the Lord thy God. Thou shalt not do any work therein, thou nor thy son, nor thy daughter, nor thy man-servant nor thy maid-servant, nor thy ox, nor thy ass, nor any of thy beasts, nor the stranger that is within thy gates: that thy man-servant and thy maid-servant may rest, even as thyself.

Remember that thou also didst serve in Egypt, and the Lord thy God brought thee out from thence with a strong hand, and a stretched out arm. Therefore hath he commanded thee that thou shouldst observe the sabbath day.—*Deut.* v. 12-15.

And if the people of the land bring in things to sell, or any things for use, to sell them on the sabbath day, that we would not buy them of them on the sabbath, or on the holy day.—2 *Esd.* x. 31.

If thou turn away thy foot from the sabbath, from doing thy own will in my holy day, and call the sabbath delightful, and the holy of the Lord glorious, and glorify him, while thou dost not thy own ways, and thy own will is not found, to speak a word:

Then shalt thou be delighted in the Lord, and I will lift thee up above the high places of the earth, and will feed thee with the inheritance of Jacob thy father. For the mouth of the Lord hath spoken it.—*Is.* lviii. 13, 14.

Thus saith the Lord: Take heed to your souls, and carry no burdens on the sabbath day: and bring them not in by the gates of Jerusalem.

And do not bring burdens out of your houses on the sabbath day, neither do ye any work: sanctify the sabbath day, as I commanded your fathers.—*Jer.* xvii. 21, 22.

But he (Jesus) said to them: What man shall there be among you, that hath one sheep: and if the same fall into a pit on the sabbath day, will he not take hold on it, and lift it up?

How much better is a man than a sheep? Therefore it is lawful to do a good deed on the sabbath days.—*Matt.* xii. 11, 12.

And he (Jesus) said to them: The sabbath was made for man, and not man for the sabbath.

Therefore the Son of man is Lord of the sabbath also.—*Mark* ii. 27, 28.

LOVE FOR US, GOD'S

What is a man that thou shouldst magnify him? or why dost thou set thy heart upon him?—*Job* vii. 17.

For the Lord is well pleased with his people: and he will exalt the meek unto salvation.—*Ps.* cxlix. 4.

For thou lovest all things that are, and hatest none of the things which thou hast made: for thou didst not appoint, or make any thing, hating it. . . .

But thou sparest all: because they are thine, O Lord, who lovest souls.—*Wis.* xi. 25, 27.

That thy children, O Lord, whom thou lovedst, might know that it is not the growing of fruits that nourisheth men, but thy word preserveth them that believe in thee.—*Wis.* xvi. 26.

And now thus saith the Lord that created thee, O Jacob, and formed thee, O Israel: Fear not, for I have redeemed thee, and called thee by thy name: thou art mine. . . .

Since thou becamest honorable in my eyes, thou art glorious: I have loved thee, and I will give men for thee, and people for thy life.—*Is.* xliii. 1, 4.

Even to your old age, I am the same, and to your grey hairs, I will carry you: I have made you, and I will bear: I will carry, and will save.—*Is.* xlvi. 4.

Can a woman forget her infant, so as not to have pity on the son of her womb? and if she should forget, yet will not I forget thee.—*Is.* xlix. 15.

And he said: Surely they are my people, children that will not deny: so he became their saviour.

In all their affliction he was not troubled, and the angel of his presence saved them: in his love, and in his mercy, he redeemed them, and he carried them, and lifted them up all the days of old.—*Is.* lxiii. 8, 9.

The Lord hath appeared from afar to me. Yea, I have loved thee with an everlasting love, therefore have I drawn thee, taking pity on thee.—*Jer.* xxxi. 3.

And I will espouse thee to me for ever: and I will espouse thee to me in justice, and judgment, and in mercy, and in commiserations.

And I will espouse thee to me in

faith: and thou shalt know that I am the Lord.—*Osee* ii. 19, 20.

And I was like a foster father to Ephraim, I carried them in my arms: and they knew not that I healed them.

I will draw them with the cords of Adam, with the bands of love: and I will be to them as one that taketh off the yoke on their jaws: and I put his meat to him that he might eat.—*Osee* xi. 3, 4.

I will heal their breaches, I will love them freely: for my wrath is turned away from them.—*Osee* xiv. 5.

The Lord thy God in the midst of thee is mighty, he will save: he will rejoice over thee with gladness, he will be silent in his love, he will be joyful over thee in praise.—*Soph.* iii. 17.

For thus saith the Lord of hosts: After the glory he hath sent me to the nations that have robbed you: for he that toucheth you, toucheth the apple of my eye.—*Zach.* ii. 8.

I have loved you, saith the Lord: and you have said: Wherein hast thou loved us?—*Malach.* i. 2.

For God so loved the world, as to give his only begotten Son; that whosoever believeth in him, may not perish, but may have life everlasting.—*John* iii. 16.

In that day you shall ask in my name; and I say not to you, that I will ask the Father for you:

For the Father himself loveth you, because you have loved me, and have believed that I came out from God.—*John* xvi. 26, 27.

Just Father, the world hath not known thee; but I have known thee: and these have known that thou hast sent me.

And I have made known thy name to them, and will make it known; that the love wherewith thou hast loved me, may be in them, and I in them.—*John* xvii. 25, 26.

For I am sure that neither death, nor life, nor angels, nor principalities, nor powers, nor things present, nor things to come, nor might,

Nor height, nor depth, nor any other creature, shall be able to separate us from the love of God, which is in Christ Jesus our Lord.—*Rom.* viii. 38, 39.

Behold what manner of charity the Father hath bestowed upon us, that we should be called, and should be the sons of God.—1 *John* iii. 1.

By this hath the charity of God appeared towards us, because God hath sent his only begotten Son into the world, that we may live by him.

In this is charity: not as though we had loved God, but because he hath first loved us, and sent his Son to be a propitiation for our sins.—1 *John* iv. 9, 10.

And we have known, and have believed the charity, which God hath to us. God is charity: and he that abideth in charity, abideth in God, and God in him.

In this is the charity of God perfected with us, that we may have confidence in the day of judgment. . . .

Let us therefore love God, because God first hath loved us.—1 *John* iv. 16, 17, 19.

LOVE FOR US, CHRIST'S

Come to me, all you that labor, and are burdened, and I will refresh you.—*Matt.* xi. 28.

I am the good shepherd. The good shepherd giveth his life for his sheep. . . .

As the Father knoweth me, and I know the Father: and I lay down my life for my sheep.—*John* x. 11, 15.

Now there was a certain man, sick, named Lazarus, of Bethania, of the town of Mary and of Martha her sister. . . .

His sisters therefore sent to him, saying: Lord, behold, he whom thou lovest is sick. . . .

Now Jesus loved Martha, and her sister Mary and Lazarus. . . .

And Jesus wept.

The Jews therefore said: Behold how he loved him.—*John* xi. 1, 3, 5, 35, 36.

And I, if I be lifted up from the earth, will draw all things to myself.—*John* xii. 32.

Before the festival day of the pasch, Jesus knowing that his hour was come, that he should pass out of this world to the Father: having loved his own who were in the world, he loved them unto the end.—*John* xiii. 1.

In my Father's house there are many mansions. If not, I would have told you: because I go to prepare a place for you.

And if I shall go, and prepare a place for you, I will come again, and will take you to myself; that where I am, you also may be. . . .

I will not leave you orphans, I will come to you.—*John* xiv. 2, 3, 18.

As the Father hath loved me, I also have loved you. Abide in my love.— *John* xv. 9.

Greater love than this no man hath, that a man lay down his life for his friends.

You are my friends, if you do the things that I command you.

I will not now call you servants: for the servant knoweth not what his lord doth. But I have called you friends: because all things whatsoever I have heard of my Father, I have made known to you.—*John* xv. 13-15.

Who then shall separate us from the love of Christ? Shall tribulation? or distress? or famine? or nakedness? or danger? or persecution? or the sword? . . .

But in all these things we overcome, because of him that hath loved us.— *Rom.* viii. 35, 37.

For the charity of Christ presseth us: judging this, that if one died for all, then all were dead.

And Christ died for all; that they also who live, may not now live to themselves, but unto him who died for them, and rose again.—2 *Cor.* v. 14, 15.

For you know the grace of our Lord Jesus Christ, that being rich, he became poor, for your sakes; that through his poverty you might be rich.—2 *Cor.* viii. 9.

And I live, now not I; but Christ liveth in me. And that I live now in the flesh: I live in the faith of the Son of God, who loved me, and delivered himself for me.—*Gal.* ii. 20.

Christ hath redeemed us from the curse of the law, being made a curse for us: for it is written: Cursed is every one that hangeth on a tree.—*Gal.* iii. 13.

That being rooted and founded in charity,

You may be able to comprehend, with all the saints, what is the breadth and length, and height and depth:

To know also the charity of Christ, which surpasseth all knowledge, that you may be filled unto all the fulness of God.—*Eph.* iii. 17-19.

Be ye therefore followers of God, as most dear children;

And walk in love, as Christ also hath loved us, and hath delivered himself for us, an oblation and a sacrifice to God for an odor of sweetness.—*Eph.* v. 1, 2.

For both he that sanctifieth, and they who are sanctified, are all of one. For which cause, he is not ashamed to call them brethren, saying:

I will declare thy name to my brethren; in the midst of the church will I praise thee. . . .

For no where doth he take hold of the angels: but of the seed of Abraham he taketh hold.—*Heb.* ii. 11, 12, 16.

In this we have known the charity of God, because he hath laid down his life for us: and we ought to lay down our lives for the brethren.—1 *John* iii. 16.

LOVE FOR SINNERS, CHRIST'S

See also: Mercy of God to repentant sinners—page 316.

And it came to pass, as he was sitting at meat in the house, behold many publicans and sinners came, and sat down with Jesus and his disciples.

And the Pharisees seeing it, said to his disciples: Why doth your master eat with publicans and sinners?

But Jesus hearing it, said: They that are in health, need not a physician, but they that are ill.

Go then, and learn what this meaneth, I will have mercy, and not sacrifice. For I am not come to call the just, but sinners.—*Matt.* ix. 10-13.

And behold, a woman that was in the city, a sinner, when she knew that he sat at meat in the Pharisee's house, brought an alabaster box of ointment;

And standing behind at his feet, she

beg: n to wash his feet with tears, and wiped them with the hairs of her head, and kissed his feet, and anointed them with the ointment. . . .

And turning to the woman, he said unto Simon: Dost thou see this woman? I entered into thy house, thou gavest me no water for my feet; but she with tears hath washed my feet, and with her hair hath wiped them. . . .

Wherefore I say to thee: Many sins are forgiven her, because she hath loved much. But to whom less is forgiven, he loveth less.

And he said to her: Thy sins are forgiven thee.—*Luke* vii. 37, 38, 44, 47, 48.

The Son of man came not to destroy souls, but to save.—*Luke* ix. 56.

Now the publicans and sinners drew near unto him, to hear him.

And the Pharisees and the scribes murmured, saying: This man receiveth sinners, and eateth with them.

And he spoke to them this parable, saying:

What man of you that hath an hundred sheep: and if he shall lose one of them, doth he not leave the ninety-nine in the desert, and go after that which was lost, until he find it?

And when he hath found it, lay it upon his shoulders, rejoicing:

And coming home, call together his friends and neighbors, saying to them: Rejoice with me, because I have found my sheep that was lost?

I say to you, that even so, there shall be joy in heaven upon one sinner that doth penance, more than upon ninety-nine just, who need not penance.—*Luke* xv. 1-7.

And rising up he (the prodigal son) came to his father. And when he was yet a great way off, his father saw him, and was moved with compassion, and running to him, fell upon his neck, and kissed him.

And the son said to him: Father, I have sinned against heaven, and before thee; I am not now worthy to be called thy son.

And the father said to his servants: Bring forth quickly the first robe, and put it on him, and put a ring on his hand, and shoes on his feet:

And bring hither the fatted calf, and kill it, and let us eat and make merry:

Because this my son was dead, and is come to life again: was lost, and is found.—*Luke* xv. 20-24.

For the Son of man is come to seek and to save that which was lost.—*Luke* xix. 10.

And when he (Jesus) drew near, seeing the city, he wept over it.—*Luke* xix. 41.

For why did Christ, when as yet we were weak, according to the time, die for the ungodly?

For scarce for a just man will one die; yet perhaps for a good man some one would dare to die.

But God commendeth his charity towards us; because when as yet we were sinners, according to the time,

Christ died for us; much more therefore, being now justified by his blood, shall we be saved from wrath through him.—*Rom.* v. 6-9.

A faithful saying, and worthy of all acceptation, that Christ Jesus came into this world to save sinners, of whom I am the chief.—1 *Tim.* i. 15.

LOVE FOR GOD

See also: Charity—page 46.

So Jacob served seven years for Rachel: and they seemed but a few days, because of the greatness of his love.—*Gen.* xxix. 20.

Thou shalt love the Lord thy God with thy whole heart, and with thy whole soul, and with thy whole strength. —*Deut.* vi. 5.

And now, Israel, what doth the Lord thy God require of thee, but that thou fear the Lord thy God, and walk in his ways, and love him, and serve the Lord thy God, with all thy heart, and with all thy soul?—*Deut.* x. 12.

I will love thee, O Lord, my strength: The Lord is my firmament, my refuge, and my deliverer.—*Ps.* xvii. 2, 3.

You that love the Lord, hate evil.— *Ps.* xcvi. 10.

I have loved, because the Lord will hear the voice of my prayer.—*Ps.* cxiv. 1.

Put me as a seal upon thy heart, as a

seal upon thy arm, for love is strong as death.—*Cant.* viii. 6.

The love of God is honorable wisdom.—*Ecclus.* i. 14.

They that fear the Lord, will not be incredulous to his word: and they that love him, will keep his way.

They that fear the Lord, will seek after the things that are well pleasing to him: and they that love him, shall be filled with his law.—*Ecclus.* ii. 18, 19.

He that loveth father or mother more than me, is not worthy of me; and he that loveth son or daughter more than me, is not worthy of me.—*Matt.* x. 37.

And one of them, a doctor of the law, asked him, tempting him:

Master, which is the great commandment in the law?

Jesus said to him: Thou shalt love the Lord thy God with thy whole heart, and with thy whole soul, and with thy whole mind.

This is the greatest and the first commandment.

And the second is like to this: Thou shalt love thy neighbor as thyself.

On these two commandments dependeth the whole law, and the prophets.—*Matt.* xxii. 35-40.

I am come to cast fire on the earth: and what will I, but that it be kindled?—*Luke* xii. 49.

If you love me, keep my commandments.

. . . He that hath my commandments, and keepeth them; he it is that loveth me.

. . . Jesus answered, and said to him: If any one love me, he will keep my word.—*John* xiv. 15, 21, 23.

When therefore they had dined, Jesus saith to Simon Peter: Simon, son of John, lovest thou me more than these? He saith to him: Yea, Lord, thou knowest that I love thee. He saith to him: Feed my lambs.—*John* xxi. 15.

And we know that to them that love God, all things work together unto good, to such as, according to his purpose, are called to be saints.—*Rom.* viii. 28.

But if any man love God, the same is known by him.—*1 Cor.* viii. 3.

If any man love not our Lord Jesus Christ, let him be anathema, maranatha.—*1 Cor.* xvi. 22.

Grace be with all them that love our Lord Jesus Christ in incorruption.—*Eph.* vi. 24.

That the trial of your faith (much more precious than gold which is tried by the fire) may be found unto praise and glory and honor, at the appearing of Jesus Christ:

Whom having not seen, you love.—*1 Peter* i. 7, 8.

If any man say, I love God, and hateth his brother; he is a liar. For he that loveth not his brother, whom he seeth, how can he love God, whom he seeth not?

And this commandment we have from God, that he who loveth God, love also his brother.—*1 John* iv. 20, 21.

LOVE FOR GOD REWARDED

I am the Lord thy God, mighty, jealous, visiting the iniquity of the fathers upon the children, unto the third and fourth generation of them that hate me.

And showing mercy unto thousands to them that love me, and keep my commandments.—*Ex.* xx. 5, 6.

And thou shalt know that the Lord thy God, he is a strong and faithful God, keeping his covenant and mercy to them that love him, and to them that keep his commandments, unto a thousand generations.—*Deut.* vii. 9.

So let all thy enemies perish, O Lord: but let them that love thee shine, as the sun shineth in his rising.—*Judges* v. 31.

The Lord keepeth all them that love him; but all the wicked he will destroy.—*Ps.* cxliv. 20.

I love them that love me: and they that in the morning early watch for me, shall find me.—*Prov.* viii. 17.

They that trust in him, shall understand the truth: and they that are faithful in love shall rest in him: for grace and peace is to his elect.—*Wis.* iii. 9.

All wisdom is from the Lord God. . . .

And he poured her out upon all his works, and upon all flesh, according to his gift, and hath given her to them that love him.—*Ecclus.* i. 1, 10.

He that loveth God, shall obtain pardon for his sins by prayer, and shall refrain himself from them, and shall be heard in the prayer of days.—*Ecclus.* iii. 4.

For their hope is on him that saveth them, and the eyes of the Lord are upon them that love him.—*Ecclus.* xxxiv. 15.

And Daniel said: Thou hast remembered me, O God, and thou hast not forsaken them that love thee.—*Dan.* xiv. 37.

Wherefore I say to thee: Many sins are forgiven her, because she hath loved much. But to whom less is forgiven, he loveth less.—*Luke* vii. 47.

And he that loveth me, shall be loved of my Father: and I will love him, and will manifest myself to him. . . .

Jesus answered, and said to him (Jude): If any one love me, he will keep my word, and my Father will love him, and we will come to him, and will make our abode with him.—*John* xiv. 21, 23.

In that day you shall ask in my name; and I say not to you, that I will ask the Father for you:

For the Father himself loveth you, because you have loved me, and have believed that I came out from God.—*John* xvi. 26, 27.

LOVE GOD, EXHORTATION TO

Therefore love the Lord thy God, and observe his precepts and ceremonies, his judgments and commandments at all times.—*Deut.* xi. 1.

This only take care of with all diligence, that you love the Lord your God.—*Jos.* xxiii. 11.

O love the Lord, all ye his saints: for the Lord will require truth, and will repay them abundantly that act proudly.—*Ps.* xxx. 24.

Ye that fear the Lord, love him, and your hearts shall be enlightened.—*Ecclus.* ii. 10.

With all thy strength love him that made thee.—*Ecclus.* vii. 32.

Love God all thy life, and call upon him for thy salvation.—*Ecclus.* xiii. 18.

Let us therefore love God, because God first hath loved us.—1 *John* iv. 19.

LOVE OF OUR NEIGHBOR

See also: Charity—page 46.

And returning to the Lord, he (Moses) said: I beseech thee: this people hath sinned a heinous sin, and they have made to themselves gods of gold; either forgive them this trespass,

Or if thou do not, strike me out of the book that thou hast written.—*Ex.* xxxii. 31, 32.

With three things my spirit is pleased, which are approved before God and men:

The concord of brethren, and the love of neighbors, and man and wife that agree well together.—*Ecclus.* xxv. 1, 2.

Have we not all one father? hath not one God created us? why then doth every one of us despise his brother, violating the covenant of our fathers?—*Malach.* ii. 10.

And the scribe said to him: Well, Master, thou hast said in truth, that there is one God, and there is no other besides him.

And that he should be loved with the whole heart, and with the whole understanding, and with the whole soul, and with the whole strength; and to love one's neighbor as one's self, is a greater thing than all holocausts and sacrifices.

And Jesus seeing that he had answered wisely, said to him: Thou art not far from the kingdom of God.—*Mark* xii. 32-34.

By this shall all men know that you are my disciples, if you have love one for another.—*John* xiii. 35.

For I wished myself to be an anathema from Christ, for my brethren, who are my kinsmen according to the flesh.—*Rom.* ix. 3.

Owe no man any thing, but to love one another. For he that loveth his neighbor, hath fulfilled the law.

For, Thou shalt not commit adultery: Thou shalt not kill: Thou shalt not steal: Thou shalt not bear false witness: Thou shalt not covet: and if there be any other commandment, it is comprised in this word: Thou shalt love thy neighbor as thyself.

The love of our neighbor worketh no evil. Love therefore is the fulfilling of the law.—*Rom.* xiii. 8-10.

For all the law is fulfilled in one word: Thou shalt love thy neighbor as thyself.—*Gal.* v. 14.

Bear ye one another's burdens; and so you shall fulfil the law of Christ.—*Gal.* vi. 2.

But as touching the charity of brotherhood, we have no need to write to you: for yourselves have learned of God to love one another.—1 *Thess.* iv. 9.

If then you fulfil the royal law, according to the scriptures, Thou shalt love thy neighbor as thyself; you do well.—*James* ii. 8.

He that loveth his brother, abideth in the light, and there is no scandal in him.—1 *John* ii. 10.

In this the children of God are manifest, and the children of the devil. Whosoever is not just, is not of God, nor he that loveth not his brother.

For this is the declaration, which you have heard from the beginning, that you should love one another.—1 *John* iii. 10, 11.

We know that we have passed from death to life, because we love the brethren. He that loveth not, abideth in death.—1 *John* iii. 14.

In this we have known the charity of God, because he hath laid down his life for us: and we ought to lay down our lives for the brethren.—1 *John* iii. 16.

Dearly beloved, let us love one another, for charity is of God. And every one that loveth is born of God, and knoweth God.

He that loveth not, knoweth not God: for God is charity.—1 *John* iv. 7, 8.

My dearest, if God hath so loved us; we also ought to love one another.

No man hath seen God at any time. If we love one another, God abideth in us, and his charity is perfected in us.

In this we know that we abide in him, and he in us: because he hath given us of his spirit.—1 *John* iv. 11-13.

If any man say, I love God, and hateth his brother, he is a liar. For he that loveth not his brother, whom he seeth, how can he love God, whom he seeth not?—1 *John* iv. 20.

Whosoever believeth that Jesus is the Christ, is born of God. And every one that loveth him who begot, loveth him also who is born of him.

In this we know that we love the children of God: when we love God, and keep his commandments.—1 *John* v. 1, 2.

LOVE OF OUR NEIGHBOR COMMANDED BY GOD, THE

Seek not revenge, nor be mindful of the injury of thy citizens. Thou shalt love thy friend as thyself. I am the Lord.—*Lev.* xix. 18.

If a stranger dwell in your land, and abide among you, do not upbraid him:

But let him be among you as one of the same country: and you shall love him as yourselves: for you were strangers in the land of Egypt. I am the Lord your God.—*Lev.* xix. 33, 34.

And one of them, a doctor of the law, asked him, tempting him:

Master, which is the great commandment in the law?

Jesus said to him: Thou shalt love the Lord thy God with thy whole heart, and with thy whole soul, and with thy whole mind.

This is the greatest and the first commandment.

And the second is like to this: Thou shalt love thy neighbor as thyself.

On these two commandments dependeth the whole law and the prophets.—*Matt.* xxii. 35-40.

A new commandment I give unto you: That you love one another, as I have loved you, that you also love one another.—*John* xiii. 34.

This is my commandment, that you love one another, as I have loved you.—*John* xv. 12.

And this is his commandment, that we should believe in the name of his Son Jesus Christ: and love one another, as he hath given commandment unto us.—1 *John* iii. 23.

And this commandment we have from God, that he who loveth God, love also his brother.—1 *John* iv. 21.

LOVE OF OUR NEIGHBOR, EXHORTATION TO THE

And do you therefore love strangers, because you also were strangers in the land of Egypt.—*Deut.* x. 19.

Love thy neighbor, and be joined to him with fidelity.—*Ecclus.* xxvii. 18.

Loving one another with the charity of brotherhood, with honor, preventing one another.—*Rom.* xii. 10.

Owe no man any thing, but to love one another. For he that loveth his neighbor, hath fulfilled the law.—*Rom.* xiii. 8.

I therefore, a prisoner in the Lord, beseech you that you walk worthy of the vocation in which you are called,

With all humility and mildness, with patience, supporting one another in charity.—*Eph.* iv. 1, 2.

Be ye therefore followers of God, as most dear children;

And walk in love, as Christ also hath loved us, and hath delivered himself for us, an oblation, and a sacrifice to God, for an odor of sweetness.—*Eph.* v. 1, 2.

I beseech thee for my son, whom I have begotten in my bonds, Onesimus, . . .

Whom I have sent back to thee. And do thou receive him as my own bowels. . . .

For perhaps he therefore departed for a season from thee, that thou mightest receive him again for ever:

Not now as a servant, but instead of a servant, a most dear brother, especially to me: but how much more to thee both in the flesh and in the Lord?—*Phil.* i. 10, 12, 15, 16.

Purifying your souls in the obedience of charity, with a brotherly love, from a sincere heart love one another earnestly.—1 *Peter* i. 22.

My little children, let us not love in word, nor in tongue, but in deed, and in truth.—1 *John* iii. 18.

Dearly beloved, let us love one another, for charity is of God.—1 *John* iv. 7.

And now I beseech thee, lady, not as writing a new commandment to thee, but that which we have had from the beginning, that we love one another.— 2 *John* i. 5.

LOVE OF OUR ENEMIES

See also: Forgiveness of injuries— page 158.

If thou meet thy enemy's ox or ass going astray, bring it back to him.

If thou see the ass of him that hateth thee, lie underneath his burden, thou shalt not pass by, but shalt lift him up with him.—*Ex.* xxiii. 4, 5.

If thy enemy be hungry, give him to eat: if he thirst, give him water to drink:

For thou shalt heap hot coals upon his head, and the Lord will reward thee. —*Prov.* xxv. 21, 22.

You have heard that it hath been said, Thou shalt love thy neighbor, and hate thy enemy.

But I say to you, Love your enemies: do good to them that hate you: and pray for them that persecute and calumniate you:

That you may be the children of your Father who is in heaven, who maketh his sun to rise upon the good and bad, and raineth upon the just and the unjust.

For if you love them that love you, what reward shall you have? do not even the publicans this?

And if you salute your brethren only, what do you more? do not also the heathens this?—*Matt.* v. 43-47.

And if you love them that love you, what thanks are to you? for sinners also love those that love them.

And if you do good to them who do good to you, what thanks are to you? for sinners also do this. . . .

But love ye your enemies: do good, and lend, hoping for nothing thereby: and your reward shall be great, and you shall be the sons of the Highest; for he is kind to the unthankful, and to the evil.—*Luke* vi. 32, 33, 35.

But if thy enemy be hungry, give him to eat; if he thirst, give him to drink.

For, doing this, thou shalt heap coals of fire upon his head.

Be not overcome by evil, but overcome evil by good.—*Rom.* xii. 20, 21.

LUKEWARMNESS

See also: Indifference to our spiritual interests—page 237.

Jesus said to him: No man, putting his hand to the plough, and looking back, is fit for the kingdom of God.— *Luke* ix. 62.

I know thy works, that thou art neither cold nor hot. I would thou wert cold or hot.

But because thou art lukewarm, and neither cold nor hot, I will begin to vomit thee out of my mouth.—*Apoc.* iii. 15, 16.

MAJESTY OF GOD, THE

And he said: I am the God of thy father, the God of Abraham, the God of Isaac, and the God of Jacob. Moses hid his face: for he durst not look at God.—*Ex.* iii. 6.

And now the third day was come, and the morning appeared: and behold, thunders began to be heard, and lightning to flash, and a very thick cloud to cover the mount, and the noise of the trumpet sounded exceeding loud, and the people that was in the camp, feared.

. . . And all mount Sinai was on a smoke: because the Lord was come down upon it in fire, and the smoke arose from it as out of a furnace: and all the mount was terrible. . . .

And the Lord came down upon mount Sinai, in the very top of the mount, and he called Moses unto the top thereof. And when he was gone up thither,

He said unto him: Go down, and charge the people; lest they should have a mind to pass the limits, to see the Lord, and a very great multitude of them should perish.—*Ex.* xix. 16, 18, 20, 21.

And all the people saw the voices and the flames, and the sound of the trumpet, and the mount smoking: and being terrified, and struck with fear, they stood afar off.

Saying to Moses: Speak thou to us, and we will hear: let not the Lord speak to us, lest we die.—*Ex.* xx. 18, 19.

And when Moses was gone up, a cloud covered the mount.

And the glory of the Lord dwelt upon Sinai, covering it with a cloud six days: and the seventh day he called him out of the midst of the cloud.

And the sight of the glory of the Lord was like a burning fire upon the top of the mount, in the eyes of the children of Israel.—*Ex.* xxiv. 15-17.

And again he (God) said: Thou canst not see my face: for man shall not see me and live.—*Ex.* xxxiii. 20.

Behold the Lord our God hath shown us his majesty and his greatness, we have heard his voice out of the midst of the fire, and have proved this day that God speaking with man, man hath lived.

Why shall we die, therefore, and why shall this exceeding great fire consume us: for if we hear the voice of the Lord our God any more, we shall die.

What is all flesh, that it should hear the voice of the living God, who speaketh out of the midst of the fire, as we have heard, and be able to live?—*Deut.* v. 24-26.

O Lord, when thou wentest out of Seir, and passedst by the regions of Edom, the earth trembled, and the heavens dropped water.

The mountains melted before the face of the Lord, and Sinai, before the face of the Lord, the God of Israel.—*Judges* v. 4, 5.

And the men of Bethsames said: Who shall be able to stand before the Lord, this holy God? and to whom shall he go up from us?—1 *Kings* vi. 20.

O God, when thou didst go forth in the sight of thy people, when thou didst pass through the desert:

The earth was moved, and the heavens dropped at the presence of the God of Sinai, at the presence of the God of Israel.—*Ps.* lxvii. 8, 9.

And blessed be the name of his majesty for ever: and the whole earth shall be filled with his majesty. So be it. So be it.—*Ps.* lxxi. 19.

The waters saw thee, O God, the waters saw thee: and they were afraid, and the depths were troubled.—*Ps.* lxxvi. 17.

Bless the Lord, O my soul: O Lord, my God, thou art exceedingly great.

Thou hast put on praise and beauty: and art clothed with light as with a garment.—*Ps.* ciii. 1, 2.

At the presence of the Lord the earth was moved, at the presence of the God of Jacob.—*Ps.* cxiii. 7.

And who shall show forth the power of his majesty?—*Ecclus.* xviii. 4.

He hath established the good things of every one. And who shall be filled with beholding his glory?—*Ecclus.* xlii. 26.

And they shall go into the holes of rocks, and into the caves of the earth, from the face of the fear of the Lord, and from the glory of his majesty, when he shall rise up to strike the earth.—*Is.* ii. 19.

In the year that king Ozias died, I saw the Lord sitting upon a throne high and elevated: and his train filled the temple. . . .
And I said: Woe is me, because I have held my peace, because I am a man of unclean lips, and I dwell in the midst of a people that hath unclean lips, and I have seen with my eyes the King, the Lord of hosts.—*Is.* vi. 1, 5.

Which in his times he shall show, who is the Blessed and only Mighty, the King of kings, and Lord of lords;
Who only hath immortality, and inhabiteth light inaccessible, whom no man hath seen, nor can see: to whom be honor and empire everlasting. Amen.—1 *Tim.* vi. 15, 16.

For our God is a consuming fire.—*Heb.* xii. 29.

And I saw a great white throne, and one sitting upon it, from whose face the earth and heaven fled away, and there was no place found for them.—*Apoc.* xx. 11.

MALICE OF MEN, GOD IS ABOVE THE REACH OF THE

Look up to heaven, and see, and behold the sky, that it is higher than thee.
If thou sin, what shalt thou hurt him? and if thy iniquities be multiplied, what shalt thou do against him? . . .
Thy wickedness may hurt a man that is like thee: and thy justice may help the son of man.—*Job* xxxv. 5, 6, 8.

Why have the Gentiles raged, and the people devised vain things?
The kings of the earth stood up and the princes met together, against the Lord, and against his Christ.
Let us break their bonds asunder: and let us cast away their yoke from us.
He that dwelleth in heaven, shall laugh at them: and the Lord shall deride them.—*Ps.* ii. 1-4.

For they have intended evils against thee: they have devised counsels which they have not been able to establish.
For thou shalt make them turn their back: in thy remnants thou shalt prepare their face.—*Ps.* xx. 12, 13.

But what have you to do with me, O Tyre, and Sidon, and all the coast of the Philistines? will you revenge yourselves on me? and if you revenge yourselves on me, I will very soon return you a recompense upon your own head.—*Joel* iii. 4.

What do ye devise against the Lord? he will make an utter end: there shall not rise a double affliction.—*Nahum* i. 9.

Pilate therefore saith to him: Speakest thou not to me? knowest thou not that I have power to crucify thee, and I have power to release thee?
Jesus answered: Thou shouldst not have any power against me, unless it were given thee from above.—*John* xix. 10, 11.

Therefore doth the Father love me: because I lay down my life, that I may take it again.
No man taketh it away from me: but I lay it down of myself, and I have power to lay it down: and I have power to take it up again. This commandment have I received of my Father.—*John* x. 17, 18.

MAN, THE BROTHERHOOD OF

See: Brotherhood—page 43.

MAN, THE DIGNITY OF

And he (God) said: Let us make man to our image and likeness: and let him have dominion over the fishes of the sea, and the fowls of the air, and the beasts, and the whole earth, and every creeping creature that moveth upon the earth.
And God created man to his own image: to the image of God he created him: male and female he created them. —*Gen.* i. 26, 27.

And the Lord God formed man of the slime of the earth: and breathed into his face the breath of life, and man became a living soul.—*Gen.* ii. 7.

And God blessed Noe and his sons. And he said to them: Increase and multiply, and fill the earth.

And let the fear and dread of you be upon all the beasts of the earth, and upon all the fowls of the air, and all that move upon the earth: all the fishes of the sea are delivered into your hand.—*Gen.* ix. 1, 2.

What is man that thou art mindful of him? or the son of man, that thou visitest him?

Thou hast made him a little less than the angels, thou hast crowned him with glory and honor:

And hast set him over the works of thy hands.

Thou hast subjected all things under his feet, all sheep and oxen: moreover the beasts also of the fields.

The birds of the air, and the fishes of the sea, that pass through the paths of the sea.—*Ps.* viii. 5-9.

For God created man incorruptible, and to the image of his own likeness he made him.—*Wis.* ii. 23.

God of my fathers, and Lord of mercy, who hast made all things with thy word,

And by thy wisdom, hast appointed man, that he should have dominion over the creature that was made by thee,

That he should order the world according to equity and justice, and execute justice with an upright heart.—*Wis.* ix. 1-3.

God created man of the earth, and made him after his own image.

And he turned him into it again, and clothed him with strength according to himself.

He gave him the number of his days, and time, and gave him power over all things that are upon the earth.

He put the fear of him upon all flesh, and he had dominion over beasts and fowls.

He created of him a helpmate like to himself: he gave them counsel, and a tongue, and eyes, and ears, and a heart to devise: and he filled them with the knowledge of understanding.

He created in them the science of the spirit, he filled their heart with wisdom, and showed them both good and evil.—*Ecclus.* xvii. 1-6.

The man indeed ought not to cover his head, because he is the image and glory of God.—*1 Cor.* xi. 7.

MAN, THE EQUALITY OF

See: Equal in the sight of God; all men are—page 125.

MAN'S DEPENDENCE UPON GOD

See: Dependence—page 106.

MANLINESS

And the days of David drew nigh that he should die, and he charged his son Solomon, saying:

I am going the way of all flesh: take thou courage, and show thyself a man.—*3 Kings* ii. 1, 2.

And David said to Solomon his son: Act like a man, and take courage, and do: fear not, and be not dismayed.—*1 Paral.* xxviii. 20.

Expect the Lord, do manfully, and let thy heart take courage, and wait thou for the Lord.—*Ps.* xxvi. 14.

Do ye manfully, and let your heart be strengthened, all ye that hope in the Lord.—*Ps.* xxx. 25.

Watch ye, stand fast in the faith, do manfully, and be strengthened.—*1 Cor.* xvi. 13.

MARRIAGE

Then the angel Raphael said to him (Tobias):

Hear me, and I will show thee who they are, over whom the devil can prevail.

For they who in such manner receive matrimony, as to shut out God from themselves and from their mind, and to give themselves to their lust, as the horse and mule, which have not understanding, over them the devil hath power.

But thou, when thou shalt take her, go into the chamber, and for three days keep thyself continent from her, and give thyself to nothing else but to prayers with her. . . .

And when the third night is past, thou shalt take the virgin with the fear of the Lord, moved rather for love of children than for lust, that in the seed of Abraham, thou mayst obtain a blessing in children.—*Tob.* vi. 16-18, 22.

Then Tobias exhorted the virgin, and said to her: Sara, arise, and let us pray to God to-day and to-morrow, and the next day: because for these three nights we are joined to God: and when the third night is over, we will be in our own wedlock.

For we are the children of saints, and we must not be joined together like heathens that know not God.—*Tob.* viii. 4, 5.

And now, Lord, thou knowest, that not for fleshly lust do I take my sister to wife, but only for the love of posterity, in which thy name may be blessed for ever and ever.—*Tob.* viii. 9.

It is better therefore that two should be together, than one: for they have the advantage of their society:

If one fall, he shall be supported by the other: woe to him that is alone, for when he falleth, he hath none to lift him up.—*Eccles.* iv. 9, 10.

Marriage honorable in all, and the bed undefiled.—*Heb.* xiii. 4.

MARRIAGE, INDISSOLUBILITY OF

See: Part II—page 716.

MARRIAGES, MIXED

Make no covenant with the men of those countries. . . .

Neither shalt thou take of their daughters a wife for thy son, lest after they themselves have committed fornication, they make thy sons also to commit fornication with their gods.—*Ex.* xxxiv. 15, 16.

Neither shalt thou make marriages with them (the Chanaanites). Thou shalt not give thy daughter to his son, nor take his daughter for thy son:

For she will turn away thy son from following me, that he may rather serve strange gods, and the wrath of the Lord will be kindled, and will quickly destroy thee.—*Deut.* vii. 3, 4.

But if you will embrace the errors of these nations that dwell among you, and make marriages with them, and join friendships:

Know ye for a certainty that the Lord your God will not destroy them before your face, but they shall be a pit and a snare in your way, and a stumbling-block at your side, and stakes in your eyes, till he take you away and destroy you from off this excellent land, which he hath given you.—*Jos.* xxiii. 12, 13.

Then Samson went down to Thamnatha, and seeing there a woman of the daughters of the Philistines,

He came up, and told his father and his mother, saying: I saw a woman in Thamnatha of the daughters of the Philistines: I beseech you, take her for me to wife.

And his father and mother said to him: Is there no woman among the daughters of thy brethren, or among all my people, that thou wilt take a wife of the Philistines, who are uncircumcised? And Samson said to his father: Take this woman for me, for she hath pleased my eyes.—*Judges* xiv. 1-3.

And Esdras the priest stood up, and said to them: You have transgressed, and taken strange wives, to add to the sins of Israel.—1 *Esd.* x. 10.

MARRIAGE, MUTUAL DUTIES OF HUSBAND AND WIFE IN

And the Lord God built the rib which he took from Adam into a woman: and brought her to Adam.

And Adam said: This is now bone of my bones, and flesh of my flesh; she shall be called woman, because she was taken out of man.

Wherefore a man shall leave father and mother, and shall cleave to his wife: and they shall be two in one flesh. —*Gen.* ii. 22-24.

Let thy vein be blessed, and rejoice with the wife of thy youth:

Let her be thy dearest hind, and most agreeable fawn: let her breasts inebriate thee at all times; be thou delighted continually with her love.—*Prov.* v. 18, 19.

Live joyfully with the wife whom thou lovest, all the days of thy unsteady life, which are given to thee under the sun, all the time of thy vanity: for this is thy portion in life, and in thy labor wherewith thou laborest under the sun. —*Eccles.* ix. 9.

Depart not from a wise and good wife, whom thou hast gotten in the fear of the Lord: for the grace of her modesty is above gold.—*Ecclus.* vii. 21.

With three things my spirit is pleased, which are approved before God and men:

The concord of brethren, and the love of neighbors, and man and wife that agree well together.—*Ecclus.* xxv. 1, 2.

Feeble hands, and disjointed knees, a woman that doth not make her husband happy.—*Ecclus.* xxv. 32.

Happy is the husband of a good wife: for the number of his years is double.

A virtuous woman rejoiceth her husband, and shall fulfil the years of his life in peace.

A good wife is a good portion, she shall be given in the portion of them that fear God, to a man for his good deeds.—*Ecclus.* xxvi. 1-3.

He that possesseth a good wife, beginneth a possession: she is a help like to himself, and a pillar of rest.—*Ecclus.* xxxvi. 26.

A friend and companion meeting together in season, but above them both is a wife with her husband.—*Ecclus.* xl. 23.

Because the Lord hath been witness between thee, and the wife of thy youth, whom thou hast despised: yet she was thy partner, and the wife of thy covenant.

Did not one make her, and she is the residue of his spirit? And what doth one seek, but the seed of God? Keep then your spirit, and despise not the wife of thy youth.—*Malach.* ii. 14, 15.

Let the husband render the debt to his wife, and the wife also in like manner to the husband.

The wife hath not power of her own body, but the husband. And in like manner, the husband also hath not power of his own body, but the wife.

Defraud not one another, except, perhaps, by consent for a time, that you may give yourselves to prayer; and return together again, lest Satan tempt you for your incontinency.—1 *Cor.* vii. 3-5.

Let women be subject to their husbands, as to the Lord:

Because the husband is the head of the wife, as Christ is the head of the church. He is the saviour of his body.

Therefore as the church is subject to Christ, so also let the wives be to their husbands in all things.

Husbands, love your wives, as Christ also loved the church, and delivered himself up for it. . . .

So also ought men to love their wives, as their own bodies. He that loveth his wife, loveth himself.

For no man ever hateth his own flesh; but nourisheth and cherisheth it, as also Christ doth the church:

Because we are members of his body, of his flesh, and of his bones.

For this cause shall a man leave his father and mother, and shall cleave to his wife, and they shall be two in one flesh. . . .

Nevertheless, let every one of you in particular love his wife as himself: and let the wife fear her husband.—*Eph.* v. 22-25, 28-31, 33.

Wives, be subject to your husbands, as it behoveth in the Lord.

Husbands, love your wives, and be not bitter towards them.—*Col.* iii. 18, 19.

That they may teach the young women to be wise, to love their husbands, to love their children,

To be discreet, chaste, sober, having a care of the house, gentle, obedient to their husbands, that the word of God be not blasphemed.—*Titus* ii. 4, 5.

In like manner also, let wives be subject to their husbands: that if any believe not the word, they may be won without the word, by the conversation of the wives.

Considering your chaste conversation with fear.

Whose adorning, let it not be the outward plaiting of the hair, or the wearing of gold, or the putting on of apparel:

But the hidden man of the heart in the incorruptibility of a quiet and a meek spirit, which is rich in the sight of God.

For after this manner heretofore the holy women also, who trusted in God, adorned themselves, being in subjection to their own husbands. . . .

Ye husbands, likewise dwelling with them according to knowledge, giving honor to the female, as to the weaker vessel, and as to the co-heirs of the grace of life: that your prayers be not hindered.—1 *Peter* iii. 1-5, 7.

MARTYRS, CONSTANCY OF THE

But the souls of the just are in the hand of God, and the torment of death shall not touch them. . . .

And though in the sight of men, they suffered torments, their hope is full of immortality.

Afflicted in few things, in many they shall be well rewarded: because God hath tried them, and found them worthy of himself.

As gold in the furnace, he hath proved them, and as a victim of a holocaust, he hath received them, and in time, there shall be respect had to them.—*Wis.* iii. 1, 4-6.

And many of the people of Israel determined with themselves, that they would not eat unclean things: and they chose rather to die, than to be defiled with unclean meats.

And they would not break the holy law of God, and they were put to death. —1 *Mach.* i. 65, 66.

Eleazar, one of the chief of the scribes, a man advanced in years and of a comely countenance, was pressed to open his mouth to eat swine's flesh.

But he, choosing rather a most glorious death than a hateful life, went forward voluntarily to the torment.

And considering in what manner he was come to it, patiently bearing, he determined not to do any unlawful things for the love of life. . . .

Wherefore by departing manfully out of this life, I shall show myself worthy of my old age:

And I shall leave an example of fortitude to young men, if with a ready mind and constancy I suffer an honorable death, for the most venerable and most holy laws. And having spoken thus, he was forthwith carried to execution. . . .

Thus did this man die, leaving not only to young men, but also to the whole nation, the memory of his death for an example of virtue and fortitude. —2 *Mach.* vi. 18-20, 27, 28, 31.

It came to pass also that seven brethren, together with their mother, were apprehended, and compelled by the king to eat swine's flesh against the law, for which end they were tormented with whips and scourges.

But one of them, who was the eldest, said thus: What wouldst thou ask, or learn, of us? we are ready to die rather than to transgress the laws of God, received from our fathers.— 2 *Mach.* vii. 1, 2.

Blessed are they that suffer persecution for justice' sake: for theirs is the kingdom of heaven.—*Matt.* v. 10.

For he that will save his life, shall lose it: and he that shall lose his life for my sake, shall find it.—*Matt.* xvi. 25.

And I say to you, my friends: Be not afraid of them who kill the body, and after that, have no more that they can do.

But I will show you whom you shall fear: fear ye him, who after he hath killed, hath power to cast into hell. Yea, I say to you, fear him.—*Luke* xii. 4, 5.

And I say to you, Whosoever shall confess me before men, him shall the Son of man also confess before the angels of God.—*Luke* xii. 8.

Amen, amen, I say to you, unless the grain of wheat, falling into the ground, die,

Itself remaineth alone. But if it die, it bringeth forth much fruit. He that loveth his life shall lose it; and he that hateth his life in this world, keepeth it unto life eternal.—*John* xii. 24, 25.

And now, behold, being bound in the spirit, I go to Jerusalem: not knowing the things which shall befall me there:

Save that the Holy Ghost in every city witnesseth to me, saying: That bands and afflictions wait for me at Jerusalem.

But I fear none of these things, neither do I count my life more precious than myself, so that I may consummate my course, and the ministry of the word which I received from the Lord Jesus, to testify the gospel of the grace of God.—*Acts* xx. 22-24.

Then Paul answered and said: What do you mean, weeping, and afflicting my heart? For I am ready, not only to be bound, but to die also in Jerusalem, for the name of the Lord Jesus.—*Acts* xxi. 13.

Who then shall separate us from the love of Christ? Shall tribulation? or distress? or famine? or nakedness? or danger? or persecution? or the sword? (As it is written: For thy sake we are put to death all the day long. We are accounted as sheep for the slaughter.)

But in all these things we overcome, because of him that hath loved us.—*Rom.* viii. 35-37.

Women received their dead raised to life again.

But others were racked, not accepting deliverance, that they might find a better resurrection.

And others had trial of mockeries and stripes, moreover also of bands and prisons.

They were stoned, they were cut asunder, they were tempted, they were put to death by the sword, they wandered about in sheepskins, in goatskins, being in want, distressed, afflicted: Of whom the world was not worthy. —*Heb.* xi. 35-38.

Dearly beloved, think not strange the burning heat which is to try you, as if some new thing happened to you;

But if you partake of the sufferings of Christ, rejoice that when his glory shall be revealed, you may also be glad with exceeding joy.—*1 Peter* iv. 12, 13.

And when he (the Lamb) had opened the fifth seal, I saw under the altar, the souls of them that were slain for the word of God, and for the testimony which they held.

And they cried with a loud voice, saying: How long, O Lord, (holy and true,) dost thou not judge and revenge our blood on them that dwell on the earth?

And white robes were given to every one of them, one; and it was said to them, that they should rest for a little while, till their fellow-servants and their brethren, who are to be slain, even as they, should be filled up.—*Apoc.* vi. 9-11.

MASTER, GOD OUR

And the Lord God took man, and put him into the paradise of pleasure, to dress it, and to keep it.

And he commanded him, saying: Of every tree of paradise thou shalt eat:

But of the tree of knowledge of good and evil, thou shalt not eat. For in what day soever thou shalt eat of it, thou shalt die the death.—*Gen.* ii. 15-17.

The Lord ruleth me, and I shall want nothing.—*Ps.* xxii. 1.

For this is God, our God unto eternity, and for ever and ever: he shall rule us for evermore.—*Ps.* xlvii. 15.

Shall not my soul be subject to God? for from him is my salvation.—*Ps.* lxi. 2.

But be thou, O my soul, subject to God: for from him is my patience.—*Ps.* lxi. 6.

O Lord, for I am thy servant: I am thy servant, and the son of thy handmaid. Thou hast broken my bonds.—*Ps.* cxv. 16.

I am thine, save thou me: for I have sought thy justifications.—*Ps.* cxviii. 94.

And now, thus saith the Lord that created thee, O Jacob, and formed thee, O Israel: Fear not, for I have redeemed thee, and called thee by thy name: thou art mine.—*Is.* xliii. 1.

Cannot I do with you as this potter, O house of Israel, saith the Lord? behold, as clay is in the hand of the potter, so are you in my hand, O house of Israel.—*Jer.* xviii. 6.

Behold, all souls are mine: as the soul of the father, so also the soul of the son is mine.—*Ezech.* xviii. 4.

The son honoreth the father, and the servant his master: if then I be a father, where is my honor? and if I be a master, where is my fear? saith the Lord of hosts.—*Malach.* i. 6.

But which of you having a servant ploughing, or feeding cattle, will say to him, when he is come from the field: Immediately go, sit down to meat:

And will not rather say to him: Make ready my supper, and gird thyself, and serve me, whilst I eat and drink, and afterwards thou shalt eat and drink?

Doth he thank that servant, for doing the things which he commanded him?

I think not. So you also, when you shall have done all these things that are commanded you, say: We are unprofitable servants; we have done that which we ought to do.—*Luke* xvii. 7-10.

O man, who art thou, that repliest against God? ·Shall the thing formed, say to him that formed it: Why hast thou made me thus?

Or hath not the potter power over the clay, of the same lump, to make one vessel unto honor, and another unto dishonor?—*Rom.* ix. 20, 21.

Or know you not, that your members are the temple of the Holy Ghost, who is in you, whom you have from God; and you are not your own?

For you are bought with a great price. Glorify and bear God in your body.—1 *Cor.* vi. 19, 20.

Masters, do to your servants that which is just and equal: knowing that you also have a master in heaven.—*Col.* iv. 1.

MASTER, CHRIST OUR

Neither be ye called masters; for one is your master, Christ.—*Matt.* xxiii. 10.

You call me Master and Lord; and you say well, for so I am.—*John* xiii. 13.

For none of us liveth to himself; and no man dieth to himself.

For whether we live, we live unto the Lord; or whether we die, we die unto the Lord. Therefore, whether we live, or whether we die, we are the Lord's.

For to this end Christ died and rose again; that he might be Lord both of the dead and of the living.—*Rom.* xiv. 7-9.

For all things are yours. . . . And you are Christ's; and Christ is God's.—1 *Cor.* iii. 22, 23.

For he that is called in the Lord, being a bondman, is the freeman of the Lord. Likewise he that is called, being free, is the bondman of Christ.

You are bought with a price; be not made the bond-slaves of men.—1 *Cor.* vii. 22, 23.

MASTER OF LIFE AND DEATH, GOD IS

See ye that I alone am, and there is no other God besides me: I will kill and I will make to live: I will strike and I will heal, and there is none that can deliver out of my hand.—*Deut.* xxxii. 39.

The Lord killeth and maketh alive, he bringeth down to hell and bringeth back again.—1 *Kings* ii. 6.

Our God is the God of salvation: and of the Lord, of the Lord are the issues from death.—*Ps.* lxvii. 21.

For it was neither herb, nor mollifying plaster, that healed them, but thy word, O Lord, which healeth all things.

For it is thou, O Lord, that hast power of life and death, and leadest down to the gates of death, and bringest back again.—*Wis.* xvi. 12, 13.

Thus saith the Lord God, that created the heavens, and stretched them out: that established the earth, and the things that spring out of it: that giveth breath to the people upon it, and spirit to them that tread thereon.—*Is.* xlii. 5.

But you denied the Holy One and the Just, and desired a murderer to be granted unto you.

But the author of life you killed, whom God hath raised from the dead, of which we are witnesses.—*Acts* iii. 14, 15.

MASTER OF ALL THINGS, GOD IS

If therefore you will hear my voice, and keep my covenant, you shall be my peculiar possession above all people: for all the earth is mine.—*Ex.* xix. 5.

Behold, heaven is the Lord's, thy God, and the heaven of heaven, the earth and all things that are therein.—*Deut.* x. 14.

Thine, O Lord, is magnificence, and power, and glory, and victory: and to thee is praise: for all that is in heaven and in earth is thine: thine is the kingdom, O Lord, and thou art above all princes.

Thine are riches, and thine is glory, thou hast dominion over all, in thy hand is power and might: in thy hand, greatness, and the empire of all things. . . .

Who am I, and what is my people, that we should be able to promise thee all these things? all things are thine: and we have given thee what we re-received of thy hand.

. . . O Lord our God, all this store that we have prepared to build thee a house, for thy holy name, is from thy

hand, and all things are thine.—
1 *Paral.* xxix. 11, 12, 14, 16.

Thou hast made heaven and earth, and all things that are under the cope of heaven.

Thou art Lord of all, and there is none that can resist thy majesty.—*Esther* xiii. 10, 11.

For he beholdeth the ends of the world: and looketh on all things that are under heaven.

Who made a weight for the winds, and weighed the waters by measure.

When he gave a law for the rain, and a way for the sounding storms.—*Job* xxviii. 24-26.

Who hath given me before, that I should repay him? All things that are under heaven are mine.—*Job* xli. 2.

The earth is the Lord's, and the fulness thereof: the world, and all they that dwell therein.—*Ps.* xxiii. 1.

For all the beasts of the woods are mine: the cattle on the hills, and the oxen.

I know all the fowls of the air: and with me is the beauty of the field.

If I should be hungry, I would not tell thee: for the world is mine, and the fulness thereof.—*Ps.* xlix. 10-12.

Thine is the day, and thine is the night: thou hast made the morning light and the sun.—*Ps.* lxxiii. 16.

Thine are the heavens, and thine is the earth: the world and the fulness thereof thou hast founded.—*Ps.* lxxxviii. 12.

For in his hand are all the ends of the earth: and the heights of the mountains are his.

For the sea is his, and he made it: and his hands formed the dry land.—*Ps.* xciv. 4, 5.

The Lord hath made all things for himself.—*Prov.* xvi. 4.

And how could any thing endure, if thou wouldst not? or be preserved, if not called by thee.

But thou sparest all: because they are thine, O Lord, who lovest souls.—*Wis.* xi. 26, 27.

For thy power is the beginning of justice: and because thou art Lord of all, thou makest thyself gracious to all.—*Wis.* xii. 16.

MASTERS TO THEIR SERVANTS, DUTIES OF

Hurt not the servant that worketh faithfully, nor the hired man that giveth thee his life.

Let a wise servant be dear to thee as thy own soul, defraud him not of liberty, nor leave him needy.—*Ecclus.* vii. 22, 23.

If thou have a faithful servant, let him be to thee as thy own soul: treat him as a brother: because in the blood of thy soul thou hast gotten him.—*Ecclus.* xxxiii. 31.

And you, masters, do the same things to them (servants), forbearing threatenings, knowing that the Lord both of them and you, is in heaven; and there is no respect of persons with him.—*Eph.* vi. 9.

Masters, do to your servants that which is just and equal: knowing that you also have a master in heaven.—*Col.* iv. 1.

MEANNESS OF DISPOSITION, OR MISERLINESS

Let not thy hand be stretched out to receive, and shut when thou shouldst give.—*Ecclus.* iv. 36.

There is one that is enriched by living sparingly, and this is the portion of his reward.

In that he saith: I have found me rest, and now I will eat of my goods alone:

And he knoweth not what time shall pass, and that death approacheth, and that he must leave all to others, and shall die.—*Ecclus.* xi. 18-20.

Riches are not comely for a covetous man and a niggard, and what should an envious man do with gold?—*Ecclus.* xiv. 3.

Against him that is niggardly of his bread, the city will murmur, and the testimony of his niggardliness is true.—*Ecclus.* xxxi. 29.

He that hath the substance of this world, and shall see his brother in need, and shall shut up his bowels from him: how doth the charity of God abide in him?—1 *John* iii. 17.

MEDDLING IN THE AFFAIRS OF OTHERS, AGAINST

The lips of a fool intermeddle with strife: and his mouth provoketh quarrels.—*Prov.* xviii. 6.

As he that taketh a dog by the ears, so is he that passeth by in anger, and meddleth with another man's quarrel. —*Prov.* xxvi. 17.

Strive not in a matter which doth not concern thee, and sit not in judgment with sinners.

My son, meddle not with many matters.—*Ecclus.* xi. 9, 10.

But we entreat you, brethren, that you abound more:

And that you use your endeavor to be quiet, and that you do your own business, and work with your own hands, as we commanded you.—1 *Thess.* iv. 10, 11.

For we have heard there are some among you who walk disorderly, working not at all, but curiously meddling.

Now we charge them that are such, and beseech them by the Lord Jesus Christ, that, working with silence, they would eat their own bread.—2 *Thess.* iii. 11, 12.

And withal being idle, they learn to go about from house to house: and are not only idle, but tattlers also, and busybodies, speaking things which they ought not.—1 *Tim.* v. 13.

MEDIATOR, CHRIST OUR

Being justified, therefore, by faith, let us have peace with God, through our Lord Jesus Christ:

By whom also we have access through faith, into this grace, wherein we stand, and glory in the hope of the glory of the sons of God.—*Rom.* v. 1, 2.

Who is he that shall condemn? Christ Jesus that died; yea, that is risen also again; who is at the right hand of God, who also maketh intercession for us.—*Rom.* viii. 34.

But now in Christ Jesus, you, who sometime were afar off, are made nigh by the blood of Christ. . . .

For by him we have access both in one Spirit to the Father.—*Eph.* ii. 13, 18.

Because in him it hath well pleased the Father, that all fulness should dwell;

And through him, to reconcile all things unto himself, making peace through the blood of his cross, both as to the things that are on earth, and the things that are in heaven.—*Col.* i. 19, 20.

For there is one God, and one mediator of God and men, the man Christ Jesus:

Who gave himself a redemption for all, a testimony in due times.—1 *Tim.* ii. 5, 6.

But this, for that he continueth for ever, hath an everlasting priesthood,

Whereby he is able also to save for ever them that come to God by him; always living to make intercession for us.—*Heb.* vii. 24, 25.

But now he hath obtained a better ministry, by how much also he is a mediator of a better testament, which is established on better promises.—*Heb.* viii. 6.

And therefore he is the mediator of the new testament: that by means of his death, for the redemption of those transgressions, which were under the former testament, they that are called, may receive the promise of eternal inheritance.—*Heb.* ix. 15.

But you are come to mount Sion, and to the city of the living God, the heavenly Jerusalem, and to the company of many thousands of angels, . . .

And to Jesus, the mediator of the new testament, and to the sprinkling of blood which speaketh better than that of Abel.—*Heb.* xii. 22, 24.

My little children, these things I write to you, that you may not sin. But if any man sin, we have an advocate with the Father, Jesus Christ the just:

And he is the propitiation for our sins: and not for ours only, but also for those of the whole world.—1 *John* ii. 1, 2.

MEDITATION

Blessed is the man who hath not walked in the counsel of the ungodly, nor stood in the way of sinners, nor sat in the chair of pestilence.

But his will is in the law of the Lord,

and on his law he shall meditate day and night.—*Ps.* i. 1, 2.

I set the Lord always in my sight: for he is at my right hand, that I be not moved.—*Ps.* xv. 8.

And the words of my mouth shall be such as may please: and the meditation of my heart always in thy sight. O Lord, my helper, and my redeemer. —*Ps.* xviii. 15.

If I have remembered thee upon my bed,

I will meditate on thee in the morning: because thou hast been my helper. —*Ps.* lxii. 7, 8.

I thought upon the days of old: and I had in my mind the eternal years.

And I meditated in the night with my own heart: and I was exercised, and I swept my spirit. . . .

And I will meditate on all thy works: and will be employed in thy inventions. —*Ps.* lxxvi. 6, 7, 13.

I will meditate on thy commandments: and I will consider thy ways.

I will think of thy justifications: I will not forget thy words.—*Ps.* cxviii. 15, 16.

For thy testimonies are my meditation: and thy justifications my counsel. . . .

I meditated also on thy commandments, which I loved. . . .

I have thought on my ways: and turned my feet unto thy testimonies.— *Ps.* cxviii. 24, 47, 59.

Unless thy law had been my meditation, I had then perhaps perished in my abjection. . . .

My eyes to thee have prevented the morning: that I might meditate on thy words.—*Ps.* cxviii. 92, 148.

I remembered the days of old, I meditated on all thy works: I meditated upon the works of thy hands.— *Ps.* cxlii. 5.

Blessed is the man that shall continue in wisdom, and that shall meditate in his justice, and in his mind shall think of the all-seeing eye of God. —*Ecclus.* xiv. 22.

And he (the wise man) shall direct his counsel, and his knowledge, and in his secrets shall he meditate.—*Ecclus.* xxxix. 10.

I will yet meditate, that I may de-clare: for I am filled, as with a holy transport.—*Ecclus.* xxxix. 16.

With desolation is all the land made desolate; because there is none that considereth in the heart.—*Jer.* xii. 11.

Therefore, behold, I will allure her, and will lead her into the wilderness: and I will speak to her heart.—*Osee* ii. 14.

But Mary kept all these words, pondering them in her heart.—*Luke* ii. 19.

MEDITATION, EXHORTATION TO PRACTISE

And these words which I command thee this day, shall be in thy heart:

And thou shalt tell them to thy children, and thou shalt meditate upon them, sitting in thy house, and walking on thy journey, sleeping and rising. —*Deut.* vi. 6, 7.

Lay up these my words in your hearts and minds, and hang them for a sign on your hands, and place them between your eyes.

Teach your children that they meditate on them, when thou sittest in thy house, and when thou walkest on the way, and when thou liest down and risest up.—*Deut.* xi. 18, 19.

Remember the days of old, think upon every generation: ask thy father, and he will declare to thee: thy elders, and they will tell thee.—*Deut.* xxxii. 7.

Let not the book of this law depart from thy mouth: but thou shalt meditate on it day and night, that thou mayst observe and do all things that are written in it: then shalt thou direct thy way, and understand it.—*Jos.* i. 8.

Seek not the things that are too high for thee, and search not into things above thy ability: but the things that God hath commanded thee, think on them always, and in many of his works be not curious.—*Ecclus.* iii. 22.

Let thy thoughts be upon the precepts of God, and meditate continually on his commandments: and he will give thee a heart, and the desire of wisdom shall be given to thee.—*Ecclus.* vi. 37.

And let the thought of God be in thy mind, and all thy discourse on the commandments of the Highest.—*Ecclus.* ix. 23.

And he (Jesus) cometh to his disciples, and findeth them asleep, and he saith to Peter: What? Could you not watch one hour with me?—*Matt.* xxvi. 40.

For the rest, brethren, whatsoever things are true, whatsoever modest, whatsoever just, whatsoever holy, whatsoever lovely, whatsoever of good fame, if there be any virtue, if any praise of discipline, think on these things.—*Philipp.* iv. 8.

Meditate upon these things, be wholly in these things: that thy profiting may be manifest to all.—1 *Tim.* iv. 15.

MEEK, THE

He will guide the mild in judgment: he will teach the meek his ways.—*Ps.* xxiv. 9.

I will bless the Lord at all times, his praise shall be always in my mouth.

In the Lord shall my soul be praised: let the meek hear and rejoice.—*Ps.* xxxiii. 2, 3.

It is better to be humbled with the meek, than to divide spoils with the proud.—*Prov.* xvi. 19.

But he shall judge the poor with justice, and shall reprove with equity for the meek of the earth.—*Is.* xi. 4.

Seek the Lord, all ye meek of the earth, you that have wrought his judgment: seek the just, seek the meek: if by any means, you may be hid in the day of the Lord's indignation.—*Soph.* ii. 3.

MEEKNESS PLEASING TO GOD

For thy power, O Lord, is not in a multitude, nor is thy pleasure in the strength of horses, nor from the beginning have the proud been acceptable to thee: but the prayer of the humble and the meek hath always pleased thee.—*Judith* ix. 16.

O Lord, remember David, and all his meekness.—*Ps.* cxxxi. 1.

For the fear of the Lord is wisdom and discipline: and that which is agreeable to him,

Is faith and meekness: and he will fill up his treasures.—*Ecclus.* i. 34, 35.

MEEKNESS REWARDED BY GOD

But the meek shall inherit the land, and shall delight in abundance of peace.—*Ps.* xxxvi. 11.

Thou hast caused judgment to be heard from heaven: the earth trembled and was still,

When God arose in judgment, to save all the meek of the earth.—*Ps.* lxxv. 9, 10.

The Lord lifteth up the meek, and bringeth the wicked down even to the ground.—*Ps.* cxlvi. 6.

For the Lord is well pleased with his people: and he will exalt the meek unto salvation.—*Ps.* cxlix. 4.

He shall scorn the scorners, and to the meek, he will give grace.—*Prov.* iii. 34.

God hath overturned the thrones of proud princes, and hath set up the meek in their stead.—*Ecclus.* x. 17.

And in that day, the deaf shall hear the words of the book, and out of darkness and obscurity, the eyes of the blind shall see.

And the meek shall increase their joy in the Lord, and the poor men shall rejoice in the Holy One of Israel.—*Is.* xxix. 18, 19.

Blessed are the meek: for they shall possess the land.—*Matt.* v. 4.

MEEKNESS, EXHORTATION TO

My son, do thy works in meekness, and thou shalt be beloved above the glory of men.—*Ecclus.* iii. 19.

Be meek to hear the word, that thou mayst understand: and return a true answer with wisdom.—*Ecclus.* v. 13.

My son, keep thy soul in meekness, and give it honor, according to its desert.—*Ecclus.* x. 31.

You have heard that it hath been said,

An eye for an eye, and a tooth for a tooth.

But I say to you not to resist evil: but if one strike thee on thy right cheek, turn to him also the other:

And if a man will contend with thee in judgment, and take away thy coat, let go thy cloak also unto him.

And whosoever will force thee one mile, go with him other two.—*Matt.* v. 38-41.

Take up my yoke upon you, and learn of me, because I am meek, and humble of heart: and you shall find rest to your souls.—*Matt.* xi. 29.

Brethren, and if a man be overtaken in any fault, you, who are spiritual, instruct such a one, in the spirit of meekness, considering thyself, lest thou also be tempted.—*Gal.* vi. 1.

Wherefore, casting away all uncleanness, and abundance of naughtiness, with meekness, receive the ingrafted word, which is able to save your souls. —*James* i. 21.

Whose adorning, let it not be the outward plaiting of the hair, or the wearing of gold, or the putting on of apparel:

But the hidden man of the heart, in the incorruptibility of a quiet and a meek spirit, which is rich in the sight of God.—1 *Peter* iii. 3, 4.

MEEKNESS OF CHRIST, THE

Take up my yoke upon you, and learn of me, because I am meek, and humble of heart.—*Matt.* xi. 29.

That it might be fulfilled which was spoken by Isaias the prophet, saying:

Behold my servant whom I have chosen, my beloved, in whom my soul hath been well pleased. I will put my spirit upon him, and he shall show judgment to the Gentiles.

He shall not contend, nor cry out, neither shall any man hear his voice in the streets.

The bruised reed he shall not break: and smoking flax he shall not extinguish: till he send forth judgment unto victory.—*Matt.* xii. 17-20.

And when they drew nigh to Jerusalem, and were come to Bethphage, unto mount Olivet, then Jesus sent two disciples,

Saying to them: Go ye into the village that is over against you, and immediately you shall find an ass tied, and a colt with her: loose them and bring them to me. . . .

Now all this was done that it might be fulfilled, which was spoken by the prophet, saying:

Tell ye the daughter of Sion: Behold thy king cometh to thee, meek, and sitting upon an ass, and a colt, the foal of her that is used to the yoke.—*Matt.* xxi. 1, 2, 4, 5.

And he sent messengers before his face: and going, they entered into a city of the Samaritans, to prepare for him.

And they received him not, because his face was of one going to Jerusalem.

And when his disciples James and John had seen this, they said: Lord, wilt thou that we command fire to come down from heaven and consume them?

And turning, he rebuked them, saying: You know not of what spirit you are.

The Son of man came not to destroy souls, but to save. And they went into another town.—*Luke* ix. 52-56.

You have condemned and put to death the Just One, and he resisted you not.—*James* v. 6.

For unto this are you called: because Christ also suffered for us, leaving you an example, that you should follow his steps. . . .

Who, when he was reviled, did not revile: when he suffered, he threatened not: but delivered himself to him that judged him unjustly.—1 *Peter* ii. 21, 23.

MERCY OF GOD, THE

And I will have mercy on whom I will, and I will be merciful to whom it shall please me.—*Ex.* xxxiii. 19.

O the Lord, the Lord God, merciful and gracious, patient, and of much compassion, and true,

Who keepest mercy unto thousands: who takest away iniquity, and wickedness, and sin, and no man of himself is innocent before thee.—*Ex.* xxxiv. 6, 7.

And David said to Gad: I am in a great strait: but it is better that I should fall into the hands of the Lord (for his mercies are many) than into the hands of men.—2 *Kings* xxiv. 14.

And I wish that God would speak with thee, and would open his lips to thee,

That he might show thee the secrets of wisdom, and that his law is manifold, and thou mightest understand that he exacteth much less of thee, than thy iniquity deserveth.—*Job* xi. 5, 6.

He shall have mercy on him, and shall say: Deliver him, that he may not go down to corruption: I have found wherein I may be merciful to him.—*Job* xxxiii. 24.

And thy mercy will follow me all the days of my life.—*Ps.* xxii. 6.

For thy mercy is before my eyes; and I am well pleased with thy truth.—*Ps.* xxv. 3.

I will be glad, and rejoice in thy mercy. For thou hast regarded my humility, thou hast saved my soul out of distress.—*Ps.* xxx. 8.

In the day time, the Lord hath commanded his mercy; and a canticle to him in the night.—*Ps.* xli. 9.

God hath spoken once, these two things have I heard, that power belongeth to God,

And mercy to thee, O Lord; for thou wilt render to every man according to his works.—*Ps.* lxi. 12, 13.

Will God then cast off for ever? or will he never more be favorable again?

Or will he cut off his mercy for ever, from generation to generation?

Or will God forget to show mercy? or will he in his anger shut up his mercies?—*Ps.* lxxvi. 8-10.

Mercy and truth have met each other: justice and peace have kissed.—*Ps.* lxxxiv. 11.

For thou hast said: Mercy shall be built up for ever in the heavens: thy truth shall be prepared in them. . . .

Justice and judgment are the preparation of thy throne. Mercy and truth shall go before thy face.—*Ps.* lxxxviii. 3, 15.

Lord, where are thy ancient mercies, according to what thou didst swear to David in thy truth?—*Ps.* lxxxviii. 50.

Thou shalt arise, and have mercy on Sion: for it is time to have mercy on it, for the time is come.—*Ps.* ci. 14.

Bless the Lord, O my soul, and never forget all he hath done for thee.

Who forgiveth all thy iniquities: who healeth all thy diseases.

Who redeemeth thy life from destruction: who crowneth thee with mercy and compassion.—*Ps.* cii. 2-4.

The Lord is compassionate and merciful: long-suffering and plenteous in mercy.

He will not always be angry; nor will he threaten for ever.—*Ps.* cii. 8, 9.

Let the mercies of the Lord give glory to him, and his wonderful works to the children of men.—*Ps.* cvi. 15.

But thou hast mercy upon all, because thou canst do all things, and overlookest the sins of men for the sake of repentance.—*Wis.* xi. 24.

Therefore God is patient in them and poureth forth his mercy upon them. . . .

Therefore hath he filled up his mercy in their favor, and hath shown them the way of justice.

The compassion of man is towards his neighbor: but the mercy of God is upon all flesh.

He hath mercy, and teacheth, and correcteth, as a shepherd doth his flock.—*Ecclus.* xviii. 9, 11-13.

Grace is like a paradise in blessings, and mercy remaineth for ever.—*Ecclus.* xl. 17.

Let your soul rejoice in his mercy, and you shall not be confounded in his praise.—*Ecclus.* li. 37.

Therefore the Lord waiteth, that he may have mercy on you; and therefore shall he be exalted, sparing you: because the Lord is the God of judgment: blessed are all they that wait for him.—*Is.* xxx. 18.

Give praise, O ye heavens, and rejoice, O earth, ye mountains, give praise with jubilation: because the Lord hath comforted his people, and will have mercy on his poor ones.—*Is.* xlix. 13.

For the mountains shall be moved, and the hills shall tremble; but my mercy shall not depart from thee, and the covenant of my peace shall not be moved: said the Lord that hath mercy on thee.—*Is.* liv. 10.

Go, and cry in the ears of Jerusalem, saying: Thus saith the Lord: I have remembered thee, pitying thy youth, and the love of thy espousals, when thou followedst me in the desert, in a land that is not sown.—*Jer.* ii. 2.

But let him that glorieth, glory in this, that he understandeth and knoweth me, for I am the Lord that exercise mercy, and judgment, and justice in the earth: for these things please me, saith the Lord.—*Jer.* ix. 24.

In the midst of the years, thou shalt make it (thy work) known: when thou art angry, thou wilt remember mercy.—*Hab.* iii. 2.

Be ye therefore merciful, as your Father also is merciful.—*Luke* vi. 36.

Blessed be the God and Father of our Lord Jesus Christ, the Father of mercies, and the God of all comfort.—2 *Cor.* i. 3.

MERCY OF GOD, THE POWER AND EXCELLENCE OF THE

For wrath is in his indignation; and life in his good will.—*Ps.* xxix. 6.

For thy mercy is better than lives: thee my lips shall praise.—*Ps.* lxii. 4.

Brethren are a help in the time of trouble, but mercy shall deliver more than they.—*Ecclus.* xl. 24.

But when the goodness and kindness of God our Saviour appeared:

Not by the works of justice, which we have done, but according to his mercy, he saved us, by the laver of regeneration, and renovation of the Holy Ghost. —*Titus* iii. 4, 5.

MERCY OF GOD, GREATNESS OF THE

But as for me, in the multitude of thy mercy,

I will come into thy house.—*Ps.* v. 8.

He loveth mercy and judgment; the earth is full of the mercy of the Lord. *Ps.* xxxii. 5.

O, how hast thou multiplied thy mercy, O God!—*Ps.* xxxv. 8.

I will give praise to thee, O Lord, among the people: I will sing a psalm to thee among the nations.

For thy mercy is magnified even to the heavens: and thy truth unto the clouds.—*Ps.* lvi. 10, 11.

His mercy and truth who shall search?—*Ps.* lx. 8.

Praise ye his name: for the Lord is sweet, his mercy endureth for ever, and his truth to generation and generation. —*Ps.* xcix. 4, 5.

For according to the height of the heaven above the earth: he hath strengthened his mercy towards them that fear him. . . .

But the mercy of the Lord is from eternity and unto eternity upon them that fear him.—*Ps.* cii. 11, 17.

For thy mercy is great above the

heavens: and thy truth even unto the clouds.—*Ps.* cvii. 5.

The earth, O Lord, is full of thy mercy: teach me thy justifications.— *Ps.* cxviii. 64.

Many, O Lord, are thy mercies; quicken me, according to thy judgment.—*Ps.* cxviii. 156.

The Lord is sweet to all: and his tender mercies are over all his works. —*Ps.* cxliv. 9.

For according to his greatness, so also is his mercy with him.—*Ecclus.* ii. 23.

And who shall show forth the power of his majesty? or who shall be able to declare his mercy?—*Ecclus.* xviii. 4.

For a small moment have I forsaken thee, but with great mercies will I gather thee.

In a moment of indignation, have I hid my face a little while from thee, but with everlasting kindness have I had mercy on thee, said the Lord thy Redeemer.—*Is.* liv. 7, 8.

The mercies of the Lord that we are not consumed: because his commiserations have not failed.

They are new every morning, great is thy faithfulness.—*Lam.* iii. 22, 23.

But God (who is rich in mercy), for his exceeding charity wherewith he loved us,

Even when we were dead in sins, hath quickened us together in Christ (by whose grace you are saved). . . .

That he might show in the ages to come, the abundant riches of his grace, in his bounty towards us in Christ Jesus.—*Eph.* ii. 4, 5, 7.

MERCY OF GOD, ACKNOWLEDGMENT OF THE

O Lord, thou hast crowned us, as with a shield of thy good will.—*Ps.* v. 13.

Blessed be the Lord, for he hath shown his wonderful mercy to me in a fortified city.—*Ps.* xxx. 22.

We have received thy mercy, O God, in the midst of thy temple.—*Ps.* xlvii. 10.

For thy mercy is great towards me: and thou hast delivered my soul out of the lower hell.—*Ps.* lxxxv. 13.

The mercies of the Lord I will sing for ever.—*Ps.* lxxxviii. 2.

We are filled in the morning with thy mercy: and we have rejoiced, and are delighted all our days.—*Ps.* lxxxix. 14.

It is good to give praise to the Lord: and to sing to thy name, O most High.

To show forth thy mercy in the morning, and thy truth in the night.—*Ps.* xci. 2, 3.

If I said: My foot is moved: thy mercy, O Lord, assisted me.—*Ps.* xciii. 18.

He hath remembered his mercy and his truth towards the house of Israel. —*Ps.* xcvii. 3.

He hath not dealt with us according to our sins: nor rewarded us according to our iniquities.—*Ps.* cii. 10.

Give glory to the Lord, for he is good: for his mercy endureth for ever.

Let them say so who have been redeemed by the Lord, whom he hath redeemed from the hand of the enemy: and gathered out of the countries.—*Ps.* cvi. 1, 2.

The Lord is merciful and just, and our God showeth mercy. . . .

Turn, O my soul, into thy rest: for the Lord hath been bountiful to thee.

For he hath delivered my soul from death: my eyes from tears, my feet from falling.—*Ps.* cxiv. 5, 7, 8.

O praise the Lord, all ye nations: praise him, all ye people.

For his mercy is confirmed upon us: and the truth of the Lord remaineth for ever.—*Ps.* cxvi. 1, 2.

But thou, our God, art gracious and true, patient, and ordering all things in mercy.—*Wis.* xv. 1.

Give thanks whilst thou art living, whilst thou art alive and in health, thou shalt give thanks, and shalt praise God, and shalt glory in his mercies.— *Ecclus.* xvii. 27.

I remembered thy mercy, O Lord, and thy works, which are from the beginning of the world.—*Ecclus.* li. 11.

Give praise, O ye heavens, for the Lord hath shown mercy: shout with joy, ye ends of the earth: ye mountains, resound with praise, thou, O forest, and every tree therein: for the Lord hath redeemed Jacob, and Israel shall be glorified.—*Is.* xliv. 23.

I will remember the tender mercies of the Lord, the praise of the Lord, for all the things that the Lord hath bestowed upon us, and for the multitude of his good things to the house of Israel, which he hath given them according to his kindness, and according to the multitude of his mercies.—*Is.* lxiii. 7.

And thou hast dealt with us, O Lord our God, according to all thy goodness, and according to all that great mercy of thine.—*Bar.* ii. 27.

O Lord God, Creator of all things, dreadful and strong, just and merciful, who alone art the good king,

Who alone art gracious, who alone art just, and almighty, and eternal.— *2 Mach.* i. 24, 25.

Blessed be the God and Father of our Lord Jesus Christ, who, according to his great mercy, hath regenerated us unto a lively hope, by the resurrection of Jesus Christ from the dead,

Unto an inheritance, incorruptible and undefiled, and that cannot fade, reserved in heaven for you.—1 *Peter* i. 3, 4.

MERCY AND FAVOR TO US, GOD'S SPECIAL

See: Favor to us, God's special— page 141.

MERCY AND FAVOR TO HIS OWN PEOPLE, GOD'S SPECIAL

In thy mercy, thou hast been a leader to the people which thou hast redeemed: and in thy strength, thou hast carried them to thy holy habitation.—*Ex.* xv. 13.

You have seen what I have done to the Egyptians, how I have carried you upon the wings of eagles, and have taken you to myself.

If therefore you will hear my voice, and keep my covenant, you shall be my peculiar possession above all people: for all the earth is mine.

And you shall be to me a priestly kingdom, and a holy nation. These are the words thou shalt speak to the children of Israel.—*Ex.* xix. 4-6.

Salvation is of the Lord: and thy blessing is upon thy people.—*Ps.* iii. 9.

The Lord is the strength of his people, and the protector of the salvation of his anointed.—*Ps.* xxvii. 8.

The Lord will give strength to his people: the Lord will bless his people with peace.—*Ps.* xxviii. 10.

Blessed is the nation whose God is the Lord: the people whom he hath chosen for his inheritance.—*Ps.* xxxii. 12.

Mountains are round about it (Jerusalem): so the Lord is round about his people, from henceforth now and for ever.—*Ps.* cxxiv. 2.

For the Lord is well pleased with his people: and he will exalt the meek unto salvation.—*Ps.* cxlix. 4.

For in all things thou didst magnify thy people, O Lord, and didst honor them, and didst not despise them, but didst assist them at all times, and in every place.—*Wis.* xix. 20.

Thou hast been favorable to the nation, O Lord, thou hast been favorable to the nation: art thou glorified? thou hast removed all the ends of the earth far off.—*Is.* xxvi. 15.

But thou, Israel, art my servant, Jacob, whom I have chosen, the seed of Abraham, my friend. . . .

Fear not, for I am with thee: turn not aside, for I am thy God: I have strengthened thee, and have helped thee, and the right hand of my just one hath upheld thee.

Behold, all that fight against thee, shall be confounded and ashamed, they shall be as nothing, and the men shall perish that strive against thee. . . .

For I am the Lord thy God, who take thee by the hand, and say to thee: Fear not, I have helped thee.—*Is.* xli. 8, 10, 11, 13.

And now hear, O Jacob, my servant, and Israel, whom I have chosen.

Thus saith the Lord that made and formed thee, thy helper from the womb: Fear not, O my servant Jacob, and thou most righteous whom I have chosen.

For I will pour out waters upon the thirsty ground, and streams upon the dry land: I will pour out my spirit upon thy seed, and my blessing upon thy stock.

And they shall spring up among the herbs, as willows beside the running waters.—*Is.* xliv. 1-4.

Even to your old age, I am the same, and to your grey hairs, I will carry you: I have made you, and I will bear: I will carry, and will save.—*Is.* xlvi. 4.

And thou shalt be a crown of glory in the hand of the Lord, and a royal diadem in the hand of thy God.

Thou shalt no more be called Forsaken; and thy land shall no more be called Desolate: but thou shalt be called My pleasure in her, and thy land, inhabited. Because the Lord hath been well pleased with thee: and thy land shall be inhabited.—*Is.* lxii. 3, 4.

And he said: Surely they are my people, children that will not deny: so he became their saviour.

In all their affliction he was not troubled, and the angel of his presence saved them: in his love and in his mercy he redeemed them, and he carried them, and lifted them up, all the days of old.—*Is.* lxiii. 8, 9.

And dost thou seek great things for thyself? Seek not: for behold I will bring evil upon all flesh, saith the Lord! but I will give thee thy life, and save thee in all places whithersoever thou shalt go.—*Jer.* xlv. 5.

And I will espouse thee to me for ever: and I will espouse thee to me in justice, and judgment, and in mercy, and in commiserations.

And I will espouse thee to me in faith: and thou shalt know that I am the Lord.—*Osee* ii. 19, 20.

And you shall know that I am in the midst of Israel: and I am the Lord your God, and there is none besides: and my people shall not be confounded for ever.—*Joel* ii. 27.

In that day it shall be said to Jerusalem: Fear not: to Sion: Let not thy hands be weakened.

The Lord thy God in the midst of thee is mighty, he will save: he will rejoice over thee with gladness, he will be silent in his love, he will be joyful over thee in praise.—*Soph.* iii. 16, 17.

And if I shall go, and prepare a place for you, I will come again, and will take you to myself; that where I am, you also may be.—*John* xiv. 3.

MERCY OF GOD TO THE JUST, THE

I am the Lord thy God, mighty, jealous, visiting the iniquity of the fathers upon the children, unto the third and fourth generation of them that hate me:

And showing mercy unto thousands to them that love me, and keep my commandments.—*Ex.* xx. 5, 6.

The innocent in hands, and clean of heart, who hath not taken his soul in vain, nor sworn deceitfully to his neighbor.

He shall receive a blessing from the Lord, and mercy from God his Saviour. —*Ps.* xxiii. 4, 5.

I have found David my servant: with my holy oil I have anointed him. . . .

And my truth and my mercy shall be with him: and in my name shall his horn be exalted. . . .

I will keep my mercy for him for ever: and my covenant faithful to him. . . .

But my mercy I will not take away from him: nor will I suffer my truth to fail.—*Ps.* lxxxviii. 21, 25, 29, 34.

For according to the height of the heaven above the earth: he hath strengthened his mercy towards them that fear him.—*Ps.* cii. 11.

He hath mercy on him that receiveth the discipline of mercy, and that maketh haste in his judgments.—*Ecclus.* xviii. 14.

Till he have judged the cause of his people, and he shall delight the just with his mercy.—*Ecclus.* xxxv. 25.

Blessed are the merciful: for they shall obtain mercy.—*Matt.* v. 7.

And his mercy is from generation unto generations, to them that fear him.—*Luke* i. 50.

See then the goodness and the severity of God: towards them indeed that are fallen, the severity; but towards thee, the goodness of God, if thou abide in goodness, otherwise thou also shalt be cut off.—*Rom.* xi. 22.

MERCY OF GOD TO THE UNJUST, THE

But thou, being master of power, judgest with tranquillity; and with great favor disposest of us: for thy power is at hand, when thou wilt.

But thou hast taught thy people by such works, that they must be just and humane, and hast made thy children to be of a good hope: because in judging, thou givest place for repentance for sins.—*Wis.* xii. 18, 19.

But I say to you, Love your enemies: do good to them that hate you: and pray for them that persecute and calumniate you:

That you may be the children of your Father who is in heaven, who maketh his sun to rise upon the good, and bad, and raineth upon the just and the unjust.—*Matt.* v. 44, 45.

Jerusalem, Jerusalem, thou that killest the prophets, and stonest them that are sent unto thee, how often would I have gathered together thy children, as the hen doth gather her chickens under her wings, and thou wouldst not?— *Matt.* xxiii. 37.

But love ye your enemies: do good, and lend, hoping for nothing thereby: and your reward shall be great, and you shall be the sons of the Highest; for he is kind to the unthankful, and to the evil.—*Luke* vi. 35.

For why did Christ, when as yet we were weak, according to the time, die for the ungodly?

For scarce for a just man will one die; yet perhaps for a good man, some one would dare to die.

But God commendeth his charity towards us; because when as yet we were sinners, according to the time, Christ died for us.—*Rom.* v. 6-9.

MERCY OF GOD TO REPENTANT SINNERS, THE

See also: Forgiveness of sins—page 157.

And having waited yet seven other days, he (Noah) again sent forth the dove out of the ark.

And she came to him in the evening, carrying a bough of an olive-tree, with green leaves, in her mouth.—*Gen.* viii. 10, 11.

And when thou shalt seek there the Lord thy God, thou shalt find him: yet so, if thou seek him with all thy heart, and all the affliction of thy soul. . . .

Because the Lord thy God is a merciful God: he will not leave thee, nor altogether destroy thee, nor forget the covenant, by which he swore to thy fathers.—*Deut.* iv. 29, 31.

For the Lord your God is merciful, and will not turn away his face from you, if you return to him.—2 *Paral.* xxx. 9.

Be converted therefore, ye sinners, and do justice before God, believing that he will show his mercy to you.—*Tob.* xiii. 8.

A sacrifice to God is an afflicted spirit: a contrite and humbled heart, O God, thou wilt not despise.—*Ps.* l. 19.

O God, thou hast cast us off, and hast destroyed us; thou hast been angry, and hast had mercy on us.—*Ps.* lix. 3.

Thou hast mitigated all thy anger: thou hast turned away from the wrath of thy indignation. . . .

Thou wilt turn, O God, and bring us to life: and thy people shall rejoice in thee.—*Ps.* lxxxiv. 4, 7.

He will not always be angry; nor will he threaten for ever.—*Ps.* cii. 9.

I shall not die, but live: and shall declare the works of the Lord.

The Lord chastising hath chastised me: but he hath not delivered me over to death.—*Ps.* cxvii. 17, 18.

For the Highest hateth sinners, and hath mercy on the penitent.—*Ecclus.* xii. 3.

But to the penitent, he hath given the way of justice.—*Ecclus.* xvii. 20.

How great is the mercy of the Lord, and his forgiveness to them that turn to him!—*Ecclus.* xvii. 28.

And they called upon the Lord, who is merciful, and spreading their hands, they lifted them up to heaven: and the holy Lord God quickly heard their voice.

He was not mindful of their sins, neither did he deliver them up to their enemies, but he purified them by the hand of Isaias, the holy prophet.—*Ecclus.* xlviii. 22, 23.

For a small moment have I forsaken thee, but with great mercies will I gather thee.

In a moment of indignation, have I hid my face a little while from thee, but with everlasting kindness, have I had mercy on thee, said the Lord thy Redeemer.—*Is.* liv. 7, 8.

Let the wicked forsake his way, and the unjust man his thoughts, and let him return to the Lord, and he will have mercy on him, and to our God: for he is bountiful to forgive.—*Is.* lv. 7.

For I will not contend for ever, neither will I be angry unto the end: because the spirit shall go forth from my face, and breathings I will make.

For the iniquity of his covetousness I was angry, and I struck him: I hid my face from thee, and was angry: and he went away wandering in his own heart.

I saw his ways, and I healed him, and brought him back, and restored comforts to him, and to them that mourn for him.—*Is.* lvii. 16-18.

For in my wrath have I struck thee, and in my reconciliation, have I had mercy upon thee.—*Is.* lx. 10.

It is commonly said: If a man put away his wife, and she go from him, and marry another man, shall he return to her any more? Shall not that woman be polluted, and defiled? but thou hast prostituted thyself to many lovers: nevertheless, return to me, saith the Lord, and I will receive thee.—*Jer.* iii. 1.

Now therefore saith the Lord: Be converted to me with all your heart, in fasting, and in weeping, and in mourning.

And rend your hearts, and not your garments, and turn to the Lord your God: for he is gracious and merciful, patient, and rich in mercy, and ready to repent of the evil.

Who knoweth but he will return, and forgive, and leave a blessing behind him, sacrifice and libation to the Lord your God?—*Joel* ii. 12-14.

Who is a God like to thee, who takest away iniquity, and passest by the sin of the remnant of thy inheritance? he will send his fury in no more, because he delighteth in mercy.—*Mich.* vii. 18.

Turn ye to me, saith the Lord of hosts: and I will turn to you, saith the Lord of hosts.—*Zach.* i. 3.

For thus saith the Lord of hosts: As I purposed to afflict you, when your fathers had provoked me to wrath, saith the Lord,

And I had no mercy: so turning again, I have thought in these days to do good to the house of Juda, and Jerusalem: fear not.—*Zach.* viii. 14, 15.

And he (the penitent thief) said to Jesus: Lord, remember me, when thou shalt come into thy kingdom.

And Jesus said to him: Amen, I say to thee, this day thou shalt be with me in paradise.—*Luke* xxiii. 42, 43.

MERCY OF GOD TO THOSE IN SORROW AND DISTRESS, THE

So going in he (the angel) saluted him, and said: Joy be to thee always.

And Tobias said: What manner of joy shall be to me, who sit in darkness, and see not the light of heaven?

And the young man said to him: Be of good courage, thy cure from God is at hand.—*Tob.* v. 11-13.

But yet thou stretchest not forth thy hand to their consumption: and if they shall fall down, thou wilt save.—*Job* xxx. 24.

How great troubles hast thou shown me, many and grievous: and turning, thou hast brought me to life, and hast brought me back again from the depths of the earth:

Thou hast multiplied thy magnificence; and turning to me, thou hast comforted me.—*Ps.* lxx. 20, 21.

According to the multitude of my sorrows in my heart, thy comforts have given joy to my soul.—*Ps.* xciii. 19.

The Lord doth mercies, and judgment for all that suffer wrong.—*Ps.* cii. 6.

They were hungry and thirsty: their soul fainted in them.

And they cried to the Lord in their tribulation: and he delivered them out of their distresses.

And he led them into the right way, that they might go to a city of habitation.

Let the mercies of the Lord give glory to him: and his wonderful works to the children of men.

For he hath satisfied the empty soul, and hath filled the hungry soul with good things.

Such as sat in darkness and in the shadow of death: bound in want and in iron. . . .

And their heart was humbled with labors: they were weakened, and there was none to help them.

Then they cried to the Lord in their affliction: and he delivered them out of their distresses.

And he brought them out of darkness, and the shadow of death; and broke their bonds in sunder.—*Ps.* cvi. 5-10, 12-14.

The sorrows of death have compassed me: and the perils of hell have found me.

I met with trouble and sorrow: and I called upon the name of the Lord.

O Lord, deliver my soul. The Lord is merciful and just, and our God showeth mercy.

. . . Turn, O my soul, into thy rest: for the Lord hath been bountiful to thee.

For he hath delivered my soul from death: my eyes from tears, my feet from falling.—*Ps.* cxiv. 3-5, 7, 8.

For he was mindful of us in our affliction: for his mercy endureth for ever.

And he redeemed us from our enemies: for his mercy endureth for ever. —*Ps.* cxxxv. 23, 24.

The Lord lifteth up all that fall: and setteth up all that are cast down.—*Ps.* cxliv. 14.

Blessed is he who hath the God of Jacob for his helper, whose hope is in the Lord his God.

. . . Who keepeth truth for ever: who executeth judgment for them that suffer wrong: who giveth food to the hungry.

The Lord looseth them that are fettered: the Lord enlighteneth the blind.

The Lord lifteth up them that are cast down: the Lord loveth the just.

The Lord keepeth the strangers, he will support the fatherless and the widow.—*Ps.* cxlv. 5, 7-9.

Praise ye the Lord, because psalm is

good: to our God be joyful and comely praise. . . .

Who healeth the broken of heart, and bindeth up their bruises.—*Ps.* cxlvi. 1, 3.

For God is compassionate and merciful, and will forgive sins in the day of tribulation: and he is a protector to all that seek him in truth.—*Ecclus.* ii. 13.

The mercy of God is beautiful in the time of affliction, as a cloud of rain, in the time of drought.—*Ecclus.* xxxv. 26.

O Lord, thou art my God, I will exalt thee, and give glory to thy name. . . .

Because thou hast been a strength to the poor, a strength to the needy in his distress: a refuge from the whirlwind, a shadow from the heat. For the blast of the mighty, is like a whirlwind beating against a wall.—*Is.* xxv. 1, 4.

Give praise, O ye heavens, and rejoice, O earth, ye mountains, give praise with jubilation: because the Lord hath comforted his people, and will have mercy on his poor ones.—*Is.* xlix. 13.

O poor little one, tossed with tempest, without all comfort, behold I will lay thy stones in order, and will lay thy foundations with sapphires.—*Is.* liv. 11.

As one whom the mother caresseth, so will I comfort you, and you shall be comforted in Jerusalem.—*Is.* lxvi. 13.

For I have inebriated the weary soul: and I have filled every hungry soul.—*Jer.* xxxi. 25.

For the Lord will not cast off for ever.

For if he hath cast off, he will also have mercy, according to the multitude of his mercies.

For he hath not willingly afflicted, nor cast off the children of men.—*Lam.* iii. 31-33.

The Lord is good and giveth strength in the day of trouble: and knoweth them that hope in him.—*Nahum* i. 7.

The bruised reed he shall not break; and smoking flax he shall not extinguish; till he send forth judgment unto victory.—*Matt.* xii. 20.

You have heard of the patience of Job, and you have seen the end of the Lord, that the Lord is merciful and compassionate.—*James* v. 11.

MERCY OF GOD, HOPE IN THE

He hath chastised us for our iniquities: and he will save us for his own mercy. . . .

Be converted, therefore, ye sinners, and do justice before God, believing that he will show his mercy to you.—*Tob.* xiii. 5, 8.

But I, as a fruitful olive-tree in the house of God, have hoped in the mercy of God for ever, yea, for ever and ever. —*Ps.* li. 10.

The Lord taketh pleasure in them that fear him: and in them that hope in his mercy.—*Ps.* cxlvi. 11.

Ye that fear the Lord, wait for his mercy: and go not aside from him, lest ye fall.—*Ecclus.* ii. 7.

In their affliction, they will rise early to me: Come, and let us return to the Lord:

For he hath taken us, and he will heal us: he will strike, and he will cure us.

He will revive us after two days: on the third day, he will raise us up, and we shall live in his sight. We shall know, and we shall follow on, that we may know the Lord. His going forth is prepared as the morning light, and he will come to us, as the early and the latter rain to the earth.—*Osee* vi. 1-3.

For we have not a high priest, who cannot have compassion on our infirmities: but one tempted in all things, like as we are, without sin.

Let us go therefore with confidence to the throne of grace: that we may obtain mercy, and find grace in seasonable aid.—*Heb.* iv. 15, 16.

MERCY OF GOD, OUR NEED OF THE

See also: Help, our need of God's —page 202.

Look thou upon me, and have mercy on me; for I am alone and poor.—*Ps.* xxiv. 16.

Remember not our former iniquities: let thy mercies speedily prevent us, for we are become exceeding poor.—*Ps.* lxxviii. 8.

Behold, as the eyes of servants are on the hands of their masters,

As the eyes of the handmaid are on

the hands of her mistress: so are our eyes unto the Lord our God, until he have mercy on us.—*Ps.* cxxii. 2.

The mercies of the Lord that we are not consumed: because his commiserations have not failed.—*Lam.* iii. 22.

MERCY OF GOD, WE SHOULD PRAY FOR THE

But forasmuch as the Lord is patient, let us be penitent for this same thing, and with many tears, let us beg his pardon:

For God will not threaten like man, nor be inflamed to anger like the son of man.

And therefore let us humble our souls before him, and continuing in an humble spirit, in his service:

Let us ask the Lord with tears, that according to his will, so he would show his mercy to us: that as our heart is troubled by their (the enemy's) pride, so also we may glorify in our humility. —*Judith* viii. 14-17.

His flesh is consumed with punishments, let him return to the days of his youth.

He shall pray to God, and he will be gracious to him: and he shall see his face with joy, and he will render to man his justice.—*Job* xxxiii. 25, 26.

And now, beseech ye the face of God, that he may have mercy on you (for by your hand hath this been done), if by any means he will receive your faces, saith the Lord of hosts.—*Malach.* i. 9.

Let us go therefore with confidence to the throne of grace: that we may obtain mercy, and find grace in seasonable aid.—*Heb.* iv. 16.

MERCY OF GOD OUR PLEA AND OUR HOPE, THE

Turn to me, O Lord, and deliver my soul: O save me, for thy mercy's sake. —*Ps.* vi. 5.

Remember, O Lord, thy bowels of compassion; and thy mercies, that are from the beginning of the world. . . .

According to thy mercy, remember thou me: for thy goodness' sake, O Lord.—*Ps.* xxiv. 6, 7.

Have mercy on me, O God, according to thy great mercy.

And according to the multitude of thy tender mercies, blot out my iniquity.—*Ps.* l. 3.

In the multitude of thy mercy, hear me, in the truth of thy salvation. . . .

Hear me, O Lord, for thy mercy is kind; look upon me, according to the multitude of thy tender mercies.—*Ps.* lxviii. 14, 17.

Have mercy on me, O Lord, for I have cried to thee, all the day.

Give joy to the soul of thy servant, for to thee, O Lord, I have lifted up my soul.

For thou, O Lord, art sweet and mild; and plenteous in mercy to all that call upon thee.—*Ps.* lxxxv. 3-5.

Help me, O Lord my God; save me according to thy mercy.—*Ps.* cviii. 26.

Put us not to confusion, but deal with us according to thy meekness, and according to the multitude of thy mercies.—*Dan.* iii. 42.

O Lord, to us belongeth confusion of face, to our princes, and to our fathers that have sinned.

But to thee, the Lord our God, mercy and forgiveness, for we have departed from thee.—*Dan.* ix. 8, 9.

Incline, O my God, thy ear, and hear: open thy eyes, and see our desolation, and the city upon which thy name is called: for it is not for our justifications, that we present our prayers before thy face, but for the multitude of thy tender mercies.—*Dan.* ix. 18.

MERCY OF GOD, EXAMPLES OF THE

I will establish my covenant with you, and all flesh shall be no more destroyed with the waters of a flood, neither shall there be from henceforth a flood to waste the earth.

And God said: This is the sign of the covenant which I give between me and you, and to every living soul that is with you, for perpetual generations.

I will set my bow in the clouds, and it shall be the sign of a covenant between me, and between the earth.

And when I shall cover the sky with clouds, my bow shall appear in the clouds:

And I will remember my covenant

with you, and with every living soul that beareth flesh: and there shall no more be waters of a flood to destroy all flesh.—*Gen.* ix. 11-15.

Now after a long time, the king of Egypt died: and the children of Israel groaning, cried out because of the works: and their cry went up unto God from the works.

And he heard their groaning, and remembered the covenant which he made with Abraham, Isaac, and Jacob.

And the Lord looked upon the children of Israel, and he knew them.—*Ex.* ii. 23-25.

But the Lord's portion is his people: Jacob, the lot of his inheritance.

He found him in a desert land, in a place of horror, and of vast wilderness: he led him about, and taught him: and he kept him as the apple of his eye.

As the eagle enticing her young to fly, and hovering over them, he spread his wings, and hath taken him and carried him on his shoulders.—*Deut.* xxxii. 9-11.

Yea, when they had made also to themselves a molten calf, and had said: This is thy God, that brought thee out of Egypt: and had committed great blasphemies:

Yet thou, in thy many mercies, didst not leave them in the desert: the pillar of the cloud departed not from them by day, to lead them in the way, and the pillar of fire by night, to show them the way by which they should go.

And thou gavest them thy good Spirit to teach them, and thy manna, thou didst not withhold from their mouth, and thou gavest them water for their thirst.

Forty years didst thou feed them in the desert, and nothing was wanting to them: their garments did not grow old, and their feet were not worn.

. . . But after they had rest, they returned to do evil in thy sight: and thou leftest them in the hand of their enemies, and they had dominion over them. Then they returned, and cried to thee: and thou heardest from heaven, and deliveredst them many times in thy mercies.—2 *Esd.* ix. 18-21. 28.

But he is merciful, and will forgive their sins: and will not destroy them.

And many a time did he turn away his anger: and did not kindle all his wrath.

And he remembered that they are flesh: a wind that goeth, and returneth not.—*Ps.* lxxvii. 38, 39.

And the word of the Lord came to me, saying:

Son of man, make known to Jerusalem her abominations.

And thou shalt say: Thus saith the Lord God to Jerusalem: . . .

And when thou wast born, in the day of thy nativity, thy navel was not cut, neither wast thou washed with water for thy health, nor salted with salt, nor swaddled with clouts.

No eye had pity on thee, to do any of these things for thee, out of compassion to thee: but thou wast cast out upon the face of the earth in the abjection of thy soul, in the day that thou wast born.

And passing by thee, I saw that thou wast trodden under foot in thy own blood; and I said to thee, when thou wast in thy blood: Live: I have said to thee: Live in thy blood.

. . . And I washed thee with water, and cleansed away thy blood from thee: and I anointed thee with oil.

And I clothed thee with embroidery, and shod thee with violet-colored shoes: and I girded thee about with fine linen, and clothed thee with fine garments.

I decked thee also with ornaments, and put bracelets on thy hands, and a chain about thy neck.

And I put a jewel upon thy forehead, and earrings in thy ears, and a beautiful crown upon thy head.

And thou wast adorned with gold, and silver, and wast clothed with fine linen, and embroidered work, and many colors: thou didst eat fine flour and honey and oil, and wast made exceeding beautiful: and wast advanced to be a queen.

And thy renown went forth among the nations for thy beauty: for thou wast perfect through my beauty, which I had put upon thee, saith the Lord God.—*Ezech.* xvi. 1-6, 9-14.

And the men of Ninive believed in God: and they proclaimed a fast, and put on sackcloth from the greatest to the least. . . .

And God saw their works, that they were turned from their evil way: and God had mercy with regard to the evil, which he had said that he would do them, and he did it not.—*Jonas* iii. 5, 10.

And the scribes and Pharisees bring unto him a woman taken in adultery: and they set her in the midst,

And said to him: Master, this woman was even now taken in adultery.

Now Moses in the law commanded us to stone such a one. But what sayest thou? . . .

He that is without sin among you, let him first cast a stone at her. . . .

Then Jesus lifting up himself, said to her: Woman, where are they that accused thee? Hath no man condemned thee?

Who said: No man, Lord. And Jesus said: Neither will I condemn thee. Go, and now sin no more.—*John* viii. 3-5, 7, 10, 11.

Nevertheless he left not himself without testimony, doing good from heaven, giving rains and fruitful seasons, filling our hearts with food and gladness.—*Acts* xiv. 16.

But when the fulness of time was come, God sent his Son, made of a woman, made under the law:

That he might redeem them who were under the law: that we might receive the adoption of sons.

And because you are sons, God hath sent the Spirit of his Son into your hearts, crying: Abba, Father.

Therefore now he is not a servant, but a son. And if a son, an heir also through God.—*Gal.* iv. 4-7.

But God (who is rich in mercy), for his exceeding charity, wherewith he loved us,

Even when we were dead in sins, hath quickened us together in Christ (by whose grace you are saved),

And hath raised us up together, and hath made us sit together in the heavenly places, through Christ Jesus.

That he might show in the ages to come the abundant riches of his grace, in his bounty towards us in Christ Jesus.—*Eph.* ii. 4-7.

Giving thanks to God the Father, who hath made us worthy to be partakers of the lot of the saints in light:

Who hath delivered us from the power of darkness, and hath translated us into the kingdom of the Son of his love,

In whom we have redemption through his blood, the remission of sins.—*Col.* i. 12-14.

And you, when you were dead in your sins, and the uncircumcision of your flesh; he hath quickened together with him, forgiving you all offences:

Blotting out the handwriting of the decree that was against us, which was contrary to us. And he hath taken the same out of the way, fastening it to the cross.—*Col.* ii. 13, 14.

But when the goodness and kindness of God our Saviour appeared:

Not by the works of justice which we have done, but according to his mercy, he saved us, by the laver of regeneration, and renovation of the Holy Ghost;

Whom he hath poured forth upon us abundantly, through Jesus Christ our Saviour:

That, being justified by his grace, we may be heirs, according to hope of life everlasting.—*Titus* iii. 4-7.

Wherefore it behoved him in all things to be made like unto his brethren, that he might become a merciful and faithful high priest before God, that he might be a propitiation for the sins of the people.

For in that, wherein he himself hath suffered and been tempted, he is able to succor them also that are tempted.—*Heb.* ii. 17, 18.

And whereas indeed he was the Son of God, he learned obedience by the things which he suffered:

And being consummated, he became, to all that obey him, the cause of eternal salvation.—*Heb.* v. 8, 9.

For it is impossible that with the blood of oxen and goats sin should be taken away.

Wherefore when he cometh into the world, he saith: Sacrifice and oblation thou wouldest not: but a body thou hast fitted to me:

Holocausts for sin did not please thee. Then said I: Behold I come: in the head of the book it is written of me: that I should do thy will, O God.—*Heb.* x. 4-7.

MERCY OF GOD, A PRAYER FOR THE

We have sinned with our fathers, we have done unjustly, we have committed iniquity:

Have thou mercy on us, because thou art good, or punish our iniquities by chastising us thyself, and deliver not them that trust in thee to a people that knoweth not thee.—*Judith* vii. 19, 20.

O Lord, rebuke me not in thy indignation, nor chastise me in thy wrath.

Have mercy on me, O Lord, for I am weak: heal me, O Lord, for my bones are troubled.

And my soul is troubled exceedingly: but thou, O Lord, how long?

Turn to me, O Lord, and deliver my soul: O save me, for thy mercy's sake. —*Ps.* vi. 2-5.

Show forth thy wonderful mercies; thou who savest them that trust in thee. —*Ps.* xvi. 7.

Look thou upon me, and have mercy on me; for I am alone and poor.

The troubles of my heart are multiplied: deliver me from my necessities. —*Ps.* xxiv. 16, 17.

Extend thy mercy to them that know thee, and thy justice to them that are right in heart.—*Ps.* xxxv. 11.

Withhold not thou, O Lord, thy tender mercies from me: thy mercy and thy truth have always upheld me.—*Ps.* xxxix. 12.

I said: O Lord, be thou merciful to me: heal my soul, for I have sinned against thee.—*Ps.* xl. 5.

Have mercy on me, O God, according to thy great mercy.

And according to the multitude of thy tender mercies, blot out my iniquity.—*Ps.* l. 3.

May God have mercy on us, and bless us: may he cause the light of his countenance to shine upon us, and may he have mercy on us.

That we may know thy way upon earth: thy salvation in all nations.—*Ps.* lxvi. 2, 3.

Remember not our former iniquities: let thy mercies speedily prevent us, for we are become exceeding poor.—*Ps.* lxxviii. 8.

Convert us, O God our saviour: and turn off thy anger from us.

Wilt thou be angry with us for ever: or wilt thou extend thy wrath from generation to generation? . . .

Show us, O Lord, thy mercy; and grant us thy salvation.—*Ps.* lxxxiv. 5, 6, 8.

Have mercy on me, O Lord, for I have cried to thee all the day.

Give joy to the soul of thy servant, for to thee, O Lord, I have lifted up my soul.

For thou, O Lord, art sweet and mild: and plenteous in mercy to all that call upon thee.—*Ps.* lxxxv. 3-5.

O! let thy mercy be for my comfort, according to thy word unto thy servant.

Let thy tender mercies come unto me, and I shall live. . . .

Deal with thy servant according to thy mercy: and teach me thy justifications.—*Ps.* cxviii. 76, 77, 124.

Have mercy on us, O Lord, have mercy on us: for we are greatly filled with contempt.—*Ps.* cxxii. 3.

The Lord will repay for me: thy mercy, O Lord, endureth for ever: O despise not the works of thy hands.— *Ps.* cxxxvii. 8.

Cause me to hear thy mercy in the morning; for in thee have I hoped.— *Ps.* cxlii. 8.

Have mercy upon us, O God of all, and behold us, and show us the light of thy mercies.—*Ecclus.* xxxvi. 1.

And now, O Lord Almighty, the God of Israel, the soul in anguish, and the troubled spirit crieth to thee:

Hear, O Lord, and have mercy, for thou art a merciful God, and have pity on us: for we have sinned before thee.

For thou remainest for ever, and shall we perish everlastingly?—*Bar.* iii. 1-3.

Put us not to confusion, but deal with us according to thy meekness, and according to the multitude of thy mercies.

And deliver us according to thy wonderful works, and give glory to thy name, O Lord.—*Dan.* iii. 42, 43.

Between the porch and the altar, the priests, the Lord's ministers, shall weep, and shall say: Spare, O Lord, spare thy people: and give not thy inheritance to reproach, that the heathen should rule over them.—*Joel* ii. 17.

And as he went out of Jericho, with his disciples and a very great multitude, Bartimeus, the blind man, the son of Timeus, sat by the wayside begging.

Who, when he had heard that it was Jesus of Nazareth, began to cry out, and to say: Jesus, son of David, have mercy on me.—*Mark* x. 46, 47.

And as he entered into a certain town, there met him ten men that were lepers, who stood afar off;

And lifted up their voice, saying: Jesus, master, have mercy on us.—*Luke* xvii. 12, 13.

And the publican, standing afar off, would not so much as lift up his eyes towards heaven; but struck his breast, saying: O God, be merciful to me a sinner.—*Luke* xviii. 13.

MERCY TO ONE ANOTHER, WE SHOULD SHOW

He that taketh away mercy from his friend, forsaketh the fear of the Lord. —*Job* vi. 14.

The sinner shall borrow, and not pay again; but the just showeth mercy and shall give.—*Ps.* xxxvi. 21.

For God loveth mercy and truth: the Lord will give grace and glory.—*Ps.* lxxxiii. 12.

To the righteous a light is risen up in darkness: he is merciful, and compassionate, and just.—*Ps.* cxi. 4.

A merciful man doth good to his own soul: but he that is cruel casteth off even his own kindred.—*Prov.* xi. 17.

Deceitful souls go astray in sins: the just are merciful, and show mercy.—*Prov.* xiii. 13.

He that believeth in the Lord, loveth mercy.

They err that work evil: but mercy and truth prepare good things.—*Prov.* xiv. 21, 22.

To do mercy and judgment, pleaseth the Lord more than victims.—*Prov.* xxi. 3.

He that is inclined to mercy, shall be blessed: for of his bread, he hath given to the poor.—*Prov.* xxii. 9.

He shall return thanks, that offereth fine flour: and he that doth mercy, offereth sacrifice.—*Ecclus.* xxxv. 4.

For I desired mercy, and not sacrifice; and the knowledge of God, more than holocausts.—*Osee* vi. 6.

I will show thee, O man, what is good, and what the Lord requireth of thee: Verily, to do judgment, and to love mercy, and to walk solicitous with thy God.—*Mich.* vi. 8.

Go then, and learn what this meaneth, I will have mercy, and not sacrifice. For I am not come to call the just, but sinners.—*Matt.* ix. 13.

And if you knew what this meaneth: I will have mercy, and not sacrifice: You would never have condemned the innocent.—*Matt.* xii. 7.

Religion clean and undefiled before God and the Father, is this: to visit the fatherless and widows in their tribulation: and to keep one's self unspotted from this world.—*James* i. 27.

For judgment without mercy to him that hath not done mercy. And mercy exalteth itself above judgment.—*James* ii. 13.

MERCY TO ONE ANOTHER, EXHORTATION TO SHOW

Say not: I will do to him, as he hath done to me: I will render to every one according to his work.—*Prov.* xxiv. 29.

Thus saith the Lord of hosts, saying: Judge ye true judgment, and show ye mercy and compassion every man to his brother.—*Zach.* vii. 9.

Be ye therefore merciful, as your Father also is merciful.—*Luke* vi. 36.

And Jesus answering said: A certain man went down from Jerusalem to Jericho, and fell among robbers, who also stripped him, and having wounded him, went away, leaving him half dead.

And it chanced that a certain priest went down the same way: and seeing him, passed by.

In like manner also a Levite, when he was near the place and saw him, passed by.

But a certain Samaritan being on his

journey, came near him; and seeing him, was moved with compassion.

And going up to him, bound up his wounds, pouring in oil and wine: and setting him upon his own beast, brought him to an inn, and took care of him. . . .

Which of these three in thy opinion, was neighbor to him that fell among the robbers?

But he said: He that showed mercy to him. And Jesus said to him: Go, and do thou in like manner.—*Luke* x. 30-34, 36, 37.

And be ye kind one to another; merciful, forgiving one another, even as God hath forgiven you in Christ.—*Eph.* iv. 32.

Put ye on, therefore, as the elect of God, holy and beloved, the bowels of mercy, benignity, humility, modesty, patience.—*Col.* iii. 12.

And in fine, be ye all of one mind, having compassion one of another, being lovers of the brotherhood, merciful, modest, humble.—1 *Peter* iii. 8.

MERCY WE SHOW TO OTHERS, GOD WILL REWARD THE

And he (Saul) said to David: Thou art more just than I: for thou hast done good to me, and I have rewarded thee with evil.

And thou hast shown this day what good things thou hast done to me: how the Lord delivered me into thy hand, and thou hast not killed me.

For who, when he hath found his enemy, will let him go well away? But the Lord reward thee for this good turn, for what thou hast done to me this day. —1 *Kings* xxiv. 18-20.

Acceptable is the man that showeth mercy, and lendeth: he shall order his words with judgment: because he shall not be moved for ever.—*Ps.* cxi. 5, 6.

Let not mercy and truth leave thee, put them about thy neck, and write them in the tables of thy heart:

And thou shalt find grace and good understanding before God and men.— *Prov.* iii. 3, 4.

By mercy and faith sins are purged away.—*Prov.* xv. 27.

By mercy and truth iniquity is redeemed.—*Prov.* xvi. 6.

He that followeth justice and mercy, shall find life, justice and glory.—*Prov.* xxi. 21.

In judging, be merciful to the fatherless as a father, and as a husband to their mother.

And thou shalt be as the obedient son of the most High, and he will have mercy on thee more than a mother.— *Ecclus.* iv. 10, 11.

The sinner shall not escape in his rapines, and the patience of him that showeth mercy shall not be put off.— *Ecclus.* xvi. 14.

For from the merciful, all these (*i.e.* evil) things shall be taken away, and they shall not wallow in sins.—*Ecclus.* xxiii. 16.

Blessed are the merciful: for they shall obtain mercy.—*Matt.* v. 7.

MERITS, WE MUST STRIVE TO ACQUIRE

Remember me, O my God, for this thing, and wipe not out my kindness, which I have done, relating to the house of my God and his ceremonies.—2 *Esd.* xiii. 14.

For thus saith the Lord to the men of Juda and Jerusalem: Break up anew your fallow ground, and sow not upon thorns.—*Jer.* iv. 3.

Sow for yourselves in justice, and reap in the mouth of mercy, break up your fallow ground: but the time to seek the Lord is, when he shall come that shall teach you justice.—*Osee* x.12.

Lay not up to yourselves treasures on earth: where the rust, and moth consume, and where thieves break through and steal.

But lay up to yourselves treasures in heaven: where neither the rust nor moth doth consume, and where thieves do not break through, nor steal.—*Matt.* vi. 19, 20.

For he that hath, to him shall be given, and he shall abound: but he that hath not, from him shall be taken away that also which he hath.—*Matt.* xiii. 12.

Make to yourselves bags which grow not old, a treasure in heaven, which faileth not: where no thief approacheth, nor moth corrupteth.—*Luke* xii. 33.

Charge the rich of this world not to be high-minded, nor to trust in the uncertainty of riches, but in the living God (who giveth us abundantly all things to enjoy),

To do good, to be rich in good works, to give easily, to communicate to others,

To lay up in store for themselves a good foundation against the time to come, that they may lay hold on the true life.—1 *Tim.* vi. 17-19.

MERITS, NOW IS THE TIME TO ACQUIRE

See: Life, the time for gaining merit —page 282.

MERITS, LOST

Moreover, if the just man shall turn away from his justice, and shall commit iniquity: I will lay a stumbling-block before him, he shall die, because thou hast not given him warning: he shall die in his sin, and his justices which he hath done, shall not be remembered.—*Ezech.* iii. 20.

But if the just man turn himself away from his justice, and do iniquity, according to all the abominations which the wicked man useth to work, shall he live? all his justices which he hath done, shall not be remembered: in the prevarication, by which he hath prevaricated, and in his sin, which he hath committed, in them he shall die.—*Ezech.* xviii. 24.

Thou therefore, O son of man, say to the children of thy people: The justice of the just shall not deliver him, in what day soever he shall sin; and the wickedness of the wicked shall not hurt him, in what day soever he shall turn from his wickedness: and the just shall not be able to live in his justice, in what day soever he shall sin.

Yea, if I shall say to the just that he shall surely live, and he, trusting in his justice, commit iniquity: all his justices shall be forgotten, and in his iniquity which he hath committed, in the same shall he die.—*Ezech.* xxxiii. 12, 13.

MILDNESS

A mild answer breaketh wrath: but a harsh word stirreth up fury.—*Prov.* xv. 1.

By patience a prince shall be appeased, and a soft tongue shall break hardness.—*Prov.* xxv. 15.

A sweet word multiplieth friends, and appeaseth enemies, and a gracious tongue in a good man aboundeth.—*Ecclus.* vi. 5.

But the fruit of the Spirit is charity, joy, peace, patience, benignity, goodness, longanimity,

Mildness, faith, modesty, continency, chastity. Against such there is no law. —*Gal.* v. 22, 23.

I therefore, a prisoner in the Lord, beseech you that you walk worthy of the vocation in which you are called, With all humility and mildness, with patience, supporting one another in charity.—*Eph.* iv. 1, 2.

But thou, O man of God, fly these things: and pursue justice, godliness, faith, charity, patience, mildness.— 1 *Tim.* vi. 11.

But the servant of the Lord must not wrangle: but be mild towards all men, apt to teach, patient.—2 *Tim.* ii. 24.

Admonish them to be subject to princes and powers, to obey at a word, to be ready to every good work.

To speak evil of no man, not to be litigious, but gentle: showing all mildness towards all men.—*Titus* iii. 1, 2.

MILDNESS OF CHRIST, THE

See: Meekness of Christ—page 311.

MISCHIEF MAKER, THE

Six things there are, which the Lord hateth, and the seventh his soul detesteth. . . .

A deceitful witness that uttereth lies, and him that soweth discord among brethren.—*Prov.* vi. 16, 19.

A fool worketh mischief, as it were for sport: but wisdom is prudence to a man.—*Prov.* x. 23.

A perverse man stirreth up quarrels, and one full of words separateth princes.—*Prov.* xvi. 28.

He that concealeth a transgression, seeketh friendships: he that repeateth it again, separateth friends.—*Prov.* xvii. 9.

Meddle not with him that revealeth secrets, and walketh deceitfully, and openeth wide his lips.—*Prov.* xx. 19.

When the wood faileth, the fire shall go out: and when the talebearer is taken away, contentions shall cease. . . .

The words of a talebearer are, as it were, simple, but they reach to the innermost parts of the belly.—*Prov.* xxvi. 20, 22.

Accuse not a servant to his master, lest he curse thee, and thou fall.—*Prov.* xxx. 10.

Take heed to thyself of a mischievous man, for he worketh evils: lest he bring upon thee reproach for ever.—*Ecclus.* xi. 35.

He that hateth babbling, extinguisheth evil.—*Ecclus.* xix. 5.

Rehearse not again a wicked and harsh word, and thou shalt not fare the worse. . . .

Hast thou heard a word against thy neighbor? let it die within thee, trusting that it will not burst thee.—*Ecclus.* xix. 7, 10.

The whisperer and the double-tongued is accursed: for he hath troubled many that were at peace.

The tongue of a third person hath disquieted many, and scattered them from nation to nation.—*Ecclus.* xxviii. 15, 16.

Repeat not the word which thou hast heard, and disclose not the thing that is secret; so shalt thou be truly without confusion, and shalt find favor before all men.—*Ecclus.* xlii. 1.

Now I beseech you, brethren, to mark them who make dissensions and offences, contrary to the doctrine which you have learned, and avoid them.— *Rom.* xvi. 17.

And withal, being idle, they learn to go about from house to house: and are not only idle, but tattlers also, and busy-bodies, speaking things which they ought not.—1 *Tim.* v. 13.

MISCHIEF MAKER, PUNISHMENT OF THE

Why dost thou glory in malice, thou that art mighty in iniquity?

All the day long thy tongue hath devised injustice: as a sharp razor, thou hast wrought deceit.

Thou hast loved malice more than goodness: and iniquity rather than to speak righteousness.

Thou hast loved all the words of ruin, O deceitful tongue.

Therefore will God destroy thee for ever: he will pluck thee out, and remove thee from thy dwelling place: and thy root out of the land of the living.—*Ps.* li. 3-7.

A man that is an apostate, an unprofitable man, walketh with a perverse mouth,

He winketh with the eyes, presseth with the foot, speaketh with the finger.

With a wicked heart, he deviseth evil, and at all times he soweth discord.

To such a one his destruction shall presently come, and he shall suddenly be destroyed, and shall no longer have any remedy.—*Prov.* vi. 12-15.

He that diggeth a pit, shall fall into it: and he that rolleth a stone, it shall return to him.—*Prov.* xxvi. 27.

Be not called a whisperer, and be not taken in thy tongue, and confounded.

For confusion and repentance is upon a thief, and an evil mark of disgrace upon the double-tongued, but to the whisperer, hatred, and enmity, and reproach.—*Ecclus.* v. 16, 17.

The talebearer shall defile his own soul, and shall be hated by all: and he that shall abide with him, shall be hateful: the silent and wise man shall be honored.—*Ecclus.* xxi. 31.

If one cast a stone on high, it will fall upon his own head; and the deceitful stroke will wound the deceitful.

He that diggeth a pit, shall fall into it: and he that setteth a stone for his neighbor, shall stumble upon it: and he that layeth a snare for another, shall perish in it.

A mischievous counsel shall be rolled back upon the author, and he shall not know from whence it cometh to him.— *Ecclus.* xxvii. 28-30.

MISERLINESS

See: Meanness—page 307.

MISERY, ACKNOWLEDGMENT OF MAN'S

See: Acknowledgment—page 13.

MISERY A CLAIM TO GOD'S MERCY, OUR

Have mercy on me, O Lord, for I am weak: heal me, O Lord, for my bones are troubled.

And my soul is troubled exceedingly: but thou, O Lord, how long?—*Ps.* vi. 3, 4.

Have mercy on me, O Lord: see my humiliation which I suffer from my enemies.—*Ps.* ix. 14.

Look thou upon me, and have mercy on me; for I am alone and poor.

The troubles of my heart are multiplied: deliver me from my necessities.

See my abjection and my labor; and forgive me all my sins.—*Ps.* xxiv. 16-18.

Remember what my substance is; for hast thou made all the children of men in vain?—*Ps.* lxxxviii. 48.

But thou, O Lord, do with me for thy name's sake: because thy mercy is sweet.

Do thou deliver me, for I am poor and needy, and my heart is troubled within me.—*Ps.* cviii. 21, 22.

MISFORTUNES OF OTHERS, REJOICING AT THE

See: Rejoicing—page 470.

MODERATION IN EATING AND DRINKING

See: Frugality—page 164.

MODESTY

Let your modesty be known to all men. The Lord is nigh.—*Philipp.* iv. 5.

For the rest, brethren, whatsoever things are true, whatsoever modest, whatsoever just, whatsoever holy, whatsoever lovely, whatsoever of good fame, if there be any virtue, if any praise of discipline, think on these things.—*Philipp.* iv. 8.

Put ye on, therefore, as the elect of God, holy and beloved, the bowels of mercy, benignity, humility, modesty, patience.—*Col.* iii. 12.

It behoveth, therefore, a bishop to be blameless, the husband of one wife, sober, prudent, of good behavior, chaste, given to hospitality, a teacher,

Not given to wine, no striker, but modest.—*1 Tim.* iii. 2, 3.

And in fine, be ye all of one mind, having compassion one of another, being lovers of the brotherhood, merciful, modest, humble.—*1 Peter* iii. 8.

But with modesty and fear, having a good conscience: that whereas they speak evil of you, they may be ashamed who falsely accuse your good conversation in Christ.—*1 Peter* iii. 16.

MOTHERHOOD A DUTY AND A BLESSING

Praise the Lord, ye children: praise ye the name of the Lord. . . .

Who maketh a barren woman to dwell in a house, the joyful mother of children.—*Ps.* cxii. 1, 9.

Behold, the inheritance of the Lord are children: the reward, the fruit of the womb.—*Ps.* cxxvi. 3.

For Adam was first formed; then Eve.

And Adam was not seduced; but the woman, being seduced, was in the transgression.

Yet she shall be saved through childbearing; if she continue in faith, and love, and sanctification, with sobriety.—*1 Tim.* ii. 13-15.

I will therefore that the younger should marry, bear children, be mistresses of families, give no occasion to the adversary to speak evil.—*1 Tim.* v. 14.

MORTAL SIN

See: Sin, mortal—Part II, page 735.

MORTIFICATION

See: Self-Denial—page 509.

MURDER

Thou shalt not kill.—*Ex.* xx. 13.

The murderer riseth at the very break of day, he killeth the needy and the poor man: but in the night he will be as a thief. . . .

If the morning suddenly appear, it is to them the shadow of death: and they walk in darkness, as if it were in light.—*Job* xxiv. 14, 17.

Deliver me from blood, O God, thou God of my salvation: and my tongue shall extol thy justice.—*Ps.* l. 16.

Six things there are which the Lord hateth, and the seventh, his soul detesteth:

Haughty eyes, a lying tongue, hands that shed innocent blood.—*Prov.* vi. 16, 17.

A man indeed killeth through malice, and when the spirit is gone forth, it shall not return, neither shall he call back the soul that is received:

But it is impossible to escape thy hand.—*Wis.* xvi. 14, 15.

You have heard that it was said to them of old: Thou shalt not kill. And whosoever shall kill, shall be in danger of the judgment.—*Matt.* v. 21.

But let none of you suffer as a murderer, or a thief, or a railer, or a coveter of other men's things.—1 *Peter* iv. 15.

MURDER, PUNISHMENT OF

And Cain said to Abel his brother: Let us go forth abroad. And when they were in the field, Cain rose up against his brother Abel, and slew him.

And the Lord said to Cain: Where is thy brother Abel? And he answered, I know not: am I my brother's keeper?

And he said to him: What hast thou done? the voice of thy brother's blood crieth to me from the earth.

Now, therefore, cursed shalt thou be upon the earth, which hath opened her mouth and received the blood of thy brother at thy hand.

When thou shalt till it, it shall not yield to thee its fruit: a fugitive and a vagabond shalt thou be upon the earth. —*Gen.* iv. 8-12.

For I will require the blood of your lives at the hand of every beast, and at the hand of man, at the hand of every man, and of his brother, will I require the life of man.

Whosoever shall shed man's blood, his blood shall be shed: for man was made to the image of God.—*Gen.* ix. 5, 6.

He that striketh a man with a will to kill him, shall be put to death.—*Ex.* xxi. 12.

If a man kill his neighbor on set purpose, and by lying in wait for him: thou shalt take him away from my altar, that he may die.—*Ex.* xxi. 14.

He that striketh and killeth a man, dying, let him die.—*Lev.* xxiv. 17.

The murderer shall be punished by witnesses: none shall be condemned upon the evidence of one man.

You shall not take money of him that is guilty of blood, but he shall die forthwith.

. . . Defile not the land of your habitation, which is stained with the blood of the innocent: neither can it otherwise be expiated, but by his blood that hath shed the blood of another.— *Num.* xxxv. 30, 31, 33.

But thou, O God, shalt bring them down into the pit of destruction.

Bloody and deceitful men shall not live out half their days.—*Ps.* liv. 24.

A man that doth violence to the blood of a person, if he flee even to the pit, no man will stay him.—*Prov.* xxviii. 17.

Being filled with all iniquity, malice, fornication, avarice, wickedness, full of envy, murder. . . .

Who having known the justice of God, did not understand that they who do such things, are worthy of death; and not only they that do them, but they also that consent to them that do them.—*Rom.* i. 29, 32.

Now the works of the flesh are manifest, which are fornication, uncleanness, immodesty, luxury,

. . . Envies, murders, drunkenness, revellings and such like. Of the which I foretell you, as I have foretold to you, that they who do such things shall not obtain the kingdom of God.—*Gal.* v. 19, 21.

Whosoever hateth his brother, is a murderer. And you know that no murderer hath eternal life abiding in himself.—1 *John* iii. 15.

But the fearful and unbelieving, and the abominable, and murderers . . . they shall have their portion in the pool burning with fire and brimstone, which is the second death.—*Apoc.* xxi. 8.

Blessed are they that wash their robes in the blood of the Lamb: that they may have a right to the tree of life, and may enter in by the gates into the city.

Without are dogs, and sorcerers, and unchaste, and murderers, and servers of idols, and every one that loveth and maketh a lie.—*Apoc.* xxii. 14, 15.

MURMURING

Say not: What thinkest thou is the cause that former times were better than they are now? for this manner of question is foolish.—*Eccles.* vii. 11.

Keep yourselves, therefore, from murmuring, which profiteth nothing, and refrain your tongue from detraction, for an obscure speech shall not go for nought: and the mouth that belieth, killeth the soul.—*Wis.* i. 11.

And they that erred in spirit, shall know understanding, and they that murmured, shall learn the law.—*Is.* xxix. 24.

Why hath a living man murmured, man suffering for his sins?—*Lam.* iii. 39.

These are murmurers, full of complaints, walking according to their own desires, and their mouth speaketh proud things, admiring persons, for gain's sake.—*Jude* i. 16.

MURMURING AGAINST GOD

And all the congregation of the children of Israel murmured against Moses and Aaron in the wilderness.

And the children of Israel said to them: Would to God we had died by the hand of the Lord in the land of Egypt, when we sat over the flesh pots, and ate bread to the full. Why have you brought us into this desert, that you might destroy all the multitude with famine?

. . . And Moses said: In the evening the Lord will give you flesh to eat, and in the morning, bread to the full: for he hath heard your murmurings, with which you have murmured against him, for what are we? your murmuring is not against us, but against the Lord.—*Ex.* xvi. 2, 3, 8.

In all these things, Job sinned not by his lips, nor spoke he any foolish thing against God.—*Job* i. 22.

Now this is the thing in which thou art not justified: I will answer thee, that God is greater than man.

Dost thou strive against him, because he hath not answered thee to all words?—*Job* xxxiii. 12, 13.

Lift not up your horn on high: speak not iniquity against God.

For neither from the east, nor from the west, nor from the desert hills: for God is the judge.

One he putteth down, and another he lifteth up.—*Ps.* lxxiv. 6-8.

The folly of a man supplanteth his steps: and he fretteth in his mind against God.—*Prov.* xix. 3.

In the good day enjoy good things, and beware beforehand of the evil day: for God hath made both the one and the other, that man may not find against him any just complaint.—*Eccles.* vii. 15.

Say not: It is through God, that she (wisdom) is not with me: for do not thou the things that he hateth.—*Ecclus.* xv. 11.

Woe to him that gainsayeth his maker, a sherd of the earthen pots: shall the clay say to him that fashioned it: What art thou making, and thy work is without hands?—*Is.* xlv. 9.

You have wearied the Lord with your words, and you said: Wherein have we wearied him? In that you say: Every one that doth evil, is good in the sight of the Lord, and such please him: or surely where is the God of judgment? —*Malach.* ii. 17.

Your words have been unsufferable to me, saith the Lord.

And you have said: What have we spoken against thee? You have said: He laboreth in vain that serveth God, and what profit is it that we have kept his ordinances, and that we have walked sorrowful before the Lord of hosts?

Wherefore now we call the proud people happy, for they that work wickedness are built up, and they have tempted God, and are preserved.—*Malach.* iii. 13-15.

Neither let us tempt Christ: as some of them tempted, and perished by the serpents.

Neither do you murmur: as some of them murmured, and were destroyed by the destroyer.—1 *Cor.* x. 9, 10.

MURMURING AGAINST GOD PUNISHED

In the meantime there arose a murmuring of the people against the Lord, as it were repining at their fatigue. And when the Lord heard it, he was angry. And the fire of the Lord being kindled against them, devoured them that were at the uttermost part of the camp.—*Num.* xi. 1.

And the Lord spoke to Moses and Aaron, saying:

How long doth this wicked multitude murmur against me? I have heard the murmurings of the children of Israel.

Say therefore to them: As I live, saith the Lord: According as you have spoken in my hearing, so will I do to you.

In the wilderness shall your carcasses lie.

All you that were numbered from twenty years old and upward, and have murmured against me,

Shall not enter into the land, over which I lifted up my hand, to make you dwell therein, except Caleb, the son of Jephone, and Josue, the son of Nun.—*Num.* xiv. 26-30.

But they that did not receive the trials with the fear of the Lord, but uttered their impatience and the reproach of their murmuring against the Lord,

Were destroyed by the destroyer, and perished by serpents.—*Judith* viii. 24, 25.

And they spoke ill of God; they said: Can God furnish a table in the wilderness?

Because he struck the rock, and the waters gushed out, and the streams overflowed.

Can he also give bread, or provide a table for his people?

Therefore the Lord heard, and was angry: and a fire was kindled against Jacob, and wrath came up against Israel.

Because they believed not in God: and trusted not in his salvation.—*Ps.* lxxvii. 19-22.

Give not thy mouth to cause thy flesh to sin: and say not before the angel: There is no providence: lest God be angry at thy words, and destroy all the works of thy hands.—*Eccles.* v. 5.

MUTABILITY OF CREATED THINGS

Man, born of a woman, living for a short time, is filled with many miseries.

Who cometh forth like a flower, and is destroyed, and fleeth as a shadow, and never continueth in the same state. —*Job* xiv. 1, 2.

In the beginning, O Lord, thou foundedst the earth: and the heavens are the works of thy hands.

They shall perish, but thou remainest: and all of them shall grow old like a garment:

And as a vesture, thou shalt change them, and they shall be changed.—*Ps.* ci. 26, 27.

From the morning until the evening, the time shall be changed, and all these are swift in the eyes of God.— *Ecclus.* xviii. 26.

MYSTERIES OF GOD ARE ABOVE OUR UNDERSTANDING, THE

See also: Ways of God are unsearchable, the—page 584.

Then Job answered the Lord, and said: . . .

Who is this that hideth counsel without knowledge? Therefore I have spoken unwisely, and things that above measure exceeded my knowledge.—*Job* xlii. 1, 3.

As it is not good for a man to eat much honey, so he that is a searcher of majesty, shall be overwhelmed by glory. —*Prov.* xxv. 27.

All things are hard: man cannot explain them by word. The eye is not filled with seeing, neither is the ear filled with hearing.—*Eccles.* i. 8.

What needeth a man to seek things that are above him, whereas he knoweth not what is profitable for him in his life, in all the days of his pilgrimage, and the time that passeth like a shadow? Or who can tell him what shall be after him under the sun?— *Eccles.* vii. 1.

Only this I have found, that God made man right, and he hath entangled himself with an infinity of questions. Who is as the wise man? and who hath known the resolution of the word?— *Eccles.* vii. 30.

As thou knowest not what is the way of the spirit, nor how the bones are joined together in the womb of her that is with child: so thou knowest not the works of God, who is the maker of all. —*Eccles.* xi. 5.

For the corruptible body is a load upon the soul, and the earthly habitation presseth down the mind that museth upon many things.

And hardly do we guess aright at things that are upon earth: and with labor do we find the things that are before us. But the things that are in heaven, who shall search out?

And who shall know thy thought, except thou give wisdom, and send thy Holy Spirit from above?—*Wis.* ix. 15-17.

Seek not the things that are too high for thee, and search not into things above thy ability: but the things that God hath commanded thee, think on them always, and in many of his works, be not curious.

For it is not necessary for thee to see with thy eyes those things that are hid.

In unnecessary matters be not over curious, and in many of his works, thou shalt not be inquisitive.

For many things are shown to thee above the understanding of men.

And the suspicion of them hath deceived many, and hath detained their minds in vanity.—*Ecclus.* iii. 22-26.

NAME OF GOD, THE

Moses said to God: Lo, I shall go to the children of Israel, and say to them: The God of your fathers hath sent me to you. If they should say to me: What is his name? what shall I say to them?

God said to Moses: I am who am. He said: Thus shalt thou say to the children of Israel: He who is, hath sent me to you.—*Ex.* iii. 13, 14.

And the Lord spoke to Moses, saying: I am the Lord,

That appeared to Abraham, to Isaac, and to Jacob, by the name of God Almighty; and my name Adonai, I did not show them.—*Ex.* vi. 2, 3.

I will declare thy name to my brethren: in the midst of the church, will I praise thee.—*Ps.* xxi. 23.

According to thy name, O God, so also is thy praise unto the ends of the earth.—*Ps.* xlvii. 11.

Blessed be he that cometh in the name of the Lord.

We have blessed you out of the house of the Lord.—*Ps.* cxvii. 26.

Thy name, O Lord, is for ever: thy memorial, O Lord, unto all generations. —*Ps.* cxxxiv. 13.

And thou hast delivered me, according to the multitude of the mercy of thy name, from them that did roar, prepared to devour.—*Ecclus.* li. 4.

Our redeemer, the Lord of hosts is his name, the Holy One of Israel.—*Is.* xlvii. 4.

For all people will walk, every one, in the name of his god: but we will walk in the name of the Lord our God for ever and ever.—*Mich.* iv. 5.

Then they that feared the Lord, spoke every one with his neighbor: and the Lord gave ear, and heard it: and a book of remembrance was written before him for them that fear the Lord, and think on his name.

And they shall be my special possession, saith the Lord of hosts, in the day that I do judgment: and I will spare them, as a man spareth his son that serveth him.—*Malach.* iii. 16, 17.

Thus therefore shall you pray: Our Father, who art in heaven, hallowed be thy name.—*Matt.* vi. 9.

Father, glorify thy name. A voice therefore came from heaven: I have both glorified it, and will glorify it again.—*John* xii. 28.

NAME OF GOD IS GREAT, AND GOOD, AND GLORIOUS, THE

Now therefore our God we give thanks to thee, and we praise thy glorious name.—1 *Paral.* xxix. 13.

Nations from afar shall come to thee (Jerusalem): and shall bring gifts, and shall adore the Lord in thee, and shall esteem thy land as holy.

For they shall call upon the great name in thee.—*Tob.* xiii. 14, 15.

O Lord our Lord, how admirable is thy name in the whole earth!

For thy magnificence is elevated above the heavens.—*Ps.* viii. 2.

I will praise thee for ever, because thou hast done it: and I will wait on thy name, for it is good in the sight of thy saints.—*Ps.* li. 11.

I will freely sacrifice to thee, and will give praise, O God, to thy name: because it is good.—*Ps.* liii. 8.

From the rising of the sun unto the going down of the same, the name of the Lord is worthy of praise.—*Ps.* cxii. 3.

Praise ye the Lord, for the Lord is good: sing ye to his name, for it is sweet.—*Ps.* cxxxiv. 3.

Young men and maidens: let the old with the younger, praise the name of the Lord:

For his name alone is exalted.—*Ps.* cxlviii. 12, 13.

Thy name is as oil poured out: therefore young maidens have loved thee. —*Cant.* i. 2.

And you say in that day: Praise ye the Lord, and call upon his name: make his works known among thy people: remember that his name is high.— *Is.* xii. 4.

There is none like to thee, O Lord: thou art great, and great is thy name in might.—*Jer.* x. 6.

Therefore hear ye the word of the Lord, all Juda, you that dwell in the land of Egypt: Behold I have sworn by my great name, saith the Lord: that my name shall no more be named in the mouth of any man of Juda, in the land of Egypt, saying: The Lord God liveth.—*Jer.* xliv. 26.

Blessed art thou, O Lord, the God of our fathers, and thy name is worthy of praise, and glorious for ever.—*Dan.* iii. 26.

For from the rising of the sun even to the going down, my name is great among the Gentiles, and in every place there is sacrifice, and there is offered to my name a clean oblation: for my name is great among the Gentiles, saith the Lord of hosts.—*Malach.* i. 11.

NAME OF GOD IS HOLY, THE

Profane not my holy name, that I may be sanctified in the midst of the children of Israel. I am the Lord who sanctify you.—*Lev.* xxii. 32.

Let them give praise to thy great name: for it is terrible and holy.—*Ps.* xcviii. 3.

Bless the Lord, O my soul: and let all that is within me bless his holy name.—*Ps.* cii. 1.

Glory ye in his holy name.—*Ps.* civ. 3.

Save us, O Lord our God: and gather us from among the nations:

That we may give thanks to thy holy name, and may glory in thy praise.— *Ps.* cv. 47.

Holy and terrible is his name.—*Ps.* cx. 9.

For thou hast magnified thy holy name above all.—*Ps.* cxxxvii. 2.

For men, serving either their affection, or their kings, gave the incommunicable name to stones and wood.— *Wis.* xiv. 21.

He set his eye upon their hearts, to show them the greatness of his works:

That they might praise the name which he hath sanctified.—*Ecclus.* xvii. 7, 8.

And when they entered among the nations whither they went, they profaned my holy name, when it was said of them: This is the people of the Lord, and they are come forth out of his land.

And I have regarded my own holy name, which the house of Israel hath profaned among the nations to which they went in. . . .

And I will sanctify my great name, which was profaned among the Gentiles, which you have profaned in the midst of them.—*Ezech.* xxxvi. 20, 21, 23.

And I will make my holy name known in the midst of my people Israel, and my holy name shall be profaned no more: and the Gentiles shall know that I am the Lord, the Holy One of Israel.—*Ezech.* xxxix. 7.

Therefore, thus saith the Lord God: Now will I bring back the captivity of Jacob, and will have mercy on all the house of Israel: and I will be jealous for my holy name.—*Ezech.* xxxix. 25.

Because he that is mighty, hath done great things to me; and holy is his name.—*Luke* i. 49.

But the sure foundation of God standeth firm, having this seal: the Lord knoweth who are his; and let every one depart from iniquity, who nameth the name of the Lord.—2 *Tim.* ii. 19.

NAME OF GOD IS TERRIBLE, THE

Let them give praise to thy great name: for it is terrible and holy.— *Ps.* xcviii. 3.

Holy and terrible is his name.—*Ps.* cx. 9.

Cursed is the deceitful man that hath in his flock a male, and making a vow, offereth in sacrifice that which is feeble to the Lord: for I am a great King, saith the Lord of hosts, and my name is dreadful among the Gentiles.— *Malach.* i. 14.

NAME OF GOD IS OUR STRENGTH AND SHIELD, THE

And David said to the Philistine: Thou comest to me with a sword, and with a spear, and with a shield: but I come to thee in the name of the Lord of hosts, the God of the armies of Israel, which thou hast defied.—1 *Kings* xvii. 45.

And let them trust in thee, who know thy name: for thou hast not forsaken them that seek thee, O Lord.— *Ps.* ix. 11.

May the Lord hear thee in the day of tribulation: may the name of the God of Jacob protect thee.—*Ps.* xix. 2.

We will rejoice in thy salvation; and in the name of our God, we shall be exalted.—*Ps.* xix. 6.

Through thee we will push down our enemies with the horn: and through thy name we will despise them that rise up against us.—*Ps.* xliii. 6.

Save me, O God, by thy name, and judge me in thy strength.—*Ps.* liii. 3.

Blessed is the people that knoweth jubilation.

They shall walk, O Lord, in the light of thy countenance: and in thy name they shall rejoice all the day.—*Ps.* lxxxviii. 16, 17.

And my truth and my mercy shall be with him: and in my name shall his horn be exalted.—*Ps.* lxxxviii. 25.

Our help is in the name of the Lord, who made heaven and earth.—*Ps.* cxxiii. 8.

The name of the Lord is a strong tower: the just runneth to it, and shall be exalted.—*Prov.* xviii. 10.

And it shall come to pass, that every one that shall call upon the name of the Lord, shall be saved.—*Joel* ii. 32.

NAME OF GOD, WE SHOULD LOVE THE

And all they that love thy name, shall glory in thee.—*Ps.* v. 12.

For God will save Sion, and the cities of Juda shall be built up. . . . And the seed of his servants shall possess it; and they that love his name, shall dwell therein.—*Ps.* lxviii. 36, 37.

In the night, I have remembered thy name, O Lord: and have kept thy law. —*Ps.* cxviii. 55.

And in the way of thy judgments, O Lord, we have patiently waited for thee: thy name, and thy remembrance are the desire of the soul.—*Is.* xxvi. 8.

O Lord our God, other lords besides thee have had dominion over us, only in thee, let us remember thy name.— *Is.* xxvi. 13.

NAME OF GOD, WE SHOULD FEAR THE

For thou, my God, hast heard my prayer: thou hast given an inheritance to them that fear thy name.—*Ps.* lx. 6.

Conduct me, O Lord, in thy way, and I will walk in thy truth: let my heart rejoice that it may fear thy name.—*Ps.* lxxxv. 11.

And the Gentiles shall fear thy name, O Lord, and all the kings of the earth, thy glory.—*Ps.* ci. 16.

The voice of the Lord crieth to the city, and salvation shall be to them that fear thy name.—*Mich.* vi. 9.

My covenant was with him of life and peace: and I gave him fear: and he feared me, and he was afraid before my name.—*Malach.* ii. 5.

But unto you that fear my name, the Sun of justice shall arise, and health in his wings: and you shall go forth, and shall leap like calves of the herd. —*Malach.* iv. 2.

NAME OF GOD, WE SHOULD TRUST IN THE

For in him our heart shall rejoice: and in his holy name we have trusted. —*Ps.* xxxii. 21.

Blessed is the man whose trust is in the name of the Lord; and who hath not had regard to vanities, and lying follies.—*Ps.* xxxix. 5.

I will praise thee for ever, because thou hast done it: and I will wait on thy name, for it is good in the sight of thy saints.—*Ps.* li. 11.

Thus will I bless thee all my life long: and in thy name I will lift up my hands.—*Ps.* lxii. 5.

Who is there among you that feareth the Lord, that heareth the voice of his servant, that hath walked in darkness, and hath no light? let him hope in the name of the Lord, and lean upon his God.—*Is.* l. 10.

And I will leave in the midst of thee a poor and needy people: and they shall hope in the name of the Lord.—*Soph.* iii. 12.

NAME OF GOD, WE SHOULD INVOKE THE

Because I will invoke the name of the Lord: give ye magnificence to our God.—*Deut.* xxxii. 3.

Begin ye to the Lord with timbrels, sing ye to the Lord with cymbals, tune unto him a new psalm, extol and call upon his name.—*Judith* xvi. 2.

Some trust in chariots, and some in horses: but we will call upon the name of the Lord our God.

They are bound, and have fallen; but we are risen, and are set upright.—*Ps.* xix. 8, 9.

We will praise thee, O God: we will praise, and we will call upon thy name. —*Ps.* lxxiv. 2.

And we depart not from thee, thou shalt quicken us: and we will call upon thy name.—*Ps.* lxxix. 19.

Give glory to the Lord, and call upon his name: declare his deeds among the Gentiles.—*Ps.* civ. 1.

The sorrows of death have compassed me: and the perils of hell have found me.

I met with trouble and sorrow: and I called upon the name of the Lord. O Lord, deliver my soul.—*Ps.* cxiv. 3, 4.

I will take the chalice of salvation; and I will call upon the name of the Lord.—*Ps.* cxv. 13.

And you shall say in that day: Praise ye the Lord, and call upon his name: make his works known among the people: remember that his name is high.—*Is.* xii. 4.

And every one that calleth upon my name, I have created him for my glory, I have formed him, and made him.— *Is.* xliii. 7.

And it shall come to pass, that every one that shall call upon the name of the Lord, shall be saved.—*Joel* ii. 32.

Because then I will restore to the people a chosen lip that all may call upon the name of the Lord, and may serve him with one shoulder.—*Soph.* iii. 9.

NAME OF GOD, PRAISING THE

Now therefore, our God, we give thanks to thee, and we praise thy glorious name.—1 *Paral.* xxix. 13.

Be thy name, O God of Israel, blessed for ever.—*Tob.* iii. 23.

I will give glory to the Lord, according to his justice: and will sing to the name of the Lord, the most high.—*Ps.* vii. 18.

In God shall we glory all the day long: and in thy name we will give praise for ever.—*Ps.* xliii. 9.

I will freely sacrifice to thee, and will give praise, O God, to thy name: because it is good.—*Ps.* liii. 8.

So will I sing a psalm to thy name for ever and ever: that I may pay my vows from day to day.—*Ps.* lx. 9.

I will praise the name of God with a canticle: and I will magnify him with praise.

And it shall please God better than a young calf, that bringeth forth horns and hoofs.—*Ps.* lxviii. 31, 32.

Let his name be blessed for evermore: his name continueth before the sun. . . .

And blessed be the name of his majesty for ever.—*Ps.* lxxi. 17, 19.

All the nations thou hast made shall come and adore before thee, O Lord: and they shall glorify thy name.—*Ps.* lxxxv. 9.

I will praise thee, O Lord my God, with my whole heart, and I will glorify thy name for ever.—*Ps.* lxxxv. 12.

It is good to give praise to the Lord; and to sing to thy name, O most High. —*Ps.* xci. 2.

Praise the Lord, ye children:

praise ye the name of the Lord.

Blessed be the name of the Lord, from henceforth now and for ever.

From the rising of the sun unto the going down of the same, the name of the Lord is worthy of praise.—*Ps.* cxii. 1-3.

Not to us, O Lord, not to us; but to thy name give glory.—*Ps.* cxiii. (*Heb.* cxv.) 1.

I will worship towards thy holy temple, and I will give glory to thy name.

For thy mercy and for thy truth; for thou hast magnified thy holy name above all.—*Ps.* cxxxvii. 2.

But as for the just, they shall give glory to thy name.—*Ps.* cxxxix. 14.

I will extol thee, O God, my king; and I will bless thy name for ever; yea, for ever and ever.

Every day will I bless thee: and I will praise thy name for ever; yea, for ever and ever.—*Ps.* cxliv. 1, 2.

He set his eye upon their hearts to show them the greatness of his works:

That they might praise the name which he hath sanctified.—*Ecclus.* xvii. 7, 8.

I will give glory to thy name; for thou hast been a helper and protector to me.—*Ecclus.* li. 2.

O Lord, thou art my God, I will exalt thee, and give glory to thy name: for thou hast done wonderful things, thy designs of old faithful, amen.—*Is.* xxv. 1.

Blessed be the name of the Lord from eternity and for evermore: for wisdom and fortitude are his.—*Dan.* ii. 20.

Who shall not fear thee, O Lord, and magnify thy name? For thou only art holy: for all nations shall come, and shall adore in thy sight, because thy judgments are manifest.—*Apoc.* xv. 4.

NAME OF GOD, EXHORTATION TO PRAISE THE

Praise ye his holy name: let the heart of them rejoice, that seek the Lord. . . .

Give to the Lord glory to his name. —1 *Paral.* xvi. 10, 29.

Bring to the Lord glory and honor: bring to the Lord glory to his name: adore ye the Lord in his holy court.— *Ps.* xxviii. 2.

O, magnify the Lord with me; and let us extol his name together.—*Ps.* xxxiii. 4.

Let all the earth adore thee, and sing to thee: let it sing a psalm to thy name. —*Ps.* lxv. 4.

Sing ye to the Lord, and bless his name: show forth his salvation from day to day.—*Ps.* xcv. 2.

Let them give praise to thy great name: for it is terrible and holy.—*Ps.* xcviii. 3.

Bless the Lord, O my soul: and let all that is within me bless his holy name.—*Ps.* cii. 1.

Praise ye the name of the Lord. . . .

Praise ye the Lord, for the Lord is good: sing ye to his name, for it is sweet.—*Ps.* cxxxiv. 1, 3.

My mouth shall speak the praise of the Lord: and let all flesh bless his holy name for ever; yea, for ever and ever.—*Ps.* cxliv. 21.

Young men and maidens: let the old with the younger, praise the name of the Lord: for his name alone is exalted.—*Ps.* cxlviii. 12, 13.

Let Israel rejoice in him that made him: and let the children of Sion be joyful in their king.

Let them praise his name in choir: let them sing to him with the timbrel and the psaltery.—*Ps.* cxlix. 2, 3.

Magnify his name, and give glory to him with the voice of your lips, and with the canticles of your mouths, and with harps.—*Ecclus.* xxxix. 20.

Now therefore with the whole heart and mouth, praise ye him, and bless the name of the Lord.—*Ecclus.* xxxix. 41.

Now therefore, glorify ye the Lord in instruction: the name of the Lord God of Israel in the islands of the sea.—*Is.* xxiv. 15.

NAME OF GOD, GRATITUDE TO THE

Save us, O Lord our God: and gather us from among the nations:

That we may give thanks to thy holy name, and may glory in thy praise.— *Ps.* cv. 47.

I will praise thy name continually, and will praise it with thanksgiving, and my prayer was heard.

And thou hast saved me from destruction, and hast delivered me from the evil time.

Therefore I will give thanks, and praise thee, and bless the name of the Lord.—*Ecclus.* li. 15-17.

NAME OF GOD IN VAIN, TAKING THE

Thou shalt not take the name of the Lord thy God in vain: for the Lord will not hold him guiltless, that shall take the name of the Lord his God in vain.—*Ex.* xx. 7.

Thou shalt not swear falsely by my name, nor profane the name of thy God. I am the Lord.—*Lev.* xix. 12.

Profane not my holy name, that I may be sanctified in the midst of the children of Israel. I am the Lord who sanctify you.—*Lev.* xxii. 32.

Thou shalt not take the name of the Lord thy God in vain: for he shall not be unpunished that taketh his name upon a vain thing.—*Deut.* v. 11.

Let not thy mouth be accustomed to swearing: for in it there are many falls.

And let not the naming of God be usual in thy mouth, and meddle not with the names of saints, for thou shalt not escape free from them.

For as a slave daily put to the question is never without a blue mark: so every one that sweareth, and nameth, shall not be wholly pure from sin.

A man that sweareth much, shall be filled with iniquity, and a scourge shall not depart from his house.—*Ecclus.* xxiii. 9-12.

And I will make my holy name known in the midst of my people Israel, and my holy name shall be profaned no more: and the Gentiles shall know that I am the Lord, the Holy One of Israel. —*Ezech.* xxxix. 7.

Therefore, thus saith the Lord God: Now will I bring back the captivity of Jacob, and will have mercy on all the house of Israel: and I will be jealous for my holy name.—*Ezech.* xxxix. 25.

NAME, GOD IS GOOD TO US FOR THE SAKE OF HIS

And the Lord will not forsake his people, for his great name's sake: be-cause the Lord hath sworn to make you his people.—1 *Kings* xii. 22.

He hath converted my soul.

He hath led me on the paths of justice, for his own name's sake.—*Ps.* xxii. 3.

For thy name's sake, O Lord, thou wilt pardon my sin: for it is great.—*Ps.* xxiv. 11.

For thou art my strength and my refuge; and for thy name's sake, thou wilt lead me, and nourish me.—*Ps.* xxx. 4.

Because he hoped in me, I will deliver him: I will protect him, because he hath known my name.—*Ps.* xc. 14.

Our fathers understood not thy wonders in Egypt: they remembered not the multitude of thy mercies:

And they provoked to wrath, going up to the sea, even the Red Sea.

And he saved them for his own name's sake: that he might make his power known.—*Ps.* cv. 7, 8.

For thy name's sake, O Lord, thou wilt quicken me in thy justice.

Thou wilt bring my soul out of trouble.—*Ps.* cxlii. 11.

For my name's sake, I will remove my wrath far off: and for my praise, I will bridle thee, lest thou shouldst perish.—*Is.* xlviii. 9.

But they provoked me, and would not hearken to me: they did not every man cast away the abominations of his eyes, neither did they forsake the idols of Egypt: and I said I would pour out my indignation upon them, and accomplish my wrath against them in the midst of the land of Egypt.

But I did otherwise for my name's sake, that it might not be violated before the nations, in the midst of whom they were, and among whom I made myself known to them, to bring them out of the land of Egypt.—*Ezech.* xx. 8, 9.

And you shall know that I am the Lord, when I shall have done well by you for my own name's sake, and not according to your evil ways, nor according to your wicked deeds, O house of Israel, saith the Lord.—*Ezech.* xx. 44.

And I have regarded my own holy name, which the house of Israel hath profaned among the nations to which they went in.

Therefore thou shalt say to the house of Israel: Thus saith the Lord God: It is not for your sake, that I will do this, O house of Israel, but for my holy name's sake, which you have profaned among the nations whither you went.—*Ezech.* xxxvi. 21, 22.

NAME, A PRAYER THAT GOD MAY BE GOOD TO US FOR THE SAKE OF HIS

Arise, O Lord, help us and redeem us, for thy name's sake.—*Ps.* xliii. 26.

Help us, O God, our saviour: and for the glory of thy name, O Lord, deliver us: and forgive us our sins for thy name's sake.—*Ps.* lxxviii. 9.

But thou, O Lord, do with me for thy name's sake: because thy mercy is sweet.—*Ps.* cviii. 21.

Give us not to be a reproach, for thy name's sake, and do not disgrace in us the throne of thy glory; remember, break not thy covenant with us.—*Jer.* xiv. 21.

Remember not the iniquities of our fathers, but think upon thy hand, and upon thy name at this time:

For thou art the Lord our God, and we will praise thee, O Lord.—*Bar.* iii. 5, 6.

Deliver us not up for ever, we beseech thee, for thy name's sake, and abolish not thy covenant. . . .

And deliver us according to thy wonderful works, and give glory to thy name, O Lord.—*Dan.* iii. 34, 43.

O Lord, hear: O Lord, be appeased: hearken and do: delay not for thy own sake, O my God: because thy name is invocated upon thy city, and upon thy people.—*Dan.* ix. 19.

Others sold all that they had left, and withal besought the Lord, that he would deliver them from the wicked Nicanor, who had sold them before he came near them:

And if not for their sakes, yet for the covenant that he had made with their fathers, and for the sake of his holy and glorious name that was invoked upon them.—*2 Mach.* viii. 14, 15.

NAME OF JESUS, THE

But I will rejoice in the Lord: and I will joy in God my Jesus.—*Hab.* iii. 18.

But while he thought on these things, behold the angel of the Lord appeared to him in his sleep, saying: Joseph, son of David, fear not to take unto thee Mary thy wife, for that which is conceived in her, is of the Holy Ghost.

And she shall bring forth a son: and thou shalt call his name Jesus. For he shall save his people from their sins.—*Matt.* i. 20, 21.

And in his name the Gentiles shall hope.—*Matt.* xii. 21.

And the angel said to her: Fear not, Mary, for thou hast found grace with God.

Behold thou shalt conceive in thy womb, and shalt bring forth a son; and thou shalt call his name Jesus.—*Luke* i. 30, 31.

And after eight days were accomplished, that the child should be circumcised, his name was called Jesus, which was called by the angel, before he was conceived in the womb.—*Luke* ii. 21.

He humbled himself, becoming obedient unto death, even to the death of the cross.

For which cause God also hath exalted him, and hath given him a name which is above all names:

That in the name of Jesus, every knee should bow, of those that are in heaven, on earth, and under the earth. —*Philipp.* ii. 8-10.

Wherefore also we pray always for you; that our God would make you worthy of his vocation, and fulfil all the good pleasure of his goodness, and the work of faith in power:

That the name of our Lord Jesus may be glorified in you, and you in him, according to the grace of our God, and of the Lord Jesus Christ.—*2 Thess.* i. 11, 12.

And we charge you, brethren, in the name of our Lord Jesus Christ, that you withdraw yourselves from every brother walking disorderly, and not according to the tradition which they have received of us.—*2 Thess.* iii. 6.

I write unto you, little children, be

cause your sins are forgiven you for his name's sake.—*1 John* ii. 12.

NAME OF JESUS, POWER OF THE

And these signs shall follow them that believe: In my name they shall cast out devils: they shall speak with new tongues.

They shall take up serpents; and if they shall drink any deadly thing, it shall not hurt them: they shall lay their hands upon the sick, and they shall recover.—*Mark* xvi. 17, 18.

And the seventy-two returned with joy, saying: Lord, the devils also are subject to us in thy name.—*Luke* x. 17.

But these are written that you may believe that Jesus is the Christ, the Son of God: and that believing, you may have life in his name.—*John* xx. 31.

But Peter said to them: Do penance, and be baptized, every one of you, in the name of Jesus Christ, for the remission of your sins: and you shall receive the gift of the Holy Ghost.—*Acts* ii. 38.

But Peter said: Silver and gold I have none; but what I have, I give thee: In the name of Jesus Christ of Nazareth, arise, and walk.—*Acts* iii. 6.

Be it known to you all, and to all the people of Israel, that by the name of our Lord Jesus Christ of Nazareth, whom you crucified, whom God hath raised from the dead, even by him, this man standeth here before you whole. . . . Neither is there salvation in any other. For there is no other name under heaven given to men, whereby we must be saved.—*Acts* iv. 10, 12.

And now, Lord, behold their threatenings, and grant unto thy servants, that with all confidence, they may speak thy word,

By stretching forth thy hand to cures, and signs, and wonders, to be done by the name of thy holy Son Jesus.—*Acts* iv. 29, 30.

To him (Jesus Christ) all the prophets give testimony, that by his name, all receive remission of sins, who believe in him.—*Acts* x. 43.

And it came to pass, as we went to prayer, a certain girl, having a pythonical spirit, met us, who brought to her masters much gain by divining.

This same, following Paul and us, cried out saying: These men are the servants of the most high God, who preach unto you the way of salvation. And this she did many days. But Paul, being grieved, turned, and said to the spirit: I command thee, in the name of Jesus Christ, to go out from her. And he went out the same hour.—*Acts* xvi. 16-18.

NAME OF JESUS, WE SHOULD SANCTIFY OUR ACTIONS BY DOING THEM IN THE

For whosoever shall give you to drink a cup of water in my name, because you belong to Christ: amen I say to you, he shall not lose his reward.—*Mark* ix. 40.

All whatsoever you do in word or in work, do all in the name of the Lord Jesus Christ, giving thanks to God and the Father by him.—*Col.* iii. 17.

NAME OF JESUS, WE SHOULD PRAY IN THE

And whatsoever you shall ask the Father in my name, that will I do: that the Father may be glorified in the Son. If you shall ask me any thing in my name, that I will do.—*John* xiv. 13, 14.

Amen, amen, I say to you: if you ask the Father any thing in my name, he will give it you.

Hitherto you have not asked any thing in my name. Ask, and you shall receive; that your joy may be full.—*John* xvi. 23, 24.

Giving thanks always for all things, in the name of our Lord Jesus Christ, to God and the Father.—*Eph.* v. 20.

NAME, THE VALUE OF A GOOD

The light of the eyes rejoiceth the soul: a good name maketh the bones fat.—*Prov.* xv. 30.

A good name is better than great riches: and good favor is above silver and gold.—*Prov.* xxii. 1.

A good name is better than precious ointments.—*Eccles.* vii. 2.

Take care of a good name: for this shall continue with thee, more than a thousand treasures precious and great.

A good life hath its number of days: but a good name shall continue for ever.—*Ecclus.* xli. 15, 16.

NEAR TO HIS PEOPLE, GOD IS

See also: Presence of God in our midst—page 413.

Neither is there any other nation so great, that hath gods so nigh them, as our God is present to all our petitions. —*Deut.* iv. 7.

No man shall be able to resist you all the days of thy life: as I have been with Moses, so I will be with thee: I will not leave thee nor forsake thee.— *Jos.* i. 5.

And the spirit of God came upon Azarias, the son of Oded,

And he went out to meet Asa, and said to him: Hear ye me, Asa, and all Juda and Benjamin: The Lord is with you, because you have been with him. If you seek him, you shall find: but if you forsake him, he will forsake you. —*2 Paral.* xv. 1, 2.

The Lord of armies is with us: the God of Jacob is our protector.—*Ps.* xlv. 8.

Mountains are round about it (Jerusalem): so the Lord is round about his people from henceforth now and for ever.—*Ps.* cxxiv. 2.

The Lord is nigh unto all them that call upon him: to all that call upon him in truth.—*Ps.* cxliv. 18.

Fear not, for I am with thee: turn not aside, for I am thy God: I have strengthened thee, and have helped thee, and the right hand of my just one hath upheld thee. . . .

For I am the Lord thy God who take thee by the hand, and say to thee: Fear not, I have helped thee.—*Is.* xli. 10, 13.

And now thus saith the Lord that created thee, O Jacob, and formed thee, O Israel: Fear not, for I have redeemed thee, and called thee by thy name: thou art mine.

When thou shalt pass through the waters, I will be with thee, and the rivers shall not cover thee: when thou shalt walk in the fire, thou shalt not be burnt, and the flames shall not burn in thee. . . .

Fear not, for I am with thee.—*Is.* xliii. 1, 2, 5.

And you shall know that I am in the midst of Israel: and I am the Lord your God, and there is none besides: and my people shall not be confounded for ever.—*Joel* ii. 27.

Seek ye good, and not evil, that you may live: and the Lord, the God of hosts will be with you, as you have said. —*Amos* v. 14.

The Lord hath taken away thy judgment, he hath turned away thy enemies: the king of Israel, the Lord. is in the midst of thee, thou shalt fear evil no more.—*Soph.* iii. 15.

Sing praise, and rejoice, O daughter of Sion: for behold I come, and I will dwell in the midst of thee: saith the Lord.—*Zach.* ii. 10.

The things which you have both learned, and received, and heard, and seen in me, these do ye, and the God of peace shall be with you.—*Philipp.* iv. 9.

NEAR US, ESPECIALLY WHEN WE NEED HIM MOST, GOD IS

I set the Lord always in my sight: for he is at my right hand, that I be not moved.—*Ps.* xv. 8.

For though I should walk in the midst of the shadow of death, I will fear no evils, for thou art with me.

Thy rod and thy staff, they have comforted me.—*Ps.* xxii. 4.

He shall cry to me, and I will hear him: I am with him in tribulation, I will deliver him, and I will glorify him. —*Ps.* xc. 15.

They that persecute me, have drawn nigh to iniquity; but they are gone far off from thy law.

Thou art near, O Lord: and all thy ways are truth.—*Ps.* cxviii. 150, 151.

O Lord, Lord, the strength of my salvation: thou hast overshadowed my head in the day of battle.—*Ps.* cxxxix. 8.

If thou sleep, thou shalt not fear: thou shalt rest, and thy sleep shall be sweet.

Be not afraid of sudden fear, nor of the power of the wicked falling upon thee.

For the Lord will be at thy side, and will keep thy foot, that thou be not taken.—*Prov.* iii. 24-26.

Even to your old age I am the same, and to your grey hairs I will carry you: I have made you, and I will bear: I will carry and will save.—*Is.* xlvi. 4.

And I will make thee to this people as a strong wall of brass: and they shall fight against thee, and shall not prevail: for I am with thee, to save thee, and to deliver thee, saith the Lord.

And I will deliver thee out of the hand of the wicked, and I will redeem thee out of the hand of the mighty.—*Jer.* xv. 20, 21.

But the Lord is with me as a strong warrior: therefore they that persecute me shall fall and shall be weak.—*Jer.* xx. 11.

I have called upon thy name, O Lord, from the lowest pit.

Thou hast heard my voice: turn not away thy ear from my sighs and cries.

Thou drewest near in the day when I called upon thee, thou saidst: Fear not. —*Lam.* iii. 55-57.

But I am the Lord thy God from the land of Egypt: and thou shalt know no God but me, and there is no saviour beside me.

I knew thee in the desert, in the land of the wilderness.—*Osee* xiii. 4, 5.

The Lord thy God in the midst of thee is mighty, he will save.—*Soph.* iii. 17.

And when he entered into the boat, his disciples followed him:

And behold a great tempest arose in the sea, so that the boat was covered with waves, but he was asleep.

And they came to him, and awaked him, saying: Lord, save us, we perish.

And Jesus saith to them: Why are you fearful, O ye of little faith? Then rising up, he commanded the winds, and the sea, and there came a great calm.—*Matt.* viii. 23-26.

And when it was late, the ship was in the midst of the sea, and himself (Jesus) alone on the land.

And seeing them laboring in rowing (for the wind was against them), and about the fourth watch of the night, he cometh to them, walking upon the sea, and he would have passed by them.

But they, seeing him walking upon the sea, thought it was an apparition, and they cried out.

For they all saw him, and were troubled. And immediately he spoke with them, and said to them: Have a good heart, it is I, fear ye not.

And he went up to them into the ship, and the wind ceased: and they were far more astonished within themselves.—*Mark* vi. 47-51.

And the patriarchs, through envy, sold Joseph into Egypt; and God was with him,

And delivered him out of all his tribulations.—*Acts* vii. 9, 10.

That they should seek God, if happily they may feel after him or find him, although he be not far from every one of us:

For in him, we live, and move, and are.—*Acts* xvii. 27, 28.

And the Lord said to Paul in the night, by a vision: Do not fear, but speak; and hold not thy peace,

Because I am with thee: and no man shall set upon thee, to hurt thee.—*Acts* xviii. 9, 10.

Let your modesty be known to all men. The Lord is nigh.—*Philipp.* iv. 5.

At my first answer, no man stood with me, but all forsook me: may it not be laid to their charge.

But the Lord stood by me, and strengthened me, that by me the preaching may be accomplished, and that all the Gentiles may hear: and I was delivered out of the mouth of the lion.—*2 Tim.* iv. 16, 17.

NEAR TO GOD, WE SHOULD DRAW

See also: Come to the Lord, invitation to—page 56.

He hath loved the people, all the saints are in his hand: and they that approach to his feet, shall receive of his doctrine.—*Deut.* xxxiii. 3.

The Lord render unto thee for thy work, and mayst thou receive a full reward of the Lord, the God of Israel, to whom thou art come, and under whose wings thou art fled.—*Ruth* ii. 12.

Wait on God with patience: join thyself to God, and endure, that thy life may be increased in the latter end.— *Ecclus.* ii. 3.

But now in Christ Jesus, you, who some time were afar off, are made nigh by the blood of Christ.

For he is our peace, who hath made

both one, and breaking down the middle wall of partition, the enmities in his flesh.—*Eph.* ii. 13, 14.

Having therefore, brethren, a confidence in the entering into the holies by the blood of Christ;

. . . Let us draw near with a true heart, in fulness of faith, having our hearts sprinkled from an evil conscience, and our bodies washed with clean water.—*Heb.* x. 19, 22.

Draw nigh to God, and he will draw nigh to you. Cleanse your hands, ye sinners: and purify your hearts, ye double minded.—*James* iv. 8.

NEAR TO GOD, WE SHOULD KEEP

See also: Presence of God, we should keep ourselves in the—page 413.

And I will rejoice under the covert of thy wings:

My soul hath stuck close to thee: thy right hand hath received me.—*Ps.* lxii. 8, 9.

But it is good for me to adhere to my God, to put my hope in the Lord God:

That I may declare all thy praises, in the gates of the daughter of Sion.— *Ps.* lxxii. 28.

And Peter answering, said to Jesus: Lord, it is good for us to be here: if thou wilt, let us make here three tabernacles, one for thee, and one for Moses, and one for Elias.—*Matt.* xvii. 4.

Abide in me, and I in you. As the branch cannot bear fruit of itself, unless it abide in the vine, so neither can you, unless you abide in me.

I am the vine, you the branches: he that abideth in me, and I in him, the same beareth much fruit: for without me, you can do nothing.

If any one abide not in me, he shall be cast forth as a branch, and shall wither, and they shall gather him up, and cast him into the fire, and he burneth.

If you abide in me, and my words abide in you, you shall ask whatever you will, and it shall be done unto you. —*John* xv. 4-7.

As therefore you have received Jesus Christ the Lord, walk ye in him;

Rooted and built up in him, and confirmed in the faith, as also you have learned, abounding in him, in thanksgiving.—*Col.* ii. 6, 7.

And now, little children, abide in him, that when he shall appear, we may have confidence, and not be confounded by him at his coming.—1 *John* ii. 28.

Whosoever abideth in him, sinneth not; and whosoever sinneth, hath not seen him, nor known him.—1 *John* iii. 6.

NEED OF GOD, OUR

See also: Dependence upon God, man's—page 106.

But I am needy and poor; O God, help me.

Thou art my helper and my deliverer: O Lord, make no delay.—*Ps.* lxix. 6.

For behold they that go far from thee, shall perish: thou hast destroyed all them that are disloyal to thee.—*Ps.* lxxii. 27.

If it had not been that the Lord was with us, let Israel now say:

If it had not been that the Lord was with us,

When men rose up against us, perhaps they had swallowed us up alive.

When their fury was enkindled against us, perhaps the water had swallowed us up.

Our soul hath passed through a torrent: perhaps our soul had passed through a water insupportable.—*Ps.* cxxiii. 1-5.

I stretched forth my hands to thee; my soul is as earth without water unto thee.

Hear me speedily, O Lord; my spirit hath fainted away.

Turn not away thy face from me, lest I be like unto them that go down into the pit.—*Ps.* cxlii. 6, 7.

As the branch cannot bear fruit of itself, unless it abide in the vine, so neither can you, unless you abide in me.

I am the vine, you the branches: he that abideth in me, and I in him, the same beareth much fruit: for without me, you can do nothing.—*John* xv. 4, 5.

For it is God who worketh in you

both to will and to accomplish, according to his good will.—*Philipp.* ii. 13.

NEEDS, GOD KNOWS OUR

And when you are praying, speak not much, as the heathens. For they think that in their much speaking they may be heard.

Be not you therefore like to them, for your Father knoweth what is needful for you, before you ask him.—*Matt.* vi. 7, 8.

Be not solicitous, therefore, saying, What shall we eat? or what shall we drink, or wherewith shall we be clothed? For after all these things do the heathens seek. For your Father knoweth that you have need of all these things.

Seek ye, therefore, first the kingdom of God, and his justice, and all these things shall be added unto you.—*Matt.* vi. 31-33.

NEGLECT OF GOD'S GRACE

See: Grace, abuse of—page 178.

NEUTRAL IN THE BATTLE OF LIFE, WE CANNOT BE

For the bed is straitened, so that one must fall out, and a short covering cannot cover both.—*Is.* xxviii. 20.

He that is not with me, is against me: and he that gathereth not with me, scattereth.—*Matt.* xii. 30.

Either make the tree good and its fruit good: or make the tree evil, and its fruit evil. For by the fruit, the tree is known.—*Matt.* xii. 33.

John answered him, saying: Master, we saw one casting out devils in thy name, who followeth not us, and we forbade him.

But Jesus said: Do not forbid him. For there is no man that doth a miracle in my name, and can soon speak ill of me.

For he that is not against you, is for you.—*Mark* ix. 37-39.

No servant can serve two masters: for either he will hate the one, and love the other; or he will hold to the one, and despise the other. You cannot serve God and mammon.—*Luke* xvi. 13.

For the flesh lusteth against the spirit: and the spirit against the flesh; for these are contrary one to another: so that you do not the things that you would.—*Gal.* v. 17.

I have fought a good fight, I have finished my course, I have kept the faith.—*2 Tim.* iv. 7.

NEW LAW IS THE FULFILMENT AND PERFECTION OF THE OLD, THE

See: Covenant of the New Law—page 85.

NEW SPIRIT, WE SHOULD PUT ON A

And I will give them one heart, and will put a new spirit in their bowels: and I will take away the stony heart out of their flesh, and will give them a heart of flesh:

That they may walk in my commandments, and keep my judgments, and do them: and that they may be my people, and I may be their God.—*Ezech.* xi. 19, 20.

Cast away from you all your transgressions, by which you have transgressed, and make to yourselves a new heart, and a new spirit: and why will you die, O house of Israel?—*Ezech.* xviii. 31.

And I will give you a new heart, and put a new spirit within you: and I will take away the stony heart out of your flesh, and will give you a heart of flesh.

And I will put my spirit in the midst of you: and I will cause you to walk in my commandments, and to keep my judgments, and do them.—*Ezech.* xxxvi. 26, 27.

For we are buried together with him by baptism into death; that as Christ is risen from the dead by the glory of the Father, so we also may walk in newness of life.

For if we have been planted together in the likeness of his death, we shall be also in the likeness of his resurrection.

Knowing this, that our old man is crucified with him, that the body of sin may be destroyed to the end that we may serve sin no longer.—*Rom.* vi. 4-6.

But now we are loosed from the law

of death, wherein we were detained; so that we should serve in newness of spirit, and not in the oldness of the letter.—*Rom.* vii. 6.

And be not conformed to this world; but be reformed in the newness of your mind, that you may prove what is the good, and the acceptable, and the perfect will of God.—*Rom.* xii. 2.

Now we have received not the spirit of this world, but the Spirit that is of God; that we may know the things that are given us from God.—1 *Cor.* ii. 12.

Purge out the old leaven, that you may be a new paste, as you are unleavened. For Christ our pasch is sacrificed.

Therefore let us feast, not with the old leaven, nor with the leaven of malice and wickedness; but with the unleavened bread of sincerity and truth. —1 *Cor.* v. 7, 8.

If then any be in Christ a new creature, the old things are passed away, behold all things are made new.—2 *Cor.* v. 17.

For as many of you as have been baptized in Christ, have put on Christ. —*Gal.* iii. 27.

For in Christ Jesus, neither circumcision availeth anything, nor uncircumcision, but a new creature.—*Gal.* vi. 15.

But you have not so learned Christ; If so be that you have heard him, and have been taught in him, as the truth is in Jesus:

To put off, according to former conversation, the old man, who is corrupted according to the desire of error.

And be renewed in the spirit of your mind:

And put on the new man, who according to God, is created in justice and holiness of truth.—*Eph.* iv. 20-24.

Lie not one to another: stripping yourselves of the old man with his deeds,

And putting on the new, him who is renewed unto knowledge, according to the image of him that created him.— *Col.* iii. 9, 10.

Wherefore, having the loins of your mind girt up, being sober, trust perfectly in the grace which is offered you in the revelation of Jesus Christ,

As children of obedience, not fashioned according to the former desires of your ignorance:

But according to him that hath called you, who is holy, be you also in all manner of conversation holy.—1 *Peter* i. 13-15.

NEW SPIRIT, A PRAYER THAT GOD MAY GIVE US A

Create a clean heart in me, O God: and renew a right spirit within my bowels.—*Ps.* l. 12.

Convert us, O Lord, to thee, and we shall be converted: renew our days, as from the beginning.—*Lam.* v. 21.

OBEDIENCE TO GOD

See also: Subjection of man's will to God—page 547.

And the Lord said to Abram: Go forth out of thy country, and from thy kindred, and out of thy father's house, and come into the land which I shall show thee. . . .

So Abram went out as the Lord had commanded him, and Lot went with him: Abram was seventy-five years old when he went forth from Haran.—*Gen.* xii. 1, 4.

After these things, God tempted Abraham, and said to him: Abraham, Abraham. And he answered: Here I am.

He said to him: Take thy only begotten son, Isaac, whom thou lovest, and go into the land of vision: and there thou shalt offer him for an holocaust upon one of the mountains which I will show thee.

So Abraham rising up in the night, saddled his ass: and took with him two young men, and Isaac his son: and when he had cut wood for the holocaust, he went his way to the place which God had commanded him. . . .

And they came to the place which God had shown him, where he built an altar, and laid the wood in order upon it: and when he had bound Isaac his son, he laid him on the altar, upon the pile of wood.

And he put forth his hand and took the sword, to sacrifice his son.

And behold an angel of the Lord

from heaven called to him, saying: Abraham, Abraham. And he answered: Here I am.

And he said to him: Lay not thy hand upon the boy, neither do thou any thing to him: now I know that thou fearest God, and hast not spared thy only begotten son for my sake.—*Gen.* xxii. 1-3, 9-12.

And Samuel said: Doth the Lord desire holocausts and victims, and not rather that the voice of the Lord should be obeyed? For obedience is better than sacrifices: and to hearken, rather than to offer the fat of rams.

Because it is like the sin of witchcraft, to rebel: and like the crime of idolatry, to refuse to obey.—*1 Kings* xv. 22, 23.

Keep thy foot, when thou goest into the house of God, and draw nigh to hear. For much better is obedience, than the victims of fools, who know not what evil they do.—*Eccles.* iv. 17.

And the Lord gave strength also to Caleb, and his strength continued even to his old age, so that he went up to the high places of the land, and his seed obtained it for an inheritance:

That all the children of Israel might see, that it is good to obey the holy God.—*Ecclus.* xlvi. 11, 12.

But this thing I commanded them, saying: Hearken to my voice, and I will be your God, and you shall be my people: and walk ye in all the way that I have commanded you, that it may be well with you.—*Jer.* vii. 23.

Whether it be good or evil, we will obey the voice of the Lord our God, to whom we send thee: that it may be well with us, when we shall hearken to the voice of the Lord our God.—*Jer.* xlii. 6.

It is good for a man, when he hath borne the yoke from his youth.—*Lam.* iii. 27.

The son honoreth the father, and the servant, his master: if then I be a father, where is my honor? and if I be a master, where is my fear? saith the Lord of hosts.—*Malach.* i. 6.

Then he saith to them: Render therefore to Cæsar the things that are Cæsar's; and to God, the things that are God's.—*Matt.* xxii. 21.

Amen, amen I say to you: If any man keep my word, he shall not see death for ever.—*John* viii. 51.

And calling them, they charged them not to speak at all, nor teach in the name of Jesus.

But Peter and John answering, said to them: If it be just in the sight of God to hear you rather than God, judge ye.—*Acts* iv. 18, 19.

But Peter and the apostles answering, said: We ought to obey God rather than men.—*Acts* v. 29.

And we are witnesses of these things and the Holy Ghost, whom God hath given to all that obey him.—*Acts* v. 32.

And falling on the ground, he heard a voice saying to him: Saul, Saul, why persecutest thou me?

Who said: Who art thou, Lord? And he: I am Jesus, whom thou persecutest. It is hard for thee to kick against the goad.

And he trembling and astonished, said: Lord, what wilt thou have me to do?—*Acts* ix. 4-6.

Moreover we have had fathers of our flesh, for instructors, and we reverenced them: shall we not much more obey the Father of spirits, and live?—*Heb.* xii. 9.

OBEDIENCE OF THE LOWER CREATION TO GOD

The pillars of heaven tremble, and dread at his beck.—*Job* xxvi. 11.

When God bloweth, there cometh frost, and again the waters are poured out abundantly.

Corn desireth clouds, and the clouds spread their light:

Which go round about, whithersoever the will of him that governeth them shall lead them, to whatsoever he shall command them upon the face of the whole earth:

Whether in one tribe, or in his own land, or in what place soever of his mercy he shall command them to be found.—*Job* xxxvii. 10-13.

I set my bounds around it, and made it bars and doors:

And I said: Hitherto thou shalt come, and shalt go no further, and here thou shalt break thy swelling waves.—*Job* xxxviii. 10, 11.

He hath made the moon for seasons: the sun knoweth his going down.

Thou hast appointed darkness, and it is night.—*Ps.* ciii. 19, 20.

For ever, O Lord, thy word standeth firm in heaven.

. . . By thy ordinance the day goeth on: for all things serve thee.—*Ps.* cxviii. 89, 91.

Praise the Lord from the earth, ye dragons, and all ye deeps:

Fire, hail, snow, ice, stormy winds, which fulfil his word.—*Ps.* cxlviii. 7, 8.

But snow and ice endured the force of fire, and melted not: that they might know that fire burning in the hail, and flashing in the rain, destroyed the fruits of the enemies. . . .

For the creature serving thee, the Creator, is made fierce against the unjust for their punishment; and abateth its strength for the benefit of them that trust in thee.—*Wis.* xvi. 22, 24.

For every creature according to its kind was fashioned again as from the beginning, obeying thy commandments, that thy children might be kept without hurt.—*Wis.* xix. 6.

Why doth one day excel another, and one light another, and one year another year, when all come of the sun?

By the knowledge of the Lord they were distinguished, the sun being made, and keeping his commandment.—*Ecclus.* xxxiii. 7, 8.

At his word, the waters stood as a heap: and at the words of his mouth, the receptacles of water.—*Ecclus.* xxxix. 22.

Fire, hail, famine, and death, all these were created for vengeance.

The teeth of beasts, and scorpions, and serpents, and the sword taking vengeance upon the ungodly unto destruction.

In his commandments they shall feast, and they shall be ready upon earth, when need is, and when their time is come, they shall not transgress his word.—*Ecclus.* xxxix. 35-37.

All these things live, and remain for ever, and for every use all things obey him.—*Ecclus.* xlii. 24.

The sun, when he appeareth showing forth at his rising, an admirable instrument, the work of the most High. . . .

Great is the Lord that made him, and at his words he hath hastened his course. . . .

The glory of the stars is the beauty of heaven; the Lord enlighteneth the world on high.

By the words of the holy one, they shall stand in judgment, and shall never fail in their watches. . . .

By his commandment he maketh the snow to fall apace, and sendeth forth swiftly the lightnings of his judgment.

Through this are the treasures opened, and the clouds fly out like birds. . . .

At his sight shall the mountains be shaken, and at his will the south wind shall blow.

. . . At his word the wind is still, and with his thought he appeaseth the deep.—*Ecclus.* xliii. 2, 5, 10, 11, 14, 15, 17, 25.

My hand also hath founded the earth, and my right hand hath measured the heavens: I shall call them, and they shall stand together.—*Is.* xlviii. 13.

I have set the sand a bound for the sea, an everlasting ordinance, which it shall not pass over: and the waves thereof shall toss themselves, and shall not prevail: they shall swell, and shall not pass over it.—*Jer.* v. 22.

He that sendeth forth light, and it goeth: and hath called it, and it obeyeth him with trembling.

And the stars have given light in their watches, and rejoiced:

They were called, and they said: Here we are: and with cheerfulness they have shined forth to him that made them.—*Bar.* iii. 33-35.

The sun, and the moon, and the stars being bright, and sent forth for profitable uses, are obedient.

In like manner, the lightning, when it breaketh forth, is easy to be seen: and after the same manner, the wind bloweth in every country.

And the clouds, when God commandeth them to go over the whole world, do that which is commanded them.

The fire also being sent from above

to consume mountains and woods, doth as it is commanded.—*Bar.* vi. 59-62.

And when he entered into the boat, his disciples followed him:

And behold a great tempest arose in the sea, so that the boat was covered with waves, but he was asleep.

And they came to him, and awaked him, saying: Lord, save us, we perish.

And Jesus saith to them: Why are you fearful, O ye of little faith? Then rising up, he commanded the winds and the sea, and there came a great calm.

But the men wondered, saying: What manner of man is this, for the winds and the sea obey him?—*Matt.* viii. 23-27.

OBEDIENCE TO PARENTS

See also: Parents, respect and love for—page 360.

If a man have a stubborn and unruly son, who will not hear the commandments of his father or mother, and being corrected, slighteth obedience:

They shall take him, and bring him to the ancients of his city, and to the gate of judgment,

And shall say to them: This our son is rebellious and stubborn, he slighteth hearing our admonitions, he giveth himself to revelling, and to debauchery and banquetings:

The people of the city shall stone him: and he shall die, that you may take away the evil out of the midst of you, and all Israel hearing it, may be afraid. —*Deut.* xxi. 18-21.

My son, hear the instruction of thy father, and forsake not the law of thy mother:

That grace may be added to thy head, and a chain of gold to thy neck.—*Prov.* i. 8, 9.

My son, keep the commandments of thy father, and forsake not the law of thy mother.

Bind them in thy heart continually, and put them about thy neck.

When thou walkest, let them go with thee: when thou sleepest, let them keep thee; and when thou wakest, talk with them.

Because the commandment is a lamp, and the law, a light, and reproofs of instruction are the way of life.—*Prov.* vi. 20-23.

Hearken to thy father, that begot thee: and despise not thy mother when she is old.—*Prov.* xxiii. 22.

He that honoreth his father, shall enjoy a long life: and he that obeyeth the father, shall be a comfort to his mother.

He that feareth the Lord, honoreth his parents, and will serve them as his masters, that brought him into the world.—*Ecclus.* iii. 7, 8.

Children, obey your parents in the Lord, for this is just.

Honor thy father and thy mother, which is the first commandment with a promise:

That it may be well with thee, and thou mayst be long-lived upon earth.— *Eph.* vi. 1-3.

Children, obey your parents in all things: for this is well pleasing to the Lord.—*Col.* iii. 20.

OBEDIENCE TO SUPERIORS

The mind of the just studieth obedience: the mouth of the wicked overfloweth with evils.—*Prov.* xv. 28.

An obedient man shall speak of victory.—*Prov.* xxi. 28.

OBEDIENCE TO ECCLESIASTICAL SUPERIORS

And the Lord spoke to Moses, saying:

This is the rite of a leper, when he is to be cleansed: he shall be brought to the priest.—*Lev.* xiv. 1, 2.

But he that will be proud, and refuse to obey the commandment of the priest, who ministereth at that time to the Lord thy God, and the decree of the judge, that man shall die, and thou shalt take away the evil from Israel.— *Deut.* xvii. 12.

And Jesus saith to him (the leper): See thou tell no man: but go, show thyself to the priest, and offer the gift which Moses commanded for a testimony unto them.—*Matt.* viii. 4.

Then Jesus spoke to the multitudes and to his disciples,

Saying: The scribes and the Pharisees have sitten on the chair of Moses.

All things therefore whatsoever they shall say to you, observe and do: but according to their works, do ye not; for they say, and do not.—*Matt.* xxiii. 1-3.

He that heareth you, heareth me; and he that despiseth you, despiseth me; and he that despiseth me, despiseth him that sent me.—*Luke* x. 16.

Obey your prelates, and be subject to them. For they watch, as being to render an account of your souls; that they may do this with joy, and not with grief. For this is not expedient for you.—*Heb.* xiii. 17.

In like manner, ye young men, be subject to the ancients.—1 *Peter* v. 5.

OBEDIENCE TO LAY SUPERIORS

And they (the Pharisees) sent to him their disciples with the Herodians, saying: Master, we know that thou art a true speaker, and teachest the way of God in truth, neither carest thou for any man: for thou dost not regard the person of men.

Tell us therefore what dost thou think, is it lawful to give tribute to Cæsar, or not?

But Jesus knowing their wickedness, said: Why do you tempt me, ye hypocrites?

Show me the coin of the tribute. And they offered him a penny.

And Jesus saith to them: Whose image and inscription is this?

They say to him: Cæsar's. Then he saith to them: Render therefore to Cæsar the things that are Cæsar's; and to God, the things that are God's.—*Matt.* xxii. 16-21.

Let every soul be subject to higher powers: for there is no power but from God: and those that are, are ordained of God.

Therefore he that resisteth the power, resisteth the ordinance of God. And they that resist, purchase to themselves damnation. . . .

Wherefore be subject of necessity, not only for wrath, but also for conscience' sake.

For therefore also you pay tribute. For they are the ministers of God, serving unto this purpose.

Render therefore to all men their dues. Tribute, to whom tribute is due: custom, to whom custom: fear, to whom fear: honor, to whom honor.—*Rom.* xiii. 1, 2, 5-7.

Servants, be obedient to them that are your lords, according to the flesh, with fear and trembling, in the simplicity of your heart, as to Christ:

Not serving to the eye, as it were pleasing men, but, as the servants of Christ, doing the will of God from the heart,

With a good will serving, as to the Lord, and not to men.

Knowing that whatsoever good thing any man shall do, the same shall he receive from the Lord, whether he be bond, or free.—*Eph.* vi. 5-8.

Servants, obey in all things your masters according to the flesh, not serving to the eye, as pleasing men, but in simplicity of heart, fearing God.

Whatsoever you do, do it from the heart, as to the Lord, and not to men:

Knowing that you shall receive of the Lord the reward of inheritance. Serve ye the Lord Christ.—*Col.* iii. 22-24.

Whosoever are servants under the yoke, let them count their masters worthy of all honor; lest the name of the Lord and his doctrine be blasphemed.

But they that have believing masters, let them not despise them, because they are brethren; but serve them the rather because they are faithful and beloved, who are partakers of the benefit. These things teach and exhort.—1 *Tim.* vi. 1, 2.

Exhort servants to be obedient to their masters, in all things pleasing, not gainsaying;

Not defrauding, but in all things showing good fidelity, that they may adorn the doctrine of God our Saviour in all things.—*Titus* ii. 9, 10.

Admonish them to be subject to princes and powers, to obey at a word, to be ready to every good work.—*Titus* iii. 1.

Be ye subject therefore to every human creature for God's sake: whether it be to the king as excelling;

Or to governors as sent by him for the punishment of evil-doers, and for the praise of the good:

For so is the will of God, that by doing well, you may put to silence the ignorance of foolish men:

As free, and not as making liberty a cloak for malice, but as the servants of God.—1 *Peter* ii. 13-16.

Servants, be subject to your masters with all fear, not only to the good and gentle, but also to the froward.—1 *Peter* ii. 18.

OBEDIENCE OF CHRIST, THE

And going a little further, he fell upon his face, praying, and saying: My Father, if it be possible, let this chalice pass from me. Nevertheless, not as I will, but as thou wilt. . . .

Again the second time he went, and prayed, saying: My Father, if this chalice may not pass away, but I must drink it, thy will be done.—*Matt.* xxvi. 39, 42.

And he went down with them, and came to Nazareth, and was subject to them.—*Luke* ii. 51.

Jesus saith to them (the disciples): My meat is to do the will of him that sent me, that I may perfect his work. —*John* iv. 34.

Because I came down from heaven, not to do my own will, but the will of him that sent me.—*John* vi. 38.

I will not now speak many things with you. For the prince of this world cometh, and in me he hath not any thing.

But that the world may know, that I love the Father: and as the Father hath given me commandment, so do I. —*John* xiv. 30, 31

If you keep my commandments, you shall abide in my love; as I also have kept my Father's commandments, and do abide in his love.—*John* xv. 10.

Jesus therefore said to Peter: Put up thy sword into the scabbard. The chalice which my Father hath given me, shall I not drink it?—*John* xviii. 11.

For as by the disobedience of one man, many were made sinners; so also by the obedience of one, many shall be made just.—*Rom.* v. 19.

He humbled himself, becoming obedient unto death, even to the death of the cross.—*Philipp.* ii. 8.

And whereas indeed he was the Son of God, he learned obedience by the things which he suffered.—*Heb.* v. 8.

Wherefore when he cometh into the world, he saith: Sacrifice and oblation thou wouldest not: but a body thou hast fitted to me:

Holocausts for sin did not please thee.

Then said I: Behold I come: in the head of the book it is written of me: that I should do thy will, O God.— *Heb.* x. 5-7.

OBSTINACY

See: Self-will—page 511.

OBSTINACY IN SIN

See also: Impenitence—page 232.

And Pharao seeing that the rain and the hail and the thunders were ceased, increased his sin.

And his heart was hardened, and the heart of his servants, and it was made exceeding hard: neither did he let the children of Israel go, as the Lord had commanded by the hand of Moses.—*Ex.* ix. 34, 35.

They kept not the covenant of God: and in his law they would not walk.

And they forgot his benefits, and his wonders that he had shown them. . . .

And they added yet more sin against him: they provoked the most High to wrath in the place without water.—*Ps.* lxxvii. 10, 11, 17.

The wicked man impudently hardeneth his face: but he that is righteous, correcteth his way.—*Prov.* xxi. 29.

A wicked heart shall be laden with sorrows, and the sinner will add sin to sin.—*Ecclus.* iii. 29.

For what shall I strike you any more, you that increase transgression? the whole head is sick, and the whole heart is sad.—*Is.* i. 5.

The show of their countenance hath answered them: and they have proclaimed abroad their sin, as Sodom, and they have not hid it: woe to their souls, for evils are rendered to them.—*Is.* iii. 9.

Thou hast been wearied in the multitude of thy ways: yet thou saidst not:

I will rest: thou hast found life of thy hand, therefore thou hast not asked.—*Is.* lvii. 10.

Thus saith the Lord: Stand ye on the ways, and see, and ask for the old paths, which is the good way, and walk ye in it: and you shall find refreshment for your souls. And they said: We will not walk.

And I appointed watchmen over you, saying: Hearken ye to the sound of the trumpet. And they said: We will not hearken.—*Jer.* vi. 16, 17.

I struck you with a burning wind, and with mildew, the palmerworm hath eaten up your many gardens, and your vineyards: your olive groves, and fig groves: yet you returned not to me, saith the Lord.

I sent death upon you in the way of Egypt, I slew your young men with the sword, even to the captivity of your horses: and I made the stench of your camp to come up into your nostrils; yet you returned not to me, saith the Lord.

I destroyed some of you, as God destroyed Sodom and Gomorrha, and you were as a firebrand plucked out of the burning: yet you returned not to me, saith the Lord.—*Amos* iv. 9-11.

The just Lord is in the midst thereof, he will not do iniquity: in the morning, in the morning, he will bring his judgment to light, and it shall not be hid: but the wicked man hath not known shame.—*Soph.* iii. 5.

Then Jesus answered and said: O unbelieving and perverse generation, how long shall I be with you? How long shall I suffer you?—*Matt.* xvii. 16.

And you will not come to me, that you may have life.—*John* v. 40.

OBSTINACY IN SIN, PUNISHMENT OF

God hath given him place for penance, and he abuseth it unto pride: but his eyes are upon his ways.

They are lifted up for a little while, and shall not stand, and shall be brought down as all things, and shall be taken away, and as the tops of the ears of corn they shall be broken.—*Job* xxiv. 23, 24.

Except you will be converted, he will brandish his sword: he hath bent his bow, and made it ready.

And in it he hath prepared the instruments of death, he hath made ready his arrows for them that burn.—*Ps.* vii. 13, 14.

But God shall break the heads of his enemies: the hairy crown of them that walk on in their sins.—*Ps.* lxvii. 22.

A hard heart shall fear evil at the last: and he that loveth danger, shall perish in it.—*Ecclus.* iii. 27.

He that rejoiceth in iniquity, shall be censured: . . .

. . . And he that is delighted with wickedness, shall be condemned.—*Ecclus.* xix. 5, 6.

All thy lovers have forgotten thee, and will not seek after thee: for I have wounded thee with the wound of an enemy, with a cruel chastisement: by reason of the multitude of thy iniquities, thy sins are hardened.

Why criest thou for thy affliction? thy sorrow is incurable: for the multitude of thy iniquity, and for thy hardened sins I have done these things to thee.—*Jer.* xxx. 14, 15.

Again therefore Jesus said to them: I go, and you shall seek me, and you shall die in your sin. Whither I go, you cannot come.—*John* viii. 21.

For the earth that drinketh in the rain which cometh often upon it, and bringeth forth herbs meet for them by whom it is tilled, receiveth blessing from God.

But that which bringeth forth thorns and briers, is reprobate, and very near unto a curse, whose end is to be burnt. —*Heb.* vi. 7, 8.

OBSTINACY IN SIN, EXHORTATION AGAINST

Be not hasty to depart from his face, and do not continue in an evil work: for he will do all that pleaseth him.— *Eccles.* viii. 3.

Be not without fear about sin forgiven, and add not sin upon sin.— *Ecclus.* v. 5.

Nor bind sin to sin: for even in one thou shalt not be unpunished.—*Ecclus.* vii. 8.

Wherefore, as the Holy Ghost saith: To-day, if you shall hear his voice,

Harden not your hearts, as in the provocation; in the day of temptation, in the desert. . . .

But exhort one another every day, whilst it is called to-day, that none of you be hardened through the deceitfulness of sin.—*Heb.* iii. 7, 8, 13.

OCCASIONS OF SIN, WE MUST AVOID THE

Now the serpent was more subtle than any of the beasts of the earth which the Lord God had made. And he said to the woman: Why hath God commanded you, that you should not eat of every tree of paradise?

And the woman answered him, saying: Of the fruit of the trees that are in paradise, we do eat:

But of the fruit of the tree which is in the midst of paradise, God hath commanded us that we should not eat; and that we should not touch it, lest perhaps we die. . . .

And the woman saw that the tree was good to eat, and fair to the eyes, and delightful to behold: and she took of the fruit thereof, and did eat, and gave to her husband who did eat.—*Gen.* iii. 1-3, 6.

Go not up, for the Lord is not with you: lest you fall before your enemies. —*Num.* xiv. 42.

Be not delighted in the paths of the wicked, neither let the way of evil men please thee.

Flee from it, pass not by it: go aside, and forsake it.—*Prov.* iv. 14, 15.

A hard heart shall fear evil at the last: and he that loveth danger, shall perish in it.—*Ecclus.* iii. 27.

Look not upon a woman that hath a mind for many: lest thou fall into her snares.

Use not much the company of her that is a dancer, and hearken not to her, lest thou perish by the force of her charms.

Gaze not upon a maiden, lest her beauty be a stumbling-block to thee. . . .

Look not round about thee in the ways of the city, nor wander up and down in the streets thereof.

Turn away thy face from a woman dressed up, and gaze not about upon another's beauty.

For many have perished by the beauty of a woman, and hereby lust is enkindled as a fire. . . .

Many by admiring the beauty of another man's wife, have become reprobate, for her conversation burneth as fire.

Sit not at all with another man's wife, nor repose upon the bed with her:

And strive not with her over wine, lest thy heart decline towards her, and by thy blood thou fall into destruction. —*Ecclus.* ix. 3-5, 7-9, 11-13.

He that toucheth pitch, shall be defiled with it: and he that hath fellowship with the proud, shall put on pride. —*Ecclus.* xiii. 1.

Go not in the way of ruin, and thou shalt not stumble against the stones: trust not thyself to a rugged way, lest thou set a stumbling-block to thy soul. —*Ecclus.* xxxii. 25.

Behold not everybody's beauty: and tarry not among women.—*Ecclus.* xlii. 12.

And if thy right eye scandalize thee, pluck it out, and cast it from thee. For it is expedient for thee that one of thy members should perish, rather than that thy whole body be cast into hell.

And if thy right hand scandalize thee, cut it off, and cast it from thee: for it is expedient for thee, that one of thy members should perish, rather than that thy whole body go into hell.— *Matt.* v. 29, 30.

OLD AGE

Cast me not off in the time of old age: when my strength shall fail, do not thou forsake me. . . .

And unto old age and gray hairs: O God, forsake me not.—*Ps.* lxx. 9, 18.

But my horn shall be exalted like that of the unicorn; and my old age in plentiful mercy.—*Ps.* xci. 11.

They (the just) shall still increase in a fruitful old age: and shall be well treated, that they may show,

That the Lord our God is righteous, and there is no iniquity in him.—*Ps.* xci. 15, 16.

If a man live many years, and have

rejoiced in them all, he must remember the darksome time, and the many days: which when they shall come, the things past shall be accused of vanity.—*Eccles.* xi. 8.

Remember thy Creator in the days of thy youth, before the time of affliction come, and the years draw nigh, of which thou shalt say: They please me not:

Before the sun, and the light, and the moon and the stars be darkened, and the clouds return after the rain:

When the keepers of the house shall tremble, and the strong men shall stagger, and the grinders shall be idle in a small number, and they that look through the holes shall be darkened:

And they shall shut the doors in the street, when the grinder's voice shall be low, and they shall rise up at the voice of the bird, and all the daughters of music shall grow deaf.

And they shall fear high things, and they shall be afraid in the way, the almond-tree shall flourish, the locust shall be made fat, and the caper-tree shall be destroyed: because man shall go into the house of his eternity, and the mourners shall go round about in the street.—*Eccles.* xii. 1-5.

For venerable old age is not that of long time, nor counted by the number of years: but the understanding of a man is gray hairs.

And a spotless life is old age.—*Wis.* iv. 8, 9.

Even to your old age I am the same, and to your gray hairs I will carry you: I have made you, and I will bear: I will carry and will save.—*Is.* xlvi. 4.

But speak thou the things that become sound doctrine:

That the aged men be sober, chaste, prudent, sound in faith, in love, in patience.

The aged women, in like manner, in holy attire, not false accusers, not given to much wine, teaching well.— *Titus* ii. 1-3.

OLD AGE, THE DIGNITY OF

In the ancient is wisdom, and in length of days, prudence.—*Job* xii. 12.

Old age is a crown of dignity, when it is found in the ways of justice.— *Prov.* xvi. 31.

The joy of young men is their strength: and the dignity of old men, their gray hairs.—*Prov.* xx. 29.

O how comely is judgment for a gray head, and for ancients to know counsel!

O how comely is wisdom for the aged, and understanding and counsel to men of honor!

Much experience is the crown of old men, and the fear of God is their glory. —*Ecclus.* xxv. 6-8.

OLD AGE, RESPECT FOR

Rise up before the hoary head, and honor the person of the aged man: and fear the Lord thy God. I am the Lord. —*Lev.* xix. 32.

Make thyself affable to the congregation of the poor, and humble thy soul to the ancient.—*Ecclus.* iv. 7.

Despise not a man in his old age; for we also shall become old.—*Ecclus.* viii. 7.

Speak, thou that art elder: for it becometh thee,

To speak the first word with careful knowledge.—*Ecclus.* xxxii. 4, 5.

In the company of great men, take not upon thee: and when the ancients are present, speak not much.

Before a storm goeth lightning; and before shamefacedness goeth favor; and for thy reverence, good grace shall come to thee.—*Ecclus.* xxxii. 13, 14.

An ancient man rebuke not, but entreat him as a father: . . .

Old women, as mothers.—1 *Tim.* v. 1, 2.

OMISSION, SINS OF

See also: Life, useless and void of good, a—page 284.

Give them (the priests) their portion, as it is commanded thee, of the first fruits and of purifications: and for thy negligences, purify thyself with a few. —*Ecclus.* vii. 34.

But thou hast not called upon me, O Jacob, neither hast thou labored about me, O Israel.

Thou hast not offered me the ram of thy holocaust, nor hast thou glorified me with thy victims: I have not caused thee to serve with oblations, nor wearied thee with incense.

Thou hast brought me no sweet cane with money, neither hast thou filled me with the fat of thy victims. But thou hast made me to serve with thy sins, thou hast wearied me with thy iniquities.—*Is.* xliii. 22-24.

Behold this was the iniquity of Sodom thy sister, pride, fulness of bread, and abundance, and the idleness of her, and of her daughters: and they did not put forth their hand to the needy, and to the poor.—*Ezech.* xvi. 49.

Then shall he say to them also that shall be on his left hand: Depart from me, you cursed, into everlasting fire which was prepared for the devil and his angels.

For I was hungry, and you gave me not to eat: I was thirsty, and you gave me not to drink.

I was a stranger, and you took me not in: naked, and you covered me not: sick and in prison, and you did not visit me.

Then they also shall answer him, saying: Lord, when did we see thee hungry, or thirsty, or a stranger, or naked, or sick, or in prison, and did not minister to thee?

Then he shall answer them, saying: Amen I say to you, as long as you did it not to one of these least, neither did you do it to me.

And these shall go into everlasting punishment.—*Matt.* xxv. 41-46.

To him therefore who knoweth to do good, and doth it not, to him it is sin.—*James* iv. 17.

OMNIPOTENCE OF GOD, THE

See also: Greatness of God, the—page 185.

And the Lord said to Abraham: Why did Sara laugh, saying: Shall I who am an old woman bear a child indeed?

Is there any thing hard to God? according to appointment I will return to thee at this same time, life accompanying, and Sara shall have a son.—*Gen.* xviii. 13, 14.

See ye that I alone am, and there is no other God besides me: I will kill, and I will make to live: I will strike, and I will heal, and there is none that can deliver out of my hand.—*Deut.* xxxii. 39.

The Lord killeth and maketh alive, he bringeth down to hell, and bringeth back again.

The Lord maketh poor and maketh rich, he humbleth and he exalteth.

He raiseth up the needy from the dust, and lifteth up the poor from the dung hill: that he may sit with princes, and hold the throne of glory. For the poles of the earth are the Lord's, and upon them he hath set the world.—1 *Kings* ii. 6-8.

And Jonathan said to the young man that bore his armor: Come, let us go over to the garrison of these uncircumcised, it may be the Lord will do for us, because it is easy for the Lord to save either by many, or by few.—1 *Kings* xiv. 6.

He is wise in heart, and mighty in strength: who hath resisted him, and hath had peace?—*Job* ix. 4.

If he pull down, there is no man that can build up: if he shut up a man, there is none that can open.

If he withhold the waters, all things shall be dried up: and if he send them out, they shall overturn the earth.—*Job* xii. 14, 15.

For he is alone, and no man can turn away his thought: and whatsoever his soul hath desired, that hath he done.—*Job* xxiii. 13.

Who shall declare the powers of the Lord? who shall set forth all his praises?—*Ps.* cv. 2.

But our God is in heaven: he hath done all things whatsoever he would.—*Ps.* cxiii. (*Heb.* cxv.) 3.

Be not hasty to depart from his face, and do not continue in an evil work: for he will do all that pleaseth him:

And his word is full of power: neither can any man say to him: Why dost thou so?—*Eccles.* viii. 3, 4.

For the wisdom of God is great, and he is strong in power, seeing all men without ceasing.—*Ecclus.* xv. 19.

And who shall show forth the power of his majesty? or who shall be able to declare his mercy?—*Ecclus.* xviii. 4.

For the Lord of hosts hath decreed, and who can disannul it? and his hand is stretched out: and who shall turn it away?—*Is.* xiv. 27.

Behold the Lord is mighty and strong, as a storm of hail: a destroying whirlwind, as the violence of many waters overflowing and sent forth upon a spacious land.—*Is.* xxviii. 2.

And from the beginning I am the same, and there is none that can deliver out of my hand: I will work, and who shall turn it away?—*Is.* xliii. 13.

Behold the hand of the Lord is not shortened that it cannot save, neither is his ear heavy that it cannot hear.—*Is.* lix. 1.

Behold, I am the Lord, the God of all flesh: shall any thing be hard for me? —*Jer.* xxxii. 27.

Thus saith the Lord of hosts: If it seem hard in the eyes of the remnant of this people in those days: shall it be hard in my eyes, saith the Lord of hosts?—*Zach.* viii. 6.

But when they saw the army coming to meet them, they said to Judas: How shall we, being few, be able to fight against so great a multitude and so strong, and we are ready to faint with fasting to-day?

And Judas said: It is an easy matter for many to be shut up in the hands of a few: and there is no difference in the sight of the God of heaven, to deliver with a great multitude, or with a small company.—1 *Mach.* iii. 17, 18.

For, said he (Judas), they trust in their weapons, and in their boldness: but we trust in the Almighty Lord, who at a beck can utterly destroy both them that come against us, and the whole world.—2 *Mach.* viii. 18.

And think not to say within yourselves, We have Abraham for our father. For I tell you that God is able of these stones to raise up children to Abraham.—*Matt.* iii. 9.

And Jesus beholding, said to them: With men this is impossible: but with God all things are possible.—*Matt.* xix. 26.

Because no word shall be impossible with God.—*Luke* i. 37.

OMNIPOTENCE OF GOD, ACKNOWLEDGMENT OF THE

Who is like to thee among the strong, O Lord? who is like to thee, glorious in holiness, terrible and praiseworthy, doing wonders?—*Ex.* xv. 11.

Lord God, thou hast begun to show unto thy servant thy greatness, and most mighty hand, for there is no other God either in heaven or earth, that is able to do thy works, or to be compared to thy strength.—*Deut.* iii. 24.

Thou art great, O Lord, for ever, and thy kingdom is unto all ages:

For thou scourgest, and thou savest: thou leadest down to hell, and bringest up again: and there is none that can escape thy hand.—*Tob.* xiii. 1, 2.

O Adonai, Lord, great art thou, and glorious in thy power, and no one can overcome thee.

Let all thy creatures serve thee: because thou hast spoken, and they were made: thou didst send forth thy spirit, and they were created, and there is no one that can resist thy voice.—*Judith* xvi. 16, 17.

O Lord, Lord, almighty king, for all things are in thy power, and there is none that can resist thy will, if thou determine to save Israel.

Thou hast made heaven and earth, and all things that are under the cope of heaven.

Thou art Lord of all, and there is none that can resist thy majesty.— *Esther* xiii. 9-11.

I know that thou canst do all things, and no thought is hid from thee.—*Job* xlii. 2.

Be thou exalted, O Lord, in thy own strength: we will sing and praise thy power.—*Ps.* xx. 14.

Great is our Lord, and great is his power: and of his wisdom there is no number.—*Ps.* cxlvi. 5.

For thy almighty hand, which made the world of matter without form, was not unable to send upon ¹them a multitude of bears, or fierce lions,

Or unknown beasts of a new kind, full of rage: either breathing out a fiery vapor, or sending forth a stinking smoke, or shooting horrible sparks out of their eyes:

¹The enemies of the Israelites.

Whereof not only the hurt might be able to destroy them, but also the very sight might kill them through fear.

Yea, and without these, they might have been slain with one blast, persecuted by their own deeds, and scattered by the breath of thy power. . . .

For great power always belonged to thee alone: and who shall resist the strength of thy arm?

For the whole world before thee is as the least grain of the balance, and as a drop of the morning dew that falleth down upon the earth:

But thou hast mercy upon all, because thou canst do all things, and overlookest the sins of men for the sake of repentance.—*Wis.* xi. 18-24.

For thy power is the beginning of justice: and because thou art Lord of all, thou makest thyself gracious to all.

For thou showest thy power, when men will not believe thee to be absolute in power, and thou convincest the boldness of them that know thee not.

But thou, being master of power, judgest with tranquillity; and with great favor disposest of us: for thy power is at hand, when thou wilt.—*Wis.* xii. 16-18.

For it is thou, O Lord, that hast power of life and death, and leadest down to the gates of death, and bringest back again: . . .

But it is impossible to escape thy hand.—*Wis.* xvi. 13, 15.

Alas, alas, alas, O Lord God, behold thou hast made heaven and earth by thy great power, and thy stretched out arm: no word shall be hard to thee.—*Jer.* xxxii. 17.

For behold, our God whom we worship is able to save us from the furnace of burning fire, and to deliver us out of thy hands, O king.—*Dan.* iii. 17.

Now at the end of the days, I, Nabuchodonosor, lifted up my eyes to heaven, and my sense was restored to me: and I blessed the most High, and I praised and glorified him that liveth for ever: for his power is an everlasting power, and his kingdom is to all generations.

And all the inhabitants of the earth are reputed as nothing before him: for he doth according to his will, as well with the powers of heaven, as among the inhabitants of the earth: and there is none that can resist his hand, and say to him: Why hast thou done it?—*Dan.* iv. 31, 32.

Now to him who is able to do all things more abundantly than we desire or understand, according to the power that worketh in us;

To him be glory in the church, and in Christ Jesus unto all generations, world without end. Amen.—*Eph.* iii. 20, 21.

OMNIPOTENCE OF GOD, MANIFESTATIONS OF THE

See also: Greatness and power of God shown by his works—page 187.

And God said: Be light made. And light was made.—*Gen.* i. 3.

And Moses said: There are six hundred thousand footmen of this people, and sayest thou: I will give them flesh to eat a whole month?

Shall then a multitude of sheep and oxen be killed, that it may suffice for their food? or shall the fishes of the sea be gathered together to fill them?

And the Lord answered him: Is the hand of the Lord unable? Thou shalt presently see whether my word shall come to pass or no. . . .

And a wind going out from the Lord, taking quails up beyond the sea, brought them, and cast them into the camp for the space of one day's journey, on every side of the camp round about, and they flew in the air two cubits high above the ground.—*Num.* xi. 21-23, 31.

Who shaketh the earth out of her place, and the pillars thereof tremble.

Who commandeth the sun and it riseth not: and shutteth up the stars as it were under a seal.

Who alone spreadeth out the heavens, and walketh upon the waves of the sea. . . .

Who doth things great and incomprehensible, and wonderful, of which there is no number.—*Job* ix. 6-8, 10.

Didst thou since thy birth, command the morning, and show the dawning of the day its place?

And didst thou hold the extremities

of the earth, shaking them, and hast thou shaken the ungodly out of it? . . .

Who can declare the order of the heavens, or who can make the harmony of heaven to sleep?—*Job* xxxviii. 12, 13, 37.

Thou who preparest the mountains by thy strength, being girded with power: who troublest the depth of the sea, the noise of its waves.—*Ps.* lxiv. 7, 8.

O Lord God of hosts, who is like to thee? thou art mighty, O Lord, and thy truth is round about thee.

Thou rulest the power of the sea: and appeasest the motion of the waves thereof.

Thou hast humbled the proud one, as one that is slain: with the arm of thy strength, thou hast scattered thy enemies.—*Ps.* lxxxviii. 9-11.

Whatsoever the Lord pleased, he hath done, in heaven, in earth, in the sea, and in all the deeps.

He bringeth up clouds from the end of the earth: he hath made lightnings for the rain.

He bringeth forth winds out of his stores: He slew the first-born of Egypt, from man even unto beast.

He sent forth signs and wonders in the midst of thee, O Egypt: upon Pharao, and upon all his servants.—*Ps.* cxxxiv. 6-9.

Praise ye him, O sun and moon: praise him, all ye stars and light.

Praise him, ye heavens of heavens: and let all the waters that are above the heavens praise the name of the Lord.

For he spoke, and they were made: he commanded, and they were created.

He hath established them for ever, and for ages of ages: he hath made a decree, and it shall not pass away.—*Ps.* cxlviii. 3-6.

God of my fathers, and Lord of mercy, who hast made all things with thy word.—*Wis.* ix. 1.

Is my hand shortened, and become little, that I cannot redeem? or is there no strength in me to deliver? Behold at my rebuke I will make the sea a desert, I will turn the rivers into dry land: the fishes shall rot for want of water, and shall die for thirst.

I will clothe the heavens with darkness, and will make sackcloth their covering.—*Is.* l. 2, 3.

OMNIPRESENCE OF GOD

See also: Hidden from God, we cannot be—page 206.

The Lord behold and judge between [1]us, when we shall be gone one from the other.

If thou afflict my daughters, and if thou bring in other wives over them: none is witness of our speech but God, who is present and beholdeth.—*Gen.* xxxi. 49, 50.

Whither shall I go from thy spirit? or whither shall I flee from thy face?

If I ascend into heaven, thou art there: if I descend into hell, thou art present.

If I take my wings early in the morning, and dwell in the uttermost parts of the sea:

Even there also shall thy hand lead me; and thy right hand shall hold me. —*Ps.* cxxxviii. 7-10.

For the spirit of the Lord hath filled the whole world: and that which containeth all things, hath knowledge of the voice.—*Wis.* i. 7.

Am I, think ye, a God at hand, saith the Lord, and not a God afar off?

Shall a man be hid in secret places, and I not see him, saith the Lord? do not I fill heaven and earth, saith the Lord?—*Jer.* xxiii. 23, 24.

OMNISCIENCE OF GOD, THE

1st. God Knows All Things

Do not multiply to speak lofty things, boasting: let old matters depart from your mouth: for the Lord is a God of all knowledge, and to him are thoughts prepared.—1 *Kings* ii. 3.

But deliver us by thy hand, and help me, who have no other helper but thee, O Lord, who hast the knowledge of all things.—*Esther* xiv. 14.

With him is strength and wisdom: he knoweth both the deceiver, and him that is deceived.—*Job* xii. 16.

[1]Laban speaking to Jacob, when the latter fled from him, and was overtaken in mount Galaad.

Can man be compared with God, even though he were of perfect knowledge?—*Job* xxii. 2.

Times are not hid from the Almighty: but they that know him, know not his days.—*Job* xxiv. 1.

O God, thou knowest my foolishness; and my offences are not hidden from thee.—*Ps.* lxviii. 6.

Lord, thou hast proved me, and known me:

Thou hast known my sitting down, and my rising up.

Thou hast understood my thoughts afar off: my path and my line thou hast searched out.

And thou hast foreseen all my ways: for there is no speech in my tongue.

Behold, O Lord, thou hast known all things, the last, and those of old: thou hast formed me, and hast laid thy hand upon me.

Thy knowledge is become wonderful to me: it is high, and I cannot reach to it.—*Ps.* cxxxviii. 1-6.

For all things were known to the Lord God, before they were created: so also after they were perfected, he beholdeth all things.—*Ecclus.* xxiii. 29.

For the Lord knoweth all knowledge, and hath beheld the signs of the world, he declareth the things that are past, and the things that are to come, and revealeth the traces of hidden things.—*Ecclus.* xlii. 19.

Nor can he be diminished, and he hath no need of any counsellor.—*Ecclus.* xlii. 22.

He revealeth deep and hidden things, and knoweth what is in darkness: and light is with him.—*Dan.* ii. 22.

Then Susanna cried out with a loud voice, and said: O eternal God, who knowest hidden things, who knowest all things before they come to pass,

Thou knowest that ¹they have borne false witness against me.—*Dan.* xiii. 42, 43.

To the Lord was his own work known from the beginning of the world.—*Acts* xv. 18.

But to us God hath revealed them by his Spirit. For the Spirit of God

searcheth all things, yea, the deep things of God.—1 *Cor.* ii. 10.

For if our heart reprehend us, God is greater than our heart, and knoweth all things.—1 *John* iii. 20.

Unto the angel of the church of Ephesus, write:

These things saith he, who holdeth the seven stars in his right hand, who walketh in the midst of the seven golden candlesticks:

I know thy works, and thy labor, and thy patience, and how thou canst not bear them that are evil, and thou hast tried them who say they are apostles, and are not, and hast found them liars:

And thou hast patience, and hast endured for my name, and hast not fainted.—*Apoc.* ii. 1-3.

And to the angel of the church of Thyatira write: These things saith the Son of God, who hath his eyes like to a flame of fire, and his feet like to fine brass.

I know thy works, and thy faith, and thy charity, and thy ministry, and thy patience, and thy last works which are more than the former.—*Apoc.* ii. 18, 19.

And to the angel of the church of Sardis, write: These things saith he, that hath the seven spirits of God and the seven stars: I know thy works, that thou hast the name of being alive: and thou art dead.—*Apoc.* iii. 1.

And to the angel of the church of Laodicea write: These things saith the Amen, the faithful and true witness, who is the beginning of the creation of God:

I know thy works, that thou art neither cold nor hot. . . .

Because thou sayest: I am rich, and made wealthy, and have need of nothing: and knowest not that thou art wretched, and miserable, and poor, and blind, and naked.—*Apoc.* iii. 14, 15, 17.

2d. God Sees All Things

See also: Hidden from God, we cannot be—page 206.

Hast thou eyes of flesh: or shalt thou see as man seeth?—*Job* x. 4.

He discovereth deep things out of darkness, and bringeth up to light the shadow of death.—*Job* xii. 22.

¹The two wicked elders, who falsely accused her.

The eye of the adulterer observeth darkness, saying: No eye shall see me: and he will cover his face.

He diggeth through houses in the dark, as in the day they had appointed for themselves, and they have not known the light. . . .

God hath given him place for penance, and he abuseth it unto pride: but his eyes are upon his ways.—*Job* xxiv. 15, 16, 23.

Hell is naked before him, and there is no covering for destruction.—*Job* xxvi. 6.

For he beholdeth the ends of the world: and looketh on all things that are under heaven.—*Job* xxviii. 24.

Doth not he consider my ways, and number all my steps?—*Job* xxxi. 4.

The Lord hath looked from heaven: he hath beheld all the sons of men.

From his habitation which he hath prepared, he hath looked upon all that dwell on the earth.—*Ps.* xxxii. 13, 14.

And they have said: The Lord shall not see: neither shall the God of Jacob understand.

Understand, ye senseless among the people: and, you fools, be wise at last.

He that planted the ear, shall he not hear? or he that formed the eye, doth he not consider?—*Ps.* xciii. 7-9.

I have kept thy commandments and thy testimonies: because all my ways are in thy sight.—*Ps.* cxviii. 168.

For the Lord is high, and looketh on the low: and the high he knoweth afar off.—*Ps.* cxxxvii. 6.

And I said: Perhaps darkness shall cover me: and night shall be my light in my pleasures.

But darkness shall not be dark to thee, and night shall be light as the day: the darkness thereof and the light thereof are alike to thee.—*Ps.* cxxxviii. 11, 12.

Thy eyes did see my imperfect being, and in thy book all shall be written. —*Ps.* cxxxviii. 16.

The eyes of the Lord in every place behold the good and the evil.—*Prov.* xv. 3.

All the ways of a man are open to his eyes: the Lord is the weigher of spirits. —*Prov.* xvi. 2.

Laugh no man to scorn in the bitterness of his soul: for there is one that humbleth and exalteth, God who seeth all.—*Ecclus.* vii. 12.

Blessed is the man that shall continue in wisdom, and that shall meditate in his justice, and in his mind shall think of the all seeing eye of God.— *Ecclus.* xiv. 22.

For the wisdom of God is great, and he is strong in power, seeing all men without ceasing.

The eyes of the Lord are towards them that fear him, and he knoweth all the work of man.—*Ecclus.* xv. 19, 20.

Their ways are always before him, they are not hidden from his eyes. . . .

And all their works are as the sun in the sight of God: and his eyes are continually upon their ways.

Their covenants were not hid by their iniquity, and all their iniquities are in the sight of God.—*Ecclus.* xvii. 13, 16, 17.

Darkness compasseth me about, and the walls cover me, and no man seeth me: whom do I fear? the most High will not remember my sins.

And he understandeth not that his eye seeth all things. . . .

And he knoweth not that the eyes of the Lord are far brighter than the sun, beholding round about all the ways of men, and the bottom of the deep, and looking into the hearts of men, into the most hidden parts.—*Ecclus.* xxiii. 26-28.

The works of all flesh are before him, and there is nothing hid from his eyes.

He seeth from eternity to eternity, and there is nothing wonderful before him.—*Ecclus.* xxxix. 24, 25.

For my eyes are upon all their ways: they are not hid from my face, and their iniquity hath not been hid from my eyes.—*Jer.* xvi. 17.

Because they have acted folly in Israel, and have committed adultery with the wives of their friends. and have spoken lying words in my name, which I commanded them not: I am the judge and the witness, saith the Lord.—*Jer.* xxix. 23.

Great in counsel, and incomprehensible in thought: whose eyes are open upon all the ways of the children of Adam, to render unto every one according to his ways, and according to the fruit of his devices.—*Jer.* xxxii. 19.

Neither is there any creature invisible in his sight: but all things are naked and open to his eyes, to whom our speech is.—*Heb.* iv. 13.

OPPORTUNITIES, REGRET FOR LOST

What shall I say, or what shall he answer for me, whereas he himself hath done it? I will recount to thee all my years in the bitterness of my soul.—*Is.* xxxviii. 15.

Strive to enter by the narrow gate; for many, I say to you, shall seek to enter, and shall not be able.

But when the master of the house shall be gone in, and shall shut the door, you shall begin to stand without, and knock at the door, saying: Lord, open to us. And he answering, shall say to you: I know you not, whence you are.
. . . There shall be weeping and gnashing of teeth, when you shall see Abraham, and Isaac, and Jacob, and all the prophets, in the kingdom of God, and you yourselves thrust out.—*Luke* xiii. 24, 25, 28.

ORDERLINESS, OR REGULARITY

Wherefore, my brethren, when you come together to eat, wait for one another.

If any man be hungry, let him eat at home; that you come not together unto judgment.

And the rest I will set in order, when I come.—1 *Cor.* xi. 33, 34.

But let all things be done decently, and according to order.—1 *Cor.* xiv. 40.

ORPHANS, GOD IS THE PROTECTOR AND AVENGER OF

You shall not hurt a widow or an orphan.

If you hurt them they will cry out to me, and I will hear their cry:

And my rage shall be enkindled, and I will strike you with the sword, and your wives shall be widows, and your children, fatherless.—*Ex.* xxii. 22-24.

He doth judgment to the fatherless and the widow, loveth the stranger, and giveth him food and raiment.—*Deut.* x. 18.

To thee is the poor man left: thou wilt be a helper to the orphan. . . .

The Lord hath heard the desire of the poor: thy ear hath heard the preparation of their heart.

To judge for the fatherless and for the humble, that man may no more presume to magnify himself upon earth.—*Ps.* ix. (*Heb.* x.) 14, 17, 18.

For my father and my mother have left me: but the Lord hath taken me up.—*Ps.* xxvi. 10.

Sing ye to God, sing a psalm to his name, make a way for him who ascendeth upon the west: the Lord is his name . . . who is the father of orphans, and the judge of widows. God in his holy place.—*Ps.* lxvii. 5, 6.

The Lord keepeth the strangers, he will support the fatherless and the widow: and the ways of sinners he will destroy.—*Ps.* cxlv. 9.

He will not despise the prayers of the fatherless; nor the widow, when she poureth out her complaint.

Do not the widow's tears run down the cheek, and her cry against him that causeth them to fall?

For from the cheek they go up even to heaven, and the Lord that heareth, will not be delighted with them.—*Ecclus.* xxxv. 17-19.

Leave thy fatherless children: I will make them live: and thy widows shall hope in me.—*Jer.* xlix. 11.

And I will come to you in judgment, and will be a speedy witness against sorcerers, and adulterers, and false swearers, and them that oppress the hireling in his wages, the widows, and the fatherless: and oppress the stranger, and have not feared me, saith the Lord of hosts.—*Malach.* iii. 5.

ORPHANS, PROHIBITION AGAINST DOING WRONG TO

Thou shalt not pervert the judgment of the stranger nor of the fatherless, neither shalt thou take away the widow's raiment for a pledge.—*Deut.* xxiv. 17.

Cursed be he that perverteth the judgment of the stranger, of the fatherless, and the widow: and all the people shall say: Amen.—*Deut.* xxvii. 19.

If I have lifted up my hand against the fatherless, even when I saw myself superior in the gate:

Let my shoulder fall from its joint, and let my arm with its bones be broken.—*Job* xxxi. 21, 22.

Touch not the bounds of little ones: and enter not into the field of the fatherless:

For their near kinsman is strong: and he will judge their cause against thee.—*Prov.* xxiii. 10, 11.

Thus saith the Lord of hosts, saying: Judge ye true judgment, and show ye mercy and compassion every man to his brother.

And oppress not the widow, and the fatherless, and the stranger, and the poor: and let not a man devise evil in his heart against his brother.—*Zach.* vii. 9, 10.

ORPHANS, WE SHOULD BE ESPECIALLY KIND TO

When thou hast reaped the corn in thy field, and hast forgot, and left a sheaf, thou shalt not return to take it away: but thou shalt suffer the stranger, and the fatherless and the widow to take it away: that the Lord thy God may bless thee in all the works of thy hands.

If thou have gathered the fruit of thy olive-trees, thou shalt not return to gather whatsoever remaineth on the trees: but shalt leave it for the stranger, for the fatherless, and the widow.

If thou make the vintage of thy vineyard, thou shalt not gather the clusters that remain, but they shall be for the stranger, the fatherless and the widow.—*Deut.* xxiv. 19-21.

In judging be merciful to the fatherless as a father, and as a husband to their mother.

And thou shalt be as the obedient son of the most High, and he will have mercy on thee more than a mother.—*Ecclus.* iv. 10, 11.

Religion clean and undefiled before God and the Father is this: to visit the fatherless and widows in their tribulation: and to keep one's self unspotted from this world.—*James* i. 27.

OSTENTATION

Take heed that you do not your justice before men, to be seen by them: otherwise you shall not have a reward of your Father who is in heaven.

Therefore when thou dost an almsdeed, sound not a trumpet before thee, as the hypocrites do in the synagogues, and in the streets, that they may be honored by men. Amen I say to you, they have received their reward.

But when thou dost alms, let not thy left hand know what thy right hand doth. That thy alms may be in secret, and thy Father, who seeth in secret, will reward thee.

And when ye pray, you shall not be as the hypocrites, that love to stand and pray in the synagogues and corners of the streets that they may be seen by men: Amen I say to you, they have received their reward. . . .

And when you fast, be not as the hypocrites, sad. For they disfigure their faces, that they may appear unto men to fast. Amen I say to you, they have received their reward.

But thou, when thou fastest, anoint thy head, and wash thy face;

That thou appear not to men to fast, but to thy Father, who is in secret: and thy Father, who seeth in secret, will repay thee.—*Matt.* vi. 1-5, 16-18.

And all their works [1] they do for to be seen of men. For they make their phylacteries broad, and enlarge their fringes.—*Matt.* xxiii. 5.

PARDON OF SINS, PRAYER FOR

See: Forgiveness of sins—page 155.

PARENTS, OBEDIENCE TO

See: Obedience to—page 347.

PARENTS, RESPECT AND LOVE FOR

Honor thy father and thy mother, that thou mayst be longlived upon the land which the Lord thy God will give thee.—*Ex.* xx. 12.

Let every one fear his father and his mother.—*Lev.* xix. 3.

Honor thy father and mother, as the

[1] The scribes and Pharisees.

Lord thy God hath commanded thee, that thou mayst live a long time, and it may be well with thee in the land which the Lord thy God will give thee. —*Deut.* v. 16.

Then Bethsabee came to king Solomon, to speak to him for Adonias: and the king arose to meet her, and bowed to her, and sat down upon his throne: and a throne was set for the king's mother, and she sat on his right hand. And she said to him: I desire one small petition of thee, do not put me to confusion. And the king said to her: My mother, ask: for I must not turn away thy face.—*3 Kings* ii. 19, 20.

But his (Tobias') mother wept, and was quite disconsolate, and said: Woe, woe is me, my son; why did we send thee to go to a strange country, the light of our eyes, the staff of our old age, the comfort of our life, the hope of our posterity?—*Tob.* x. 4.

A wise son heareth the doctrine of his father: but he that is a scorner, heareth not when he is reproved.—*Prov.* xiii. 1.

A fool laugheth at the instruction of his father: but he that regardeth reproofs shall become prudent.—*Prov.* xv. 5.

Children's children are the crown of old men: and the glory of children are their fathers.—*Prov.* xvii. 6.

He that stealeth any thing from his father or from his mother: and saith, This is no sin, is the partner of a murderer.—*Prov.* xxviii. 24.

There is a generation that curseth their father, and doth not bless their mother.

A generation that are pure in their own eyes, and yet are not washed from their filthiness.—*Prov.* xxx. 11, 12.

Children, hear the judgment of your father, and so do that you may be saved.

For God hath made the father honorable to the children: and seeking the judgment of the mothers, hath confirmed it upon the children.—*Ecclus.* iii. 2, 3.

And he that honoreth his mother, is as one that layeth up a treasure.

He that honoreth his father, shall have joy in his own children, and in the day of his prayer, he shall be heard.

He that honoreth his father shall enjoy a long life: and he that obeyeth the father, shall be a comfort to his mother.

He that feareth the Lord, honoreth his parents, and will serve them as his masters, that brought him into the world.—*Ecclus.* iii. 5-8.

The father's blessing establisheth the houses of the children: but the mother's curse rooteth up the foundation.

Glory not in the dishonor of thy father: for his shame is no glory to thee.

For the glory of a man is from the honor of his father, and a father without honor is the disgrace of the son.— *Ecclus.* iii. 11-13.

PARENTS, EXHORTATION TO HONOR AND LOVE

Therefore when Tobias thought that his prayer was heard that he might die, he called to him Tobias his son,

And said to him: Hear, my son, the words of my mouth, and lay them as a foundation in thy heart.

When God shall take my soul, thou shalt bury my body: and thou shalt honor thy mother all the days of her life:

For thou must be mindful what and how great perils she suffered for thee in her womb.—*Tob.* iv. 1-4.

My son, hear the instruction of thy father, and forsake not the law of thy mother.—*Prov.* i. 8.

Hearken to thy father that begot thee: and despise not thy mother when she is old.

. . . Let thy father and thy mother be joyful, and let her rejoice that bore thee.—*Prov.* xxiii. 22, 25.

Honor thy father in work and word, and all patience,

That a blessing may come upon thee from him, and his blessing may remain in the latter end.—*Ecclus.* iii. 9, 10.

Son, support the old age of thy father, and grieve him not in his life;

And if his understanding fail, have patience with him, and despise him not, when thou art in thy strength: for the relieving of the father shall not be forgotten. . . .

And in justice thou shalt be built up, and in the day of affliction, thou shalt be remembered: and thy sins shall melt away as the ice in the fair warm weather.—*Ecclus.* iii. 14, 15, 17.

With thy whole heart,

Honor thy father, and forget not the groanings of thy mother:

Remember that thou hadst not been born but through them: and make a return to them as they have done for thee.—*Ecclus.* vii. 28-30.

PARENTS, PUNISHMENT OF FAILURE TO HONOR ONE'S

He that striketh his father or mother, shall be put to death. . . .

He that curseth his father or mother, shall die the death.—*Ex.* xxi. 15, 17.

He that curseth his father or mother, dying let him die: he hath cursed his father and mother, let his blood be upon him.—*Lev.* xx. 9.

Cursed be he that honoreth not his father and mother: and all the people shall say: Amen.—*Deut.* xxvii. 16.

No good shall come to the deceitful son.—*Prov.* xiv. 15.

He that afflicteth his father, and chaseth away his mother, is infamous and unhappy.—*Prov.* xix. 26.

He that curseth his father and mother, his lamp shall be put out in the midst of darkness.—*Prov.* xx. 20.

The eye that mocketh at his father, and that despiseth the labor of his mother in bearing him, let the ravens of the brooks pick it out, and the young eagles eat it.—*Prov.* xxx. 17.

The father's blessing establisheth the houses of the children: but the mother's curse rooteth up the foundation.—*Ecclus.* iii. 11.

Of what an evil fame is he that forsaketh his father: and he is cursed of God that angereth his mother.—*Ecclus.* iii. 18.

Remember thy father and thy mother, for thou sittest in the midst of great men:

Lest God forget thee in their sight, and thou, by thy daily custom, be infatuated and suffer reproach: and wish that thou hadst not been born, and curse the day of thy nativity.—*Ecclus.* xxiii. 18, 19.

PARENTS TO THEIR CHILDREN, THE DUTY OF

1st. Teaching Them

Lay up these my words in your hearts and minds. . . .

Teach your children that they meditate on them, when thou sittest in thy house, and when thou walkest on the way, and when thou liest down and risest up.—*Deut.* xi. 18, 19.

And when he (Tobias) was a man, he took to wife Anna, of his own tribe, and had a son by her, whom he called after his own name,

And from his infancy he taught him to fear God, and to abstain from all sin.—*Tob.* i. 9, 10.

Instruct thy son, and he shall refresh thee, and shall give delight to thy soul.—*Prov.* xxix. 17.

Hast thou children? instruct them, and bow down their neck from their childhood.—*Ecclus.* vii. 25.

A son ill taught is the confusion of the father; and a foolish daughter shall be to his loss.—*Ecclus.* xxii. 3.

He that instructeth his son, shall be praised in him, and shall glory in him in the midst of them of his household.

He that teacheth his son, maketh his enemy jealous, and in the midst of his friends he shall glory in him.

His father is dead, and he is as if he were not dead: for he hath left one behind him that is like himself.

While he lived, he saw and rejoiced in him: and when he died, he was not sorrowful, neither was he confounded before his enemies.—*Ecclus.* xxx. 2-5.

Instruct thy son, and labor about him, lest his lewd behavior be an offence to thee.—*Ecclus.* xxx. 13.

2d. Correcting Them

He that spareth the rod, hateth his son: but he that loveth him, correcteth him betimes.—*Prov.* xiii. 24.

Chastise thy son, despair not: but to the killing of him, set not thy soul.—*Prov.* xix. 18.

Folly is bound up in the heart of a

child, and the rod of correction shall drive it away.—*Prov.* xxii. 15.

Withhold not correction from a child: for if thou strike him with the rod, he shall not die.

Thou shalt beat him with the rod, and deliver his soul from hell.—*Prov.* xxiii. 13, 14.

The rod and reproof give wisdom: but the child that is left to his own will, bringeth his mother to shame.—*Prov.* xxix. 15.

He that loveth his son, frequently chastiseth him, that he may rejoice in his latter end, and not grope after the doors of his neighbors.—*Ecclus.* xxx. 1.

A horse not broken, becometh stubborn, and a child left to himself will become headstrong.

Give thy son his way, and he shall make thee afraid: play with him, and he shall make thee sorrowful. . . .

Give him not liberty in his youth, and wink not at his devices.

Bow down his neck while he is young, and beat his sides while he is a child, lest he grow stubborn, and regard thee not, and so be a sorrow of heart to thee. —*Ecclus.* xxx. 8, 9, 11, 12.

Fathers, provoke not your children to indignation, lest they be discouraged. —*Col.* iii. 21.

3d. Watchfulness and Care Over Them

Hast thou daughters? have a care of their body, and show not thy countenance gay towards them.

Marry thy daughter well, and thou shalt do a great work, and give her to a wise man.—*Ecclus.* vii. 26, 27.

On a daughter that turneth not away herself, set a strict watch: lest, finding an opportunity, she abuse herself.

Take heed of the impudence of her eyes, and wonder not if she slight thee.

She will open her mouth as a thirsty traveller to the fountain, and will drink of every water near her, and will sit down by every hedge, and open her quiver against every arrow, until she fail.—*Ecclus.* xxvi. 13-15.

And beware of thy own children, and take heed of them of thy household.— *Ecclus.* xxxii. 26.

The father waketh for the daughter when no man knoweth, and the care for her taketh away his sleep, when she is young, lest she pass away the flower of her age, and when she is married, lest she should be hateful:

In her virginity, lest she should be corrupted, and be found with child in her father's house: and having a husband, lest she should misbehave herself, or at the least, become barren.—*Ecclus.* xlii. 9, 10.

Keep a sure watch over a shameless daughter: lest at any time she make thee become a laughing-stock to thy enemies, and a by-word in the city, and a reproach among the people, and make thee ashamed before all the multitude.—*Ecclus.* xlii. 11.

But if any widow have children or grand-children, let her learn first to govern her own house, and to make a return of duty to her parents: for this is acceptable before God.—1 *Tim.* v. 4.

But if any man have not care of his own, and especially of those of his house, he hath denied the faith, and is worse than an infidel.—1 *Tim.* v. 8.

4th. Bringing Them Up in the Fear of God and in Obedience to His Laws

And the Lord said: Can I hide from Abraham what I am about [1]to do: . . .

For I know that he will command his children, and his household after him, to keep the way of the Lord, and do judgment and justice: that for Abraham's sake the Lord may bring to effect all the things he hath spoken unto him.—*Gen.* xviii. 17, 19.

And command your children that they do justice and almsdeeds, and that they be mindful of God, and bless him at all times in truth, and with all their power.—*Tob.* xiv. 11.

And you, fathers, provoke not your children to anger; but bring them up in the discipline and correction of the Lord.—*Eph.* vi. 4.

PARENTS TO THEIR CHILDREN, PUNISHMENT OF FAILURE IN THE DUTY OF

And the Lord said to Samuel: Behold I do a thing in Israel: and who-

[1]The impending destruction of Sodom and Gomorrha.

soever shall hear it, both his ears shall tingle.

In that day I will raise up against Heli all the things I have spoken concerning his house: I will begin, and I will make an end.

For I have foretold unto him that I will judge his house for ever, for iniquity, because he knew that his sons did wickedly, and did not chastise them. —1 *Kings* iii. 11-13.

The children will complain of an ungodly father, because for his sake they are in reproach.—*Ecclus.* xli. 10.

PARENTS SHOULD ALWAYS MAINTAIN THEIR AUTHORITY

Give not to son or wife, brother or friend, power over thee while thou livest; and give not thy estate to another, lest thou repent, and thou entreat for the same.

As long as thou livest, and hast breath in thee, let no man change thee.

For it is better that thy children should ask of thee, than that thou look toward the hands of thy children.

In all thy works, keep the pre-eminence.

Let no stain sully thy glory. In the time when thou shalt end the days of thy life, and in the time of thy decease, distribute thy inheritance.—*Ecclus.* xxxiii. 20-24.

PASSION OF CHRIST, THE

When a man hath committed a crime, for which he is to be punished with death, and being condemned to die, is hanged on a gibbet:

His body shall not remain upon the tree, but shall be buried the same day: for he is accursed of God that hangeth on a tree.—*Deut.* xxi. 22, 23.

Have pity on me, have pity on me, at least you my friends, because the hand of the Lord hath touched me.—*Job* xix. 21.

O God, my God, look upon me: why hast thou forsaken me?—*Ps.* xxi. 2.

But I am a worm, and no man: the reproach of men, and the outcast of the people.

All they that saw me, have laughed me to scorn: they have spoken with the lips, and wagged the head.—*Ps.* xxi. 7, 8.

My friends and my neighbors have drawn near, and stood against me.

And they that were near me, stood afar off: And they that sought my soul, used violence.

And they that sought evils to me, spoke vain things, and studied deceits all the day long.

But I, as a deaf man, heard not: and as a dumb man not opening his mouth.

And I became as a man that heareth not: and that hath no reproofs in his mouth.—*Ps.* xxxvii. 12-15.

I was dumb, and was humbled, and kept silence from good things: and my sorrow was renewed.—*Ps.* xxxviii. 3.

For even the man of my peace, in whom I trusted, who ate my bread, hath greatly supplanted me.—*Ps.* xl. 10.

For if my enemy had reviled me, I would verily have borne with it.

And if he that hated me had spoken great things against me, I would perhaps have hidden myself from him.

But thou, a man of one mind, my guide and my familiar,

Who didst take sweetmeats together with me: in the house of God we walked with consent.—*Ps.* liv. 13-15.

My heart hath expected reproach and misery. And I looked for one that would grieve together with me, but there was none: and for one that would comfort me, and I found none.

And they gave me gall for my food, and in my thirst, they gave me vinegar to drink.—*Ps.* lxviii. 21, 22.

They have spoken against me with deceitful tongues; and they have compassed me about with words of hatred; and have fought against me without cause.

Instead of making me a return of love, they detracted me: but I gave myself to prayer.

And they repaid me evil for good: and hatred for my love.—*Ps.* cviii. 3-5.

Go forth, ye daughters of Sion, and seeking Solomon in the diadem, wherewith his mother crowned him in the day of his espousals, and in the day of the joy of his heart.—*Cant.* iii. 11.

Let us see then if his words be true, and let us prove what shall happen to him, and we shall know what his end shall be.

For if he be the true son of God, he will defend him, and will deliver him from the hands of his enemies.

Let us examine him by outrages and tortures, that we may know his meekness, and try his patience.

Let us condemn him to a most shameful death: for there shall be respect had unto him by his words.

These things they thought, and were deceived: for their own malice blinded them.—*Wis.* ii. 17-21.

For blessed is the wood, by which justice cometh.—*Wis.* xiv. 7.

He will crown thee with a crown of tribulation.—*Is.* xxii. 18.

To whom have you likened me, and made me equal, and compared me, and made me like?—*Is.* xlvi. 5.

O all ye that pass by the way, attend, and see if there be any sorrow like to my sorrow.—*Lam.* i. 12.

He shall give his cheek to him that striketh him, he shall be filled with reproaches.—*Lam.* iii. 30.

Out of thee shall come forth one that imagineth evil against the Lord, contriving treachery in his mind.—*Nahum* i. 11.

Then Jesus came with them into a country place which is called Gethsemani; and he said to his disciples: Sit you here, till I go yonder, and pray.

And taking with him Peter and the two sons of Zebedee, he began to grow sorrowful, and to be sad.

Then he saith to them: My soul is sorrowful even unto death: stay you here, and watch with me.

And going a little further, he fell upon his face, praying and saying: My Father, if it be possible, let this chalice pass from me. Nevertheless not as I will, but as thou wilt.—*Matt.* xxvi. 36-39.

And he that betrayed him, gave them a sign, saying: Whomsoever I shall kiss, that is he, hold him fast.

And forthwith coming to Jesus, he said: Hail, Rabbi. And he kissed him.

And Jesus said to him: Friend, whereto art thou come? Then they came up, and laid hands on Jesus, and held him.—*Matt.* xxvi. 48-50.

Then the high-priest rent his garments, saying: He hath blasphemed; what further need have we of witnesses? Behold, now you have heard the blasphemy:

What think you? But they answering, said: He is guilty of death.

Then did they spit in his face, and buffeted him: and others struck his face with the palms of their hands,

Saying: Prophesy unto us, O Christ, who is he that struck thee?—*Matt.* xxvi. 65-68.

Now upon the solemn day, the governor was accustomed to release to the people one prisoner, whom they would.

And he had then a notorious prisoner, that was called Barabbas.

They therefore being gathered together, Pilate said: Whom will you that I release to you, Barabbas, or Jesus that is called Christ? . . .

But the chief priests and ancients persuaded the people, that they should ask Barabbas, and make Jesus away.

And the governor answering, said to them:

Whether will you of the two to be released unto you? But they said: Barabbas. Pilate saith to them: What shall I do then with Jesus, that is called Christ? They say all: Let him be crucified.

The governor said to them: Why, what evil hath he done? But they cried out the more, saying: Let him be crucified.—*Matt.* xxvii. 15-17, 20-23.

Then he released to them Barabbas, and having scourged Jesus, delivered him unto them to be crucified.

Then the soldiers of the governor taking Jesus into the hall, gathered together unto him the whole band;

And stripping him, they put a scarlet cloak about him.

And platting a crown of thorns, they put it upon his head, and a reed in his right hand. And bowing the knee before him, they mocked him, saying: Hail, king of the Jews.

And spitting upon him, they took the reed, and struck his head.

And after they had mocked him, they took off the cloak from him, and put on him his own garments, and led him away to crucify him.

And going out, they found a man of Cyrene, named Simon: him they forced to take up his cross.

And they came to the place that is called Golgotha, which is the place of Calvary.

And they gave him wine to drink, mingled with gall. And when he had tasted, he would not drink.

And after they had crucified him, they divided his garments, casting lots. —*Matt.* xxvii. 26-35.

Now from the sixth hour there was darkness over the whole earth, until the ninth hour.

And about the ninth hour Jesus cried with a loud voice, saying: Eli, Eli, lamma sabacthani? that is, My God, my God, why hast thou forsaken me? . . .

And Jesus again crying with a loud voice, yielded up the ghost.—*Matt.* xxvii. 45, 46, 50.

And he was withdrawn away from them a stone's cast; and kneeling down, he prayed,

Saying: Father, if thou wilt, remove this chalice from me: but yet, not my will, but thine be done.

And there appeared to him an angel from heaven, strengthening him. And being in an agony, he prayed the longer.

And his sweat became as drops of blood, trickling down upon the ground. —*Luke* xxii. 41-44.

And Herod with his army set him at nought, and mocked him, putting on him a white garment, and sent him back to Pilate.—*Luke* xxiii. 11.

Now is my soul troubled. And what shall I say? Father, save me from this hour. But for this cause, I came unto this hour.—*John* xii. 27.

Jesus therefore said to Peter: Put up thy sword into the scabbard. The chalice which my Father hath given me, shall I not drink it?—*John* xviii. 11.

(Jesus therefore came forth, bearing the crown of thorns and the purple garment.) And he (Pilate) saith to them: Behold the Man.—*John* xix. 5.

And they took Jesus, and led him forth.

And bearing his own cross, he went forth to that place which is called Calvary, but in Hebrew, Golgotha.

Where they crucified him, and with him two others, one on each side, and Jesus in the midst.—*John* xix. 16-18.

Christ hath redeemed us from the curse of the law, being made a curse for us: for it is written: Cursed is every one that hangeth on a tree.—*Gal.* iii. 13.

Because Christ also suffered for us, leaving you an example that you should follow his steps.

Who did no sin, neither was guile found in his mouth.

Who, when he was reviled, did not revile: when he suffered, he threatened not: but delivered himself to him that judged him unjustly.

Who his own self bore our sins in his body upon the tree: that we, being dead to sins, should live to justice: by whose stripes you were healed.—1 *Peter* ii. 21-24.

PASSION OF CHRIST, PROPH-ECIES OF THE

See: Part II—page 796.

PASTORS, WE SHOULD SUPPORT OUR

And the Lord said to Aaron: Behold I have given thee the charge of my first-fruits. All things that are sanctified by the children of Israel, I have delivered to thee and to thy sons for the priestly office, by everlasting ordinances. . . .

But the first-fruits which the children of Israel shall vow and offer, I have given to thee and to thy sons, and to thy daughters, by a perpetual law. . . .

Every thing that the children of Israel shall give by vow, shall be thine. —*Num.* xviii. 8, 11, 14.

And I have given to the sons of Levi all the tithes of Israel for a possession, for the ministry wherewith they serve me in the tabernacle of the covenant.— *Num.* xviii. 21.

Honor God with all thy soul, and give honor to the priests, and purify thyself with thy arms.

Give them their portion, as it is

commanded thee, of the first-fruits and of purifications: and for thy negligences, purify thyself with a few.—*Ecclus.* vii. 33, 34.

And in the same house remain, eating and drinking such things as they have: for the laborer is worthy of his hire.—*Luke* x. 7.

For it hath pleased them of Macedonia and Achaia to make a contribution for the poor of the saints that are in Jerusalem.

For it hath pleased them; and they are their debtors. For if the Gentiles have been made partakers of their spiritual things, they ought also in carnal things to minister to them.—*Rom.* xv. 26, 27.

Who serveth as a soldier at any time at his own charges? Who planteth a vineyard, and eateth not of the fruit thereof? Who feedeth the flock, and eateth not of the milk of the flock?

Speak I these things according to man? Or doth not the law also say these things? . . .

If we have sown unto you spiritual things, is it a great matter if we reap your carnal things? . . .

Know you not, that they who work in the holy place, eat the things that are of the holy place; and they that serve the altar, partake with the altar?

So also the Lord ordained that they who preach the gospel, should live by the gospel.—1 *Cor.* ix. 7, 8, 11, 13, 14.

Or did I commit a fault, humbling myself, that you might be exalted? Because I preached unto you the gospel of God freely?

I have taken from other churches, receiving wages of them for your ministry.—2 *Cor.* xi. 7, 8.

Let the priests that rule well be esteemed worthy of double honor: especially they who labor in the word and doctrine:

For the scripture saith: Thou shalt not muzzle the ox that treadeth out the corn: and, The laborer is worthy of his reward.—1 *Tim.* v. 17, 18.

PATH OF RECTITUDE, THE

Then if any of thy people Israel . . . shall pray, and shall spread forth his hands in this house,

Hear thou from heaven, from thy high dwelling place, and forgive, and render to every one according to his ways. . . .

That they may fear thee, and walk in thy ways all the days that they live upon the face of the land, which thou hast given to our fathers.—2 *Paral.* vi. 29-31.

My foot hath followed his steps, I have kept his way, and have not declined from it.

I have not departed from the commandments of his lips, and the words of his mouth, I have hid in my bosom. —*Job* xxiii. 11, 12.

For the sake of the words of thy lips, I have kept hard ways.

Perfect thou my goings in thy paths: that my footsteps be not moved.—*Ps.* xvi. 4, 5.

He hath converted my soul.

He hath led me on the paths of justice, for his own name's sake.—*Ps.* xxii. 3.

My foot hath stood in the direct way: in the churches, I will bless thee, O Lord.—*Ps.* xxv. 12.

He will keep the salvation of the righteous, and protect them that walk in simplicity.

Keeping the paths of justice, and guarding the ways of saints.—*Prov.* ii. 7, 8.

If wisdom shall enter into thy heart, and knowledge please thy soul:

Counsel shall keep thee, and prudence shall preserve thee,

That thou mayst be delivered from the evil way, . . .

That thou mayst walk in a good way: and mayst keep the paths of the just.— *Prov.* ii. 10-12, 20.

In the path of justice is life: but the by-way leadeth to death.—*Prov.* xii. 28.

Woe to them that have lost patience, and that have forsaken the right ways, and have gone aside into crooked ways.

And what will they do, when the Lord shall begin to examine?—*Ecclus.* ii. 16, 17.

When I was yet young, before I wandered about, I sought for wisdom openly in my prayer. . . .

My heart delighted in her, my foot walked in the right way, from my youth up I sought after her.—*Ecclus.* li. 18, 20.

The way of the just is right, the path of the just is right to walk in.—*Is.* xxvi. 7.

And a path and a way shall be there, and it shall be called the holy way: the unclean shall not pass over it, and this shall be unto you a straight way so that fools shall not err therein:

. . . But they shall walk there that shall be delivered.—*Is.* xxxv. 8, 9.

For if thou hadst walked in the way of God, thou hadst surely dwelt in peace for ever.—*Bar.* iii. 13.

And they have not known his justices, nor walked by the ways of God's commandments, neither have they entered by the paths of his truth and justice.—*Bar.* iv. 13.

Through the bowels of the mercy of our God, in which the Orient from on high hath visited us:

To enlighten them that sit in darkness, and in the shadow of death: to direct our feet into the way of peace.—*Luke* i. 78, 79.

PATH OF RECTITUDE, EXHORTATION TO WALK IN THE

Keep therefore and do the things which the Lord God hath commanded you: you shall not go aside, neither to the right hand, nor to the left.

But you shall walk in the way that the Lord your God hath commanded, that you may live, and it may be well with you, and your days may be long in the land of your possession.—*Deut.* v. 32, 33.

Let our hearts also be perfect with the Lord our God, that we may walk in his statutes, and keep his commandments, as at this day.—*3 Kings* viii. 61.

Let thy eyes look straight on, and let thy eyelids go before thy steps.

Make straight the path for thy feet, and all thy ways shall be established.

Decline not to the right hand, nor to the left: turn away thy foot from evil. For the Lord knoweth the ways that are on the right hand: but those are perverse, which are on the left hand. But he will make thy courses straight, he will bring forward thy ways in peace.—*Prov.* iv. 25-27.

Rejoice therefore, O young man, in thy youth, and let thy heart be in that which is good in the days of thy youth, and walk in the ways of thy heart, and in the sight of thy eyes: and know that for all these God will bring thee into judgment.—*Eccles.* xi. 9.

Be steadfast in the way of the Lord, and in the truth of thy judgment, and in knowledge, and let the word of peace and justice keep with thee.—*Ecclus.* v. 12.

And thy ears shall hear the word of one admonishing thee behind thy back: This is the way, walk ye in it: and go not aside, neither to the right hand, nor to the left.—*Is.* xxx. 21.

Thus saith the Lord: Stand ye on the ways, and see, and ask for the old paths, which is the good way, and walk ye in it: and you shall find refreshment for your souls.—*Jer.* vi. 16.

But this thing I commanded them, saying: Hearken to my voice, and I will be your God, and you shall be my people: and walk ye in all the way that I have commanded you, that it may be well with you.—*Jer.* vii. 23.

Set thee up a watch tower, make to thee bitterness: direct thy heart into the right way, wherein thou hast walked: return, O virgin of Israel, return to these thy cities.—*Jer.* xxxi. 21.

PATH TO HEAVEN IS NARROW AND HARD, THE

Enter ye in at the narrow gate. . . .

How narrow is the gate, and strait is the way that leadeth to life: and few there are that find it!—*Matt.* vii. 13, 14.

And a certain man said to him: Lord, are they few that are saved? But he said to them:

Strive to enter by the narrow gate; for many, I say to you, shall seek to enter, and shall not be able.—*Luke* xiii. 23, 24.

PATH TO HELL IS BROAD AND EASY, THE

Enter ye in at the narrow gate: for wide is the gate, and broad is the way that leadeth to destruction, and many there are who go in thereat.—*Matt.* vii. 13.

PATIENCE IN SUFFERING AND UNDER DIFFICULTIES

But now the scourge is come upon thee, and thou faintest: it hath touched thee, and thou art troubled.

Where is thy fear, thy fortitude, thy patience, and the perfection of thy ways?—*Job* iv. 5, 6.

But be thou, O my soul, subject to God: for from him is my patience.—*Ps.* lxi. 6.

For thou art my patience, O Lord: my hope, O Lord, from my youth.—*Ps.* lxx. 5.

A patient man shall bear for a time, and afterwards joy shall be restored to him.—*Ecclus.* i. 29.

Woe to them that have lost patience, and that have forsaken the right ways, and have gone aside into crooked ways.

And what will they do, when the Lord shall begin to examine?—*Ecclus.* ii. 16, 17.

They that fear the Lord, keep his commandments, and will have patience even until his visitation.—*Ecclus.* ii. 21.

In your patience you shall possess your souls.—*Luke* xxi. 19.

Who will render to every man according to his works.

To them indeed who according to patience in good work seek glory and honor and incorruption, eternal life.—*Rom.* ii. 6, 7.

But we glory also in tribulations, knowing that tribulation worketh patience;

And patience, trial; and trial, hope;

And hope confoundeth not: because the charity of God is poured forth in our hearts by the Holy Ghost, who is given to us.—*Rom.* v. 3-5.

But the fruit of the Spirit is charity, joy, peace, patience, benignity, goodness, longanimity.—*Gal.* v. 22.

For patience is necessary for you: that doing the will of God, you may receive the promise.

For yet a little, and a very little while, and he that is to come, will come, and will not delay.—*Heb.* x. 36, 37.

And therefore we also having so great a cloud of witnesses over our head, laying aside every weight and sin which surrounds us, let us run by patience to the fight proposed to us.—*Heb.* xii. 1.

My brethren, count it all joy, when you shall fall into divers temptations;

Knowing that the trying of your faith worketh patience.

And patience hath a perfect work; that you may be perfect and entire, failing in nothing.—*James* i. 2-4.

Take, my brethren, for an example of suffering evil, of labor and patience, the prophets, who spoke in the name of the Lord.

Behold, we account them blessed who have endured. You have heard of the patience of Job, and you have seen the end of the Lord, that the Lord is merciful and compassionate.—*James* v. 10, 11.

For what glory is it, if committing sin, and being buffeted for it, you endure? But if, doing well, you suffer patiently; this is thankworthy before God.

For unto this are you called: because Christ also suffered for us, leaving you an example that you should follow his steps.—1 *Peter* ii. 20, 21.

PATIENCE IN SUFFERING, EXHORTATION TO

Wait on God with patience: join thyself to God, and endure, that thy life may be increased in the latter end.

Take all that shall be brought upon thee: and in thy sorrow endure, and in thy humiliation keep patience.

For gold and silver are tried in the fire, but acceptable men in the furnace of humiliation.—*Ecclus.* ii. 3-5.

My children, suffer patiently the wrath that is come upon you: for thy enemy hath persecuted thee, but thou shalt quickly see his destruction: and thou shalt get up upon his neck.—*Bar.* iv. 25.

Rejoicing in hope. Patient in tribulation. Instant in prayer.—*Rom.* xii. 12.

But in all things let us exhibit ourselves as the ministers of God, in much patience, in tribulation, in necessities, in distresses.—2 *Cor.* vi. 4.

Therefore we also, from the day that we heard it, cease not to pray for you, and to beg that you may be filled with the knowledge of his will, in all wisdom and spiritual understanding. . . .

Strengthened with all might, according to the power of his glory, in all patience and long-suffering with joy.—*Col.* i. 9, 11.

PATIENCE IN DEALING WITH OTHERS

He that is patient, is governed with much wisdom: but he that is impatient, exalteth his folly.—*Prov.* xiv. 29.

A passionate man stirreth up strifes: he that is patient, appeaseth those that are stirred up.—*Prov.* xv. 18.

The patient man is better than the valiant: and he that ruleth his spirit, than he that taketh cities.—*Prov.* xvi. 32.

The learning of a man is known by patience: and his glory is to pass over wrongs.—*Prov.* xix. 11.

By patience, a prince shall be appeased, and a soft tongue shall break hardness.—*Prov.* xxv. 15.

Better is the patient man, than the presumptuous.—*Eccles.* vii. 9.

The sinner shall not escape in his rapines, and the patience of him that showeth mercy, shall not be put off.—*Ecclus.* xvi. 14.

PATIENCE IN OUR DEALINGS WITH OTHERS, EXHORTATION TO

You have heard that it hath been said, An eye for an eye, and a tooth for a tooth.

But I say to you, not to resist evil: but if one strike thee on thy right cheek, turn to him also the other:

And if a man will contend with thee in judgment, and take away thy coat, let go thy cloak also unto him.

And whosoever will force thee one mile, go with him other two.—*Matt.* v. 38-41.

I therefore, a prisoner in the Lord, beseech you that you walk worthy of the vocation in which you are called,

With all humility and mildness, with patience supporting one another in charity.—*Eph.* iv. 1, 2.

Put ye on therefore, as the elect of God, holy and beloved, the bowels of mercy, benignity, humility, modesty, patience:

Bearing with one another, and forgiving one another.—*Col.* iii. 12, 13.

And we beseech you, brethren, rebuke the unquiet, comfort the feebleminded, support the weak, be patient towards all men.—*1 Thess.* v. 14.

But thou, O man of God, fly these things: and pursue justice, godliness, faith, charity, patience, mildness.—*1 Tim.* vi. 11.

But the servant of God must not wrangle: but be mild towards all men, apt to teach, patient.—*2 Tim.* ii. 24.

PATIENCE OF CHRIST, THE

See: Meekness of Christ, the—page 311.

PATIENCE OF GOD, THE

But forasmuch as the Lord is patient, let us be penitent for this same thing, and with many tears, let us beg his pardon:

For God will not threaten like man, nor be inflamed to anger like the son of man.—*Judith* viii. 14, 15.

God is a just judge, strong and patient: is he angry every day?—*Ps.* vii. 12.

And thou, O Lord, art a God of compassion, and merciful, patient, and of much mercy, and true.—*Ps.* lxxxv. 15.

But thou, our God, art gracious and true, patient, and ordering all things in mercy.—*Wis.* xv. 1.

Say not: I have sinned, and what harm hath befallen me? for the most High is a patient rewarder.—*Ecclus.* v. 4.

The number of the days of men, at the most, are a hundred years: as a drop of water of the sea are they esteemed: and as a pebble of the sand, so are a few years compared to eternity.

Therefore God is patient in them, and poureth forth his mercy upon them.—*Ecclus.* xviii. 8, 9.

Therefore the Lord waiteth, that he may have mercy on you: and therefore shall he be exalted, sparing you: because the Lord is the God of judgment:

The Lord be with you all.—2 *Thess.* iii. 16.

PEACE WITH GOD

Blessed are all they that love thee, and that rejoice in thy peace.—*Tob.* xiii. 18.

I will hear what the Lord God will speak in me: for he will speak peace unto his people:

And unto his saints: and unto them that are converted to the heart.—*Ps.* lxxxiv. 9.

For the peace of God is over all the face of the earth.—*Ecclus.* xxxviii. 8.

How beautiful upon the mountains are the feet of him that bringeth good tidings, and that preacheth peace!—*Is.* lii. 7.

Being justified therefore by faith, let us have peace with God, through our Lord Jesus Christ.—*Rom.* v. 1.

For he is our peace, who hath made both one, and breaking down the middle wall of partition, the enmities in his flesh. . . .

And coming, he preached peace to you that were afar off, and peace to them that were nigh.—*Eph.* ii. 14, 17.

Because in him it hath well pleased the Father, that all fulness should dwell;

And through him, to reconcile all things unto himself, making peace through the blood of his cross, both as to the things that are on earth, and the things that are in heaven.—*Col.* i. 19, 20.

And let the peace of Christ rejoice in your hearts, wherein also you are called in one body: and be ye thankful. —*Col.* iii. 15.

PEACE WITH ONE ANOTHER

See also: Concord, living in— page 70.

Who is the man that desireth life: who loveth to see good days?

Keep thy tongue from evil, and thy lips from speaking guile.

Turn away from evil and do good: seek after peace, and pursue it.—*Ps.* xxxiii. 13-15.

In his days shall justice spring up, and abundance of peace, till the moon be taken away.—*Ps.* lxxi. 7.

With them that hated peace, I was peaceable: when I spoke to them, they fought against me without cause.—*Ps.* cxix. 7.

Deceit is in the heart of them that think evil things: but joy followeth them that take counsels of peace.— *Prov.* xii. 20.

Blessed are the peacemakers: for they shall be called the children of God. —*Matt.* v. 9.

For God is not the God of dissension, but of peace: as also I teach in all the churches of the saints.—1 *Cor.* xiv. 33.

And the fruit of justice is sown in peace, to them that make peace.—*James* iii. 18.

PEACE WITH ONE ANOTHER, EXHORTATION TO HAVE

Be in peace with many, but let one of a thousand be thy counsellor.— *Ecclus.* vi. 6.

Thus saith the Lord of hosts: The fast of the fourth month, and the fast of the fifth, and the fast of the seventh, and the fast of the tenth shall be to the house of Juda joy, and gladness, and great solemnities: only love ye truth and peace.—*Zach.* viii. 19.

If therefore thou offer thy gift at the altar, and there thou remember that thy brother hath any thing against thee;

Leave there thy offering before the altar, and go first to be reconciled to thy brother: and then coming, thou shalt offer thy gift.

Be at agreement with thy adversary betimes, whilst thou art in the way with him: lest perhaps the adversary deliver thee to the judge, and the judge deliver thee to the officer, and thou be cast into prison.

Amen I say to thee, thou shalt not go out from thence till thou repay the last farthing.—*Matt.* v. 23-26.

Salt is good. But if the salt become unsavory; wherewith will you season it? Have salt in you, and have peace among you.—*Mark* ix. 49.

Being of one mind one towards another.—*Rom.* xii. 16.

If it be possible, as much as is in you, have peace with all men.—*Rom.* xii. 18.

blessed are all they that wait for him.— *Is.* xxx. 18.

The Lord is patient, and great in power, and will not cleanse and acquit the guilty.—*Nahum* i. 3.

Then Jesus answered and said: O unbelieving and perverse generation, how long shall I be with you? How long shall I suffer you?—*Matt.* xvii. 16.

Or despisest thou the riches of his goodness, and patience, and longsuffering? Knowest thou not that the benignity of God leadeth thee to penance? —*Rom.* ii. 4.

But for this cause have I obtained mercy: that in me first Christ Jesus might show forth all patience, for the information of them that shall believe in him unto life everlasting.—1 *Tim.* i. 16.

And account the longsuffering of our Lord, salvation; as also our most dear brother Paul, according to the wisdom given him, hath written to you.— 2 *Peter* iii. 15.

PATIENCE OF GOD IN DEALING WITH SINNERS, EXAMPLES OF THE

But they and our fathers dealt proudly, and hardened their necks, and hearkened not to thy commandments.

And they would not hear, and they remembered not thy wonders, which thou hadst done for them. And they hardened their necks, and gave the head to return to their bondage, as it were by contention. But thou, a forgiving God, gracious and merciful, longsuffering, and full of compassion, didst not forsake them.

Yea, when they had made also to themselves a molten calf, and had said: This is thy God, that brought thee out of Egypt: and had committed great blasphemies:

Yet thou, in thy many mercies, didst not leave them in the desert: the pillar of the cloud departed not from them by day to lead them in the way, and the pillar of fire by night to show them the way by which they should go.

And thou gavest them thy good Spirit to teach them, and thy manna thou didst not withhold from their

mouth, and thou gavest them water for their thirst.

Forty years didst thou feed them in the desert, and nothing was wanting to them: their garments did not grow old, and their feet were not worn. . . .

And thou didst forbear with them for many years, and didst testify against them by thy spirit by the hand of thy prophets: and they heard not, and thou didst deliver them into the hand of the people of the lands.

Yet in thy very many mercies thou didst not utterly consume them, nor forsake them: because thou art a merciful and gracious God.—2 *Esd.* ix. 16-21, 30, 31.

But he is merciful, and will forgive their sins: and will not destroy them.

And many a time did he turn away his anger: and did not kindle all his wrath. And he remembered that they are flesh: a wind that goeth, and returneth not.—*Ps.* lxxvii. 38, 39.

For because sentence is not speedily pronounced against the evil, the children of men commit evils without any fear.

But though a sinner do evil a hundred times, and by patience be borne withal, I know from thence that it shall be well with them that fear God, who dread his face.—*Eccles.* viii. 11, 12.

O how good and sweet is thy spirit, O Lord, in all things!

And therefore thou chastisest them that err, by little and little: and admonishest them, and speakest to them, concerning the things wherein they offend: that leaving their wickedness they may believe in thee, O Lord.—*Wis.* xii. 1, 2.

Yet even those thou sparedst as men, and didst send wasps, forerunners of thy host, to destroy them by little and little.

Not that thou wast unable to bring the wicked under the just by war, or by cruel beasts, or by one rough word to destroy them at once:

But executing thy judgments by degrees, thou gavest them place of repentance, not being ignorant that they were a wicked generation, and their malice natural, and that their thought could never be changed.—*Wis.* xii. 8-10.

But thou hast taught thy people by such works, that they must be just and humane, and hast made thy children to be of a good hope: because in judging thou givest place for repentance of sins.

For if thou didst punish the enemies of thy servants, and that deserved to die, with so great deliberation, giving them time and place whereby they might be changed from their wickedness:

With what circumspection hast thou judged thy own children, to whose parents thou hast sworn, and made covenants of good promises?—*Wis.* xii. 19-21.

For whom hast thou been solicitous and afraid, that thou hast lied, and hast not been mindful of me, nor thought on me in thy heart? for I am silent, and as one that seeth not, and thou hast forgotten me.—*Is.* lvii. 11.

I will not execute the fierceness of my wrath: I will not return to destroy Ephraim: because I am God, and not man: the holy one in the midst of thee, and I will not enter into the city.—*Osee* xi. 9.

Thy eyes are too pure to behold evil, and thou canst not look on iniquity. Why lookest thou upon them that do unjust things, and holdest thy peace when the wicked devoureth the man that is more just than himself?—*Hab.* i. 13.

He spoke also this parable: A certain man had a fig-tree planted in his vineyard, and he came seeking fruit on it, and found none.

And he said to the dresser of the vineyard: Behold, for these three years I come seeking fruit on this fig-tree, and I find none. Cut it down therefore: why cumbereth it the ground?

But he answering, said to him: Lord, let it alone this year also, until I dig about it, and dung it.

And if happily it bear fruit: but if not, then after that thou shalt cut it down.—*Luke* xiii. 6-9.

And he began to speak to the people this parable: A certain man planted a vineyard, and let it out to husbandmen: and he was abroad for a long time.

And at the season he sent a servant to the husbandmen, that they should give him of the fruit of the vineyard. Who, beating him, sent him away empty.

And again he sent another servant. But they beat him also, and treating him reproachfully, sent him away empty.

And again he sent the third: and they wounded him also, and cast him out.

Then the lord of the vineyard said: What shall I do? I will send my beloved son: it may be, when they see him, they will reverence him.—*Luke* xx. 9-13.

What if God, willing to show his wrath, and to make his power known, endured with much patience vessels of wrath, fitted for destruction,

That he might show the riches of his glory on the vessels of mercy, which he hath prepared unto glory?—*Rom.* ix. 22, 23.

But to Israel, he saith: All the day long have I spread my hands to a people that believeth not, and contradicteth me.—*Rom.* x. 21.

The Lord delayeth not his promise, as some imagine, but dealeth patiently for your sake, not willing that any should perish, but that all should return to penance.—2 *Peter* iii. 9.

PEACE THE GIFT OF GOD

For when he granteth peace, who is there that can condemn?—*Job* xxxiv. 29.

The Lord will give strength to his people: the Lord will bless his people with peace.—*Ps.* xxviii. 10.

And I said: Who will give me wings like a dove, and I will fly, and be at rest?—*Ps.* liv. 7.

The old error is passed away: thou wilt keep peace: peace, because we have hoped in thee.—*Is.* xxvi. 3.

Lord, thou wilt give us peace: for thou hast wrought all our works for us.—*Is.* xxvi. 12.

I created the fruit of the lips, peace, peace to him that is far off, and to him that is near, said the Lord, and I healed him.—*Is.* lvii. 19.

And when you come into the house, salute it, saying: Peace be to this house.

And if that house be worthy, your peace shall come upon it; but if it be not worthy, your peace shall return to you.—*Matt.* x. 12, 13.

And rising up, he rebuked the wind, and said to the sea: Peace, be still. And the wind ceased: and there was made a great calm.—*Mark* iv. 39.

And suddenly there was with the angel a multitude of the heavenly army, praising God, and saying:

Glory to God in the highest; and on earth, peace to men of good will.—*Luke* ii. 13, 14.

Now whilst they were speaking these things, Jesus stood in the midst of them, and saith to them: Peace be to you; it is I, fear not.—*Luke* xxiv. 36.

Peace I leave with you, my peace I give unto you: not as the world giveth, do I give unto you. Let not your heart be troubled, nor let it be afraid.—*John* xiv. 27.

God sent the word to the children of Israel, preaching peace by Jesus Christ (he is Lord of all).—*Acts* x. 36.

Now the God of peace be with you all. Amen.—*Rom.* xv. 33.

But the fruit of the Spirit is charity, joy, peace, patience, benignity, goodness, longanimity.—*Gal.* v. 22.

PEACE OF THE JUST, THE

Submit thyself then to him (God), and be at peace: and thereby thou shalt have the best fruit.—*Job* xxii. 21.

In peace, in the selfsame I will sleep, and I will rest:

For thou, O Lord, singularly hast settled me in hope.—*Ps.* iv. 9, 10.

Let them rejoice and be glad, who are well pleased with my justice, and let them say always: The Lord be magnified, who delights in the peace of his servant.—*Ps.* xxxiv. 27.

Much peace have they that love thy law, and to them there is no stumbling-block.—*Ps.* cxviii. 165.

I am a wall: and my breasts are as a tower, since I am become in his presence as one finding peace.—*Cant.* viii. 10.

O that thou hadst hearkened to my commandments: thy peace had been as a river, and thy justice as the waves of the sea.—*Is.* xlviii. 18.

All thy children shall be taught of the Lord: and great shall be the peace of thy children.—*Is.* liv. 13.

And I am not troubled, following thee for my pastor, and I have not desired the day of man, thou knowest.—*Jer.* xvii. 16.

For if thou hadst walked in the way of God, thou hadst surely dwelt in peace for ever.—*Bar.* iii. 13.

Through the bowels of the mercy of our God, in which the Orient from on high hath visited us:

To enlighten them that sit in darkness, and in the shadow of death: to direct our feet into the way of peace.—*Luke* i. 78, 79.

These things I have spoken to you, that in me you may have peace. In the world you shall have distress: but have confidence, I have overcome the world.—*John* xvi. 33.

PEACE, A PRAYER FOR

The Lord turn his countenance to thee, and give thee peace.—*Num.* vi. 26.

Give to the king thy judgment, O God; and to the king's son thy justice. . . .

Let the mountains receive peace for the people: and the hills justice.—*Ps.* lxxi. 2, 3.

Pray ye for the things that are for the peace of Jerusalem: and abundance for them that love thee.

Let peace be in thy strength: and abundance in thy towers.

For the sake of my brethren, and of my neighbors, I spoke peace of thee.—*Ps.* cxxi. 6-8.

May he grant us joyfulness of heart, and that there be peace in our days in Israel for ever.—*Ecclus.* l. 25.

Grace to you, and peace from God our Father, and from the Lord Jesus Christ.—*Rom.* i. 7.

And the peace of God, which surpasseth all understanding, keep your hearts and minds in Christ Jesus.—*Philipp.* iv. 7.

Now the Lord of peace himself give you everlasting peace in every pl

blessed are all they that wait for him.— *Is.* xxx. 18.

The Lord is patient, and great in power, and will not cleanse and acquit the guilty.—*Nahum* i. 3.

Then Jesus answered and said: O unbelieving and perverse generation, how long shall I be with you? How long shall I suffer you?—*Matt.* xvii. 16.

Or despisest thou the riches of his goodness, and patience, and longsuffering? Knowest thou not that the benignity of God leadeth thee to penance? —*Rom.* ii. 4.

But for this cause have I obtained mercy: that in me first Christ Jesus might show forth all patience, for the information of them that shall believe in him unto life everlasting.—1 *Tim.* i. 16.

And account the longsuffering of our Lord, salvation; as also our most dear brother Paul, according to the wisdom given him, hath written to you.— 2 *Peter* iii. 15.

PATIENCE OF GOD IN DEALING WITH SINNERS, EXAMPLES OF THE

But they and our fathers dealt proudly, and hardened their necks, and hearkened not to thy commandments.

And they would not hear, and they remembered not thy wonders, which thou hadst done for them. And they hardened their necks, and gave the head to return to their bondage, as it were by contention. But thou, a forgiving God, gracious and merciful, longsuffering, and full of compassion, didst not forsake them.

Yea, when they had made also to themselves a molten calf, and had said: This is thy God, that brought thee out of Egypt: and had committed great blasphemies:

Yet thou, in thy many mercies, didst not leave them in the desert: the pillar of the cloud departed not from them by day to lead them in the way, and the pillar of fire by night to show them the way by which they should go.

And thou gavest them thy good Spirit to teach them, and thy manna thou didst not withhold from their mouth, and thou gavest them water for their thirst.

Forty years didst thou feed them in the desert, and nothing was wanting to them: their garments did not grow old, and their feet were not worn. . . .

And thou didst forbear with them for many years, and didst testify against them by thy spirit by the hand of thy prophets: and they heard not, and thou didst deliver them into the hand of the people of the lands.

Yet in thy very many mercies thou didst not utterly consume them, nor forsake them: because thou art a merciful and gracious God.—2 *Esd.* ix. 16-21, 30, 31.

But he is merciful, and will forgive their sins: and will not destroy them.

And many a time did he turn away his anger: and did not kindle all his wrath. And he remembered that they are flesh: a wind that goeth, and returneth not.—*Ps.* lxxvii. 38, 39.

For because sentence is not speedily pronounced against the evil, the children of men commit evils without any fear.

But though a sinner do evil a hundred times, and by patience be borne withal, I know from thence that it shall be well with them that fear God, who dread his face.—*Eccles.* viii. 11, 12.

O how good and sweet is thy spirit, O Lord, in all things!

And therefore thou chastisest them that err, by little and little: and admonishest them, and speakest to them, concerning the things wherein they offend: that leaving their wickedness they may believe in thee, O Lord.—*Wis.* xii. 1, 2.

Yet even those thou sparedst as men, and didst send wasps, forerunners of thy host, to destroy them by little and little.

Not that thou wast unable to bring the wicked under the just by war, or by cruel beasts, or by one rough word to destroy them at once:

But executing thy judgments by degrees, thou gavest them place of repentance, not being ignorant that they were a wicked generation, and their malice natural, and that their thought could never be changed.—*Wis.* xii. 8-10.

But thou hast taught thy people by such works, that they must be just and humane, and hast made thy children to be of a good hope: because in judging thou givest place for repentance of sins.

For if thou didst punish the enemies of thy servants, and that deserved to die, with so great deliberation, giving them time and place whereby they might be changed from their wickedness:

With what circumspection hast thou judged thy own children, to whose parents thou hast sworn, and made covenants of good promises?—*Wis.* xii. 19-21.

For whom hast thou been solicitous and afraid, that thou hast lied, and hast not been mindful of me, nor thought on me in thy heart? for I am silent, and as one that seeth not, and thou hast forgotten me.—*Is.* lvii. 11.

I will not execute the fierceness of my wrath: I will not return to destroy Ephraim: because I am God, and not man: the holy one in the midst of thee, and I will not enter into the city.—*Osee* xi. 9.

Thy eyes are too pure to behold evil, and thou canst not look on iniquity. Why lookest thou upon them that do unjust things, and holdest thy peace when the wicked devoureth the man that is more just than himself?—*Hab.* i. 13.

He spoke also this parable: A certain man had a fig-tree planted in his vineyard, and he came seeking fruit on it, and found none.

And he said to the dresser of the vineyard: Behold, for these three years I come seeking fruit on this fig-tree, and I find none. Cut it down therefore: why cumbereth it the ground?

But he answering, said to him: Lord, let it alone this year also, until I dig about it, and dung it.

And if happily it bear fruit: but if not, then after that thou shalt cut it down.—*Luke* xiii. 6-9.

And he began to speak to the people this parable: A certain man planted a vineyard, and let it out to husbandmen: and he was abroad for a long time.

And at the season he sent a servant to the husbandmen, that they should give him of the fruit of the vineyard. Who, beating him, sent him away empty.

And again he sent another servant. But they beat him also, and treating him reproachfully, sent him away empty.

And again he sent the third: and they wounded him also, and cast him out.

Then the lord of the vineyard said: What shall I do? I will send my beloved son: it may be, when they see him, they will reverence him.—*Luke* xx. 9-13.

What if God, willing to show his wrath, and to make his power known, endured with much patience vessels of wrath, fitted for destruction,

That he might show the riches of his glory on the vessels of mercy, which he hath prepared unto glory?—*Rom.* ix. 22, 23.

But to Israel, he saith: All the day long have I spread my hands to a people that believeth not, and contradicteth me.—*Rom.* x. 21.

The Lord delayeth not his promise, as some imagine, but dealeth patiently for your sake, not willing that any should perish, but that all should return to penance.—2 *Peter* iii. 9.

PEACE THE GIFT OF GOD

For when he granteth peace, who is there that can condemn?—*Job* xxxiv. 29.

The Lord will give strength to his people: the Lord will bless his people with peace.—*Ps.* xxviii. 10.

And I said: Who will give me wings like a dove, and I will fly, and be at rest?—*Ps.* liv. 7.

The old error is passed away: thou wilt keep peace: peace, because we have hoped in thee.—*Is.* xxvi. 3.

Lord, thou wilt give us peace: for thou hast wrought all our works for us —*Is.* xxvi. 12.

I created the fruit of the lips, peace, peace to him that is far off, and to him that is near, said the Lord, and I healed him.—*Is.* lvii. 19.

And when you come into the house, salute it, saying: Peace be to this house.

And if that house be worthy, your peace shall come upon it; but if it be not worthy, your peace shall return to you.—*Matt.* x. 12, 13.

And rising up, he rebuked the wind, and said to the sea: Peace, be still. And the wind ceased: and there was made a great calm.—*Mark* iv. 39.

And suddenly there was with the angel a multitude of the heavenly army, praising God, and saying:

Glory to God in the highest; and on earth, peace to men of good will.—*Luke* ii. 13, 14.

Now whilst they were speaking these things, Jesus stood in the midst of them, and saith to them: Peace be to you; it is I, fear not.—*Luke* xxiv. 36.

Peace I leave with you, my peace I give unto you: not as the world giveth, do I give unto you. Let not your heart be troubled, nor let it be afraid.—*John* xiv. 27.

God sent the word to the children of Israel, preaching peace by Jesus Christ (he is Lord of all).—*Acts* x. 36.

Now the God of peace be with you all. Amen.—*Rom.* xv. 33.

But the fruit of the Spirit is charity, joy, peace, patience, benignity, goodness, longanimity.—*Gal.* v. 22.

PEACE OF THE JUST, THE

Submit thyself then to him (God), and be at peace: and thereby thou shalt have the best fruit.—*Job* xxii. 21.

In peace, in the selfsame I will sleep, and I will rest:

For thou, O Lord, singularly hast settled me in hope.—*Ps.* iv. 9, 10.

Let them rejoice and be glad, who are well pleased with my justice, and let them say always: The Lord be magnified, who delights in the peace of his servant.—*Ps.* xxxiv. 27.

Much peace have they that love thy law, and to them there is no stumbling-block.—*Ps.* cxviii. 165.

I am a wall: and my breasts are as a tower, since I am become in his presence as one finding peace.—*Cant.* viii. 10.

O that thou hadst hearkened to my commandments: thy peace had been as a river, and thy justice as the waves of the sea.—*Is.* xlviii. 18.

All thy children shall be taught of the Lord: and great shall be the peace of thy children.—*Is.* liv. 13.

And I am not troubled, following thee for my pastor, and I have not desired the day of man, thou knowest.—*Jer.* xvii. 16.

For if thou hadst walked in the way of God, thou hadst surely dwelt in peace for ever.—*Bar.* iii. 13.

Through the bowels of the mercy of our God, in which the Orient from on high hath visited us:

To enlighten them that sit in darkness, and in the shadow of death: to direct our feet into the way of peace.—*Luke* i. 78, 79.

These things I have spoken to you, that in me you may have peace. In the world you shall have distress: but have confidence, I have overcome the world.—*John* xvi. 33.

PEACE, A PRAYER FOR

The Lord turn his countenance to thee, and give thee peace.—*Num.* vi. 26.

Give to the king thy judgment, O God; and to the king's son thy justice. . . .

Let the mountains receive peace for the people: and the hills justice.—*Ps.* lxxi. 2, 3.

Pray ye for the things that are for the peace of Jerusalem: and abundance for them that love thee.

Let peace be in thy strength: and abundance in thy towers.

For the sake of my brethren, and of my neighbors, I spoke peace of thee.—*Ps.* cxxi. 6-8.

May he grant us joyfulness of heart, and that there be peace in our days in Israel for ever.—*Ecclus.* l. 25.

Grace to you, and peace from God our Father, and from the Lord Jesus Christ.—*Rom.* i. 7.

And the peace of God, which surpasseth all understanding, keep your hearts and minds in Christ Jesus.—*Philipp.* iv. 7.

Now the Lord of peace himself give you everlasting peace in every place.

The Lord be with you all.—2 *Thess.* iii. 16.

PEACE WITH GOD

Blessed are all they that love thee, and that rejoice in thy peace.—*Tob.* xiii. 18.

I will hear what the Lord God will speak in me: for he will speak peace unto his people:

And unto his saints: and unto them that are converted to the heart.—*Ps.* lxxxiv. 9.

For the peace of God is over all the face of the earth.—*Ecclus.* xxxviii. 8.

How beautiful upon the mountains are the feet of him that bringeth good tidings, and that preacheth peace!—*Is.* lii. 7.

Being justified therefore by faith, let us have peace with God, through our Lord Jesus Christ.—*Rom.* v. 1.

For he is our peace, who hath made both one, and breaking down the middle wall of partition, the enmities in his flesh. . . .

And coming, he preached peace to you that were afar off, and peace to them that were nigh.—*Eph.* ii. 14, 17.

Because in him it hath well pleased the Father, that all fulness should dwell;

And through him, to reconcile all things unto himself, making peace through the blood of his cross, both as to the things that are on earth, and the things that are in heaven.—*Col.* i. 19, 20.

And let the peace of Christ rejoice in your hearts, wherein also you are called in one body: and be ye thankful.—*Col.* iii. 15.

PEACE WITH ONE ANOTHER

See also: Concord, living in—page 70.

Who is the man that desireth life: who loveth to see good days?

Keep thy tongue from evil, and thy lips from speaking guile.

Turn away from evil and do good: seek after peace, and pursue it.—*Ps.* xxxiii. 13-15.

In his days shall justice spring up, and abundance of peace, till the moon be taken away.—*Ps.* lxxi. 7.

With them that hated peace, I was peaceable: when I spoke to them, they fought against me without cause.—*Ps.* cxix. 7.

Deceit is in the heart of them that think evil things: but joy followeth them that take counsels of peace.—*Prov.* xii. 20.

Blessed are the peacemakers: for they shall be called the children of God.—*Matt.* v. 9.

For God is not the God of dissension, but of peace: as also I teach in all the churches of the saints.—1 *Cor.* xiv. 33.

And the fruit of justice is sown in peace, to them that make peace.—*James* iii. 18.

PEACE WITH ONE ANOTHER, EXHORTATION TO HAVE

Be in peace with many, but let one of a thousand be thy counsellor.—*Ecclus.* vi. 6.

Thus saith the Lord of hosts: The fast of the fourth month, and the fast of the fifth, and the fast of the seventh, and the fast of the tenth shall be to the house of Juda joy, and gladness, and great solemnities: only love ye truth and peace.—*Zach.* viii. 19.

If therefore thou offer thy gift at the altar, and there thou remember that thy brother hath any thing against thee;

Leave there thy offering before the altar, and go first to be reconciled to thy brother: and then coming, thou shalt offer thy gift.

Be at agreement with thy adversary betimes, whilst thou art in the way with him: lest perhaps the adversary deliver thee to the judge, and the judge deliver thee to the officer, and thou be cast into prison.

Amen I say to thee, thou shalt not go out from thence till thou repay the last farthing.—*Matt.* v. 23-26.

Salt is good. But if the salt become unsavory; wherewith will you season it? Have salt in you, and have peace among you.—*Mark* ix. 49.

Being of one mind one towards another.—*Rom.* xii. 16.

If it be possible, as much as is in you, have peace with all men.—*Rom.* xii. 18.

Therefore let us follow after the things that are of peace; and keep the things that are of edification, one towards another.—*Rom.* xiv. 19.

For the rest, brethren, rejoice, be perfect, take exhortation, be of one mind, have peace; and the God of peace and of love shall be with you.—*2 Cor.* xiii. 11.

I therefore, a prisoner in the Lord, beseech you that you walk worthy of the vocation in which you are called. . . .

Careful to keep the unity of the Spirit in the bond of peace.—*Eph.* iv. 1, 3.

But flee thou youthful desires, and pursue justice, faith, charity and peace, with them that call on the Lord out of a pure heart.—*2 Tim.* ii. 22.

Follow peace with all men, and holiness: without which no man shall see God.—*Heb.* xii. 14.

PENANCE, OR ATONEMENT FOR SIN, THE EFFICACY OF

And this shall be to you an everlasting ordinance: The seventh month, the tenth day of the month, you shall afflict your souls, and shall do no work, whether it be one of your own country, or a stranger that sojourneth among you.

Upon this day shall be the expiation for you, and the cleansing from all your sins: you shall be cleansed before the Lord.

For it is a sabbath of rest, and you shall afflict your souls by a perpetual religion.

And the priest that is anointed, and whose hands are consecrated to do the office of the priesthood in his father's stead, shall make atonement.—*Lev.* xvi. 29-32.

And if they be converted in their heart in the land to which they were led captive, and do penance, and pray to thee in the land of their captivity, saying: We have sinned, we have done wickedly, we have dealt unjustly: . . .

Then hear thou from heaven, that is, from thy firm dwelling place, their prayers, and do judgment, and forgive thy people, although they have sinned. —*2 Paral.* vi. 37, 39.

If I shut up heaven, and there fall no rain, or if I give orders, and command the locust to devour the land, or if I send pestilence among my people:

And my people, upon whom my name is called, being converted, shall make supplication to me, and seek out my face, and do penance for their most wicked ways: then will I hear from heaven, and will forgive their sins, and will heal their land.—*2 Paral.* vii. 13, 14.

But if the wicked do penance for all his sins which he hath committed, and keep all my commandments, and do judgment and justice, living he shall live, and shall not die.—*Ezech.* xviii. 21.

And if I shall say to the wicked: Thou shalt surely die: and he do penance for his sin, and do judgment, and justice,

And if that wicked man restore the pledge, and render what he had robbed, and walk in the commandments of life, and do no unjust thing: he shall surely live, and shall not die.—*Ezech.* xxxiii. 14, 15.

And Jonas began to enter into the city one day's journey: and he cried, and said: Yet forty days, and Ninive shall be destroyed.

And the men of Ninive believed in God: and they proclaimed a fast, and put on sackcloth, from the greatest to the least. . . .

And God saw their works, that they were turned from their evil way: and God had mercy with regard to the evil which he had said that he would do to them, and he did it not.—*Jonas* iii. 4, 5, 10.

PENANCE, OR ATONEMENT FOR SIN, THE NECESSITY OF

And the Lord spoke to Moses, saying: Upon the tenth day of this seventh month shall be the day of atonement, it shall be most solemn, and shall be called holy: and you shall afflict your souls on that day, and shall offer a holocaust to the Lord.

You shall do no servile work in the time of this day: because it is a day of propitiation, that the Lord your God may be merciful unto you.

Every soul that is not afflicted on

this day, shall perish from among his people.—*Lev.* xxiii. 26-29.

Then Job answered the Lord, and said: . . . Who is this that hideth counsel without knowledge? Therefore I have spoken unwisely, and things that above measure exceed my knowledge. . . . Therefore I reprehend myself, and do penance in dust and ashes.—*Job* xlii. 1, 3, 6.

If we do not penance, we shall fall into the hands of the Lord, and not into the hands of men.—*Ecclus.* ii. 22.

But unless you shall do penance, you shall all likewise perish.—*Luke* xiii. 3.

And God indeed having winked at the times of this ignorance, now declareth unto men, that all should everywhere do penance.

Because he hath appointed a day, wherein he will judge the world in equity, by the man whom he hath appointed; giving faith to all, by raising him up from the dead.—*Acts* xvii. 30, 31.

PENANCE, EXHORTATION TO DO

Therefore will I judge every man according to his ways, O house of Israel, saith the Lord God. Be converted, and do penance for all your iniquities: and iniquity shall not be your ruin.—*Ezech.* xviii. 30.

And in those days cometh John the Baptist, preaching in the desert of Judea.

And saying: Do penance: for the kingdom of heaven is at hand.—*Matt.* iii. 1, 2.

From that time Jesus began to preach, and to say: Do penance, for the kingdom of heaven is at hand.—*Matt.* iv. 17.

But I have somewhat against thee, because thou hast left thy first charity.

Be mindful, therefore, from whence thou art fallen: and do penance, and do the first works. Or else I come to thee, and will move thy candlestick out of its place, except thou do penance.—*Apoc.* ii. 4, 5.

But I have against thee a few things: because thou hast there them that hold the doctrine of Balaam, who taught Balac to cast a stumbling-block before the children of Israel, to eat, and to commit fornication:

So hast thou also them that hold the doctrine of the Nicolaites.

In like manner, do penance: if not, I will come to thee quickly, and will fight against them with the sword of my mouth.—*Apoc.* ii. 14-16.

Be watchful and strengthen the things that remain, which are ready to die. For I find not thy works full before my God.

Have in mind therefore in what manner thou hast received and heard: and observe, and do penance.—*Apoc.* iii. 2, 3.

Such as I love, I rebuke and chastise. Be zealous therefore, and do penance.— *Apoc.* iii. 19.

PEOPLE, GOD IS NEAR TO HIS

See: Near, God is—page 340.

PEOPLE, GOD'S SPECIAL MERCY AND FAVOR TO HIS

See: Mercy to his people, God's— page 314.

PERFECTION

O Lord God of Abraham, and of Isaac, and of Israel, our fathers, keep for ever this will of their heart, and let this mind remain always for the worship of thee.

And give to Solomon, my son, a perfect heart, that he may keep thy commandments, thy testimonies, and thy ceremonies, and do all things.—1 *Paral.* xxix. 18, 19.

Jesus saith to him (the rich young man): If thou wilt be perfect, go, sell what thou hast, and give to the poor, and thou shalt have treasure in heaven: and come, follow me.—*Matt.* xix. 21.

I am the true vine; and my Father is the husbandman.

Every branch in me, that beareth not fruit, he will take away; and every one that beareth fruit, he will purge it, that it may bring forth more fruit.—*John* xv. 1, 2.

This also we pray for, your perfection.—2 *Cor.* xiii. 9.

Whom we preach, admonishing every man, and teaching every man in all wisdom, that we may present every man perfect in Christ Jesus.—*Col.* i. 28.

But above all these things, have charity, which is the bond of perfection.—*Col.* iii. 14.

Epaphras saluteth you, who is one of you, a servant of Christ Jesus, who is always solicitous for you in prayers, that you may stand perfect and full in all the will of God.—*Col.* iv. 12.

All scripture, inspired of God, is profitable to teach, to reprove, to correct, to instruct in justice,

That the man of God may be perfect, furnished to every good work.—*2 Tim.* iii. 16, 17.

My brethren, count it all joy, when you shall fall into divers temptations;

Knowing that the trying of your faith worketh patience.

And patience hath a perfect work; that you may be perfect and entire, failing in nothing.—*James* i. 2-4.

PERFECTION, WE SHOULD STRIVE AFTER

And after he (Abraham) began to be ninety and nine years old, the Lord appeared to him: and said unto him: I am the Almighty God: walk before me, and be perfect.—*Gen.* xvii. 1.

Thou shalt be perfect, and without spot before the Lord thy God.—*Deut.* xviii. 13.

Let our hearts also be perfect with the Lord our God, that we may walk in his statutes, and keep his commandments, as at this day.—*3 Kings* viii. 61.

Be you therefore perfect, as also your heavenly Father is perfect.—*Matt.* v. 48.

For the rest, brethren, rejoice, be perfect, take exhortation, be of one mind, have peace; and the God of peace and of love shall be with you.—*2 Cor.* xiii. 11.

PERJURY

Thou shalt not swear falsely by my name, nor profane the name of thy God. I am the Lord.—*Lev.* xix. 12.

And I turned, and lifted up my eyes: and I saw, and behold a volume flying. . . . And he (the angel) said to me:

This is the curse that goeth forth over the face of the earth: for every thief shall be judged, as is there written: and every one that sweareth, in like manner shall be judged by it.

I will bring it forth, saith the Lord of hosts: and it shall come to the house of the thief, and to the house of him that sweareth falsely by my name: and it shall remain in the midst of his house, and shall consume it, with the timber thereof, and the stones thereof.—*Zach.* v. 1, 3, 4.

And let none of you imagine evil in your hearts against his friend: and love not a false oath: for all these are the things that I hate, saith the Lord. —*Zach.* viii. 17.

And I will come to you in judgment, and will be a speedy witness against sorcerers, and adulterers, and false swearers; . . . saith the Lord of hosts. —*Malach.* iii. 5.

Again you have heard that it was said to them of old, Thou shalt not forswear thyself: but thou shalt perform thy oaths to the Lord.—*Matt.* v. 33.

PERSECUTION FOR THE SAKE OF CHRIST, SUFFERING

See also: Martyrs, constancy of the —page 304.

Blessed are they that suffer persecution for justice' sake: for theirs is the kingdom of heaven.

Blessed are ye when they shall revile you, and persecute you, and speak all that is evil against you, untruly, for my sake:

Be glad and rejoice, for your reward is very great in heaven. For so they persecuted the prophets that were before you.—*Matt.* v. 10-12.

Blessed shall you be when men shall hate you, and when they shall separate you, and shall reproach you, and cast out your name as evil, for the Son of man's sake.

Be glad in that day and rejoice; for behold, your reward is great in heaven. —*Luke* vi. 22, 23.

Think ye, that I am come to give peace on earth? I tell you, no; but separation.

For there shall be from henceforth

five in one house divided: three against two, and two against three.

The father shall be divided against the son, and the son against his father, the mother against the daughter, and the daughter against the mother, the mother-in-law against her daughter-in-law, and the daughter-in-law against her mother-in-law.—*Luke* xii. 51-53.

And calling in the apostles, after they had scourged them, they charged them that they should not speak at all in the name of Jesus; and they dismissed them.

And they indeed went from the presence of the council, rejoicing that they were accounted worthy to suffer reproach for the name of Jesus.—*Acts* v. 40, 41.

And the Lord said to him (Ananias): Go thy way; for this man is to me a vessel of election, to carry my name before the Gentiles, and kings, and the children of Israel.

For I will show him how great things he must suffer for my name's sake.—*Acts* ix. 15, 16.

For I think that God hath set forth us apostles, the last, as it were men appointed to death: we are made a spectacle to the world, and to angels, and to men.

We are fools for Christ's sake, but you are wise in Christ; we are weak, but you are strong; you are honorable, but we without honor.

Even unto this hour we both hunger and thirst, and are naked, and are buffeted, and have no fixed abode;

And we labor, working with our own hands: we are reviled, and we bless; we are persecuted, and we suffer it.

We are blasphemed, and we entreat; we are made as the refuse of this world, the offscouring of all even until now.— 1 *Cor.* iv. 9-13.

They are the ministers of Christ (I speak as one less wise): I am more; in many more labors, in prisons more frequently, in stripes above measure, in deaths often.

Of the Jews five times did I receive forty stripes, save one.

Thrice was I beaten with rods, once I was stoned, thrice I suffered ship-wreck, a night and a day I was in the depth of the sea.—2 *Cor.* xi. 23-25.

For which cause I please myself in my infirmities, in reproaches, in necessities, in persecutions, in distresses, for Christ. For when I am weak, then am I powerful.—2 *Cor.* xii. 10.

Now we, brethren, as Isaac was, are the children of promise.

But as then he that was born according to the flesh, persecuted him that was after the spirit; so also it is now.— *Gal.* iv. 28, 29.

And in nothing be ye terrified by the adversaries: which to them is a cause of perdition, but to you of salvation, and this from God:

For unto you it is given for Christ, not only to believe in him, but also to suffer for him.—*Philipp.* i. 28, 29.

But thou hast fully known my, . . . Persecutions, afflictions: such as came upon me at Antioch, at Iconium, and at Lystra: what persecutions I endured, and out of them all the Lord delivered me.—2 *Tim.* iii. 10, 11.

And all that will live godly in Christ Jesus, shall suffer persecution.—2 *Tim.* iii. 12.

But call to mind the former days, wherein, being illuminated, you endured a great fight of afflictions.

And on the one hand indeed, by reproaches and tribulations, were made a gazing stock; and on the other, became companions of them that were used in such sort.

For you both had compassion on them that were in bands, and took with joy the being stripped of your own goods, knowing that you have a better and a lasting substance.

Do not therefore lose your confidence, which hath a great reward.—*Heb.* x. 32-35.

But if also you suffer any thing for justice' sake, blessed are ye. And be not afraid of their fear, and be not troubled.—1 *Peter* iii. 14.

If you be reproached for the name of Christ, you shall be blessed: for that which is of the honor, glory and power of God, and that which is his Spirit, resteth upon you.

But let none of you suffer as a murderer, or a thief, or a railer, or a coveter of other men's things.

But if as a Christian, let him not be ashamed, but let him glorify God in that name.—1 *Peter* iv. 14-16.

Fear none of those things which thou shalt suffer. Behold, the devil will cast some of you into prison, that you may be tried: and you shall have tribulation ten days. Be thou faithful unto death: and I will give thee the crown of life.—*Apoc.* ii. 10.

PERSECUTION OF THE CHURCH

See: Church—page 54.

PERSEVERANCE, THE NECESSITY OF

Woe to them that are faint-hearted, who believe not God: and therefore they shall not be protected by him.

Woe to them that have lost patience, and that have forsaken the right ways, and have gone aside into crooked ways.

And what will they do, when the Lord shall begin to examine?—*Ecclus.* ii. 15-17.

Yea, if I shall say to the just, that he shall surely live, and he, trusting in his justice, commit iniquity: all his justices shall be forgotten, and in his iniquity, which he hath committed, in the same shall he die. . . .

For when the just shall depart from his justice, and commit iniquities, he shall die in them.—*Ezech.* xxxiii. 13,18.

Jesus said to him: No man putting his hand to the plough, and looking back, is fit for the kingdom of God.—*Luke* ix. 62.

Now I make known unto you, brethren, the gospel which I preached to you, which also you have received, and wherein you stand;

By which also you are saved, if you hold fast after what manner I preached unto you, unless you have believed in vain.—1 *Cor.* xv. 1, 2.

I know thy works, and thy labor, and thy patience, and how thou canst not bear them that are evil, and thou hast tried them who say they are apostles, and are not, and hast found them liars:

And thou hast patience, and hast en-dured for my name, and hast not fainted.

But I have somewhat against thee, because thou hast left thy first charity.

Be mindful, therefore, from whence thou art fallen: and do penance, and do the first works. Or else I come to thee, and will move thy candlestick out of its place, except thou do penance.—*Apoc.* ii. 2-5.

PERSEVERANCE, THE REWARD OF

For we are the children of saints, and look for that life which God will give to those that never change their faith from him.—*Tob.* ii. 18.

But he that shall persevere to the end, he shall be saved.—*Matt.* xxiv. 13.

Then Jesus said to those Jews who believed him: If you continue in my word, you shall be my disciples indeed.

And you shall know the truth, and the truth shall make you free.—*John* viii. 31, 32.

I have glorified thee on the earth; I have finished the work which thou gavest me to do.

And now, glorify thou me, O Father, with thyself, with the glory which I had, before the world was, with thee.—*John* xvii. 4, 5.

And you, whereas you were some time alienated and enemies in mind in evil works:

Yet now he hath reconciled in the body of his flesh through death, to present you holy and unspotted, and blameless before him:

If so ye continue in the faith, grounded and settled, and immovable from the hope of the gospel which you have heard, which is preached in all the creation that is under heaven, whereof I, Paul, am made a minister.—*Col.* i. 21-23.

I have fought a good fight, I have finished my course, I have kept the faith.

As to the rest, there is laid up for me a crown of justice, which the Lord, the just judge, will render to me in that day: and not only to me, but to them also that love his coming. —2 *Tim.* iv. 7, 8.

And Moses indeed was faithful in all

his house as a servant, for a testimony of those things which were to be said: But Christ, as the Son, in his own house: which house are we, if we hold fast the confidence and glory of hope unto the end.—*Heb.* iii. 5, 6.

For we are made partakers of Christ: yet so, if we hold the beginning of his substance firm unto the end.—*Heb.* iii. 14.

Fear none of those things which thou shalt suffer. Behold, the devil will cast some of you into prison that you may be tried: and you shall have tribulation ten days. Be thou faithful unto death: and I will give thee the crown of life.—*Apoc.* ii. 10.

And he that shall overcome, and keep my works unto the end, I will give him power over the nations.—*Apoc.* ii. 26.

PERSEVERANCE, EXHORTATION TO

And know the justices and judgments of God, and stand firm in the lot set before thee, and in prayer to the most high God.—*Ecclus.* xvii. 24.

Let nothing hinder thee from praying always, and be not afraid to be justified even to death: for the reward of God continueth for ever.—*Ecclus.* xviii. 22.

Who (Barnabas), when he was come, and had seen the grace of God, rejoiced: and he exhorted them all with purpose of heart to continue in the Lord.—*Acts* xi. 23.

And when they (Paul and Barnabas) had preached the gospel to that city, and had taught many, they returned again to Lystra, and to Iconium, and to Antioch:

Confirming the souls of the disciples, and exhorting them to continue in the faith: and that through many tribulations we must enter into the kingdom of God.—*Acts* xiv. 20, 21.

Therefore, my beloved brethren, be ye steadfast and unmovable; always abounding in the work of the Lord, knowing that your labor is not in vain in the Lord.—1 *Cor.* xv. 58.

Watch ye, stand fast in the faith, do manfully, and be strengthened.—1 *Cor.* xvi. 13.

And in doing good, let us not fail.

For in due time we shall reap, not failing.—*Gal.* vi. 9.

Therefore, my dearly beloved brethren, and most desired, my joy and my crown; so stand fast in the Lord, my dearly beloved.—*Philipp.* iv. 1.

But prove all things; hold fast that which is good.—1 *Thess.* v. 21.

But you, brethren, be not weary in well doing.—2 *Thess.* iii. 13.

And we desire that every one of you show forth the same carefulness to the accomplishing of hope unto the end:

That you become not slothful, but followers of them, who through faith and patience, shall inherit the promises. —*Heb.* vi. 11, 12.

Do not therefore lose your confidence, which hath a great reward.

For patience is necessary for you; that, doing the will of God, you may receive the promise.

For yet a little, and a very little while, and he that is to come, will come, and will not delay.—*Heb.* x. 35-37.

Look to yourselves, that you lose not the things which you have wrought: but that you may receive a full reward. —2 *John* i. 8.

But you, my beloved, building yourselves upon your most holy faith, praying in the Holy Ghost,

Keep yourselves in the love of God, waiting for the mercy of our Lord Jesus Christ, unto life everlasting.— *Jude* i. 20, 21.

Yet that, which you have, hold fast till I come.—*Apoc.* ii. 25.

Behold, I come quickly: hold fast that which thou hast, that no man take thy crown.—*Apoc.* iii. 11.

PERSEVERANCE THE GIFT OF GOD

So that nothing is wanting to you in any grace, waiting for the manifestation of our Lord Jesus Christ.

Who also will confirm you unto the end without crime, in the day of the coming of our Lord Jesus Christ.— 1 *Cor.* i. 7, 8.

Being confident of this very thing, that he, who hath begun a good work in you, will perfect it unto the day of Christ Jesus.—*Philipp.* i. 6.

Now to him who is able to preserve you without sin, and to present you spotless before the presence of his glory, with exceeding joy, in the coming of our Lord Jesus Christ,

To the only God our Saviour through Jesus Christ our Lord, be glory and magnificence, empire and power, before all ages, and now, and for all ages of ages. Amen.—*Jude* i. 24, 25.

PERSEVERANCE, A PRAYER FOR

O Lord God of Abraham, and of Isaac, and of Israel, our fathers, keep for ever this will of their heart, and let this mind remain always for the worship of thee.—*1 Paral.* xxix. 18.

Command thy strength, O God: confirm, O God, what thou hast wrought in us.—*Ps.* lxvii. 29.

And may the God of peace himself sanctify you in all things; that your whole spirit, and soul, and body, may be preserved blameless in the coming of our Lord Jesus Christ.

He is faithful who hath called you, who also will do it.—*1 Thess.* v. 23, 24.

PHYSICIAN OF OUR SOUL AND BODY, GOD IS THE

If thou wilt hear the voice of the Lord thy God, and do what is right before him, and obey his commandments, and keep all his precepts, none of the evils that I laid upon Egypt, will I bring upon thee: for I am the Lord thy healer.—*Ex.* xv. 26.

Bless the Lord, O my soul, and never forget all that he hath done for thee.

Who forgiveth all thy iniquities: who healeth all thy diseases.—*Ps.* cii. 2, 3.

Their soul abhorred all manner of meat: and they drew nigh even to the gates of death.

And they cried to the Lord in their affliction: and he delivered them out of their distresses.

He sent his word, and healed them: and delivered them from their destructions.—*Ps.* cvi. 18-20.

For he that turned to [1]it, was not

[1]The brazen serpent raised by Moses in the desert.

healed by that which he saw, but by thee, the Saviour of all.—*Wis.* xvi. 7.

But not even the teeth of venomous serpents overcame thy children: for thy mercy came and healed them. . . .

For it was neither herb, nor mollifying plaster that healed them, but thy word, O Lord, which healeth all things. —*Wis.* xvi. 10, 12.

Honor the physician for the need thou hast of him: for the most High hath created him.

For all healing is from God.—*Ecclus.* xxxviii. 1, 2.

Heal me, O Lord, and I shall be healed: save me, and I shall be saved: for thou art my praise.—*Jer.* xvii. 14.

Behold I will close their wounds and give them health, and I will cure them: and I will reveal to them the prayer of peace and truth.—*Jer.* xxxiii. 6.

PLEASURES, VANITY OF

I said in my heart: I will go, and abound with delights, and enjoy good things. And I saw that this also was vanity. . . .

And whatsoever my eyes desired, I refused them not: and I withheld not my heart from enjoying every pleasure, and delighting itself in the things which I had prepared: and esteemed this my portion, to make use of my own labor.

And when I turned myself to all the works which my hands had wrought, and to the labors wherein I had labored in vain, I saw in all things vanity, and vexation of mind, and that nothing was lasting under the sun.—*Eccles.* ii. 1, 10, 11.

Remove anger from thy heart, and put away evil from thy flesh. For youth and pleasure are vain.—*Eccles.* xi. 10.

Good things that are hidden in a mouth that is shut, are as messes of meat set about a grave.

What good shall an offering do to an idol? for it can neither eat, nor smell: So is he that is persecuted by the Lord, bearing the reward of his iniquity.—*Ecclus.* xxx. 18-20.

For she that liveth in pleasures, is dead while she is living.—*1 Tim.* v. 6.

POLITENESS

A man amiable in society, shall be more friendly than a brother.—*Prov.* xviii. 24.

Make thyself affable to the congregation of the poor, and humble thy soul to the ancient, and bow thy head to a great man.—*Ecclus.* iv. 7.

Art thou set at a great table? be not the first to open thy mouth upon it.

Say not: There are many things which are upon it. . . .

Stretch not out thy hand first, lest being disgraced with envy thou be put to confusion.

Be not hasty in a feast. . . .

Use as a frugal man the things that are set before thee: lest, if thou eatest much, thou be hated.

Leave off first, for manner's sake: and exceed not, lest thou offend.

And if thou sittest among many, reach not thy hand out first of all: and be not the first to ask for drink.—*Ecclus.* xxxi. 12, 13, 16, 17, 19-21.

Wherefore have a shame of these things I am now going to speak of. . . .

Of leaning with thy elbow over meat. . . .

Of silence before them that salute thee.—*Ecclus.* xli. 19, 24, 25.

POOR, THE

Fear not, my son; we lead indeed a poor life, but we shall have many good things if we fear God, and depart from all sin, and do that which is good.— *Tob.* iv. 23.

Let not the humble be turned away with confusion: the poor and needy shall praise thy name.—*Ps.* lxxiii. 21.

Riches make many friends: but from the poor man, even they whom he had, depart.

. . . The brethren of the poor man, hate him: moreover also his friends have departed far from him.—*Prov.* xix. 4, 7.

The rich and poor have met one another: the Lord is the maker of them both.—*Prov.* xxii. 2.

The poor man and the creditor have met one another: the Lord is the enlightener of them both.—*Prov.* xxix. 13.

The poor man is glorified by his discipline and fear.—*Ecclus.* x. 33.

For it is easy in the eyes of God on a sudden to make the poor man rich.— *Ecclus.* xi. 23.

The rich man hath done wrong, and yet he will fume: but the poor is wronged, and must hold his peace. . . .

When a rich man is shaken, he is kept up by his friends: but when a poor man is fallen down, he is thrust away even by his acquaintance.

When a rich man hath been deceived, he hath many helpers: he hath spoken proud things, and they have justified him.

The poor man was deceived, and he is rebuked also: he hath spoken wisely, and could have no place.

The rich man spoke, and all held their peace, and what he said they extol even to the clouds.

The poor man spoke, and they say: Who is this? and if he stumble, they will overthrow him.—*Ecclus.* xiii. 4, 25-29.

Three sorts my soul hateth, and I am greatly grieved at their life:

A poor man that is proud: a rich man that is a liar: an old man that is a fool, and doting.—*Ecclus.* xxv. 3, 4.

Better is a poor man who is sound, and strong of constitution, than a rich man who is weak and afflicted with evils.—*Ecclus.* xxx. 14.

And in that day the deaf shall hear the words of the book, and out of darkness and obscurity the eyes of the blind shall see.

And the meek shall increase their joy in the Lord, and the poor men shall rejoice in the Holy One of Israel.—*Is.* xxix. 18, 19.

There was a certain rich man, who was clothed in purple and fine linen; and feasted sumptuously every day.

And there was a certain beggar, named Lazarus, who lay at his gate, full of sores,

Desiring to be filled with the crumbs that fell from the rich man's table, and no one did give him; moreover the dogs came, and licked his sores.

And it came to pass, that the beggar died, and was carried by the angels into

Abraham's bosom. And the rich man also died: and he was buried in hell.

And lifting up his eyes, when he was in torments, he saw Abraham afar off, and Lazarus in his bosom:

And he cried, and said: Father Abraham, have mercy on me, and send Lazarus, that he may dip the tip of his finger in water, to cool my tongue: for I am tormented in this flame.

And Abraham said to him: Son, remember that thou didst receive good things in thy lifetime, and likewise Lazarus evil things, but now he is comforted; and thou art tormented.—*Luke* xvi. 19-25.

Now we make known unto you, brethren, the grace of God, that hath been given in the churches of Macedonia.

That in much experience of tribulation, they have had abundance of joy; and their very deep poverty hath abounded unto the riches of their simplicity.—*2 Cor.* viii. 1, 2.

But let the brother of low condition glory in his exaltation.—*James* i. 9.

POOR ARE ALWAYS WITH US, THE

There will not be wanting poor in the land of thy habitation: therefore I command thee to open thy hand to thy needy and poor brother, that liveth in the land.—*Deut.* xv. 11.

For the poor you have always with you: and whensoever you will, you may do them good: but me you have not always.—*Mark* xiv. 7.

POOR ARE PLEASING TO GOD, THE

He shall spare the poor and needy: . . . And their names shall be honorable in his sight.—*Ps.* lxxi. 13, 14.

Better is the poor man that walketh in his simplicity, than a rich man that is perverse in his lips, and unwise.—*Prov.* xix. 1.

Better is the poor man walking in his simplicity, than the rich in crooked ways.—*Prov.* xxviii. 6.

Behold I have refined thee, but not as silver, I have chosen thee in the furnace of poverty.—*Is.* xlviii. 10.

Blessed are the poor in spirit: for theirs is the kingdom of heaven.—*Matt.* v. 3.

And he, lifting up his eyes on his disciples, said: Blessed are ye, poor, for yours is the kingdom of heaven.

Blessed are ye that hunger now: for you shall be filled. Blessed are ye that weep now: for you shall laugh.—*Luke* vi. 20, 21.

Hearken, my dearest brethren: hath not God chosen the poor in this world, rich in faith, and heirs of the kingdom, which God hath promised to them that love him?—*James* ii. 5.

POOR, GOD IS MINDFUL OF THE

For the poor man shall not be forgotten to the end: the patience of the poor shall not perish for ever.—*Ps.* ix. 19.

The Lord is in his holy temple, the Lord's throne is in heaven.

His eyes look on the poor man: his eyelids examine the sons of men.—*Ps.* x. 5.

Who is as the Lord our God, who dwelleth on high:

And looketh down on the low things in heaven and in earth?

Raising up the needy from the earth, and lifting up the poor out of the dunghill:

That he may place him with princes, with the princes of his people.—*Ps.* cxii. 5-8.

For God will not except any man's person; neither will he stand in awe of any man's greatness: for he made the little and the great, and he hath equally care of all.—*Wis.* vi. 8.

But to whom shall I have respect, but to him that is poor and little, and of a contrite heart, and that trembleth at my words?—*Is.* lxvi. 2.

POOR, GOD IS THE HELPER AND PROTECTOR OF THE

But he shall save the needy from the sword of their mouth, and the poor from the hand of the violent.

And to the needy there shall be hope, but iniquity shall draw in her mouth.—*Job* v. 15, 16.

He shall deliver the poor out of his distress, and shall open his ear in affliction.—*Job* xxxvi. 15.

And the Lord is become a refuge for the poor: a helper in due time in tribulation.—*Ps.* ix. 10.

To thee is the poor man left: thou wilt be a helper to the orphan.—*Ps.* ix. (*Heb.* x.) 14.

By reason of the misery of the needy, and the groans of the poor, now will I arise, saith the Lord.

I will set him in safety; I will deal confidently in his regard.—*Ps.* xi. 6.

For the Lord is in the just generation: you have confounded the counsel of the poor man, but the Lord is his hope.—*Ps.* xiii. 6.

All my bones shall say: Lord, who is like to thee?

Who deliverest the poor from the hand of them that are stronger than he; the needy and the poor from them that strip him.—*Ps.* xxxiv. 10.

But I am a beggar and poor: the Lord is careful for me.

Thou art my helper and my protector: O my God, be not slack.—*Ps.* xxxix. 18.

He shall judge the poor of the people, and he shall save the children of the poor: and he shall humble the oppressor.—*Ps.* lxxi. 4.

For he shall deliver the poor from the mighty: and the needy that had no helper.

He shall spare the poor and needy: and he shall save the souls of the poor.

He shall redeem their souls from usuries and iniquity.—*Ps.* lxxi. 12-14.

I know that the Lord will do justice to the needy, and will revenge the poor. —*Ps.* cxxxix. 13.

And there shall come forth a rod out of the root of Jesse, and a flower shall rise up out of his root. . . .

But he shall judge the poor with justice, and shall reprove with equity for the meek of the earth.—*Is.* xi. 1, 4.

And what shall be answered to the messengers of the nations? That the Lord hath founded Sion, and the poor of his people shall hope in him.—*Is.* xiv. 32.

O Lord, thou art my God, I will exalt thee, and give glory to thy name: for thou hast done wonderful things, thy designs of old faithful, amen⸱ . . .

Because thou hast been a strength to the poor, a strength to the needy in his distress: a refuge from the whirlwind, a shadow from the heat. For the blast of the mighty is like a whirlwind beating against a wall.—*Is.* xxv. 1, 4.

Sing ye to the Lord, praise the Lord: because he hath delivered the soul of the poor out of the hand of the wicked. —*Jer.* xx. 13.

POOR, GOD HEARS THE CRY AND PRAYER OF THE

Sing ye to the Lord who dwelleth in Sion: declare his ways among the Gentiles:

For requiring their blood he hath remembered them: he hath not forgotten the cry of the poor.—*Ps.* ix. 12, 13.

The Lord hath heard the desire of the poor: thy ear hath heard the preparation of their heart.—*Ps.* ix. (*Heb.* x.) 17.

Let all the seed of Israel fear him: because he hath not slighted nor despised the supplication of the poor man. —*Ps.* xxi. 25.

Let the poor see and rejoice: seek ye God, and your soul shall live.

For the Lord hath heard the poor: and hath not despised his prisoners.— *Ps.* lxviii. 33, 34.

The prayer out of the mouth of the poor shall reach the ears of God, and judgment shall come for him speedily. —*Ecclus.* xxi. 6.

The Lord will not accept any person against a poor man, and he will hear the prayer of him that is wronged.

He will not despise the prayers of the fatherless; nor the widow, when she poureth out her complaint.

Do not the widow's tears run down the cheek, and her cry against him that causeth them to fall?

For from the cheek they go up even to heaven, and the Lord that heareth, will not be delighted with them.— *Ecclus.* xxxv. 16-19.

The needy and the poor seek for waters, and there are none: their tongue hath been dry with thirst. I, the Lord, will hear them, I, the God of Israel, will not forsake them.—*Is.* xli. 17.

POOR, GOD PROVIDES FOR THE

The poor shall eat, and shall be filled: and they shall praise the Lord, that seek him: their hearts shall live for ever and ever.—*Ps.* xxi. 27.

In thy sweetness, O God, thou hast provided for the poor.—*Ps.* lxvii. 11.

Blessing I will bless her widow: I will satisfy her poor with bread.—*Ps.* cxxxi. 15.

And the first-born of the poor shall be fed, and the poor shall rest with confidence.—*Is.* xiv. 30.

He hath filled the hungry with good things; and the rich he hath sent empty away.—*Luke* i. 53.

POOR, WE SHOULD HELP THE

See: Almsgiving—page 23.

POOR, WE SHOULD DO JUSTICE TO THE

Judge for the needy and fatherless: do justice to the humble and the poor.

Rescue the poor; and deliver the needy out of the hand of the sinner.—*Ps.* lxxxi. 3, 4.

The just taketh notice of the cause of the poor: the wicked is void of knowledge.—*Prov.* xxix. 7.

Open thy mouth for the dumb, and for the causes of all the children that pass.

Open thy mouth, decree that which is .just, and do justice to the needy and poor.—*Prov.* xxxi. 8, 9.

Bow down thy ear cheerfully to the poor, and pay what thou owest, and answer him peaceable words with mildness.—*Ecclus.* iv. 8.

Shalt thou reign, because thou comparest thyself to the cedar? did not thy father eat and drink, and do judgment and justice, and it was then well with him?

He judged the cause of the poor and needy for his own good: was it not therefore, because he knew me, saith the Lord?—*Jer.* xxii. 15, 16.

POOR, AGAINST DEFRAUDING THE

Thou shalt not calumniate thy neighbor, nor oppress him by violence. The wages of him that hath been hired by thee, shall not abide with thee until the morning.—*Lev.* xix. 13.

Thou shalt not refuse the hire of the needy and the poor, whether he be thy brother, or a stranger that dwelleth with thee in the land, and is within thy gates:

But thou shalt pay him the price of his labor the same day, before the going down of the sun, because he is poor, and with it maintaineth his life: lest he cry against thee to the Lord, and it be reputed to thee for a sin.—*Deut.* xxiv. 14, 15.

If any man hath done any work for thee, immediately pay him his hire, and let not the wages of thy hired servant stay with thee at all.—*Tob.* iv. 15.

He that offereth sacrifice of the goods of the poor, is as one that sacrificeth the son in the presence of his father.

The bread of the needy is the life of the poor: he that defraudeth them thereof, is a man of blood.

He that taketh away the bread gotten by sweat, is like him that killeth his neighbor.

He that sheddeth blood, and he that defraudeth the laborer of his hire, are brothers.—*Ecclus.* xxxiv. 24-27.

Behold the hire of the laborers, who have reaped down your fields, which by fraud, has been kept back by you, crieth: and the cry of them hath entered into the ears of the Lord of sabaoth.—*James* v. 4.

POOR, OPPRESSION OF THE

If thou lend money to any of my people that is poor, that dwelleth with thee, thou shalt not be hard upon them as an extortioner, nor oppress them with usuries.—*Ex.* xxii. 25.

If I have lifted up my hand against the fatherless, even when I saw myself superior in the gate:

Let my shoulder fall from its joint, and let my arm with its bones, be broken.—*Job* xxxi. 21, 22.

He that oppresseth the poor, upbraideth his Maker: but he that hath pity on the poor, honoreth him.—*Prov.* xiv. 31.

A poor man that oppresseth the poor, is like a violent shower, which bringeth a famine.—*Prov.* xxviii. 3.

Thy princes are faithless, companions of thieves: they all love bribes, they run after rewards. They judge not for the fatherless: and the widow's cause cometh not in to them.—*Is.* i. 23.

Woe to them that make wicked laws: and when they write, write injustice:

To oppress the poor in judgment, and do violence to the cause of the humble of my people: that widows might be their prey, and that they might rob the fatherless.

What will you do in the day of visitation, and of the calamity which cometh from afar? to whom will ye flee for help? and where will ye leave your glory?—*Is.* x. 1-3.

And oppress not the widow, and the fatherless, and the stranger, and the poor: and let not a man devise evil in his heart against his brother.—*Zach.* vii. 10.

And I will come to you in judgment, and will be a speedy witness against sorcerers, and adulterers, and false swearers, and them that oppress the hireling in his wages, the widows, and the fatherless: and oppress the stranger, and have not feared me, saith the Lord of hosts.—*Malach.* iii. 5.

POOR, PUNISHMENT OF OPPRESSION OF THE

He shall be punished for all that he did, and yet shall not be consumed: according to the multitude of his devices so also shall he suffer.

Because he broke in and stripped the poor: he hath violently taken away a house which he did not build.—*Job* xx. 18, 19.

Times are not hid from the Almighty: but they that know him, know not his days.

Some have removed landmarks, have taken away flocks by force, and fed them.

They have driven away the ass of the fatherless, and have taken away the widow's ox for a pledge.

They have overturned the way of the poor, and have oppressed together the meek of the earth.

. . . They reap the field that is not their own, and gather the vintage of

his vineyard whom by violence they have oppressed.

They send men away naked, taking away their clothes who have no covering in the cold:

Who are wet with the showers of the mountains, and having no covering, embrace the stones.

They have violently robbed the fatherless, and stripped the poor common people.

From the naked, and them that go without clothing, and from the hungry, they have taken away the ears of corn.

They have taken their rest at noon among the stores of them, who after having trodden the wine presses, suffer thirst.

Out of the cities they have made men to groan, and the soul of the wounded hath cried out, and God doth not suffer it to pass unrevenged.—*Job* xxiv. 1-4, 6-12.

May his days be few: and his bishopric let another take. . . .

Because he remembered not to show mercy,

But persecuted the poor man and the beggar; and the broken in heart, to put him to death.—*Ps.* cviii. 8, 16, 17.

I know that the Lord will do justice to the needy, and will revenge the poor.—*Ps.* cxxxix. 13.

He that oppresseth the poor, to increase his own riches, shall himself give to one that is richer, and shall be in need.—*Prov.* xxii. 16.

Do no violence to the poor, because he is poor: and do not oppress the needy in the gate:

Because the Lord will judge his cause, and will afflict them that have afflicted his soul.—*Prov.* xxii. 22, 23.

They are grown gross and fat: and have most wickedly transgressed my words. They have not judged the cause of the widow, they have not managed the cause of the fatherless, and they have not judged the judgment of the poor.

Shall I not visit for these things, saith the Lord? or shall not my soul take revenge on such a nation?—*Jer.* v. 28, 29.

Therefore because you robbed the poor, and took the choice prey from him: you shall build houses with square stone, and shall not dwell in them: you shall plant most delightful vineyards, and shall not drink the wine of them.

Because I know your manifold crimes, and your grievous sins: enemies of the just, taking bribes, and oppressing the poor in the gate.—*Amos* v. 11, 12.

Hear this, you that crush the poor, and make the needy of the land to fail,

Saying: When will the month be over, and we shall sell our wares: and the sabbath, and we shall open the corn: that we may lessen the measure, and increase the sicle, and may convey in deceitful balances,

That we may possess the needy for money, and the poor for a pair of shoes, and may sell the refuse of the corn?

The Lord hath sworn against the pride of Jacob: Surely I will never forget all their works.

Shall not the land tremble for this, and every one mourn that dwelleth therein: and rise up altogether as a river, and be cast out, and run down as the river of Egypt?—*Amos* viii. 4-8.

POOR, DESPISING THE

If I have despised him that was perishing for want of clothing, and the poor man that had no covering. . . .

Let my shoulder fall from its joint, and let my arm with its bones, be broken.—*Job* xxxi. 19, 22.

The poor man shall be hateful even to his own neighbor: but the friends of the rich are many.

He that despiseth his neighbor sinneth: but he that showeth mercy to the poor, shall be blessed.—*Prov.* xiv. 20. 21.

He that despiseth the poor, reproacheth his Maker.—*Prov.* xvii. 5.

Many honor the person of him that is mighty, and are friends of him that giveth gifts.

The brethren of the poor man hate him: moreover also his friends have departed far from him.—*Prov.* xix. 6, 7.

Make thyself affable to the congregation of the poor. . . .

Bow down thy ear cheerfully to the poor, and pay what thou owest, and answer him peaceable words with mildness.—*Ecclus.* iv. 7, 8.

Despise not a just man that is poor, and do not magnify a sinful man that is rich.—*Ecclus.* x. 26.

Deal thy bread to the hungry, and bring the needy and the harborless into thy house: when thou shalt see one naked, cover him, and despise not thy own flesh.—*Is.* lviii. 7.

For if there shall come into your assembly a man having a golden ring, in fine apparel, and there shall come in also a poor man in mean attire,

And you shall have respect to him that is clothed with the fine apparel, and shall say to him: Sit thou here well; but say to the poor man: Stand thou there, or sit under my footstool:

Do you not judge within yourselves, and are become judges of unjust thoughts?

Hearken, my dearest brethren: hath not God chosen the poor in this world, rich in faith, and heirs of the kingdom which God hath promised to them that love him?

But you have dishonored the poor man. . . .

If then you fulfil the royal law according to the scriptures, Thou shalt love thy neighbor as thyself; you do well.

But if you have respect to persons, you commit sin, being reproved by the law as transgressors.—*James* ii. 2-6, 8, 9.

POOR, REFUSING AID TO THE

If one of thy brethren that dwelleth within the gates of thy city in the land which the Lord thy God will give thee, come to poverty: thou shalt not harden thy heart, nor close thy hand,

But shalt open it to the poor man, thou shalt lend him that which thou perceivest he hath need of.

Beware lest perhaps a wicked thought steal in upon thee, and thou say in thy heart: The seventh year of remission draweth nigh; and thou turn away thy eyes from thy poor brother, denying to lend him that which he asketh: lest he cry against thee to the Lord, and it become a sin unto thee.

But thou shalt give to him: neither

shalt thou do anything craftily in relieving his necessities: that the Lord thy God my bless thee at all times, and in all things to which thou shalt put thy hand.—*Deut.* xv. 7-10.

If I have denied to the poor what they desired, and have made the eyes of the widow wait:

If I have eaten my morsel alone, and the fatherless hath not eaten thereof:

(For from my infancy mercy grew up with me: and it came out with me from my mother's womb:)

If I have despised him that was perishing for want of clothing, and the poor man that had no covering:

If his sides have not blessed me, and if he were not warmed with the fleece of my sheep:

If I have lifted up my hand against the fatherless, even when I saw myself superior in the gate:

Let my shoulder fall from its joint, and let my arm with its bones be broken.—*Job* xxxi. 16-22.

He that stoppeth his ear against the cry of the poor, shall also cry himself and shall not be heard.—*Prov.* xxi. 13.

He that giveth to the poor, shall not want: he that despiseth his entreaty, shall suffer indigence.—*Prov.* xxviii. 27.

Son, defraud not the poor of alms, and turn not away thy eyes from the poor.

Despise not the hungry soul: and provoke not the poor in his want.

Afflict not the heart of the needy, and defer not to give to him that is in distress.

Reject not the petition of the afflicted: and turn not away thy face from the needy.

Turn not away thy eyes from the poor for fear of anger: and leave not to them that ask of thee to curse thee behind thy back.

For the prayer of him that curseth thee in the bitterness of his soul, shall be heard, for he that made him, will hear him.—*Ecclus.* iv. 1-6.

For there is no good for him that is always occupied in evil, and that giveth no alms: for the Highest hateth sinners, and hath mercy on the penitent. —*Ecclus.* xii. 3.

Behold, this was the iniquity of So-dom, thy sister, pride, fulness of bread, and abundance, and the idleness of her, and of her daughters: and they did not put forth their hand to the needy and to the poor.—*Ezech.* xvi. 49.

He that hath the substance of this world, and shall see his brother in need, and shall shut up his bowels from him: how doth the charity of God abide in him?—1 *John* iii. 17.

POOR, A PRAYER FOR THE

Arise, O Lord God, let thy hand be exalted: forget not the poor. . . .

To thee is the poor man left: thou wilt be a helper to the orphan.—*Ps.* ix. (*Heb.* x.) 12, 14.

Deliver not up to beasts the souls that confess to thee: and forget not to the end the souls of thy poor. . . .

Let not the humble be turned away with confusion: the poor and needy shall praise thy name.—*Ps.*lxxiii.19,21.

POVERTY, ACKNOWLEDGMENT OF OUR

Look thou upon me, and have mercy on me; for I am alone and poor.—*Ps.* xxiv. 16.

But I am a beggar, and poor: the Lord is careful for me.—*Ps.* xxxix. 18.

But I am poor and sorrowful: thy salvation, O God, hath set me up.—*Ps.* lxviii. 30.

But I am needy and poor; O God, help me.

Thou art my helper and my deliverer: O Lord, make no delay.—*Ps.* lxix. 6.

Remember not our former iniquities: let thy mercies speedily prevent us, for we are become exceeding poor.—*Ps.* lxxviii. 8.

Incline thy ear, O Lord, and hear me: for I am needy and poor.—*Ps.* lxxxv. 1.

I am poor, and in labors from my youth: and being exalted, have been humbled and troubled.—*Ps.* lxxxvii. 16.

POVERTY OF CHRIST, THE

Rejoice greatly, O daughter of Sion, shout for joy, O daughter of Jerusalem: behold thy King will come to thee, the just and saviour: he is poor, and riding upon an ass, and upon a colt, the foal of an ass.—*Zach.* ix. 9.

And a certain scribe came, and said to him: Master, I will follow thee whithersoever thou shalt go.

And Jesus saith to him: The foxes have holes, and the birds of the air nests: but the Son of man hath not where to lay his head.—*Matt.* viii. 19, 20.

And she brought forth her first-born son, and wrapped him up in swaddling clothes, and laid him in a manger; because there was no room for them in the inn.—*Luke* ii. 7.

For, this day is born to you a Saviour, who is Christ the Lord, in the city of David.

And this shall be a sign unto you. You shall find the infant wrapped in swaddling clothes, and laid in a manger.—*Luke* ii. 11, 12.

And the Jews wondered, saying: How doth this man know letters, having never learned?—*John* vii. 15.

For you know the grace of our Lord Jesus Christ, that being rich, he became poor, for your sakes; that through his poverty you might be rich.—2 *Cor.* viii. 9.

POWER OF GOD, THE

See: Omnipotence of God, the—page 353.

POWER IS NOT SHORTENED, GOD'S

And Moses said: There are six hundred thousand footmen of this people, and sayest thou: I will give them flesh to eat a whole month?

Shall then a multitude of sheep and oxen be killed, that it may suffice for their food? or shall the fishes of the sea be gathered together to fill them?

And the Lord answered him: Is the hand of the Lord unable? Thou shalt presently see whether my word shall come to pass, or no.—*Num.* xi. 21-23.

Is my hand shortened and become little, that I cannot redeem? or is there no strength in me to deliver? Behold at my rebuke I will make the sea a desert, I will turn the rivers into dry land: the fishes shall rot for want of water, and shall die for thirst.—*Is.* l. 2.

Behold the hand of the Lord is not shortened, that it cannot save, neither is his ear heavy that it cannot hear.—*Is.* lix. 1.

POWER IS FROM GOD, ALL

See: Authority is from God—page 34.

POWERLESSNESS BEFORE GOD, MAN'S

See ye that I alone am, and there is no other God besides me: I will kill, and I will make to live: I will strike, and I will heal, and there is none that can deliver out of my hand.—*Deut.* xxxii. 39.

The bow of the mighty is overcome, and the weak are girt with strength. . . .

He will keep the feet of his saints, and the wicked shall be silent in darkness, because no man shall prevail by his own strength.—1 *Kings* ii. 4, 9.

If he shall overturn all things, or shall press them together, who shall contradict him?—*Job* xi. 10.

If he pull down, there is no man that can build up: if he shut up a man, there is none that can open.

If he withhold the waters, all things shall be dried up: and if he send them out, they shall overturn the earth.—*Job* xii. 14, 15.

For it is no longer in the power of man to enter into judgment with God.—*Job* xxxiv. 23.

If thou sin, what shalt thou hurt him? and if thy iniquities be multiplied, what shalt thou do against him?—*Job* xxxv. 6.

Thou perhaps hast made the heavens with him, which are most strong, as if they were of molten brass.—*Job* xxxvii. 18.

And I said: Hitherto thou shalt come, and shalt go no further, and here thou shalt break thy swelling waves.

Didst thou since thy birth command the morning, and show the dawning of the day its place? . . .

Shalt thou be able to join together the shining stars the Pleiades, or canst thou stop the turning about of Arcturus?

Canst thou bring forth the day star in its time, and make the evening star to rise upon the children of the earth? . . .

Canst thou lift up thy voice to the clouds, that an abundance of waters may cover thee?

Canst thou send lightnings, and will they go, and will they return and say to thee: Here we are?—*Job* xxxviii. 11, 12, 31, 32, 34, 35.

And hast thou an arm like God, and canst thou thunder with a voice like him?—*Job* xl. 4.

I will not stir him (the leviathan) up, like one that is cruel: for who can resist my countenance?—*Job* xli. 1.

Why have the Gentiles raged, and the people devised vain things?

The kings of the earth stood up, and the princes met together, against the Lord, and against his Christ.

Let us break their bonds asunder: and let us cast away their yoke from us.

He that dwelleth in heaven shall laugh at them: and the Lord shall deride them.—*Ps.* ii. 1-4.

For they have intended evils against thee: they have devised counsels which they have not been able to establish.

For thou shalt make them turn their back: in thy remnants thou shalt prepare their face.—*Ps.* xx. 12, 13.

The Lord bringeth to nought the counsels of nations; and he rejecteth the devices of people, and casteth away the counsels of princes.

But the counsel of the Lord standeth for ever: the thoughts of his heart to all generations.—*Ps.* xxxii. 10, 11.

Let God arise, and let his enemies be scattered: and let them that hate him, flee from before his face.

As smoke vanisheth, so let them vanish away: as wax melteth before the fire, so let the wicked perish at the presence of God.—*Ps.* lxvii. 2, 3.

Who is the man that shall live, and not see death: that shall deliver his soul from the hand of hell?—*Ps.* lxxxviii. 49.

They that go down to the sea in ships, doing business in the great waters:

These have seen the works of the Lord, and his wonders in the deep.

He said the word, and there arose a storm of wind: and the waves thereof were lifted up.

They mount up to the heavens, and they go down to the depths: their soul pined away with evils.

They were troubled, and reeled like a drunken man; and all their wisdom was swallowed up.—*Ps.* cvi. 23-27.

Unless the Lord build the house, they labor in vain that build it.

Unless the Lord keep the city, he watcheth in vain that keepeth it.—*Ps.* cxxvi. 1.

Who hath ascended up into heaven, and descended? who hath held the wind in his hands? who hath bound up the waters together as in a garment? who hath raised up all the borders of the earth? what is his name, and what is the name of his son, if thou knowest? —*Prov.* xxx. 4.

I have learned that all the works which God hath made, continue for ever: we cannot add any thing, nor take away from those things which God hath made, that he may be feared. —*Eccles.* iii. 14.

Be not hasty to depart from his face, and do not continue in an evil work: for he will do all that pleaseth him:

And his word is full of power: neither can any man say to him: Why dost thou so?—*Eccles.* viii. 3, 4.

It is not in man's power to stop the spirit, neither hath he power in the day of death.—*Eccles.* viii. 8.

As the potter's clay is in his hand, to fashion and order it:

All his ways are according to his ordering: so man is in the hand of him that made him, and he will render to him according to his judgment.—*Ecclus.* xxxiii. 13, 14.

What will you do in the day of visitation, and of the calamity which cometh from afar? to whom will ye flee for help? and where will ye leave your glory?—*Is.* x. 3.

Nations shall make a noise like the noise of waters overflowing, but he shall rebuke him, and he shall flee far off: and he shall be carried away as the dust of the mountains before the wind, and as a whirlwind before a tempest.—*Is.* xvii. 13.

Thou shalt bring down the tumult of strangers, as heat in thirst: and as with heat under a burning cloud, thou shalt make the branch of the mighty to wither away.—*Is.* xxv. 5.

And from the beginning I am the same, and there is none that can deliver out of my hand: I will work, and who shall turn it away?—*Is.* xliii. 13.

Woe to him that gainsayeth his maker, a sherd of the earthen pots: shall the clay say to him that fashioneth it: What art thou making, and thy work is without hands.—*Is.* xlv. 9.

Cannot I do with you as this potter, O house of Israel, saith the Lord? behold, as clay is in the hand of the potter, so are you in my hand, O house of Israel.—*Jer.* xviii. 6.

For who is like to me? and who shall bear up against me? and who is that shepherd that can withstand my countenance?—*Jer.* l. 44.

For I will be like a lioness to Ephraim, and like a lion's whelp to the house of Juda: I, I will catch, and go: I will take away, and there is none that can rescue.—*Osee* v. 14.

But what have you to do with me, O Tyre, and Sidon, and all the coast of the Philistines? will you revenge yourselves on me? and if you revenge yourselves on me, I will very soon return you a recompense upon your own head.—*Joel* iii. 4.

Who can stand before the face of his indignation? and who shall resist in the fierceness of his anger? his indignation is poured out like fire: and the rocks are melted by him. . . .

What do ye devise against the Lord? he will make an utter end: there shall not rise a double affliction.—*Nahum* i. 6, 9.

Then Jesus saith to him (Peter): Put up again thy sword into its place: for all that take the sword, shall perish with the sword.

Thinkest thou that I cannot ask my Father, and he will give me presently more than twelve legions of angels?—*Matt.* xxvi. 52, 53.

Therefore doth the Father love me: because I lay down my life, that I may take it again.

No man taketh it away from me: but I lay it down of myself, and I have power to lay it down: and I have power to take it up again. This commandment have I received of my Father.—*John* x. 17, 18.

Jesus therefore, knowing all things that should come upon him, went forth, and said to them: Whom seek ye?

They answered him: Jesus of Nazareth. Jesus saith to them: I am he. And Judas also, who betrayed him, stood with them.

As soon, therefore, as he had said to them: I am he; they went backward, and fell to the ground.—*John* xviii. 4-6.

Pilate therefore saith to him: Speakest thou not to me? knowest thou not that I have power to crucify thee, and I have power to release thee?

Jesus answered: Thou shouldst not have any power against me, unless it were given thee from above. Therefore, he that hath delivered me to thee, hath the greater sin.—*John* xix. 10, 11.

Do we provoke the Lord to jealousy? Are we stronger than he?—*1 Cor.* x. 22.

POWERLESSNESS, ACKNOWLEDGMENT TO GOD OF MAN'S

O Lord God of our fathers, thou art God in heaven, and rulest over all the kingdoms and nations, in thy hand is strength and power, and no one can resist thee.—*2 Paral.* xx. 6.

And Tobias the elder, opening his mouth, blessed the Lord, and said: Thou art great, O Lord, for ever, and thy kingdom is unto all ages:

For thou scourgest, and thou savest: thou leadest down to hell, and bringest up again: and there is none that can escape thy hand.—*Tob.* xiii. 1, 2.

O Adonai, Lord, great art thou, and glorious in thy power, and no one can overcome thee.

Let all thy creatures serve thee: because thou hast spoken, and they were made: thou didst send forth thy spirit, and they were created, and there is no one that can resist thy voice.—*Judith* xvi. 16, 17.

Are thy days as the days of man, and are thy years as the times of men:

That thou shouldst inquire after my iniquity, and search after my sin?

And shouldst know that I have done no wicked thing, whereas there is no man that can deliver out of thy hand.—*Job* x. 5-7.

Against a leaf, that is carried away with the wind, thou showest thy power, and thou pursuest a dry straw.—*Job* xiii. 25.

The days of man are short, and the number of his months is with thee: thou hast appointed his bounds which cannot be passed.—*Job* xiv. 5.

Thou art terrible, and who shall resist thee? from that time thy wrath.—*Ps.* lxxv. 8.

O grant us help from trouble: for vain is the help of man.—*Ps.* cvii. 13.

Yea, and without these, they might have been slain with one blast, persecuted by their own deeds, and scattered by the breath of thy power: but thou hast ordered all things in measure, and number, and weight.

For great power always belonged to thee alone: and who shall resist the strength of thy arm?

For the whole world before thee is as the least grain of the balance, and as a drop of the morning dew, that falleth down upon the earth. . . .

And how could anything endure, if thou wouldst not? or be preserved, if not called by thee.—*Wis.* xi. 21-23, 26.

For who shall say to thee: What hast thou done? or who shall withstand thy judgment? or who shall come before thee to be a revenger of wicked men? or who shall accuse thee, if the nations perish, which thou hast made?—*Wis.* xii. 12.

But it is impossible to escape thy hand.—*Wis.* xvi. 15.

PRACTICAL IN OUR FAITH, WE MUST BE

See also: Service of God, sincerity in the—page 513.

But to the sinner God hath said: Why dost thou declare my justices, and take my covenant in thy mouth?

Seeing thou hast hated discipline: and hast cast my words behind thee. . . .

These things hast thou done, and I was silent. Thou thoughtest unjustly that I should be like to thee: but I will reprove thee, and set before thy face.

Understand these things, you that forget God; lest he snatch you away, and there be none to deliver you.—*Ps.* xlix. 16, 17, 21, 22.

And they loved him with their mouth: and with their tongue they lied unto him:

But their heart was not right with him: nor were they counted faithful in his covenant.—*Ps.* lxxvii. 36, 37.

He hath commanded no man to do wickedly, and he hath given no man license to sin:

For he desireth not a multitude of faithless and unprofitable children.—*Ecclus.* xv. 21, 22.

He that believeth God, taketh heed to the commandments.—*Ecclus.* xxxii. 28.

And seeing many of the Pharisees and Sadducees coming to his baptism, he (John) said to them: Ye brood of vipers, who hath showed you to flee from the wrath to come?

Bring forth therefore fruit worthy of penance.

And think not to say within yourselves, We have Abraham for our father. For I tell you that God is able of these stones to raise up children to Abraham.

For now the axe is laid to the root of the trees. Every tree therefore that doth not yield good fruit, shall be cut down and cast into the fire.—*Matt.* iii. 7-10.

For I tell you, that unless your justice abound more than that of the scribes and Pharisees, you shall not enter into the kingdom of heaven.—*Matt.* v. 20.

Wherefore by their fruits you shall know them.

Not every one that saith to me, Lord, Lord, shall enter into the kingdom of heaven: but he that doth the will of my Father who is in heaven, he shall enter into the kingdom of heaven.

Many will say to me in that day: Lord, Lord, have we not prophesied in thy name, and cast out devils in thy name, and done many miracles in thy name?

And then will I profess unto them, I never knew you: depart from me, you that work iniquity.—*Matt.* vii. 20-23.

And I say to you that many shall come from the east and the west, and shall sit down with Abraham, and Isaac, and Jacob, in the kingdom of heaven:

But the children of the kingdom shall be cast out into the exterior darkness: there shall be weeping and gnashing of teeth.—*Matt.* viii. 11, 12.

And he spoke to them many things in parables, saying: Behold the sower went forth to sow. . . .

And others fell upon good ground: and they brought forth fruit, some an hundredfold, some sixtyfold, and some thirtyfold.

. . . But he that received the seed upon good ground, is he that heareth the word, and understandeth, and beareth fruit, and yieldeth the one an hundredfold, and another sixty, and another thirty.—*Matt.* xiii. 3, 8, 23.

He said unto them: Therefore every scribe instructed in the kingdom of heaven, is like to a man that is a householder, who bringeth forth out of his treasure new things and old.—*Matt.* xiii. 52.

And why call you me, Lord, Lord; and do not the things which I say?—*Luke* vi. 46.

And it came to pass, as he spoke these things, a certain woman from the crowd, lifting up her voice, said to him: Blessed is the womb that bore thee, and the paps that gave thee suck.

But he said: Yea rather, blessed are they who hear the word of God, and keep it.—*Luke* xi. 27, 28.

For not the hearers of the law are just before God, but the doers of the law shall be justified.—*Rom.* ii. 13.

For it is not he is a Jew, who is so outwardly; nor is that circumcision which is outwardly in the flesh:

But he is a Jew, that is one inwardly; and the circumcision is that of the heart, in the spirit, not in the letter; whose praise is not of men, but of God.—*Rom.* ii. 28, 29.

For all are not Israelites that are of Israel:

Neither are all they that are the seed of Abraham, children; but in Isaac shall thy seed be called:

That is to say, not they that are the children of the flesh, are the children of God; but they that are the children of the promise, are accounted for the seed.—*Rom.* ix. 6-8.

For the kingdom of God is not in speech, but in power.—1 *Cor.* iv. 20.

They profess that they know God: but in their works, they deny him; being abominable and incredulous, and to every good work reprobate.—*Titus* i. 16.

It is a faithful saying: and these things I will have thee affirm constantly: that they, who believe in God, may be careful to excel in good works. These things are good and profitable unto men.—*Titus* iii. 8.

I give thanks to my God, always making a remembrance of thee in my prayers.

Hearing of thy charity and faith, which thou hast in the Lord Jesus, and towards all the saints:

That the communication of thy faith may be made evident in the acknowledgment of every good work, that is in you in Christ Jesus.—*Phile.* i. 4-6.

But be ye doers of the word, and not hearers only, deceiving your own selves.

For if a man be a hearer of the word, and not a doer, he shall be compared to a man beholding his own countenance in a glass.

For he beheld himself, and went his way, and presently forgot what manner of man he was.

But he that hath looked into the perfect law of liberty, and hath continued therein, not becoming a forgetful hearer, but a doer of the work; this man shall be blessed in his deed.

And if any man think himself to be religious, not bridling his tongue, but deceiving his own heart, this man's religion is vain.

Religion clean and undefiled before God and the Father is this: to visit the fatherless and widows in their tribulation: and to keep one's self unspotted from this world.—*James* i. 22-27.

And this is the declaration which we have heard from him, and declare unto you: That God is light, and in him there is no darkness.

If we say that we have fellowship with him, and walk in darkness, we lie, and do not the truth.

But if we walk in the light, as he also is in the light, we have fellowship one with another, and the blood of Jesus Christ his Son cleanseth us from all sin.—1 *John* i. 5-7.

And by this we know that we have known him, if we keep his commandments.

He who saith that he knoweth him, and keepeth not his commandments, is a liar, and the truth is not in him.

But he that keepeth his word, in him, in very deed, the charity of God is perfected; and by this we know that we are in him.

He that saith he abideth in him, ought himself also to walk, even as he walked.—1 *John* ii. 3-6.

PRACTICAL IN OUR FAITH, EX-HORTATION TO BE

And Moses called all Israel, and said to them: Hear, O Israel, the ceremonies and judgments, which I speak in your ears this day: learn them, and fulfil them in work.—*Deut.* v. 1.

Be not hasty in thy tongue: and slack and remiss in thy works.—*Ecclus.* iv. 34.

Try your own selves if you be in the faith; prove ye yourselves.—2 *Cor.* xiii. 5.

I therefore a prisoner in the Lord, beseech you that you walk worthy of the vocation in which you are called. —*Eph.* iv. 1.

Only let your conversation be worthy of the gospel of Christ.—*Philipp.* i. 27.

The things which you have both learned, and received, and heard, and seen in me, these do ye, and the God of peace shall be with you.—*Philipp.* iv. 9.

Therefore we also, from the day that we heard it, cease not to pray for you, and to beg that you may be filled with the knowledge of his will, in all wisdom, and spiritual understanding:

That you may walk worthy of God, in all things pleasing; being fruitful in every good work, and increasing in the knowledge of God.—*Col.* i. 9, 10.

As therefore you have received Jesus Christ the Lord, walk ye in him;

Rooted and built up in him, and confirmed in the faith, as also you have learned, abounding in him in thanksgiving.—*Col.* ii. 6, 7.

As you know in what manner, entreating and comforting you, (as a father doth his children,)

We testified to every one of you, that you would walk worthy of God, who hath called you unto his kingdom and glory.—1 *Thess.* ii. 11, 12.

And you, employing all care, minister in your faith, virtue; and in virtue, knowledge;

And in knowledge, abstinence; and in abstinence, patience; and in patience, godliness;

And in godliness, love of brotherhood; and in love of brotherhood, charity.

For if these things be with you and abound, they will make you to be neither empty nor unfruitful in the knowledge of our Lord Jesus Christ.— 2 *Peter* i. 5-8.

My little children, let us not love in word, nor in tongue, but in deed, and in truth.—1 *John* iii. 18.

PRAISE GOD, EXHORTATION TO

Ye that fear the Lord, praise him: all ye the seed of Jacob, glorify him.— *Ps.* xxi. 24.

Sing to the Lord, O ye his saints: and give praise to the memory of his holiness.—*Ps.* xxix. 5.

O magnify the Lord with me; and let us extol his name together.—*Ps.* xxxiii. 4.

Sing praises to our God, sing ye: sing praises to our king, sing ye.

For God is the king of all the earth: sing ye wisely.—*Ps.* xlvi. 7, 8.

Offer to God the sacrifice of praise: and pay thy vows to the most High.— *Ps.* xlix. 14.

Let the people, O God, confess to thee: let all the people give praise to thee.—*Ps.* lxvi. 6.

Let the heavens and the earth praise him; the sea, and everything that creepeth therein.—*Ps.* lxviii. 35.

Come, let us praise the Lord with

joy: let us joyfully sing to God our saviour.

Let us come before his presence with thanksgiving, and make a joyful noise to him with psalms.—*Ps.* xciv. 1, 2.

Praise the Lord, ye children: praise ye the name of the Lord.—*Ps.* cxii. 1.

O praise ye the Lord, for he is good: for his mercy endureth for ever.—*Ps.* cxvii. 29.

Praise ye the name of the Lord: O you his servants, praise the Lord:

You that stand in the house of the Lord, in the courts of the house of our God.

Praise ye the Lord, for the Lord is good: sing ye to his name, for it is sweet.—*Ps.* cxxxiv. 1-3.

Praise ye the Lord, because psalm is good: to our God be joyful and comely praise.

. . . Sing ye to the Lord with praise: sing to our God upon the harp. —*Ps.* cxlvi. 1, 7.

Praise ye the Lord from the heavens: praise ye him in the high places.

Praise ye him, all his angels: praise ye him, all his hosts.

Praise ye him, O sun and moon: praise him, all ye stars and light.

Praise him, ye heavens of heavens: and let all the waters that are above the heavens praise the name of the Lord.

For he spoke, and they were made: he commanded, and they were created. —*Ps.* cxlviii. 1-5.

Sing ye to the Lord a new canticle: let his praise be in the church of the saints. . . .

Let them praise his name in choir: let them sing to him with the timbrel and the psaltery.—*Ps.* cxlix. 1, 3.

Praise ye the Lord in his holy places: praise ye him in the firmament of his power.

Praise ye him for his mighty acts: praise ye him according to the multitude of his greatness. . . .

Praise him on high sounding cymbals: praise him on cymbals of joy: let every spirit praise the Lord. Alleluia. —*Ps.* cl. 1, 2, 5.

Give thanks whilst thou art living, whilst thou art alive and in health, thou shalt give thanks, and shalt praise

God, and shalt glory in his mercies.— *Ecclus.* xvii. 27.

Now therefore with the whole heart and mouth praise ye him, and bless the name of the Lord.—*Ecclus.* xxxix. 41.

And you shall say in that day: Praise ye the Lord, and call upon his name: make his works known among the people: remember that his name is high.

Sing ye to the Lord, for he hath done great things: show this forth in all the earth.

Rejoice, and praise, O thou habitation of Sion: for great is he that is in the midst of thee, the Holy One of Israel.—*Is.* xii. 4, 5, 6.

Give praise, O ye heavens, for the Lord hath shown mercy: shout with joy, ye ends of the earth: ye mountains, resound with praise, thou, O forest, and every tree therein: for the Lord hath redeemed Jacob, and Israel shall be glorified.—*Is.* xliv. 23.

All ye works of the Lord, bless the Lord: praise and exalt him above all for ever.

O ye angels of the Lord, bless the Lord: praise and exalt him above all for ever. . . .

O ye sons of men, bless the Lord: praise and exalt him above all for ever.

O let Israel bless the Lord: let them praise and exalt him above all for ever.

O ye priests of the Lord, bless the Lord: praise and exalt him above all for ever.

O ye servants of the Lord, bless the Lord: praise and exalt him above all for ever.

O ye spirits and souls of the just, bless the Lord: praise and exalt him above all for ever.

O ye holy and humble of heart, bless the Lord: praise and exalt him above all for ever. . . .

O all ye religious, bless the Lord the God of gods: praise him, and give him thanks, because his mercy endureth for ever and ever.—*Dan.* iii. 57, 58, 82-87, 90.

And be not drunk with wine, wherein is luxury; but be ye filled with the holy Spirit,

Speaking to yourselves in psalms,

and hymns, and spiritual canticles, singing, and making melody in your hearts to the Lord.—*Eph.* v. 18, 19.

Let the word of Christ dwell in you abundantly, in all wisdom: teaching and admonishing one another in psalms, hymns and spiritual canticles, singing in grace in your hearts to God.—*Col.* iii. 16.

By him therefore let us offer the sacrifice of praise always to God, that is to say, the fruit of lips confessing to his name.—*Heb.* xiii. 15.

And a voice came out from the throne, saying: Give praise to our God, all ye his servants; and you that fear him, little and great.—*Apoc.* xix. 5.

PRAISE, GOD IS WORTHY OF ALL

I will call on the Lord, who is worthy to be praised: and I shall be saved from my enemies.—*2 Kings* xxii. 4.

Great is the Lord, and exceedingly to be praised in the city of our God, in his holy mountain.—*Ps.* xlvii. 2.

For the Lord is great, and exceedingly to be praised: he is to be feared above all gods.—*Ps.* xcv. 4.

From the rising of the sun unto the going down of the same, the name of the Lord is worthy of praise.

The Lord is high above all nations; and his glory above the heavens.—*Ps.* cxii. 3, 4.

Great is the Lord, and greatly to be praised: and of his greatness there is no end.—*Ps.* cxliv. 3.

Blessed art thou, O Lord the God of our fathers: and worthy to be praised, and glorified, and exalted above all for ever: and blessed is the holy name of thy glory: and worthy to be praised, and exalted above all in all ages.

Blessed art thou in the holy temple of thy glory: and exceedingly to be praised, and exceeding glorious for ever.

Blessed art thou on the throne of thy kingdom, and exceedingly to be praised, and exalted above all for ever. . . .

Blessed art thou in the firmament of heaven: and worthy of praise, and glorious for ever.—*Dan.* iii. 52-54, 56.

Thou art worthy, O Lord our God,

to receive glory, and honor, and power: because thou hast created all things; and for thy will they were, and have been created.—*Apoc.* iv. 11.

The Lamb that was slain is worthy to receive power, and divinity, and wisdom, and strength, and honor, and glory, and benediction.—*Apoc.* v. 12.

PRAISES OF GOD, THE

Out of the mouth of infants and of sucklings thou hast perfected praise, because of thy enemies, that thou mayst destroy the enemy and the avenger.—*Ps.* viii. 3.

The sacrifice of praise shall glorify me: and there is the way by which I will show him the salvation of God.—*Ps.* xlix. 23.

Who shall declare the powers of the Lord? who shall set forth all his praises?—*Ps.* cv. 2.

The praise of him is above heaven and earth: and he hath exalted the horn of his people.—*Ps.* cxlviii. 14.

Praise is not seemly in the mouth of a sinner.—*Ecclus.* xv. 9.

Sing ye to the Lord a new song, his praise is from the ends of the earth: you that go down to the sea, and all that are therein: ye islands, and ye inhabitants of them.—*Is.* xlii. 10.

PRAISING GOD

See also: Glorifying God—page 166.

Save us, O God our saviour: and gather us together, and deliver us from the nations, that we may give glory to thy holy name, and may rejoice in singing thy praises.—*1 Paral.* xvi. 35.

Thine, O Lord, is magnificence, and power, and glory, and victory: and to thee is praise: for all that is in heaven, and in earth, is thine: thine is the kingdom, O Lord, and thou art above all princes.

Thine are riches, and thine is glory, thou hast dominion over all, in thy hand is power and might: in thy hand greatness, and the empire of all things.

Now therefore, our God, we give thanks to thee, and we praise thy glorious name.—*1 Paral.* xxix. 11-13.

I will give praise to thee, O Lord,

with my whole heart: I will relate all thy wonders.—*Ps.* ix. 2.

I will declare thy name to my brethren: in the midst of the church will I praise thee.—*Ps.* xxi. 23.

The Lord is my helper and my protector: in him hath my heart confided, and I have been helped.

And my flesh hath flourished again, and with my will I will give praise to him.—*Ps.* xxvii. 7.

Rejoice in the Lord, O ye just: praise becometh the upright.—*Ps.* xxxii. 1.

I will bless the Lord at all times, his praise shall be always in my mouth.—*Ps.* xxxiii. 2.

Blessed be the Lord the God of Israel from eternity to eternity. So be it. So be it.—*Ps.* xl. 14.

O Lord, thou wilt open my lips: and my mouth shall declare thy praise.—*Ps.* l. 17.

I will give praise to thee, O Lord, among the people: I will sing a psalm to thee among the nations.

For thy mercy is magnified even to the heavens: and thy truth unto the clouds.

Be thou exalted, O God, above the heavens: and thy glory above all the earth.—*Ps.* lvi. 10-12.

I will praise the name of God with a canticle: and I will magnify him with praise.

And it shall please God better than a young calf, that bringeth forth horns and hoofs.—*Ps.* lxviii. 31, 32.

We will praise thee, O God: we will praise, and we will call upon thy name. We will relate thy wondrous works.—*Ps.* lxxiv. 2.

I will praise thee, O Lord my God, with my whole heart, and I will glorify thy name for ever.—*Ps.* lxxxv. 12.

It is good to give praise to the Lord: and to sing to thy name, O most High.

To show forth thy mercy in the morning, and thy truth in the night.—*Ps.* xci. 2, 3.

I will sing to the Lord as long as I live: I will sing praise to my God, while I have my being.—*Ps.* ciii. 33.

My heart is ready, O God, my heart is ready: I will sing, and will give praise with my glory. . . .

I will praise thee, O Lord, among the people: and I will sing unto thee among the nations.

For thy mercy is great above the heavens: and thy truth even unto the clouds.

Be thou exalted, O God, above the heavens, and thy glory over all the earth.—*Ps.* cvii. 2, 4-6.

I will praise thee, O Lord, with my whole heart; in the council of the just, and in the congregation.—*Ps.* cx. 1.

I will sacrifice to thee the sacrifice of praise, and I will call upon the name of the Lord.—*Ps.* cxv. 17.

Thou art my God, and I will praise thee: thou art my God, and I will exalt thee.

I will praise thee, because thou hast heard me, and art become my salvation. —*Ps.* cxvii. 28.

Seven times a day I have given praise to thee, for the judgments of thy justice.—*Ps.* cxviii. 164.

I will praise thee, O Lord, with my whole heart: for thou hast heard the words of my mouth.

I will sing praise to thee in the sight of the angels.—*Ps.* cxxxvii. 1.

I will extol thee, O God my king: and I will bless thy name for ever; yea, for ever and ever.

Every day will I bless thee: and I will praise thy name for ever; yea, for ever and ever.—*Ps.* cxliv. 1, 2.

Praise the Lord, O my soul, in my life I will praise the Lord: I will sing to my God, as long as I shall be.—*Ps.* cxlv. 2.

In all his works, he (David) gave thanks to the holy one, and to the most High, with words of glory.

With his whole heart he praised the Lord, and loved God that made him: and he gave him power against his enemies.—*Ecclus.* xlvii. 9, 10.

My soul shall praise the Lord, even to death.—*Ecclus.* li. 8.

They shall give glory to the Lord, and shall declare his praise in the islands.—*Is.* xlii. 12.

And the multitudes that went before, and that followed, cried, saying: Hosanna to the son of David: Blessed is he that cometh in the name of the

Lord: Hosanna in the highest.—*Matt.* xxi. 9.

To the only God our Saviour, through Jesus Christ, our Lord, be glory and magnificence, empire and power, before all ages, and now, and for all ages of ages. Amen.—*Jude* i. 25.

And the four living creatures had each of them six wings; and round about and within they are full of eyes. And they rested not, day and night, saying: Holy, holy, holy, Lord God Almighty, who was, and who is, and who is to come.—*Apoc.* iv. 8.

And every creature which is in heaven, and on the earth, and under the earth, and such as are in the sea, and all that are in them: I heard all saying: To him that sitteth on the throne, and to the Lamb, benediction, and honor, and glory, and power, for ever and ever.—*Apoc.* v. 13.

PRAYER

And he (Jacob) saw in his sleep a ladder standing upon the earth, and the top thereof touching heaven: the angels also of God ascending and descending by it;

And the Lord leaning upon the ladder, saying to him: I am the Lord God of Abraham thy father, and the God of Isaac.—*Gen.* xxviii. 12, 13.

To thee, O Lord, I turn my face, to thee I direct my eyes.—*Tob.* iii. 14.

Prayer is good with fasting and alms, more than to lay up treasures of gold. —*Tob.* xii. 8.

When thou didst pray with tears, and didst bury the dead, and didst leave thy dinner, and hide the dead by day in thy house, and bury them by night, I offered thy prayer to the Lord.—*Tob.* xii. 12.

For this shall every one that is holy pray to thee in a seasonable time.

And yet in a flood of many waters, they shall not come nigh unto him.— *Ps.* xxxi. 6.

In the daytime the Lord hath commanded his mercy; and a canticle to him in the night. With me is prayer to the God of my life.

I will say to God: Thou art my support. Why hast thou forgotten me? and why go I mourning, whilst my enemy afflicteth me?—*Ps.* xli. 9, 10.

Let my prayer be directed as incense in thy sight; the lifting up of my hands, as evening sacrifice.—*Ps.* cxl. 2.

I cried to the Lord with my voice: with my voice I made supplication to the Lord.

In his sight I pour out my prayer, and before him I declare my trouble.—*Ps.* cxli. 2, 3.

He (the wise man) will give his heart to resort early to the Lord that made him, and he will pray in the sight of the most High.

He will open his mouth in prayer, and will make supplication for his sins. . . .

And he will pour forth the words of his wisdom as showers, and in his prayer, he will confess to the Lord.— *Ecclus.* xxxix. 6, 7, 9.

You covet, and have not: you kill, and envy, and cannot obtain. You contend and war, and you have not, because you ask not.—*James* iv. 2.

And when he had opened the book, the four living creatures, and the four and twenty ancients fell down before the Lamb, having every one of them, harps, and golden vials full of odors, which are the prayers of saints.—*Apoc.* v. 8.

And another angel came, and stood before the altar, having a golden censer; and there was given to him much incense, that he should offer of the prayers of all saints upon the golden altar, which is before the throne of God.

And the smoke of the incense of the prayers of the saints ascended up before God from the hand of the angel.—*Apoc.* viii. 3, 4.

PRAYER, EFFICACY OF

See also: Prayers, God hears our— page 403.

And they turned themselves from thence, and went their way to Sodom: but Abraham as yet stood before the Lord.

And drawing nigh, he said: Wilt thou destroy the just with the wicked?

If there be fifty just men in the city, shall they perish withal? and wilt thou not spare that place for the sake of the fifty just, if they be therein?

Far be it from thee to do this thing, and to slay the just with the wicked, and for the just to be in like case as the wicked, this is not beseeming thee: thou who judgest all the earth, wilt not make this judgment.

And the Lord said to him: If I find in Sodom fifty just within the city, I will spare the whole place for their sake.

And Abraham answered, and said: Seeing I have once begun, I will speak to my Lord, whereas I am dust and ashes.

What if there be five less than fifty just persons? wilt thou for five and forty destroy the whole city? And he said: I will not destroy it, if I find five and forty.

And again he said to him: But if forty be found there, what wilt thou do? He said: I will not destroy it for the sake of forty.

Lord, saith he, be not angry, I beseech thee, if I speak: What if thirty shall be found there? He answered: I will not do it, if I find thirty there.

Seeing, saith he, I have once begun, I will speak to my Lord. What if twenty be found there? He said: I will not destroy it for the sake of twenty.

I beseech thee, saith he, be not angry, Lord, if I speak yet once more: What if ten should be found there? And he said: I will not destroy it for the sake of ten.—Gen. xviii. 22-32.

Moses said to Aaron: Take the censer, and putting fire in it from the altar, put incense upon it, and go quickly to the people to pray for them: for already wrath is gone out from the Lord, and the plague rageth.

When Aaron had done this, and had run to the midst of the multitude which the burning fire was now destroying, he offered the incense:

And standing between the dead and the living, he prayed for the people, and the plague ceased.—Num. xvi. 46-48.

Praising I will call upon the Lord: and I shall be saved from my enemies.—Ps. xvii. 4.

And they cried to the Lord in their affliction: and he delivered them out of their distresses.

He sent his word, and healed them: and delivered them from their destructions.—Ps. cvi. 19, 20.

For the Lord will judge his people, and will be entreated in favor of his servants.—Ps. cxxxiv. 14.

For a blameless man made haste to pray for the people, bringing forth the shield of his ministry, prayer, and by incense making supplication, withstood the wrath, and put an end to the calamity, showing that he was thy servant.

And he overcame the disturbance, not by strength of body, nor with force of arms, but with a word he subdued him that punished them, alleging the oaths and covenant made with the fathers.—Wis. xviii. 21, 22.

For who hath continued in his commandment, and hath been forsaken? or who hath called upon him, and he despised him?—Ecclus. ii. 12.

He that loveth God, shall obtain pardon for his sins by prayer, and shall refrain himself from them, and shall be heard in the prayer of days.—Ecclus. iii. 4.

Be of good comfort, my children, cry to the Lord, and he will deliver you out of the hand of the princes your enemies.—Bar. iv. 21.

Ask, and it shall be given you: seek, and you shall find: knock, and it shall be opened to you.

For every one that asketh, receiveth: and he that seeketh, findeth: and to him that knocketh, it shall be opened.

Or what man is there among you, of whom, if his son shall ask bread, will he reach him a stone?

Or if he shall ask him a fish, will he reach him a serpent?

If you then being evil, know how to give good gifts to your children: how much more will your Father who is in heaven, give good things to them that ask him?—Matt. vii. 7-11.

And behold a leper came and adored him, saying: Lord, if thou wilt, thou canst make me clean.

And Jesus stretching forth his hand, touched him, saying: I will, be thou made clean. And forthwith his leprosy was cleansed.—Matt. viii. 2, 3.

But this kind (of devil) is not cast out, but by prayer and fasting.—*Matt.* xvii. 20.

Again I say to you, that if two of you shall consent upon earth, concerning any thing whatsoever they shall ask, it shall be done to them by my Father who is in Heaven.—*Matt.* xviii. 19.

And all things whatsoever you shall ask in prayer, believing, you shall receive.—*Matt.* xxi. 22.

Because I go to the Father: and whatsoever you shall ask the Father in my name, that will I do: that the Father may be glorified in the Son. If you shall ask me any thing in my name, that I will do.—*John* xiv. 13, 14.

If you abide in me, and my words abide in you, you shall ask whatever you will, and it shall be done unto you. —*John* xv. 7.

And in that day you shall not ask me any thing. Amen, amen, I say to you: if you ask the Father any thing in my name, he will give it you.

Hitherto you have not asked any thing in my name. Ask, and you shall receive; that your joy may be full.— *John* xvi. 23, 24.

For there is no distinction of the Jew and the Greek: for the same is Lord over all, rich unto all that call upon him.

For whosoever shall call upon the name of the Lord, shall be saved.—*Rom.* x. 12, 13.

Put you on the armor of God, that you may be able to stand against the deceits of the devil.

For our wrestling is not against flesh and blood; but against principalities and powers, against the rulers of the world of this darkness, against the spirits of wickedness in the high places.

Therefore take unto you the armor of God, that you may be able to resist in the evil day, and to stand in all things perfect.—*Eph.* vi. 11-13.

Confess therefore your sins one to another: and pray one for another, that you may be saved. For the continual prayer of a just man availeth much.

Elias was a man passible like unto us: and with prayer he prayed that it might not rain upon the earth, and it rained not for three years and six months.

And he prayed again: and the heaven gave rain, and the earth brought forth her fruit.—*James* v. 16-18.

Dearly beloved, if our heart do not reprehend us, we have confidence towards God:

And whatsoever we shall ask, we shall receive of him: because we keep his commandments, and do those things which are pleasing in his sight.— 1 *John* iii. 21, 22.

PRAYER, THE PROPER KIND OF

Trust in him, all ye congregation of people: pour out your hearts before him. God is our helper for ever.—*Ps.* lxi. 9.

I entreated thy face with all my heart: have mercy on me according to thy word.—*Ps.* cxviii. 58.

Make thy prayer before the face of the Lord, and offend less.—*Ecclus.* xvii. 22.

Before prayer, prepare thy soul: and be not as a man that tempteth God.— *Ecclus.* xviii. 23.

Let us lift up our hearts with our hands to the Lord in the heavens.— *Lam.* iii. 41.

But thou, when thou shalt pray, enter into thy chamber, and having shut the door, pray to thy Father in secret: and thy Father who seeth in secret, will repay thee.

And when you are praying, speak not much, as the heathens. For they think that in their much speaking they may be heard.

Be not you therefore like to them, for your Father knoweth what is needful for you, before you ask him.—*Matt.* vi. 6-8.

Therefore I say unto you, all things whatsoever you ask when ye pray, believe that you shall receive; and they shall come unto you.—*Mark* xi. 24.

Likewise the Spirit also helpeth our infirmity. For we know not what we should pray for as we ought; but the Spirit himself asketh for us with unspeakable groanings.

And he that searcheth the hearts, knoweth what the Spirit desireth; because he asketh for the saints according to God.—*Rom.* viii. 26, 27.

I will, therefore, that men pray in every place, lifting up pure hands, without anger and contention.—1 *Tim.* ii. 8.

But if any of you want wisdom, let him ask of God, who giveth to all men abundantly, and upbraideth not; and it shall be given him.

But let him ask in faith, nothing wavering.—*James* i. 5, 6.

And this is the confidence which we have towards him: That whatsoever we shall ask according to his will, he heareth us.—1 *John* v. 14.

PRAYER, THE WRONG KIND OF

Be not full of words in a multitude of ancients, and [1]repeat not the word in thy prayer.—*Ecclus.* vii. 15.

And when ye pray, you shall not be as the hypocrites, that love to stand and pray in the synagogues and corners of the streets, that they may be seen by men: Amen I say to you, they have received their reward. . . .

And when you are praying, speak not much, as the heathens. For they think that in their much speaking they may be heard.—*Matt.* vi. 5, 7.

Hypocrites, well hath Isaias prophesied of you, saying:

This people honoreth me with their lips; but their heart is far from me.

And in vain do they worship me, teaching doctrines and commandments of men.—*Matt.* xv. 7-9.

But let him ask in faith, nothing wavering. For he that wavereth is like a wave of the sea, which is moved and carried about by the wind.

Therefore let not that man think that he shall receive any thing of the Lord.—*James* i. 6, 7.

You ask, and receive not; because you ask amiss: that you may consume it on your concupiscences.—*James* iv. 3.

PRAYER, PERSEVERANCE IN

He (Jacob) remained alone: and behold a man wrestled with him till morning. . . .

And he said to him: Let me go, for

[1]That is, make not much babbling by repetition of words; but aim more at fervor of heart.

it is break of day. He answered: I will not let thee go except thou bless me. . . .

But he said: Thy name shall not be called Jacob, but Israel: for if thou hast been strong against God, how much more shalt thou prevail against men?—*Gen.* xxxii. 24, 26, 28.

And when Moses lifted up his hands, Israel overcame: but if he let them down a little, Amalec overcame.

And Moses' hands were heavy: so they took a stone, and put under him, and he sat on it: and Aaron and Hur stayed up his hands on both sides. And it came to pass that his hands were not weary until sunset.—*Ex.* xvii. 11, 12.

Know ye that the Lord will hear your prayers, if you continue with perseverance in fastings and prayers in the sight of the Lord.—*Judith* iv. 11.

I will bless the Lord at all times, his praise shall be always in my mouth.—*Ps.* xxxiii. 2.

But I have cried to God: and the Lord will save me.

Evening and morning, and at noon I will speak and declare: and he shall hear my voice.—*Ps.* liv. 17, 18.

O Lord, the God of my salvation: I have cried in the day, and in the night before thee.

. . . All the day I cried to thee, O Lord: I stretched out my hands to thee.—*Ps.* lxxxvii. 2, 10.

To thee have I lifted up my eyes, who dwellest in heaven.

Behold as the eyes of servants are on the hands of their masters,

As the eyes of the handmaid are on the hands of her mistress: so are our eyes unto the Lord our God, until he have mercy on us.—*Ps.* cxxii. 1, 2.

The prayer of him that humbleth himself, shall pierce the clouds: and till it come nigh, he will not be comforted: and he will not depart till the most High behold.—*Ecclus.* xxxv. 21.

And behold a woman of Chanaan, who came out of those coasts, crying out, said to him: Have mercy on me, O Lord, thou son of David: my daughter is grievously troubled by a devil.

Who answered her not a word. And his disciples came and besought him, saying: Send her away, for she crieth after us:

And he answering, said: I was not sent but to the sheep that are lost of the house of Israel.

But she came and adored him, saying: Lord, help me.

Who answering, said: It is not good to take the bread of the children, and to cast it to the dogs.

But she said: Yea, Lord; for the whelps also eat of the crumbs that fall from the table of their masters.

Then Jesus answering, said to her: O woman, great is thy faith: be it done to thee as thou wilt: and her daughter was cured from that hour.—*Matt.* xv. 22-28.

And behold two blind men sitting by the wayside, heard that Jesus passed by, and they cried out, saying: O Lord, thou son of David, have mercy on us.

And the multitude rebuked them that they should hold their peace. But they cried out the more, saying: O Lord, thou son of David, have mercy on us. . . .

And Jesus having compassion on them, touched their eyes. And immediately they saw, and followed him.—*Matt.* xx. 30, 31, 34.

And leaving them, he (Jesus) went again: and he prayed the third time, saying the selfsame word.—*Matt.* xxvi. 44.

And it came to pass in those days, that he (Jesus) went out into a mountain to pray, and he passed the whole night in the prayer of God.—*Luke* vi. 12.

And he said to them: Which of you shall have a friend, and shall go to him at midnight, and shall say to him: Friend, lend me three loaves,

Because a friend of mine is come off his journey to me, and I have not what to set before him.

And he from within should answer, and say: Trouble me not, the door is now shut, and my children are with me in bed; I cannot rise and give thee.

Yet if he shall continue knocking, I say to you, although he will not rise and give him, because he is his friend; yet, because of his importunity, he will rise, and give him as many as he needeth.—*Luke* xi. 5-8.

And he spoke also a parable to them, that we ought always to pray, and not to faint,

Saying: There was a judge in a certain city, who feared not God, nor regarded man.

And there was a certain widow in that city, and she came to him, saying: Avenge me of my adversary.

And he would not for a long time. But afterwards he said within himself: Although I fear not God, nor regard man,

Yet because this widow is troublesome to me, I will avenge her, lest continually coming she weary me.

And the Lord said: Hear what the unjust judge saith.

And will not God revenge his elect who cry to him day and night: and will he have patience in their regard?

I say to you that he will quickly revenge them.—*Luke* xviii. 1-8.

And there appeared to him (Jesus) an angel from heaven, strengthening him. And being in an agony, he prayed the longer.—*Luke* xxii. 43.

All these (the apostles) were persevering with one mind in prayer with the women, and Mary the mother of Jesus, and with his brethren.—*Acts* i. 14.

PRAYER, EXHORTATION TO PERSEVERANCE IN

And know the justices and judgments of God, and stand firm in the lot set before thee, and in prayer to the most high God.—*Ecclus.* xvii. 24.

Let nothing hinder thee from praying always, and be not afraid to be justified even to death: for the reward of God continueth for ever.—*Ecclus.* xviii. 22.

Watch ye, therefore, praying at all times, that you may be accounted worthy to escape all these things that are to come, and to stand before the Son of man.—*Luke* xxi. 36.

Rejoicing in hope. Patient in tribulation. Instant in prayer.—*Rom.* xii. 12.

By all prayer and supplication, praying at all times in the spirit; and in the same watching with all instance and supplication for all the saints.—*Eph.* vi. 18.

Be instant in prayer; watching in it with thanksgiving.—*Col.* iv. 2.

Pray without ceasing.—1 *Thess.* v. 17.

But the end of all is at hand. Be prudent therefore, and watch in prayers.—1 *Peter* iv. 7.

PRAYERS, GOD HEARS OUR

See also: Cry of the distressed reaches God, the—page 94.

Neither is there any other nation so great, that hath gods so nigh them, as our God is present to all our petitions. —*Deut.* iv. 7.

And the priest and the Levites rose up, and blessed the people: and their voice was heard: and their prayer came to the holy dwelling place of heaven.— 2 *Paral.* xxx. 27.

At that time the prayers of ¹them both were heard in the sight of the glory of the most high God:

And the holy angel of the Lord, Raphael, was sent to heal them both, whose prayers at one time were rehearsed in the sight of the Lord.—*Tob.* iii. 24, 25.

I have cried to the Lord with my voice: and he hath heard me from his holy hill.—*Ps.* iii. 5.

When I called upon him, the God of my justice heard me: when I was in distress, thou hast enlarged me. . . .

Know ye also that the Lord hath made his holy one wonderful: the Lord will hear me, when I shall cry unto him.—*Ps.* iv. 2, 4.

Depart from me, all ye workers of iniquity: for the Lord hath heard the voice of my weeping.

The Lord hath heard my supplication: the Lord hath received my prayer. —*Ps.* vi. 9, 10.

Let all the seed of Israel fear him: because he hath not slighted nor despised the supplication of the poor man.

Neither hath he turned away his face from me: and when I cried to him, he heard me.—*Ps.* xxi. 25.

Blessed be the Lord, for he hath heard the voice of my supplication.— *Ps.* xxvii. 6.

But I said in the excess of my mind: I am cast away from before thy eyes.

¹The elder Tobias and Sara.

Therefore thou hast heard the voice of my prayer, when I cried to thee.— *Ps.* xxx. 23.

I sought the Lord, and he heard me; and he delivered me from all my troubles. . . .

This poor man cried, and the Lord heard him: and saved him out of all his troubles.—*Ps.* xxxiii. 5, 7.

With expectation I have waited for the Lord, and he was attentive to me.

And he heard my prayers, and brought me out of the pit of misery and the mire of dregs.

And he set my foot upon a rock, and directed my steps.—*Ps.* xxxix. 2, 3.

Offer to God the sacrifice of praise: and pay thy vows to the most High.

And call upon me in the day of trouble: I will deliver thee, and thou shalt glorify me.—*Ps.* xlix. 14, 15.

But I have cried to God: and the Lord will save me.

Evening and morning, and at noon I will speak and declare: and he shall hear my voice.

He shall redeem my soul in peace from them that draw near to me: for among many they were with me.

God shall hear, and the Eternal shall humble them.—*Ps.* liv. 17-20.

I will cry to God the most High; to God who hath done good to me.

He hath sent from heaven, and delivered me: he hath made them a reproach that trod upon me. God hath sent his mercy and his truth.—*Ps.* lvi. 3, 4.

For thou, my God, hast heard my prayer: thou hast given an inheritance to them that fear thy name.—*Ps.* lx. 6.

Come and hear, all ye that fear God, and I will tell you what great things he hath done for my soul.

I cried to him with my mouth: and I extolled him with my tongue. . . .

Therefore hath God heard me, and hath attended to the voice of my supplication.

Blessed be God, who hath not turned away my prayer, nor his mercy from me.—*Ps.* lxv. 16, 17, 19, 20.

I cried to the Lord with my voice; to God with my voice, and he gave ear to me.

In the day of my trouble I sought

God, with my hands lifted up to him in the night, and I was not deceived.—*Ps.* lxxvi. 2, 3.

Thou calledst upon me in affliction, and I delivered thee: I heard thee in the secret place of tempest: I proved thee at the waters of contradiction.—*Ps.* lxxx. 8

For thou, O Lord, art sweet and mild: and plenteous in mercy to all that call upon thee. . . .

I have called upon thee in the day of my trouble: because thou hast heard me.—*Ps.* lxxxv. 5, 7.

Moses and Aaron among his priests: and Samuel among them that call upon his name.

They called upon the Lord, and he heard them. . . .

Thou didst hear them, O Lord our God: thou wast a merciful God to them.—*Ps.* xcviii. 6, 8.

I have loved, because the Lord will hear the voice of my prayer.

Because he hath inclined his ear unto me: and in my days I will call upon him.—*Ps.* cxiv. 1, 2.

In my trouble I called upon the Lord: and the Lord heard me, and enlarged me. . . .

I will give glory to thee, because thou hast heard me: and art become my salvation.—*Ps.* cxvii. 5, 21.

The Lord is nigh unto all them that call upon him: to all that call upon him in truth.

He will do the will of them that fear him: and he will hear their prayer, and save them.—*Ps.* cxliv. 18, 19.

I called upon the Lord, the father of my Lord, that he would not leave me in the day of my trouble, and in the time of the proud without help.

I will praise thy name continually, and will praise it with thanksgiving, and my prayer was heard.

And thou hast saved me from destruction, and hast delivered me from the evil time.

Therefore I will give thanks and praise thee, and bless the name of the Lord.—*Ecclus.* li. 14-17.

Thus saith the Lord, who will do, and will form it, and prepare it, the Lord is his name.

Cry to me, and I will hear thee: and I will show thee great things, and sure things which thou knowest not.—*Jer.* xxxiii. 2, 3.

And Jonas prayed to the Lord his God out of the belly of the fish.

And he said: I cried out of my affliction to the Lord, and he heard me: I cried out of the belly of hell, and thou hast heard my voice.—*Jonas* ii. 2, 3.

And this is the confidence which we have towards him: That, whatsoever we shall ask according to his will, he heareth us.

And we know that he heareth us whatsoever we ask: we know that we have the petitions which we request of him.—1 *John* v. 14, 15.

PRAYERS OF THE JUST, GOD HEARS THE

See: Just, prayers of the—page 263.

PRAYERS OF THE WICKED NOT ACCEPTABLE TO GOD, THE

See: Wicked, prayers of the—page 600.

PRAY, EXHORTATION TO

Be subject to the Lord, and pray to him.—*Ps.* xxxvi. 7.

Neglect not to pray, and to give alms.—*Ecclus.* vii. 10.

Love God all thy life, and call upon him for thy salvation.—*Ecclus.* xiii. 18.

Make thy prayer before the face of the Lord, and offend less.—*Ecclus.* xvii. 22.

My son, hast thou sinned? do so no more: but for thy former sins also pray that they may be forgiven thee.—*Ecclus.* xxi. 1.

But above all these things, pray to the most High, that he may direct thy way in truth.—*Ecclus.* xxxvii. 19.

My son, in thy sickness, neglect not thyself, but pray to the Lord, and he shall heal thee.—*Ecclus.* xxxviii. 9.

And now pray ye to the God of all, who hath done great things in all the earth, who hath increased our days from our mother's womb, and hath done with us according to his mercy.—*Ecclus.* l. 24.

And now beseech ye the face of God,

that he may have mercy on you (for by your hand hath this been done), if by any means, he will receive your faces, saith the Lord of hosts.—*Malach.* i. 9.

Ask, and it shall be given you: seek, and you shall find: knock, and it shall be opened to you.—*Matt.* vii. 7.

Watch ye, and pray, that ye enter not into temptation. The spirit indeed is willing, but the flesh weak.—*Matt.* xxvi. 41.

Be nothing solicitous; but in every thing, by prayer and supplication, with thanksgiving, let your petitions be made known to God.—*Philipp.* iv. 6.

I will therefore that men pray in every place, lifting up pure hands, without anger and contention.—1 *Tim.* ii. 8.

Let us go therefore with confidence to the throne of grace: that we may obtain mercy, and find grace in seasonable aid.—*Heb.* iv. 16.

PRAYING FOR ONE ANOTHER

Now therefore restore the man his wife, for he is a prophet: and he shall pray for thee, and thou shalt live: but if thou wilt not restore her, know that thou shalt surely die, thou and all that are thine. . . .

And when Abraham prayed, God healed Abimelech and his wife, and his handmaids, and they bore children.—*Gen.* xx. 7, 17.

And again the Lord said to Moses: See that this people is stiffnecked:

Let me alone, that my wrath may be kindled against them, and that I may destroy them, and I will make of thee a great nation.

But Moses besought the Lord his God, saying: Why, O Lord, is thy indignation enkindled against thy people, whom thou hast brought out of the land of Egypt, with great power, and with a mighty hand? . . .

Let thy anger cease, and be appeased upon the wickedness of thy people. . . .

And the Lord was appeased from doing the evil which he had spoken against his people.—*Ex.* xxxii. 9-12, 14.

And far from me be this sin against the Lord, that I should cease to pray for you, and I will teach you the good and right way.—1 *Kings* xii. 23.

And Ozias and the ancients said to her (Judith): All things which thou hast spoken are true, and there is nothing to be reprehended in thy words.

Now therefore pray for us, for thou art a holy woman, and one fearing God. —*Judith* viii. 28, 29.

We therefore at all times without ceasing, both in our festivals and other days, wherein it is convenient, remember you in the sacrifices that we offer, and in our observances, as it is meet and becoming to remember brethren.— 1 *Mach.* xii. 11.

To the brethren the Jews that are throughout Egypt, the brethren, the Jews that are in Jerusalem, and in the land of Judea, send health and good peace. . . .

And now here we are praying for you.—2 *Mach.* i. 1, 6.

Then some of the friends of Heliodorus forthwith begged of Onias, that he would call upon the most High to grant him his life, who was ready to give up the ghost.

So the high priest, considering that the king might perhaps suspect that some mischief had been done to Heliodorus by the Jews, offered a sacrifice of health for the recovery of the man.

And when the high priest was praying, the same young men in the same clothing stood by Heliodorus, and said to him: Give thanks to Onias the priest: because for his sake the Lord hath granted thee life.—2 *Mach.* iii. 31-33.

Peter therefore was kept in prison. But prayer was made without ceasing by the church unto God for him.—*Acts* xii. 5.

For God is my witness, whom I serve in my spirit in the gospel of his Son, that without ceasing, I make a commemoration of you.—*Rom.* i. 9.

Wherefore I also, hearing of your faith that is in the Lord Jesus, and of your love towards all the saints,

Cease not to give thanks for you, making commemoration of you in my prayers.—*Eph.* i. 15, 16.

I give thanks to my God in every remembrance of you,

Always in all my prayers making supplication for you all, with joy.—*Philipp.* i. 3, 4.

We give thanks to God, and the Father of our Lord Jesus Christ, praying always for you.—*Col.* i. 3.

Therefore we also, from the day that we heard it, cease not to pray for you, and to beg that you may be filled with the knowledge of his will, in all wisdom and spiritual understanding:

That you may walk worthy of God, in all things pleasing; being fruitful in every good work, and increasing in the knowledge of God.—*Col.* i. 9, 10.

Epaphras saluteth you, who is one of you, a servant of Christ Jesus, who is always solicitous for you in prayers, that you may stand perfect, and full in all the will of God.—*Col.* iv. 12.

We give thanks to God always for you all; making a remembrance of you in our prayers without ceasing.— 1 *Thess.* i. 2.

Wherefore also we pray always for you; that our God would make you worthy of his vocation, and fulfil all the good pleasure of his goodness, and the work of faith in power.—2 *Thess.* i. 11.

I give thanks to God, whom I serve from my forefathers, with a pure conscience, that without ceasing, I have a remembrance of thee in my prayers, night and day.—2 *Tim.* i. 3.

I give thanks to my God, always making a remembrance of thee in my prayers.—*Phile.* i. 4.

Dearly beloved, concerning all things, I make it my prayer, that thou mayst proceed prosperously, and fare well as thy soul doth prosperously.—3 *John* i. 2.

PRAY FOR ONE ANOTHER, EXHORTATION TO

[1]Wherefore lift up thy prayer for the remnant that is left.—*Is.* xxxvii. 4.

And they said to Jeremias the prophet: Let our supplication fall before thee: and pray thou for us to the Lord thy God for all this remnant, for we are left but a few of many, as thy eyes do behold us.—*Jer.* xlii. 2.

And they said: Behold we have sent you money, buy with it holocausts, and

[1]The envoys of Ezechias beseeching Isaias.

frankincense, and make meat offerings, and offerings for sin at the altar of the Lord our God. . . .

And pray ye for us to the Lord our God: for we have sinned against the Lord our God, and his wrath is not turned away from us even to this day.— *Bar.* i. 10, 13.

But I say to you, Love your enemies: do good to them that hate you: and pray for them that persecute and calumniate you.—*Matt.* v. 44.

I beseech you, therefore, brethren, through our Lord Jesus Christ, and by the charity of the Holy Ghost, that you help me in your prayers for me to God. —*Rom.* xv. 30.

You helping withal in prayer for us: that for this gift obtained for us, by the means of many persons, thanks may be given by many in our behalf.—2 *Cor.* i. 11.

By all prayer and supplication praying at all times in the spirit; and in the same watching with all instance and supplication for all the saints:

And for me, that speech may be given me, that I may open my mouth with confidence, to make known the mystery of the gospel.—*Eph.* vi. 18, 19.

Praying withal for us also, that God may open unto us a door of speech to speak the mystery of Christ (for which also I am bound);

That I may make it manifest as I ought to speak.—*Col.* iv. 3, 4.

Brethren, pray for us.—1 *Thess.* v. 25.

For the rest, brethren, pray for us, that the word of God may run, and may be glorified, even as among you;

And that we may be delivered from importunate and evil men; for all men have not faith.—2 *Thess.* iii. 1, 2.

I desire therefore, first of all, that supplications, prayers, intercessions, and thanksgivings be made for all men:

For kings, and for all that are in high station: that we may lead a quiet and a peaceable life in all piety and chastity.

For this is good and acceptable in the sight of God our Saviour.—1 *Tim.* ii. 1-3.

Pray for us. . . .

And I beseech you the more to do

this, that I may be restored to you the sooner.—*Heb.* xiii. 18, 19.

Confess therefore your sins one to another: and pray one for another, that you may be saved. For the continual prayer of a just man availeth much.—*James* v. 16.

PRAYERS OF CHRIST, THE

And having dismissed the multitude, he went into a mountain alone to pray. And when it was evening, he was there alone.—*Matt.* xiv. 23.

Then Jesus came with them into a country place which is called Gethsemani; and he said to his disciples: Sit you here, till I go yonder and pray. . . .

And going a little further, he fell upon his face, praying, and saying: My Father, if it be possible, let this chalice pass from me. Nevertheless, not as I will, but as thou wilt. . . .

Again the second time, he went and prayed, saying: My Father, if this chalice may not pass away, but I must drink it, thy will be done. . . .

And leaving them, he went again: and he prayed the third time, saying the selfsame word.—*Matt.* xxvi. 36, 39, 42, 44.

And he retired into the desert, and prayed.—*Luke* v. 16.

And it came to pass in those days, that he went out into a mountain to pray, and he passed the whole night in the prayer of God.—*Luke* vi. 12.

And it came to pass, as he was alone praying, his disciples also were with him: and he asked them, saying: Whom do the people say that I am?—*Luke* ix. 18.

And it came to pass, that as he was in a certain place praying, when he ceased, one of his disciples said to him: Lord, teach us to pray, as John also taught his disciples.—*Luke* xi. 1.

I pray for them: I pray not for the world, but for them whom thou hast given me: because they are thine. . . .

I pray not that thou shouldst take them out of the world, but that thou shouldst keep them from evil. . . .

And not for them only do I pray, but for them also who through their word, shall believe in me;

That they all may be one, as thou, Father, in me, and I in thee; that they also may be one in us; that the world may believe that thou hast sent me.—*John* xvii. 9, 15, 20, 21.

Who in the days of his flesh, with a strong cry and tears, offering up prayers and supplications to him that was able to save him from death, was heard for his reverence.—*Heb.* v. 7.

PRAYER OF ONE IN SORROW AND DISTRESS, A

See also: Cry of one in distress, a—page 92.

Then Tobias sighed, and began to pray with tears:

. . .And now, O Lord, do with me according to thy will, and command my spirit to be received in peace: for it is better for me to die, than to live.—*Tob.* iii. 1, 6.

O Lord God of heaven and earth, behold their pride, and look on our low condition, and have regard to the face of thy saints, and show that thou forsakest not them that trust in thee, and that thou humblest them that presume of themselves, and glory in their own strength.—*Judith* vi. 15.

Hear my supplication, and be merciful to thy lot and inheritance, and turn our mourning into joy, that we may live, and praise thy name, O Lord, and shut not the mouths of them that sing to thee.—*Esther* xiii. 17.

O my Lord, who alone art our king, help me a desolate woman, and who have no other helper but thee.

My danger is in my hands. . . .

Remember, O Lord, and show thyself to us in the time of our tribulation, and give me boldness, O Lord, king of gods, and of all power. . . .

But deliver us by thy hand, and help me, who have no other helper but thee, O Lord, who hast the knowledge of all things. . . .

O God, who art mighty above all, hear the voice of them that have no other hope, and deliver us from the hand of the wicked, and deliver me from my fear.—*Esther* xiv. 3, 4, 12, 14, 19.

Thy hands have made me, and fashioned me wholly round about, and dost thou thus cast me down headlong on a sudden?

Remember, I beseech thee, that thou hast made me as the clay, and thou wilt bring me into dust again.—*Job* x. 8, 9.

Have mercy on me, O Lord, for I am weak: heal me, O Lord, for my bones are troubled.

And my soul is troubled exceedingly: but thou, O Lord, how long?

Turn to me, O Lord, and deliver my soul: O save me, for thy mercy's sake. —*Ps.* vi. 3-5.

Have mercy on me, O Lord: see my humiliation which I suffer from my enemies.—*Ps.* ix. 14.

How long, O Lord, wilt thou forget me unto the end? how long dost thou turn away thy face from me?

How long shall I take counsels in my soul, sorrow in my heart all the day?

How long shall my enemy be exalted over me?

Consider, and hear me, O Lord my God.

Enlighten my eyes, that I never sleep in death: lest at any time my enemy say: I have prevailed against him.—*Ps.* xii. 1-5.

Have mercy on me, O Lord, for I am afflicted: my eye is troubled with wrath, my soul, and my belly:

For my life is wasted with grief: and my years in sighs.

My strength is weakened through poverty, and my bones are disturbed....

My lots are in thy hands.

Deliver me out of the hands of my enemies; and from them that persecute me.

. . . Let me not be confounded, O Lord, for I have called upon thee.—*Ps.* xxx. 10, 11, 16, 18.

Rebuke me not, O Lord, in thy indignation; nor chastise me in thy wrath.

For thy arrows are fastened in me: and thy hand hath been strong upon me.

There is no health in my flesh, because of thy wrath: there is no peace for my bones, because of my sins.

For my iniquities are gone over my head: and as a heavy burden, are become heavy upon me.

. . . I am become miserable, and am bowed down even to the end:

I walked sorrowful all the day long. . . .

I am afflicted and humbled exceedingly: I roared with the groaning of my heart.

Lord, all my desire is before thee, and my groaning is not hidden from thee.

My heart is troubled, my strength hath left me, and the light of my eyes itself is not with me. . . .

For I am ready for scourges: and my sorrow is continually before me. . . .

Forsake me not, O Lord my God: do not thou depart from me.—*Ps.* xxxvii. 2-5, 7, 9-11, 18, 22.

For evils without number have surrounded me; my iniquities have overtaken me, and I was not able to see.

They are multiplied above the hairs of my head: and my heart hath forsaken me.

Be pleased, O Lord, to deliver me: look down, O Lord, to help me.—*Ps.* xxxix. 13, 14.

Arise, why sleepest thou, O Lord? arise, and cast us not off to the end.

Why turnest thou thy face away? and forgettest our want and our trouble?

For our soul is humbled down to the dust: our belly cleaveth to the earth.

Arise, O Lord, help us and redeem us for thy name's sake.—*Ps.* xliii. 23-26.

Have mercy on me, O God, for man hath trodden me under foot; all the day long he hath afflicted me fighting against me.

My enemies have trodden on me all the day long; for they are many that make war against me.—*Ps.* lv. 2, 3.

Save me, O God: for the waters are come in even unto my soul.

I stick fast in the mire of the deep: and there is no sure standing.

I am come into the depth of the sea: and a tempest hath overwhelmed me.

I have labored with crying; my jaws are become hoarse: my eyes have failed, whilst I hope in my God. . . .

Draw me out of the mire, that I may not stick fast: deliver me from them that hate me, and out of the deep waters.

Let not the tempest of water drown me, nor the deep swallow me up: and let not the pit shut her mouth upon me.

Hear me, O Lord, for thy mercy is

kind; look upon me according to the multitude of thy tender mercies.

And turn not away thy face from thy servant: for I am in trouble, hear me speedily.

Attend to my soul, and deliver it: save me because of my enemies.—*Ps.* lxviii. 2-4, 15-19.

Have mercy on me, O Lord, for I have cried to thee all the day. . . .

I have called upon thee in the day of my trouble: because thou hast heard me.—*Ps.* lxxxv. 3, 7.

Hear, O Lord, my prayer: and let my cry come to thee.

Turn not away thy face from me: in the day when I am in trouble, incline thy ear to me.

In what day soever I shall call upon thee, hear me speedily.

For my days are vanished like smoke: and my bones are grown dry like fuel for the fire.

I am smitten as grass, and my heart is withered: because I forgot to eat my bread.

Through the voice of my groaning, my bone hath cleaved to my flesh.—*Ps.* ci. 2-6.

But thou, O Lord, do with me for thy name's sake: because thy mercy is sweet.

Do thou deliver me, for I am poor and needy, and my heart is troubled within me.

I am taken away like the shadow when it declineth, and I am shaken off as locusts.—*Ps.* cviii. 21-23.

The sorrows of death have compassed me: and the perils of hell have found me.

I met with trouble and sorrow: and I called upon the name of the Lord. O Lord, deliver my soul.—*Ps.* cxiv. 3, 4.

Out of the depths I have cried to thee, O Lord: Lord, hear my voice.

Let thy ears be attentive to the voice of my supplication.

If thou, O Lord, wilt mark iniquities: Lord, who shall stand it.

For with thee there is merciful forgiveness: and by reason of thy law, I have waited for thee, O Lord.—*Ps.* cxxix. 1-4.

I cried to the Lord with my voice:

with my voice I made supplication to the Lord.

In his sight I pour out my prayer, and before him I declare my trouble. . . .

I looked on my right hand, and beheld, and there was no one that would know me.

Flight hath failed me: and there is no one that hath regard to my soul.

I cried to thee, O Lord: I said: Thou art my hope, my portion in the land of the living.

Attend to my supplication: for I am brought very low.

Deliver me from my persecutors; for they are stronger than I.—*Ps.* cxli. 2, 3. 5-7.

Hear, O Lord, my prayer: give ear to my supplication in thy truth: hear me in thy justice. . . .

For the enemy hath persecuted my soul: he hath brought down my life to the earth.

He hath made me to dwell in darkness, as those that have been dead of old: and my spirit is in anguish within me: my heart within me is troubled. . . .

I stretched forth my hands to thee: my soul is as earth without water unto thee.

Hear me speedily, O Lord; my spirit hath fainted away.

Turn not away thy face from me, lest I be like unto them that go down into the pit.

Cause me to hear thy mercy in the morning; for in thee have I hoped.—*Ps.* cxlii. 1, 3, 4, 6-8.

They compassed me on every side, and there was no one that would help me. I looked for the succor of men, and there was none.

. . . I called upon the Lord, the father of my Lord, that he would not leave me in the day of my trouble, and in the time of the proud without help. . . .

And thou hast saved me from destruction, and hast delivered me from the evil time.—*Ecclus.* li. 10, 14, 16.

I will cry like a young swallow, I will meditate like a dove: my eyes are weakened looking upward: Lord, I suffer violence, answer thou for me.—*Is.* xxxviii. 14.

Look down upon us, O Lord, from thy holy house, and incline thy ear, and hear us.

Open thy eyes, and behold: for the dead that are in hell, whose spirit is taken away from their bowels, shall not give glory and justice to the Lord:

But the soul that is sorrowful for the greatness of evil she hath done, and goeth bowed down, and feeble, and the eyes that fail, and the hungry soul, giveth glory and justice to thee the Lord.

For it is not for the justices of our fathers, that we pour out our prayers, and beg mercy in thy sight, O Lord our God:

But because thou hast sent out thy wrath, and thy indignation upon us, as thou hast spoken by the hand of thy servants, the prophets.—*Bar.* ii. 16-20.

And now, O Lord Almighty, the God of Israel, the soul in anguish, and the troubled spirit crieth to thee:

Hear, O Lord, and have mercy, for thou art a merciful God, and have pity on us: for we have sinned before thee.

For thou remainest for ever, and shall we perish everlastingly?

O Lord Almighty, the God of Israel, hear now the prayer of the dead of Israel, and of their children, that have sinned before thee, and have not hearkened to the voice of the Lord their God, wherefore evils have cleaved fast to us.

Remember not the iniquities of our fathers, but think upon thy hand, and upon thy name at this time:

For thou art the Lord our God, and we will praise thee, O Lord.—*Bar.* iii. 1-6.

When my soul was in distress within me, I remembered the Lord: that my prayer may come to thee, unto thy holy temple.—*Jonas* ii. 8.

PRAYER THAT GOD WILL LISTEN TO US, A

But have regard to the prayer of thy servant, and to his supplications, O Lord my God: hear the hymn and the prayer, which thy servant prayeth before thee this day.—*3 Kings* viii. 28.

For thou art my God: let thy eyes, I beseech thee, be open, and let thy ears be attentive to the prayer, that is made in this place.—*2 Paral.* vi. 40.

Let thy ears be attentive, and thy eyes open, to hear the prayer of thy servant, which I pray before thee now, night and day, for the children of Israel thy servants: and I confess the sins of the children of Israel, by which they have sinned against thee: I and my father's house have sinned.—*2 Esd.* i. 6.

O God of the heavens, creator of the waters, and Lord of the whole creation, hear me a poor wretch, making supplication to thee, and presuming of thy mercy.—*Judith* ix. 17.

When I called upon him, the God of my justice heard me: when I was in distress, thou hast enlarged me. Have mercy on me: and hear my prayer.—*Ps.* iv. 2.

Give ear, O Lord, to my words, understand my cry.

Hearken to the voice of my prayer, O my King and my God.

For to thee will I pray: O Lord, in the morning thou shalt hear my voice.—*Ps.* v. 2-4.

Hear, O Lord, my justice: attend to my supplication.

Give ear unto my prayer, which proceedeth not from deceitful lips. . .

I have cried to thee, for thou, O God, hast heard me: O incline thy ear unto me, and hear my words.—*Ps.* xvi. 1, 6.

May the Lord hear thee in the day of tribulation: may the name of the God of Jacob protect thee.—*Ps.* xix. 2.

O Lord, save the king: and hear us in the day that we shall call upon thee.—*Ps.* xix. 9.

Hear, O Lord, my voice, with which I have cried to thee: have mercy on me, and hear me.—*Ps.* xxvi. 7.

Unto thee will I cry, O Lord; O my God, be not thou silent to me: lest if thou be silent to me, I become like them that go down into the pit.

Hear, O Lord, the voice of my supplication, when I pray to thee; when I lift up my hands to thy holy temple.—*Ps.* xxvii. 1, 2.

Hear my prayer, O Lord, and my supplication: give ear to my tears.

Be not silent: for I am a stranger with thee, and a sojourner, as all my fathers were.—*Ps.* xxxviii. 13.

Hear, O God, my prayer, and despise not my supplication: be attentive to me, and hear me.—*Ps.* liv. 2, 3.

Hear, O God, my supplication: be attentive to my prayer.

To thee have I cried from the ends of the earth: when my heart was in anguish, thou hast exalted me on a rock.—*Ps.* lx. 2, 3.

Hear, O God, my prayer, when I make supplication to thee: deliver my soul from the fear of the enemy.—*Ps.* lxiii. 2.

O hear my prayer: all flesh shall come to thee.—*Ps.* lxiv. 3.

But as for me, my prayer is to thee, O Lord; for the time of thy good pleasure, O God.

In the multitude of thy mercy, hear me, in the truth of thy salvation. . . .

Hear me, O Lord, for thy mercy is kind. . . .

And turn not away thy face from thy servant: for I am in trouble, hear me speedily.—*Ps.* lxviii. 14, 17, 18.

O Lord God of hosts, hear my prayer: give ear, O God of Jacob.—*Ps.* lxxxiii. 9.

Incline thy ear, O Lord, and hear me: for I am needy and poor. . . .

Give ear, O Lord, to my prayer: and attend to the voice of my petition.

I have called upon thee in the day of my trouble: because thou hast heard me.—*Ps.* lxxxv. 1, 6, 7.

O Lord, the God of my salvation: I have cried in the day, and in the night before thee.

Let my prayer come in before thee: incline thy ear to my petition.—*Ps.* lxxxvii. 2, 3.

Return, O Lord, how long? and be entreated in favor of thy servants.—*Ps.* lxxxix. 13.

Hear, O Lord, my prayer: and let my cry come to thee.

Turn not away thy face from me: in the day when I am in trouble, incline thy ear to me. In what day soever I shall call upon thee, hear me speedily. —*Ps.* ci. 2, 3.

Hear thou my voice, O Lord, accord-

ing to thy mercy: and quicken me, according to thy judgment. . . .

Let my supplication, O Lord, come near in thy sight. . . .

Let my request come in before thee; deliver thou me according to thy word. —*Ps.* cxviii. 149, 169, 170.

In what day soever I shall call upon thee, hear me: thou shalt multiply strength in my soul.—*Ps.* cxxxvii. 3.

I have cried to thee, O Lord, hear me: hearken to my voice, when I cry to thee.

Let my prayer be directed as incense in thy sight; the lifting up of my hands, as evening sacrifice.—*Ps.* cxl. 1, 2.

Now therefore, O our God, hear the supplication of thy servant, and his prayers: and show thy face upon thy sanctuary which is desolate, for thy own sake.

Incline, O my God, thy ear, and hear: open thy eyes, and see our desolation, and the city upon which thy name is called: for it is not for our justifications that we present our prayers before thy face, but for the multitude of thy tender mercies.

O Lord, hear: O Lord, be appeased: hearken and do: delay not, for thy own sake, O my God: because thy name is invocated upon thy city, and upon thy people.—*Dan.* ix. 17-19.

PRAYER THAT GOD WILL LOOK DOWN UPON US IN PITY, A

See also: Mercy of God, a prayer for the—page 323.

The Lord show his face to thee, and have mercy on thee.

The Lord turn his countenance to thee, and give thee peace.—*Num.* vi. 25, 26.

O God, my God, look upon me: why hast thou forsaken me?—*Ps.* xxi. 2.

Look thou upon me, and have mercy on me; for I am alone and poor.—*Ps.* xxiv. 16.

Make thy face to shine upon thy servant; save me in thy mercy.—*Ps.* xxx. 17.

Be pleased, O Lord, to deliver me:

look down, O Lord, to help me.—*Ps.* xxxix. 14.

Hear me, O Lord, for thy mercy is kind; look upon me according to the multitude of thy tender mercies.

And turn not away thy face from thy servant: for I am in trouble, hear me speedily.—*Ps.* lxviii. 17, 18.

Turn again, O God of hosts, look down from heaven, and see, and visit this vineyard:

And perfect the same, which thy right hand hath planted: and upon the son of man, whom thou hast confirmed for thyself.—*Ps.* lxxix. 15, 16.

O look upon me, and have mercy on me: give thy command to thy servant, and save the son of thy handmaid.—*Ps.* lxxxv. 16.

Look upon thy servants, and upon their works: and direct their children. —*Ps.* lxxxix. 16.

Look thou upon me, and have mercy on me, according to the judgment of them that love thy name.—*Ps.* cxviii. 132.

Look down from heaven, and behold from thy holy habitation and the place of thy glory: where is thy zeal, and thy strength, the multitude of thy bowels, and of thy mercies? they have held back themselves from me.—*Is.* lxiii. 15.

Look down upon us, O Lord, from thy holy house, and incline thy ear, and hear us.—*Bar.* ii. 16.

PREACHING

Moses said: I beseech thee, Lord, I am not eloquent from yesterday and the day before: and since thou hast spoken to thy servant, I have more impediment and slowness of tongue.

The Lord said to him: Who made man's mouth? or who made the dumb and the deaf, the seeing and the blind? did not I?

Go therefore, and I will be in thy mouth: and I will teach thee what thou shalt speak.—*Ex.* iv. 10-12.

He (Balaam) answered him: Can I speak anything else but what the Lord commandeth?—*Num.* xxiii. 12.

I have declared thy justice in a great church, lo, I will not restrain my lips: O Lord, thou knowest it.

I have not hid thy justice within my heart: I have declared thy truth and thy salvation. I have not concealed thy mercy and thy truth from a great council.—*Ps.* xxxix. 10, 11.

The Lord shall give the word to them that preach good tidings with great power.—*Ps.* lxvii. 12.

How beautiful upon the mountains are the feet of him that bringeth good tidings, and that preacheth peace: of him that showeth forth good, that preacheth salvation, that sayeth to Sion: Thy God shall reign!—*Is.* lii. 7.

But they that are learned, shall shine as the brightness of the firmament: and they that instruct many to justice, as stars for all eternity.—*Dan.* xii. 3.

Behold upon the mountains the feet of him that bringeth good tidings, and that preacheth peace.—*Nahum* i. 15.

How then shall they call on him, in whom they have not believed? Or how shall they believe him, of whom they have not heard? And how shall they hear without a preacher?

And how shall they preach unless they be sent, as it is written: How beautiful are the feet of them that preach the gospel of peace, of them that bring glad tidings of good things! . . .

Faith then cometh by hearing; and hearing by the word of Christ.—*Rom.* x. 14, 15, 17.

For if I preach the gospel, it is no glory to me, for a necessity lieth upon me: for woe is unto me if I preach not the gospel.

For if I do this thing willingly, I have a reward: but if against my will, a dispensation is committed to me.—1 *Cor.* ix. 16, 17.

For if the trumpet give an uncertain sound, who shall prepare himself to the battle?

So likewise you, except you utter by the tongue plain speech, how shall it be known what is said? For you shall be speaking into the air.—1 *Cor.* xiv. 8, 9.

For we preach not ourselves, but Jesus Christ, our Lord; and ourselves your servants through Jesus.—2 *Cor.* iv. 5.

Praying withal for us also, that God may open unto us a door of speech, to speak the mystery of Christ (for which also I am bound;)

That I may make it manifest as I ought to speak.—*Col.* iv. 3, 4.

Take heed to thyself and to doctrine: be earnest in them. For in doing this, thou shalt both save thyself and them that hear thee.—1 *Tim.* iv. 16.

Carefully study to present thyself approved unto God, a workman that needeth not to be ashamed, rightly handling the word of truth.—2 *Tim.* ii. 15.

I charge thee before God and Jesus Christ, who shall judge the living and the dead, by his coming and his kingdom:

Preach the word: be instant, in season, out of season: reprove, entreat, rebuke in all patience and doctrine.

For there shall be a time, when they will not endure sound doctrine; but, according to their own desires, they will heap to themselves teachers, having itching ears:

And will indeed turn away their hearing from the truth, but will be turned unto fables.

But be thou vigilant, labor in all things, do the work of an evangelist, fulfil thy ministry.—2 *Tim.* iv. 1-5.

But hath in due times manifested his word in preaching, which is committed to me, according to the commandment of God our Saviour.—*Titus* i. 3.

My brethren, if any of you err from the truth, and one convert him:

He must know that he who causeth a sinner to be converted from the error of his way, shall save his soul from death, and shall cover a multitude of sins.—*James* v. 19, 20.

PRESENCE OF GOD IN OUR MIDST, THE

See also: Near to his people, God is —page 340.

And when Jacob awaked out of sleep, he said: Indeed the Lord is in this place, and I knew it not.—*Gen.* xxviii. 16.

I will set my tabernacle in the midst of you, and my soul shall not cast you off.

I will walk among you, and will be your God, and you shall be my people. —*Lev.* xxvi. 11, 12.

Rejoice, and praise, O thou **habitation** of Sion: for great is he that is in the midst of thee, the Holy One of Israel.—*Is.* xii. 6.

For where there are two or three gathered together in my name, there am I in the midst of them.—*Matt.* xviii. 20.

And [1]they drew nigh to the town, whither they were going: and he made as though he would go farther.

But they constrained him, saying: Stay, with us, because it is towards evening, and the day is now far spent. And he went in with them. . . .

And they said one to another: Was not our heart burning within us, whilst he spoke in the way, and opened to us the scriptures?—*Luke* xxiv. 28, 29, 32.

For you are the temple of the living God; as God saith: I will dwell in them, and walk among them; and I will be their God, and they shall be my people. —2 *Cor.* vi. 16.

PRESENCE OF GOD, WE SHOULD KEEP OURSELVES IN THE

See also: Near to God, we should keep—page 342.

And after he (Abram) began to be ninety and nine years old, the Lord appeared to him: and said unto him: I am the Almighty God: walk before me, and be perfect.—*Gen.* xvii. 1.

And all the days of thy life, have God in thy mind: and take heed thou never consent to sin, nor transgress the commandments of the Lord our God.— *Tob.* iv. 6.

In the morning I will stand before thee, and will see: because thou art not a God that willest iniquity.—*Ps.* v. 5.

I set the Lord always in my sight: for he is at my right hand, that I be not moved.—*Ps.* xv. 8.

And the words of my mouth shall be such as may please: and the meditation of my heart always in thy sight.

O Lord, my helper, and my redeemer. —*Ps.* xviii. 15.

Come, let us praise the Lord with joy: let us joyfully sing to God our saviour.

[1]The two disciples on the way to Emmaus, meeting Jesus.

Let us come before his presence with thanksgiving, and make a joyful noise to him with psalms.—*Ps.* xciv. 1, 2.

Sing joyfully to God, all the earth: serve ye the Lord with gladness.

Come in before his presence with exceeding great joy.—*Ps.* xcix. 2.

I am a wall: and my breasts are as a tower, since I am become in his presence as one finding peace.—*Cant.* viii. 10.

PRESERVER, GOD OUR

See also: Protector, God our—page 447.

Thou hast granted me life and mercy, and thy visitation hath preserved my spirit.—*Job* x. 12.

Thou, O Lord, wilt preserve us: and keep us from this generation for ever.—*Ps.* xi. 8.

You that love the Lord, hate evil: the Lord preserveth the souls of his saints, he will deliver them out of the hand of the sinner.—*Ps.* xcvi. 10.

If it had not been that the Lord was with us, let Israel now say:

If it had not been that the Lord was with us,

When men rose up against us, perhaps they had swallowed us up alive.

When their fury was enkindled against us, perhaps the waters had swallowed us up. . . .

Blessed be the Lord, who hath not given us to be a prey to their teeth.

Our soul hath been delivered as a sparrow out of the snare of the fowlers.

The snare is broken, and we are delivered.—*Ps.* cxxiii. 1-4, 6, 7.

I will give glory to thy name: for thou hast been a helper and protector to me.

And hast preserved my body from destruction, from the snare of an unjust tongue, and from the lips of them that forge lies, and in the sight of them that stood by, thou hast been my helper.—*Ecclus.* li. 2, 3.

I pray not that thou shouldst take them out of the world, but that thou shouldst keep them from evil.—*John* xvii. 15.

But God is faithful, who will strengthen and keep you from evil.—2 *Thess.* iii. 3.

Now to him who is able to preserve you without sin, and to present you spotless before the presence of his glory, with exceeding joy, in the coming of our Lord Jesus Christ,

To the only God our Saviour, through Jesus Christ our Lord, be glory and magnificence, empire and power, before all ages, and now, and for all ages of ages. Amen.—*Jude* i. 24, 25.

PRESUMPTION

Blessed is the man that is always fearful: but he that is hardened in mind, shall fall into evil.—*Prov.* xxviii. 14.

Better is the patient man than the presumptuous.—*Eccles.* vii. 9.

The fear of the Lord driveth out sin:

For he that is without fear, cannot be justified: for the wrath of his high spirits is his ruin.—*Ecclus.* i. 27, 28.

Son, when thou comest to the service of God, stand in justice and in fear, and prepare thy soul for temptation.—*Ecclus.* ii. 1.

A wise man will fear in every thing, and in the days of sins, will beware of sloth.—*Ecclus.* xviii. 27.

And he will repay vengeance to the Gentiles, till he have taken away the multitude of the proud, and broken the sceptres of the unjust,

Till he have rendered to men according to their deeds: and according to the works of Adam, and according to his presumption.—*Ecclus.* xxxv. 23, 24.

O wicked presumption, whence camest thou to cover the earth with thy malice, and deceitfulness?—*Ecclus.* xxxvii. 3.

PRESUMING UPON GOD'S MERCY, AGAINST

Serve ye the Lord with fear: and rejoice unto him with trembling.—*Ps.* ii. 11.

If the just man receive in the earth, how much more the wicked and the sinner.—*Prov.* xi. 31.

All these things have I considered in my heart, that I might carefully understand them: there are just men and wise men, and their works are in the hand of God: and yet man knoweth not whether he be worthy of love or hatred.—*Eccles.* ix. 1.

Say not: I have sinned, and what harm hath befallen me? for the most High is a patient rewarder.

Be not without fear about sin forgiven, and add not sin upon sin:

And say not: The mercy of the Lord is great, he will have mercy on the multitude of my sins.

For mercy and wrath quickly come from him, and his wrath looketh upon sinners.—*Ecclus.* v. 4-7.

Sanctify the Lord of hosts himself: and let him be your fear, and let him be your dread.

And he shall be a sanctification to you.—*Is.* viii. 13, 14.

Thou wilt say then: The branches were broken off, that I might be grafted in.

Well: because of unbelief they were broken off. But thou standest by faith: be not high-minded, but fear.

For if God hath not spared the natural branches, fear lest perhaps he also spare not thee.

See then the goodness and the severity of God: towards them indeed that are fallen, the severity; but towards thee, the goodness of God, if thou abide in goodness, otherwise thou also shalt be cut off.—*Rom.* xi. 19-22.

Wherefore, my dearly beloved, (as you have always obeyed, not as in my presence only, but much more now in my absence,) with fear and trembling work out your salvation.—*Philipp.* ii. 12.

Therefore receiving an immovable kingdom, we have grace; whereby let us serve, pleasing God, with fear and reverence.

For our God is a consuming fire.—*Heb.* xii. 28, 29.

And if you invoke as Father him who, without respect of persons, judgeth according to every one's work: converse in fear during the time of your sojourning here.—1 *Peter* i. 17.

And if the just man shall scarcely be saved, where shall the ungodly and the sinner appear?—1 *Peter* iv. 18.

Wherefore, brethren, labor the more, that by good works, you may make sure your calling and election. For doing these things, you shall not sin at any time.—2 *Peter* i. 10.

PRESUMING UPON OUR OWN STRENGTH OR RESOURCES

The Lord said to me: Say to them: Go not up, and fight not, for I am not with you: lest you fall before your enemies.

I spoke, and you hearkened not: but resisting the commandment of the Lord, and swelling with pride, you went up into the mountain.

And the Amorrhite that dwelt in the mountains, coming out, and meeting you, chased you, as bees do: and made slaughter of you from Seir as far as Horma.—*Deut.* i. 42-44.

And after he had afflicted and proved thee, at the last, he had mercy on thee,

Lest thou shouldst say in thy heart: My own might, and the strength of my own hand have achieved all these things for me.

But remember the Lord thy God, that he hath given thee strength, that he might fulfil his covenant, concerning which he swore to thy fathers, as this present day showeth.—*Deut.* viii. 16-18.

O Lord God of heaven and earth, behold their pride, and look on our low condition, and have regard to the face of thy saints, and show that thou forsakest not them that trust on thee, and that thou humblest them that presume of themselves, and glory in their own strength.—*Judith* vi. 15.

The just shall see, and fear, and shall laugh at him, and say: Behold the man that made not God his helper:

But trusted in the abundance of his riches: and prevailed in his vanity.—*Ps.* li. 8, 9.

He that is good, shall draw grace from the Lord: but he that trusteth in his own devices, doth wickedly.—*Prov.* xii. 2.

He that trusteth in his own heart, is a fool: but he that walketh wisely, he shall be saved.—*Prov.* xxviii. 26.

Follow not in thy strength the desires of thy heart:

And say not: How mighty am I?

and who shall bring me under for my deeds? for God will surely take revenge. —*Ecclus.* v. 2, 3.

Say not: What need I, and what good shall I have by this?

Say not: I am sufficient for myself: and what shall I be made worse by this? —*Ecclus.* xi. 25, 26.

And thou hast trusted in thy wickedness, and hast said: There is none that seeth me. Thy wisdom and thy knowledge, this hath deceived thee. And thou hast said in thy heart: I am, and besides me there is no other.

Evil shall come upon thee, and thou shalt not know the rising thereof: and calamity shall fall violently upon thee, which thou canst not keep off: misery shall come upon thee suddenly, which thou shalt not know.—*Is.* xlvii. 10, 11.

Then Jesus saith to them: All you shall be scandalized in me this night. For it is written: I will strike the shepherd, and the sheep of the flock shall be dispersed. . . .

And Peter answering, said to him: Although all shall be scandalized in thee, I will never be scandalized.

Jesus said to him: Amen I say to thee, that in this night before the cock crow, thou wilt deny me thrice.

Peter saith to him: Yea, though I should die with thee, I will not deny thee. And in like manner said all the disciples.—*Matt.* xxvi. 31, 33-35.

PRESUMING UPON OUR OWN STRENGTH OR RESOURCES, THE UNREASONABLE- NESS OF

He will keep the feet of his saints, and the wicked shall be silent in darkness, because no man shall prevail by his own strength.—1 *Kings* ii. 9.

Wilt thou make void my judgment: and condemn me, that thou mayst be justified?

And hast thou an arm like God, and canst thou thunder with a voice like him?

Clothe thyself with beauty, and set thyself up on high, and be glorious, and put on goodly garments.

Scatter the proud in thy indignation, and behold every arrogant man, and humble him.

Look on all that are proud, and confound them, and crush the wicked in their place.

Hide them in the dust together, and plunge their faces into the pit.

Then I will confess that thy right hand is able to save thee.—*Job* xl. 3-9.

They that trust in their own strength, and glory in the multitude of their riches,

No brother can redeem, nor shall man redeem: he shall not give to God his ransom,

Nor the price of the redemption of his soul: and shall labor for ever.—*Ps.* xlviii. 7-9.

Who is the man that shall live, and not see death: that shall deliver his soul from the hand of hell?—*Ps.* lxxxviii. 49.

And such confidence we have, through Christ, towards God.

Not that we are sufficient to think any thing of ourselves, as of ourselves: but our sufficiency is from God.— 2 *Cor.* iii. 4, 5.

But we have this treasure in earthen vessels, that the excellency may be of the power of God, and not of us.— 2 *Cor.* iv. 7.

PRESUMING UPON OUR OWN WISDOM OR KNOWLEDGE

Then Job answered the Lord, and said:

I know that thou canst do all things, and no thought is hid from thee.

Who is this that hideth counsel without knowledge? Therefore I have spoken unwisely, and things that above measure exceeded my knowledge.—*Job* xlii. 1-3.

Have confidence in the Lord with all thy heart, and lean not upon thy own prudence.

In all thy ways think on him, and he will direct thy steps.

Be not wise in thy own conceit: fear God, and depart from evil.—*Prov.* iii. 5-7.

Seek not the things that are too high for thee, and search not into things above thy ability: but the things that

God hath commanded thee, think on them always, and in many of his works be not curious.

For it is not necessary for thee to see with thy eyes those things that are hid.

In unnecessary matters be not over curious, and in many of his works thou shalt not be inquisitive.

For many things are shown to thee above the understanding of men.

And the suspicion of them hath deceived many, and hath detained their minds in vanity.—*Ecclus.* iii. 22-26.

PRESUMING UPON OUR OWN WISDOM OR KNOWLEDGE, THE UNREASONABLE- NESS OF

Shall any one teach God knowledge, who judgeth those that are high?—*Job* xxi. 22.

Can man be compared with God, even though he were of perfect knowledge? —*Job* xxii. 2.

To whom hast thou given counsel? perhaps to him that hath no wisdom, and thou hast shown thy very great prudence.

Whom hast thou desired to teach? was it not him that made life?—*Job* xxvi. 3, 4.

The steps of man are guided by the Lord: but who is the man that can understand his own way?—*Prov.* xx. 24.

PRESUMING UPON OUR OWN JUSTICE OR MERIT

Hear, O Israel; Thou shalt go over the Jordan this day; to possess nations very great, and stronger than thyself, cities great, and walled up to the sky. . . .

Say not in thy heart, when the Lord thy God shall have destroyed them in thy sight: For my justice hath the Lord brought me in to possess this land, whereas these nations are destroyed for their wickedness.

For it is not for thy justices, and the uprightness of thy heart, that thou shalt go in to possess their lands: but because they have done wickedly, they are destroyed at thy coming in: and

that the Lord might accomplish his word, which he promised by oath to thy fathers Abraham, Isaac, and Jacob.— *Deut.* ix. 1, 4, 5.

Justify not thyself before God, for he knoweth the heart.—*Ecclus.* vii. 5.

And thou hast said: I am without sin and am innocent: and therefore let thy anger be turned away from me. Behold, I will contend with thee in judgment, because thou hast said: I have not sinned.—*Jer.* ii. 35.

For I am with thee, saith the Lord, to save thee: for I will utterly consume all the nations, among which I have scattered thee: but I will not utterly consume thee: but I will chastise thee in judgment, that thou mayst not seem to thyself innocent.—*Jer.* xxx. 11.

For I bear them (the Jews) witness, that they have a zeal of God, but not according to knowledge.

For they, not knowing the justice of God, and seeking to establish their own, have not submitted themselves to the justice of God.—*Rom.* x. 2, 3.

But I chastise my body, and bring it into subjection: lest perhaps, when I have preached to others, I myself should become a castaway.—1 *Cor.* ix. 27.

Wherefore, he that thinketh himself to stand, let him take heed lest he fall. —1 *Cor.* x. 12.

PRESUMING UPON OUR OWN JUSTICE OR MERIT, THE UN- REASONABLENESS OF

O the Lord, the Lord God, merciful and gracious, patient and of much compassion, and true,

Who keepest mercy unto thousands: who takest away iniquity, and wickedness, and sin, and no man of himself is innocent before thee.—*Ex.* xxxiv. 6, 7.

Shall man be justified in comparison of God, or shall a man be more pure than his maker?

Behold they that serve him are not steadfast, and in his angels he found wickedness:

How much more shall they that dwell in houses of clay, who have an earthly foundation, be consumed, as with the moth?—*Job* iv. 17-19.

What am I, then, that I should answer him, and have words with him?

I, who although I should have any just thing, would not answer, but would make supplication to my judge.

And if he should hear me when I call, I should not believe that he had heard my voice. . . .

If I would justify myself, my own mouth shall condemn me: if I would show myself innocent, he shall prove me wicked. . . .

For I shall not answer a man that is like myself: nor one that may be heard with me equally in judgment.—*Job* ix. 14-16, 20, 32.

What is man that he should be without spot, and he that is born of a woman, that he should appear just?

Behold among his saints none is unchangeable, and the heavens are not pure in his sight.

How much more is man abominable and unprofitable, who drinketh iniquity like water?—*Job* xv. 14-16.

Can man be justified compared with God, or he that is born of a woman, appear clean?

Behold even the moon doth not shine, and the stars are not pure in his sight.

How much less man that is rottenness, and the son of man who is a worm?—*Job* xxv. 4-6.

And enter not into judgment with thy servant: for in thy sight no man living shall be justified.—*Ps.* cxlii. 2.

Who can say: My heart is clean, I am pure from sin?—*Prov.* xx. 9.

For there is no just man upon earth, that doth good, and sinneth not.—*Eccles.* vii. 21.

And the scribes and Pharisees bring unto him a woman taken in adultery: and they set her in the midst,

And said to him: Master, this woman was even now taken in adultery.

Now Moses in the law commanded us to stone such a one. But what sayest thou? . . .

When therefore they continued asking him, he lifted up himself, and said to them: He that is without sin among you, let him first cast a stone at her.—*John* viii. 3-5, 7.

For I am not conscious to myself of any thing, yet am I not hereby justified; but he that judgeth me, is the Lord.—1 *Cor.* iv. 4.

For not he who commendeth himself, is approved, but he whom God commendeth.—2 *Cor.* x. 18.

For in many things we all offend. If any man offend not in word, the same is a perfect man.—*James* iii. 2.

If we say that we have no sin, we deceive ourselves, and the truth is not in us.—1 *John* i. 8.

PRIDE

For thy power, O Lord, is not in a multitude, nor is thy pleasure in the strength of horses, nor from the beginning have the proud been acceptable to thee: but the prayer of the humble and the meek hath always pleased thee. —*Judith* ix. 16.

A vain man is lifted up into pride, and thinketh himself born free like a wild ass's colt.—*Job* xi. 12.

The wicked man is proud all his days, and the number of the years of his tyranny is uncertain.—*Job* xv. 20.

The Lord hath heard the desire of the poor: thy ear hath heard the preparation of their heart.

To judge for the fatherless and for the humble, that man may no more presume to magnify himself upon earth.—*Ps.* ix. (*Heb.* x.) 17, 18.

Where pride is, there also shall be reproach: but where humility is, there also is wisdom.—*Prov.* xi. 2.

It is better to be humbled with the meek, than to divide spoils with the proud.—*Prov.* xvi. 19.

Pride was not made for men: nor wrath for the race of women.—*Ecclus.* x. 22.

Three sorts my soul hateth, and I am greatly grieved at their life:

A poor man that is proud: a rich man that is a liar: an old man that is a fool and doting.—*Ecclus.* xxv. 3, 4.

We have heard of the pride of Moab, he is exceeding proud: his pride and his arrogancy, and his indignation is more than his strength.—*Is.* xvi. 6.

We have heard the pride of Moab, he is exceeding proud: his haughtiness, and his arrogancy, and his pride, and the loftiness of his heart.

I know, saith the Lord, his boasting,

and that the strength thereof is not according to it, neither hath it endeavored to do according as it was able.—*Jer.* xlviii. 29, 30.

The Lord hath sworn against the pride of Jacob: surely I will never forget all their works.—*Amos* viii. 7.

PRIDE, THE FOLLY OF

What is a man that thou shouldst magnify him? or why dost thou set thy heart upon him?—*Job* vii. 17.

What is man that thou art mindful of him? or the son of man that thou visitest him?—*Ps.* viii. 5.   ,

Lord, what is man that thou art made known to him? or the son of man, that thou makest account of him?

Man is like to vanity: his days pass away like a shadow.—*Ps.* cxliii. 3, 4.

The proud and the arrogant is called ignorant, who in anger worketh pride.—*Prov.* xxi. 24.

Shall the axe boast itself against him that cutteth with it? or shall the saw exalt itself against him by whom it is drawn? or as if a rod should lift itself up against him that lifteth it up, and a staff exalt itself, which is but wood.—*Is.* x. 15.

Thus he (Antiochus) that seemed to himself to command even the waves of the sea, being proud above the condition of man, and to weigh the heights of the mountains in a balance, now being cast down to the ground, was carried in a litter, bearing witness to the manifest power of God in himself:

So that worms swarmed out of the body of this man, and whilst he lived in sorrow and pain, his flesh fell off, and the filthiness of his smell was noisome to the army.

And the man that thought a little before, he could reach to the stars of heaven, no man could endure to carry, for the intolerable stench.

And by this means, being brought from his great pride, he began to come to the knowledge of himself, being admonished by the scourge of God, his pains increasing every moment.

And when he himself could not now abide his own stench, he spoke thus: It is just to be subject to God, and that a mortal man should not equal himself to God.—*2 Mach.* ix. 8-12.

For who distinguisheth thee? Or what hast thou that thou hast not received? And if thou hast received, why dost thou glory, as if thou hadst not received it?—*1 Cor.* iv. 7.

For if any man think himself to be something, whereas he is nothing, he deceiveth himself.—*Gal.* vi. 3.

PRIDE OF LIFE

And thy heart was lifted up with thy beauty: thou hast lost thy wisdom in thy beauty, I have cast thee to the ground: I have set thee before the face of kings, that they might behold thee.—*Ezech.* xxviii. 17.

You that rejoice in a thing of nought: you that say: Have we not taken unto us horns by our own strength?—*Amos* vi. 14.

PRIDE OF LIFE, THE FOLLY OF

See also: Powerlessness, before God, man's—page 389.

In the sweat of thy face shalt thou eat bread, till thou return to the earth, out of which thou wast taken: for dust thou art, and into dust thou shalt return. . . .

And the Lord God sent him out of the paradise of pleasure, to till the earth from which he was taken.—*Gen.* iii. 19, 23.

Naked came I out of my mother's womb, and naked shall I return thither: the Lord gave, and the Lord hath taken away: as it hath pleased the Lord, so is it done.—*Job* i. 21.

Remember, I beseech thee, that thou hast made me as the clay, and thou wilt bring me into dust again.—*Job* x. 9.

I have said to rottenness: Thou art my father; to worms, my mother and my sister.—*Job* xvii. 14.

All flesh shall perish together, and man shall return into ashes.—*Job* xxxiv. 15.

Where wast thou when I laid the foundations of the earth? tell me, if thou hast understanding.—*Job* xxxviii. 4.

What profit is there in my blood, whilst I go down to corruption?

Shall dust confess to thee, or declare thy truth?—*Ps.* xxix. 10.

For he knoweth our frame.

He remembereth that we are dust: man's days are as grass, as the flower of the field, so shall he flourish.

For the spirit shall pass in him, and he shall not be: and he shall know his place no more.—*Ps.* cii. 14-16.

And all things go to one place: of earth they were made, and into earth they return together.—*Eccles.* iii. 20.

What hath pride profited us? or what advantage hath the boasting of riches brought us?

All those things are passed away like a shadow, and like a post that runneth on,

And as a ship that passeth through the waves: whereof when it is gone by, the trace cannot be found, nor the path of its keel in the waters:

Or as when a bird flieth through the air, of the passage of which no mark can be found, but only the sound of the wings beating the light air, and parting it by the force of her flight; she moved her wings, and hath flown through, and there is no mark found afterwards of her way:

Or as when an arrow is shot at a mark, the divided air presently cometh together again, so that the passage thereof is not known:

So we also being born, forthwith ceased to be: and have been able to show no mark of virtue: but are consumed in our wickedness.

Such things as these the sinners said in hell.—*Wis.* v. 8-14.

For all men have one entrance into life, and the like going out.—*Wis.* vii. 6.

Why is earth and ashes proud? . . .

For when a man shall die, he shall inherit serpents, and beasts, and worms. —*Ecclus.* x. 9, 13.

What is brighter than the sun; yet it shall be eclipsed. Or what is more wicked than that which flesh and blood hath invented? and this shall be reproved.

He beholdeth the power of the height of heaven: and all men are earth and ashes.—*Ecclus.* xvii. 30, 31.

What is man, and what is his grace?

and what is his good, or what is his evil?

The number of the days of men at the most are a hundred years: as a drop of water of the sea are they esteemed; and as a pebble of the sand, so are a few years compared to eternity.—*Ecclus.* xviii. 7, 8.

And all men are from the ground, and out of the earth, from whence Adam was created.—*Ecclus.* xxxiii. 10.

And fear not the words of a sinful man, for his glory is dung and worms:

To-day he is lifted up, and to-morrow he shall not be found, because he is returned into his earth; and his thought is come to nothing.—1 *Mach.* ii. 62, 63.

For we brought nothing into this world: and certainly we can carry nothing out.—1 *Tim.* vi. 7.

Behold, now you that say: To-day or to-morrow we will go into such a city, and there we will spend a year, and will traffic, and make our gain.

Whereas you know not what shall be on the morrow.

For what is your life? It is a vapor which appeareth for a little while, and afterwards shall vanish away. For that you should say: If the Lord will, and if we shall live, we will do this or that.

But now you rejoice in your arrogancies. All such rejoicing is wicked. —*James* iv. 13-16.

PRIDE OF INTELLECT

And the serpent said to the woman: No, you shall not die the death.

For God doth know that in what day soever you shall eat thereof, your eyes shall be opened, and you shall be as gods, knowing good and evil.—*Gen.* iii. 4, 5.

Therefore men shall fear him, and all that seem to themselves to be wise, shall not dare to behold him.—*Job* xxxvii. 24.

Lord, my heart is not exalted: nor are my eyes lofty.

Neither have I walked in great matters, nor in wonderful things above me. —*Ps.* cxxx. 1.

As it is not good for a man to eat much honey, so he that is a searcher of

majesty, shall be overwhelmed by glory.
—*Prov.* xxv. 27.

Where there is no hearing, pour not out words, and be not lifted up out of season with thy wisdom.—*Ecclus.* xxxii. 6.

And it shall come to pass, that when the Lord shall have performed all his works in mount Sion, and in Jerusalem, I will visit the fruit of the proud heart of the king of Assyria, and the glory of the haughtiness of his eyes.

For he hath said: By the strength of my own hand, I have done it, and by my own wisdom, I have understood.—*Is.* x. 12, 13.

'Behold thou art wiser than Daniel: no secret is hid from thee.

In thy wisdom and thy understanding thou hast made thyself strong: and hast gotten gold and silver into thy treasures.

By the greatness of thy wisdom, and by thy traffic, thou hast increased thy strength: and thy heart is lifted up with thy strength.—*Ezech.* xxviii. 3-5.

At that time Jesus answered and said: I confess to thee, O Father, Lord of heaven and earth, because thou hast hid these things from the wise and prudent, and hast revealed them to little ones.

Yea, Father; for so hath it seemed good in thy sight.—*Matt.* xi. 25, 26.

For the weapons of our warfare are not carnal, but mighty to God unto the pulling down of fortifications, destroying counsels,

And every height that exalteth itself against the knowledge of God, and bringing into captivity every understanding unto the obedience of Christ.—*2 Cor.* x. 4, 5.

Who is a wise man, and endued with knowledge among you? Let him show, by a good conversation, his work in the meekness of wisdom.—*James* iii. 13.

PRIDE OF INTELLECT, THE FOLLY OF

See also: Knowledge, the littleness of man's—page 272.

Peradventure thou wilt comprehend ¹That is, in thy own conceit.

the steps of God, and wilt find out the Almighty perfectly?

He is higher than heaven, and what wilt thou do? he is deeper than hell, and how wilt thou know?—*Job* xi 7, 8.

Hast thou heard God's counsel, and shall his wisdom be inferior to thee?—*Job* xv. 8.

His spirit shall go forth, and he shall return into his earth: in that day, all their thoughts shall perish.—*Ps.* cxlv. 4.

What needeth a man to seek things that are above him, whereas he knoweth not what is profitable for him in his life, in all the days of his pilgrimage, and the time that passeth like a shadow? Or who can tell him what shall be after him under the sun? . . .

Only this I have found, that God made man right, and he hath entangled himself with an infinity of questions. Who is as the wise man? and who hath known the resolution of the word?—*Eccles.* vii. 1, 30.

And I understood that man can find no reason of all those works of God that are done under the sun: and the more he shall labor to seek, so much the less shall he find: yea, though the wise man shall say that he knoweth it, he shall not be able to find it.—*Eccles.* viii. 17.

For I am thy servant, and the son of thy handmaid, a weak man, and of short time, and falling short of the understanding of judgment and laws. . . .

For who among men is he that can know the counsel of God? or who can think what the will of God is?

For the thoughts of mortal men are fearful, and our counsels uncertain. . . . .

And hardly do we guess aright at things that are upon earth: and with labor do we find the things that are before us. But the things that are in heaven, who shall search out?

And who shall know thy thought, except thou give wisdom, and send thy Holy Spirit from above?—*Wis.* ix. 5, 13, 14, 16, 17.

Seek not the things that are too high for thee, and search not into things above thy ability: but the things that God hath commanded thee, think on them always, and in many of his works be not curious.

For it is not necessary for thee to see with thy eyes those things that are hid.

In unnecessary matters, be not over curious, and in many of his works, thou shalt not be inquisitive.

For many things are shown to thee above the understanding of men.

And the suspicion of them hath deceived many, and hath detained their minds in vanity.—*Ecclus*. iii. 22-26.

But the foolish things of the world hath God chosen, that he may confound the wise.—1 *Cor*. i. 27.

Let no man deceive himself: if any man among you seem to be wise in this world, let him become a fool, that he may be wise.

For the wisdom of this world is foolishness with God. For it is written: I will catch the wise in their own craftiness.

And again: The Lord knoweth the thoughts of the wise, that they are vain. —1 *Cor*. iii. 18-20.

And if any man think that he knoweth any thing, he hath not yet known as he ought to know.—1 *Cor*. viii. 2.

PRIDE, SPIRITUAL

Say not in thy heart, when the Lord thy God shall have destroyed them in thy sight: For my justice hath the Lord brought me in to possess this land, whereas these nations are destroyed for their wickedness.

For it is not for thy justices, and the uprightness of thy heart, that thou shalt go in to possess their lands: but because they have done wickedly, they are destroyed at thy coming in: and that the Lord might accomplish his word, which he promised by oath to thy fathers Abraham, Isaac and Jacob.

Know therefore that the Lord thy God giveth thee not this excellent land in possession for thy justices, for thou art a very stiff-necked people.—*Deut*. ix. 4-6.

And if I be wicked, woe unto me: and if just, I shall not lift up my head, being filled with affliction and misery. —*Job* x. 15.

And thou hast said: I am without sin, and am innocent: and therefore let thy anger be turned away from me. Behold, I will contend with thee in judgment, because thou hast said: I have not sinned.—*Jer*. ii. 35.

Doth he thank that servant, for doing the things which he commanded him?

I think not. So you also, when you shall have done all these things, that are commanded you, say: We are unprofitable servants; we have done that which we ought to do.—*Luke* xvii. 9, 10.

And to some who trusted in themselves as just, and despised others, he spoke also this parable:

Two men went up into the temple to pray: the one a Pharisee, and the other a publican.

The Pharisee standing, prayed thus with himself: O God, I give thee thanks that I am not, as the rest of men, extortioners, unjust, adulterers, as also is this publican.

I fast twice in a week: I give tithes of all that I possess.

And the publican standing afar off, would not so much as lift up his eyes towards heaven; but struck his breast, saying: O God, be merciful to me a sinner.

I say to you, this man went down into his house justified, rather than the other: because every one that exalteth himself, shall be humbled: and he that humbleth himself, shall be exalted.— *Luke* xviii. 9-14.

PRIDE, THE FOLLY OF SPIRITUAL

See also: Acknowledgment of sin —page 14.

What am I then, that I should answer him, and have words with him?

I, who although I should have any just thing, would not answer, but would make supplication to my judge.

And if he should hear me when I call, I should not believe that he had heard my voice. . . .

If I would justify myself, my own mouth shall condemn me: if I would show myself innocent, he shall prove me wicked.—*Job* ix. 14-16, 20.

I feared all my works, knowing that thou didst not spare the offender.—*Job* ix. 28.

Can man be justified compared with God, or he that is born of a woman appear clean?

Behold even the moon doth not shine, and the stars are not pure in his sight. How much less man that is rottenness, and the son of man, who is a worm?—*Job* xxv. 4-6.

And enter not into judgment with thy servant: for in thy sight no man living shall be justified.—*Ps.* cxlii. 2.

All these things have I considered in my heart, that I might carefully understand them: there are just men and wise men, and their works are in the hand of God: and yet man knoweth not whether he be worthy of love, or hatred. —*Eccles.* ix. 1.

And Jesus said to him: Why dost thou call me good? None is good, but God alone.—*Luke* xviii. 19.

What then? Do we excel them? No, not so. For we have charged both Jews and Greeks, that they are all under sin.

As it is written: There is not any man just.

. . . For all have sinned, and do need the glory of God.

Being justified freely by his grace, through the redemption that is in Christ Jesus.—*Rom.* iii. 9, 10, 23, 24.

But he that glorieth, let him glory in the Lord.

For not he who commendeth himself is approved, but he whom God commendeth.—*2 Cor.* x. 17, 18.

Wherefore, my dearly beloved, (as you have always obeyed, not as in my presence only, but much more now in my absence,) with fear and trembling work out your salvation.—*Philipp.* ii. 12.

Not by the works of justice, which we have done, but according to his mercy, he saved us, by the laver of regeneration, and renovation of the Holy Ghost; Whom he hath poured forth upon us abundantly, through Jesus Christ our Saviour:

That being justified by his grace, we may be heirs, according to hope of life everlasting.—*Titus* iii. 5-7.

And if the just man shall scarcely be saved, where shall the ungodly and the sinner appear?—*1 Peter* iv. 18.

PRIDE IS REBELLION AGAINST GOD

But the soul that committeth any thing through pride, whether he be born in the land, or a stranger (because he hath been rebellious against the Lord), shall be cut off from among his people: For he hath contemned the word of the Lord, and made void his precept: therefore shall he be destroyed, and shall bear his iniquity.—*Num.* xv. 30, 31.

May the Lord destroy all deceitful lips, and the tongue that speaketh proud things.

Who have said: We will magnify our tongue; our lips are our own; who is Lord over us?—*Ps.* xi. 4, 5.

The beginning of the pride of man, is to fall off from God:

Because his heart is departed from him that made him: for pride is the beginning of all sin.—*Ecclus.* x. 14, 15.

And thou hast trusted in thy wickedness, and hast said: There is none that seeth me. Thy wisdom and thy knowledge, this hath deceived thee. And thou hast said in thy heart: I am, and besides me there is no other.—*Is.* xlvii. 10.

And the word of the Lord came to me, saying:

Son of man, say to the prince of Tyre: Thus saith the Lord God: Because thy heart is lifted up, and thou hast said: I am God, and I sit in the chair of God, in the heart of the sea: whereas thou art a man, and not God: and hast set thy heart as if it were the heart of God.

. . . Therefore thus saith the Lord God: Because thy heart is lifted up as the heart of God:

. . . They shall kill thee, and bring thee down: and thou shalt die the death of them that are slain in the heart of the sea.

Wilt thou yet say before them that slay thee: I am God; whereas thou art a man, and not God, in the hand of them that slay thee?—*Ezech.* xxviii. 1, 2, 5, 8, 9.

Thou also his son, O Baltasar, hast

not humbled thy heart, whereas thou knewest all these things.

But hast lifted thyself up against the Lord of heaven: . . . but the God who hath thy breath in his hand, and all thy ways, thou hast not glorified.—*Dan.* v. 22, 23.

For the weapons of our warfare are not carnal, but mighty to God unto the pulling down of fortifications, destroying counsels,

And every height that exalteth itself against the knowledge of God, and bringing into captivity every understanding unto the obedience of Christ. —2 *Cor.* x. 4, 5.

PRIDE IS THE SOURCE OF ALL OTHER SINS

Never suffer pride to reign in thy mind, or in thy words: for from it all perdition took its beginning.—*Tob.* iv. 14

Among the proud, there are always contentions: but they that do all things with counsel, are ruled by wisdom.—*Prov.* xiii. 10.

The congregation of the proud shall not be healed: for the plant of wickedness shall take root in them, and it shall not be perceived.—*Ecclus.* iii. 30.

The beginning of the pride of man, is to fall off from God:

Because his heart is departed from him that made him: for pride is the beginning of all sin: he that holdeth it, shall be filled with maledictions, and it shall ruin him in the end.—*Ecclus.* x. 14, 15.

Behold [1]this was the iniquity of Sodom thy sister, pride, fulness of bread, and abundance, and the idleness of her, and of her daughters: and they did not put forth their hand to the needy and to the poor.

And they were lifted up, and committed abominations before me: and I took them away, as thou hast seen.—*Ezech.* xvi. 49, 50.

PRIDE, GRIEVOUSNESS OF THE SIN OF

But the soul that committeth any thing through pride, whether he be born

[1]That is: these were the steps by which the Sodomites came to fall into those abominations, for which they were destroyed.

in the land, or a stranger (because he hath been rebellious against the Lord), shall be cut off from among his people:

For he hath contemned the word of the Lord, and made void his precept: therefore shall he be destroyed, and shall bear his iniquity.—*Num.*xv.30,31.

The fear of the Lord hateth evil: I hate arrogance, and pride, and every wicked way, and a mouth with a double tongue.—*Prov.* viii. 13.

Every proud man is an abomination to the Lord: even though hand should be joined to hand, he is not innocent.—*Prov.* xvi. 5.

Pride is hateful before God and men: and all iniquity of nations is execrable. —*Ecclus.* x. 7.

The Lord God hath sworn by his own soul, saith the Lord the God of hosts: I detest the pride of Jacob, and I hate his houses, and I will deliver up the city, with the inhabitants thereof.—*Amos* vi. 8.

Now the Pharisees, who were covetous, heard all these things: and they derided him (Jesus).

And he said to them: You are they who justify yourselves before men, but God knoweth your hearts; for that which is high to men, is an abomination before God.—*Luke* xvi. 14, 15.

But now you rejoice in your arrogancies. All such rejoicing is wicked. —*James* iv. 16.

PRIDE, EXHORTATION AGAINST

Take heed, and beware, lest at any time thou forget the Lord thy God, and neglect his commandments, and judgments and ceremonies, which I command thee this day:

Lest after thou hast eaten and art filled, hast built goodly houses and dwelt in them, . . .

Thy heart be lifted up, and thou remember not the Lord thy God, who brought thee out of the land of Egypt, out of the house of bondage: . . .

Lest thou shouldst say in thy heart: My own might, and the strength of my own hand have achieved all these things for me.—*Deut.* viii. 11, 12, 14, 17.

Never suffer pride to reign in thy mind, or in thy words: for from it all perdition took its beginning.—*Tob.* iv. 14.

Extol not thyself in the thoughts of thy soul like a bull: lest thy strength be quashed by folly,

And it eat up thy leaves, and destroy thy fruit, and thou be left as a dry tree in the wilderness.—*Ecclus.* vi. 2, 3.

Say not: What need I, and what good shall I have by this?

Say not: I am sufficient for myself: and what shall I be made worse by this? —*Ecclus.* xi. 25, 26.

Hear ye, and give ear: Be not proud, for the Lord hath spoken. . . .

But if you will not hear this, my soul shall weep in secret for your pride: weeping, it shall weep, and my eyes shall run down with tears, because the flock of the Lord is carried away captive.—*Jer.* xiii. 15, 17.

PRIDE, PUNISHMENT OF

O love the Lord, all ye his saints: for the Lord will require truth, and will repay them abundantly that act proudly. —*Ps.* xxx. 24.

For pride is the beginning of all sin: he that holdeth it, shall be filled with maledictions, and it shall ruin him in the end.—*Ecclus.* x. 15.

Mockery and reproach are of the proud, and vengeance as a lion shall lie in wait for him.—*Ecclus.* xxvii. 31.

And it shall come to pass, that when the Lord shall have performed all his works in mount Sion and in Jerusalem, I will visit the fruit of the proud heart of the king of Assyria, and the glory of the haughtiness of his eyes.

For he hath said: By the strength of my own hand I have done it, and by my own wisdom I have understood. . . .

Therefore the sovereign Lord, the Lord of hosts, shall send leanness among his fat ones: and under his glory shall be kindled a burning, as it were the burning of a fire.—*Is.* x. 12, 13, 16.

When thou wast mad against me, thy pride came up to my ears: therefore I will put a ring in thy nose, and a bit between thy lips, and I will turn thee back by the way by which thou camest. —*Is.* xxxvii. 29.

And thou hast trusted in thy wicked-ness, and hast said: There is none that seeth me. Thy wisdom, and thy knowledge, this hath deceived thee. And thou hast said in thy heart: I am, and besides me there is no other.

Evil shall come upon thee, and thou shalt not know the rising thereof: and calamity shall fall violently upon thee, which thou canst not keep off: misery shall come upon thee suddenly, which thou shalt not know.—*Is.* xlvii. 10, 11.

Arise, arise, put on strength, O thou arm of the Lord, arise as in the days of old, in the ancient generations. Hast thou not struck the proud one, and wounded the dragon?—*Is.* li. 9.

And he (Jesus) said to them: I saw Satan, like lightning, falling from heaven.—*Luke* x. 18.

PROUD TORMENTED BY GOD, THE

And for pride thou wilt take me as a lioness, and returning thou tormentest me wonderfully.—*Job* x. 16.

As much as she hath glorified herself, and lived in delicacies, so much torment and sorrow give ye to her; because she saith in her heart: I sit a queen, and am no widow; and sorrow I shall not see.—*Apoc.* xviii. 7.

PROUD HUMBLED BY GOD, THE

For thou wilt save the humble people; but wilt bring down the eyes of the proud.—*Ps.* xvii. 28.

Thou hast humbled the proud one, as one that is slain: with the arm of thy strength, thou hast scattered thy enemies.—*Ps.* lxxxviii. 11.

Thou hast rebuked the proud: they are cursed who decline from thy commandments.—*Ps.* cxviii. 21.

Humiliation followeth the proud: and glory shall uphold the humble of spirit. —*Prov.* xxix. 23.

Injuries and wrongs will waste riches: and the house that is very rich shall be brought to nothing by pride: so the substance of the proud shall be rooted out.—*Ecclus.* xxi. 5.

The lofty eyes of man are humbled, and the haughtiness of men shall be made to stoop: and the Lord alone shall be exalted in that day.

Because the day of the Lord of hosts shall be upon every one that is proud and high-minded, and upon every one that is arrogant, and he shall be humbled.—*Is.* ii. 11, 12.

And I will visit the evils of the world, and against the wicked, for their iniquity: and I will make the pride of infidels to cease, and will bring down the arrogancy of the mighty.—*Is.* xiii. 11.

How art thou fallen from heaven, O Lucifer, who didst rise in the morning? how art thou fallen to the earth, that didst wound the nations?

And thou saidst in thy heart: I will ascend into heaven, I will exalt my throne above the stars of God, I will sit in the mountain of the covenant, in the sides of the north.

I will ascend above the height of the clouds, I will be like the most High.

But yet thou shalt be brought down to hell, into the depth of the pit.

They that shall see thee, shall turn toward thee, and behold thee. Is this the man that troubled the earth, that shook kingdoms?

. . . Thy pride is brought down to hell, thy carcass is fallen down: under thee shall the moth be strewed, and worms shall be thy covering.—*Is.* xiv. 12-16, 11.

Who hath taken this counsel against Tyre, that was formerly crowned, whose merchants were princes, and her traders the nobles of the earth?

The Lord of hosts hath designed it, to pull down the pride of all glory, and bring to disgrace all the glorious ones of the earth.—*Is.* xxiii. 8, 9.

We have heard the pride of Moab, he is exceeding proud: his haughtiness, and his arrogancy, and his pride, and the loftiness of his heart. . . .

Upon all the housetops of Moab, and in the streets thereof, general mourning: because I have broken Moab, as a useless vessel, saith the Lord.

How is it overthrown, and they have howled! How hath Moab bowed down the neck, and is confounded! And Moab shall be a derision, and an example to all round about him. . . .

And Moab shall cease to be a people: because he hath gloried against the Lord.—*Jer.* xlviii. 29, 38, 39, 42.

Thy arrogancy hath deceived thee, and the pride of thy heart: O thou that dwellest in the clefts of the rock, and endeavorest to lay hold on the height of the hill: but though thou shouldst make thy nest as high as an eagle, I will bring thee down from thence, saith the Lord.—*Jer.* xlix. 16.

And the proud one shall fall, he shall fall down, and there shall be none to lift him up: and I will kindle a fire in his cities, and it shall devour all round about him.—*Jer.* l. 32.

Therefore I, Nabuchodonosor, do now praise, and magnify, and glorify the King of heaven: because all his works are true, and his ways judgments, and them that walk in pride he is able to abase.—*Dan.* iv. 34.

But when his (Nabuchodonosor's) heart was lifted up, and his spirit hardened unto pride, he was put down from the throne of his kingdom, and his glory was taken away.

And he was driven out from the sons of men, and his heart was made like the beasts, and his dwelling was with the wild asses, and he did eat grass like an ox, and his body was wet with the dew of heaven: till he knew that the most High ruled in the kingdom of men, and that he will set over it whomsoever it shall please him.—*Dan.* v. 20, 21.

The pride of thy heart hath lifted thee up, who dwellest in the clefts of the rocks, and settest up thy throne on high: who sayest in thy heart: Who shall bring me down to the ground?

Though thou be exalted as an eagle, and though thou set thy nest among the stars: thence will I bring thee down, saith the Lord.—*Abdias* i. 3, 4.

And as wine deceiveth him that drinketh it: so shall the proud man be, and he shall not be honored: who hath enlarged his desire like hell: and is himself like death, and he is never satisfied: but will gather together unto him all nations, and heap together unto him all people.—*Hab.* ii. 5.

This is the glorious city that dwelt in security: that said in her heart: I am, and there is none beside me: how is she become a desert, a place for beasts to lie down in? every one that passeth by

her, shall hiss, and wag his hand.—
Soph. ii. 15.

Thus he (Antiochus) that seemed to himself to command even the waves of the sea, being proud above the condition of man, and to weigh the heights of the mountains in a balance, now being cast down to the ground, was carried in a litter, bearing witness to the manifest power of God in himself. . . .

And the man that thought a little before he could reach to the stars of heaven, no man could endure to carry, for the intolerable stench.

And by this means, being brought from his great pride, he began to come to the knowledge of himself, being admonished by the scourge of God, his pains increasing every moment.

And when he himself could not now abide his own stench, he spoke thus: It is just to be subject to God, and that a mortal man should not equal himself to God.—2 *Mach.* ix. 8, 10, 11, 12.

And many that are first, shall be last: and the last shall be first.—*Matt.* xix. 30.

He hath showed might in his arm: he hath scattered the proud in the conceit of their heart.

He hath put down the mighty from their seat, and hath exalted the humble. —*Luke* i. 51, 52.

Because every one that exalteth himself, shall be humbled; and he that humbleth himself, shall be exalted.— *Luke* xiv. 11.

And upon a day appointed, Herod, being arrayed in kingly apparel, sat in the judgment seat, and made an oration to them.

And the people made acclamation, saying: It is the voice of a god, and not of a man.

And forthwith an angel of the Lord struck him, because he had not given the honor to God: and being eaten up by worms, he gave up the ghost.—*Acts* xii. 21-23.

PROUD DESTROYED BY GOD, THE

But the soul that committeth any thing through pride, whether he be born in the land, or a stranger (because he hath been rebellious against the Lord),

shall be cut off from among his people:

For he hath contemned the word of the Lord, and made void his precept: therefore shall he be destroyed, and shall bear his iniquity.—*Num.* xv. 30, 31.

If his pride mount up even to heaven, and his head touch the clouds:

In the end he shall be destroyed like a dung hill, and they that had seen him, shall say: Where is he?

As a dream that fleeth away, he shall not be found, he shall pass as a vision of the night.

The eyes that had seen him, shall see him no more, neither shall his place any more behold him.—*Job* xx. 6-9.

The Lord will destroy the house of the proud: and will strengthen the borders of the widow.—*Prov.* xv. 25.

Pride goeth before destruction: and the spirit is lifted up before a fall.— *Prov.* xvi. 18.

Before destruction, the heart of a man is exalted: and before he be glorified, it is humbled.—*Prov.* xviii. 12.

God hath overturned the thrones of proud princes, and hath set up the meek in their stead.

God hath made the roots of proud nations to wither, and hath planted the humble of these nations. . . .

God hath abolished the memory of the proud, and hath preserved the memory of them that are humble in mind. —*Ecclus.* x. 17, 18, 21.

And he will repay vengeance to the Gentiles, till he have taken away the multitude of the proud, and broken the sceptres of the unjust.—*Ecclus.* xxxv. 23.

And the word of the Lord came to me, saying:

Son of man, say to the prince of Tyre: Thus saith the Lord God: Because thy heart is lifted up, and thou hast said: I am God, and I sit in the chair of God, in the heart of the sea: whereas thou art a man, and not God: and hast set thy heart as if it were the heart of God. . . .

Therefore, thus saith the Lord God: Because thy heart is lifted up as the heart of God:

Therefore behold, I will bring upon

thee strangers, the strongest of the nations: and they shall draw their swords against the beauty of thy wisdom, and they shall defile thy beauty.

They shall kill thee, and bring thee down: and thou shalt die the death of them that are slain in the heart of the sea.

Wilt thou yet say before them that slay thee: I am God; whereas thou art a man, and not God, in the hand of them that slay thee?

Thou shalt die the death of the uncircumcised by the hand of strangers: for I have spoken it, saith the Lord God.—*Ezech.* xxviii. 1, 2, 6-10.

Thou also his son, O Baltasar, hast not humbled thy heart, whereas thou knewest all these things:

But hast lifted thyself up against the Lord of heaven: . . . but the God who hath thy breath in his hand, and all thy ways, thou hast not glorified.

Wherefore he hath sent the part of the hand which hath written this that is set down.

And this is the writing that is written: Mane, Thecel, Phares. . . .

The same night Baltasar the Chaldean king was slain.—*Dan.* v. 22-25, 30.

Therefore, as I live, saith the Lord of hosts, the God of Israel, Moab shall be as Sodom, and the children of Ammon as Gomorrha, the dryness of thorns, and heaps of salt, and a desert even for ever: the remnant of my people shall make a spoil of them, and the residue of my nation shall possess them.

This shall befall them for their pride: because they have blasphemed, and have been magnified against the people of the Lord of hosts.—*Soph.* ii. 9, 10.

For behold, the day shall come kindled as a furnace: and all the proud, and all that do wickedly shall be stubble: and the day that cometh, shall set them on fire, saith the Lord of hosts, it shall not leave them root, nor branch. —*Malach.* iv. 1.

But when Nicanor understood that Judas was in the places of Samaria, he purposed to set upon him with all violence on the sabbath day.

And when the Jews that were constrained to follow him, said: Do not act so fiercely and barbarously, but give honor to the day that is sanctified: and reverence him that beholdeth all things:

That unhappy man asked, if there were a mighty One in heaven, that had commanded the sabbath day to be kept.

And when they answered: There is the living Lord himself in heaven, the mighty One, that commanded the seventh day to be kept,

Then he said: And I am mighty upon the earth, and I command to take arms, and to do the king's business. Nevertheless he prevailed not to accomplish his design.

So Nicanor, being puffed up with exceeding great pride, thought to set up a public monument of his victory over Judas. . . .

And when the battle was over, and they (the Jews) were returning with joy, they understood that Nicanor was slain in his armor.—*2 Mach.* xv. 1-6, 28.

PROUD, A PRAYER THAT GOD MAY PUNISH THE

O Lord God of heaven and earth, behold their pride, and look on our low condition, and have regard to the face of thy saints, and show that thou forsakest not them that trust on thee, and that thou humblest them that presume of themselves, and glory in their own strength.—*Judith* vi. 15.

May the Lord destroy all deceitful lips, and the tongue that speaketh proud things.

Who have said: We will magnify our tongue; our lips are our own; who is Lord over us?—*Ps.* xi. 4, 5.

Lift up thy hands against their pride unto the end; see what things the enemy hath done wickedly in the sanctuary. . . .

Forget not the voices of thy enemies: the pride of them that hate thee, ascendeth continually.—*Ps.* lxxiii. 3, 23.

Lift up thyself, thou that judgest the earth: render a reward to the proud.— *Ps.* xciii. 2.

PRIESTHOOD, SACREDNESS OF THE

And the Lord spoke to Moses, saying: Say to Aaron: Whosoever of thy seed throughout their families, hath a blemish, he shall not offer bread to his God.

Neither shall he approach to minister to him: If he be blind, if he be lame, if he have a little, or a great, or a crooked nose,

If his foot, or if his hand be broken,

If he be crooked-backed, or blear-eyed, or have a pearl in his eye, or a continual scab, or a dry scurf in his body, or a rupture:

Whosoever of the seed of Aaron the priest, hath a blemish, he shall not approach to offer sacrifices to the Lord, nor bread to his God.

He shall eat nevertheless of the loaves, that are offered in the sanctuary,

Yet so that he enter not within the veil, nor approach to the altar, because he hath a blemish, and he must not defile my sanctuary. I am the Lord who sanctify them.—*Lev.* xxi. 16-23.

And when he (Ozias) was made strong, his heart was lifted up to his destruction, and he neglected the Lord his God: and going into the temple of the Lord, he had a mind to burn incense upon the altar of incense.

And immediately Azarias the priest, going in after him, and with him fourscore priests of the Lord, most valiant men,

Withstood the king, and said: It doth not belong to thee, Ozias, to burn incense to the Lord, but to the priests, that is, to the sons of Aaron, who are consecrated for this ministry: go out of the sanctuary, do not despise: for this thing shall not be accounted to thy glory by the Lord God.

And Ozias was angry, and holding in his hand the censer to burn incense, threatened the priests. And presently there rose a leprosy in his forehead, before the priests, in the house of the Lord at the altar of incense.—*2 Paral.* xxvi. 16-19.

PRIESTHOOD A GREAT PRIVILEGE, THE

Is it a small thing unto you, that the God of Israel hath spared you from all the people, and joined you to himself, that you should serve him in the service of the tabernacle, and should stand before the congregation of the people, and should minister to him?—*Num.* xvi. 9.

The Lord is the portion of my inheritance and of my cup: it is thou that wilt restore my inheritance to me.

The lines are fallen unto me in goodly places: for my inheritance is goodly to me.—*Ps.* xv. 5, 6.

Thou hast anointed my head with oil; and my chalice which inebriateth me, how goodly is it!

And thy mercy will follow me all the days of my life.

And that I may dwell in the house of the Lord unto length of days.—*Ps.* xxii. 5, 6.

One thing I have asked of the Lord, this will I seek after; that I may dwell in the house of the Lord all the days of my life.

That I may see the delight of the Lord, and may visit his temple.—*Ps.* xxvi. 4.

Blessed is he whom thou hast chosen and taken to thee: he shall dwell in thy courts. We shall be filled with the good things of thy house; holy is thy temple.—*Ps.* lxiv. 5.

How lovely are thy tabernacles, O Lord of hosts! my soul longeth and fainteth for the courts of the Lord.

My heart and my flesh have rejoiced in the living God. . . .

Blessed are they that dwell in thy house, O Lord: they shall praise thee for ever and ever. . . .

For better is one day in thy courts above thousands.

I have chosen to be an abject in the house of my God, rather than to dwell in the tabernacles of sinners.—*Ps.* lxxxiii. 2, 3, 5, 11.

What shall I render to the Lord, for all the things that he hath rendered to me?

I will take the chalice of salvation; and I will call upon the name of the Lord.—*Ps.* cxv. 12, 13.

And he (God) said: It is a small thing that thou shouldst be my servant to raise up the tribes of Jacob, and to convert the dregs of Israel. Behold, I have given thee to be the light of the Gentiles, that thou mayst be my salvation even to the farthest part of the earth.—*Is.* xlix. 6.

I will not now call you servants: for the servant knoweth not what his lord doth. But I have called you friends: because all things whatsoever I have heard of my Father, I have made known to you.—*John* xv. 15.

PRIEST, CHRIST OUR HIGH

The Lord hath sworn, and he will not repent: Thou art a priest for ever, according to the order of Melchisedech.—*Ps.* cix. 4.

Wherefore it behoved him in all things to be made like unto his brethren, that he might become a merciful and faithful high priest before God, that he might be a propitiation for the sins of the people.—*Heb.* ii. 17.

Wherefore, holy brethren, partakers of the heavenly vocation, consider the apostle and high priest of our confession, Jesus.—*Heb.* iii. 1.

Having therefore a great high priest that hath passed into the heavens, Jesus the Son of God: let us hold fast our confession.

For we have not a high priest, who cannot have compassion on our infirmities: but one tempted in all things like as we are, without sin.—*Heb.* iv. 14, 15.

And whereas indeed he was the Son of God, he learned obedience by the things which he suffered:

And being consummated, he became, to all that obey him, the cause of eternal salvation.

Called by God a high priest according to the order of Melchisedech.—*Heb.* v. 8-10.

Where the forerunner, Jesus, is entered for us, made a high priest for ever according to the order of Melchisedech.—*Heb.* vi. 20.

But this, for that he continueth for ever, hath an everlasting priesthood,

Whereby he is able also to save for ever them that come to God by him; always living to make intercession for us.

For it was fitting that we should have such a high priest, holy, innocent, undefiled, separated from sinners, and made higher than the heavens;

Who needeth not daily (as the other priests) to offer sacrifices first for his own sins, and then for the people's: for this he did once, in offering himself.—*Heb.* vii. 24-27.

Now of the things which we have spoken, this is the sum: We have such an high priest, who is set on the right hand of the throne of majesty in the heavens,

A minister of the holies, and of the true tabernacle, which the Lord hath pitched, and not man.

For every high priest is appointed to offer gifts and sacrifices: wherefore it is necessary that he also should have something to offer.—*Heb.* viii. 1-3.

But Christ, being come an high priest of the good things to come, by a greater and more perfect tabernacle not made with hand, that is, not of this creation:

Neither by the blood of goats, or of calves, but by his own blood, entered once into the holies, having obtained eternal redemption.—*Heb.* ix. 11, 12.

Having therefore, brethren, a confidence in the entering into the holies by the blood of Christ;

A new and living way which he hath dedicated for us through the veil, that is to say, his flesh,

And a high priest over the house of God.—*Heb.* x. 19-21.

PRIEST, THE

And the Lord said to Aaron: You shall possess nothing in their land, neither shall you have a portion among them: I am thy portion and inheritance in the midst of the children of Israel.—*Num.* xviii. 20.

Send forth thy light and thy truth: they have conducted me, and brought me unto thy holy hill, and into thy tabernacles.

And I will go in to the altar of God: to God who giveth joy to my youth.—*Ps.* xlii. 3, 4.

In thy tabernacle I shall dwell for ever: I shall be protected under the covert of thy wings.—*Ps.* lx. 5.

For what have I in heaven? and besides thee, what do I desire upon earth?

For thee my flesh and my heart hath fainted away: thou art the God of my heart, and the God that is my portion for ever.—*Ps.* lxxii. 25, 26.

The Lord hath sworn, and he will not repent: Thou art a priest for ever, according to the order of Melchisedech.—*Ps.* cix. 4.

How beautiful upon the mountains are the feet of him that bringeth good tidings, and that preacheth peace: of him that showeth forth good, that preacheth salvation, that saith to Sion: Thy God shall reign!—*Is.* lii. 7.

Behold upon the mountains the feet of him that bringeth good tidings, and that preacheth peace.—*Nahum* i. 15.

You are the salt of the earth. But if the salt lose its savor, wherewith shall it be salted? It is good for nothing any more but to be cast out, and to be trodden on by men.

You are the light of the world. A city seated on a mountain cannot be hid.

Neither do men light a candle and put it under a bushel, but upon a candlestick, that it may shine to all that are in the house.

So let your light shine before men, that they may see your good works, and glorify your Father who is in heaven.—*Matt.* v. 13-16.

Paul, a servant of Jesus Christ, called to be an apostle, separated unto the gospel of God.—*Rom.* i. 1.

For we are God's coadjutors: you are God's husbandry; you are God's building.—1 *Cor.* iii. 9.

For Christ therefore we are ambassadors, God as it were exhorting by us.—2 *Cor.* v. 20.

For this Melchisedech was king of Salem, priest of the most high God, who met Abraham returning from the slaughter of the kings, and blessed him:

To whom also Abraham divided the tithes of all: who first indeed by interpretation, is king of justice: and then also king of Salem, that is, king of peace:

Without father, without mother, without genealogy, having neither beginning of days, nor end of life, but likened unto the Son of God, continueth a priest for ever.

Now consider how great this man is, to whom also Abraham the patriarch gave tithes out of the principal things.—*Heb.* vii. 1-4.

PRIEST IS CHOSEN BY GOD, THE

You shall be holy unto me, because I the Lord am holy, and I have separated you from other people, that you should be mine.—*Lev.* xx. 26.

Is it a small thing unto you, that the God of Israel hath spared you from all the people, and joined you to himself, that you should serve him in the service of the tabernacle, and should stand before the congregation of the people, and should minister to him?—*Num.* xvi. 9.

For the Lord thy God hath chosen him (the priest) of all thy tribes, to stand, and to minister to the name of the Lord, him and his sons for ever.—*Deut.* xviii. 5.

My sons, be not negligent: the Lord hath chosen you to stand before him, and to minister to him, and to worship him, and to burn incense to him.—2 *Paral.* xxix. 11.

Blessed is he whom thou hast chosen and taken to thee: he shall dwell in thy courts.—*Ps.* lxiv. 5.

And he chose his servant David, and took him from the flocks of sheep: he brought him from following the ewes great with young,

To feed Jacob his servant, and Israel his inheritance.—*Ps.* lxxvii. 70, 71.

He chose him (Aaron) out of all men living, to offer sacrifice to God, incense, and a good savor, for a memorial to make reconciliation for his people:

And he gave him power in his commandments, in the covenants of his judgments, that he should teach Jacob his testimonies, and give light to Israel in his law.—*Ecclus.* xlv. 20, 21.

You are my witnesses, saith the Lord, and my servant whom I have chosen: that you may know and believe me, and understand that I myself am.—*Is.* xliii. 10.

Then he saith to his disciples, The harvest indeed is great, but the laborers are few.

Pray ye therefore the Lord of the harvest, that he send forth laborers into his harvest.—*Matt.* ix. 37, 38.

And going up into a mountain, he called unto him whom he would himself: and they came to him.—*Mark* iii. 13.

Amen, amen, I say to you: He that entereth not by the door into the sheepfold, but climbeth up another way, the same is a thief and a robber.

But he that entereth in by the door, is the shepherd of the sheep. . . .

I am the door.—*John* x. 1, 2, 9.

You have not chosen me: but I have chosen you; and have appointed you, that you should go, and should bring forth fruit; and your fruit should remain.—*John* xv. 16.

I have manifested thy name to the men whom thou hast given me out of the world. Thine they were, and to me thou gavest them; and they have kept thy word. . . .

I pray for them: I pray not for the world, but for them whom thou hast given me: because they are thine. . . .

As thou hast sent me into the world, I also have sent them into the world.— *John* xvii. 6, 9, 18.

How then shall they call on him, in whom they have not believed? Or how shall they believe him, of whom they have not heard? And how shall they hear, without a preacher?

And how shall they preach, unless they be sent?—*Rom.* x. 14, 15.

Not that we are sufficient to think any thing of ourselves, as of ourselves: but our sufficiency is from God.

Who also hath made us fit ministers of the new testament, not in the letter, but in the spirit.—*2 Cor.* iii. 5, 6.

But all things are of God, who hath reconciled us to himself by Christ; and hath given to us the ministry of reconciliation.

For God indeed was in Christ, reconciling the world to himself, not imputing to them their sins; and he hath placed in us the word of reconciliation.

For Christ therefore we are ambassadors, God as it were exhorting by us. —*2 Cor.* v. 18-20.

I therefore, a prisoner in the Lord, beseech you, that you walk worthy of the vocation in which you are called. —*Eph.* iv. 1.

Wherefore also we pray always for you; that our God would make you worthy of his vocation, and fulfil all the good pleasure of his goodness and the work of faith in power.—*2 Thess.* i. 11.

I give him thanks who hath strengthened me, even to Christ Jesus our Lord, for that he hath counted me faithful, putting me in the ministry.— *1 Tim.* i. 12.

Be not thou therefore ashamed of the testimony of our Lord, nor of me his prisoner: but labor with the gospel, according to the power of God,

Who hath delivered us, and called us by his holy calling, not according to our works, but according to his own purpose and grace, which was given us in Christ Jesus, before the times of the world.—*2 Tim.* i. 8, 9.

For every high priest taken from among men, is ordained for men in the things that appertain to God, that he may offer up gifts and sacrifices for sins. . . .

Neither doth any man take the honor to himself, but he that is called by God, as Aaron was.

So Christ also did not glorify himself, that he might be made a high priest: but he that said unto him: Thou art my Son, this day have I begotten thee.

As he saith also in another place: Thou art a priest for ever, according to the order of Melchisedech.—*Heb.* v. 1, 4-6.

PRIEST, THE WORK OR DUTY OF THE

1st. To Guide Souls

And he (David) fed them in the innocence of his heart: and conducted them by the skilfulness of his hands.— *Ps.* lxxvii. 72.

I the Lord have called thee in justice, and taken thee by the hand, and preserved thee. And I have given thee for a covenant of the people, for a light of the Gentiles:

That thou mightest open the eyes of the blind, and bring forth the prisoner out of prison, and them that sit in darkness out of the prison house.—*Is.* xlii. 6, 7.

Go through, go through the gates, prepare the way for the people, make the road plain, pick out the stones, and lift up the standard to the people.—*Is.* lxii. 10.

The law of truth was in his mouth, and iniquity was not found in his lips: he walked with me in peace, and in equity, and turned many away from iniquity.—*Malach.* ii. 6.

But he that entereth in by the door, is the shepherd of the sheep.

To him the porter openeth; and the sheep hear his voice: and he calleth his own sheep by name, and leadeth them out.

And when he hath let out his own sheep, he goeth before them: and the sheep follow him, because they know his voice.—*John* x. 2-4.

2d. To Teach and Preach

I will teach the unjust thy ways: and the wicked shall be converted to thee.—*Ps.* l. 15.

He chose him (Aaron) out of all men living. . . .

And he gave him power in his commandments, in the covenants and his judgments, that he should teach Jacob his testimonies, and give light to Israel in his law.—*Ecclus.* xlv. 20, 21.

Get thee up upon a high mountain, thou that bringest good tidings to Sion: lift up thy voice with strength, thou that bringest good tidings to Jerusalem; lift it up, fear not. Say to the cities of Juda: Behold your God:

Behold the Lord God shall come with strength, and his arm shall rule: Behold his reward is with him, and his work is before him.—*Is.* xl. 9, 10.

The spirit of the Lord is upon me, because the Lord hath anointed me: he hath sent me to preach to the meek, to heal the contrite of heart, and to preach a release to the captives, and deliverance to them that are shut up.

To proclaim the acceptable year of the Lord, and the day of vengeance of our God: to comfort all that mourn.—*Is.* lxi. 1, 2.

And the Lord said to me: Say not: I am a child: for thou shalt go to all that I shall send thee: and whatsoever I shall command thee, thou shalt speak.

Be not afraid at their presence: for I am with thee, to deliver thee, saith the Lord.—*Jer.* i. 7, 8.

That which I tell you in the dark, speak ye in the light: and that which you hear in the ear, preach ye upon the house tops.—*Matt.* x. 27.

And I said: Who art thou, Lord? And the Lord answered: I am Jesus, whom thou persecutest.

But rise up, and stand upon thy feet: for to this end have I appeared to thee, that I may make thee a minister, and a witness of those things which thou hast seen, and of those things wherein I will appear to thee,

Delivering thee from the people, and from the nations, unto which now I send thee:

To open their eyes, that they may be converted from darkness to light, and from the power of Satan to God, that they may receive forgiveness of sins, and a lot among the saints, by the faith that is in me.—*Acts* xxvi. 15-18.

To me, the least of all the saints, is given this grace, to preach among the Gentiles, the unsearchable riches of Christ,

And to enlighten all men, that they may see what is the dispensation of the mystery which hath been hidden from eternity in God, who created all things.—*Eph.* iii. 8, 9.

To whom God would make known the riches of the glory of this mystery among the Gentiles, which is Christ, in you the hope of glory.

Whom we preach, admonishing every man, and teaching every man in all wisdom, that we may present every man perfect in Christ Jesus.—*Col.* i. 27, 28.

Praying withal for us also, that God may open unto us a door of speech, to speak the mystery of Christ; (for which also I am bound;)

That I may make it manifest as I ought to speak.—*Col.* iv. 3, 4.

These things proposing to the brethren, thou shalt be a good minister of Christ Jesus, nourished up in the words of faith, and of the good doctrine which thou hast attained unto. . . .

These things command and teach. . . .

Take heed to thyself and to doctrine: be earnest in them. For in doing this, thou shalt both save thyself and them that hear thee.—1 *Tim.* iv. 6, 11, 16.

3d. To Rebuke

Cry, cease not, lift up thy voice like a trumpet, and show my people their wicked doings, and the house of Jacob their sins.—*Is.* lviii. 1.

But the servant of the Lord must not wrangle: but be mild towards all men, apt to teach, patient,

With modesty, admonishing them that resist the truth: if peradventure God may give them repentance to know the truth.—2 *Tim.* ii. 24, 25.

Preach the word: be instant in season, out of season: reprove, entreat, rebuke in all patience and doctrine.—2 *Tim.* iv. 2.

These things speak, and exhort and rebuke with all authority. Let no man despise thee.—*Titus* ii. 15.

4th. To Watch Over and Guard Souls

And a lion cried out: I am upon the watch-tower of the Lord, standing continually by day: and I am upon my ward, standing whole nights. . . .

The burden of Duma calleth to me out of Seir: Watchman, what of the night? watchman, what of the night? —*Is.* xxi. 8, 11.

He shall feed his flock like a shepherd: he shall gather together the lambs with his arm, and shall take them up in his bosom, and he himself shall carry them that are with young.—*Is.* xl. 11.

Upon thy walls, O Jerusalem, I have appointed watchmen all the day and all the night, they shall never hold their peace. You that are mindful of the Lord, hold not your peace.—*Is.* lxii. 6.

What man of you that hath a hundred sheep: and if he shall lose one of them, doth he not leave the ninety-nine in the desert, and go after that which was lost, until he find it?

And when he hath found it, lay it upon his shoulders, rejoicing?—*Luke* xv. 4, 5.

The good shepherd giveth his life for his sheep.

But the hireling, and he that is not the shepherd, whose own the sheep are not, seeth the wolf coming, and leaveth the sheep, and flieth: and the wolf catcheth, and scattereth the sheep:

And the hireling flieth, because he is a hireling: and he hath no care for the sheep.

I am the good shepherd; and I know mine, and mine know me.—*John* x. 11-14.

But be thou vigilant, labor in all things, do the work of an evangelist, fulfil thy ministry.—2 *Tim.* iv. 5.

5th. To Feed Souls

And he chose his servant David, and took him from the flocks of sheep: he brought him from following the ewes great with young,

To feed Jacob his servant, and Israel his inheritance.

And he fed them in the innocence of his heart: and conducted them by the skilfulness of his hands.—*Ps.* lxxvii. 70-72.

He shall feed his flock like a shepherd: he shall gather together the lambs with his arm, and shall take them up in his bosom, and he himself shall carry them that are with young.—*Is.* xl. 11.

And I will give you pastors according to my own heart, and they shall feed you with knowledge and doctrine. —*Jer.* iii. 15.

And I will set up pastors over them, and they shall feed them: they shall fear no more, and they shall not be dismayed: and none shall be wanting of their number, saith the Lord.—*Jer.* xxiii. 4.

And the word of the Lord came to me, saying:

Son of man, prophesy concerning the shepherds of Israel: prophesy, and say to the shepherds: Thus saith the Lord God: Woe to the shepherds of Israel, that fed themselves: should not the flocks be fed by the shepherds?—*Ezech.* xxxiii. 1, 2.

Feed the flock of God which is among you, taking care of it, not by constraint, but willingly, according to God: not for filthy lucre's sake, but voluntarily.—1 *Peter* v. 2.

6th. To Comfort and to Heal

The spirit of the Lord is upon me, because the Lord hath anointed me: he hath sent me to preach to the meek, to heal the contrite of heart, and to preach a release to the captives, and deliverance to them that are shut up: . . . to comfort all that mourn:

To appoint to the mourners of Sion, and to give them a crown for ashes, the oil of joy for mourning, a garment of praise for the spirit of grief.—*Is.* lxi. 1-3.

These twelve Jesus sent: commanding them, saying: Go ye not into the way of the Gentiles, and into the city of the Samaritans enter ye not.

But go ye rather to the lost sheep of the house of Israel.

And going, preach, saying: The kingdom of heaven is at hand.

Heal the sick, raise the dead, cleanse the lepers, cast out devils: freely have you received, freely give.—*Matt.* x. 5-8.

For every high priest taken from among men, is ordained for men in the things that appertain to God, that he may offer up gifts and sacrifices for sins:

Who can have compassion on them that are ignorant and that err: because he himself also is compassed with infirmity.—*Heb.* v. 1, 2.

7th. To Give Good Example

So let your light shine before men, that they may see your good works, and glorify your Father who is in heaven.—*Matt.* v. 16.

For we are the good odor of Christ unto God, in them that are saved, and in them that perish.—2 *Cor.* ii. 15.

Let no man despise thy youth: but be thou an example of the faithful in word, in conversation, in charity, in faith, in chastity.—1 *Tim.* iv. 12.

In all things show thyself an example of good works, in doctrine, in integrity, in gravity,

The sound word that cannot be blamed: that he who is on the contrary part, may be afraid, having no evil to say of us.—*Titus* ii. 7, 8,

8th. To Pray and Offer Sacrifice for Others

For a blameless man (Aaron) made haste to pray for the people, bringing forth the shield of his ministry, prayer, and by incense making supplication, withstood the wrath, and put an end to the calamity, showing that he was thy servant.—*Wis.* xviii. 21.

He chose him (Aaron) out of all men living, to offer sacrifice to God, incense, and a good savor, for a memorial to make reconciliation for his people.—*Ecclus.* xlv. 20.

Remember that I have stood in thy sight, to speak good for them, and to turn away thy indignation from them.—*Jer.* xviii. 20.

For every high priest taken from among men, is ordained for men in the things that appertain to God, that he may offer up gifts and sacrifices for sins:

Who can have compassion on them that are ignorant and that err: because he himself also is compassed with infirmity.

And therefore he ought, as for the people, so also for himself, to offer for sins.—*Heb.* v. 1-3.

For every high priest is appointed to offer gifts and sacrifices: wherefore it is necessary that he (Jesus) also should have something to offer.—*Heb.* viii. 3.

9th. To Praise God

Praise ye the name of the Lord: O you his servants, praise the Lord:

You that stand in the house of the Lord, in the courts of the house of our God.—*Ps.* cxxxiv. 1, 2.

O ye priests of the Lord, bless the Lord: praise and exalt him above all for ever.

O ye servants of the Lord, bless the Lord: praise and exalt him above all for ever.—*Dan.* iii. 84, 85.

PRIEST, THE RESPONSIBILITY OF THE

Watch ye in the charge of the sanctuary, and in the ministry of the altar: lest indignation rise upon the children of Israel.—*Num.* xviii. 5.

And far from me be this sin against the Lord, that I should cease to pray for you, and I will teach you the good and right way.—1 *Kings* xii. 23.

Cursed be he that doth the work of the Lord ¹deceitfully.—*Jer.* xlviii. 10.

Son of man, I have made thee a watchman to the house of Israel: and thou shalt hear the word out of my mouth, and shalt tell it them from me.

If, when I say to the wicked, Thou shalt surely die: thou declare it not to him, nor speak to him, that he may be converted from his wicked way, and live: the same wicked man shall die in his iniquity, but I will require his blood at thy hand.

But if thou give warning to the wicked, and he be not converted from his wickedness, and from his evil way: he indeed shall die in his iniquity, but thou hast delivered thy soul.

Moreover if the just man shall turn away from his justice, and shall commit iniquity: I will lay a stumbling-block before him, he shall die, because thou hast not given him warning: he shall die in his sin, and his justices which he hath done, shall not be remembered: but I will require his blood at thy hand.

But if thou warn the just man, that the just may not sin, and he doth not sin: living he shall live, because thou hast warned him, and thou hast delivered thy soul.—*Ezech.* iii. 17-21.

And there shall be like people like priest: and I will visit their ways upon them, and I will repay them their devices.—*Osee* iv. 9.

And unto whomsoever much is given, of him much shall be required: and to whom they have committed much, of him they will demand the more.—*Luke* xii. 48.

To the Greeks and to the barbarians, to the wise and to the unwise, I am a debtor;

So (as much as is in me) I am ready to preach the gospel to you also that are at Rome.—*Rom.* i. 14, 15.

For if I preach the gospel, it is no glory to me, for a necessity lieth upon me: for woe is unto me if I preach not the gospel.

¹In the Greek, negligently.

For if I do this thing willingly, I have a reward: but if against my will, a dispensation is committed to me.—1 *Cor.* ix. 16, 17.

Keep the good thing committed to thy trust by the Holy Ghost, who dwelleth in us.—2 *Tim.* i. 14.

Obey your prelates, and be subject to them. For they watch, as being to render an account of your souls; that they may do this with joy, and not with grief. For this is not expedient for you.—*Heb.* xiii. 17.

Be ye not many masters, my brethren, knowing that you receive the greater judgment.—*James* iii. 1.

PRIEST, THE FIDELITY OF THE

I have glorified thee on the earth; I have finished the work which thou gavest me to do.—*John* xvii. 4.

But I fear none of these things, neither do I count my life more precious than myself, so that I may consummate my course, and the ministry of the word which I received from the Lord Jesus, to testify the gospel of the grace of God.—*Acts* xx. 24.

Then Paul answered, and said: What do you mean weeping and afflicting my heart? For I am ready not only to be bound, but to die also in Jerusalem, for the name of the Lord Jesus.—*Acts* xxi. 13.

For I say to you, Gentiles: as long indeed as I am the apostle of the Gentiles, I will honor my ministry,

If, by any means, I may provoke to emulation them who are my flesh, and may save some of them.—*Rom.* xi. 13, 14.

Let a man so account of us as of the ministers of Christ, and the dispensers of the mysteries of God.

Here now it is required among the dispensers, that a man be found faithful.—1 *Cor.* iv. 1, 2.

And say to Archippus: Take heed to the ministry which thou hast received in the Lord, that thou fulfil it.—*Col.* iv. 17.

But as we were approved by God that the gospel should be committed to us: even so we speak, not as pleasing men, but God, who proveth our hearts.

For neither have we used, at any time, the speech of flattery, as you know; nor taken an occasion of covetousness, God is witness:

Nor sought we glory of men, neither of you, nor of others.—1 *Thess.* ii. 4-6.

These things proposing to the brethren, thou shalt be a good minister of Christ Jesus, nourished up in the words of faith, and of the good doctrine which thou hast attained unto.—1 *Tim.* iv. 6.

O Timothy, keep that which is committed to thy trust, avoiding the profane novelties of words, and oppositions of knowledge falsely so called.

Which some promising, have erred concerning the faith.—1 *Tim.* vi. 20, 21.

Carefully study to present thyself approved unto God, a workman that needeth not to be ashamed, rightly handling the word of truth.—2 *Tim.* ii. 15.

But be thou vigilant, labor in all things, do the work of an evangelist, fulfil thy ministry.—2 *Tim.* iv. 5.

PRIEST, THE HUMILITY OF THE

Therefore, neither he that planteth is any thing, nor he that watereth; but God that giveth the increase.—1 *Cor.* iii. 7.

But I chastise my body, and bring it into subjection: lest perhaps, when I have preached to others, I myself should become a castaway.—1 *Cor.* ix. 27.

For we preach not ourselves, but Jesus Christ our Lord; and ourselves your servants through Jesus.—2 *Cor.* iv. 5.

PRIEST, THE LEARNING OF THE

And that you may have knowledge to discern between holy and unholy, between unclean and clean:

And may teach the children of Israel all my ordinances which the Lord hath spoken to them by the hand of Moses.—*Lev.* x. 10, 11.

And I will give you pastors according to my own heart, and they shall feed you with knowledge and doctrine.—*Jer.* iii. 15.

My people have been silent, because they had no knowledge: because thou hast rejected knowledge, I will reject

thee, that thou shalt not do the office of priesthood to me: and thou hast forgotten the law of thy God, I also will forget thy children.—*Osee* iv. 6.

For the lips of the priest shall keep knowledge, and they shall seek the law at his mouth: because he is the angel of the Lord of hosts.—*Malach.* ii. 7.

You are the light of the world. A city seated on a mountain cannot be hid.

Neither do men light a candle, and put it under a bushel, but upon a candlestick, that it may shine to all that are in the house.

So let your light shine before men, that they may see your good works, and glorify your Father who is in heaven. —*Matt.* v. 14-16.

Behold I send you as sheep in the midst of wolves. Be ye therefore wise as serpents, and simple as doves.—*Matt.* x. 16.

Now the end of the commandment is charity, from a pure heart, and a good conscience, and an unfeigned faith.

From which things some going astray, are turned aside unto vain babbling:

Desiring to be teachers of the law, understanding neither the things they say, nor whereof they affirm.—1 *Tim.* i. 5-7.

Let no man despise thy youth: but be thou an example of the faithful in word, in conversation. . . .

Till I come, attend unto reading, to exhortation, and to doctrine. . . .

Meditate upon these things, be wholly in these things: that thy profiting may be manifest to all.

Take heed to thyself and to doctrine: be earnest in them. For in doing this thou shalt both save thyself and them that hear thee.—1 *Tim.* iv. 12, 13, 15, 16.

Carefully study to present thyself approved unto God, a workman that needeth not to be ashamed, rightly handling the word of truth.—2 *Tim.* ii. 15.

Embracing that faithful word which is according to doctrine, that he may be able to exhort in sound doctrine, and to convince the gainsayers.—*Titus* i. 9.

In all things show thyself an example

of good works, in doctrine, in integrity, in gravity,

The sound word that cannot be blamed: that he who is on the contrary part, may be afraid, having no evil to say of us.—*Titus* ii. 7, 8.

PRIEST, THE SANCTITY OF THE

And the men of Bethsames said: Who shall be able to stand before the Lord this holy God? and to whom shall he go up from us?—1 *Kings* vi. 20.

And I said to them (the priests): You are the holy ones of the Lord, and the vessels are holy, and the silver and gold, that is freely offered to the Lord the God of our fathers.—1 *Esd.* viii. 28.

Lord, who shall dwell in thy tabernacle? or who shall rest in thy holy hill?

He that walketh without blemish, and worketh justice:

He that speaketh truth in his heart, who hath not used deceit in his tongue:

Nor hath done evil to his neighbor: nor taken up a reproach against his neighbors.—*Ps.* xiv. 1-3.

Who shall ascend into the mountain of the Lord: or who shall stand in his holy place?

The innocent in hands, and clean of heart, who hath not taken his soul in vain, nor sworn deceitfully to his neighbor.

He shall receive a blessing from the Lord, and mercy from God his Saviour. —*Ps.* xxiii. 3-5.

And he chose his servant David, and took him from the flocks of sheep: he brought him from following the ewes great with young,

To feed Jacob his servant, and Israel his inheritance.

And he fed them in the innocence of his heart: and conducted them by the skilfulness of his hands.—*Ps.* lxxvii. 70-72.

I will clothe her priests with salvation: and her saints shall rejoice with exceeding great joy.—*Ps.* cxxxi. 16.

When he (Simon the high priest) went up to the holy altar, he honored the vesture of holiness.—*Ecclus.* l. 12.

The law of truth was in his (Levi's) mouth, and iniquity was not found in his lips: he walked with me in peace and in equity, and turned many away from iniquity.—*Malach.* ii. 6.

And he (Judas) chose priests without blemish, whose will was set upon the law of God:

And they cleansed the holy places, and took away the stones that had been defiled into an unclean place.—1 *Mach.* iv. 42, 43.

And for them do I sanctify myself, that they also may be sanctified in truth.—*John* xvii. 19.

But we renounce the hidden things of dishonesty, not walking in craftiness, nor adulterating the word of God; but by manifestation of the truth commending ourselves to every man's conscience, in the sight of God.—2 *Cor.* iv. 2.

You are witnesses, and God also, how holily, and justly, and without blame, we have been to you that have believed. —1 *Thess.* ii. 10.

All scripture, inspired of God, is profitable to teach, to reprove, to correct, to instruct in justice,

That the man of God may be perfect, furnished to every good work.—2 *Tim.* iii. 16, 17.

PRIEST COMMANDED BY GOD, THE SANCTITY OF THE

Seven days shalt thou expiate the altar and sanctify it, and it shall be most holy. Every one that shall touch it, shall be holy.—*Ex.* xxix. 37.

And Moses said to Aaron: This is what the Lord hath spoken: I will be sanctified in them that approach to me, and I will be glorified in the sight of all the people.—*Lev.* x. 3.

For I am the Lord your God: be holy, because I am holy. Defile not your souls by any creeping thing, that moveth upon the earth.—*Lev.* xi. 44.

You shall be holy unto me, because I the Lord am holy, and I have separated you from other people, that you should be mine.—*Lev.* xx. 26.

The Lord said also to Moses: Speak to the priests the sons of Aaron, and thou shalt say to them. . . .

They shall be holy to their God, and shall not profane his name: for they offer the burnt offering of the Lord, and the bread of their God, and therefore they shall be holy; . . . because they are consecrated to their God,

And offer the loaves of proposition. Let them therefore be holy, because I also am holy, the Lord, who sanctify them.—*Lev.* xxi. 1, 6-8.

Depart, depart, go ye out from thence, touch no unclean thing: go out of the midst of her, be ye clean, you that carry the vessels of the Lord.—*Is.* lii. 11.

PRIEST, EXHORTATION TO THE SANCTITY OF THE

Now therefore arise, O Lord God, into thy resting place, thou and the ark of thy strength: let thy priests, O Lord God, put on salvation, and thy saints rejoice in good things.—*2 Paral.* vi. 41.

Arise, O Lord, into thy resting place: thou and the ark, which thou hast sanctified.

Let thy priests be clothed with justice: and let thy saints rejoice.—*Ps.* cxxxi. 8, 9.

But in all things let us exhibit ourselves as the ministers of God, in much patience, . . .

In chastity, in knowledge, in long-suffering, in sweetness, in the Holy Ghost, in charity unfeigned; . . .

As sorrowful, yet always rejoicing; as needy, yet enriching many; as having nothing, and possessing all things. —*2 Cor.* vi. 4, 6, 10.

I therefore, a prisoner in the Lord, beseech you that you walk worthy of the vocation in which you are called.—*Eph.* iv. 1.

Neglect not the grace that is in thee, which was given thee by prophecy, with imposition of the hands of the priesthood.—*1 Tim.* iv. 14.

But thou, O man of God, fly these things: and pursue justice, godliness, faith, charity, patience, mildness.

Fight the good fight of faith: lay hold on eternal life, whereunto thou art called, and hast confessed a good confession before many witnesses.

I charge thee before God, who quickeneth all things, and before Christ Jesus, who gave testimony under Pontius Pilate, a good confession,

That thou keep the commandment without spot, blameless, unto the coming of our Lord Jesus Christ.—*1 Tim.* vi. 11-14.

PRIEST, THE SELF-DENIAL OF THE

To Levi also he (Moses) said: Thy perfection and thy doctrine be to thy 'holy man, whom thou hast proved in the temptation, and judged at the waters of contradiction:

Who hath said to his father and to his mother: I do not know you; and to his brethren: I know you not: and their own children they have not known. These have kept thy word, and observed thy covenant,

Thy judgments, O Jacob, and thy law, O Israel: they shall put incense in thy wrath and holocaust upon thy altar.—*Deut.* xxxiii. 8-10.

Do not possess gold, nor silver, nor money in your purses:

Nor scrip for your journey, nor two coats, nor shoes, nor a staff; for the workman is worthy of his meat.—*Matt.* x. 9, 10.

He that loveth father or mother more than me, is not worthy of me; and he that loveth son or daughter more than me, is not worthy of me.

And he that taketh not up his cross, and followeth me, is not worthy of me. —*Matt.* x. 37, 38.

Then Jesus said to his disciples: If any man will come after me, let him deny himself, and take up his cross, and follow me.—*Matt.* xvi. 24.

Then Peter answering, said to him: Behold we have left all things, and have followed thee: what therefore shall we have?

And Jesus said to them: Amen, I say to you, that you, who have followed me, in the regeneration, when the Son of man shall sit on the seat of his majesty, you also shall sit on twelve seats, judging the twelve tribes of Israel.

And every one that hath left house, or brethren, or sisters, or father, or mother, or wife, or children, or lands for my name's sake, shall receive a hundredfold, and shall possess life everlasting. —*Matt.* xix. 27-29.

¹Aaron and his successors in the priesthood.

They are not of the world, as I also am not of the world.—*John* xvii. 16.

But Peter said: Silver and gold I have none; but what I have, I give thee: In the name of Jesus Christ of Nazareth, arise, and walk.—*Acts.* iii. 6.

But I chastise my body, and bring it into subjection: lest perhaps, when I have preached to others, I myself should become a castaway.—1 *Cor.* ix. 27.

In all things we suffer tribulation, but are not distressed; we are straitened, but are not destitute; . . .

Always bearing about in our body the mortification of Jesus, that the life also of Jesus may be made manifest in our bodies.—2 *Cor.* iv. 8, 10.

For we rejoice that we are weak, and you are strong.—2 *Cor.* xiii. 9.

But God forbid that I should glory, save in the cross of our Lord Jesus Christ; by whom the world is crucified to me, and I to the world.—*Gal.* vi. 14.

But the things that were gain to me, the same I have counted loss for Christ.

Furthermore I count all things to be but loss for the excellent knowledge of Jesus Christ my Lord; for whom I have suffered the loss of all things, and count them but as dung, that I may gain Christ: . . .

That I may know him, and the power of his resurrection, and the fellowship of his sufferings, being made conformable to his death,

If by any means I may attain to the resurrection which is from the dead.— *Philipp.* iii. 7, 8, 10, 11.

Who now rejoice in my sufferings for you, and fill up those things that are wanting of the sufferings of Christ, in my flesh, for his body, which is the church.—*Col.* i. 24.

PRIEST, THE SOBRIETY OF THE

The Lord also said to Aaron:

You shall not drink wine, nor any thing that may make drunk, thou nor thy sons, when you enter into the tabernacle of the testimony, lest you die: because it is an everlasting precept through your generations.—*Lev.* x. 8, 9.

It behoveth therefore a bishop to be blameless . . . sober, prudent, of good behavior . . .

Not given to wine.—1 *Tim.* iii. 2, 3.

But be thou vigilant, labor in all things, do the work of an evangelist, fulfil thy ministry. Be sober.—2 *Tim.* iv. 5.

For a bishop must be without crime, as the steward of God: not proud, not subject to anger, not given to wine. . . .

But given to hospitality, gentle, sober, just, holy, continent.—*Titus* i. 7, 8.

PRIEST, THE ZEAL OF THE

For the zeal of thy house hath eaten me up: and the reproaches of them that reproached thee are fallen upon me.— *Ps.* lxviii. 10.

Jesus saith to them: My meat is to do the will of him that sent me, that I may perfect his work.—*John* iv. 34.

And when they were come to him (Paul), and were together, he said to them: You know from the first day that I came into Asia, in what manner I have been with you, for all the time,

Serving the Lord with all humility, and with tears, and temptations which befell me by the conspiracies of the Jews;

How I have kept back nothing that was profitable to you, but have preached it to you, and taught you publicly, and from house to house.—*Acts* xx. 18-20.

And Agrippa said to Paul: In a little thou persuadest me to become a Christian.

And Paul said: I would to God, that both in a little and in much, not only thou, but also all that hear me, this day, should become such as I also am, except these bonds.—*Acts* xxvi. 28, 29.

For I long to see you, that I may impart unto you some spiritual grace, to strengthen you:

That is to say, that I may be comforted together in you, by that which is common to us both, your faith and mine.—*Rom.* i. 11, 12.

Brethren, the will of my heart, indeed, and my prayer to God, is for them unto salvation.—*Rom.* x. 1.

For whereas I was free as to all, I made myself the servant of all, that I might gain the more. . . .

To the weak I became weak, that I might gain the weak. I became all things to all men, that I might save all.

And I do all things for the gospel's sake: that I may be made partaker thereof.—1 *Cor.* ix. 19, 22, 23.

Therefore, seeing we have this ministration, according as we have obtained mercy, we faint not.—2 *Cor.* iv. 1.

Besides those things which are without: my daily instance, the solitude for all the churches.

Who is weak, and I am not weak? Who is scandalized, and I am not on fire?—2 *Cor.* xi. 28, 29.

For I seek not the things that are yours, but you. . . .

But I most gladly will spend, and be spent myself, for your souls; although loving you more, I be loved less.—2 *Cor.* xii. 14, 15.

And many of the brethren in the Lord, growing confident by my bands, are much more bold to speak the word of God without fear.

Some indeed, even out of envy and contention; but some also for good will, preach Christ.

Some out of charity, knowing that I am set for the defence of the gospel.

And some out of contention preach Christ not sincerely: supposing that they raise affliction to my bands.

But what then? So that by all means, whether by occasion, or by truth, Christ be preached: in this also I rejoice, yea, and will rejoice.—*Philipp.* i. 14-18.

So desirous of you, we would gladly impart unto you, not only the gospel of God, but also our own souls: because you were become most dear unto us. . . .

For what is our hope, or joy, or crown of glory? Are not you, in the presence of our Lord Jesus Christ at his coming?

For you are our glory and joy.—1 *Thess.* ii. 8, 19, 20.

Therefore we were comforted, brethren, in you, in all our necessity and tribulation, by your faith,

Because now we live, if you stand in the Lord.

For what thanks can we return to God for you, in all the joy wherewith we rejoice for you before our God,

Night and day more abundantly praying that we may see your face, and may accomplish those things that are wanting to your faith?—1 *Thess.* iii. 7-10.

Labor as a good soldier of Christ Jesus.

No man, being a soldier to God, entangleth himself with secular businesses; that he may please him to whom he hath engaged himself.—2 *Tim.* ii. 3, 4.

I charge thee, before God and Jesus Christ, who shall judge the living and the dead, by his coming, and his kingdom:

Preach the word: be instant, in season, out of season: reprove, entreat, rebuke in all patience and doctrine. . . .

But be thou vigilant, labor in all things, do the work of an evangelist, fulfil thy ministry.—2 *Tim.* iv. 1, 2, 5.

I have no greater grace than this, to hear that my children walk in truth.— 3 *John* i. 4.

PRIEST, MOTIVES FOR THE ZEAL OF THE

But they that are learned, shall shine as the brightness of the firmament: and they that instruct many to justice, as stars for all eternity.—*Dan.* xii. 3.

Then he saith to his disciples, The harvest indeed is great, but the laborers are few.

Pray ye therefore the Lord of the harvest, that he send forth laborers into his harvest.—*Matt.* ix. 37, 38.

Do not you say, There are yet four months, and then the harvest cometh? Behold, I say to you, lift up your eyes, and see the countries; for they are white already to harvest.

And he that reapeth, receiveth wages, and gathereth fruit unto life everlasting: that both he that soweth, and he that reapeth, may rejoice together. —*John* iv. 35, 36.

But having the same spirit of faith, as it is written: I believed, for which cause I have spoken; we also believe, for which cause we speak also.—2 *Cor.* iv. 13.

My brethren, if any of you err from the truth, and one convert him:

He must know that he who causeth a sinner to be converted from the error of his way, shall save his soul from death, and shall cover a multitude of sins.—*James* v. 19, 20.

PRIEST, THE REWARD OF THE GOOD

They that are planted in the house of the Lord, shall flourish in the courts of the house of our God.

They shall still increase in a fruitful old age: and shall be well treated, that they may show,

That the Lord our God is righteous, and there is no iniquity in him.—*Ps.* xci. 14-16.

I have glorified thee on the earth; I have finished the work which thou gavest me to do.

And now glorify thou me, O Father, with thyself, with the glory which I had, before the world was, with thee.—*John* xvii. 4, 5.

Father, I will that where I am, they also whom thou hast given me, may be with me; that they may see my glory which thou hast given me, because thou hast loved me before the creation of the world.—*John* xvii. 24.

For they that have ministered well, shall purchase to themselves a good degree, and much confidence in the faith which is in Christ Jesus.—1*Tim.*iii.13.

I have fought a good fight. I have finished my course, I have kept the faith.

As to the rest, there is laid up for me a crown of justice, which the Lord the just judge will render to me in that day: and not only to me, but to them also that love his coming.—2 *Tim.* iv. 7, 8.

Feed the flock of God, which is among you, taking care of it, not by constraint, but willingly, according to God: not for filthy lucre's sake, but voluntarily: . . .

And when the prince of pastors shall appear, you shall receive a never fading crown of glory.—1 *Peter* v. 2, 4.

PRIEST, RESPECT AND REVERENCE FOR THE

And David said to Abisai: Kill him (Saul) not: for who shall put forth his hand against the Lord's anointed, and shall be guiltless?—1 *Kings* xxvi. 9.

David said to ¹him: Why didst thou not fear to put out thy hand to kill the Lord's anointed?—2 *Kings* i. 14.

And he (Eliseus) went up from thence to Bethel: and as he was going up by the way, little boys came out of the city, and mocked him, saying: Go up, thou bald head; go up, thou bald head.

And looking back, he saw them, and cursed them in the name of the Lord: and there came forth two bears out of the forest, and tore of them two and forty boys.—4 *Kings* ii. 23, 24.

Blessed be he that cometh in the name of the Lord.

We have blessed you out of the house of the Lord.—*Ps.* cxvii. 26.

He that receiveth you, receiveth me: and he that receiveth me, receiveth him that sent me.—*Matt.* x. 40.

He that heareth you, heareth me; and he that despiseth you, despiseth me; and he that despiseth me, despiseth him that sent me.—*Luke* x. 16.

Amen, amen, I say to you, he that receiveth whomsoever I send, receiveth me; and he that receiveth me, receiveth him that sent me.—*John* xiii. 20.

Let no man despise thy youth: but be thou an example of the faithful in word, in conversation, in charity, in faith, in chastity.—1 *Tim.* iv. 12.

These things speak, and exhort and rebuke with all authority. Let no man despise thee.—*Titus* ii. 15.

Moreover we have had fathers of our flesh, for instructors, and we reverenced them: shall we not much more obey the Father of spirits, and live?—*Heb.* xii. 9.

PRIEST, EXHORTATION TO RESPECT AND REVERENCE FOR THE

Touch ye not my anointed: and do no evil to my prophets.—*Ps.* civ. 15.

With all thy soul, fear the Lord, and reverence his priests.

With all thy strength love him that made thee: and forsake not his ministers.

Honor God with all thy soul, and give honor to the priests, and purify

¹The Amalecite who pretended to David that he had killed Saul on Mount Gelboe.

thyself with thy arms.—*Ecclus.* vii. 31-33.

Let a man so account of us as of the ministers of Christ, and the dispensers of the mysteries of God.—1 *Cor.* iv. 1.

Now if Timothy come, see that he be with you without fear, for he worketh the work of the Lord, as I also do.

Let no man therefore despise him, but conduct ye him on his way in peace: that he may come to me.—1 *Cor.* xvi. 10, 11.

But I have thought it necessary to send to you Epaphroditus, my brother and fellow laborer, and fellow soldier, but your apostle, and he that hath ministered to my wants. . . .

Receive him therefore with all joy in the Lord; and treat with honor such as he is.—*Philipp.* ii. 25, 29.

And we beseech you, brethren, to know them who labor among you, and are over you in the Lord, and admonish you:

That you esteem them more abundantly in charity, for their work's sake. Have peace with them.—1 *Thess.* v. 12, 13.

Let the priests that rule well, be esteemed worthy of double honor: especially they who labor in the word and doctrine.—1 *Tim.* v. 17.

Remember your prelates who have spoken the word of God to you; whose faith follow, considering the end of their conversation.—*Heb.* xiii. 7.

PRIEST, THE PRAYER OF CHRIST FOR THE

I have manifested thy name to the men whom thou hast given me out of the world.

Thine they were, and to me thou gavest them; and they have kept thy word.

Now they have known, that all things which thou hast given me, are from thee:

Because the words which thou gavest me, I have given to them; and they have received them, and have known in very deed that I came out from thee, and they have believed that thou didst send me.

I pray for them: I pray not for the world, but for them whom thou hast given me: because they are thine. . . .

And now I am not in the world, and these are in the world, and I come to thee.

Holy Father, keep them in thy name, whom thou hast given me; that they may be one, as we also are. . . .

I have given them thy word, and the world hath hated them, because they are not of the world; as I also am not of the world.

I pray not that thou shouldst take them out of the world, but that thou shouldst keep them from evil.

They are not of the world, as I also am not of the world.

Sanctify them in truth. Thy word is truth.

As thou hast sent me into the world, I also have sent them into the world,

And for them do I sanctify myself, that they also may be sanctified in truth.

And not for them only do I pray, but for them also who through their word, shall believe in me;

That they all may be one, as thou, Father, in me, and I in thee; that they also may be one in us; that the world may believe that thou hast sent me. . . .

Father, I will that where I am, they also whom thou hast given me, may be with me; that they may see my glory which thou hast given me, because thou hast loved me before the creation of the world.

. . . And I have made known thy name to them, and will make it known; that the love wherewith thou hast loved me, may be in them, and I in them.—*John* xvii. 6-9, 11, 14-21, 24, 26.

PRIEST, THE BAD AND UNFAITHFUL

Now the sons of Heli were children of Belial, not knowing the Lord,

Nor the office of the priests to the people: but whosoever had offered a sacrifice, the servant of the priest came, while the flesh was in boiling, with a flesh-hook of three teeth in his hand,

And thrust it into the kettle, or into the caldron, or into the pot, or into the pan: and all that the flesh-hook brought up, the priest took to himself. Thus did they to all Israel that came to Silo. . . .

Wherefore the sin of the young men was exceeding great before the Lord: because they withdrew men from the sacrifice of the Lord.—1 *Kings* ii 12-14, 17.

I saw the wicked buried: who also when they were yet living were in the holy place, and were praised in the city as men of just works: but this also is vanity.—*Eccles.* viii. 10.

But these also have been ignorant through wine, and through drunkenness have erred: the priest and the prophet have been ignorant through drunkenness, they are swallowed up with wine, they have gone astray in drunkenness, they have not known him that seeth, they have been ignorant of judgment.—*Is.* xxviii. 7.

His watchmen are all blind, they are all ignorant: dumb dogs not able to bark, seeing vain things, sleeping and loving dreams.

And most impudent dogs, they never had enough: the shepherds themselves knew no understanding: all have turned aside into their own way, every one after his own gain, from the first even to the last.

Come, let us take wine, and be filled with drunkenness: and it shall be as to-day, so also to-morrow, and much more.—*Is.* lvi. 10-12.

Because the pastors have done foolishly, and have not sought the Lord: therefore have they not understood, and all their flock is scattered.—*Jer.* x. 21.

My people have been a lost flock, their shepherds have caused them to go astray, and have made them wander in the mountains: they have gone from mountain to hill, they have forgotten their resting place.—*Jer.* l. 6.

Her priests have despised my law, and have defiled my sanctuaries: they have put no difference between holy and profane: nor have distinguished between the polluted and the clean: and they have turned away their eyes from my sabbaths, and I was profaned in the midst of them.—*Ezech.* xxii. 26.

Son of man, prophesy concerning the shepherds of Israel: prophesy, and say to the shepherds:

Thus saith the Lord God: Woe to the shepherds of Israel, that fed themselves: should not the flocks be fed by the shepherds?

You ate the milk, and you clothed yourselves with the wool, and you killed that which was fat: but my flock you did not feed.

The weak you have not strengthened, and that which was sick you have not healed, that which was broken you have not bound up, and that which was driven away you have not brought again, neither have you sought that which was lost: but you ruled over them with rigor and with a high hand.

And my sheep were scattered, because there was no shepherd: and they became the prey of all the beasts of the field, and were scattered. . . .

Was it not enough for you to feed upon good pastures? but you must also tread down with your feet the residue of your pastures: and when you drank the clearest water, you troubled the rest with your feet.

And my sheep were fed with that which you had trodden with your feet: and they drank what your feet had troubled.—*Ezech.* xxxiv. 2-5, 18, 19.

Her princes have judged for bribes, and her priests have taught for hire, and her prophets divined for money: and they leaned upon the Lord, saying: Is not the Lord in the midst of us? no evil shall come upon us.

Therefore, because of you, Sion shall be ploughed as a field, and Jerusalem shall be as a heap of stones, and the mountain of the temple as the high places of the forests.—*Mich.* iii. 11, 12.

To you, O priests, that despise my name, and have said: Wherein have we despised thy name? You offer polluted bread upon my altar, and you say: Wherein have we polluted thee? In that you say: The table of the Lord is contemptible.

If you offer the blind for sacrifice, is it not evil? and if you offer the lame and the sick, is it not evil? offer it to thy prince, if he will be pleased with it, or if he will regard thy face, saith the Lord of hosts.—*Malach.* i. 7, 8.

Insomuch that the priests were not now occupied about the offices of the altar, but despising the temple, and neglecting the sacrifices, hastened to be partakers of the games, and of the unlawful allowance thereof, and of the exercise of the discus.

And setting nought by the honors of their fathers, they esteemed the Grecian glories for the best:

For the sake of which they incurred a dangerous contention, and followed earnestly their ordinances, and in all things they coveted to be like them, who were their enemies and murderers.—2 *Mach.* iv. 14-16.

You are the salt of the earth. But if the salt lose its savor, wherewith shall it be salted? It is good for nothing any more but to be cast out, and to be trodden on by men.—*Matt.* v. 13.

Beware of false prophets, who come to you in the clothing of sheep, but inwardly they are ravening wolves.

By their fruits you shall know them. Do men gather grapes of thorns, or figs of thistles?—*Matt.* vii. 15, 16.

Then Jesus spoke to the multitudes and to his disciples,

Saying: The scribes and the Pharisees have sitten on the chair of Moses.

All things therefore whatsoever they shall say to you, observe and do: but according to their works, do ye not; for they say, and do not.

For they bind heavy and insupportable burdens, and lay them on men's shoulders; but with a finger of their own they will not move them. . . .

But woe to you scribes and Pharisees, hypocrites; because you shut the kingdom of heaven against men, for you yourselves do not enter in; and those that are going in, you suffer not to enter.—*Matt.* xxiii. 1-4, 13.

Woe to you, lawyers, for you have taken away the key of knowledge: you yourselves have not entered in, and those that were entering in, you have hindered.—*Luke* xi. 52.

Jesus answered them: Have not I chosen you twelve; and one of you is a devil?

Now he meant Judas Iscariot, the son of Simon: for this same was about to betray him, whereas he was one of the twelve.—*John* vi. 71, 72.

But the hireling, and he that is not the shepherd, whose own the sheep are not, seeth the wolf coming, and leaveth the sheep, and flieth: and the wolf catcheth and scattereth the sheep:

And the hireling flieth, because he is a hireling: and he hath no care for the sheep.—*John* x. 12, 13.

(But if thou) Art confident that thou thyself art a guide of the blind, a light of them that are in darkness,

An instructor of the foolish, a teacher of infants, having the form of knowledge and of truth in the law.

Thou therefore that teachest another, teachest not thyself: thou that preachest that men should not steal, stealest:

Thou that sayest, men should not commit adultery, committest adultery: thou that abhorrest idols, committest sacrilege:

Thou that makest thy boast of the law, by transgression of the law dishonorest God.

(For the name of God through you is blasphemed among the Gentiles, as it is written.)

Circumcision profiteth indeed, if thou keep the law; but if thou be a transgressor of the law, thy circumcision is made, uncircumcision.—*Rom.* ii. 19-25.

PRIESTS, PUNISHMENT OF BAD AND UNFAITHFUL

Remember them, O Lord my God, that defile the priesthood, and the law of priests and Levites.—2 *Esd.* xiii. 29.

He leadeth away priests without glory, and overthroweth nobles.—*Job* xii. 19.

Thus saith the Lord God of hosts: Go, get thee in to him that dwelleth in the tabernacle, to Sobna, who is over the temple: and thou shalt say to him: . . .

Behold the Lord will cause thee to be carried away, as a cock is carried away, and he will lift thee up as a garment.

He will crown thee with a crown of tribulation. . . .

And I will drive thee out from thy station, and depose thee from thy ministry.—*Is.* xxii. 15, 17-19.

For from the least of them even to the greatest, all are given to covetousness: and from the prophet even to the priest, all are guilty of deceit.

And they healed the breach of the daughter of my people disgracefully, saying: Peace, peace: and there was no peace.

They were confounded, because they committed abomination: yea, rather they were not confounded with confusion, and they knew not how to blush: wherefore they shall fall among them that fall: in the time of their visitation, they shall fall down, saith the Lord.—*Jer.* vi. 13-15.

Woe to the pastors, that destroy and tear the sheep of my pasture, saith the Lord.

Therefore thus saith the Lord the God of Israel to the pastors that feed my people: You have scattered my flock, and driven them away, and have not visited them: behold I will visit upon you for the evil of your doings, saith the Lord.—*Jer.* xxiii. 1, 2.

For the prophet and the priest are defiled: and in my house I have found their wickedness, saith the Lord.

Therefore their way shall be as a slippery way in the dark: for they shall be driven on, and fall therein: for I will bring evils upon them, the year of their visitation, saith the Lord.—*Jer.* xxiii. 11, 12.

Therefore, ye shepherds, hear the word of the Lord:

As I live, saith the Lord God, forasmuch as my flocks have Leen made a spoil, and my sheep are become a prey to all the beasts of the field, because there was no shepherd: for my shepherds did not seek after my flock, but the shepherds fed themselves, and fed not my flocks:

Therefore, ye shepherds, hear the word of the Lord:

Thus saith the Lord God: Behold I myself come upon the shepherds, I will require my flock at their hand, and I will cause them to cease from feeding the flock any more, neither shall the shepherds feed themselves any more: and I will deliver my flock from their mouth, and it shall no more be meat for them.—*Ezech.* xxxiv. 7-10.

Hear ye this, O priests, and hearken, O ye house of Israel, and give ear, O house of the king: for there is a judgment against you, because you have been a snare to them whom you should have watched over, and a net spread upon Thabor.

And you have turned aside victims into the depth: and I am the teacher of them all.—*Osee* v. 1, 2.

For behold I will raise up a shepherd in the land, who shall not visit what is forsaken, nor seek what is scattered, nor heal what is broken, nor nourish that which standeth, and he shall eat the flesh of the fat ones, and break their hoofs.

O shepherd, and idol, that forsaketh the flock: the sword upon his arm, and upon his right eye: his arm shall quite wither away, and his right eye shall be utterly darkened.—*Zach.* xi. 16, 17.

And now, O ye priests, this commandment is to you.

If you will not hear, and if you will not lay it to heart, to give glory to my name, saith the Lord of hosts: I will send poverty upon you, and will curse your blessings, yea I will curse them, because you have not laid it to heart.

. . . But you have departed out of the way, and have caused many to stumble at the law: you have made void the covenant of Levi, saith the Lord of hosts.

Therefore have I also made you contemptible and base before all people, as you have not kept my ways, and have accepted persons in the law.—*Malach.* ii. 1, 2, 8, 9.

Many will say to me in that day: Lord, Lord, have we not prophesied in thy name, and cast out devils in thy name, and done many miracles in thy name?

And then will I profess unto them, I never knew you: depart from me, you that work iniquity.—*Matt.* vii. 22, 23.

PROCRASTINATION

Say not to thy friend: Go, and come again: and to-morrow I will give to thee: when thou canst give at present.—*Prov.* iii. 28.

Delay not to be converted to the Lord,

and defer it not from day to day. For his wrath shall come on a sudden, and in the time of vengeance he will destroy thee.—*Ecclus.* v. 8, 9.

But he said to another: Follow me. And he said: Lord, suffer me first to go, and to bury my father.

And Jesus said to him: Let the dead bury their dead: but go thou, and preach the kingdom of God.

And another said: I will follow thee, Lord; but let me first take my leave of them that are at my house.

Jesus said to him: No man putting his hand to the plough, and looking back, is fit for the kingdom of God.—*Luke* ix. 59-62.

PRODIGALITY

Make not thyself poor by borrowing to contribute to feasts, when thou hast nothing in thy purse: for thou shalt be an enemy to thy own life.—*Ecclus.* xviii. 33.

And he (Jesus) said: A certain man had two sons:

And the younger of them said to his father: Father, give me the portion of substance that falleth to me. And he divided unto them his substance.

And not many days after, the younger son, gathering all together, went abroad into a far country: and there wasted his substance, living riotously.

And after he had spent all, there came a mighty famine in that country; and he began to be in want.

And he went, and cleaved to one of the citizens of that country. And he sent him into his farm to feed swine.

And he would fain have filled his belly with the husks the swine did eat; and no man gave unto him.—*Luke* xv. 11-16.

PROFANITY

See: Cursing—page 95.

Also: Name of God, taking in vain the—page 337.

PROTECTOR, GOD OUR

See also: Preserver, God our—page 414.

Now when these things were done, the word of the Lord came to Abram by a vision, saying: Fear not, Abram, I am thy protector, and thy reward exceeding great.—*Gen.* xv. 1.

And I will be thy (Jacob's) keeper whithersoever thou goest, and will bring thee back into this land: neither will I leave thee, till I shall have accomplished all that I have said.—*Gen.* xxviii. 15.

The Lord will fight for you, and you shall hold your peace.—*Ex.* xiv. 14.

The Lord is my firmament, my refuge, and my deliverer.

My God is my helper, and in him will I put my trust.

My protector, and the horn of my salvation, and my support. . . .

He sent from on high, and took me, and received me out of many waters.

He delivered me from my strongest enemies, and from them that hated me: for they were too strong for me.

They prevented me in the day of my affliction: and the Lord became my protector.

And he brought me forth into a large place: he saved me, because he was well pleased with me.—*Ps.* xvii. 3, 17-20.

As for my God, his way is undefiled: the words of the Lord are fire tried: he is the protector of all that trust in him.—*Ps.* xvii. 31.

The Lord is my light and my salvation, whom shall I fear?

The Lord is the protector of my life: of whom shall I be afraid? . . .

For he hath hidden me in his tabernacle; in the day of evils, he hath protected me in the secret place of his tabernacle.—*Ps.* xxvi. 1, 5.

The Lord is my helper and my protector: in him hath my heart confided, and I have been helped.

And my flesh hath flourished again, and with my will I will give praise to him.

The Lord is the strength of his people, and the protector of the salvation of his anointed.—*Ps.* xxvii. 7, 8.

Our soul waiteth for the Lord: for he is our helper and protector.—*Ps.* xxxii. 20.

With the Lord shall the steps of a man be directed, and he shall like well his way.

When he shall fall, he shall not be

bruised, for the Lord putteth his hand under him.—*Ps.* xxxvi. 23, 24.

But the salvation of the just is from the Lord, and he is their protector in the time of trouble.—*Ps.* xxxvi. 39.

The Lord of armies is with us: the God of Jacob is our protector.—*Ps.* xlv. 8.

For behold God is my helper: and the Lord is the protector of my soul.—*Ps.* liii. 6.

For our protection is of the Lord, and of our king, the holy one of Israel. —*Ps.* lxxxviii. 19.

He that dwelleth in the aid of the most High, shall abide under the protection of the God of Jacob.

He shall say to the Lord: Thou art my protector, and my refuge: my God, in him will I trust.

For he hath delivered me from the snare of the hunters: and from the sharp word.

He will overshadow thee with his shoulders: and under his wings thou shalt trust.

His truth shall compass thee with a shield: thou shalt not be afraid of the terror of the night.

. . . A thousand shall fall at thy side, and ten thousand at thy right hand: but it shall not come nigh thee. . . .

There shall no evil come to thee: nor shall the scourge come near thy dwelling.

For he hath given his angels charge over thee; to keep thee in all thy ways.

In their hands they shall bear thee up: lest thou dash thy foot against a stone.—*Ps.* xc. 1-5, 7, 10-12.

Behold he shall neither slumber nor sleep, that keepeth Israel.

The Lord is thy keeper, the Lord is thy protection upon thy right hand.

The sun shall not burn thee by day: nor the moon by night.

The Lord keepeth thee from all evil: may the Lord keep thy soul.—*Ps.* cxx. 4-7.

Often have they fought against me from my youth, let Israel now say.

Often have they fought against me from my youth: but they could not prevail over me.—*Ps.* cxxviii. 1, 2.

For God is compassionate and merci-

ful, and will forgive sins in the day of tribulation: and he is a protector to all that seek him in truth.—*Ecclus.* ii. 13.

The eyes of the Lord are upon them that fear him, he is their powerful protector, and strong stay, a defence from the heat, and a cover from the sun at noon,

A preservation from stumbling, and a help from falling.—*Ecclus.* xxxiv. 19, 20.

In the shadow of his hand he hath protected me, and hath made me as a chosen arrow: in his quiver he hath hidden me.—*Is.* xlix. 2.

I, I myself will comfort you: who art thou, that thou shouldst be afraid of a mortal man, and of the son of man, who shall wither away like grass?

And thou hast forgotten the Lord thy maker, who stretched out the heavens, and founded the earth: and thou hast been afraid continually all the day at the presence of his fury who afflicted thee, and had prepared himself to destroy thee: where is now the fury of the oppressor? . . .

I have put my words in thy mouth, and have protected thee in the shadow of my hand.—*Is.* li. 12, 13, 16.

But we had in ourselves the answer of death, that we should not trust in ourselves, but in God, who raiseth the dead.

Who hath delivered, and doth deliver us out of so great dangers: in whom we trust that he will yet also deliver us.— *2 Cor.* i. 9, 10.

And who is he that can hurt you, if you be zealous of good?

But if also you suffer any thing for justice' sake, blessed are ye. And be not afraid of their fear, and be not troubled.—1 *Peter* iii. 13, 14.

PROTECTOR, ACKNOWLEDGMENT THAT GOD IS OUR

But thou, O Lord, art my protector, my glory, and the lifter up of my head. . . .

I have slept and have taken my rest: and I have risen up, because the Lord hath protected me.—*Ps.* iii. 4, 6.

And thou hast given me the protection of thy salvation: and thy right hand hath held me up.—*Ps.* xvii. 36.

Thou wilt bring me out of this snare, which they have hidden for me: for thou art my protector.—*Ps.* xxx. 5.

In thy tabernacle I shall dwell for ever: I shall be protected under the covert of thy wings.—*Ps.* lx. 5.

And I will rejoice under the covert of thy wings: my soul hath stuck close to thee: thy right hand hath received me.—*Ps.* lxii. 8, 9.

Thou hast protected me from the assembly of the malignant; from the multitude of the workers of iniquity.—*Ps.* lxiii. 3.

By thee have I been confirmed from the womb: from my mother's womb thou art my protector.—*Ps.* lxx. 6.

If I shall walk in the midst of tribulation, thou wilt quicken me: and thou hast stretched forth thy hand against the wrath of my enemies: and thy right hand hath saved me.—*Ps.* cxxxvii. 7.

For thou hast possessed my reins: thou hast protected me from my mother's womb.—*Ps.* cxxxviii. 13.

I will give glory to thy name: for thou hast been a helper and protector to me. . . .

And thou hast delivered me, according to the multitude of the mercy of thy name, from them that did roar, prepared to devour.

Out of the hands of them that sought my life, and from the gates of afflictions, which compassed me about:

From the oppression of the flame which surrounded me, and in the midst of the fire, I was not burnt.

From the depth of the belly of hell, and from an unclean tongue, and from lying words, from an unjust king, and from a slanderous tongue.—*Ecclus.* li. 2, 4-7.

PROTECTION OF GOD, A PRAYER FOR THE

And Tobias answering, said: May you have a good journey, and God be with you in your way, and his angel accompany you.—*Tob.* v. 21.

Deliver me, O Lord, and set me beside thee, and let any man's hand fight against me.—*Job* xvii. 3.

O Lord my God, in thee have I put my trust: save me from all them that persecute me, and deliver me.

Lest at any time he seize upon my soul like a lion, while there is no one to redeem me, nor to save.—*Ps.* vii. 2, 3.

From them that resist thy right hand, keep me, as the apple of thy eye.

Protect me under the shadow of thy wings. From the face of the wicked who have afflicted me.—*Ps.* xvi. 8, 9.

May the Lord hear thee in the day of tribulation: may the name of the God of Jacob protect thee.

May he send thee help from the sanctuary: and defend thee out of Sion.—*Ps.* xix. 2, 3.

Bow down thy ear to me: make haste to deliver me.

Be thou unto me a God, a protector, and a house of refuge, to save me.—*Ps.* xxx. 3.

Be thou unto me a God, a protector, and a place of strength: that thou mayst make me safe.

For thou art my firmament and my refuge. Deliver me, O my God, out of the hand of the sinner, and out of the hand of the transgressor of the law, and of the unjust.—*Ps.* lxx. 3, 4.

O Lord, deliver my soul from wicked lips, and a deceitful tongue.—*Ps.* cxix. 2.

May the Lord keep thy soul.

May the Lord keep thy coming in and thy going out; from henceforth now and for ever.—*Ps.* cxx. 7, 8.

Keep me, O Lord, from the hand of the wicked: and from unjust men deliver me.

Who have proposed to supplant my steps.—*Ps.* cxxxix. 5.

But to thee, O Lord, Lord, are my eyes: in thee have I put my trust, take not away my soul.

Keep me from the snare, which they have laid for me, and from the stumbling-blocks of them that work iniquity.—*Ps.* cxl. 8, 9.

Put forth thy hand from on high, take me out, and deliver me from many waters: from the hand of strange children:

Whose mouth hath spoken vanity: and their right hand is the right hand of iniquity.—*Ps.* cxliii. 7, 8.

O Lord, have mercy on us: for we have waited for thee: be thou our arm in the morning, and our salvation in the time of trouble.—*Is.* xxxiii. 2.

And in his prayer, he (Judas Machabeus) said after this manner: Thou, O Lord, who didst send thy angel in the time of Ezechias king of Juda, and didst kill a hundred and eighty-five thousand of the army of Sennacherib:

Send now also, O Lord of heaven, thy good angel before us, for the fear and dread of the greatness of thy arm,

That they may be afraid, who come with blasphemy against thy holy people. —*2 Mach.* xv. 22-24.

PROVIDENCE OF GOD, THE

There is no other God like the God of the rightest: he that is mounted upon the heaven is thy helper. By his magnificence the clouds run hither and thither.

His dwelling is above, and 'underneath are the everlasting arms.—*Deut.* xxxiii. 26, 27.

For all thy ways are prepared, and in thy providence thou hast placed thy judgments.—*Judith* ix. 5.

In the good day enjoy good things, and beware beforehand of the evil day: for God hath made both the one and the other, that man may not find against him any just complaint.—*Eccles.* vii. 15.

Good things and evil, life and death, poverty and riches, are from God.—*Ecclus.* xi. 14.

The works of God are done in judgment from the beginning, and from the making of them he distinguished their parts, and their beginnings in their generations.

He beautified their works for ever, they have neither hungered, nor labored, and they have not ceased from their works.

Nor shall any of them straiten his neighbor at any time. . . .

After this, God looked upon the earth, and filled it with his goods.—*Ecclus.* xvi. 26-28, 30.

Or, is it not lawful for me to do what I will? is thy eye evil, because I am good?—*Matt.* xx. 15.

¹That is: though the dwelling of God be above in heaven, His arms are always stretched out to help us here below.

PROVIDENCE OF GOD CARING FOR US, THE

That thou mayst consider in **thy** heart, that as a man traineth up **his** son, so the Lord thy God hath **trained** thee up.—*Deut.* viii. 5.

Thou hast granted me life and mercy, and thy visitation hath preserved **my** spirit.—*Job* x. 12.

But I am a beggar and poor: **the** Lord is careful for me.—*Ps.* xxxix. 18.

He will overshadow thee with **his** shoulders: and under his wings thou shalt trust. . . .

For he hath given his angels charge over thee; to keep thee in all thy ways.

In their hands they shall bear **thee** up: lest thou dash thy foot against a stone.—*Ps.* xc. 4, 11, 12.

He hath given food to them that **fear** him. He will be mindful for ever of his covenant.—*Ps.* cx. 5.

Praise the Lord, for he is good: for his mercy endureth for ever. . . .

Who giveth food to all flesh: for his mercy endureth for ever.—*Ps.* cxxxv. 1, 25.

The eyes of all hope in thee, O Lord: and thou givest them meat in due season.

Thou openest thy hand, and fillest with blessing every living creature.— *Ps.* cxliv. 15, 16.

Who keepeth truth for ever: who executeth judgment for them that suffer wrong: who giveth food to the hungry. —*Ps.* cxlv. 7.

And how could any thing endure, if thou wouldst not? or be preserved, if not called by thee?—*Wis.* xi. 26.

For there is no other God but thou, who hast care of all, that thou shouldst show that thou dost not give judgment unjustly.—*Wis.* xii. 13.

And for raiment, why are you solicitous? Consider the lilies of the field, how they grow: they labor not, neither do they spin.

But I say to you, that not even Solomon in all his glory was arrayed as one of these.

And if the grass of the field, which is to-day, and to-morrow is cast into the oven, God doth so clothe: how much more you, O ye of little faith!

Be not solicitous therefore, saying, What shall we eat: or what shall we drink, or wherewith shall we be clothed? For after all these things do the heathens seek. For your Father knoweth that you have need of all these things.

Seek ye therefore first the kingdom of God, and his justice, and all these things shall be added unto you.—*Matt.* vi. 28-33.

Are not two sparrows sold for a farthing? and not one of them shall fall on the ground without your Father. But the very hairs of your head are all numbered.

Fear not therefore: better are you than many sparrows.—*Matt.* x. 29-31.

Casting all your care upon him, for he hath care of you.—1 *Peter* v. 7.

PROVIDENCE OF GOD ORDERING THE ELEMENTS AND ALL THINGS FOR THE WELFARE OF MAN, THE

And the Lord smelled a sweet savor, and said: I will no more curse the earth for the sake of man. . . .

All the days of the earth, seed time and harvest, cold and heat, summer and winter, night and day, shall not cease. —*Gen.* viii. 21, 22.

Wherefore I will pray to the Lord, and address my speech to God: . . .

Who giveth rain upon the face of the earth, and watereth all things with waters.—*Job* v. 8, 10.

For he beholdeth the ends of the world: and looketh on all things that are under heaven.

Who made a weight for the winds, and weighed the waters by measure.

When he gave a law for the rain, and a way for the sounding storms.—*Job* xxviii. 24-26.

He lifteth up the drops of rain, and poureth out showers like floods:

Which flow from the clouds that cover all above.

If he will spread out clouds as his tent,

And lighten with his light from above, he shall cover also the ends of the sea.

For by these he judgeth people, and giveth food to many mortals.—*Job* xxxvi. 27-31.

He commandeth the snow to go down upon the earth, and the winter rain, and the shower of his strength.

He sealeth up the hand of all men, that every one may know his works.

Then the beast shall go into his covert, and shall abide in his den.

Out of the inner parts shall a tempest come, and cold out of the north.

When God bloweth, there cometh frost, and again the waters are poured out abundantly.

Corn desireth clouds, and the clouds spread their light:

Which go round about, whithersoever the will of him that governeth them shall lead them, to whatsoever he shall command them upon the face of the whole earth:

Whether in one tribe, or in his own land, or in what place soever of his mercy he shall command them to be found.—*Job* xxxvii. 6-13.

Thou hast visited the earth, and hast plentifully watered it; thou hast many ways enriched it.

The river of God is filled with water, thou hast prepared their food: for so is its preparation. . . .

Thou shalt bless the crown of the year of thy goodness: and thy fields shall be filled with plenty.

The beautiful places of the wilderness shall grow fat: and the hills shall be girded about with joy.

The rams of the flock are clothed, and the vales shall abound with corn: they shall shout, yea, they shall sing a hymn.—*Ps.* lxiv. 10, 12-14.

Let the people, O God, confess to thee: let all the people give praise to thee: the earth hath yielded her fruit.— *Ps.* lxvi. 6, 7.

Thou rulest the power of the sea: and appeasest the motion of the waves thereof.—*Ps.* lxxxviii. 10.

Thou waterest the hills from thy upper rooms: the earth shall be filled with the fruit of thy works:

Bringing forth grass for cattle, and herb for the service of men.

That thou mayst bring bread out of the earth: and that wine may cheer the heart of man.

That he may make the face cheerful with oil: and that bread may strengthen man's heart. . . .

He hath made the moon for seasons: the sun knoweth his going down.

Thou hast appointed darkness, and it is night: in it shall all the beasts of the woods go about.

. . . The sun ariseth, and they are gathered together: and they shall lie down in their dens.

Man shall go forth to his work, and to his labor, until the evening.—Ps. ciii. 13-15, 19, 20, 22, 23.

Thou hast founded the earth, and it continueth.

By thy ordinance the day goeth on: for all things serve thee.—Ps. cxviii. 90, 91.

Sing ye to the Lord with praise: sing to our God upon the harp.

Who covereth the heaven with clouds, and prepareth rain for the earth.

Who maketh grass to grow on the mountains, and herbs for the service of men.—Ps. cxlvi. 7, 8.

Again, another designing to sail, and beginning to make his voyage through the raging waves, calleth upon a piece of wood (an idol) more frail than the wood that carrieth him. . . .

But thy providence, O Father, governeth it: for thou hast made a way even in the sea, and a most sure path among the waves,

Showing that thou art able to save out of all things, yea, though a man went to sea without art.

But that the works of thy wisdom might not be idle: therefore men also trust their lives even to a little wood, and passing over the sea by ship are saved.—Wis. xiv. 1, 3-5.

Let them that sail on the sea, tell the dangers thereof: and when we hear with our ears, we shall admire. . . .

Through him is established the end of their journey, and by his word all things are regulated.—Ecclus. xliii. 26, 28.

And they have not said in their heart: Let us fear the Lord our God, who giveth us the early and the latter rain in due season: who preserveth for us the fulness of the yearly harvest.—Jer. v. 24.

Seek him that maketh Arcturus, and Orion, and that turneth darkness into morning, and that changeth day into night: that calleth the waters of the sea, and poureth them out upon the face of the earth: The Lord is his name. —Amos v. 8.

That you may be the children of your Father who is in heaven, who maketh his sun to rise upon the good and bad, and raineth upon the just and the unjust.—Matt. v. 45.

Nevertheless he left not himself without testimony, doing good from heaven, giving rains and fruitful seasons, filling our hearts with food and gladness. —Acts xiv. 16.

PROVIDENCE OF GOD CARING FOR THE BRUTE CREATION, THE

Who provideth food for the raven, when her young ones cry to God, wandering about, because they have no meat?—Job xxxviii. 41.

Thou sendest forth springs in the vales: between the midst of the hills the waters shall pass.

All the beasts of the field shall drink: the wild asses shall expect in their thirst.

. . . Thou hast appointed darkness, and it is night: in it shall all the beasts of the woods go about:

The young lions roaring after their prey, and seeking their meat from God.

The sun ariseth, and they are gathered together: and they shall lie down in their dens. . . .

All expect of thee that thou give them food in season.

What thou givest to them they shall gather up: when thou openest thy hand, they shall all be filled with good.

But if thou turnest away thy face, they shall be troubled: thou shalt take away their breath, and they shall fail, and shall return to their dust.—Ps. ciii. 10, 11, 20-22, 27-29.

The eyes of all hope in thee, O Lord: and thou givest them meat in due season.

Thou openest thy hand, and fillest with blessing every living creature.— Ps. cxliv. 15, 16.

Sing ye to the Lord with praise: sing to our God upon the harp. . . .

Who giveth to beasts their food: and to the young ravens that call upon him.—*Ps.* cxlvi. 7, 9.

Go to the ant, O sluggard, and consider her ways, and learn wisdom:

Which, although she hath no guide, nor master, nor captain,

Provideth her meat for herself in the summer, and gathereth her food in the harvest.—*Prov.* vi. 6-8.

Behold the birds of the air, for they neither sow, nor do they reap, nor gather into barns: and your heavenly Father feedeth them. Are not you of much more value than they?—*Matt.* vi. 26.

Are not two sparrows sold for a farthing? and not one of them shall fall on the ground without your Father.—*Matt.* x. 29.

Are not five sparrows sold for two farthings, and not one of them is forgotten before God?—*Luke* xii. 6.

PROVIDENCE OF GOD IN HIS DEALINGS WITH MEN, EXAMPLES OF THE

And he (Joseph) said mildly to them: Come nearer to me. And when they were come near him, he said: I am Joseph, your brother, whom you sold into Egypt.

Be not afraid, and let it not seem to you a hard case, that you sold me into these countries: for God sent me before you into Egypt for your preservation. . . .

Not by your counsel was I sent hither, but by the will of God: who hath made me as it were a father to Pharao, and lord of his whole house, and governor in all the land of Egypt.—*Gen.* xlv. 4, 5, 8.

And he (Joseph) answered them: Fear not: can we resist the will of God?

You thought evil against me: but God turned it into good, that he might exalt me, as at present you see, and might save many people.—*Gen.* l. 19, 20.

And the Lord said to Moses: Arise in the morning, and stand before Pharao, and thou shalt say to him: Thus saith the Lord, the God of the Hebrews: Let my people go to sacrifice to me. . . .

For now I will stretch out my hand to strike thee and thy people with pestilence, and thou shalt perish from the earth.

And therefore have I raised thee, that I may show my power in thee, and my name may be spoken of throughout all the earth.—*Ex.* ix. 13, 15, 16.

And in the wilderness (as thou hast seen) the Lord thy God hath carried thee, as a man is wont to carry his little son, all the way that you have come, until you came to this place.—*Deut.* i. 31.

But the Lord's portion is his people: Jacob, the lot of his inheritance.

He found him in a desert land, in a place of horror and of vast wilderness: he led him about, and taught him: and he kept him as the apple of his eye.

As the eagle enticing her young to fly, and hovering over them, he spread his wings, and hath taken him and carried him on his shoulders.—*Deut.* xxxii. 9-11.

Give glory to the Lord, ye children of Israel, and praise him in the sight of the Gentiles:

Because he hath therefore scattered you among the Gentiles, who know not him, that you may declare his wonderful works, and make them know that there is no other almighty God besides him.—*Tob.* xiii. 3, 4.

PROVIDENCE OF GOD, DENYING THE

Give not thy mouth to cause thy flesh to sin: and say not before the angel: There is no providence: lest God be angry at thy words, and destroy all the works of thy hands.—*Eccles.* v. 5.

And it shall come to pass at that time, that I will search Jerusalem with lamps, and will visit upon the men that are settled on their lees: that say in their hearts: The Lord will not do good, nor will he do evil.—*Soph.* i. 12.

You have wearied the Lord with your words, and you said: Wherein have we wearied him? In that you say: Every one that doth evil, is good in the sight of the Lord, and such please him: or surely where is the God of judgment?—*Malach.* ii. 17.

PRUDENCE

But a net is spread in vain before the eyes of them that have wings.—*Prov. i. 17.*

The wisdom of a discreet man is to understand his way: and the imprudence of fools erreth.—*Prov. xiv. 8.*

In the heart of the prudent resteth wisdom, and it shall instruct all the ignorant.—*Prov. xiv. 33.*

The prudent man saw the evil, and hid himself: the simple passed on, and suffered loss.—*Prov. xxii. 3.*

According to thy power beware of thy neighbor, and treat with the wise and prudent.—*Ecclus. ix. 21.*

He that is hasty to give credit, is light of heart, and shall be lessened. . . .

And believe not every word. There is one that slippeth with the tongue, but not from his heart.—*Ecclus. xix. 4, 16.*

Behold I send you as sheep in the midst of wolves. Be ye therefore wise as serpents, and simple as doves.—*Matt. x. 16.*

Brethren, do not become children in sense: but in malice be children, and in sense be perfect.—*1 Cor. xiv. 20.*

But the end of all is at hand. Be prudent therefore, and watch in prayers. —*1 Peter iv. 7.*

PRUDENCE, THE VALUE OF

Blessed is the man that findeth wisdom and is rich in prudence:

The purchasing thereof is better than the merchandise of silver, and her fruit than the chiefest and purest gold.

She is more precious than all riches: and all the things that are desired, are not to be compared with her.—*Prov. iii. 13-15.*

Get wisdom, because it is better than gold: and purchase prudence, for it is more precious than silver.—*Prov. xvi. 16.*

PRUDENCE IN CONDUCT

Among the proud there are always contentions: but they that do all things with counsel, are ruled by wisdom. . . .

The prudent man doth all things with counsel: but he that is a fool, layeth open his folly.—*Prov. xiii. 10, 16.*

The innocent believeth every word: the discreet man considereth his steps. —*Prov. xiv. 15.*

He that trusteth in his own heart, is a fool: but he that walketh wisely, he shall be saved.—*Prov. xxviii. 26.*

Before a stranger, do no matter of counsel: for thou knowest not what he will bring forth.—*Ecclus. viii. 21.*

Strive not in a matter which doth not concern thee, and sit not in judgment with sinners.

My son, meddle not with many matters.—*Ecclus. xi. 9, 10.*

If thou be invited by one that is mightier, withdraw thyself: for so he will invite thee the more.

Be not troublesome to him, lest thou be put back: and keep not far from him, lest thou be forgotten.

Affect not to speak with him as an equal: and believe not his many words: for by much talk he will sift thee, and smiling, will examine thee concerning thy secrets. . . .

Take heed to thyself, and attend diligently to what thou hearest: for thou walkest in danger of thy ruin.

When thou hearest those things, see as it were in sleep, and thou shalt awake.—*Ecclus. xiii. 12-14, 16, 17.*

Give not to son or wife, brother or friend, power over thee while thou livest; and give not thy estate to another, lest thou repent, and thou entreat for the same.

As long as thou livest, and hast breath in thee, let no man change thee.

For it is better that thy children should ask of thee, than that thou look toward the hands of thy children.

In all thy works keep the pre-eminence.

Let no stain sully thy glory. In the time when thou shalt end the days of thy life, and in the time of thy decease, distribute thy inheritance.—*Ecclus. xxxiii. 20-24.*

Consult not with him that layeth a snare for thee, and hide thy counsel from them that envy thee.

Every counsellor giveth out counsel, but there is one that is a counsellor for himself.

Beware of a counsellor. And know

before what need he hath: for he will devise to his own mind:

Lest he thrust a stake into the ground, and say to thee:

Thy way is good; and then stand on the other side to see what shall befall thee.

Treat not with a man without religion concerning holiness, nor with an unjust man, concerning justice, nor with a woman touching her of whom she is jealous, nor with a coward concerning war, nor with a merchant about traffic, nor with a buyer of selling, nor with an envious man of giving thanks,

Nor with the ungodly of piety, nor with the dishonest of honesty, nor with the field laborer of every work,

Nor with him that worketh by the year of the finishing of the year, nor with an idle servant of much business: give no heed to these in any matter of counsel.—*Ecclus.* xxxvii. 7-14.

In all thy works let the true word go before thee, and steady counsel before every action.—*Ecclus.* xxxvii. 20.

Where there are many hands, shut up, and deliver all things in number, and weight: and put all in writing that thou givest out or receivest in.—*Ecclus.* xlii. 7.

See therefore, brethren, how you walk circumspectly: not as unwise,

But as wise: redeeming the time, because the days are evil.—*Eph.* v. 15, 16.

Walk with wisdom towards them that are without, redeeming the time.—*Col.* iv. 5.

PRUDENCE IN WORDS

See also: Tongue; control of the—page 560.

The mouth of the just shall meditate wisdom: and his tongue shall speak judgment.—*Ps.* xxxvi. 30.

A fool uttereth all his mind: a wise man deferreth, and keepeth it till afterwards.—*Prov.* xxix. 11.

All things have their season, and in their times all things pass under heaven. . . .

A time to keep silence, and a time to speak.—*Eccles.* iii. 1, 7.

Speak not any thing rashly, and let not thy heart be hasty to utter a word before God. For God is in heaven, and thou upon earth: therefore let thy words be few.

Dreams follow many cares: and in many words shall be found folly.—*Eccles.* v. 1, 2.

The heart of a wise man understandeth time and answer.—*Eccles.* viii. 5.

Before thou hear, answer not a word: and interrupt not others in the midst of their discourse.—*Ecclus.* xi. 8.

Before judgment prepare thee justice, and learn before thou speak.—*Ecclus.* xviii. 19.

There is one that holdeth his peace, that is found wise: and there is another that is hateful, that is bold in speech.

There is one that holdeth his peace, because he knoweth not what to say: and there is another that holdeth his peace, knowing the proper time.

A wise man will hold his peace till he see opportunity: but a babbler, and a fool, will regard no time.—*Ecclus.* xx. 5-7.

The lips of the unwise will be telling foolish things: but the words of the wise shall be weighed in a balance.

The heart of fools is in their mouth: and the mouth of wise men is in their heart.—*Ecclus.* xxi. 28, 29.

Let not thy mouth be accustomed to indiscreet speech: for therein is the word of sin.—*Ecclus.* xxiii. 17.

Praise not a man before he speaketh, for this is the trial of men.—*Ecclus.* xxvii. 8.

Speak, thou that art elder: for it becometh thee,

To speak the first word with careful knowledge.—*Ecclus.* xxxii. 4, 5.

Young man, scarcely speak in thy own cause.

If thou be asked twice, let thy answer be short.

In many things be as if thou wert ignorant, and hear in silence, and withal seeking.

In the company of great men take not upon thee: and when the ancients are present, speak not much.—*Ecclus.* xxxii. 10-13.

He that cleareth up a question, shall prepare what to say, and so having prayed he shall be heard, and shall keep discipline, and then he shall answer.—*Ecclus.* xxxiii. 4.

Let your speech be always in grace, seasoned with salt: that you may know how you ought to answer every man.—*Col.* iv. 6.

You know, my dearest brethren. And let every man be swift to hear, but slow to speak, and slow to anger.—*James* i. 19.

PRUDENCE IN WORDS COMMENDED

In the multitude of words, there shall not want sin: but he that refraineth his lips is most wise.—*Prov.* x. 19.

A man rejoiceth in the sentence of his mouth: and a word in due time is best.—*Prov.* xv. 23.

Well ordered words are as a honeycomb: sweet to the soul, and health to the bones.—*Prov.* xvi. 24.

He that setteth bounds to his words, is knowing and wise: and the man of understanding is of a precious spirit.—*Prov.* xvii. 27.

To speak a word in due time is like apples of gold on beds of silver.—*Prov.* xxv. 11.

A man wise in words shall make himself beloved: but the graces of fools shall be poured out.—*Ecclus.* xx. 13.

A wise man shall advance himself with his words, and a prudent man shall please the great ones.—*Ecclus.* xx. 29.

PRUDENCE IN WORDS, THE NECESSITY OF

In the multitude of words there shall not want sin: but he that refraineth his lips is most wise.—*Prov.* x. 19.

The lip of truth shall be steadfast for ever: but he that is a hasty witness, frameth a lying tongue.—*Prov.* xii. 19.

Whosoever speaketh ill of any thing, bindeth himself for the time to come: but he that feareth the commandment, shall dwell in peace.—*Prov.* xiii. 13.

He that answereth before he heareth, showeth himself to be a fool and worthy of confusion.—*Prov.* xviii. 13.

The things which thy eyes have seen, utter not hastily in a quarrel: lest afterward thou mayst not be able to make amends, when thou hast dishonored thy friend.

Treat thy cause with thy friend, and discover not the secret to a stranger:

Lest he insult over thee, when he hath heard it, and cease not to upbraid thee.—*Prov.* xxv. 8-10.

Open not thy heart to every man: lest he repay thee with an evil turn, and speak reproachfully to thee.—*Ecclus.* viii. 22.

A man full of tongue is terrible in his city, and he that is rash in his word, shall be hateful.—*Ecclus.* ix. 25.

Tell not thy mind to friend or foe: and if there be a sin with thee, disclose it not.

For he will hearken to thee, and will watch thee, and as it were defending thy sin, he will hate thee, and so will he be with thee always.—*Ecclus.* xix. 8, 9.

He that useth many words, shall hurt his own soul.—*Ecclus.* xx. 8.

PUNISHMENT, ACKNOWLEDGMENT THAT WE DESERVE

See: Acknowledgment—page 13.

PUNISHMENT OR REWARD GIVEN BY GOD ACCORDING TO OUR DESERTS

See: Rewards or punishes—page 487.

PUNISHMENT OF SINNERS, GOD TAKES HIS TIME IN THE

See: Time, God takes his—page 556.

PURITY

See: Chastity—page 47.

PURITY OF HEART

See: Heart—page 194.

PURITY OF INTENTION

See: Intention—page 246.

QUARRELS

See also: Dissensions—page 116.

Strive not against a man without cause, when he hath done thee no evil.—*Prov.* iii. 30.

A mild answer breaketh wrath: but a harsh word stirreth up fury.—*Prov.* xv. 1.

A perverse man stirreth up quarrels: and one full of words, separateth princes.—*Prov.* xvi. 28.

Better is a dry morsel with joy, than a house full of victims with strife.—*Prov.* xvii. 1.

An evil man always seeketh quarrels: but a cruel angel shall be sent against him.—*Prov.* xvii. 11.

He that studieth discords, loveth quarrels: and he that exalteth his door, seeketh ruin.—*Prov.* xvii. 19.

The lips of a fool intermeddle with strife: and his mouth provoketh quarrels.—*Prov.* xviii. 6.

A foolish son is the grief of his father: and a wrangling wife is like a roof continually dropping through.—*Prov.* xix. 13.

It is an honor for a man to separate himself from quarrels: but all fools are meddling with reproaches.—*Prov.* xx. 3.

It is better to dwell in a wilderness, than with a quarrelsome and passionate woman.—*Prov.* xxi. 19.

As he that taketh a dog by the ears, so is he that passeth by in anger, and meddleth with another man's quarrel.—*Prov.* xxvi. 17.

Roofs dropping through in a cold day, and a contentious woman, are alike.

He that retaineth her, is as he that would hold the wind, and shall call in the oil of his right hand.—*Prov.* xxvii. 15, 16.

And he that strongly squeezeth the paps to bring out milk, straineth out butter: and he that violently bloweth his nose, bringeth out blood: and he that provoketh wrath, bringeth forth strife.—*Prov.* xxx. 33.

In the quarrels of the proud is the shedding of blood: and their cursing is a grievous hearing.—*Ecclus.* xxvii. 16.

Refrain from strife, and thou shalt diminish thy sins:

For a passionate man kindleth strife, and a sinful man will trouble his friends, and bring in debate in the midst of them that are at peace.—*Ecclus.* xxviii. 10, 11.

A hasty contention kindleth a fire: and a hasty quarrel sheddeth blood: and a tongue that beareth witness bringeth death.—*Ecclus.* xxviii. 13.

But the servant of God must not wrangle: but be mild towards all men, apt to teach, patient.—2 *Tim.* ii. 24.

QUERULOUSNESS

See: Murmuring—page 330.

QUESTION GOD'S DOINGS, WE MUST NOT

See also: Ways of God—page 584.

And Job answered, and said:

Indeed I know it is so, and that man cannot be justified compared with God.

If he will contend with him, he cannot answer him one for a thousand.

He is wise in heart, and mighty in strength: who hath resisted him, and hath had peace?—*Job* ix. 1-4.

If he examine on a sudden, who shall answer him? or who can say: Why dost thou so? . . .

What am I then, that I should answer him, and have words with him?

I, who although I should have any just thing, would not answer, but would make supplication to my judge.—*Job* ix. 12, 14, 15.

Shall any one teach God knowledge, who judgeth those that are high?—*Job* xxi. 22.

To whom hast thou given counsel? perhaps to him that hath no wisdom, and thou hast shown thy very great prudence.

Whom hast thou desired to teach? was it not him that made life?—*Job* xxvi. 3, 4.

For it is no longer in the power of man to enter into judgment with God.—*Job* xxxiv. 23.

And the Lord answering Job out of the whirlwind, said: . . .

Wilt thou make void my judgment: and condemn me, that thou mayst be justified?—*Job* xl. 1, 3.

What needeth a man to seek things that are above him, whereas he knoweth not what is profitable for him in his life, in all the days of his pilgrimage, and the time that passeth like a shadow? . . .

Only this I have found, that God made man right, and he hath entangled himself with an infinity of questions.—*Eccles.* vii. 1, 30.

And his word is full of power: neither can any man say to him: Why dost thou so?—*Eccles.* viii. 4.

For who shall say to thee: What hast thou done? or who shall withstand thy judgment? or who shall come before thee to be a revenger of wicked men? or who shall accuse thee, if the nations perish, which thou hast made?—*Wis.* xii. 12.

Woe to him that gainsayeth his maker, a sherd of the earthen pots: shall the clay say to him that fashioneth it: What art thou making, and thy work is without hands?

Woe to him that sayeth to his father: Why begettest thou? and to the woman: Why dost thou bring forth?—*Is.* xlv. 9, 10.

And all the inhabitants of the earth are reputed as nothing before him: for he doth according to his will, as well with the powers of heaven, as among the inhabitants of the earth: and there is none that can resist his hand, and say to him: Why hast thou done it?—*Dan.* iv. 32.

Therefore he hath mercy on whom he will; and whom he will, he hardeneth.

Thou wilt say therefore to me: Why doth he then find fault? for who resisteth his will?

O man, who art thou that repliest against God? Shall the thing formed say to him that formed it: Why hast thou made me thus?

Or hath not the potter power over the clay, of the same lump to make one vessel unto honor, and another unto dishonor?—*Rom.* ix. 18-21.

REASON FOR OUR FAITH, WE SHOULD BE ABLE TO GIVE A

Incline thy ear, and hear the words of the wise: and apply thy heart to my doctrine. . . .

That thy trust may be in the Lord, wherefore I have also shown it to thee this day. . . .

That I might show thee the certainty, and the words of truth, to answer out of these to them that sent thee.—*Prov.* xxii. 17, 19, 21.

Study wisdom, my son, and make my heart joyful, that thou mayst give an answer to him that reproacheth.—*Prov.* xxvii. 11.

To you therefore, O kings, are these my words, that you may learn wisdom, and not fall from it.

For they that have kept just things justly, shall be justified: and they that have learned these things, shall find what to answer.—*Wis.* vi. 10, 11.

Be meek to hear the word, that thou mayst understand: and return a true answer with wisdom.

If thou have understanding, answer thy neighbor: but if not, let thy hand be upon thy mouth, lest thou be surprised in an unskilful word, and be confounded.—*Ecclus.* v. 13, 14.

Let not the discourse of the ancients escape thee, for they have learned of their fathers:

For of them thou shalt learn understanding, and to give an answer in time of need.—*Ecclus.* viii. 11, 12.

Be not ashamed to inform the unwise and foolish, and the aged, that are judged by young men: and thou shalt be well instructed in all things, and well approved in the sight of all men living.—*Ecclus.* xlii. 8.

Walk with wisdom towards them that are without, redeeming the time.

Let your speech be always in grace seasoned with salt: that you may know how you ought to answer every man.—*Col.* iv. 5, 6.

For a bishop must be without crime, as the steward of God: . . .

Embracing that faithful word which is according to doctrine, that he may be able to exhort in sound doctrine, and to convince the gainsayers.—*Titus* i. 7, 9.

But sanctify the Lord Christ in your hearts, being ready always to satisfy every one that asketh you a reason of that hope which is in you.—1 *Peter* iii. 15.

REBELLION AGAINST GOD

Because it is like the sin of witchcraft, to rebel: and like the crime of idolatry, to refuse to obey.—1 *Kings* xv. 23.

O children of Israel, fight not against the Lord the God of your fathers, for it is not good for you.—2 *Paral.* xiii. 12.

They spend their days in wealth, and in a moment they go down to hell.

Who have said to God: Depart from us, we desire not the knowledge of thy ways.

Who is the Almighty, that we should serve him? and what doth it profit us, if we pray to him?—*Job* xxi. 13-15.

The kings of the earth stood up, and the princes met together, against the Lord, and against his Christ.

Let us break their bonds asunder: and let us cast away their yoke from us.

He that dwelleth in heaven shall laugh at them: and the Lord shall deride them.—*Ps.* ii. 2-4.

May the Lord destroy all deceitful lips, and the tongue that speaketh proud things.

Who have said: We will magnify our tongue; our lips are our own; who is Lord over us?—*Ps.* xi. 4, 5.

For behold they that go far from thee shall perish: thou hast destroyed all them that are disloyal to thee.—*Ps.* lxxii. 27.

But the wicked shall be punished according to their own devices: who have neglected the just, and have revolted from the Lord.—*Wis.* iii. 10.

That the nations might know his power, that it is not easy to fight against God.—*Ecclus.* xlvi. 8.

Of old thou hast broken my yoke, thou hast burst my bands, and thou saidst: I will not serve.—*Jer.* ii. 20.

See ye the word of the Lord: Am I become a wilderness to Israel, or a lateward springing land? why then have my people said: We are revolted, we will come to thee no more?—*Jer.* ii. 31.

REBELLION AGAINST GOD, SIN IS

See: Sin is rebellion against God— page 522.

REDEEMER, THE

Thou art beautiful above the sons of men: grace is poured abroad in thy lips, therefore hath God blessed thee for ever.—*Ps.* xliv. 3.

Let his name be blessed for evermore: his name continueth before the sun.

And in him shall all the tribes of the earth be blessed: all nations shall magnify him.—*Ps.* lxxi. 17.

The stone which the builders rejected; the same is become the head of the corner.—*Ps.* cxvii. 22.

Behold, God is my saviour, I will deal confidently, and will not fear: because the Lord is my strength, and my praise, and he is become my salvation. —*Is.* xii. 2.

I am, I am the Lord: and there is no saviour besides me.—*Is.* xliii. 11.

But I am the Lord thy God from the land of Egypt: and thou shalt know no God but me, and there is no saviour beside me.—*Osee* xiii. 4.

But I will rejoice in the Lord: and I will joy in God my Jesus.—*Hab.* iii. 18.

And all nations shall know that there is one that redeemeth and delivereth Israel.—1 *Mach.* iv. 11.

And she shall bring forth a son: and thou shalt call his name Jesus. For he shall save his people from their sins.—*Matt.* i. 21.

Therefore having yet one son, most dear to him; he also sent him unto them last of all, saying: They will reverence my son.

But the husbandmen said one to another: This is the heir; come let us kill him; and the inheritance shall be ours.

And laying hold on him, they killed him, and cast him out of the vineyard. . . .

And have you not read this Scripture, The stone which the builders rejected, the same is made the head of the corner.—*Mark* xii. 6-8, 10.

For the Son of man is come to seek and to save that which was lost.— *Luke* xix. 10.

The next day, John saw Jesus coming to him, and he saith: Behold the Lamb of God, behold him who taketh away the sin of the world.—*John* i. 29.

And I, if I be lifted up from the earth, will draw all things to myself. —*John* xii. 32.

And if any man hear my words, and keep them not, I do not judge him: for

I came not to judge the world, but to save the world.—*John* xii. 47.

The God of our fathers hath raised up Jesus, whom you put to death, hanging him upon a tree.

Him hath God exalted with his right hand, to be Prince and Saviour, to give repentance to Israel, and remission of sins.—*Acts* v. 30, 31.

For there is one God, and one mediator of God and men, the man Christ Jesus;

Who gave himself a redemption for all, a testimony in due times.—1 *Tim.* ii. 5, 6.

Who being the brightness of his glory, and the figure of his substance, and upholding all things by the word of his power, making purgation of sins, sitteth on the right hand of the majesty on high.—*Heb.* i. 3.

And he is the propitiation for our sins: and not for ours only, but also for those of the whole world.—1 *John* ii. 2.

And from Jesus Christ, who is the faithful witness, the first begotten of the dead, and the prince of the kings of the earth, who hath loved us, and washed us from our sins in his own blood,

And hath made us a kingdom, and priests to God and his Father, to him be glory and empire for ever and ever. Amen.—*Apoc.* i. 5, 6.

REDEEMER, FIGURES OF CHRIST THE

So Abraham rising up in the night, saddled his ass: and took with him two young men, and Isaac his son: and when he had cut wood for the holocaust, he went his way to the place which God had commanded him. . . .

And he took the wood for the holocaust, and laid it upon Isaac his son: and he himself carried in his hands fire and a sword. . . .

And they came to the place which God had shown him, where he built an altar, and laid the wood in order upon it: and when he had bound Isaac his son, he laid him on the altar, upon the pile of wood.

And he put forth his hand, and took the sword, to sacrifice his son.—*Gen.* xxii. 3, 6, 9, 10.

Speak ye to the whole assembly of the children of Israel, and say to them: On the tenth day of this month, let every man take a lamb by their families and houses. . . .

And it shall be a lamb without blemish, a male, of one year: according to which rite also you shall take a kid.

And you shall keep it until the fourteenth day of this month: and the whole multitude of the children of Israel shall sacrifice it in the evening.

And they shall take of the blood thereof, and put it upon both the side posts, and on the upper door posts of the houses, wherein they shall eat it. . . .

In one house shall it be eaten, neither shall you carry forth of the flesh thereof out of the house, neither shall you break a bone thereof. . . .

And the blood shall be unto you for a sign in the houses where you shall be: and I shall see the blood, and shall pass over you: and the plague shall not be upon you to destroy you, when I shall strike the land of Egypt.—*Ex.* xii. 3, 5-7, 46, 13.

And he (Moses) took the blood, and sprinkled it upon the people, and he said: This is the blood of the covenant which the Lord hath made with you concerning all these words.—*Ex.* xxiv. 8.

But that whose lot was to be the emissary goat, he shall present alive before the Lord, that he may pour out prayers upon him, and let him go into the wilderness. . . .

After he hath cleansed the sanctuary, and the tabernacle, and the altar, then let him offer the living goat:

And putting both hands upon his head, let him confess all the iniquities of the children of Israel, and all their offences and sins: and praying that they may light on his head, he shall turn him out by a man ready for it, into the desert.

And when the goat hath carried all their iniquities into an uninhabited land, and shall be let go into the desert,

Aaron shall return into the tabernacle of the testimony.—*Lev.* xvi. 10, 20-23.

And the Lord said to him: Make a brazen serpent, and set it up for a sign: whosoever being struck shall look on it, shall live.

Moses therefore made a brazen serpent, and set it up for a sign: which when they that were bitten looked upon, they were healed.—*Num.* xxi. 8, 9.

For when the fierce rage of beasts came upon these, they were destroyed with the bitings of crooked serpents.

But thy wrath endured not for ever, but they were troubled for a short time, for their correction, having a sign of salvation, to put them in remembrance of the commandment of thy law.

For he that turned to it, was not healed by that which he saw, but by thee, the Saviour of all.—*Wis.* xvi. 5-7.

REDEEMER, LONGING OF THE WORLD FOR THE COMING OF THE

I shall see him, but not now: I shall behold him, but not near. A star shall rise out of Jacob, and a sceptre shall spring up from Israel.—*Num.* xxiv. 17.

Send forth, O Lord, the lamb, the ruler of the earth, from Petra of the desert, to the mount of the daughter of Sion.—*Is.* xvi. 1.

In that day man shall bow down himself to his Maker, and his eyes shall look to the Holy One of Israel.—*Is.* xvii. 7.

Drop down dew, ye heavens, from above, and let the clouds rain the just: let the earth be opened, and bud forth a saviour.—*Is.* xlv. 8.

For Sion's sake I will not hold my peace, and for the sake of Jerusalem, I will not rest till her just one come forth as brightness, and her saviour be lighted as a lamp.—*Is.* lxii. 1.

O that thou wouldst rend the heavens, and wouldst come down: the mountains would melt away at thy presence.—*Is.* lxiv. 1.

And I will move all nations: and the desired of all nations shall come.— *Aggeus* ii. 8.

REDEEMER, A PRAYER FOR THE COMING OF THE

See: Redeemer, longing of the world for the—page 461.

REDEEMER, PROMISE OF THE COMING OF THE

See also: Part II—page 725.

The sceptre shall not be taken away from Juda, nor a ruler from his thigh, till he come that is to be sent, and he shall be the expectation of nations.— *Gen.* xlix. 10.

I shall see him, but not now: I shall behold him, but not near. A star shall rise out of Jacob, and a sceptre shall spring up from Israel.—*Num.* xxiv. 17.

Therefore the Lord himself shall give you a sign. Behold a virgin shall conceive, and bear a son, and his name shall be called Emmanuel.—*Is.* vii. 14.

Say to the faint-hearted: Take courage, and fear not: behold your God will bring the revenge of recompense: God himself will come, and will save you.— *Is.* xxxv. 4.

Behold my servant, I will uphold him: my elect, my soul delighteth in him: I have given my spirit upon him, he shall bring forth judgment to the Gentiles.

He shall not cry, nor have respect to person, neither shall his voice be heard abroad.

The bruised reed he shall not break, and smoking flax he shall not quench; he shall bring forth judgment unto truth.

He shall not be sad, nor troublesome, till he set judgment in the earth: and the islands shall wait for his law.—*Is.* xlii. 1-4.

The Spirit of the Lord is upon me, because the Lord hath anointed me: he hath sent me to preach to the meek, to heal the contrite of heart, and to preach a release to the captives, and deliverance to them that are shut up.

To proclaim the acceptable year of the Lord, and the day of vengeance of our God: to comfort all that mourn:

To appoint to the mourners of Sion, and to give them a crown for ashes, the oil of joy for mourning, a garment of praise for the spirit of grief: and they shall be called in it the mighty ones of justice, the planting of the Lord to glorify him.—*Is.* lxi. 1-3.

For Sion's sake I will not hold my peace, and for the sake of Jerusalem, I will not rest till her just one come forth as brightness, and her saviour be lighted as a lamp.

And the Gentiles shall see thy just one, and all kings thy glorious one: and thou shalt be called by a new name, which the mouth of the Lord shall name.—*Is.* lxii. 1, 2.

Behold the Lord hath made it to be heard in the ends of the earth, tell the daughter of Sion: Behold thy Saviour cometh: behold his reward is with him, and his work before him.

And they shall call them, The holy people, the redeemed of the Lord.—*Is.* lxii. 11, 12.

I will deliver them out of the hand of death. I will redeem them from death: O death, I will be thy death; O hell, I will be thy bite.—*Osee* xiii. 14.

And thou Bethlehem Ephrata, art a little one among the thousands of Juda: out of thee shall he come forth unto me, that is to be the ruler in Israel: and his going forth is from the beginning, from the days of eternity.—*Mich.* v. 2.

For thus saith the Lord of hosts: yet a little while, and I will move the heaven and the earth, and the sea, and the dry land.

And I will move all nations: and the desired of all nations shall come: and I will fill this house with glory: saith the Lord of hosts.—*Aggeus* ii. 7, 8.

Rejoice greatly, O daughter of Sion, shout for joy, O daughter of Jerusalem: behold thy King will come to thee, the just and saviour: he is poor, and riding upon an ass, and upon a colt the foal of an ass.—*Zach.* ix. 9.

REDEEMER, THE COMING OF THE

See also: Incarnation, the—page 233.

For a child is born to us, and a son is given to us, and the government is upon his shoulder: and his name shall be called, Wonderful, Counsellor, God the Mighty, the Father of the world to come, the Prince of peace.

His empire shall be multiplied, and there shall be no end of peace: he shall sit upon the throne of David, and upon his kingdom; to establish it and strengthen it with judgment and with justice, from henceforth and for ever: the zeal of the Lord of hosts will perform this.—*Is.* ix. 6, 7.

Afterwards he was seen upon earth, and conversed with men.—*Bar.* iii. 38.

And we declare unto you, that the promise which was made to our fathers,

This same God hath fulfilled to our children, raising up Jesus, as in the second psalm also is written: Thou art my Son, this day have I begotten thee.—*Acts* xiii. 32, 33.

But when the fulness of the time was come, God sent his Son, made of a woman, made under the law:

That he might redeem them who were under the law: that we might receive the adoption of sons.—*Gal.* iv. 4, 5.

God, who, at sundry times and in divers manners, spoke in times past to the fathers by the prophets, last of all,

In these days hath spoken to us by his Son, whom he hath appointed heir of all things, by whom also he made the world.—*Heb.* i. 1, 2.

REDEMPTION, NEED OF THE

See also: Corruption of the world—page 82.

They that trust in their own strength, and glory in the multitude of their riches.

No brother can redeem, nor shall man redeem: he shall not give to God his ransom,

Nor the price of the redemption of his soul: and shall labor for ever.—*Ps.* xlviii. 7-9.

For all have sinned, and do need the glory of God.

Being justified freely by his grace, through the redemption, that is in Christ Jesus.—*Rom.* iii. 23, 24.

For which cause be mindful. . . .

That you were at that time without Christ, being aliens from the conversation of Israel, and strangers to the testament, having no hope of the promise, and without God in this world. But now in Christ Jesus, you, who sometime were afar off, are made nigh by the blood of Christ.—*Eph.* ii. 12, 13.

And you, whereas you were sometime alienated and enemies in mind in evil works:

Yet now he hath reconciled in the body of his flesh through death, to present you holy and unspotted, and blameless before him.—*Col.* i. 21, 22.

REDEMPTION, HOPE OF THE

But God will redeem my soul from the hand of hell, when he shall receive me.—*Ps.* xlviii. 16.

From the morning watch even until night, let Israel hope in the Lord.

Because with the Lord there is mercy: and with him plentiful redemption.

And he shall redeem Israel from all his iniquities.—*Ps.* cxxix. 6-8.

For their hope is on him that saveth them.—*Ecclus.* xxxiv. 15.

Looking for the blessed hope and coming of the glory of the great God and our Saviour Jesus Christ,

Who gave himself for us, that he might redeem us from all iniquity, and might cleanse to himself a people acceptable, a pursuer of good works.—*Titus* ii. 13, 14.

REDEMPTION, ACKNOWLEDG-MENT OF THE

Into thy hands I commend my spirit: thou hast redeemed me, O Lord, the God of truth.—*Ps.* xxx. 6.

He hath sent redemption to his people: he hath commanded his covenant for ever.—*Ps.* cx. 9.

And we have seen, and do testify, that the Father hath sent his Son to be the Saviour of the world.—*1 John* iv. 14.

Thou art worthy, O Lord, to take the book, and to open the seals thereof; because thou wast slain, and hast redeemed us to God, in thy blood, out of every tribe, and tongue, and people, and nation.—*Apoc.* v. 9.

REDEMPTION, GRATITUDE FOR THE

Bless the Lord, O my soul: and let all that is within me bless his holy name.

Bless the Lord, O my soul, and never forget all he hath done for thee.

Who forgiveth all thy iniquities: who healeth all thy diseases.

Who redeemeth thy life from destruction: who crowneth thee with mercy and compassion.—*Ps.* cii. 1-4.

Give glory to the Lord, for he is good: for his mercy endureth for ever.

Let them say so that have been redeemed by the Lord, whom he hath redeemed from the hand of the enemy: and gathered out of the countries.—*Ps.* cvi. 1, 2.

Blessed be the Lord God of Israel; because he hath visited and wrought the redemption of his people:

And hath raised up a horn of salvation to us, in the house of David, his servant.—*Luke* i. 68, 69.

REDEMPTION, PRICE OF THE

See also: Passion of Christ, the—page 364.

I. The Humiliation of Christ

But I am a worm, and no man: the reproach of men, and the outcast of the people.

All they that saw me have laughed me to scorn: they have spoken with the lips, and wagged the head.—*Ps.* xxi. 7, 8.

I have given my body to the strikers, and my cheeks to them that plucked them: I have not turned away my face from them that rebuked me, and spit upon me.—*Is.* l. 6.

So shall his visage be inglorious among men, and his form among the sons of men.—*Is.* lii. 14.

Despised, and the most abject of men, a man of sorrows, and acquainted with infirmity: and his look was as it were hidden and despised, whereupon we esteemed him not.—*Is.* liii. 3.

He shall give his cheek to him that striketh him, he shall be filled with reproaches.—*Lam.* iii. 30.

For let this mind be in you, which was also in Christ Jesus:

Who being in the form of God, thought it not robbery to be equal with God:

But emptied himself, taking the form of a servant, being made in the likeness of men, and in habit found as a man.

He humbled himself, becoming obedient unto death, even to the death of the cross.—*Philipp.* ii. 5-8.

Looking on Jesus, the author and finisher of faith, who having joy set before him, endured the cross, despising the shame, and now sitteth on the right hand of the throne of God.

For think diligently upon him that endured such opposition from sinners against himself; that you be not wearied, fainting in your minds.—*Heb.* xii. 2, 3.

II. Christ Bearing Our Sins

Surely he hath borne our infirmities and carried our sorrows: and we have thought him as it were a leper, and as one struck by God and afflicted:

. . . And was reputed with the wicked: and he hath borne the sins of many, and hath prayed for the transgressors.—*Is.* liii. 4, 12.

Because his soul hath labored, he shall see and be filled: by his knowledge shall this my just servant justify many, and he shall bear their iniquities.—*Is.* liii. 11.

Him, who knew no sin, he hath made sin for us, that we might be made the justice of God in him.—2 *Cor.* v. 21.

Christ hath redeemed us from the curse of the law, being made a curse for us: for it is written: Cursed is every one that hangeth on a tree.—*Gal.* iii. 13.

Who his own self bore our sins in his body upon the tree: that we, being dead to sins, should live to justice: by whose stripes you were healed.—1 *Peter* ii. 24.

III. The Sorrows of Christ

I was dumb, and was humbled, and kept silence from good things: and my sorrow was renewed.—*Ps.* xxxviii. 3.

For if my enemy had reviled me, I would verily have borne with it.

And if he that hated me had spoken great things against me, I would perhaps have hidden myself from him.

But thou a man of one mind, my guide, and my familiar,

Who didst take sweetmeats together with me: in the house of God we walked with consent.—*Ps.* liv. 13-15.

My heart hath expected reproach and misery.

And I looked for one that would grieve together with me, but there was none: and for one that would comfort me, and I found none.—*Ps.* lxviii. 21.

Instead of making me a return of love, they detracted me: but I gave myself to prayer.

And they repaid me evil for good: and hatred for my love.—*Ps.* cviii. 4, 5.

Despised, and the most abject of men, a man of sorrows, and acquainted with infirmity.—*Is.* liii. 3.

O all ye that pass by the way, attend, and see if there be any sorrow like to my sorrow: for he hath made a vintage of me, as the Lord spoke in the day of his fierce anger.—*Lam.* i. 12.

And taking with him Peter and the two sons of Zebedee, he began to grow sorrowful and to be sad.

Then he saith to them: My soul is sorrowful even unto death: stay you here, and watch with me.—*Matt.* xxvi. 37, 38.

And about the ninth hour Jesus cried with a loud voice, saying: Eli, Eli, lamma sabacthani? that is, My God, my God, why hast thou forsaken me?—*Matt.* xxvii. 46.

And as he was yet speaking, behold a multitude; and he that was called Judas, one of the twelve, went before them, and drew near to Jesus, for to kiss him.

And Jesus said to him: Judas, dost thou betray the Son of man with a kiss? —*Luke* xxii. 47, 48.

IV. The Sufferings of Christ

Go forth, ye daughters of Sion, and see king Solomon in the diadem, wherewith his mother crowned him in the day of his espousals, and in the day of the joy of his heart.—*Cant.* iii. 11.

From the sole of the foot unto the top of the head, there is no soundness therein: wounds and bruises and swelling sores: they are not bound up, nor dressed, nor fomented with oil.—*Is.* i. 6.

Surely he hath borne our infirmities and carried our sorrows: and we have thought him as it were a leper, and as one struck by God and afflicted.

But he was wounded for our iniquities, he was bruised for our sins: the chastisement of our peace was upon him, and by his bruises we are healed. —*Is.* liii. 4, 5.

Ought not Christ to have suffered these things, and so to enter into his glory?—*Luke* xxiv. 26.

And you, when you were dead in your sins, and the uncircumcision of your flesh; he hath quickened together with him, forgiving you all offences:

Blotting out the handwriting of the decree that was against us, which was contrary to us. And he hath taken the same out of the way, fastening it to the cross.—*Col.* ii. 13, 14.

And whereas indeed he was the Son of God, he learned obedience by the things which he suffered:

And being consummated, he became to all that obey him, the cause of eternal salvation.—*Heb.* v. 8, 9.

For unto this are you called: because Christ also suffered for us, leaving you an example that you should follow his steps. . . .

Who his own self bore our sins in his body upon the tree: that we, being dead to sins, should live to justice: by whose stripes you were healed.—1 *Peter* ii. 21, 24.

V. The Shedding of His Blood

And taking the chalice, he gave thanks, and gave to them, saying: Drink ye all of this.

For this is my blood of the new testament, which shall be shed for many unto remission of sins.—*Matt.* xxvi. 27, 28.

Take heed to yourselves, and to the whole flock, wherein the Holy Ghost hath placed you bishops, to rule the church of God, which he hath purchased with his own blood.—*Acts* xx. 28.

In whom we have redemption through his blood, the remission of sins, according to the riches of his grace.— *Eph.* i. 7.

Because in him, it hath well pleased the Father, that all fulness should dwell;

And through him to reconcile all things unto himself, making peace through the blood of his cross, both as to the things that are on earth, and the things that are in heaven.—*Col.* i. 19, 20.

But Christ, being come a high priest of the good things to come, by a greater and more perfect tabernacle not made with hand, that is, not of this creation:

Neither by the blood of goats, or of calves, but by his own blood, entered once into the holies, having obtained eternal redemption.

For if the blood of goats and of oxen, and the ashes of a heifer being sprinkled, sanctify such as are defiled, to the cleansing of the flesh:

How much more shall the blood of Christ, who by the Holy Ghost offered himself unspotted unto God, cleanse our conscience from dead works, to serve the living God? . . .

And almost all things, according to the law, are cleansed with blood: and without shedding of blood there is no remission.—*Heb.* ix. 11-14, 22.

Wherefore Jesus also, that he might sanctify the people by his own blood, suffered without the gate. — *Heb.* xiii. 12.

Knowing that you were not redeemed with corruptible things as gold or silver, from your vain conversation of the tradition of your fathers:

But with the precious blood of Christ, as of a lamb unspotted and undefiled. —1 *Peter* i. 18, 19.

Thou art worthy, O Lord, to take the book, and to open the seals thereof; because thou wast slain, and hast redeemed us to God, in thy blood, out of every tribe, and tongue, and people, and nation.—*Apoc.* v. 9.

VI. The Sacrifice of His Life

Even as the Son of man is not come to be ministered unto, but to minister, and to give his life a redemption for many.—*Matt.* xx. 28.

And as Moses lifted up the serpent in the desert, so must the Son of man be lifted up:

That whosoever believeth in him, may not perish; but may have life everlasting.—*John* iii. 14, 15.

I am the good shepherd. The good shepherd giveth his life for his sheep.

. . . As the Father knoweth me, and I know the Father: and I lay down my life for my sheep. . . .

Therefore doth the Father love me: because I lay down my life, that I may take it again.

No man taketh it away from me: but I lay it down of myself, and I have power to lay it down: and I have power to take it up again. This commandment have I received of my Father.—*John* x. 11, 15, 17, 18.

But one of them, named Caiphas, being the high priest that year, said to them: You know nothing.

Neither do you consider that it is expedient for you that one man should die for the people, and that the whole nation perish not.

And this he spoke not of himself: but being the high priest of that year, he prophesied that Jesus should die for the nation.

And not only for the nation, but to gather together in one the children of God, that were dispersed.—*John* xi. 49-52.

Amen, amen I say to you, unless the grain of wheat falling into the ground, die,

Itself remaineth alone. But if it die, it bringeth forth much fruit.—*John* xii. 24, 25.

He humbled himself, becoming obedient unto death, even to the death of the cross.—*Philipp.* ii. 8.

But we see Jesus, who was made a little lower than the angels, for the suffering of death, crowned with glory and honor: that, through the grace of God, he might taste death for all.—*Heb.* ii. 9.

And therefore he is the mediator of the new testament: that by means of his death, for the redemption of those transgressions, which were under the former testament, they that are called may receive the promise of eternal inheritance.

For where there is a testament, the death of the testator must of necessity come in.

For a testament is of force after men are dead: otherwise it is as yet of no strength, whilst the testator liveth.—*Heb.* ix. 15-17.

But now once at the end of ages, he hath appeared for the destruction of sin, by the sacrifice of himself.

And as it is appointed unto men once to die, and after this the judgment:

So also Christ was offered once to exhaust the sins of many.—*Heb.* ix. 26-28.

REDEMPTION, FRUIT OF THE

I. Freedom from Sin and the Devil

Thou hast ascended on high, thou hast led captivity captive; thou hast received gifts in men.—*Ps.* lxvii. 19.

Our soul hath been delivered as a sparrow out of the snare of the fowlers. The snare is broken, and we are delivered.—*Ps.* cxxiii. 7.

Blessed be the Lord God of Israel; because he hath visited and wrought the redemption of his people:

And hath raised up a horn of salvation to us, in the house of David his servant. . . .

Salvation from our enemies, and from the hand of all that hate us: . . .

The oath, which he swore to Abraham our father, that he would grant to us,

That being delivered from the hand of our enemies, we may serve him without fear,

In holiness and justice before him, all our days.—*Luke* i. 68, 69, 71, 73-75.

To open their eyes, that they may be converted from darkness to light, and from the power of Satan to God.—*Acts* xxvi. 18.

But thanks be to God, that you were the servants of sin, but have obeyed from the heart unto that form of doctrine, into which you have been delivered.

Being then freed from sin, we have been made servants of justice. . . .

But now being made free from sin, and become servants to God, you have your fruit unto sanctification, and the end life everlasting.—*Rom.* vi. 17, 18, 22.

Grace be to you, and peace from God the Father, and from our Lord Jesus Christ,

Who gave himself for our sins, that he might deliver us from this present wicked world, according to the will of God and our Father.—*Gal.* i. 3, 4.

Giving thanks to God the Father, who hath made us worthy to be partakers of the lot of the saints in light:

Who hath delivered us from the power of darkness, and hath translated us into the kingdom of the Son of his love. —*Col.* i. 12, 13.

Therefore because the children are partakers of flesh and blood, he also himself in like manner hath been partaker of the same: that, through death, he might destroy him who had the empire of death, that is to say, the devil:

And might deliver them, who through the fear of death were all their lifetime subject to servitude.—*Heb.* ii. 14, 15.

He that committeth sin is of the devil: for the devil sinneth from the beginning. For this purpose, the Son of God appeared, that he might destroy the works of the devil.—1 *John* iii. 8.

II. Forgiveness of Sins

Be it known therefore to you, men, brethren, that through him forgiveness of sins is preached to you: and from all the things, from which you could not be justified by the law of Moses.—*Acts* xiii. 38.

To open their eyes, that they may be converted from darkness to light, and from the power of Satan to God, that they may receive forgiveness of sins, and a lot among the saints, by the faith that is in me.—*Acts* xxvi. 18.

Being justified freely by his grace, through the redemption that is in Christ Jesus,

Whom God hath proposed to be a propitiation, through faith in his blood, to the showing of his justice, for the remission of former sins.—*Rom.* iii. 24, 25.

In whom we have redemption through his blood, the remission of sins.—*Col.* i. 14.

Who gave himself for us, that he might redeem us from all iniquity, and might cleanse to himself a people acceptable, a pursuer of good works.— *Titus* ii. 14.

But now once at the end of ages, he hath appeared for the destruction of sin, by the sacrifice of himself.

And as it is appointed unto men once to die, and after this the judgment:

So also Christ was offered once to exhaust the sins of many.—*Heb.* ix. 26-28.

And you know that he appeared to take away our sins, and in him there is no sin.—1 *John* iii. 5.

Grace be unto you, and peace from him that is, and that was, and that is to come, . . .

And from Jesus Christ, who is the faithful witness, the first begotten of the dead, and the prince of the kings of the earth, who hath loved us, and washed us from our sins in his own blood.—*Apoc.* i. 4, 5.

III. Peace and Reconciliation with God

In his days shall justice spring up, and abundance of peace, till the moon be taken away.—*Ps.* lxxi. 7.

Being justified therefore by faith, let us have peace with God, through our Lord Jesus Christ:

By whom also we have access through faith into this grace, wherein we stand, and glory in the hope of the glory of the sons of God. . . .

For if, when we were enemies, we were reconciled to God by the death of his Son; much more, being reconciled, shall we be saved by his life.—*Rom.* v. 1, 2, 10.

But all things are of God, who hath reconciled us to himself by Christ; and hath given to us the ministry of reconciliation.

For God indeed was in Christ, reconciling the world to himself, not imputing to them their sins; and he hath placed in us the word of reconciliation. —2 *Cor.* v. 18, 19.

For he is our peace, who hath made both one, and breaking down the middle wall of partition, the enmities in his flesh:

Making void the law of commandments contained in decrees; that he might make the two in himself into one new man, making peace;

And might reconcile both to God in one body by the cross, killing the enmities in himself.

And coming, he preached peace to you that were afar off, and peace to them that were nigh.—*Eph.* ii. 14-17.

Because in him, it hath well pleased the Father, that all fulness should dwell;

And through him to reconcile all things unto himself, making peace through the blood of his cross, both as to the things that are on earth, and the things that are in heaven.

And you, whereas you were sometime alienated and enemies in mind in evil works:

Yet now he hath reconciled in the body of his flesh through death, to present you holy and unspotted, and blameless before him.—*Col.* i. 19-22.

IV. The Light of Faith

See also: Faith the gift of God—page 134.

To open their eyes, that they may be converted from darkness to light, and from the power of Satan to God.—*Acts* xxvi. 18.

For God, who commanded the light to shine out of darkness, hath shined in our hearts, to give the light of the knowledge of God, in the face of Christ Jesus.—*2 Cor.* iv. 6.

Again a new commandment I write unto you, which thing is true both in him and in you; because the darkness is passed, and the true light now shineth.—*1 John* ii. 8.

V. Justification

Being justified freely by his grace, through the redemption, that is in Christ Jesus.—*Rom.* iii. 24.

For as by the disobedience of one man, many were made sinners; so also by the obedience of one, many shall be made just.—*Rom.* v. 19.

And such some of you were; but you are washed, but you are sanctified; but you are justified in the name of our Lord Jesus Christ, and the Spirit of our God.—*1 Cor.* vi. 11.

In the which will, we are sanctified by the oblation of the body of Jesus Christ once. . . .

For by one oblation he hath perfected for ever them that are sanctified. —*Heb.* x. 10, 14.

VI. Adoption of Children of God

And now thus saith the Lord that created thee, O Jacob, and formed thee, O Israel: Fear not, for I have redeemed thee, and called thee by thy name: thou art mine.—*Is.* xliii. 1.

For you have not received the spirit of bondage again in fear; but you have received the spirit of adoption of sons, whereby we cry: Abba (Father).— *Rom.* viii. 15.

But when the fulness of the time was come, God sent his Son, made of a woman, made under the law:

That he might redeem them who were under the law: that we might receive the adoption of sons.—*Gal.* iv. 4, 5.

Who hath predestinated us unto the adoption of children through Jesus Christ unto himself: according to the purpose of his will.—*Eph.* i. 5.

Behold what manner of charity the Father hath bestowed upon us, that we should be called, and should be the sons of God.—*1 John* iii. 1.

VII. All Spiritual Gifts and Blessings

He that spared not even his own Son, but delivered him up for us all, how hath he not also, with him, given us all things?—*Rom.* viii. 32.

For by him we have access both in one Spirit to the Father.

Now therefore you are no more strangers and foreigners; but you are fellow citizens with the saints, and the domestics of God.—*Eph.* ii. 18, 19.

But to every one of us is given grace, according to the measure of the giving of Christ.

Wherefore he saith: Ascending on high, he led captivity captive; he gave gifts to men.—*Eph.* iv. 7, 8.

Grace be unto you, and peace from him that is, and that was, and that is to come, . . .

And from Jesus Christ, who is the faithful witness, the first begotten of the dead, and the prince of the kings ot the earth, who hath loved us, and washed us from our sins in his own blood,

And hath made us a kingdom, and priests to God and his Father, to him be glory and empire for ever and ever. Amen.—*Apoc.* i. 4-6.

VIII. Everlasting Life

And as Moses lifted up the serpent in the desert, so must the Son of man be lifted up:

That whosoever believeth in him, may not perish; but may have life everlasting.

For God so loved the world, as to give his only begotten Son; that whosoever believeth in him, may not perish, but may have life everlasting.—*John* iii. 14-16.

I am come that they may have life, and may have it more abundantly.—*John* x. 10.

For if by one man's offence, death reigned through one; much more they who receive abundance of grace, and of the gift, and of justice, shall reign in life through one, Jesus Christ. . . .

That as sin hath reigned to death; so also grace might reign by justice unto life everlasting, through Jesus Christ our Lord.—*Rom.* v. 17, 21.

For by a man came death, and by a man, the resurrection of the dead.

And as in Adam all die, so also in Christ, all shall be made alive.—1 *Cor.* xv. 21, 22.

For God hath not appointed us unto wrath, but unto the purchasing of salvation by our Lord Jesus Christ,

Who died for us; that, whether we watch or sleep, we may live together with him.—1 *Thess.* v. 9, 10.

But is now made manifest by the illumination of our Saviour Jesus Christ, who hath destroyed death, and hath brought to light life and incorruption by the gospel.—2 *Tim.* i. 10.

But when the goodness and kindness of God our Saviour appeared:

Not by the works of justice, which we have done, but according to his mercy, he saved us, by the laver of regeneration, and renovation of the Holy Ghost: . . .

That, being justified by his grace, we may be heirs, according to hope of life everlasting.—*Titus* iii. 4, 5, 7.

And whereas indeed he was the Son of God, he learned obedience by the things which he suffered:

And being consummated, he became, to all that obey him, the cause of eternal salvation.—*Heb.* v. 8, 9.

Who is on the right hand of God, swallowing down death, that we might be made heirs of life everlasting.—1 *Peter* iii. 22.

IX. The Happiness of Heaven

That they may receive forgiveness of sins, and a lot among the saints, by the faith that is in me.—*Acts* xxvi. 18.

Giving thanks to God the Father, who hath made us worthy to be partakers of the lot of the saints in light:

Who hath delivered us from the power of darkness, and hath translated us into the kingdom of the Son of his love.—*Col.* i. 12, 13.

But we ought to give thanks to God always for you, brethren, beloved of God, for that God hath chosen you first-fruits unto salvation, in sanctification of the spirit, and faith of the truth:

Whereunto also he hath called you by our gospel, unto the purchasing of the glory of our Lord Jesus Christ.—2 *Thess.* ii. 12, 13.

Blessed be the God and Father of our Lord Jesus Christ, who according to his great mercy, hath regenerated us unto a lively hope, by the resurrection of Jesus Christ from the dead,

Unto an inheritance incorruptible, and undefiled, and that cannot fade, reserved in heaven for you.—1 *Peter* i. 3, 4.

REFUGE, GOD OUR

And he (David) said: The Lord is my rock, and my strength, and my saviour.

God is my strong one, in him will I trust: my shield, and the horn of my salvation: he lifteth me up, and is my refuge: my saviour, thou wilt deliver me from iniquity.—2 *Kings* xxii. 2, 3.

I will love thee, O Lord, my strength: The Lord is my firmament, my refuge, and my deliverer.

My God is my helper, and in him will I put my trust.

My protector, and the horn of my salvation, and my support.—*Ps.* xvii. 2, 3.

Bow down thy ear to me: make haste to deliver me.

Be thou unto me a God, a protector, and a house of refuge, to save me.

For thou art my strength and my refuge; and for thy name's sake thou wilt lead me, and nourish me.—*Ps.* xxx. 3, 4.

Thou art my refuge from the trouble which hath encompassed me: my joy, deliver me from them that surround me.—*Ps.* xxxi. 7.

Our God is our refuge and strength: a helper in troubles, which have found us exceedingly.

Therefore we will not fear, when the earth shall be troubled; and the mountains shall be removed into the heart of the sea.—*Ps.* xlv. 2, 3.

But I will sing thy strength: and will extol thy mercy in the morning.

For thou art become my support, and my refuge, in the day of my trouble.

Unto thee, O my helper, will I sing, for thou art God my defence: my God, my mercy.—*Ps.* lviii. 17, 18.

Be thou unto me a God, a protector, and a place of strength: that thou mayst make me safe.

For thou art my firmament and my refuge.—*Ps.* lxx. 3.

Lord, thou hast been our refuge from generation to generation.—*Ps.* lxxxix. 1.

He shall say to the Lord: Thou art my protector, and my refuge: my God, in him will I trust. . . .

Because thou, O Lord, art my hope: thou hast made the most High thy refuge.—*Ps.* xc. 2, 9.

Deliver me from my enemies, O Lord, to thee have I fled.—*Ps.* cxlii. 9.

O Lord, thou art my God, I will exalt thee, and give glory to thy name: for thou hast done wonderful things, thy designs of old faithful, amen. . . .

Because thou hast been a strength to the poor, a strength to the needy in his distress: a refuge from the whirlwind, a shadow from the heat. For the blast of the mighty, is like a whirlwind beating against a wall.—*Is.* xxv. 1, 4.

O Lord, my might and my strength, and my refuge in the day of tribulation.—*Jer.* xvi. 19.

Heal me, O Lord, and I shall be healed: save me, and I shall be saved: for thou art my praise.—*Jer.* xvii. 14.

REGRET FOR LOST INNOCENCE

See: Innocence, lost—page 245.

REGRET FOR LOST OPPORTUNITIES

See: Opportunities, regret for lost—page 359.

REJECTS NO ONE THAT SEEKS HIM, GOD

All that the Father giveth to me, shall come to me; and him that cometh to me, I will not cast out.—*John* vi. 37.

And he that loveth me, shall be loved of my Father: and I will love him, and will manifest myself to him.—*John* xiv. 21.

And Peter opening his mouth, said: In very deed I perceive, that God is not a respecter of persons.

But in every nation, he that feareth him, and worketh justice, is acceptable to him.—*Acts* x. 34, 35.

For when the Gentiles, who have not the law, do by nature those things that are of the law; these having not the law, are a law to themselves:

Who show the works of the law written in their hearts, their conscience bearing witness to them, and their thoughts between themselves accusing, or also defending one another,

In the day when God shall judge the secrets of men by Jesus Christ, according to my gospel.—*Rom.* ii. 14-16.

REJECTION OF GOD'S GRACE

See: Grace, abuse of God's—page 178.

REJOICE IN THE LORD, EXHORTATION TO

See: Joy, spiritual—page 249.

REJOICING AT THE MISFORTUNE OF OTHERS

For what shall I do, when God shall rise to judge? and when he shall examine, what shall I answer him? . . .

If I have been glad at the downfall of him that hated me, and have rejoiced that evil had found him.—*Job* xxxi. 14, 29.

He that despiseth the poor, reproacheth his Maker; and he that rejoiceth at another man's ruin, shall not be unpunished.—*Prov.* xvii. 5.

When thy enemy shall fall, be not glad, and in his ruin let not thy heart rejoice:

Lest the Lord see, and it displease him, and he turn away his wrath from him.—*Prov.* xxiv. 17, 18.

Rejoice not at the death of thy enemy; knowing that we all die, and are not willing that others should rejoice at our death.—*Ecclus.* viii. 8.

They shall perish in a snare that are delighted with the fall of the just: and sorrow shall consume them before they die.—*Ecclus.* xxvii. 32.

RELAPSE INTO SIN

As a dog that returneth to his vomit, so is the fool that repeateth his folly.—*Prov.* xxvi. 11.

He that washeth himself after touching the dead, if he toucheth him again, what doth his washing avail?

So a man that fasteth for his sins, and doth the same again, what doth his humbling himself profit him? who will hear his prayer?—*Ecclus.* xxxiv. 30, 31.

How exceeding base art thou become, going the same ways over again!—*Jer.* ii. 36.

And when an unclean spirit is gone out of a man, he walketh through dry places seeking rest, and findeth none.

Then he saith: I will return into my house from whence I came out. And coming, he findeth it empty, swept, and garnished.

Then he goeth, and taketh with him seven other spirits more wicked than himself, and they enter in and dwell there: and the last state of that man is made worse than the first. So shall it be also to this wicked generation.—*Matt.* xii. 43-45.

Afterwards, Jesus findeth him in the temple, and saith to him: Behold thou art made whole: sin no more, lest some worse thing happen to thee.—*John* v. 14.

But now, after that you have known God, or rather are known by God: how turn you again to the weak and needy elements, which you desire to serve again?—*Gal.* iv. 9.

Stand fast, and be not held again under the yoke of bondage.—*Gal.* v. 1.

For it is impossible for those who who were once illuminated, have tasted also the heavenly gift, and were made partakers of the Holy Ghost,

Have moreover tasted the good word of God, and the powers of the world to come,

And are fallen away: to be renewed again to penance, crucifying again to themselves the Son of God, and making him a mockery.

For the earth that drinketh in the rain which cometh often upon it, and bringeth forth herbs meet for them by whom it is tilled, receiveth blessing from God.

But that which bringeth forth thorns and briars, is reprobate, and very near unto a curse, whose end is to be burnt. —*Heb.* vi. 4-8.

For if, flying from the pollutions of the world, through the knowledge of our Lord and Saviour Jesus Christ, they be again entangled in them and overcome: their latter state is become unto them worse than the former.

For it had been better for them not to have known the way of justice, than after they have known it, to turn back from that holy commandment which was delivered to them.

For, that of the true proverb has happened to them: The dog is returned to his vomit: and, The sow that was washed, to her wallowing in the mire. —*2 Peter* ii. 20-22.

RELIGIOUSNESS

Religiousness shall keep and justify the heart, it shall give joy and gladness. —*Ecclus.* i. 18.

O all ye religious, bless the Lord, the God of gods: praise him, and give him thanks, because his mercy endureth for ever and ever.—*Dan.* iii. 90.

But avoid foolish and old wives'

fables: and exercise thyself unto godliness.

For bodily exercise is profitable to little: but godliness is profitable to all things, having promise of the life that now is, and of that which is to come.—1 *Tim.* iv. 7, 8.

And if any man think himself to be religious, not bridling his tongue, but deceiving his own heart, this man's religion is vain.

Religion clean and undefiled before God and the Father, is this: to visit the fatherless and widows in their tribulation: and to keep one's self unspotted from this world.—*James* i. 26, 27.

REMEMBERS ALL THINGS, GOD

Although thou conceal these things in thy heart, yet I know that thou rememberest all things.—*Job* x. 13.

They have sinned deeply, as in the days of Gabaa: he will remember their iniquity, and will visit their sin.—*Osee* ix. 9.

The Lord hath sworn against the pride of Jacob: surely I will never forget all their works.—*Amos* viii. 7.

Therefore, my beloved brethren, be ye steadfast and unmovable; always abounding in the work of the Lord, knowing that your labor is not in vain in the Lord.—1 *Cor.* xv. 58.

For God is not unjust, that he should forget your work, and the love which you have shown in his name, you who have ministered, and do minister to the saints.—*Heb.* vi. 10.

REMEMBRANCE OF GOD

See also: Presence of God, we should keep ourselves in the—page 413.

And all the days of thy life, have God in thy mind: and take heed thou never consent to sin, nor transgress the commandments of the Lord our God.—*Tob.* iv. 6.

If I have remembered thee upon my bed, I will meditate on thee in the morning: because thou hast been my helper.—*Ps.* lxii. 7, 8.

I remembered God, and was delighted, and was exercised, and my spirit swooned away.—*Ps.* lxxvi. 4.

Remember thy Creator in the days of thy youth, before the time of affliction come, and the years draw nigh of which thou shalt say: They please me not.—*Eccles.* xii. 1.

And let the thought of God be in thy mind, and all thy discourse on the commandments of the Highest.—*Ecclus.* ix. 23.

Blessed is the man that shall continue in wisdom, and that shall meditate in his justice, and in his mind shall think of the all seeing eye of God.—*Ecclus.* xiv. 22.

And in the way of thy judgments, O Lord, we have patiently waited for thee: thy name, and thy remembrance are the desire of the soul.—*Is.* xxvi. 8.

REMORSE

For I know my iniquity, and my sin is always before me.—*Ps.* l. 5.

Thy wrath hath come upon me: and thy terrors have troubled me.

They have come round about me like water all the day: they have compassed me about together.—*Ps.* lxxxvii. 17, 18.

And thou mourn at the last, when thou shalt have spent thy flesh and thy body, and say:

Why have I hated instruction, and my heart consented not to reproof,

And have not heard the voice of them that taught me, and have not inclined my ear to masters?

I have almost been in all evil, in the midst of the church and of the congregation.—*Prov.* v. 11-14.

These, seeing it, shall be troubled with terrible fear, and shall be amazed at the suddenness of their unexpected salvation.

Saying within themselves, repenting, and groaning for anguish of spirit: These are they, whom we had some time in derision, and for a parable of reproach.

We fools esteemed their life madness, and their end without honor.

Behold how they are numbered among the children of God, and their lot is among the saints.

Therefore we have erred from the way of truth, and the light of justice hath not shined unto us, and the sun of understanding hath not risen upon us.

We wearied ourselves in the way of iniquity and destruction, and have walked through hard ways, but the way of the Lord we have not known.

What hath pride profited us? or what advantage hath the boasting of riches brought us?

All those things are passed away like a shadow, and like a post that runneth on.

. . . So we also being born, forthwith ceased to be: and have been able to show no mark of virtue: but are consumed in our wickedness.

Such things as these the sinners said in hell.—*Wis.* v. 2-9, 13, 14.

For whether absent or present, they were tormented alike.

For a double affliction came upon them, and a groaning for the remembrance of things past.—*Wis.* xi. 12, 13.

Blessed is the man that hath not slipped by a word out of his mouth, and is not pricked with the remorse of sin.

Happy is he that hath had no sadness of his mind, and who is not fallen from his hope.—*Ecclus.* xiv. 1, 2.

I will recount to thee all my years in the bitterness of my soul.—*Is.* xxxviii. 15.

Thy own wickedness shall reprove thee, and thy apostasy shall rebuke thee. Know thou, and see that it is an evil and a bitter thing for thee, to have left the Lord thy God, and that my fear is not with thee, saith the Lord, the God of hosts.—*Jer.* ii. 19.

And though they be hid in the top of Carmel, I will search and take them away from thence: and though they hide themselves from my eyes in the depth of the sea, there will I command the serpent, and he shall bite them.—*Amos* ix. 3.

Then Judas, who betrayed him, seeing that he was condemned, repenting himself, brought back the thirty pieces of silver to the chief priests and ancients,

Saying: I have sinned in betraying innocent blood. But they said: What is that to us? look thou to it.

And casting down the pieces of silver in the temple, he departed: and went, and hanged himself with a halter.—*Matt.* xxvii. 3-5.

And if thy hand scandalize thee, cut it off: it is better for thee to enter into life, maimed, than having two hands, to go into hell, into unquenchable fire:

Where their worm dieth not, and the fire is not extinguished.—*Mark* ix. 42, 43.

REPENTANCE, TRUE

See also: Sin, hatred of—page 526.

And: Sin, sorrow for—page 527.

And when thou shalt seek there the Lord thy God, thou shalt find him: yet so, if thou seek him with all thy heart, and all the affliction of thy soul.—*Deut.* iv. 29.

Then if they do penance in their heart, in the place of captivity, and being converted, make supplication to thee in their captivity, saying: We have sinned, we have done unjustly, we have committed wickedness:

And return to thee with all their heart, and all their soul, in the land of their enemies, to which they had been led captives. . . .

Then hear thou in heaven, in the firmament of thy throne, their prayers, and their supplications, and do judgment for them.—*3 Kings* viii. 47-49.

Be converted therefore, ye sinners, and do justice before God, believing that he will show his mercy to you.—*Tob.* xiii. 8.

For I am ready for scourges: and my sorrow is continually before me.

For I will declare my iniquity: and I will think for my sin.—*Ps.* xxxvii. 18, 19.

I will hear what the Lord God will speak in me: for he will speak peace unto his people:

And unto his saints: and unto them that are converted to the heart.—*Ps.* lxxxiv. 9.

Be not without fear about sin forgiven, and add not sin upon sin.—*Ecclus.* v. 5.

And I will give them a heart to know me, that I am the Lord: and they shall be my people, and I will be their God: because they shall return to me with their whole heart.—*Jer.* xxiv. 7.

Let us search our ways, and seek, and return to the Lord.

Let us lift up our hearts with our hands to the Lord in the heavens.—*Lam.* iii. 40, 41.

For as it was your mind to go astray from God; so when you return again you shall seek him ten times as much.—*Bar.* iv. 28.

Bring forth therefore fruits worthy of penance; and do not begin to say, We have Abraham for our father. For I say unto you, that God is able of these stones to raise up children to Abraham.—*Luke* iii. 8.

REPENTANCE, FALSE

The Lord is only for them that wait upon him in the way of truth and justice.

The most High approveth not the gifts of the wicked: neither hath he respect to the oblations of the unjust, nor will he be pacified for sins by the multitude of their sacrifices.—*Ecclus.* xxxiv. 22, 23.

He that washeth himself after touching the dead, if he toucheth him again, what doth his washing avail?

So a man that fasteth for his sins, and doth the same again, what doth his humbling himself profit him? who will hear his prayer?—*Ecclus.* xxxiv. 30, 31.

Cry, cease not, lift up thy voice like a trumpet, and show my people their wicked doings, and the house of Jacob their sins.

For they seek me from day to day, and desire to know my ways, as a nation that hath done justice, and hath not forsaken the judgment of their God: they ask of me the judgments of justice: they are willing to approach to God.

Why have we fasted, and thou hast not regarded: have we humbled our souls, and thou hast not taken notice?

Behold in the day of your fast your own will is found, and you exact of all your debtors.

Behold you fast for debates and strife, and strike with the fist wickedly. Do not fast as you have done until this day, to make your cry to be heard on high.

Is this such a fast as I have chosen: for a man to afflict his soul for a day? is this it, to wind his head about like a circle, and to spread sackcloth and ashes? wilt thou call this a fast, and a day acceptable to the Lord?—*Is.* lviii. 1-5.

REPENTANCE, NECESSITY OF

Except you will be converted, he will brandish his sword: he hath bent his bow, and made it ready.

And in it he hath prepared the instruments of death, he hath made ready his arrows for them that burn.—*Ps.* vii. 13, 14.

If we do not penance, we shall fall into the hands of the Lord, and not into the hands of men.—*Ecclus.* ii. 22.

Bring forth therefore fruit worthy of penance.

And think not to say within yourselves, We have Abraham for our father. For I tell you that God is able of these stones to raise up children to Abraham.

For now the axe is laid to the root of the trees. Every tree therefore that doth not yield good fruit, shall be cut down, and cast into the fire.—*Matt.* iii. 8-10.

But unless you shall do penance, you shall all likewise perish.—*Luke* xiii. 3.

Now when they had heard these things, they had compunction in their heart, and said to Peter, and to the rest of the apostles: What shall we do, men and brethren?

But Peter said to them: Do penance, and be baptized every one of you in the name of Jesus Christ, for the remission of your sins: and you shall receive the gift of the Holy Ghost.—*Acts* ii. 37, 38.

Be penitent, therefore, and be converted, that your sins may be blotted out.—*Acts* iii. 19.

REPENTANCE, GOD CALLS US TO

O how good and sweet is thy spirit, O Lord, in all things!

And therefore thou chastisest them that err, by little and little: and admonishest them, and speakest to them, concerning the things wherein they offend: that leaving their wickedness, they may believe in thee, O Lord.—*Wis.* xii. 1, 2.

And the Lord, the God of hosts, in that day shall call to weeping, and to mourning, to baldness, and to girding with sackcloth.—*Is.* xxii. 12.

Is it my will that a sinner should die, saith the Lord God, and not that he should be converted from his ways, and live? . . .

Be converted, and do penance for all your iniquities: and iniquity shall not be your ruin.—*Ezech.* xviii. 23, 30.

And God indeed having winked at the times of this ignorance, now declareth unto men, that all should everywhere do penance.

Because he hath appointed a day, wherein he will judge the world in equity, by the man whom he hath appointed; giving faith to all, by raising him up from the dead.—*Acts* xvii. 30, 31.

REPENTANCE, NOW IS THE TIME FOR

But thou hast taught thy. people by such works, that they must be just and humane, and hast made thy children to be of a good hope: because in judging thou givest place for repentance for sins.

For if thou didst punish the enemies of thy servants, and that deserved to die, with so great deliberation, giving them time and place whereby they might be changed from their wickedness:

With what circumspection hast thou judged thy own children, to whose parents thou hast sworn, and made covenants of good promises?—*Wis.* xii. 19-21.

Seek ye the Lord, while he may be found: call upon him, while he is near.—*Is.* lv. 6.

Jesus therefore said to them: yet a little while I am with you: and then I go to him that sent me.

You shall seek me, and shall not find me: and where I am, thither you cannot come.—*John* vii. 33, 34.

Let us go therefore with confidence to the throne of grace: that we may obtain mercy, and find grace in seasonable aid.—*Heb.* iv. 16.

REPENTANCE, EFFICACY OF

If heaven shall be shut up, and there shall be no rain, because of their sins, and they praying in this place, shall do penance to thy name, and shall be converted from their sins, by occasion of their afflictions:

Then hear thou them in heaven, and forgive the sins of thy servants, and of thy people Israel: and show them the good way wherein they should walk, and give rain upon thy land, which thou hast given to thy people in possession.—3 *Kings* viii. 35, 36.

Whatsoever curse or imprecation shall happen to any man of thy people Israel: when a man shall know the wound of his own heart, and shall spread forth his hands in this house,

Then hear thou in heaven, in the place of thy dwelling, and forgive, and do so as to give to every one according to his ways, as thou shalt see his heart (for thou only knowest the heart of all the children of men).—3 *Kings* viii. 38, 39.

A sacrifice to God is an afflicted spirit: a contrite and humbled heart, O God, thou wilt not despise.—*Ps.* l. 19.

But thou hast mercy upon all, because thou canst do all things, and overlookest the sins of men for the sake of repentance.—*Wis.* xi. 24.

But to the penitent he hath given the way of justice, and he hath strengthened them that were fainting in patience, and hath appointed to them the lot of truth.—*Ecclus.* xvii. 20.

For thus saith the High and the Eminent that inhabiteth eternity: and his name is Holy, who dwelleth in the high and holy place, and with a contrite and humble spirit, to revive the spirit of the humble, and to revive the heart of the contrite.—*Is.* lvii. 15.

Is there no balm in Galaad? or is there no physician there? Why then is not the wound of the daughter of my people closed?—*Jer.* viii. 22.

If that nation against which I have spoken, shall repent of their evil, I also will repent of the evil that I have thought to do to them.—*Jer.* xviii. 8.

You shall seek me, and shall find me: when you shall seek me with all your heart.—*Jer.* xxix. 13.

But if the wicked do penance for all his sins which he hath committed, and keep all my commandments, and do judgment, and justice, living he shall live, and shall not die.

I will not remember all his iniquities that he hath done: in his justice which he hath wrought, he shall live. . . .

Because he considereth and turneth away himself from all his iniquities which he hath wrought, he shall surely live, and not die. . . .

Be converted, and do penance for all your iniquities: and iniquity shall not be your ruin.

Cast away from you all your transgressions, by which you have transgressed, and make to yourselves a new heart, and a new spirit: and why will you die, O house of Israel?

For I desire not the death of him that dieth, saith the Lord God, return ye and live.—*Ezech.* xviii. 21, 22, 28, 30-32.

And if I shall say to the wicked: Thou shalt surely die: and he do penance for his sin, and do judgment and justice,

And if that wicked man restore the pledge, and render what he had robbed, and walk in the commandments of life, and do no unjust thing: he shall surely live, and shall not die.

None of his sins, which he hath committed, shall be imputed to him: he hath done judgment and justice, he shall surely live.—*Ezech.* xxxiii. 14-16.

And one of those robbers who were hanged, blasphemed him, saying: If thou be Christ, save thyself and us.

But the other answering, rebuked him, saying: Neither dost thou fear God, seeing thou art under the same condemnation?

And we indeed justly, for we receive the due reward of our deeds; but this man hath done no evil.

And he said to Jesus: Lord, remember me when thou shalt come into thy kingdom.

And Jesus said to him: Amen I say to thee, this day thou shalt be with me in paradise.—*Luke* xxiii. 39-43.

Be penitent, therefore, and be converted, that your sins may be blotted out.—*Acts* iii. 19.

For the sorrow that is according to God, worketh penance, steadfast unto salvation.—2 *Cor.* vii. 10.

Blessed are they that wash their robes in the blood of the Lamb: that they may have a right to the tree of life, and may enter in by the gates into the city.—*Apoc.* xxii. 14.

REPUTATION, THE VALUE OF A GOOD

See: Name, value of a good—page 339.

RESIGNATION TO GOD'S WILL

See: Will of God, conformity to the —page 604.

RESOLUTIONS, GOOD

As long as breath remaineth in me, and the spirit of God in my nostrils,

My lips shall not speak iniquity, neither shall my tongue contrive lying.

. . . Till I die, I will not depart from my innocence.—*Job* xxvii. 3-5.

And I said, Now have I begun: this is the change of the right hand of the most High.—*Ps.* lxxvi. 11.

I will keep thy justifications: O! do not thou utterly forsake me.—*Ps.* cxvi̇. 8.

I have sworn and am determined to keep the judgments of thy justice.—*Ps.* cxviii. 106.

RESPECT FOR PRIESTS

See: Priests—page 430.

RESPECT FOR HOLY PLACES

See: House of God, reverence and respect for the—page 215.

RESPECT FOR HOLY THINGS

And when Aaron and his sons have wrapped up the sanctuary and the vessels thereof at the removing of the camp, then shall the sons of Caath enter in to carry the things wrapped up: and they shall not touch the vessels of the sanctuary, lest they die.—*Num.* iv. 15.

Now therefore, if thou have any thing at hand, though it were but five loaves, give me, or whatsoever thou canst find.

And the priest answered David, saying: I have no common bread at hand, but only holy bread, if the young men be clean, especially from women. . . .

The priest therefore gave him hallowed bread: for there was no bread there, but only the loaves of proposition, which had been taken away from before the face of the Lord, that hot loaves might be set up.—1 *Kings* xxi. 3, 4, 6.

And when they came to the floor of Nachon, Oza put forth his hand to the ark of God, and took hold of it: because the oxen kicked and made it lean aside.

And the indignation of the Lord was enkindled against Oza, and he struck him for his rashness: and he died there before the ark of God. . . .

And David was afraid of the Lord that day, saying: How shall the ark of the Lord come to me?

And he would not have the ark of the Lord brought in to himself, into the city of David: but he caused it to be carried into the house of Obededom the Gethite. —2 *Kings* vi. 6, 7, 9, 10.

Give not that which is holy to dogs; neither cast ye your pearls before swine, lest perhaps they trample them under their feet, and turning upon you, they tear you.—*Matt.* vii. 6.

REST FROM THE TROUBLES AND LABOR OF THIS LIFE

And the Lord said: My face shall go before thee, and I will give thee rest.— *Ex.* xxxiii. 14.

There the wicked cease from tumult, and there the wearied in strength are at rest.—*Job* iii. 17.

The life of man upon earth is a warfare, and his days are like the days of a hireling.

As a servant longeth for the shade, as the hireling looketh for the end of his work;

So I also have had empty months, and have numbered to myself wearisome nights.—*Job* vii. 1-3.

All that I have shall go down into the deepest pit: thinkest thou that there at least I shall have rest?—*Job* xvii 16.

And I said: Who will give me wings like a dove, and I will fly, and be at rest?—*Ps.* liv. 7.

Blessed is the man whom thou shalt instruct, O Lord: and shalt teach him out of thy law.

That thou mayst give him rest from the evil days: till a pit be dug for the wicked.—*Ps.* xciii. 12, 13.

Turn, O my soul, into thy rest: for the Lord hath been bountiful to thee. —*Ps.* cxiv. 7.

Seeing it is a just thing with God to repay tribulation to them that trouble you:

And to you who are troubled, rest with us when the Lord Jesus shall be revealed from heaven, with the angels of his power.—2 *Thess.* i. 6, 7.

REST FROM THE LABOR AND TROUBLES OF THIS LIFE
THE REWARD OF SERVING GOD

If thou wilt put away from thee the iniquity that is in thy hand, and let not injustice remain in thy tabernacle. . . .

And thou shalt have confidence, hope being set before thee, and being buried, thou shalt sleep secure.

Thou shalt rest, and there shall be none to make thee afraid: and many shall entreat thy face.—*Job* xi. 14, 18, 19.

Forty years long was I offended with that generation, and I said: These always err in heart.

And these men have not known my ways: so I swore in my wrath, that they shall not enter into my rest.—*Ps.* xciv. 10, 11.

They that trust in him, shall understand the truth: and they that are faithful in love, shall rest in him: for grace and peace is to his elect.—*Wis.* iii. 9.

When thou shalt pour out thy soul

to the hungry, and shalt satisfy the afflicted soul, then shall thy light rise up in darkness, and thy darkness shall be as the noon-day.

And the Lord will give thee rest continually, and will fill thy soul with brightness, and deliver thy bones, and thou shalt be like a watered garden, and like a fountain of water, whose waters shall not fail.—*Is.* lviii. 10, 11.

Take up my yoke upon you, and learn of me, because I am meek, and humble of heart: and you shall find rest to your souls.—*Matt.* xi. 29.

For we, who have believed, shall enter into rest; as he said: As I have sworn in my wrath; If they shall enter into my rest; and this indeed when the works from the foundation of the world were finished. . . .

There remaineth therefore a day of rest for the people of God.

For he that is entered into his rest, the same also hath rested from his works, as God did from his.

Let us hasten therefore to enter into that rest; lest any man fall into the same example of unbelief.—*Heb.* iv. 3, 9-11.

And I heard a voice from heaven, saying to me: Write: Blessed are the dead who die in the Lord. From henceforth now, saith the Spirit, that they may rest from their labors; for their works follow them.—*Apoc.* xiv. 13.

RESTITUTION

If any man steal an ox or a sheep, and kill or sell it: he shall restore five oxen for one ox, and four sheep for one sheep. . . .

If that which he stole, be found with him, alive, either ox, or ass, or sheep: he shall restore double.—*Ex.* xxii. 1, 4.

If a man seduce a virgin not yet espoused, and lie with her: he shall endow her, and have her to wife.

If the maid's father will not give her to him, he shall give money, according to the dowry, which virgins are wont to receive.—*Ex.* xxii. 16, 17.

The Lord spoke to Moses, saying:

Whosoever shall sin, and despising the Lord, shall deny to his neighbor the thing delivered to his keeping, which was committed to his trust; or shall by force extort any thing, or commit oppression;

Or shall find a thing lost, and denying it, shall also swear falsely, or shall do any other of the many things, wherein men are wont to sin:

Being convicted of the offence, he shall restore

All that he would have gotten by fraud, in the principal, and the fifth part besides to the owner, whom he wronged.—*Lev.* vi. 1-5.

Say to the children of Israel: When a man or woman shall have committed any of all the sins that men are wont to commit, and by negligence shall have transgressed the commandment of the Lord, and offended,

They shall confess their sin, and restore the principal itself, and the fifth part over and above, to him against whom they have sinned.

But if there be no one to receive it, they shall give it to the Lord, and it shall be the priest's, besides the ram that is offered for expiation, to be an atoning sacrifice.—*Num.* v. 6-8.

And if I shall say to the wicked: Thou shalt surely die: and he do penance for his sin, and do judgment and justice,

And if that wicked man restore the pledge, and render what he had robbed, and walk in the commandments of life, and do no unjust thing, he shall surely live, and shall not die.—*Ezech.* xxxiii. 14, 15.

But Zacheus standing, said to the Lord: Behold, Lord, the half of my goods I give to the poor; and if I have wronged any man of any thing, I restore him fourfold.

Jesus said to him: This day is salvation come to this house, because he also is a son of Abraham.—*Luke* xix. 8, 9.

RESURRECTION OF THE DEAD, THE

See: Part II—page 728.

RETURNING TO GOD

If thou wilt return to the Almighty, thou shalt be built up, and shalt put away iniquity far from thy tabernacle. . . .

Then shalt thou abound in delights in the Almighty, and shalt lift up thy face to God.

Thou shalt pray to him, and he will hear thee, and thou shalt pay vows.

Thou shalt decree a thing, and it shall come to thee, and light shall shine in thy ways.—*Job* xxii. 23, 26-28.

Return, you rebellious children, and I will heal your rebellions. Behold we come to thee: for thou art the Lord our God.—*Jer.* iii. 22.

But even until this day, when Moses is read, the veil is upon their heart.

But when they shall be converted to the Lord, the veil shall be taken away. —2 *Cor.* iii. 15, 16.

RETURN TO GOD, EXHORTATION TO

Return to the Lord, and turn away from thy injustice, and greatly hate abomination.—*Ecclus.* xvii. 23.

Return as you had deeply revolted, O children of Israel.—*Is.* xxxi. 6.

Remember this, and be ashamed: return, ye transgressors, to the heart.—*Is.* xlvi. 8.

It is commonly said: If a man put away his wife, and she go from him, and marry another man, shall he return to her any more? shall not that woman be polluted, and defiled? but thou hast prostituted thyself to many lovers: nevertheless return to me, saith the Lord, and I will receive thee.—*Jer.* iii. 1.

Go, and proclaim these words towards the north, and thou shalt say: Return, O rebellious Israel, saith the Lord, and I will not turn away my face from you: for I am holy, saith the Lord, and I will not be angry for ever.—*Jer.* iii. 12.

Let us search our ways, and seek, and return to the Lord.—*Lam.* iii. 40.

For from the days of your fathers, you have departed from my ordinances, and have not kept them: Return to me, and I will return to you, saith the Lord of hosts.—*Malach.* iii. 7.

REVENGE

Revenge is mine, and I will repay them in due time.—*Deut.* xxxii. 35.

If I have been glad at the downfall of him that hated me, and have rejoiced that evil had found him.

For I have not given my mouth to sin, by wishing a curse to his soul. . . .

Let thistles grow up to me instead of wheat, and thorns instead of barley. —*Job* xxxi. 29, 30, 40.

O Lord my God, if I have done this thing, if there be iniquity in my hands:

If I have rendered to them that repaid me evils, let me deservedly fall empty before my enemies.

Let the enemy pursue my soul, and take it, and tread down my life on the earth, and bring down my glory to the dust.—*Ps.* vii. 4-6.

The Lord is the God to whom revenge belongeth: the God of revenge hath acted freely.—*Ps.* xciii. 1.

He that seeketh to revenge himself, shall find vengeance from the Lord, and he will surely keep his sins in remembrance.

Forgive thy neighbor, if he hath hurt thee: and then shall thy sins be forgiven to thee when thou prayest.

Man to man reserveth anger, and doth he seek remedy of God?

He hath no mercy on a man like himself, and doth he entreat for his own sins?

He that is but flesh, nourisheth anger, and doth he ask forgiveness of God? who shall obtain pardon for his sins?—*Ecclus.* xxviii. 1-5.

REVENGE FORBIDDEN BY GOD

See also: Forgiving injuries—page 158.

Seek not revenge, nor be mindful of the injury of thy citizens.—*Lev.* xix. 18.

You have heard that it hath been said, An eye for an eye, and a tooth for a tooth.

But I say to you, not to resist evil: but if one strike thee on thy right cheek, turn to him also the other.—*Matt.* v. 38, 39.

REVENGE, EXHORTATION AGAINST

Say not: I will return evil: wait for the Lord, and he will deliver thee.—*Prov.* xx. 22.

Say not: I will do to him as he hath

done to me: I will render to every one according to his work.—*Prov.* xxiv. 29.

Rejoice not at the death of thy enemy; knowing that we all die, and are not willing that others should rejoice at our death.—*Ecclus.* viii. 8.

Remember not any injury done thee by thy neighbor, and do thou nothing by deeds of injury.—*Ecclus.* x. 6.

Remember thy last things, and let enmity cease.—*Ecclus.* xxviii. 6.

Bless them that persecute you: bless, and curse not. . . .

To no man rendering evil for evil. . . .

Revenge not yourselves, my dearly beloved; but give place unto wrath, for it is written: Revenge is mine, I will repay, saith the Lord.

But if thy enemy be hungry, give him to eat; if he thirst, give him to drink. For, doing this, thou shalt heap coals of fire upon his head.

Be not overcome by evil, but overcome evil by good.—*Rom.* xii. 14, 17, 19-21.

See that none render evil for evil to any man; but ever follow that which is good towards each other, and towards all men.—1 *Thess.* v. 15.

Not rendering evil for evil, nor railing for railing, but contrariwise, blessing: for unto this are you called, that you may inherit a blessing.—1 *Peter* iii. 9.

REWARD, GOD OUR

Now when these things were done, the word of the Lord came to Abram by a vision, saying: Fear not, Abram, I am thy protector, and thy reward exceeding great.—*Gen.* xv. 1.

The Lord is the portion of my inheritance and of my cup: it is thou that wilt restore my inheritance to me. The lines are fallen unto me in goodly places: for my inheritance is goodly to me.—*Ps.* xv. 5, 6.

O Lord, my portion, I have said, I would keep thy law.—*Ps.* cxviii. 57.

REWARD GOD GIVES TO THOSE WHO SERVE HIM, THE

I. Certainty of the Reward, The

Do you therefore take courage, and let not your hands be weakened: for there shall be a reward for your work.— 2 *Paral.* xv. 7.

For we are the children of saints, and look for that life which God will give to those that never change their faith from him.—*Tob.* ii. 18.

Delight in the Lord, and he will give thee the requests of thy heart.—*Ps.* xxxvi. 4.

He will not deprive of good things them that walk in innocence: O Lord of hosts, blessed is the man that trusteth in thee.—*Ps.* lxxxiii. 13.

I have inclined my heart to do thy justifications for ever, for the reward.— *Ps.* cxviii. 112.

The wicked man maketh an unsteady work; but to him that soweth justice, there is a faithful reward.—*Prov.* xi. 18.

He that walketh uprightly, shall be saved: he that is perverse in his ways, shall fall at once.—*Prov.* xxviii. 18.

If thou followest justice, thou shalt obtain her: and shalt put her on as a long robe of honor, and thou shalt dwell with her: and she shall protect thee for ever, and in the day of acknowledgment, thou shalt find a strong foundation.— *Ecclus.* xxvii. 9.

And he that reapeth, receiveth wages, and gathereth fruit unto life everlasting: that both he that soweth, and he that reapeth, may rejoice together.— *John* iv. 36.

If any man minister to me, let him follow me; and where I am, there also shall my minister be. If any man minister to me, him will my Father honor. —*John* xii. 26.

In my Father's house there are many mansions. If not, I would have told you: because I go to prepare a place for you.

And if I shall go, and prepare a place for you, I will come again, and will take you to myself; that where I am, you also may be.—*John* xiv. 2, 3.

Whatsoever you do, do it from the heart, as to the Lord, and not to men: Knowing that you shall receive of the Lord the reward of inheritance. Serve ye the Lord Christ.—*Col.* iii. 23, 24.

I have fought a good fight, I have finished my course, I have kept the faith. As to the rest, there is laid up for me a crown of justice, which the Lord the just judge will render to me in that day: and not only to me, but to them also that love his coming.—*2 Tim.* iv. 7, 8.

For God is not unjust, that he should forget your work, and the love which you have shown in his name, you who have ministered, and do minister to the saints.—*Heb.* vi. 10.

Blessed is the man that endureth temptation; for when he hath been proved, he shall receive the crown of life, which God hath promised to them that love him.—*James* i. 12.

II. Greatness of the Reward

And Amasias said to the man of God: What will then become of the hundred talents which I have given to the soldiers of Israel? and the man of God answered him: The Lord is rich enough to be able to give thee much more than this.—*2 Paral.* xxv. 9.

Fear not, my son: we lead indeed a poor life, but we shall have many good things, if we fear God, and depart from all sin, and do that which is good.—*Tob.* iv. 23.

O how great is the multitude of thy sweetness, O Lord, which thou hast hidden for them that fear thee!

Which thou hast wrought for them that hope in thee, in the sight of the sons of men.—*Ps.* xxx. 20.

Afflicted in few things, in many they shall be well rewarded: because God hath tried them, and found them worthy of himself.—*Wis.* iii. 5.

Let nothing hinder thee from praying always, and be not afraid to be justified even to death: for the reward of God continueth for ever.—*Ecclus.* xviii. 22.

From the beginning of the world they have not heard, nor perceived with the ears: the eye hath not seen, O God, besides thee, what things thou hast prepared for them that wait for thee.—*Is.* lxiv. 4.

Blessed are ye when they shall revile you, and persecute you, and speak all that is evil against you, untruly, for my sake:

Be glad and rejoice, for your reward is very great in heaven.—*Matt.* v. 11, 12.

But he said to him: Son, thou art al-ways with me, and all I have is thine. —*Luke* xv. 31.

For I reckon that the sufferings of this time, are not worthy to be compared with the glory to come, that shall be revealed in us.—*Rom.* viii. 18.

But, as it is written: That eye hath not seen, nor ear heard, neither hath it entered into the heart of man, what things God hath prepared for them that love him.—1 *Cor.* ii. 9.

Know you not that they that run in the race, all run indeed, but one receiveth the prize? So run that you may obtain.

And every one that striveth for the mastery, refraineth himself from all things: and they indeed that they may receive a corruptible crown; but we, an incorruptible one.—1 *Cor.* ix. 24, 25.

Blessed be the God and Father of our Lord Jesus Christ, who, according to his great mercy, hath regenerated us unto a lively hope, by the resurrection of Jesus Christ from the dead,

Unto an inheritance incorruptible, and undefiled, and that cannot fade, reserved in heaven for you.—1 *Peter* i. 3, 4.

And when the prince of pastors shall appear, you shall receive a never fading crown of glory.—1 *Peter* v. 4.

III. Reward Even in This Life

Blessed is the man that hath not walked in the counsel of the ungodly, nor stood in the way of sinners, nor sat in the chair of pestilence.

But his will is in the law of the Lord, and on his law he shall meditate day and night.

And he shall be like a tree which is planted near the running waters, which shall bring forth its fruit, in due season.

And his leaf shall not fall off: and all whatsoever he shall do, shall prosper. —*Ps.* i. 1-3.

The just shall flourish like the palm-tree: he shall grow up like the cedar of Libanus.

. . . They shall still increase in a fruitful old age: and shall be well treated, that they may show,

That the Lord our God is righteous, and there is no iniquity in him.—*Ps.* xci. 13, 15, 16.

Blessed are all they that fear the Lord: that walk in his ways.

For thou shalt eat the labors of thy hands: blessed art thou, and it shall be well with thee.

Thy wife as a fruitful vine, on the sides of thy house.

Thy children as olive plants, round about thy table.

Behold, thus shall the man be blessed that feareth the Lord.—*Ps.* cxxvii. 1-4.

That which the wicked feareth, shall come upon him: to the just, their desire shall be given.—*Prov.* x. 24.

The justice of the upright, shall make his way prosperous: and the wicked man shall fall by his own wickedness.

The justice of the righteous, shall deliver them: and the unjust shall be caught in their own snares.—*Prov.* xi. 5, 6.

God hath given to a man that is good in his sight, wisdom, and knowledge, and joy: but to the sinner he hath given vexation, and superfluous care, to heap up, and to gather together, and to give it to him that hath pleased God. —*Eccles.* ii. 26.

But the Lord hath made all things, and to the godly he hath given wisdom. —*Ecclus.* xliii. 37.

If you be willing, and will hearken to me, you shall eat the good things of the land.—*Is.* i. 19.

IV. The Blessing of God

For thou wilt bless the just.

O Lord, thou hast crowned us, as with a shield of thy good will.— *Ps.* v. 13.

The Lord hath been mindful of us, and hath blessed us.

He hath blessed the house of Israel: he hath blessed the house of Aaron.

He hath blessed all that fear the Lord, both little and great.—*Ps.* cxiii. (*Heb.* cxv.) 12, 13.

Want is from the Lord in the house of the wicked: but the habitations of the just shall be blessed.—*Prov.* iii. 33.

The blessing of the Lord maketh men rich: neither shall affliction be joined to them.—*Prov.* x. 22.

The blessing of God maketh haste to reward the just, and in a swift hour his blessing beareth fruit.—*Ecclus.* xi. 24.

V. They Become His Chosen People

If therefore you will hear my voice, and keep my covenant, you shall be my peculiar possession above all people: for all the earth is mine.—*Ex.* xix. 5.

Seek ye good, and not evil, that you may live: and the Lord the God of hosts will be with you, as you have said.— *Amos* v. 14.

Then they that feared the Lord spoke every one with his neighbor: and the Lord gave ear, and heard it: and a book of remembrance was written before him for them that fear the Lord, and think on his name.

And they shall be my special possession, saith the Lord of hosts, in the day that I do judgment: and I will spare them, as a man spareth his son that serveth him.

And you shall return, and shall see the difference between the just and the wicked: and between him that serveth God, and him that serveth him not.— *Malach.* iii. 16-18.

Blessed are the peacemakers: for they shall be called the children of God.—*Matt.* v. 9.

And one said unto him: Behold thy mother and thy brethren stand without, seeking thee.

But he answering him that told him, said: Who is my mother, and who are my brethren?

And stretching forth his hand towards his disciples, he said: Behold my mother, and my brethren.

For whosoever shall do the will of my Father, that is in heaven, he is my brother, and sister, and mother.—*Matt.* xii. 47-50.

Then Jesus said to those Jews who believed him: If you continue in my word, you shall be my disciples indeed.

And you shall know the truth, and the truth shall make you free.—*John* viii. 31, 32.

The things which you have both learned and received, and heard, and seen in me, these do ye, and the God of peace shall be with you.—*Philipp.* iv. 9.

And I heard a great voice from the throne, saying: Behold the tabernacle of God with men, and he will dwell with them. And they shall be his people; and God himself with them shall be their God. . . .

He that shall overcome, shall possess these things, and I will be his God; and he shall be my son.—*Apoc.* xxi. 3, 7.

VI. Peace and Security and Refreshment

The just shall be in everlasting remembrance: he shall not fear the evil hearing.

His heart is ready to hope in the Lord: his heart is strengthened, he shall not be moved, until he look over his enemies.—*Ps.* cxi. 7, 8.

But he that shall hear me, shall rest without terror, and shall enjoy abundance, without fear of evils.—*Prov.* i. 33.

My son, forget not my law, and let thy heart keep my commandments.

For they shall add to thee length of days, and years of life and peace.—*Prov.* iii. 1, 2.

And my people shall sit in the beauty of peace, and in the tabernacles of confidence, and in wealthy rest.—*Is.* xxxii. 18.

O that thou hadst hearkened to my commandments: thy peace had been as a river, and thy justice as the waves of the sea.—*Is.* xlviii. 18.

Thus saith the Lord: Stand ye on the ways, and see, and ask for the old paths, which is the good way, and walk ye in it: and you shall find refreshment for your souls.—*Jer.* vi. 16.

Come to me, all you that labor, and are burdened, and I will refresh you. Take up my yoke upon you, and learn of me, because I am meek, and humble of heart: and you shall find rest to your souls.—*Matt.* xi. 28, 29.

But glory, and honor, and peace to every one that worketh good, to the Jew first, and also to the Greek.—*Rom.* ii. 10.

VII. The Grace of God in This Life

They that trust in him shall understand the truth: and they that are faithful in love shall rest in him: for grace and peace is to his elect.—*Wis.* iii. 9.

For happy is the barren: and the undefiled, that hath not known bed in sin: she shall have fruit in the visitation of holy souls.

And the eunuch, that hath not wrought iniquity with his hands, nor thought wicked things against God: for the precious gift of faith shall be given to him, and a most acceptable lot in the temple of God.—*Wis.* iii. 13, 14.

The gift of God abideth with the just, and his advancement shall have success for ever.—*Ecclus.* xi. 17.

Because thou hast kept the word of my patience, I will also keep thee from the hour of temptation, which shall come upon the whole world to try them that dwell upon the earth.—*Apoc.* iii. 10.

VIII. Happiness of the Just

See: Just, happiness of the—page 262.

IX. Eternal Life

He asked life of thee: and thou hast given him length of days for ever and ever.—*Ps.* xx. 5.

Who is the man that desireth life: who loveth to see good days?

Keep thy tongue from evil, and thy lips from speaking guile.

Turn away from evil and do good: seek after peace, and pursue it.—*Ps.* xxxiii. 13-15.

Decline from evil and do good, and dwell for ever and ever.

For the Lord loveth judgment, and will not forsake his saints: they shall be preserved for ever.—*Ps.* xxxvi. 27, 28.

Bless the Lord, O my soul, and never forget all he hath done for thee. . . .

Who satisfieth thy desire with good things: thy youth shall be renewed like the eagle's.—*Ps.* cii. 2, 5.

I shall not die, but live: and shall declare the works of the Lord.—*Ps.* cxvii. 17.

But the souls of the just are in the hand of God, and the torment of death shall not touch them.

In the sight of the unwise they seemed to die: and their departure was taken for misery:

And their going away from us, for utter destruction: but they are in peace.

And though in the sight of men they suffered torments, their hope is full of immortality.—*Wis.* iii. 1-4.

But the just shall live for evermore: and their reward is with the Lord, and the care of them with the most High.—*Wis.* v. 16.

It is great glory to follow the Lord: for length of days shall be received from him.—*Ecclus.* xxiii. 38.

And every one that hath left house, or brethren, or sisters, or father, or mother, or wife, or children, or lands for my name's sake, shall receive an hundred-fold, and shall possess life everlasting.—*Matt.* xix. 29.

And these shall go into everlasting punishment: but the just, into life everlasting.—*Matt.* xxv. 46.

Amen, amen I say to you: If any man keep my word, he shall not see death for ever.—*John* viii. 51.

My sheep hear my voice: and I know them, and they follow me.

And I give them life everlasting; and they shall not perish for ever, and no man shall pluck them out of my hand.—*John* x. 27, 28.

He that loveth his life shall lose it; and he that hateth his life in this world, keepeth it unto life eternal.—*John* xii. 25.

Who will render to every man according to his works.

To them indeed, who, according to patience in good work, seek glory and honor and incorruption, eternal life.—*Rom.* ii. 6, 7.

For if we have been planted together in the likeness of his death, we shall be also in the likeness of his resurrection. . . .

Now if we be dead with Christ, we believe that we shall live also together with Christ.—*Rom.* vi. 5, 8.

And this is the promise which he hath promised us, life everlasting.—1 *John* ii. 25.

He, that hath an ear, let him hear what the Spirit saith to the churches: To him, that overcometh, I will give to eat of the tree of life, which is in the paradise of my God.—*Apoc.* ii. 7.

He, that hath an ear, let him hear what the Spirit saith to the churches: He that shall overcome, shall not be hurt by the second death.—*Apoc.* ii. 11.

Blessed and holy is he that hath part in the first resurrection. In these the second death hath no power; but they shall be priests of God and of Christ, and shall reign with him a thousand years.—*Apoc.* xx. 6.

X. The Happiness and Glory of Heaven

Lord, who shall dwell in thy tabernacle? or who shall rest in thy holy hill?

He that walketh without blemish, and worketh justice:

He that speaketh truth in his heart, who hath not used deceit in his tongue:

Nor hath done evil to his neighbor: nor taken up a reproach against his neighbors.

. . . He that hath not put out his money to usury, nor taken bribes against the innocent:

He that doth these things, shall not be moved for ever.—*Ps.* xiv. 1-3, 5.

For thou hast prevented him with blessings of sweetness: thou hast set on his head a crown of precious stones . . .

His glory is great in thy salvation: glory and great beauty shalt thou lay upon him.

For thou shalt give him to be a blessing for ever and ever: thou shalt make him joyful in gladness with thy countenance.—*Ps.* xx. 4, 6, 7.

But the just shall inherit the land, and shall dwell therein for evermore.—*Ps.* xxxvi. 29.

He hath distributed, he hath given to the poor: his justice remaineth for ever and ever: his horn shall be exalted in glory.—*Ps.* cxi. 9.

Open ye to me the gates of justice: I will go in to them, and give praise to the Lord. This is the gate of the Lord, the just shall enter into it.—*Ps.* cxvii. 19, 20.

But as for the just, they shall give glory to thy name: and the upright shall dwell with thy countenance.—*Ps.* cxxxix. 14.

The just shall shine, and shall run to and fro like sparks among the reeds.

They shall judge nations, and rule over people, and their Lord shall reign for ever.—*Wis.* iii. 7, 8.

Behold how they are numbered among the children of God, and their lot is among the saints. . . .

Therefore shall they receive a kingdom of glory, and a crown of beauty at the hand of the Lord: for with his right hand he will cover them, and with his holy arm he will defend them.— *Wis.* v. 5, 17.

He that feareth God, will do good: and he that possesseth justice, shall lay hold on her (*i.e.* wisdom). . . .

She shall heap upon him a treasure of joy and gladness, and shall cause him to inherit an everlasting name.— *Ecclus.* xv. 1, 6.

Open ye the gates, and let the just nation, that keepeth the truth, enter in. —*Is.* xxvi. 2.

He that walketh in justices, and speaketh truth, that casteth away avarice by oppression, and shaketh his hands from all bribes, that stoppeth his ears lest he hear blood, and shutteth his eyes, that he may see no evil.

He shall dwell on high, the fortifications of rocks shall be his highness: bread is given him, his waters are sure.

His eyes shall see the king in his beauty, they shall see the land far off. —*Is.* xxxiii. 15-17.

For thus saith the Lord to the eunuchs, They that shall keep my sabbaths, and shall choose the things that please me, and shall hold fast my covenant:

I will give to them in my house, and within my walls, a place, and a name better than sons and daughters: I will give them an everlasting name which shall never perish.

And the children of the stranger that adhere to the Lord, to worship him, and to love his name, to be his servants: every one that keepeth the sabbath from profaning it, and that holdeth fast my covenant:

I will bring them into my holy mount, and will make them joyful in my house of prayer: their holocausts and their victims shall please me upon my altar: for my house shall be called the house of prayer, for all nations.— *Is.* lvi. 4-7.

Deal thy bread to the hungry, and bring the needy and the harborless into thy house: when thou shalt see one naked, cover him, and despise not thy own flesh.

Then shall thy light break forth as the morning, and thy health shall speed-ily arise, and thy justice shall go before thy face, and the glory of the Lord shall gather thee up. . . .

When thou shalt pour out thy soul to the hungry, and shalt satisfy the afflicted soul, then shall thy light rise up in darkness, and thy darkness shall be as the noonday.

And the Lord will give thee rest continually, and will fill thy soul with brightness, and deliver thy bones, and thou shalt be like a watered garden, and like a fountain of water whose waters shall not fail.—*Is.* lviii. 7, 8, 10, 11.

God will clothe thee with the double garment of justice, and will set a crown on thy head of everlasting honor.

For God will show his brightness in thee, to every one under heaven.

For thy name shall be named to thee by God for ever: the peace of justice, and honor of piety.—*Bar.* v. 2-4.

Blessed are the poor in spirit: for theirs is the kingdom of heaven.

Blessed are the meek: for they shall possess the land.

Blessed are they that mourn: for they shall be comforted. . . .

Blessed are the clean of heart: for they shall see God. . . .

Blessed are they that suffer persecution for justice' sake: for theirs is the kingdom of heaven.—*Matt.* v. 3-5, 8, 10.

Suffer both to grow until the harvest, and in the time of the harvest I will say to the reapers: Gather up first the cockle, and bind it into bundles to burn, but the wheat gather ye into my barn. —*Matt.* xiii. 30.

Then shall the just shine as the sun, in the kingdom of their Father.—*Matt.* xiii. 43.

His lord said to him: Well done, good and faithful servant, because thou hast been faithful over a few things, I will place thee over many things: enter thou into the joy of thy lord.—*Matt.* xxv. 21.

Then shall the king say to them, that shall be on his right hand: Come, ye blessed of my Father, possess you the kingdom prepared for you from the foundation of the world.—*Matt.* xxv. 34.

Whose fan is in his hand, and he will purge his floor, and will gather the wheat into his barn; but the chaff he will burn with unquenchable fire.—*Luke* iii. 17.

But our conversation is in heaven; from whence also we look for the Saviour, our Lord Jesus Christ,

Who will reform the body of our lowness, made like to the body of his glory, according to the operation whereby also he is able to subdue all things unto himself.—*Philipp.* iii. 20, 21.

When Christ shall appear, who is your life, then you also shall appear with him in glory.—*Col* iii. 4.

And we will not have you ignorant, brethren, concerning them that are asleep, that you be not sorrowful, even as others who have no hope.

For if we believe that Jesus died, and rose again; even so them who have slept through Jesus, will God bring with him. . . .

Then we who are alive, who are left, shall be taken up together with them in the clouds to meet Christ, into the air, and so shall we be always with the Lord.—1 *Thess.* iv. 12, 13, 16.

Wherefore, brethren, labor the more, that by good works you may make sure your calling and election. For doing these things, you shall not sin at any time.

For so an entrance shall be ministered to you abundantly into the everlasting kingdom of our Lord and Saviour Jesus Christ.—2 *Peter* i. 10, 11.

He, that hath an ear, let him hear what the Spirit saith to the churches: To him that overcometh, I will give the hidden manna, and will give him a white counter, and in the counter, a new name written, which no man knoweth, but he that receiveth it.

. . . And he that shall overcome, and keep my works unto the end I will give him power over the nations.—*Apoc.* ii. 17, 26.

But thou hast a few names in Sardis, which have not defiled their garments: and they shall walk with me in white, because they are worthy.

He that shall overcome, shall thus be clothed in white garments, and I will not blot out his name out of the book of life, and I will confess his name before my Father, and before his angels.—*Apoc.* iii. 4, 5.

He that shall overcome, I will make him a pillar in the temple of my God; and he shall go out no more; and I will write upon him the name of my God, and the name of the city of my God, the new Jerusalem, which cometh down out of heaven from my God, and my new name. . . .

To him that shall overcome, I will give to sit with me in my throne: as I also have overcome, and am set down with my Father in his throne.—*Apoc.* iii. 12, 21.

And one of the ancients answered, and said to me: These that are clothed in white robes, who are they? and whence came they?

And I said to him: My Lord, thou knowest. And he said to me: These are they who are come out of great tribulation, and have washed their robes, and have made them white in the blood of the Lamb.

Therefore they are before the throne of God, and they serve him day and night in his temple: and he, that sitteth on the throne, shall dwell over them.

They shall no more hunger nor thirst, neither shall the sun fall on them, nor any heat.

For the Lamb, which is in the midst of the throne, shall rule them, and shall lead them to the fountains of the waters of life, and God shall wipe away all tears from their eyes.—*Apoc.* vii. 13-17.

And I, John, saw the holy city, the new Jerusalem, coming down out of heaven from God, prepared as a bride adorned for her husband. . . .

And God shall wipe away all tears from their eyes: and death shall be no more, nor mourning, nor crying, nor sorrow shall be any more, for the former things are passed away. . . .

He that shall overcome, shall possess these things, and I will be his God; and he shall be my son.—*Apoc.* xxi. 2, 4, 7.

And they shall see his face: and his name shall be on their foreheads.

And night shall be no more: and they shall not need the light of the lamp, nor the light of the sun, because the Lord God shall enlighten them, and they shall reign for ever and ever.— *Apoc.* xxii. 4, 5.

XI. Prayer that God May Reward the Just

The Lord render unto thee for thy work, and mayst thou receive a full reward of the Lord the God of Israel, to whom thou art come, and under whose wings thou art fled.—*Ruth* ii. 12.

Father, I will that where I am, they also whom thou hast given me, may be with me; that they may see my glory which thou hast given me, because thou hast loved me before the creation of the world.—*John* xvii. 24.

REWARDS OR PUNISHES US ACCORDING TO OUR DESERTS, GOD

See also: Justice of God, the— page 266.

For he will render to a man his work, and according to the ways of every one, he will reward them.—*Job* xxxiv. 11.

For thou wilt render to every man according to his works.—*Ps.* lxi. 13.

By the fruit of his own mouth shall a man be filled with good things, and according to the works of his hands it shall be repaid him.—*Prov.* xii. 14.

If thou say: I have not strength enough: he that seeth into the heart, he understandeth, and nothing deceiveth the keeper of thy soul, and he shall render to a man according to his works. —*Prov.* xxiv. 12.

For it is easy before God in the day of death, to reward every one according to his ways.—*Ecclus.* xi. 28.

According as his mercy is, so his correction judgeth a man according to his works.

The sinner shall not escape in his rapines, and the patience of him that showeth mercy shall not be put off.

All mercy shall make a place for every man according to the merit of his works, and according to the wisdom of his sojournment.—*Ecclus.* xvi. 13-15.

And he will repay vengeance to the Gentiles, till he have taken away the multitude of the proud, and broken the sceptres of the unjust,

Till he have rendered to men according to their deeds: and according to the works of Adam, and according to his presumption.—*Ecclus.* xxxv. 23, 24.

Say to the just man that it is well, for he shall eat the fruit of his doings.

Woe to the wicked unto evil: for the reward of his hands shall be given him. —*Is.* iii. 10, 11.

Great in counsel, and incomprehensible in thought: whose eyes are open upon all the ways of the children of Adam, to render unto every one according to his ways, and according to the fruit of his devices.—*Jer.* xxxii. 19.

The soul that sinneth, the same shall die: the son shall not bear the iniquity of the father, and the father shall not bear the iniquity of the son: the justice of the just shall be upon him, and the wickedness of the wicked shall be upon him. . . .

Therefore will I judge every man according to his ways, O house of Israel, saith the Lord God.—*Ezech.* xviii. 20, 30.

Therefore there is a judgment of the Lord with Juda, and a visitation for Jacob: he will render to him according to his ways, and according to his devices.—*Osee* xii. 2.

And you shall return, and shall see the difference between the just and the wicked: and between him that serveth God, and him that serveth him not.— *Malach.* iii. 18.

For the Son of man shall come in the glory of his Father with his angels: and then will he render to every man according to his works.—*Matt.* xvi. 27.

Wonder not at this; for the hour cometh, wherein all that are in the graves shall hear the voice of the Son of God.

And they that have done good things, shall come forth unto the resurrection of life; but they that have done evil, unto the resurrection of judgment.— *John* v. 28, 29.

But according to thy hardness and impenitent heart, thou treasurest up to thyself wrath, against the day of wrath, and revelation of the just judgment of God.

Who will render to every man according to his works.

To them indeed, who according to patience in good work, seek glory and honor and incorruption, eternal life:

But to them that are contentious, and who obey not the truth, but give credit to iniquity, wrath and indignation.—*Rom.* ii. 5-8.

And every man shall receive his own reward, according to his own labor.—1 *Cor.* iii. 8.

For we must all be manifested before the judgment seat of Christ, that every one may receive the proper things of the body, according as he hath done, whether it be good or evil.—2 *Cor.* v. 10.

Be not deceived, God is not mocked.

For what things a man shall sow, those also shall he reap. For he that soweth in his flesh, of the flesh also shall reap corruption. But he that soweth in the spirit, of the spirit shall reap life everlasting.

And in doing good, let us not fail. For in due time we shall reap, not failing.—*Gal.* vi. 7-9.

Alexander the coppersmith hath done me much evil: the Lord will reward him according to his works.—2 *Tim.* iv. 14.

And if you invoke as Father him who, without respect of persons, judgeth according to every one's work: converse in fear during the time of your sojourning here.—1 *Peter* i. 17.

And all the churches shall know that I am he that searcheth the reins and hearts, and I will give to every one of you according to your works.—*Apoc.* ii. 23.

And I saw the dead, great and small, standing in the presence of the throne, and the books were opened; and another book was opened, which is the book of life; and the dead were judged by those things which were written in the books, according to their works.

And the sea gave up the dead that were in it, and death and hell gave up their dead that were in them; and they were judged every one according to their works. . . .

And whosoever was not found written in the book of life, was cast into the pool of fire.—*Apoc.* xx. 12, 13, 15.

Behold, I come quickly; and my re-ward is with me, to render to every man according to his works.—*Apoc.* xxii. 12.

RICH, THE

Their storehouses full, flowing out of this into that.

Their sheep fruitful in young, abounding in their goings forth: their oxen fat.

There is no breach of wall, nor passage, nor crying out in their streets.

They have called the people happy, that hath these things: but happy is that people whose God is the Lord.—*Ps.* cxliii. 13-15.

The rich and poor have met one another: the Lord is the maker of them both.—*Prov.* xxii. 2.

Better is the poor man walking in his simplicity, than the rich in crooked ways.—*Prov.* xxviii. 6.

The rich man seemeth to himself wise: but the poor man that is prudent shall search him out.—*Prov.* xxviii. 11.

Three sorts my soul hateth, and I am greatly grieved at their life:

A poor man that is proud: a rich man that is a liar: an old man that is a fool, and doting.—*Ecclus.* xxv. 3, 4.

Woe to you that are wealthy in Sion, and to you that have confidence in the mountain of Samaria: ye great men, heads of the people, that go in with state into the house of Israel.

. . . You that sleep upon beds of ivory, and are wanton on your couches: that eat the lambs out of the flock, and the calves out of the midst of the herd;

You that sing to the sound of the psaltery: they have thought themselves to have instruments of music like David;

That drink wine in bowls, and anoint themselves with the best ointments: and they are not concerned for the affliction of Joseph.

Wherefore now they shall go captive at the head of them that go into captivity: and the faction of the luxurious ones shall be taken away.—*Amos* vi. 1, 4-7.

He hath filled the hungry with good things; and the rich he hath sent empty away.—*Luke* i. 53.

But woe to you that are rich: for you have your consolation.—*Luke* vi. 24.

There was a certain rich man, who was clothed in purple and fine linen; and feasted sumptuously every day.

And there was a certain beggar, named Lazarus, who lay at his gate, full of sores,

Desiring to be filled with the crumbs that fell from the rich man's table, and no one did give him; moreover the dogs came, and licked his sores.

And it came to pass, that the beggar died, and was carried by the angels into Abraham's bosom. And the rich man also died: and he was buried in hell.

And lifting up his eyes when he was in torments, he saw Abraham afar off, and Lazarus in his bosom:

And he cried, and said: Father Abraham, have mercy on me, and send Lazarus, that he may dip the tip of his finger in water, to cool my tongue: for I am tormented in this flame.

And Abraham said to him: Son, remember that thou didst receive good things in thy lifetime, and likewise Lazarus evil things, but now he is comforted; and thou art tormented.

And besides all this, between us and you, there is fixed a great chaos: so that they who would pass from hence to you, cannot, nor from thence, come hither.—*Luke* xvi. 19-26.

But let the brother of low condition, glory in his exaltation:

And the rich, in his being low; because as the flower of the grass shall he pass away.

For the sun rose with a burning heat, and parched the grass, and the flower thereof fell off, and the beauty of the shape thereof perished: so also shall the rich man fade away in his ways.—*James* i. 9-11.

He that hath the substance of this world, and shall see his brother in need, and shall shut up his bowels from him: how doth the charity of God abide in him?—1 *John* iii. 17.

RICH, ADULATION AND SUBSERVIENCE TO THE

The poor man shall be hateful even to his own neighbor: but the friends of the rich are many.—*Prov.* xiv. 20.

For laughter they make bread, and wine that the living may feast: and all things obey money.—*Eccles.* x. 19.

Despise not a just man that is poor, and do not magnify a sinful man that is rich.—*Ecclus.* x. 26.

When a rich man is shaken, he is kept up by his friends: but when a poor man is fallen down, he is thrust away even by his acquaintance.

When a rich man hath been deceived, he hath many helpers: he hath spoken proud things, and they have justified him. . . .

The rich man spoke, and all held their peace, and what he said they extol even to the clouds.—*Ecclus.* xiii. 25, 26, 28.

My brethren, have not the faith of our Lord Jesus Christ of glory, with respect of persons.

For if there shall come into your assembly a man having a golden ring, in fine apparel, and there shall come in also a poor man in mean attire,

And you have respect to him that is clothed with the fine apparel, and shall say to him: Sit thou here well; but say to the poor man: Stand thou there, or sit under my footstool:

Do you not judge within yourselves, and are become judges of unjust thoughts?—*James* ii. 1-4.

RICHES, THE DANGER OF

Give me neither beggary, nor riches: give me only the necessaries of life:

Lest perhaps being filled, I should be tempted to deny, and say: Who is the Lord? or being compelled by poverty, I should steal, and forswear the name of my God.—*Prov.* xxx. 8, 9.

For gold and silver hath destroyed many, and hath reached even to the heart of kings, and perverted them.—*Ecclus.* viii. 3.

And if thou be rich, thou shalt not be free from sin: for if thou pursue after, thou shalt not overtake: and if thou run before, thou shalt not escape.—*Ecclus.* xi. 10.

Riches are not comely for a covetous man and a niggard, and what should an envious man do with gold?—*Ecclus.* xiv. 3.

Injuries and wrongs will waste riches: and the house that is very rich shall be brought to nothing by pride: so the substance of the proud shall be rooted out. —*Ecclus*. xxi. 5.

Many have been brought to fall for gold, and the beauty thereof hath been their ruin.

Gold is a stumbling-block to them that sacrifice to it: woe to them that eagerly follow after it, and every fool shall perish by it.—*Ecclus*. xxxi. 6, 7.

I spoke to thee in thy prosperity: and thou saidst: I will not hear: this hath been thy way from thy youth, because thou hast not heard my voice.—*Jer*. xxii. 21.

According to their pastures they were filled, and were made full: and they lifted up their heart, and have forgotten me.—*Osee* xiii. 6.

And he spoke to them many things in parables, saying: Behold the sower went forth to sow. . . .

And others fell among thorns; and the thorns grew up and choked them. . . .

And he that received the seed among thorns, is he that heareth the word, and the care of this world and the deceitfulness of riches choketh up the word, and he becometh fruitless.—*Matt*. xiii. 3, 7, 22.

Jesus saith to him: If thou wilt be perfect, go, sell what thou hast, and give to the poor, and thou shalt have treasure in heaven: and come follow me.

And when the young man had heard this word, he went away sad: for he had great possessions.

Then Jesus said to his disciples: Amen, I say to you, that a rich man shall hardly enter into the kingdom of heaven.

And again I say to you: It is easier for a camel to pass through the eye of a needle, than for a rich man to enter into the kingdom of heaven.—*Matt*. xix. 21-24.

And Jesus looking round about, saith to his disciples: How hardly shall they that have riches, enter into the kingdom of God!

And the disciples were astonished at his words. But Jesus again answering, saith to them: Children, how hard is it for them that trust in riches, to enter into the kingdom of God?—*Mark* x. 23, 24.

For they that will become rich, fall into temptation, and into the snare of the devil, and into many unprofitable and hurtful desires, which drown men into destruction and perdition.

For the desire of money is the root of all evils; which some coveting, have erred from the faith, and have entangled themselves in many sorrows.—1 *Tim*. vi. 9, 10.

Go to now, ye rich men, weep and howl in your miseries, which shall come upon you.

Your riches are corrupted: and your garments are motheaten.

Your gold and silver is cankered: and the rust of them shall be for a testimony against you, and shall eat your flesh like fire. You have stored up to yourselves wrath against the last days. —*James* v. 1-3.

RICHES, THE VANITY OF

The riches which he hath swallowed, he shall vomit up, and God shall draw them out of his belly.—*Job* xx. 15.

The rich man, when he shall sleep, shall take away nothing with him: he shall open his eyes, and find nothing.—*Job* xxvii. 19.

I am brought to nothing: as a wind, thou hast taken away my desire: and my prosperity hath passed away like a cloud.—*Job* xxx. 15.

Better is a little to the just, than the great riches of the wicked.

For the arms of the wicked shall be broken in pieces; but the Lord strengtheneth the just.—*Ps*. xxxvi. 16, 17.

Behold thou hast made my days measurable: and my substance is as nothing before thee.

And indeed all things are vanity: every man living.

Surely man passeth as an image: yea, and he is disquieted in vain.

He storeth up: and he knoweth not for whom he shall gather these things. —*Ps*. xxxviii. 6, 7.

They that trust in their own strength, and glory in the multitude of their riches,

No brother can redeem, nor shall man

redeem: he shall not give to God his ransom,

Nor the price of the redemption of his soul: and shall labor for ever. . . .

The senseless and the fool shall perish together:

And they shall leave their riches to strangers: and their sepulchres shall be their houses for ever.—*Ps.* xlviii. 7-9, 11, 12.

Be not thou afraid, when a man shall be made rich, and when the glory of his house shall be increased.

For when he shall die he shall take nothing away; nor shall his glory descend with him.

. . . He shall go in to the generations of his fathers: and he shall never see light.—*Ps.* xlviii. 17, 18, 20.

The just shall see and fear, and shall laugh at him, and say: Behold the man that made not God his helper:

But trusted in the abundance of his riches: and prevailed in his vanity.—*Ps.* li. 8, 9.

All the foolish of heart were troubled. They have slept their sleep; and all the men of riches have found nothing in their hands.—*Ps.* lxxv. 6.

Riches shall not profit in the day of revenge: but justice shall deliver from death.—*Prov.* xi. 4.

He that trusteth in his riches shall fall: but the just shall spring up as a green leaf.—*Prov.* xi. 28.

The inheritance gotten hastily in the beginning, in the end shall be without a blessing.—*Prov.* xx. 21.

I heaped together for myself silver and gold, and the wealth of kings, and provinces: I made me singing men, and singing women, and the delights of the sons of men, cups and vessels to serve to pour out wine:

And I surpassed in riches all that were before me in Jerusalem: my wisdom also remained with me. . . .

And when I turned myself to all the works which my hands had wrought, and to the labors wherein I had labored in vain, I saw in all things vanity, and vexation of mind, and that nothing was lasting under the sun.—*Eccles.* ii. 8, 9, 11.

Considering, I found also another vanity under the sun:

There is but one, and he hath not a second, no child, no brother, and yet he ceaseth not to labor, neither are his eyes satisfied with riches, neither doth he reflect, saying: For whom do I labor, and defraud my soul of good things? in this also is vanity, and a grievous vexation.—*Eccles.* iv. 7, 8.

Where there are great riches, there are also many to eat them. And what doth it profit the owner, but that he seeth the riches with his eyes?—*Eccles.* v. 10.

There is also another grievous evil, which I have seen under the sun: riches kept to the hurt of the owner.

For they are lost with very great affliction: he hath begotten a son, who shall be in extremity of want.

As he came forth naked from his mother's womb, so shall he return, and shall take nothing away with him of his labor.

A most deplorable evil: as he came, so shall he return. What then doth it profit him that he hath labored for the wind?—*Eccles.* v. 12-15.

What hath pride profited us? or what advantage hath the boasting of riches brought us?

All those things are passed away like a shadow, and like a post that runneth on,

And as a ship that passeth through the waves: whereof, when it is gone by, the trace cannot be found, nor the path of its keel in the waters:

Or as when a bird flieth through the air, of the passage of which no mark can be found, but only the sound of the wings beating the light air, and parting it by the force of her flight; she moved her wings, and hath flown through, and there is no mark found afterwards of her way:

Or as when an arrow is shot at a mark, the divided air presently cometh together again, so that the passage thereof is not known.—*Wis.* v. 8-12.

There is one that is enriched by living sparingly, and this is the portion of his reward.

In that he saith: I have found me rest, and now I will eat of my goods alone:

And he knoweth not what time shall

pass, and that death approacheth, and that he must leave all to others, and shall die.—*Ecclus.* xi. 18-20.

The riches of the unjust shall be dried up like a river, and shall pass away with a noise like a great thunder in rain.—*Ecclus.* xl. 13.

Where are the princes of the nations, and they that rule over the beasts that are upon the earth?

. . . That hoard up silver and gold, wherein men trust, and there is no end of their getting? who work in silver and are solicitous, and their works are unsearchable.

They are cut off, and are gone down to hell, and others are risen up in their place.—*Bar.* iii. 16, 18, 19.

Their silver shall be cast forth, and their gold shall become a dung hill. Their silver and their gold shall not be able to deliver them in the day of the wrath of the Lord. They shall not satisfy their soul, and their bellies shall not be filled: because it hath been the stumbling-block of their iniquity.—*Ezech.* vii. 19.

Neither shall their silver and their gold be able to deliver them in the day of the wrath of the Lord: all the land shall be devoured by the fire of his jealousy, for he shall make even a speedy destruction of all them that dwell in the land.—*Soph.* i. 18.

Lay not up to yourselves treasures on earth: where the rust and moth consume, and where thieves break through and steal.—*Matt.* vi. 19.

And he spoke a similitude to them, saying: The land of a certain rich man brought forth plenty of fruits.

And he thought within himself, saying: What shall I do, because I have no room where to bestow my fruits?

And he said: This will I do: I will pull down my barns, and will build greater; and into them will I gather all things that are grown to me, and my goods.

And I will say to my soul: Soul, thou hast much goods laid up for many years, take thy rest; eat, drink, make good cheer.

But God said to him: Thou fool, this night do they require thy soul of thee:

and whose shall those things be which thou hast provided?

So is he that layeth up treasure for himself, and is not rich towards God.—*Luke* xii. 16-21.

For we brought nothing into this world: and certainly we can carry nothing out.—1 *Tim.* vi. 7.

Because thou sayest: I am rich, and made wealthy, and have need of nothing: and knowest not, that thou art wretched, and miserable, and poor, and blind, and naked.—*Apoc.* iii. 17.

RICHES, THE LOVE OF

See also: Covetousness—page 86.

For what shall I do when God shall rise to judge? and when he shall examine, what shall I answer him? . . .

If I have thought gold my strength, and have said to fine gold: My confidence:

If I have rejoiced over my great riches, and because my hand had gotten much.—*Job* xxxi. 14, 24, 25.

Trust not in iniquity, and cover not robberies: if riches abound, set not your heart upon them.—*Ps.* lxi. 11.

A covetous man shall not be satisfied with money: and he that loveth riches, shall reap no fruit from them: so this also is vanity.—*Eccles.* v. 9.

Do not transgress against thy friend deferring money, nor despise thy dear brother for the sake of gold.—*Ecclus.* vii. 20.

There is not a more wicked thing than to love money: for such a one setteth even his own soul to sale: because while he liveth he hath cast away his bowels.—*Ecclus.* x. 10.

Through poverty many have sinned: and he that seeketh to be enriched, turneth away his eye.—*Ecclus.* xxvii. 1.

Watching for riches consumeth the flesh, and the thought thereof driveth away sleep.—*Ecclus.* xxxi. 1.

He that loveth gold, shall not be justified: and he that followeth after corruption, shall be filled with it.

Many have been brought to fall for gold, and the beauty thereof hath been their ruin.

Gold is a stumbling-block to them that sacrifice to it: woe to them that eagerly follow after it, and every fool shall perish by it.—*Ecclus.* xxxi. 5-7.

No man can serve two masters. For either he will hate the one, and love the other: or he will sustain the one, and despise the other. You cannot serve God and mammon.—*Matt.* vi. 24.

Then went one of the twelve, who was called Judas Iscariot, to the chief priests,

And said to them: What will you give me, and I will deliver him unto you? But they appointed him thirty pieces of silver.

And from henceforth he sought opportunity to betray him.—*Matt.* xxvi. 14-16.

Then one of his disciples, Judas Iscariot, he that was about to betray him, said:

Why was not this ointment sold for three hundred pence, and given to the poor?

Now he said this, not because he cared for the poor; but because he was a thief, and having the purse, carried the things that were put therein.—*John* xii. 4-6.

Deacons in like manner chaste, not double tongued, not given to much wine, not greedy of filthy lucre.—1 *Tim.* iii. 8.

But they that will become rich, fall into temptation, and into the snare of the devil, and into many unprofitable and hurtful desires, which drown men into destruction and perdition.

For the desire of money is the root of all evils; which some coveting, have erred from the faith, and have entangled themselves in many sorrows.— 1 *Tim.* vi. 9, 10.

RICHES, THE RIGHT USE OF

And every man to whom God hath given riches, and substance, and hath given him power to eat thereof, and to enjoy his portion, and to rejoice of his labor: this is the gift of God.—*Eccles.* v. 18.

Wisdom with riches is more profitable, and bringeth more advantage to them that see the sun.

For as wisdom is a defence, so money is a defence: but learning and wisdom

excel in this, that they give life to him that possesseth them.—*Eccles.* vii. 12, 13.

Riches are good to him that hath no sin in his conscience: and poverty is very wicked in the mouth of the ungodly.—*Ecclus.* xiii. 30.

Remember poverty in the time of abundance, and the necessities of poverty in the day of riches.—*Ecclus.* xviii. 25.

Blessed is the rich man that is found without blemish: and that hath not gone after gold, nor put his trust in money nor in treasures.

Who is he, and we will praise him? for he hath done wonderful things in his life.

Who hath been tried thereby, and made perfect, he shall have glory everlasting. He that could have transgressed, and hath not transgressed: and could do evil things, and hath not done them:

Therefore are his goods established in the Lord, and all the church of the saints shall declare his alms.—*Ecclus.* xxxi. 8-11.

And I say to you: Make unto you friends of the mammon of iniquity; that when you shall fail, they may receive you into everlasting dwellings.— *Luke* xvi. 9.

Charge the rich of this world not to be high-minded, nor to trust in the uncertainty of riches, but in the living God, (who giveth us abundantly all things to enjoy,)

To do good, to be rich in good works, to give easily, to communicate to others,

To lay up in store for themselves a good foundation against the time to come, that they may lay hold on the true life.—1 *Tim.* vi. 17-19.

RICHES, ILL-GOTTEN

See: Goods, ill-gotten—page 171.

RICHES, TRUE

And now what is my hope? is it not the Lord? and my substance is with thee.—*Ps.* xxxviii. 8.

With me (wisdom) are riches and glory, glorious riches, and justice.

For my fruit is better than gold and

the precious stone, and my blossoms than choice silver.

I walk in the way of justice, in the midst of the paths of judgment,

That I may enrich them that love me, and may fill their treasures.—*Prov.* viii. 18-21.

The blessing of the Lord maketh men rich: neither shall affliction be joined to them.—*Prov.* x. 22.

And if riches be desired in life, what is richer than wisdom, which maketh all things?—*Wis.* viii. 5.

Place thy treasure in the commandments of the most High, and it shall bring thee more profit than gold.—*Ecclus.* xxix. 14.

And there shall be faith in thy times: riches of salvation, wisdom and knowledge: the fear of the Lord is his treasure.—*Is.* xxxiii. 6.

Lay not up to yourselves treasures on earth: where the rust and moth consume, and where thieves break through and steal.

But lay up to yourselves treasures in heaven: where neither the rust nor moth doth consume, and where thieves do not break through nor steal.

For where thy treasure is, there is thy heart also.—*Matt.* vi. 19-21.

Jesus saith to him: If thou wilt be perfect, go, sell what thou hast, and give to the poor, and thou shalt have treasure in heaven: and come, follow me.—*Matt.* xix. 21.

Sell what you possess, and give alms. Make to yourselves bags which grow not old, a treasure in heaven which faileth not: where no thief approacheth, nor moth corrupteth.—*Luke* xii. 33.

I give thanks to my God always for you, for the grace of God that is given you in Christ Jesus,

That in all things you are made rich in him, in all utterance, and in all knowledge.—1 *Cor.* i. 4, 5.

But in all things let us exhibit ourselves as the ministers of God, in much patience, in tribulation, in necessities, in distresses; . . .

As sorrowful, yet always rejoicing; as needy, yet enriching many; as having nothing, and possessing all things.—2 *Cor.* vi. 4, 10.

Charge the rich of this world not to be high-minded, nor to trust in the uncertainty of riches, but in the living God, (who giveth us abundantly all things to enjoy,)

To do good, to be rich in good works, . . . To lay up in store for themselves a good foundation against the time to come, that they may lay hold on the true life.—1 *Tim.* vi. 17-19.

I know thy tribulation and thy poverty, but thou art rich: and thou art blasphemed by them that say they are Jews and are not, but are the synagogue of Satan.—*Apoc.* ii. 9.

I counsel thee to buy of me gold firetried, that thou mayst be made rich; and mayst be clothed in white garments, and that the shame of thy nakedness may not appear; and anoint thy eyes with eyesalve, that thou mayst see.—*Apoc.* iii. 18.

RULERS, THE DUTY AND RESPONSIBILITY OF

See also: Judges—page 252.

And now, O ye kings, understand: receive instruction, you that judge the earth.—*Ps.* ii. 10.

Hear therefore, ye kings, and understand: learn, ye that are judges of the ends of the earth.

Give ear, you that rule the people, and that please yourselves in multitudes of nations:

For power is given you by the Lord, and strength by the most High, who will examine your works, and search out your thoughts:

Because being ministers of his kingdom, you have not judged rightly, nor kept the law of justice, nor walked according to the will of God.

Horribly and speedily will he appear to you: for a most severe judgment shall be for them that bear rule.

For to him that is little, mercy is granted: but the mighty shall be mightily tormented.

For God will not except any man's person, neither will be stand in awe of any man's greatness: for he made the little and the great, and he hath equally care of all.

But a greater punishment is ready for the more mighty.

To you therefore, O kings, are these

my words, that you may learn wisdom, and not fall from it.—*Wis.* vi. 2-10.

Have they made thee ruler? be not lifted up: be among them as one of them.

Have care of them, and so sit down, and when thou hast acquitted thyself of all thy charge, take thy place:

That thou mayst rejoice for them, and receive a crown as an ornament of grace, and get the honor of the contribution.—*Ecclus.* xxxii. 1-3.

SABBATH, SANCTITY OF THE

See: Lord's day, the—page 290.

SACRAMENT, THE BLESSED

See: Eucharist, the Holy—page 129.

SACRAMENTS, THE

Thou hast visited the earth, and hast plentifully watered it; thou hast many ways enriched it.

The river of God is filled with water, thou hast prepared their food: for so is its preparation.—*Ps.* lxiv. 10.

You shall draw waters with joy out of the saviour's fountains.—*Is.* xii. 3.

In that day there shall be a fountain open to the house of David, and to the inhabitants of Jerusalem: for the washing of the sinner, and of the unclean woman.—*Zach.* xiii. 1.

SACRIFICE THAT PLEASES GOD, THE

Offer up the sacrifice of justice, and trust in the Lord: many say, Who showeth us good things?—*Ps.* iv. 6.

For if thou hadst desired sacrifice, I would indeed have given it: with burnt offerings thou wilt not be delighted.

A sacrifice to God is an afflicted spirit: a contrite and humbled heart, O God, thou wilt not despise.—*Ps.* l. 18, 19.

I will sacrifice to thee the sacrifice of praise, and I will call upon the name of the Lord.—*Ps.* cxv. 17.

The beginning of a good way is to do justice; and this is more acceptable with God, than to offer sacrifices.—*Prov.* xvi. 5.

It is a wholesome sacrifice to take heed to the commandments, and to depart from all iniquity.

And to depart from injustice, is to offer a propitiatory sacrifice for injustices, and a begging of pardon for sins.

He shall return thanks, that offereth fine flour: and he that doth mercy, offereth sacrifice.

To depart from iniquity is that which pleaseth the Lord, and to depart from injustice, is an entreaty for sins.—*Ecclus.* xxxv. 2-5.

The oblation of the just maketh the altar fat, and is an odor of sweetness in the sight of the most High.

The sacrifice of the just is acceptable, and the Lord will not forget the memorial thereof.—*Ecclus.* xxxv. 8, 9.

What shall I offer to the Lord that is worthy? wherewith shall I kneel before the high God? shall I offer holocausts unto him, and calves of a year old?

May the Lord be appeased with thousands of rams, or with many thousands of fat he goats? shall I give my first born for my wickedness, the fruit of my body for the sin of my soul?

I will show thee, O man, what is good, and what the Lord requireth of thee: Verily, to do judgment, and to love mercy, and to walk solicitous with thy God.—*Mich.* vi. 6-8.

Who is there among you, that will shut the doors, and will kindle the fire on my altar gratis? I have no pleasure in you, saith the Lord of hosts: and I will not receive a gift of your hand.

For from the rising of the sun even to the going down, my name is great among the Gentiles, and in every place there is sacrifice, and there is offered to my name a clean oblation: for my name is great among the Gentiles, saith the Lord of hosts.—*Malach.* i. 10, 11.

And do not forget to do good, and to impart; for by such sacrifices God's favor is obtained.—*Heb.* xiii. 16.

Be you also as living stones built up, a spiritual house, a holy priesthood, to offer up spiritual sacrifices, acceptable to God by Jesus Christ.—1 *Peter* ii. 5.

SADNESS

See also: Sorrowing, the—page 540.

Why art thou sad, O my soul? and why dost thou trouble me?

Hope in God, for I will still give

praise to him: the salvation of my countenance, and my God.—*Ps.* xli. 6.

Upon the rivers of Babylon, there we sat and wept: when we remembered Sion:

On the willows in the midst thereof we hung up our instruments. For there they that led us into captivity required of us the words of songs.

And they that carried us away, said: Sing ye to us a hymn of the songs of Sion.

How shall we sing the song of the Lord in a strange land?—*Ps.* cxxxvi. 1-4.

Grief in the heart of a man shall bring him low, but with a good word he shall be made glad.—*Prov.* xii. 25.

A glad heart maketh a cheerful countenance: but by grief of mind the spirit is cast down.—*Prov.* xv. 13.

A joyful mind maketh age flourishing: a sorrowful spirit drieth up the bones.—*Prov.* xvii. 22.

As a moth doth by a garment, and a worm by the wood: so the sadness of a man consumeth the heart.—*Prov.* xxv. 20.

The affliction of an hour maketh one forget great delights, and in the end of a man is the disclosing of his works.—*Ecclus.* xi. 29.

Happy is he that hath had no sadness of his mind, and who is not fallen from his hope.—*Ecclus.* xiv. 2.

The sadness of the heart is every plague. . . .

And a man will chose any plague, but the plague of the heart.—*Ecclus.* xxv. 17, 18.

Give not up thy soul to sadness, and afflict not thyself in thy own counsel. . . .

Have pity on thy own soul, pleasing God, and contain thyself: gather up thy heart in his holiness: and drive away sadness far from thee.

For sadness hath killed many, and there is no profit in it.

Envy and anger shorten a man's days, and pensiveness will bring old age before the time.—*Ecclus.* xxx. 22, 24-26.

For of sadness cometh death, and it overwhelmeth the strength, and the sorrow of the heart boweth down the neck. . . .

Give not up thy heart to sadness, but drive it from thee: and remember the latter end.—*Ecclus.* xxxviii. 19, 21.

SAINTS, THE, PROTECTED BY GOD

And he (Moses) said: The Lord came from Sinai, and from Seir he rose up to us: he hath appeared from mount Pharan, and with him thousands of saints. In his right hand a fiery law.

He hath loved the people, all the saints are in his hand: and they that approach to his feet, shall receive of his doctrine.—*Deut.* xxxiii. 2, 3.

He will keep the feet of his saints, and the wicked shall be silent in darkness, because no man shall prevail by his own strength.—1 *Kings* ii. 9.

For the Lord loveth judgment, and will not forsake his saints: they shall be preserved for ever.—*Ps.* xxxvi. 28.

You that love the Lord, hate evil; the Lord preserveth the souls of his saints, he will deliver them out of the hand of the sinner.—*Ps.* xcvi. 10.

Precious in the sight of the Lord is the death of his saints.—*Ps.* cxv. 15.

For his soul pleased God: therefore he hastened to bring him out of the midst of iniquities: but the people see this, and understand not, nor lay up such things in their hearts:

That the grace of God, and his mercy is with his saints, and that he hath respect to his chosen.—*Wis.* iv. 14, 15.

SAINTS, THE HAPPINESS OF THE

He shall call heaven from above, and the earth, to judge his people.

Gather ye together his saints to him: who set his covenant before sacrifices.—*Ps.* xlix. 4, 5.

With thee is the principality in the day of thy strength: in the brightness of the saints: from the womb before the day star I begot thee.—*Ps.* cix. 3.

Let thy priests be clothed with justice: and let thy saints rejoice. . . .

I will clothe her priests with salvation: and her saints shall rejoice with exceeding great joy.—*Ps.* cxxxi. 9, 16.

The saints shall rejoice in glory: they shall be joyful in their beds.—*Ps.* cxlix. 5.

Go forth, ye daughters of Sion, and see king Solomon in the diadem, wherewith his mother crowned him in the day of his espousals, and in the day of the joy of his heart.—*Cant.* iii. 11.

Moses was beloved of God and men: whose memory is in benediction.

He made him like the saints in glory. —*Ecclus.* xlv. 1, 2.

That being rooted and founded in charity,

You may be able to comprehend, with all the saints, what is the breadth, and length, and height, and depth:

To know also the charity of Christ, which surpasseth all knowledge, that you may be filled unto all the fulness of God.—*Eph.* iii. 17-19.

Giving thanks to God the Father, who hath made us worthy to be partakers of the lot of the saints in light. —*Col.* i. 12.

After this I saw a great multitude, which no man could number, of all nations, and tribes, and peoples, and tongues, standing before the throne, and in sight of the Lamb, clothed with white robes, and palms in their hands. . . .

And one of the ancients answered, and said to me: These that are clothed in white robes, who are they? and whence came they?

And I said to him: My Lord, thou knowest. And he said to me: These are they who are come out of great tribulation, and have washed their robes, and have made them white in the blood of the Lamb.

Therefore they are before the throne of God, and they serve him day and night in his temple: and he, that sitteth on the throne, shall dwell over them.

They shall no more hunger, nor thirst, neither shall the sun fall on them, nor any heat.

For the Lamb, which is in the midst of the throne, shall rule them, and shall lead them to the fountains of the waters of life, and God shall wipe away all tears from their eyes.—*Apoc.* vii. 9, 13-17.

SAINTS PRAISE AND GIVE GLORY TO GOD, THE

Sing to the Lord, O ye his saints: and give praise to the memory of his holiness.—*Ps.* xxix. 5.

Let all thy works, O Lord, praise thee: and let thy saints bless thee.

They shall speak of the glory of thy kingdom: and shall tell of thy power:

To make thy might known to the sons of men: and the glory of the magnificence of thy kingdom.—*Ps.* cxliv. 10-12.

The saints shall rejoice in glory: they shall be joyful in their beds.

The high praises of God shall be in their mouth.—*Ps.* cxlix. 5, 6.

Hath not the Lord made the saints to declare all his wonderful works, which the Lord Almighty hath firmly settled to be established for his glory? —*Ecclus.* xlii. 17.

After this I saw a great multitude, which no man could number, of all nations, and tribes, and peoples, and tongues, standing before the throne, and in sight of the Lamb, clothed with white robes, and palms in their hands:

And they cried with a loud voice, saying: Salvation to our God, who sitteth upon the throne, and to the Lamb. —*Apoc.* vii. 9, 10.

SAINTS ARE WORTHY OF HONOR AND REVERENCE, THE

But to me thy friends, O God, are made exceedingly honorable: their principality is exceedingly strengthened.— *Ps.* cxxxviii. 17.

The saints shall rejoice in glory: they shall be joyful in their beds.

The high praises of God shall be in their mouth: and two-edged swords in their hands:

To execute vengeance upon the nations, chastisements among the people:

To bind their kings with fetters, and their nobles with manacles of iron.

To execute upon them the judgment that is written: this glory is to all his saints.—*Ps.* cxlix. 5-9.

As gold in the furnace he hath proved them, and as a victim of a holocaust he hath received them, and in time

there shall be respect had to them.—
Wis. iii. 6.

And let not the naming of God be usual in thy mouth, and meddle not with the names of saints, for thou shalt not escape free from them.—*Ecclus.* xxiii. 10.

Know you not that the saints shall judge this world? And if the world shall be judged by you, are you unworthy to judge the smallest matters?

Know you not that we shall judge angels? how much more things of this world?—1 *Cor.* vi. 2, 3.

Now therefore you are no more strangers and foreigners; but you are fellow citizens with the saints, and the domestics of God.—*Eph.* ii. 19.

SAINTS, GOD IS GLORIFIED IN HIS

God is wonderful in his saints: the God of Israel is he who will give power and strength to his people. Blessed be God.—*Ps.* lxvii. 36.

God, who is glorified in the assembly of the saints: great and terrible above all them that are about him.—*Ps.* lxxxviii. 8.

And to you who are troubled, rest with us when the Lord Jesus shall be revealed from heaven, with the angels of his power. . . .

When he shall come to be glorified in his saints, and to be made wonderful in all them who have believed; because our testimony was believed upon you in that day.—2 *Thess.* i. 7, 10.

SAINTS, THE COMMUNION OF

See: Part II—page 732.

SALVATION, THE IMPORTANCE OF

For what doth it profit a man, if he gain the whole world, and suffer the loss of his own soul? Or what exchange shall a man give for his soul?—*Matt.* xvi. 26.

But yet rejoice not in this, that spirits are subject unto you; but rejoice in this, that your names are written in heaven.—*Luke* x. 20.

But Martha was busy about much serving. Who stood and said: Lord, hast thou no care that my sister hath left me alone to serve? speak to her therefore, that she help me.

And the Lord answering, said to her: Martha, Martha, thou art careful, and art troubled about many things:

But one thing is necessary. Mary hath chosen the best part, which shall not be taken away from her.—*Luke* x. 40-42.

While we look not at the things which are seen, but at the things which are not seen. For the things which are seen, are temporal; but the things which are not seen, are eternal.—2 *Cor.* iv. 18.

Therefore ought we more diligently to observe the things which we have heard, lest perhaps we should let them slip.

For if the word, spoken by angels, became steadfast, and every transgression and disobedience received a just recompense of reward:

How shall we escape if we neglect so great salvation? which having begun to be declared by the Lord, was confirmed unto us by them that heard him.—*Heb.* ii. 1-3.

SALVATION, GOD OUR

Neither is my house so great with God, that he should make with me an eternal covenant, firm in all things and assured. For he is all my salvation, and all my will: neither is there ought thereof that springeth not up.—2 *Kings* xxiii. 5.

Bring out the sword, and shut up the way against them that persecute me: say to my soul: I am thy salvation.—*Ps.* xxxiv. 3.

I will give glory to thee because thou hast heard me: and art become my salvation.—*Ps.* cxvii. 21.

Behold, God is my saviour, I will deal confidently, and will not fear: because the Lord is my strength, and my praise, and he is become my salvation.—*Is.* xii. 2.

O Lord, have mercy on us: for we have waited for thee: be thou our arm in the morning, and our salvation in the time of trouble.—*Is.* xxxiii. 2.

SALVATION IS FROM GOD

Salvation is of the Lord: and thy blessing is upon thy people.—*Ps.* iii. 9.

But the salvation of the just is from the Lord, and he is their protector in the time of trouble.—*Ps.* xxxvi. 39.

Shall not my soul be subject to God? for from him is my salvation. . . .

In God is my salvation and my glory: he is the God of my help, and my hope is in God.—*Ps.* lxi. 2, 8.

But God is our king before ages: he hath wrought salvation in the midst of the earth.—*Ps.* lxxiii. 12.

I will fill him with length of days; and I will show him my salvation.— *Ps.* xc. 16.

He hath remembered his mercy and his truth toward the house of Israel.

All the ends of the earth have seen the salvation of our God.—*Ps.* xcvii. 3.

Love God all thy life, and call upon him for thy salvation.—*Ecclus.* xiii. 18.

For at his commandment favor is shown, and there is no diminishing of his salvation.—*Ecclus.* xxxix. 23.

I am, I am the Lord: and there is no saviour besides me.—*Is.* xliii. 11.

Israel is saved in the Lord with an eternal salvation: you shall not be confounded, and you shall not be ashamed for ever and ever.—*Is.* xlv. 17.

I am the door. By me, if any man enter in, he shall be saved: and he shall go in, and go out, and shall find pastures.—*John* x. 9.

Jesus saith to him (Thomas): I am the way, and the truth, and the life. No man cometh to the Father, but by me.—*John* xiv. 6.

These things Jesus spoke, and lifting up his eyes to heaven, he said: Father, the hour is come, glorify thy Son, that thy Son may glorify thee.

As thou hast given him power over all flesh, that he may give eternal life to all whom thou hast given him.— *John* xvii. 1, 2.

For by grace you are saved through faith, and that not of yourselves, for it is the gift of God;

Not of works, that no man may glory.—*Eph.* ii. 8, 9.

But we ought to give thanks to God always for you, brethren, beloved of God, for that God hath chosen you firstfruits unto salvation, in sanctification of the spirit, and faith of the truth.—2 *Thess.* ii. 12.

SALVATION IS FROM GOD, ACKNOWLEDGMENT THAT

My heart hath rejoiced in the Lord, and my horn is exalted in my God: my mouth is enlarged over my enemies: because I have joyed in thy salvation. —1 *Kings* ii. 1.

I will rejoice in thy salvation: the Gentiles have stuck fast in the destruction which they prepared.

Their foot hath been taken in the very snare which they hid.—*Ps.* ix. 16.

But I am poor and sorrowful: thy salvation, O God, hath set me up.— *Ps.* lxviii. 30.

He shall cry out to me: Thou art my father: my God, and the support of my salvation.—*Ps.* lxxxviii, 27.

I looked for thy salvation, O Lord: and I loved thy commandments. . . .

I have longed for thy salvation, O Lord; and thy law is my meditation.— *Ps.* cxviii. 166, 174.

Now thou dost dismiss thy servant, O Lord, according to thy word in peace;

Because my eyes have seen thy salvation,

Which thou hast prepared before the face of all peoples.—*Luke* ii. 29-31.

SANCTITY OF GOD, THE

The Lord spoke to Moses, saying:

Speak to all the congregation of the children of Israel, and thou shalt say to them: Be ye holy, because I the Lord your God am holy.—*Lev.* xix. 1, 2.

Shall man be justified in comparison of God, or shall a man be more pure than his maker?—*Job* iv. 17.

Behold among his saints none is unchangeable, and the heavens are not pure in his sight.—*Job* xv. 15.

Can man be justified compared with God, or he that is born of a woman appear clean?

Behold even the moon doth not shine, and the stars are not pure in his sight. —*Job* xxv. 4, 5.

Once have I sworn by my holiness: I will not lie unto David: his seed shall endure for ever.—*Ps.* lxxxviii. 36, 37.

Rejoice, ye just, in the Lord: and give praise to the remembrance of his holiness.—*Ps.* xcvi. 12.

Exalt ye the Lord our God, and adore at his holy mountain: for the Lord our God is holy.—*Ps.* xcviii. 9.

God hath spoken in his holiness.— *Ps.* cvii. 8.

Go, and proclaim these words towards the north, and thou shalt say: Return, O rebellious Israel, saith the Lord, and I will not turn away my face from you: for I am holy, saith the Lord, and I will not be angry for ever.—*Jer.* iii. 12.

The Lord God hath sworn by his holiness, that lo, the days shall come upon you, when they shall lift you up on pikes, and what shall remain of you in boiling pots.—*Amos* iv. 2.

Be you therefore perfect, as also your heavenly Father is perfect.—*Matt.* v. 48.

SANCTITY OF GOD, ACKNOWLEDGMENT OF THE

Who is like to thee, among the strong, O Lord? who is like to thee, glorious in holiness, terrible and praiseworthy, doing wonders?—*Ex.* xv. 11.

There is none holy as the Lord is: for there is none beside thee, and there is none strong like our God.—1 *Kings* ii. 2.

In the morning I will stand before thee, and will see: because thou art not a God that willest iniquity.

Neither shall the wicked dwell near thee: nor shall the unjust abide before thy eyes.

Thou hatest all the workers of iniquity: thou wilt destroy all that speak a lie.

The bloody and the deceitful man the Lord will abhor.—*Ps.* v. 5-7.

Generation and generation shall praise thy works: and they shall declare thy power.

They shall speak of the magnificence of the glory of thy holiness: and shall tell thy wondrous works.—*Ps.* cxliv. 4, 5.

And they (the seraphim) cried one to another, and said: Holy, holy, holy, the Lord God of hosts, all the earth is full of his glory.—*Is.* vi. 3.

Thy eyes are too pure to behold evil, and thou canst not look on iniquity. Why lookest thou upon them that do unjust things, and holdest thy peace when the wicked devoureth the man that is more just than himself?—*Hab.* i. 13.

And the four living creatures had each of them six wings; and round about and within they are full of eyes. And they rested not day and night, saying: Holy, holy, holy, Lord God Almighty, who was, and who is, and who is to come.—*Apoc.* iv. 8.

Who shall not fear thee, O Lord, and magnify thy name? For thou only art holy: for all nations shall come, and shall adore in thy sight, because thy judgments are manifest.—*Apoc.* xv. 4.

SANCTITY OF CHRIST, THE

And the angel answering, said to her: The Holy Ghost shall come upon thee, and the power of the most High shall overshadow thee. And therefore also the Holy which shall be born of thee, shall be called the Son of God.—*Luke* i. 35.

And it came to pass that when Elisabeth heard the salutation of Mary, the infant leaped in her womb. And Elisabeth was filled with the Holy Ghost: And she cried out with a loud voice, and said: Blessed art thou among women, and blessed is the fruit of thy womb.—*Luke* i. 41, 42.

Which of you shall convince me of sin? If I say the truth to you, why do you not believe me?—*John* viii. 46.

But you denied the Holy One and the Just, and desired a murderer to be granted unto you.—*Acts* iii. 14.

And now, Lord, behold their threatenings, and grant unto thy servants, that with all confidence they may speak thy word,

By stretching forth thy hand to cures, and signs, and wonders to be done by the name of thy holy Son Jesus.—*Acts* iv. 29, 30.

SANCTITY OF GOD'S HOUSE

See: House of God—page 214.

SANCTITY, PERSONAL

And I shall be perfect with him: and shall keep myself from my iniquity.—2 *Kings* xxii. 24.

Preserve my soul, for I am holy: save thy servant, O my God, that trusteth in thee.—*Ps.* lxxxv. 2.

They that fear the Lord, will prepare their hearts, and in his sight will sanctify their souls.—*Ecclus.* ii. 20.

Health of the soul in holiness of justice, is better than all gold and silver: and a sound body, than immense revenues.—*Ecclus.* xxx. 15.

But godliness with contentment is great gain.—1 *Tim.* vi. 6.

And every one that hath this hope in him, sanctifieth himself, as he also is holy.—1 *John* iii. 3.

SANCTITY, GOD CALLS US TO PERSONAL

To all that are at Rome, the beloved of God, called to be saints.—*Rom.* i. 7.

As he chose us in him before the foundation of the world, that we should be holy and unspotted in his sight in charity.—*Eph.* i. 4.

For this is the will of God, your sanctification; that you should abstain from fornication;

That every one of you should know how to possess his vessel in sanctification and honor. . . .

For God hath not called us unto uncleanness, but unto sanctification.—1 *Thess.* iv. 3, 4, 7.

But we ought to give thanks to God always for you, brethren, beloved of God, for that God hath chosen you firstfruits unto salvation, in sanctification of the spirit, and faith of the truth. —2 *Thess.* ii. 12.

For the grace of God our Saviour hath appeared to all men;

Instructing us, that, denying ungodliness and worldly desires, we should live soberly, and justly, and godly in this world,

Looking for the blessed hope and coming of the glory of the great God and our Saviour Jesus Christ.—*Titus* ii. 11-13.

SANCTITY, EXHORTATION TO PERSONAL

The Lord spoke to Moses, saying: Speak to all the congregation of the children of Israel, and thou shalt say to them:

Be ye holy, because I the Lord your God am holy.—*Lev.* xix. 1, 2.

Sanctify yourselves, and be ye holy, because I am the Lord your God.

Keep my precepts, and do them. I am the Lord that sanctify you. . . .

You shall be holy unto me, because I the Lord am holy, and I have separated you from other people, that you should be mine.—*Lev.* xx. 7, 8, 26.

But avoid foolish and old wives' fables: and exercise thyself unto godliness.

For bodily exercise is profitable to little: but godliness is profitable to all things, having promise of the life that now is, and of that which is to come.— 1 *Tim.* iv. 7, 8.

But thou, O man of God, fly these things: and pursue justice, godliness, faith, charity, patience, mildness.— 1 *Tim.* vi. 11.

Follow peace with all men, and holiness: without which no man shall see God.—*Heb.* xii. 14.

But according to him that hath called you, who is holy, be you also in all manner of conversation, holy:

Because it is written: You shall be holy, for I am holy.—1 *Peter* i. 15, 16.

And you, employing all care, minister in your faith, virtue; and in virtue, knowledge;

And in knowledge, abstinence; and in abstinence, patience; and in patience, godliness;

And in godliness, love of brotherhood; and in love of brotherhood, charity.

For if these things be with you and abound, they will make you to be neither empty nor unfruitful in the knowledge of our Lord Jesus Christ.— 2 *Peter* i. 5-8.

SAVED, THE, OR THE ELECT

See also: Saints, the—page 496.

And these are thy servants, and thy people: whom thou hast redeemed by thy great strength, and by thy mighty hand.—2 *Esd.* i. 10.

They that are planted in the house of the Lord shall flourish in the courts of the house of our God.

They shall still increase in a fruitful old age: and shall be well treated, that they may show,

That the Lord our God is righteous, and there is no iniquity in him.—*Ps.* xci. 14-16.

Give glory to the Lord, for he is good: for his mercy endureth for ever.

Let them say so that have been redeemed by the Lord, whom he hath redeemed from the hand of the enemy: and gathered out of the countries.

From the rising and from the setting of the sun, from the north, and from the sea.—*Ps.* cvi. 1-3.

They that trust in him, shall understand the truth: and they that are faithful in love shall rest in him: for grace and peace is to his elect.—*Wis.* iii. 9.

Behold how they are numbered among the children of God, and their lot is among the saints.—*Wis.* v. 5.

And they shall say in that day: Lo, this is our God, we have waited for him, and he will save us: this is the Lord, we have patiently waited for him, we shall rejoice and be joyful in his salvation.—*Is.* xxv. 9.

In that day the Lord of hosts shall be a crown of glory, and a garland of joy to the residue of his people.—*Is.* xxviii. 5.

And my people shall sit in the beauty of peace, and in the tabernacles of confidence, and in wealthy rest.—*Is.* xxxii. 18.

And the redeemed of the Lord shall return, and shall come into Sion with praise, and everlasting joy shall be upon their heads: they shall obtain joy and gladness, and sorrow and mourning shall flee away.—*Is.* xxxv. 10.

Israel is saved in the Lord with an eternal salvation: you shall not be confounded, and you shall not be ashamed for ever and ever.—*Is.* xlv. 17.

Amen I say to you, there hath not risen among them that are born of women, a greater than John the Baptist: yet he that is the lesser in the kingdom of heaven is greater than he. —*Matt.* xi. 11.

And Jesus answering, said to them: You err, not knowing the Scriptures, nor the power of God.

For in the resurrection they shall neither marry nor be married; but shall be as the angels of God in heaven.— *Matt.* xxii. 29, 30.

Fear not, little flock, for it hath pleased your Father to give you a kingdom.—*Luke* xii. 32.

When one of them that sat at table with him, had heard these things, he said to him: Blessed is he that shall eat bread in the kingdom of God.—*Luke* xiv. 15.

But they that shall be accounted worthy of that world, and of the resurrection from the dead, shall neither be married, nor take wives.

Neither can they die any more: for they are equal to the angels, and are the children of God, being the children of the resurrection.—*Luke* xx. 35, 36.

These shall fight with the Lamb, and the Lamb shall overcome them, because he is Lord of lords, and King of kings, and they that are with him are called, and elect, and faithful.—*Apoc.* xvii. 14.

And he said to me: Write: Blessed are they that are called to the marriage supper of the Lamb. And he saith to me: These words of God are true.—*Apoc.* xix. 9.

Blessed and holy is he that hath part in the first resurrection. In these the second death hath no power; but they shall be priests of God and of Christ; and shall reign with him a thousand years.—*Apoc.* xx. 6.

There shall not enter into it (the new Jerusalem) any thing defiled, or that worketh abomination or maketh a lie, but they that are written in the book of life of the Lamb.—*Apoc.* xxi. 27.

SAVED, THE SMALL NUMBER OF THE

How narrow is the gate, and strait is the way that leadeth to life: and few there are that find it!—*Matt.* vii. 14.

So shall the last be first, and the first last. For many are called, but few are chosen.—*Matt.* xx. 16.

Strive to enter by the narrow gate; for many, I say to you, shall seek to enter, and shall not be able.—*Luke* xiii. 24.

SAVED, A PRAYER TO BE

Save us, O God our saviour: and gather us together, and deliver us from the nations, that we may give glory to thy holy name, and may rejoice in singing thy praises.—1 *Paral.* xvi. 35.

Who will grant me this, that thou mayst protect me in hell, and hide me till thy wrath pass, and appoint me a time when thou wilt remember me?—*Job* xiv. 13.

I will not fear thousands of the people, surrounding me: arise, O Lord; save me, O my God.—*Ps.* iii. 7.

Turn to me, O Lord, and deliver my soul: O save me for thy mercy's sake.—*Ps.* vi. 5.

But thou, O Lord, remove not thy help to a distance from me; look towards my defence.

Deliver, O God, my soul from the sword: my only one from the hand of the dog.

Save me from the lion's mouth; and my lowness from the horns of the unicorns.—*Ps.* xxi. 20-22.

Keep thou my soul, and deliver me: I shall not be ashamed, for I have hoped in thee.—*Ps.* xxiv. 20.

But as for me, I have walked in my innocence: redeem me, and have mercy on me.—*Ps.* xxv. 11.

Save, O Lord, thy people, and bless thy inheritance: and rule them, and exalt them for ever.—*Ps.* xxvii. 9.

Make thy face to shine upon thy servant; save me in thy mercy.

Let me not be confounded, O Lord, for I have called upon thee.—*Ps.* xxx. 17, 18.

Save me, O God: for the waters are come in even unto my soul. . . .

Draw me out of the mire, that I may not stick fast: deliver me from them that hate me, and out of the deep waters.

Let not the tempest of water drown me, nor the deep swallow me up: and let not the pit shut her mouth upon me.

. . . Attend to my soul, and deliver it: save me because of my enemies.—*Ps.* lxviii. 2, 15, 16, 19.

Stir up thy might, and come to save us.

Convert us, O God: and show us thy face, and we shall be saved.—*Ps.* lxxix. 3, 4.

Show us, O Lord, thy mercy; and grant us thy salvation.—*Ps.* lxxxiv. 8.

Preserve my soul, for I am holy: save thy servant, O my God, that trusteth in thee. . . .

O look upon me, and have mercy on me: give thy command to thy servant, and save the son of thy handmaid.—*Ps.* lxxxv. 2, 16.

Remember us, O Lord, in the favor of thy people: visit us with thy salvation.

That we may see the good of thy chosen, that we may rejoice in the joy of thy nation: that thou mayst be praised with thy inheritance.—*Ps.* cv. 4, 5.

Be thou exalted, O God, above the heavens, and thy glory over all the earth: that thy beloved may be delivered.

Save with thy right hand and hear me.—*Ps.* cvii. 6, 7.

Help me, O Lord my God; save me according to thy mercy.

And let them know that this is thy hand: and that thou, O Lord, hast done it.—*Ps.* cviii. 26, 27.

I am thine, save thou me: for I have sought thy justifications. . .

Let thy hand be with me to save me; for I have chosen thy precepts. . . .

I have gone astray like a sheep that is lost: seek thy servant, because I have not forgotten thy commandments.—*Ps.* cxviii. 94, 173, 176.

Bring my soul out of prison, that I may praise thy name: the just wait for me, until thou reward me.—*Ps.* cxli. 8.

O Lord, have mercy on us: for we have waited for thee: be thou our arm in the morning, and our salvation in the time of trouble.—*Is.* xxxiii. 2.

Heal me, O Lord, and I shall be healed: save me, and I shall be saved: for thou art my praise.—*Jer.* xvii. 14.

And lead us not into temptation. But deliver us from evil. Amen.—*Matt.* vi. 13.

And behold a great tempest arose in the sea, so that the boat was covered with waves, but he was asleep.

And they came to him, and awaked him, saying: Lord, save us, we perish. —*Matt.* viii. 24, 25.

And he said to Jesus: Lord, remember me, when thou shalt come into thy kingdom.—*Luke* xxiii. 42.

SCANDAL

See also: Leading others into evil— page 276.

Wherefore the sin of the [1]young men was exceeding great before the Lord: because they withdrew men from the sacrifice of the Lord.—*1 Kings* ii. 17.

Sitting, thou didst speak against thy brother, and didst lay a scandal against thy mother's son: these things hast thou done, and I was silent.

Thou thoughtest unjustly that I should be like to thee: but I will reprove thee, and set before thy face.— *Ps.* xlix. 20, 21.

Let not them be ashamed for me, who look for thee, O Lord, the Lord of hosts.

Let them not be confounded on my account, who seek thee, O God of Israel.—*Ps.* lxviii. 7.

If the Ethiopian can change his skin, or the leopard his spots: you also may do well, when you have learned evil.—*Jer.* xiii. 23.

But woe is to you scribes and Pharisees, hypocrites; because you shut the kingdom of heaven against men, for you yourselves do not enter in; and those that are going in, you suffer not to enter.—*Matt.* xxiii. 13.

Thou that makest thy boast of the law, by trangression of the law dishonorest God.

(For the name of God through you is blasphemed among the Gentiles, as it is written).—*Rom.* ii. 23, 24.

Let us not therefore judge one another any more. But judge this rather, that you put not a stumbling-block or a scandal in your brother's way. . . .

It is good not to eat flesh, and not

[1]The two wicked sons of the high priest Heli.

to drink wine, nor any thing whereby thy brother is offended, or scandalized, or made weak.—*Rom.* xiv. 13, 21.

Your glorying is not good. Know you not that a little leaven corrupteth the whole lump?—*1 Cor.* v. 6.

But take heed lest perhaps this your liberty become a stumbling-block to the weak.

For if a man see him that hath knowledge sit at meat in the idol's temple, shall not his conscience, being weak, be emboldened to eat those things which are sacrificed to idols?

And through thy knowledge shall the weak brother perish, for whom Christ hath died?

Now when you sin thus against the brethren, and wound their weak conscience, you sin against Christ.

Wherefore, if meat scandalize my brother, I will never eat flesh, lest I should scandalize my brother.—*1 Cor.* viii. 9-13.

You did run well, who hath hindered you, that you should not obey the truth? . . .

I have confidence in you in the Lord: that you will not be of another mind: but he that troubleth you, shall bear the judgment, whosoever he be. . . .

I would they were even cut off, who trouble you.—*Gal.* v. 7, 10, 12.

SCANDAL, THE PUNISHMENT OF

If thy brother the son of thy mother, or thy son, or daughter, or thy wife that is in thy bosom, or thy friend, whom thou lovest as thy own soul, would persuade thee secretly, saying: Let us go, and serve strange gods, which thou knowest not, nor thy fathers. . . .

Consent not to him, hear him not, neither let thy eye spare him to pity and conceal him,

But thou shalt presently put him to death. Let thy hand be first upon him. and afterwards the hands of all the people.

With stones shall he be stoned to death: because he would have withdrawn thee from the Lord thy God, who brought thee out of the land of Egypt, from the house of bondage:

That all Israel hearing may fear, and

may do no more any thing like this.—*Deut.* xiii. 6, 8-11.

Nevertheless, 'because thou hast given occasion to the enemies of the Lord to blaspheme, for this thing, the child that is born to thee, shall surely die.—*2 Kings* xii. 14.

The Son of man shall send his angels, and they shall gather out of his kingdom all scandals, and them that work iniquity.

And shall cast them into the furnace of fire: there shall be weeping and gnashing of teeth.—*Matt.* xiii. 41, 42.

But he that shall scandalize one of these little ones that believe in me, it were better for him that a millstone should be hanged about his neck, and that he should be drowned in the depth of the sea.

Woe to the world because of scandals. For it must needs be that scandals come: but nevertheless woe to that man by whom the scandal cometh.

And if thy hand, or thy foot scandalize thee, cut it off, and cast it from thee. It is better for thee to go into life maimed or lame, than having two hands or two feet, to be cast into everlasting fire.

And if thy eye scandalize thee, pluck it out, and cast it from thee. It is better for thee having one eye to enter into life, than having two eyes to be cast into hell fire.—*Matt.* xviii. 6-9.

SCOFFER, THE

For every mocker is an abomination to the Lord, and his communication is with the simple. . . .

He shall scorn the scorners, and to the meek he will give grace.—*Prov.* iii. 32, 34.

Rebuke not a scorner lest he hate thee.

Rebuke a wise man, and he will love thee.—*Prov.* ix. 8.

If thou be wise, thou shalt be so to thyself: and if a scorner, thou alone shalt bear the evil.—*Prov.* ix. 12.

A wise son heareth the doctrine of his father: but he that is a scorner, heareth not when he is reproved.—*Prov.* xiii. 1.

'Nathan upbraiding David for his sin against Urias the Hethite.

Good instruction shall give grace: in the way of scorners is a deep pit.—*Prov.* xiii. 15.

A scorner seeketh wisdom, and findeth it not: the learning of the wise is easy.—*Prov.* xiv. 6.

Judgments are prepared for scorners; and striking hammers for the bodies of fools.—*Prov.* xix. 29.

Cast out the scoffer, and contention shall go out with him, and quarrels and reproaches shall cease.—*Prov.* xxii. 10.

Mockery and reproach are of the proud, and vengeance as a lion shall lie in wait for him.—*Ecclus.* xxvii. 31.

A friend that is a mocker, is like a stallion horse: he neigheth under every one that sitteth upon him.—*Ecclus.* xxxiii. 6.

And now do not mock, lest your bonds be tied strait. For I have heard of the Lord the God of hosts a consumption and a cutting short upon all the earth.—*Is.* xxviii. 22.

For he that did prevail hath failed, the scorner is consumed, and they are all cut off that watched for iniquity.—*Is.* xxix. 20.

But you, my dearly beloved, be mindful of the words which have been spoken before by the apostles of our Lord Jesus Christ,

Who told you that in the last time there should come mockers, walking according to their own desires in ungodlinesses.—*Jude* i. 17, 18.

SEARCHER OF HEARTS, GOD THE

And the Lord said to Samuel: Look not on his countenance, nor on the height of his stature: because I have rejected him, nor do I judge according to the look of man: for man seeth those things that appear, but the Lord beholdeth the heart.—*1 Kings* xvi. 7.

And thou my son Solomon, know the God of thy father, and serve him with a perfect heart, and a willing mind: for the Lord searcheth all hearts, and understandeth all the thoughts of minds.—*1 Paral.* xxviii. 9.

For behold my witness is in heaven, and he that knoweth my conscience is on high.—*Job* xvi. 20.

The Lord is in his holy temple, the Lord's throne is in heaven.

His eyes look on the poor man: his eyelids examine the sons of men.—*Ps.* x. 5.

If we have forgotten the name of our God, and if we have spread forth our hands to a strange god:

Shall not God search out these things: for he knoweth the secrets of the heart.—*Ps.* xliii. 21, 22.

The Lord knoweth the thoughts of men, that they are vain.—*Ps.* xciii. 11.

Hell and destruction are before the Lord: how much more the hearts of the children of men?—*Prov.* xv. 11.

All the ways of a man are open to his eyes: the Lord is the weigher of spirits.—*Prov.* xvi. 2.

Every way of a man seemeth right to himself: but the Lord weigheth the hearts.—*Prov.* xxi. 2.

If thou say: I have not strength enough: he that seeth into the heart, he understandeth, and nothing deceiveth the keeper of thy soul, and he shall render to a man according to his works.—*Prov.* xxiv. 12.

For the spirit of wisdom is benevolent, and will not acquit the evil speaker from his lips: for God is witness of his reins, and he is a true searcher of his heart, and a hearer of his tongue.—*Wis.* i. 6.

For power is given you by the Lord, and strength by the most High, who will examine your works, and search out your thoughts.—*Wis.* vi. 4.

Justify not thyself before God, for he knoweth the heart.—*Ecclus.* vii. 5.

And in all these things the heart is senseless: and every heart is understood by him.—*Ecclus.* xvi. 20.

And he knoweth not that the eyes of the Lord are far brighter than the sun, beholding round about all the ways of men, and the bottom of the deep, and looking into the hearts of men, into the most hidden parts.—*Ecclus.* xxiii. 28.

He that searched out the deep, and the heart of men: and considered their crafty devices. . . .

No thought escapeth him, and no word can hide itself from him.—*Ecclus.* xlii. 18, 20.

Woe to you that are deep of heart,

to hide your counsel from the Lord: and their works are in the dark, and they say: Who seeth us, and who knoweth us?

This thought of yours is perverse: as if the clay should think against the potter, and the work should say to the maker thereof: Thou madest me not: or the thing framed should say to him that fashioned it: Thou understandest not.—*Is.* xxix. 15, 16.

The heart is perverse above all things, and unsearchable, who can know it?

I am the Lord who search the heart, and prove the reins: who give to every one according to his way, and according to the fruit of his devices.—*Jer.* xvii. 9, 10.

And behold some of the scribes said within themselves: He blasphemeth.

And Jesus seeing their thoughts, said: Why do you think evil in your hearts?—*Matt.* ix. 3, 4.

And the scribes and Pharisees watched if he would heal on the sabbath; that they might find an accusation against him.

But he knew their thoughts; and said to the man who had the withered hand: Arise, and stand forth in the midst.—*Luke* vi. 7, 8.

And there entered a thought into them (the disciples), which of them should be greater.

But Jesus, seeing the thoughts of their heart, took a child and set him by him.—*Luke* ix. 46, 47.

And he said to them (the Pharisees): You are they who justify yourselves before men, but God knoweth your hearts; for that which is high to men, is an abomination before God.—*Luke* xvi. 15.

But Jesus did not trust himself unto them, for that he knew all men,

And because he needed not that any should give testimony of man: for he knew what was in man.—*John* ii. 24, 25.

And he that searcheth the hearts, knoweth what the Spirit desireth; because he asketh for the saints according to God.—*Rom.* viii. 27.

And to the angel of the church of Thyatira write: These things saith the Son of God, who hath his eyes like to a flame of fire, and his feet like to fine brass. . . .

And all the churches shall know that I am he that searcheth the reins and hearts, and I will give to every one of you according to your works.—*Apoc.* ii. 18, 23.

SEARCHER OF HEARTS, ACKNOWLEDGMENT THAT GOD IS THE

Whatsoever curse or imprecation shall happen to any man of thy people Israel: when a man shall know the wound of his own heart, and shall spread forth his hands in this house,

Then hear thou in heaven, in the place of thy dwelling, and forgive, and do so as to give to every one according to his ways, as thou shalt see his heart (for thou only knowest the heart of all the children of men).—*3 Kings* viii. 38, 39.

I know that thou canst do all things, and no thought is hid from thee.—*Job* xlii. 2.

The wickedness of sinners shall be brought to nought: and thou shalt direct the just: the searcher of hearts and reins is God.—*Ps.* vii. 10.

Lord, thou hast proved me, and known me: thou hast known my sitting down, and my rising up.

Thou hast understood my thoughts afar off: my path and my line thou hast searched out.

And thou hast foreseen all my ways: for there is no speech in my tongue.—*Ps.* cxxxviii. 1-4.

And praying, they said: Thou, Lord, who knowest the hearts of all men, show whether of these two thou hast chosen,

To take the place of this ministry and apostleship, from which Judas hath by transgression fallen, that he might go to his own place.—*Acts* i. 24, 25.

SEEKING AFTER GOD

Who will grant me that I might know and find him, and come even to his throne?—*Job* xxiii. 3.

We can not find him worthily: he is great in strength, and in judgment, and in justice, and he is ineffable.—*Job* xxxvii. 23.

My heart hath said to thee: My face hath sought thee: thy face, O Lord, will I still seek.—*Ps.* xxvi. 8.

Let all that seek thee rejoice and be glad in thee: and let such as love thy salvation say always: The Lord be magnified.—*Ps.* xxxix. 17.

Glory ye in his holy name: let the heart of them rejoice that seek the Lord.—*Ps.* civ. 3.

Blessed are they that search his testimonies: that seek him with their whole heart.—*Ps.* cxviii. 2.

With my whole heart have I sought after thee: let me not stray from thy commandments.—*Ps.* cxviii. 10.

Evil men think not on judgment: but they that seek after the Lord, take notice of all things.—*Prov.* xxviii. 5.

I have not spoken in secret, in a dark place of the earth: I have not said to the seed of Jacob: Seek me in vain. I am the Lord that speak justice, that declare right things.—*Is.* xlv. 19.

And now we follow thee with all our heart, and we fear thee, and seek thy face.

Put us not to confusion, but deal with us according to thy meekness, and according to the multitude of thy mercies.—*Dan.* iii. 41, 42.

When Jesus therefore was born in Bethlehem of Juda, in the days of king Herod, behold, there came wise men from the east to Jerusalem,

Saying, Where is he that is born king of the Jews? For we have seen his star in the east, and are come to adore him.—*Matt.* ii. 1, 2.

And hath made of one, all mankind, to dwell upon the whole face of the earth, determining appointed times, and the limits of their habitation.

That they should seek God, if happily they may feel after him, or find him, although he be not far from every one of us.—*Acts* xvii. 26, 27.

SEEKING AFTER GOD, THE REWARD OF

And when thou shalt seek there the Lord thy God, thou shalt find him: yet so, if thou seek him with all thy heart, and all the affliction of thy soul.—*Deut.* iv. 29.

And thou my son Solomon, know the God of thy father, and serve him with a perfect heart, and a willing mind. . . . If thou seek him, thou shalt find him: but if thou forsake him, he will cast thee off for ever.—1 *Paral.* xxviii. 9.

And when in their distress, they shall return to the Lord the God of Israel, and shall seek him, they shall find him. —2 *Paral.* xv. 4.

For with all their heart they swore, and with all their will they sought him, and they found him, and the Lord gave them rest round about.—2 *Paral.* xv. 15.

And Ezechias prayed for them, saying: The Lord who is good will show mercy,

To all them who, with their whole heart, seek the Lord the God of their fathers.—2 *Paral.* xxx. 18, 19.

The hand of our God is upon all them that seek him in goodness: and his power and strength, and wrath upon all them that forsake him.—1 *Esd.* viii. 22.

And let them trust in thee who know thy name: for thou hast not forsaken them that seek thee, O Lord.—*Ps.* ix. 11.

The poor shall eat and shall be filled: and they shall praise the Lord that seek him: their hearts shall live for ever and ever.—*Ps.* xxi. 27.

Who shall ascend into the mountain of the Lord: or who shall stand in his holy place?

The innocent in hands, and clean of heart, who hath not taken his soul in vain, nor sworn deceitfully to his neighbor.

He shall receive a blessing from the Lord, and mercy from God his Saviour. This is the generation of them that seek him, of them that seek the face of the God of Jacob.—*Ps.* xxiii. 3-6.

The rich have wanted, and have suffered hunger: but they that seek the Lord, shall not be deprived of any good. —*Ps.* xxxiii. 11.

I love them that love me: and they that in the morning early watch for me, shall find me. . . .

He that shall find me, shall find life, and shall have salvation from the Lord. —*Prov.* viii. 17, 35.

I am a wall: and my breasts are as a tower since I am become in his pres-ence as one finding peace.—*Cant.* viii. 10.

For God is compassionate and merciful, and will forgive sins in the day of tribulation: and he is a protector to all that seek him in truth.—*Ecclus.* ii. 13.

He that feareth the Lord, will receive his discipline: and they that will seek him early, shall find a blessing.— *Ecclus.* xxxii. 18.

You shall seek me, and shall find me: when you shall seek me with all your heart.—*Jer.* xxix. 13.

The Lord is good to them that hope in him, to the soul that seeketh him.— *Lam.* iii. 25.

SEEK AFTER GOD, EXHORTATION TO

Give therefore your hearts and your souls, to seek the Lord your God.— 1 *Paral.* xxii. 19.

Let the poor see and rejoice: seek ye God, and your soul shall live.—*Ps.* lxviii. 33.

Seek ye the Lord, and be strengthened: seek his face evermore.—*Ps.* civ. 4.

Think of the Lord in goodness, and seek him in simplicity of heart.

For he is found by them that tempt him not: and he showeth himself to them that have faith in him.—*Wis.* i. 1, 2.

Seek ye the Lord, while he may be found: call upon him, while he is near. —*Is.* lv. 6.

For thus saith the Lord to the house of Israel: Seek ye me, and you shall live. . . .

Seek ye the Lord, and live.—*Amos.* v. 4, 6.

Seek the Lord, all ye meek of the earth, you that have wrought his judgment: seek the just, seek the meek: if by any means you may be hid in the day of the Lord's indignation.—*Soph.* ii. 3.

Be not solicitous, therefore, saying, What shall we eat: or what shall we drink, or wherewith shall we be clothed?

For after all these things do the heathens seek. For your Father knoweth that you have need of all these things.

Seek ye therefore first the kingdom

of God, and his justice, and all these things shall be added unto you.—*Matt.* vi. 31-33.

SEEKING GOD'S DOCTRINE AND TRUTH

He hath loved the people, all the saints are in his hand: and they that approach to his feet, shall receive of his doctrine.—*Deut.* xxxiii. 3.

If I have erred, teach thou me: if I have spoken iniquity, I will add no more.—*Job* xxxiv. 32.

In his hands he hideth the light, and commandeth it to come again.

He showeth his friend concerning it, that it is his possession, and that he may come up to it.—*Job* xxxvi. 32, 33.

Show, O Lord, thy ways to me, and teach me thy paths.

Direct me in thy truth, and teach me; for thou art God my Saviour; and on thee have I waited all the day long. —*Ps.* xxiv. 4, 5.

Send forth thy light and thy truth: they have conducted me, and brought me unto thy holy hill, and into thy tabernacles.

And I will go in to the altar of God: to God who giveth joy to my youth.— *Ps.* xlii. 3, 4.

Conduct me, O Lord, in thy way, and I will walk in thy truth: let my heart rejoice that it may fear thy name.— *Ps.* lxxxv. 11.

SEEKING GOD'S WILL AND LAW

All the ways of the Lord are mercy and truth, to them that seek after his covenant and his testimonies.—*Ps.* xxiv. 10.

Blessed is the man whom thou shalt instruct, O Lord: and shalt teach him out of thy law.—*Ps.* xciii. 12.

Set before me for a law the way of thy justifications, O Lord: and I will always seek after it.

Give me understanding, and I will search thy law; and I will keep it with my whole heart.

Lead me unto the path of thy commandments; for this same I have desired.—*Ps.* cxviii. 33-35.

The iniquity of the proud hath been multiplied over me: but I will seek thy commandments with my whole heart.—*Ps.* cxviii. 69.

Make the way known to me, wherein I should walk: for I have lifted up my soul to thee. . . .

Teach me to do thy will, for thou art my God.—*Ps.* cxlii. 8, 10.

They that fear the Lord, will seek after the things that are well pleasing to him: and they that love him, shall be filled with his law.—*Ecclus.* ii. 19.

He that seeketh the law, shall be filled with it: and he that dealeth deceitfully, shall meet with a stumbling-block therein.—*Ecclus.* xxxii. 19.

I cannot of myself do any thing. As I hear, so I judge: and my judgment is just; because I seek not my own will, but the will of him that sent me.—*John* v. 30.

SELF-CONTROL

The patient man is better than the valiant: and he that ruleth his spirit, than he that taketh cities.—*Prov.* xvi. 32.

Have pity on thy own soul, pleasing God, and contain thyself: gather up thy heart in his holiness: and drive away sadness far from thee.—*Ecclus.* xxx. 24.

My son, prove thy soul in thy life: and if it be wicked, give it no power.— *Ecclus.* xxxvii. 30.

SELF-DENIAL

And he that taketh not up his cross, and followeth me, is not worthy of me. —*Matt.* x. 38.

And whosoever doth not carry his cross, and come after me, cannot be my disciple.—*Luke* xiv. 27.

So likewise every one of you that doth not renounce all that he possesseth, cannot be my disciple.—*Luke* xiv. 33.

Who said to them: Amen, I say to you, there is no man that hath left house, or parents, or brethren, or wife, or children, for the kingdom of God's sake,

Who shall not receive much more in this present time, and in the world to come life everlasting.—*Luke* xviii. 29, 30.

Now if we be dead with Christ, we

believe that we shall live also together with Christ.—*Rom.* vi. 8.

For if you live according to the flesh, you shall die: but if by the Spirit you mortify the deeds of the flesh, you shall live.—*Rom.* viii. 13.

Know you not that they that run in the race, all run indeed, but one receiveth the prize? So run that you may obtain.

And every one that striveth for the mastery, refraineth himself from all things: and they indeed that they may receive a corruptible crown; but we an incorruptible one.—1 *Cor.* ix. 24, 25.

But I chastise my body, and bring it into subjection: lest perhaps, when I have preached to others, I myself should become a castaway.—1 *Cor.* ix. 27.

I die daily, I protest by your glory, brethren, which I have in Christ Jesus our Lord.—1 *Cor.* xv. 31.

Always bearing about in our body the mortification of Jesus, that the life also of Jesus may be made manifest in our bodies.—2 *Cor.* iv. 10.

With Christ I am nailed to the cross. And I live, now not I; but Christ liveth in me.—*Gal.* ii. 19, 20.

And they that are Christ's, have crucified their flesh, with the vices and concupiscences.—*Gal.* v. 24.

But God forbid that I should glory, save in the cross of our Lord Jesus Christ; by whom the world is crucified to me, and I to the world.—*Gal.* vi. 14.

Who now rejoice in my sufferings for you, and fill up those things that are wanting of the sufferings of Christ, in my flesh, for his body, which is the church.—*Col.* i. 24.

SELF-DENIAL, EXHORTATION TO

Then Jesus said to his disciples: If any man will come after me, let him deny himself, and take up his cross, and follow me.

For he that will save his life, shall lose it: and he that shall lose his life for my sake, shall find it.

For what doth it profit a man, if he gain the whole world, and suffer the loss of his own soul? Or what exchange shall a man give for his soul?—*Matt.* xvi. 24-26.

And he said to all: If any man will come after me, let him deny himself, and take up his cross daily, and follow me.—*Luke* ix. 23.

I beseech you therefore, brethren, by the mercy of God, that you present your bodies a living sacrifice, holy, pleasing unto God, your reasonable service.—*Rom.* xii. 1.

If then you be dead with Christ from the elements of this world, why do you yet decree as though living in the world?—*Col.* ii. 20.

Mortify therefore your members which are upon the earth; fornication, uncleanness, lust, evil concupiscence, and covetousness, which is the service of idols.—*Col.* iii. 5.

SELF-PRAISE

See: Boasting—page 41.

SELF-SUFFICIENCY

Have confidence in the Lord with all thy heart, and lean not upon thy own prudence. . . .

Be not wise in thy own conceit.— *Prov.* iii. 5, 7.

He that trusteth in his own heart, is a fool; but he that walketh wisely, he shall be saved.—*Prov.* xxviii. 26.

Follow not in thy strength the desires of thy heart:

And say not: How mighty am I? and who shall bring me under for my deeds? for God will surely take revenge.— *Ecclus.* v. 2, 3.

Say not: What need I, and what good shall I have by this?

Say not: I am sufficient for myself: and what shall I be made worse by this? —*Ecclus.* xi. 25, 26.

Woe to you, apostate children, saith the Lord, that you would take counsel, and not of me: and would begin a web, and not by my spirit, that you might add sin upon sin:

Who walk to go down into Egypt, and have not asked at my mouth, hoping for help in the strength of Pharao, and trusting in the shadow of Egypt.—*Is.* xxx. 1, 2.

I know, O Lord, that the way of a

man is not his: neither is it in a man to walk, and to direct his steps.—*Jer.* x. 23.

And such confidence we have, through Christ, towards God.

Not that we are sufficient to think any thing of ourselves, as of ourselves: but our sufficiency is from God.—*2 Cor.* iii. 4, 5.

SELF-WILL, OR OBSTINACY

The rod and reproof give wisdom: but the child that is left to his own will, bringeth his mother to shame.—*Prov.* xxix. 15.

A horse not broken becometh stubborn, and a child left to himself will become headstrong.—*Ecclus.* xxx. 8.

Know also this, that, in the last days, shall come dangerous times.

Men shall be lovers of themselves, . . .

Traitors, stubborn, puffed up, and lovers of pleasures more than of God. —*2 Tim.* iii. 1, 2, 4.

SELF, DISTRUST OF

See: Distrust of self—page 117.

SELF, FORGETFULNESS OF

See: Forgetfulness of self—page 155.

SELFISHNESS

Let not thy hand be stretched out to receive, and shut when thou shouldst give.—*Ecclus.* iv. 36.

There is one that is enriched by living sparingly, and this is the portion of his reward.

In that he saith: I have found me rest, and now I will eat of my goods alone:

And he knoweth not what time shall pass, and that death approacheth, and that he must leave all to others, and shall die.—*Ecclus.* xi. 18-20.

Against him that is niggardly of his bread, the city will murmur, and the testimony of his niggardliness is true. —*Ecclus.* xxxi. 29.

For all seek the things that are their own; not the things that are Jesus Christ's.—*Philipp.* ii. 21.

SENSITIVENESS

But do not apply thy heart to all words that are spoken: lest perhaps thou hear thy servant reviling thee.

For thy conscience knoweth that thou also hast often spoken evil of others.— *Eccles.* vii. 22, 23.

SERVANTS, THE DUTY OF

See: Obedience to lay superiors— page 348.

SERVICE OF GOD, THE

But yet they shall serve him (the king of Egypt), that they may know the difference between my service, and the service of a kingdom of the earth.— *2 Paral.* xii. 8.

Son, when thou comest to the service of God, stand in justice and in fear, and prepare thy soul for temptation.— *Ecclus.* ii. 1.

Your words have been unsufferable to me, saith the Lord.

And you have said: What have we spoken against thee? You have said: He laboreth in vain that serveth God, and what profit is it that we have kept his ordinances, and that we have walked sorrowful before the Lord of hosts? . . .

And you shall return, and shall see the difference between the just and the wicked: and between him that serveth God, and him that serveth him not.— *Malach.* iii. 13, 14, 18.

The kingdom of heaven is like unto a treasure hidden in a field. Which a man having found, hid it, and for joy thereof goeth, and selleth all that he hath, and buyeth that field.

Again the kingdom of heaven is like to a merchant seeking good pearls.

Who when he had found one pearl of great price, went his way, and sold all that he had, and bought it.—*Matt.* xiii. 44-46.

Know you not, that to whom you yield yourselves servants to obey, his servants you are whom you obey, whether it be of sin unto death, or of obedience unto justice.—*Rom.* vi. 16.

But we are confident, and have a good will to be absent rather from the body, and to be present with the Lord.

And therefore we labor, whether absent or present, to please him.—2 *Cor.* v. 8, 9.

SERVICE OF GOD A DUTY OF JUSTICE, THE

And now, Israel, what doth the Lord thy God require of thee, but that thou fear the Lord thy God, and walk in his ways, and love him, and serve the Lord thy God, with all thy heart, and with all thy soul:

And keep the commandments of the Lord, and his ceremonies, which I command thee this day, that it may be well with thee?—*Deut.* x. 12, 13.

Who am I, and what is my people, that we should be able to promise thee all these things? all things are thine: and we have given thee what we received of thy hand.—1 *Paral.* xxix. 14.

Then Jesus saith to him: Begone, Satan: for it is written, The Lord thy God shalt thou adore, and him only shalt thou serve.—*Matt.* iv. 10.

But which of you having a servant ploughing, or feeding cattle, will say to him, when he is come from the field: Immediately go, sit down to meat:

And will not rather say to him: Make ready my supper, and gird thyself, and serve me whilst I eat and drink, and afterwards thou shalt eat and drink?

Doth he thank that servant, for doing the things which he commanded him?

I think not. So you also, when you shall have done all these things that are commanded you, say: We are unprofitable servants; we have done that which we ought to do.—*Luke* xvii. 7-10.

For the charity of Christ presseth us: judging this, that if one died for all, then all are dead.

And Christ died for all, that they also who live, may not now live to themselves, but unto him who died for them, and rose again.—2 *Cor.* v. 14, 15.

SERVICE OF GOD A PRIVILEGE, THE

See also: Happiness in serving God —page 193.

But it is good for me to adhere to my God, to put my hope in the Lord God:

That I may declare all thy praises, in the gates of the daughter of Sion.—*Ps.* lxxii. 28.

It is great glory to follow the Lord: for length of days shall be received from him.—*Ecclus.* xxiii. 38.

Take up my yoke upon you, and learn of me, because I am meek and humble of heart: and you shall find rest to your souls.

For my yoke is sweet and my burden light.—*Matt.* xi. 29, 30.

SERVICE OF GOD SHOULD BE A WILLING SERVICE, THE

So Jacob served seven years for Rachel: and they seemed but a few days, because of the greatness of his love.—*Gen.* xxix. 20.

Set aside with you firstfruits to the Lord. Let every one that is willing and hath a ready heart, offer them to the Lord.—*Ex.* xxxv. 5.

And thou my son Solomon, know the God of thy father, and serve him with a perfect heart, and a willing mind: for the Lord searcheth all hearts, and understandeth all the thoughts of minds.—1 *Paral.* xxviii. 9.

Delight in the Lord, and he will give thee the requests of thy heart.—*Ps.* xxxvi. 4.

Sing joyfully to God, all the earth: serve ye the Lord with gladness.

Come in before his presence with exceeding great joy.—*Ps.* xcix. 2.

I have inclined my heart to do thy justifications for ever, for the reward. —*Ps.* cxviii. 112.

My soul hath kept thy testimonies: and hath loved them exceedingly.—*Ps.* cxviii. 167.

My son, give me thy heart: and let thy eyes keep my ways.—*Prov.* xxiii. 26.

Give glory to God with a good heart: and diminish not the firstfruits of thy hands.

In every gift show a cheerful countenance, and sanctify thy tithes with joy. —*Ecclus.* xxxv. 10, 11.

May God be gracious to you, and remember his covenant that he made with Abraham, and Isaac, and Jacob, his faithful servants:

And give you all a heart to worship

him, and to do his will with a great heart, and a willing mind.—2 *Mach.* i. 2, 3.

SERVICE OF GOD, EARNEST-NESS IN THE

And now, Israel, what doth the Lord thy God require of thee, but that thou fear the Lord thy God, and walk in his ways, and love him, and serve the Lord thy God, with all thy heart, and with all thy soul.—*Deut.* x. 12.

This day the Lord thy God hath commanded thee to do these commandments and judgments: and to keep and fulfil them with all thy heart, and with all thy soul.—*Deut.* xxvi. 16.

Therefore fear the Lord, and serve him in truth and with your whole heart, for you have seen the great works which he hath done among you.— 1 *Kings* xii. 24.

Lord God of Israel, there is no God like thee in heaven above, or on earth beneath: who keepest covenant and mercy with thy servants that have walked before thee with all their heart. —3 *Kings* viii. 23.

Hearken therefore, my children, to your father: serve the Lord in truth, and seek to do the things that please him:

And command your children that they do justice and almsdeeds, and that they be mindful of God, and bless him at all times in truth, and with all their power.—*Tob.* xiv. 10, 11.

Give me understanding, and I will search thy law; and I will keep it with my whole heart.—*Ps.* cxviii. 34.

Cursed be he that doth the work of the Lord ¹deceitfully.—*Jer.* xlviii. 10.

And now we follow thee with all our heart, and we fear thee, and seek thy face.—*Dan.* iii. 41.

Jesus said to him: No man putting his hand to the plough, and looking back, is fit for the kingdom of God.— *Luke* ix. 62.

In carefulness not slothful. In spirit fervent. Serving the Lord.—*Rom.* xii. 11.

Know you not that they that run in the race, all run indeed, but one receiv-

¹In the Greek, negligently.

eth the prize? So run that you may obtain.

And every one that striveth for the mastery, refraineth himself from all things: and they indeed that they may receive a corruptible crown; but we an incorruptible one.

I therefore so run, not as at an uncertainty: I so fight, not as one beating the air.—1 *Cor.* ix. 24-26.

Brethren, I do not count myself to have apprehended. But one thing I do: forgetting the things that are behind, and stretching forth myself to those that are before,

I press towards the mark, to the prize of the supernal vocation of God, in Christ Jesus.—*Philipp.* iii. 13, 14.

Whatsoever you do, do it from the heart, as to the Lord, and not to men:

Knowing that you shall receive of the Lord the reward of inheritance. Serve ye the Lord Christ.—*Col.* iii. 23, 24.

SERVICE OF GOD, SINCERITY IN THE

See also: Practical in our faith— page 392.

Adore not any strange god. The Lord his name is Jealous, he is a jealous God.—*Ex.* xxxiv. 14.

Now therefore fear the Lord, and serve him with a perfect and most sincere heart: and put away the gods which your fathers served in Mesopotamia and in Egypt, and serve the Lord.—*Jos.* xxiv. 14.

Therefore fear the Lord, and serve him in truth and with your whole heart, for you have seen the great works which he hath done among you.— 1 *Kings* xii. 24.

Hearken, therefore, my children, to your father: serve the Lord in truth, and seek to do the things that please him.—*Tob.* xiv. 10.

The Lord is only for them that wait upon him in the way of truth and justice.—*Ecclus.* xxxiv. 22.

Is not this rather the fast that I have chosen? loose the hands of wickedness, undo the bundles that oppress, let them that are broken go free, and break asunder every burden.

Deal thy bread to the hungry, and bring the needy and the harborless into thy house: when thou shalt see one naked, cover him, and despise not thy own flesh.

Then shall thy light break forth as the morning, and thy health shall speedily arise, and thy justice shall go before thy face, and the glory of the Lord shall gather thee up.—*Is.* lviii. 6-8.

For I am the Lord that love judgment, and hate robbery in a holocaust. —*Is.* lxi. 8.

No man can serve two masters. For either he will hate the one, and love the other: or he will sustain the one, and despise the other. You cannot serve God and mammon.—*Matt.* vi. 24.

That being delivered from the hand of our enemies, we may serve him without fear,

In holiness and justice before him, all our days.—*Luke* i. 74, 75.

But the hour cometh, and now is, when the true adorers shall adore the Father in spirit and in truth. For the Father also seeketh such to adore him.

God is a spirit; and they that adore him, must adore him in spirit and in truth.—*John* iv. 23, 24.

For our glory is this, the testimony of our conscience, that in simplicity of heart and sincerity of God, and not in carnal wisdom, but in the grace of God, we have conversed in this world: and more abundantly towards you.—*2 Cor.* i. 12.

And this I pray, that your charity may more and more abound in knowledge, and in all understanding:

That you may approve the better things, that you may be sincere and without offence unto the day of Christ,

Filled with the fruit of justice, through Jesus Christ, unto the glory and praise of God.—*Philipp.* i. 9-11.

SERVICE OF GOD, HYPOCRISY IN THE

And they loved him with their mouth: and with their tongue they lied unto him:

But their heart was not right with him: nor were they counted faithful in his covenant.—*Ps.* lxxvii. 36, 37.

Be not incredulous to the fear of the Lord: and come not to him with a double heart.

Be not a hypocrite in the sight of men, and let not thy lips be a stumbling-block to thee.

Watch over them, lest thou fall, and bring dishonor upon thy soul,

And God discover thy secrets, and cast thee down in the midst of the congregation.

Because thou camest to the Lord wickedly, and thy heart is full of guile and deceit.—*Ecclus.* i. 36-40.

A heart that goeth two ways shall not have success, and the perverse of heart shall be scandalized therein.—*Ecclus.* iii. 28.

And the Lord said: Forasmuch as this people draw near me with their mouth, and with their lips glorify me, but their heart is far from me, and they have feared me with the commandment and doctrines of men:

Therefore behold I will proceed to cause an admiration in this people, by a great and wonderful miracle: for wisdom shall perish from their wise men, and the understanding of their prudent men shall be hid.—*Is.* xxix. 13, 14.

Why have we fasted, and thou hast not regarded: have we humbled our souls, and thou hast not taken notice? Behold in the day of your fast your own will is found, and you exact of all your debtors.

Behold you fast for debates and strife, and strike with the fist wickedly. Do not fast as you have done until this day, to make your cry to be heard on high.

Is this such a fast as I have chosen: for a man to afflict his soul for a day? is this it, to wind his head about like a circle, and to spread sackcloth and ashes? wilt thou call this a fast, and a day acceptable to the Lord?—*Is.* lviii. 3-5.

Behold you put your trust in lying words, which shall not profit you:

To steal, to murder, to commit adultery, to swear falsely, to offer to Baalim, and to go after strange gods, which you know not.

And you have come, and stood before me in this house, in which my name is called upon, and have said: We are delivered, because we have done all these abominations.

Is this house, then, in which my name hath been called upon, in your eyes become a den of robbers? I, I am he: I have seen it, saith the Lord.—*Jer.* vii. 8-11.

For I tell you, that unless your justice abound more than that of the scribes and Pharisees, you shall not enter into the kingdom of heaven.—*Matt.* v. 20.

But he (Jesus) answering, said to them: Well did Isaias prophesy of you hypocrites, as it is written: This people honoreth me with their lips, but their heart is far from me.

And in vain do they worship me, teaching doctrines and precepts of men.

For leaving the commandment of God, you hold the tradition of men, the washing of pots and of cups: and many other things you do like to these. —*Mark* vii. 6-8.

SERVICE WE RENDER TO GOD MUST BE REASONABLE, THE

Therefore glorify ye the Lord in instruction: the name of the Lord God of Israel in the islands of the sea.—*Is.* xxiv. 15.

I beseech you therefore, brethren, by the mercy of God, that you present your bodies a living sacrifice, holy, pleasing unto God, your reasonable service.—*Rom.* xii. 1.

SERVICE OF GOD, THE FOLLY OF ABANDONING THE

See also: Forsaking the law of God —page 160.

Be astonished, O ye heavens, at this, and ye gates thereof, be very desolate, saith the Lord.

For my people have done two evils. They have forsaken me, the fountain of living water, and have digged to themselves cisterns, broken cisterns, that can hold no water.—*Jer.* ii. 12, 13.

O Lord, the hope of Israel: all that forsake thee shall be confounded: they that depart from thee, shall be written in the earth: because they have for-saken the Lord, the vein of living waters.—*Jer.* xvii. 13.

Thou hast forsaken the fountain of wisdom:

For if thou hadst walked in the way of God, thou hadst surely dwelt in peace for ever.—*Bar.* iii. 12, 13.

I and my sons, and my brethren, will obey the law of our fathers.

God be merciful unto us: it is not profitable for us to forsake the law, and the justices of God.—1 *Mach.* ii. 20, 21.

SERVICE, GOD STANDS NOT IN NEED OF OUR

See also: God needs not our goods.—page 171.

What doth it profit God if thou be just? or what dost thou give him if thy way be unspotted?—*Job* xxii. 3.

Whose helper art thou? is it of him that is weak? and dost thou hold up the arm of him that has no strength?

To whom hast thou given counsel? perhaps to him that hath no wisdom, and thou hast shown thy very great prudence.—*Job* xxvi. 2, 3.

Look up to heaven and see, and behold the sky, that it is higher than thee.

If thou sin, what shalt thou hurt him? and if thy iniquities be multiplied, what shalt thou do against him?

And if thou do justly, what shalt thou give him, or what shall he receive of thy hand?

Thy wickedness may hurt a man that is like thee: and thy justice may help the son of man.—*Job* xxxv. 5-8.

So you also, when you shall have done all these things that are commanded you, say: We are unprofitable servants; we have done that which we ought to do.—*Luke* xvii. 10.

But Jesus did not trust himself unto them, for that he knew all men,

And because he needed not that any should give testimony of man: for he knew what was in man.—*John* ii. 24, 25.

SERVING GOD, THE HAPPINESS OF

See: Happiness—page 193.

SERVING GOD, THE REWARD OF

See: Reward—page 480.

SERVE GOD BY DOING WRONG, WE CANNOT

See also: Wicked not acceptable to God, the offerings of the—page 599.

Hath God any need of your lie, that you should speak deceitfully for him?—*Job* xiii. 7.

Say not: He hath caused me to err: for he hath no need of wicked men.—*Ecclus.* xv. 12.

He hath commanded no man to do wickedly, and he hath given no man license to sin:

For he desireth not a multitude of faithless and unprofitable children.—*Ecclus.* xv. 21, 22.

Do not offer wicked gifts, for such he will not receive.

And look not upon an unjust sacrifice, for the Lord is judge, and there is not with him respect of person.—*Ecclus.* xxxv. 14, 15.

SERVE GOD, THE PUNISHMENT OF REFUSAL TO

Because thou didst not serve the Lord thy God with joy and gladness of heart, for the abundance of all things:

Thou shalt serve thy enemy, whom the Lord will send upon thee, in hunger, and thirst, and nakedness, and in want of all things: and he shall put an iron yoke upon thy neck, till he consume thee.—*Deut.* xxviii. 47, 48.

And when the Lord saw that they were humbled, the word of the Lord came to Semeias, saying: Because they are humbled, I will not destroy them, and I will give them a little help, and my wrath shall not fall upon Jerusalem by the hand of Sesac.

But yet they shall serve him, that they may know the difference between my service, and the service of a kingdom of the earth.—*2 Paral.* xii. 7, 8.

For the nation and the kingdom that will not serve him, shall perish: and the Gentiles shall be wasted with desolation.—*Is.* lx. 12.

And they that are saved of you shall remember me amongst the nations to which they are carried captives: because I have broken their heart that was faithless, and revolted from me: and their eyes that went a fornicating after their idols: and they shall be displeased with themselves because of the evils which they have committed in all their abominations.

And they shall know that I the Lord have not spoken in vain that I would do this evil to them.—*Ezech.* vi. 9, 10.

SERVE GOD, EXHORTATION TO

Yet so that you observe attentively, and in work fulfil the commandment and the law which Moses the servant of the Lord commanded you: that you love the Lord your God, and walk in all his ways, and keep all his commandments, and cleave to him, and serve him with all your heart, and with all your soul.—*Jos.* xxii. 5.

And thou my son Solomon, know the God of thy father, and serve him with a perfect heart and a willing mind: for the Lord searcheth all hearts, and understandeth all the thoughts of minds. If thou seek him, thou shalt find him: but if thou forsake him, he will cast thee off for ever.—*1 Paral.* xxviii. 9.

Harden not your necks, as your fathers did: yield yourselves to the Lord, and come to his sanctuary, which he hath sanctified for ever: serve the Lord the God of your fathers, and the wrath of his indignation shall be turned away from you.—*2 Paral.* xxx. 8.

Hearken therefore, my children, to your father: serve the Lord in truth, and seek to do the things that please him.—*Tob.* xiv. 10.

Serve ye the Lord with fear: and rejoice unto him with trembling.—*Ps.* ii. 11.

My son, give me thy heart: and let thy eyes keep my ways.—*Prov.* xxiii. 26.

All you that thirst, come to the waters: and you that have no money, make haste, buy, and eat: come ye, buy wine and milk without money, and without any price.

Why do you spend money for that which is not bread, and your labor for that which doth not satisfy you? Hearken diligently to me, and eat that which is good, and your soul shall be delighted in fatness.

Incline your ear and come to me: hear and your soul shall live, and I will make an everlasting covenant with you, the faithful mercies of David.—*Is.* lv. 1-3.

Take up my yoke upon you, and learn of me, because I am meek, and humble of heart: and you shall find rest to your souls.

For my yoke is sweet, and my burden light.—*Matt.* xi. 29, 30.

Labor not for the meat which perisheth, but for that which endureth unto life everlasting, which the Son of man will give you. For him hath God, the Father, sealed.—*John* vi. 27.

Serve ye the Lord Christ.—*Col.* iii. 24.

Therefore receiving an immovable kingdom, we have grace; whereby let us serve, pleasing God, with fear and reverence.

For our God is a consuming fire.—*Heb.* xii. 28, 29.

SHEPHERD, THE GOOD

The Lord ¹ruleth me: and I shall want nothing. He hath set me in a place of pasture.

He hath brought me up, on the water of refreshment.—*Ps.* xxii. 1, 2.

And he took away his own people as sheep: and guided them in the wilderness like a flock.—*Ps.* lxxvii. 52.

But we thy people, and the sheep of thy pasture, will give thanks to thee for ever. We will show forth thy praise, unto generation and generation.—*Ps.* lxxviii. 13.

For he is the Lord our God: and we are the people of his pasture and the sheep of his hand.—*Ps.* xciv. 7.

Know ye that the Lord he is God: he made us, and not we ourselves.

We are his people and the sheep of his pasture.—*Ps.* xcix. 3.

I have gone astray like a sheep that is lost: seek thy servant, because I have not forgotten thy commandments.—*Ps.* cxviii. 176.

He hath mercy, and teacheth, and correcteth, as a shepherd doth his flock.—*Ecclus.* xviii. 13.

¹In Hebrew, "is my shepherd."

He shall feed his flock like a shepherd: he shall gather together the lambs with his arm, and shall take them up in his bosom, and he himself shall carry them that are with young.—*Is.* xl. 11.

They shall not hunger, nor thirst, neither shall the heat nor the sun strike them: for he that is merciful to them, shall be their shepherd, and at the fountains of waters he shall give them drink.—*Is.* xlix. 10.

And I am not troubled, following thee for my pastor, and I have not desired the day of man, thou knowest.—*Jer.* xvii. 16.

For thus saith the Lord God: Behold I myself will seek my sheep, and will visit them.

As the shepherd visiteth his flock in the day when he shall be in the midst of his sheep that were scattered, so will I visit my sheep, and will deliver them out of all the places where they have been scattered in the cloudy and dark days. . . .

I will feed them in the most fruitful pastures, and their pastures shall be in the high mountains of Israel: there shall they rest on the green grass, and be fed in fat pastures upon the mountains of Israel.

I will feed my sheep: and I will cause them to lie down, saith the Lord God.

I will seek that which was lost: and that which was driven away, I will bring again: and I will bind up that which was broken, and I will strengthen that which was weak, and that which was fat and strong I will preserve: and I will feed them in judgment.

. . . And I will set up one shepherd over them, and he shall feed them, even my servant David: he shall feed them, and he shall be their shepherd. . . .

And you my flocks, the flocks of my pasture are men: and I am the Lord your God, saith the Lord God.—*Ezech.* xxxiv. 11, 12, 14-16, 23, 31.

And seeing the multitudes, he (Jesus) had compassion on them: because they were distressed, and lying like sheep that have no shepherd.—*Matt.* ix. 36.

What think you? If a man have a hundred sheep, and one of them should go astray: doth he not leave the ninety-nine in the mountains, and go to seek that which is gone astray?

And if it so be that he find it: Amen I say to you, he rejoiceth more for that, than for the ninety-nine that went not astray.—*Matt.* xviii. 12, 13.

What man of you that hath a hundred sheep: and if he shall lose one of them, doth he not leave the ninety-nine in the desert, and go after that which was lost, until he find it?

And when he hath found it, lay it upon his shoulders, rejoicing:

And coming home, call together his friends and neighbors, saying to them: Rejoice with me, because I have found my sheep that was lost?

I say to you, that even so there shall be joy in heaven upon one sinner that doth penance, more than upon ninety-nine just who need not penance. —*Luke* xv. 4-7.

But he that entereth in by the door is the shepherd of the sheep.

To him the porter openeth; and the sheep hear his voice: and he calleth his own sheep by name, and leadeth them out.

And when he hath let out his own sheep, he goeth before them: and the sheep follow him, because they know his voice.—*John* x. 2-4.

I am the good shepherd. The good shepherd giveth his life for his sheep. . . .

I am the good shepherd; and I know mine, and mine know me.

As the Father knoweth me, and I know the Father: and I lay down my life for my sheep.

And other sheep I have, that are not of this fold: them also I must bring, and they shall hear my voice, and there shall be one fold and one shepherd. . . .

My sheep hear my voice: and I know them, and they follow me.

And I give them life everlasting; and they shall not perish for ever, and no man shall pluck them out of my hand.—*John* x. 11, 14-16, 27, 28.

And may the God of peace, who brought again from the dead the great pastor of the sheep, our Lord Jesus Christ, in the blood of the everlasting testament,

Fit you in all goodness, that you may do his will; doing in you that which is well pleasing in his sight, through Jesus Christ, to whom is glory for ever and ever. Amen.—*Heb.* xiii. 20, 21.

For you were as sheep going astray; but you are now converted to the shepherd and bishop of your souls.—1 *Peter* ii. 25.

SICK, VISITING THE

Be not slow to visit the sick: for by these things thou shalt be confirmed in love.—*Ecclus.* vii. 39.

Then shall the king say to them that shall be on his right hand: Come, ye blessed of my Father, possess you the kingdom prepared for you from the foundation of the world.

For I was hungry, and you gave me to eat: . . . sick, and you visited me.

. . . Then shall the just answer him, saying: Lord, when did we see thee hungry, and fed thee? . . .

Or when did we see thee sick or in prison, and came to thee?

And the king answering, shall say to them: Amen I say to you, as long as you did it to one of these my least brethren, you did it to me.—*Matt.* xxv. 34-37, 39, 40.

SICKNESS

He rebuketh also by sorrow in the bed, and he maketh all his bones to wither.—*Job* xxxiii. 19.

The thinking beforehand turneth away the understanding, and a grievous sickness maketh the soul sober.—*Ecclus.* xxxi. 2.

Now there was a certain man sick, named Lazarus, of Bethania, of the town of Mary and of Martha her sister. . . .

His sisters therefore sent to him, saying: Lord, behold, he whom thou lovest is sick.

And Jesus hearing it, said to them: This sickness is not unto death, but for the glory of God: that the Son of God may be glorified by it.—*John* xi. 1, 3, 4.

And he said to me: My grace is sufficient for thee: for power is made perfect in infirmity. Gladly therefore will

I glory in my infirmities, that the power of Christ may dwell in me.—*2 Cor.* xii. 9.

SICKNESS, CONDUCT IN

Humble thyself before thou art sick, and in the time of sickness show thy conversation.—*Ecclus.* xviii. 21.

Honor the physician for the need thou hast of him: for the most High hath created him. . . .

The most High hath created medicines out of the earth, and a wise man will not abhor them.

Was not bitter water made sweet with wood?

The virtue of these things is come to the knowledge of men, and the most High hath given knowledge to men, that he may be honored in his wonders.

By these he shall cure and shall allay their pains, and of these the apothecary shall make sweet confections, and shall make up ointments of health, and of his works there shall be no end.—*Ecclus.* xxxviii. 1, 4-7.

My son, in thy sickness neglect not thyself, but pray to the Lord, and he shall heal thee.

Turn away from sin and order thy hands aright, and cleanse thy heart from all offence.

Give a sweet savor, and a memorial of fine flour, and make a fat offering, and then give place to the physician.

For the Lord created him: and let him not depart from thee, for his works are necessary.

For there is a time when thou must fall into their hands:

And they shall beseech the Lord, that he would prosper what they give for ease and remedy, for their conversation.—*Ecclus.* xxxviii. 9-14.

Is any man sick among you? Let him bring in the priests of the church, and let them pray over him, anointing him with oil in the name of the Lord.

And the prayer of faith shall save the sick man: and the Lord shall raise him up: and if he be in sins, they shall be forgiven him.—*James* v. 14, 15.

SILENCE, THE VALUE OF

Even a fool, if he will hold his peace shall be counted wise: and if he close his lips, a man of understanding.—*Prov.* xvii. 28.

He that keepeth his mouth and his tongue, keepeth his soul from distress.—*Prov.* xxi. 23.

And there is a judgment that is not allowed to be good: and there is one that holdeth his peace, he is wise.—*Ecclus.* xix. 28.

There is one that holdeth his peace, that is found wise: and there is another that is hateful, that is bold in speech.

There is one that holdeth his peace, because he knoweth not what to say: and there is another that holdeth his peace, knowing the proper time.

A wise man will hold his peace till he see opportunity: but a babbler, and a fool, will regard no time.—*Ecclus.* xx. 5-7.

Hear in silence, and for thy reverence good grace shall come to thee.

Young man, scarcely speak in thy own cause.

If thou be asked twice, let thy answer be short.

In many things be as if thou wert ignorant, and hear in silence and withal seeking.

In the company of great men, take not upon thee: and when the ancients are present, speak not much.—*Ecclus.* xxxii. 9-13.

Let the woman learn in silence, with all subjection.

But I suffer not a woman to teach, nor to use authority over the man: but to be in silence.—*1 Tim.* ii. 11, 12.

SILENCE OF CHRIST, THE

My friends and my neighbors have drawn near, and stood against me.

And they that were near me, stood afar off: And they that sought my soul, used violence.

And they that sought evils to me spoke vain things, and studied deceits all the day long.

But I, as a deaf man, heard not: and as a dumb man not opening his mouth.

And I became as a man that heareth not: and that hath no reproofs in his mouth.—*Ps.* xxxvii. 12-15.

I was dumb, and was humbled, and

kept silence from good things: and my sorrow was renewed.—*Ps.* xxxviii. 3.

He was offered because it was his own will, and he opened not his mouth: he shall be led as a sheep to the slaughter, and shall be dumb as a lamb before his shearer, and he shall not open his mouth.—*Is.* liii. 7.

And the high priest rising up, said to him: Answerest thou nothing to the things which these witness against thee?

But Jesus held his peace.—*Matt.* xxvi. 62, 63.

And when he was accused by the chief priests and ancients, he answered nothing.

Then Pilate saith to him: Dost not thou hear how great testimonies they allege against thee?

And he answered him to never a word; so that the governor wondered exceedingly.—*Matt.* xxvii. 12-14.

And Herod seeing Jesus, was very glad; for he was desirous of a long time to see him, because he had heard many things of him; and he hoped to see some sign wrought by him.

And he questioned him in many words. But he answered him nothing.

And the chief priests and the scribes stood by, earnestly accusing him.

And Herod with his army set him at nought, and mocked him, putting on him a white garment, and sent him back to Pilate.—*Luke* xxiii. 8-11.

For unto this are you called: because Christ also suffered for us, leaving you an example that you should follow his steps. . . .

Who, when he was reviled, did not revile: when he suffered, he threatened not: but delivered himself to him that judged him unjustly.—1 *Peter* ii. 21, 23.

SIMONY

And when Simon saw, that by the imposition of the hands of the apostles, the Holy Ghost was given, he offered them money,

Saying: Give me also this power, that on whomsoever I shall lay my hands, he may receive the Holy Ghost.

But Peter said to him:

Keep thy money to thyself, to perish with thee, because thou hast thought that the gift of God may be purchased with money.

Thou hast no part nor lot in this matter. For thy heart is not right in the sight of God.

Do penance therefore for this thy wickedness; and pray to God, that perhaps this thought of thy heart may be forgiven thee.

For I see thou art in the gall of bitterness, and in the bonds of iniquity.—*Acts* viii. 18-23.

SIMPLICITY

Let him weigh me in a just balance, and let God know my simplicity.—*Job* xxxi. 6.

The simplicity of the just shall guide them: and the deceitfulness of the wicked shall destroy them.—*Prov.* xi. 3.

Better is the poor man, that walketh in his simplicity, than a rich man that is perverse in his lips, and unwise.—*Prov.* xix. 1.

The just that walketh in his simplicity, shall leave behind him blessed children.—*Prov.* xx. 7.

Love justice, you that are the judges of the earth. Think of the Lord in goodness, and seek him in simplicity of heart.—*Wis.* i. 1.

Better is a man that hath less wisdom, and wanteth understanding, with the fear of God, than he that aboundeth in understanding, and transgresseth the law of the most High.—*Ecclus.* xix. 21.

And Jesus calling unto him a little child, set him in the midst of them,

And said: Amen I say to you, unless you be converted, and become as little children, you shall not enter into the kingdom of heaven.

Whosoever therefore shall humble himself as this little child, he is the greater in the kingdom of heaven.—*Matt.* xviii. 2-4.

But Jesus, calling them together, said: Suffer children to come to me, and forbid them not: for of such is the kingdom of God.

Amen, I say to you: Whosoever shall not receive the kingdom of God as a child, shall not enter into it.—*Luke* xviii. 16, 17.

And continuing daily with one accord in the temple, and breaking bread from house to house, they took their meat with gladness and simplicity of heart.—*Acts* ii. 46.

For our glory is this, the testimony of our conscience, that in simplicity of heart and sincerity of God, and not in carnal wisdom, but in the grace of God, we have conversed in this world; and more abundantly towards you.— 2 *Cor.* i. 12.

Now we make known unto you, brethren, the grace of God, that hath been given in the churches of Macedonia.

That in much experience of tribulation, they have had abundance of joy; and their very deep poverty hath abounded unto the riches of their simplicity.—2 *Cor.* viii. 1, 2.

And he that ministereth seed to the sower, will both give you bread to eat, and will multiply your seed, and increase the growth of the fruits of your justice:

That being enriched in all things, you may abound unto all simplicity, which worketh through us thanksgiving to God.—2 *Cor.* ix. 10, 11.

But I fear lest, as the serpent seduced Eve by his subtilty, so your minds should be corrupted, and fall from the simplicity that is in Christ.— 2 *Cor.* xi. 3.

Wherefore laying away all malice, and all guile, and dissimulations, and envies, and all detractions,

As newborn babes, desire the rational milk without guile, that thereby you may grow unto salvation.—1 *Peter* ii. 1, 2.

SIMPLICITY PLEASING TO GOD

I know, my God, that thou provest hearts, and lovest simplicity, wherefore I also in the simplicity of my heart, have joyfully offered all these things: and I have seen with great joy thy people, which are here present, offer thee their offerings.—1 *Paral.* xxix. 17.

God will not cast away the simple, nor reach out his hand to the evildoer.—*Job* viii. 20.

He that is mocked by his friends as I, shall call upon God, and he will hear him: for the simplicity of the just man is laughed to scorn.—*Job* xii. 4.

The Lord is the keeper of little ones: I was humbled, and he delivered me. —*Ps.* cxiv. 6.

He will keep the salvation of the righteous, and protect them that walk in simplicity.

Keeping the paths of justice, and guarding the ways of saints. . . .

For they that are upright, shall dwell in the earth, and the simple shall continue in it.—*Prov.* ii. 7, 8, 21.

SIN

Who can understand sins? from my secret ones cleanse me, O Lord.—*Ps.* xviii. 13.

For evils without number have surrounded me; my iniquities have overtaken me, and I was not able to see.

They are multiplied above the hairs of my head: and my heart hath forsaken me.—*Ps.* xxxix. 13.

Trust not in iniquity, and cover not robberies.—*Ps.* lxi. 11.

Stolen waters are sweeter, and hidden bread is more pleasant.—*Prov.* ix. 17.

Justice exalteth a nation: but sin maketh nations miserable.—*Prov.* xiv. 34.

Better is a little with justice, than great revenues with iniquity.—*Prov.* xvi. 8.

Be not without fear about sin forgiven, and add not sin upon sin.— *Ecclus.* v. 5.

For a wicked soul shall destroy him that hath it, and maketh him to be a joy to his enemies, and shall lead him into the lot of the wicked.—*Ecclus.* vi. 4.

Flee from sins as from the face of a serpent: for if thou comest near them, they will take hold of thee.

The teeth thereof are the teeth of a lion, killing the souls of men.

All iniquity is like a two-edged sword, there is no remedy for the wound thereof.—*Ecclus.* xxi. 2-4.

The lion always lieth in wait for prey: so do sins for them that work iniquities.—*Ecclus.* xxvii. 11.

He that loveth gold, shall not be justified: and he that followeth after corruption, shall be filled with it.—*Ecclus.* xxxi. 5.

For wickedness is kindled as a fire, it shall devour the brier and the thorn: and shall kindle in the thicket of the forest, and it shall be wrapped up in smoke ascending on high.—*Is.* ix. 18.

Though thou wash thyself with nitre, and multiply to thyself the herb borith, thou art stained in thy iniquity before me, saith the Lord God.—*Jer.* ii. 22.

Susanna sighed, and said: I am straitened on every side: for if I do this thing, it is death to me: and if I do it not, I shall not escape your hands.

But it is better for me to fall into your hands without doing it, than to sin in the sight of the Lord.—*Dan.* xiii. 22, 23.

And fear ye not them that kill the body, and are not able to kill the soul: but rather fear him that can destroy both soul and body in hell.—*Matt.* x. 28.

And because iniquity hath abounded, the charity of many shall grow cold.— *Matt.* xxiv. 12.

Now the sting of death is sin: and the power of sin is the law.—1 *Cor.* xv. 56.

And you, when you were dead in your offences and sins,

Wherein in time past you walked according to the course of this world, according to the prince of the power of this air, of the spirit that now worketh on the children of unbelief:

In which also we all conversed in time past, in the desires of our flesh, fulfilling the will of the flesh and of our thoughts, and were by nature children of wrath, even as the rest.—*Eph.* ii. 1-3.

But exhort one another every day, whilst it is called to-day, that none of you be hardened through the deceitfulness of sin.—*Heb.* iii. 13.

SIN, MORTAL

See: Part II—page 735.

SIN, VENIAL

See: Part II—page 735.

SIN IS REBELLION AGAINST GOD

After these things Moses and Aaron went in, and said to Pharao: Thus saith the Lord God of Israel: Let my people go that they may sacrifice to me in the desert.

But he answered: Who is the Lord, that I should hear his voice, and let Israel go? I know not the Lord, neither will I let Israel go.—*Ex.* v. 1, 2.

Whom hast thou reproached, and whom hast thou blasphemed? against whom hast thou exalted thy voice, and lifted up thy eyes on high? against the holy one of Israel.—4 *Kings* xix. 22.

For he hath stretched out his hand against God, and hath strengthened himself against the Almighty.

He hath run against him with his neck raised up, and is armed with a fat neck.—*Job* xv. 25, 26.

They spend their days in wealth, and in a moment they go down to hell.

Who have said to God: Depart from us, we desire not the knowledge of thy ways.

Who is the Almighty, that we should serve him? and what doth it profit us if we pray to him?—*Job* xxi. 13-15.

He hath struck them, as being wicked, in open sight.

Who as it were on purpose have revolted from him, and would not understand all his ways:

So that they caused the cry of the needy to come to him, and he heard the voice of the poor.—*Job* xxxiv. 26-28.

May the Lord destroy all deceitful lips, and the tongue that speaketh proud things.

Who have said: We will magnify our tongue; our lips are our own; who is Lord over us?—*Ps.* xi. 4, 5.

Thy own wickedness shall reprove thee, and thy apostasy shall rebuke thee. Know thou, and see that it is an evil and a bitter thing for thee, to have left the Lord thy God, and that my fear is not with thee, saith the Lord the God of hosts.

Of old time thou hast broken my yoke, thou hast burst my bands, and thou saidst: I will not serve.—*Jer.* ii. 19, 20.

But the heart of this people is become hard of belief and provoking, they are revolted and gone away.

And they have not said in their heart: Let us fear the Lord our God, who giveth us the early and the latter rain in due season: who preserveth for us the fulness of the yearly harvest.—*Jer.* v. 23, 24.

Thus saith the Lord: Stand ye on the ways, and see, and ask for the old paths, which is the good way, and walk ye in it: and you shall find refreshment for your souls. And they said: We will not walk.

And I appointed watchmen over you, saying: Hearken ye to the sound of the trumpet. And they said: We will not hearken.—*Jer.* vi. 16, 17.

The son honoreth the father, and the servant his master: if then I be a father, where is my honor? and if I be a master, where is my fear? saith the Lord of hosts.—*Malach.* i. 6.

And it was the parasceve of the pasch, about the sixth hour, and he (Pilate) saith to the Jews: Behold your king.

But they cried out: Away with him; away with him; crucify him. Pilate saith to them: Shall I crucify your king? The chief priests answered: We have no king but Cæsar.—*John* xix. 14, 15.

SIN IS INGRATITUDE TO GOD

They have sinned against him, and are none of his children in their filth: they are a wicked and perverse generation.

Is this the return thou makest to the Lord, O foolish and senseless people? Is not he thy father, that hath possessed thee, and made thee, and created thee?—*Deut.* xxxii. 5, 6.

The beloved grew fat, and kicked: he grew fat, and thick and gross, he forsook God who made him, and departed from God his saviour. . . .

Thou hast forsaken the God that begot thee, and hast forgotten the Lord that created thee.—*Deut.* xxxii. 15, 18.

The tabernacles of robbers abound, and they provoke God boldly; whereas it is he that hath given all into their hands.—*Job* xii. 6.

For even the man of my peace, in whom I trusted, who ate my bread, hath greatly supplanted me.—*Ps.* xl. 10.

My heart hath expected reproach and misery.

And I looked for one that would grieve together with me, but there was none: and for one that would comfort me, and I found none.

And they gave me gall for my food, and in my thirst they gave me vinegar to drink.—*Ps.* lxviii. 21, 22.

And they turned back and tempted God: and grieved the holy one of Israel.—*Ps.* lxxvii. 41.

They have spoken against me with deceitful tongues; and they have compassed me about with words of hatred; and have fought against me without cause.

Instead of making me a return of love, they detracted me: but I gave myself to prayer.

And they repaid me evil for good: and hatred for my love.—*Ps.* cviii. 3-5.

Hear, O ye heavens, and give ear, O earth, for the Lord hath spoken. I have brought up children, and exalted them: but they have despised me.

The ox knoweth his owner, and the ass his master's crib: but Israel hath not known me, and my people hath not understood.

Woe to the sinful nation, a people laden with iniquity, a wicked seed, ungracious children: they have forsaken the Lord, they have blasphemed the Holy One of Israel, they are gone away backwards.—*Is.* i. 2-4.

What is there that I ought to do more to my vineyard, that I have not done to it? was it that I looked that it should bring forth grapes, and it hath brought forth wild grapes?—*Is.* v. 4.

And he said: Surely they are my people, children that will not deny: so he became their saviour.

In all their affliction he was not troubled, and the angel of his presence saved them: in his love, and in his mercy he redeemed them, and he carried them and lifted them up all the days of old.

But they provoked to wrath, and afflicted the spirit of his Holy One: and he was turned to be their enemy, and he fought against them.—*Is.* lxiii. 8-10.

Yet I planted thee a chosen vineyard, all true seed: how then art thou turned unto me into that which is good for nothing, O strange vineyard?—*Jer.* ii. 21.

For you have forgotten God, who brought you up, and you have grieved Jerusalem that nursed you.—*Bar.* iv. 8.

And they shall say to him: What are these wounds in the midst of thy hands? And he shall say: With these I was wounded in the house of them that loved me.—*Zach.* xiii. 6.

SIN, THE MALICE OF

And the Lord said: The cry of Sodom and Gomorrha is multiplied, and their sin is become exceedingly grievous.—*Gen.* xviii. 20.

For he doth not now bring on his fury, neither doth he revenge wickedness exceedingly.—*Job* xxxv. 15.

Who can understand sins?—*Ps.* xviii. 13.

And he (the Lord) said: Hear ye therefore, O house of David: Is it a small thing for you to be grievous to men, that you are grievous to my God also?—*Is.* vii. 13.

Upon whom have you jested? upon whom have you opened your mouth wide, and put out your tongue? are not you wicked children, a false seed? —*Is.* lvii. 4.

Be astonished, O ye heavens, at this, and ye gates thereof, be very desolate, saith the Lord.

For my people have done two evils. They have forsaken me, the fountain of living water, and have digged to themselves cisterns, broken cisterns, that can hold no water.—*Jer.* ii. 12, 13.

Thy own wickedness shall reprove thee, and thy apostasy shall rebuke thee. Know thou, and see that it is an evil and a bitter thing for thee, to have left the Lord thy God, and that my fear is not with thee, saith the Lord the God of hosts.

Of old time thou hast broken my yoke, thou hast burst my bands, and thou saidst: I will not serve.—*Jer.* ii. 19, 20.

Shall a man afflict God? for you afflict me. And you have said: Wherein do we afflict thee? in tithes and in first-fruits.

And you are cursed with want, and you afflict me, even the whole nation of you.—*Malach.* iii. 8, 9.

Then went one of the twelve, who was called Judas Iscariot, to the chief priests,

And said to them: What will you give me, and I will deliver him unto you?

But they appointed him thirty pieces of silver. And from thenceforth he sought opportunity to betray him. . . .

And he that betrayed him, gave them a sign, saying: Whomsoever I shall kiss, that is he, hold him fast.

And forthwith coming to Jesus, he said: Hail, Rabbi. And he kissed him. —*Matt.* xxvi. 14-16, 48, 49.

And the governor answering, said to them: Whether will you of the two to be released unto you? But they said, Barabbas.

Pilate saith to them: What shall I do then with Jesus that is called Christ? They say all: Let him be crucified.— *Matt.* xxvii. 21, 22.

And grieve not the holy Spirit of God: whereby you are sealed unto the day of redemption.—*Eph.* iv. 30.

And have no fellowship with the unfruitful works of darkness, but rather reprove them.

For the things that are done by them in secret, it is a shame even to speak of.—*Eph.* v. 11, 12.

A man making void the law of Moses, dieth without any mercy under two or three witnesses:

How much more, do you think he deserveth worse punishments, who hath trodden under foot the Son of God, and hath esteemed the blood of the testament unclean, by which he was sanctified, and hath offered an affront to the Spirit of grace?—*Heb.* x. 28, 29.

SIN, THE FOLLY OF

See also: Sinner, blindness of the— page 535.

And Jacob said to him: Sell me thy first birthright.

He answered: Lo, I die, what will the first birthright avail me.

Jacob said: Swear therefore to me. Esau swore to him, and sold his first birthright.

And so taking bread and the pottage of lentils, he ate, and drank, and went his way; making little account of having sold his first birthright.—*Gen.* xxv. 31-34.

But they that commit sin and iniquity, are enemies to their own soul. —*Tob.* xii. 10.

O God my God, look upon me: why hast thou forsaken me?

Far from my salvation are the words of my sins.—*Ps.* xxi. 2.

Men shall not be strengthened by wickedness: and the root of the just shall not be moved.—*Prov.* xii. 3.

It is not in man's power to stop the spirit, neither hath he power in the day of death, . . . neither shall wickedness save the wicked.—*Eccles.* viii. 8.

Who will justify him that sinneth against his own soul? and who will honor him that dishonoreth his own soul?—*Ecclus.* x. 32.

Be astonished, O ye heavens, at this, and ye gates thereof, be very desolate, saith the Lord.

For my people have done two evils. They have forsaken me, the fountain of living water, and have digged to themselves cisterns, broken cisterns, that can hold no water.—*Jer.* ii. 12, 13.

Your iniquities have turned these things away, and your sins have withholden good things from you.—*Jer.* v. 25.

What fruit therefore had you then in those things of which you are now ashamed? For the end of them is death. —*Rom.* vi. 21.

SIN, THE HATRED OF GOD FOR

I am the Lord thy God, mighty, jealous, visiting the iniquity of the fathers upon the children, unto the third and fourth generation of tnem that hate me.—*Ex.* xx. 5.

Let the fear of the Lord be with you, and do all things with diligence: for there is no iniquity with the Lord our God, nor respect of persons, nor desire of gifts.—2 *Paral.* xix. 7.

And as long as they sinned not in the sight of their God, it was well with them: for their God hateth iniquity.— *Judith* v. 21.

Therefore, ye men of understanding, hear me: far from God be wickedness, and iniquity from the Almighty.—*Job* xxxiv. 10.

In the morning I will stand before thee, and will see: because thou art not a God that willest iniquity.—*Ps.* v. 5.

The way of the wicked is an abomination to the Lord: he that followeth justice is beloved by him.—*Prov.* xv. 9.

But to God the wicked and his wickedness are hateful alike.—*Wis.* xiv. 9.

Say not: It is through God, that she (wisdom) is not with me: for do not thou the things that he hateth. . . .

The Lord hateth all abomination of error, and they that fear him shall not love it. . . .

He hath commanded no man to do wickedly, and he hath given no man license to sin.—*Ecclus.* xv. 11, 13, 21.

For the wrath of God is revealed from heaven against all ungodliness and injustice of those men that detain the truth of God in injustice.—*Rom.* i. 18.

SIN SEPARATES US FROM GOD

Behold the hand of the Lord is not shortened that it cannot save, neither is his ear heavy that it cannot hear.

But your iniquities have divided between you and your God, and your sins have hid his face from you that he should not hear.—*Is.* lix. 1, 2.

We have done wickedly, and provoked thee to wrath: therefore thou art inexorable.

Thou hast covered in thy wrath, and hast struck us: thou hast killed and hast not spared.

Thou hast set a cloud before thee, that our prayer may not pass through. —*Lam.* iii. 42-44.

SIN, THE SLAVERY OF

Direct my steps according to thy word: and let no iniquity have dominion over me.—*Ps.* cxviii. 133.

For wisdom will not enter into a

malicious soul, nor dwell in a body subject to sins.—*Wis.* i. 4.

Jesus answered them: Amen, amen I say unto you: that whosoever committeth sin, is the servant of sin.—*John* viii. 34.

Let not sin therefore reign in your mortal body, so as to obey the lusts thereof.

Neither yield ye your members as instruments of iniquity unto sin. . . .

Know you not, that to whom you yield yourselves servants to obey, his servants you are whom you obey, whether it be of sin unto death, or of obedience unto justice.—*Rom.* vi. 12, 13, 16.

For, speaking proud words of vanity, they allure by the desires of fleshly riotousness, those who for a little while escape, such as converse in error:

Promising them liberty, whereas they themselves are the slaves of corruption. For by whom a man is overcome, of the same also he is the slave. —*2 Peter* ii. 18, 19.

SIN, FREEDOM FROM THE SLAVERY OF

I am the Lord your God: who have brought you out of the land of the Egyptians, that you should not serve them, and who have broken the chains of your necks, that you might go upright.—*Lev.* xxvi. 13.

Who can understand sins? from my secret ones cleanse me, O Lord: and from those of others spare thy servant.

If they shall have no dominion over me, then shall I be without spot: and I shall be cleansed from the greatest sin.—*Ps.* xviii. 13, 14.

Our soul hath been delivered as a sparrow out of the snare of the fowlers. The snare is broken, and we are delivered.—*Ps.* cxxiii. 7.

For we that are dead to sin, how shall we live any longer therein?—*Rom.* vi. 2.

Knowing this, that our old man is crucified with him, that the body of sin may be destroyed, to the end that we may serve sin no longer.—*Rom.* vi. 6.

For sin shall not have dominion over you; for you are not under the law, but under grace.—*Rom.* vi. 14.

But thanks be to God, that you were the servants of sin, but have obeyed from the heart, unto that form of doctrine, into which you have been delivered.

Being then freed from sin, we have been made servants of justice.—*Rom.* vi. 17, 18.

Having therefore these promises, dearly beloved, let us cleanse ourselves from all defilement of the flesh and of the spirit, perfecting sanctification in the fear of God.—*2 Cor.* vii. 1.

Giving thanks to God the Father, who hath made us worthy to be partakers of the lot of the saints in light:

Who hath delivered us from the power of darkness, and hath translated us into the kingdom of the Son of his love.—*Col.* i. 12, 13.

With modesty admonishing them that resist the truth: if peradventure God may give them repentance to know the truth,

And they may recover themselves from the snares of the devil, by whom they are held captive at his will.—2 *Tim.* ii. 25, 26.

SIN, HATRED OF

You that love the Lord, hate evil.—*Ps.* xcvi. 10.

By thy commandments I have had understanding: therefore have I hated every way of iniquity.—*Ps.* cxviii. 104.

I have hated and abhorred iniquity; but I have loved thy law.—*Ps.* cxviii. 163.

And you shall remember your wicked ways, and your doings that were not good: and your iniquities, and your wicked deeds shall displease you.—*Ezech.* xxxvi. 31.

Seek ye good, and not evil, that you may live: and the Lord the God of hosts will be with you, as you have said.

Hate evil, and love good, and establish judgment in the gate: it may be the Lord the God of hosts may have mercy on the remnant of Joseph.—*Amos* v. 14, 15.

Let love be without dissimulation. Hating that which is evil, cleaving to that which is good.—*Rom.* xii. 9.

SIN, SORROW FOR

See also: Contrite of heart—page 79.

And: Repentance, true—page 473.

My eyes have sent forth springs of water: because they have not kept thy law.—*Ps.* cxviii. 136.

I will recount to thee all my years in the bitterness of my soul.—*Is.* xxxviii. 15.

But the soul that is sorrowful for the greatness of evil she hath done, and goeth bowed down, and feeble, and the eyes that fail, and the hungry soul giveth glory and justice to thee the Lord.—*Bar.* ii. 18.

Now therefore saith the Lord: Be converted to me with all your heart, in fasting, and in weeping, and in mourning.

And rend your hearts, and not your garments, and turn to the Lord your God: for he is gracious and merciful, patient and rich in mercy, and ready to repent of the evil.—*Joel* ii. 12, 13.

And Peter remembered the word of Jesus which he had said: Before the cock crow, thou wilt deny me thrice. And going forth, he wept bitterly.—*Matt.* xxvi. 75.

For the sorrow that is according to God worketh penance, steadfast unto salvation; but the sorrow of the world worketh death.—2 *Cor.* vii. 10.

Cleanse your hands, ye sinners: and purify your hearts, ye double-minded. Be afflicted, and mourn, and weep: let your laughter be turned into mourning, and your joy into sorrow. Be humbled in the sight of the Lord, and he will exalt you.—*James* iv. 8-10.

SIN, TURNING AWAY FROM

See also: Amendment of life—page 27.

And he said to man: Behold the fear of the Lord, that is wisdom: and to depart from evil, is understanding.—*Job* xxviii. 28.

He hath delivered his soul from going into destruction, that it may live and see the light.—*Job* xxxiii. 28.

The path of the just departeth from evils: he that keepeth his soul keepeth his way.—*Prov.* xvi. 17.

He that hideth his sins, shall not prosper: but he that shall confess, and forsake them, shall obtain mercy.—*Prov.* xxviii. 13.

It is a wholesome sacrifice to take heed to the commandments, and to depart from all iniquity.

And to depart from injustice, is to offer a propitiatory sacrifice for injustices, and a begging of pardon for sins. . . .

To depart from iniquity is that which pleaseth the Lord, and to depart from injustice, is an entreaty for sins.—*Ecclus.* xxxv. 2, 3, 5.

SIN, EXHORTATION TO TURN AWAY FROM

Who is the man that desireth life: who loveth to see good days?

Keep thy tongue from evil, and thy lips from speaking guile.

Turn away from evil and do good: seek after peace and pursue it.—*Ps.* xxxiii. 13-15.

Decline from evil and do good, and dwell for ever and ever.—*Ps.* xxxvi. 27.

Be not wise in thy own conceit: fear God, and depart from evil.—*Prov.* iii. 7.

Be not without fear about sin forgiven, and add not sin upon sin.—*Ecclus.* v. 5.

Nor bind sin to sin: for even in one thou shalt not be unpunished.—*Ecclus.* vii. 8.

Abide not in the works of sinners. But trust in God, and stay in thy place.—*Ecclus.* xi. 22.

Return to the Lord, and turn away from thy injustice, and greatly hate abomination.—*Ecclus.* xvii. 23.

Turn away from sin and order thy hands aright, and cleanse thy heart from all offence.—*Ecclus.* xxxviii. 10.

Say to them: As I live, saith the Lord God, I desire not the death of the wicked, but that the wicked turn from his way, and live. Turn ye, turn ye from your evil ways: and why will you die, O house of Israel?—*Ezech.* xxxiii. 11.

But the sure foundation of God standeth firm, having this seal: the Lord knoweth who are his; and let every one depart from iniquity who nameth the name of the Lord.—2 *Tim.* ii. 19.

SIN, AVOIDING

And all the days of thy life have God in thy mind: and take heed thou never consent to sin, nor transgress the commandments of the Lord our God.—*Tob.* iv. 6.

Beware thou turn not aside to iniquity: for this thou hast begun to follow after misery.—*Job* xxxvi. 21.

I have restrained my feet from every evil way: that I may keep thy words. —*Ps.* cxviii. 101.

Seek not death in the error of your life, neither procure ye destruction by the works of your hands.—*Wis.* i. 12.

A wise heart, and which hath understanding, will abstain from sins, and in the works of justice shall have success.—*Ecclus.* iii. 32.

Son, observe the time, and fly from evil.—*Ecclus.* iv. 23.

Do no evils, and no evils shall lay hold of thee.—*Ecclus.* vii. 1.

Say not: It is through God, that she (wisdom) is not with me: for do not thou the things that he hateth.— *Ecclus.* xv. 11.

And their eye saw the majesty of his glory, and their ears heard his glorious voice, and he said to them: Beware of all iniquity.—*Ecclus.* xvii. 11.

Flee from sins as from the face of a serpent: for if thou comest near them, they will take hold of thee.—*Ecclus.* xxi. 2.

Awake, ye just, and sin not. For some have not the knowledge of God, I speak it to your shame.—1 *Cor.*xv.34.

From all appearance of evil refrain yourselves.—1 *Thess.* v. 22.

SIN, A PRAYER FOR DELIVERANCE AND PRESERVATION FROM

Who can understand sins? from my secret ones cleanse me, O Lord: and from those of others spare thy servant. —*Ps.* xviii. 13, 14.

Deliver thou me from all my iniquities: thou hast made me a reproach to the fool.—*Ps.* xxxviii. 9.

For evils without number have sur-rounded me; my iniquities have overtaken me, and I was not able to see.

They are multiplied above the hairs of my head: and my heart hath forsaken me.

Be pleased, O Lord, to deliver me: look down, O Lord, to help me.—*Ps.* xxxix. 13, 14.

Let my heart be undefiled in thy justifications, that I may not be confounded.—*Ps.* cxviii. 80.

Direct my steps according to thy word: and let no iniquity have dominion over me.—*Ps.* cxviii. 133.

And may the God of peace himself sanctify you in all things; that your whole spirit, and soul, and body, may be preserved blameless in the coming of our Lord Jesus Christ.—1 *Thess.* v. 23.

SIN, WITHDRAWING OTHERS FROM

The just considereth seriously the house of the wicked, that he may withdraw the wicked from evil.—*Prov.* xxi. 12.

The law of truth was in his (Levi's) mouth, and iniquity was not found in his lips: he walked with me in peace, and in equity, and turned many away from iniquity.—*Malach.* ii. 6.

My brethren, if any of you err from the truth, and one convert him:

He must know that he who causeth a sinner to be converted from the error of his way, shall save his soul from death, and shall cover a multitude of sins.—*James* v. 19, 20.

SIN, CERTAINTY OF THE PUNISHMENT OF

But if you do not what you say, no man can doubt but you sin against God: and know ye, that your sin shall overtake you.—*Num.* xxxii. 23.

Nor bind sin to sin: for even in one thou shalt not be unpunished.—*Ecclus.* vii. 8.

The sinner shall not escape in his rapines, and the patience of him that showeth mercy shall not be put off.— *Ecclus.* xvi. 14.

Sin shall be destroyed with the sinner.—*Ecclus.* xxvii. 3.

In those days they shall say no more: The fathers have eaten a sour grape, and the teeth of the children are set on edge.

But every one shall die for his own iniquity: every man that shall eat the sour grape, his teeth shall be set on edge.—*Jer.* xxxi. 29, 30.

Behold all souls are mine: as the soul of the father, so also the soul of the son is mine: the soul that sinneth, the same shall die.—*Ezech.* xviii. 4.

The soul that sinneth, the same shall die: the son shall not bear the iniquity of the father, and the father shall not bear the iniquity of the son: the justice of the just shall be upon him, and the wickedness of the wicked shall be upon him.—*Ezech.* xviii. 20.

Yea, if I shall say to the just that he shall surely live, and he, trusting in his justice, commit iniquity: all his justices shall be forgotten, and in his iniquity, which he hath committed, in the same shall he die.—*Ezech.* xxxiii. 13.

Now this I say, brethren, that flesh and blood cannot possess the kingdom of God: neither shall corruption possess incorruption.—1 *Cor.* xv. 50.

For know you this and understand, that no fornicator, or unclean, or covetous person (which is a serving of idols), hath inheritance in the kingdom of Christ and of God.

Let no man deceive you with vain words. For because of these things cometh the anger of God upon the children of unbelief.—*Eph.* v. 5, 6.

For this is the will of God, your sanctification; that you should abstain from fornication;

That every one of you should know how to possess his vessel in sanctification and honor:

Not in the passion of lust, like the Gentiles that know not God:

And that no man overreach, nor circumvent his brother in business: because the Lord is the avenger of all these things, as we have told you before, and have testified.—1 *Thess.* iv. 3-6.

For if we sin wilfully after having the knowledge of the truth, there is now left no sacrifice for sins,

But a certain dreadful expectation of judgment, and the rage of a fire which shall consume the adversaries.

A man making void the law of Moses, dieth without any mercy under two or three witnesses:

How much more, do you think he deserveth worse punishments, who hath trodden under foot the Son of God, and hath esteemed the blood of the testament unclean, by which he was sanctified, and hath offered an affront to the Spirit of grace?

For we know him that hath said: Vengeance belongeth to me, and I will repay. And again: The Lord shall judge his people.

It is a fearful thing to fall into the hands of the living God.—*Heb.* x. 26-31.

SIN, THE PUNISHMENT OF

See also: Wicked, punishment of the —page 589.

I. In this Life

To the woman also he said: I will multiply thy sorrows, and thy conceptions: in sorrow shalt thou bring forth children, and thou shalt be under thy husband's power, and he shall have dominion over thee.

And to Adam he said: Because thou hast hearkened to the voice of thy wife, and hast eaten of the tree, whereof I commanded thee that thou shouldst not eat, cursed is the earth in thy work; with labor and toil shalt thou eat thereof all the days of thy life.

Thorns and thistles shall it bring forth to thee; and thou shalt eat the herbs of the earth.

In the sweat of thy face shalt thou eat bread till thou return to the earth, out of which thou wast taken: for dust thou art, and into dust thou shalt return.—*Gen.* iii. 16-19.

And the Lord said to Cain: Where is thy brother Abel? And he answered, I know not: am I my brother's keeper?

And he said to him: What hast thou done? the voice of thy brother's blood crieth to me from the earth.

Now, therefore, cursed shalt thou be upon the earth, which hath opened her mouth and received the blood of thy brother at thy hand.

When thou shalt till it, it shall not

yield to thee its fruit: a fugitive and a vagabond shalt thou be upon the earth. —*Gen.* iv. 9-12.

And God seeing that the wickedness of men was great on the earth, and that all the thought of their heart was bent upon evil at all times,

It repented him that he had made man on the earth. And being touched inwardly with sorrow of heart,

He said: I will destroy man, whom I have created, from the face of the earth, from man even to beasts, from the creeping thing even to the fowls of the air, for it repenteth me that I have made them.—*Gen.* vi. 5-7.

And the Lord said: The cry of Sodom and Gomorrha is multiplied, and their sin is become exceedingly grievous. . . .

And the Lord rained upon Sodom and Gomorrha brimstone and fire from the Lord out of heaven.

And he destroyed these cities, and all the country about, all the inhabitants of the cities, and all things that spring from the earth. . . .

And Abraham got up early in the morning, and in the place where he had stood before with the Lord,

He looked towards Sodom and Gomorrha, and the whole land of that country: and he saw the ashes rise up from the earth as the smoke of a furnace.—*Gen.* xviii. 20; xix. 24, 25, 27, 28.

And when they came to the floor of Nachon, Oza put forth his hand to the ark of God, and took hold of it: because the oxen kicked and made it lean aside.

And the indignation of the Lord was enkindled against Oza, and he struck him for his rashness: and he died there before the ark of God.—2 *Kings* vi. 6, 7.

There is no health in my flesh, because of thy wrath: there is no peace for my bones, because of my sins.

For my iniquities are gone over my head: and as a heavy burden are become heavy upon me.—*Ps.* xxxvii. 4, 5.

I was dumb, and I opened not my mouth, because thou hast done it. Remove thy scourges from me.

The strength of thy hand hath made me faint in rebukes: thou hast corrected man for iniquity.

And thou hast made his soul to waste away like a spider: surely in vain is any man disquieted.—*Ps.* xxxviii. 10-12.

For whereas wickedness is fearful, it beareth witness of its condemnation: for a troubled conscience always forcasteth grievous things.—*Wis.* xvii. 10.

For Jerusalem is ruined, and Juda is fallen: because their tongue, and their devices are against the Lord, to provoke the eyes of his majesty.

The show of their countenance hath answered them: and they have proclaimed abroad their sin as Sodom, and they have not hid it: woe to their souls, for evils are rendered to them.—*Is.* iii. 8, 9.

There is none that calleth upon thy name: that riseth up, and taketh hold of thee: thou hast hid thy face from us, and hast crushed us in the hand of our iniquity.—*Is.* lxiv. 7.

Thy ways, and thy devices have brought these things upon thee: this is thy wickedness, because it is bitter, because it hath touched thy heart.—*Jer.* iv. 18.

But the heart of this people is become hard of belief and provoking, they are revolted and gone away.

And they have not said in their heart: Let us fear the Lord our God, who giveth us the early and the latter rain in due season: who preserveth for us the fulness of the yearly harvest.

Your iniquities have turned these things away, and your sins have withholden good things from you.—*Jer.* v. 23-25.

So that the Lord could no longer bear, because of the evil of your doings, and because of the abominations which you have committed: therefore your land is become a desolation, and an astonishment, and a curse, without an inhabitant, as at this day.

Because you have sacrificed to idols, and have sinned against the Lord: and have not obeyed the voice of the Lord, and have not walked in his law, and in his commandments, and in his testimonies: therefore, are these evils come upon you, as at this day.—*Jer.* xliv. 22, 23.

Our fathers have sinned, and are not: and we have borne their iniquities. . . .

The crown is fallen from our head: woe to us, because we have sinned.—*Lam.* v. 7, 16.

But exhort one another every day, whilst it is called to-day, that none of you be hardened through the deceitfulness of sin.—*Heb.* iii. 13.

II. In the Life to Come

And the Lord answered him (Moses): He that hath sinned against me, him will I strike out of my book.—*Ex.* xxxii. 33.

If thou, O Lord, wilt mark iniquities: Lord, who shall stand it.—*Ps.* cxxix. 3.

Clemency prepareth life: and the pursuing of evil things, death.—*Prov.* xi. 19.

He that soweth iniquity shall reap evils, and with the rod of his anger he shall be consumed.—*Prov.* xxii. 8.

Seek not death in the error of your life, neither procure ye destruction by the works of your hands.—*Wis.* i. 12.

And Pilate seeing that he prevailed nothing, but that rather a tumult was made; taking water washed his hands before the people, saying: I am innocent of the blood of this just man; look you to it.

And the whole people answering, said: His blood be upon us and upon our children.—*Matt.* xxvii. 24, 25.

Who, having known the justice of God, did not understand that they who do such things, are worthy of death; and not only they that do them, but they also that consent to them that do them.—*Rom.* i. 32.

What fruit therefore had you then in those things, of which you are now ashamed? For the end of them is death. . . .

For the wages of sin is death. But the grace of God, life everlasting, in Christ Jesus our Lord.—*Rom.* vi. 21, 23.

Then when concupiscence hath conceived, it bringeth forth sin. But sin, when it is completed, begetteth death.—*James* i. 15.

There shall not enter into it (the new Jerusalem) any thing defiled, or that worketh abomination, or maketh a lie, but they that are written in the book of life of the Lamb.—*Apoc.* xxi. 27.

SINS ARE KNOWN TO GOD, OUR

And the Lord said: The cry of Sodom and Gomorrha is multiplied, and their sin is become exceedingly grievous.

I will go down and see whether they have done according to the cry that is come to me: or whether it be not so, that I may know.—*Gen.* xviii. 20, 21.

For he knoweth the vanity of men, and when he seeth iniquity, doth he not consider it?—*Job* xi. 11.

With him is strength and wisdom: he knoweth both the deceiver, and him that is deceived. . . .

He discovereth deep things out of darkness, and bringeth up to light the shadow of death.—*Job* xii. 16, 22.

The eye of the adulterer observeth darkness, saying: No eye shall see me: and he will cover his face.

He diggeth through houses in the dark, as in the day they had appointed for themselves, and they have not known the light. . . .

God hath given him place for penance, and he abuseth it unto pride: but his eyes are upon his ways.—*Job* xxiv. 15, 16, 23.

For his eyes are upon the ways of men, and he considereth all their steps.

There is no darkness, and there is no shadow of death, where they may be hid who work iniquity.—*Job* xxxiv. 21, 22.

O God, thou knowest my foolishness; and my offences are not hidden from thee.—*Ps.* lxviii. 6.

Thou hast set our iniquities before thy eyes: our life in the light of thy countenance.—*Ps.* lxxxix. 8.

How long shall sinners, O Lord: how long shall sinners glory? . . .

They have slain the widow and the stranger: and they have murdered the fatherless.

And they have said: The Lord shall not see: neither shall the God of Jacob understand.

Understand, ye senseless among the people: and, you fools, be wise at last.

He that planted the ear, shall he not hear? or he that formed the eye, doth he not consider?

He that chastiseth nations, shall he not rebuke: he that teacheth man knowledge?—*Ps.* xciii. 3, 6-10.

And all their works are as the sun in the sight of God: and his eyes are continually upon their ways.

Their covenants were not hid by their iniquity, and all their iniquities are in the sight of God.—*Ecclus.* xvii. 16, 17.

Every man that passeth beyond his own bed, despising his own soul, and saying: Who seeth me?

Darkness compasseth me about, and the walls cover me, and no man seeth me: whom do I fear? the most High will not remember my sins.

And he understandeth not that his eye seeth all things, for such a man's fear driveth from him the fear of God, and the eyes of men fearing him:

And he knoweth not that the eyes of the Lord are far brighter than the sun, beholding round about all the ways of men, and the bottom of the deep and looking into the hearts of men, into the most hidden parts.

For all things were known to the Lord God, before they were created: so also after they were perfected he beholdeth all things.—*Ecclus.* xxiii. 25-29.

No thought escapeth him, and no word can hide itself from him.—*Ecclus.* xlii. 20.

For my eyes are upon all their ways: they are not hid from my face, and their iniquity hath not been hid from my eyes.—*Jer.* xvi. 17.

Because they have acted folly in Israel, and have committed adultery with the wives of their friends, and have spoken lying words in my name, which I commanded them not: I am the judge and the witness, saith the Lord.—*Jer.* xxix. 23.

Because I know your manifold crimes, and your grievous sins: enemies of the just, taking bribes, and oppressing the poor in the gate.—*Amos* v. 12.

For her sins have reached unto heaven, and the Lord hath remembered her iniquities.—*Apoc.* xviii. 5.

SINS OF THE WICKED TURN AGAINST THEM, THE

But if you do not what you say, no man can doubt but you sin against God: and know ye, that your sin shall overtake you.—*Num.* xxxii. 23.

On the contrary I have seen those who work iniquity, and sow sorrows, and reap them,

Perishing by the blast of God, and consumed by the spirit of his wrath.—*Job* iv. 8, 9.

Shall not the light of the wicked be extinguished, and the flame of his fire not shine? . . .

The step of his strength shall be straitened, and his own counsel shall cast him down headlong.

For he hath thrust his feet into a net, and walketh in its meshes.—*Job* xviii. 5, 7, 8.

Behold he hath been in labor with injustice; he hath conceived sorrow, and brought forth iniquity.

He hath opened a pit and dug it: and he is fallen into the hole he made.

His sorrow shall be turned on his own head: and his iniquity shall come down upon his crown.—*Ps.* vii. 15-17.

I will rejoice in thy salvation: the Gentiles have stuck fast in the destruction which they prepared.

Their foot hath been taken in the very snare which they hid.

The Lord shall be known when he executeth judgments: the sinner hath been caught in the works of his own hands.—*Ps.* ix. 16, 17.

And they themselves lie in wait for their own blood, and practise deceits against their own souls.—*Prov.* i. 18.

Because they have hated instruction, and received not the fear of the Lord,

Nor consented to my counsel, but despised all my reproof.

Therefore they shall eat the fruit of their own way, and shall be filled with their own devices.—*Prov.* i. 29-31.

His own iniquities catch the wicked, and he is fast bound with the ropes of his own sins.—*Prov.* v. 22.

The simplicity of the just shall guide them: and the deceitfulness of the wicked shall destroy them. . . .

The justice of the upright shall make

his way prosperous: and the wicked man shall fall by his own wickedness.

The justice of the righteous shall deliver them: and the unjust shall be caught in their own snares.—*Prov.* xi. 3, 5, 6.

Justice keepeth the way of the innocent: but wickedness overthroweth the sinner.—*Prov.* xiii. 6.

The robberies of the wicked shall be their downfall, because they would not do judgment.—*Prov.* xxi. 7.

He that soweth iniquity shall reap evils, and with the rod of his anger he shall be consumed.—*Prov.* xxii. 8.

He that diggeth a pit, shall fall into it: and he that rolleth a stone, it shall return to him.—*Prov.* xxvi. 27.

A snare shall entangle the wicked man when he sinneth: and the just shall praise and rejoice.—*Prov.* xxix. 6.

He that diggeth a pit, shall fall into it: and he that breaketh a hedge, a serpent shall bite him.

He that removeth stones, shall be hurt by them: and he that cutteth trees, shall be wounded by them.—*Eccles.* x. 8, 9.

Seek not death in the error of your life, neither procure ye destruction by the works of your hands.—*Wis.* i. 12.

These things they thought, and were deceived: for their own malice blinded them.—*Wis.* ii. 21.

But the wicked shall be punished according to their own devices: who have neglected the just, and have revolted from the Lord.—*Wis.* iii. 10.

That they might know that by what things a man sinneth, by the same also he is tormented.—*Wis.* xi. 17.

Wherefore thou hast also greatly tormented them who in their life have lived foolishly and unjustly, by the same things which they worshipped.—*Wis.* xii. 23.

For whereas wickedness is fearful, it beareth witness of its condemnation: for a troubled conscience always forecasteth grievous things.—*Wis.* xvii. 10.

A sinner is caught in his own vanity, and the proud and the evil speakers shall fall thereby.—*Ecclus.* xxiii. 8.

If one cast a stone on high, it will fall upon his own head: and the deceitful stroke will wound the deceitful.

He that diggeth a pit, shall fall into it: and he that setteth a stone for his neighbor, shall stumble upon it: and he that layeth a snare for another, shall perish in it.

A mischievous counsel shall be rolled back upon the author, and he shall not know from whence it cometh to him.—*Ecclus.* xxvii. 28-30.

For our iniquities are multiplied before thee, and our sins have testified against us: for our wicked doings are with us, and we have known our iniquities.—*Is.* lix. 12.

But as for them whose heart walketh after their scandals and abominations, I will lay their way upon their head, saith the Lord God.—*Ezech.* xi. 21.

According to the multitude of them so have they sinned against me: I will change their glory into shame.

They shall eat the sins of my people, a..d shall lift up their souls to their iniquity.

And there shall be like people like priest: and I will visit their ways upon them, and I will repay them their devices.—*Osee* iv. 7-9.

For they shall sow wind, and reap a whirlwind.—*Osee* viii. 7.

You have ploughed wickedness, you have reaped iniquity, you have eaten the fruit of lying.—*Osee* x. 13.

Be not deceived, God is not mocked. For what things a man shall sow, those also shall he reap. For he that soweth in his flesh, of the flesh also shall reap corruption. But he that soweth in the spirit, of the spirit shall reap life everlasting.—*Gal.* vi. 7, 8.

SINS CANNOT HURT GOD, OUR

See: Malice of men, God is above the reach of the—page 300.

SINCERITY

See also: Truth, love of—page 567.

He that walketh sincerely, walketh confidently: but he that perverteth his ways, shall be manifest.—*Prov.* x. 9.

A perverse heart is abominable to the Lord: and his will is in them that walk sincerely.—*Prov.* xi. 20.

Therefore let us feast, not with the old leaven, nor with the leaven of malice and wickedness; but with the unleavened bread of sincerity and truth. —1 *Cor.* v. 8.

SINCERITY IN THE SERVICE OF GOD

See: Service of God, sincerity in the —page 513.

SINNER, THE

See also: Wicked, the—page 586.

But they provoked thee to wrath, and departed from thee, and threw thy law behind their backs.—2 *Esd.* ix. 26.

Behold among his saints none is unchangeable, and the heavens are not pure in his sight.

How much more is man abominable, and unprofitable, who drinketh iniquity like water?—*Job* xv. 15, 16.

But to the sinner God hath said: Why dost thou declare my justices, and take my covenant in thy mouth?

Seeing thou hast hated discipline: and hast cast my words behind thee. . . .

Thy mouth hath abounded with evil, and thy tongue framed deceits. . . .

These things hast thou done, and I was silent.

Thou thoughtest unjustly that I should be like to thee: but I will reprove thee, and set before thy face.

Understand these things, you that forget God; lest he snatch you away, and there be none to deliver you.— *Ps.* xlix. 16, 17, 19, 21, 22.

Who by his power ruleth for ever: his eyes behold the nations; let not them that provoke him be exalted in themselves.—*Ps.* lxv. 7.

Salvation is far from sinners; because they have not sought thy justifications.—*Ps.* cxviii. 155.

Justice keepeth the way of the innocent: but wickedness overthroweth the sinner.

One is as it were rich, when he hath nothing: and another is as it were poor, when he hath great riches.—*Prov.* xiii. 6, 7.

He that deviseth to do evils, shall be called a fool—*Prov.* xxiv. 8.

The lovers of evil things deserve to have no better things to trust in, both they that make them, and they that love them, and they that worship them.— *Wis.* xv. 6.

For his heart is ashes, and his hope vain earth, and his life more base than clay.—*Wis.* xv. 10.

Error and darkness are created with sinners: and they that glory in evil things, grow old in evil.—*Ecclus.* xi. 16.

Praise is not seemly in the mouth of a sinner.—*Ecclus.* xv. 9.

Anger and fury are both of them abominable, and the sinful man shall be subject to them.—*Ecclus.* xxvii. 33.

For what shall I strike you any more, you that increase transgression? the whole head is sick, and the whole heart is sad.—*Is.* i. 5.

But thou hast made me to serve with thy sins, thou hast wearied me with thy iniquities. . . .

Put me in remembrance, and let us plead together: tell me if thou hast any thing to justify thyself.—*Is.* xliii. 24, 26.

My people have been a lost flock: . . . they have gone from mountain to hill, they have forgotten their resting place.

All that found them, have devoured them: and their enemies said: We have not sinned in so doing: because they have sinned against the Lord the beauty of justice, and against the Lord the hope of their fathers.—*Jer.* l. 6, 7.

Whosoever abideth in him, sinneth not; and whosoever sinneth, hath not seen him, nor known him. . . .

He that committeth sin is of the devil: for the devil sinneth from the beginning. . . .

Whosoever is born of God, committeth not sin: for his seed abideth in him, and he cannot sin, because he is born of God.

In this the children of God are manifest, and the children of the devil. Whosoever is not just, is not of God, nor he that loveth not his brother.— 1 *John* iii. 6, 8-10.

Dearly beloved, follow not that which is evil, but that which is good. He that doth good, is of God: he that doth evil, hath not seen God.—3 *John* i. 11.

And to the angel of the church of Sardis, write: These things saith he, that hath the seven spirits of God, and the seven stars: I know thy works, that thou hast the name of being alive: and thou art dead.—*Apoc.* iii. 1.

SINNER, FOLLY AND BLIND-NESS OF THE

Neither are they content not to return thanks for benefits received, and to violate in themselves the laws of humanity, but they think they can also escape the justice of God who seeth all things.—*Esther* xvi. 4.

Thou hast set their heart far from understanding, therefore they shall not be exalted.—*Job* xvii. 4.

The eye of the adulterer observeth darkness, saying: No eye shall see me: and he will cover his face.

He diggeth through houses in the dark, as in the day they had appointed for themselves, and they have not known the light.

If the morning suddenly appear, it is to them the shadow of death: and they walk in darkness as if it were in light.—*Job* xxiv. 15-17.

O ye sons of men, how long will you be dull of heart? why do you love vanity, and seek after lying?—*Ps.* iv. 3.

The sinner hath provoked the Lord, according to the multitude of his wrath he will not seek him:

God is not before his eyes: his ways are filthy at all times.

Thy judgments are removed from his sight: he shall rule over all his enemies.

For he hath said in his heart: I shall not be moved from generation to generation, and shall be without evil. . . .

For he hath said in his heart: God hath forgotten, he hath turned away his face not to see to the end. . . .

Wherefore hath the wicked provoked God? for he hath said in his heart: He will not require it.

Thou seest it, for thou considerest labor and sorrow: that thou mayst deliver them into thy hands.—*Ps.* ix. (*Heb.* x.) 4-6, 11, 13, 14.

Draw me not away together with the wicked; and with the workers of iniquity destroy me not:

Who speak peace with their neighbor, but evils are in their hearts. . . .

Because they have not understood the works of the Lord, and the operations of his hands: thou shalt destroy them, and shalt not build them up.—*Ps.* xxvii. 3, 5.

And man when he was in honor did not understand; he is compared to senseless beasts, and is become like to them.—*Ps.* xlviii. 13.

And they said: How doth God know? and is there knowledge in the most High?

Behold these are sinners; and yet abounding in the world, they have obtained riches.—*Ps.* lxxii. 11, 12.

They have not known nor understood: they walk on in darkness: all the foundations of the earth shall be moved.—*Ps.* lxxxi. 5.

How long shall sinners, O Lord: how long shall sinners glory?

Shall they utter, and speak iniquity: shall all speak who work injustice? . . .

And they have said: The Lord shall not see: neither shall the God of Jacob understand.

Understand, ye senseless among the people: and, you fools, be wise at last.

He that planted the ear, shall he not hear? or he that formed the eye, doth he not consider?

He that chastiseth nations, shall he not rebuke: he that teacheth man knowledge?—*Ps.* xciii. 3, 4, 7-10.

They made also a calf in Horeb: and they adored the graven thing.

And they changed their glory into the likeness of a calf that eateth grass.—*Ps.* cv. 19, 20.

And I said: Perhaps darkness shall cover me: and night shall be my light in my pleasures.

But darkness shall not be dark to thee, and night shall be light as the day: the darkness thereof, and the light thereof are alike to thee.—*Ps.* cxxxviii. 11, 12.

Such also is the way of an adulterous woman, who eateth, and wipeth her mouth, and saith: I have done no evil. —*Prov.* xxx. 20.

But let our strength be the law of justice: for that which is feeble, is found to be nothing worth. . . .

These things they thought, and were deceived: for their own malice blinded them.

And they knew not the secrets of

God, nor hoped for the wages of justice, nor esteemed the honor of holy souls.—*Wis.* ii. 11, 21, 22.

Therefore we have erred from the way of truth, and the light of justice hath not shined unto us, and the sun of understanding hath not risen upon us.

We wearied ourselves in the way of iniquity and destruction, and have walked through hard ways, but the way of the Lord we have not known.—*Wis.* v. 6, 7.

For regarding not wisdom, they did not only slip in this, that they were ignorant of good things, but they left also unto men a memorial of their folly, so that in the things in which they sinned, they could not so much as lie hid.—*Wis.* x. 8.

But they have fled from the praise of God, and from his blessing.—*Wis.* xv. 19.

In the treasures of wisdom is understanding, and religiousness of knowledge: but to sinners wisdom is an abomination.—*Ecclus.* i. 26.

Every man that passeth beyond his own bed, despising his own soul, and saying: Who seeth me?

Darkness compasseth me about, and the walls cover me, and no man seeth me: whom do I fear? the most High will not remember my sins.

And he understandeth not that his eye seeth all things, for such a man's fear driveth from him the fear of God, and the eyes of men fearing him:

And he knoweth not that the eyes of the Lord are far brighter than the sun, beholding round about all the ways of men, and the bottom of the deep, and looking into the hearts of men, into the most hidden parts.—*Ecclus.* xxiii. 25-28.

A sinful man will flee reproof, and will find an excuse according to his will.—*Ecclus.* xxxii. 21.

The harp, and the lyre, and the timbrel, and the pipe, and wine are in your feasts: and the work of the Lord you regard not, nor do you consider the works of his hands.

Therefore is my people led away captive, because they had not knowledge, and their nobles have perished with famine, and their multitude were dried up with thirst.—*Is.* v. 12, 13.

Woe to you that call evil good, and good evil: that put darkness for light, and light for darkness: that put bitter for sweet, and sweet for bitter.

Woe to you that are wise in your own eyes, and prudent in your own conceits.—*Is.* v. 20, 21.

Wherefore hear the word of the Lord, ye scornful men, who rule over my people that is in Jerusalem.

For you have said: We have entered into a league with death, and we have made a covenant with hell. When the overflowing scourge shall pass through, it shall not come upon us: for we have placed our hope in lies, and by falsehood we are protected. . . .

And your league with death shall be abolished, and your covenant with hell shall not stand: when the overflowing scourge shall pass, you shall be trodden down by it.

Whensoever it shall pass through, it shall take you away: because in the morning early it shall pass through, in the day and in the night, and vexation alone shall make you understand what you hear.—*Is.* xxviii. 14, 15, 18, 19.

Woe to you that are deep of heart, to hide your counsel from the Lord: and their works are in the dark, and they say: Who seeth us, and who knoweth us?

This thought of yours is perverse: as if the clay should think against the potter, and the work should say to the maker thereof: Thou madest me not: or the thing framed should say to him that fashioned it: Thou understandest not.—*Is.* xxix. 15, 16.

And thou hast trusted in thy wickedness, and hast said: There is none that seeth me. Thy wisdom, and thy knowledge, this hath deceived thee. And thou hast said in thy heart: I am, and besides me there is no other.—*Is.* xlvii. 10.

For my foolish people have not known me: they are foolish and senseless children: they are wise to do evil, but to do good they have no knowledge. —*Jer.* iv. 22.

Hear, O foolish people, and without understanding: who have eyes, and see not: and ears, and hear not.—*Jer.* v. 21.

They have sown wheat, and reaped

thorns: they have received an inheritance, and it shall not profit them: you shall be ashamed of your fruits, because of the fierce wrath of the Lord.—*Jer.* xii. 13.

Thou hast forsaken the fountain of wisdom.—*Bar.* iii. 12.

And he said to me: Surely thou seest, O son of man, what the ancients of the house of Israel do in the dark, every one in private in his chamber: for they say: The Lord seeth us not, the Lord hath forsaken the earth.—*Ezech.* viii. 12.

And every one that heareth these my words, and doth them not, shall be like a foolish man that built his house upon the sand,

And the rain fell, and the floods came, and the winds blew, and they beat upon that house, and it fell, and great was the fall thereof.—*Matt.* vii. 26, 27.

And this is the judgment: because the light is come into the world, and men loved darkness rather than the light: for their works were evil.

For every one that doth evil hateth the light, and cometh not to the light, that his works may not be reproved.—*John* iii. 19, 20.

But these men, as irrational beasts, naturally tending to the snare and to destruction, blaspheming those things which they know not, shall perish in their corruption,

Receiving the reward of their injustice, counting for a pleasure the delights of a day: stains and spots, sporting themselves to excess, rioting in their feasts with you. . . .

Leaving the right way, they have gone astray, having followed the way of Balaam of Bosor, who loved the wages of iniquity.—*2 Peter* ii. 12, 13, 15.

Because thou sayest: I am rich, and made wealthy, and have need of nothing: and knowest not, that thou art wretched, and miserable, and poor, and blind, and naked.—*Apoc.* iii. 17.

SINNER IS GOD'S ENEMY, THE

Thou shalt fly lying. The innocent and just person thou shalt not put to death: because I abhor the wicked.—*Ex.* xxiii. 7.

God will not cast away the simple, nor reach out his hand to the evildoer.—*Job* viii. 20.

I made a covenant with my eyes, that I would not so much as think upon a virgin.

For what part should God from above have in me, and what inheritance the Almighty from on high?

Is not destruction to the wicked, and aversion to them that work iniquity?—*Job* xxxi. 1-3.

Thou hatest all the workers of iniquity: thou wilt destroy all that speak a lie.

The bloody and the deceitful man the Lord will abhor.—*Ps.* v. 7.

Thou hast despised all them that fall off from thy judgments; for their thought is unjust.—*Ps.* cxviii. 118.

A perverse heart is abominable to the Lord: and his will is in them that walk sincerely.—*Prov.* xi. 20.

But to God the wicked and his wickedness are hateful alike.—*Wis.* xiv. 9.

For there is no good for him that is always occupied in evil, and that giveth no alms: for the Highest hateth sinners, and hath mercy on the penitent.—*Ecclus.* xii. 3.

You have wearied the Lord with your words, and you said: Wherein have we wearied him? In that you say: Every one that doth evil, is good in the sight of the Lord, and such please him: or surely where is the God of judgment?—*Malach.* ii. 17.

If we say that we have fellowship with him, and walk in darkness, we lie, and do not the truth.—*1 John* i. 6.

SINNER AN ENEMY TO HIS OWN SOUL, THE

But they that commit sin and iniquity, are enemies to their own soul.—*Tob.* xii. 10.

Can the rush be green without moisture? or a sedge-bush grow without water?

When it is yet in flower, and is not plucked up with the hand, it withereth before all herbs.

Even so are the ways of all that forget God, and the hope of the hypocrite shall perish.

His folly shall not please him, and his trust shall be like the spider's web.

He shall lean upon his house, and it shall not stand: he shall prop it up, and it shall not rise.—*Job* viii. 11-15.

He is wise in heart, and mighty in strength: who hath resisted him, and hath had peace?—*Job* ix. 4.

Can he be healed that loveth not judgment?—*Job* xxxiv. 17.

The Lord trieth the just and the wicked: but he that loveth iniquity hateth his own soul.—*Ps.* x. 6.

But he that shall sin against me, shall hurt his own soul. All that hate me love death.—*Prov.* viii. 36.

For wisdom will not enter into a malicious soul, nor dwell in a body subject to sins.

For the Holy Spirit of discipline will flee from the deceitful, and will withdraw himself from thoughts that are without understanding, and he shall not abide when iniquity cometh in.—*Wis.* i. 4, 5.

For God made not death, neither hath he pleasure in the destruction of the living.

For he created all things that they might be: and he made the nations of the earth for health: and there is no poison of destruction in them, nor kingdom of hell upon the earth. . . .

But the wicked with works and words have called it to them: and esteeming it a friend, have fallen away, and have made a covenant with it: because they are worthy to be of the part thereof.—*Wis.* i. 13, 14, 16.

Who will justify him that sinneth against his own soul? and who will honor him that dishonoreth his own soul?—*Ecclus.* x. 32.

He that is evil to himself, to whom will he be good? and he shall not take pleasure in his goods.—*Ecclus.* iv. 5.

And he that sinneth against his own soul, shall be despised.—*Ecclus.* xix. 4.

Destruction is thy own, O Israel: thy help is only in me.—*Osee* xiii. 9.

They that are vain observe vanities, forsake their own mercy.—*Jonas* ii. 9.

And you will not come to me that you may have life.—*John* v. 40.

SLANDER

See: Detraction—page 110.

SLAVES AND SLAVERY

If thou buy a Hebrew servant, six years shall he serve thee: in the seventh, he shall go out free for nothing.

With what raiment he came in, with the like let him go out: if having a wife, his wife also shall go out with him.—*Ex.* xxi. 2, 3.

Let a wise servant be dear to thee as thy own soul, defraud him not of liberty, nor leave him needy.—*Ecclus.* vii. 23.

If thou have a faithful servant, let him be to thee as thy own soul: treat him as a brother: because in the blood of thy soul thou hast gotten him.—*Ecclus.* xxxiii. 31.

For perhaps he therefore departed for a season from thee, that thou mightest receive him again for ever:

Not now as a servant, but instead of a servant, a most dear brother, especially to me: but how much more to thee both in the flesh and in the Lord?—*Phile.* i. 15, 16.

SLOTH

See: Laziness, page 275.

SOLICITUDE, VAIN OR WORLDLY

When the wicked man is dead, there shall be no hope any more: and the expectation of the solicitous shall perish.—*Prov.* xi. 7.

Therefore I say to you, be not solicitous for your life, what you shall eat, nor for your body, what you shall put on. Is not the life more than the meat: and the body more than the raiment?

Behold the birds of the air, for they neither sow, nor do they reap, nor gather into barns: and your heavenly Father feedeth them. Are not you of much more value than they?

And which of you by taking thought, can add to his stature one cubit?

And for raiment why are you solicitous? Consider the lilies of the field, how they grow: they labor not, neither do they spin.

But I say to you, that not even Solomon in all his glory was arrayed as one of these.

And if the grass of the field, which is to-day, and to-morrow is cast into the oven, God doth so clothe: how much more you, O ye of little faith?

Be not solicitous therefore, saying, What shall we eat: or what shall we drink, or wherewith shall we be clothed?

For after all these things do the heathens seek. For your Father knoweth that you have need of all these things.

Seek ye therefore first the kingdom of God, and his justice, and all these things shall be added unto you.

Be not solicitous therefore for to-morrow; for the morrow will be solicitous for itself. Sufficient for the day is the evil thereof.—*Matt.* vi. 25-34.

Labor not for the meat which perisheth, but for that which endureth unto life everlasting, which the Son of man will give you. For him hath God, the Father, sealed.—*John* vi. 27.

Let not your heart be troubled. You believe in God, believe also in me.— *John* xiv. 1.

Be nothing solicitous; but in every thing, by prayer and supplication, with thanksgiving, let your petitions be made known to God.—*Philipp.* iv. 6.

SOPHISTRY

There is a man that is subtle and a teacher of many, and yet is unprofitable to his own soul.—*Ecclus.* xxxvii. 21.

He that speaketh sophistically, is hateful: he shall be destitute of every thing.—*Ecclus.* xxxvii. 23.

There is an exquisite subtilty, and the same is unjust.

And there is one that uttereth an exact word telling the truth.—*Ecclus.* xix. 22, 23.

SORROW FOR SIN

See: Sin, sorrow for—page 527.

SORROWS AND TRIBULATIONS, GOD COMFORTS US IN OUR

See: Tribulations—page 562.

SORROWS AND AFFLICTIONS ARE KNOWN TO GOD, OUR

See also: Cry of the distressed reaches God, the—page 94.

Lord, all my desire is before thee, and my groaning is not hidden from thee.—*Ps.* xxxvii. 10.

Praise the Lord, for he is good: for his mercy endureth for ever. . . .

For he was mindful of us in our affliction: for his mercy endureth for ever.—*Ps.* cxxxv. 1, 23.

SORROW INTO JOY, GOD TURNS OUR

But this every one is sure of that worshippeth thee, that his life, if it be under trial, shall be crowned: and if it be under tribulation, it shall be delivered: and if it be under correction, it shall be allowed to come to thy mercy.

For thou art not delighted in our being lost: because after a storm thou makest a calm, and after tears and weeping thou pourest in joyfulness.— *Tob.* iii. 21, 22.

If thou wilt put away from thee the iniquity that is in thy hand, and let not injustice remain in thy tabernacle: . . .

Thou shalt also forget misery, and remember it only as waters that are passed away.

And brightness like that of the noonday, shall arise to thee at evening: and when thou shalt think thyself consumed, thou shalt rise as the day star. —*Job* xi. 14, 16, 17.

In the evening weeping shall have place, and in the morning gladness. . . .

Thou hast turned for me my mourning into joy: thou hast cut my sackcloth, and hast compassed me with gladness.—*Ps.* xxix. 6, 12.

We have passed through fire and water, and thou hast brought us out into a refreshment.—*Ps.* lxv. 12.

How great troubles hast thou shown me, many and grievous: and turning thou hast brought me to life, and hast brought me back again from the depths of the earth:

Thou hast multiplied thy magnificence; and turning to me, thou hast comforted me.—*Ps.* lxx. 20, 21.

They that sow in tears shall reap in joy.

Going they went and wept, casting their seeds.

But coming they shall come with joyfulness, carrying their sheaves.—*Ps.* cxxv. 5-7.

He shall cast death down headlong for ever: and the Lord God shall wipe away tears from every face, and the reproach of his people he shall take away from off the whole earth: for the Lord hath spoken it.

And they shall say in that day: Lo, this is our God, we have waited for him, and he will save us: this is the Lord, we have patiently waited for him, we shall rejoice and be joyful in his salvation.—*Is.* xxv. 8, 9.

The spirit of the Lord is upon me, because the Lord hath anointed me: he hath sent me to preach to the meek, to heal the contrite of heart, and to preach a release to the captives, and deliverance to them that are shut up.

To proclaim the acceptable year of the Lord, and the day of vengeance of our God: to comfort all that mourn:

To appoint to the mourners of Sion, and to give them a crown for ashes, the oil of joy for mourning, a garment of praise for the spirit of grief: and they shall be called in it the mighty ones of justice, the planting of the Lord to glorify him.—*Is.* lxi. 1-3.

Then shall the virgin rejoice in the dance, the young men and old men together: and I will turn their mourning into joy, and will comfort them, and make them joyful after their sorrow.—*Jer.* xxxi. 13.

For my hope is in the Eternal that he will save you: and joy is come upon me from the Holy One, because of the mercy which shall come to you from our everlasting Saviour.

For I sent you forth with mourning and weeping: but the Lord will bring you back to me with joy and gladness for ever.—*Bar.* iv. 22, 23.

Blessed are they that mourn: for they shall be comforted.—*Matt.* v. 5.

Blessed are ye that hunger now: for you shall be filled. Blessed are ye that weep now: for you shall laugh.—*Luke* vi. 21.

Amen, amen I say to you, that you shall lament and weep, but the world shall rejoice; and you shall be made sorrowful, but your sorrow shall be turned into joy.

A woman, when she is in labor, hath sorrow, because her hour is come; but when she hath brought forth the child, she remembereth no more the anguish, for joy that a man is born into the world.

So also you now indeed have sorrow; but I will see you again, and your heart shall rejoice; and your joy no man shall take from you.—*John* xvi. 20-22.

That our hope for you may be steadfast: knowing that as you are partakers of the sufferings, so shall you be also of the consolation.—*2 Cor.* i. 7.

Wherein you shall greatly rejoice, if now you must be for a little time made sorrowful in divers temptations:

That the trial of your faith (much more precious than gold which is tried by the fire) may be found unto praise and glory and honor at the appearing of Jesus Christ.—*1 Peter* i. 6, 7.

And God shall wipe away all tears from their eyes: and death shall be no more, nor mourning, nor crying, nor sorrow shall be any more, for the former things are passed away.—*Apoc.* xxi. 4.

SORROWING, THE

See also: Sadness—page 495.

But she said to them: Call me not Noemi (that is, beautiful,) but call me Mara, (that is, bitter,) for the Almighty hath quite filled me with bitterness.

I went out full, and the Lord hath brought me back empty. Why then do you call me Noemi, whom the Lord hath humbled and the Almighty hath afflicted?—*Ruth* i. 20, 21.

Wherefore I will pray to the Lord, and address my speech to God: . . .

Who setteth up the humble on high, and comforteth with health those that mourn.—*Job* v. 8, 11.

I have labored in my groanings,

every night I will wash my bed: I will water my couch with my tears.—*Ps.* vi. 7.

Is there no balm in Galaad? or is there no physician there? Why then is not the wound of the daughter of my people closed?—*Jer.* viii. 22.

O all ye that pass by the way, attend, and see if there be any sorrow like to my sorrow: for he hath made a vintage of me, as the Lord spoke in the day of his fierce anger.—*Lam.* i. 12.

Blessed are they that mourn: for they shall be comforted.—*Matt.* v. 5.

Come to me, all you that labor, and are burdened, and I will refresh you. —*Matt.* xi. 28.

But in all things let us exhibit ourselves as the ministers of God, in much patience, in tribulation, in necessities, in distresses;

. . . As sorrowful, yet always rejoicing; as needy, yet enriching many; as having nothing, and possessing all things.—2 *Cor.* vi. 4, 10.

Is any of you sad? Let him pray. —*James* v. 13.

SORROWING AND AFFLICTED, WE SHOULD COMFORT THE

See: Comfort the afflicted—page 56.

SOUL, THE

And he said: Let us make man to our image and likeness. . . .

And God created man to his own image: to the image of God he created him.—*Gen.* i. 26, 27.

And the Lord God formed man of the slime of the earth: and breathed into his face the breath of life, and man became a living soul.—*Gen.* ii. 7.

Keep thou my soul, and deliver me: I shall not be ashamed, for I have hoped in thee.—*Ps.* xxiv. 20.

For the price of a harlot is scarce one loaf: but the woman catcheth the precious soul of a man.—*Prov.* vi. 26.

Where there is no knowledge of the soul, there is no good: and he that is hasty with his feet shall stumble.— *Prov.* xix. 2.

My son, prove thy soul in thy life: and if it be wicked, give it no power. —*Ecclus.* xxxvii. 30.

SOUL, VALUE OF THE

But he that possesseth a mind, loveth his own soul.—*Prov.* xix. 8.

My son, keep thy soul in meekness, and give it honor according to its desert.

Who will justify him. that sinneth against his own soul? and who will honor him that dishonoreth his own soul?—*Ecclus.* x. 31, 32.

For what shall it profit a man, if he gain the whole world, and suffer the loss of his soul?

Or what shall a man give in exchange for his soul?—*Mark* viii. 36, 37.

SOUL WITHOUT GOD, THE WRETCHEDNESS OF A

Behold thou dost cast me out this day from the face of the earth, and I shall be hidden from thy face, and I shall be a vagabond and a fugitive on the earth.—*Gen.* iv. 14.

And my wrath shall be kindled against them in that day: and I will forsake them, and will hide my face from them, and they shall be devoured: all evils and afflictions shall find them, so that they shall say in that day: In truth it is because God is not with me, that these evils have found me.— *Deut.* xxxi. 17.

I stretched forth my hands to thee: my soul is as earth without water unto thee. Hear me speedily, O Lord: my spirit hath fainted away.

Turn not away thy face from me, lest I be like unto them that go down into the pit.—*Ps.* cxlii. 6, 7.

When you shall be as an oak with the leaves falling off, and as a garden without water.

And your strength shall be as the ashes of tow, and your work as a spark: and both shall burn together, and there shall be none to quench it.—*Is.* i. 30, 31.

To what shall I compare thee? or to what shall I liken thee, O daughter of Jerusalem? to what shall I equal thee, that I may comfort thee, O virgin daughter of Sion? for great as the sea is thy destruction: who shall heal thee?—*Lam.* ii. 13.

Yea, and woe to them, when I shall depart from them.—*Osee* ix. 12.

Jesus answered: He it is to whom I shall reach bread dipped. And when he had dipped the bread, he gave it to Judas Iscariot, the son of Simon.

And after the morsel, Satan entered into him. And Jesus said to him: That which thou dost, do quickly. . . .

He therefore having received the morsel, went out immediately. And it was night.—*John* xiii. 26, 27, 30.

SPEAKING TO GOD

And Abraham answered, and said: Seeing I have once begun, I will speak to my Lord, whereas I am dust and ashes.—*Gen.* xviii. 27.

With me is prayer to the God of my life. I will say to God: Thou art my support.

Why hast thou forgotten me? and why go I mourning, whilst my enemy afflicteth me?—*Ps.* xli. 9, 10.

SPEAKING TO US, GOD

What is all flesh, that it should hear the voice of the living God, who speaketh out of the midst of the fire, as we have heard, and be able to live?—*Deut.* v. 26.

And the Lord came and stood: and he called, as he had called the other times: Samuel, Samuel. And Samuel said: Speak, Lord, for thy servant heareth.—1 *Kings* iii. 10.

Hear, O my people, and I will speak: O Israel, and I will testify to thee: I am God thy God.—*Ps.* xlix. 7.

I will hear what the Lord God will speak in me: for he will speak peace unto his people:

And unto his saints: and unto them that are converted to the heart.—*Ps.* lxxxiv. 9.

To-day if you shall hear his voice, harden not your hearts.—*Ps.* xciv. 8.

God hath spoken in his holiness.—*Ps.* cvii. 8.

Behold my beloved speaketh to me.—*Cant.* ii. 10.

Therefore, behold I will allure her, and will lead her into the wilderness: and I will speak to her heart.—*Osee* ii. 14.

And [1]they said one to another: Was

[1]The two disciples on the way to Emmaus.

not our heart burning within us, whilst he spoke in the way, and opened to us the scriptures?—*Luke* xxiv. 32.

Behold, I stand at the gate, and knock. If any man shall hear my voice, and open to me the door, I will come in to him, and will sup with him, and he with me.—*Apoc.* iii. 20.

SPIRITUAL LIFE, THE

All the glory of the king's daughter is within in golden borders.—*Ps.* xliv. 14.

Labor not for the meat which perisheth, but that which endureth unto life everlasting, which the Son of man will give you. For him hath God, the Father, sealed.—*John* vi. 27.

There is now therefore no condemnation to them that are in Christ Jesus, who walk not according to the flesh. . . .

For they that are according to the flesh, mind the things that are of the flesh; but they that are according to the spirit, mind the things that are of the spirit.

For the wisdom of the flesh is death; but the wisdom of the spirit is life and peace.

. . . But you are not in the flesh, but in the spirit, if so be that the Spirit of God dwell in you. Now if any man have not the Spirit of Christ, he is none of his.—*Rom.* viii. 1, 5, 6, 9.

For we walk by faith, and not by sight.—2 *Cor.* v. 7.

For though we walk in the flesh, we do not war according to the flesh.

For the weapons of our warfare are not carnal, but mighty to God unto the pulling down of fortifications, destroying counsels,

And every height that exalteth itself against the knowledge of God, and bringing into captivity every understanding unto the obedience of Christ. —2 *Cor.* x. 3-5.

I say then, walk in the spirit, and you shall not fulfil the lusts of the flesh.

For the flesh lusteth against the spirit: and the spirit against the flesh; for these are contrary one to another: so that you do not the things that you would. . . .

STEALING 543

If we live in the Spirit, let us also walk in the Spirit.—*Gal.* v. 16, 17, 25.

For what things a man shall sow, those also shall he reap. For he that soweth in his flesh, of the flesh also shall reap corruption. But he that soweth in the spirit, of the spirit shall reap life everlasting.—*Gal.* vi. 8.

To put off, according to former conversation, the old man, who is corrupted according to the desire of error.

And be renewed in the spirit of your mind:

And put on the new man, who according to God is created in justice and holiness of truth.—*Eph.* iv. 22-24.

Therefore if you be risen with Christ, seek the things that are above; where Christ is sitting at the right hand of God:

Mind the things that are above, not the things that are upon the earth.

For you are dead; and your life is hid with Christ in God.

When Christ shall appear, who is your life, then you also shall appear with him in glory.—*Col.* iii. 1-4.

For the grace of God our Saviour hath appeared to all men;

Instructing us, that, denying ungodliness and worldly desires, we should live soberly, and justly, and godly in this world,

Looking for the blessed hope and coming of the glory of the great God and our Saviour Jesus Christ.—*Titus* ii. 11-13.

Be you also as living stones built up, a spiritual house, a holy priesthood, to offer up spiritual sacrifices, acceptable to God by Jesus Christ.—1 *Peter* ii. 5.

In like manner also let wives be subject to their husbands: that if any believe not the word, they may be won without the word, by the conversation of the wives.

. . . Whose adorning, let it not be the outward plaiting of the hair, or the wearing of gold, or the putting on of apparel:

But the hidden man of the heart in the incorruptibility of a quiet and a meek spirit, which is rich in the sight of God.—1 *Peter* iii. 1, 3, 4.

SPIRITUAL OR UNSEEN WORLD, THE

While we look not at the things which are seen, but at the things which are not seen. For the things which are seen, are temporal; but the things which are not seen, are eternal.—2 *Cor.* iv. 18.

For we walk by faith, and not by sight.—2 *Cor.* v. 7.

Therefore, if you be risen with Christ, seek the things that are above; where Christ is sitting at the right hand of God:

Mind the things that are above, not the things that are upon the earth.—*Col.* iii. 1, 2.

SPIRITUAL THINGS, UNDERSTANDING OF

See: Understanding of spiritual things—page 571.

STEALING

See also: Goods, ill-gotten—page 171.

Thou shalt not steal.—*Ex.* xx. 15.

The robberies of the wicked shall be their downfall, because they would not do judgment.—*Prov.* xxi. 7.

He that stealeth any thing from his father, or from his mother: and saith, This is no sin, is the partner of a murderer.—*Prov.* xxviii. 24.

A thief is better than a man that is always lying: but both of them shall inherit destruction.—*Ecclus.* xx. 27.

And I turned and lifted up my eyes: and I saw, and behold a volume flying. . . .

And he (the angel) said to me: This is the curse that goeth forth over the face of the earth: for every thief shall be judged as is there written: and every one that sweareth in like manner shall be judged by it.

I will bring it forth, saith the Lord of hosts: and it shall come to the house of the thief, and to the house of him that sweareth falsely by my name: and it shall remain in the midst of his house, and shall consume it, with the timber thereof, and the stones thereof.—*Zach.* v. 1, 3, 4.

Know you not that the unjust shall not possess the kingdom of God? Do not err: neither fornicators, nor idolaters, nor adulterers,

. . . Nor thieves, nor covetous . . . nor extortioners, shall possess the kingdom of God.—1 *Cor.* vi. 9, 10.

He that stole, let him now steal no more; but rather let him labor, working with his hands the thing which is good, that he may have something to give to him that suffereth need.—*Eph.* iv. 28.

But let none of you suffer as a murderer, or a thief, or a railer, or a coveter of other men's things.—1 *Peter* iv. 15.

STRAYING AWAY FROM GOD

See: Wandering—page 580.

STRENGTH, GOD OUR

And he (David) said: The Lord is my rock, and my strength, and my saviour.

God is my strong one, in him will I trust: my shield, and the horn of my salvation: he lifteth me up, and is my refuge: my saviour, thou wilt deliver me from iniquity.—2 *Kings* xxii. 2, 3.

I will love thee, O Lord, my strength. —*Ps.* xvii. 2.

The Lord is the strength of his people, and the protector of the salvation of his anointed.—*Ps.* xxvii. 8.

For thou art my strength and my refuge; and for thy name's sake thou wilt lead me, and nourish me.—*Ps.* xxx. 4.

For thou art God my strength: why hast thou cast me off? and why do I go sorrowful whilst the enemy afflicteth me?—*Ps.* xlii. 2.

Our God is our refuge and strength: a helper in troubles, which have found us exceedingly.—*Ps.* xlv. 2.

For thou hast been my hope; a tower of strength against the face of the enemy.—*Ps.* lx. 4.

Be thou unto me a God, a protector, and a place of strength: that thou mayst make me safe.

For thou art my firmament and my refuge.—*Ps.* lxx. 3.

For thou art the glory of their strength: and in thy good pleasure shall our horn be exalted.—*Ps.* lxxxviii. 18.

Being pushed I was overturned that I might fall: but the Lord supported me.

The Lord is my strength and my praise: and he is become my salvation. —*Ps.* cxvii. 13, 14.

Behold God is my saviour, I will deal confidently, and will not fear: because the Lord is my strength, and my praise, and he is become my salvation.—*Is.* xii. 2.

Because thou hast been a strength to the poor, a strength to the needy in his distress: a refuge from the whirlwind, a shadow from the heat.—*Is.* xxv. 4.

And I said: I have labored in vain, I have spent my strength without cause and in vain: therefore my judgment is with the Lord, and my work with my God.

And now saith the Lord, that formed me from the womb to be his servant, that I may bring back Jacob unto him, and Israel will not be gathered together: and I am glorified in the eyes of the Lord, and my God is made my strength.—*Is.* xlix. 4, 5.

And the Lord shall be the hope of his people, and the strength of the children of Israel.—*Joel* iii. 16.

The Lord God is my strength: and he will make my feet like the feet of harts: and he the conqueror will lead me upon my high places singing psalms.—*Hab.* iii. 19.

STRENGTH IS FROM GOD, ALL

O Lord God of our fathers, thou art God in heaven, and rulest over all the kingdoms and nations, in thy hand is strength and power, and no one can resist thee.—2 *Paral.* xx. 6.

And he (Nehemias) said to them: Go, eat fat meats, and drink sweet wine, and send portions to them that have not prepared for themselves: because it is the holy day of the Lord, and be not sad: for the joy of the Lord is our strength.—2 *Esd.* viii. 10.

Through God we shall do mightily: and he shall bring to nothing them that afflict us.—*Ps.* lix. 14.

Seek ye the Lord, and be strengthened: seek his face evermore.—*Ps.* civ. 4.

The right hand of the Lord hath wrought strength: the right hand of the Lord hath exalted me: the right hand of the Lord hath wrought strength.—*Ps.* cxvii. 16.

Counsel and equity is mine, prudence is mine, strength is mine.—*Prov.* viii. 14.

Hear therefore, ye kings, and understand: learn, ye that are judges of the ends of the earth. . . .

For power is given you by the Lord, and strength by the most High, who will examine your works, and search out your thoughts.—*Wis.* vi. 2, 4.

And Judas said: It is an easy matter for many to be shut up in the hands of a few: and there is no difference in the sight of the God of heaven to deliver with a great multitude, or with a small company:

For the success of war is not in the multitude of the army, but strength cometh from heaven.—1 *Mach.* iii. 18, 19.

But we have this treasure in earthen vessels, that the excellency may be of the power of God, and not of us.— 2 *Cor.* iv. 7.

Finally, brethren, be strengthened in the Lord, and in the might of his power. —*Eph.* vi. 10.

I can do all things in him who strengtheneth me.—*Philipp.* iv. 13.

STRENGTH, GOD GIVES US

For who is God but the Lord? or who is God but our God?

God who hath girt me with strength; and made my way blameless. . . .

And thou hast girded me with strength unto battle; and hast subdued under me them that rose up against me. —*Ps.* xvii. 32, 33, 40.

The Lord will give strength to his people: the Lord will bless his people with peace.—*Ps.* xxviii. 10.

For the arms of the wicked shall be broken in pieces; but the Lord strengtheneth the just.—*Ps.* xxxvi. 17.

God is wonderful in his saints: the God of Israel is he who will give power and strength to his people. Blessed be God.—*Ps.* lxvii. 36.

For my hand shall help him: and my arm shall strengthen him.—*Ps.* lxxxviii. 22.

But to the penitent he hath given the way of justice, and he hath strengthened them that were fainting in patience, and hath appointed to them the lot of truth.—*Ecclus.* xvii. 20.

It is he that giveth strength to the weary, and increaseth force and might to them that are not.—*Is.* xl. 29.

Fear not, for I am with thee: turn not aside, for I am thy God: I have strengthened thee, and have helped thee, and the right hand of my just one hath upheld thee.—*Is.* xli. 10.

The Lord is good and giveth strength in the day of trouble: and knoweth them that hope in him.—*Nahum* i. 7.

I will strengthen them in the Lord, and they shall walk in his name, saith the Lord.—*Zach.* x. 12.

But God is faithful, who will strengthen and keep you from evil.— 2 *Thess.* iii. 3.

I give him thanks who hath strengthened me, even to Christ Jesus our Lord, for that he hath counted me faithful, putting me in the ministry.— 1 *Tim.* i. 12.

STRENGTH, A PRAYER FOR

Restore unto me the joy of thy salvation, and strengthen me with a perfect spirit.—*Ps.* l. 14.

My soul hath slumbered through heaviness: strengthen thou me in thy words.—*Ps.* cxviii. 28.

Uphold me according to thy word, and I shall live: and let me not be confounded in my expectation.—*Ps.* cxviii. 116.

For this cause I bow my knees to the Father of our Lord Jesus Christ,

Of whom all paternity in heaven and earth is named,

That he would grant you, according to the riches of his glory, to be strengthened by his Spirit with might unto the inward man.—*Eph.* iii. 14-16.

Now our Lord Jesus Christ himself, and God and our Father, who hath loved us, and hath given us everlasting consolation, and good hope in grace,

Exhort your hearts, and confirm you in every good work and word.—2 *Thess.* ii. 15, 16.

STRENGTH IS VAIN, RELIANCE UPON HUMAN

He will keep the feet of his saints, and the wicked shall be silent in darkness, because no man shall prevail by his own strength.—1 *Kings* ii. 9.

For what is my strength, that I can hold out? or what is my end that I should keep patience?

My strength is not the strength of stones, nor is my flesh of brass.

Behold there is no help for me in myself, and my familiar friends also are departed from me.—*Job* vi. 11-13.

The king is not saved by a great army: nor shall the giant be saved by his own great strength.

Vain is the horse for safety: neither shall he be saved by the abundance of his strength.—*Ps.* xxxii. 16, 17.

For I will not trust in my bow: neither shall my sword save me.

But thou hast saved us from them that afflict us: and hast put them to shame that hate us.—*Ps.* xliii. 7, 8.

They that trust in their own strength, and glory in the multitude of their riches,

No brother can redeem, nor shall man redeem: he shall not give to God his ransom,

Nor the price of the redemption of his soul: and shall labor for ever.—*Ps.* xlviii. 7-9.

O grant us help from trouble: for vain is the help of man.

Through God we shall do mightily: and he will bring our enemies to nothing.—*Ps.* cvii. 13, 14.

It is good to confide in the Lord, rather than to have confidence in man.

It is good to trust in the Lord, rather than to trust in princes.—*Ps.* cxvii. 8, 9.

Unless the Lord build the house, they labor in vain that build it.

Unless the Lord keep the city, he watcheth in vain that keepeth it.—*Ps.* cxxvi. 1.

Put not your trust in princes: in the children of men, in whom there is no salvation.—*Ps.* cxlv. 2, 3.

The horse is prepared for the day of battle: but the Lord giveth safety.—*Prov.* xxi. 31.

I turned me to another thing, and I saw that under the sun, the race is not to the swift, nor the battle to the strong, nor bread to the wise, nor riches to the learned, nor favor to the skilful: but time and chance in all.—*Eccles.* ix. 11.

And my life was drawing near to hell beneath.

They compassed me on every side, and there was no one that would help me. I looked for the succor of men, and there was none.—*Ecclus.* li. 9, 10.

But we had in ourselves the answer of death, that we should not trust in ourselves, but in God who raiseth the dead.—2 *Cor.* i. 9.

STRENGTH, PUNISHMENT OF RELIANCE UPON HUMAN

And if thou think that battles consist in the strength of the army, God will make thee to be overcome by the enemies: for it belongeth to God both to help, and to put to flight.—2 *Paral.* xxv. 8.

Some trust in chariots, and some in horses: but we will call upon the name of the Lord our God.

They are bound, and have fallen; but we are risen, and are set upright.—*Ps.* xix. 8, 9.

The just shall see and fear, and shall laugh at him, and say: Behold the man that made not God his helper:

But trusted in the abundance of his riches: and prevailed in his vanity.—*Ps.* li. 8, 9.

The ancient giants did not obtain pardon for their sins, who were destroyed trusting to their own strength.—*Ecclus.* xvi. 8.

Woe to you, apostate children, saith the Lord, that you would take counsel, and not of me; and would begin a web, and not by my spirit, that you might add sin upon sin:

Who walk to go down into Egypt, and have not asked at my mouth, hoping for help in the strength of Pharao, and trusting in the shadow of Egypt.

And the strength of Pharao shall be to your confusion and the confidence of the shadow of Egypt to your shame.—*Is.* xxx. 1-3.

Woe to them that go down to Egypt for help, trusting in horses, and putting their confidence in chariots, because they are many: and in horsemen, because they are very strong: and have not trusted in the Holy One of Israel, and have not sought after the Lord. . . .

Egypt is man, and not God: and their horses, flesh, and not spirit: and the Lord shall put down his hand, and the helper shall fall, and he that is helped shall fall, and they shall all be confounded together.—*Is.* xxxi. 1, 3.

Thus saith the Lord: Cursed be the man that trusteth in man, and maketh flesh his arm, and whose heart departeth from the Lord.—*Jer.* xvii. 5.

For because thou hast trusted in thy bulwarks, and in thy treasures, thou also shalt be taken: and Chamos shall go into captivity, his priests, and his princes together.

And the spoiler shall come upon every city, and no city shall escape: and the valleys shall perish, and the plains shall be destroyed, for the Lord hath spoken.—*Jer.* xlviii. 7, 8.

STUBBORNNESS

See: Self-will—page 511.

SUBJECTION TO GOD OF MAN'S WILL

See also: Obedience to God—page 344.

Submit thyself then to him, and be at peace: and thereby thou shalt have the best fruits.—*Job* xxii. 21.

Be subject to the Lord and pray to him.—*Ps.* xxxvi. 7.

Shall not my soul be subject to God? for from him is my salvation.—*Ps.* lxi. 2.

But be thou, O my soul, subject to God: for from him is my patience.—*Ps.* lxi. 6.

Be subject therefore to God, but resist the devil, and he will fly from you.—*James* iv. 7.

SUCCESS IN EVIL

See: Wicked, prosperity of the—page 595.

SUFFERING, LOVE OF

If I must needs glory, I will glory of the things that concern my infirmity.—*2 Cor.* xi. 30.

And he said to me: My grace is sufficient for thee: for power is made perfect in infirmity. Gladly therefore will I glory in my infirmities, that the power of Christ may dwell in me.

For which cause I please myself in my infirmities, in reproaches, in necessities, in persecutions, in distresses, for Christ. For when I am weak, then am I powerful.—*2 Cor.* xii. 9, 10.

With Christ I am nailed to the cross.—*Gal.* ii. 19.

But God forbid that I should glory, save in the cross of our Lord Jesus Christ; by whom the world is crucified to me, and I to the world.—*Gal.* vi. 14.

For unto you it is given for Christ, not only to believe in him, but also to suffer for him.—*Philipp.* i. 29.

Furthermore I count all things to be but loss for the excellent knowledge of Jesus Christ my Lord; for whom I have suffered the loss of all things, and count them but as dung, that I may gain Christ: . . .

That I may know him, and the power of his resurrection, and the fellowship of his sufferings, being made conformable to his death,

If by any means I may attain to the resurrection which is from the dead.—*Philipp.* iii. 8, 10, 11.

Who now rejoice in my sufferings for you, and fill up those things that are wanting of the sufferings of Christ, in my flesh, for his body, which is the church.—*Col.* i. 24.

Let us go forth therefore to him without the camp, bearing his reproach.—*Heb.* xiii. 13.

SUFFERING, THE VALUE OF

And though in the sight of men they suffered torments, their hope is full of immortality.

Afflicted in few things, in many they shall be well rewarded: because God hath tried them, and found them worthy of himself.—*Wis.* iii. 4, 5.

Ought not Christ to have suffered

these things, and so to enter into his glory?—*Luke* xxiv. 26.

For the Spirit himself giveth testimony to our spirit, that we are the sons of God.

And if sons, heirs also; heirs indeed of God, and joint heirs with Christ: yet so, if we suffer with him, that we may be also glorified with him.

For I reckon that the sufferings of this time are not worthy to be compared with the glory to come, that shall be revealed in us.—*Rom.* viii. 16-18.

Always bearing about in our body the mortification of Jesus, that the life also of Jesus may be made manifest in our bodies. . . .

For that which is at present momentary and light of our tribulation, worketh for us above measure exceedingly an eternal weight of glory.—2 *Cor.* iv. 10, 17.

And lest the greatness of the revelations should exalt me, there was given me a sting of my flesh, an angel of Satan, to buffet me.

For which thing thrice I besought the Lord, that it might depart from me.

And he said to me: My grace is sufficient for thee: for power is made perfect in infirmity. Gladly therefore will I glory in my infirmities, that the power of Christ may dwell in me.— 2 *Cor.* xii. 7-9.

A faithful saying: for if we be dead with him, we shall live also with him. If we suffer, we shall also reign with him.—2 *Tim.* ii. 11, 12.

For this is thankworthy, if for conscience towards God, a man endure sorrows, suffering wrongfully.

For what glory is it, if committing sin, and being buffeted for it, you endure? But if doing well you suffer patiently; this is thankworthy before God.

For unto this are you called: because Christ also suffered for us, leaving you an example that you should follow his steps.—1 *Peter* ii. 19-21.

For it is better doing well (if such be the will of God) to suffer, than doing ill.—1 *Peter* iii. 17.

Christ therefore having suffered in the flesh, be you also armed with the same thought: for he that hath suffered in the flesh, hath ceased from sins:

That now he may live the rest of his time in the flesh, not after the desires of men, but according to the will of God.—1 *Peter* iv. 1, 2.

Dearly beloved, think not strange the burning heat which is to try you, as if some new thing happened to you;

But if you partake of the sufferings of Christ, rejoice that when his glory shall be revealed, you may also be glad with exceeding joy.—1 *Peter* iv. 12, 13.

Wherefore let them also that suffer according to the will of God, commend their souls in good deeds to the faithful Creator.—1 *Peter* iv. 19.

But the God of all grace, who hath called us unto his eternal glory in Christ Jesus, after you have suffered a little, will himself perfect you, and confirm you, and establish you.—1 *Peter* v. 10.

SUFFERING, A LIFE OF

See: Life of suffering—page 282.

SUICIDE

Thou shalt not kill.—*Ex.* xx. 13.

See ye that I alone am, and there is no other God besides me: I will kill and I will make to live: I will strike, and I will heal, and there is none that can deliver out of my hand.—*Deut.* xxxii. 39.

For it is thou, O Lord, that hast power of life and death, and leadest down to the gates of death, and bringest back again:

A man indeed killeth through malice, and when the spirit is gone forth, it shall not return, neither shall he call back the soul that is received.—*Wis.* xvi. 13, 14.

Then Judas who betrayed him, seeing that he was condemned, repenting himself, brought back the thirty pieces of silver to the chief priests and ancients,

Saying: I have sinned in betraying innocent blood. But they said: What is that to us? look thou to it.

And casting down the pieces of silver in the temple, he departed: and went and hanged himself with an halter.— *Matt.* xxvii. 3-5.

SUPERIORS TO SUBJECTS, THE DUTY OF

See: Masters, the duty of—page 307.

SUPERSTITIOUS PRACTICES

You shall not divine nor observe dreams. . . .

Go not aside after wizards, neither ask any thing of soothsayers, to be defiled by them: I am the Lord your God.—*Lev.* xix. 26, 31.

The soul that shall go aside after magicians, and soothsayers, and shall commit fornication with them, I will set my face against that soul, and destroy it out of the midst of its people.—*Lev.* xx. 6.

A man, or woman, in whom there is a pythonical or divining spirit, dying let them die: they shall stone them: their blood be upon them.—*Lev.* xx. 27.

Neither let there be found among you any one that shall expiate his son or daughter, making them to pass through the fire: or that consulteth soothsayers, or observeth dreams and omens, neither let there be any wizard,

Nor charmer, nor any one that consulteth pythonic spirits, or fortune tellers, or that seeketh the truth from the dead.

For the Lord abhorreth all these things, and for these abominations he will destroy them at thy coming.—*Deut.* xviii. 10-12.

And Saul saw the army of the Philistines, and was afraid, and his heart was very much dismayed.

And he consulted the Lord, and he answered him not, neither by dreams, nor by priests, nor by prophets.

And Saul said to his servants: Seek me a woman that hath a divining spirit, and I will go to her, and inquire by her. And his servants said to him: There is a woman that hath a divining spirit at Endor.—1 *Kings* xxviii. 5-7.

And when they shall say to you: Seek of pythons, and of diviners, who mutter in their enchantments: should not the people seek of their God, for the living to the dead?—*Is.* viii. 19.

Stand now with thy enchanters, and with the multitude of thy sorceries, in which thou hast labored from thy youth,

if so be it may profit thee any thing, or if thou mayst become stronger.

Thou hast failed in the multitude of thy counsels: let now the astrologers stand and save thee, they that gazed at the stars, and counted the months, that from them they might tell the things that shall come to thee.

Behold they are as stubble, fire hath burnt them, they shall not deliver themselves from the power of the flames: there are no coals wherewith they may be warmed, nor fire, that they may sit thereat.—*Is.* xlvii. 12-14.

But Paul standing in the midst of the Areopagus, said: Ye men of Athens, I perceive that in all things you are too superstitious.—*Acts* xvii. 22.

SURETY FOR ANOTHER

See: Bond, giving—page 42.

SWEARING

The person that sweareth, and uttereth with his lips, that he would do either evil or good, and bindeth the same with an oath, and his word, and having forgotten it afterwards understandeth his offence,

Let him do penance for his sin.—*Lev.* v. 4, 5.

Let not thy mouth be accustomed to swearing: for in it there are many falls. . . .

For as a slave daily put to the question is never without a blue mark: so every one that sweareth, and nameth, shall not be wholly pure from sin.

A man that sweareth much, shall be filled with iniquity, and a scourge shall not depart from his house.

And if he make it void, his sin shall be upon him: and if he dissemble it, he offendeth double:

And if he swear in vain, he shall not be justified: for his house shall be filled with his punishment.—*Ecclus.* xxiii. 9, 11-14.

The speech that sweareth much shall make the hair of the head stand upright: and its irreverence shall make one stop his ears.—*Ecclus.* xxvii. 15.

And I turned and lifted up my eyes· and I saw, and behold a volume flying. . . .

And he (the angel) said to me: This

is the curse that goeth forth over the face of the earth: for every thief shall be judged as is there written: and every one that sweareth in like manner shall be judged by it.—*Zach.* v. 1, 3.

Again you have heard that it was said to them of old, Thou shalt not forswear thyself: but thou shalt perform thy oaths to the Lord.

But I say to you not to swear at all, neither by heaven, for it is the throne of God:

Nor by the earth, for it is his footstool: nor by Jerusalem, for it is the city of the great king:

Neither shalt thou swear by thy head, because thou canst not make one hair white or black.

But let your speech be yea, yea: no, no: and that which is over and above these, is of evil.—*Matt.* v. 33-37.

He therefore that sweareth by the altar, sweareth by it, and by all things that are upon it:

And whosoever shall swear by the temple, sweareth by it, and by him that dwelleth in it:

And he that sweareth by heaven, sweareth by the throne of God, and by him that sitteth thereon.—*Matt.* xxiii. 20-22.

But above all things, my brethren, swear not, neither by heaven, nor by the earth, nor by any other oath. But let your speech be, yea, yea: no, no: that you fall not under judgment.—*James* v. 12.

When Michael the archangel, disputing with the devil, contended about the body of Moses, he durst not bring against him the judgment of railing speech, but said: The Lord command thee.—*Jude* i. 9.

SWEARING, FALSE

See: Perjury—page 377.

SYMPATHY FOR THOSE IN DISTRESS

See: Comfort the afflicted, we should —page 56.

TALE-BEARING

See: Mischief-maker—page 326.

TEACHER, GOD OUR

That thou mightest know that the Lord he is God, and there is no other besides him.

From heaven he made thee to hear his voice, that he might teach thee.— *Deut.* iv. 35, 36.

And he hath not said: Where is God, who made me, who hath given songs in the night?

Who teacheth us more than the beasts of the earth, and instructeth us more than the fowls of the air.—*Job* xxxv. 10, 11.

Thou hast made known to me the ways of life, thou shalt fill me with joy with thy countenance: at thy right hand are delights even to the end.—*Ps.* xv. 11.

He will guide the mild in judgment: he will teach the meek his ways.—*Ps.* xxiv. 9.

I will give thee understanding, and I will instruct thee in this way, in which thou shalt go: I will fix my eyes upon thee.—*Ps.* xxxi. 8.

For behold thou hast loved truth: the uncertain and hidden things of thy wisdom thou hast made manifest to me. —*Ps.* l. 8.

Thou hast taught me, O God, from my youth: and till now I will declare thy wonderful works.—*Ps.* lxx. 17.

Blessed is the man whom thou shalt instruct, O Lord: and shalt teach him out of thy law.—*Ps.* xciii. 12.

Therefore hath he filled up his mercy in their favor, and hath shown them the way of justice.—*Ecclus.* xviii. 11.

And many people shall go, and say: Come and let us go up to the mountain of the Lord, and to the house of the God of Jacob, and he will teach us his ways, and we will walk in his paths: for the law shall come forth from Sion, and the word of the Lord from Jerusalem.—*Is.* ii. 3.

For he will instruct him in judgment: his God will teach him.—*Is.* xxviii. 26.

Thus saith the Lord thy redeemer, the Holy One of Israel: I am the Lord thy God that teach thee profitable things, that govern thee in the way that thou walkest.—*Is.* xlviii. 17.

All thy children shall be taught of the Lord: and great shall be the peace of thy children.—*Is.* liv. 13.

Hear ye this, O priests, and hearken, O ye house of Israel, and give ear, O house of the king: for there is a judgment against you, because you have been a snare to them whom you should have watched over, and a net spread upon Thabor.

And you have turned aside victims into the depth: and I am the teacher of them all.—*Osee* v. 1, 2.

But the Paraclete, the Holy Ghost, whom the Father will send in my name, he will teach you all things, and bring all things to your mind, whatsoever I shall have said to you.—*John* xiv. 26.

But when he, the Spirit of truth, is come, he will teach you all truth. For he shall not speak of himself; but what things soever he shall hear, he shall speak; and the things that are to come, he shall show you.—*John* xvi. 13.

TEACHER, CHRIST OUR

And the Lord will give you spare bread, and short water: and will not cause thy teacher to flee away from thee any more, and thy eyes shall see thy teacher.

And thy ears shall hear the word of one admonishing thee behind thy back: This is the way, walk ye in it: and go not aside neither to the right hand, nor to the left.—*Is.* xxx. 20, 21.

Sow for yourselves in justice, and reap in the mouth of mercy, break up your fallow ground: but the time to seek the Lord is, when he shall come that shall teach you justice.—*Osee* x. 12.

And you, O children of Sion, rejoice, and be joyful in the Lord your God: because he hath given you a teacher of justice, and he will make the early and the latter rain to come down to you as in the beginning.—*Joel* ii. 23.

And seeing the multitudes, he went up into a mountain, and when he was set down, his disciples came unto him.

And opening his mouth, he taught them.—*Matt.* v. 1, 2.

And it came to pass when Jesus had fully ended these words, the people were in admiration at his doctrine.

For he was teaching them as one having power, and not as the scribes and Pharisees.—*Matt.* vii. 28, 29.

Take up my yoke upon you, and learn of me, because I am meek, and humble of heart: and you shall find rest to your souls.—*Matt.* xi. 29.

And he went down into Capharnaum, a city of Galilee, and there he taught them on the sabbath days.

And they were astonished at his doctrine: for his speech was with power.—*Luke* iv. 31, 32.

Jesus saith to him (Thomas): I am the way, and the truth, and the life. No man cometh to the Father, but by me.—*John* xiv. 6.

TEACH US, A PRAYER TO GOD TO

Then hear thou from heaven, O Lord, and forgive the sins of thy servants and of thy people Israel, and teach them the good way, in which they may walk.—*2 Paral.* vi. 27.

Show, O Lord, thy ways to me, and teach me thy paths.

Direct me in thy truth, and teach me; for thou art God my Saviour; and on thee have I waited all the day long.—*Ps.* xxiv. 4, 5.

Blessed art thou, O Lord: teach me thy justifications.—*Ps.* cxviii. 12.

Teach me goodness and discipline and knowledge; for I have believed thy commandments.—*Ps.* cxviii. 66.

TEACHING OTHERS THE WAY OF GOD

See: Instructing—page 245.

TEMPERANCE

See: Frugality or moderation in eating and drinking—page 164.

TEMPLE OF GOD, THE

See: House of God, the—page 214.

TEMPORAL LOSS IS TO BE PRE- FERRED TO ETERNAL LOSS

And if thy right eye scandalize thee, pluck it out and cast it from thee. For it is expedient for thee that one of thy members should perish, rather than that thy whole body be cast into hell.

And if thy right hand scandalize thee, cut it off, and cast it from thee: for it is expedient for thee, that one of thy members should perish, rather than that thy whole body go into hell.—*Matt. v.* 29, 30.

And fear ye not them that kill the body, and are not able to kill the soul: but rather fear him that can destroy both soul and body in hell.—*Matt. x.* 28.

For whosoever will save his life, shall lose it: and whosoever shall lose his life for my sake and the gospel, shall save it.

For what shall it profit a man, if he gain the whole world, and suffer the loss of his soul?

Or what shall a man give in exchange for his soul?—*Mark viii.* 35-37.

And if thy hand scandalize thee, cut it off: it is better for thee to enter into life, maimed, than having two hands to go into hell, into unquenchable fire:

Where their worm dieth not, and the fire is not extinguished.

And if thy foot scandalize thee, cut it off. It is better for thee to enter lame into life everlasting, than having two feet, to be cast into the hell of unquenchable fire:

Where their worm dieth not, and the fire is not extinguished.

And if thy eye scandalize thee, pluck it out. It is better for thee with one eye to enter into the kingdom of God, than having two eyes to be cast into the hell of fire:

Where their worm dieth not, and the fire is not extinguished.—*Mark ix.* 42-47.

And I say to you, my friends: Be not afraid of them who kill the body, and after that have no more that they can do.

But I will show you whom you shall fear: fear ye him, who after he hath killed, hath power to cast into hell. Yea, I say to you, fear him.—*Luke xii.* 4, 5.

Furthermore I count all things to be but loss for the excellent knowledge of Jesus Christ my Lord; for whom I have suffered the loss of all things, and count

them but as dung, that I may gain Christ.—*Philipp. iii.* 8.

But call to mind the former days, wherein, being illuminated, you endured a great fight of afflictions. . . .

For you both had compassion on them that were in bands, and took with joy the being stripped of your own goods, knowing that you have a better and a lasting substance.

Do not therefore lose your confidence, which hath a great reward.—*Heb. x.* 32, 34, 35.

By faith Moses, when he was grown up, denied himself to be the son of Pharao's daughter;

Rather choosing to be afflicted with the people of God, than to have the pleasure of sin for a time,

Esteeming the reproach of Christ greater riches than the treasure of the Egyptians. For he looked unto the reward.—*Heb. xi.* 24-26.

Women received their dead raised to life again. But others were racked, not accepting deliverance, that they might find a better resurrection.—*Heb. xi.* 35.

TEMPORAL NECESSITIES, A PRAYER FOR

Two things I have asked of thee, deny them not to me before I die.

Remove far from me vanity, and lying words. Give me neither beggary, nor riches: give me only the necessaries of life:

Lest perhaps being filled, I should be tempted to deny, and say: Who is the Lord? or being compelled by poverty, I should steal, and forswear the name of my God.—*Prov. xxx.* 7-9.

Give us this day our daily bread.—*Luke xi.* 3.

And may my God supply all your want, according to his riches in glory in Christ Jesus.—*Philipp. iv.* 19.

TEMPTATIONS

And because thou wast acceptable to God, it was necessary that temptation should prove thee.—*Tob. xii.* 13.

The life of man upon earth is a warfare, and his days are like the days of a hireling.—*Job vii.* 1.

Son, when thou comest to the service of God, stand in justice and in fear, and prepare thy soul for temptation.—*Ecclus.* ii. 1.

Then Jesus was led by the spirit into the desert, to be tempted by the devil.—*Matt.* iv. 1.

Watch ye, and pray that you enter not into temptation. The spirit indeed is willing, but the flesh is weak.—*Mark* xiv. 38.

And the Lord said: Simon, Simon, behold Satan hath desired to have you, that he may sift you as wheat.—*Luke* xxii. 31.

But I fear lest, as the serpent seduced Eve by his subtlety, so your minds should be corrupted, and fall from the simplicity that is in Christ.—2 *Cor.* xi. 3.

For the flesh lusteth against the spirit: and the spirit against the flesh; for these are contrary one to another: so that you do not the things that you would.—*Gal.* v. 17.

My brethren, count it all joy, when you shall fall into divers temptations;

Knowing that the trying of your faith worketh patience.

And patience hath a perfect work; that you may be perfect and entire, failing in nothing.—*James* i. 2-4.

Blessed is the man that endureth temptation; for when he hath been proved, he shall receive the crown of life, which God hath promised to them that love him.

Let no man, when he is tempted, say that he is tempted by God. For God is not a tempter of evils, and he tempteth no man.

But every man is tempted by his own concupiscence, being drawn away and allured.

Then when concupiscence hath conceived, it bringeth forth sin. But sin, when it is completed, begetteth death.—*James* i. 12-15.

Wherein you shall greatly rejoice, if now you must be for a little time made sorrowful in divers temptations:

That the trial of your faith (much more precious than gold which is tried by the fire) may be found unto praise and glory and honor at the appearing of Jesus Christ.—1 *Peter* i. 6, 7.

Be sober and watch: because your adversary the devil, as a roaring lion, goeth about seeking whom he may devour.—1 *Peter* v. 8.

TEMPTATIONS, RESISTING

See: Devil and his temptations —page 112.

TEMPTATION, GOD OUR HELP IN

Fear them not: for the Lord your God will fight for you.—*Deut.* iii. 22.

If thou say in thy heart: These nations are more than I, how shall I be able to destroy them?

Fear not, but remember what the Lord thy God did to Pharao and to all the Egyptians.—*Deut.* vii. 17, 18.

Hear, O Israel, you join battle this day against your enemies, let not your heart be dismayed, be not afraid, do not give back, fear ye them not:

Because the Lord your God is in the midst of you, and will fight for you against your enemies, to deliver you from danger.—*Deut.* xx. 3, 4.

He sent from on high, and took me, and drew me out of many waters.

He delivered me from my most mighty enemy, and from them that hated me: for they were too strong for me.

He prevented me in the day of my affliction, and the Lord became my stay.

And he brought me forth into a large place, he delivered me, because I pleased him.—2 *Kings* xxii. 17-20.

For by thee I shall be delivered from temptation; and through my God I shall go over a wall.—*Ps.* xvii. 30.

And thou hast girded me with strength unto battle; and hast subdued under me them that rose up against me. —*Ps.* xvii. 40.

Through thee we will push down our enemies with the horn: and through thy name we will despise them that rise up against us.—*Ps.* xliii. 6.

Thou calledst upon me in affliction, and I delivered thee: I heard thee in the secret place of tempest.—*Ps.* lxxx. 8.

For my hand shall help him: and my arm shall strengthen him.

The enemy shall have no advantage over him: nor the son of iniquity have power to hurt him.—*Ps.* lxxxviii. 22, 23.

Often have they fought against me from my youth, let Israel now say.

Often have they fought against me from my youth: but they could not prevail over me.—*Ps.* cxxviii. 1, 2.

No evils shall happen to him that feareth the Lord, but in temptation God will keep him, and deliver him from evils.—*Ecclus.* xxxiii. 1.

And they shall fight against thee, and shall not prevail: for I am with thee, saith the Lord, to deliver thee.—*Jer.* i. 19.

And when he entered into the boat, his disciples followed him:

And behold a great tempest arose in the sea, so that the boat was covered with waves, but he was asleep.

And they came to him, and awaked him, saying: Lord, save us, we perish.

And Jesus saith to them: Why are you fearful, O ye of little faith? Then rising up he commanded the winds, and the sea, and there came a great calm. —*Matt.* viii. 23-26.

And the Lord said: Simon, Simon, behold Satan hath desired to have you, that he may sift you as wheat:

But I have prayed for thee, that thy faith fail not: and thou, being once converted, confirm thy brethren.—*Luke* xxii. 31, 32.

I pray not that thou shouldst take them out of the world, but that thou shouldst keep them from evil.—*John* xvii. 15.

I find then a law, that when I have a will to do good, evil is present with me.

For I am delighted with the law of God, according to the inward man:

But I see another law in my members, fighting against the law of my mind, and captivating me in the law of sin, that is in my members.

Unhappy man that I am, who shall deliver me from the body of this death?

The grace of God, by Jesus Christ our Lord.—*Rom.* vii. 21-25.

Let no temptation take hold on you, but such as is human. And God is faithful, who will not suffer you to be tempted above that which you are able: but will make also with temptation issue, that you may be able to bear it.— 1 *Cor.* x. 13.

Now thanks be to God, who always maketh us to triumph in Christ Jesus, and manifesteth the odor of his knowledge by us in every place.—2 *Cor.* ii. 14.

But God is faithful, who will strengthen and keep you from evil.— 2 *Thess.* iii. 3.

For in that, wherein he himself hath suffered and been tempted, he is able to succor them also that are tempted.— *Heb.* ii. 18.

For we have not a high priest, who cannot have compassion on our infirmities: but one tempted in all things like as we are, without sin.

Let us go therefore with confidence to the throne of grace: that we may obtain mercy, and find grace in seasonable aid.—*Heb.* iv. 15, 16.

The Lord knoweth how to deliver the godly from temptation, but to reserve the unjust unto the day of judgment to be tormented.—2 *Peter* ii. 9.

You are of God, little children, and have overcome him (Antichrist). Because greater is he that is in you, than he that is in the world.—1 *John* iv. 4.

TEMPTATION, A PRAYER IN

Consider, and hear me, O Lord my God.

Enlighten my eyes that I never sleep in death: lest at any time my enemy say: I have prevailed against him.—*Ps.* xii. 4, 5.

O God, come to my assistance; O Lord, make haste to help me.

Let them be confounded and ashamed that seek my soul:

Let them be turned backward, and blush for shame that desire evils to me.

Let them be presently turned away blushing for shame that say to me: 'Tis well, 'tis well.—*Ps.* lxix. 2-4.

O Lord, father and sovereign ruler of my life, leave me not to their counsel: nor suffer me to fall by them. . . .

Lest my ignorances increase, and my offences be multiplied, and my sins abound, and I fall before my adversaries, and my enemy rejoice over me.

O Lord, father, and God of my life, leave me not to their devices.

Give me not haughtiness of my eyes, and turn away from me all coveting.

Take from me the greediness of the belly, and let not the lusts of the flesh take hold of me, and give me not over to a shameless and foolish mind.—*Ecclus.* xxiii. 1, 3-6.

Send now also, O Lord of heaven, thy good angel before us, for the fear and dread of the greatness of thy arm,

That they may be afraid, who come with blasphemy against thy holy people.—2 *Mach.* xv. 23, 24.

And lead us not into temptation. But deliver us from evil. Amen.—*Matt.* vi. 13.

And the God of peace crush Satan under your feet speedily. The grace of our Lord Jesus Christ be with you.—*Rom.* xvi. 20.

TEMPTING GOD

Then all the multitude of the children of Israel setting forward from the desert of Sin, by their mansions, according to the word of the Lord, encamped in Raphidim, where there was no water for the people to drink.

And they chided with Moses, and said: Give us water, that we may drink. And Moses answered them: Why chide you with me? Wherefore do you tempt the Lord?

. . . And he called the name of that place Temptation, because of the chiding of the children of Israel, and for that they tempted the Lord, saying: Is the Lord amongst us or not?—*Ex.* xvii. 1, 2, 7.

Thou shalt not tempt the Lord thy God, as thou temptedst him in the place of temptation.—*Deut.* vi. 16.

And they tempted God in their hearts, by asking meat for their desires.

And they spoke ill of God: they said: Can God furnish a table in the wilderness?

Because he struck the rock, and the waters gushed out, and the streams overflowed.

Can he also give bread, or provide a table for his people?

Therefore the Lord heard, and was angry: and a fire was kindled against Jacob, and wrath came up against Israel.—*Ps.* lxxvii. 18-21.

How often did they provoke him in the desert: and move him to wrath in the place without water?

And they turned back and tempted God: and grieved the holy one of Israel.—*Ps.* lxxvii. 40, 41.

Yet they tempted, and provoked the most high God: and they kept not his testimonies.—*Ps.* lxxvii. 56.

To-day if you shall hear his voice, harden not your hearts:

As in the provocation, according to the day of temptation in the wilderness: where your fathers tempted me, they proved me, and saw my works.—*Ps.* xciv. 8, 9.

And they coveted their desire in the desert: and they tempted God in the place without water.—*Ps.* cv. 14.

For he is found by them that tempt him not: and he showeth himself to them that have faith in him.—*Wis.* i. 2.

A hard heart shall fear evil at the last: and he that loveth danger shall perish in it.—*Ecclus.* iii. 27.

Before prayer prepare thy soul: and be not as a man that tempteth God.—*Ecclus.* xviii. 23.

Then the devil took him up into the holy city, and set him upon the pinnacle of the temple,

And said to him: If thou be the Son of God, cast thyself down, for it is written: That he hath given his angels charge over thee, and in their hands shall they bear thee up, lest perhaps thou dash thy foot against a stone.

Jesus said to him: It is written again: Thou shalt not tempt the Lord thy God.—*Matt.* iv. 5-7.

But Jesus knowing their wickedness, said: Why do you tempt me, ye hypocrites?—*Matt.* xxii. 18.

And the Pharisees came forth, and began to question with him, asking him a sign from heaven, tempting him.

And sighing deeply in spirit, he saith: Why doth this generation seek a sign? Amen, I say to you, a sign shall not be given to this generation.—*Mark* viii. 11, 12.

Neither let us tempt Christ: as some of them tempted, and perished by the serpents.—*1 Cor.* x. 9.

THANKFULNESS TO GOD

See: Gratitude to God—page 183.

THANKSGIVING TO GOD, A PRAYER OF

See: Gratitude to God, a prayer of—page 184.

THOUGHTS, BAD

I made a covenant with my eyes, that I would not so much as think upon a virgin.

For what part should God from above have in me, and what inheritance the Almighty from on high?—*Job* xxxi. 1, 2.

They have thought and spoken wickedness: they have spoken iniquity on high.—*Ps.* lxxii. 8.

Deceit is in the heart of them that think evil things: but joy followeth them that take counsels of peace.—*Prov.* xii. 20.

Evil thoughts are an abomination to the Lord: and pure words most beautiful shall be confirmed by him.—*Prov.* xv. 26.

The thought of a fool is sin.—*Prov.* xxiv. 9.

For perverse thoughts separate from God.—*Wis.* i. 3.

For inquisition shall be made into the thoughts of the ungodly: and the hearing of his words shall come to God, to the chastising of his iniquities.—*Wis.* i. 9.

And the eunuch that hath not wrought iniquity with his hands, nor thought wicked things against God: for the precious gift of faith shall be given to him, and a most acceptable lot in the temple of God.—*Wis.* iii. 14.

Wash thy heart from wickedness, O Jerusalem, that thou mayst be saved: how long shall hurtful thoughts abide in thee?—*Jer.* iv. 14.

But the things which proceed out of the mouth, come forth from the heart, and those things defile a man.

For from the heart come forth evil thoughts, murders, adulteries, fornications, thefts, false testimonies, blasphemies.

These are the things that defile a man. But to eat with unwashed hands doth not defile a man.—*Matt.* xv. 18-20.

THOUGHTS, GOOD

For the thought of man shall give praise to thee: and the remainders of the thought shall keep holiday to thee. —*Ps.* lxxv. 11.

THOUGHTS ARE KNOWN TO GOD, OUR

See: Searcher of hearts, God is the —page 507.

THOUGHTLESSNESS

And man when he was in honor did not understand; he is compared to senseless beasts, and is become like to them.—*Ps.* xlviii. 13.

The just perisheth, and no man layeth it to heart, and men of mercy are taken away, because there is none that understandeth; for the just man is taken away from before the face of evil. —*Is.* lvii. 1.

With desolation is all the land made desolate; because there is none that considereth in the heart.—*Jer.* xii. 11.

TIME IN HIS DEALINGS WITH US, GOD TAKES HIS OWN

And they came to her (Judith), and she said to them: What is this word, by which Ozias hath consented to give up the city to the Assyrians, if within five days there come no aid to us?

And who are you that tempt the Lord?

This is not a word that may draw down mercy, but rather that may stir up wrath, and enkindle indignation.

You have set a time for the mercy of the Lord, and you have appointed him a day, according to your pleasure.

But forasmuch as the Lord is patient, let us be penitent for this same thing, and with many tears let us beg his pardon.—*Judith* viii. 10-14.

Times are not hid from the Almighty: but they that know him, know not his days.—*Job* xxiv. 1.

And the Lord is become a refuge for the poor: a helper in due time in tribulation.—*Ps.* ix. 10.

But as for me, my prayer is to thee, O Lord; for the time of thy good pleasure, O God.—*Ps.* lxviii. 14.

My eyes have failed for thy word, saying: When wilt thou comfort me?—*Ps.* cxviii. 82.

All the works of the Lord are good, and he will furnish every work in due time.

It is not to be said: This is worse than that: for all shall be well approved in their time.—*Ecclus.* xxxix. 39, 40.

Work your work before the time, and he will give you your reward in his time.—*Ecclus.* li. 38.

How long, O Lord, shall I cry, and thou wilt not hear? shall I cry out to thee suffering violence, and thou wilt not save?—*Hab.* i. 2.

But he (Jesus) said to them: It is not for you to know the times or moments, which the Father hath put in his own power.—*Acts* i. 7.

And in doing good, let us not fail. For in due time we shall reap, not failing.—*Gal.* vi. 9.

TIME IN PUNISHING THE SINNER, GOD TAKES HIS

See also: Wicked, temporal prosperity of the—page 595.

Yea when thou shalt say: He considereth not: be judged before him, and expect him.

For he doth not now bring on his fury, neither doth he revenge wickedness exceedingly.—*Job* xxxv. 14, 15.

These things thou hast done, and I was silent.

Thou thoughtest unjustly that I should be like to thee: but I will reprove thee, and set before thy face.

Understand these things, you that forget God; lest he snatch you away, and there be none to deliver you.—*Ps.* xlix. 21, 22.

How long shall sinners, O Lord: how long shall sinners glory?

Shall they utter, and speak iniquity: shall all speak who work injustice?—*Ps.* xciii. 3, 4.

For because sentence is not speedily pronounced against the evil, the children of men commit evils without any fear.

But though a sinner do evil a hundred times and by patience be borne withal, I know from thence that it shall be well with them that fear God, who dread his face.—*Eccles.* viii. 11, 12.

Say not: I have sinned, and what harm hath befallen me? for the most High is a patient rewarder.—*Ecclus.* v. 4.

Thy eyes are too pure to behold evil, and thou canst not look on iniquity. Why lookest thou upon them that do unjust things, and holdest thy peace when the wicked devoureth the man that is more just than himself?—*Hab.* i. 13.

You have wearied the Lord with your words, and you said: Wherein have we wearied him? In that you say: Every man that doth evil, is good in the sight of the Lord, and such please him: or surely where is the God of judgment?—*Malach.* ii. 17.

For, not as with other nations (whom the Lord patiently expecteth, that when the day of judgment shall come, he may punish them in the fulness of their sins:)

Doth he also deal with us, so as to suffer our sins to come to their height, and then take vengeance on us.—2 *Mach.* vi. 14, 15.

And the servants of the goodman of the house coming, said to him: Sir, didst thou not sow good seed in thy field? whence then hath it cockle?

And he said to them: An enemy hath done this. And the servants said to him: Wilt thou that we go and gather it up?

And he said: No, lest perhaps gathering up the cockle, you root up the wheat also together with it.

Suffer both to grow until the harvest, and in the time of the harvest I will say to the reapers: Gather up first the cockle, and bind it into bundles to burn, but the wheat gather ye into my barn.—*Matt.* xiii. 27-30.

The Lord delayeth not his promise, as

some imagine, but dealeth patiently for your sake, not willing that any should perish, but that all should return to penance.—2 *Peter* iii. 9.

TONGUE, THE

Death and life are in the power of the tongue: they that love it, shall eat the fruits thereof.—*Prov.* xviii. 21.

As the dressing of a tree showeth the fruit thereof, so a word out of the thought of the heart of man.—*Ecclus.* xxvii. 7.

If thou blow the spark, it shall burn as a fire: and if thou spit upon it, it shall be quenched: both come out of the mouth.—*Ecclus.* xxviii. 14.

A wicked word shall change the heart: out of which four manner of things arise, good and evil, life and death: and the tongue is continually the ruler of them.—*Ecclus.* xxxvii. 21.

A good man out of the good treasure of his heart bringeth forth that which is good: and an evil man out of the evil treasure bringeth forth that which is evil. For out of the abundance of the heart the mouth speaketh.—*Luke* vi. 45.

Even so the tongue is indeed a little member, and boasteth great things. Behold how small a fire kindleth a great wood.

And the tongue is a fire, a world of iniquity. The tongue is placed among our members, which defileth the whole body, and inflameth the wheel of our nativity, being set on fire by hell.

For every nature of beasts, and of birds, and of serpents, and of the rest, is tamed, and hath been tamed by the nature of man:

But the tongue no man can tame, an unquiet evil, full of deadly poison.

By it we bless God and the Father: and by it we curse men, who are made after the likeness of God.

Out of the same mouth proceedeth blessing and cursing. My brethren, these things ought not so to be.

Doth a fountain send forth, out of the same hole, sweet and bitter water?

Can the fig-tree, my brethren, bear grapes; or the vine, figs? So neither can the salt water yield sweet.—*James* iii. 5-12.

TONGUE, BAD USE OF THE

See also: Conversations, evil—page 79.

For there is no truth in their mouth: their heart is vain.

Their throat is an open sepulchre: they deal deceitfully with their tongues: judge them, O God.—*Ps.* v. 10, 11.

His mouth is full of cursing, and of bitterness, and of deceit: under his tongue are labor and sorrow.—*Ps.* ix. (*Heb.* x.) 7.

They are all gone aside, they are become unprofitable together: there is none that doth good, no not one.

Their throat is an open sepulchre: with their tongues they acted deceitfully; the poison of asps is under their lips.

Their mouth is full of cursing and bitterness; their feet are swift to shed blood. Destruction and unhappiness in their ways: and the way of peace they have not known: there is no fear of God before their eyes.—*Ps.* xiii. 3.

Thy mouth hath abounded with evil, and thy tongue framed deceits.

Sitting thou didst speak against thy brother, and didst lay a scandal against thy mother's son: these things thou hast done, and I was silent.

Thou thoughtest unjustly that I should be like to thee: but I will reprove thee, and set before thy face.

Understand these things, you that forget God; lest he snatch you away, and there be none to deliver you.—*Ps.* xlix. 19-22.

Why dost thou glory in malice, thou that art mighty in iniquity?

All the day long thy tongue hath devised injustice: as a sharp razor, thou has wrought deceit. . . .

Thou hast loved all the words of ruin, O deceitful tongue.

Therefore will God destroy thee for ever: he will pluck thee out, and remove thee from thy dwelling place: and thy root out of the land of the living.—*Ps.* li. 3, 4, 6, 7.

Scatter them by thy power; and bring them down, O Lord, my protector:

For the sin of their mouth, and the

word of their lips: and let them be taken in their pride.

And for their cursing and lying they shall be talked of, when they are consumed: when they are consumed by thy wrath, and they shall be no more.

And they shall know that God will rule Jacob, and all the ends of the earth.—*Ps.* lviii. 12-14.

They have thought and spoken wickedness: they have spoken iniquity on high.

They have set their mouth against heaven: and their tongue hath passed through the earth.—*Ps.* lxxii. 8, 9.

For the spirit of wisdom is benevolent, and will not acquit the evil speaker from his lips: for God is witness of his reins, and he is a true searcher of his heart, and a hearer of his tongue. . . .

Therefore he that speaketh unjust things cannot be hid, neither shall the chastising judgment pass him by.

For inquisition shall be made into the thoughts of the ungodly: and the hearing of his words shall come to God, to the chastising of his iniquities.—*Wis.* i. 6, 8, 9.

For who is there that hath not offended with his tongue?—*Ecclus.* xix. 17.

And you rose up against me with your mouth, and have derogated from me by your words: I have heard them.

Thus saith the Lord God: When the whole earth shall rejoice, I will make thee a wilderness.—*Ezech.* xxxv. 13, 14.

But I say unto you, that every idle word that men shall speak, they shall render an account for it in the day of judgment.

For by thy words thou shalt be justified, and by thy words, thou shalt be condemned.—*Matt.* xii. 36, 37.

TONGUE, PROPER USE OF THE

See also: Conversations, good—page 80.

And the words of my mouth shall be such as may please: and the meditation of my heart always in thy sight.

O Lord, my helper, and my redeemer. —*Ps.* xviii. 15.

And my tongue shall meditate thy justice, thy praise all the day long.—*Ps.* xxxiv. 28.

The mouth of the just shall meditate wisdom: and his tongue shall speak judgment.—*Ps.* xxxvi. 30.

My mouth shall show forth thy justice; thy salvation all the day long.—*Ps.* lxx. 15.

My lips shall greatly rejoice, when I shall sing to thee; and my soul which thou hast redeemed.

Yea and my tongue shall meditate on thy justice all the day: when they shall be confounded and put to shame that seek evils to me.—*Ps.* lxx. 23, 24.

The mouth of the just is a vein of life: and the mouth of the wicked covereth iniquity.—*Prov.* x. 11.

The tongue of the just is as choice silver: but the heart of the wicked is nothing worth.—*Prov.* x. 20.

The mouth of the just shall bring forth wisdom: the tongue of the perverse shall perish.

The lips of the just consider what is acceptable: and the mouth of the wicked uttereth perverse things.—*Prov.* x. 31, 32.

By the fruit of his own mouth shall a man be filled with good things.—*Prov.* xii. 14.

The tongue of the wise adorneth knowledge: but the mouth of fools bubbleth out folly. . . .

A peaceable tongue is a tree of life: but that which is immoderate, shall crush the spirit. . . .

The lips of the wise shall disperse knowledge: the heart of fools shall be unlike.—*Prov.* xv. 2, 4, 7.

For by the tongue wisdom is discerned: and understanding, and knowledge, and learning by the word of the wise, and steadfastness in the works of justice.—*Ecclus.* iv. 29.

A sweet word multiplieth friends, and appeaseth enemies, and a gracious tongue in a good man aboundeth.—*Ecclus.* vi. 5.

The law of truth was in his (Levi's) mouth, and iniquity was not found in his lips: he walked with me in peace, and in equity, and turned many away from iniquity.—*Malach.* ii. 6.

TONGUE, CONTROL OF THE

See also: Prudence in words— page 455.

I said: I will take heed to my ways: that I sin not with my tongue.

I have set a guard to my mouth, when the sinner stood against me.—*Ps.* xxxviii. 2.

Set a watch, O Lord, before my mouth: and a door round about my lips.

Incline not my heart to evil words; to make excuses in sins.

With men that work iniquity: and I will not communicate with the choicest of them.—*Ps.* cxl. 3, 4.

Even a fool, if he will hold his peace shall be counted wise: and if he close his lips, a man of understanding.— *Prov.* xvii. 28.

He that keepeth his mouth and his tongue, keepeth his soul from distress. —*Prov.* xxi. 23.

Blessed is the man that hath not slipped by a word out of his mouth, and is not pricked with the remorse of sin. —*Ecclus.* xiv. 1.

A wise man will hold his peace till he see opportunity: but a babbler, and a fool, will regard no time.—*Ecclus.* xx. 7.

For in many things we all offend. If any man offend not in word, the same is a perfect man. He is able also with a bridle to lead about the whole body.—*James* iii. 2.

TONGUE, NECESSITY OF CONTROL OF THE

He that keepeth his mouth, keepeth his soul: but he that hath no guard on his speech shall meet with evils.—*Prov.* xiii. 3.

As a city that lieth open and is not compassed with walls, so is a man that cannot refrain his own spirit in speaking.—*Prov.* xxv. 28.

Hast thou seen a man hasty to speak? folly is rather to be looked for, than his amendment.—*Prov.* xxix. 20.

And believe not every word. There is one, that slippeth with the tongue, but not from his heart.—*Ecclus.* xix. 16.

He that useth many words, shall hurt his own soul.—*Ecclus.* xx. 8.

Who will set a guard before my mouth, and a sure seal upon my lips, that I fall not by them, and that my tongue destroy me not?—*Ecclus.* xxii. 33.

And if any man think himself to be religious, not bridling his tongue, but deceiving his own heart, this man's religion is vain.—*James* i. 26.

TONGUE, EXHORTATION TO CONTROL THE

Who is the man that desireth life: who loveth to see good days?

Keep thy tongue from evil, and thy lips from speaking guile.—*Ps.* xxxiii. 13, 14.

Remove from thee a froward mouth, and let detracting lips be far from thee.—*Prov.* iv. 24.

Be not a hypocrite in the sight of men, and let not thy lips be a stumbling-block to thee.

Watch over them, lest thou fall, and bring dishonor upon thy soul.—*Ecclus.* i. 37, 38.

Hear, O ye children, the discipline of the mouth: and he that will keep it shall not perish by his lips, nor be brought to fall into most wicked works. —*Ecclus.* xxiii. 7.

Hedge in thy ears with thorns, hear not a wicked tongue, and make doors and bars to thy mouth.

Melt down thy gold and silver, and make a balance for thy words, and a just bridle for thy mouth:

And take heed lest thou slip with thy tongue, and fall in the sight of thy enemies who lie in wait for thee, and thy fall be incurable unto death.— *Ecclus.* xxviii. 28-30.

But shun profane and vain babblings: for they grow much towards ungodliness. . . .

And avoid foolish and unlearned questions, knowing that they beget strifes.—2 *Tim.* ii. 16, 23.

TONGUE, THE DANGER AND EVIL OF A WICKED AND FOOLISH

O Lord, deliver my soul from wicked lips, and a deceitful tongue.

What shall be given to thee, or what

shall be added to thee, to a deceitful tongue?—*Ps.* cxix. 2, 3.

They have sharpened their tongues like a serpent: the venom of asps is under their lips.—*Ps.* cxxxix. 4.

A man full of tongue shall not be established in the earth: evil shall catch the unjust man unto destruction.—*Ps.* cxxxix. 12.

The mouth of the wicked covereth iniquity

. . . Wise men lay up knowledge: but the mouth of the fool is next to confusion. . . .

In the multitude of words there shall not want sin: but he that refraineth his lips is most wise.—*Prov.* x. 11, 14, 19.

The tongue of the perverse shall perish.

The lips of the just consider what is acceptable: and the mouth of the wicked uttereth perverse things.—*Prov.* x. 31, 32.

For the sins of the lips ruin draweth nigh to the evil man: but the just shall escape out of distress.—*Prov.* xii. 13.

The tongue of the wise adorneth knowledge: but the mouth of fools bubbleth out folly.

. . . A peaceable tongue is a tree of life: but that which is immoderate, shall crush the spirit.—*Prov.* xv. 2, 4.

He that is of a perverse heart, shall not find good: and he that perverteth his tongue, shall fall into evil.—*Prov.* xvii. 20.

The mouth of a fool is his destruction: and his lips are the ruin of his soul.

The words of the double tongued are as if they were harmless: and they reach even to the inner parts of the bowels.—*Prov.* xviii. 7, 8.

A deceitful tongue loveth not truth: and a slippery mouth worketh ruin.—*Prov.* xxvi. 28.

Honor and glory is in the word of the wise, but the tongue of the fool is his ruin.—*Ecclus.* v. 15.

A man full of tongue is terrible in his city, and he that is rash in his word shall be hateful.—*Ecclus.* ix. 25.

The slipping of a false tongue is as one that falleth on the pavement: so the fall of the wicked shall come speedily.—*Ecclus.* xx. 20.

Let not thy mouth be accustomed to indiscreet speech: for therein is the word of sin.—*Ecclus.* xxiii. 17.

As the climbing of a sandy way is to the feet of the aged, so is a wife full of tongue to a quiet man.—*Ecclus.* xxv. 27.

The tongue of a third person hath disquieted many, and scattered them from nation to nation.

It hath destroyed the strong cities of the rich, and hath overthrown the houses of great men.

It hath cut in pieces the forces of people, and undone strong nations.

The tongue of a third person hath cast out valiant women, and deprived them of their labors.

He that hearkeneth to it, shall never have rest, neither shall he have a friend in whom he may repose.

The stroke of a whip maketh a blue mark: but the stroke of the tongue will break the bones.—*Ecclus.* xxviii. 16-21.

Many have fallen by the edge of the sword, but not so many as have perished by their own tongue.

Blessed is he that is defended from a wicked tongue, that hath not passed into the wrath thereof, and that hath not drawn the yoke thereof, and hath not been bound in its bands. For its yoke is a yoke of iron: and its bands are bands of brass.

The death thereof is a most evil death: and hell is preferable to it.—*Ecclus.* xxviii. 22-25.

And take heed lest thou slip with thy tongue, and fall in the sight of thy enemies who lie in wait for thee, and thy fall be incurable unto death.—*Ecclus.* xxviii. 30.

TRIALS AND TRIBULATIONS

See also: Suffering, love of—page 547.

But she said to them: Call me not Noemi, (that is, beautiful,) but call me Mara, (that is, bitter,) for the Almighty hath quite filled me with bitterness.

I went out full, and the Lord hath brought me back empty. Why then do you call me Noemi, whom the Lord hath humbled and the Almighty hath afflicted?—*Ruth* i. 20, 21.

I expected good things, and evils are come upon me: I waited for light, and darkness broke out.—*Job* xxx. 26.

The Lord trieth the just and the wicked.—*Ps.* x. 6.

The furnace trieth the potter's vessels, and the trial of affliction just men. —*Ecclus.* xxvii. 6.

Many shall be chosen, and made white, and shall be tried as fire: and the wicked shall deal wickedly, and none of the wicked shall understand, but the learned shall understand.—*Dan.* xii. 10.

In all things we suffer tribulation, but are not distressed; we are straitened, but are not destitute;

We suffer persecution, but are not forsaken; we are cast down, but we perish not:

Always bearing about in our body the mortification of Jesus, that the life also of Jesus may be made manifest in our bodies.—2 *Cor.* iv. 8-10.

And all that will live godly in Christ Jesus, shall suffer persecution.—2 *Tim.* iii. 12.

TRIBULATIONS COME FROM THE HANDS OF GOD

Now it happened one day, that being wearied with burying, he (Tobias) came to his house, and cast himself down by the wall, and slept.

And as he was sleeping, hot dung out of a swallow's nest fell upon his eyes, and he was made blind.

Now this trial the Lord therefore permitted to happen to him, that an example might be given to posterity of his patience, as also of holy Job.—*Tob.* ii. 10-12.

And Tobias said: I bless thee, O Lord God of Israel, because thou hast chastised me, and thou hast saved me: and behold, I see Tobias my son.—*Tob.* xi. 17.

Blessed is the man whom God correcteth: refuse not therefore the chastising of the Lord:

For he woundeth, and cureth: he striketh, and his hands shall heal.—*Job* v. 17, 18.

For the arrows of the Lord are in me, the rage whereof drinketh up my spirit, and the terrors of the Lord war against me.—*Job* vi. 4.

But he knoweth my way, and has tried me as gold that passeth through the fire.—*Job* xxiii. 10.

He rebuketh also by sorrow in the bed, and he maketh all his bones to wither.

Bread becometh abominable to him in his life, and to his soul the meat which before he desired.—*Job* xxxiii. 19, 20.

Thou hast proved my heart, and visited it by night, thou hast tried me by fire: and iniquity hath not been found in me.—*Ps.* xvi. 3.

For thou hast humbled us in the place of affliction: and the shadow of death hath covered us.—*Ps.* xliii. 20.

For thou, O God, hast proved us: thou hast tried us by fire, as silver is tried.

Thou hast brought us into a net, thou hast laid afflictions on our back.—*Ps.* lxv. 10, 11.

The Lord chastising hath chastised me: but he hath not delivered me over to death.—*Ps.* cxvii. 18.

I know, O Lord, that thy judgments are equity: and in thy truth thou hast humbled me.—*Ps.* cxviii. 75.

My son, reject not the correction of the Lord: and do not faint when thou art chastised by him:

For whom the Lord loveth, he chastiseth: and as a father in the son he pleaseth himself.—*Prov.* iii. 11, 12.

As silver is tried by fire, and gold in the furnace: so the Lord trieth the hearts.—*Prov.* xvii. 3.

For when they were tried, and chastised with mercy, they knew how the wicked were judged with wrath, and tormented.

For thou didst admonish and try them as a father: but the others, as a severe king, thou didst examine and condemn.—*Wis.* xi. 10, 11.

In their affliction they will rise early to me: Come, and let us return to the Lord:

For he hath taken us, and he will heal us: he will strike, and he will cure us.—*Osee* vi. 1, 2.

TRIBULATIONS ARE FOR OUR ADVANTAGE

And because thou wast acceptable to God, it was necessary that temptation should prove thee.—*Tob.* xii. 13.

But esteeming these very punishments to be less than our sins deserve, let us believe that these scourges of the Lord, with which like servants we are chastised, have happened for our amendment, and not for our destruction.—*Judith* viii. 27.

Blessed is the man whom God correcteth: refuse not therefore the chastising of the Lord.—*Job* v. 17.

Before I was humbled I offended; therefore have I kept thy word.—*Ps.* cxviii. 67.

It is good for me that thou hast humbled me, that I may learn thy justifications.—*Ps.* cxviii. 71.

O how good and sweet is thy spirit, O Lord, in all things!

And therefore thou chastisest them that err, by little and little: and admonishest them, and speakest to them, concerning the things wherein they offend; that leaving their wickedness, they may believe in thee, O Lord.—*Wis.* xii. 1, 2.

I am the true vine; and my Father is the husbandman.

Every branch in me, that beareth not fruit, he will take away: and every one that beareth fruit, he will purge it, that it may bring forth more fruit.—*John* xv. 1, 2.

Confirming the souls of the disciples, and exhorting them to continue in the faith: and that through many tribulations we must enter into the kingdom of God.—*Acts* xiv. 21.

But we glory also in tribulations, knowing that tribulation worketh patience;

And patience, trial; and trial hope;

And hope confoundeth not: because the charity of God is poured forth in our hearts, by the Holy Ghost, who is given to us.—*Rom.* v. 3-5.

But whilst we are judged, we are chastised by the Lord, that we be not condemned with this world.—1 *Cor.* xi. 32.

And lest the greatness of the revelations should exalt me, there was given me a sting of my flesh, an angel of Satan, to buffet me.

For which thing thrice I besought the Lord, that it might depart from me.

And he said to me: My grace is sufficient for thee: for power is made perfect in infirmity. Gladly therefore will I glory in my infirmities, that the power of Christ may dwell in me.

For which cause I please myself in my infirmities, in reproaches, in necessities, in persecutions, in distresses, for Christ. For when I am weak, then am I powerful.—2 *Cor.* xii. 7-10.

Persevere under discipline. God dealeth with you as with his sons; for what son is there, whom the father doth not correct?

But if you be without chastisement, whereof all are made partakers, then are you bastards, and not sons.—*Heb.* xii. 7, 8.

Now all chastisement for the present indeed seemeth not to bring with it joy, but sorrow: but afterwards it will yield, to them that are exercised by it, the most peaceable fruit of justice.—*Heb.* xii. 11.

My brethren, count it all joy, when you shall fall into divers temptations;

Knowing that the trying of your faith worketh patience.

And patience hath a perfect work; that you may be perfect and entire; failing in nothing.—*James* i. 2-4.

I know thy tribulation and thy poverty, but thou art rich: and thou art blasphemed by them that say they are Jews and are not, but are the synagogue of Satan.—*Apoc.* ii. 9.

TRIBULATIONS ARE TO BE BORNE WITH PATIENCE AND RESIGNATION

For whereas he (Tobias) had always feared God from his infancy, and kept his commandments, he repined not against God because the evil of blindness had befallen him,

But continued immovable in the fear of God, giving thanks to God all the days of his life.—*Tob.* ii. 13, 14.

So Isaac, so Jacob, so Moses, and all

that have pleased God, passed through many tribulations, remaining faithful.

But they that did not receive the trials with the fear of the Lord, but uttered their impatience and the reproach of their murmuring against the Lord,

Were destroyed by the destroyer, and perished by serpents.—*Judith* viii. 23-25.

Blessed is the man whom God correcteth: refuse not therefore the chastising of the Lord.—*Job* v. 17.

For the sake of the words of thy lips, I have kept hard ways.—*Ps.* xvi. 4.

We have rejoiced for the days in which thou hast humbled us: for the years in which we have seen evils.—*Ps.* lxxxix. 15.

My son, reject not the correction of the Lord: and do not faint when thou art chastised by him:

For whom the Lord loveth, he chastiseth: and as a father in the son he pleaseth himself.—*Prov.* iii. 11, 12.

Son, when thou comest to the service of God, stand in justice and in fear, and prepare thy soul for temptation.

Humble thy heart, and endure: incline thy ear, and receive the words of understanding: and make not haste in the time of clouds.

Wait on God with patience: join thyself to God, and endure, that thy life may be increased in the latter end.

Take all that shall be brought upon thee: and in thy sorrow endure, and in thy humiliation keep patience.

For gold and silver are tried in the fire, but acceptable men in the furnace of humiliation.—*Ecclus.* ii. 1-5.

Rejoicing in hope. Patient in tribulation. Instant in prayer.—*Rom.* xii. 12.

But God forbid that I should glory, save in the cross of our Lord Jesus Christ; by whom the world is crucified to me, and I to the world.—*Gal.* vi. 14.

Furthermore I count all things to be but loss for the excellent knowledge of Jesus Christ my Lord; for whom I have suffered the loss of all things, and count them but as dung, that I may gain Christ: . . .

That I may know him, and the power of his resurrection, and the fellowship of his sufferings, being made conformable to his death.—*Philipp.* iii. 8, 10.

And we sent Timothy, our brother, and the minister of God in the gospel of Christ, to confirm you and exhort you concerning your faith:

That no man should be moved in these tribulations: for yourselves know, that we are appointed thereunto. —1 *Thess.* iii. 2, 3.

Take, my brethren, for an example of suffering evil, of labor and patience, the prophets, who spoke in the name of the Lord.

Behold, we account them blessed who have endured. You have heard of the patience of Job, and you have seen the end of the Lord, that the Lord is merciful and compassionate.—*James* v. 10, 11.

For this is thankworthy, if for conscience towards God, a man endure sorrows, suffering wrongfully.

For what glory is it, if committing sin, and being buffeted for it, you endure? But if doing well, you suffer patiently; this is thankworthy before God.

For unto this are you called: because Christ also suffered for us, leaving you an example that you should follow his steps.—1 *Peter* ii. 19-21.

Be you humbled therefore under the mighty hand of God, that he may exalt you in the time of visitation.—1 *Peter* v. 6.

TRIBULATIONS, IF BORNE WELL, ARE REWARDED BY GOD

But this every one is sure of that worshippeth thee, that his life, if it be under trial, shall be crowned: and if it be under tribulation, it shall be delivered: and if it be under correction, it shall be allowed to come to thy mercy. —*Tob.* iii. 21.

They that sow in tears shall reap in joy.

Going they went and wept, casting their seeds.

But coming they shall come with joyfulness, carrying their sheaves.—*Ps.* cxxv. 5-7.

But the souls of the just are in the hand of God, and the torment of death shall not touch them. . . .

And though in the sight of men they suffered torments, their hope is full of immortality.

Afflicted in few things, in many they shall be well rewarded: because God hath tried them, and found them worthy of himself.

As gold in the furnace he hath proved them, and as a victim of a holocaust he hath received them, and in time there shall be respect had to them.—*Wis.* iii. 1, 4-6.

Blessed are they that mourn: for they shall be comforted.—*Matt.* v. 5.

Blessed are they that suffer persecution for justice' sake: for theirs is the kingdom of heaven.

Blessed are ye when they shall revile you, and persecute you, and speak all that is evil against you, untruly, for my sake:

Be glad and rejoice, for your reward is very great in heaven.—*Matt.* v. 10-12.

That our hope for you may be steadfast: knowing that as you are partakers of the sufferings, so shall you be also of the consolation.—2 *Cor.* i. 7.

For that which is at present momentary and light of our tribulation, worketh for us above measure exceedingly an eternal weight of glory.—2 *Cor.* iv. 17.

So that we ourselves also glory in you in the churches of God, for your patience and faith, and in all your persecutions and tribulations, which you endure,

For an example of the just judgment of God, that you may be counted worthy of the kingdom of God, for which also you suffer.

Seeing it is a just thing with God to repay tribulation to them that trouble you:

And to you who are troubled, rest with us when the Lord Jesus shall be revealed from heaven, with the angels of his power.—2 *Thess.* i. 4-7.

A faithful saying: for if we be dead with him, we shall live also with him.

If we suffer, we shall also reign with him.—2 *Tim.* ii. 11, 12.

Fear none of those things which thou shalt suffer. Behold, the devil will cast some of you into prison that you may be tried: and you shall have tribulation ten days. Be thou faithful unto death: and I will give thee the crown of life.—*Apoc.* ii. 10.

And one of the ancients answered, and said to me: These that are clothed in white robes, who are they? and whence came they?

And I said to him: My Lord, thou knowest. And he said to me: These are they who are come out of great tribulation, and have washed their robes, and have made them white in the blood of the Lamb.

Therefore they are before the throne of God, and they serve him day and night in his temple: and he, that sitteth on the throne, shall dwell over them.

They shall no more hunger nor thirst, neither shall the sun fall on them, nor any heat.

For the Lamb, which is in the midst of the throne, shall rule them, and shall lead them to the fountains of the waters of life, and God shall wipe away all tears from their eyes.—*Apoc.* vii. 13-17.

TRIBULATIONS ARE ONLY TRANSITORY

See also: Sorrow into joy, God turns our—page 539.

But this every one is sure of that worshippeth thee, that his life, if it be under trial, shall be crowned: and if it be under tribulation, it shall be delivered: and if it be under correction, it shall be allowed to come to thy mercy.

For thou art not delighted in our being lost: because after a storm thou makest a calm, and after tears and weeping thou pourest in joyfulness.—*Tob.* iii. 21, 22.

And Tobias said: I bless thee, O Lord God of Israel, because thou hast chastised me, and thou hast saved me: and behold I see Tobias my son.—*Tob.* xi. 17.

Blessed is the man whom God correcteth: refuse not therefore the chastising of the Lord:

For he woundeth, and cureth: he striketh, and his hands shall heal.—*Job* v. 17, 18.

Many are the afflictions of the just;

but out of them all will the Lord deliver them.—*Ps.* xxxiii. 20.

He shall cry to me, and I will hear him: I am with him in tribulation, I will deliver him, and I will glorify him. —*Ps.* xc. 15.

She (wisdom) will bring upon him fear and dread and trial: and she will scourge him with the affliction of her discipline, till she try him by her laws, and trust his soul.

Then she will strengthen him, and make a straight way to him, and give him joy.—*Ecclus.* iv. 19, 20.

For a small moment have I forsaken thee, but with great mercies will I gather thee.

In a moment of indignation have I hid my face a little while from thee, but with everlasting kindness have I had mercy on thee, said the Lord thy Redeemer.—*Is.* liv. 7, 8.

In their affliction they will rise early to me: Come, and let us return to the Lord:

For he hath taken us, and he will heal us: he will strike, and he will cure us.

He will revive us after two days: on the third day he will raise us up, and we shall live in his sight. We shall know, and we shall follow on, that we may know the Lord. His going forth is prepared as the morning light, and he will come to us as the early and the latter rain to the earth.—*Osee* vi. 1-3.

For that which is at present momentary and light of our tribulation, worketh for us above measure exceedingly an eternal weight of glory.

While we look not at the things which are seen, but at the things which are not seen. For the things which are seen, are temporal; but the things which are not seen, are eternal.—2 *Cor.* iv. 17, 18.

But the God of all grace, who hath called us unto his eternal glory in Christ Jesus, after you have suffered a little, will himself perfect you, and confirm you, and establish you.—1 *Peter* v. 10.

TRIBULATIONS, THE VALUE OF

See: Suffering, the value of—page 547.

TRIBULATIONS, GOD COMFORTS US IN OUR

See also: Comforter, God our— page 57.

Wherefore I will pray to the Lord, and address my speech to God: . . .

Who setteth up the humble on high, and comforteth with health those that mourn.—*Job* v. 8, 11.

According to the multitude of my sorrows in my heart, thy comforts have given joy to my soul.—*Ps.* xciii. 19.

Be thou mindful of thy word to thy servant, in which thou hast given me hope.

This hath comforted me in my humiliation: because thy word hath enlivened me.—*Ps.* cxviii. 49, 50.

I remembered, O Lord, thy judgments of old: and I was comforted.— *Ps.* cxviii. 52.

O! let thy mercy be for my comfort, according to thy word unto thy servant. —*Ps.* cxviii. 76.

If I shall walk in the midst of tribulation, thou wilt quicken me: and thou hast stretched forth thy hand against the wrath of my enemies: and thy right hand hath saved me.—*Ps.* cxxxvii. 7.

Come to me, all you that labor, and are burdened, and I will refresh you. —*Matt.* xi. 28.

Blessed be the God and Father of our Lord Jesus Christ, the Father of mercies, and the God of all comfort.

Who comforteth us in all our tribulation; that we also may be able to comfort them who are in all distress, by the exhortation wherewith we also are exhorted by God.

For as the sufferings of Christ abound in us: so also by Christ doth our comfort abound.—2 *Cor.* i. 3-5.

Now we make known unto you, brethren, the grace of God, that hath been given in the churches of Macedonia.

That in much experience of tribulation, they have had abundance of joy; and their very deep poverty hath abounded unto the riches of their simplicity.—2 *Cor.* viii. 1, 2.

And you became followers of us, and of the Lord; receiving the word in much tribulation, with joy of the Holy Ghost.—*1 Thess.* i. 6.

And you have forgotten the consolation, which speaketh to you, as unto children, saying: My son, neglect not the discipline of the Lord; neither be thou wearied whilst thou art rebuked by him.

For whom the Lord loveth, he chastiseth; and he scourgeth every son whom he receiveth.—*Heb.* xii. 5, 6.

TRUST IN GOD

See: Confidence in God—page 71.

TRUTH, THE

Mercy and truth have met each other: justice and peace have kissed.

Truth is sprung out of the earth: and justice hath looked down from heaven.—*Ps.* lxxxiv. 11, 12.

The lip of truth shall be steadfast for ever: but he that is a hasty witness, frameth a lying tongue.—*Prov.* xii. 19.

They err that work evil: but mercy and truth prepare good things.—*Prov.* xiv. 22.

By mercy and truth iniquity is redeemed.—*Prov.* xvi. 6.

Then Jesus said to those Jews, who believed him: If you continue in my word, you shall be my disciples indeed.

And you shall know the truth, and the truth shall make you free.—*John* viii. 31, 32.

Sanctify them in truth. Thy word is truth.—*John* xvii. 17.

Pilate saith to him (Jesus): What is truth? And when he said this, he went out again to the Jews, and saith to them: I find no cause in him.—*John* xviii. 38.

Stand therefore, having your loins girt about with truth, and having on the breastplate of justice.—*Eph.* vi. 14.

TRUTH, RESISTING THE

See: Blindness of heart, wilful—page 39.

TRUTH, LOVE OF THE

Lord, who shall dwell in thy tabernacle? or who shall rest in thy holy hill? . . .

He that speaketh truth in his heart, who hath not used deceit in his tongue.—*Ps.* xiv. 1, 3.

O love the Lord, all ye his saints: for the Lord will require truth, and will repay them abundantly that act proudly.—*Ps.* xxx. 24.

Lying men shall not be mindful of her (wisdom): but men that speak truth shall be found with her, and shall advance, even till they come to the sight of God.—*Ecclus.* xv. 8.

Birds resort unto their like: so truth will return to them that practise her.—*Ecclus.* xxvii. 10.

The law of truth was in his (Levi's) mouth, and iniquity was not found in his lips: he walked with me in peace, and in equity, and turned many away from iniquity.—*Malach.* ii. 6.

For we can do nothing against the truth; but for the truth.—*2 Cor.* xiii. 8.

TRUTH, EXHORTATION TO LOVE AND PRACTICE OF THE

Who is the man that desireth life: who loveth to see good days?

Keep thy tongue from evil, and thy lips from speaking guile.—*Ps.* xxxiii. 13, 14.

Let not mercy and truth leave thee, put them about thy neck, and write them in the tables of thy heart:

And thou shalt find grace and good understanding before God and men.—*Prov.* iii. 3, 4.

For thy soul be not ashamed to say the truth.

For there is a shame that bringeth sin, and there is a shame that bringeth glory and grace.—*Ecclus.* iv. 24, 25.

These then are the things, which you shall do: Speak ye truth every one to his neighbor: judge ye truth and judgment of peace in your gates.—*Zach.* viii. 16.

Thus saith the Lord of hosts: The fast of the fourth month, and the fast of the fifth, and the fast of the seventh, and the fast of the tenth shall be to the house of Juda, joy and gladness, and great solemnities: only love ye truth and peace.—*Zach.* viii. 19.

But doing the truth in charity, we may in all things grow up in him who is the head, even Christ. . . .

Wherefore putting away lying, speak ye the truth every man with his neighbor; for we are members one of another.—*Eph.* iv. 15, 25.

TRUTH, GOD LOVES THE

For behold thou hast loved truth: the uncertain and hidden things of thy wisdom thou hast made manifest to me. —*Ps.* l. 8.

For God loveth mercy and truth: the Lord will give grace and glory.—*Ps.* lxxxiii. 12.

The Lord is only for them that wait upon him in the way of truth and justice.—*Ecclus.* xxxiv. 22.

Pilate therefore said to him: Art thou a king then? Jesus answered: Thou sayest that I am a king. For this was I born, and for this came I into the world; that I should give testimony to the truth. Every one that is of the truth, heareth my voice.—*John* xviii. 37.

TRUTH OF GOD, THE

See also: Fidelity of God, the— page 150.

For thy mercy is before my eyes; and I am well pleased with thy truth.—*Ps.* xxv. 3.

O Lord, thy mercy is in heaven, and thy truth reacheth even to the clouds. —*Ps.* xxxv. 6.

Withhold not thou, O Lord, thy tender mercies from me: thy mercy and thy truth have always upheld me.—*Ps.* xxxix. 12.

For thy mercy is magnified even to the heavens: and thy truth unto the clouds.—*Ps.* lvi. 11.

He abideth for ever in the sight of God: his mercy and truth who shall search?—*Ps.* lx. 8.

The mercies of the Lord I will sing for ever.

I will show forth thy truth with my mouth to generation and generation.

For thou hast said: Mercy shall be built up for ever in the heavens: thy truth shall be prepared in them.—*Ps.* lxxxviii. 2, 3.

The heavens shall confess thy wonders, O Lord: and thy truth in the church of the saints.—*Ps.* lxxxviii. 6.

O Lord God of hosts, who is like to thee? thou art mighty, O Lord, and thy truth is round about thee. . . .

Justice and judgment are the preparation of thy throne.

Mercy and truth shall go before thy face.—*Ps.* lxxxviii. 9, 15.

But my mercy I will not take away from him (David): nor will I suffer my truth to fail.—*Ps.* lxxxviii. 34.

His truth shall compass thee with a shield: thou shalt not be afraid of the terror of the night.—*Ps.* xc. 5.

It is good to give praise to the Lord: and to sing to thy name, O most High.

To show forth thy mercy in the morning, and thy truth in the night.—*Ps.* xci. 2, 3.

He shall judge the world with justice, and the people with his truth.— *Ps.* xcv. 13.

He hath remembered his mercy and his truth toward the house of Israel.

All the ends of the earth have seen the salvation of our God.— *Ps.* xcvii. 3.

Praise ye his name: for the Lord is sweet, his mercy endureth for ever, and his truth to generation and generation.—*Ps.* xcix. 5.

O praise the Lord, all ye nations: praise him, all ye people.

For his mercy is confirmed upon us: and the truth of the Lord remaineth for ever.—*Ps.* cxvi. 1, 2.

For ever, O Lord, thy word standeth firm in heaven.

Thy truth unto all generations: thou hast founded the earth, and it continueth.—*Ps.* cxviii. 89, 90.

He that hath received his testimony, hath set to his seal that God is true.— *John* iii. 33.

Jesus saith to him (Thomas): I am the way, and the truth, and the life. No man cometh to the Father, but by me.—*John* xiv. 6.

But God is true; and every man a liar, as it is written, That thou mayst be justified in thy words, and mayst overcome when thou art judged.—*Rom.* iii. 4.

TURN TO GOD, EXHORTATION TO

See: Converted to God—page 80.

TURNING AWAY FROM GOD

See also: Wandering—page 580.

But such as turn aside into bonds, the Lord shall lead out with the workers of iniquity: peace upon Israel. —*Ps.* cxxiv. 5.

Be not hasty to depart from his face, and do not continue in an evil work: for he will do all that pleaseth him.— *Eccles.* viii. 3.

The beginning of the pride of man, is to fall off from God:

Because his heart is departed from him that made him.—*Ecclus.* x. 14, 15.

And he that passeth over from justice to sin, God hath prepared such a one for the sword.—*Ecclus.* xxvi. 27.

Thus saith the Lord: Cursed be the man that trusteth in man, and maketh flesh his arm, and whose heart departeth from the Lord.—*Jer.* xvii. 5.

And they have turned their backs to me, and not their faces: when I taught them early in the morning, and instructed them, and they would not hearken to receive instruction.—*Jer.* xxxii. 33.

Woe to them, for they have departed from me: they shall be wasted because they have transgressed against me: and I redeemed them: and they have spoken lies against me.—*Osee* vii. 13.

And I will stretch out my hand upon Juda, and upon all the inhabitants of Jerusalem: and I will destroy out of this place the remnant of Baal, and the names of the wardens of the temples with the priests: . . .

And them that turn away from following after the Lord, and that have not sought the Lord, nor searched after him.—*Soph.* i. 4, 6.

Take heed, brethren, lest perhaps there be in any of you an evil heart of unbelief, to depart from the living God. —*Heb.* iii. 12.

UNBELIEF

See: Incredulity—page 236.

UNBELIEVERS

See: Infidels—page 239.

UNBELIEVERS, A PRAYER FOR

Have mercy upon us, O God of all, and behold us, and show us the light of thy mercies:

And send thy fear upon the nations, that have not sought after thee: that they may know that there is no God beside thee, and that they may show forth thy wonders.

Lift up thy hand over the strange nations, that they may see thy power.

For as thou hast been sanctified in us in their sight, so thou shalt be magnified among them in our presence,

That they may know thee, as we also have known thee, that there is no God beside thee, O Lord.

Renew thy signs, and work new miracles.

Glorify thy hand, and thy right arm. —*Ecclus.* xxxvi. 1-7.

UNCHASTITY

See also: Adultery—page 20.

Then the angel Raphael said to him (Tobias): Hear me, and I will show thee who they are, over whom the devil can prevail.

For they who in such manner receive matrimony, as to shut out God from themselves, and from their mind, and to give themselves to their lust, as the horse and mule, which have not understanding, over them the devil hath power.—*Tob.* vi. 16, 17.

His own iniquities catch the wicked, and he is fast bound with the ropes of his own sins.—*Prov.* v. 22.

He that loveth gold, shall not be justified: and he that followeth after corruption, shall be filled with it.—*Ecclus.* xxxi. 5.

And thou didst bow thyself to women: and by thy body thou wast brought under subjection.

Thou hast stained thy glory, and defiled thy seed, so as to bring wrath upon thy children, and to have thy folly kindled.—*Ecclus.* xlvii. 21, 22.

Fornication, and wine, and drunkenness take away the understanding.— *Osee* iv. 11.

Wherefore God gave them up to the

desires of their heart, unto uncleanness, to dishonor their own bodies among themselves.

Who changed the truth of God into a lie; and worshipped and served the creature rather than the Creator, who is blessed for ever. Amen.

For this cause God delivered them up to shameful affections. For their women have changed the natural use into that use which is against nature.

And in like manner, the men also, leaving the natural use of the women, have burned in their lusts one towards another, men with men working that which is filthy, and receiving in themselves the recompense which was due to their error.

And as they liked not to have God in their knowledge, God delivered them up to a reprobate sense, to do those things which are not convenient.—*Rom.* i. 24-28.

For what things a man shall sow, those also shall he reap. For he that soweth in his flesh, of the flesh also shall reap corruption. But he that soweth in the spirit, of the spirit shall reap life everlasting.—*Gal.* vi. 8.

For, speaking proud words of vanity, they allure by the desires of fleshly riotousness, those who for a little while escape, such as converse in error:

Promising them liberty, whereas they themselves are the slaves of corruption. For by whom a man is overcome, of the same also he is the slave.—2 *Peter* ii. 18, 19.

UNCHASTITY, THE PUNISHMENT OF

Juda therefore said to Onan his son: Go in to thy brother's wife and marry her, that thou mayst raise seed to thy brother.

He knowing that the children should not be his, when he went in to his brother's wife, spilled his seed upon the ground, lest children should be born in his brother's name.

And therefore the Lord slew him, because he did a detestable thing.—*Gen.* xxxviii. 8-10.

Every soul that shall commit any of these abominations, shall perish from the midst of his people.—*Lev.* xviii. 29.

For if you live according to the flesh, you shall die: but if by the Spirit you mortify the deeds of the flesh, you shall live.—*Rom.* viii. 13.

Know you not that the unjust shall not possess the kingdom of God? Do not err: neither fornicators, nor idolaters, nor adulterers,

Nor the effeminate, nor liers with mankind, . . . shall possess the kingdom of God.—1 *Cor.* vi. 9, 10.

Now the works of the flesh are manifest, which are fornication, uncleanness, immodesty, luxury. . . .

Of the which I foretell you, as I have foretold to you, that they who do such things shall not obtain the kingdom of God.—*Gal.* v. 19, 21.

For know you this and understand, that no fornicator, or unclean, or covetous person (which is a serving of idols), hath inheritance in the kingdom of Christ and of God.—*Eph.* v. 5.

The Lord knoweth how to deliver the godly from temptation, but to reserve the unjust unto the day of judgment to be tormented.

And especially them who walk after the flesh in the lust of uncleanness. . . .

But these men, as irrational beasts, naturally tending to the snare and to destruction, blaspheming those things which they know not, shall perish in their corruption,

Receiving the reward of their injustice, counting for a pleasure the delights of a day: stains and spots, sporting themselves to excess, rioting in their feasts with you:

Having eyes full of adultery and of sin that ceaseth not: alluring unstable souls, having their heart exercised with covetousness, children of malediction. . . .

These are fountains without water, and clouds tossed with whirlwinds, to whom the mist of darkness is reserved. —2 *Peter* ii. 9, 10, 12-14, 17.

As Sodom and Gomorrha, and the neighboring cities, in like manner, having given themselves to fornication, and going after other flesh, were made an example, suffering the punishment of eternal fire.—*Jude* i. 7.

Blessed are they that wash their robes in the blood of the Lamb: that they may have a right to the tree of life, and may enter in by the gates into the city.

Without are dogs, and sorcerers, and unchaste, and murderers, and servers of idols, and every one that loveth and maketh a lie.—*Apoc.* xxii. 14, 15.

UNCHASTITY, EXHORTATION AGAINST

Remove anger from thy heart, and put away evil from thy flesh. For youth and pleasure are vain.—*Eccles.* xi. 10.

Go not after thy lusts, but turn away from thy own will.

If thou give to thy soul her desires, she will make thee a joy to thy enemies. —*Ecclus.* xviii. 30, 31.

Let us walk honestly, as in the day: not in rioting and drunkenness, not in chambering and impurities, not in contention and envy:

But put ye on the Lord Jesus Christ, and make not provision for the flesh in its concupiscences.—*Rom.* xiii. 13, 14.

Know you not that your bodies are the members of Christ? Shall I then take the members of Christ, and make them the members of a harlot? God forbid.

Or know you not, that he who is joined to a harlot, is made one body? For they shall be, saith he, two in one flesh. . . .

Fly fornication. Every sin that a man doth, is without the body; but he that committeth fornication, sinneth against his own body.—1 *Cor.* vi. 15, 16, 18.

Neither let us commit fornication, as some of them committed fornication, and there fell in one day three and twenty thousand.—1 *Cor.* x. 8.

I say then, walk in the spirit, and you shall not fulfil the lusts of the flesh.

For the flesh lusteth against the spirit: and the spirit against the flesh; for these are contrary one to another: so that you do not the things that you would.—*Gal.* v. 16, 17.

But fornication, and all uncleanness, or covetousness, let it not so much as be named among you, as becometh saints:

Or obscenity, or foolish talking, or scurrility, which is to no purpose; but rather giving of thanks.—*Eph.* v. 3, 4.

Mortify therefore your members which are upon the earth; fornication, uncleanness, lust, evil concupiscence, and covetousness, which is the service of idols.

For which things the wrath of God cometh upon the children of unbelief. —*Col.* iii. 5, 6.

For this is the will of God, your sanctification; that you should abstain from fornication;

That every one of you should know how to possess his vessel in sanctification and honor:

Not in the passion of lust, like the Gentiles that know not God.—1 *Thess.* iv. 3-5.

UNDERSTANDING OF SPIRITUAL THINGS

I will bless the Lord, who hath given me understanding: moreover my reins also have corrected me even till night. —*Ps.* xv. 7.

Thy hands have made me and formed me: give me understanding, and I will learn thy commandments.—*Ps.* cxviii. 73.

By thy commandments I have had understanding: therefore have I hated every way of iniquity.—*Ps.* cxviii. 104.

Thy testimonies are justice for ever: give me understanding, and I shall live.—*Ps.* cxviii. 144.

Where there is no knowledge of the soul, there is no good: and he that is hasty with his feet shall stumble.— *Prov.* xix. 2.

They that trust in him, shall understand the truth: and they that are faithful in love shall rest in him: for grace and peace is to his elect.—*Wis.* iii. 9.

In the treasures of wisdom is understanding, and religiousness of knowledge: but to sinners wisdom is an abomination.—*Ecclus.* i. 26.

For if it shall please the great Lord, he will fill him with the spirit of understanding.—*Ecclus.* xxxix. 8.

For I desired mercy, and not sacrifice: and the knowledge of God more than holocausts.—*Osee* vi. 6.

Now we have received not the spirit of this world, but the Spirit that is of God; that we may know the things that are given us from God. . . .

But the sensual man perceiveth not these things that are of the Spirit of God; for it is foolishness to him, and he cannot understand, because it is spiritually examined.

But the spiritual man judgeth all things; and he himself is judged of no man.—*1 Cor.* ii. 12, 14, 15.

And this I pray, that your charity may more and more abound in knowledge, and in all understanding:

That you may approve the better things, that you may be sincere and without offence unto the day of Christ,

Filled with the fruit of justice, through Jesus Christ, unto the glory and praise of God.—*Philipp.* i. 9-11.

Therefore we also, from the day that we heard it, cease not to pray for you, and to beg that you may be filled with the knowledge of his will, in all wisdom, and spiritual understanding:

That you may walk worthy of God, in all things pleasing; being fruitful in every good work, and increasing in the knowledge of God.—*Col.* i. 9, 10.

And we know that the Son of God is come: and he hath given us understanding that we may know the true God, and may be in his true Son. This is the true God and life eternal.—*1 John* v. 20.

UNDERSTANDING, GOD IS ABOVE OUR

See also: Greatness of God, the—page 185.

Peradventure thou wilt comprehend the steps of God, and wilt find out the Almighty perfectly?

He is higher than heaven, and what wilt thou do? he is deeper than hell, and how wilt thou know?

The measure of him is longer than the earth, and broader than the sea.—*Job* xi. 7-9.

All men see him, every one beholdeth afar off.

Behold, God is great, exceeding our knowledge: the number of his years is inestimable.—*Job* xxxvi. 25, 26.

What shall we be able to do to glorify him? for the Almighty himself is above all his works.—*Ecclus.* xliii. 30.

To whom then have you likened God? or what image will you make for him? —*Is.* xl. 18.

UNION WITH GOD OUR HAPPI- NESS AND OUR SALVATION

See also: Dwelling in us, God— page 119.

And after six days Jesus taketh unto him Peter and James, and John his brother, and bringeth them up into a high mountain apart:

And he was transfigured before them. And his face did shine as the sun: and his garments became white as snow.

And behold there appeared to them Moses and Elias talking with him.

And Peter answering, said to Jesus: Lord, it is good for us to be here: if thou wilt, let us make here three tabernacles, one for thee, and one for Moses, and one for Elias.—*Matt.* xvii. 1-4.

I am the true vine; and my Father is the husbandman.

Every branch in me, that beareth not fruit, he will take away: and every one that beareth fruit, he will purge it, that it may bring forth more fruit. . . .

Abide in me, and I in you. As the branch cannot bear fruit of itself, unless it abide in the vine, so neither can you, unless you abide in me.

I am the vine; you the branches: he that abideth in me, and I in him, the same beareth much fruit: for without me you can do nothing.

If any one abide not in me, he shall be cast forth as a branch, and shall wither, and they shall gather him up, and cast him into the fire, and he burneth.

If you abide in me, and my words abide in you, you shall ask whatever you will, and it shall be done unto you. —*John* xv. 1, 2, 4-7.

But he who is joined to the Lord, is one spirit.—*1 Cor.* vi. 17.

UNSELFISHNESS

See: Forgetfulness of self—page 155.

UNWORTHINESS OF GOD AND HIS FAVORS, MAN'S

And king David came and sat before the Lord, and said: Who am I, O Lord God, and what is my house, that thou shouldst give such things to me?—1 *Paral.* xvii. 16.

What is a man that thou shouldst magnify him? or why dost thou set thy heart upon him?—*Job* vii. 17.

What am I then, that I should answer him, and have words with him?

I, who although I should have any just thing, would not answer, but would make supplication to my judge.

And if he should hear me when I call, I should not believe that he had heard my voice.—*Job* ix. 14-16.

What is man that thou art mindful of him? or the son of man that thou visitest him?—*Ps.* viii. 5.

Lord, what is man, that thou art made known to him? or the son of man, that thou makest account of him?—*Ps.* cxliii. 3.

UNWORTHINESS OF GOD AND HIS FAVORS, ACKNOWLEDGMENT OF OUR

I am not worthy of the least of all thy mercies, and of thy truth which thou hast fulfilled to thy servant.—*Gen.* xxxii. 10.

O God of the heavens, creator of the waters, and Lord of the whole creation, hear me a poor wretch, making supplication to thee, and presuming of thy mercy.—*Judith* ix. 17.

I indeed baptize you in water unto penance, but he that shall come after me, is mightier than I, whose shoes I am not worthy to bear; he shall baptize you in the Holy Ghost and fire.—*Matt.* iii. 11.

And Jesus saith to him: I will come and heal him.

And the centurion making answer, said: Lord, I am not worthy that thou shouldst enter under my roof: but only say the word, and my servant shall be healed.—*Matt.* viii. 7, 8.

And he (the Baptist) preached, saying: There cometh after me one mightier than I, the latchet of whose shoes I am not worthy to stoop down and loose.—*Mark* i. 7.

Which when Simon Peter saw, he fell down at Jesus' knees, saying: Depart from me, for I am a sinful man, O Lord.—*Luke* v. 8.

I will arise, and will go to my father, and say to him: Father, I have sinned against heaven, and before thee:

I am not worthy to be called thy son: make me as one of thy hired servants.—*Luke* xv. 18, 19.

USURY

If thou lend money to any of my people that is poor, that dwelleth with thee, thou shalt not be hard upon them as an extortioner, nor oppress them with usuries.—*Ex.* xxii. 25.

If thy brother be impoverished, and weak of hand, and thou receive him as a stranger and sojourner, and he live with thee,

Take not usury of him nor more than thou gavest: fear thy God, that thy brother may live with thee.

Thou shalt not give him thy money upon usury, nor exact of him any increase of fruits.—*Lev.* xxv. 35-37.

Lord, who shall dwell in thy tabernacle? or who shall rest in thy holy hill? . . .

He that hath not put out his money to usury, nor taken bribes against the innocent.—*Ps.* xiv. 1, 5.

He that heapeth together riches by usury and loan, gathereth them for him that will be bountiful to the poor.—*Prov.* xxviii. 8.

Know you not that the unjust shall not possess the kingdom of God? Do not err: neither fornicators, nor idolators, nor adulterers,

. . . Nor thieves, nor covetous, . . . nor extortioners, shall possess the kingdom of God.—1 *Cor.* vi. 9, 10.

VAIN IS THE RELIANCE UPON HUMAN STRENGTH

See: Strength, reliance upon human —page 546.

VAINGLORY

Glory not in apparel at any time, and be not exalted in the day of thy honor: for the works of the Highest only are wonderful, and his works are glorious, and secret, and hidden.—*Ecclus.* xi. 4.

Thus saith the Lord: Let not the wise man glory in his wisdom, and let not the strong man glory in his strength, and let not the rich man glory in his riches:

But let him that glorieth glory in this, that he understandeth and knoweth me, for I am the Lord that exercise mercy, and judgment, and justice in the earth: for these things please me, saith the Lord.—*Jer.* ix. 23, 24.

For the wisdom of this world is foolishness with God. For it is written: I will catch the wise in their own craftiness.

And again: The Lord knoweth the thoughts of the wise, that they are vain.

Let no man therefore glory in men.—1 *Cor.* iii. 19-21.

For who distinguisheth thee? Or what hast thou that thou hast not received? And if thou hast received, why dost thou glory, as if thou hadst not received it?—1 *Cor.* iv. 7.

But he that glorieth, let him glory in the Lord.

For not he who commendeth himself, is approved, but he, whom God commendeth.—2 *Cor.* x. 17, 18.

Let us not be made desirous of vainglory, provoking one another, envying one another.—*Gal.* v. 26.

For if any man think himself to be something, whereas he is nothing, he deceiveth himself.—*Gal.* vi. 3.

But God forbid that I should glory, save in the cross of our Lord Jesus Christ; by whom the world is crucified to me, and I to the world.—*Gal.* vi. 14.

Let nothing be done through contention, neither by vainglory: but in humility, let each esteem others better than themselves.—*Philipp.* ii. 3.

VANITY

And the Lord said to Samuel: Look not on his countenance, nor on the height of his stature: because I have rejected him, nor do I judge according to the look of man: for man seeth those things that appear, but the Lord beholdeth the heart.—1 *Kings* xvi. 7.

O ye sons of men, how long will you be dull of heart? why do you love vanity, and seek after lying?—*Ps.* iv. 3.

Behold thou hast made my days measurable: and my substance is as nothing before thee. And indeed all things are vanity: every man living.—*Ps.* xxxviii. 6.

Favor is deceitful, and beauty is vain: the woman that feareth the Lord, she shall be praised.—*Prov.* xxxi. 30.

Vanity of vanities, said Ecclesiastes: vanity of vanities, and all is vanity.—*Eccles.* i. 2.

Praise not a man for his beauty, neither despise a man for his look. . . .

Glory not in apparel at any time, and be not exalted in the day of thy honor: for the works of the Highest only are wonderful, and his works are glorious, and secret, and hidden.—*Ecclus.* xi. 2, 4.

A sinner is caught in his own vanity, and the proud and the evil speakers shall fall thereby.—*Ecclus.* xxiii. 8.

Look not upon a woman's beauty, and desire not a woman for beauty.—*Ecclus.* xxv. 28.

They that are vain observe vanities, forsake their own mercy.—*Jonas* ii. 9.

VANITY OF THE THINGS OF THIS LIFE

See: Life, emptiness of this—page 279.

VENIAL SIN

See: Part II—page 735.

VERACITY OF GOD, THE

See: Truth of God—page 568.

VICTORY OVER SIN AND DEATH

See also: Devil and his temptations, gaining the mastery over the—page 112.

And when this mortal hath put on immortality, then shall come to pass the saying that is written: Death is swallowed up in victory.

O death, where is thy victory? O death, where is thy sting?

Now the sting of death is sin: and the power of sin is the law.

But thanks be to God, who hath given us the victory through our Lord Jesus Christ.—1 *Cor.* xv. 54-57.

VIRGIN MARY, EXCELLENCE OF THE BLESSED

I will put enmities between thee and the woman, and thy seed and her seed: she shall crush thy head, and thou shalt lie in wait for her heel.—*Gen.* iii. 15.

And Ozias the prince of the people of Israel, said to her (Judith): Blessed art thou, O daughter, by the Lord the most high God, above all women upon the earth. . . .

Because he hath so magnified thy name this day, that thy praise shall not depart out of the mouth of men who shall be mindful of the power of the Lord for ever, for that thou hast not spared thy life, by reason of the distress and tribulation of thy people, but hast prevented our ruin in the presence of our God. . . .

Blessed art thou by thy God in every tabernacle of Jacob, for in every nation which shall hear thy name, the God of Israel shall be magnified on occasion of thee.—*Judith* xiii. 23, 25, 31.

And when she was come out to him (the high priest), they all blessed her with one voice, saying: Thou art the glory of Jerusalem, thou art the joy of Israel, thou art the honor of our people.—*Judith* xv. 10.

Hearken, O daughter, and see, and incline thy ear: and forget thy people and thy father's house.

And the king shall greatly desire thy beauty; for he is the Lord thy God, and him they shall adore.—*Ps.* xliv. 11, 12.

All the glory of the king's daughter is within in golden borders, clothed round about with varieties.

After her shall virgins be brought to the king: her neighbors shall be brought to thee.

They shall be brought with gladness and rejoicing: they shall be brought into the temple of the king.—*Ps.* xliv. 14-16.

Many daughters have gathered together riches: thou hast surpassed them all.—*Prov.* xxxi. 29.

I am the flower of the field, and the lily of the valleys.

As the lily among thorns, so is my love among the daughters.—*Cant.* ii. 1, 2.

I am the mother of fair love, and of fear, and of knowledge, and of holy hope.—*Ecclus.* xxiv. 24.

And the angel being come in, said unto her: Hail, full of grace, the Lord is with thee: blessed art thou among women.

Who having heard, was troubled at his saying, and thought with herself what manner of salutation this should be.

And the angel said to her: Fear not, Mary, for thou hast found grace with God.

Behold thou shalt conceive in thy womb, and shalt bring forth a son; and thou shalt call his name Jesus.—*Luke* i. 28-31.

And it came to pass, that when Elizabeth heard the salutation of Mary, the infant leaped in her womb. And Elizabeth was filled with the Holy Ghost:

And she cried out with a loud voice, and said: Blessed art thou among women, and blessed is the fruit of thy womb.

And whence is this to me, that the mother of my Lord should come to me?

For behold as soon as the voice of thy salutation sounded in my ears, the infant in my womb leaped for joy.

And blessed art thou that hast believed, because those things shall be accomplished that were spoken to thee by the Lord.—*Luke* i. 41-45.

And Mary said: My soul doth magnify the Lord.

And my spirit hath rejoiced in God my Saviour.

Because he hath regarded the humility of his handmaid; for behold from henceforth all generations shall call me blessed.

Because he that is mighty, hath done great things to me; and holy is his name.—*Luke* i. 46-49.

And it came to pass, as he spoke these things, a certain woman from the crowd, lifting up her voice, said to him: Blessed is the womb that bore thee, and the paps that gave thee suck.—*Luke* xi. 27.

And the third day, there was a marriage in Cana of Galilee: and the mother of Jesus was there.

And Jesus also was invited, and his disciples, to the marriage.

And the wine failing, the mother of Jesus saith to him: They have no wine.

And Jesus saith to her: Woman, what is that to me and to thee? my hour is not yet come.

His mother saith to the waiters: Whatsoever he shall say to you, do ye. —*John* ii. 1-5.

But when the fulness of the time was come, God sent his Son, made of a woman, made under the law:

That he might redeem them who were under the law: that we might receive the adoption of sons.—*Gal.* iv. 4, 5.

And a great sign appeared in heaven: A woman clothed with the sun, and the moon under her feet, and on her head a crown of twelve stars.—*Apoc.* xii. 1.

VIRGIN MARY, VIRGINITY OF THE BLESSED

Therefore the Lord himself shall give you a sign. Behold a virgin shall conceive, and bear a son, and his name shall be called Emmanuel.—*Is.* vii. 14.

How long wilt thou be dissolute in deliciousness, O wandering daughter? for the Lord hath created a new thing upon the earth: A woman shall compass a man.—*Jer.* xxxi. 22.

Now the generation of Christ was in this wise. When as his mother Mary was espoused to Joseph, before they came together, she was found with child, of the Holy Ghost.

Whereupon Joseph her husband, being a just man, and not willing publicly to expose her, was minded to put her away privately.

But while he thought on these things, behold the angel of the Lord appeared to him in his sleep, saying: Joseph, son of David, fear not to take unto thee Mary thy wife, for that which is conceived in her, is of the Holy Ghost.

And she shall bring forth a son: and thou shalt call his name Jesus. For he shall save his people from their sins.

Now all this was done that it might be fulfilled which the Lord spoke by the prophet, saying:

Behold a virgin shall be with child, and bring forth a son, and they shall call his name Emmanuel, which being interpreted is, God with us.

And Joseph rising up from sleep, did as the angel of the Lord had commanded him, and took unto him his wife.

And he knew her not till she brought forth her first-born son: and he called his name Jesus.—*Matt.* i. 18-25.

And the angel said to her: Fear not, Mary, for thou hast found grace with God.

Behold thou shalt conceive in thy womb, and shalt bring forth a son; and thou shalt call his name Jesus. . . .

And Mary said to the angel: How shall this be done, because I know not man?

And the angel answering, said to her: The Holy Ghost shall come upon thee, and the power of the most High shall overshadow thee. And therefore also the Holy which shall be born of thee shall be called the Son of God.— *Luke* i. 30, 31, 34, 35.

VIRGIN MARY, THE IMMACULATE CONCEPTION OF THE BLESSED

What is the matter, Esther? I am thy brother, fear not.

Thou shalt not die: for this law is not made for thee, but for all others. —*Esther* xv. 12, 13.

As the lily among thorns, so is my love among the daughters.—*Cant.* ii. 2.

Thou art all fair, O my love, and there is not a spot in thee.—*Cant.* iv. 7.

My sister, my spouse, is a garden enclosed, a garden enclosed, a fountain sealed up.—*Cant.* iv. 12.

Thou art beautiful, O my love, sweet and comely as Jerusalem: terrible as an army set in array.—*Cant.* vi. 3.

One is my dove, my perfect one is but one, she is the only one of her mother, the chosen of her that bore her. The daughters saw her, and declared her most blessed: the queens and concubines, and they praised her.—*Cant.* vi. 8.

Who is she that cometh forth as the

morning rising, fair as the moon, bright as the sun, terrible as an army set in array?—*Cant.* vi. 9.

And the angel being come in, said unto her: Hail, full of grace, the Lord is with thee: blessed art thou among women.

Who having heard, was troubled at his saying, and thought with herself what manner of salutation this should be.

And the angel said to her: Fear not, Mary, for thou hast found grace with God.—*Luke* i. 28-30.

VIRGIN MARY, SORROWS OF THE BLESSED

For the zeal of thy house hath eaten me up; and the reproaches of them that reproached thee are fallen upon me.—*Ps.* lxviii. 10.

Therefore have I said: Depart from me, I will weep bitterly: labor not to comfort me, for the devastation of the daughter of my people.—*Is.* xxii. 4.

My sorrow is above sorrow, my heart mourneth within me.—*Jer.* viii. 18.

Thus saith the Lord: A voice was heard on high of lamentation, of mourning, and weeping, of Rachel weeping for her children, and refusing to be comforted for them, because they are not.—*Jer.* xxxi. 15.

Weeping she hath wept in the night, and her tears are on her cheeks: there is none to comfort her among all them that were dear to her: all her friends have despised her, and are become her enemies.—*Lam.* i. 2.

O all ye that pass by the way, attend, and see if there be any sorrow like to my sorrow: for he hath made a vintage of me, as the Lord spoke in the day of his fierce anger.—*Lam.* i. 12.

And Simeon blessed them, and said to Mary his mother: Behold this child is set for the fall, and for the resurrection of many in Israel, and for a sign which shall be contradicted;

And thy own soul a sword shall pierce, that, out of many hearts, thoughts may be revealed.—*Luke* ii. 34, 35.

And having fulfilled the days, when they returned, the child Jesus remained

in Jerusalem; and his parents knew it not.

And thinking that he was in the company, they came a day's journey, and sought him among their kinsfolks and acquaintance.

And not finding him, they returned into Jerusalem, seeking him.

And it came to pass that, after three days, they found him in the temple, sitting in the midst of the doctors, hearing them, and asking them questions.

And all that heard him were astonished at his wisdom and his answers.

And seeing him, they wondered. And his mother said to him: Son, why hast thou done so to us? behold thy father and I have sought thee sorrowing.

And he said to them: How is it that you sought me? did you not know, that I must be about my father's business?—*Luke* ii. 43-49.

Now there stood by the cross of Jesus, his mother, and his mother's sister, Mary of Cleophas, and Mary Magdalen.—*John* xix. 25.

VIRGIN MARY, OUR MOTHER

Now there stood by the cross of Jesus, his mother, and his mother's sister, Mary of Cleophas, and Mary Magdalen.

When Jesus therefore had seen his mother and the disciple standing whom he loved, he saith to his mother: Woman, behold thy son.

After that, he saith to the disciple: Behold thy mother. And from that hour, the disciple took her to his own.—*John* xix. 25-27.

VIRGINITY

See: Part II—page 738.

VOCATION TO THE PRIESTHOOD

See: Priest is chosen by God—page 431.

VOICE OF GOD, LISTENING TO THE

See: Listening—page 289.

VOWS MADE BY SERVANTS OF GOD

And he (Jacob) made a vow, saying: If God shall be with me, and shall keep me in the way by which I walk, and shall give me bread to eat, and raiment to put on,

And I shall return prosperously to my father's house: the Lord shall be my God:

And this stone, which I have set up for a title, shall be called the house of God: and of all things that thou shalt give to me, I will offer tithes to thee.—*Gen.* xxviii. 20-22.

As Anna had her heart full of grief, she prayed to the Lord, shedding many tears,

And she made a vow, saying: O Lord of hosts, if thou wilt look down on the affliction of thy servant, and wilt be mindful of me, and not forget thy handmaid, and will give to thy servant a man child: I will give him to the Lord all the days of his life, and no razor shall come upon his head.—1 *Kings* i. 10, 11.

So will I sing a psalm to thy name for ever and ever: that I may pay my vows from day to day.—*Ps.* lx. 9.

I will pay my vows to the Lord before all his people.—*Ps.* cxv. 14.

But Paul, when he had stayed yet many days, taking his leave of the brethren, sailed thence into Syria (and with him Priscilla and Aquila), having shorn his head in Cenchra: for he had a vow.—*Acts* xviii. 18.

VOWS ARE PLEASING TO GOD

These things shall you offer to the Lord in your solemnities: besides your vows and voluntary oblations for holocaust, for sacrifice, for libation, and for victims of peace offerings.—*Num.* xxix. 39.

Offer to God the sacrifice of praise: and pay thy vows to the most High.

And call upon me in the day of trouble: I will deliver thee, and thou shalt glorify me.—*Ps.* xlix. 14, 15.

In me, O God, are vows to thee, which I will pay, praises to thee:

Because thou hast delivered my soul from death, my feet from falling: that I may please in the sight of God, in the light of the living.—*Ps.* lv. 12, 13.

A hymn, O God, becometh thee in Sion: and a vow shall be paid to thee in Jerusalem.—*Ps.* lxiv. 2.

Vow ye, and pay to the Lord your God: all you that are round about him bring presents. To him that is terrible. —*Ps.* lxxv. 12.

O Lord, remember David, and all his meekness.

How he swore to the Lord, he vowed a vow to the God of Jacob:

If I shall enter into the tabernacle of my house: if I shall go up into the bed wherein I lie:

If I shall give sleep to my eyes, or slumber to my eyelids,

Or rest to my temples: until I find out a place for the Lord, a tabernacle for the God of Jacob.—*Ps.* cxxxi. 1-5.

The victims of the wicked are abominable to the Lord: the vows of the just are acceptable.—*Prov.* xv. 8.

And the Lord shall be known by Egypt, and the Egyptians shall know the Lord in that day, and shall worship him with sacrifices and offerings: and they shall make vows to the Lord, and perform them.—*Is.* xix. 21.

VOWS ONCE MADE ARE TO BE FULFILLED

And the Lord spoke to Moses, saying:

Speak to the children of Israel, and thou shalt say to them: The man that shall have made a vow, and promised his soul to God, shall give the price according to estimation. . . .

But a beast that may be sacrificed to the Lord, if any one shall vow, shall be holy,

And cannot be changed, that is to say, neither a better for a worse, nor a worse for a better. And if he shall change it: both that which was changed, and that for which it was changed, shall be consecrated to the Lord.—*Lev.* xxvii. 1, 2, 9, 10.

And the Lord spoke to Moses, saying:

Speak to the children of Israel, and thou shalt say to them: When a man, or woman, shall make a vow to be sanctified, and will consecrate themselves to the Lord:

They shall abstain from wine, and from every thing that may make a man drunk. They shall not drink vinegar of wine, or of any other drink, nor any thing that is pressed out of the grape: nor shall they eat grapes either fresh or dried.

All the days that they are consecrated to the Lord by vow: they shall eat nothing that cometh of the vineyard, from the raisin even to the kernel.—*Num.* vi. 1-4.

And Moses told the children of Israel all that the Lord had commanded him:

And he said to the princes of the tribes of the children of Israel: This is the word that the Lord hath commanded:

If any man make a vow to the Lord, or bind himself by an oath: he shall not make his word void, but shall fulfil all that he promised.—*Num.* xxx. 1-3.

When thou hast made a vow to the Lord thy God, thou shalt not delay to pay it: because the Lord thy God will require it. And if thou delay, it shall be imputed to thee for a sin.

If thou wilt not promise, thou shalt be without sin.

But that which is once gone out of thy lips, thou shalt observe, and shalt do as thou hast promised to the Lord thy God, and hast spoken with thy own will and with thy own mouth.—*Deut.* xxiii. 21-23.

With thee is my praise in a great church: I will pay my vows in the sight of them that fear him.—*Ps.* xxi. 26.

Offer to God the sacrifice of praise: and pay thy vows to the most High.—*Ps.* xlix. 14.

I will go into thy house with burnt offerings: I will pay thee my vows, which my lips have uttered,

And my mouth hath spoken, when I was in trouble.—*Ps.* lxv. 13, 14.

It is ruin to a man to devour holy ones, and after vows to retract.—*Prov.* xx. 25.

If thou hast vowed any thing to God, defer not to pay it: for an unfaithful and foolish promise displeaseth him: but whatsoever thou hast vowed, pay it.

And it is much better not to vow, than after a vow not to perform the things promised.—*Eccles.* v. 3, 4.

But I with the voice of praise will sacrifice to thee: I will pay whatsoever I have vowed for my salvation to the Lord.—*Jonas* ii. 10.

But the younger widows avoid. For when they have grown wanton in Christ, they will marry:

Having damnation, because they have made void their first faith.—1 *Tim.* v. 11, 12.

WAITING FOR GOD AND HIS MERCY

Direct me in thy truth, and teach me; for thou art God my Saviour; and on thee have I waited all the day long. . . .

The innocent and the upright have adhered to me: because I have waited on thee.—*Ps.* xxiv. 5, 21.

Our soul waiteth for the Lord: for he is our helper and protector.—*Ps.* xxxii. 20.

I waited for him that hath saved me from pusillanimity of spirit, and a storm.—*Ps.* liv. 9.

O God my God, to thee do I watch at break of day.

For thee my soul hath thirsted; for thee my flesh, O how many ways!—*Ps.* lxii. 2.

I looked for thy salvation, O Lord: and I loved thy commandments.—*Ps.* cxviii. 166.

To thee have I lifted up my eyes, who dwellest in heaven.

Behold as the eyes of servants are on the hands of their masters,

As the eyes of the handmaid are on the hands of her mistress: so are our eyes unto the Lord our God, until he have mercy on us.—*Ps.* cxxii. 1, 2.

And I will wait for the Lord, who hath hid his face from the house of Jacob, and I will look for him.—*Is.* viii. 17.

And in the way of thy judgments, O Lord, we have patiently waited for thee: thy name, and thy remembrance are the desire of the soul.—*Is.* xxvi. 8.

Therefore the Lord waiteth that he may have mercy on you: and therefore shall he be exalted sparing you: because the Lord is the God of judgment: blessed are all they that wait for him. —*Is.* xxx. 18.

O Lord, have mercy on us: for we have waited for thee: be thou our arm in the morning, and our salvation in the time of trouble.—*Is.* xxxiii. 2.

The Lord is my portion, said my soul: therefore will I wait for him. . . .

It is good to wait with silence for the salvation of God.—*Lam.* iii. 24, 26.

But I will look towards the Lord, I will wait for God my Saviour: my God will hear me.—*Mich.* vii. 7.

For the grace of God our Saviour hath appeared to all men;

Instructing us, that, denying ungodliness and worldly desires, we should live soberly, and justly, and godly in this world,

Looking for the blessed hope and coming of the glory of the great God and our Saviour Jesus Christ.—*Titus* ii. 11-13.

WAITING FOR GOD AND HIS MERCY, THE REWARD OF

Neither let my enemies laugh at me: for none of them that wait on thee shall be confounded.—*Ps.* xxiv. 3.

Expect the Lord and keep his way: and he will exalt thee to inherit the land: when the sinners shall perish thou shalt see.—*Ps.* xxxvi. 34.

With expectation I have waited for the Lord, and he was attentive to me.

And he heard my prayers, and brought me out of the pit of misery and the mire of dregs.

And he set my feet upon a rock, and directed my steps.—*Ps.* xxxix. 2, 3.

Reward them that patiently wait for thee, that thy prophets may be found faithful: and hear the prayers of thy servants.—*Ecclus.* xxxvi. 18.

I remembered thy mercy, O Lord, and thy works, which are from the beginning of the world.

How thou deliverest them that wait for thee, O Lord, and savest them out of the hands of the nations.—*Ecclus.* li. 11. 12.

And they shall say in that day: Lo, this is our God, we have waited for him, and he will save us: this is the Lord, we have patiently waited for him, we shall rejoice and be joyful in his salvation.—*Is.* xxv. 9.

And thou shalt know that I am the Lord, for they shall not be confounded that wait for him.—*Is.* xlix. 23.

From the beginning of the world they have not heard, nor perceived with the ears: the eye hath not seen, O God, besides thee, what things thou hast prepared for them that wait for thee.—*Is.* lxiv. 4.

WAIT FOR GOD AND HIS MERCY, EXHORTATION TO

Let us humbly wait for his consolation, and the Lord our God will require our blood of the afflictions of our enemies, and he will humble all the nations that shall rise up against us, and bring them to disgrace.—*Judith* viii. 20.

Expect the Lord, do manfully, and let thy heart take courage, and wait thou for the Lord.—*Ps.* xxvi. 14.

Wait on God with patience: join thyself to God, and endure, that thy life may be increased in the latter end.—*Ecclus.* ii. 3.

Ye that fear the Lord, wait for his mercy: and go not aside from him, lest ye fall.—*Ecclus.* ii. 7.

Humble thyself to God, and wait for his hands.—*Ecclus.* xiii. 9.

Be patient therefore, brethren, until the coming of the Lord. Behold, the husbandman waiteth for the precious fruit of the earth: patiently bearing till he receive the early and latter rain.

Be you therefore also patient, and strengthen your hearts: for the coming of the Lord is at hand.—*James* v. 7, 8.

But you, my beloved, building yourselves upon your most holy faith, praying in the Holy Ghost,

Keep yourselves in the love of God, waiting for the mercy of our Lord Jesus Christ, unto life everlasting.—*Jude* i. 20, 21.

WANDERING AWAY FROM GOD

See also: Turning away from God—page 569.

Lo, I have gone far off flying away; and I abode in the wilderness.—*Ps.* liv. 8.

For behold they that go far from thee shall perish: thou hast destroyed all them that are disloyal to thee.—*Ps.* lxxii. 27.

I have gone astray like a sheep that

is lost: seek thy servant, because I have not forgotten thy commandments.—*Ps.* cxviii. 176.

Ye that fear the Lord, wait for his mercy: and go not aside from him, lest ye fall.—*Ecclus.* ii. 7.

But if he go astray, she (wisdom) will forsake him, and deliver him into the hands of his enemy.—*Ecclus.* iv. 22.

All we like sheep have gone astray, every one hath turned aside into his own way: and the Lord hath laid on him the iniquity of us all.—*Is.* liii. 6.

Thus saith the Lord: What iniquity have your fathers found in me, that they are gone far from me, and have walked after vanity, and are become vain?—*Jer.* ii. 5.

My people have been a lost flock, their shepherds have caused them to go astray, and have made them wander in the mountains: they have gone from mountain to hill, they have forgotten their resting place.—*Jer.* l. 6.

WARFARE, THIS LIFE IS A

See: Life, a warfare—page 199.

WATCHFULNESS

I said: I will take heed to my ways: that I sin not with my tongue.

I have set a guard to my mouth, when the sinner stood against me.—*Ps.* xxxviii. 2.

If the spirit of him that hath power, ascend upon thee, leave not thy place: because care will make the greatest sins to cease.—*Eccles. x.* 4.

I sleep, and my heart watcheth: the voice of my beloved knocking: Open to me, my sister, my love, my dove, my undefiled: for my head is full of dew, and my locks of the drops of the nights.—*Cant. v.* 2.

A wise man will fear in every thing, and in the days of sins will beware of sloth.—*Ecclus.* xviii. 27.

My soul hath desired thee in the night: yea, and with my spirit within me in the morning early I will watch to thee.—*Is.* xxvi. 9.

Have in mind therefore in what manner thou hast received and heard: and observe, and do penance. If then thou shalt not watch, I will come to thee as

a thief, and thou shalt not know at what hour I will come to thee.—*Apoc.* iii. 3.

Behold, I come as a thief. Blessed is he that watcheth, and keepeth his garments, lest he walk naked, and they see his shame.—*Apoc.* xvi. 15.

WATCHFULNESS, EXHORTATATION TO

Keep thyself therefore, and thy soul carefully. Forget not the words that thy eyes have seen, and let them not go out of thy heart all the days of thy life.—*Deut.* iv. 9.

With all watchfulness keep thy heart, because life issueth out from it.—*Prov.* iv. 23.

My son, prove thy soul in thy life: and if it be wicked, give it no power.—*Ecclus.* xxxvii. 30.

Watch ye therefore, because you know not what hour your Lord will come.—*Matt.* xxiv. 42.

And he cometh to his disciples, and findeth them asleep, and he saith to Peter: What? Could you not watch one hour with me?

Watch ye, and pray that ye enter not into temptation. The spirit indeed is willing, but the flesh weak.—*Matt.* xxvi. 40, 41.

Take ye heed, watch and pray. For ye know not when the time is.

Even as a man who going into a far country, left his house; and gave authority to his servants over every work, and commanded the porter to watch.

Watch ye therefore, (for you know not when the lord of the house cometh: at even, or at midnight, or at the cock crowing, or in the morning,)

Lest coming on a sudden, he find you sleeping,

And what I say to you, I say to all: Watch.—*Mark* xiii. 33-37.

Let your loins be girt, and lamps burning in your hands.

And you yourselves like to men who wait for their lord, when he shall return from the wedding; that when he cometh and knocketh, they may open to him immediately.

Blessed are those servants, whom the Lord when he cometh, shall find watching. Amen I say to you, that he will gird himself, and make them sit down to meat, and passing will minister unto them.

And if he shall come in the second watch, or come in the third watch, and find them so, blessed are those servants.

But this know ye, that if the householder did know at what hour the thief would come, he would surely watch, and would not suffer his house to be broken open.

Be you then also ready: for at what hour you think not, the Son of man will come.—*Luke* xii. 35-40.

And take heed to yourselves, lest perhaps your hearts be overcharged with surfeiting and drunkenness, and the cares of this life, and that day come upon you suddenly. . . .

Watch ye, therefore, praying at all times, that you may be accounted worthy to escape all these things that are to come, and to stand before the Son of man.—*Luke* xxi. 34, 36.

Watch ye, stand fast in the faith, do manfully, and be strengthened.— 1 *Cor.* xvi. 13.

By all prayer and supplication praying at all times in the spirit; and in the same watching with all instance and supplication for all the saints.—*Eph.* vi. 18.

For all you are the children of light, and children of the day: we are not of the night, nor of darkness.

Therefore, let us not sleep, as others do; but let us watch, and be sober.— 1 *Thess.* v. 5, 6.

But be thou vigilant, labor in all things, do the work of an evangelist, fulfil thy ministry. Be sober.—2 *Tim.* iv. 5.

But the end of all is at hand. Be prudent therefore, and watch in prayers.— 1 *Peter* iv. 7.

Be sober and watch: because your adversary the devil, as a roaring lion, goeth about seeking whom he may devour.—1 *Peter* v. 8.

Look to yourselves, that you lose not the things which you have wrought: but that you may receive a full reward. —2 *John* i. 8.

Be watchful and strengthen the things that remain, which are ready to die. For I find not thy works full before my God.—*Apoc.* iii. 2.

WATCHFULNESS OF GOD OVER US, THE

See: Providence of God—page 450.

WATER, HOLY

And he (the priest) shall take holy water in an earthen vessel, and he shall cast a little earth of the pavement of the tabernacle into it.—*Num.* v. 17.

And the Lord spoke to Moses, saying: Take the Levites out of the midst of the children of Israel, and thou shalt purify them,

According to this rite: Let them be sprinkled with the water of purification, and let them shave all the hairs of their flesh.—*Num.* viii. 5-8.

And a man that is clean shall gather up the ashes of the cow, and shall pour them forth without the camp in a most clean place, that they may be reserved for the multitude of the children of Israel, and for a water of aspersion: because the cow was burnt for sin. . . .

He that toucheth the corpse of a man, and is therefore unclean seven days,

Shall be sprinkled with this water on the third day, and on the seventh, and so shall be cleansed. If he were not sprinkled on the third day, he cannot be cleansed on the seventh.

Every one that toucheth the corpse of a man, and is not sprinkled with this mixture, shall profane the tabernacle of the Lord, and shall perish out of Israel: because he was not sprinkled with the water of expiation, he shall be unclean, and his uncleanness shall remain upon him.—*Num.* xix. 9, 11-13.

WATER OF ETERNAL LIFE, THE

And Moses and Aaron leaving the multitude, went into the tabernacle of the covenant, and fell flat upon the ground, and cried to the Lord, and said: O Lord God, hear the cry of this people, and open to them thy treasure, a fountain of living water, that being satisfied, they may cease to murmur. —*Num.* xx. 6.

You shall draw waters with joy out of the saviour's fountains.—*Is.* xii. 3.

For my people have done two evils. They have forsaken me, the fountain of living water, and have digged to themselves cisterns, broken cisterns, that can hold no water.—*Jer.* ii. 13.

O Lord, the hope of Israel: all that forsake thee shall be confounded: they that depart from thee, shall be written in the earth: because they have forsaken the Lord, the vein of living waters.—*Jer.* xvii. 13.

And it shall come to pass in that day, that the mountains shall drop down sweetness, and the hills shall flow with milk: and waters shall flow through all the rivers of Juda: and a fountain shall come forth of the house of the Lord, and shall water the torrent of thorns.—*Joel* iii. 18.

Jesus answered, and said to her: If thou didst know the gift of God, and who he is that saith to thee, Give me to drink; thou perhaps wouldst have asked of him, and he would have given thee living water.

. . . Jesus answered, and said to her: Whosoever drinketh of this water, shall thirst again; but he that shall drink of the water, that I will give him, shall not thirst for ever.

But the water that I will give him, shall become in him a fountain of water, springing up into life everlasting.—*John* iv. 10, 13, 14.

And on the last, and great day of the festivity, Jesus stood and cried, saying: If any man thirst, let him come to me, and drink.

He that believeth in me, as the scripture saith, Out of his belly shall flow rivers of living water.—*John* vii. 37, 38.

But one of the soldiers with a spear opened his side, and immediately there came out blood and water.—*John* xix. 34.

They shall no more hunger nor thirst, neither shall the sun fall on them, nor any heat.

For the Lamb, which is in the midst of the throne, shall rule them, and shall lead them to the fountains of the waters of life, and God shall wipe away all tears from their eyes.—*Apoc.* vii. 16, 17.

And he said to me: It is done. I am Alpha and Omega; the beginning and the end. To him that thirsteth, I will give of the fountain of the water of life, freely.—*Apoc.* xxi. 6.

And he (the angel) showed me a river of water of life, clear as crystal, proceeding from the throne of God and of the Lamb. . . .

And the spirit and the bride say: Come. And he that heareth, let him say: Come. And he that thirsteth, let him come: and he that will, let him take the water of life, freely.—*Apoc.* xxii. 1, 17.

WAYS OF GOD ARE JUST, THE

See also: Judgments of God, the— page 260.

Then Tobias sighed, and began to pray with tears,

Saying: Thou art just, O Lord, and all thy judgments are just, and all thy ways mercy, and truth, and judgment.—*Tob.* iii. 1, 2.

As for my God, his way is undefiled: the words of the Lord are fire tried: he is the protector of all that trust in him.—*Ps.* xvii. 31.

All the ways of the Lord are mercy and truth, to them that seek after his covenant and his testimonies.—*Ps.* xxiv. 10.

Thou art near, O Lord: and all thy ways are truth.—*Ps.* cxviii. 151.

The Lord is just in all his ways: and holy in all his works.—*Ps.* cxliv. 17.

And you have said: The way of the Lord is not right. Hear ye, therefore, O house of Israel: Is it my way that is not right, and are not rather your ways perverse?—*Ezech.* xviii. 25.

For thou art just in all that thou hast done to us, and all thy works are true, and thy ways right, and all thy judgments true.—*Dan.* iii. 27.

Who is wise, and he shall understand these things? prudent, and he shall know these things? for the ways of the Lord are right, and the just shall walk in them: but the transgressors shall fall in them.—*Osee* xiv. 10.

And I saw as it were a sea of glass mingled with fire, and them that had overcome the beast, and his image, and the number of his name, standing on the sea of glass, having the harps of God:

And singing the canticle of Moses, the servant of God, and the canticle of the Lamb, saying: Great and wonderful are thy works, O Lord God Almighty; just and true are thy ways, O King of ages.—*Apoc.* xv. 2, 3.

WAYS OF GOD ARE NOT AS OUR WAYS, THE

Thou hast multiplied thy wonderful works, O Lord my God: and in thy thoughts there is no one like to thee.—*Ps.* xxxix. 6.

There is also another vanity, which is done upon the earth. There are just men to whom evils happen, as though they had done the works of the wicked: and there are wicked men, who are as secure, as though they had the deeds of the just: but this also I judge most vain.—*Eccles.* viii. 14.

For my thoughts are not your thoughts: nor your ways my ways, saith the Lord.

For as the heavens are exalted above the earth, so are my ways exalted above your ways, and my thoughts above your thoughts.—*Is.* lv. 8, 9.

Thy eyes are too pure to behold evil, and thou canst not look on iniquity. Why lookest thou upon them that do unjust things, and holdest thy peace when the wicked devoureth the man that is more just than himself?—*Hab.* i. 13.

For the foolishness of God is wiser than men; and the weakness of God is stronger than men.

. . . But the foolish things of the world hath God chosen, that he may confound the wise; and the weak things of the world hath God chosen, that he may confound the strong.

And the base things of the world, and the things that are contemptible, hath God chosen, and things that are not, that he might bring to nought things that are:

That no flesh should glory in his sight.—1 *Cor.* i. 25, 27-29.

WAYS OF GOD ARE UNSEARCH-ABLE, THE

See also: Mysteries of God, the—page 331.

Wherefore I will pray to the Lord, and address my speech to God:

Who doth great things and unsearchable and wonderful things without number.—*Job* v. 8, 9.

Peradventure thou wilt comprehend the steps of God, and wilt find out the Almighty perfectly?

He is higher than heaven, and what wilt thou do? he is deeper than hell, and how wilt thou know?

The measure of him is longer than the earth, and broader than the sea.

If he shall overturn all things, or shall press them together, who shall contradict him?—*Job* xi. 7-10.

Hast thou heard God's counsel, and shall his wisdom be inferior to thee?—*Job* xv. 8.

Shall any one teach God knowledge, who judgeth those that are high?

One man dieth strong, and hale, rich and happy.

His bowels are full of fat, and his bones are moistened with marrow.

But another dieth in bitterness of soul without any riches:

And yet they shall sleep together in the dust, and worms shall cover them. —*Job* xxi. 22-26.

Behold, God is high in his strength, and none is like him among the lawgivers.

Who can search out his ways? or who can say to him: Thou hast wrought iniquity?

Remember that thou knowest not his work, concerning which men have sung.

All men see him, every one beholdeth afar off.—*Job* xxxvi. 22-25.

This is the Lord's doing: and it is wonderful in our eyes.—*Ps.* cxvii. 23.

He hath made all things good in their time, and hath delivered the world to their consideration, so that man cannot find out the work which God hath made from the beginning to the end.—*Eccles.* iii. 11.

And I understood that man can find no reason of all those works of God that are done under the sun: and the more he shall labor to seek, so much the less shall he find: yea, though the wise man shall say, that he knoweth it, he shall not be able to find it.—*Eccles.* viii. 17.

For who among men is he that can know the counsel of God? or who can think what the will of God is?—*Wis.* ix. 13.

Who hath searched out the wisdom of God that goeth before all things?—*Ecclus.* i. 3.

And his ways who shall understand, and the storm, which no eye of man shall see?

For many of his works are hidden: but the works of his justice who shall declare? or who shall endure? for the testament is far from some, and the examination of all is in the end.—*Ecclus.* xvi. 21, 22.

Who is able to declare his works?

For who shall search out his glorious acts?

And who shall show forth the power of his majesty? or who shall be able to declare his mercy?

Nothing may be taken away, nor added, neither is it possible to find out the glorious works of God:

When a man hath done, then shall he begin: and when he leaveth off, he shall be at a loss—*Ecclus.* xviii. 2-6.

For her (wisdom's) thoughts are more vast than the sea, and her counsels more deep than the great ocean.—*Ecclus.* xxiv. 39.

Who hath forwarded the spirit of the Lord? or who hath been his counsellor, and hath taught him?

With whom hath he consulted, and who hath instructed him, and taught him the path of justice, and taught him knowledge, and showed him the way of understanding?—*Is.* xl. 13, 14.

Knowest thou not, or hast thou not heard? the Lord is the everlasting God, who hath created the ends of the earth: he shall not faint, nor labor, neither is there any searching out of his wisdom. —*Is.* xl. 28.

For who hath stood in the counsel of the Lord, and hath seen and heard his word? Who hath considered his word and heard it?—*Jer.* xxiii. 18.

O the depth of the riches of the wisdom and of the knowledge of God! How incomprehensible are his judgments, and how unsearchable his ways!

For who hath known the mind of the Lord? Or who hath been his counsellor?—*Rom.* xi. 33, 34.

For who hath known the mind of the Lord, that he may instruct him?— 1 *Cor.* ii. 16.

WAYS OF GOD ARE UNSEARCH-ABLE, ACKNOWLEDGMENT THAT THE

For thy counsel is not in man's power.—*Tob.* iii. 20.

O Lord, how great are thy works! thy thoughts are exceeding deep.

The senseless man shall not know: nor will the fool understand these things.—*Ps.* xci. 6, 7.

Thou showest mercy unto thousands, and returnest the iniquity of the fathers into the bosom of their children after them: O most mighty, great, and powerful, the Lord of hosts is thy name.

Great in counsel, and incomprehensible in thought: whose eyes are open upon all the ways of the children of Adam, to render unto every one according to his ways, and according to the fruit of his devices.—*Jer.* xxxii. 18, 19.

WAYS OF GOD, WE MUST NOT QUESTION THE

See: Question—page 457.

WEAKNESS, MAN'S

See: Powerlessness—page 389.

WEAKNESS IN SPIRITUAL THINGS, MAN'S

Have mercy on me, O Lord, for I am weak: heal me, O Lord, for my bones are troubled.—*Ps.* vi. 3.

Remember what my substance is; for hast thou made all the children of men in vain?—*Ps.* lxxxviii. 48.

My soul hath slumbered through heaviness: strengthen thou me in thy words.—*Ps.* cxviii. 28.

For a just man shall fall seven times and shall rise again: but the wicked shall fall down into evil.—*Prov.* xxiv. 16.

For there is no just man upon earth

that doth good, and sinneth not.—*Eccles.* vii. 21.

For all things cannot be in men, because the son of man is not immortal, and they are delighted with the vanity of evil.—*Ecclus.* xvii. 29.

For she is become weak unto good that dwelleth in bitterness: for evil is come down from the Lord into the gate of Jerusalem.—*Mich.* i. 12.

And he cometh to his disciples, and findeth them asleep, and he saith to Peter: What? Could you not watch one hour with me?

Watch ye, and pray that ye enter not into temptation. The spirit indeed is willing, but the flesh weak.—*Matt.* xxvi. 40, 41.

The sower went out to sow his seed. And as he sowed, some fell by the way side, and it was trodden down, and the fowls of the air devoured it.

And other some fell upon a rock: and as soon as it was sprung up, it withered away, because it had no moisture. . . .

Now they upon the rock, are they who when they hear, receive the word with joy: and these have no roots; for they believe for a while, and in time of temptation, they fall away.—*Luke* viii. 5, 6, 13.

For I know that there dwelleth not in me, that is to say, in my flesh, that which is good. For to will, is present with me; but to accomplish that which is good, I find not.

. . . For I am delighted with the law of God, according to the inward man:

But I see another law in my members, fighting against the law of my mind, and captivating me in the law of sin, that is in my members.—*Rom.* vii. 18, 22, 23.

For the flesh lusteth against the spirit: and the spirit against the flesh; for these are contrary one to another; so that you do not the things that you would.—*Gal.* v. 17.

WICKED, THE

See also: Sinner, the—page 534.

And if I be wicked, woe unto me: and if just I shall not lift up my head,

being filled with affliction and misery. —*Job* x. 15.

For there is no truth in their mouth: their heart is vain.

Their throat is an open sepulchre: they dealt deceitfully with their tongues: judge them, O God.—*Ps.* v. 10, 11.

The sinner hath provoked the Lord, according to the multitude of his wrath he will not seek him:

God is not before his eyes: his ways are filthy at all times.

Thy judgments are removed from his sight.—*Ps.* ix. (*Heb.* x.) 4, 5.

They are all gone aside, they are become unprofitable together: there is none that doth good, no not one.

Their throat is an open sepulchre: with their tongues they acted deceitfully; the poison of asps is under their lips.

Their mouth is full of cursing and bitterness; their feet are swift to shed blood.

Destruction and unhappiness in their ways: and the way of peace they have not known: there is no fear of God before their eyes.—*Ps.* xiii. 3.

The unjust hath said within himself, that he would sin: there is no fear of God before his eyes. . . .

The words of his mouth are iniquity and guile: he would not understand that he might do well.

He hath devised iniquity on his bed, he hath set himself on every way that is not good: but evil he hath not hated. —*Ps.* xxxv. 2, 4, 5.

Why dost thou glory in malice, thou that art mighty in iniquity? . . .

Thou hast loved malice more than goodness: and iniquity rather than to speak righteousness.—*Ps.* li. 3, 5.

Therefore pride hath held them fast: they are covered with their iniquity and their wickedness.

Their iniquity hath come forth, as it were from fatness: they have passed into the affection of the heart.

They have thought and spoken wickedness: they have spoken iniquity on high.

They have set their tongue against heaven: and their tongue hath passed through the earth.—*Ps.* lxxii. 6-9.

Who leave the right way, and walk by dark ways:

Who are glad when they have done evil, and rejoice in most wicked things:

Whose ways are perverse, and their steps infamous.—*Prov.* ii. 13-15.

For they sleep not except they have done evil: and their sleep is taken away unless they have made some to fall.

They eat the bread of wickedness, and drink the wine of iniquity. . . .

The way of the wicked is darksome: they know not where they fall.—*Prov.* iv. 16, 17, 19.

The work of the just is unto life: but the fruit of the wicked, unto sin. —*Prov.* x. 16.

The lamp of the wicked is sin.— *Prov.* xxi. 4.

But by the envy of the devil, death came into the world:

And they follow him that are of his side.—*Wis.* ii. 24, 25.

But the worship of God is an abomination to a sinner.—*Ecclus.* i. 32.

For the wicked life of a wicked fool is worse than death.—*Ecclus.* xxii. 12.

Woe to you that draw iniquity with cords of vanity, and sin as the rope of a cart.—*Is.* v. 18.

Their feet run to evil, and make haste to shed innocent blood: their thoughts are unprofitable thoughts: wasting and destruction are in their ways.

They have not known the way of peace, and there is no judgment in their steps: their paths are become crooked to them, every one that treadeth in them, knoweth no peace.—*Is.* lix. 7, 8.

Therefore is judgment far from us, and justice shall not overtake us. We looked for light, and behold darkness: brightness, and we have walked in the dark.

We have groped for the wall, and like the blind we have groped as if we had no eyes: we have stumbled at noon day as in darkness, we are in dark places as dead men. . . .

For our iniquities are multiplied before thee, and our sins have testified against us: for our wicked doings are with us, and we have known our iniquities. . . .

And judgment is turned away back-ward, and justice hath stood far off: because truth hath fallen down in the street, and equity could not come in. —*Is.* lix. 9, 10, 12, 14.

But this thing I commanded them, saying: Hearken to my voice, and I will be your God, and you shall be my people: and walk ye in all the way that I have commanded you, that it may be well with you.

But they hearkened not, nor inclined their ear: but walked in their own will, and in the perversity of their wicked heart: and went backward and not forward.—*Jer.* vii. 23, 24.

Thou art weighed in the balance, and art found wanting.—*Dan.* v. 27.

For many walk, of whom I have told you often (and now tell you weeping), that they are enemies of the cross of Christ;

Whose end is destruction; whose God is their belly; and whose glory is in their shame; who mind earthly things. —*Philipp.* iii. 18, 19.

These are spots in their banquets, feasting together without fear, feeding themselves, clouds without water, which are carried about by winds, trees of the autumn, unfruitful, twice dead, plucked up by the roots,

Raging waves of the sea, foaming out their own confusion; wandering stars, to whom the storm of darkness is reserved for ever.—*Jude* i. 12, 13.

WICKED, BLINDNESS AND FOLLY OF THE

See: Sinner, blindness of the— page 535.

WICKED, PUNISHMENT OF THE

See also: Sin, the punishment of— page 529.

But if you will not yet for all this obey me: I will chastise you seven times more for your sins,

And I will break the pride of your stubbornness, and I will make to you the heaven above as iron, and the earth as brass.—*Lev.* xxvi. 18, 19.

The riches which he hath swallowed he shall vomit up, and God shall draw them out of his belly. . . .

And yet his belly was not filled: and when he hath the things he coveted, he shall not be able to possess them. . . . This is the portion of a wicked man from God, and the inheritance of his doings from the Lord.—*Job* xx. 15, 20, 29.

This is the portion of a wicked man with God, and the inheritance of the violent which they shall receive of the Almighty. . . .

If he shall heap together silver as earth, and prepare raiment as clay,

He shall prepare indeed, but the just man shall be clothed with it: and the innocent shall divide the silver. . . .

A burning wind shall take him up, and carry him away, and as a whirlwind shall snatch him from his place.

And he shall cast upon him, and shall not spare: out of his hand he would willingly flee.—*Job* xxvii. 13, 16, 17, 21, 22.

From the wicked their light shall be taken away, and the high arm shall be broken.—*Job* xxxviii. 15.

But the countenance of the Lord is against them that do evil things: to cut off the remembrance of them from the earth. . . .

The death of the wicked is very evil. —*Ps.* xxxiii. 17, 22.

God shall hear, and the Eternal shall humble them.

For there is no change with them, and they have not feared God: he hath stretched forth his hand to repay.

They have defiled his covenant, they are divided by the wrath of his countenance, and his heart hath drawn near. —*Ps.* liv. 20-22.

I said to the wicked: Do not act wickedly: and to the sinners: Lift not up the horn. . . .

For in the hand of the Lord there is a cup of strong wine full of mixture. And he hath poured it out from this to that: but the dregs thereof are not emptied: all the sinners of the earth shall drink.—*Ps.* lxxiv. 5, 9.

God will repay vengeance to the ungodly, and to sinners, and keep them against the day of vengeance.—*Ecclus.* xii. 4.

Woe to you, ungodly men, who have forsaken the law of the most high Lord.

And if you be born, you shall be born in malediction: and if you die, in malediction shall be your portion.— *Ecclus.* xli. 11, 12.

Their silver shall be cast forth, and their gold shall become a dunghill. Their silver and their gold shall not be able to deliver them in the day of the wrath of the Lord. They shall not satisfy their soul, and their bellies shall not be filled: because it hath been the stumbling-block of their iniquity.— *Ezech.* vii. 19.

Therefore thus saith the Lord God: Because thou hast forgotten me, and hast cast me off behind thy back, bear thou also thy wickedness, and thy fornications.—*Ezech.* xxiii. 35.

And I will execute great vengeance upon them, rebuking them in fury: and they shall know that I am the Lord, when I shall lay my vengeance upon them.—*Ezech.* xxv. 17.

Then shall they begin to say to the mountains: Fall upon us; and to the hills: Cover us.

For if in the green wood they do these things, what shall be done in the dry?—*Luke* xxiii. 30, 31.

But to them that are contentious, and who obey not the truth, but give credit to iniquity, wrath and indignation.

Tribulation and anguish upon every soul of man that worketh evil, of the Jew first, and also of the Greek.—*Rom.* ii. 8, 9.

It is a fearful thing to fall into the hands of the living God.—*Heb.* x. 31.

And if the just man shall scarcely be saved, where shall the ungodly and the sinner appear?—1 *Peter* iv. 18.

And the kings of the earth, and the princes, and tribunes, and the rich, and the strong, and every bondman, and every freeman, hid themselves in the dens and in the rocks of mountains:

And they say to the mountains and the rocks: Fall upon us, and hide us from the face of him that sitteth upon the throne, and from the wrath of the Lamb:

For the great day of their wrath is come, and who shall be able to stand? —*Apoc.* vi. 15-17.

WICKED, PUNISHMENT OF THE

1st. In this Life

And my wrath shall be kindled against them in that day: and I will forsake them, and will hide my face from them, and they shall be devoured: all evils and afflictions shall find them, so that they shall say in that day: In truth it is because God is not with me, that these evils have found me.—*Deut.* xxxi. 17.

They that hate thee, shall be clothed with confusion: and the dwelling of the wicked shall not stand.—*Job* viii. 22.

But the eyes of the wicked shall decay, and the way to escape shall fail them, and their hope the abomination of the soul.—*Job* xi. 20.

Before his days be full, he shall perish: and his hands shall wither away.

He shall be blasted as a vine when its grapes are in the first flower, and as an olive-tree that casteth its flower.—*Job* xv. 32, 33.

Shall not the light of the wicked be extinguished, and the flame of his fire not shine?

The light shall be dark in his tabernacle, and the lamp that is over him, shall be put out.

The step of his strength shall be straitened, and his own counsel shall cast him down headlong.

For he hath thrust his feet into a net, and walketh in its meshes.

The sole of his foot shall be held in a snare, and thirst shall burn against him. —*Job* xviii. 5-9.

For I am the Lord thy God, who brought thee out of the land of Egypt: open thy mouth wide, and I will fill it.

But my people heard not my voice: and Israel hearkened not to me.

So I let them go according to the desires of their heart: they shall walk in their own inventions.—*Ps.* lxxx. 11-13.

His own iniquities catch the wicked, and he is fast bound with the ropes of his own sins.

He shall die, because he hath not received instruction, and in the multitude of his folly he shall be deceived.—*Prov.* v. 22, 23.

That which the wicked feareth, shall come upon him: to the just their desire shall be given. . . .

The expectation of the just is joy; but the hope of the wicked shall perish. —*Prov.* x. 24, 28.

The wicked man when he is come into the depth of sins, contemneth: but ignominy and reproach follow him.— *Prov.* xviii. 3.

A snare shall entangle the wicked man when he sinneth: and the just shall praise and rejoice.—*Prov.* xxix. 6.

God hath given to a man that is good in his sight, wisdom, and knowledge, and joy: but to the sinner he hath given vexation, and superfluous care, to heap up and to gather together, and to give it to him that hath pleased God: but this also is vanity, and a fruitless solicitude of the mind.—*Eccles.* ii. 26.

A wicked heart shall be laden with sorrows, and the sinner will add sin to sin.—*Ecclus.* iii. 29.

What good shall an offering do to an idol? for it can neither eat, nor smell: So is he that is persecuted by the Lord, bearing the reward of his iniquity:

He seeth with his eyes, and groaneth, as an eunuch embracing a virgin, and sighing.—*Ecclus.* xxx. 19-21.

What is there that I ought to do more to my vineyard, that I have not done to it? was it that I looked that it should bring forth grapes, and it hath brought forth wild grapes?

And now I will show you what I will do to my vineyard. I will take away the hedge thereof, and it shall be wasted: I will break down the wall thereof, and it shall be trodden down.

And I will make it desolate: it shall not be pruned, and it shall not be digged: but briers and thorns shall come up: and I will command the clouds to rain no rain upon it.—*Is.* v. 4-6.

And if they speak not according to this word, they shall not have the morning light.

And they shall pass by it, they shall fall, and be hungry: and when they shall be hungry, they will be angry, and curse their king, and their God, and look upwards.

And they shall look to the earth, and behold trouble and darkness, weakness and distress, and a mist following them, and they cannot fly away from their distress.—*Is.* viii. 20-22.

And as he that is hungry dreameth, and eateth, but when he is awake, his soul is empty: and as he that is thirsty dreameth, and drinketh, and after he is awake, is yet faint with thirst, and his soul is empty: so shall be the multitude of all the Gentiles, that have fought against mount Sion.—*Is.* xxix. 8.

For the iniquity of his covetousness I was angry, and I struck him: I hid my face from thee, and was angry: and he went away wandering in his own heart.—*Is.* lvii. 17.

And when they shall go, I will spread my net upon them: I will bring them down as the fowl of the air, I will strike them as their congregation hath heard.

Woe to them, for they have departed from me: they shall be wasted because they have transgressed against me: and I redeemed them: and they have spoken lies against me.—*Osee* vii. 12, 13.

But these men, as irrational beasts, naturally tending to the snare and to destruction, blaspheming those things which they know not, shall perish in their corruption,

Receiving the reward of their injustice, counting for a pleasure the delights of a day: stains and spots, sporting themselves to excess, rioting in their feasts with you.—*2 Peter* ii. 12,13.

2d. Dread and Disquiet

Neither shalt thou be quiet, even in those nations, nor shall there be any rest for the sole of thy foot. For the Lord will give thee a fearful heart, and languishing eyes, and a soul consumed with pensiveness:

And thy life shall be as it were hanging before thee. Thou shalt fear night and day, neither shalt thou trust thy life.

In the morning thou shalt say: Who will grant me evening? and at evening: Who will grant me morning? for the fearfulness of thy heart, wherewith thou shalt be terrified, and for those things which thou shalt see with thy eyes.—*Deut.* xxviii. 65-67.

The wicked man is proud all his days,

and the number of the years of his tyranny is uncertain.

The sound of dread is always in his ears: and when there is peace, he always suspecteth treason.

He believeth not that he may return from darkness to light, looking round about for the sword on every side.

When he moveth himself to seek bread, he knoweth that the day of darkness is ready at his hand.

Tribulation shall terrify him, and distress shall surround him, as a king that is prepared for the battle.

For he hath stretched out his hand against God, and hath strengthened himself against the Almighty.—*Job* xv. 20-25.

A gin is hidden for him in the earth, and his trap upon the path.

Fears shall terrify him on every side, and shall entangle his feet.—*Job* xviii. 10, 11.

Sing ye to God, sing a psalm to his name. make a way for him who ascendeth upon the west: the Lord is his name.

Rejoice ye before him: but the wicked shall be troubled at this presence.—*Ps.* lxvii. 5.

The wicked man fleeth, when no man pursueth: but the just, bold as a lion, shall be without dread.—*Prov.* xxviii. 1.

They shall come with fear at the thought of their sins, and their iniquities shall stand against them to convict them.—*Wis.* iv. 20.

But the wicked are like the raging sea, which cannot rest, and the waves thereof cast up dirt and mire.

There is no peace to the wicked, saith the Lord God.—*Is.* lvii. 20, 21.

They have not known the way of peace, and there is no judgment in their steps: their paths are become crooked to them, every one that treadeth in them, knoweth no peace.—*Is.* lix. 8.

We looked for peace, and no good came: for a time of healing, and behold fear.—*Jer.* viii. 15.

3d. Despair and Remorse

See also: Despair—page 109.

And Remorse—page 472.

For he hath stretched out his hand against God, and hath strengthened himself against the Almighty. . . .

He shall not believe, being vainly deceived by error, that he may be redeemed with any price.—*Job* xv. 25, 31.

When the wicked man is dead, there shall be no hope any more: and the expectation of the solicitous shall perish.—*Prov.* xi. 7.

For evil men have no hope of things to come, and the lamp of the wicked shall be put out.—*Prov.* xxiv. 20.

For a double affliction came upon them, and a groaning for the remembrance of things past.—*Wis.* xi. 13.

4th. Destroyed by God

On the contrary I have seen those who work iniquity, and sow sorrows, and reap them,

Perishing by the blast of God, and consumed by the spirit of his wrath.—*Job* iv. 8, 9.

This I know from the beginning, since man was placed upon the earth,

That the praise of the wicked is short, and the joy of the hypocrite but for a moment.

If his pride mount up even to heaven, and his head touch the clouds:

In the end he shall be destroyed like a dunghill, and they that had seen him, shall say: Where is he?

As a dream that fleeth away he shall not be found, he shall pass as a vision of the night:

The eyes that had seen him, shall see him no more, neither shall his place any more behold him.—*Job* xx. 4-9.

How often shall the lamp of the wicked be put out, and a deluge come upon them, and he shall distribute the sorrows of his wrath?

They shall be as chaff before the face of the wind, and as ashes which the whirlwind scattereth.

. . . His eyes shall see his own destruction, and he shall drink of the wrath of the Almighty. . . .

Because the wicked man is reserved to the day of destruction, and he shall be brought to the day of wrath.—*Job* xxi. 17, 18, 20, 30.

Is not destruction to the wicked, and aversion to them that work iniquity?—*Job* xxxi. 3.

For he knoweth their works: and therefore he shall bring night on them, and they shall be destroyed.

He hath struck them, as being wicked, in open sight.

Who as it were on purpose have revolted from him, and would not understand all his ways.—*Job* xxxiv. 25-27.

Thou hatest all the workers of iniquity: thou wilt destroy all that speak a lie. The bloody and the deceitful man the Lord will abhor.—*Ps.* v. 7.

Be not emulous of evil-doers; nor envy them that work iniquity.

For they shall shortly wither away as grass, and as the green herbs shall quickly fall.

. . . Cease from anger, and leave rage; have no emulation to do evil.

For evil-doers shall be cut off: but they that wait upon the Lord, they shall inherit the land.

For yet a little while, and the wicked shall not be: and thou shalt seek his place, and shalt not find it.

. . . Because the wicked shall perish. And the enemies of the Lord, presently after they shall be honored and exalted, shall come to nothing and vanish like smoke. . . .

I have seen the wicked highly exalted, and lifted up like the cedars of Libanus.

And I passed by, and lo, he was not: and I sought him, and his place was not found.—*Ps.* xxxvi. 1, 2, 8-10, 20, 35, 36.

But thou, O Lord, shalt bring them down into the pit of destruction. Bloody and deceitful men shall not live out half their days; but I will trust in thee, O Lord.—*Ps.* liv. 24.

They shall come to nothing, like water running down; he hath bent his bow till they be weakened.

Like wax that melteth they shall be taken away: fire hath fallen on them, and they shall not see the sun.

Before your thorns could know the brier: he swalloweth them up, as alive, in his wrath.—*Ps.* lvii. 8-10.

For behold they that go far from thee shall perish: thou hast destroyed all them that are disloyal to thee.—*Ps.* lxxii. 27.

When the wicked shall spring up as grass: and all the workers of iniquity shall appear:

That they may perish for ever and ever. . . .

For behold thy enemies, O Lord, for behold thy enemies shall perish: and all the workers of iniquity shall be scattered.—*Ps.* xci. 8, 10.

And he will render them their iniquity: and in their malice he will destroy them: the Lord our God will destroy them.—*Ps.* xciii. 23.

But the wicked shall be destroyed from the earth: and they that do unjustly shall be taken away from it.—*Prov.* ii. 22.

All things that are of the earth, shall return into the earth: so the ungodly shall from malediction to destruction. —*Ecclus.* xli. 13.

And they sought out all iniquities, till vengeance came upon them, and put an end to all their sins.—*Ecclus.* xlvii. 31.

And he shall destroy the wicked, and the sinners together: and they that have forsaken the Lord, shall be consumed.—*Is.* i. 28.

For he that did prevail hath failed, the scorner is consumed, and they are all cut off that watched for iniquity.—*Is.* xxix. 20.

To what shall I compare thee? or to what shall I liken thee, O daughter of Jerusalem? to what shall I equal thee, that I may comfort thee, O virgin daughter of Sion? for great as the sea is thy destruction: who shall heal thee?—*Lam.* ii. 13.

I will bring thee to nothing, and thou shalt not be, and if thou be sought for, thou shalt not be found any more for ever, saith the Lord God.—*Ezech.* xxvi. 21.

5th. Eternal Punishment

The enemies of the Lord have lied to him: and their time shall be for ever.—*Ps.* lxxx. 16.

And they shall fall after this without honor, and be a reproach among the dead for ever: for he shall burst them puffed up and speechless, and shall shake them from the foundations, and they shall be utterly laid waste: they shall be in sorrow, and their memory shall perish.—*Wis.* iv. 19.

And your strength shall be as the ashes of tow, and your work as a spark: and both shall burn together, and there shall be none to quench it.—*Is.* i. 31.

And they shall go out, and see the carcasses of the men that have transgressed against me: their worm shall not die, and their fire shall not be quenched: and they shall be a loathsome sight to all flesh.—*Is.* lxvi. 24.

And these shall go into everlasting punishment: but the just, into life everlasting.—*Matt.* xxv. 46.

Whose fan is in his hand, and he will purge his floor, and will gather the wheat into his barn; but the chaff he will burn with unquenchable fire.—*Luke* iii. 17.

Raging waves of the sea, foaming out their own confusion; wandering stars, to whom the storm of darkness is reserved for ever.—*Jude* i. 13.

And the smoke of their torments shall ascend up for ever and ever: neither have they rest day nor night, who have adored the beast, and his image, and whoever receiveth the character of his name.—*Apoc.* xiv. 11.

6th. Exclusion from Heaven

Therefore the wicked shall not rise again in judgment: nor sinners in the council of the just.—*Ps.* i. 5.

Neither shall the wicked dwell near thee: nor shall the unjust abide before thy eyes.—*Ps.* v. 6.

There the workers of iniquity are fallen, they are cast out, and could not stand.—*Ps.* xxxv. 13.

Let them be blotted out of the book of the living; and with the just let them not be written.—*Ps.* lxviii. 29.

For while the wicked thought to be able to have dominion over the holy nation, they themselves being fettered with the bonds of darkness, and a long night, shut up in their houses, lay there exiled from the eternal providence.—*Wis.* xvii. 2.

Let us have pity on the wicked, but he will not learn justice: in the land of the saints he hath done wicked things, and he shall not see the glory of the Lord.—*Is.* xxvi. 10.

And I will pick out from among you the transgressors, and the wicked, and will bring them out of the land where they sojourn, and they shall not enter into the land of Israel: and you shall know that I am the Lord.—*Ezech.* xx. 38.

And then will I profess unto them, I never knew you: depart from me, you that work iniquity.—*Matt.* vii. 23.

Now the works of the flesh are manifest, which are fornication, uncleanness, immodesty, luxury,

Idolatry, witchcrafts, enmities, contentions, emulations, wraths, quarrels, dissensions, sects,

Envies, murders, drunkenness, revellings, and such like. Of the which I foretell you, as I have foretold to you, that they who do such things shall not obtain the kingdom of God.—*Gal.* v. 19-21.

There shall not enter into it any thing defiled, or that worketh abomination or maketh a lie, but they that are written in the book of life of the Lamb. —*Apoc.* xxi. 27.

Blessed are they that wash their robes in the blood of the Lamb: that they may have a right to the tree of life, and may enter in by the gates into the city.

Without are dogs, and sorcerers, and unchaste, and murderers, and servers of idols, and every one that loveth and maketh a lie.—*Apoc.* xxii. 14, 15.

7th. The Sufferings of Hell

But transgressors shall all of them be plucked up as thorns: which are not taken away with hands.

And if a man will touch them, he must be armed with iron and with the staff of a lance: but they shall be set on fire and burnt to nothing.—*2 Kings* xxiii. 6, 7.

His bones shall be filled with the vices of his youth, and they shall sleep with him in the dust. . . .

He shall be punished for all that he did, and yet shall not be consumed: according to the multitude of his devices so also shall he suffer. . . .

When he shall be filled, he shall be straitened, he shall burn, and every sorrow shall fall upon him. . . .

All darkness is hid in his secret places: a fire that is not kindled shall devour him, he shall be afflicted when left in his tabernacle.

The heavens shall reveal his iniquity; and the earth shall rise up against him. . . .

This is the portion of a wicked man from God, and the inheritance of his doings from the Lord.—*Job* xx. 11, 18, 22, 26, 27, 29.

He shall rain snares upon sinners: fire and brimstone and storms of winds shall be the portion of their cup.—*Ps.* x. 7.

Let thy hand be found by all thy enemies: let thy right hand find out all them that hate thee.

Thou shalt make them as an oven of fire, in the time of thy anger: the Lord shall trouble them in his wrath, and fire shall devour them.—*Ps.* xx. 9, 10.

Many are the scourges of the sinner, but mercy shall encompass him that hopeth in the Lord.—*Ps.* xxxi. 10.

The wicked shall see, and shall be angry, he shall gnash with his teeth and pine away: the desire of the wicked shall perish.—*Ps.* cxi. 10.

Burning coals shall fall upon them; thou wilt cast them down into the fire: in miseries they shall not be able to stand.—*Ps.* cxxxix. 11.

But the wicked shall be punished according to their own devices: who have neglected the just, and have revolted from the Lord.—*Wis.* iii. 10.

For when they (the chosen people) were tried, and chastised with mercy, they knew how the wicked were judged with wrath and tormented.

For thou didst admonish and try them as a father: but the others, as a severe king, thou didst examine and condemn. . . .

That they might know that by what things a man sinneth, by the same also he is tormented.—*Wis.* xi. 10, 11, 17.

For the whole world was enlightened with a clear light, and none were hindered in their labors.

But over them only was spread a heavy night, an image of that darkness which was to come upon them. But they were to themselves more grievous than the darkness.—*Wis.* xvii. 19, 20.

Humble thy spirit very much: for the vengeance on the flesh of the ungodly is fire and worms.—*Ecclus.* vii. 19.

The congregation of sinners is like tow heaped together, and the end of them is a flame of fire.

The way of sinners is made plain with stones, and in their end is hell, and darkness, and pains.—*Ecclus.* xxi. 10, 11.

Therefore hath hell enlarged her soul, and opened her mouth without any bounds, and their strong ones, and their people, and their high and glorious ones shall go down into it.—*Is.* v. 14.

For behold the day shall come kindled as a furnace: and all the proud, and all that do wickedly shall be stubble: and the day that cometh shall set them on fire, saith the Lord of hosts, it shall not leave them root, nor branch. —*Malach.* iv. 1.

Suffer both to grow until the harvest, and in the time of the harvest I will say to the reapers: Gather up first the cockle, and bind it into bundles to burn, but the wheat gather ye into my barn. . . .

So shall it be at the end of the world. The angels shall go out, and shall separate the wicked from among the just.

And shall cast them into the furnace of fire: there shall be weeping and gnashing of teeth.—*Matt.* xiii. 30, 49, 50.

And the unprofitable servant cast ye out into the exterior darkness. There shall be weeping and gnashing of teeth. —*Matt.* xxv. 30.

Then shall he say to them also that shall be on his left hand: Depart from me, you cursed, into everlasting fire which was prepared for the devil and his angels.—*Matt.* xxv. 41.

For if God spared not the angels that sinned, but delivered them, drawn down by infernal ropes to the lower hell, unto torments, to be reserved unto judgment. . . .

The Lord knoweth how to deliver the godly from temptation, but to reserve the unjust unto the day of judgment to be tormented.—*2 Peter* ii. 4, 9.

These are fountains without water, and clouds tossed with whirlwinds, to whom the mist of darkness is reserved. —*2 Peter* ii. 17.

And the third angel followed them, saying with a loud voice: If any man shall adore the beast and his image, and receive his character in his forehead, or in his hand;

He also shall drink of the wine of the wrath of God, which is mingled with pure wine in the cup of his wrath, and shall be tormented with fire and brimstone in the sight of the holy angels, and in the sight of the Lamb.

And the smoke of their torments shall ascend up for ever and ever: neither have they rest day nor night.— *Apoc.* xiv. 9-11.

But the fearful, and unbelieving, and the abominable, and murderers, and whoremongers, and sorcerers, and idolators, and all liars, they shall have their portion in the pool burning with fire and brimstone, which is the second death.—*Apoc.* xxi. 8.

WICKED, CERTAINTY OF THE PUNISHMENT OF THE

But thou shalt consider with thy eyes: and shalt see the reward of the wicked. —*Ps.* xc. 8.

If the just man receive in the earth, how much more the wicked and the sinner.—*Prov.* xi. 31.

Be not hasty to depart from his face, and do not continue in an evil work: for he will do all that pleaseth him:

And his word is full of power: neither can any man say to him: Why dost thou so?—*Eccles.* viii. 3, 4.

It is not in man's power to stop the spirit, neither hath he power in the day of death, neither is he suffered to rest when war is at hand, neither shall wickedness save the wicked.—*Eccles.* viii. 8.

But for two things they shall be justly punished, because they have thought not well of God, giving heed to idols, and have sworn unjustly, in guile despising justice.

For it is not the power of them, by whom they swear, but the just vengeance of sinners always punisheth the transgression of the unjust.—*Wis.* xiv. 30, 31.

The slipping of a false tongue is as

one that falleth on the pavement: so the fall of the wicked shall come speedily.—*Ecclus.* xx. 20.

Woe to the wicked unto evil: for the reward of his hands shall be given him. —*Is.* iii. 11.

I have spread forth my hands all the day to an unbelieving people, who walk in a way that is not good after their own thoughts.

A people that continually provoke me to anger before my face. . . .

Behold it is written before me: I will not be silent, but I will render and repay into their bosom.—*Is.* lxv. 2, 3, 6.

For among my people are found wicked men, that lie in wait as fowlers, setting snares and traps to catch men.

As a net is full of birds, so their houses are full of deceit: therefore are they become great and enriched.

They are grown gross and fat: and have most wickedly transgressed my words. They have not judged the cause of the widow, they have not managed the cause of the fatherless, and they have not judged the judgment of the poor.

Shall I not visit for these things, saith the Lord? or shall not my soul take revenge on such a nation?—*Jer.* v. 26-29.

Behold the whirlwind of the Lord's indignation shall come forth, and a tempest shall break out and come upon the head of the wicked.

The wrath of the Lord shall not return till he execute it, and till he accomplish the thought of his heart: in the latter days you shall understand his counsel.—*Jer.* xxiii. 19, 20.

For acting wickedly against the laws of God doth not pass unpunished: but this the time following will declare.— 2 *Mach.* iv. 17.

But do not think that thou shalt escape unpunished, for that thou hast attempted to fight against God.— 2 *Mach.* vii. 19.

You serpents, generation of vipers, how will you flee from the judgment of hell?—*Matt.* xxiii. 33.

He (the Baptist) said therefore to the multitudes that went forth to be baptized by him: Ye offspring of vipers, who hath showed you to flee from the wrath to come?—*Luke* iii. 7.

WICKED, A PRAYER THAT GOD MAY PUNISH THE

May his belly be filled, that God may send forth the wrath of his indignation upon him, and rain down his war upon him.—*Job* xx. 23.

For there is no truth in their mouth: their heart is vain.

Their throat is an open sepulchre: they dealt deceitfully with their tongues: judge them, O God.

Let them fall from their devices: according to the multitude of their wickednesses cast them out: for they have provoked thee, O Lord.—*Ps.* v. 10, 11.

Let thy hand be found by all thy enemies: let thy right hand find out all them that hate thee.—*Ps.* xx. 9.

Let God arise, and let his enemies be scattered: and let them that hate him flee from before his face.

As smoke vanisheth, so let them vanish away: as wax melteth before the fire, so let the wicked perish at the presence of God.—*Ps.* lxvii. 2, 3.

Let them be blotted out of the book of the living; and with the just let them not be written.—*Ps.* lxviii. 29.

Lord, let thy hand be exalted, and let them not see: let the envious people see, and be confounded: and let fire devour thy enemies.—*Is.* xxvi. 11.

WICKED, GOD TAKES HIS TIME IN PUNISHING THE

See: Time—page 557.

WICKED, THE TEMPORAL PROS- PERITY OF THE

This I know from the beginning, since man was placed upon the earth,

That the praise of the wicked is short, and the joy of the hypocrite but for a moment.—*Job* xx. 4, 5.

Why then do the wicked live, are they advanced, and strengthened with riches? . . .

Their houses are secure and peaceable, and the rod of God is not upon them. . .

They spend their days in wealth, and in a moment they go down to hell.

Who have said to God: Depart from us, we desire not the knowledge of thy ways.

Who is the Almighty, that we should serve him? and what doth it profit us if we pray to him?—*Job* xxi. 7, 9, 13-15.

Envy not the man who prospereth in his way; the man who doth unjust things. . . .

For yet a little while, and the wicked shall not be: and thou shalt seek his place, and shalt not find it.—*Ps.* xxxvi. 7, 10.

Better is a little to the just, than the great riches of the wicked. . . .

Because the wicked shall perish. And the enemies of the Lord, presently after they shall be honored and exalted, shall come to nothing and vanish like smoke.—*Ps.* xxxvi. 16, 20.

I have seen the wicked highly exalted, and lifted up like the cedars of Libanus.

And I passed by, and lo, he was not: and I sought him, and his place was not found.—*Ps.* xxxvi. 35, 36.

Be not thou afraid, when a man shall be made rich, and when the glory of his house shall be increased.

For when he shall die he shall take nothing away; nor shall his glory descend with him.

For in his lifetime his soul will be blessed: and he will praise thee when thou shalt do well to him.

He shall go in to the generations of his fathers: and he shall never see light. —*Ps.* xlviii. 17-20.

But my feet were almost moved; my steps had well nigh slipped.

Because I had a zeal on occasion of the wicked, seeing the prosperity of sinners. . . .

They are not in the labor of men: neither shall they be scourged like other men.

Therefore pride hath held them fast: they are covered with their iniquity and their wickedness. . . .

Behold these are sinners; and yet abounding in the world they have obtained riches.

And I said: Then have I in vain justified my heart, and washed my hands among the innocent. . . .

I studied that I might know this thing, it is a labor in my sight:

Until I go into the sanctuary of God, and understand concerning their last ends.

But indeed for deceits thou hast put it to them: when they were lifted up, thou hast cast them down.

How are they brought to desolation? they have suddenly ceased to be: they have perished by reason of their iniquity.

As the dream of them that awake, O Lord; so in thy city thou shalt bring their image to nothing.—*Ps.* lxxii. 2, 3, 5, 6, 12, 13, 16-20.

. . . Deliver me,

And rescue me out of the hand of strange children; whose mouth hath spoken vanity: and their right hand is the right hand of iniquity:

Whose sons are as new plants in their youth:

Their daughters decked out, adorned round about after the similitude of a temple:

Their storehouses full, flowing out of this into that.

Their sheep fruitful in young, abounding in their goings forth: their oxen fat.

There is no breach of wall, nor passage, nor crying out in their streets.

They have called the people happy, that hath these things: but happy is that people whose God is the Lord.— *Ps.* cxliii. 11-15.

These things also I saw in the days of my vanity: A just man perisheth in his justice, and a wicked man liveth a long time in his wickedness.

Be not over just: and be not more wise than is necessary, lest thou become stupid.—*Eccles.* vii. 16, 17.

There is also another vanity, which is done upon the earth. There are just men to whom evils happen, as though they had done the works of the wicked: and there are wicked men, who are as secure, as though they had the deeds of the just: but this also I judge most vain.—*Eccles.* viii. 14.

For the hope of the wicked is as dust, which is blown away with the wind, and as a thin froth which is dispersed by the storm: and a smoke that is scattered abroad by the wind: and as the remembrance of a guest of one day that passeth by.—*Wis.* v. 15.

Envy not the glory and riches of a sinner: for thou knowest not what his ruin shall be.—*Ecclus.* ix. 16.

There is success in evil things to a man without discipline, and there is a finding that turneth to loss.—*Ecclus.* xx. 9.

Thou indeed, O Lord, art just, if I plead with thee, but yet I will speak what is just to thee: Why doth the way of the wicked prosper: why is it well with all them that transgress, and do wickedly?

Thou hast planted them, and they have taken root: they prosper and bring forth fruit: thou art near in their mouth, and far from their reins.—*Jer.* xii. 1, 2.

Why hast thou shown me iniquity and grievance, to see rapine and injustice before me? and there is a judgment, but opposition is more powerful. . . .

Thy eyes are too pure to behold evil, and thou canst not look on iniquity. Why lookest thou upon them that do unjust things, and holdest thy peace when the wicked devoureth the man that is more just than himself?—*Hab.* i. 3, 13.

Your words have been unsufferable to me, saith the Lord.

And you have said: What have we spoken against thee? You have said: He laboreth in vain that serveth God, and what profit is it that we have kept his ordinances, and that we have walked sorrowful before the Lord of hosts?

Wherefore now we call the proud people happy, for they that work wickedness are built up, and they have tempted God and are preserved. . . .

And you shall return, and shall see the difference between the just and the wicked: and between him that serveth God, and him that serveth him not.—*Malach.* iii. 13-15, 18.

And Abraham said to him (Dives): Son, remember that thou didst receive good things in thy lifetime, and likewise Lazarus evil things, but now he is comforted; and thou art tormented.—*Luke* xvi. 25.

WICKED, WE MUST NOT FOLLOW THE EXAMPLE OF THE

See: Example of the wicked—page 131.

WICKED, WE MUST NOT APPROVE OF OR UPHOLD THE

He that justifieth the wicked, and he that condemneth the just, both are abominable before God.—*Prov.* xvii. 15.

It is not good to accept the person of the wicked, to decline from the truth of judgment.—*Prov.* xviii. 5.

They that say to the wicked man: Thou art just: shall be cursed by the people, and the tribes shall abhor them. —*Prov.* xxiv. 24.

They that forsake the law, praise the wicked man: they that keep it, are incensed against him.—*Prov.* xxviii. 4.

Be not pleased with the wrong done by the unjust, knowing that even to hell the wicked shall not please.—*Ecclus.* ix. 17.

Despise not a just man that is poor, and do not magnify a sinful man that is rich.—*Ecclus.* x. 26.

Give to the merciful, and uphold not the sinner: God will repay vengeance to the ungodly and to sinners, and keep them against the day of vengeance.

Give to the good, and receive not a sinner.

Do good to the humble, and give not to the ungodly: hold back thy bread, and give it not to him, lest thereby he overmaster thee.

For thou shalt receive twice as much evil for all the good thou shalt have done to him: for the Highest also hateth sinners, and will repay vengeance to the ungodly.—*Ecclus.* xii. 4-7.

Woe to you that are mighty to drink wine, and stout men at drunkenness.

That justify the wicked for gifts, and take away the justice of the just from him.—*Is.* v. 22, 23.

WICKED, WE SHOULD REBUKE THE

See also: Admonition, giving—page 17.

They that say to the wicked man: Thou art just: shall be cursed by the people, and the tribes shall abhor them.

They that rebuke him, shall be praised: and a blessing shall come upon them.—*Prov.* xxiv. 24, 25.

Them that sin reprove before all: that the rest also may have fear.— 1 *Tim.* v. 20.

WICKED, VAIN IS THE HOPE OF THE

But the eyes of the wicked shall decay, and the way to escape shall fail them, and their hope the abomination of the soul.—*Job* xi. 20.

Yea when thou shalt say: He considereth not: be judged before him, and expect him.

For he doth not now bring on his fury, neither doth he revenge wickedness exceedingly.—*Job* xxxv. 14, 15.

The expectation of the just is joy; but the hope of the wicked shall perish. —*Prov.* x. 28.

When the wicked man is dead, there shall be no hope any more: and the expectation of the solicitous shall perish.—*Prov.* xi. 7.

For the hope of the wicked is as dust, which is blown away with the wind, and as a thin froth which is dispersed by the storm: and a smoke that is scattered abroad by the wind: and as the remembrance of a guest of one day that passeth by.—*Wis.* v. 15.

For his heart is ashes, and his hope vain earth, and his life more base than clay.—*Wis.* xv. 10.

Woe to him that gathereth together an evil covetousness to his house, that his nest may be on high, and thinketh he may be delivered out of the hand of evil.—*Hab.* ii. 9.

WICKED BROUGHT TO NOUGHT BY GOD, THE DESIGNS OF THE

Wherefore I will pray to the Lord, and address my speech to God: . . .

Who bringeth to nought the designs of the malignant, so that their hands cannot accomplish what they had begun:

Who catcheth the wise in their craftiness, and disappointeth the counsel of the wicked.—*Job* v. 8, 12, 13.

Why have the Gentiles raged, and the people devised vain things?

The kings of the earth stood up, and the princes met together, against the Lord, and against his Christ.

Let us break their bonds asunder: and let us cast away their yoke from us.

He that dwelleth in heaven shall laugh at them: and the Lord shall deride them.

Then shall he speak to them in his anger, and trouble them in his rage.— *Ps.* ii. 1-5.

The wickedness of sinners shall be brought to nought: and thou shalt direct the just: the searcher of hearts and reins is God.—*Ps.* vii. 10.

For they have intended evils against thee: they have devised counsels which they have not been able to establish.— *Ps.* xx. 12.

The Lord bringeth to nought the counsels of nations; and he rejecteth the devices of people, and casteth away the counsels of princes.

But the counsel of the Lord standeth for ever: the thoughts of his heart to all generations.—*Ps.* xxxii. 10, 11.

The wicked shall see, and shall be angry, he shall gnash with his teeth and pine away: the desire of the wicked shall perish.—*Ps.* cxi. 10.

For the Lord will not leave the rod of sinners upon the lot of the just: that the just may not stretch forth their hands to iniquity.—*Ps.* cxxiv. 3.

The Lord will not afflict the soul of the just with famine, and he will disappoint the deceitful practices of the wicked.—*Prov.* x. 3.

Men shall not be strengthened by wickedness: and the root of the just shall not be moved.—*Prov.* xii. 3.

WICKED TURN AGAINST THEM, THE SINS OF THE

See: Sins of the wicked—page 532.

WICKED, THE FRUITLESS RE-PENTANCE OF THE

See: Remorse—page 472.

WICKED NOT ACCEPTABLE TO GOD, THE OFFERINGS OF THE

The sacrifices of the wicked are abominable to the Lord: the vows of the just are acceptable.—*Prov.* xv. 8.

The victims of the wicked are abominable, because they are offered of wickedness.—*Prov.* xxi. 27.

The offering of him that sacrificeth of a thing wrongfully gotten, is stained, and the mockeries of the unjust are not acceptable.

The Lord is only for them that wait upon him in the way of truth and justice.

The most High approveth not the gifts of the wicked: neither hath he respect to the oblations of the unjust, nor will he be pacified for sins by the multitude of their sacrifices.

He that offereth sacrifice of the goods of the poor, is as one that sacrificeth the son in the presence of his father.—*Ecclus.* xxxiv. 21-24.

Woe to the sinful nation, a people laden with iniquity, a wicked seed, ungracious children: they have forsaken the Lord, they have blasphemed the Holy One of Israel, they are gone away backwards. . . .

To what purpose do you offer me the multitude of your victims, saith the Lord? I am full, I desire not holocausts of rams, and fat of fatlings, and blood of calves, and lambs, and buck goats.

When you came to appear before me, who required these things at your hands, that you should walk in my courts?

Offer sacrifice no more in vain: incense is an abomination to me. The new moons, and the sabbaths, and other festivals I will not abide, your assemblies are wicked.

My soul hateth your new moons, and your solemnities: they are become troublesome to me, I am weary of bearing them.—*Is.* i. 4, 11-14.

Hear, O earth: Behold I will bring evils upon this people, the fruits of their own thoughts: because they have not heard my words, and they have cast away my law.

To what purpose do you bring me frankincense from Saba, and the sweet-smelling cane from a far country? your holocausts are not acceptable, nor are your sacrifices pleasing to me.—*Jer.* vi. 19, 20.

What is the meaning that my beloved hath wrought much wickedness in my house? shall the holy flesh take away from thee thy crimes, in which thou hast boasted?—*Jer.* xi. 15.

Thus saith the Lord to his people, that have loved to move their feet, and have not rested, and have not pleased the Lord: He will now remember their iniquities, and visit their sins.

. . . When they fast I will not hear their prayers: and if they offer holocausts and victims, I will not receive them: for I will consume them by the sword, and by famine, and by the pestilence.—*Jer.* xiv. 10, 12.

I hate, and have rejected your festivities: and I will not receive the odor of your assemblies.

And if you offer me holocausts, and your gifts, I will not receive them: neither will I regard the vows of your fat beasts.—*Amos* v. 21, 22.

And Aggeus said: If one that is unclean by occasion of a soul touch any of all these things, shall it be defiled? And the priests answered, and said: It shall be defiled.

And Aggeus answered, and said: So is this people, and so is this nation before my face, saith the Lord, and so is all the work of their hands: and all that they have offered there, shall be defiled.—*Aggeus* ii. 14, 15.

Who is there among you, that will shut the doors, and will kindle the fire on my altar gratis? I have no pleasure in you, saith the Lord of hosts: and I will not receive a gift of your hand. . . .

And you have said: Behold of our labor, and you puffed it away, saith the Lord of hosts, and you brought in of rapine the lame, and the sick, and brought in an offering: shall I accept it at your hands, saith the Lord?—*Malach.* i. 10, 13.

WICKED NOT ACCEPTABLE TO GOD, THE PRAYERS OF THE

For what is the hope of the hypocrite, if through covetousness he take by violence, and God deliver not his soul?

Will God hear his cry, when distress shall come upon him?

Or can he delight himself in the Almighty, and call upon God at all times? —*Job* xxvii. 8-10.

If I have looked at iniquity in my heart, the Lord will not hear me.—*Ps.* lxv. 18.

The Lord is far from the wicked: and he will hear the prayers of the just. —*Prov.* xv. 29.

He that turneth away his ears from hearing the law, his prayer shall be an abomination.—*Prov.* xxviii. 9.

And when you stretch forth your hands, I will turn away my eyes from you: and when you multiply prayer, I will not hear: for your hands are full of blood.—*Is.* i. 15.

They are returned to the former iniquities of their fathers, who refused to hear my words: so these likewise have gone after strange gods, to serve them: the house of Israel, and the house of Juda have made void my covenant, which I made with their fathers.

Wherefore thus saith the Lord: Behold I will bring in evils upon them, which they shall not be able to escape: and they shall cry to me, and I will not hearken to them.—*Jer.* xi. 10, 11.

For according to the number of thy cities were thy gods, O Juda: and according to the number of the streets of Jerusalem thou hast set up altars of confusion, altars to offer sacrifice to Baalim.

Therefore do not thou pray for this people, and do not take up praise and prayer for them: for I will not hear them in the time of their cry to me, in the time of their affliction.—*Jer.* xi. 13, 14.

When they fast, I will not hear their prayers: and if they offer holocausts and victims, I will not receive them: for I will consume them by the sword, and by famine, and by the pestilence. —*Jer.* xiv. 12.

Then shall they cry to the Lord, and he will not hear them: and he will hide his face from them at that time, as they have behaved wickedly in their devices.—*Mich.* iii. 4.

Now we know that God doth not hear sinners: but if a man be a server of God, and doth his will, him he heareth. —*John* ix. 31.

WICKED DESPISE THE JUST, THE

See: Just, despised by the wicked— page 265.

WICKEDNESS OF THE WORLD BEFORE THE REDEMPTION, THE

See: Corruption of the world— page 82.

WIDOWS, GOD THE PROTECTOR AND AVENGER OF

You shall not hurt a widow or an orphan.

If you hurt them, they will cry out to me, and I will hear their cry:

And my rage shall be enkindled, and I will strike you with the sword, and your wives shall be widows, and your children fatherless.—*Ex.* xxii. 22-24.

He (God) doth judgment to the fatherless and the widow, loveth the stranger, and giveth him food and raiment.—*Deut.* x. 18.

Rejoice ye before him: but the wicked shall be troubled at his presence, who is the father of orphans, and the judge of widows.

God in his holy place.—*Ps.* lxvii. 5, 6.

For the Lord hath chosen Sion: he hath chosen it for his dwelling.

This is my rest for ever and ever: here will I dwell, for I have chosen it.

Blessing I will bless her widow: I will satisfy her poor with bread.—*Ps.* cxxxi. 13-15.

The Lord keepeth the strangers, he will support the fatherless and the widow: and the ways of sinners he will destroy.—*Ps.* cxlv. 9.

The Lord will destroy the house of the proud: and will strengthen the borders of the widow.—*Prov.* xv. 25.

He will not despise the prayers of the fatherless; nor the widow, when she poureth out her complaint.

Do not the widow's tears run down the cheek, and her cry against him that causeth them to fall?

For from the cheek they go up even to heaven, and the Lord that heareth will not be delighted with them.—*Ecclus.* xxxv. 17-19.

Leave thy fatherless children: I will make them live: and thy widows shall hope in me.—*Jer.* xlix. 11.

And when he came nigh to the gate of the city, behold a dead man was carried out, the only son of his mother; and she was a widow: and a great multitude of the city was with her.

Whom when the Lord had seen, being moved with mercy towards her, he said to her: Weep not.

And he came near, and touched the bier. And they that carried it, stood still. And he said: Young man, I say to thee, arise.

And he that was dead, sat up, and began to speak. And he gave him to his mother.—*Luke* vii. 12-15.

But she that is a widow indeed, and desolate, let her trust in God, and continue in supplications and prayers night and day.—1 *Tim.* v. 5.

WIDOWS, A WARNING AGAINST DOING WRONG TO

Thou shalt not pervert the judgment of the stranger nor of the fatherless, neither shalt thou take away the widow's raiment for a pledge.—*Deut.* xxiv. 17.

Cursed be he that perverteth the judgment of the stranger, of the fatherless and the widow: and all the people shall say: Amen.—*Deut.* xxvii. 19.

Thy princes are faithless, companions of thieves: they all love bribes, they run after rewards. They judge not for the fatherless: and the widow's cause cometh not in to them.

Therefore saith the Lord the God of hosts, the mighty one of Israel: Ah! I will comfort myself over my adversaries: and I will be revenged of my enemies.—*Is.* i. 23, 24.

They are grown gross and fat: and have most wickedly transgressed my words. They have not judged the cause of the widow, they have not managed the cause of the fatherless, and they have not judged the judgment of the poor.

Shall I not visit for these things, saith the Lord? or shall not my soul take revenge on such a nation?—*Jer.* v. 28, 29.

Thus saith the Lord of hosts, saying: Judge ye true judgment, and show ye mercy and compassion every man to his brother.

And oppress not the widow, and the fatherless, and the stranger, and the poor.—*Zach.* vii. 9, 10.

And I will come to you in judgment, and will be a speedy witness against sorcerers, and adulterers, and false swearers, and them that oppress the hireling in his wages, the widows, and the fatherless: and oppress the stranger, and have not feared me, saith the Lord of hosts.—*Malach.* iii. 5.

WIDOWS, WE SHOULD BE ESPECIALLY KIND TO

When thou hast reaped the corn in thy field, and hast forgot and left a sheaf, thou shalt not return to take it away: but thou shalt suffer the stranger, and the fatherless and the widow to take it away: that the Lord thy God may bless thee in all the works of thy hands.

If thou have gathered the fruit of thy olive trees, thou shalt not return to gather whatsoever remaineth on the trees: but shalt leave it for the stranger, for the fatherless, and the widow.

If thou make the vintage of thy vineyard, thou shalt not gather the clusters that remain, but they shall be for the stranger, the fatherless, and the widow. —*Deut.* xxiv. 19-21.

Learn to do well: seek judgment, relieve the oppressed, judge for the fatherless, defend the widow.

And then come, and accuse me, saith the Lord: if your sins be as scarlet, they shall be made as white as snow: and if they be red as crimson, they shall be white as wool.—*Is.* i. 17, 18.

Religion clean and undefiled before

God and the Father, is this: to visit the fatherless and widows in their tribulation: and to keep one's self unspotted from this world.—*James* i. 27.

WIFE IS A BLESSING FROM GOD, A GOOD

Blessed are all they that fear the Lord: that walk in his ways.

For thou shalt eat the labors of thy hands: blessed art thou, and it shall be well with thee.

Thy wife as a fruitful vine, on the sides of thy house.

Thy children, as olive plants, round about thy table.

Behold, thus shall the man be blessed that feareth the Lord.—*Ps.* cxxvii. 1-4.

A diligent woman is a crown to her husband.—*Prov.* xii. 4.

He that hath found a good wife, hath found a good thing, and shall receive a pleasure from the Lord. He that driveth away a good wife, driveth away a good thing: but he that keepeth an adulteress, is foolish and wicked.—*Prov.* xviii. 22.

House and riches are given by parents: but a prudent wife is properly from the Lord.—*Prov.* xix. 14.

Who shall find a valiant woman? far and from the uttermost coasts is the price of her.

The heart of her husband trusteth in her, and he shall have no need of spoils.

She will render him good, and not evil, all the days of her life. . . .

She hath opened her hand to the needy, and stretched out her hands to the poor. . . .

She hath opened her mouth to wisdom, and the law of clemency is on her tongue.

She hath looked well to the paths of her house, and hath not eaten her bread idle.

Her children rose up, and called her blessed: her husband, and he praised her.—*Prov.* xxxi. 10-12, 20, 26-28.

Depart not from a wise and good wife, whom thou hast gotten in the fear of the Lord: for the grace of her modesty is above gold.—*Ecclus.* vii. 21.

Happy is the husband of a good wife: for the number of his years is double.

A virtuous woman rejoiceth her husband, and shall fulfil the years of his life in peace.

A good wife is a good portion, she shall be given in the portion of them that fear God, to a man for his good deeds. . . .

The grace of a diligent woman shall delight her husband, and shall fat his bones.

Her discipline is the gift of God.

Such is a wise and silent woman, and there is nothing so much worth as a well instructed soul.

A holy and shamefaced woman is grace upon grace.

And no price is worthy of a continent soul.

As the sun when it riseth to the world in the high places of God, so is the beauty of a good wife for the ornament of her house.—*Ecclus.* xxvi. 1-3, 16-21.

The beauty of a woman cheereth the countenance of her husband, and a man desireth nothing more.

If she have a tongue that can cure, and likewise mitigate and show mercy: her husband is not like other men.

He that possesseth a good wife, beginneth a possession: she is a help like to himself, and a pillar of rest.

Where there is no hedge, the possession shall be spoiled: and where there is no wife, he mourneth that is in want. —*Ecclus.* xxxvi. 24-27.

Children, and the building of a city shall establish a name, but a blameless wife shall be counted above them both. —*Ecclus.* xl. 19.

WIFE TO A HUSBAND, THE DUTIES OF A

See: Marriage, duties of—page 302.

WILL OF GOD, DOING THE

See also: Obedience to God—page 344.

For the sake of the words of thy lips, I have kept hard ways.—*Ps.* xvi. 4.

Sacrifice and oblation thou didst not desire; but thou hast pierced ears for me.

Burnt offering and sin offering thou didst not require: then said I, Behold I come.

In the head of the book it is written of me that I should do thy will: O my God, I have desired it, and thy law in the midst of my heart.—*Ps.* xxxix. 7-9.

Teach me to do thy will, for thou art my God.—*Ps.* cxlii. 10.

Every one therefore that heareth these my words, and doth them, shall be likened to a wise man that built his house upon a rock,

And the rain fell, and the floods came, and the winds blew, and they beat upon that house, and it fell not, for it was founded on a rock.—*Matt.* vii. 24, 25.

As he (Jesus) was yet speaking to the multitudes, behold his mother and his brethren stood without, seeking to speak to him.

And one said unto him: Behold thy mother and thy brethren stand without, seeking thee.

But he answering him that told him, said: Who is my mother, and who are my brethren?

And stretching forth his hand towards his disciples, he said: Behold my mother and my brethren.

For whosoever shall do the will of my Father, that is in heaven, he is my brother, and sister, and mother.—*Matt.* xii. 46-50.

And seeing him (Jesus), they wondered. And his mother said to him: Son why hast thou done so to us? behold thy father and I have sought thee sorrowing.

And he said to them: How is it that you sought me? did you not know, that I must be about my father's business? —*Luke* ii. 48, 49.

And that servant who knew the will of his lord, and prepared not himself, and did not according to his will, shall be beaten with many stripes.

But he that knew not, and did things worthy of stripes, shall be beaten with few stripes.—*Luke* xii. 47, 48.

In the meantime the disciples prayed him, saying: Rabbi, eat.

But he said to them: I have meat to eat, which you know not.

The disciples therefore said one to another: Hath any man brought him to eat?

Jesus saith to them: My meat is to do the will of him that sent me, that I may perfect his work.—*John* iv. 31-34.

Because I came down from heaven, not to do my own will, but the will of him that sent me.—*John* vi. 38.

Jesus answered them, and said: My doctrine is not mine, but his that sent me.

If any man will do the will of him; he shall know of the doctrine, whether it be of God, or whether I speak of myself.—*John* vii. 16, 17.

And he that sent me, is with me, and he hath not left me alone: for I do always the things that please him.—*John* viii. 29.

And may the God of peace, who brought again from the dead the great pastor of the sheep, our Lord Jesus Christ, in the blood of the everlasting testament,

Fit you in all goodness, that you may do his will; doing in you that which is well pleasing in his sight, through Jesus Christ, to whom is glory for ever and ever. Amen.—*Heb.* xiii. 20, 21.

WILL OF GOD, REWARD FOR DOING THE

If thou turn away thy foot from the sabbath, from doing thy own will in my holy day, and call the sabbath delightful, and the holy of the Lord glorious, and glorify him, while thou dost not thy own ways, and thy own will is not found, to speak a word:

Then shalt thou be delighted in the Lord, and I will lift thee up above the high places of the earth, and will feed thee with the inheritance of Jacob thy father. For the mouth of the Lord hath spoken it.—*Is.* lviii. 13, 14.

Not every one that saith to me, Lord, Lord, shall enter into the kingdom of heaven: but he that doth the will of my Father who is in heaven, he shall enter into the kingdom of heaven.—*Matt.* vii. 21.

Now we know that God doth not hear sinners: but if a man be a server of God, and doth his will, him he heareth. —*John* ix. 31.

For patience is necessary for you; that, doing the will of God, you may receive the promise.—*Heb.* x. 36.

And the world passeth away, and the concupiscence thereof: but he that doth the will of God, abideth for ever.— 1 *John* ii. 17.

WILL OF GOD, CONFORMITY TO THE

And the king (David) said to Sadoc: Carry back the ark of God into the city: if I shall find grace in the sight of the Lord, he will bring me again, and he will show me it, and his tabernacle.

But if he shall say to me: Thou pleasest me not: I am ready, let him do that which is good before him.— 2 *Kings* xv. 25, 26.

Neither is my house so great with God, that he should make with me an eternal covenant, firm in all things and assured. For he is all my salvation, and all my will: neither is there ought thereof that springeth not up.— 2 *Kings* xxiii. 5.

For whereas he (Tobias) had always feared God from his infancy, and kept his commandments, he repined not against God because the evil of blindness had befallen him,

But continued immovable in the fear of God, giving thanks to God all the days of his life.—*Tob.* ii. 13, 14.

And he said to her: Thou hast spoken like one of the foolish women: if we have received good things at the hand of God, why should we not receive evil? In all these things Job did not sin with his lips.—*Job* ii. 10.

Blessed is the man who hath not walked in the counsel of the ungodly, nor stood in the way of sinners, nor sat in the chair of pestilence.

But his will is in the law of the Lord, and on his law he shall meditate day and night.—*Ps.* i. 1, 2.

Whatsoever shall befall the just man, it shall not make him sad.—*Prov.* xii. 21.

Take all that shall be brought upon thee: and in thy sorrow endure, and in thy humiliation keep patience.—*Ecclus.* ii. 4.

Woe to him that gainsayeth his maker, a sherd of the earthen pots: shall the clay say to him that fashion-

eth it: What art thou making, and thy work is without hands?

Woe to him that saith to his father: Why begettest thou? and to the woman: Why dost thou bring forth?—*Is.* xlv. 9, 10.

And so much the more did they wonder, saying: He hath done all things well; he hath made both the deaf to hear, and the dumb to speak.—*Mark* vii. 37.

Now is my soul troubled. And what shall I say? Father, save me from this hour. But for this cause I came unto this hour.—*John* xii. 27.

Jesus therefore said to Peter: Put up thy sword into the scabbard. The chalice which my Father hath given me, shall I not drink it?—*John* xviii. 11.

Then Paul answered, and said: What do you mean weeping and afflicting my heart? For I am ready not only to be bound, but to die also in Jerusalem, for the name of the Lord Jesus.

And when we could not persuade him, we ceased, saying: The will of the Lord be done.—*Acts* xxi. 13, 14.

O man, who art thou that repliest against God? Shall the thing formed say to him that formed it: Why hast thou made me thus?

Or hath not the potter power over the clay, of the same lump, to make one vessel unto honor, and another unto dishonor?—*Rom.* ix. 20, 21.

And be not conformed to this world; but be reformed in the newness of your mind, that you may prove what is the good, and the acceptable, and the perfect will of God.—*Rom.* xii. 2.

For to me, to live is Christ: and to die is gain.—*Philipp.* i. 21

WILL OF GOD, A PRAYER OF CONFORMITY TO THE

So Samuel told him (Heli) all the words, and did not hide them from him. And he answered: It is the Lord: let him do what is good in his sight.— 1 *Kings* iii. 18.

And now, O Lord, do with me according to thy will, and command my spirit to be received in peace: for it is better for me to die, than to live.—*Tob.* iii. 6.

Naked came I out of my mother's womb, and naked shall I return thither: the Lord gave, and the Lord hath taken away: as it hath pleased the Lord so is it done: blessed be the name of the Lord.—*Job* i. 21.

Then said I, Behold I come.

In the head of the book it is written of me, that I should do thy will: O my God, I have desired it, and thy law in the midst of my heart.—*Ps.* xxxix. 8, 9.

We have rejoiced for the days in which thou hast humbled us: for the years in which we have seen evils.—*Ps.* lxxxix. 15.

My heart is ready, O God, my heart is ready: I will sing, and will give praise, with my glory.—*Ps.* cvii. 2.

Nevertheless as it shall be the will of God in heaven, so be it done.—1 *Mach.* iii. 60.

Thy will be done on earth as it is in heaven.—*Matt.* vi. 10.

And going a little further, he fell upon his face, praying, and saying: My Father, if it be possible, let this chalice pass from me. Nevertheless not as I will, but as thou wilt. . . .

Again the second time, he went and prayed, saying: My Father, if this chalice may not pass away, but I must drink it, thy will be done.—*Matt.* xxvi. 39, 42.

And Mary said: Behold the handmaid of the Lord; be it done to me according to thy word.—*Luke* i. 38.

WILL OF GOD, USELESSNESS OF OPPOSITION TO THE

See also: Powerlessness before God, man's—page 389.

And he (Joseph) answered them: Fear not: can we resist the will of God?

You thought evil against me: but God turned it into good, that he might exalt me, as at present you see, and might save many people.—*Gen.* l. 19, 20.

O Adonai, Lord, great art thou, and glorious in thy power, and no one can overcome thee.

Let all thy creatures serve thee: because thou hast spoken, and they were made: thou didst send forth thy spirit, and they were created, and there is no one that can resist thy voice.—*Judith* xvi. 16, 17.

O Lord, Lord, almighty king, for all things are in thy power, and there is none that can resist thy will, if thou determine to save Israel.

Thou hast made heaven and earth, and all things that are under the cope of heaven.

Thou art Lord of all, and there is none that can resist thy majesty.—*Esther* xiii. 9-11.

He is wise in heart, and mighty in strength: who hath resisted him, and hath had peace?—*Job* ix. 4.

For he is alone, and no man can turn away his thought: and whatsoever his soul hath desired, that hath he done.—*Job* xxiii. 13.

But our God is in heaven: he hath done all things whatsoever he would.—*Ps.* cxiii. (*Heb.* cxv.) 3.

There are many thoughts in the heart of a man: but the will of the Lord shall stand firm.—*Prov.* xix. 21.

There is no wisdom, there is no prudence, there is no counsel against the Lord.—*Prov.* xxi. 30.

For the Lord of hosts hath decreed, and who can disannul it? and his hand is stretched out: and who shall turn it away?—*Is.* xiv. 27.

Therefore shall he say: In the Lord are my justices and empire: they shall come to him, and all that resist him shall be confounded.—*Is.* xlv. 25.

Remember the former age, for I am God, and there is no God beside, neither is there the like to me:

Who show from the beginning the things that shall be at last, and from ancient times the things that as yet are not done, saying: My counsel shall stand, and all my will shall be done:

Who call a bird from the east, and from a far country the man of my own will, and I have spoken, and will bring it to pass: I have created, and I will do it.

Hear me, O ye hardhearted, who are far from justice.—*Is.* xlvi. 9-11.

So shall my word be, which shall go forth from my mouth: it shall not return to me void, but it shall do whatsoever I please, and shall prosper in the things for which I sent it.—*Is.* lv. 11.

And all the inhabitants of the earth are reputed as nothing before him: for he doth according to his will, as well with the powers of heaven, as among the inhabitants of the earth: and there is none that can resist his hand, and say to him: Why hast thou done it?—*Dan.* iv. 32.

And now, therefore, I say to you, refrain from these men, and let them alone; for if this council or this work be of men, it will come to nought:

But if it be of God, you cannot overthrow it, lest perhaps you be found even to fight against God.—*Acts* v. 38, 39.

And falling on the ground, he heard a voice saying to him: Saul, Saul, why persecutest thou me?

Who said: Who art thou, Lord? And he: I am Jesus whom thou persecutest. It is hard for thee to kick against the goad.—*Acts* ix. 4, 5.

WILL TO US, GOD HAS MADE KNOWN HIS

See also: Teacher, God our—page 550.

Thou hast made known to me the ways of life, thou shalt fill me with joy with thy countenance: at thy right hand are delights even to the end.—*Ps.* xv. 11.

He hath made his ways known to Moses: his wills to the children of Israel.—*Ps.* cii. 7.

We are happy, O Israel: because the things that are pleasing to God, are made known to us.—*Bar.* iv. 4.

For this is the will of God, your sanctification; that you should abstain from fornication;

That every one of you should know how to possess his vessel in sanctification and honor:

Not in the passion of lust, like the Gentiles that know not God:

And that no man overreach, nor circumvent his brother in business: because the Lord is the avenger of all these things, as we have told you before, and have testified.

For God hath not called us unto un-cleanness, but unto sanctification.—1 *Thess.* iv. 3-7.

WILL, GOD DESIRES AND ACCEPTS OUR GOOD

For if the will be forward, it is accepted according to that which a man hath, not according to that which he hath not.—2 *Cor.* viii. 12.

WILL, BAD

See: Desires, evil—page 107.

WILLINGNESS AND CHEERFULNESS IN DOING GOOD

See also: Service of God should be willing—page 512.

And the people rejoiced, when they promised their offerings willingly: because they offered them to the Lord with all their heart: and David the king rejoiced also with a great joy.—1 *Paral.* xxix. 9.

I know, my God, that thou provest hearts, and lovest simplicity, wherefore I also in the simplicity of my heart, have joyfully offered all these things: and I have seen with great joy thy people, which are here present, offer thee their offerings.—1 *Paral.* xxix. 17.

According to thy ability be merciful. If thou have much, give abundantly: if thou have little, take care even so to bestow willingly a little.—*Tob.* iv. 8, 9.

My son, in thy good deeds, make no complaint, and when thou givest any thing, add not grief by an evil word.

Shall not the dew assuage the heat? so also the good word is better than the gift.

Lo, is not a word better than a gift? but both are with a justified man.—*Ecclus.* xviii. 15-17.

In every gift show a cheerful countenance, and sanctify thy tithes with joy.

Give to the most High, according to what he hath given to thee, and with a good eye, do according to the ability of thy hands.—*Ecclus.* xxxv. 11, 12.

And when you fast, be not as the hypocrites, sad. For they disfigure their faces, that they may appear unto men to fast. Amen I say to you, they have received their reward.

But thou, when thou fastest anoint thy head, and wash thy face;

That thou appear not to men to fast, but to thy Father who is in secret: and thy Father who seeth in secret, will repay thee.—*Matt.* vi. 16-18.

Now this I say: He who soweth sparingly, shall also reap sparingly: and he who soweth in blessings, shall also reap blessings.

Every one as he hath determined in his heart, not with sadness, or of necessity: for God loveth a cheerful giver.— 2 *Cor.* ix. 6, 7.

And do ye all things without murmurings and hesitations;

That you may be blameless and sincere children of God, without reproof, in the midst of a crooked and perverse generation; among whom you shine as lights in the world.—*Philipp.* ii. 14, 15.

WINE, ABSTINENCE FROM

See: Abstinence—page 12.

WISDOM, TRUE

You know that I have taught you statutes and justices, as the Lord my God hath commanded me: so shall you do them in the land which you shall possess:

And you shall observe, and fulfil them in practice. For this is your wisdom, and understanding in the sight of nations, that hearing all these precepts, they may say: Behold a wise and understanding people, a great nation.—*Deut.* iv. 5, 6.

O that they would be wise and would understand, and would provide for their last end.—*Deut.* xxxii. 29.

And he said to man: Behold the fear of the Lord, that is wisdom: and to depart from evil, is understanding.—*Job* xxviii. 28.

Who is wise, and will keep these things; and will understand the mercies of the Lord?—*Ps.* cvi. 43.

Through thy commandments, thou hast made me wiser than my enemies: for it is ever with me.

I have understood more than all my teachers: because thy testimonies are my meditation.

I have had understanding above ancients: because I have sought thy commandments.

. . . By thy commandments I have had understanding: therefore have I hated every way of iniquity.—*Ps.* cxviii. 98-100, 104.

Doth not wisdom cry aloud, and prudence put forth her voice?

Standing in the top of the highest places by the way, in the midst of the paths,

Beside the gates of the city, in the very doors she speaketh, saying: . . .

My mouth shall meditate truth, and my lips shall hate wickedness.

All my words are just, there is nothing wicked nor perverse in them.

They are right to them that understand, and just to them that find knowledge.—*Prov.* viii. 1-3, 7-9.

The root of wisdom is to fear the Lord: and the branches thereof are long lived.—*Ecclus.* i. 25.

A wise heart, and which hath understanding, will abstain from sins, and in the works of justice shall have success.—*Ecclus.* iii. 32.

The perfection of the fear of God is wisdom and understanding.—*Ecclus.* xxi. 13.

A wise man hateth not the commandments and justices, and he shall not be dashed in pieces as a ship in a storm.

A man of understanding is faithful to the law of God, and the law is faithful to him.—*Ecclus.* xxxiii. 2, 3.

There is a wise man that is wise to his own soul: and the fruit of his understanding is commendable.—*Ecclus.* xxxvii. 25.

Thus saith the Lord: Let not the wise man glory in his wisdom. . . .

But let him that glorieth, glory in this, that he understandeth and knoweth me, for I am the Lord that exercise mercy, and judgment, and justice in the earth: for these things please me, saith the Lord.—*Jer.* ix. 23, 24.

For the wisdom of the flesh is death; but the wisdom of the spirit is life and peace.—*Rom.* viii. 6.

For I say, by the grace that is given me, to all that are among you, not to be more wise than it behoveth to be wise, but to be wise unto sobriety, and according as God hath divided to every one the measure of faith.—*Rom.* xii. 3.

But I would have you to be wise in good, and simple in evil.—*Rom.* xvi. 19.

For I judged not myself to know any thing among you, but Jesus Christ, and him crucified. . . .

And my speech and my preaching was not in the persuasive words of human wisdom, but in showing of the Spirit and power;

That your faith might not stand on the wisdom of men, but on the power of God.

Howbeit we speak wisdom among the perfect: yet not the wisdom of this world, neither of the princes of this world that come to nought;

But we speak the wisdom of God in a mystery, a wisdom which is hidden, which God ordained before the world, unto our glory:

Which none of the princes of the world knew; for if they had known it, they would never have crucified the Lord of glory.—1 *Cor.* ii. 2, 4-8.

See therefore, brethren, how you walk circumspectly: not as unwise,

But as wise: redeeming the time, because the days are evil.

Wherefore become not unwise, but understanding what is the will of God. —*Eph.* v. 15-17.

And this I pray, that your charity may more and more abound in knowledge, and in all understanding:

That you may approve the better things, that you may be sincere and without offence unto the day of Christ. —*Philipp.* i. 9, 10.

But the wisdom, that is from above, first indeed is chaste, then peaceable, modest, easy to be persuaded, consenting to the good, full of mercy and good fruits, without judging, without dissimulation.—*James* iii. 17.

WISDOM, THE EXCELLENCE AND VALUE OF

But where is wisdom to be found, and where is the place of understanding?

Man knoweth not the price thereof,

neither is it found in the land of them that live in delights. . . .

The finest gold shall not purchase it, neither shall silver be weighed in exchange for it.

It shall not be compared with the dyed colors of India, or with the most precious stone sardonyx, or the sapphire.

Gold or crystal cannot equal it, neither shall any vessels of gold be changed for it.

High and eminent things shall not be mentioned in comparison of it: but wisdom is drawn out of secret places.

The topaz of Ethiopia shall not be equal to it, neither shall it be compared to the cleanest dyeing.—*Job* xxviii. 12, 13, 15-19.

Blessed is the man that findeth wisdom and is rich in prudence:

The purchasing thereof is better than the merchandise of silver, and her fruit, than the chiefest and purest gold:

She is more precious than all riches: and all the things that are desired, are not to be compared with her.

Length of days is in her right hand, and in her left hand riches and glory.

Her ways are beautiful ways, and all her paths are peaceable.

She is a tree of life to them that lay hold on her: and he that shall retain her is blessed.—*Prov.* iii. 13-18.

For wisdom is better than all the most precious things: and whatsoever may be desired cannot be compared to it. . . .

With me are riches and glory, glorious riches and justice.

For my fruit is better than gold and the precious stone, and my blossoms than choice silver.—*Prov.* viii. 11, 18, 19.

And I saw that wisdom excelled folly, as much as light differeth from darkness.—*Eccles.* ii. 13.

Wisdom is better than strength, and a wise man is better than a strong man. —*Wis.* vi. 1.

Wherefore I wished, and understanding was given me: and I called upon God, and the spirit of wisdom came upon me:

And I preferred her before kingdoms

and thrones, and esteemed riches nothing in comparison of her.

Neither did I compare unto her any precious stone: for all gold in comparison of her, is as a little sand, and silver in respect to her shall be counted as clay.

I loved her above health and beauty, and chose to have her instead of light: for her light cannot be put out.—*Wis.* vii. 7-10.

For she (wisdom) is a vapor of the power of God, and a certain pure emanation of the glory of the almighty God: and therefore no defiled thing cometh into her.

For she is the brightness of eternal light, and the unspotted mirror of God's majesty, and the image of his goodness. . . . For she is more beautiful than the sun, and above all the order of the stars: being compared with the light, she is found before it.—*Wis.* vii. 25, 26, 29.

For it is she that teacheth the knowledge of God, and is the chooser of his works.

And if riches be desired in life, what is richer than wisdom, which maketh all things?

And if sense do work: who is a more artful worker than she of those things that are?

And if a man love justice: her labors have great virtues; for she teacheth temperance, and prudence, and justice, and fortitude, which are such things as men can have nothing more profitable in life.

And if a man desire much knowledge: she knoweth things past, and judgeth of things to come: she knoweth the subtilties of speeches, and the solutions of arguments: she knoweth signs and wonders before they be done, and the events of times and ages.

I purposed therefore to take her to me to live with me: knowing that she will communicate to me of her good things, and will be a comfort in my cares and grief.—*Wis.* viii. 4-9.

When I go into my house, I shall repose myself with her: for her conversation hath no bitterness, nor her company any tediousness, but joy and gladness.

Thinking these things with myself, and pondering them in my heart, that to be allied to wisdom is immortality,

And that there is great delight in her friendship, and inexhaustible riches in the works of her hands, and in the exercise of conference with her, wisdom, and glory in the communication of her words: I went about seeking, that I might take her to myself.—*Wis.* viii. 16-18.

WISDOM, THE POWER AND EFFICACY OF

Eat honey, my son, because it is good, and the honeycomb most sweet to thy throat:

So also is the doctrine of wisdom to thy soul: which when thou hast found, thou shalt have hope in the end, and thy hope shall not perish.—*Prov.* xxiv. 13, 14.

Wisdom with riches is more profitable, and bringeth more advantage to them that see the sun.

For as wisdom is a defence, so money is a defence: but learning and wisdom excel in this, that they give life to him that possesseth them.—*Eccles.* vii. 12, 13.

Now all good things came to me together with her, and innumerable riches through her hands,

And I rejoiced in all these: for this wisdom went before me, and I knew not that she was the mother of them all.

Which I have learned without guile, and communicate without envy, and her riches I hide not.

For she is an infinite treasure to men! which they that use, become the friends of God, being commended for the gift of discipline.—*Wis.* vii. 11-14.

For wisdom is more active than all active things: and reacheth everywhere by reason of her purity.

. . . And being but one, she can do all things: and remaining in herself the same, she reneweth all things, and through nations conveyeth herself into holy souls, she maketh the friends of God and prophets.

For God loveth none but him that dwelleth with wisdom.—*Wis.* vii. 24, 27, 28.

For after this cometh night, but no evil can overcome wisdom.—*Wis.* vii. 30.

She (wisdom) reacheth therefore from end to end mightily, and ordereth all things sweetly.—*Wis.* viii. 1.

Moreover by the means of her, I shall have immortality: and shall leave behind me an everlasting memory to them that come after me.—*Wis.* viii. 13.

And who shall know thy thought, except thou give wisdom, and send thy Holy Spirit from above:

And so the ways of them that are upon earth may be corrected, and men may learn the things that please thee?

For by wisdom they were healed, whosoever have pleased thee, O Lord, from the beginning.—*Wis.* ix. 17-19.

But wisdom hath delivered from sorrow them that attend upon her.—*Wis.* x. 9.

For wisdom opened the mouth of the dumb, and made the tongues of infants eloquent.—*Wis.* x. 21.

Wisdom shall distribute knowledge, and understanding of prudence: and exalteth the glory of them that hold her.—*Ecclus.* i. 24.

Wisdom inspireth life into her children, and protecteth them that seek after her, and will go before them in the way of justice.

And he that loveth her, loveth life: and they that watch for her, shall embrace her sweetness.

They that hold her fast, shall inherit life: and whithersoever she entereth, God will give a blessing.

They that serve her, shall be servants to the holy one: and God loveth them that love her.

He that hearkeneth to her, shall judge nations: and he that looketh upon her, shall remain secure.—*Ecclus.* iv. 12-16.

For the wisdom of doctrine is according to her name, and she is not manifest unto many, but with them to whom she is known, she continueth even to the sight of God.—*Ecclus.* vi. 23.

Search for her, and she shall be made known to thee, and when thou hast gotten her, let her not go:

For in the latter end thou shalt find rest in her, and she shall be turned to thy joy.

Then shall her fetters be a strong defence for thee, and a firm foundation, and her chain a robe of glory:

For in her is the beauty of life, and her bands are a healthful binding.

Thou shalt put her on as a robe of glory, and thou shalt set her upon thee as a crown of joy.—*Ecclus.* vi. 28-32.

Wisdom shall praise her own self, and shall be honored in God, and shall glory in the midst of her people. . . .

And in the multitude of the elect she shall have praise, and among the blessed she shall be blessed, saying: . . .

I am the mother of fair love, and of fear, and of knowledge, and of holy hope.

In me is all grace of the way and of the truth, in me is all hope of life and of virtue.

Come over to me, all ye that desire me, and be filled with my fruits.

For my spirit is sweet above honey, and my inheritance above honey and the honeycomb.

My memory is unto everlasting generations.

They that eat me, shall yet hunger: and they that drink me, shall yet thirst.

He that hearkeneth to me, shall not be confounded: and they that work by me, shall not sin.

They that explain me, shall have life everlasting.—*Ecclus.* xxiv. 1, 4, 24-31.

Learn where is wisdom, where is strength, where is understanding: that thou mayst know also where is length of days and life, where is the light of the eyes, and peace.—*Bar.* iii. 14.

But they that are learned shall shine as the brightness of the firmament.—*Dan.* xii. 3.

WISDOM, THE DESIRE AND LOVE OF

For if thou shalt call for wisdom, and incline thy heart to prudence:

If thou shalt seek her as money, and shalt dig for her as for a treasure:

Then shalt thou understand the fear of the Lord, and shalt find the knowledge of God.—*Prov.* ii. 3-5.

If wisdom shall enter into thy heart, and knowledge please thy soul:

Counsel shall keep thee, and prudence shall preserve thee,

That thou mayst be delivered from the evil way, and from the man that speaketh perverse things.—*Prov.* ii. 10-12.

Blessed is the man that heareth me, and that watcheth daily at my gates, and waiteth at the posts of my doors.

He that shall find me, shall find life, and shall have salvation from the Lord.

But he that shall sin against me, shall hurt his own soul. All that hate me love death.—*Prov.* viii. 34-36.

Wisdom is glorious, and never fadeth away, and is easily seen by them that love her, and is found by them that seek her.

She preventeth them that covet her, so that she first showeth herself unto them.

He that awaketh early to seek her, shall not labor: for he shall find her sitting at his door.

To think therefore upon her, is perfect understanding: and he that watcheth for her, shall quickly be secure.

For she goeth about seeking such as are worthy of her, and she showeth herself to them cheerfully in the ways, and meeteth them with all providence.

For the beginning of her is the most true desire of discipline.

And the care of discipline is love: and love is the keeping of her laws: and the keeping of her laws is the firm foundation of incorruption:

And incorruption bringeth near to God.

Therefore the desire of wisdom bringeth to the everlasting kingdom.—*Wis.* vi. 13-21.

Wherefore I wished, and understanding was given me: and I called upon God, and the spirit of wisdom came upon me.—*Wis.* vii. 7.

Her have I loved, and have sought her out from my youth, and have desired to take her for my spouse, and I became a lover of her beauty.—*Wis.* viii. 2.

In the treasures of wisdom is understanding, and religiousness of knowledge: but to sinners wisdom is an abomination.—*Ecclus.* i. 26.

Son, if thou desire wisdom, keep justice, and God will give her to thee.—*Ecclus.* i. 33.

Let thy thoughts be upon the precepts of God, and meditate continually on his commandments: and he will give thee a heart, and the desire of wisdom shall be given to thee.—*Ecclus.* vi. 37.

When I was yet young, before I wandered about, I sought for wisdom openly in my prayer.

I prayed for her before the temple, and unto the very end I will seek after her, and she flourished as a grape soon ripe.

My heart delighted in her, my foot walked in the right way, from my youth up I sought after her.

I bowed down my ear a little, and received her.—*Ecclus.* li. 18-21.

But if any of you want wisdom, let him ask of God, who giveth to all men abundantly, and upbraideth not; and it shall be given him.—*James* i. 5.

WISDOM, EXHORTATION TO LOVE AND SEEK

Wisdom preacheth abroad, she uttereth her voice in the streets:

At the head of multitudes she crieth out, in the entrance of the gates of the city she uttereth her words, saying:

O children, how long will you love childishness, and fools covet those things which are hurtful to themselves, and the unwise hate knowledge?

Turn ye at my reproof: behold I will utter my spirit to you, and will show you my words. . . .

But he that shall hear me, shall rest without terror, and shall enjoy abundance, without fear of evils.—*Prov.* i. 20-23, 33.

Get wisdom, get prudence: forget not, neither decline from the words of my mouth.

Forsake her not, and she shall keep thee: love her, and she shall preserve thee.

The beginning of wisdom, get wisdom, and with all thy possession purchase prudence.

Take hold on her, and she shall exalt thee: thou shalt be glorified by her, when thou shalt embrace her.—*Prov.* iv. 5-8.

Say to wisdom: Thou art my sister: and call prudence thy friend.—*Prov.* vii. 4.

Doth not wisdom cry aloud, and prudence put forth her voice?

Standing in the top of the highest places by the way, in the midst of the paths,

Beside the gates of the city, in the very doors she speaketh, saying. . . .

Receive my instruction, and not money: choose knowledge rather than gold.—*Prov.* viii. 1-3, 10.

Wisdom hath built herself a house, she hath hewn her out seven pillars.

She hath slain her victims, mingled her wine, and set forth her table.

She hath sent her maids to invite to the tower, and to the walls of the city:

Whosoever is a little one, let him come to me. And to the unwise she said:

Come, eat my bread, and drink the wine which I have mingled for you.

Forsake childishness, and live, and walk by the ways of prudence.—*Prov.* ix. 1-6.

Get wisdom, because it is better than gold: and purchase prudence, for it is more precious than silver.—*Prov.* xvi. 16.

Study wisdom, my son, and make my heart joyful, that thou mayst give an answer to him that reproacheth.—*Prov.* xxvii. 11.

Give ear, my son, and take wise counsel, and cast not away my advice.

Put thy feet into her fetters, and thy neck into her chains:

Bow down thy shoulder, and bear her, and be not grieved with her bands.

Come to her with all thy mind, and keep her ways with all thy power.

Search for her, and she shall be made known to thee, and when thou hast gotten her, let her not go:

For in the latter end thou shalt find rest in her, and she shall be turned to thy joy.—*Ecclus.* vi. 24-29.

Wisdom shall praise her own self, and shall be honored in God, and shall glory in the midst of her people. . . .

And in the multitude of the elect she shall have praise, and among the blessed she shall be blessed, saying: . . .

Come over to me, all ye that desire me, and be filled with my fruits.

For my spirit is sweet above honey, and my inheritance above honey and the honeycomb.—*Ecclus.* xxiv. 1, 4, 26, 27.

Draw near to me, ye unlearned, and gather yourselves together into the house of discipline.

Why are ye slow? and what do you say of these things? your souls are exceeding thirsty.

I have opened my mouth, and have spoken: buy her for yourselves without silver,

And submit your neck to the yoke, and let your soul receive discipline: for she is near at hand to be found.—*Ecclus.* li. 31-34.

WISDOM IS FROM GOD, ALL

But where is wisdom to be found, and where is the place of understanding? . . .

The depth saith: It is not in me: and the sea saith: It is not with me. . . .

Whence then cometh wisdom? and where is the place of understanding? . . .

God understandeth the way of it, and he knoweth the place thereof.—*Job* xxviii. 12, 14, 20, 23.

Who hath put wisdom in the heart of man? or who gave the cock understanding?—*Job* xxxviii. 36.

He that chastiseth nations, shall he not rebuke: he that teacheth man knowledge?—*Ps.* xciii. 10.

And God hath given to me to speak as I would, and to conceive thoughts worthy of those things that are given me: because he is the guide of wisdom, and the director of the wise:

For in his hand are both we, and our words, and all wisdom, and the knowledge and skill of works.

For he hath given me the true knowledge of the things that are: to know the disposition of the whole world, and the virtues of the elements,

The beginning, and ending, and midst of the times, the alterations of their courses, and the changes of seasons,

The revolutions of the year, and the dispositions of the stars,

The natures of living creatures, and rage of wild beasts, the force of winds, and reasonings of men, the diversities of plants, and the virtues of roots,

And all such things as are hid and not foreseen, I have learned: for wisdom, which is the worker of all things, taught me.—*Wis.* vii. 15-21.

All wisdom is from the Lord God, and hath been always with him, and is before all time. . . .

Wisdom hath been created before all things, and the understanding of prudence from everlasting.

. . . He created her in the Holy Ghost, and saw her, and numbered her, and measured her.—*Ecclus.* i. 1, 4, 9.

Wisdom and discipline, and the knowledge of the law are with God.—*Ecclus.* xi. 15.

For wisdom came forth from God.—*Ecclus.* xv. 10.

Wisdom shall praise her own self, and shall be honored in God, and shall glory in the midst of her people. . . .

And in the multitude of the elect she shall have praise, and among the blessed she shall be blessed, saying:

I came out of the mouth of the most High, the first born before all creatures.—*Ecclus.* xxiv. 1, 4, 5.

Learn where is wisdom, where is strength, where is understanding: that thou mayst know also where is length of days and life, where is the light of the eyes, and peace.—*Bar.* iii. 14.

Who hath gone up into heaven, and taken her, and brought her down from the clouds?

Who hath passed over the sea, and found her, and brought her preferably to chosen gold?

There is none that is able to know her ways, nor that can search out her paths:

But he that knoweth all things, knoweth her, and hath found her out with his understanding: he that prepared the earth for evermore, and filled it with cattle and fourfooted beasts.—*Bar.* iii. 29-32.

To God, the only wise, through Jesus Christ, to whom be honor and glory for ever and ever. Amen.—*Rom.* xvi. 27.

That their hearts may be comforted, being instructed in charity, and unto all riches of fulness of understanding, unto the knowledge of the mystery of God the Father and of Christ Jesus:

In whom are hid all the treasures of wisdom and knowledge.—*Col.* ii. 2, 3.

WISDOM THE GIFT OF GOD

But, as I see, there is a spirit in men, and the inspiration of the Almighty giveth understanding.—*Job* xxxii. 8.

I will bless the Lord, who hath given me understanding.—*Ps.* xv. 7.

I will give thee understanding, and I will instruct thee in this way, in which thou shalt go: I will fix my eyes upon thee.—*Ps.* xxxi. 8.

Because the Lord giveth wisdom: and out of his mouth cometh prudence and knowledge.—*Prov.* ii. 6.

Wherefore I wished, and understanding was given me: and I called upon God, and the spirit of wisdom came upon me.—*Wis.* vii. 7.

Thinking these things with myself, and pondering them in my heart, that to be allied to wisdom is immortality. . . .

And as I knew that I could not otherwise be continent, except God gave it, and this also was a point of wisdom, to know whose gift it was: I went to the Lord, and besought him.—*Wis.* viii. 17, 21.

God created man of the earth, and made him after his own image. . . .

He created of him a helpmate like to himself: he gave them counsel, and a tongue, and eyes, and ears, and a heart to devise: and he filled them with the knowledge of understanding.

He created in them the science of the spirit, he filled their heart with wisdom, and showed them both good and evil.—*Ecclus.* xvii. 1, 5, 6.

For if it shall please the great Lord, he will fill him with the spirit of understanding.—*Ecclus.* xxxix. 8.

To him that giveth me wisdom, will I give glory.—*Ecclus.* li. 23.

And speaking, he (Daniel) said: Blessed be the name of the Lord from eternity and for evermore: for wisdom and fortitude are his.

And he changeth times and ages:

taketh away kingdoms and establisheth them, giveth wisdom to the wise, and knowledge to them that have understanding.

He revealeth deep and hidden things, and knoweth what is in darkness: and light is with him.—*Dan.* ii. 20-22.

Lay it up therefore in your hearts, not to meditate before how you shall answer:

For I will give you a mouth and wisdom, which all your adversaries shall not be able to resist and gainsay. —*Luke* xxi. 14, 15.

But if any of you want wisdom, let him ask of God, who giveth to all men abundantly, and upbraideth not; and it shall be given him.—*James* i. 5.

WISDOM GIVEN TO THE JUST, BUT REFUSED TO THE WICKED

For wisdom will not enter into a malicious soul, nor dwell in a body subject to sins.—*Wis.* i. 4.

And who shall know thy thought, except thou give wisdom, and send thy Holy Spirit from above:

And so the ways of them that are upon earth may be corrected, and men may learn the things that please thee?

For by wisdom they were healed, whosoever have pleased thee, O Lord, from the beginning.—*Wis.* ix. 17-19.

All wisdom is from the Lord God, and hath been always with him, and is before all time.

. . . And he poured her out upon all his works, and upon all flesh according to his gift, and hath given her to them that love him.—*Ecclus.* i. 1, 10.

The fear of the Lord is the beginning of wisdom, and was created with the faithful in the womb, it walketh with chosen women, and is known with the just and faithful.—*Ecclus.* i. 16.

Son, if thou desire wisdom, keep justice, and God will give her to thee.— *Ecclus.* i. 33.

But the Lord hath made all things, and to the godly he hath given wisdom. —*Ecclus.* xliii. 37.

There were the giants, those renowned men that were from the beginning, of great stature, expert in war.

The Lord chose not them, neither did they find the way of knowledge: therefore did they perish.

And because they had not wisdom, they perished through their folly.— *Bar.* iii. 26-28.

WISDOM, A PRAYER FOR

And now, O Lord God, thou hast made thy servant king instead of David my father: and I am but a child, and know not how to go out and come in. . . .

Give therefore to thy servant an understanding heart, to judge thy people, and discern between good and evil.— 3 *Kings* iii. 7, 9.

Give me wisdom and knowledge, that I may come in and go out before thy people: for who can worthily judge this thy people, which is so great?— 2 *Paral.* i. 10.

Give to the king thy judgment, O God; and to the king's son thy justice: To judge thy people with justice, and thy poor with judgment.—*Ps.* lxxi. 2.

Thy testimonies are justice for ever: give me understanding, and I shall live. —*Ps.* cxviii. 144.

God of my fathers, and Lord of mercy, who hast made all things with thy word,

And by thy wisdom hast appointed man, that he should have dominion over the creature that was made by thee,

That he should order the world according to equity and justice, and execute justice with an upright heart:

Give me wisdom, that sitteth by thy throne, and cast me not off from among thy children.

. . . For if one be perfect among the children of men, yet if thy wisdom be not with him, he shall be nothing regarded. . . .

And hardly do we guess aright at things that are upon earth: and with labor do we find the things that are before us. But the things that are in heaven, who shall search out?

And who shall know thy thought, except thou give wisdom, and send thy Holy Spirit from above.—*Wis.* ix. 1-4, 6, 16, 17.

That the God of our Lord Jesus

Christ, the Father of glory, may give unto you the spirit of wisdom and of revelation, in the knowledge of him: The eyes of your heart enlightened, that you may know what the hope is of his calling, and what are the riches of the glory of his inheritance in the saints.—*Eph.* i. 17, 18.

WISDOM, FALSE

Wherefore I will pray to the Lord, and address my speech to God: . . . Who catcheth the wise in their craftiness, and disappointeth the counsel of the wicked.—*Job* v. 8, 13.

Be not over just: and be not more wise than is necessary, lest thou become stupid.—*Eccles.* vii. 17.

But the learning of wickedness is not wisdom: and the device of sinners is not prudence.—*Ecclus.* xix. 19.

But there is a wisdom that aboundeth in evil: and there is no understanding where there is bitterness.—*Ecclus.* xxi. 15.

He that speaketh sophistically, is hateful: he shall be destitute of every thing.

Grace is not given him from the Lord: for he is deprived of all wisdom.—*Ecclus.* xxxvii. 23, 24.

Woe to you that are wise in your own eyes, and prudent in your own conceits.—*Is.* v. 21.

For my foolish people have not known me: they are foolish and senseless children: they are wise to do evil, but to do good they have no knowledge.—*Jer.* iv. 22.

How do you say: We are wise, and the law of the Lord is with us? Indeed the lying pen of the scribes hath wrought falsehood.

The wise men are confounded, they are dismayed, and taken: for they have cast away the word of the law, and there is no wisdom in them.—*Jer.* viii. 8, 9.

Every man is become foolish by his knowledge: every founder is confounded by his idol, for what he hath cast is a lie, and there is no breath in them.—*Jer.* li. 17.

Take heed, therefore, that the light which is in thee, be not darkness.—*Luke* xi. 35.

For the wisdom of the flesh is death; but the wisdom of the spirit is life and peace.

Because the wisdom of the flesh is an enemy to God; for it is not subject to the law of God, neither can it be.—*Rom.* viii. 6, 7.

For I say, by the grace that is given me, to all that are among you, not to be more wise than it behoveth to be wise, but to be wise unto sobriety, and according as God hath divided to every one the measure of faith. . . .

Not minding high things, but consenting to the humble. Be not wise in your own conceits.—*Rom.* xii. 3, 16.

Beware lest any man cheat you by philosophy, and vain deceit; according to the tradition of men, according to the elements of the world, and not according to Christ.—*Col.* ii. 8.

But if you have bitter zeal, and there be contentions in your hearts; glory not, and be not liars against the truth.

For this is not wisdom, descending from above: but earthly, sensual, devilish.—*James* iii. 14, 15.

WISDOM OF THE WORLD, THE

The children of Agar also, that search after the wisdom that is of the earth, the merchants of Merrha, and of Theman, and the tellers of fables, and searchers of prudence and understanding: but the way of wisdom they have not known, neither have they remembered her paths.—*Bar.* iii. 23.

At that time Jesus answered and said: I confess to thee, O Father, Lord of heaven and earth, because thou hast hid these things from the wise and prudent, and hast revealed them to little ones.

Yea, Father; for so hath it seemed good in thy sight.—*Matt.* xi. 25, 26.

And the lord commended the unjust steward, forasmuch as he had done wisely: for the children of this world are wiser in their generation than the children of light.—*Luke* xvi. 8.

For it is written: I will destroy the wisdom of the wise, and the prudence of the prudent I will reject.

Where is the wise? Where is the

scribe? Where is the disputer of this world? Hath not God made foolish the wisdom of this world?

For seeing that in the wisdom of God the world, by wisdom, knew not God, it pleased God, by the foolishness of our preaching, to save them that believe.—1 *Cor.* i. 19-21.

Let no man deceive himself: if any man among you seem to be wise in this world, let him become a fool, that he may be wise.

For the wisdom of this world is foolishness with God. For it is written: I will catch the wise in their own craftiness.

And again: The Lord knoweth the thoughts of the wise, that they are vain. —1 *Cor.* iii. 18-20.

Know you not that they that run in the race, all run indeed, but one receiveth the prize? So run that you may obtain.

And every one that striveth for the mastery, refraineth himself from all things: and they indeed that they may receive a corruptible crown; but we an incorruptible one.—1 *Cor.* ix. 24, 25.

WISDOM OF GOD, THE

See also: Omniscience of God— page 356.

He is wise in heart, and mighty in strength: who hath resisted him, and hath had peace?—*Job* ix. 4.

With him is wisdom and strength, he hath counsel and understanding.—*Job* xii. 13.

Who can declare the order of the heavens, or who can make the harmony of heaven to sleep?—*Job* xxxviii. 37.

O Lord, how great are thy works! thy thoughts are exceeding deep.—*Ps.* xci. 6.

How great are thy works, O Lord? thou hast made all things in wisdom: the earth is filled with thy riches.—*Ps.* ciii. 24.

Great is our Lord, and great is his power: and of his wisdom there is no number.—*Ps.* cxlvi. 5.

The Lord by wisdom hath founded the earth, hath established the heavens by prudence.

By his wisdom the depths have broken out, and the clouds grow thick with dew.—*Prov.* iii. 19, 20.

God of my fathers, and Lord of mercy, who hast made all things with thy word,

And by thy wisdom hast appointed man, that he should have dominion over the creature that was made by thee.—*Wis.* ix. 1, 2.

Who hath searched out the wisdom of God that goeth before all things? —*Ecclus.* i. 3.

For the wisdom of God is great, and he is strong in power, seeing all men without ceasing.—*Ecclus.* xv. 19.

For her (wisdom's) thoughts are more vast than the sea, and her counsels more deep than the great ocean.— *Ecclus.* xxiv. 39.

Who hath forwarded the spirit of the Lord? or who hath been his counsellor, and hath taught him?

With whom hath he consulted, and who hath instructed him, and taught him the path of justice, and taught him knowledge, and showed him the way of understanding?

. . . Knowest thou not, or hast thou not heard? the Lord is the everlasting God, who hath created the ends of the earth: he shall not faint, nor labor, neither is there any searching out of his wisdom.—*Is.* xl. 13, 14, 28.

He that maketh the earth by his power, that prepareth the world by his wisdom, and stretcheth out the heavens by his knowledge.—*Jer.* x. 12.

O the depth of the riches of the wisdom and of the knowledge of God! How incomprehensible are his judgments, and how unsearchable his ways! —*Rom.* xi. 33.

To God the only wise, through Jesus Christ, to whom be honor and glory for ever and ever. Amen.—*Rom.* xvi. 27.

WITHDRAW FROM US FOR A WHILE, GOD SEEMS TO

See also: Desolation of spirit— page 108.

I cry to thee, and thou hearest me not: I stand up, and thou dost not regard me.—*Job* xxx. 20.

When he hideth his countenance, who is there that can behold him,

whether it regard nations, or all men?
—*Job* xxxiv. 29.

Why, O Lord, hast thou retired afar
off? why dost thou slight us in our
wants, in the time of trouble?—*Ps.* ix.
(*Heb.* x.) 1.

How long, O Lord, wilt thou forget
me unto the end? how long dost thou
turn away thy face from me?—*Ps.*
xii. 1.

O God my God, look upon me: why
hast thou forsaken me? . . .

O my God, I shall cry by day, and
thou wilt not hear: and by night, and
it shall not be reputed as folly in me.
—*Ps.* xxi. 2, 3.

And in my abundance I said: I shall
never be moved.

O Lord, in thy favor, thou gavest
strength to my beauty.

Thou turnedst away thy face from
me, and I became troubled.—*Ps.* xxix.
7, 8.

Arise, why sleepest thou, O Lord?
arise, and cast us not off to the end.

Why turnest thou thy face away? and
forgettest our want and our trouble?

For our soul is humbled down to the
dust: our belly cleaveth to the earth.—
Ps. xliii. 23-25.

Lord, why castest thou off my prayer:
why turnest thou away thy face from
me?—*Ps.* lxxxvii. 15.

And Sion said: The Lord hath forsaken me, and the Lord hath forgotten
me.—*Is.* xlix. 14.

How long, O Lord, shall I cry, and
thou wilt not hear? shall I cry out to
thee suffering violence, and thou wilt
not save?—*Hab.* i. 2.

And about the ninth hour Jesus cried
with a loud voice, saying: Eli, Eli,
lamma sabacthani? that is, My God, my
God, why hast thou forsaken me?—
Matt. xxvii. 46.

WITHDRAWING OTHERS FROM SIN

See: Sin, withdrawing others from—
page 528.

WITNESS, FALSE

Thou shalt not bear false witness
against thy neighbor.—*Ex.* xx. 16.

Thou shalt not receive the voice of
a lie: neither shalt thou join thy hand
to bear false witness for a wicked person.—*Ex.* xxiii. 1.

If a lying witness stand against a
man, accusing him of transgression, . . .

And when after most diligent inquisition, they shall find that the false witness hath told a lie against his brother:

They shall render to him as he meant
to do to his brother, and thou shalt take
away the evil out of the midst of thee:

That others hearing may fear, and
may not dare to do such things.—*Deut.*
xix. 16, 18-20.

A false witness shall not be unpunished: and he that speaketh lies, shall
perish.—*Prov.* xix. 9.

A lying witness shall perish.—*Prov.*
xxi. 28.

A man that beareth false witness
against his neighbor, is like a dart and
a sword and a sharp arrow.—*Prov.*
xxv. 18.

And they rose up against the two elders, (for Daniel had convicted them
of false witness by their own mouth,)
and they did to them as they had mali-
ciously dealt against their neighbor,

To fulfil the law of Moses: and they
put them to death, and innocent blood
was saved in that day.—*Dan.* xiii. 61, 62.

WOMAN, A GOOD

See: Wife, a good—page 602.

WOMAN, A WICKED

That thou mayst be delivered from
the strange women, and from the
stranger, who softeneth her words:

And forsaketh the guide of her
youth,

And hath forgotten the covenant of
her God: for her house inclineth unto
death, and her paths to hell.

None that go in unto her shall return
again, neither shall they take hold of
the paths of life.—*Prov.* ii. 16-19.

The sadness of the heart is every
plague: and the wickedness of a woman
is all evil.

And a man will choose any plague,
but the plague of the heart:

And any wickedness, but the wickedness of a woman. . . .

It will be more agreeable to abide with a lion and a dragon, than to dwell with a wicked woman.

The wickedness of a woman changeth her face: and she darkeneth her countenance as a bear: and showeth it like sackcloth. In the midst of her neighbors,

Her husband groaned, and hearing he sighed a little.

All malice is short to the malice of a woman, let the lot of sinners fall upon her. . . .

A wicked woman abateth the courage, and maketh a heavy countenance, and a wounded heart.—*Ecclus.* xxv. 17-19, 23-26, 31.

As a yoke of oxen that is moved to and fro, so also is a wicked woman: he that hath hold of her, is as he that taketh hold of a scorpion.—*Ecclus.* xxvi. 10.

A drunken woman is a great wrath: and her reproach and shame shall not be hid.—*Ecclus.* xxvi. 11.

Sure keeping is good over a wicked wife.—*Ecclus.* xlii. 6.

WOMAN, A BOLD OR FORWARD

A diligent woman is a crown to her husband: and she that doth things worthy of confusion, is a rottenness in his bones—*Prov.* xii. 4.

A wise daughter shall bring an inheritance to her husband: but she that confoundeth, becometh a disgrace to her father.

She that is bold shameth both her father and husband, and will not be inferior to the ungodly: and shall be disgraced by them both.—*Ecclus.* xxii. 4, 5.

As the climbing of a sandy way is to the feet of the aged, so is a wife full of tongue to a quiet man.—*Ecclus.* xxv. 27.

The fornication of a woman shall be known by the haughtiness of her eyes, and by her eyelids.

On a daughter that turneth not away herself, set a strict watch: lest finding an opportunity she abuse herself.

Take heed of the impudence of her eyes, and wonder not if she slight thee.

She will open her mouth as a thirsty traveller to the fountain, and will drink of every water near her, and will sit down by every hedge, and open her quiver against every arrow, until she fail.—*Ecclus.* xxvi. 12-15.

WOMAN, A QUARRELSOME

A foolish son is the grief of his father: and a wrangling wife is like a roof continually dropping through.—*Prov.* xix. 13.

It is better to sit in a corner of the housetop, than with a brawling woman, and in a common house.—*Prov.* xxi. 9.

It is better to dwell in a wilderness, than with a quarrelsome and passionate woman.—*Prov.* xxi. 19.

Roofs dropping through in a cold day, and a contentious woman are alike.—*Prov.* xxvii. 15.

Pride was not made for men: nor wrath for the race of women.—*Ecclus.* x. 22.

And there is no anger above the anger of a woman.—*Ecclus.* xxv. 23.

WOMEN IN CHURCH, PROPER CONDUCT OF

But every woman praying or prophesying with her head not covered, disgraceth her head: for it is all one as if she were shaven.

For if a woman be not covered, let her be shorn. But if it be a shame to a woman to be shorn or made bald, let her cover her head. . . .

Therefore ought the woman to have a ¹power over her head, because of the angels.—1 *Cor.* xi. 5, 6, 10.

Let women keep silence in the churches: for it is not permitted them to speak, but to be subject, as also the law saith.

But if they would learn any thing, let them ask their husbands at home. For it is a shame for a woman to speak in the church.—1 *Cor.* xiv. 34, 35.

I will therefore that men pray in every place, lifting up pure hands, without anger and contention.

In like manner women also in decent apparel: adorning themselves with modesty and sobriety, not with plaited hair, or gold, or pearls, or costly attire,

¹A veil or covering, as a sign that she is under the power of her husband.

But as it becometh women professing godliness, with good works.

Let the woman learn in silence, with all subjection.

But I suffer not a woman to teach, nor to use authority over the man: but to be in silence.—*1 Tim.* ii. 8-12.

WORD OF GOD, THE

For ever, O Lord, thy word standeth firm in heaven.—*Ps.* cxviii. 89.

Thy word is exceedingly refined: and thy servant hath loved it.—*Ps.* cxviii. 140.

Judge my judgment and redeem me: quicken thou me for thy word's sake. —*Ps.* cxviii. 154.

Praise the Lord, O Jerusalem: praise thy God, O Sion. . . .

Who sendeth forth his speech to the earth: his word runneth swiftly.—*Ps.* cxlvii. 12, 15.

The word of God on high is the fountain of wisdom, and her ways are everlasting commandments.—*Ecclus.*i.5.

The grass is withered, and the flower is fallen: but the word of the Lord endureth for ever.—*Is.* xl. 8.

Heaven and earth shall pass away, but my words shall not pass away.— *Luke* xxi. 33.

He that despiseth me, and receiveth not my words, hath one that judgeth him; the word that I have spoken, the same shall judge him in the last day. —*John* xii. 48.

WORD OF GOD, THE POWER OF THE

By the word of the Lord the heavens were established; and all the power of them by the spirit of his mouth:

Gathering together the waters of the sea, as in a vessel; laying up the depths in storehouses. . . .

For he spoke and they were made: he commanded and they were created. —*Ps.* xxxii. 6, 7, 9.

He sendeth his crystal like morsels: who shall stand before the face of his cold?

He shall send out his word, and shall melt them: his wind shall blow, and the waters shall run.—*Ps.* cxlvii. 17, 18.

Be not hasty to depart from his face, and do not continue in an evil work: for he will do all that pleaseth him:

And his word is full of power: neither can any man say to him: Why dost thou so?—*Eccles.* viii. 3, 4.

God of my fathers, and Lord of mercy, who hast made all things with thy word.—*Wis.* ix. 1.

For it was neither herb, nor mollifying plaster that healed them, but thy word, O Lord, which healeth all things. —*Wis.* xvi. 12.

That thy children, O Lord, whom thou lovedst, might know that it is not the growing of fruits that nourisheth men, but thy word preserveth them that believe in thee.—*Wis.* xvi. 26.

Through him is established the end of their journey, and by his word all things are regulated.—*Ecclus.* xliii. 28.

And as the rain and the snow come down from heaven, and return no more thither, but soak the earth, and water it, and make it to spring, and give seed to the sower, and bread to the eater:

So shall my word be, which shall go forth from my mouth: it shall not return to me void, but it shall do whatsoever I please, and shall prosper in the things for which I sent it.—*Is.* lv. 10, 11.

It is the spirit that quickeneth: the flesh profiteth nothing. The words that I have spoken to you, are spirit and life.—*John* vi. 64.

Then Jesus said to the twelve: Will you also go away?

And Simon Peter answered him: Lord, to whom shall we go? thou hast the words of eternal life.—*John* vi. 68, 69.

Now you are clean by reason of the word, which I have spoken to you.— *John* xv. 3.

And take unto you the helmet of salvation, and the sword of the Spirit (which is the word of God.)—*Eph.* vi. 17.

Be mindful that the Lord Jesus Christ is risen again from the dead, of the seed of David, according to my gospel.

Wherein I labor even unto bands, as an evil-doer; but the word of God is not bound.—*2 Tim.* ii. 8, 9.

For the word of God is living and effectual, and more piercing than any two edged sword; and reaching unto the division of the soul and the spirit, of the joints also and the marrow, and is a discerner of the thoughts and intents of the heart.—*Heb.* iv. 12.

By faith we understand that the world was framed by the word of God; that from invisible things visible things might be made.—*Heb.* xi. 3.

Wherefore casting away all uncleanness, and abundance of naughtiness, with meekness receive the ingrafted word, which is able to save your souls. —*James* i. 21.

Purifying your souls in the obedience of charity, with a brotherly love, from a sincere heart love one another earnestly:

Being born again not of corruptible seed, but incorruptible, by the word of God who liveth and remaineth for ever.—1 *Peter* i. 22, 23.

For this they are wilfully ignorant of, that the heavens were before, and the earth out of water, and through water consisting by the word of God. —2 *Peter* iii. 5.

WORD OF GOD IS TRUE, THE

See also: Truth of God—page 568.

And now, O Lord God, thou art God, and thy words shall be true: for thou hast spoken to thy servant these good things.—2 *Kings* vii. 28.

The beginning of thy words is truth: all the judgments of thy justice are for ever.—*Ps.* cxviii. 160.

The Lord is faithful in all his words: and holy in all his works.—*Ps.* cxliv. 13.

Sanctify them in truth. Thy word is truth.—*John* xvii. 17.

WORD OF GOD IS JUST AND GOOD, THE

The words of the Lord are pure words: as silver tried by the fire, purged from the earth, refined seven times.—*Ps.* xi. 7.

As for my God, his way is undefiled: the words of the Lord are fire tried: he is the protector of all that trust in him. —*Ps.* xvii. 31.

For the word of the Lord is right, and all his works are done with faithfulness.—*Ps.* xxxii. 4.

All my words are just, there is nothing wicked nor perverse in them.

They are right to them that understand, and just to them that find knowledge.—*Prov.* viii. 8, 9.

Every word of God is fire tried: he is a buckler to them that hope in him. —*Prov.* xxx. 5.

The house of Jacob saith: Is the spirit of the Lord straitened, or are these his thoughts? Are not my words good to him that walketh uprightly?— *Mich.* ii. 7.

WORD OF GOD OUR COMFORT AND STRENGTH, THE

Be thou mindful of thy word to thy servant, in which thou hast given me hope.

This hath comforted me in my humiliation: because thy word hath enlivened me.—*Ps.* cxviii. 49, 50.

My soul hath fainted after thy salvation: and in thy word I have very much hoped.—*Ps.* cxviii. 81.

How sweet are thy words to my palate! more than honey to my mouth.— *Ps.* cxviii. 103.

WORD OF GOD OUR LIGHT AND OUR GUIDE, THE

By what doth a young man correct his way? by observing thy words.—*Ps.* cxviii. 9.

Thy word is a lamp to my feet, and a light to my paths.—*Ps.* cxviii. 105.

The declaration of thy words giveth light: and giveth understanding to little ones.—*Ps.* cxviii. 130.

WORD OF GOD, OUR NEED OF THE

He afflicted thee with want, and gave thee manna for thy food, which neither thou nor thy fathers knew: to show that not in bread alone doth man live, but in every word that proceedeth from the mouth of God.—*Deut.* viii. 3.

Behold the days come, saith the Lord, and I will send forth a famine into the land: not a famine of bread, nor a thirst of water, but of hearing the word of the Lord.

And they shall move from sea to sea, and from the north to the east: they shall go about seeking the word of the Lord, and shall not find it.—*Amos*. viii. 11, 12.

And the tempter coming, said to him: If thou be the Son of God, command that these stones be made bread.

Who answered and said: It is written, Not in bread alone doth man live, but in every word that proceedeth from the mouth of God.—*Matt*. iv. 3, 4.

WORD OF GOD, RECEIVING THE

Thy words have I hidden in my heart, that I may not sin against thee.—*Ps*. cxviii. 11.

Princes have persecuted me without cause: and my heart hath been in awe of thy words.

I will rejoice at thy words, as one that hath found great spoil.—*Ps*. cxviii. 161, 162.

Thy words were found, and I did eat them, and thy word was to me a joy and gladness of my heart: for thy name is called upon me, O Lord God of hosts.—*Jer*. xv. 16.

And he spoke to them many things in parables, saying: Behold the sower went forth to sow.

And whilst he soweth some fell by the way side, and the birds of the air came and ate them up. . . .

And others fell upon good ground: and they brought forth fruit, some an hundredfold, some sixtyfold, and some thirtyfold. . . .

But he that received the seed upon good ground, is he that heareth the word, and understandeth, and beareth fruit, and yieldeth the one an hundredfold, and another sixty, and another thirty.—*Matt*. xiii. 3, 4, 8, 23.

And it came to pass, as he spoke these things, a certain woman from the crowd, lifting up her voice, said to him: Blessed is the womb that bore thee, and the paps that gave thee suck.

But he said: Yea rather, blessed are they who hear the word of God, and keep it.—*Luke* xi. 27, 28.

He that is of God, heareth the words of God. Therefore you hear them not, because you are not of God.—*John* viii. 47.

Therefore we also give thanks to God without ceasing: because, that when you had received of us the word of the hearing of God, you received it not as the word of men, but (as it is indeed) the word of God, who worketh in you that have believed.—1 *Thess*. ii. 13.

WORD OF GOD, EXHORTATION TO RECEIVE THE

And these words which I command thee this day, shall be in thy heart.—*Deut*. vi. 6.

Lay up these my words in your hearts and minds, and hang them for a sign on your hands, and place them between your eyes.

Teach your children that they meditate on them, when thou sittest in thy house, and when thou walkest on the way, and when thou liest down and risest up.

Thou shalt write them upon the posts and the doors of thy house.—*Deut*. xi. 18-20.

Receive the law of his mouth, and lay up his words in thy heart.—*Job* xxii. 22.

My son, hearken to my words, and incline thy ear to my sayings.

Let them not depart from thy eyes, keep them in the midst of thy heart:

For they are life to those that find them, and health to all flesh.—*Prov*. iv. 20-22.

Let the word of Christ dwell in you abundantly, in all wisdom: teaching and admonishing one another in psalms, hymns, and spiritual canticles, singing in grace in your hearts to God. —*Col*. iii. 16.

Wherefore casting away all uncleanness, and abundance of naughtiness, with meekness receive the ingrafted word, which is able to save your souls. —*James* i. 21.

WORDS, EVIL AND UNKIND

See also: Conversations, evil— page 79.

Be ye angry, and sin not: the things you say in your hearts, be sorry for them upon your beds.—*Ps*. iv. 5.

Incline not my heart to evil words; to make excuses in sins.—*Ps.* cxl. 4.

Therefore he that speaketh unjust things cannot be hid, neither shall the chastising judgment pass him by.

For inquisition shall be made into the thoughts of the ungodly: and the hearing of his words shall come to God, to the chastising of his iniquities.—*Wis.* i. 8, 9.

A wicked word shall change the heart: out of which four manner of things arise, good and evil, life and death: and the tongue is continually the ruler of them.—*Ecclus.* xxxvii. 21.

For by thy words thou shalt be justified, and by thy words thou shalt be condemned.—*Matt.* xii. 37.

WORDS, IDLE

See: Idle—page 226.

WORDS, KIND

See: Kind—page 269.

WORDS OF CHRIST ON THE CROSS, THE SEVEN

And about the ninth hour Jesus cried with a loud voice, saying: Eli, Eli, lamma sabacthani? that is, My God, my God, why hast thou forsaken me?—*Matt.* xxvii. 46.

And Jesus said: Father, forgive them, for they know not what they do.—*Luke* xxiii. 34.

And Jesus said to him: Amen I say to thee, this day thou shalt be with me in paradise.—*Luke* xxiii. 43.

And Jesus crying with a loud voice, said: Father, into thy hands I commend my spirit. And saying this, he gave up the ghost.—*Luke* xxiii. 46.

When Jesus therefore had seen his mother and the disciple standing whom he loved, he saith to his mother: Woman, behold thy son.

After that, he saith to the disciple: Behold thy mother.—*John* xix. 26, 27.

Afterwards, Jesus knowing that all things were now accomplished, that the scripture might be fulfilled, said: I thirst.—*John* xix. 28.

Jesus therefore, when he had taken the vinegar, said: It is consummated. And bowing his head, he gave up the ghost.—*John* xix. 30.

WORK AND FIGHT TO GAIN HEAVEN, WE MUST

See: Heaven—page 195.

WORKS OF GOD, THE

For the word of the Lord is right, and all his works are done with faithfulness.—*Ps.* xxxii. 4.

Thou hast multiplied thy wonderful works, O Lord my God: and in thy thoughts there is no one like to thee. I have declared and I have spoken: they are multiplied above number.—*Ps.* xxxix. 6.

Come and behold ye the works of the Lord: what wonders he hath done upon earth.—*Ps.* xlv. 9.

Come and see the works of God; who is terrible in his counsels over the sons of men.—*Ps.* lxv. 5.

May the glory of the Lord endure for ever: the Lord shall rejoice in his works.—*Ps.* ciii. 31.

Let the mercies of the Lord give glory to him, and his wonderful works to the children of men.—*Ps.* cvi. 31.

Let all thy works, O Lord, praise thee: and let thy saints bless thee.—*Ps.* cxliv. 10.

For many of his works are hidden: but the works of his justice who shall declare? or who shall endure? for the testament is far from some, and the examination of all is in the end.—*Ecclus.* xvi. 22.

O how desirable are all his works, and what we can know is but as a spark!—*Ecclus.* xlii. 23.

What shall we be able to do to glorify him? for the Almighty himself is above all his works.

. . . There are many things hidden from us that are greater than these: for we have seen but a few of his works.

But the Lord hath made all things, and to the godly he hath given wisdom.—*Ecclus.* xliii. 30, 36, 37.

The harp, and the lyre, and the timbrel, and the pipe, and wine are in your feasts: and the work of the Lord you regard not, nor do you consider the works of his hands.—*Is.* v. 12.

WORKS OF GOD ARE WONDERFUL AND GREAT, THE

Wherefore I will pray to the Lord, and address my speech to God: Who doth great things and unsearchable and wonderful things without number.—*Job* v. 8, 9.

Hearken to these things, Job: Stand, and consider the wondrous works of God.—*Job* xxxvii. 14.

Blessed be the Lord, the God of Israel, who alone doth wonderful things.—*Ps.* lxxi. 18.

Sing ye to the Lord a new canticle: because he hath done wonderful things. —*Ps.* xcvii. 1.

Remember his marvellous works which he hath done; his wonders, and the judgments of his mouth.—*Ps.* civ. 5.

They that go down to the sea in ships, doing business in the great waters: These have seen the works of the Lord, and his wonders in the deep.— *Ps.* cvi. 23, 24.

Great are the works of the Lord: sought out according to all his wills. . . .

He hath made a remembrance of his wonderful works, being a merciful and gracious Lord. . . .

He will show forth to his people the power of his works.—*Ps.* cx. 2, 4, 6.

This is the Lord's doing: and it is wonderful in our eyes.—*Ps.* cxvii. 23.

Glory not in apparel at any time, and be not exalted in the day of thy honor: for the works of the Highest only are wonderful, and his works are glorious, and secret, and hidden.—*Ecclus.* xi. 4.

The works of God are done in judgment from the beginning, and from the making of them he distinguished their parts, and their beginnings in their generations.

He beautified their works for ever, they have neither hungered, nor labored, and they have not ceased from their works.

Neither shall any of them straiten his neighbor at any time.—*Ecclus.* xvi. 26-28.

Who is able to declare his works?

For who shall search out his glorious acts?

. . . Nothing may be taken away, nor added, neither is it possible to find out the glorious works of God: When a man hath done, then shall he begin: and when he leaveth off, he shall be at a loss.—*Ecclus.* xviii. 2, 3, 5, 6.

The sun giving light hath looked upon all things, and full of the glory of the Lord is his work.

. . . He hath beautified the glorious works of his wisdom: and he is from eternity to eternity, and to him nothing may be added.—*Ecclus.* xlii. 16, 21.

Fear not, O land, be glad and rejoice: for the Lord hath done great things.— *Joel* ii. 21.

WORKS OF GOD ARE WONDERFUL AND GREAT, ACKNOWLEDGMENT THAT THE

Say unto God, How terrible are thy works, O Lord! in the multitude of thy strength thy enemies shall lie to thee.—*Ps.* lxv. 3.

O Lord, how great are thy works! thy thoughts are exceeding deep.—*Ps.* xci. 6.

How great are thy works, O Lord? thou hast made all things in wisdom: the earth is filled with thy riches.—*Ps.* ciii. 24.

I will praise thee, for thou art fearfully magnified: wonderful are thy works, and my soul knoweth right well. —*Ps.* cxxxviii. 14.

O Lord, thou art my God, I will exalt thee, and give glory to thy name: for thou hast done wonderful things, thy designs of old faithful, amen.—*Is.* xxv. 1.

And I saw as it were a sea of glass mingled with fire, and them that had overcome the beast, and his image, and the number of his name, standing on the sea of glass, having the harps of God:

And singing the canticle of Moses, the servant of God, and the canticle of the Lamb, saying: Great and wonderful are thy works, O Lord God Almighty; just and true are thy ways, O King of ages.—*Apoc.* xv. 2, 3.

WORKS OF GOD ARE GOOD, ALL THE

And God saw all the things that he had made, and they were very good.—*Gen.* i. 31.

The works of God are perfect, and all his ways are judgments: God is faithful and without any iniquity, he is just and right.—*Deut.* xxxii. 4.

For thou hast given me, O Lord, a delight in thy doings: and in the works of thy hands I shall rejoice.—*Ps.* xci. 5.

The Lord is faithful in all his words: and holy in all his works.—*Ps.* cxliv. 13.

Magnify his name, and give glory to him with the voice of your lips, and with the canticles of your mouths, and with harps, and in praising him, you shall say in this manner:

All the works of the Lord are exceeding good.

. . . All the works of the Lord are good, and he will furnish every work in due time.

It is not to be said: This is worse than that: for all shall be well approved in their time.—*Ecclus.* xxxix. 20, 21, 39. 40.

All things are double, one against another, and he hath made nothing defective.—*Ecclus.* xlii. 25.

For thou art just in all that thou hast done to us, and all thy works are true, and thy ways right, and all thy judgments true.—*Dan.* iii. 27.

And he (Jesus) charged them that they should tell no man. But the more he charged them, so much the more a great deal did they publish it.

And so much the more did they wonder, saying: He hath done all things well; he hath made both the deaf to hear, and the dumb to speak.—*Mark* vii. 36, 37.

WORKS OF GOD, WE SHOULD PROCLAIM THE

For it is good to hide the secret of a king: but honorable to reveal and confess the works of God.—*Tob.* xii. 7.

It is time therefore that I return to him that sent me: but bless ye God, and publish all his wonderful works.—*Tob.* xii. 20.

I will wash my hands among the innocent; and will compass thy altar, O Lord:

That I may hear the voice of thy praise: and tell of all thy wondrous works.—*Ps.* xxv. 6, 7.

Come and hear, all ye that fear God, and I will tell you what great things he hath done for my soul.—*Ps.* lxv. 16.

We will praise thee, O God: we will praise, and we will call upon thy name.

We will relate thy wondrous works.—*Ps.* lxxiv. 2.

Give glory to the Lord, and call upon his name: declare his deeds among the Gentiles.

Sing to him, yea sing praises to him: relate all his wondrous works.—*Ps.* civ. 1, 2.

I shall not die, but live: and shall declare the works of the Lord.—*Ps.* cxvii. 17.

Generation and generation shall praise thy works: and they shall declare thy power.

They shall speak of the magnificence of the glory of thy holiness: and shall tell thy wondrous works.

And they shall speak of the might of thy terrible acts: and shall declare thy greatness.—*Ps.* cxliv. 4-6.

He set his eye upon their hearts to show them the greatness of his works:

That they might praise the name which he hath sanctified: and glory in his wondrous acts, that they might declare the glorious things of his works.—*Ecclus.* xvii. 7, 8.

I will now remember the works of the Lord, and I will declare the things I have seen. By the words of the Lord are his works. . . .

Hath not the Lord made the saints to declare all his wonderful works, which the Lord Almighty hath firmly settled to be established for his glory?—*Ecclus.* xlii. 15, 17.

And you shall say in that day: Praise ye the Lord, and call upon his name: make his works known among the people: remember that his name is high.

Sing ye to the Lord, for he hath done great things: show this forth in all the earth.—*Is.* xii. 4, 5.

And when he (Jesus) went up into the ship, he that had been troubled with the devil, began to beseech him that he might be with him.

And he admitted him not, but saith to him: Go into thy house to thy friends, and tell them how great things the Lord hath done for thee, and hath had mercy on thee.

And he went his way, and began to publish in Decapolis how great things Jesus had done for him: and all men wondered.—*Mark* v. 18-20.

WORKS OF GOD SHOW FORTH HIS GREATNESS AND POWER, THE

See: Greatness of God shown by His works—page 185.

WORKS, GOOD

See also: Practical in our religion—page 392.

When thou didst pray with tears, and didst bury the dead, and didst leave thy dinner, and hide the dead by day in thy house, and bury them by night, I offered thy prayer to the Lord.—*Tob.* xii. 12.

Who is the man that desireth life: who loveth to see good days?

Keep thy tongue from evil, and thy lips from speaking guile.

Turn away from evil and do good: seek after peace and pursue it.—*Ps.* xxxiii. 13-15.

The work of the just is unto life: but the fruit of the wicked, unto sin.—*Prov.* x. 16.

Every work that is corruptible shall fail in the end: and the worker thereof shall go with it.

And every excellent work shall be justified: and the worker thereof shall be honored therein.—*Ecclus.* xiv. 20, 21.

And he (Jesus) said: So is the kingdom of God, as if a man should cast seed into the earth,

And should sleep, and rise, night and day, and the seed should spring, and grow up whilst he knoweth not.

For the earth of itself bringeth forth fruit, first the blade, then the ear, afterwards the full corn in the ear.

And when the fruit is brought forth, immediately he putteth in the sickle, because the harvest is come.—*Mark* iv. 26-29.

In this is my Father glorified; that you bring forth very much fruit, and become my disciples.—*John* xv. 8.

For we are his workmanship, created in Christ Jesus in good works, which God hath prepared that we should walk in them.—*Eph.* ii. 10.

Now our Lord Jesus Christ himself, and God and our Father, who hath loved us, and hath given us everlasting consolation, and good hope in grace,

Exhort your hearts, and confirm you in every good work and word.—*2 Thess.* ii. 15, 16.

Let us be glad and rejoice, and give glory to him; for the marriage of the Lamb is come, and his wife hath prepared herself.

And it is granted to her that she should clothe herself with fine linen, glittering and white. For the fine linen are the justifications of saints.—*Apoc.* xix. 7, 8.

WORKS ARE NECESSARY FOR SALVATION, GOOD

See: Part II—page 740.

WORKS REWARDED BY GOD, GOOD

See also: Reward God gives to those who serve Him, the—page 480.

If thou do well, shalt thou not receive? but if ill, shall not sin forthwith be present at the door?—*Gen.* iv. 7.

For he will render to a man his work, and according to the ways of every one he will reward them.—*Job* xxxiv. 11.

And the Lord will reward me according to my justice; and will repay me according to the cleanness of my hands:

Because I have kept the ways of the Lord; and have not done wickedly against my God.—*Ps.* xvii. 21, 22.

The judgments of the Lord are true, justified in themselves.

More to be desired than gold and many precious stones: and sweeter than honey and the honeycomb.

For thy servant keepeth them, and in keeping them there is a great reward.—*Ps.* xviii. 10-12.

By the fruit of his own mouth shall a man be filled with good things, and according to the works of his hands it shall be repaid him.—*Prov.* xii. 14.

All mercy shall make a place for every man according to the merit of his works, and according to the wisdom of his sojournment.—*Ecclus.* xvi. 15.

Work your work before the time, and he will give you your reward in his time.—*Ecclus.* li. 38.

Then shall the king say to them that shall be on his right hand: Come, ye blessed of my Father, possess you the kingdom prepared for you from the foundation of the world.

For I was hungry, and you gave me to eat; I was thirsty, and you gave me to drink; I was a stranger, and you took me in:

Naked, and you covered me: sick, and you visited me: I was in prison, and you came to me.

Then shall the just answer him, saying: Lord, when did we see thee hungry, and fed thee; thirsty, and gave thee drink?

And when did we see thee a stranger, and took thee in? or naked, and covered thee?

Or when did we see thee sick or in prison, and came to thee?

And the king answering, shall say to them: Amen I say to you, as long as you did it to one of these my least brethren, you did it to me.—*Matt.* xxv. 34-40.

And they that have done good things, shall come forth unto the resurrection of life; but they that have done evil, unto the resurrection of judgment.—*John* v. 29.

But in every nation, he that feareth him, and worketh justice, is acceptable to him.—*Acts* x. 35.

Who will render to every man according to his works.

To them indeed, who according to patience in good works, seek glory and honor and incorruption, eternal life.—*Rom.* ii. 6, 7.

But glory, and honor, and peace to every one that worketh good, to the Jew first, and also to the Greek.

For there is no respect of persons with God.—*Rom.* ii. 10, 11.

And every man shall receive his own reward, according to his own labor.—1 *Cor.* iii. 8.

Every man's work shall be manifest; for the day of the Lord shall declare it, because it shall be revealed in fire; and the fire shall try every man's work, of what sort it is.

If any man's work abide, which he hath built thereupon, he shall receive a reward.—1 *Cor.* iii. 13, 14.

Therefore, my beloved brethren, be ye steadfast and unmovable; always abounding in the work of the Lord, knowing that your labor is not in vain in the Lord.—1 *Cor.* xv. 58.

And in doing good, let us not fail. For in due time we shall reap, not failing.—*Gal.* vi. 9.

Knowing that whatsoever good thing any man shall do, the same shall he receive from the Lord, whether he be bond, or free.—*Eph.* vi. 8.

For God is not unjust, that he should forget your work, and the love which you have shown in his name, you who have ministered, and do minister to the saints.—*Heb.* vi. 10.

Wherefore, brethren, labor the more, that by good works you may make sure your calling and election. For doing these things, you shall not sin at any time.

For so an entrance shall be ministered to you abundantly into the everlasting kingdom of our Lord and Saviour Jesus Christ.—2 *Peter* i. 10, 11.

WORKS, EXHORTATION TO THE PRACTICE OF GOOD

Thou shalt not appear empty in the sight of the Lord.—*Ecclus.* xxxv. 6.

By a voice he saith: Hear me, [1]ye divine offspring, and bud forth as the rose planted by the brooks of waters.

Give ye a sweet odor as frankincense. Send forth flowers, as the lily, and yield a smell, and bring forth leaves in grace, and praise with canticles, and bless the Lord in his works.—*Ecclus.* xxxix. 17-19.

Seek ye good, and not evil, that you may live: and the Lord the God of

[1]The children of Israel, the people of God.

hosts will be with you, as you have said.

Hate evil, and love good, and establish judgment in the gate: it may be the Lord the God of hosts may have mercy on the remnant of Joseph.—*Amos* v. 14, 15.

But to them first that are at Damascus, and at Jerusalem, and unto all the country of Judea, and to the Gentiles did I preach, that they should do penance, and turn to God, doing works worthy of penance.—*Acts* xxvi. 20.

For the rest, brethren, whatsoever things are true, whatsoever modest, whatsoever just, whatsoever holy, whatsoever lovely, whatsoever of good fame, if there be any virtue, if any praise of discipline, think on these things.

The things which you have both learned, and received, and heard, and seen in me, these do ye, and the God of peace shall be with you.—*Philipp.* iv. 8, 9.

That you may walk worthy of God, in all things pleasing; being fruitful in every good work, and increasing in the knowledge of God.—*Col.* i. 10.

It is a faithful saying: and these things I will have thee affirm constantly: that they, who believe in God, may be careful to excel in good works. These things are good and profitable unto men.—*Titus* iii. 8.

And let our men also learn to excel in good works for necessary uses: that they be not unfruitful.—*Titus* iii. 14.

And let us consider one another, to provoke unto charity and to good works. —*Heb.* x. 24.

And do not forget to do good, and to impart; for by such sacrifices God's favor is obtained.—*Heb.* xiii. 16.

Wherefore let them also that suffer according to the will of God, commend their souls in good deeds to the faithful Creator.—1 *Peter* iv. 19.

And you, employing all care, minister in your faith, virtue; and in virtue, knowledge;

And in knowledge, abstinence; and in abstinence, patience; and in patience, godliness;

And in godliness, love of brotherhood; and in love of brotherhood, charity.

For if these things be with you and abound, they will make you to be neither empty nor unfruitful in the knowledge of our Lord Jesus Christ.

For he that hath not these things with him, is blind, and groping, having forgotten that he was purged from his old sins.—2 *Peter* i. 5-9.

WORLD IS GOD'S ENEMY, THE

The world cannot hate you; but me it hateth: because I give testimony of it, that the works thereof are evil.—*John* vii. 7.

And he (Jesus) said to them: You are from beneath, I am from above. You are of this world, I am not of this world.—*John* viii. 23.

Now is the judgment of the world: now shall the prince of this world be cast out.—*John* xii. 31.

And I will ask the Father, and he shall give you another Paraclete, that he may abide with you for ever.

The spirit of truth, whom the world cannot receive, because it seeth him not, nor knoweth him: but you shall know him; because he shall abide with you, and shall be in you.—*John* xiv. 16, 17.

I will not now speak many things with you. For the prince of this world cometh, and in me he hath not any thing.—*John* xiv. 30.

If the world hate you, know ye, that it hath hated me before you.

If you had been of the world, the world would love its own: but because you are not of the world, but I have chosen you out of the world, therefore the world hateth you.

Remember my word that I said to you: The servant is not greater than his master. If they have persecuted me, they will also persecute you: if they have kept my word, they will keep yours also.

But all these things they will do to you for my name's sake: because they know not him that sent me.—*John* xv. 18-21.

But I tell you the truth: it is expedient for you that I go: for if I go not, the Paraclete will not come to you; but if I go, I will send him to you.

And when he is come, he will convince the world of sin, and of justice, and of judgment.

Of sin: because they believed not in me.

And of justice: because I go to the Father; and you shall see me no longer.

And of judgment: because the prince of this world is already judged.—*John* xvi. 7-11.

These things I have spoken to you, that in me you may have peace. In the world you shall have distress: but have confidence, I have overcome the world. —*John* xvi. 33.

I pray for them: I pray not for the world, but for them whom thou hast given me: because they are thine.— *John* xvii. 9.

I have given them thy word, and the world hath hated them, because they are not of the world; as I also am not of the world.—*John* xvii. 14.

Just Father, the world hath not known thee; but I have known thee: and these have known that thou hast sent me.—*John* xvii. 25.

Adulterers, know you not that the friendship of this world is the enemy of God? Whosoever therefore will be a friend of this world, becometh an enemy of God.—*James* iv. 4.

Wonder not, brethren, if the world hate you.—1 *John* iii. 13.

And every spirit that dissolveth Jesus, is not of God: and this is Antichrist, of whom you have heard that he cometh, and he is now already in the world.

You are of God, little children, and have overcome him. Because greater is he that is in you, than he that is in the world.

They are of the world: therefore of the world they speak, and the world heareth them.—1 *John* iv. 3-5.

WORLD CAN NEVER SATISFY US, THE

Hell and destruction are never filled: so the eyes of men are never satisfied. —*Prov.* xxvii. 20.

All the labor of man is for his mouth, but his soul shall not be filled.—*Eccles.* vi. 7.

WORLD, VANITY OF THE THINGS OF THIS

See: Vanity—page 574.

And: Life, its emptiness—page 279.

WORLD, THE WISDOM OF THE

See: Wisdom of the world—page 615.

WORLD DESPISES THE JUST, THE

See: Just despised by the world— page 265.

WORLD, LOVE OF THE

See: Worldliness—page 628.

WORLDLINESS

Thou hast hated them that regard vanities, to no purpose.—*Ps.* xxx. 7.

Yea and they have counted our life a pastime, and the business of life to be gain, and that we must be getting every way, even out of evil.—*Wis.* xv. 12.

The sower went out to sow his seed. And as he sowed, some fell by the wayside, and it was trodden down, and the fowls of the air devoured it. . . .

And other some fell among thorns, and the thorns growing up with it, choked it. . . .

And that which fell among thorns, are they who have heard, and going their way, are choked with the cares and riches and pleasures of this life, and yield no fruit.—*Luke* viii. 5, 7, 14.

And be not conformed to this world; but be reformed in the newness of your mind, that you may prove what is the good, and the acceptable, and the perfect will of God.—*Rom.* xii. 2.

And if our gospel be also hid, it is hid to them that are lost,

In whom the god of this world hath blinded the minds of unbelievers that the light of the gospel of the glory of Christ, who is the image of God, should not shine unto them.—2 *Cor.* iv. 3, 4.

If then you be dead with Christ from the elements of this world, why do you yet decree as living in the world?—*Col.* ii. 20.

For she that liveth in pleasures, is dead while she is living.—1 *Tim.* v. 6.

Religion clean and undefiled before God and the Father, is this: to visit the fatherless and widows in their tribulation: and to keep one's self unspotted from this world.—*James* i. 27.

Adulterers, know you not that the friendship of this world is the enemy of God? Whosoever therefore will be a friend of this world, becometh an enemy of God.—*James* iv. 4.

Love not the world, nor the things which are in the world. If any man love the world, the charity of the Father is not in him.

For all that is in the world, is the concupiscence of the flesh, and the concupiscence of the eyes, and the pride of life, which is not of the Father, but is of the world.

And the world passeth away, and the concupiscence thereof: but he that doth the will of God, abideth for ever.— 1 *John* ii. 15-17.

WORLDLY MINDED, THE

Who turning, said to Peter: Go behind me, Satan, thou art a scandal unto me: because thou savorest not the things that are of God, but the things that are of men.—*Matt.* xvi. 23.

He that cometh from above, is above all. He that is of the earth, of the earth he is, and of the earth he speaketh. He that cometh from heaven, is above all.—*John* iii. 31.

How can you believe, who receive glory one from another: and the glory which is from God alone, you do not seek?—*John* v. 44.

And he (Jesus) said to them: You are from beneath, I am from above. You are of this world, I am not of this world.

Therefore I said to you, that you shall die in your sins. For if you believe not that I am he, you shall die in your sin.—*John* viii. 23, 24.

For they that are according to the flesh, mind the things that are of the flesh; but they that are according to the spirit, mind the things that are of the spirit.

For the wisdom of the flesh is death; but the wisdom of the spirit is life and peace. . . . And they who are in the flesh, cannot please God.—*Rom.* viii. 5, 6, 8.

Now we have received not the spirit of this world, but the Spirit that is of God; that we may know the things that are given us from God. . . .

But the sensual man perceiveth not these things that are of the Spirit of God; for it is foolishness to him, and he cannot understand, because it is spiritually examined.—1 *Cor.* ii. 12, 14.

For all seek the things that are their own; not the things that are Jesus Christ's.—*Philipp.* ii. 21.

Therefore, if you be risen with Christ, seek the things that are above; where Christ is sitting at the right hand of God:

Mind the things that are above, not the things that are upon the earth.— *Col.* iii. 1, 2.

WRATH OF GOD, THE

See: Anger of God—page 30.

YOUNG MEN

The parables of Solomon, the son of David, king of Israel.

To know wisdom, and instruction: . . .

To give subtilty to little ones, to the young man knowledge and understanding.—*Prov.* i. 1, 2, 4.

The joy of young men is their strength: and the dignity of old men, their grey hairs.—*Prov.* xx. 29.

My son, from thy youth up receive instruction, and even to thy grey hairs thou shalt find wisdom.—*Ecclus.* vi. 18.

I write unto you, young men, because you have overcome the wicked one. . . .

I write unto you, young men, because you are strong, and the word of God abideth in you, and you have overcome the wicked one.—1 *John* ii. 13, 14.

YOUNG MEN, PROPER CONDUCT FOR

Young man, scarcely speak in thy own cause.

If thou be asked twice, let thy answer be short.

In many things be as if thou wert ignorant, and hear in silence and withal seeking.

In the company of great men take

not upon thee: and when the ancients are present, speak not much.

Before a storm goeth lightning: and before shamefacedness goeth favor: and for thy reverence good grace shall come to thee.

And at the time of rising be not slack: but be first to run home to thy house, and there withdraw thyself, and there take thy pastime.

And do what thou hast a mind, but not in sin or proud speech.

And for all these things bless the Lord, that made thee, and that replenisheth thee with all his good things.—*Ecclus.* xxxii. 10-17.

Young men, in like manner, exhort that they be sober.—*Titus* ii. 6.

In like manner, ye young men, be subject to the ancients.—1 *Peter* v. 5.

YOUTH, THOUGHTLESSNESS OF

The sins of my youth and my ignorances do not remember.—*Ps.* xxiv. 7.

Three things are hard to me, and the fourth I am utterly ignorant of.

The way of an eagle in the air, the way of a serpent upon a rock, the way of a ship in the midst of the sea, and the way of a man in youth.—*Prov.* xxx. 18, 19.

YOUTH DOES NOT LAST LONG

Remove anger from thy heart, and put away evil from thy flesh. For youth and pleasure are vain.—*Eccles.* xi. 10.

Remember thy Creator in the days of thy youth, before the time of affliction come, and the years draw nigh of which thou shalt say: They please me not.—*Eccles.* xii. 1.

YOUTH, WE SHOULD FORM GOOD HABITS IN

His bones shall be filled with the vices of his youth, and they shall sleep with him in the dust.—*Job* xx. 11.

By what doth a young man correct his way? by observing thy words.—*Ps.* cxviii. 9.

It is a proverb: A young man according to his way, even when he is old he will not depart from it.—*Prov.* xxii. 6.

Rejoice therefore, O young man, in thy youth, and let thy heart be in that which is good in the days of thy youth, and walk in the ways of thy heart, and in the sight of thy eyes: and know that for all these God will bring thee into judgment.—*Eccles.* xi. 9.

The things that thou hast not gathered in thy youth, how shalt thou find them in thy old age?—*Ecclus.* xxv. 5.

If the Ethiopian can change his skin, or the leopard his spots: you also may do well, when you have learned evil.—*Jer.* xiii. 23.

It is good for a man, when he hath borne the yoke from his youth.—*Lam.* iii. 27.

ZEAL FOR THE HONOR OF GOD

And when he was come thither, he abode in a cave: and behold the word of the Lord came unto him, and he said to him: What dost thou here, Elias?

And he answered: With zeal have I been zealous for the Lord God of hosts: for the children of Israel have forsaken thy covenant: they have thrown down thy altars, they have slain thy prophets with the sword, and I alone am left, and they seek my life to take it away.—3 *Kings* xix. 9, 10.

For the zeal of thy house hath eaten me up: and the reproaches of them that reproached thee are fallen upon me.—*Ps.* lxviii. 10.

My zeal hath made me pine away: because my enemies forgot thy words.—*Ps.* cxviii. 139.

Have I not hated them, O Lord, that hated thee: and pined away because of thy enemies?

I have hated them with a perfect hatred: and they are become enemies to me.—*Ps.* cxxxviii. 21, 22.

Thus therefore shall you pray: Our Father who art in heaven, hallowed be thy name.

Thy kingdom come. Thy will be done on earth as it is in heaven.—*Matt.* vi. 9, 10.

ZEAL IN DOING GOOD

For I have determined to follow her (wisdom): I have had a zeal for good, and shall not be confounded.—*Ecclus.* li. 24.

Blessed are they that hunger and thirst after justice: for they shall have their fill.—*Matt.* v. 6.

I am come to cast fire on the earth: and what will I, but that it be kindled?—*Luke* xii. 49.

And the lord commended the unjust steward, forasmuch as he had done wisely: for the children of this world are wiser in their generation than the children of light.—*Luke* xvi. 8.

To the weak I became weak, that I might gain the weak. I became all things to all men, that I might save all. And I do all things for the gospel's sake: that I may be made partaker thereof.—1 *Cor.* ix. 22, 23.

Besides those things which are without: my daily instance, the solicitude for all the churches.

Who is weak, and I am not weak? Who is scandalized, and I am not on fire?—2 *Cor.* xi. 28, 29.

But I most gladly will spend and be spent myself for your souls; although loving you more, I be loved less.—2 *Cor.* xii. 15.

But be zealous for that which is good in a good thing always: and not only when I am present with you.—*Gal.* iv. 18.

Brethren, I do not count myself to have apprehended. But one thing I do: forgetting the things that are behind, and stretching forth myself to those that are before,

I press towards the mark, to the prize of the supernal vocation of God in Christ Jesus.—*Philipp.* iii. 13, 14.

My brethren, if any of you err from the truth, and one convert him:

He must know that he who causeth a sinner to be converted from the error of his way, shall save his soul from death, and shall cover a multitude of sins.—*James* v. 19, 20.

And who is he that can hurt you, if you be zealous of good?—1 *Peter* iii. 13.

Such as I love, I rebuke and chastise. Be zealous therefore, and do penance.—*Apoc.* iii. 19.

ZEAL OF THE PRIEST

See: Priest, zeal of the—page 440.

ZEAL OF CHRIST, THE

And Jesus went about all the cities, and towns, teaching in their syna-gogues, and preaching the gospel of the kingdom, and healing every disease, and every infirmity.

And seeing the multitudes, he had compassion on them: because they were distressed, and lying like sheep that have no shepherd.

Then he saith to his disciples, The harvest indeed is great, but the laborers are few.

Pray ye therefore the Lord of the harvest, that he send forth laborers into his harvest.—*Matt.* ix. 35-38.

And rising very early, going out, he (Jesus) went into a desert place: and there he prayed.

And Simon, and they that were with him, followed after him.

And when they had found him, they said to him: All seek for thee.

And he saith to them: Let us go into the neighboring towns and cities, that I may preach there also; for to this purpose am I come.—*Mark* i. 35-38.

And with many such parables, he spoke to them the word, according as they were able to hear.

And without parable he did not speak unto them; but apart he explained all things to his disciples.

And he saith to them that day, when evening was come: Let us pass over to the other side:

And sending away the multitude, they take him even as he was in the ship: and there were other ships with him.

And there arose a great storm of wind, and the waves beat into the ship, so that the ship was filled.

And he was in the hinder part of the ship, sleeping upon a pillow.—*Mark* iv. 33-38.

And the apostles coming together unto Jesus, related to him all things that they had done and taught.

And he said to them: Come apart into a desert place, and rest a little. For there were many coming and going: and they had not so much as time to eat.

And going up into a ship, they went into a desert place apart.

And they saw them going away, and many knew: and they ran flocking thither on foot from all the cities, and were there before them.

And Jesus going out saw a great multitude: and he had compassion on them, because they were as sheep not having a shepherd, and he began to teach them many things.

And when the day was now far spent, his disciples came to him, saying: This is a desert place, and the hour is now past.

. . . And when he had dismissed them, he went up to the mountain to pray.—*Mark* vi. 30-35, 46.

And it came to pass that, after three days, they found him in the temple, sitting in the midst of the doctors, hearing them, and asking them questions.

And all that heard him were astonished at his wisdom and his answers.

And seeing him, they wondered. And his mother said to him: Son, why hast thou done so to us? behold thy father and I have sought thee sorrowing.

And he said to them: How is it that you sought me? did you not know, that I must be about my father's business? —*Luke* ii. 46-49.

And I have a baptism wherewith I am to be baptized: and how am I straitened until it be accomplished?— *Luke* xii. 50.

And the pasch of the Jews was at hand, and Jesus went up to Jerusalem.

And he found in the temple them that sold oxen and sheep and doves, and the changers of money sitting.

And when he had made, as it were, a scourge of little cords, he drove them all out of the temple, the sheep also and the oxen, and the money of the changers he poured out, and the tables he overthrew.

And to them that sold doves he said: Take these things hence, and make not the house of my Father a house of traffic.

And his disciples remembered that it was written: The zeal of thy house hath eaten me up.—*John* ii. 13-17.

He cometh therefore to a city of Samaria, which is called Sichar, near the land which Jacob gave to his son Joseph.

Now Jacob's well was there. Jesus therefore being wearied with his journey, sat thus on the well. It was about the sixth hour. . . .

In the mean time the disciples prayed him, saying: Rabbi, eat.

But he said to them: I have meat to eat, which you know not.

The disciples therefore said one to another: Hath any man brought him to eat?

Jesus saith to them: My meat is to do the will of him that sent me, that I may perfect his work.

Do not you say, There are yet four months, and then the harvest cometh? Behold, I say to you, lift up your eyes, and see the countries; for they are white already to harvest.—*John* iv. 5, 6, 31-35.

ZEAL, IMPRUDENT OR WRONG

From that time Jesus began to show to his disciples, that he must go to Jerusalem, and suffer many things from the ancients and scribes and chief priests, and be put to death, and the third day rise again.

And Peter taking him, began to rebuke him, saying: Lord, be it far from thee, this shall not be unto thee.

Who turning, said to Peter: Go behind me, Satan, thou art a scandal unto me: because thou savorest not the things that are of God, but the things that are of men.—*Matt.* xvi. 21-23.

And when Jesus was in Bethania, in the house of Simon the leper,

There came to him a woman having an alabaster box of precious ointment, and poured it on his head as he was at table.

And the disciples seeing it, had indignation, saying: To what purpose is this waste?

For this might have been sold for much, and given to the poor.—*Matt.* xxvi. 6-9.

Then Jesus saith to them: All you shall be scandalized in me this night. For it is written: I will strike the shepherd, and the sheep of the flock shall be dispersed.

But after I shall be risen again, I will go before you into Galilee.

And Peter answering, said to him:

Although all shall be scandalized in thee, I will never be scandalized.

Jesus said to him: Amen, I say to thee, that in this night before the cock crow, thou wilt deny me thrice.

Peter saith to him: Yea, though I should die with thee, I will not deny thee. And in like manner said all the disciples.—*Matt.* xxvi. 31-35.

Then they came up, and laid hands on Jesus, and held him.

And behold one of them that were with Jesus, stretching forth his hand, drew out his sword: and striking the servant of the high priest, cut off his ear.

Then Jesus saith to him: Put up thy sword into its place: for all that take the sword shall perish with the sword.

Thinkest thou that I cannot ask my Father, and he will give me presently more than twelve legions of angels?

How then shall the scriptures be fulfilled, that so it must be done?—*Matt.* xxvi. 50-54.

And he (Jesus) sent messengers before his face; and going, they entered into a city of the Samaritans, to prepare for him.

And they received him not, because his face was of one going to Jerusalem.

And when his disciples James and John had seen this, they said: Lord, wilt thou that we command fire to come down from heaven, and consume them?

And turning, he rebuked them, saying: You know not of what spirit you are.

The Son of man came not to destroy souls, but to save. And they went into another town.—*Luke* ix. 52-56.

For I bear them witness, that they have a zeal of God, but not according to knowledge.

For they, not knowing the justice of God, and seeking to establish their own, have not submitted themselves to the justice of God.—*Rom.* x. 2, 3.

[1]They are zealous in your regard not well: but they would exclude you, that you might be zealous for them.—*Gal.* iv. 17.

But if you have bitter zeal, and there be contentions in your hearts; glory not, and be not liars against the truth.

For this is not wisdom, descending from above: but earthly, sensual, devilish.

For where envying and contention is, there is inconstancy, and every evil work.—*James* iii. 14-16.

[1]St. Paul refers to the Judaizing Christians.

PART II

DOCTRINAL

PART II.—DOCTRINAL

ABSOLUTION OF THE PRIEST, THE

See: Penance, the sacrament of, Part II—page 719.

ANGELS ARE PURE SPIRITS, THE

And the angel said to them: Peace be to you, fear not.

For when I was with you, I was there by the will of God: bless ye him, and sing praises to him.

I seemed indeed to eat and to drink with you: but I use an invisible meat and drink, which cannot be seen by men.—*Tob.* xii. 17-19.

Who makest thy angels spirits: and thy ministers a burning fire.—*Ps.*ciii.4.

And to the angels indeed he saith: He that maketh his angels spirits, and his ministers a flame of fire.—*Heb.* i. 7.

But to which of the angels said he at any time: Sit on my right hand, until I make thy enemies thy footstool? Are they not all ministering spirits, sent to minister for them, who shall receive the inheritance of salvation?—*Heb.* i. 13, 14.

And from the throne proceeded lightnings, and voices, and thunders; and there were seven lamps burning before the throne, which are the seven spirits of God.—*Apoc.* iv. 5.

ANGELS, THE GREAT NUMBER OF THE

I beheld till thrones were placed, and the Ancient of days sat: his garment was white as snow, and the hair of his head like clean wool: his throne like flames of fire: the wheels of it like a burning fire.

A swift stream of fire issued forth from before him: thousands of thousands ministered to him, and ten thousand times a hundred thousand stood before him: the judgment sat, and the books were opened.—*Dan.* vii. 9, 10.

Then Jesus saith to him (Peter):

Put up again thy sword into its place: for all that take the sword shall perish with the sword.

Thinkest thou that I cannot ask my Father, and he will give me presently more than twelve legions of angels?—*Matt.* xxvi. 52, 53.

And I beheld, and I heard the voice of many angels round about the throne, and the living creatures, and the ancients; and the number of them was thousands of thousands.—*Apoc.* v. 11.

ANGELS, THE NINE CHOIRS OF

1st. Seraphim

In the year that king Ozias died, I saw the Lord sitting upon a throne high and elevated: and his train filled the temple.

Upon it stood the Seraphim: the one had six wings, and the other had six wings: with two they covered his face, and with two they covered his feet, and with two they flew.—*Is.* vi. 1, 2.

2d. Cherubim

And he cast out Adam; and placed before the paradise of pleasure Cherubim, and a flaming sword, turning every way, to keep the way of the tree of life.—*Gen.* iii. 24.

He bowed the heavens, and came down, and darkness was under his feet.

And he ascended upon the cherubim, and he flew; he flew upon the wings of the winds.—*Ps.* xvii. 10, 11.

And the sound of the wings of the cherubim was heard even to the outward court as the voice of God Almighty speaking. . . .

And the cherubim lifting up their wings, were raised from the earth before me: and as they went out, the wheels also followed: and it stood in the entry of the east gate of the house of the Lord: and the glory of the God of Israel was over them.

This is the living creature, which I saw under the God of Israel by the river Chobar: and I understood that they were cherubim.—*Ezech.* x. 5, 19, 20.

3d. Thrones

For in him were all things created in heaven and on earth, visible and invisible, whether thrones, or dominations, or principalities, or powers: all things were created by him and in him. —*Col.* i. 16.

4th. Dominations

Above all principality, and power, and virtue, and dominion, and every name that is named, not only in this world, but also in that which is to come.—*Eph.* i. 21.

For in him were all things created in heaven and on earth, visible and invisible, whether thrones, or dominations, or principalities, or powers: all things were created by him and in him.—*Col.* i. 16.

5th and 6th. Principalities and Powers

For I am sure that neither death, nor life, nor angels, nor principalities, nor powers, nor things present, nor things to come, nor might,

Nor height, nor depth, nor any other creature, shall be able to separate us from the love of God, which is in Christ Jesus our Lord.—*Rom.* viii. 38, 39.

And above all principality, and power, and virtue, and dominion, and every name that is named, not only in this world, but also in that which is to come.—*Eph.* i. 21.

That the manifold wisdom of God may be made known to the principalities and powers in heavenly places through the church.—*Eph.* iii. 10.

For in him were all things created in heaven and on earth, visible and invisible, whether thrones, or dominations, or principalities, or powers: all things were created by him and in him. —*Col.* i. 16.

Who is on the right hand of God, swallowing down death, that we might be made heirs of life everlasting: being gone into heaven, the angels and powers and virtues being made subject to him.—1 *Peter* iii. 22.

7th. Virtues

Above all principality, and power, and virtue, and dominion, and every name that is named, not only in this world, but also in that which is to come.—*Eph.* i. 21.

Who is on the right hand of God, swallowing down death, that we might be made heirs of life everlasting: being gone into heaven, the angels and powers and virtues being made subject to him.—1 *Peter* iii. 22.

8th. Archangels

For the Lord himself shall come down from heaven with commandment, and with the voice of an archangel, and with the trumpet of God: and the dead who are in Christ, shall rise first.— 1 *Thess.* iv. 15.

When Michael the archangel, disputing with the devil, contended about the body of Moses, he durst not bring against him the judgment of railing speech, but said: The Lord command thee.—*Jude* i. 9.

9th. Angels

For I am sure that neither death, nor life, nor angels, nor principalities, nor powers, nor things present, nor things to come, nor might,

Nor height, nor depth, nor any other creature, shall be able to separate us from the love of God, which is in Christ Jesus our Lord.—*Rom.* viii. 38, 39.

Who is on the right hand of God, swallowing down death, that we might be made heirs of life everlasting: being gone into heaven, the angels and powers and virtues being made subject to him.—1 *Peter* iii. 22.

ANGELS SEE AND PRAISE GOD IN HEAVEN, THE

For I am the angel Raphael, one of the seven, who stand before the Lord. —*Tob.* xii. 15.

Adore him, all you his angels.—*Ps.* xcvi. 7.

Praise ye him, all his angels: praise ye him, all his hosts.—*Ps.* cxlviii. 2.

In the year that king Ozias died, I saw the Lord sitting upon a throne high and elevated: and his train filled the temple.

Upon it stood the Seraphim: the one had six wings, and the other had six wings: with two they covered his face, and with two they covered his feet, and with two they flew.

And they cried one to another, and said: Holy, holy, holy, the Lord God of hosts, all the earth is full of his glory. —*Is.* vi. 1-3.

See that you despise not one of these little ones: for I say to you, that their angels in heaven always see the face of my Father who is in heaven.—*Matt.* xviii. 10.

And again, when he bringeth in the first begotten into the world, he saith: And let all the angels of God adore him.—*Heb.* i. 6.

To whom it was revealed, that not to themselves, but to you they ministered those things which are now declared to you by them that have preached the gospel to you, the Holy Ghost being sent down from heaven, on whom the angels desire to look.—1 *Peter* i. 12.

And from the throne proceeded lightnings, and voices, and thunders; and there were seven lamps burning before the throne, which are the seven spirits of God.—*Apoc.* iv. 5.

And I beheld, and I heard the voice of many angels round about the throne, and the living creatures, and the ancients; and the number of them was thousands of thousands,

Saying with a loud voice: The Lamb that was slain is worthy to receive power, and divinity, and wisdom, and strength, and honor, and glory, and benediction.—*Apoc.* v. 11, 12.

ANGELS ACCOMPANY CHRIST, THE

For the Son of man shall come in the glory of his Father with his angels: and then will he render to every man according to his works.—*Matt.* xvi. 27.

And he saith to him (Nathanael): Amen, amen I say to you, you shall see the heaven opened, and the angels of God ascending and descending upon the Son of man.—*John* i. 51.

And to you who are troubled, rest with us when the Lord Jesus shall be revealed from heaven, with the angels of his power.—2 *Thess.* i. 7.

ANGELS ARE WORTHY OF REVERENCE AND HONOR, THE

Behold I will send my angel, who shall go before thee, and keep thee in thy journey, and bring thee into the place that I have prepared.

Take notice of him, and hear his voice, and do not think him one to be contemned: for he will not forgive when thou hast sinned, and my name is in him.

But if thou wilt hear his voice, and do all that I speak, I will be an enemy to thy enemies, and will afflict them that afflict thee.—*Ex.* xxiii. 20-22.

And when Josue was in the field of the city of Jericho, he lifted up his eyes, and saw a man standing over against him, holding a drawn sword, and he went to him, and said: Art thou one of ours, or of our adversaries?

And he answered: No: but I am prince of the host of the Lord, and now I am come.

Josue fell on his face to the ground. And worshipping, said: What saith my lord to his servant?

Loose, saith he, thy shoes from off thy feet: for the place whereon thou standest is holy. And Josue did as was commanded him.—*Jos.* v. 13-16.

And Gedeon seeing that it was the angel of the Lord, said: Alas, my Lord God: for I have seen the angel of the Lord face to face.

And the Lord said to him: Peace be with thee: fear not, thou shalt not die. —*Judges* vi. 22, 23.

Therefore ought the woman to have a power (*i.e.* a veil) over her head, because of the angels.—1 *Cor.* xi. 10.

Whereas angels who are greater in strength and power, bring not against themselves a railing judgment. —2 *Peter* ii. 11.

ANGELS OUR COMPANIONS IN HEAVEN, THE

But you are come to mount Sion, and to the city of the living God, the heavenly Jerusalem, and to the com-

pany of many thousands of angels.—
Heb. xii. 22.

ANGELS OUR GUARDIANS, THE

Behold I will send my angel, who shall go before thee, and keep thee in thy journey, and bring thee into the place that I have prepared.—*Ex.* xxiii. 20.

The angel of the Lord shall encamp round about them that fear him: and shall deliver them.—*Ps.* xxxiii. 8.

For he hath given his angels charge over thee; to keep thee in all thy ways. In their hands they shall bear thee up: lest thou dash thy foot against a stone.—*Ps.* xc. 11, 12.

And he (the angel) said to me: Fear not, Daniel: for from the first day that thou didst set thy heart to understand, to afflict thyself in the sight of thy God, thy words have been heard: and I am come for thy words.

But the ¹prince of the kingdom of the Persians resisted me one and twenty days: and behold Michael, one of the chief princes, came to help me, and I remained there by the king of the Persians. . . .

And he said: Dost thou know wherefore I am come to thee? and now I will return, to fight against the prince of the Persians. When I went forth, there appeared the prince of the Greeks coming.

But I will tell thee what is set down in the scripture of truth: and none is my helper in all these things, but Michael your prince.—*Dan.* x. 12, 13, 20, 21.

But at that time shall Michael rise up, the great prince, who standeth for the children of thy people: and a time shall come such as never was from the time that nations began even until that time. And at that time shall thy people be saved, every one that shall be found written in the book.—*Dan.* xii. 1.

But when you see the multitude behind, and before, adoring them (the idols), say you in your hearts: Thou oughtest to be adored, O Lord.

¹That is, the angel guardian of Persia: who according to his office, seeking the spiritual good of the Persians, was desirous that many of the Jews should remain among them.

For my angel is with you: And I myself will demand an account of your souls.—*Bar.* vi. 5, 6.

I saw by night, and behold a man riding upon a red horse, and he stood among the myrtle-trees, that were in the bottom: and behind him were horses, red, speckled, and white.

And I said: What are these, my Lord? and the angel that spoke in me, said to me: I will show thee what these are:

And the man that stood among the myrtle-trees answered and said: These are they, whom the Lord hath sent to walk through the earth.

And they answered the angel of the Lord, that stood among the myrtle-trees, and said: We have walked through the earth, and behold all the earth is inhabited, and is at rest.—*Zach.* i. 8-11.

And the angel of the Lord protested to Jesus (the high priest), saying:

Thus saith the Lord of hosts: If thou wilt walk in my ways, and keep my charge, thou also shalt judge my house, and shalt keep my courts, and I will give thee some of them that are now present here to walk with thee.—*Zach.* iii. 6, 7.

See that you despise not one of these little ones: for I say to you, that their angels in heaven always see the face of my Father who is in heaven.—*Matt.* xviii. 10.

But to which of the angels said he at any time: Sit on my right hand, until I make thy enemies thy footstool?

Are they not all ministering spirits, sent to minister for them, who shall receive the inheritance of salvation?—*Heb.* i. 13, 14.

ANGELS ARE INTERESTED IN OUR WELFARE, THE

So I say to you, there shall be joy before the angels of God upon one sinner doing penance.—*Luke* xv. 10.

ANGELS OFFER OUR PRAYERS TO GOD, THE

When thou didst pray with tears, and didst bury the dead, and didst leave thy dinner, and hide the dead by day in thy house, and bury them by night, I offered thy prayer to the Lord. . . .

For I am the angel Raphael, one of the seven, who stand before the Lord.—*Tob.* xii. 12, 15.

And when he had opened the book, the four living creatures, and the four and twenty ancients fell down before the Lamb, having every one of them harps, and golden vials full of odors, which are the prayers of saints.—*Apoc.* v. 8.

And another angel came, and stood before the altar, having a golden censer; and there was given to him much incense, that he should offer of the prayers of all saints upon the golden altar, which is before the throne of God.

And the smoke of the incense of the prayers of the saints ascended up before God from the hand of the angel.—*Apoc.* viii. 3, 4.

ANGELS SENT BY GOD TO HELP AND PROTECT US, THE

And Jacob blessed the sons of Joseph, and said. . . .

The angel that delivereth me from all evils, bless these boys.—*Gen.* xlviii. 15, 16.

And the angel of God, who went before the camp of Israel, removing, went behind them: and together with him the pillar of the cloud, leaving the forepart,

Stood behind, between the Egyptians' camp and the camp of Israel: and it was a dark cloud, and enlightening the night, so that they could not come at one another all the night.—*Ex.* xiv. 19, 20.

But go thou, and lead this people whither I have told thee: my angel shall go before thee.—*Ex.* xxxii. 34.

In the mean time Moses sent messengers from Cades to the king of Edom, to say: Thus saith thy brother Israel: Thou knowest all the labor that hath come upon us:

In what manner our fathers went down into Egypt, and there we dwelt a long time, and the Egyptians afflicted us and our fathers.

And how we cried to the Lord, and he heard us, and sent an angel, who hath brought us out of Egypt.—*Num.* xx. 14-16.

And the angel of the Lord came again the second time, and touched him (Elias), and said to him: Arise, eat: for thou hast yet a great way to go.

And he arose, and ate, and drank, and walked in the strength of that food forty days and forty nights, unto the mount of God, Horeb.—*3 Kings* xix. 7, 8.

At that time the prayers of them both were heard in the sight of the glory of the most high God:

And the holy angel of the Lord, Raphael was sent to heal them both, whose prayers at one time were rehearsed in the sight of the Lord.—*Tob.* iii. 24, 25.

Then Tobias called to him his son, and said to him: What can we give to this holy man, that is come with thee?

Tobias answering, said to his father: Father, what wages shall we give him? or what can be worthy of his benefits?

He conducted me and brought me safe again, he received the money of Gabelus, he caused me to have my wife, and he chased from her the evil spirit, he gave joy to her parents, myself he delivered from being devoured by the fish, thee also he hath made to see the light of heaven, and we are filled with all good things through him. What can we give him sufficient for these things?

. . . And the angel said to them: Peace be to you, fear not.

For when I was with you, I was there by the will of God: bless ye him, and sing praises to him. . . .

It is time therefore that I return to him that sent me: but bless ye God, and publish all his wonderful works.—*Tob.* xii. 1-3, 17, 18, 20.

But as the same Lord liveth, his angel hath been my keeper both going hence, and abiding there, and returning from thence hither: and the Lord hath not suffered me his handmaid to be defiled, but hath brought me back to you without pollution of sin, rejoicing for his victory, for my escape, and for your deliverance.—*Judith* xiii. 20.

But the angel of the Lord went down

with Azarias and his companions into the furnace: and he drove the flame of the fire out of the furnace,

And made the midst of the furnace like the blowing of a wind bringing dew, and the fire touched them not at all, nor troubled them, nor did them any harm.—*Dan.* iii. 49, 50.

Now there was in Judea a prophet called Habacuc, and he had boiled pottage, and had broken bread in a bowl: and was going into the field, to carry it to the reapers.

And the angel of the Lord said to Habacuc: Carry the dinner which thou hast into Babylon to Daniel, who is in the lion's den.

And Habacuc said: Lord, I never saw Babylon, nor do I know the den.

And the angel of the Lord took him by the top of his head, and carried him by the hair of his head, and set him in Babylon over the den in the force of his spirit.

And Habacuc cried, saying: O Daniel, thou servant of God, take the dinner that God hath sent thee. . . .

And Daniel arose and ate. And the angel of the Lord presently set Habacuc again in his own place.—*Dan.* xiv. 32-36, 38.

But when they were in the heat of the engagement there appeared to the enemies from heaven five men upon horses, comely with golden bridles, conducting the Jews:

Two of whom took Machabeus between them, and covered him on every side with their arms, and kept him safe: but cast darts and fireballs against the enemy, so that they fell down, being both confounded with blindness, and filled with trouble.—*2 Mach.* x. 29, 30.

And when they were going forth together with a willing mind, there appeared at Jerusalem a horseman going before them in white clothing, with golden armor, shaking a spear. . . .

So they went on courageously, having a helper from heaven, and the Lord who showed mercy to them.—*2 Mach.* xi. 8, 10.

Now there is at Jerusalem a pond, called Probatica, which in Hebrew is named Bethsaida, having five porches. In these lay a great multitude of sick, of blind, of lame, of withered; waiting for the moving of the water.

And an angel of the Lord descended at certain times into the pond; and the water was moved. And he that went down first into the pond after the motion of the water, was made whole, of whatsoever infirmity he lay under.—*John* v. 2-4.

And they laid hands on the apostles, and put them in the common prison.

But an angel of the Lord by night opening the doors of the prison, and leading them out, said:

Go, and standing speak in the temple to the people all the words of this life. . . .

But when the ministers came, and opening the prison, found them not there, they returned and told,

Saying: The prison indeed we found shut with all diligence, and the keepers standing before the doors; but opening it, we found no man within.—*Acts* v. 18-20, 22, 23.

And when Herod would have brought him forth, the same night Peter was sleeping between two soldiers, bound with two chains: and the keepers before the door kept the prison.

And behold an angel of the Lord stood by him: and a light shined in the room: and he striking Peter on the side, raised him up, saying: Arise quickly. And the chains fell off from his hands.

And the angel said to him: Gird thyself, and put on thy sandals. And he did so.

And he said to him: Cast thy garment about thee, and follow me.

And going out, he followed him, and he knew not that it was true which was done by the angel: but thought he saw a vision.

And passing through the first and the second ward, they came to the iron gate that leadeth to the city, which of itself opened to them. And going out, they passed on through one street: and immediately the angel departed from him.

And Peter coming to himself, said: Now I know in very deed, that the Lord hath sent his angel, and hath delivered me out of the hand of Herod, and from all the expectation of the people of the Jews.—*Acts* xii. 6-11.

And now I exhort you to be of good cheer. For there shall be no loss of any man's life among you, but only of the ship.

For an angel of God, whose I am, and whom I serve, stood by me this night,

Saying: Fear not, Paul, thou must be brought before Cæsar; and behold, God hath given thee all them that sail with thee.—*Acts* xxvii. 22-24.

ANGELS EMPLOYED AS MESSENGERS AND MINISTERS OF GOD, THE

And the angel of the Lord having found her, by a fountain of water in the wilderness, which is in the way to Sur in the desert,

He said to her: Agar, handmaid of Sarai, whence comest thou? and whither goest thou? And she answered: I flee from the face of Sarai, my mistress.

And the angel of the Lord said to her: Return to thy mistress, and humble thyself under her hand.—*Gen.* xvi. 7-9.

And when he (Abraham) had lifted up his eyes, there appeared to him three men standing near him: and as soon as he saw them he ran to meet them from the door of his tent, and adored down to the ground. . . .

And when the men rose up from thence, they turned their eyes towards Sodom: and Abraham walked with them, bringing them on the way.—*Gen.* xviii. 2, 16.

And the two angels came to Sodom in the evening, and Lot was sitting in the gate of the city. And seeing them, he rose up and went to meet them: and worshipped prostrate to the ground. . . .

And they said to Lot: Hast thou here any of thine? son-in-law, or sons, or daughters, all that are thine bring them out of this city:

For we will destroy this place, because their cry is grown loud before the Lord, who hath sent us to destroy them.—*Gen.* xix. 1, 12, 13.

And God heard the voice of the boy: and an angel of God called to Agar from heaven, saying: What art thou doing, Agar? fear not: for God hath heard the voice of the boy, from the place wherein he is.

Arise, take up the boy, and hold him by the hand: for I will make him a great nation.—*Gen.* xxi. 17, 18.

And they came to the place which God had shown him, where he built an altar, and laid the wood in order upon it: and when he had bound Isaac his son, he laid him on the altar upon the pile of wood.

And he put forth his hand and took the sword, to sacrifice his son.

And behold an angel of the Lord from heaven called to him, saying: Abraham, Abraham. And he answered: Here I am.

And he said to him: Lay not thy hand upon the boy, neither do thou any thing to him: now I know that thou fearest God, and hast not spared thy only begotten son for my sake.—*Gen.* xxii. 9-12.

And the angel of God said to me in my sleep: Jacob? And I answered: Here I am. . . .

I am the God of Bethel, where thou didst anoint the stone, and make a vow to me. Now therefore arise, and go out of this land, and return into thy native country.—*Gen.* xxxi. 11, 13.

Jacob also went on the journey he had begun: and the angels of God met him.

And when he saw them, he said: These are the camps of God, and he called the name of that place Mahanaim, that is, Camps.—*Gen.* xxxii. 1, 2.

And when all things were brought over that belonged to him,

He (Jacob) remained alone: and behold a man wrestled with him till morning.

And when he saw that he could not overcome him, he touched the sinew of his thigh, and forthwith it shrank.

And he said to him: Let me go, for it is break of day. He answered: I will not let thee go except thou bless me.

And he said: What is thy name? He answered: Jacob.

¹But he said: Thy name shall not be called Jacob, but Israel: for if thou hast been strong against God, how much more shalt thou prevail against men?—*Gen.* xxxii. 23-28.

And an angel of the Lord stood in the way against Balaam, who sat on the ass, and had two servants with him. . . .

Forthwith the Lord opened the eyes of Balaam, and he saw the angel standing in the way with a drawn sword, and he worshipped him falling flat on the ground. . . .

The angel said: Go with these men, and see thou speak no other thing than what I shall command thee. He went therefore with the princes.—*Num.* xxii. 22, 31, 35.

And an angel of the Lord went up from Galgal to the place of weepers, and said: I made you go out of Egypt, and have brought you into the land for which I swore to your fathers: and I promised that I would not make void my covenant with you for ever:

On condition that you should not make a league with the inhabitants of this land, but should throw down their altars: and you would not hear my voice: why have you done this? . . .

And when the angel of the Lord spoke these words to all the children of Israel, they lifted up their voice, and wept.—*Judges* ii. 1, 2, 4.

And an angel of the Lord came, and sat under an oak, that was in Ephra, and belonged to Joas the father of the family of Ezri. And when Gedeon his son was threshing and cleansing wheat by the winepress, to flee from Madian,

The angel of the Lord appeared to him, and said: The Lord is with thee, O most valiant of men. . . .

And the angel of the Lord said to him: Take the flesh and the unleavened loaves, and lay them upon that rock, and pour out the broth thereon. And when he had done so,

The angel of the Lord put forth the tip of the rod, which he held in his hand, and touched the flesh and the unleavened loaves: and there arose a fire from the rock, and consumed the flesh and the unleavened loaves: and the angel of the Lord vanished out of his sight.

And Gedeon seeing that it was the angel of the Lord, said: Alas, my Lord God: for I have seen the angel of the Lord face to face.—*Judges* vi. 11, 12, 20-22.

Now there was a certain man of Saraa, and of the race of Dan, whose name was Manue, and his wife was barren.

And an angel of the Lord appeared to her, and said: Thou art barren and without children: but thou shalt conceive and bear a son.

. . . Then Manue prayed to the Lord, and said: I beseech thee, O Lord, that the man of God, whom thou didst send, may come again, and teach us what we ought to do concerning the child that shall be born.

And the Lord heard the prayer of Manue, and the angel of the Lord appeared again to his wife as she was sitting in the field.—*Judges* xiii. 2, 3, 8, 9.

And an angel of the Lord spoke to Elias the Thesbite, saying: Arise, and go up to meet the messengers of the king of Samaria, and say to them: Is there not a God in Israel, that ye go to consult Beelzebub the god of Accaron? —*4 Kings* i. 3.

And the angel of the Lord spoke to Elias, saying: Go down with him, fear not. He arose therefore, and went down with him to the king.—*4 Kings* i. 15.

And it came to pass that night, that an angel of the Lord came, and slew in the camp of the Assyrians a hundred and eighty-five thousand.— *4 Kings* xix. 35.

And he (the Lord) sent an angel to Jerusalem, to strike it: and as he was striking it, the Lord beheld, and took pity for the greatness of the evil: and said to the angel that destroyed: It is enough, now stop thy hand. And the angel of the Lord stood by the thrashing floor of Ornan the Jebusite.

And David lifting up his eyes, saw

¹This was an angel as the prophet Osee tells us in xii. 3, 4: saying: "In the womb he (Jacob) supplanted his brother: and by his strength he had success with an angel. And he prevailed over the angel, and was strengthened: he wept, and made supplication to him: he found him in Bethel, and there he spoke with us."

the angel of the Lord standing between heaven and earth, with a drawn sword in his hand, turned against Jerusalem: and both he and the ancients clothed in haircloth, fell down flat on the ground. . . .

And the angel of the Lord commanded Gad to tell David, to go up, and build an altar to the Lord God in the thrashing floor of Ornan the Jebusite. . . .

Now when Ornan looked up, and saw the angel, he and his four sons hid themselves: for at that time he was thrashing wheat in the floor. . . .

And the Lord commanded the angel: and he put up his sword again into the sheath.—1 *Paral.* xxi. 15, 16, 18, 20, 27.

Bless the Lord, all ye his angels: you that are mighty in strength, and execute his word, hearkening to the voice of his orders.

Bless the Lord, all ye his hosts: you ministers of his that do his will.—*Ps.* cii. 20, 21.

As I was yet speaking in prayer, behold the man Gabriel, whom I had seen in the vision at the beginning, flying swiftly touched me at the time of the evening sacrifice.

And he instructed me, and spoke to me, and said: O Daniel, I am now come forth to teach thee, and that thou mightest understand.—*Dan.* ix. 21, 22.

And I lifted up my eyes, and I saw: and behold a man clothed in linen, and his loins were girded with the finest gold:

And his body was like the chrysolite, and his face as the appearance of lightning, and his eyes as a burning lamp: and his arms, and all downward even to his feet, like in appearance to glittering brass: and the voice of his word like the voice of a multitude. . . .

And he said to me: Daniel, thou man of desires, understand the words that I speak to thee, and stand upright: for I am sent now to thee. . . .

But I am come to teach thee what things shall befall thy people in the latter days, for as yet the vision is for many days.—*Dan.* x. 5, 6, 11, 14.

But while he thought on these things, behold the angel of the Lord appeared to him in his sleep, saying: Joseph, son of David, fear not to take unto thee Mary thy wife, for that which is conceived in her is of the Holy Ghost.—*Matt.* i. 20.

And after they (the wise men) were departed, behold an angel of the Lord appeared in sleep to Joseph, saying: Arise, and take the child and his mother, and fly into Egypt: and be there until I shall tell thee. For it will come to pass that Herod will seek the child to destroy him.—*Matt.* ii. 13.

But when Herod was dead, behold an angel of the Lord appeared in sleep to Joseph in Egypt,

Saying: Arise, and take the child and his mother, and go into the land of Israel. For they are dead that sought the life of the child.—*Matt.* ii. 19, 20.

Then the devil left him (Jesus); and behold angels came and ministered to him.—*Matt.* iv. 11.

The Son of man shall send his angels, and they shall gather out of his kingdom all scandals, and them that work iniquity.

And shall cast them into the furnace of fire: there shall be weeping and gnashing of teeth.

. . . So shall it be at the end of the world. The angels shall go out, and shall separate the wicked from among the just.

And shall cast them into the furnace of fire: there shall be weeping and gnashing of teeth.—*Matt.* xiii. 41, 42, 49, 50.

And he shall send his angels with a trumpet, and a great voice: and they shall gather together his elect from the four winds, from the farthest parts of the heavens to the utmost bounds of them.—*Matt.* xxiv. 31.

Thinkest thou that I cannot ask my Father, and he will give me presently more than twelve legions of angels?—*Matt.* xxvi. 53.

And in the end of the sabbath, when it began to dawn towards the first day of the week, came Mary Magdalen and the other Mary, to see the sepulchre.

And behold there was a great earthquake. For an angel of the Lord descended from heaven, and coming, rolled back the stone, and sat upon it.

And his countenance was as lightning, and his raiment as snow. . . .

And the angel answering, said to the women: Fear not you; for I know that you seek Jesus who was crucified.

He is not here, for he is risen, as he said. Come, and see the place where the Lord was laid.

And going quickly, tell ye his disciples that he is risen: and behold he will go before you into Galilee, there you shall see him.

Lo, I have foretold it to you.—*Matt.* xxviii. 1-3, 5-7.

And there appeared to him an angel of the Lord, standing on the right side of the altar of incense.

And Zachary seeing him, was troubled, and fear fell upon him.

But the angel said to him: Fear not, Zachary, for thy prayer is heard; and thy wife Elizabeth shall bear thee a son, and thou shalt call his name John. . . .

And Zachary said to the angel: Whereby shall I know this? for I am an old man, and my wife is advanced in years.

And the angel answering, said to him: I am Gabriel, who stand before God; and am sent to speak to thee, and to bring thee these good tidings.—*Luke* i. 11-13, 18, 19.

And in the sixth month, the angel Gabriel was sent from God into a city of Galilee, called Nazareth,

To a virgin espoused to a man whose name was Joseph, of the house of David; and the virgin's name was Mary.

And the angel being come in, said unto her: Hail, full of grace, the Lord is with thee: blessed art thou among women. . . .

Behold thou shalt conceive in thy womb, and shalt bring forth a son; and thou shalt call his name Jesus. . . .

And Mary said to the angel: How shall this be done, because I know not man?

And the angel answering, said to her: The Holy Ghost shall come upon thee, and the power of the most High shall overshadow thee. And therefore also

the Holy which shall be born of thee shall be called the Son of God.—*Luke* i. 26-28, 31, 34, 35.

And there were in the same country shepherds watching, and keeping the night watches over their flock.

And behold an angel of the Lord stood by them, and the brightness of God shone round about them; and they feared with a great fear.

And the angel said to them: Fear not; for, behold, I bring you good tidings of great joy, that shall be to all the people:

For, this day, is born to you a Saviour, who is Christ the Lord, in the city of David.

And this shall be a sign unto you. You shall find the infant wrapped in swaddling clothes, and laid in a manger.

And suddenly there was with the angel a multitude of the heavenly army, praising God, and saying:

Glory to God in the highest; and on earth peace to men of good will.—*Luke* ii. 8-14.

And it came to pass, that the beggar died, and was carried by the angels into Abraham's bosom. And the rich man also died: and he was buried in hell.—*Luke* xvi. 22.

And he (Jesus) was withdrawn away from them a stone's cast; and kneeling down, he prayed.

Saying: Father, if thou wilt, remove this chalice from me: but yet not my will, but thine be done.

And there appeared to him an angel from heaven, strengthening him. And being in an agony, he prayed the longer. —*Luke* xxii. 41-43.

But Mary stood at the sepulchre without, weeping. Now as she was weeping, she stooped down, and looked into the sepulchre,

And she saw two angels in white, sitting, one at the head, and one at the feet, where the body of Jesus had been laid.

They say to her: Woman, why weepest thou? She saith to them: Because they have taken away my Lord; and I know not where they have laid him.—*John* xx. 11-13.

And while they were beholding him

going up to heaven, behold two men stood by them in white garments.

Who also said: Ye men of Galilee, why stand you looking up to heaven? This Jesus who is taken up from you into heaven, shall so come, as you have seen him going into heaven.—*Acts* i. 10, 11.

Now an angel of the Lord spoke to Philip, saying: Arise, go towards the south, to the way that goeth down from Jerusalem into Gaza: this is desert.—*Acts* viii. 26.

This man (Cornelius) saw in a vision manifestly, about the ninth hour of the day, an angel of God coming in unto him, and saying to him: Cornelius.

And he, beholding him, being seized with fear, said: What is it, Lord? And he said to him: Thy prayers and thy alms are ascended for a memorial in the sight of God.

And now send men to Joppe, and call hither one Simon, who is surnamed Peter.—*Acts* x. 3-5.

And upon a day appointed, Herod being arrayed in kingly apparel, sat in the judgment seat, and made an oration to them.

And the people made acclamation, saying: It is the voice of a god, and not of a man.

And forthwith an angel of the Lord struck him, because he had not given the honor to God: and being eaten up by worms, he gave up the ghost.—*Acts* xii. 21-23.

The Revelation of Jesus Christ, which God gave unto him, to make known to his servants the things which must shortly come to pass: and signified, sending by his angel to his servant John.—*Apoc.* i. 1.

And there was a great battle in heaven, Michael and his angels fought with the dragon, and the dragon fought and his angels:

And they prevailed not, neither was their place found any more in heaven. —*Apoc.* xii. 7, 8.

And he (the angel) said to me: These words are most faithful and true. And the Lord God of the spirits of the prophets sent his angel to show his servants the things which must be done shortly.—*Apoc.* xxii. 6.

ANGELS, THE FALLEN

See: Devil, Part I—page 111.

APOSTLES, THE CALLING OF THE

And Jesus walking by the sea of Galilee, saw two brethren, Simon who is called Peter, and Andrew his brother, casting a net into the sea (for they were fishers).

And he saith to them: Come ye after me, and I will make you to be fishers of men.

And they immediately leaving their nets, followed him.

And going on from thence, he saw other two brethren, James the son of Zebedee, and John his brother, in a ship with Zebedee their father, mending their nets: and he called them.

And they forthwith left their nets and father and followed him.—*Matt.* iv. 18-22.

And passing by the sea of Galilee, he saw Simon and Andrew his brother, casting nets into the sea (for they were fishermen).

And Jesus said to them: Come after me, and I will make you to become fishers of men.

And immediately leaving their nets, they followed him.

And going on from thence a little farther, he saw James the son of Zebedee, and John his brother, who also were mending their nets in the ship:

And forthwith he called them. And leaving their father Zebedee in the ship with his hired men, they followed him. —*Mark* i. 16-20.

The next day again John stood, and two of his disciples.

And beholding Jesus walking, he saith: Behold the Lamb of God.

And the two disciples heard him speak, and they followed Jesus.

And Jesus turning, and seeing them following him, saith to them: What seek you? Who said to him, Rabbi, (which is to say, being interpreted, Master,) where dwellest thou?

He saith to them: Come and see. They came, and saw where he abode, and they stayed with him that day: now it was about the tenth hour.

And Andrew, the brother of Simon Peter, was one of the two who had heard of John, and followed him.

He findeth first his brother Simon, and saith to him: We have found the Messias, which is, being interpreted, the Christ.

And he brought him to Jesus. And Jesus looking upon him, said: Thou art Simon the son of Jona: thou shalt be called Cephas, which is interpreted Peter.

On the following day, he would go forth into Galilee, and he findeth Philip. And Jesus saith to him: Follow me.

Now Philip was of Bethsaida, the city of Andrew and Peter.

Philip findeth Nathanael, and saith to him: We have found him of whom Moses in the law, and the prophets did write, Jesus the son of Joseph of Nazareth.

And Nathanael said to him: Can any thing of good come from Nazareth? Philip saith to him: Come and see.

Jesus saw Nathanael coming to him: and he saith of him: Behold an Israelite indeed, in whom there is no guile.

Nathanael saith to him: Whence knowest thou me? Jesus answered, and said to him: Before that Philip called thee, when thou wast under the fig-tree, I saw thee.

Nathanael answered him, and said: Rabbi, thou art the Son of God, thou art the king of Israel.—*John* i. 35-49.

And when Jesus passed on from thence, he saw a man sitting in the custom house, named Matthew; and he saith to him: Follow me. And he arose up and followed him.—*Matt.* ix. 9.

And when he was passing by, he saw Levi the son of Alpheus sitting at the receipt of custom; and he saith to him: Follow me. And rising up, he followed him.—*Mark* ii. 14.

And after these things he went forth, and saw a publican named Levi, sitting at the receipt of custom, and he said to him: Follow me.

And leaving all things, he rose up and followed him.—*Luke* v. 27, 28.

And having called his twelve disciples together, he gave them power over unclean spirits, to cast them out, and to heal all manner of diseases, and all manner of infirmities.

And the names of the twelve apostles are these: The first, Simon who is called Peter, and Andrew his brother,

James the son of Zebedee, and John his brother, Philip and Bartholomew, Thomas and Matthew the publican, and James the son of Alpheus, and Thaddeus,

Simon the Cananean,

And going up into a mountain, he called unto him whom he would himself: and they came to him.

And he made that twelve should be with him, and that he might send them to preach.

And he gave them power to heal sicknesses, and to cast out devils.

And to Simon he gave the name Peter:

And James the son of Zebedee, and John the brother of James; and he named them Boanerges, which is, The sons of thunder:

And when day was come, he called unto him his disciples; and he chose twelve of them (whom also he named apostles):

Simon, whom he surnamed Peter, and Andrew his brother, James and John, Philip and Bartholomew,

Matthew and Thomas, James the son of Alpheus, and Simon who is called Zelotes,

And Jude the brother of James, and Judas Iscariot, who was the traitor.—*Luke* vi. 13-16.

and Judas Iscariot, who also betrayed him.

These twelve Jesus sent: commanding them, saying: Go ye not into the way of the Gentiles, and into the city of the Samaritans enter ye not. But go ye rather to the lost sheep of the house of Israel.—*Matt.* x. 1-6.

And Andrew and Philip, and Bartholomew and Matthew, and Thomas and James of Alpheus, and Thaddeus, and Simon the Cananean: And Judas Iscariot, who also betrayed him.—*Mark* iii. 13-19.

And they (the apostles) appointed two, Joseph, called Barsabas, who was surnamed Justus, and Matthias.

And praying, they said: Thou, Lord, who knowest the hearts of all men, show whether of these two thou hast chosen,

To take the place of this ministry and apostleship, from which Judas hath by transgression fallen, that he might go to his own place.

And they gave them lots, and the lot fell upon Matthias, and he was numbered with the eleven apostles.—*Acts* i. 23-26.

And as he (Saul) went on his journey, it came to pass that he drew nigh to Damascus; and suddenly a light from heaven shined round about him.

And falling on the ground, he heard a voice saying to him: Saul, Saul, why persecutest thou me?

Who said: Who art thou, Lord? And he: I am Jesus whom thou persecutest. It is hard for thee to kick against the goad.

And he trembling and astonished, said: Lord, what wilt thou have me to do?

And the Lord said to him: Arise, and go into the city, and there it shall be told thee what thou must do. . . .

And the Lord said to him (Ananias): Arise, and go into the street that is called Straight, and seek in the house of Judas, one named Saul of Tarsus. For behold he prayeth. . . .

And the Lord said to him: Go thy way; for this man is to me a vessel of election, to carry my name before the Gentiles, and kings, and the children of Israel.—*Acts* ix. 3-7, 11, 15.

But contrariwise, when they had seen that to me was committed the gospel of the uncircumcision, as to Peter was that of the circumcision.

(For he who wrought in Peter to the apostleship of the circumcision, wrought in me also among the Gentiles.)—*Gal.* ii. 7, 8.

APOSTLES, THE COMMISSION OF THE

Then calling together the twelve apostles, he gave them power and authority over all devils, and to cure diseases.

And he sent them to preach the kingdom of God, and to heal the sick.

And he said to them: Take nothing for your journey; neither staff, nor scrip, nor bread, nor money; neither have two coats.

And whatsoever house you shall enter into, abide there, and depart not from thence.

And whosoever will not receive you, when ye go out of that city, shake off even the dust of your feet, for a testimony against them.

And going out, they went about through the towns, preaching the gospel, and healing everywhere.—*Luke* ix. 1-6.

And Jesus coming, spoke to them, saying: All power is given to me in heaven and in earth.

Going therefore, teach ye all nations; baptizing them in the name of the Father, and of the Son, and of the Holy Ghost.

Teaching them to observe all things whatsoever I have commanded you: and behold I am with you all days, even to the consummation of the world.—*Matt.* xxviii. 18-20.

And he said to them: Go ye into the whole world, and preach the gospel to every creature.

He that believeth and is baptized, shall be saved: but he that believeth not shall be condemned.—*Mark* xvi. 15, 16.

He said therefore to them again: Peace be to you. As the Father hath sent me, I also send you.

When he had said this, he breathed on them; and he said to them: Receive ye the Holy Ghost.

Whose sins you shall forgive, they are forgiven them; and whose sins you shall retain, they are retained.—*John* xx. 21-23.

But you shall receive the power of the Holy Ghost coming upon you, and you shall be witnesses unto me in Jerusalem, and in all Judea, and Samaria, and even to the uttermost part of the earth.—*Acts* i. 8.

And we are witnesses of all things that he did in the land of the Jews and in Jerusalem, whom they killed, hanging him upon a tree.

. . . And he commanded us to preach to the people, and to testify that it is he who was appointed by God, to be judge of the living and of the dead.—*Acts* x. 39, 42.

Then Paul and Barnabas said boldly: To you it behoved us first to speak the word of God: but because you reject it, and judge yourselves unworthy of eternal life, behold we turn to the Gentiles.

For so the Lord hath commanded us: I have set thee to be the light of the Gentiles; that thou mayst be for salvation unto the utmost part of the earth. —*Acts* xiii. 46, 47.

BAPTISM, THE SACRAMENT OF

1st. Its Existence

And Jesus coming, spoke to them, saying: All power is given to me in heaven and in earth.

Going therefore, teach ye all nations; baptizing them in the name of the Father, and of the Son, and of the Holy Ghost.—*Matt.* xxviii. 18, 19.

And he said to them: Go ye into the whole world, and preach the gospel to every creature.

He that believeth and is baptized, shall be saved: but he that believeth not shall be condemned.—*Mark* xvi. 15, 16.

Jesus answered: Amen, amen I say to thee, unless a man be born again of water and the Holy Ghost, he cannot enter into the kingdom of God.—*John* iii. 5.

2d. Administered and Alluded to

Now when they had heard these things, they had compunction in their heart, and said to Peter, and to the rest of the apostles: What shall we do, men and brethren?

But Peter said to them: Do penance, and be baptized every one of you in the name of Jesus Christ, for the remission of your sins: and you shall receive the gift of the Holy Ghost. . . . They therefore that received his word, were baptized; and there were added in that day about three thousand souls.—*Acts* ii. 37, 38, 41.

And as they went on their way, they came to a certain water; and the eunuch said: See, here is water: what doth hinder me from being baptized?

And Philip said: If thou believest with all thy heart, thou mayst. And he answering, said: I believe that Jesus Christ is the Son of God.

And he commanded the chariot to stand still; and they went down into the water, both Philip and the eunuch: and he baptized him.—*Acts* viii. 36-38.

Then Peter answered: Can any man forbid water, that these should not be baptized, who have received the Holy Ghost, as well as we?

And he commanded them to be baptized in the name of the Lord Jesus Christ.—*Acts* x. 47, 48.

And Crispus, the ruler of the synagogue, believed in the Lord, with all his house; and many of the Corinthians hearing, believed, and were baptized.—*Acts* xviii. 8.

And it came to pass, while Apollo was at Corinth, that Paul having passed through the upper coasts, came to Ephesus, and found certain disciples.

And he said to them: Have you received the Holy Ghost since ye believed? But they said to him: We have not so much as heard whether there be a Holy Ghost.

And he said: In what then were you baptized? Who said: In John's baptism.

Then Paul said: John baptized the people with the baptism of penance, saying: That they should believe in him who was to come after him, that is to say, in Jesus.

Having heard these things, they were baptized in the name of the Lord Jesus. —*Acts* xix. 1-5.

For in one Spirit were we all baptized into one body, whether Jews or Gentiles, whether bond or free; and in one Spirit we have all been made to drink.—1 *Cor.* xii. 13.

Husbands, love your wives, as Christ also loved the church, and delivered himself up for it:

That he might sanctify it, cleansing it by the laver of water in the word of life:

That he might present it to himself a glorious church, not having spot or wrinkle, or any such thing; but that it should be holy, and without blemish.— *Eph.* v. 25-27.

Let us draw near with a true heart in fulness of faith, having our hearts sprinkled from an evil conscience, and our bodies washed with clean water.— *Heb.* x. 22.

In which also coming he preached to those spirits that were in prison:

Which had been some time incredulous, when they waited for the patience of God in the days of Noe, when the ark was a building: wherein a few, that is, eight souls, were saved by water.

Whereunto baptism being of the like form, now saveth you also: not the putting away of the filth of the flesh, but the examination of a good conscience towards God by the resurrection of Jesus Christ.—1 *Peter* iii. 19-21.

BAPTISM, THE NECESSITY OF

Jesus answered, and said to him: Amen, amen I say to thee, unless a man be born again, he cannot see the kingdom of God.

Nicodemus saith to him: How can a man be born when he is old? can he enter a second time into his mother's womb, and be born again?

Jesus answered: Amen, amen I say to thee, unless a man be born again of water and the Holy Ghost, he cannot enter into the kingdom of God.

That which is born of the flesh, is flesh; and that which is born of the Spirit, is spirit.

Wonder not, that I said to thee, you must be born again.—*John* iii. 3-7.

BAPTISM OF INFANTS, THE

1st. Compare

But Jesus said to them: Suffer the little children, and forbid them not to come to me: for the kingdom of heaven is for such.—*Matt.* xix. 14.

But Jesus, calling them together, said: Suffer children to come to me, and forbid them not: for of such is the kingdom of God.—*Luke* xviii. 16.

With

Jesus answered: Amen, amen I say to thee, unless a man be born again of water and the Holy Ghost, he cannot enter into the kingdom of God.—*John* iii. 5.

2d. Probably Inferred

And they preached the word of the Lord to him (the keeper of the prison) and to all that were in his house.

And he, taking them the same hour of the night, washed their stripes, and himself was baptized, and all his house immediately.—*Acts* xvi. 32, 33.

And I baptized also the household of Stephanus; besides, I know not whether I baptized any other.—1 *Cor.* i. 16.

BAPTISM, THE EFFECTS OF

Jesus answered: Amen, amen I say to thee, unless a man be born again of water and the Holy Ghost, he cannot enter into the kingdom of God.—*John* iii. 5.

But Peter said to them: Do penance, and be baptized every one of you in the name of Jesus Christ, for the remission of your sins: and you shall receive the gift of the Holy Ghost.—*Acts* ii. 38.

And now why tarriest thou? Rise up, and be baptized, and wash away thy sins, invoking his name.—*Acts* xxii. 16.

Know you not that all we, who are baptized in Christ Jesus, are baptized in his death?

For we are buried together with him by baptism into death; that as Christ is risen from the dead by the glory of the Father, so we also may walk in newness of life.

For if we have been planted together in the likeness of his death, we shall be also in the likeness of his resurrection. . . .

So do you also reckon, that you are dead to sin, but alive unto God, in Christ Jesus our Lord.—*Rom.* vi. 3-5, 11.

For you are all the children of God by faith in Christ Jesus.

For as many of you as have been baptized in Christ, have put on Christ.—*Gal.* iii. 26, 27.

In whom also you are circumcised with circumcision not made by hand, in despoiling of the body of the flesh, but in the circumcision of Christ:

Buried with him in baptism, in whom also you are risen again by the faith of the operation of God, who hath raised him up from the dead.—*Col.* ii. 11, 12.

Not by the works of justice, which we have done, but according to his mercy, he saved us, by the laver of regeneration, and renovation of the Holy Ghost;

Whom he hath poured forth upon us abundantly, through Jesus Christ our Saviour:

That, being justified by his grace, we may be heirs, according to hope of life everlasting.—*Titus* iii. 5-7.

BAPTISM OF DESIRE, THOUGH ONLY IMPLICIT, CAN SUPPLY THE PLACE OF SACRAMENTAL BAPTISM WHEN THE LATTER IS IMPOSSIBLE

Wash yourselves, be clean, take away the evil of your devices from my eyes: cease to do perversely,

Learn to do well: seek judgment, relieve the oppressed, judge for the fatherless, defend the widow.

And then come, and accuse me, saith the Lord: if your sins be as scarlet, they shall be made as white as snow:

and if they be red as crimson, they shall be white as wool.—*Is.* i. 16-18.

But if the wicked do penance for all his sins which he hath committed, and keep all my commandments, and do judgment, and justice, living he shall live, and shall not die.

I will not remember all his iniquities that he hath done: in his justice which he hath wrought, he shall live.—*Ezech.* xviii. 21, 22.

All that the Father giveth to me shall come to me; and him that cometh to me, I will not cast out.—*John* vi. 37.

Jesus answered, and said to him: If any one love me, he will keep my word, and my Father will love him, and we will come to him, and will make our abode with him.—*John* xiv. 23.

And Peter opening his mouth, said: In very deed I perceive, that God is not a respecter of persons.

But in every nation, he that feareth him, and worketh justice, is acceptable to him.—*Acts* x. 34, 35.

BAPTISM OF BLOOD—MARTYRDOM—CAN SUPPLY THE PLACE OF SACRAMENTAL BAPTISM

Every one therefore that shall confess me before men, I will also confess him before my Father who is in heaven.—*Matt.* x. 32.

He that findeth his life, shall lose it: and he that shall lose his life for me, shall find it.—*Matt.* x. 39.

CEREMONIES AND VESTMENTS, THE USE OF

And thou shalt make a holy vesture for Aaron thy brother for glory and for beauty.

And thou shalt speak to all the wise of heart, whom I have filled with the spirit of wisdom, that they may make Aaron's vestments, in which he being consecrated may minister to me.

And these shall be the vestments that they shall make: A rational and an ephod, a tunic and a strait linen garment, a mitre and a girdle. They shall make the holy vestments for thy brother Aaron and his sons, that they may do the office of priesthood unto me.—*Ex.* xxviii. 2-4.

And thou shalt bring Aaron and his sons to the door of the tabernacle of the testimony. And when thou hast washed the father and his sons with water,

Thou shalt clothe Aaron with his vestments, that is, with the linen garment and the tunic, and the ephod and the rational, which thou shalt gird with the girdle.

And thou shalt put the mitre upon his head, and the holy plate upon the mitre,

And thou shalt pour the oil of unction upon his head: and by this rite shall he be consecrated.

Thou shalt bring his sons also and shalt put on them the linen tunics, and gird them with a girdle:

To wit, Aaron and his children, and thou shalt put mitres upon them: and they shall be priests to me by a perpetual ordinance.—*Ex.* xxix. 4-9.

The Lord spoke to Moses in the desert of Sinai, the second year after they were come out of the land of Egypt, in the first month, saying:

Let the children of Israel make the phase in its due time,

The fourteenth day of this month in the evening, according to all the ceremonies and justifications thereof.—*Num.* ix. 1-3.

For what other nation is there so renowned that hath ceremonies, and just judgments, and all the law, which I will set forth this day before your eyes?—*Deut.* iv. 8.

In all his works he (David) gave thanks to the holy one, and to the most High with words of glory. . . .

And he set singers before the altar, and by their voices he made sweet melody.

And to the festivals he added beauty, and set in order the solemn times even to the end of his life, that they should praise the holy name of the Lord, and magnify the holiness of God in the morning.—*Ecclus.* xlvii. 9, 11, 12.

And when the priests shall have entered in, they shall not go out of the holy places into the outward court: but there they shall lay their vestments, wherein they minister, for they are holy: and they shall put on other garments, and so they shall go forth to the people.—*Ezech.* xlii. 14.

They shall enter into my sanctuary, and they shall come near to my table, to minister unto me, and to keep my ceremonies.

And when they shall enter in at the gates of the inner court, they shall be clothed with linen garments: neither shall any woollen come upon them, when they minister in the gates of the inner court and within.

They shall have linen mitres on their heads, and linen breeches on their loins, and they shall not be girded with any thing that causeth sweat.

And when they shall go forth to the outward court to the people, they shall put off their garments wherein they ministered, and lay them up in the store chamber of the sanctuary, and they shall clothe themselves with other garments: and they shall not sanctify the people with their vestments.—*Ezech.* xliv. 16-19.

But let all things be done decently, and according to order.—1 *Cor.* xiv. 40.

CHRIST IS THE TRUE SON OF GOD

The Lord hath said to me: Thou art my son, this day have I begotten thee.

Ask of me, and I will give thee the Gentiles for thy inheritance, and the utmost parts of the earth for thy possession.—*Ps.* ii. 7, 8.

And Jesus being baptized, forthwith came out of the water: and lo, the heavens were opened to him: and he saw the Spirit of God descending as a dove, and coming upon him,

And behold a voice from heaven, saying: This is my beloved Son, in whom I am well pleased.—*Matt.* iii. 16, 17.

Jesus saith to them: But whom do you say that I am?

Simon Peter answered and said: Thou art Christ, the Son of the living God.

And Jesus answering, said to him: Blessed art thou, Simon Bar-Jona: because flesh and blood hath not revealed it to thee, but my Father who is in heaven.—*Matt.* xvi. 15-17.

And the high priest said to him: I adjure thee by the living God, that thou tell us if thou be the Christ the Son of God.

Jesus saith to him: Thou hast said it. Nevertheless I say to you, hereafter you shall see the Son of man sitting on the right hand of the power of God, and coming in the clouds of heaven.—*Matt.* xxvi. 63, 64.

But hereafter the Son of man shall be sitting on the right hand of the power of God.

Then said they all: Art thou then the Son of God? Who said: You say that I am.

And they said: What need we any further testimony? for we ourselves have heard it from his own mouth.—*Luke* xxii. 69-71.

And the Word was made flesh, and dwelt among us, (and we saw his glory, the glory as it were of the only begotten of the Father,) full of grace and truth.—*John* i. 14.

And I knew him not; but he who sent me to baptize with water, said to me: He upon whom thou shalt see the Spirit descending, and remaining upon him, he it is that baptizeth with the Holy Ghost.

And I saw, and I gave testimony, that this is the Son of God.—*John* i. 33, 34.

For God so loved the world, as to give his only begotten Son; that whosoever believeth in him, may not perish, but may have life everlasting.—*John* iii. 16.

Jesus heard that they had cast him (the man born blind) out: and when he had found him, he said to him: Dost thou believe in the Son of God?

He answered, and said: Who is he, Lord, that I may believe in him?

And Jesus said to him: Thou hast both seen him; and it is he that talketh with thee.

And he said: I believe, Lord. And falling down, he adored him.—*John* ix. 35-38.

The Jews answered him (Pilate): We have a law; and according to the law he ought to die, because he made himself the Son of God.—*John* xix. 7.

Many other signs also did Jesus in the sight of his disciples, which are not written in this book.

But these are written, that you may believe that Jesus is the Christ, the Son of God: and that believing, you may have life in his name.—*John* xx. 30, 31.

And we declare unto you, that the promise which was made to our fathers,

This same God hath fulfilled to our children, raising up Jesus, as in the second psalm also is written: Thou art my Son, this day have I begotten thee. —*Acts* xiii. 32, 33.

He that spared not even his own Son, but delivered him up for us all, how hath he not also, with him, given us all things?—*Rom.* viii. 32.

God, who, at sundry times and in divers manners, spoke in times past to the fathers by the prophets, last of all,

In these days hath spoken to us by his Son, whom he hath appointed heir of all things, by whom also he made the world. . . .

For to which of the angels hath he said at any time, Thou art my Son, to-day have I begotten thee? And again, I will be to him a Father, and he shall be to me a Son?

And again, when he bringeth in the first begotten into the world, he saith: And let all the angels of God adore him.—*Heb.* i. 1, 2, 5, 6.

By this hath the charity of God appeared towards us, because God hath sent his only begotten Son into the world, that we may live by him. . . .

And we have seen, and do testify, that the Father hath sent his Son to be the Saviour of the world.

Whosoever shall confess that Jesus is the Son of God, God abideth in him, and he in God.—1 *John* iv. 9, 14, 15.

And we know that the Son of God is come: and he hath given us understanding that we may know the true God, and may be in his true Son. This is the true God and life eternal.— 1 *John* v. 20.

CHRIST IS EQUAL TO GOD THE FATHER

But Jesus answered them: My Father worketh until now; and I work.

Hereupon therefore the Jews sought

the more to kill him, because he did not only break the sabbath, but also said God was his Father, making himself equal to God. Then Jesus answered, and said to them:

Amen, amen, I say unto you, the Son cannot do any thing of himself, but what he seeth the Father doing: for what things soever he doth, these the Son also doth in like manner. . . .

For as the Father raiseth up the dead, and giveth life: so the Son also giveth life to whom he will. . . .

That all men may honor the Son, as they honor the Father. He who honoreth not the Son, honoreth not the Father, who hath sent him.—*John* v. 17-19, 21, 23.

I and the Father are one.—*John* x. 30.

Jesus saith to him: Have I been so long a time with you; and have you not known me? Philip, he that seeth me seeth the Father also. How sayest thou, Show us the Father?

Do you not believe, that I am in the Father and the Father in me? The words that I speak to you, I speak not of myself. But the Father who abideth in me, he doth the works.

Believe you not that I am in the Father, and the Father in me?—*John* xiv. 9-11.

All things whatsoever the Father hath, are mine. Therefore I said, that he (the Holy Spirit) shall receive of mine, and show it to you.—*John* xvi. 15.

And all my things are thine, and thine are mine; and I am glorified in them.

And now I am not in the world, and these are in the world, and I come to thee. Holy Father, keep them in thy name whom thou hast given me; that they may be one, as we also are.—*John* xvii. 10, 11.

That they all may be one, as thou, Father, in me, and I in thee; that they also may be one in us; that the world may believe that thou hast sent me.

And the glory which thou hast given me, I have given to them; that they may be one, as we also are one —*John* xvii. 21, 22.

For let this mind be in you, which was also in Christ Jesus:

Who being in the form of God, thought it not robbery to be equal with God.—*Philipp.* ii. 5, 6.

CHRIST IS TRUE GOD

For a child is born to us, and a son is given to us, and the government is upon his shoulder: and his name shall be called, Wonderful, Counsellor, God the Mighty, the Father of the world to come, the Prince of Peace.—*Is.* ix. 6.

But while he thought on these things, behold the angel of the Lord appeared to him in his sleep, saying: Joseph, son of David, fear not to take unto thee Mary thy wife, for that which is conceived in her, is of the Holy Ghost.

And she shall bring forth a son: and thou shalt call his name Jesus. For he shall save his people from their sins.

Now all this was done that it might be fulfilled which the Lord spoke by the prophet, saying:

Behold a virgin shall be with child, and bring forth a son, and they shall call his name Emmanuel, which being interpreted is, God with us.—*Matt.* i. 20-23.

In the beginning was the Word, and the Word was with God, and the Word was God.

The same was in the beginning with God.

All things were made by him: and without him was made nothing that was made.

. . . He was in the world, and the world was made by him, and the world knew him not.—*John* i. 1-3, 10.

They said therefore to him: Who art thou? Jesus said to them: The beginning, who also speak unto you.—*John* viii. 25.

The Jews therefore said to him: Thou art not yet fifty years old, and hast thou seen Abraham?

Jesus said to them: Amen, amen I say to you, before Abraham was made, I am.—*John* viii. 57, 58.

I and the Father are one.

The Jews then took up stones to stone him.

Jesus answered them: Many good works I have showed you from my

Father; for which of those works do you stone me?

The Jews answered him: For a good work we stone thee not, but for blasphemy; and because that thou, being a man, makest thyself God.—*John* x. 30-33.

Thomas answered, and said to him: My Lord, and my God.

Jesus saith to him: Because thou hast seen me, Thomas, thou hast believed: blessed are they that have not seen, and have believed.—*John* xx. 28, 29.

But you denied the Holy One and the Just, and desired a murderer to be granted unto you.

But the author of life you killed, whom God hath raised from the dead, of which we are witnesses.—*Acts* iii. 14, 15.

God sent the word to the children of Israel, preaching peace by Jesus Christ: (he is Lord of all.)—*Acts* x. 36.

For I wished myself to be an anathema from Christ, for my brethren, who are my kinsmen according to the flesh: . . .

Whose are the fathers, and of whom is Christ, according to the flesh, who is over all things, God blessed for ever. Amen.—*Rom.* ix. 3, 5.

Who is the image of the invisible God, the first born of every creature:

For in him were all things created in heaven and on earth, visible and invisible, whether thrones, or dominations, or principalities, or powers: all things were created by him and in him.

And he is before all, and by him all things consist.—*Col.* i. 15-17.

For in him dwelleth all the fulness of the Godhead corporeally.—*Col.* ii. 9.

God, who, at sundry times and in divers manners, spoke in times past to the fathers by the prophets, last of all,

In these days hath spoken to us by his Son, whom he hath appointed heir of all things, by whom also he made the world.

Who being the brightness of his glory, and the figure of his substance, and upholding all things by the word of his power, making purgation of sins, sitteth on the right hand of the majesty on high. . . .

And to the angels indeed he saith: He that maketh his angels spirits, and his ministers a flame of fire.

But to the Son: Thy throne, O God, is for ever and ever: a sceptre of justice is the sceptre of thy kingdom.—*Heb.* i. 1-3, 7, 8.

Simon Peter, servant and apostle of Jesus Christ, to them that have obtained equal faith with us in the justice of our God and Saviour Jesus Christ.—*2 Peter* i. 1.

In this we have known the charity of God, because he hath laid down his life for us: and we ought to lay down our lives for the brethren.—*1 John* iii. 16.

And we know that the Son of God is come: and he hath given us understanding that we may know the true God, and may be in his true Son. This is the true God and life eternal.—*1 John* v. 20.

I will therefore admonish you, though ye once knew all things, that Jesus, having saved the people out of the land of Egypt, did afterwards destroy them that believed not:

And the angels who kept not their principality, but forsook their own habitation, he hath reserved under darkness in everlasting chains, unto the judgment of the great day.—*Jude* i. 5, 6.

And in the midst of the seven golden candlesticks, one like to the Son of man, clothed with a garment down to the feet, and girt about the paps with a golden girdle. . . .

And when I had seen him, I fell at his feet as dead. And he laid his right hand upon me, saying: Fear not. I am the First and the Last,

And alive, and was dead, and behold I am living for ever and ever, and have the keys of death and of hell.—*Apoc.* i. 13, 17, 18.

CHRIST IS TRUE MAN

And she shall bring forth a son: and thou shalt call his name Jesus. For he shall save his people from their sins.

Now all this was done that it might be fulfilled which the Lord spoke by the prophet, saying:

Behold a virgin shall be with child, and bring forth a son, and they shall call his name Emmanuel, which being interpreted is, God with us.

And Joseph rising up from sleep, did as the angel of the Lord had commanded him, and took unto him his wife.

And he knew her not till she brought forth her first-born son: and he called his name Jesus.—*Matt.* i. 21-25.

And it came to pass, that when they were there, her days were accomplished, that she should be delivered.

And she brought forth her first-born son, and wrapped him up in swaddling clothes, and laid him in a manger; because there was no room for them in the inn.—*Luke* ii. 6, 7.

And the Word was made flesh, and dwelt among us, (and we saw his glory, the glory as it were of the only begotten of the Father,) full of grace and truth. —*John* i. 14.

But when the fulness of the time was come, God sent his Son, made of a woman, made under the law:

That he might redeem them who were under the law: that we might receive the adoption of sons.—*Gal.* iv. 4, 5.

Therefore because the children are partakers of flesh and blood, he also himself in like manner hath been partaker of the same: that, through death, he might destroy him who had the empire of death, that is to say, the devil. . . .

For no where doth he take hold of the angels: but of the seed of Abraham he taketh hold.

Wherefore it behoved him in all things to be made like unto his brethren, that he might become a merciful and faithful high priest before God, that he might be a propitiation for the sins of the people.—*Heb.* ii. 14, 16, 17.

CHRIST IS THE REDEEMER OF THE WORLD

Surely he hath borne our infirmities and carried our sorrows: and we have thought him as it were a leper, and as one struck by God and afflicted.

But he was wounded for our iniquities, he was bruised for our sins: the chastisement of our peace was upon him, and by his bruises we are healed.

All we like sheep have gone astray, every one hath turned aside into his own way: and the Lord hath laid on him the iniquity of us all. . . .

And the Lord was pleased to bruise him in infirmity: if he shall lay down his life for sin, he shall see a longlived seed, and the will of the Lord shall be prosperous in his hand.

Because his soul hath labored, he shall see and be filled: by his knowledge shall this my just servant justify many, and he shall bear their iniquities. . . .

And he hath borne the sins of many, and hath prayed for the transgressors. —*Is.* liii. 4-6, 10, 11, 12.

Even as the Son of man is not come to be ministered unto, but to minister, and to give his life a redemption for many.—*Matt.* xx. 28.

For this is my blood of the new testament, which shall be shed for many unto remission of sins.—*Matt.* xxvi. 28.

The next day, John saw Jesus coming to him, and he saith: Behold the Lamb of God, behold him who taketh away the sin of the world.— *John* i. 29.

For God so loved the world, as to give his only begotten Son; that whosoever believeth in him, may not perish, but may have life everlasting.

For God sent not his Son into the world, to judge the world, but that the world may be saved by him.—*John* iii. 16, 17.

And if any man hear my words, and keep them not, I do not judge him: for I am come not to judge the world, but to save the world.—*John* xii. 47.

For all have sinned, and do need the glory of God.

Being justified freely by his grace, through the redemption, that is in Christ Jesus,

Whom God hath proposed to be a propitiation, through faith in his blood, to the showing of his justice, for the remission of former sins.—*Rom.* iii. 23-25.

For I delivered unto you first of all, which I also received: how that Christ died for our sins, according to the scriptures.—*1 Cor.* xv. 3.

Christ hath redeemed us from the curse of the law, being made a curse for us: for it is written: Cursed is every one that hangeth on a tree:

That the blessing of Abraham might come on the Gentiles through Christ Jesus: that we may receive the promise of the Spirit by faith.—*Gal.* iii. 13, 14.

But now in Christ Jesus, you, who some time were afar off, are made nigh by the blood of Christ.

For he is our peace, who hath made both one, and breaking down the middle wall of partition, the enmities in his flesh:

. . . And might reconcile both to God in one body by the cross, killing the enmities in himself.—*Eph.* ii. 13, 14, 16.

And walk in love, as Christ also hath loved us, and hath delivered himself for us, an oblation and a sacrifice to God for an odor of sweetness.—*Eph.* v. 2.

Because in him, it hath well pleased the Father, that all fulness should dwell:

And through him to reconcile all things unto himself, making peace through the blood of his cross, both as to the things that are on earth, and the things that are in heaven.

And you, whereas you were sometime alienated and enemies in mind in evil works:

Yet now he hath reconciled in the body of his flesh through death, to present you holy and unspotted, and blameless before him.—*Col.* i. 19-22.

Looking for the blessed hope and coming of the glory of the great God and our Saviour Jesus Christ,

Who gave himself for us, that he might redeem us from all iniquity, and might cleanse to himself a people acceptable, a pursuer of good works.—*Titus* ii. 13, 14.

Therefore because the children are partakers of flesh and blood, he also himself in like manner hath been partaker of the same: that, through death, he might destroy him who had the empire of death, that is to say, the devil. . . .

Wherefore it behoved him in all things to be made like unto his brethren, that he might become a merciful and faithful high priest before God,

that he might be a propitiation for the sins of the people.—*Heb.* ii. 14, 17.

But Christ, being come a high priest of the good things to come, by a greater and more perfect tabernacle not made with hand, that is, not of this creation:

Neither by the blood of goats, or of calves, but by his own blood, entered once into the holies, having obtained eternal redemption.

For if the blood of goats and of oxen, and the ashes of a heifer being sprinkled, sanctify such as are defiled, to the cleansing of the flesh:

How much more shall the blood of Christ, who by the Holy Ghost offered himself unspotted unto God, cleanse our conscience from dead works, to serve the living God?

And therefore he is the mediator of the new testament: that by means of his death, for the redemption of those transgressions, which were under the former testament, they that are called may receive the promise of eternal inheritance.—*Heb.* ix. 11-15.

Knowing that you were not redeemed with corruptible things as gold or silver, from your vain conversation of the tradition of your fathers:

But with the precious blood of Christ, as of a lamb unspotted and undefiled.—1 *Peter* i. 18, 19.

Who his own self bore our sins in his body upon the tree: that we, being dead to sins, should live to justice: by whose stripes you were healed.—1 *Peter* ii. 24.

And we have seen, and do testify, that the Father hath sent his Son to be the Saviour of the world.—1 *John* iv. 14.

And they sung a new canticle, saying: Thou art worthy, O Lord, to take the book, and to open the seals thereof; because thou wast slain, and hast redeemed us to God, in thy blood, out of every tribe, and tongue, and people, and nation,

And hast made us to our God a kingdom and priests, and we shall reign on the earth.—*Apoc.* v. 9, 10.

CHRIST DIED FOR ALL MEN

For God so loved the world, as to give his only begotten Son; that whosoever believeth in him, may not perish, but may have life everlasting.

For God sent not his Son into the world, to judge the world, but that the world may be saved by him.—*John* iii. 16, 17.

Therefore, as by the offence of one (Adam), unto all men to condemnation; so also by the justice of one (Christ), unto all men to justification of life.—*Rom.* v. 18.

For the charity of Christ presseth us: judging this, that if one died for all, then all were dead.

And Christ died for all; that they also who live, may not now live to themselves, but unto him who died for them, and rose again.—2 *Cor.* v. 14, 15.

For this is good and acceptable in the sight of God our Saviour,

Who will have all men to be saved, and to come to the knowledge of the truth.

For there is one God, and one mediator of God and men, the man Christ Jesus:

Who gave himself a redemption for all, a testimony in due times.—1 *Tim.* ii. 3-6.

For therefore we labor and are reviled, because we hope in the living God, who is the Saviour of all men, especially of the faithful.—1 *Tim.* iv. 10.

But we see Jesus, who was made a little lower than the angels, for the suffering of death, crowned with glory and honor: that, through the grace of God, he might taste death for all.—*Heb.* ii. 9.

My little children, these things I write to you, that you may not sin. But if any man sin, we have an advocate with the Father, Jesus Christ the just:

And he is the propitiation for our sins: and not for ours only, but also for those of the whole world.—1 *John* ii. 1, 2.

CHRIST DIED EVEN FOR THE REPROBATE

For if, because of thy meat, thy brother be grieved, thou walkest not now according to charity. Destroy not him with thy meat, for whom Christ died.—*Rom.* xiv. 15.

For if a man see him that hath knowledge sit at meat in the idol's temple, shall not his conscience, being weak, be emboldened to eat those things which are sacrificed to idols?

And through thy knowledge shall the weak brother perish, for whom Christ hath died?—1 *Cor.* viii. 10, 11.

But there were also false prophets among the people, even as there shall be among you lying teachers, who shall bring in sects of perdition, and deny the Lord who bought them: bringing upon themselves swift destruction.—2 *Peter* ii. 1.

TESTIMONIES TO CHRIST

1st. Testimony of God the Father

And Jesus being baptized, forthwith came out of the water: and lo, the heavens were opened to him: and he saw the Spirit of God descending as a dove, and coming upon him.

And behold a voice from heaven, saying: This is my beloved Son, in whom I am well pleased.—*Matt.* iii. 16, 17.

And as he was yet speaking, behold a bright cloud overshadowed them. And lo, a voice out of the cloud, saying: This is my beloved Son, in whom I am well pleased: hear ye him.—*Matt.* xvii. 5.

For he (Jesus) received from God the Father, honor and glory: this voice coming down to him from the excellent glory: This is my beloved Son, in whom I am well pleased; hear ye him.

And this voice we heard brought from heaven, when we were with him in the holy mount.—2 *Peter* i. 17, 18.

2d. Testimony of Christ Himself

Again the high priest asked him, and said to him: Art thou the Christ the Son of the blessed God?

And Jesus said to him: I am. And you shall see the Son of man sitting on the right hand of the power of God, and coming with the clouds of heaven. —*Mark* xiv. 61, 62.

3d. Testimony of the Scriptures

Search the scriptures, for you think in them to have life everlasting; and the same are they that give testimony of me.—*John* v. 39.

Many other signs also did Jesus in the sight of his disciples, which are not written in this book.

But these are written, that you may believe that Jesus is the Christ, the Son of God: and that believing, you may have life in his name.—*John* xx. 30, 31.

For with much vigor he (Apollo) convinced the Jews openly, showing by the scriptures, that Jesus is the Christ. —*Acts* xviii. 28.

4th. Testimony of the Prophets

Think not that I will accuse you to the Father. There is one that accuseth you, Moses, in whom you trust.

For if you did believe Moses, you would perhaps believe me also; for he wrote of me.

But if you do not believe his writings, how will you believe my words?— *John* v. 45-47.

To him (Jesus) all the prophets give testimony, that by his name all receive remission of sins, who believe in him.— *Acts* x. 43.

And when they had appointed him (Paul) a day, there came very many to him unto his lodgings; to whom he expounded, testifying the kingdom of God, and persuading them concerning Jesus, out of the law of Moses and the prophets, from morning until evening. —*Acts* xxviii. 23.

5th. Testimony of John the Baptist

I indeed baptize you in water unto penance, but he that shall come after me, is mightier than I, whose shoes I am not worthy to bear; he shall baptize you in the Holy Ghost and fire.

Whose fan is in his hand, and he will thoroughly cleanse his floor and gather his wheat into the barn; but the chaff he will burn with unquenchable fire.— *Matt.* iii. 11, 12.

And they asked him, and said to him: Why then dost thou baptize, if thou be not Christ, nor Elias, nor the prophet?

John answered them, saying: I baptize with water; but there hath stood one in the midst of you, whom you know not.

The same is he that shall come after me, who is preferred before me: the latchet of whose shoe I am not worthy to loose.—*John* i. 25-27.

The next day, John saw Jesus coming to him, and he saith: Behold the Lamb of God, behold him who taketh away the sin of the world.

This is he, of whom I said: After me there cometh a man, who is preferred before me: because he was before me. . . .

And John gave testimony, saying: I saw the Spirit coming down, as a dove from heaven, and he remained upon him.

And I knew him not; but he who sent me to baptize with water, said to me: He upon whom thou shalt see the Spirit descending, and remaining upon him, he it is that baptizeth with the Holy Ghost.

And I saw, and I gave testimony, that this is the Son of God.—*John* i. 29, 30, 32-34.

6th. Testimony of the Apostles

And when they were come up into the boat, the wind ceased.

And they that were in the boat came and adored him, saying: Indeed thou art the Son of God.—*Matt.* xiv. 32, 33.

And Jesus came into the quarters of Cesarea Philippi: and he asked his disciples, saying: Whom do men say that the Son of man is?

But they said: Some John the Baptist, and other some Elias, and others Jeremias, or one of the prophets.

Jesus saith to them: But whom do you say that I am?

Simon Peter answered and said: Thou art Christ, the Son of the living God.—*Matt.* xvi. 13-16.

Nathanael answered him, and said: Rabbi, thou art the Son of God, thou art the king of Israel.—*John* i. 49.

Then Jesus said to the twelve: Will you also go away?

And Simon Peter answered him: Lord, to whom shall we go? thou hast the words of eternal life.

And we have believed and have known, that thou art the Christ, the Son of God.—*John* vi. 68-70.

Then he saith to Thomas: Put in

thy finger hither, and see my hands; and bring hither thy hand, and put it into my side; and be not faithless, but believing.

Thomas answered, and said to him: My Lord, and my God.—*John* xx. 27, 28.

7th. Testimony of the Angels

And the angel said to her: Fear not, Mary, for thou hast found grace with God.

Behold thou shalt conceive in thy womb, and shalt bring forth a son; and thou shalt call his name Jesus.

He shall be great, and shall be called the Son of the most High; and the Lord God shall give unto him the throne of David his father; and he shall reign in the house of Jacob for ever.

And of his kingdom there shall be no end.

And Mary said to the angel: How shall this be done, because I know not man?

And the angel answering, said to her: The Holy Ghost shall come upon thee, and the power of the most High shall overshadow thee. And therefore also the Holy which shall be born of thee shall be called the Son of God.— *Luke* i. 30-35.

And there were in the same country shepherds watching, and keeping the night watches over their flock.

And behold an angel of the Lord stood by them, and the brightness of God shone round about them; and they feared with a great fear.

And the angel said to them: Fear not; for, behold, I bring you good tidings of great joy, that shall be to all the people:

For, this day is born to you a Saviour, who is Christ the Lord, in the city of David.

And this shall be a sign unto you. You shall find the infant wrapped in swaddling clothes, and laid in a manger. —*Luke* ii. 8-12.

8th. Testimony of the Demons

And when he was come on the other side of the water, into the country of the Gerasens, there met him two that were possessed with devils, coming out of the sepulchres, exceeding fierce, so that none could pass by that way.

And behold, they cried out, saying: What have we to do with thee, Jesus, Son of God? art thou come hither to torment us before the time.—*Matt.* viii. 28, 29.

And as he went out of the ship, immediately there met him out of the monuments a man with an unclean spirit. . . .

And seeing Jesus afar off, he ran and adored him.

And crying with a loud voice, he said: What have I to do with thee, Jesus, the Son of the most high God? I adjure thee by God that thou torment me not.—*Mark* v. 2, 6, 7.

And there was in their synagogue a man with an unclean spirit; and he cried out,

Saying: What have we to do with thee, Jesus of Nazareth? art thou come to destroy us? I know who thou art, the Holy One of God.—*Mark* i. 23, 24.

And the unclean spirits, when they saw him, fell down before him: and they cried, saying:

Thou art the Son of God. And he strictly charged them that they should not make him known.—*Mark* iii. 11, 12.

And devils went out from many, crying out and saying: Thou art the Son of God. And rebuking them he suffered them not to speak, for they knew that he was Christ.—*Luke* iv. 41.

9th. Testimony of Jews, Samaritans, and Pagans

Jesus said to her (Martha): I am the resurrection and the life: he that believeth in me, although he be dead, shall live:

And every one that liveth, and believeth in me, shall not die for ever. Believest thou this?

She saith to him: Yea, Lord, I have believed that thou art Christ, the Son of the living God, who art come into this world.—*John* xi. 25-27.

The woman therefore left her water pot, and went her way into the city, and saith to the men there:

Come, and see a man who has told

me all things whatsoever I have done. Is not he the Christ? . . .

So when the Samaritans were come to him, they desired that he would tarry there. And he abode there two days. And many more believed in him because of his own word.

And they said to the woman: We now believe, not for thy saying: for we ourselves have heard him, and know that this is indeed the Saviour of the world. —*John* iv. 28, 29, 40-42.

Now the centurion and they that were with him watching Jesus, having seen the earthquake, and the things that were done, were sore afraid, saying: Indeed this was the Son of God.—*Matt.* xxvii. 54.

And Philip said: If thou believest with all thy heart, thou mayst (be baptized). And he (the eunuch of Ethiopia) answering, said: I believe that Jesus Christ is the Son of God.—*Acts* viii. 37.

10th. Testimony of the Enemies of Christ

The chief priests therefore, and the Pharisees, gathered a council, and said: What do we, for this man doth many miracles?

If we let him alone so, all will believe in him; and the Romans will come, and take away our place and nation.—*John* xi. 47, 48.

The Jews answered him (Pilate): We have a law; and according to the law he ought to die, because he made himself the Son of God.—*John* xix. 7.

But they commanded them (Peter and John) to go aside out of the council; and they conferred among themselves,

Saying: What shall we do to these men? for indeed a known miracle hath been done by them, to all the inhabitants of Jerusalem: it is manifest, and we cannot deny it.

But that it may be no farther spread among the people, let us threaten them that they speak no more in this name to any man.

And calling them, they charged them not to speak at all, nor teach in the name of Jesus.—*Acts* iv. 15-18.

CHRIST, THE REDEEMER, PROPHECIES OF THE COMING OF

I will put enmities between thee (the serpent) and the woman, and thy seed and her seed: she shall crush thy head, and thou shalt lie in wait for her heel. —*Gen.* iii. 15.

And the Lord saith to Abram: . . . I will bless them that bless thee, and curse them that curse thee, and in thee shall all the kindred of the earth be blessed.—*Gen.* xii. 3.

And the Lord said: Can I hide from Abraham what I am about to do:

Seeing he shall become a great and mighty nation, and in him all the nations of the earth shall be blessed?—*Gen.* xviii. 17, 18.

By my own self have I sworn, saith the Lord: because thou hast done this thing, and hast not spared thy only begotten son for my sake:

I will bless thee, and I will multiply thy seed as the stars of heaven, and as the sand that is by the sea shore: thy seed shall possess the gates of their enemies.

And in thy seed shall all the nations of the earth be blessed, because thou hast obeyed my voice.—*Gen.* xxii. 16-18.

And the Lord appeared to him (Isaac) and said: Go not down into Egypt, but stay in the land that I shall tell thee. . . .

And I will multiply thy seed like the stars of heaven: and I will give to thy posterity all these countries: and in thy seed shall all the nations of the earth be blessed.—*Gen.* xxvi. 2, 4.

And he (Jacob) saw in his sleep a ladder standing upon the earth, and the top thereof touching heaven: the angels also of God ascending and descending by it;

And the Lord leaning upon the ladder, saying to him: I am the Lord God of Abraham thy father, and the God of Isaac; the land wherein thou sleepest, I will give to thee and to thy seed.

And thy seed shall be as the dust of the earth: thou shalt spread abroad to the west, and to the east, and to the north, and to the south: and in thee and thy seed all the tribes of the earth shall be blessed.—*Gen.* xxviii. 12-14.

The sceptre shall not be taken away from Juda, nor a ruler from his thigh, till he come that is to be sent, and he shall be the expectation of nations.—*Gen.* xlix. 10.

The blessings of thy father are strengthened with the blessings of his fathers: until the desire of the everlasting hills should come; may they be upon the head of Joseph, and upon the crown of the Nazarite among his brethren.—*Gen.* xlix. 26.

I shall see him, but not now: I shall behold him, but not near. A star shall rise out of Jacob, and a sceptre shall spring up from Israel. . . .

And taking up his parable, again he (Balaam) said: Alas, who shall live when God shall do these things?

They shall come in galleys from Italy, they shall overcome the Assyrians, and shall waste the Hebrews, and at the last they themselves also shall perish.—*Num.* xxiv. 17, 23, 24.

The Lord thy God will raise up to thee a prophet of thy nation and of thy brethren like unto me: him thou shalt hear.—*Deut.* xviii. 15.

Therefore the Lord himself shall give you a sign. Behold a virgin shall conceive; and bear a son, and his name shall be called Emmanuel.—*Is.* vii. 14.

For a child is born to us, and a son is given to us, and the government is upon his shoulder: and his name shall be called, Wonderful, Counsellor, God the Mighty, the Father of the world to come, the Prince of Peace.

His empire shall be multiplied, and there shall be no end of peace: he shall sit upon the throne of David, and upon his kingdom; to establish it and strengthen it with judgment and with justice, from henceforth and for ever: the zeal of the Lord of hosts will perform this.—*Is.* ix. 6, 7.

And there shall come forth a rod out of the root of Jesse, and a flower shall rise up out of his root.

And the spirit of the Lord shall rest upon him: the spirit of wisdom, and of understanding, the spirit of counsel, and of fortitude, the spirit of knowledge, and of godliness.

And he shall be filled with the spirit of the fear of the Lord. He shall not judge according to the sight of the eyes, nor reprove according to the hearing of the ears.

But he shall judge the poor with justice, and shall reprove with equity for the meek of the earth: and he shall strike the earth with the rod of his mouth, and with the breath of his lips he shall slay the wicked.

And justice shall be the girdle of his loins: and faith the girdle of his reins. —*Is.* xi. 1-5.

[1]And there shall come a redeemer to Sion, and to them that return from iniquity in Jacob, saith the Lord.—*Is.* lix. 20.

For Sion's sake I will not hold my peace, and for the sake of Jerusalem, I will not rest till her just one come forth as brightness, and her saviour be lighted as a lamp.

And the Gentiles shall see thy just one, and all kings thy glorious one: and thou shalt be called by a new name, which the mouth of the Lord shall name.—*Is.* lxii. 1, 2.

Behold the Lord hath made it to be heard in the ends of the earth, tell the daughter of Sion: Behold thy Saviour cometh: behold his reward is with him, and his work before him.—*Is.* lxii. 11.

In those days, and at that time, I will make the bud of justice to spring forth unto David, and he shall do judgment and justice in the earth.

In those days shall Juda be saved, and Jerusalem shall dwell securely: and this is the name that they shall call him, The Lord our just one.—*Jer.* xxxiii, 15, 16.

This is our God, and there shall no other be accounted of in comparison of him.

He found out all the way of knowledge, and gave it to Jacob his servant, and to Israel his beloved.

Afterwards he was seen upon earth,

[1]St. Paul refers to this in *Romans* xi. 26, 27. "And so all Israel should be saved, as it is written : There shall come out of Sion, he that shall deliver, and shall turn away ungodliness from Jacob.
And this is to them my covenant: when I shall take away their sins."

and conversed with men.—*Bar.* iii. 36-38.

And I will set up one shepherd over them, and he shall feed them, even my servant David: he shall feed them, and he shall be their shepherd.—*Ezech.* xxxiv. 23.

And I will raise up for them a bud of renown: and they shall be no more consumed with famine in the land, neither shall they bear any more the reproach of the Gentiles.—*Ezech.* xxxiv. 29.

Seventy weeks are shortened upon thy people, and upon thy holy city, that transgression may be finished, and sin may have an end, and iniquity may be abolished; and everlasting justice may be brought; and vision and prophecy may be fulfilled; and the saint of saints may be anointed.

Know thou therefore, and take notice; that from the going forth of the word, to build up Jerusalem again, unto Christ the prince, there shall be seven weeks, and sixty-two weeks.—*Dan.* ix. 24, 25.

And thou, Bethlehem Ephrata, are a little one among the thousands of Juda: out of thee shall he come forth unto me that is to be the ruler in Israel: and his going forth is from the beginning, from the days of eternity.—*Mich.* v. 2.

For thus saith the Lord of hosts: Yet one little while, and I will move the heaven and the earth, and the sea, and the dry land.

And I will move all nations: and the desired of all nations shall come: and I will fill this house with glory: saith the Lord of hosts. . . .

Great shall be the glory of this last house more than of the first, saith the Lord of hosts: and in this place I will give peace, saith the Lord of hosts.—*Aggeus* ii. 7, 8, 10.

Hear, O Jesus thou high priest, thou and thy friends that dwell before thee, for they are portending men: for behold I will bring my servant the Orient.—*Zach.* iii. 8.

Rejoice greatly, O daughter of Sion, shout for joy, O daughter of Jerusalem: behold thy King will come to thee, the just and saviour: he is poor, and riding upon an ass, and upon a colt the foal of an ass.—*Zach.* ix. 9.

Behold I send my angel, and he shall prepare the way before my face. And presently the Lord, whom you seek, and the angel of the testament, whom you desire, shall come to his temple. Behold he cometh, saith the Lord of hosts.

And who shall be able to think of the day of his coming? and who shall stand to see him? for he is like a refining fire, and like the fuller's herb.—*Malach.* iii. 1, 2.

CHRIST, PROPHECIES OF THE PASSION OF

Now all this was done, that the scriptures of the prophets might be fulfilled.—*Matt.* xxvi. 56.

Then Jesus took unto him the twelve, and said to them: Behold we go up to Jerusalem, and all things shall be accomplished which were written by the prophets concerning the Son of man.

For he shall be delivered to the Gentiles, and shall be mocked, and scourged, and spit upon:

And after they have scourged him, they will put him to death; and the third day he shall rise again.—*Luke* xviii. 31-33.

O God my God, look upon me: why hast thou forsaken me?

Far from my salvation are the words of my sins. . . .

But I am a worm, and no man: the reproach of men, and the outcast of the people.

All they that saw me have laughed me to scorn: they have spoken with the lips, and wagged the head.

He hoped in the Lord, let him deliver him: let him save him, seeing he delighted in him. . . .

For many dogs have encompassed me: the council of the malignant hath besieged me.

They have dug my hands and feet. They have numbered all my bones.

And they have looked and stared upon me. They parted my garments amongst them; and upon my vesture they cast lots.—*Ps.* xxi. 2, 7-9, 17-19.

[1]For even the man of my peace, in whom I trusted, who ate my bread, hath greatly supplanted me.—*Ps.* xl. 10.

For the zeal of thy house hath eaten me up: and the reproaches of them that reproached thee are fallen upon me. . . .

In thy sight are all they that afflict me; my heart hath expected reproach and misery.

And I looked for one that would grieve together with me, but there was none: and for one that would comfort me, and I found none.

And they gave me gall for my food, and in my thirst they gave me vinegar to drink.—*Ps.* lxviii. 10, 21, 22.

The stone which the builders rejected; the same is become the head of the corner.—*Ps.* cxvii. 22.

The ox knoweth his owner, and the ass his master's crib: but Israel hath not known me, and my people hath not understood.

. . . For what shall I strike you any more, you that increase transgression? the whole head is sick, and the whole heart is sad.

From the sole of the foot unto the top of the head, there is no soundness therein: wounds and bruises and swelling sores: they are not bound up, nor dressed, nor fomented with oil.—*Is.* i. 3, 5, 6.

I have given my body to the strikers, and my cheeks to them that plucked them: I have not turned away my face from them that rebuked me, and spit upon me.—*Is.* l. 6.

As many have been astonished at thee, so shall his visage be inglorious among men, and his form among the sons of men.—*Is.* lii. 14.

Who hath believed our report? and to whom is the arm of the Lord revealed?

And he shall grow up as a tender plant before him, and as a root out of a thirsty ground: there is no beauty in him, nor comeliness: and we have seen him, and there was no sightliness, that we should be desirous of him:

Despised, and the most abject of men,

a man of sorrows, and acquainted with infirmity: and his look was as it were hidden and despised, whereupon we esteemed him not.

Surely he hath borne our infirmities and carried our sorrows: and we have thought him as it were a leper, and as one struck by God and afflicted.

But he was wounded for our iniquities, he was bruised for our sins: the chastisement of our peace was upon him, and by his bruises we are healed.

All we like sheep have gone astray, every one hath turned aside into his own way: and the Lord hath laid on him the iniquity of us all.

He was offered because it was his own will, and he opened not his mouth: he shall be led as a sheep to the slaughter, and shall be dumb as a lamb before his shearer, and he shall not open his mouth.

He was taken away from distress, and from judgment: who shall declare his generation? because he is cut off out of the land of the living: for the wickedness of my people have I struck him. . . .

And the Lord was pleased to bruise him in infirmity: if he shall lay down his life for sin, he shall see a long-lived seed, and the will of the Lord shall be prosperous in his hand.

Because his soul hath labored, he shall see and be filled: by his knowledge shall this my just servant justify many, and he shall bear their iniquities.

Therefore will I distribute to him very many, and he shall divide the spoils of the strong, because he hath delivered his soul unto death, and was reputed with the wicked: and he hath borne the sins of many, and hath prayed for the transgressors.—*Is.* liii. 1-8, 10, 11, 12.

And after sixty-two weeks Christ shall be slain: and the people that shall deny him shall not be his. And a people with their leader that shall come, shall destroy the city and the sanctuary: and the end thereof shall be waste, and after the end of the war the appointed desolation.—*Dan.* ix. 26.

And I said to them: If it be good in your eyes, bring hither my wages: and

---

[1]Jesus tells us that this refers to the treachery of Judas: for He says in *John* xiii. 18, "I speak not of you all: I know whom I have chosen. But that the Scripture may be fulfilled: He that eateth bread with me, shall lift up his heel against me."

if not, be quiet. And they weighed for my wages thirty pieces of silver.

And the Lord said to me: Cast it to the statuary, a handsome price, that I was prized at by them. And I took the thirty pieces of silver, and I cast them into the house of the Lord to the statuary.—*Zach.* xi. 12, 13.

And they shall look upon me, whom they have pierced: and they shall mourn for him as one mourneth for an only son, and they shall grieve over him, as the manner is to grieve for the death of the first born.—*Zach.* xii. 10.

And they shall say to him: What are these wounds in the midst of thy hands? And he shall say: With these I was wounded in the house of them that loved me.

Awake, O sword, against my shepherd, and against the man that cleaveth to me, saith the Lord of hosts: strike the shepherd, and the sheep shall be scattered: and I will turn my hand to the little ones.—*Zach.* xiii. 6, 7.

And Simeon blessed them, and said to Mary his mother: Behold this child is set for the fall, and for the resurrection of many in Israel, and for a sign which shall be contradicted.—*Luke* ii. 34.

CHRIST'S PASSION PROPHESIED BY HIMSELF

See: Prophecies of Christ, His passion—Appendix, page 796.

CHRIST, THE PROPHECIES OF THE OLD TESTAMENT ARE FULFILLED IN

Do not think that I am come to destroy the law, or the prophets. I am not come to destroy, but to fulfil.—*Matt.* v. 17.

How then shall the scriptures be fulfilled, that so it must be done?

In that same hour Jesus said to the multitudes: You are come out as it were to a robber with swords and clubs to apprehend me. I sat daily with you, teaching in the temple, and you laid not hands on me.

Now all this was done, that the scriptures of the prophets might be fulfilled. —*Matt.* xxvi. 54-56.

Blessed be the Lord God of Israel; because he hath visited and wrought the redemption of his people:

And hath raised up a horn of salvation to us, in the house of David his servant:

As he spoke by the mouth of his holy prophets, who are from the beginning.—*Luke* i. 68-70.

Then Jesus took unto him the twelve, and said to them: Behold, we go up to Jerusalem, and all things shall be accomplished which were written by the prophets concerning the Son of man.—*Luke* xviii. 31.

Then he (Jesus) said to them: O foolish, and slow of heart to believe in all things which the prophets have spoken.

Ought not Christ to have suffered these things, and so to enter into his glory?

And beginning at Moses and all the prophets, he expounded to them in all the scriptures, the things that were concerning him.—*Luke* xxiv. 25-27.

And he (Jesus) said to them: These are the words which I spoke to you, while I was yet with you, that all things must needs be fulfilled, which are written in the law of Moses, and in the prophets, and in the psalms, concerning me.

Then he opened their understanding, that they might understand the scriptures.

And he said to them: Thus it is written, and thus it behoved Christ to suffer, and to rise again from the dead, the third day:

And that penance and remission of sins should be preached in his name, unto all nations, beginning at Jerusalem.—*Luke* xxiv. 44-47.

For if you did believe Moses, you would perhaps believe me also; for he wrote of me.—*John* v. 46.

And many resorted to him (Jesus), and they said: John indeed did no sign.

But all things whatsoever John said of this man, were true. And many believed in him.—*John* x. 41, 42.

But those things which God before had showed by the mouth of all the prophets, that his Christ should suffer, he hath so fulfilled.—*Acts* iii. 18.

For they that inhabited Jerusalem, and the rulers thereof, not knowing him, nor the voices of the prophets, which are read every sabbath, judging him have fulfilled them.

And finding no cause of death in him, they desired of Pilate, that they might kill him.

And when they had fulfilled all things that were written of him, taking him down from the tree, they laid him in a sepulchre.—*Acts* xiii. 27-29.

But being aided by the help of God, I stand unto this day, witnessing both to small and great, saying no other thing than those which the prophets, and Moses did say should come to pass:

That Christ should suffer, and that he should be the first that should rise from the dead, and should show light to the people, and to the Gentiles.—*Acts* xxvi. 22, 23.

Of which salvation the prophets have inquired and diligently searched, who prophesied of the grace to come in you.

Searching what or what manner of time the Spirit of Christ in them did signify: when it foretold those sufferings that are in Christ, and the glories that should follow.—1 *Peter* i. 10, 11.

THE PROPHECIES AND THEIR FULFILMENT CONCERNING CHRIST

Now the generation of Christ was in this wise. When as his mother Mary was espoused to Joseph, before they came together, she was found with child, of the Holy Ghost.

Whereupon Joseph her husband, being a just man, and not willing publicly to expose her, was minded to put her away privately.

But while he thought on these things, behold the angel of the Lord appeared to him in his sleep, saying: Joseph, son of David, fear not to take unto thee Mary thy wife, for that which is conceived in her, is of the Holy Ghost.

And she shall bring forth a son: and thou shalt call his name Jesus. For he shall save his people from their sins.

Now all this was done that it might be fulfilled which the Lord spoke by the prophet, saying:

Behold a virgin shall be with child, and bring forth a son, and they shall call his name Emmanuel, which being interpreted is, God with us.

And Joseph rising up from sleep, did as the angel of the Lord had commanded him, and took unto him his wife.

And he knew her not till she brought forth her first-born son: and he called his name Jesus.—*Matt.* i. 18-25.

Therefore the Lord himself shall give you a sign. Behold a virgin shall conceive, and bear a son, and his name shall be called Emmanuel.—*Is.* vii. 14.

And king Herod hearing this, was troubled, and all Jerusalem with him.

And assembling together all the chief priests and the scribes of the people, he inquired of them where Christ should be born.

But they said to him: In Bethlehem of Juda. For so it is written by the prophet:

And thou Bethlehem the land of Juda art not the least among the princes of Juda: for out of thee shall come forth the captain that shall rule my people Israel.—*Matt.* ii. 3-6.

And thou, Bethlehem Ephrata, art a little one among the thousands of Juda: out of thee shall he come forth unto me that is to be the ruler in Israel: and his going forth is from the beginning, from the days of eternity.—*Mich.* v. 2.

And after they (the wise men) were departed, behold an angel of the Lord appeared in sleep to Joseph, saying: Arise, and take the child and his mother, and fly into Egypt: and be there until I shall tell thee. For it will come to pass that Herod will seek the child to destroy him.

Who arose, and took the child and his mother by night, and retired into Egypt: and he was there until the death of Herod:

That it might be fulfilled which the Lord spoke by the prophet, saying: Out of Egypt have I called my son.—*Matt.* ii. 13-15.

As the morning passeth, so hath the king of Israel passed away. Because Israel was a child, and I loved him: and I called my son out of Egypt.—*Osee* xi. 1.

Then Herod perceiving that he was deluded by the wise men, was exceeding angry; and sending killed all the men children that were in Bethlehem, and in all the borders thereof, from two years old and under, according to the time which he had diligently inquired of the wise men.

Then was fulfilled that which was spoken by Jeremias the prophet, saying:

A voice in Rama was heard, lamentation and great mourning; Rachel bewailing her children, and would not be comforted, because they are not.—*Matt.* ii. 16-18.

Thus saith the Lord: A voice was heard on high of lamentation, of mourning, and weeping, of Rachel weeping for her children, and refusing to be comforted for them, because they are not.—*Jer.* xxxi. 15.

And coming he dwelt in a city called Nazareth: that it might be fulfilled which was said by the prophets: That he shall be called a Nazarene.—*Matt.* ii. 23.

And in those days cometh John the Baptist preaching in the desert of Judea.

And saying: Do penance: for the kingdom of heaven is at hand.

For this is he that was spoken of by Isaias the prophet, saying: A voice of one crying in the desert, Prepare ye the way of the Lord, make straight his paths.—*Matt.* iii. 1-3.

As it is written in Isaias the prophet: Behold I send my angel before thy face, who shall prepare the way before thee.

A voice of one crying in the desert: Prepare ye the way of the Lord, make straight his paths.—*Mark* i. 2, 3.

And he (John) came into all the country about the Jordan, preaching the baptism of penance for the remission of sins;

As it was written in the book of the sayings of Isaias the prophet: A voice of one crying in the wilderness: Prepare ye the way of the Lord, make straight his paths.

Every valley shall be filled; and every mountain and hill shall be brought low; and the crooked shall be made straight; and the rough ways plain;

And all flesh shall see the salvation of God.—*Luke* iii. 3-6.

Behold I send my angel, and he shall prepare the way before my face.—*Malach.* iii. 1.

The voice of one crying in the desert: Prepare ye the way of the Lord, make straight in the wilderness the paths of our God.

Every valley shall be exalted, and every mountain and hill shall be made low, and the crooked shall become straight, and the rough ways plain.

And the glory of the Lord shall be revealed, and all flesh together shall see, that the mouth of the Lord hath spoken.—*Is.* xl. 3-5.

And leaving the city Nazareth, he (Jesus) came and dwelt in Capharnaum on the sea coast, in the borders of Zabulon and of Nephthalim;

That it might be fulfilled which was said by Isaias the prophet:

Land of Zabulon and land of Nephthalim, the way of the sea beyond the Jordan, Galilee of the Gentiles:

The people that sat in darkness, hath seen great light: and to them that sat in the region of the shadow of death, light is sprung up.—*Matt.* iv. 13-16.

At the first time the land of Zabulon, and the land of Nephthali was lightly touched: and at the last the way of the sea beyond the Jordan of the Galilee of the Gentiles was heavily loaded.

The people that walked in darkness, have seen a great light: to them that dwelt in the region of the shadow of death, light is risen.—*Is.* ix. 1, 2.

And when evening was come, they brought to him (Jesus) many that were possessed with devils: and he cast out the spirits with his word: and all that were sick he healed:

That it might be fulfilled, which was spoken by the prophet Isaias, saying: He took our infirmities, and bore our diseases.—*Matt.* viii. 16, 17.

Surely he hath borne our infirmities and carried our sorrows: and we have thought him as it were a leper, and as one struck by God and afflicted.—*Is.* liii. 4.

And the Pharisees going out made a consultation against him, how they might destroy him.

But Jesus knowing it, retired from thence: and many followed him, and he healed them all. And he charged them that they should not make him known.

That it might be fulfilled which was spoken by Isaias the prophet, saying:

Behold my servant whom I have chosen, my beloved in whom my soul hath been well pleased. I will put my spirit upon him, and he shall show judgment to the Gentiles.

He shall not contend, nor cry out, neither shall any man hear his voice in the streets.

The bruised reed he shall not break: and smoking flax he shall not extinguish: till he send forth judgment unto victory. And in his name the Gentiles shall hope.—*Matt.* xii. 14-21.

Behold my servant, I will uphold him: my elect, my soul delighteth in him: I have given my spirit upon him, he shall bring forth judgment to the Gentiles.

He shall not cry, nor have respect to person, neither shall his voice be heard abroad.

The bruised reed he shall not break, and smoking flax he shall not quench: he shall bring forth judgment unto truth.

He shall not be sad, nor troublesome, till he set judgment in the earth: and the islands shall wait for his law.—*Is.* xlii. 1-4.

All these things Jesus spoke in parables to the multitudes: and without parables he did not speak to them.

That it might be fulfilled which was spoken by the prophet, saying: I will open my mouth in parables, I will utter things hidden from the foundation of the world.—*Matt.* xiii. 34, 35.

I will open my mouth in parables: I will utter propositions from the beginning.—*Ps.* lxxvii. 2.

¹A wicked and adulterous generation seeketh after a sign: and a sign shall not be given it, but the sign of Jonas the prophet.—*Matt.* xvi. 4.

And the multitudes running together, he began to say: This generation is a wicked generation: it asketh a sign, and a sign shall not be given it, but the sign of Jonas the prophet.

For as Jonas was a sign to the Ninivites; so shall the Son of man also be to this generation.—*Luke* xi. 29, 30.

Now the Lord prepared a great fish to swallow up Jonas: and Jonas was in the belly of the fish three days and three nights.—*Jonas* ii. 1.

And when they drew nigh to Jerusalem, and were come to Bethphage, unto mount Olivet, then Jesus sent two disciples,

Saying to them: Go ye into the village that is over against you, and immediately you shall find an ass tied, and a colt with her: loose them and bring them to me.

And if any man shall say anything

¹Also Matt xii. 39, 40.

Behold the Lord hath made it to be heard in the ends of the earth, tell the daughter of Sion: Behold thy Saviour

to you, say ye, that the Lord hath need of them: and forthwith he will let them go.

Now all this was done that it might be fulfilled which was spoken by the prophet, saying:

Tell ye the daughter of Sion: Behold thy king cometh to thee, meek, and sitting upon an ass, and a colt the foal of her that is used to the yoke.—*Matt.* xxi. 1-5.

And on the next day, a great multitude that was come to the festival day, when they had heard that Jesus was coming to Jerusalem,

Took branches of palm-trees, and went forth to meet him, and cried: Hosanna, blessed is he that cometh in the name of the Lord, the king of Israel.

And Jesus found a young ass, and sat upon it, as it is written:

Fear not, daughter of Sion: behold, thy king cometh, sitting on an ass's colt.

These things his disciples did not know at the first; but when Jesus was glorified, then they remembered that these things were written of him, and that they had done these things to him. —*John* xii. 12-16.

cometh: behold his reward is with him, and his work before him.—*Is.* lxii. 11.

Rejoice greatly, O daughter of Sion, shout for joy, O daughter of Jerusalem: behold thy King will come to thee, the just and saviour: he is poor, and riding upon an ass, and upon a colt the foal of an ass.—*Zach.* ix. 9.

Jesus saith to them: Have you never read in the Scriptures: The stone which the builders rejected, the same is become the head of the corner? By the Lord this has been done; and it is wonderful in our eyes.—*Matt.* xxi. 42.

Be it known to you all, and to all the people of Israel, that by the name of our Lord Jesus Christ of Nazareth, whom you crucified, whom God hath raised from the dead, even by him this man standeth here before you whole.

This is the stone which was rejected by you the builders, which is become the head of the corner.—*Acts* iv. 10, 11.

The stone which the builders rejected; the same is become the head of the corner.

This is the Lord's doing: and it is wonderful in our eyes.—*Ps.* cxvii. 22, 23.

But when it was evening, he sat down with his twelve disciples.

And whilst they were eating, he said: Amen I say to you, that one of you is about to betray me. . . .

The Son of man indeed goeth, as it is written of him: but woe to that man by whom the Son of man shall be betrayed: it were better for him, if that man had not been born.—*Matt.* xxvi. 20, 21, 24.

I speak not of you all: I know whom I have chosen. But that the scripture may be fulfilled: He that eateth bread with me, shall lift up his heel against me.—*John* xiii. 18.

Men, brethren, the scripture must needs be fulfilled, which the Holy Ghost spoke before by the mouth of David concerning Judas, who was the leader of them that apprehended Jesus:

Who was numbered with us, and had obtained part of this ministry.—*Acts* i. 16, 17.

For even the man of my peace, in whom I trusted, who ate my bread, hath greatly supplanted me.—*Ps.* xl. 10.

Then Jesus saith to them: All you shall be scandalized in me this night. For it is written: I will strike the shepherd, and the sheep of the flock shall be dispersed.—*Matt.* xxvi. 31.

Awake, O sword, against my shepherd, and against the man that cleaveth to me, saith the Lord of hosts: strike the shepherd, and the sheep shall be scattered: and I will turn my hand to the little ones.—*Zach.* xiii. 7.

But the chief priests having taken the pieces of silver, said: It is not lawful to put them into the corbona, because it is the price of blood.

And after they had consulted together, they bought with them the potter's field, to be a burying place for strangers.

For this cause that field was called Haceldama, that is, The field of blood, even to this day.

Then was fulfilled that which was spoken by Jeremias the prophet, saying: And they took the thirty pieces of silver, the price of him that was prized, whom they prized of the children of Israel.

And they gave them unto the potter's field, as the Lord appointed to me.—*Matt.* xxvii. 6-10.

And I said to them: If it be good in your eyes, bring hither my wages: and if not, be quiet. And they weighed for my wages thirty pieces of silver.

And the Lord said to me: Cast it to the ¹statuary, a handsome price, that I was prized at by them.

And I took the thirty pieces of silver, and I cast them into the house of the Lord to the statuary.—*Zach.* xi. 12, 13.

And after they had crucified him, they divided his garments, casting lots; that it might be fulfilled which was spoken by the prophet, saying: They divided my garments among them; and upon my vesture they cast lots.—*Matt.* xxvii. 35.

The soldiers therefore, when they had crucified him, took his garments, (and they made four parts, to every soldier a part,) and also his coat. Now the coat was without seam, woven from the top throughout.

They parted my garments amongst them; and upon my vesture they cast lots.—*Ps.* xxi. 19.

¹The Hebrew word signifies also a potter.

They said then one to another: Let us not cut it, but let us cast lots for it, whose it shall be; that the scripture might be fulfilled, saying: They have parted my garments among them, and upon my vesture they have cast lot. And the soldiers indeed did these things.—*John* xix. 23, 24.

Despised, and the most abject of men, a man of sorrows, and acquainted with infirmity: and his look was as it were hidden and despised, whereupon we esteemed him not.

Surely he hath borne our infirmities and carried our sorrows; and we have thought him as it were a leper, and as one struck by God and afflicted.

But he was wounded for our iniquities, he was bruised for our sins: the chastisement of our peace was upon him, and by his bruises we are healed.—*Is* liii. 3-5.

And they asked him, saying: Why then do the Pharisees and scribes say that Elias must come first?

Who answering, said to them: Elias, when he shall come first, shall restore all things; and as it is written of the Son of man, that he must suffer many things and be despised.—*Mark* ix. 10, 11.

And with him they crucify two thieves; the one on his right hand, and the other on his left.

And the scripture was fulfilled, which saith: And with the wicked he was reputed.—*Mark* xv. 27, 28.

For I say to you, that this that is written must yet be fulfilled in me: And with the wicked was he reckoned. For the things concerning me have an end.—*Luke* xxii. 37.

Therefore will I distribute to him very many, and he shall divide the spoils of the strong, because he hath delivered his soul unto death, and was reputed with the wicked: and he hath borne the sins of many, and hath prayed for the transgressors.—*Is.* liii. 12.

And he came to Nazareth where he was brought up: and he went into the synagogue, according to his custom, on the sabbath day; and he rose up to read.

And the book of Isaias the prophet was delivered unto him. And as he unfolded the book, he found the place where it was written:

The Spirit of the Lord is upon me. Wherefore he hath anointed me to preach the gospel to the poor, he hath sent me to heal the contrite of heart,

To preach deliverance to the captives, and sight to the blind, to set at liberty them that are bruised, to preach the acceptable year of the Lord, and the day of reward.

And when he had folded the book, he restored it to the minister, and sat

The spirit of the Lord is upon me, because the Lord hath anointed me: he hath sent me to preach to the meek, to heal the contrite of heart, and to preach a release to the captives, and deliverance to them that are shut up.

To proclaim the acceptable year of the Lord, and the day of vengeance of our God: to comfort all that mourn.—*Is.* lxi. 1, 2.

down. And the eyes of all in the synagogue were fixed on him.

And he began to say to them: This day is fulfilled this scripture in your ears.—*Luke* iv. 16-21.

And he found in the temple them that sold oxen and sheep and doves, and the changers of money sitting.

And when he had made, as it were, a scourge of little cords, he drove them all out of the temple, the sheep also and the oxen, and the money of the changers he poured out, and the tables he overthrew.

For the zeal of thy house hath eaten me up: and the reproaches of them that reproached thee are fallen upon me.—*Ps.* lxviii. 10.

And to them that sold doves he said: Take these things hence, and make not the house of my Father a house of traffic.

And his disciples remembered that it was written:

The zeal of thy house hath eaten me up.—*John* ii. 14-17.

No man can come to me, except the Father, who hath sent me, draw him; and I will raise him up in the last day.

It is written in the prophets: And they shall all be taught of God. Every one that hath heard of the Father, and hath learned, cometh to me.—*John* vi. 44, 45.

All thy children shall be taught of the Lord: and great shall be the peace of thy children.—*Is.* liv. 13.

And whereas he had done so many miracles before them, they believed not in him:

That the saying of Isaias the prophet might be fulfilled, which he said: Lord, who hath believed our hearing? and to whom hath the arm of the Lord been revealed?

Who hath believed our report? and to whom is the arm of the Lord revealed.—*Is.* liii. 1.

Therefore they could not believe, because Isaias said again:

He hath blinded their eyes, and hardened their heart, that they should not see with their eyes, nor understand with their heart, and be converted, and I should heal them.

These things said Isaias, when he saw his glory, and spoke of him.—*John* xii. 37-41.

And he (the Lord) said: Go, and thou shalt say to this people: Hearing, hear, and understand not: and see the vision, and know it not.

Blind the heart of this people, and make their ears heavy, and shut their eyes: lest they see with their eyes, and hear with their ears, and understand with their heart, and be converted and I heal them.—*Is.* vi. 9, 10.

If I had not done among them the works that no other man hath done, they would not have sin; but now they have both seen and hated both me and my Father.

But that the word may be fulfilled which is written in their law: They hated me without cause.—*John* xv. 24, 25.

Consider my enemies for they are multiplied, and have hated me with an unjust hatred.—*Ps.* xxiv. 19.

Afterwards, Jesus knowing that all things were now accomplished, that the scripture might be fulfilled, said: I thirst.

Now there was a vessel set there full of vinegar. And they, putting a sponge full of vinegar about hyssop, put it to his mouth.—*John* xix. 28, 29.

And they came to the place that is called Golgoth, which is the place of Calvary.

And they gave him wine to drink mingled with gall. And when he had tasted, he would not drink.—*Matt.* xxvii. 33, 34.

And they gave me gall for my food, and in my thirst they gave me vinegar to drink.—*Ps.* lxviii. 22.

The soldiers therefore came; and they broke the legs of the first, and of the other that was crucified with him.

But after they were come to Jesus, when they saw that he was already dead, they did not break his legs.

But one of the soldiers with a spear opened his side, and immediately there came out blood and water.

And he that saw it, hath given testimony; and his testimony is true. And he knoweth that he saith true; that you also may believe.

For these things were done, that the scripture might be fulfilled: You shall not break a bone of him.

And again another scripture saith: They shall look on him whom they pierced.—*John* xix. 32-37.

In one house shall it (the paschal lamb) be eaten, neither shall you carry forth of the flesh thereof out of the house, neither shall you break a bone thereof.—*Ex.* xii. 46.

They shall not leave any thing thereof until morning, nor break a bone thereof, they shall observe all the ceremonies of the phase.—*Num.* ix. 12.

And I will pour out upon the house of David, and upon the inhabitants of Jerusalem, the spirit of grace, and of prayers: and they shall look upon me, whom they have pierced: and they shall mourn for him as one mourneth for an only son, and they shall grieve over him, as the manner is to grieve for the death of the first born.—*Zach.* xii. 10.

This same being delivered up, by the determinate counsel and foreknowledge of God, you by the hands of wicked men have crucified and slain.

Whom God hath raised up, having loosed the sorrows of hell, as it was impossible that he should be holden by it.

For David saith concerning him: I foresaw the Lord before my face: because he is at my right hand, that I may not be moved.

For this my heart hath been glad,

I set the Lord always in my sight: for he is at my right hand, that I be not moved.

Therefore my heart hath been glad,

and my tongue hath rejoiced: moreover my flesh also shall rest in hope.

Because thou wilt not leave my soul in hell, nor suffer thy Holy One to see corruption.

Thou hast made known to me the ways of life: thou shalt make me full of joy with thy countenance.

Ye men, brethren, let me freely speak to you of the patriarch David; that he died, and was buried; and his sepulchre is with us to this present day.

Whereas therefore he was a prophet, and knew that God hath sworn to him with an oath, that of the fruit of his loins one should sit upon his throne.

Foreseeing this, he spoke of the resurrection of Christ. For neither was he left in hell, neither did his flesh see corruption.—*Acts* ii. 23-31.

And we declare unto you, that the promise which was made to our fathers,

This same God hath fulfilled to our children, raising up Jesus, as in the second psalm also is written: Thou art my Son, this day have I begotten thee.

And to show that he raised him up from the dead, not to return now any more to corruption, he said thus: I will give you the holy things of David faithful.

And therefore, in another place also, he saith: Thou shalt not suffer thy holy one to see corruption.

For David, when he had served in his generation, according to the will of God, slept: and was laid unto his fathers, and saw corruption.

But he whom God hath raised from the dead, saw no corruption.—*Acts* xiii. 32-37.

Be penitent, therefore, and be converted, that your sins may be blotted out.

That when the times of refreshment shall come from the presence of the Lord, and he shall send him who hath been preached unto you, Jesus Christ,

Whom heaven indeed must receive, until the times of the restitution of all things, which God hath spoken by the mouth of his holy prophets, from the beginning of the world.

For Moses said: A prophet shall the Lord your God raise up unto you of

and my tongue hath rejoiced: moreover my flesh also shall rest in hope.

Because thou wilt not leave my soul in hell; nor wilt thou give thy holy one to see corruption.

Thou hast made known to me the ways of life, thou shalt fill me with joy with thy countenance: at thy right hand are delights even to the end.—*Ps.* xv. 8-11.

Incline your ear and come to me: hear and your soul shall live, and I will make an everlasting covenant with you, the faithful mercies of David.—*Is.* lv. 3.

The Lord thy God will raise up te thee a prophet of thy nation and of thy brethren like unto me: him thou shalt hear. . . .

your brethren, like unto me: him you shall hear according to all things whatsoever he shall speak to you.

And it shall be, that every soul which will not hear that prophet, shall be destroyed from among the people.—*Acts* iii. 19-23.

You are the children of the prophets, and of the testament which God made to our fathers, saying to Abraham: And in thy seed shall all the kindreds of the earth be blessed.

To you first God, raising up his Son, hath sent him to bless you; that every one may convert himself from his wickedness.—*Acts* iii. 25, 26.

Who having heard it, with one accord lifted up their voice to God, and said: Lord, thou art he that didst make heaven and earth, the sea, and all things that are in them.

Who, by the Holy Ghost, by the mouth of our father David, thy servant, hast said: Why did the Gentiles rage, and the people meditate vain things?

The kings of the earth stood up, and the princes assembled together against the Lord and his Christ.

For of a truth there assembled together in this city against thy holy child Jesus, whom thou hast anointed, Herod, and Pontius Pilate, with the Gentiles and the people of Israel,

To do what thy hand and thy counsel decreed to be done.—*Acts* iv. 24-28.

And the place of the scripture which he (the eunuch of Ethiopia) was reading was this: He was led as a sheep to the slaughter; and like a lamb without voice before his shearer, so openeth he not his mouth.

In humility his judgment was taken away. His generation who shall declare, for his life shall be taken from the earth?

And the eunuch answering Philip, said: I beseech thee, of whom doth the prophet speak this? of himself, or of some other man?

Then Philip, opening his mouth, and beginning at this scripture, preached unto him Jesus.—*Acts* viii. 32-35.

And he that will not hear his words, which he shall speak in my name, I will be the revenger.—*Deut.* xviii. 15, 19.

I will bless them that bless thee, and curse them that curse thee, and in thee shall all the kindred of the earth be blessed.—*Gen.* xii. 3.

And in thy seed shall all the nations of the earth be blessed, because thou hast obeyed my voice.—*Gen.* xxii. 18.

Why have the Gentiles raged, and the people devised vain things?

The kings of the earth stood up, and the princes met together, against the Lord, and against his Christ.—*Ps.* ii. 1, 2.

He was offered because it was his own will, and he opened not his mouth: he shall be led as a sheep to the slaughter, and shall be dumb as a lamb before his shearer, and he shall not open his mouth.

He was taken away from distress, and from judgment: who shall declare his generation? because he is cut off out of the land of the living: for the wickedness of my people have I struck him.—*Is.* liii. 7, 8.

For Christ did not please himself, but as it is written: The reproaches of them that reproached thee, fell upon me.—*Rom.* xv. 3.

For the zeal of thy house hath eaten me up: and the reproaches of them that reproached thee are fallen upon me. —*Ps.* lxviii. 10.

For it is evident that our Lord sprung out of Juda: in which tribe Moses spoke nothing concerning priests.

And it is yet far more evident: if according to the similitude of Melchisedech there ariseth another priest,

Who is made not according to the law of a carnal commandment, but according to the power of an indissoluble life:

For he testifieth: Thou art a priest for ever, according to the order of Melchisedech.—*Heb.* vii. 14-17.

The Lord hath sworn, and he will not repent: Thou art a priest for ever according to the order of Melchisedech. —*Ps.* cix. 4.

Wherefore when he cometh into the world, he saith: Sacrifice and oblation thou wouldest not: but a body thou hast fitted to me:

Holocausts for sin did not please thee.

Then said I: Behold I come: in the head of the book, it is written of me: that I should do thy will, O God.

In saying before, Sacrifices, and oblations, and holocausts for sin thou wouldest not, neither are they pleasing to thee, which are offered according to the law.

Then said I: Behold, I come to do thy will, O God: he taketh away the first, that he may establish that which followeth.

In the which will, we are sanctified by the oblation of the body of Jesus Christ once.—*Heb.* x. 5-10.

Sacrifice and oblation thou didst not desire; but thou hast pierced ears for me.

Burnt offering and sin offering thou didst not require: then said I, Behold I come.

In the head of the book it is written of me that I should do thy will: O my God, I have desired it, and thy law in the midst of my heart.—*Ps.* xxxix. 7-9.

For unto this are you called: because Christ also suffered for us, leaving you an example that you should follow his steps.

Who did no sin, neither was guile found in his mouth.

Who, when he was reviled, did not revile: when he suffered, he threatened not: but delivered himself to him that judged him unjustly.

Who his own self bore our sins in his body upon the tree: that we, being dead to sins, should live to justice: by whose stripes you were healed.—1 *Peter* ii. 21-24.

But he was wounded for our iniquities, he was bruised for our sins: the chastisement of our peace was upon him, and by his bruises we are healed. . . .

And he shall give the ungodly for his burial, and the rich for his death: because he hath done no iniquity, neither was there deceit in his mouth.—*Is.* liii. 5, 9.

CHURCH INSTITUTED BY CHRIST, THE

And I say to thee: That thou art Peter; and upon this rock I will build my church, and the gates of hell shall not prevail against it.

And I will give to thee the keys of the kingdom of heaven. And whatsoever thou shalt bind upon earth, it shall be bound also in heaven: and whatsoever thou shalt loose on earth, it shall be loosed also in heaven.—*Matt.* xvi. 18, 19.

And Jesus coming, spoke to them, saying: All power is given to me in heaven and in earth.

Going therefore, teach ye all nations; baptizing them in the name of the Father, and of the Son, and of the Holy Ghost.

Teaching them to observe all things whatsoever I have commanded you: and behold I am with you all days, even to the consummation of the world.— *Matt.* xxviii. 18-20.

And he said to them: Go ye into the whole world, and preach the gospel to every creature.

He that believeth and is baptized, shall be saved: but he that believeth not shall be condemned.—*Mark* xvi. 15, 16.

When therefore they had dined, Jesus saith to Simon Peter: Simon, son of John, lovest thou me more than these? He saith to him: Yea, Lord, thou knowest that I love thee. He saith to him: Feed my lambs.

He saith to him again: Simon, son of John, lovest thou me? He saith to him: Yea, Lord, thou knowest that I love thee. He saith to him: Feed my lambs.

He said to him the third time: Simon, son of John, lovest thou me? Peter was grieved, because he had said to him the third time: Lovest thou me? And he said to him: Lord, thou knowest all things: thou knowest that I love thee. He said to him: Feed my sheep. —*John* xxi. 15-17.

And he hath subjected all things under his feet, and hath made him (Christ) head over all the church,

Which is his body, and the fulness of him who is filled all in all.—*Eph.* i. 22, 23.

And he gave some apostles, and some prophets, and other some evangelists, and other some pastors and doctors,

For the perfecting of the saints, for the work of the ministry, for the edifying of the body of Christ.—*Eph.* iv. 11, 12.

Because the husband is the head of the wife, as Christ is the head of the Church. He is the saviour of his body.

Therefore as the church is subject to Christ, so also let the wives be to their husbands in all things.—*Eph.* v. 23, 24.

CHURCH ESTABLISHED AND WORKING, THE

And with very many other words did he (Peter) testify and exhort them, saying: Save yourselves from this perverse generation.

They therefore that received his word, were baptized; and there were added in that day about three thousand souls.

And they were persevering in the doctrine of the apostles, and in the communication of the breaking of bread, and in prayers.

. . . And continuing daily with one accord in the temple, and breaking bread from house to house, they took their meat with gladness and simplicity of heart;

Praising God, and having favor with all the people. And the Lord increased daily together such as should be saved. —*Acts* ii. 40-42, 46, 47.

And as they (Peter and John) were speaking to the people, the priests, and the officer of the temple, and the Sadducees, came upon them,

Being grieved that they taught the people, and preached in Jesus the resurrection from the dead.

But many of them who had heard the word, believed; and the number of the men was made five thousand.—*Acts* iv. 1, 2, 4.

And when they had prayed, the place was moved wherein they were assembled; and they were all filled with the Holy Ghost, and they spoke the word of God with confidence.

And the multitude of believers had

but one heart and one soul: neither did any one say that aught of the things which he possessed, was his own; but all things were common unto them.

And with great power did the apostles give testimony of the resurrection of Jesus Christ our Lord; and great grace was in them all.—*Acts* iv. 31-33.

And there came great fear upon the whole church, and upon all that heard these things.

And by the hands of the apostles were many signs and wonders wrought among the people. And they were all with one accord in Solomon's porch.

But of the rest no man durst join himself unto them; but the people magnified them.

And the multitude of men and women who believed in the Lord, was more increased.—*Acts* v. 11-14.

But one came and told them: Behold, the men whom you put in prison, are in the temple standing, and teaching the people. . . .

And when they had brought them, they set them before the council. And the high priest asked them,

Saying: Commanding, we commanded you, that you should not teach in this name; and behold, you have filled Jerusalem with your doctrine, and you have a mind to bring the blood of this man upon us.

But Peter and the apostles answering, said: We ought to obey God rather than men. . . .

And every day they ceased not in the temple, and from house to house, to teach and preach Christ Jesus.—*Acts* v. 25, 27-29, 42.

And in those days, the number of the disciples increasing, there arose a murmuring of the Greeks against the Hebrews, for that their widows were neglected in the daily ministration.

Then the twelve calling together the multitude of the disciples, said: It is not reason that we should leave the word of God, and serve tables.

Wherefore, brethren, look ye out among you seven men of good reputation, full of the Holy Ghost and wisdom, whom we may appoint over this business.

But we will give ourselves continually to prayer, and to the ministry of the word.

And the saying was liked by all the multitude. And they chose Stephen, a man full of faith, and of the Holy Ghost, and Philip, and Prochorus, and Nicanor, and Timon, and Parmenas, and Nicolas, a proselyte of Antioch.

These they set before the apostles; and they praying, imposed hands upon them.

And the word of the Lord increased; and the number of the disciples was multiplied in Jerusalem exceedingly: a great multitude also of the priests obeyed the faith.—*Acts* vi. 1-7.

And at that time there was raised a great persecution against the church which was at Jerusalem; and they were all dispersed through the countries of Judea, and Samaria, except the apostles. . . .

They therefore that were dispersed, went about preaching the word of God. —*Acts* viii. 1, 4.

While Peter was yet speaking these words, the Holy Ghost fell on all them that heard the word.

And the faithful of the circumcision, who came with Peter, were astonished, for that the grace of the Holy Ghost was poured out upon the Gentiles also.

For they heard them speaking with tongues, and magnifying God.

Then Peter answered: Can any man forbid water, that these should not be baptized, who have received the Holy Ghost, as well as we?

And he commanded them to be baptized in the name of the Lord Jesus Christ.—*Acts* x. 44-48.

Now they who had been dispersed by the persecution that arose on occasion of Stephen, went about as far as Phenice and Cyprus and Antioch, speaking the word to none, but to the Jews only.

But some of them were men of Cyprus and Cyrene, who, when they were entered into Antioch, spoke also to the Greeks, preaching the Lord Jesus.

And the hand of the Lord was with them: and a great number believing, were converted to the Lord.

And the tidings came to the ears of the church that was at Jerusalem, touching these things: and they sent Barnabas as far as Antioch.

Who, when he was come, and had seen the grace of God, rejoiced: and he exhorted them all with purpose of heart to continue in the Lord.

For he was a good man, and full of the Holy Ghost and of faith. And a great multitude was added to the Lord.

And Barnabas went to Tarsus to seek Saul: whom, when he had found, he brought to Antioch.

And they conversed there in the church a whole year; and they taught a great multitude, so that at Antioch the disciples were first named Christians.—*Acts* xi. 19-26.

But the word of the Lord increased and multiplied.

And Barnabas and Saul returned from Jerusalem, ¹having fulfilled their ministry, taking with them John, who was surnamed Mark.—*Acts* xii. 24, 25.

Now there were in the church which was at Antioch, prophets and doctors, among whom was Barnabas, and Simon who was called Niger, and Lucius of Cyrene, and Manahen, who was the foster brother of Herod the tetrach, and Saul.

And as they were ministering to the Lord, and fasting, the Holy Ghost said to them: Separate me Saul and Barnabas, for the work whereunto I have taken them.

Then they, fasting and praying, and imposing their hands upon them, sent them away.—*Acts* xiii. 1-3.

Then Paul and Barnabas said boldly (to the Jews of Antioch in Pisidia): To you it behoved us first to speak the word of God: but because you reject it, and judge yourselves unworthy of eternal life, behold we turn to the Gentiles.

For so the Lord hath commanded us: I have set thee to be the light of the Gentiles; that thou mayst be for salvation unto the utmost part of the earth.

And the Gentiles hearing it, were glad, and glorified the word of the

¹They were sent to Jerusalem to convey the alms collected by the church at Antioch. *Acts* xi. 29, 30.

Lord: and as many as were ordained to life everlasting, believed.

And the word of the Lord was published throughout the whole country.— *Acts* xiii. 46-49.

And some coming down from Judea, taught the brethren: That except you be circumcised after the manner of Moses, you cannot be saved.

And when Paul and Barnabas had no small contest with them, they determined that Paul and Barnabas, and certain others of the other side, should go up to the apostles and priests to Jerusalem about this question.

. . . And when they were come to Jerusalem, they were received by the church, and by the apostles and ancients, declaring how great things God had done with them.

But there arose some of the sect of the Pharisees that believed, saying: They must be circumcised, and be commanded to observe the law of Moses.

And the apostles and ancients assembled to consider of this matter. . . .

Then it pleased the apostles and ancients, with the whole church, to choose men of their own company, and to send to Antioch, with Paul and Barnabas, namely, Judas, who was surnamed Barsabas, and Silas, chief men among the brethren.

Writing by their hands: The apostles and ancients, brethren, to the brethren of the Gentiles that are at Antioch, and in Syria and Cilicia, greeting.

Forasmuch as we have heard, that some going out from us have troubled you with words, subverting your souls; to whom we gave no commandment:

It hath seemed good to us, being assembled together, to choose out men, and to send them unto you, with our well beloved Barnabas and Paul. . . .

For it hath seemed good to the Holy Ghost and to us, to lay no further burden upon you than these necessary things:

That you abstain from things sacrificed to idols, and from blood, and from things strangled, and from fornication; from which things keeping yourselves, you shall do well. Fare ye well.—*Acts* xv. 1, 2, 4-6, 22-25, 28, 29.

And as they (Paul and Silas) passed

through the cities, they delivered unto them the decrees for to keep, that were decreed by the apostles and ancients who were at Jerusalem.

And the churches were confirmed in faith, and increased in number daily.—*Acts* xvi. 4, 5.

We have found this (Paul) to be a pestilent man, and raising seditions among all the Jews throughout the world, and author of the sedition of the sect of the Nazarenes.—*Acts* xxiv. 5.

But we desire to hear of thee what thou thinkest; for as concerning this sect, we know that it is everywhere contradicted.—*Acts* xxviii. 22.

And God indeed hath set some in the church; first apostles, secondly prophets, thirdly doctors; after that miracles; then the graces of healings, helps, governments, kinds of tongues, interpretations of speeches.—1 *Cor.* xii. 28.

If therefore the whole church come together into one place, and all speak with tongues, and there come in unlearned persons or infidels, will they not say that you are mad?

But if all prophesy, and there come in one that believeth not, or an unlearned person, he is convinced of all, he is judged of all.

The secrets of his heart are made manifest; and so, falling down on his face, he will adore God, affirming that God is among you indeed.

How is it, then, brethren? When you come together, every one of you hath a psalm, hath a doctrine, hath a revelation, hath a tongue, hath an interpretation: let all things be done to edification.

If any speak with a tongue, let it be by two, or at the most by three, and in course, and let one interpret.

But if there be no interpreter, let him hold his peace in the church, and speak to himself and to God.

And let the prophets speak, two or three; and let the rest judge.

But if any thing be revealed to another sitting, let the first hold his peace.

For you may all prophesy one by one; that all may learn, and all may be exhorted. . . .

Let women keep silence in the churches: for it is not permitted them to speak, but to be subject, as also the law saith.—1 *Cor.* xiv. 23-31, 34.

And he gave some apostles, and some prophets, and other some evangelists, and other some pastors and doctors,

For the perfecting of the saints, for the work of the ministry, for the edifying of the body of Christ.—*Eph.* iv. 11, 12.

CHURCH IS OF GOD, THE

Take heed to yourselves, and to the whole flock, wherein the Holy Ghost hath placed you bishops, to rule the church of God, which he hath purchased with his own blood.—*Acts* xx. 28.

Be without offence to the Jews, and to the Gentiles, and to the church of God.—1 *Cor.* x. 32.

What, have you not houses to eat and to drink in? Or despise ye the church of God; and put them to shame that have not? What shall I say to you? Do I praise you? In this I praise you not.—1 *Cor.* xi. 22.

And he hath subjected all things under his feet, and hath made him head over all the church,

Which is his body, and the fulness of him who is filled all in all.—*Eph.* i. 22, 23.

But if I tarry long, that thou mayst know how thou oughtest to behave thyself in the house of God, which is the church of the living God, the pillar and ground of the truth.—1 *Tim.* iii. 15.

CHURCH, THE UNITY OF THE

See also: Pope, or Chief Pastor—page 720.

And other sheep I have, that are not of this fold: them also I must bring, and they shall hear my voice, and there shall be one fold and one shepherd.—*John* x. 16.

And this he (Caiphas) spoke not of himself: but being the high priest of that year, he prophesied that Jesus should die for the nation.

And not only for the nation, but to gather together in one the children of God, that were dispersed.—*John* xi. 51, 52.

And now I am not in the world, and these are in the world, and I come to thee. Holy Father, keep them in thy name whom thou hast given me; that they may be one, as we also are. . . .

And not for them only do I pray, but for them also who through their word shall believe in me;

That they all may be one, as thou, Father, in me, and I in thee; that they also may be one in us; that the world may believe that thou hast sent me.— *John* xvii. 11, 20, 21.

For as in one body we have many members, but all the members have not the same office:

So we being many, are one body in Christ, and every one members one of another.—*Rom.* xii. 4, 5.

For we, being many, are one bread, one body, all that partake of one bread. —1 *Cor.* x. 17.

For as the body is one, and hath many members; and all the members of the body, whereas they are many, yet are one body, so also is Christ.

For in one Spirit were we all baptized into one body, whether Jews or Gentiles, whether bond or free; and in one Spirit we have all been made to drink. . . .

But now there are many members indeed, yet one body. . . .

Now you are the body of Christ, and members of member.—1 *Cor.* xii. 12, 13, 20, 27.

But though we, or an angel from heaven, preach a gospel to you besides that which we have preached to you, let him be anathema.

As we said before, so now I say again: if any one preach to you a gospel, besides that which you have received, let him be anathema.—*Gal.* i. 8, 9.

And he hath subjected all things under his feet, and hath made him head over all the church,

Which is his body, and the fulness of him who is filled all in all.—*Eph.* i. 22, 23.

Now therefore you are no more strangers and foreigner; but you are fellow citizens with the saints, and the domestics of God,

Built upon the foundation of the apostles and prophets, Jesus Christ himself being the chief corner stone:

In whom all the building, being framed together, groweth up into a holy temple in the Lord.

In whom you also are built together into an habitation of God in the Spirit. —*Eph.* ii. 19-22.

One body and one Spirit; as you are called in one hope of your calling. One Lord, one faith, one baptism.— *Eph.* iv. 4, 5.

But doing the truth in charity, we may in all things grow up in him who is the head, even Christ:

From whom the whole body, being compacted and fitly joined together, by what every joint supplieth, according to the operation in the measure of every part, maketh increase of the body, unto the edifying of itself in charity.—*Eph.* iv. 15, 16.

And he is the head of the body, the church, who is the beginning, the first born from the dead; that in all things he may hold the primacy.—*Col.* i. 18.

Let no man seduce you, willing in humility, and religion of angels, walking in the things which he hath not seen, in vain puffed up by the sense of his flesh,

And not holding the head, from which the whole body, by joints and bands, being supplied with nourishment and compacted, groweth unto the increase of God.—*Col.* ii. 18, 19.

And let the peace of Christ rejoice in your hearts, wherein also you are called in one body: and be ye thankful.—*Col.* iii. 15.

CHURCH, THE HOLINESS OF THE

1st. In its Founder and Head, Christ

And he hath subjected all things under his feet, and hath made him head over all the church,

Which is his body, and the fulness of him who is filled all in all.—*Eph.* i. 22, 23.

Now therefore you are no more strangers and foreigners; but you are fellow citizens with the saints, and the domestics of God,

Built upon the foundation of the

apostles and prophets, Jesus Christ himself being the chief corner stone:

In whom all the building being framed together, groweth up into a holy temple in the Lord.

In whom you also are built together into an habitation of God in the Spirit. —*Eph.* ii. 19-22.

And he is the head of the body, the church, who is the beginning, the first born from the dead; that in all things he may hold the primacy.—*Col.* i. 18.

2d. In its Doctrine

Going therefore, teach ye all nations; baptizing them in the name of the Father, and of the Son, and of the Holy Ghost.

Teaching them to observe all things whatsoever I have commanded you: and behold I am with you all days, even to the consummation of the world.— *Matt.* xxviii. 19, 20.

3d. Declared

Husbands, love your wives, as Christ also loved the church, and delivered himself up for it:

That he might sanctify it, cleansing it by the laver of water in the word of life:

That he might present it to himself a glorious church, not having spot or wrinkle, or any such thing; but that it should be holy, and without blemish.— *Eph.* v. 25-27.

CHURCH, CATHOLICITY OF THE

1st. Prophesied in the Old Testament

Ask of me, and I will give thee the Gentiles for thy inheritance, and the utmost parts of the earth for thy possession.—*Ps.* ii. 8.

There are no speeches nor languages, where their voices are not heard.

Their sound hath gone forth into all the earth: and their words unto the ends of the world.—*Ps.* xviii. 4, 5.

All the ends of the earth shall remember, and shall be converted to the Lord:

And all the kindreds of the Gentiles shall adore in his sight.—*Ps.* xxi. 28.

And he shall rule from sea to sea, and from the river unto the ends of the earth.

. . . The kings of Tharsis and the islands shall offer presents: the kings of the Arabians and of Saba shall bring gifts:

And all the kings of the earth shall adore him: all nations shall serve him. —*Ps.* lxxi. 8, 10, 11.

And in the last days the mountain of the house of the Lord shall be prepared on the top of mountains, and it shall be exalted above the hills, and all nations shall flow unto it.

And many people shall go, and say: Come and let us go up to the mountain of the Lord, and to the house of the God of Jacob, and he will teach us his ways, and we will walk in his paths: for the law shall come forth from Sion, and the word of the Lord from Jerusalem.—*Is.* ii. 2, 3.

And he (the Lord) said: It is a small thing that thou shouldst be my servant to raise up the tribes of Jacob, and to convert the dregs of Israel. Behold, [1]I have given thee to be the light of the Gentiles, that thou mayst be my salvation even to the farthest part of the earth.—*Is.* xlix. 6.

Behold these shall come from afar, and behold these from the north and from the sea, and these from the south country. . . .

Lift up thy eyes round about, and see all these are gathered together, they are come to thee: as I live, saith the Lord, thou shalt be clothed with all these as with an ornament, and as a bride thou shalt put them about thee.—*Is.* xlix. 12, 18.

Lift up thy eyes round about, and see: all these are gathered together, they are come to thee: thy sons shall come from afar, and thy daughters shall rise up at thy side.

Then shalt thou see, and abound, and thy heart shall wonder and be enlarged, when the multitude of the sea shall be converted to thee, the strength of the Gentiles shall come to thee.—*Is.* lx. 4, 5.

[1]That this refers to the church, we are told in *Acts* xiii. 46, 47. "Then Paul and Barnabas said boldly: To you it behoved us first to speak the word of God: but because you reject it, and judge yourselves unworthy of eternal life, behold we turn to the Gentiles."

For so the Lord hath commanded us: I have set thee to be the light of the Gentiles; that thou mayst be for salvation unto the utmost part of the earth.

Then thou sawest, till a stone was cut out of a mountain without hands: and it struck the statue upon the feet thereof that were of iron and of clay, and broke them in pieces.

Then was the iron, the clay, the brass, the silver, and the gold broken to pieces together, and became like the chaff of a summer's thrashing floor, and they were carried away by the wind: and there was no place found for them: but the stone that struck the statue, became a great mountain, and filled the whole earth.

This is the dream: we will also tell the interpretation thereof before thee, O king. . . .

But in the days of those kingdoms the God of heaven will set up a kingdom that shall never be destroyed, and his kingdom shall not be delivered up to another people, and it shall break in pieces, and shall consume all these kingdoms, and itself shall stand for ever.—*Dan.* ii. 34-36, 44.

And it shall come to pass in the last days, that the mountain of the house of the Lord shall be prepared in the top of mountains, and high above the hills: and people shall flow to it.

And many nations shall come in haste, and say: Come, let us go up to the mountain of the Lord, and to the house of the God of Jacob: and he will teach us of his ways, and we will walk in his paths: for the law shall go forth out of Sion, and the word of the Lord out of Jerusalem.—*Mich.* iv. 1, 2.

Rejoice greatly, O daughter of Sion, shout for joy, O daughter of Jerusalem: behold thy King will come to thee, the just and saviour: he is poor, and riding upon an ass, and upon a colt the foal of an ass.

And I will destroy the chariot out of Ephraim, and the horse out of Jerusalem, and the bow of war shall be broken: and he shall speak peace to the Gentiles, and his power shall be from sea to sea, and from the rivers even to the end of the earth.—*Zach.* ix. 9, 10.

For from the rising of the sun even to the going down, my name is great among the Gentiles, and in every place there is sacrifice, and there is offered to my name a clean oblation: for my name is great among the Gentiles, saith the Lord of hosts.—*Malach.* i. 11.

2d. Prophesied by Christ Himself

And this gospel of the kingdom, shall be preached in the whole world, for a testimony to all nations, and then shall the consummation come.—*Matt.* xxiv. 14.

And unto all nations the gospel must first be preached.—*Mark* xiii. 10.

There shall be weeping and gnashing of teeth, when you shall see Abraham and Isaac and Jacob, and all the prophets, in the kingdom of God, and you yourselves thrust out.

And there shall come from the east and the west, and the north and the south; and shall sit down in the kingdom of God.—*Luke* xiii. 28, 29.

And he (Christ) said to them: Thus it is written, and thus it behoved Christ to suffer, and to rise again from the dead, the third day:

And that penance and remission of sins should be preached in his name, unto all nations, beginning at Jerusalem.—*Luke* xxiv. 46, 47.

3d. The Commission Given to the Apostles to Preach to all Nations

Going therefore, teach ye all nations; baptizing them in the name of the Father, and of the Son, and of the Holy Ghost.

Teaching them to observe all things whatsoever I have commanded you: and behold I am with you all days, even to the consummation of the world.—*Matt.* xxviii. 19, 20.

And he said to them: Go ye into the whole world, and preach the gospel to every creature.

He that believeth and is baptized, shall be saved: but he that believeth not shall be condemned.—*Mark* xvi. 15, 16.

But you shall receive the power of the Holy Ghost coming upon you, and you shall be witnesses unto me in Jerusalem, and in all Judea, and Samaria, and even to the uttermost part of the earth.—*Acts* i. 8.

By whom we have received grace and apostleship for obedience to the faith, in all nations, for his name.—*Rom.* i. 5.

4th. Declared

Faith then cometh by hearing; and hearing by the word of Christ.

But I say: Have they not heard? Yes, verily, their sound hath gone forth into all the earth, and their words unto the ends of the whole world.—*Rom.* x. 17, 18.

If so ye continue in the faith, grounded and settled, and immovable from the hope of the gospel which you have heard, which is preached in all the creation that is under heaven, whereof I Paul am made a minister.—*Col.* i. 23.

5th. Deduced

Compare

I desire, therefore, first of all, that supplications, prayers, intercessions, and thanksgivings be made for all men. . . .

For this is good and acceptable in the sight of God our Saviour,

Who will have all men to be saved, and to come to the knowledge of the truth.—1 *Tim.* ii. 1, 3, 4.

With

But without faith it is impossible to please God. For he that cometh to God, must believe that he is, and is a rewarder to them that seek him.—*Heb.* xi. 6.

How then shall they call on him, in whom they have not believed? Or how shall they believe him, of whom they have not heard? And how shall they hear without a preacher?

And how shall they preach unless they be sent, as it is written: How beautiful are the feet of them that preach the gospel of peace, of them that bring glad tidings of good things!—*Rom.* x. 14, 15.

CHURCH, APOSTOLICITY OF THE

And I say to thee: That thou art Peter; and upon this rock I will build my church, and the gates of hell shall not prevail against it.—*Matt.* xvi. 18.

And Jesus coming, spoke to them, saying: All power is given to me in heaven and in earth.

Going therefore, teach ye all nations; baptizing them in the name of the Father, and of the Son, and of the Holy Ghost.

Teaching them to observe all things whatsoever I have commanded you: and behold I am with you all days, even to the consummation of the world. —*Matt.* xxviii. 18-20.

And he said to them: Go ye into the whole world, and preach the gospel to every creature.

He that believeth and is baptized, shall be saved: but he that believeth not shall be condemned.—*Mark* xvi. 15, 16.

He said therefore to them again: Peace be to you. As the Father hath sent me, I also send you.—*John* xx. 21.

But though we, or an angel from heaven, preach a gospel to you besides that which we have preached to you, let him be anathema.—*Gal.* i. 8.

And God indeed hath set some in the church; first apostles, secondly prophets, thirdly doctors; after that miracles; then the graces of healings, helps, governments, kinds of tongues, interpretation of speeches.

Are all apostles? Are all prophets? Are all doctors?—1 *Cor.* xii. 28, 29.

And he gave some apostles, and some prophets, and other some evangelists, and other some pastors and doctors,

For the perfecting of the saints, for the work of the ministry, for the edifying of the body of Christ:

Until we all meet into the unity of faith, and of the knowledge of the Son of God, unto a perfect man, unto the measure of the age of the fulness of Christ;

That henceforth we be no more children tossed to and fro, and carried about with every wind of doctrine by the wickedness of men, by cunning craftiness, by which they lie in wait to deceive.—*Eph.* iv. 11-14.

And when they (Paul and Barnabas) had ordained to them priests in every church, and had prayed with fasting, they commended them to the Lord, in whom they believed.—*Acts* xiv. 22.

For which cause I admonish thee, that thou stir up the grace of God which is in thee, by the imposition of my hands.—2 *Tim.* i. 6.

For this cause I left thee in Crete, that thou shouldest set in order the things that are wanting, and shouldest ordain priests in every city, as I also appointed thee.—*Titus* i. 5.

CHURCH, AUTHORITY OF THE

1st. Authority of the Priests in the Old Law

If thou perceive that there be among you a hard and doubtful matter in judgment between blood and blood, cause and cause, leprosy and leprosy: and thou see that the words of the judges within thy gates do vary: arise, and go up to the place, which the Lord thy God shall choose.

And thou shalt come to the priests of the Levitical race, and to the judge, that shall be at that time: and thou shalt ask of them, and they shall show thee the truth of the judgment.

And thou shalt do whatsoever they shall say, that preside in the place, which the Lord shall choose, and what they shall teach thee,

According to his law; and thou shalt follow their sentence: neither shalt thou decline to the right hand nor to the left hand.—*Deut.* xvii. 8-11.

2d. Declared by Christ

He that receiveth you, receiveth me: and he that receiveth me, receiveth him that sent me.—*Matt.* x. 40.

And if he will not hear them: tell the church. And if he will not hear the church, let him be to thee as the heathen and publican.—*Matt.* xviii. 17.

Amen I say to you, whatsoever you shall bind upon earth, shall be bound also in heaven; and whatsoever you shall loose upon earth, shall be loosed also in heaven.—*Matt.* xviii. 18.

And Jesus coming, spoke to them, saying: All power is given to me in heaven and in earth.

Going therefore, teach ye all nations; baptizing them in the name of the Father, and of the Son, and of the Holy Ghost.

Teaching them to observe all things whatsoever I have commanded you: and behold I am with you all days, even to the consummation of the world.—*Matt.* xxviii. 18-20.

He that heareth you, heareth me; and he that despiseth you, despiseth me; and he that despiseth me, despiseth him that sent me.—*Luke* x. 16.

For he whom God hath sent, speaketh the words of God: for God doth not give the Spirit by measure.—*John* iii. 34.

Amen, amen I say to you, he that receiveth whomsoever I send, receiveth me; and he that receiveth me, receiveth him that sent me.—*John* xiii. 20.

As thou hast sent me into the world, I also have sent them into the world.— *John* xvii. 18.

He said therefore to them again: Peace be to you. As the Father hath sent me, I also send you.

When he had said this, he breathed on them; and he said to them: Receive ye the Holy Ghost.

Whose sins you shall forgive, they are forgiven them; and whose sins you shall retain, they are retained.—*John* xx. 21-23.

3d. Declared by the Apostles

For Christ sent me not to baptize, but to preach the gospel: not in wisdom of speech, lest the cross of Christ should be made void.—1 *Cor.* i. 17.

We are of God. He that knoweth God, heareth us. He that is not of God, heareth us not. By this we know the spirit of truth, and the spirit of error.—1 *John* iv. 6.

4th. Exercised by the Apostles

For it hath seemed good to the Holy Ghost and to us, to lay no further burden upon you than these necessary things:

That you abstain from things sacrificed to idols, and from blood, and from things strangled, and from fornication; from which things keeping yourselves, you shall do well. Fare ye well.—*Acts* xv. 28, 29.

It is absolutely heard, that there is fornication among you, and such fornication as the like is not among the heathens; that one should have his father's wife. . . .

I indeed, absent in body, but present in spirit, have already judged, as though I were present, him that hath so done.—1 *Cor.* v. 1, 3.

For to this end also did I write, that I may know the experiment of you, whether you be obedient in all things.

And to whom you have pardoned any thing, I also. For, what I have pardoned, if I have pardoned any thing, for your sakes have I done it in the person of Christ.—2 *Cor.* ii. 9, 10.

And if any man obey not our word by this epistle, note that man, and do not keep company with him, that he may be ashamed:

Yet do not esteem him as an enemy, but admonish him as a brother.—2 *Thess.* iii. 14, 15.

These things speak, and exhort and rebuke with all authority. Let no man despise thee.—*Titus* ii. 15.

Remember your prelates who have spoken the word of God to you; whose faith follow, considering the end of their conversation. . . .

Obey your prelates, and be subject to them. For they watch as being to render an account of your souls; that they may do this with joy, and not with grief. For this is not expedient for you.—*Heb.* xiii. 7, 17.

In like manner, ye young men, be subject to the ancients.—1 *Peter* v. 5.

5th. The Necessity of Authority in the Church

For whosoever shall call upon the name of the Lord, shall be saved.

How then shall they call on him, in whom they have not believed? Or how shall they believe him, of whom they have not heard? And how shall they hear, without a preacher?

And how shall they preach unless they be sent, as it is written: How beautiful are the feet of them that preach the gospel of peace, of them that bring glad tidings of good things! —*Rom.* x. 13-15.

And he gave some apostles, and some prophets, and other some evangelists, and other some pastors and doctors,

For the perfecting of the saints, for the work of the ministry, for the edifying of the body of Christ:

Until we all meet into the unity of faith, and of the knowledge of the Son of God unto a perfect man, unto the measure of the age of the fulness of Christ;

That henceforth we be no more children tossed to and fro, and carried about with every wind of doctrine by the wickedness of men, by cunning craftiness, by which they lie in wait to deceive.

But doing the truth in charity, we may in all things grow up in him who is the head, even Christ.—*Eph.* iv. 11-15.

CHURCH, INFALLIBILITY OF THE

1st. Prophesied

And a path and a way shall be there, and it shall be called the holy way: the unclean shall not pass over it, and this shall be unto you a straight way, so that fools shall not err therein.—*Is.* xxxv. 8.

And there shall come a redeemer to Sion, and to them that return from iniquity in Jacob, saith the Lord.

This is my covenant with them, saith the Lord: My spirit that is in thee, and my words that I have put in thy mouth, shall not depart out of thy mouth, nor out of the mouth of thy seed, nor out of the mouth of thy seed's seed, saith the Lord, from henceforth and for ever.—*Is.* lix. 20, 21.

2d. Promised by Christ

And I say to thee: That thou art Peter; and upon this rock I will build my church, and the gates of hell shall not prevail against it.—*Matt.* xvi. 18.

Going therefore, teach ye all nations; baptizing them in the name of the Father, and of the Son, and of the Holy Ghost.

Teaching them to observe all things whatsoever I have commanded you: and behold I am with you all days, even to the consummation of the world.—*Matt.* xxviii. 19, 20.

And the Lord said: Simon, Simon, behold Satan hath desired to have you, that he may sift you as wheat:

But I have prayed for thee, that thy faith fail not: and thou, being once converted, confirm thy brethren.—*Luke* xxii. 31, 32.

And I will ask the Father, and he shall give you another Paraclete, that he may abide with you for ever.

The spirit of truth, whom the world cannot receive, because it seeth him not, nor knoweth him: but you shall know him; because he shall abide with you, and shall be in you. . . .

But the Paraclete, the Holy Ghost, whom the Father will send in my name, he will teach you all things, and bring all things to your mind, whatsoever I shall have said to you.—*John* xiv. 16, 17, 26.

But when he, the Spirit of truth, is come, he will teach you all truth. For he shall not speak of himself; but what things soever he shall hear, he shall speak; and the things that are to come, he shall show you.—*John* xvi. 13.

3d. Declared by the Apostles

And he gave some apostles, and some prophets, and other some evangelists, and other some pastors and doctors,

For the perfecting of the saints, for the work of the ministry, for the edifying of the body of Christ:

Until we all meet into the unity of faith, and of the knowledge of the Son of God, unto a perfect man, unto the measure of the age of the fulness of Christ;

That henceforth we be no more children tossed to and fro, and carried about with every wind of doctrine by the wickedness of men, by cunning craftiness, by which they lie in wait to deceive.—*Eph.* iv. 11-14.

Therefore as the church is subject to Christ, so also let the wives be to their husbands in all things.

Husbands, love your wives, as Christ also loved the church, and delivered himself up for it:

That he might sanctify it, cleansing it by the laver of water in the word of life:

That he might present it to himself a glorious church, not having spot or wrinkle, or any such thing; but that it should be holy, and without blemish.—*Eph.* v. 24-27.

But if I tarry long, that thou mayst know how thou oughtest to behave thyself in the house of the living God, which is the pillar and ground of the truth.—1 *Tim.* iii. 15.

4th. Having an Infallible Head, Christ

Now you are the body of Christ, and members of member.—1 *Cor.* xii. 27.

And he hath subjected all things under his feet, and hath made him head over all the church,

Which is his body, and the fulness of him who is filled all in all.—*Eph.* i. 22, 23.

Now therefore you are no more strangers and foreigners; but you are fellow citizens with the saints, and the domestics of God,

Built upon the foundation of the apostles and prophets, Jesus Christ himself being the chief corner stone:

In whom all the building, being framed together, groweth up into an holy temple in the Lord.—*Eph.* ii. 19-21.

But doing the truth in charity, we may in all things grow up in him who is the head, even Christ.—*Eph.* iv. 15.

Because the husband is the head of the wife, as Christ is the head of the church. He is the saviour of his body. . . .

For no man ever hateth his own flesh; but nourisheth and cherisheth it, as also Christ doth the church:

Because we are members of his body, of his flesh, and of his bones.—*Eph.* v. 23, 29, 30.

And he is the head of the body, the church, who is the beginning, the first born from the dead; that in all things he may hold the primacy.—*Col.* i. 18.

CHURCH, PERPETUITY OF THE

1st. Prophesied

For a child is born to us, and a son is given to us, and the government is upon his shoulder: and his name shall be called, Wonderful, Counsellor, God the Mighty, the Father of the world to come, the Prince of Peace.

His empire shall be multiplied, and there shall be no end of peace: he shall sit upon the throne of David, and upon his kingdom; to establish it and strengthen it with judgment and with justice, from henceforth and for ever: the zeal of the Lord of hosts will perform this.—*Is.* ix. 6, 7.

And there shall come a redeemer to Sion, and to them that return from iniquity in Jacob, saith the Lord.

This is my covenant with them, saith the Lord: My spirit that is in thee, and my words that I have put in thy mouth, shall not depart out of thy mouth, nor out of the mouth of thy seed, nor out of the mouth of thy seed's seed, saith the Lord, from henceforth and for ever.—*Is.* lix. 20, 21.

For thus saith the Lord: There shall not to cut off from David a man to sit upon the throne of the house of Israel.

Neither shall there be cut off from the priests and Levites a man before my face to offer holocausts, and to burn sacrifices, and to kill victims continually.

And the word of the Lord came to Jeremias, saying:

Thus saith the Lord: If my covenant with the day can be made void, and my covenant with the night, that there should not be day and night in their season:

Also my covenant with David my servant may be made void, that he should not have a son to reign upon his throne, and with the Levites and priests my ministers.

As the stars of heaven cannot be numbered, nor the sand of the sea be measured: so will I multiply the seed of David my servant, and the Levites my ministers.—*Jer.* xxxiii. 17-22.

And my servant David shall be king over them, and they shall have one shepherd: they shall walk in my judgments, and shall keep my commandments, and shall do them. . . .

And I will make a covenant of peace with them, it shall be an everlasting covenant with them: and I will establish them, and will multiply them, and will set my sanctuary in the midst of them for ever.

And my tabernacle shall be with them: and I will be their God, and they shall be my people.

And the nations shall know that I am the Lord the sanctifier of Israel, when my sanctuary shall be in the midst of them for ever.—*Ezech.* xxxvii. 24, 26-28.

But in the days of those kingdoms the God of heaven will set up a kingdom that shall never be destroyed, and his kingdom shall not be delivered up to another people, and it shall break in pieces, and shall consume all these kingdoms, and itself shall stand for ever.—*Dan.* ii. 44.

I beheld therefore in the vision of the night, and lo, one like the son of man came with the clouds of heaven, and he came even to the Ancient of days: and they presented him before him.

And he gave him power, and glory, and a kingdom: and all peoples, tribes and tongues shall serve him: his power is an everlasting power, that shall not be taken away: and his kingdom that shall not be destroyed.—*Dan.* vii. 13, 14.

In that day, saith the Lord, I will gather up her that halteth: and her that I had cast out, I will gather up: and her whom I had afflicted.

And I will make her that halted, a remnant: and her that had been afflicted, a mighty nation: and the Lord will reign over them in mount Sion, from this time now and for ever.— *Mich.* iv. 6, 7.

And the angel said to her: Fear not, Mary, for thou hast found grace with God.

Behold thou shalt conceive in thy womb, and shalt bring forth a son; and thou shalt call his name Jesus.

He shall be great, and shall be called the Son of the most High; and the Lord God shall give unto him the throne of David his father; and he shall reign in the house of Jacob for ever.

And of his kingdom there shall be no end.—*Luke* i. 30-33.

2d. Promised by Christ

And I say to thee: That thou art Peter; and upon this rock I will build my church, and the gates of hell shall not prevail against it.—*Matt.* xvi. 18.

And Jesus coming, spoke to them, saying: All power is given to me in heaven and in earth.

Going therefore, teach ye all nations; baptizing them in the name of the Father, and of the Son, and of the Holy Ghost.

Teaching them to observe all things whatsoever I have commanded you: and behold I am with you all days, even to the consummation of the world.— *Matt.* xxviii. 18-20.

And I will ask the Father, and he shall give you another Paraclete, that he may abide with you for ever.

The spirit of truth, whom the world cannot receive, because it seeth him not, nor knoweth him: but you shall know him; because he shall abide with you, and shall be in you.—*John* xiv. 16, 17.

3d. Declared by the Apostle

And he gave some apostles, and some prophets, and other some evangelists, and other some pastors and doctors,

For the perfecting of the saints, for the work of the ministry, for the edifying of the body of Christ:

Until we all meet into the unity of faith, and of the knowledge of the Son of God, unto a perfect man, unto the measure of the age of the fulness of Christ;

That henceforth we be no more children tossed to and fro, and carried about with every wind of doctrine by the wickedness of men, by cunning craftiness, by which they lie in wait to deceive.—*Eph.* iv. 11-14.

CHURCH, VISIBILITY OF THE

1st. Prophesied

And in the last days the mountain of the house of the Lord shall be prepared on the top of mountains, and it shall be exalted above the hills, and all nations shall flow unto it.

And many people shall go, and say: Come and let us go up to the mountain of the Lord, and to the house of the God of Jacob, and he will teach us his ways, and we will walk in his paths: for the law shall come forth from Sion, and the word of the Lord from Jerusalem.—*Is.* ii. 2, 3.

2d. Declared

You are the light of the world. A city seated on a mountain cannot be hid.—*Matt.* v. 14.

[1]The same passage occurs also in *Mich.* iv. 1, 2.

COMMUNION OF SAINTS, THE

See: Saints—page 732.

CONFESSION OF SINS

1st. In the Old Law

And the Lord spoke to Moses, saying: Say to the children of Israel: When a man or woman shall have committed any of all the sins that men are wont to commit, and by negligence shall have transgressed the commandment of the Lord, and offended,

They shall confess their sin, and restore the principal itself, and the fifth part over and above, to him against whom they have sinned.—*Num.* v. 5-7.

And in the four and twentieth day of the month, the children of Israel came together with fasting, and with sackcloth, and earth upon them.

And the seed of the children of Israel separated themselves from every stranger: and they stood, and confessed their sins, and the iniquities of their fathers. —2 *Esd.* ix. 1, 2.

If as a man I have hid my sin, and have concealed my iniquity in my bosom: . . .

Let thistles grow up to me instead of wheat, and thorns instead of barley. —*Job* xxxi. 33, 40.

He that hideth his sins, shall not prosper: but he that shall confess, and forsake them, shall obtain mercy.—*Prov.* xxviii. 13.

Be not ashamed to confess thy sins, but submit not thyself to every man for sin.—*Ecclus.* iv. 31.

Then went out to him (John the Baptist) Jerusalem and all Judea, and all the country about Jordan:

And were baptized by him in the Jordan, confessing their sins.—*Matt.* iii. 5, 6.

2d. In the New Law

And many of them that believed, came confessing and declaring their deeds.—*Acts* xix. 18.

Confess therefore your sins one to another: and pray one for another, that you may be saved. For the continual prayer of a just man availeth much.—*James* v. 16.

If we confess our sins, he is faithful

and just, to forgive us our sins, and to cleanse us from all iniquity.—1 *John* i. 9.

3d. The Obligation of Confessing our Sins Implied in the Power Given to the Apostles of Forgiving or Retaining Sins

And I will give to thee the keys of the kingdom of heaven. And whatsoever thou shalt bind upon earth, it shall be bound also in heaven: and whatsoever thou shalt loose on earth, it shall be loosed also in heaven.—*Matt.* xvi. 19.

Amen I say to you, whatsoever you shall bind upon earth, shall be bound also in heaven; and whatsoever you shall loose upon earth, shall be loosed also in heaven.—*Matt.* xviii. 18.

He said therefore to them again: Peace be to you. As the Father hath sent me, I also send you.

When he had said this, he breathed on them; and he said to them; Receive ye the Holy Ghost.

Whose sins you shall forgive, they are forgiven them; and whose sins you shall retain, they are retained.—*John* xx. 21-23.

CONFIRMATION, THE SACRAMENT OF

Now when the apostles, who were in Jerusalem, had heard that Samaria had received the word of God, they sent unto them Peter and John.

Who, when they were come, prayed for them, that they might receive the Holy Ghost.

For he was not as yet come upon any of them; but they were only baptized in the name of the Lord Jesus.

Then they laid their hands upon them, and they received the Holy Ghost.

And when Simon saw, that by the imposition of the hands of the apostles, the Holy Ghost was given, he offered them money,

Saying: Give me also this power, that on whomsoever I shall lay my hands, he may receive the Holy Ghost. —*Acts* viii. 14-19.

And it came to pass, while Apollo was at Corinth, that Paul having passed through the upper coasts, came to Ephesus, and found certain disciples.

And he said to them: Have you received the Holy Ghost since ye believed? But they said to him: We have not so much as heard whether there be a Holy Ghost.

. . . And when Paul had imposed his hands on them, the Holy Ghost came upon them, and they spoke with tongues and prophesied.—*Acts* xix. 1, 2, 6.

Probably Referred to

Now he that confirmeth us with you in Christ, and that hath anointed us, is God:

Who also hath sealed us, and given the pledge of the Spirit in our hearts. —2 *Cor.* i. 21, 22.

DEACONS

And in those days, the number of the disciples increasing, there arose a murmuring of the Greeks against the Hebrews, for that their widows were neglected in the daily ministration.

Then the twelve calling together the multitude of the disciples, said: It is not reason that we should leave the word of God, and serve tables.

Wherefore, brethren, look ye out among you seven men of good reputation, full of the Holy Ghost and wisdom, whom we may appoint over this business.

But we will give ourselves continually to prayer, and to the ministry of the word.

And the saying was liked by all the multitude. And they chose Stephen, a man full of faith, and of the Holy Ghost, and Philip, and Prochorus, and Nicanor, and Timon, and Parmenas, and Nicolas, a proselyte of Antioch.

These they set before the apostles; and they praying, imposed hands upon them.—*Acts* vi. 1-6.

Paul and Timothy, the servants of Jesus Christ; to all the saints in Christ Jesus, who are at Philippi, with the bishops and deacons.—*Philipp.* i. 1.

Deacons in like manner chaste, not

double tongued, not given to much wine, not greedy of filthy lucre:

Holding the mystery of faith in a pure conscience.

And let these also first be proved: and so let them minister, having no crime.—1 *Tim.* iii. 8-10.

DEAD, PRAYING FOR THE

A gift hath grace in the sight of all the living, and restrain not ¹grace from the dead.—*Ecclus.* vii. 37.

And making a gathering, he (Judas) sent twelve thousand drachms of silver to Jerusalem for sacrifice to be offered for the sins of the dead, thinking well and religiously concerning the resurrection,

(For if he had not hoped that they that were slain should rise again, it would have seemed superfluous and vain to pray for the dead,)

And because he considered that they who had fallen asleep with godliness, had great grace laid up for them.

It is therefore a holy and wholesome thought to pray for the dead, that they may be loosed from sins.—2 *Mach.* xii. 43-46.

EPISCOPACY

Take heed to yourselves, and to the whole flock, wherein the Holy Ghost hath placed you bishops, to rule the church of God, which he hath purchased with his own blood.—*Acts* xx. 28.

Against a priest receive not an accusation, but under two or three witnesses.—1 *Tim.* v. 19.

For this cause I left thee in Crete, that thou shouldest set in order the things that are wanting, and shouldest ordain priests in every city, as I also appointed thee.—*Titus* i. 5.

The ancients therefore that are among you, I beseech, who am myself also an ancient, and a witness of the sufferings of Christ: as also a partaker of that glory which is to be revealed in time to come:

Feed the flock of God which is among you, taking care of it, not by con-

¹That is, withhold not from them the benefit of alms, prayers, and sacrifices.

straint, but willingly, according to God: not for filthy lucre's sake, but voluntarily:

Neither as lording it over the clergy, but being made a pattern of the flock from the heart.

And when the prince of pastors shall appear, you shall receive a never-fading crown of glory.—1 *Peter* v. 1-4.

EUCHARIST, THE HOLY

1st. Prefigured

But Melchisedech the king of Salem, bringing forth bread and wine, for he was the priest of the most high God,

Blessed him, and said: Blessed be Abram by the most high God, who created heaven and earth.—*Gen.* xiv. 18, 19.

And the Lord said to Moses: Behold I will rain bread from heaven for you: let the people go forth, and gather what is sufficient for every day: that I may prove them whether they will walk in my law, or not. . . .

And when the people of Israel saw it, they said one to another: Manhu! which signifieth: What is this! for they knew not what it was. And Moses said to them: This is the bread, which the Lord hath given you to eat.—*Ex.* xvi. 4, 15.

Instead of which things thou didst feed thy people with the food of angels, and gavest them bread from heaven prepared without labor; having in it all that is delicious, and the sweetness of every taste.—*Wis.* xvi. 20.

And the Lord spoke to Moses, saying:

. . . Thou shalt take also fine flour, and shalt bake twelve loaves thereof, two tenths shall be in every loaf:

And thou shalt set them six and six one against another upon the most clean table before the Lord:

And thou shalt put upon them the clearest frankincense, that the bread may be for a memorial of the oblation of the Lord.

Every sabbath they shall be changed before the Lord, being received of the children of Israel by an everlasting covenant:

And they shall be Aaron's and his

sons', that they may eat them in the holy place: because it is most holy of the sacrifices of the Lord by a perpetual right.—*Lev.* xxiv. 1, 5-9.

And David said to Achimelech the priest:

. . . Now therefore if thou have any thing at hand, though it were but five loaves, give me, or whatsoever thou canst find.

And the priest answered David, saying: I have no common bread at hand, but only holy bread, if the young men be clean, especially from women? . . .

The priest therefore gave him hallowed bread: for there was no bread there, but only the loaves of proposition, which had been taken away from before the face of the Lord, that hot loaves might be set up.—1 *Kings* xxi. 2, 3, 4, 6.

And he (Elias) cast himself down, and slept in the shadow of the juniper tree: and behold an angel of the Lord touched him, and said to him: Arise and eat.

He looked, and behold there was at his head a hearth cake, and a vessel of water: and he ate and drank, and he fell asleep again. . . .

And he arose, and ate, and drank, and walked in the strength of that food forty days and forty nights, unto the mount of God, Horeb.—3 *Kings* xix. 5, 6, 8.

2d. Prophesied

For what is the good thing of him, and what is his beautiful thing, but the corn of the elect, and wine springing forth virgins?—*Zach.* ix. 17.

For from the rising of the sun even to the going down, my name is great among the Gentiles, and in every place there is sacrifice, and there is offered to my name a clean oblation: for my name is great among the Gentiles, saith the Lord of hosts.—*Malach.* i. 11.

3d. Promised by Christ

I am the bread of life.

Your fathers did eat manna in the desert, and are dead.

This is the bread which cometh down from heaven; that if any man eat of it, he may not die.

I am the living bread which came down from heaven.

If any man eat of this bread, he shall live for ever; and the bread that I will give, is my flesh, for the life of the world.

The Jews therefore strove among themselves, saying: How can this man give us his flesh to eat?

Then Jesus said to them: Amen, amen I say unto you: Except you eat the flesh of the Son of man, and drink his blood, you shall not have life in you.

He that eateth my flesh, and drinketh my blood, hath everlasting life: and I will raise him up in the last day.

For my flesh is meat indeed: and my blood is drink indeed.

He that eateth my flesh, and drinketh my blood, abideth in me, and I in him.

As the living Father hath sent me, and I live by the Father; so he that eateth me, the same also shall live by me.

This is the bread that came down from heaven. Not as your fathers did eat manna, and are dead. He that eateth this bread, shall live for ever.

These things he said, teaching in the synagogue, in Capharnaum.—*John* vi. 48-60.

I will not leave you orphans, I will come to you.—*John* xiv. 18.

4th. Prepared

And he said to them: With desire I have desired to eat this pasch with you, before I suffer.—*Luke* xxii. 15.

Before the festival day of the pasch, Jesus knowing that his hour was come, that he should pass out of this world to the Father: having loved his own who were in the world, he loved them unto the end.—*John* xiii. 1.

5th. Instituted

And whilst they were at supper, Jesus took bread, and blessed, and broke: and gave to his disciples, and said: Take ye, and eat. This is my body.

And taking the chalice, he gave thanks, and gave to them, saying: Drink ye all of this.

For this is my blood of the new testament, which shall be shed for many unto remission of sins.—*Matt.* xxvi. 26-28.

And whilst they were eating, Jesus took bread; and blessing, broke, and gave to them, and said: Take ye. This is my body.

And having taken the chalice, giving thanks, he gave it to them. And they all drank of it.

And he said to them: This is my blood of the new testament, which shall be shed for many.—*Mark* xiv. 22-24.

And taking bread, he gave thanks, and brake; and gave to them, saying: This is my body, which is given for you. Do this for a commemoration of me.

In like manner the chalice also, after he had supped, saying: This is the chalice, the new testament in my blood, which shall be shed for you.—*Luke* xxii. 19, 20.

For I have received of the Lord that which also I delivered unto you, that the Lord Jesus, the same night in which he was betrayed, took bread,

And giving thanks, broke, and said: Take ye, and eat: this is my body, which shall be delivered for you: this do for the commemoration of me.

In like manner also the chalice, after he had supped, saying: This chalice is the new testament in my blood: this do ye, as often as you shall drink, for the commemoration of me.

For as often as you shall eat this bread, and drink the chalice, you shall show the death of the Lord, until he come.—1 *Cor.* xi. 23-26.

6th. Celebrated and Received

The chalice of benediction which we bless, is it not the communion of the blood of Christ? And the bread, which we break, is it not the partaking of the body of the Lord?

For we, being many, are one bread, one body, all that partake of one bread. —1 *Cor.* x. 16, 17.

You cannot drink the chalice of the Lord, and the chalice of devils: you cannot be partakers of the table of the Lord, and of the table of devils.— 1 *Cor.* x. 21.

Therefore whosoever shall eat this bread, or drink the chalice of the Lord unworthily, shall be guilty of the body and of the blood of the Lord.

But let a man prove himself: and so let him eat of that bread, and drink of the chalice.

For he that eateth and drinketh unworthily, eateth and drinketh judgment to himself, not discerning the body of the Lord.—1 *Cor.* xi. 27-29.

They therefore that received his word, were baptized; and there were added in that day about three thousand souls.

And they were persevering in the doctrine of the apostles, and in the communication of the breaking of bread, and in prayers.—*Acts* ii. 41, 42.

And on the first day of the week, when we were assembled to break bread, Paul discoursed with them, being to depart on the morrow: and he continued his speech until midnight.— *Acts* xx. 7.

7th. Probably Alluded to

And it came to pass, whilst 'he was at table with them, he took bread, and blessed, and brake, and gave to them.

And their eyes were opened, and they knew him: and he vanished out of their sight.—*Luke* xxiv. 30, 31.

Now there were in the church which was at Antioch, prophets and doctors, among whom was Barnabas, and Simon who was called Niger, and Lucius of Cyrene, and Manahen, who was the foster brother of Herod the tetrarch, and Saul.

And as they were ministering to the Lord, and fasting, the Holy Ghost said to them: Separate me Saul and Barnabas, for the work whereunto I have taken them.—*Acts* xiii. 1, 2.

EXTREME UNCTION, THE SACRAMENT OF

Is any man sick among you? Let him bring in the priests of the church,

'Jesus and the disciples at Emmaus.

and let them pray over him, anointing him with oil in the name of the Lord.

And the prayer of faith shall save the sick man: and the Lord shall raise him up: and if he be in sins, they shall be forgiven him.—*James* v. 14, 15.

Possibly Referred to

And they (the apostles) cast out many devils, and anointed with oil many that were sick, and healed them. —*Mark* vi. 13.

FAITH

1st. Its True Nature

Now faith is the substance of things to be hoped for, the evidence of things that appear not.—*Heb.* xi. 1.

For in Christ Jesus neither circumcision availeth any thing, nor uncircumcision: but faith that worketh by charity.—*Gal.* v. 6.

2d. Faith is not an Assurance of our Salvation

Thou wilt say then: The branches were broken off, that I might be grafted in.

Well: because of unbelief they were broken off. But thou standest by faith: be not high minded, but fear.

For if God hath not spared the natural branches, fear lest perhaps he also spare not thee.

See then the goodness and the severity of God: towards them indeed that are fallen, the severity; but towards thee, the goodness of God, if thou abide in goodness, otherwise thou also shalt be cut off.—*Rom.* xi. 19-22.

But I chastise my body, and bring it into subjection: lest perhaps, when I have preached to others, I myself should become a castaway.—1 *Cor.* ix. 27.

Wherefore he that thinketh himself to stand, let him take heed lest he fall. —1 *Cor.* x. 12.

Wherefore, my dearly beloved, (as you have always obeyed, not as in my presence only, but much more now in my absence,) with fear and trembling work out your salvation.—*Philipp.* ii. 12.

Behold, I come quickly: hold fast that which thou hast, that no man take thy crown.—*Apoc.* iii. 11.

3d. Faith is Necessary for Salvation

Behold, he that is unbelieving, his soul shall not be right in himself: but the just shall live in his faith.—*Hab.* ii. 4.

And he said to them: Go ye into the whole world, and preach the gospel to every creature.

He that believeth and is baptized, shall be saved: but he that believeth not shall be condemned.—*Mark* xvi. 15, 16.

He that believeth in him is not judged. But he that doth not believe, is already judged: because he believeth not in the name of the only begotten Son of God.—*John* iii. 18.

He that believeth in the Son, hath life everlasting; but he that believeth not the Son, shall not see life; but the wrath of God abideth on him.—*John* iii. 36.

Then calling for a light, he (the keeper of the prison) went in, and trembling, fell down at the feet of Paul and Silas.

And bringing them out, he said: Masters, what must I do, that I may be saved?

But they said: Believe in the Lord Jesus, and thou shalt be saved, and thy house.—*Acts* xvi. 29-31.

But that in the law no man is justified with God, it is manifest: because the just man liveth by faith.—*Gal.* iii. 11.

For in Christ Jesus neither circumcision availeth any thing, nor uncircumcision: but faith that worketh by charity.—*Gal.* v. 6.

But we ought to give thanks to God always for you, brethren, beloved of God, for that God hath chosen you firstfruits unto salvation, in sanctification of the spirit, and faith of the truth.— 2 *Thess.* ii. 12.

But without faith it is impossible to please God. For he that cometh to God, must believe that he is, and is a rewarder to them that seek him.—*Heb.* xi. 6.

4th. Faith Alone is not Sufficient for Salvation

See: Justification, 1st—page 711.

5th. There is Another Law besides the Law of Faith—viz., the Law of Love

And there came one of the scribes that had heard them reasoning together, and seeing that he had answered them well, asked him which was the first commandment of all.

And Jesus answered him: The first commandment of all is, Hear, O Israel: the Lord thy God is one God.

And thou shalt love the Lord thy God, with thy whole heart, and with thy whole soul, and with thy whole mind, and with thy whole strength. This is the first commandment.

And the second is like to it: Thou shalt love thy neighbor as thyself. There is no other commandment greater than these.—*Mark* xii. 28-31.

Owe no man anything, but to love one another. For he that loveth his neighbor, hath fulfilled the law.—*Rom.* xiii. 8.

For all the law is fulfilled in one word: Thou shalt love thy neighbor as thyself.—*Gal.* v. 14.

Bear ye one another's burdens; and so you shall fulfil the law of Christ.—*Gal.* vi. 2.

Little children, let no man deceive you. He that doth justice is just, even as he is just.

He that committeth sin is of the devil: for the devil sinneth from the beginning.

. . . In this the children of God are manifest, and the children of the devil. Whosoever is not just, is not of God, nor he that loveth not his brother.—1 *John* iii. 7, 8, 10.

FASTING

1st. Recommended

Prayer is good with fasting and alms more than to lay up treasures of gold.—*Tob.* xii. 8.

Sanctify ye a fast, call an assembly; gather together the ancients, all the inhabitants of the land into the house of your God: and cry ye to the Lord.—*Joel* i. 14.

Now therefore saith the Lord: Be converted to me with all your heart, in fasting, and in weeping, and in mourning.—*Joel* ii. 12.

And when you fast, be not as the hypocrites, sad. For they disfigure their faces, that they may appear unto men to fast. Amen I say to you, they have received their reward.

But thou, when thou fastest anoint thy head, and wash thy face;

That thou appear not to men to fast, but to thy Father who is in secret: and thy Father who seeth in secret, will repay thee.—*Matt.* vi. 16-18.

But in all things let us exhibit ourselves as the ministers of God, in much patience, in tribulation, in necessities, in distresses,

In stripes, in prisons, in seditions, in labors, in watchings, in fastings.—2 *Cor.* vi. 4, 5.

2d. Practised by God's Servants

And he (Moses) was there with the Lord forty days and forty nights: he neither ate bread nor drank water, and he wrote upon the tables the ten words of the covenant.—*Ex.* xxxiv. 28.

And I fell down before the Lord as before, forty days and nights neither eating bread, nor drinking water, for all your sins, which you had committed against the Lord, and had provoked him to wrath.—*Deut.* ix. 18.

And I proclaimed there a fast by the river Ahava, that we might afflict ourselves before the Lord our God, and might ask of him a right way for us and for our children, and for all our substance. . . .

And we fasted, and besought our God for this: and it fell out prosperously unto us.—1 *Esd.* viii. 21, 23.

And when I had heard these words, I (Nehemias) sat down and wept, and mourned for many days: and I fasted, and prayed before the face of the God of heaven.—2 *Esd.* i. 4.

I humbled my soul with fasting; and my prayer shall be turned into my bosom.—*Ps.* xxxiv. 13.

And I covered my soul in fasting: and it was made a reproach to me.

And I made haircloth my garment:

and I became a byword to them.—*Ps.* lxviii. 11, 12.

And I set my face to the Lord my God, to pray and make supplication with fasting, and sackcloth, and ashes. —*Dan.* ix. 3.

In those days I, Daniel, mourned the days of three weeks.

I ate no desirable bread, and neither flesh, nor wine entered into my mouth, neither was I anointed with ointment: till the days of three weeks were accomplished.—*Dan.* x. 2, 3.

And they assembled together, and came to Maspha over against Jerusalem: for in Maspha was a place of prayer heretofore in Israel.

And they fasted that day, and put on haircloth, and put ashes upon their heads: and they rent their garments.— 1 *Mach.* iii. 46, 47.

And as they were ministering to the Lord, and fasting, the Holy Ghost said to them: Separate me Saul and Barnabas, for the work whereunto I have taken them.

Then they fasting and praying, and imposing their hands upon them, sent them away.—*Acts* xiii. 2, 3.

And when they had ordained to them priests in every church, and had prayed with fasting, they commended them to the Lord, in whom they believed.—*Acts* xiv. 22.

In labor and painfulness, in much watchings, in hunger and thirst, in fastings often, in cold and nakedness.— 2 *Cor.* xi. 27.

3d. By Christ Himself

Then Jesus was led by the spirit into the desert, to be tempted by the devil. And when he had fasted forty days and forty nights, afterwards he was hungry.—*Matt.* iv. 1, 2.

And Jesus being full of the Holy Ghost, returned from the Jordan, and was led by the Spirit into the desert, For the space of forty days; and was tempted by the devil. And he ate nothing in those days; and when they were ended, he was hungry.—*Luke* iv. 1, 2.

4th. The Utility of Fasting

And the men of Ninive believed in God: and they proclaimed a fast, and put on sackcloth from the greatest to the least. . . .

And God saw their works, that they were turned from their evil way: and God had mercy with regard to the evil which he had said that he would do to them, and he did it not.—*Jonas* iii. 5, 10.

And Jesus rebuked him, and the devil went out of him, and the child was cured from that hour.

Then came the disciples to Jesus secretly, and said: Why could not we cast them out?

Jesus said to them: Because of your unbelief. . . .

But this kind is not cast out but by prayer and fasting.—*Matt.* xvii. 17-20.

FREE WILL

1st. The Existence of Free Will in Man

If thou do well, shalt thou not receive? but if ill, shall not sin forthwith be present at the door? but the lust thereof shall be under thee, and thou shalt have dominion over it.— *Gen.* iv. 7.

Behold I set forth in your sight this day a blessing and a curse:

A blessing, if you obey the commandments of the Lord your God, which I command you this day:

A curse, if you obey not the commandments of the Lord your God, but revolt from the way which now I show you, and walk after strange gods which you know not.—*Deut.* xi. 26-28.

Consider that I have set before thee this day life and good, and on the other hand, death and evil. . . .

I call heaven and earth to witness this day, that I have set before you life and death, blessing and cursing. Choose therefore life, that both thou and thy seed may live.—*Deut.* xxx. 15, 19.

But if it seem evil to you to serve the Lord, you have your choice: choose this day that which pleaseth you, whom you would rather serve, whether the gods which your fathers served in Mesopotamia, or the gods of the Amorrhites, in whose land you dwell: but as for me and my house we will serve the Lord.—*Jos.* xxiv. 15.

God made man from the beginning, and left him in the hand of his own counsel.

He added his commandments and precepts.

If thou wilt keep the commandments and perform acceptable fidelity for ever, they shall preserve thee.

He hath set fire and water before thee: stretch forth thy hand to which thou wilt.

Before man is life and death, good and evil, that which he shall choose shall be given him.—*Ecclus.* xv. 14-18.

Blessed is the rich man that is found without blemish: and that hath not gone after gold, nor put his trust in money nor in treasures.

Who is he, and we will praise him? for he hath done wonderful things in his life.

Who hath been tried thereby, and made perfect, he shall have glory everlasting. He that could have transgressed, and hath not transgressed: and could do evil things, and hath not done them.—*Ecclus.* xxxi. 8-10.

As I live, saith the Lord God, I desire not the death of the wicked, but that the wicked turn from his way, and live. Turn ye, turn ye from your evil ways: and why will you die, O house of Israel?—*Ezech.* xxxiii. 11.

2d. Free Will Can, and Often Does, Resist God's Grace

Because I called, and you refused: I stretched out my hand, and there was none that regarded.

You have despised all my counsel, and have neglected my reprehensions.

I also will laugh in your destruction, and will mock when that shall come to you which you feared.—*Prov.* i. 24-26.

What is there that I ought to do more to my vineyard, that I have not done to it? was it that I looked that it should bring forth grapes, and it hath brought forth wild grapes?—*Is.* v. 4.

I will number you in the sword, and you shall all fall by slaughter: because I called and you did not answer: I spoke, and you did not hear: and you did evil in my eyes, and you have chosen the things that displease me.—*Is.* lxv. 12.

Wherefore I also will choose their mockeries, and will bring upon them the things they feared: because I called, and there was none that would answer; I have spoken, and they heard not; and they have done evil in my eyes, and have chosen the things that displease me.—*Is.* lxvi. 4.

And now, because you have done all these works, saith the Lord: and I have spoken to you rising up early, and speaking, and you have not heard: and I have called you, and you have not answered. . . .

And I will cast you away from before my face, as I have cast away all your brethren, the whole seed of Ephraim.—*Jer.* vii. 13, 15.

But if the just man turn himself away from his justice, and do iniquity according to all the abominations which the wicked man useth to work, shall he live? All his justices which he hath done, shall not be remembered: in the prevarication, by which he hath prevaricated, and in his sin, which he hath committed, in them he shall die.—*Ezech.* xviii. 24.

Jerusalem, Jerusalem, thou that killest the prophets, and stonest them that are sent unto thee, how often would I have gathered together thy children, as the hen doth gather her chickens under her wings, and thou wouldest not? —*Matt.* xxiii. 37.

You stiff necked and uncircumcised in heart and ears, you always resist the Holy Ghost: as your fathers did, so do you also.—*Acts* vii. 51.

Follow peace with all men, and holiness: without which no man shall see God.

Looking diligently, lest any man be wanting to the grace of God; lest any root of bitterness springing up do hinder, and by it many be defiled.—*Heb.* xii. 14, 15.

GOD, THE UNITY OF

And the Lord spoke all these words:

I am the Lord thy God, who brought thee out of the land of Egypt, out of the house of bondage.

Thou shalt not have strange gods before me.—*Ex.* xx. 1-3.

Know therefore this day, and think in thy heart that the Lord he is God in heaven above, and in the earth beneath, and there is no other.—*Deut.* iv. 39.

Hear, O Israel, the Lord our God is one Lord.—*Deut.* vi. 4.

See ye that I alone am, and there is no other God besides me: I will kill, and I will make to live: I will strike, and I will heal, and there is none that can deliver out of my hand.—*Deut.* xxxii. 39.

That all the people of the earth may know, that the Lord he is God, and there is no other besides him.—*3 Kings* viii. 60.

Because he hath therefore scattered you among the Gentiles, who know not him, that you may declare his wonderful works, and make them know that there is no other almighty God besides him.—*Tob.* xiii. 4.

For who is God but the Lord? or who is God but our God?—*Ps.* xvii. 32.

For there is no other God but thou, who hast care of all, that thou shouldest show that thou dost not give judgment unjustly.—*Wis.* xii. 13.

O Lord of hosts, God of Israel, who sittest upon the cherubims, thou alone art the God of all the kingdoms of the earth, thou hast made heaven and earth. —*Is.* xxxvii. 16.

You are my witnesses, saith the Lord, and my servant whom I have chosen: that you may know, and believe me, and understand that I myself am. Before me there was no God formed, and after me there shall be none.

I am, I am the Lord: and there is no saviour besides me.—*Is.* xliii. 10, 11.

Thus saith the Lord the king of Israel, and his redeemer the Lord of hosts: I am the first, and I am the last, and besides me there is no God.

Who is like to me? let him call and declare: and let him set before me the order, since I appointed the ancient people: and the things to come, and that shall be hereafter, let them show unto them.

Fear ye not, neither be ye troubled, from that time I have made thee to hear, and have declared: you are my witnesses. Is there a God besides me, a maker, whom I have not known?— *Is.* xliv. 6-8.

And Jesus answered him: The first commandment of all is, Hear, O Israel: the Lord thy God is one God.

And thou shalt love the Lord thy God, with thy whole heart, and with thy whole soul, and with thy whole mind, and with thy whole strength. This is the first commandment.—*Mark* xii. 29, 30.

But as for the meats that are sacrificed to idols, we know that an idol is nothing in the world, and that there is no God but one.

For although there be that are called gods, even in heaven or on earth (for there be gods many, and lords many);

Yet to us there is but one God, the Father, of whom are all things, and we unto him; and one Lord Jesus Christ, by whom are all things, and we by him. —*1 Cor.* viii. 4-6.

One God and Father of all, who is above all, and through all, and in us all. —*Eph.* iv. 6.

For there is one God, and one mediator of God and men, the man Christ Jesus.—*1 Tim.* ii. 5.

GOD, THE TRINITY IN

See: Trinity—page 736.

GRACE, ACTUAL

I. The Effects of Actual Grace

1st. Illumines the Mind

The law of the Lord is unspotted, converting souls: the testimony of the Lord is faithful, giving wisdom to little ones.

The justices of the Lord are right, rejoicing hearts: the commandment of the Lord is lightsome, enlightening the eyes.—*Ps.* xviii. 8, 9.

And a certain woman named Lydia, a seller of purple, of the city of Thyatira, one that worshipped God, did hear: whose heart the Lord opened to attend to those things which were said by Paul.—*Acts* xvi. 14.

But rise up, and stand upon thy feet:

for to this end have I appeared to thee, that I may make thee a minister, and a witness of those things which thou hast seen, and of those things wherein I will appear to thee,

Delivering thee from the people, and from the nations, unto which I now send thee:

To open their eyes, that they may be converted from darkness to light, and from the power of Satan to God. —*Acts* xxvi. 16-18.

For God, who commanded the light to shine out of darkness, hath shined in our hearts, to give the light of the knowledge of the glory of God, in the face of Christ Jesus.—*2 Cor.* iv. 6.

That the God of our Lord Jesus Christ, the Father of glory, may give up to you the spirit of wisdom and of revelation, in the knowledge of him:

The eyes of your heart enlightened, that you may know what the hope is of his calling, and what are the riches of the glory of his inheritance in the saints.—*Eph.* i. 17, 18.

2d. Moves the Will

Jesus therefore answered, and said to them: Murmur not among yourselves.

No man can come to me, except the Father, who hath sent me, draw him; and I will raise him up in the last day. —*John* vi. 43, 44.

For it is God who worketh in you, both to will and to accomplish, according to his good will.—*Philipp.* ii. 13.

II. Actual Grace Can be Resisted

What is there that I ought to do more to my vineyard, that I have not done to it? was it that I looked that it should bring forth grapes, and it hath brought forth wild grapes?—*Is.* v. 4.

Jerusalem, Jerusalem, thou that killest the prophets, and stonest them that are sent unto thee, how often would I have gathered together thy children, as the hen doth gather her chickens under her wings, and thou wouldest not? —*Matt.* xxiii. 37.

But by the grace of God, I am what I am; and his grace in me hath not been void, but I have labored more abundantly than all they: yet not I, but the grace of God with me.—*1 Cor.* xv. 10.

And we helping do exhort you, that you receive not the grace of God in vain.—*2 Cor.* vi. 1.

I cast not away the grace of God.— *Gal.* ii. 21.

You are made void of Christ, you who are justified in the law: you are fallen from grace.—*Gal.* v. 4.

Looking diligently, lest any man be wanting to the grace of God; lest any root of bitterness springing up do hinder, and by it many be defiled.—*Heb.* xii. 15.

III. Actual Grace and Free Will Work Together, Hand in Hand

Perfect thou my goings in thy paths: that my footsteps be not moved.—*Ps.* xvi. 5.

Who hath been tried thereby, and made perfect, he shall have glory everlasting. He that could have transgressed, and hath not transgressed: and could do evil things, and hath not done them.—*Ecclus.* xxxi. 10.

Convert me, and I shall be converted, for thou art the Lord my God.

For after thou didst convert me, I did penance: and after thou didst show unto me, I struck my thigh: I am confounded and ashamed, because I have borne the reproach of my youth.— *Jer.* xxxi. 18, 19.

And every man shall receive his own reward, according to his own labor.

For we are God's coadjutors.—*1 Cor.* iii. 8, 9.

But by the grace of God, I am what I am; and his grace in me hath not been void, but I have labored more abundantly than all they: yet not I, but the grace of God with me.—*1 Cor.* xv. 10.

Wherefore he saith: Rise thou that sleepest, and arise from the dead: and Christ shall enlighten thee.—*Eph.* v. 14.

I can do all things in him who strengtheneth me.—*Philipp.* iv. 13.

Compare

The Lord our God be with us, as he was with our fathers, and not leave us, nor cast us off:

But may he incline our hearts to himself, that we may walk in all his ways, and keep his commandments, and his ceremonies, and all his judgments which he commanded our fathers.— 3 *Kings* viii. 57, 58.

With

I have inclined my heart to do thy justifications for ever, for the reward. —*Ps.* cxviii. 112.

Also

Convert us, O God our Saviour: and turn off thy anger from us.—*Ps.* lxxxiv. 5.

With

I have thought on my ways: and turned my feet unto thy testimonies.— *Ps.* cxviii. 59.

Also

Create a clean heart in me, O God: and renew a right spirit within my bowels.—*Ps.* l. 12.

With

Cast away from you all your transgressions, by which you have transgressed, and make to yourselves a new heart, and a new spirit: and why will you die, O house of Israel?—*Ezech.* xviii. 31.

IV. The Necessity of Actual Grace

1st. To Resist for any Length of Time Grave Temptations

Watch ye, and pray that ye enter not into temptation. The spirit indeed is willing, but the flesh weak.—*Matt.* xxvi. 41.

For I know that there dwelleth not in me, that is to say, in my flesh, that which is good. For to will, is present with me; but to accomplish that which is good, I find not.

For the good which I will, I do not; but the evil which I will not, that I do.

Now if I do that which I will not, it is no more I that do it, but sin that dwelleth in me.

I find then a law, that when I have a will to do good, evil is present with me.

For I am delighted with the law of God, according to the inward man:

But I see another law in my members, fighting against the law of my mind, and captivating me in the law of sin, that is in my members.

Unhappy man that I am, who shall deliver me from the body of this death?

The grace of God, by Jesus Christ our Lord. Therefore I myself, with the mind serve the law of God; but with the flesh, the law of sin.—*Rom.* vii. 18-25.

2d. To Observe, for any Length of Time, the Natural Law

And as I knew that I could not otherwise be continent, except God gave it, and this also was a point of wisdom, to know whose gift it was: I went to the Lord, and besought him.—*Wis.* viii. 21.

For that which I work, I understand not. For I do not that good which I will; but the evil which I hate, that I do.

. . . For I know that there dwelleth not in me, that is to say, in my flesh, that which is good. For to will is present with me; but to accomplish that which is good, I find not.

For the good which I will, I do not; but the evil which I will not, that I do.

. . . I find then a law, that when I have a will to do good, evil is present with me. . . .

Unhappy man that I am, who shall deliver me from the body of this death?

The grace of God, by Jesus Christ our Lord.—*Rom.* vii. 15, 18, 19, 21, 24, 25.

But the tongue no man can tame, an unquiet evil, full of deadly poison. —*James* iii. 8.

3d. To Perform Supernatural Works

For if by the offence of one, many died; much more the grace of God, and the gift, by the grace of one man, Jesus

Christ, hath abounded unto many.—*Rom.* v. 15.

But God, (who is rich in mercy,) for his exceeding charity wherewith he loved us,

Even when we were dead in sins, hath quickened us together in Christ, (by whose grace you are saved).—*Eph.* ii. 4, 5.

For you were heretofore darkness, but now light in the Lord. Walk then as children of the light.—*Eph.* v. 8.

I know, O Lord, that the way of a man is not his: neither is it in a man to walk, and to direct his steps.—*Jer.* x. 23.

No man can come to me, except the Father, who hath sent me, draw him; and I will raise him up in the last day.—*John* vi. 44.

Jesus saith to him (Thomas): I am the way, and the truth, and the life. No man cometh to the Father, but by me.—*John* xiv. 6.

I am the true vine; and my Father is the husbandman.

Every branch in me, that beareth not fruit, he will take away: and every one that beareth fruit, he will purge it, that it may bring forth more fruit.

Now you are clean by reason of the word, which I have spoken to you.

Abide in me, and I in you. As the branch cannot bear fruit of itself, unless it abide in the vine, so neither can you, unless you abide in me.

I am the vine; you the branches: he that abideth in me, and I in him, the same beareth much fruit: for without me you can do nothing.—*John* xv. 1-5.

Likewise the Spirit also helpeth our infirmity. For we know not what we should pray for as we ought; but the Spirit himself asketh for us with unspeakable groanings.—*Rom.* viii. 26.

So then it is not of him that willeth, nor of him that runneth, but of God that showeth mercy.—*Rom.* ix. 16.

Or who hath first given to him, and recompense shall be made him?—*Rom.* xi. 35.

For who distinguisheth thee? Or what hast thou that thou hast not received? And if thou hast received, why dost thou glory, as if thou hadst not received it?—1 *Cor.* iv. 7.

Wherefore I give you to understand, that no man, speaking by the Spirit of God, saith Anathema to Jesus. And no man can say the Lord Jesus, but by the Holy Ghost.—1 *Cor.* xii. 3.

Not that we are sufficient to think any thing of ourselves, as of ourselves: but our sufficiency is from God.—2 *Cor.* iii. 5.

For by grace you are saved through faith, and that not of yourselves, for it is the gift of God;

Not of works, that no man may glory.—*Eph.* ii. 8, 9.

For it is God who worketh in you, both to will and to accomplish, according to his good will.—*Philipp.* ii. 13.

4th. To Persevere in Justification

Watch ye, and pray that ye enter not into temptation. The spirit indeed is willing, but the flesh weak.—*Matt.* xxvi. 41.

For our wrestling is not against flesh and blood; but against principalities and powers, against the rulers of the world of this darkness, against the spirits of wickedness in the high places.

Therefore take unto you the armor of God, that you may be able to resist in the evil day, and to stand in all things perfect.—*Eph.* vi. 12, 13.

Be sober and watch: because your adversary the devil, as a roaring lion, goeth about seeking whom he may devour.

Whom resist ye, strong in faith.—1 *Peter* v. 8, 9.

5th. For Final Perseverance

Being confident of this very thing, that he, who hath begun a good work in you, will perfect it unto the day of Christ Jesus.—*Philipp.* i. 6.

But the God of all grace, who hath called us unto his eternal glory in Christ Jesus, after you have suffered a little, will himself perfect you, and confirm you, and establish you.—1 *Peter* v. 10.

V. Actual Grace is the Free Gift of God

Because by the works of the law no flesh shall be justified before him.

. . . Being justified freely by his grace, through the redemption, that is in Christ Jesus. . . .

For we account a man to be justified by faith, without the works of the law.—*Rom.* iii. 20, 24, 28.

For if Abraham were justified by works, he hath whereof to glory, but not before God. . . .

Now to him that worketh, the reward is not reckoned according to grace, but according to debt.

But to him that worketh not, yet believeth in him that justifieth the ungodly, his faith is reputed to justice, according to the purpose of the grace of God.—*Rom.* iv. 2, 4, 5.

Even so then at this present time also, there is a remnant saved according to the election of grace.

And if by grace, it is not now by works: otherwise grace is no more grace.—*Rom.* xi. 5, 6.

VI. The Universality of Actual Grace

1st. To All the Just

And of his fulness we all have received, and grace for grace.—*John* i. 16.

And God is faithful, who will not suffer you to be tempted above that which you are able: but will make also with temptation issue, that you may be able to bear it.—1 *Cor.* x. 13.

But to every one of us is given grace, according to the measure of the giving of Christ.—*Eph.* iv. 7.

2d. To Sinners

And I have sent to you all my servants the prophets, rising early, and sending and saying: Return ye every man from his wicked way, and make your ways good: and follow not strange gods, nor worship them, and you shall dwell in the land, which I gave you and your fathers: and you have not inclined your ear, nor hearkened to me.—*Jer.* xxxv. 15.

Is it my will that a sinner should die, saith the Lord God, and not that he should be converted from his ways, and live? . . .

For I desire not the death of him that dieth, saith the Lord God, return ye and live.—*Ezech.* xviii. 23, 32.

As I live, saith the Lord God, I desire not the death of the wicked, but that the wicked turn from his way, and live. Turn ye, turn ye from your evil ways: and why will you die, O house of Israel?—*Ezech.* xxxiii. 11.

I came not to call the just, but sinners to penance.—*Luke* v. 32.

What man of you that hath a hundred sheep: and if he shall lose one of them, doth he not leave the ninety-nine in the desert, and go after that which was lost, until he find it?—*Luke* xv. 4.

The Lord delayeth not his promise, as some imagine, but dealeth patiently for your sake, not willing that any should perish, but that all should return to penance.—2 *Peter* iii. 9.

3d. Even to Blinded and Obdurate Sinners

Wisdom preacheth abroad, she uttereth her voice in the streets:

At the head of multitudes she crieth out, in the entrance of the gates of the city she uttereth her words, saying:

O children, how long will you love childishness, and fools covet those things which are hurtful to themselves, and the unwise hate knowledge?

Turn ye at my reproof: behold I will utter my spirit to you, and will show you my words.

Because I called, and you refused: I stretched out my hand, and there was none that regarded.

You have despised all my counsel, and have neglected my reprehensions.—*Prov.* i. 20-25.

I have spread forth my hands all the day to an unbelieving people, who walk in a way that is not good after their own thoughts.

A people that continually provoke me to anger before my face.—*Is.* lxv. 2, 3.

Or despisest thou the riches of his goodness, and patience, and longsuffering? Knowest thou not, that the benignity of God leadeth thee to penance?—*Rom.* ii. 4.

4th. To Infidels

But thou hast mercy upon all, because thou canst do all things, and overlookest the sins of men for the sake of repentance.—*Wis.* xi. 24.

That was the true light, which enlighteneth every man that cometh into this world.—*John* i. 9.

For there is no distinction of the Jew and the Greek: for the same is Lord over all, rich unto all that call upon him.—*Rom.* x. 12.

For this is good and acceptable in the sight of God our Saviour,

Who will have all men to be saved, and to come to the knowledge of the truth.—1 *Tim.* ii. 3, 4.

And he is the propitiation for our sins: and not for ours only, but also for those of the whole world.—1 *John* ii. 2.

GRACE, HABITUAL

See: Justification—page 711.

HELL, THE ETERNITY OF

The enemies of the Lord have lied to him: and their time shall be for ever.—*Ps.* lxxx. 16.

And they shall go out, and see the carcasses of the men that have transgressed against me: their worm shall not die, and their fire shall not be quenched: and they shall be a loathsome sight to all flesh.—*Is.* lxvi. 24.

And many of those that sleep in the dust of the earth, shall awake: Some unto life everlasting, and others unto reproach, to see it always.—*Dan.* xii. 2.

I indeed baptize you in water unto penance, but he that shall come after me, is mightier than I, whose shoes I am not worthy to bear; he shall baptize you in the Holy Ghost and fire

Whose fan is in his hand, and he will thoroughly cleanse his floor, and gather his wheat into the barn; but the chaff he will burn with unquenchable fire.—*Matt.* iii. 11, 12.

Then he shall say to them also that shall be on his left hand: Depart from me, you cursed, into everlasting fire which was prepared for the devil and his angels. . . .

And these shall go into everlasting punishment: but the just, into life everlasting.—*Matt.* xxv. 41, 46.

And if thy hand scandalize thee, cut it off: it is better for thee to enter into life, maimed, than having two hands to go into hell, into unquenchable fire:

Where their worm dieth not, and the fire is not extinguished.—*Mark* ix. 42, 43.

And Abraham said to him (Dives): Son, remember that thou didst receive good things in thy lifetime, and likewise Lazarus evil things, but now he is comforted; and thou art tormented.

And besides all this, between us and you, there is fixed a great chaos: so that they who would pass from hence to you, cannot, nor from thence come hither.—*Luke* xvi. 25, 26.

And to you who are troubled, rest with us when the Lord Jesus shall be revealed from heaven, with the angels of his power:

In a flame of fire, giving vengeance to them who know not God, and who obey not the gospel of our Lord Jesus Christ.

Who shall suffer eternal punishment in destruction, from the face of the Lord, and from the glory of his power.—2 *Thess.* i. 7-9.

And the angels who kept not their principality, but forsook their own habitation, he hath reserved under darkness in everlasting chains, unto the judgment of the great day.

As Sodom and Gomorrha, and the neighboring cities, in like manner, having given themselves to fornication, and going after other flesh, were made an example, suffering the punishment of eternal fire.

In like manner these men also defile the flesh, and despise dominion, and blaspheme majesty. . . .

Raging waves of the sea, foaming out their own confusion; wandering stars to whom the storm of darkness is reserved for ever.—*Jude* i. 6-8, 13.

And the smoke of their torments shall ascend up for ever and ever: neither have they rest day nor night, who have adored the beast, and his image, and whoever receiveth the character of his name.—*Apoc.* xiv. 11.

And there came down fire from God out of heaven, and devoured them; and the devil, who seduced them, was cast into the pool of fire and brimstone, where both the beast,

And the false prophet shall be tormented day and night, for ever and ever.—*Apoc.* xx. 9, 10.

Also Inferred from

And whosoever shall speak a word against the Son of man, it shall be forgiven him: but he that shall speak against the Holy Ghost, it shall not be forgiven him, neither in this world, nor in the world to come.—*Matt.* xii. 32.

But he that shall blaspheme against the Holy Ghost, shall never have forgiveness, but shall be guilty of an everlasting sin.—*Mark* iii. 29.

Know you not that the unjust shall not possess the kingdom of God? Do not err: neither fornicators, nor idolaters, nor adulterers,

Nor the effeminate, nor liers with mankind, nor thieves, nor covetous, nor drunkards, nor railers, nor extortioners, shall possess the kingdom of God.— 1 *Cor.* vi. 9, 10.

Now this I say, brethren, that flesh and blood cannot possess the kingdom of God: neither shall corruption possess incorruption.—1 *Cor.* xv. 50.

Now the works of the flesh are manifest, which are fornication, uncleanness, immodesty, luxury,

Idolatry, witchcrafts, enmities, contentions, emulations, wraths, quarrels, dissensions, sects,

Envies, murders, drunkenness, revellings, and such like. Of the which I foretell you, as I have foretold to you, that they who do such things shall not obtain the kingdom of God.—*Gal.* v. 19-21.

HELL, PAIN OF SENSE IN
Inferred from

And fear ye not them that kill the body, and are not able to kill the soul: but rather fear him that can destroy both soul and body in hell.—*Matt.* x. 28.

The Son of man shall send his angels, and they shall gather out of his kingdom all scandals, and them that work iniquity.

And shall cast them into the furnace of fire: there shall be weeping and gnashing of teeth.—*Matt.* xiii. 41, 42.

And if thy hand scandalize thee, cut it off: it is better for thee to enter into life, maimed, than having two hands to go into hell, into unquenchable fire:

Where their worm dieth not, and the fire is not extinguished.—*Mark* ix. 42, 43.

Whose fan is in his hand, and he will purge his floor, and will gather the wheat into his barn; but the chaff he will burn with unquenchable fire.— *Luke* iii. 17.

And it came to pass, that the beggar died, and was carried by the angels into Abraham's bosom. And the rich man also died: and he was buried in hell.

And lifting up his eyes when he was in torments, he saw Abraham afar off, and Lazarus in his bosom:

And he cried, and said: Father Abraham, have mercy on me, and send Lazarus, that he may dip the tip of his finger in water, to cool my tongue: for I am tormented in this flame.

And Abraham said to him: Son, remember that thou didst receive good things in thy lifetime, and likewise Lazarus evil things, but now he is comforted; and thou art tormented.—*Luke* xvi. 22-25.

If any one abide not in me, he shall be cast forth as a branch, and shall wither, and they shall gather him up, and cast him into the fire, and he burneth.—*John* xv. 6.

For we must all be manifested before the judgment seat of Christ, that every one may receive the proper things of the body, according as he hath done, whether it be good or evil.—2 *Cor.* v. 10.

And hell and death were cast into the pool of fire. This is the second death.

And whosoever was not found written in the book of life, was cast into the pool of fire.—*Apoc.* xx. 14, 15.

But the fearful, and unbelieving, and the abominable, and murderers, and whoremongers, and sorcerers, and idolaters, and all liars, they shall have their portion in the pool burning with fire and brimstone, which is the second death.—*Apoc.* xxi. 8.

HOLY GHOST, THE

1st. His Divinity

And Jesus being baptized, forthwith came out of the water: and lo, the heavens were opened to him: and he saw the Spirit of God descending as a dove, and coming upon him.—*Matt.* iii. 16.

Going therefore, teach ye all nations; baptizing them in the name of the Father, and of the Son, and of the Holy Ghost.—*Matt.* xxviii. 19.

Jesus answered: Amen, amen I say to thee, unless a man be born again of water and the Holy Ghost, he cannot enter into the kingdom of God.—*John* iii. 5.

But Peter said: Ananias, why hath Satan tempted thy heart, that thou shouldst lie to the Holy Ghost, and by fraud keep part of the price of the land?

Whilst it remained, did it not remain to thee? and after it was sold, was it not in thy power? Why hast thou conceived this thing in thy heart? Thou hast not lied to men, but to God. —*Acts* v. 3, 4.

And hope confoundeth not: because the charity of God is poured forth in our hearts, by the Holy Ghost, who is given to us.—*Rom.* v. 5.

But you are not in the flesh, but in the spirit, if so be that the Spirit of God dwell in you. Now if any man have not the Spirit of Christ, he is none of his. . . .

And if the Spirit of him that raised up Jesus from the dead, dwell in you; he that raised up Jesus Christ from the dead, shall quicken also your mortal bodies, because of his Spirit that dwelleth in you. . . .

For whosoever are led by the Spirit of God, they are the sons of God.— *Rom.* viii. 9, 11, 14.

But to us God hath revealed them, by his Spirit. For the Spirit, searcheth all things, yea, the deep things of God.

For what man knoweth the things of a man, but the spirit of a man that is in him? So the things also that are of God no man knoweth, but the Spirit of God.—1 *Cor.* ii. 10, 11.

And such some of you were; but you are washed, but you are sanctified, but you are justified in the name of our Lord Jesus Christ, and the Spirit of our God.—1 *Cor.* vi. 11.

Or know you not, that your members are the temple of the Holy Ghost, who is in you, whom you have from God; and you are not your own?

For you are bought with a great price. Glorify and bear God in your body.—1 *Cor.* vi. 19, 20.

Wherefore I give you to understand, that no man, speaking by the Spirit of God, saith Anathema to Jesus. And no man can say the Lord Jesus, but by the Holy Ghost.—1 *Cor.* xii. 3.

And there are diversities of operations, but the same God, who worketh all in all.

. . . To one indeed, by the Spirit, is given the word of wisdom: and to another, the word of knowledge, according to the same Spirit. . . .

But all these things one and the same Spirit worketh, dividing to every one according as he will.—1 *Cor.* xii. 6, 8, 11.

For prophecy came not by the will of man at any time: but the holy men of God spoke, inspired by the Holy Ghost. —2 *Peter* i. 21.

Compare

And when they agreed not among themselves, they departed, Paul speaking this one word: Well did the Holy Ghost speak to our fathers by Isaias the prophet,

Saying: Go to this people, and say to them: With the ear you shall hear, and shall not understand; and seeing you shall see, and shall not perceive.— *Acts* xxviii. 25, 26.

With

And I heard the voice of the Lord saying: Whom shall I send? and who shall go for us? And I said: Lo, here am I, send me.

And he said: Go, and thou shalt say to this people: Hearing, hear, and understand not: and see the vision, and know it not.—*Is.* vi. 8, 9.

2d. Proceeds from the Father

For it is not you that speak, but the Spirit of your Father that speaketh in you.—*Matt.* x. 20.

And I will ask the Father, and he shall give you another Paraclete, that he may abide with you for ever.—*John* xiv. 16.

But the Paraclete, the Holy Ghost, whom the Father will send in my name, he will teach you all things, and bring all things to your mind, whatsoever I shall have said to you.—*John* xiv. 26.

But when the Paraclete cometh, whom I will send you from the Father, the Spirit of truth, who proceedeth from the Father, he shall give testimony of me.—*John* xv. 26.

3d. Proceeds also from the Son, Because

A. He is Called the Spirit of the Son

And when they were come into Mysia, they attempted to go into Bithynia, and the Spirit of Jesus suffered them not.—*Acts* xvi. 7.

And because you are sons, God hath sent the Spirit of his Son into your hearts, crying: Abba, Father.—*Gal.* iv. 6.

For I know that this shall fall out to me unto salvation, through your prayer, and the supply of the Spirit of Jesus Christ.—*Philipp.* i. 19.

Searching what or what manner of time the Spirit of Christ in them did signify: when it foretold those sufferings that are in Christ, and the glories that should follow.—1 *Peter* i. 11.

B. Is Sent by the Son

And I send the promise of my Father upon you: but stay you in the city, till you be endued with power from on high.—*Luke* xxiv. 49.

But when the Paraclete cometh, whom I will send you from the Father, the Spirit of truth, who proceedeth from the Father, he shall give testimony of me.—*John* xv. 26.

But I tell you the truth: it is expedient to you that I go: for if I go not, the Paraclete will not come to you; but if I go, I will send him to you.—*John* xvi. 7.

When he had said this, he breathed on them; and he said to them: Receive ye the Holy Ghost.—*John* xx. 22.

C. Receives from the Son

But when he, the Spirit of truth, is come, he will teach you all truth. For he shall not speak of himself; but what things soever he shall hear, he shall speak; and the things that are to come, he shall show you.

He shall glorify me; because he shall receive of mine, and shall show it to you.

All things whatsoever the Father hath, are mine. Therefore I said, that he shall receive of mine, and show it to you.—*John* xvi. 13-15.

4th. The Holy Ghost Promised to the Apostles

And I send the promise of my Father upon you: but stay you in the city, till you be endued with power from on high.—*Luke* xxiv. 49.

And I will ask the Father, and he shall give you another Paraclete, that he may abide with you for ever.

The spirit of truth, whom the world cannot receive, because it seeth him not, nor knoweth him: but you shall know him; because he shall abide with you, and shall be in you.—*John* xiv. 16, 17.

But the Paraclete, the Holy Ghost, whom the Father will send in my name, he will teach you all things, and bring all things to your mind, whatsoever I shall have said to you.—*John* xiv. 26.

But when the Paraclete cometh, whom I will send you from the Father, the Spirit of truth, who proceedeth from the Father, he shall give testimony of me.—*John* xv. 26.

But I tell you the truth: it is expedient to you that I go: for if I go not, the Paraclete will not come to you; but if I go, I will send him to you.—*John* xvi. 7.

But when he, the Spirit of truth, is come, he will teach you all truth. For he shall not speak of himself; but what things soever he shall hear, he shall speak; and the things that are to come, he shall show you.—*John* xvi. 13.

And eating together with them, he commanded them, that they should not depart from Jerusalem, but should wait for the promise of the Father, which you have heard (saith he) by my mouth.

For John indeed baptized with water, but you shall be baptized with the Holy Ghost, not many days hence.

. . . But you shall receive the power of the Holy Ghost coming upon you, and you shall be witnesses unto me in Jerusalem, and in all Judea, and Samaria, and even to the uttermost part of the earth.—*Acts* i. 4, 5, 8.

Fulfilment of the Promise

And when the days of the Pentecost were accomplished, they were all together in one place:

And suddenly there came a sound from heaven, as of a mighty wind coming, and it filled the whole house where they were sitting.

And there appeared to them parted tongues as it were of fire, and it sat upon every one of them:

And they were all filled with the Holy Ghost, and they began to speak with divers tongues, according as the Holy Ghost gave them to speak.—*Acts* ii. 1-4.

IMAGES

1st. Their Use Commanded by God

Thou shalt make also two cherubims of beaten gold, on the two sides of the oracle.

Let one cherub be on the one side, and the other on the other.

Let them cover both sides of the propitiatory, spreading their wings, and covering the oracle, and let them look one towards the other, their faces being turned towards the propitiatory wherewith the ark is to be covered.—*Ex.* xxv. 18-20.

And the Lord said to him: Make a brazen serpent, and set it up for a sign: whosoever being struck shall look on it, shall live.

Moses therefore made a brazen serpent, and set it up for a sign: which when they that were bitten looked upon, they were healed.—*Num.* xxi. 8, 9.

And for the altar of incense, he (David) gave the purest gold: and to make the likeness of the chariot of the cherubims spreading their wings, and covering the ark of the covenant of the Lord.

All these things, said he, came to me written by the hand of the Lord that I might understand all the works of this pattern.—1 *Paral.* xxviii. 18, 19.

2d. Used in His Worship in the Temple

He (Beseleel) made also the propitiatory, that is, the oracle, of the purest gold, two cubits and a half in length, and a cubit and a half in breadth.

Two cherubims also of beaten gold, which he set on the two sides of the propitiatory:

One cherub in the top of one side, and the other cherub in the top of the other side: two cherubims at the two ends of the propitiatory,

Spreading their wings, and covering the propitiatory, and looking one towards the other, and towards it.—*Ex.* xxxvii. 6-9.

And all the walls of the temple round about he (Solomon) carved with divers figures and carvings: and he made in them cherubims and palm-trees, and divers representations, as it were standing out, and coming forth from the wall.

. . . And in the entrance of the oracle he made little doors of olive-tree, and posts of five corners,

And two doors of olive-tree: and he carved upon them figures of cherubims, and figures of palm-trees, and carvings very much projecting: and he overlaid them with gold: and he covered both the cherubims and the palm-trees, and the other things with gold.— 3 *Kings* vi. 29, 31, 32.

And in the top of the base there was a round compass of half a cubit, so wrought that the laver might be set thereon, having its gravings, and divers sculptures of itself.

He engraved also in those plates, which were of brass, and in the corners, cherubims, and lions, and palm-trees, in the likeness of a man standing, so that they seemed not to be engraven, but added round about.—3 *Kings* vii. 35, 36.

And the priests brought in the ark of the covenant of the Lord into its place, into the oracle of the temple, into the holy of holies under the wings of the cherubims.

For the cherubims spread forth their wings over the place of the ark, and covered the ark, and the staves thereof above.—*3 Kings* viii. 6, 7.

And the gold of the plates with which he overlaid the house, and the beams thereof, and the posts, and the walls, and the doors was of the finest: and he graved cherubims on the walls. . . .

He made also in the house of the holy of holies two cherubims of image work: and he overlaid them with gold. . . .

He made also a veil of violet, purple, scarlet, and silk: and wrought in it cherubims.—*2 Paral.* iii. 7, 10, 14.

IMMORTALITY OF THE SOUL, BELIEF EXPRESSED IN THE OLD TESTAMENT IN THE

1st. Indirectly Declared or Insinuated

And the days of Abraham's life were a hundred and seventy-five years.

And decaying he died in a good old age, and having lived a long time, and being full of days: and was gathered to his people.—*Gen.* xxv. 7, 8.

And all his children being gathered together to comfort their father in his sorrow, he (Jacob) would not receive comfort, but said: I will go down to my son into hell, mourning.—*Gen.* xxxvii. 35.

And being asked by him (Pharao): How many are the day of the years of thy life?

He (Jacob) answered: The days of my pilgrimage are a hundred and thirty years, few, and evil, and they are not come up to the days of the pilgrimage of my fathers.—*Gen.* xlvii. 8, 9.

Who can count the dust of Jacob, and know the number of the stock of Israel? Let my soul die the death of the just, and my last end be like to them.—*Num.* xxiii. 10.

Neither let there be found among you any one that shall expiate his son or daughter, making them to pass through the fire: or that consulteth soothsayers, or observeth dreams and omens, neither let there be any wizard,

Nor charmer, nor any one that consulteth pythonic spirits, or fortune tellers, or that seeketh the truth from the dead.—*Deut.* xviii. 10, 11.

2d. Clearly Proclaimed

Who will grant me this, that thou mayst protect me in hell, and hide me till thy wrath pass, and appoint me a time when thou wilt remember me?

Shall man that is dead, thinkest thou, live again? all the days in which I am now in warfare, I expect until my change come.

Thou shalt call me, and I will answer thee: to the work of thy hands thou shalt reach out thy right hand.—*Job* xiv. 13-15.

For I know that my Redeemer liveth, and in the last day I shall rise out of the earth.

And I shall be clothed again with my skin, and in my flesh I shall see my God.

Whom I myself shall see, and my eyes shall behold, and not another: this my hope is laid up in my bosom.—*Job* xix. 25-27.

I saw under the sun in the place of judgment wickedness, and in the place of justice iniquity.

And I said in my heart: God shall judge both the just and the wicked, and then shall be the time of every thing.—*Eccles.* iii. 16, 17.

And the dust return into its earth, from whence it was, and the spirit return to God, who gave it.—*Eccles.* xii. 7.

But the souls of the just are in the hand of God, and the torment of death shall not touch them.

In the sight of the unwise they seemed to die: and their departure was taken for misery:

And their going away from us, for utter destruction: but they are in peace.

And though in the sight of men they suffered torments, their hope is full of immortality.—*Wis.* iii. 1-4.

But the just shall live for evermore: and their reward is with the Lord, and the care of them with the most High.

Therefore shall they receive a kingdom of glory, and a crown of beauty at the hand of the Lord: for with his right hand he will cover them, and with his holy arm he will defend them.—*Wis.* v. 16, 17.

Thy dead men shall live, my slain shall rise again: awake, and give praise, ye that dwell in the dust: for thy dew is the dew of the light: and the land of the giants thou shalt pull down into ruin.—*Is.* xxvi. 19.

But many of those that sleep in the dust of the earth, shall awake: Some unto life everlasting, and others unto reproach, to see it always.

But they that are learned shall shine as the brightness of the firmament: and they that instruct many to justice, as stars for all eternity.—*Dan.* xii. 2, 3.

And when he was at the last gasp, he said thus: Thou indeed, O most wicked man, destroyest us out of this present life: but the King of the world will raise us up, who die for his laws, in the resurrection of eternal life.—2 *Mach.* vii. 9.

And when he was now ready to die, he spoke thus: It is better, being put to death by men, to look for hope from God, to be raised up again by him: for, as to thee, thou shalt have no resurrection unto life.—2 *Mach.* vii. 14.

But the Creator of the world, that formed the nativity of man, and that found out the origin of all, he will restore to you again in his mercy, both breath and life, as now you despise yourselves for the sake of his laws.—2 *Mach.* vii. 23.

And making a gathering, he (Judas) sent twelve thousand drachms of silver to Jerusalem for sacrifice to be offered for the sins of the dead, thinking well and religiously concerning the resurrection,

(For if he had not hoped that they that were slain should rise again, it would have seemed superfluous and vain to pray for the dead).—2 *Mach.* xii. 43, 44.

INDULGENCES

1st. The Power Given to the Church to Grant Indulgences

And I will give to thee the keys of the kingdom of heaven. And whatsoever thou shalt bind upon earth, it shall be bound also in heaven: and whatsoever thou shalt loose on earth, it shall be loosed also in heaven.—*Matt.* xvi. 19.

Amen I say to you, whatsoever you shall bind upon earth, shall be bound also in heaven; and whatsoever you shall loose upon earth, shall be loosed also in heaven.—*Matt.* xviii. 18.

2d. The Use of this Power

It is absolutely heard, that there is fornication among you, and such fornication as the like is not among the heathens; that one should have his father's wife. . . .

I indeed, absent in body, but present in spirit, have already judged, as though I were present, him that hath so done,

In the name of our Lord Jesus Christ, you being gathered together, and my spirit, with the power of our Lord Jesus;

To deliver such a one to Satan for the destruction of the flesh, that the spirit may be saved in the day of our Lord Jesus Christ. . . .

To him who is such a one, this rebuke is sufficient, which is given by many:

So that on the contrary, you should rather forgive him and comfort him, lest perhaps such a one be swallowed up with overmuch sorrow. . . .

And to whom you have pardoned any thing, I also. For, what I have pardoned, if I have pardoned any thing, for your sakes have I done it in the person of Christ.—1 *Cor.* v. 1, 3-5; 2 *Cor.* ii. 6, 7, 10.

JUSTIFICATION

I. Faith Alone is not Sufficient for Justification

What shall it profit, my brethren, if a man say he hath faith, but hath not works? Shall faith be able to save him? . . .

So faith also, if it have not works, is dead in itself. . . .

But wilt thou know, O vain man, that faith without works is dead? . . .

Do you see that by works a man is justified; and not by faith only?

. . . For even as the body without the spirit is dead; so also faith without works is dead.—*James* ii. 14, 17, 20, 24, 26.

And if I should have prophecy and should know all mysteries, and all knowledge, and if I should have all faith, so that I could remove mountains, and have not charity, I am nothing.—1 *Cor.* xiii. 2.

For in Christ Jesus neither circumcision availeth any thing, nor uncircumcision: but faith that worketh by charity.—*Gal.* v. 6.

For he that is without fear, cannot be justified: for the wrath of his high spirits is his ruin.—*Ecclus.* i. 28.

No, I say to you: but unless you shall do penance, you shall all likewise perish.—*Luke* xiii. 3.

Be penitent, therefore, and be converted, that your sins may be blotted out.—*Acts* iii. 19.

We know that we have passed from death to life, because we love the brethren. He that loveth not, abideth in death.—1 *John* iii. 14.

II. The Faith Required for Justification is not Mere Confidence, but is Belief in All the Truths Revealed by God

1st. Not Mere Confidence

For I am not conscious to myself of any thing, yet am I not hereby justified; but he that judgeth me is the Lord.—1 *Cor.* iv. 4.

2d. But is Belief

And he said to them: Go ye into the whole world, and preach the gospel to every creature.

He that believeth and is baptized, shall be saved: but he that believeth not shall be condemned.—*Mark* xvi. 15, 16.

Jesus saith to him: Because thou hast seen me, Thomas, thou hast believed: blessed are they that have not seen, and have believed.

Many other signs also did Jesus in the sight of his disciples, which are not written in this book.

But these are written, that you may believe that Jesus is the Christ, the Son of God: and that believing, you may have life in his name.—*John* xx. 29-31.

For if thou confess with thy mouth the Lord Jesus, and believe in thy heart that God hath raised him up from the dead, thou shalt be saved.

For, with the heart, we believe unto justice; but, with the mouth, confession is made unto salvation.

For the scripture saith: Whosoever believeth in him, shall not be confounded.—*Rom.* x. 9-11.

But without faith it is impossible to please God. For he that cometh to God, must believe that he is, and is a rewarder to them that seek him.—*Heb.* xi. 6.

III. In Justification Mortal Sins are Forgiven, Wiped Out, not Merely Covered

1st. Are Blotted Out

Have mercy on me, O God, according to thy great mercy.

And according to the multitude of thy tender mercies blot out my iniquity.—*Ps.* l. 3.

I am, I am he that blot out thy iniquities for my own sake, and I will not remember thy sins.—*Is.* xliii. 25.

I have blotted out thy iniquities as a cloud, and thy sins as a mist: return to me, for I have redeemed thee.—*Is.* xliv. 22.

Be penitent, therefore, and be converted, that your sins may be blotted out.—*Acts* iii. 19.

2d. Are Taken Away

Seventy weeks are shortened upon thy people, and upon thy holy city, that transgression may be finished, and sin may have an end, and iniquity may be abolished; and everlasting justice may be brought; and vision and prophecy may be fulfilled; and the saint of saints may be anointed.—*Dan.* ix. 24.

Who is a God like to thee, who takest away iniquity, and passest by the sin of the remnant of thy inheritance? he will send his fury in no more, because he delighteth in mercy.

He will turn again, and have mercy on us: he will put away our iniquities:

and he will cast all our sins into the bottom of the sea.—*Mich.* vii. 18, 19.

And behold they brought to him one sick of the palsy lying in a bed. And Jesus, seeing their faith, said to the man sick of the palsy: Be of good heart, son, thy sins are forgiven thee.—*Matt.* ix. 2.

The next day, John saw Jesus coming to him, and he saith: Behold the Lamb of God, behold him who taketh away the sin of the world.—*John* i. 29.

3d. Are Washed Away

Wash me yet more from my iniquity, and cleanse me from my sin. . . .

Thou shalt sprinkle me with hyssop, and I shall be cleansed: thou shalt wash me, and I shall be made whiter than snow.—*Ps.* l. 4, 9.

Wash yourselves, be clean, take away the evil of your devices from my eyes: cease to do perversely,

Learn to do well: seek judgment, relieve the oppressed, judge for the fatherless, defend the widow.

And then come, and accuse me, saith the Lord: if your sins be as scarlet, they shall be made as white as snow: and if they be red as crimson, they shall be white as wool.—*Is.* i. 16-18.

But if we walk in the light, as he also is in the light, we have fellowship one with another, and the blood of Jesus Christ his Son cleanseth us from all sin.—1 *John* i. 7.

John to the seven churches which are in Asia. Grace be unto you and peace from him that is, and that was, and that is to come, and from the seven spirits which are before his throne,

And from Jesus Christ, who is the faithful witness, the first begotten of the dead, and the prince of the kings of the earth, who hath loved us, and washed us from our sins in his own blood.—*Apoc.* i. 4, 5.

4th. Justification Implies Newness of Heart

Create a clean heart in me, O God: and renew a right spirit within my bowels.—*Ps.* l. 12.

If then any be in Christ a new creature, the old things are passed away,

behold all things are made new.—2 *Cor.* v. 17.

For in Christ Jesus neither circumcision availeth anything, nor uncircumcision, but a new creature.—*Gal.* vi. 15.

Lie not one to another: stripping yourselves of the old man with his deeds,

And putting on the new, him who is renewed unto knowledge, according to the image of him that created him. —*Col.* iii. 9, 10.

IV. Justification is the Intrinsic Infusion of Sanctifying Grace in the Soul, and not Mere External Imputation of Christ's Merits

For as by the disobedience of one man, many were made sinners; so also by the obedience of one, many shall be made just.—*Rom.* v. 19.

To put off, according to former conversation, the old man, who is corrupted according to the desire of error.

And be renewed in the spirit of your mind:

And put on the new man, who according to God is created in justice and holiness of truth.—*Eph.* iv. 22-24.

Not by the works of justice, which we have done, but according to his mercy, he saved us, by the laver of regeneration, and renovation of the Holy Ghost;

Whom he hath poured forth upon us abundantly, through Jesus Christ our Saviour;

That, being justified by his grace, we may be heirs, according to hope of life everlasting.—*Titus* iii. 5-7.

V. The Effects of Justification

1st. It Makes Us Friends of God

I love them that love me: and they that in the morning early watch for me, shall find me.—*Prov.* viii. 17.

He pleased God and was beloved, and living among sinners he was translated. . . .

For his soul pleased God: therefore he hastened to bring him out of the midst of iniquities: but the people see this, and understand not, nor lay up such things in their hearts:

That the grace of God, and his mercy is with his saints, and that he hath respect to his chosen.—*Wis.* iv. 10, 14, 15.

Jesus answered, and said to him (Judas, not the Iscariot): If any one love me, he will keep my word, and my Father will love him, and we will come to him, and will make our abode with him.—*John* xiv. 23.

2d. Children of God by Adoption and Heirs of Heaven

For whosoever are led by the Spirit of God, they are the sons of God.

For you have not received the spirit of bondage again in fear; but you have received the spirit of adoption of sons, whereby we cry: Abba (Father).

For the Spirit himself giveth testimony to our spirit, that we are the sons of God.

And if sons, heirs also; heirs indeed with God, and joint heirs with Christ: yet so, if we suffer with him, that we may be also glorified with him.—*Rom.* viii. 14-17.

Behold what manner of charity the Father hath bestowed upon us, that we should be called, and should be the sons of God. . . .

Dearly beloved, we are now the sons of God; and it hath not yet appeared what we shall be. We know, that, when he shall appear, we shall be like to him: because we shall see him as he is.— 1 *John* iii. 1, 2.

Whosoever is born of God, committeth not sin: for his seed abideth in him, and he cannot sin, because he is born of God.—1 *John* iii. 9.

3d. Partakers of the Divine Nature

By whom he hath given us most great and precious promises: that by these you may be made partakers of the divine nature: flying the corruption of that concupiscence which is in the world.—2 *Peter* i. 4.

Dearly beloved, we are now the sons of God; and it hath not yet appeared what we shall be. We know, that, when he shall appear, we shall be like to him: because we shall see him as he is.— 1 *John* iii. 2.

Whosoever is born of God, committeth not sin: for his seed abideth in him, and he cannot sin, because he is born of God.—1 *John* iii. 9.

4th. Temples of the Holy Trinity

Jesus answered, and said to him: (Judas, not the Iscariot:) If any one love me, he will keep my word, and my Father will love him, and we will come to him, and will make our abode with him.—*John* xiv. 23.

Know you not, that you are the temple of God, and that the Spirit of God dwelleth in you?—1 *Cor.* iii. 16.

Or know you not, that your members are the temple of the Holy Ghost, who is in you, whom you have from God; and you are not your own?—1 *Cor.* vi. 19.

And what agreement hath the temple of God with idols? For you are the temple of the living God; as God saith: I will dwell in them, and walk among them; and I will be their God, and they shall be my people.—2 *Cor.* vi. 16.

MAN, THE ORIGIN OF

And he (God) said: Let us make man to our image and likeness: and let him have dominion over the fishes of the sea, and the fowls of the air, and the beasts, and the whole earth, and every creeping creature that moveth upon the earth.

And God created man to his own image: to the image of God he created him: male and female he created them.

And God blessed them, saying: Increase and multiply, and fill the earth, and subdue it, and rule over the fishes of the sea, and the fowls of the air, and all living creatures that move upon the earth.—*Gen.* i. 26-28.

These are the generations of the heaven and the earth, when they were created, in the day that the Lord God made the heaven and the earth:

And every plant of the field before it sprung up in the earth, and every herb of the ground before it grew: for the Lord God had not rained upon the earth; and there was not a man to till the earth.

But a spring rose out of the earth, watering all the surface of the earth.

And the Lord God formed man of

the slime of the earth: and breathed into his face the breath of life, and man became a living soul.

And the Lord God had planted a paradise of pleasure from the beginning: wherein he placed man whom he had formed. . . .

And Adam called all the beasts by their names, and all the fowls of the air, and all the cattle of the field: but for Adam there was not found a helper like himself.

Then the Lord God cast a deep sleep upon Adam: and when he was fast asleep, he took one of his ribs, and filled up flesh for it.

And the Lord God built the rīb which he took from Adam into a woman: and brought her to Adam.— *Gen.* ii. 4-8, 20-22.

And Adam knew Eve his wife: who conceived and brought forth Cain, saying: I have gotten a man through God.

And again she brought forth his brother Abel. And Abel was a shepherd, and Cain a husbandman. . . .

Adam also knew his wife again: and she brought forth a son, and called his name Seth, saying: God hath given me another seed, for Abel whom Cain slew. . . .

And the days of Adam, after he begot Seth, were eight hundred years: and he begot sons and daughters.— *Gen.* iv. 1, 2, 25; v. 4.

She (wisdom) preserved him, that was first formed by God the father of the world, when he was created alone.

And she brought him out of his sin, and gave him power to govern all things.—*Wis.* x. 1, 2.

Neither is he served with men's hands, as though he needed any thing; seeing it is he who giveth to all life, and breath, and all things:

And hath made of one, all mankind, to dwell upon the whole face of the earth, determining appointed times, and the limits of their habitation.— *Acts* xvii. 25, 26.

MASS, THE SACRIFICE OF THE

1st. Prefigured

But Melchisedech the king of Salem, bringing forth bread and wine, for he was the priest of the most high God,

Blessed him, and said: Blessed be Abram by the most high God, who created heaven and earth.—*Gen.* xiv. 18, 19.

2d. Foretold

Who is there among you, that will shut the doors, and will kindle the fire of my altar gratis? I have no pleasure in you, saith the Lord of hosts: and I will not receive a gift of your hand.

For from the rising of the sun even to the going down, my name is great among the Gentiles, and in every place there is sacrifice, and there is offered to my name a clean oblation: for my name is great among the Gentiles, saith the Lord of hosts.—*Malach.* i. 10, 11.

The Lord hath sworn, and he will not repent: Thou art a priest for ever according to the order of Melchisedech. —*Ps.* cix. 4.

3d. Instituted and Celebrated by Christ

And he said to them: With desire I have desired to eat this pasch with you, before I suffer. . . .

And taking bread, he gave thanks, and brake; and gave to them, saying: This is my body, which is given for you. Do this for a commemoration of me. In like manner the chalice also, after he had supped, saying: This is the chalice, the new testament in my blood, which shall be shed for you.— *Luke* xxii. 15, 19, 20.

For I have received of the Lord that which also I delivered unto you, that the Lord Jesus, the same night in which he was betrayed, took bread,

And giving thanks, broke, and said: Take ye, and eat: this is my body, which shall be delivered for you: this do for the commemoration of me.

In like manner also the chalice, after he had supped, saying: This chalice is the new testament in my blood: this do ye, as often as you shall drink, for the commemoration of me.

For as often as you shall eat this bread, and drink the chalice, you shall show the death of the Lord, until he come.—1 *Cor.* xi. 23-26.

4th. Attested and Alluded to

The chalice of benediction, which we bless, is it not the communion of the blood of Christ? And the bread, which we break, is it not the partaking of the body of the Lord?

For we, being many, are one bread, one body, all that partake of one bread.

Behold Israel according to the flesh: are not they, that eat of the sacrifices, partakers of the altar?

What then? Do I say, that what is offered in sacrifice to idols, is any thing? Or, that the idol is any thing?

But the things which the heathens sacrifice, they sacrifice to devils, and not to God. And I would not that you should be made partakers with devils.

You cannot drink the chalice of the Lord, and the chalice of devils: you cannot be partakers of the table of the Lord, and of the table of devils.—1 *Cor.* x. 16-21.

We have an altar, whereof they have no power to eat who serve the tabernacle.—*Heb.* xiii. 10.

And they were persevering in the doctrine of the apostles, and in the communication of the breaking of bread, and in prayers.—*Acts* ii. 42.

And as they were ministering to the Lord, and fasting, the Holy Ghost said to them: Separate me Saul and Barnabas, for the work whereunto I have taken them.—*Acts* xiii. 2.

And on the first day of the week, when we were assembled to break bread, Paul discoursed with them, being to depart on the morrow: and he continued his speech until midnight.—*Acts* xx. 7.

MATRIMONY

1st. A Sacrament in the New Law

For this cause shall a man leave his father, and mother, and shall cleave to his wife, and they shall be two in one flesh.

This is a great sacrament; but I speak in Christ and in the church.—*Eph.* v. 31, 32.

2d. Indissolubility of Matrimony in the New Law

And it hath been said, Whosoever shall put away his wife, let him give her a bill of divorce.

But I say to you, that whosoever shall put away his wife, excepting for the cause of fornication, maketh her to commit adultery: and he that shall marry her that is put away, committeth adultery.—*Matt.* v. 31, 32.

And the Pharisees coming to him asked him: Is it lawful for a man to put away his wife? tempting him.

But he answering, saith to them: What did Moses command you?

Who said: Moses permitted to write a bill of divorce, and to put her away.

To whom Jesus answering, said: Because of the hardness of your heart he wrote you that precept.

But from the beginning of the creation, God made them male and female.

For this cause a man shall leave his father and mother; and shall cleave to his wife.

And they two shall be in one flesh. Therefore now they are not two, but one flesh.

What therefore God hath joined together, let not man put asunder.

And in the house again his disciples asked him concerning the same thing.

And he saith to them: Whosoever shall put away his wife and marry another, committeth adultery against her.

And if the wife shall put away her husband, and be married to another, she committeth adultery.—*Mark* x. 2-12.

Every one that putteth away his wife, and marrieth another, committeth adultery: and he that marrieth her that is put away from her husband, committeth adultery.—*Luke* xvi. 18.

And Adam said: This now is bone of my bones, and flesh of my flesh; she shall be called woman, because she was taken out of man.

Wherefore a man shall leave father and mother, and shall cleave to his wife: and they shall be two in one flesh. —*Gen.* ii. 23, 24.

For the woman that hath an husband, whilst her husband liveth is bound to the law. But if her husband be dead, she is loosed from the law of her husband.

Therefore, whilst her husband liveth, she shall be called an adulteress, if she be with another man: but if her husband be dead, she is delivered from the law of her husband; so that she is not an adulteress, if she be with another man.—*Rom.* vii. 2, 3.

But to them that are married, not I but the Lord commandeth, that the wife depart not from her husband.

And if she depart, that she remain unmarried, or be reconciled to her husband. And let not the husband put away his wife.—1 *Cor.* vii. 10, 11.

A woman is bound by the law as long as her husband liveth; but if her husband die, she is at liberty: let her marry to whom she will; only in the Lord.—1 *Cor.* vii. 39.

For this cause shall a man leave his father and mother, and shall cleave to his wife, and they shall be two in one flesh.—*Eph.* v. 31.

MERITORIOUS, GOOD WORKS ARE

See: Works—page 738.

MERITS CAN BE LOST

See: Part I—page 326.

MIRACLES, THE POSSIBILITY OF

See also: Omnipotence of God—Part I—page 353.

And the Lord said to Abraham: Why did Sara laugh, saying: Shall I who am an old woman bear a child indeed?

Is there any thing hard to God? according to appointment I will return to thee at this same time, life accompanying, and Sara shall have a son.—*Gen.* xviii. 13, 14.

And Moses said: There are six hundred thousand footmen of this people, and sayest thou: I will give them flesh to eat a whole month?

Shall then a multitude of sheep and oxen be killed, that it may suffice for their food? or shall the fishes of the sea be gathered together to fill them?

And the Lord answered him: Is the hand of the Lord unable? Thou shalt presently see whether my word shall come to pass or no.—*Num.* xi. 21-23.

Behold the hand of the Lord is not shortened that it cannot save, neither is his ear heavy that it cannot hear.—*Is.* lix. 1.

MIRACLES ADDUCED BY CHRIST AS PROOFS OF HIS MISSION

And Jesus seeing their thoughts, said: Why do you think evil in your hearts?

Whether is easier, to say, Thy sins are forgiven thee: or to say, Arise, and walk?

But that you may know that the Son of man hath power on earth to forgive sins, (then said he to the man sick of the palsy,) Arise, take up thy bed, and go into thy house.

And he arose, and went into his house.—*Matt.* ix. 4-7.

But the Pharisees hearing it, said: This man casteth not out devils, but by Beelzebub the prince of the devils.

And Jesus knowing their thoughts, said to them: Every kingdom divided against itself shall be made desolate: and every city or house divided against itself shall not stand.

And if Satan cast out Satan, he is divided against himself: how then shall his kingdom stand?

And if I by Beelzebub cast out devils, by whom do your children cast them out? Therefore they shall be your judges.

But if I by the Spirit of God cast out devils, then is the kingdom of God come upon you.—*Matt.* xii. 24-28.

And these signs shall follow them that believe: In my name they shall cast out devils: they shall speak with new tongues.

They shall take up serpents; and if they shall drink any deadly thing, it shall not hurt them: they shall lay their hands upon the sick, and they shall recover. . . .

But they going forth preached everywhere: the Lord working withal, and confirming the word with signs that followed.—*Mark* xvi. 17, 18, 20.

And John called to him two of his disciples, and sent them to Jesus, saying: Art thou he that art to come; or look we for another? . . .

(And in that same hour, he cured many of their diseases, and hurts, and evil spirits: and to many that were blind he gave sight.)

And answering, he said to them: Go

and relate to John what you have heard and seen: the blind see, the lame walk, the lepers are made clean, the deaf hear, the dead rise again, to the poor the gospel is preached.—*Luke* vii. 19, 21, 22.

The Jews, therefore, answered, and said to him: What sign dost thou show unto us, seeing thou dost these things?

Jesus answered, and said to them: Destroy this temple, and in three days I will raise it up.

The Jews then said: Six and forty years was this temple in building; and wilt thou raise it up in three days?

But he spoke of the temple of his body.—*John* ii. 18-21.

But I have a greater testimony than that of John: for the works which the Father hath given me to perfect; the works themselves, which I do, give testimony of me, that the Father hath sent me.—*John* v. 36.

But of the people many believed in him, and said: When the Christ cometh, shall he do more miracles, than these which this man doth?—*John* vii. 31.

Jesus answered them: I speak to you, and you believe not: the works that I do in the name of my Father, they give testimony of me. . . .

If I do not the works of my Father, believe me not.

But if I do, though you will not believe me, believe the works: that you may know and believe that the Father is in me, and I in the Father.—*John* x. 25, 37, 38.

Jesus saith: Take away the stone. Martha, the sister of him that was dead, saith to him: Lord, by this time he stinketh, for he is now of four days.

Jesus saith to her: Did not I say to thee, that if thou believe, thou shalt see the glory of God?

They took therefore the stone away. And Jesus lifting up his eyes said: Father, I give thee thanks that thou hast heard me.

And I knew that thou hearest me always; but because of the people who stand about have I said it, that they may believe that thou hast sent me.

When he had said these things, he cried with a loud voice: Lazarus, come forth.

And presently he that had been dead came forth, bound feet and hands with winding bands; and his face was bound about with a napkin. Jesus said to them: Loose him, and let him go.

Many therefore of the Jews, who were come to Mary and Martha, and had seen the things that Jesus did, believed in him.—*John* xi. 39-45.

Believe you not that I am in the Father, and the Father in me?

Otherwise believe for the very works' sake.—*John* xiv. 11, 12.

MORTAL SIN

See: Sin—page 735.

ORDERS, HOLY

I. It is a Sacrament, because

1st. It Confers Grace

Neglect not the grace that is in thee, which was given thee by prophecy, with imposition of the hands of the priesthood.—1 *Tim.* iv. 14.

For which cause I admonish thee, that thou stir up the grace of God which is in thee, by the imposition of my hands.—2 *Tim.* i. 6.

2d. Instituted by Christ

And taking bread, he gave thanks, and brake; and gave to them, saying: This is my body, which is given for you. Do this for a commemoration of me.—*Luke* xxii. 19.

He said therefore to them again: Peace be to you. As the Father hath sent me, I also send you.

When he had said this, he breathed on them; and he said to them: Receive ye the Holy Ghost.

Whose sins you shall forgive, they are forgiven them; and whose sins you shall retain, they are retained.—*John* xx. 21-23.

II. Conferred by the Apostles

And when they (Paul and Barnabas) had ordained to them priests in every church, and had prayed with fasting, they commended them to the Lord, in whom they believed.—*Acts* xiv. 22.

Impose not hands lightly upon any

man, neither be partaker of other men's sins.—*1 Tim.* v. 22.

For which cause I admonish thee, that thou stir up the grace of God which is in thee, by the imposition of my hands.—*2 Tim.* i. 6.

For this cause I left thee in Crete, that thou shouldest set in order the things that are wanting, and shouldest ordain priests in every city, as I also appointed thee.—*Titus* i. 5.

III. The Manner of Conferring

And they chose Stephen, a man full of faith, and of the Holy Ghost, and Philip, and Prochorus, and Nicanor, and Timon, and Parmenas, and Nicolas, a proselyte of Antioch.

These they set before the apostles; and they praying, imposed hands upon them.—*Acts* vi. 5, 6.

And as they were ministering to the Lord, and fasting, the Holy Ghost said to them: Separate me Saul and Barnabas, for the work whereunto I have taken them.

Then they, fasting, and praying, and imposing their hands upon them, sent them away.—*Acts* xiii. 2, 3.

Neglect not the grace that is in thee, which was given thee by prophecy, with imposition of the hands of the priesthood.—*1 Tim.* iv. 14.

ORIGINAL SIN

See: Sin—page 734.

PENANCE, THE SACRAMENT OF

1st. Its Institution

And I say to thee: That thou art Peter; and upon this rock I will build my church, and the gates of hell shall not prevail against it.

And I will give to thee the keys of the kingdom of heaven. And whatsoever thou shalt bind upon earth, it shall be bound also in heaven: and whatsoever thou shalt loose on earth, it shall be loosed also in heaven.—*Matt.* xvi. 18, 19.

Amen I say to you, whatsoever you shall bind upon earth, shall be bound also in heaven; and whatsoever you shall loose upon earth, shall be loosed also in heaven.—*Matt.* xviii. 18.

He said therefore to them again: Peace be to you. As the Father hath sent me, I also send you.

When he had said this, he breathed on them; and he said to them: Receive ye the Holy Ghost.

Whose sins you shall forgive, they are forgiven them; and whose sins you shall retain, they are retained.—*John* xx. 21-23.

2d. Its Existence

But all things are of God, who hath reconciled us to himself by Christ; and hath given to us the ministry of reconciliation.

For God indeed was in Christ, reconciling the world to himself, not imputing to them their sins; and he hath placed in us the word of reconciliation. —*2 Cor.* v. 18, 19.

PENANCE OR REPENTANCE

1st. Its True Nature

And when thou shalt seek there the Lord thy God, thou shalt find him: yet so, if thou seek him with all thy heart, and all the affliction of thy soul.—*Deut.* iv. 29.

I will recount to thee all my years in the bitterness of my soul.—*Is.* xxxviii. 15.

And thou shalt say to them: Thus saith the Lord: Shall not he that falleth, rise again? and he that is turned away, shall he not turn again? . . .

I attended, and hearkened; no man speaketh what is good, there is none that doth penance for his sin, saying: What have I done?—*Jer.* viii. 4, 6.

But the soul that is sorrowful for the greatness of evil she hath done, and goeth bowed down, and feeble, and the eyes that fail, and the hungry soul giveth glory and justice to thee the Lord. —*Bar.* ii. 18.

Cast away from you all your transgressions, by which you have transgressed, and make to yourselves a new heart, and a new spirit: and why will you die, O house of Israel?—*Ezech.* xviii. 31.

Now therefore saith the Lord: Be converted to me with all your heart, in fasting, and in weeping, and in mourning.

And rend your hearts, and not your garments, and turn to the Lord your God: for he is gracious and merciful, patient and rich in mercy, and ready to repent of the evil.—*Joel* ii. 12, 13.

2d. Its Necessity

They that fear the Lord, keep his commandments, and will have patience even until his visitation,

Saying: If we do not penance, we shall fall into the hands of the Lord, and not into the hands of men.—*Ecclus.* ii. 21, 22.

Be converted, and do penance for all your iniquities: and iniquity shall not be your ruin.

Cast away from you all your transgressions, by which you have transgressed, and make to yourselves a new heart, and a new spirit: and why will you die, O house of Israel?

For I desire not the death of him that dieth, saith the Lord God, return ye and live.—*Ezech.* xviii. 30-32.

And in those days cometh John the Baptist preaching in the desert of Judea.

And saying: Do penance: for the kingdom of heaven is at hand.

. . . Bring forth therefore fruit worthy of penance. . . .

For now the axe is laid to the root of the trees. Every tree therefore that doth not yield good fruit, shall be cut down, and cast into the fire.—*Matt.* iii. 1, 2, 8, 10.

No, I say to you: but unless you shall do penance, you shall all likewise perish.—*Luke* xiii. 3.

But Peter said to them: Do penance, and be baptized every one of you in the name of Jesus Christ, for the remission of your sins: and you shall receive the gift of the Holy Ghost.—*Acts* ii. 38.

Be penitent, therefore, and be converted, that your sins may be blotted out.—*Acts* iii. 19.

3d. Its Efficacy

See: Part I—page 375.

POPE, OR CHIEF PASTOR

1st. This Superiority Conferred Upon Peter

And I say to thee: That thou art Peter; and upon this rock I will build my church, and the gates of hell shall not prevail against it.

And I will give to thee the keys of the kingdom of heaven. And whatsoever thou shalt bind upon earth, it shall be bound also in heaven: and whatsoever thou shalt loose on earth, it shall be loosed also in heaven.—*Matt.* xvi. 18, 19.

And the Lord said: Simon, Simon, behold Satan hath desired to have you, that he may sift you as wheat:

But I have prayed for thee, that thy faith fail not: and thou, being once converted, confirm thy brethren.—*Luke* xxii. 31, 32.

When therefore they had dined, Jesus saith to Simon Peter: Simon, son of John, lovest thou me more than these? He saith to him: Yea, Lord, thou knowest that I love thee. He saith to him: Feed my lambs.

He saith to him again: Simon, son of John. lovest thou me? He saith to him: Yea, Lord, thou knowest that I love thee. He saith to him: Feed my lambs.

He saith to him the third time: Simon, son of John, lovest thou me? Peter was grieved, because he had said to him the third time: Lovest thou me? And he said to him: Lord, thou knowest all things: thou knowest that I love thee. He said to him: Feed my sheep. —*John* xxi. 15-17.

2d. Some Pre-eminence Implied in Peter

And the names of the twelve apostles are these: The first, Simon who is called Peter, and Andrew his brother,

James the son of Zebedee, and John his brother, Philip and Bartholomew,

Thomas and Matthew the publican, and James the son of Alpheus, and Thaddeus, Simon the Cananean, and Judas Iscariot, who also betrayed him. —*Matt.* x. 2-4.

And he made that twelve should be

with him, and that he might send them to preach.

And he gave them power to heal sicknesses, and to cast out devils.

And to Simon he gave the name Peter:

And James the son of Zebedee, and John the brother of James; and he named them Boanerges, which is, The sons of thunder:

And Andrew and Philip, and Bartholomew and Matthew, and Thomas and James of Alpheus, and Thaddeus, and Simon the Cananean:

And Judas Iscariot, who also betrayed him.—*Mark* iii. 14-19.

And when day was come, he called unto him his disciples; and he chose twelve of them (whom also he named apostles):

Simon, whom he surnamed Peter, and Andrew his brother, James and John, Philip and Bartholomew,

Matthew and Thomas, James the son of Alpheus, and Simon who is called Zelotes,

And Jude, the brother of James, and Judas Iscariot, who was the traitor.—*Luke* vi. 13-16.

Neither went I to Jerusalem, to the apostles who were before me: but I went into Arabia, and again I returned to Damascus.

Then, after three years, I went to Jerusalem, to see Peter, and I tarried with him fifteen days.

But other of the apostles I saw none, saving James the brother of the Lord.—*Gal.* i. 17-19.

In those days Peter rising up in the midst of the brethren, said: (now the number of persons together was about an hundred and twenty:)

Men, brethren, the scripture must needs be fulfilled, which the Holy Ghost spoke before by the mouth of David concerning Judas, who was the leader of them that apprehended Jesus.—*Acts* i. 15, 16.

But Peter standing up with the eleven, lifted up his voice, and spoke to them: Ye men of Judea, and all you that dwell in Jerusalem, be this known to you, and with your ears receive my words.—*Acts* ii. 14.

Now when they had heard these things, they had compunction in their heart, and said to Peter, and to the rest of the apostles: What shall we do, men and brethren?

But Peter said to them: Do penance, and be baptized every one of you in the name of Jesus Christ, for the remission of your sins: and you shall receive the gift of the Holy Ghost.—*Acts* ii. 37, 38.

But Peter with John fastening his eyes upon him, said: Look upon us. . . .

But Peter said: Silver and gold I have none; but what I have, I give thee: In the name of Jesus Christ of Nazareth, arise, and walk.

And taking him by the right hand, he lifted him up, and forthwith his feet and soles received strength.—*Acts* iii. 4, 6, 7.

And as he held Peter and John, all the people ran to them to the porch which is called Solomon's, greatly wondering.

But Peter seeing, made answer to the people: Ye men of Israel, why wonder you at this? or why look you upon us, as if by our strength or power we had made this man to walk?—*Acts* iii. 11, 12.

And setting them in the midst, they asked: By what power, or by what name, have you done this?

Then Peter, filled with the Holy Ghost, said to them: Ye princes of the people, and ancients, hear.—*Acts* iv. 7, 8.

But Peter said: Ananias, why hath Satan tempted thy heart, that thou shouldst lie to the Holy Ghost, and by fraud keep part of the price of the land?—*Acts* v. 3.

Insomuch that they brought forth the sick into the streets, and laid them on beds and couches, that when Peter came, his shadow at the least, might overshadow any of them, and they might be delivered from their infirmities.—*Acts* v. 15.

But Peter and the apostles answering, said: We ought to obey God, rather than men.—*Acts* v. 29.

Now the church had peace throughout all Judea, and Galilee, and Samaria, and was edified, walking in the fear of the Lord, and was filled with the consolation of the Holy Ghost.

And it came to pass that Peter, as he passed through, visiting all, came to the saints who dwelt at Lydda.—*Acts* ix. 31, 32.

Peter therefore was kept in prison. But prayer was made without ceasing by the church unto God for him.—*Acts* xii. 5.

And the apostles and ancients assembled to consider of this matter.

And when there had been much disputing, Peter, rising up, said to them: Men, brethren, you know, that in former days God made choice among us, that by my mouth the Gentiles should hear the word of the gospel, and believe. —*Acts* xv. 6, 7.

PREDESTINATION, AGAINST CALVINISTIC

1st. God Will not Condemn the Innocent and the Just

For in very deed God will not condemn without cause, neither will the Almighty pervert judgment.—*Job* xxxiv. 12.

For so much then as thou art just, thou orderest all things justly: thinking it not agreeable to thy power, to condemn him who deserveth not to be punished.—*Wis.* xii. 15.

For the earth that drinketh in the rain which cometh often upon it, and bringeth forth herbs meet for them by whom it is tilled, receiveth blessing from God.

But that which bringeth forth thorns and briars, is reprobate, and very near unto a curse, whose end is to be burnt.

But, my dearly beloved, we trust better things of you, and nearer to salvation; though we speak thus.

For God is not unjust, that he should forget your work, and the love which you have shown in his name, you who have ministered, and do minister to the saints.—*Heb.* vi. 7-10.

2d. God Will not Reject Those Who Seek Him

I have not spoken in secret, in a dark place of the earth: I have not said to the seed of Jacob: Seek me in vain.

I am the Lord that speak justice, that declare right things.—*Is.* xlv. 19.

All that the Father giveth to me shall come to me; and him that cometh to me, I will not cast out.—*John* vi. 37.

And he said to me: It is done. I am Alpha and Omega; the beginning and the end. To him that thirsteth, I will give of the fountain of the water of life, freely.—*Apoc.* xxi. 6.

And the spirit and the bride say: Come. And he that heareth, let him say: Come. And he that thirsteth, let him come: and he that will, let him take the water of life, freely.—*Apoc.* xxii. 17.

3d. God Wishes All to be Saved

For thou lovest all things that are, and hatest none of the things which thou hast made: for thou didst not appoint, or make any thing hating it.— *Wis.* xi. 25.

For God hath not appointed us unto wrath, but unto the purchasing of salvation by our Lord Jesus Christ.— 1 *Thess.* v. 9.

A faithful saying, and worthy of all acceptation, that Christ Jesus came into this world to save sinners, of whom I am the chief.—1 *Tim.* i. 15.

Who will have all men to be saved, and to come to the knowledge of the truth.—1 *Tim.* ii. 4.

Who gave himself a redemption for all, a testimony in due times.—1 *Tim.* ii. 6.

For therefore we labor and are reviled, because we hope in the living God, who is the Saviour of all men, especially of the faithful.—1 *Tim.* iv. 10.

The Lord delayeth not his promise, as some imagine, but dealeth patiently for your sake, not willing that any should perish, but that all should return to penance.—2 *Peter* iii. 9.

4th. God Rewards or Punishes According to Our Works

For he will render to a man his work, and according to the ways of every one he will reward them.—*Job* xxxiv. 11.

God hath spoken once, these two things have I heard, that power belongeth to God,

And mercy to thee, O Lord; for thou

wilt render to every man according to his works.—*Ps.* lxi. 12, 13.

By the fruit of his own mouth shall a man be filled with good thirgs, and according to the works of his lands it shall be repaid him.—*Prov.* xii. 14.

If thou say: I have not strength enough: he that seeth into the heart, he understandeth, and nothing deceiveth the keeper of thy soul, and he shall render to a man according to his work —*Prov.* xxiv. 12.

For it is easy before God in the day of death to reward every one according to his ways.—*Ecclus.* xi. 28.

According as his mercy is, so his correction judgeth a man according to his works.—*Ecclus.* xvi. 13.

All mercy shall make a place for every man according to the merit of his works, and according to the wisdom of his sojournment.—*Ecclus.* xvi. 15.

And he will repay vengeance to the Gentiles, till he have taken away the multitude of the proud, and broken the sceptres of the unjust,

Till he have rendered to men according to their deeds: and according to the works of Adam, and according to his presumption.—*Ecclus.* xxxv. 23, 24.

For the Son of man shall come in the glory of his Father with his angels: and then will he render to every man according to his works.—*Matt.* xvi. 27.

For we know that the judgment of God is, according to truth, against them that do such things. . . .

Who will render to every man according to his works.—*Rom.* ii. 2, 6.

And every man shall receive his own reward, according to his own labor.— 1 *Cor.* iii. 8.

For we must all be manifested before the judgment seat of Christ, that every one may receive the proper things of the body, according as he hath done, whether it be good or evil.—2 *Cor.* v. 10.

Be not deceived, God is not mocked. For what things a man shall sow, those also shall he reap. For he that soweth in his flesh, of the flesh also shall reap corruption. But he that soweth in the spirit, of the spirit shall reap life everlasting.

And in doing good, let us not fail.

For in due time we shall reap, not failing.—*Gal.* vi. 7-9.

With a good will serving, as to the Lord, and not to men.

Knowing that whatsoever good thing any man shall do, the same shall he receive from the Lord, whether he be bond, or free.—*Eph.* vi. 7, 8.

For he that doth wrong, shall receive for that which he hath done wrongfully: and there is no respect of persons with God.—*Col.* iii. 25.

Alexander the coppersmith hath done me much evil: the Lord will reward him according to his works.—2 *Tim.* iv. 14.

And all the churches shall know that I am he that searcheth the reins and hearts, and I will give to every one of you according to your works.—*Apoc.* ii. 23.

And the sea gave up the dead that were in it, and death and hell gave up their dead that were in them; and they were judged every one according to their works.—*Apoc.* xx. 13.

Behold, I come quickly; and my reward is with me, to render to every man according to his works.—*Apoc.* xxii. 12.

PROPHECIES FULFILLED IN CHRIST, THE

See: Christ—page 666.

PUNISHMENT, TEMPORAL, OFTEN REMAINS AFTER THE GUILT OF SIN HAS BEEN FOR- GIVEN

Shown by Examples of

1st. Adam

And to Adam he (God) said: Because thou hast hearkened to the voice of thy wife, and hast eaten of the tree, whereof I commanded thee that thou shouldst not eat, cursed is the earth in thy work; with labor and toil shalt thou eat thereof all the days of thy life.

Thorns and thistles shall it bring forth to thee: and thou shalt eat the herbs of the earth.

In the sweat of thy face shalt thou eat bread till thou return to the earth, out of which thou wast taken: for dust thou art, and into dust thou shalt return.—*Gen.* iii. 17-19.

She (wisdom) preserved him, that

was first formed by God the father of the world, when he was created alone,

And she brought him out of his sin, and gave him power to govern all things.—*Wis.* x. 1, 2.

2d. Moses

And the Lord said to Moses and Aaron: Because you have not believed me, to sanctify me before the children of Israel, you shall not bring these people into the land, which I will give them.—*Num.* xx. 12.

The Lord also said to Moses: Go up into this mountain Abarim, and view from thence the land which I will give to the children of Israel.

But when thou shalt have seen it, thou also shalt go to thy people, as thy brother Aaron is gone:

Because you offended me in the desert of Sin, in the contradiction of the multitude, neither would you sanctify me before them at the waters. These are the waters of contradiction in Cades of the desert of Sin.—*Num.* xxvii. 12-14.

3d. Mary, the Sister of Moses

And Mary and Aaron spoke against Moses, because of his wife the Ethiopian,

And they said: Hath the Lord spoken by Moses only? hath he not also spoken to us in like manner? And when the Lord heard this, . . .

The cloud also that was over the tabernacle departed: and behold Mary appeared white as snow with a leprosy. . . .

And Moses cried to the Lord, saying: O God, I beseech thee heal her.

And the Lord answered him: If her father had spitten upon her face, ought she not to have been ashamed for seven days at least? Let her be separated seven days without the camp, and afterwards she shall be called again.

Mary therefore was put out of the camp seven days: and the people moved not from that place until Mary was called again.—*Num.* xii. 1, 2, 10, 13-15.

4th. David

And David said to Nathan: I have sinned against the Lord. And Nathan said to David: The Lord also hath taken away thy sin: thou shalt not die.

Nevertheless, because thou hast given occasion to the enemies of the Lord to blaspheme, for this thing, the child that is born to thee, shall surely die.—*2 Kings* xii. 13, 14.

PURGATORY

And making a gathering, he (Judas) sent twelve thousand drachms of silver to Jerusalem for sacrifice to be offered for the sins of the dead, thinking well and religiously concerning the resurrection, . . .

And because he considered that they who had fallen asleep with godliness, had great grace laid up for them.

It is therefore a holy and wholesome thought to pray for the dead, that they may be loosed from sins.—*2 Mach.* xii. 43, 45, 46.

Probably Alluded to or Implied

A gift hath grace in the sight of all the living and restrain not grace from the dead.—*Ecclus.* vii. 37.

And whosoever shall speak a word against the Son of man, it shall be forgiven him: but he that shall speak against the Holy Ghost, it shall not be forgiven him, neither in this world, nor in the world to come.—*Matt.* xii. 32.

Every man's work shall be manifest; for the day of the Lord shall declare it, because it shall be revealed in fire; and the fire shall try every man's work, of what sort it is.

If any man's work abide, which he hath built thereupon, he shall receive a reward.

If any man's work burn, he shall suffer loss; but he himself shall be saved, yet so as by fire.—*1 Cor.* iii. 13-15.

Compare

But I say unto you, that every idle word that men shall speak, they shall render an account for it in the day of judgment.—*Matt.* xii. 36.

And

There shall not enter into it (the new Jerusalem) any thing defiled, or that worketh abomination or maketh a lie, but they that are written in the book of life of the Lamb.—*Apoc.* xxi. 27.

REDEEMER, THE PROPHECIES OF THE COMING OF A

See: Christ, the Redeemer—page 657.

RELICS, VENERATION FOR

And Eliseus died, and they buried him. And the rovers from Moab came into the land the same year.

And some that were burying a man, saw the rovers, and cast the body into the sepulchre of Eliseus. And when it had touched the bones of Eliseus, the man came to life, and stood upon his feet.—*4 Kings* xiii. 20, 21.

No word could overcome him (Eliseus), and after death his body prophesied.

In his life he did great wonders, and in death he wrought miracles.—*Ecclus.* xlviii. 14, 15.

In that day the root of Jesse, who standeth for an ensign of the people, him the Gentiles shall beseech, and his sepulchre shall be glorious.—*Is.* xi. 10.

And God wrought by the hand of Paul more than common miracles.

So that even there were brought from his body to the sick, handkerchiefs and aprons, and the diseases departed from them, and the wicked spirits went out of them.—*Acts* xix. 11, 12.

RESURRECTION OF CHRIST, THE

1st. Foretold by David

Whom God hath raised up, having loosed the sorrows of hell, as it was impossible that he should be holden by it.

For David saith concerning him: [1]I foresaw the Lord before my face; because he is at my right hand, that I may not be moved.

For this my heart hath been glad, and my tongue hath rejoiced: moreover my flesh also shall rest in hope.

Because thou wilt not leave my soul in hell, nor suffer thy Holy One to see corruption.

Thou hast made known to me the ways of life: thou shalt make me full of joy with thy countenance.

Ye men, brethren, let me freely speak to you of the patriarch David;
[1]*Ps.* xv. 8-11, inclusive.

that he died, and was buried; and his sepulchre is with us to this present day.

Whereas therefore he was a prophet, and knew that God had sworn to him with an oath, that of the fruit of his loins one should sit upon his throne.

Foreseeing this, he spoke of the resurrection of Christ. For neither was he left in hell, neither did his flesh see corruption.—*Acts* ii. 24-31.

2d. Foretold by Christ Himself

Who answering said to them: An evil and adulterous generation seeketh a sign: and a sign shall not be given it, but the sign of Jonas the prophet.

For as Jonas was in the whale's belly three days and three nights: so shall the Son of man be in the heart of the earth three days and three nights.—*Matt.* xii. 39, 40.

A wicked and adulterous generation seeketh after a sign: and a sign shall not be given it, but the sign of Jonas the prophet.—*Matt.* xvi. 4.

From that time Jesus began to show to his disciples, that he must go to Jerusalem, and suffer many things from the ancients and scribes and chief priests, and be put to death, and the third day rise again.—*Matt.* xvi. 21.

And when they abode together in Galilee, Jesus said to them: The Son of man shall be betrayed into the hands of men:

And they shall kill him, and the third day he shall rise again.—*Matt.* xvii. 21, 22.

Behold we go up to Jerusalem, and the Son of man shall be betrayed to the chief priests and the scribes, and they shall condemn him to death.

And shall deliver him to the Gentiles to be mocked, and scourged, and crucified, and the third day he shall rise again.—*Matt.* xx. 18, 19.

Then Jesus saith to them: All you shall be scandalized in me this night. For it is written: I will strike the shepherd, and the sheep of the flock shall be dispersed.

But after I shall be risen again, I will go before you into Galilee.—*Matt.* xxvi. 31, 32.

And the next day, which followed the day of preparation, the chief priests and the Pharisees came together to Pilate,

Saying: Sir, we have remembered that that seducer said, while he was yet alive: After three days I will rise again.

Command therefore the sepulchre to be guarded until the third day: lest perhaps his disciples come and steal him away, and say to the people: He is risen from the dead; and the last error shall be worse than the first.—*Matt.* xxvii. 62-64.

And as they came down from the mountain, he (Jesus) charged them not to tell any man what things they had seen, till the Son of man shall be risen again from the dead.

And they kept the word to themselves; questioning together what that should mean, when he shall be risen from the dead.—*Mark* ix. 8, 9.

The Jews, therefore, answered, and said to him: What sign dost thou show unto us, seeing thou dost these things?

Jesus answered, and said to them: Destroy this temple, and in three days I will raise it up.

The Jews then said: Six and forty years was this temple in building; and wilt thou raise it up in three days?

But he spoke of the temple of his body.

When therefore he was risen again from the dead, his disciples remembered, that he had said this, and they believed the scripture, and the word that Jesus had said.—*John* ii. 18-22.

3d. Narrated and Declared

And in the end of the sabbath, when it began to dawn towards the first day of the week, came Mary Magdalen and the other Mary, to see the sepulchre.

And behold there was a great earthquake. For an angel of the Lord descended from heaven, and coming, rolled back the stone, and sat upon it.

And his countenance was as lightning, and his raiment as snow.

And for fear of him, the guards were struck with terror, and became as dead men.

And the angel answering, said to the women: Fear not you; for I know that you seek Jesus who was crucified.

He is not here, he is risen, as he said. Come, and see the place where the Lord was laid.

And going quickly, tell ye his disciples that he is risen: and behold he will go before you into Galilee; there you shall see him. Lo, I have foretold it to you.

And they went out quickly from the sepulchre with fear and great joy, running to tell his disciples.

And behold Jesus met them, saying: All hail. But they came up and took hold of his feet, and adored him.—*Matt.* xxviii. 1-9.

And when the sabbath was past, Mary Magdalen, and Mary the mother of James, and Salome, bought sweet spices, that coming, they might anoint Jesus.

And very early in the morning, the first day of the week, they come to the sepulchre, the sun being now risen.

And they said one to another: Who shall roll us back the stone from the door of the sepulchre?

And looking, they saw the stone rolled back. For it was very great.

And entering into the sepulchre, they saw a young man sitting on the right side, clothed with a white robe: and they were astonished.

Who saith to them: Be not affrighted; you seek Jesus of Nazareth, who was crucified: he is risen, he is not here, behold the place where they laid him.

But go, tell his disciples and Peter that he goeth before you into Galilee; there you shall see him, as he told you.

But they going out, fled from the sepulchre. For a trembling and fear had seized them: and they said nothing to any man; for they were afraid.

But he rising early the first day of the week, appeared first to Mary Magdalen, out of whom he had cast seven devils.—*Mark* xvi. 1-9.

And on the first day of the week, very early in the morning, they came to the sepulchre, bringing the spices which they had prepared.

And they found the stone rolled back from the sepulchre.

And going in, they found not the body of the Lord Jesus.

And it came to pass, as they were astonished in their mind at this, behold, two men stood by them in shining apparel.

And as they were afraid, and bowed down their countenance towards the ground, they said unto them: Why seek you the living with the dead?

He is not here, but is risen. Remember how he spoke unto you, when he was yet in Galilee,

Saying: The Son of man must be delivered into the hands of sinful men, and be crucified, and the third day rise again.

And they remembered his words.——*Luke* xxiv. 1-8.

And on the first day of the week, Mary Magdalen cometh early, when it was yet dark, unto the sepulchre; and she saw the stone taken away from the sepulchre.

She ran, therefore, and cometh to Simon Peter, and to the other disciple whom Jesus loved, and saith to them: They have taken away the Lord out of the sepulchre, and we know not where they have laid him.

Peter therefore went out, and that other disciple, and they came to the sepulchre.

And they both ran together, and that other disciple did outrun Peter, and came first to the sepulchre.

And when he stooped down, he saw the linen cloths lying: but yet he went not in.

Then cometh Simon Peter, following him, and went into the sepulchre, and saw the linen cloths lying,

And the napkin that had been about his head, not lying with the linen cloths, but apart, wrapped up into one place.

Then that other disciple also went in, who came first to the sepulchre: and he saw, and believed.

For as yet they knew not the scripture, that he must rise again from the dead.

The disciples therefore departed again to their home.

But Mary stood at the sepulchre without, weeping. Now as she was weeping, she stooped down, and looked into the sepulchre,

And she saw two angels in white, sitting, one at the head, and one at the feet, where the body of Jesus had been laid.

They say to her: Woman, why weepest thou? She saith to them: Because they have taken away my Lord; and I know not where they have laid him.

When she had thus said, she turned herself back, and saw Jesus standing; and she knew not that it was Jesus.

Jesus saith to her: Woman, why weepest thou? whom seekest thou? She, thinking that it was the gardener, saith to him: Sir, if thou hast taken him hence, tell me where thou hast laid him, and I will take him away.

Jesus saith to her: Mary. She turning, saith to him: Rabboni (which is to say, Master).

Jesus saith to her: Do not touch me, for I am not yet ascended to my Father. But go to my brethren, and say to them: I ascend to my Father and to your Father, to my God and your God.——*John* xx. 1-17.

Ye men of Israel, hear these words: Jesus of Nazareth, a man approved of God among you, by miracles, and wonders, and signs, which God did by him, in the midst of you, as you also know:

This same being delivered up, by the determinate counsel and foreknowledge of God, you by the hands of wicked men have crucified and slain.

Whom God hath raised up, having loosed the sorrows of hell, as it was impossible that he should be holden by it. . . .

Foreseeing this, he (David) spoke of the resurrection of Christ. For neither was he left in hell, neither did his flesh see corruption.

This Jesus hath God raised again, whereof all we are witnesses.—*Acts* ii. 22-24, 31, 32.

For I delivered unto you first of all, which I also received: how that Christ died for our sins, according to the scriptures:

And that he was buried, and that he rose again the third day, according to the scriptures:

And that he was seen by Cephas; and after that by the eleven.

Then was he seen by more than five hundred brethren at once: of whom many remain until this present, and some are fallen asleep.

After that, he was seen by James, then by all the apostles.

And last of all, he was seen also by me, as one born out of due time.—*1 Cor.* xv. 3-8.

And if Christ be not risen again, then is our preaching vain, and your faith is also vain.

Yea, and we are found false witnesses of God: because we have given testimony against God, that he hath raised up Christ; whom he hath not raised up, if the dead rise not again. . . .

And if Christ be not risen again, your faith is vain, for you are yet in your sins. . . .

But now Christ is risen from the dead, the first fruits of them that sleep. —*1 Cor.* xv. 14, 15, 17, 20.

RESURRECTION OF THE DEAD, THE

For I know that my Redeemer liveth, and in the last day I shall rise out of the earth.

And I shall be clothed again with my skin, and in my flesh I shall see my God.

Whom I myself shall see, and my eyes shall behold, and not another: this my hope is laid up in my bosom.—*Job* xix. 25-27.

Thy dead men shall live, my slain shall rise again: awake, and give praise, ye that dwell in the dust: for thy dew is the dew of the light: and the land of the giants thou shalt pull down into ruin. . . .

For behold the Lord will come out of his place, to visit the iniquity of the inhabitant of the earth against him: and the earth shall disclose her blood, and shall cover her slain no more.—*Is.* xxvi. 19, 21.

And many of those that sleep in the dust of the earth, shall awake: some unto life everlasting, and others unto reproach, to see it always.—*Dan.* xii. 2.

And when he was at the last gasp, he said thus: Thou indeed, O most wicked man, destroyest us out of this present life: but the King of the world will raise us up, who die for his laws, in the resurrection of eternal life.— *2 Mach.* vii. 9.

After him the third was made a mocking stock, and when he was required, he quickly put forth his tongue, and courageously stretched out his hands:

And said with confidence: These I have from heaven, but for the laws of God I now despise them: because I hope to receive them again from him. —*2 Mach.* vii. 10, 11.

And when he was now ready to die, he spoke thus: It is better, being put to death by men, to look for hope from God, to be raised up again by him: for, as to thee, thou shalt have no resurrection unto life.—*2 Mach.* vii. 14.

She (the mother) said to them: I know not how you were formed in my womb: for I neither gave you breath, nor soul, nor life, neither did I frame the limbs of every one of you.

But the Creator of the world, that formed the nativity of man, and that found out the origin of all, he will restore to you again in his mercy, both breath and life, as now you despise yourselves for the sake of his laws.— *2 Mach.* vii. 22, 23.

And making a gathering, he (Judas) sent twelve thousand drachms of silver to Jerusalem for sacrifice to be offered for the sins of the dead, thinking well and religiously concerning the resurrection.

(For if he had not hoped that they that were slain should rise again, it would have seemed superfluous and vain to pray for the dead.)—*2 Mach.* xii. 43, 44.

But when thou makest a feast, call the poor, the maimed, the lame, and the blind;

And thou shalt be blessed, because they have not wherewith to make thee recompense: for recompense shall be made thee at the resurrection of the just.—*Luke* xiv. 13, 14.

But they that shall be accounted worthy of that world, and of the resurrection from the dead, shall neither be married, nor take wives.

Neither can they die any more: for they are equal to the angels, and are the children of God, being the children of the resurrection.

Now that the dead rise again, Moses also showed, at the bush, when he called the Lord, The God of Abraham, and the God of Isaac, and the God of Jacob;

For he is not the God of the dead, but of the living: for all live to him. —*Luke* xx. 35-38.

Wonder not at this; for the hour cometh, wherein all that are in the graves shall hear the voice of the Son of God.

And they that have done good things, shall come forth unto the resurrection of life; but they that have done evil, unto the resurrection of judgment.— *John* v. 28, 29.

And this is the will of my Father that sent me: that every one who seeth the Son, and believeth in him, may have life everlasting, and I will raise him up in the last day. . . .

No man can come to me, except the Father, who hath sent me, draw him; and I will raise him up in the last day.

. . . He that eateth my flesh, and drinketh my blood, hath everlasting life: and I will raise him up in the last day.—*John* vi. 40, 44, 55.

Jesus saith to her: Thy brother shall rise again.

Martha saith to him: I know that he shall rise again, in the resurrection at the last day.

Jesus said to her: I am the resurrection and the life: he that believeth in me, although he be dead, shall live. —*John* xi. 23-25.

But this I confess to thee, that according to the way, which they call a heresy, so do I serve the Father and my God, believing all things which are written in the law and the prophets:

Having hope in God, which these also themselves look for, that there shall be a resurrection of the just and unjust.—*Acts* xxiv. 14, 15.

Now God hath both raised up the Lord, and will raise us up also by his power.—1 *Cor.* vi. 14.

Now if Christ be preached, that he arose again from the dead, how do some of you say, that there is no resurrection of the dead?

But if there be no resurrection of the dead, then Christ is not risen again.

And if Christ be not risen again, then is our preaching vain, and your faith is also vain.

Yea, and we are found false witnesses of God: because we have given testimony against God, that he hath raised up Christ; whom he hath not raised up, if the dead rise not again.

For if the dead rise not again, neither is Christ risen again.

And if Christ be not risen again, your faith is vain, for you are yet in your sins. . . .

But now Christ is risen from the dead, the first-fruits of them that sleep.

For by a man came death, and by a man the resurrection of the dead.

And as in Adam all die, so also in Christ all shall be made alive.—1 *Cor.* xv. 12-17, 20-22.

Otherwise what shall they do that are baptized for the dead, if the dead rise not again at all? why are they then baptized for them? . . .

If (according to man) I fought with beasts at Ephesus, what doth it profit me, if the dead rise not again? Let us eat and drink, for to-morrow we shall die.—1 *Cor.* xv. 29, 32.

But some man will say: How do the dead rise again? or with what manner of body shall they come?

Senseless man, that which thou sowest is not quickened, except it die first.

And that which thou sowest, thou sowest not the body that shall be; but bare grain, as of wheat, or of some of the rest.

But God giveth it a body as he will: and to every seed its proper body. . . .

So also is the resurrection of the dead. It is sown in corruption, it shall rise in incorruption.

It is sown in dishonor, it shall rise in glory. It is sown in weakness, it shall rise in power.

It is sown a natural body, it shall rise a spiritual body.—1 *Cor.* xv. 35-38, 42-44.

Behold, I tell you a mystery. We shall all indeed rise again: but we shall not all be changed.

In a moment, in the twinkling of an eye, at the last trumpet: for the trumpet shall sound, and the dead shall rise again incorruptible: and we shall be changed.

For this corruptible must put on incorruption; and this mortal must put on immortality.—1 *Cor.* xv. 51-53.

And we will not have you ignorant, brethren, concerning them that are asleep, that you be not sorrowful, even as others who have no hope.

For if we believe that Jesus died, and rose again; even so them who have slept through Jesus, will God bring with him.

For this we say unto you in the word of the Lord, that we who are alive, who remain unto the coming of the Lord, shall not prevent them who have slept.

For the Lord himself shall come down from heaven with commandment, and with the voice of an archangel, and with the trumpet of God: and the dead who are in Christ, shall rise first.

Then we who are alive, who are left, shall be taken up together with them in the clouds to meet Christ, into the air, and so shall we be always with the Lord.

Wherefore, comfort ye one another with these words.—1 *Thess.* iv. 12-17.

And I saw the dead, great and small, standing in the presence of the throne, and the books were opened; and another book was opened, which is the book of life; and the dead were judged by those things which were written in the books, according to their works.

And the sea gave up the dead that were in it, and death and hell gave up their dead that were in them; and they were judged every one according to their works.—*Apoc.* xx. 12, 13.

SAINTS, THE

1st. They are Like to the Angels

For in the resurrection they shall neither marry nor be married; but shall be as the angels of God in heaven. —*Matt.* xxii. 30.

But they that shall be accounted worthy of that world, and of the resurrection from the dead, shall neither be married, nor take wives.

Neither can they die any more: for they are equal to the angels, and are the children of God, being the children of the resurrection.—*Luke* xx. 35, 36.

2d. They Know What Passes Among Us

I say to you, that even so there shall be joy in heaven upon one sinner that doth penance, more than upon ninety-nine just who need not penance. . . .

So I say to you, there shall be joy before the angels of God upon one sinner doing penance.—*Luke* xv. 7, 10.

Also Probably Deduced from

We see now through a glass in a dark manner; but then face to face. Now I know in part; but then I shall know even as I am known.—1 *Cor.* xiii. 12.

Dearly beloved, we are now the sons of God; and it hath not yet appeared what we shall be. We know, that when he shall appear, we shall be like to him: because we shall see him as he is.— 1 *John* iii. 2.

3d. Their Intercession is to be Invoked, as the Prayers of God's Servants are of Help to Us

And God came to Abimelech in a dream by night, and he said to him: Lo thou shalt die for the woman thou hast taken: for she hath a husband. . . .

Now therefore restore the man his wife, for he is a prophet: and he shall pray for thee, and thou shalt live. . . .

And when Abraham prayed, God healed Abimelech and his wife, and his handmaids, and they bore children.— *Gen.* xx. 3, 7, 17.

And again the Lord said to Moses: I see that this people is stiff-necked:

Let me alone, that my wrath may be kindled against them, and that I may destroy them, and I will make of thee a great nation.

But Moses besought the Lord his God, saying: Why, O Lord, is thy indignation enkindled against thy people, whom thou hast brought out of the land of Egypt, with great power, and with a mighty hand?

Let not the Egyptians say, I beseech thee: He craftily brought them out, that he might kill them in the mountains, and destroy them from the earth: let thy anger cease, and be appeased upon the wickedness of thy people. . . .

And the Lord was appeased from doing the evil which he had spoken against his people.—*Ex.* xxxii. 9-12, 14.

The cloud also that was over the tabernacle departed: and behold Mary appeared white as snow with a leprosy. . . .

And Moses cried to the Lord, saying: O God, I beseech thee heal her.

And the Lord answered him: If her father had spi⁺ten upon her face, ought she not to have been ashamed for seven days at least? Let her be separated seven days without the camp, and afterwards she shall be called again.—*Num.* xi⁺. 10, 13, 14.

And Moses said to the Lord: . . . Forgive, I beseech thee, the sins of this people, according to the greatness of thy mercy, as thou hast been merciful to them from their going out of Egypt unto this place.

And the Lord said: I have forgiven according to thy word.—*Num.* xiv. 19, 20.

And the Lord said to Moses:

Get you out from the midst of this multitude, this moment will I destroy them. And as they were lying on the ground,

Moses said to Aaron: Take the censer, and putting fire in it from ⁺he altar, put incense upon it, and go quickly to the people to pray for them: for already wrath is gone out from the Lord, and the plague rageth.

When Aaron had done this, and had run to the midst of the multitude which the burning fire was now destroying, he offered the incense:

And standing between the dead and the living, he prayed for the people, and the plague ceased.—*Num.* xvi. 44-48.

And the Philistines heard that the children of Israel were gathered together to Masphath, and the lords of the Philistines went up against Israel. And when the children of Israel heard

this, they were afraid of the Philistines.

And they said to Samuel: Cease not to cry to the Lord our God for us, that he may save us out of the hand of the Philistines.

And Samuel took a sucking lamb, and offered it whole for a holocaust to the Lord: and Samuel cried to the Lord for Israel, and the Lord heard him.

And it came to pass, when Samuel was offering the holocaust, the Philistines began the battle against Israel: but the Lord thundered with a great thunder on that day upon the Philistines, and terrified them, and they were overthrown before the face of Israel.— 1 *Kings* vii. 7-10.

And after the Lord had spoken these words to Job, he said to Eliphaz the Themanite: My wrath is kindled against thee, and against thy two friends, because you have not spoken the thing that is right before me, as my servant Job hath.

Take unto you therefore seven oxen, and seven rams, and go to my servant Job, and offer for yourselves a holocaust: and my servant Job shall pray for you: his face I will accept, that folly be not imputed to you: for you have not spoken right things before me, as my servant Job hath.

So Eliphaz the Themanite, and Baldad the Suhite, and Sophar the Naamathite went, and did as the Lord had spoken to them, and the Lord accepted the face of Job.

The Lord also was turned at the penance of Job, when he prayed for his friends.—*Job* xlii. 7-10.

They forgot God, who saved them, who had done great things in Egypt, wondrous works in the land of Cham: terrible things in the Red Sea.

And he said that he would destroy them: had not Moses his chosen stood before him in the breach:

To turn away his wrath, lest he should destroy them.—*Ps.* cv. 21-23.

And they provoked him with their inventions: and destruction was multiplied among them.

Then Phinees stood up, and pacified

him: and the slaughter ceased.—*Ps.* cv. 29, 30.

But the just also were afterwards touched by an assault of death, and there was a disturbance of the multitude in the wilderness: but thy wrath did not long continue.

For a blameless man made haste to pray for the people, bringing forth the shield of his ministry, prayer, and by incense making supplication, withstood the wrath, and put an end to the calamity, showing that he was thy servant.

And he overcame the disturbance, not by strength of body nor with force of arms, but with a word he subdued him that punished them, alleging the oaths and covenant made with the fathers.—*Wis.* xviii. 20-22.

Then some of the friends of Heliodorus forthwith begged of Onias, that he would call upon the most High to grant him his life, who was ready to give up the ghost.

So the high priest considering that the king might perhaps suspect that some mischief had been done to Heliodorus by the Jews, offered a sacrifice of health for the recovery of the man.

And when the high priest was praying, the same young men in the same clothing stood by Heliodorus, and said to him: Give thanks to Onias the priest: because for his sake the Lord hath granted thee life.—2 *Mach.* iii. 31-33.

Confess therefore your sins one to another: and pray one for another, that you may be saved. For the continual prayer of a just man availeth much.—*James* v. 16.

Also Deduced from

I beseech you therefore, brethren, through our Lord Jesus Christ, and by the charity of the Holy Ghost, that you help me in your prayers for me to God.—*Rom.* xv. 30.

By all prayer and supplication praying at all times in the spirit; and in the same watching with all instance and supplication for all the saints:

And for me, that speech may be given me, that I may open my mouth with confidence, to make known the mystery of the gospel.—*Eph.* vi. 18, 19.

Brethren, pray for us.—1 *Thess.* v. 25.

4th. Veneration of the Saints

But to me, thy friends, O God, are made exceedingly honorable: their principality is exceedingly strengthened.—*Ps.* cxxxviii. 17.

And let not the naming of God be usual in thy mouth, and meddle not with the names of saints, for thou shalt not escape free from them.—*Ecclus.* xxiii. 10.

Blessed are they that saw thee (Elias), and were honored with thy friendship.—*Ecclus.* xlviii. 11.

5th. The Communion of Saints
I. In Heaven

Now therefore you are no more strangers and foreigners; but you are fellow citizens with the saints, and the domestics of God,

Built upon the foundation of the apostles and prophets, Jesus Christ himself being the chief corner stone:

In whom all the building, being framed together, groweth up into an holy temple in the Lord.—*Eph.* ii. 19-21.

After this there appeared also another man, admirable for age, and glory, and environed with great beauty and majesty:

Then Onias answering, said: This is a lover of his brethren, and of the people of Israel: this is he that prayeth much for the people, and for all the holy city, Jeremias the prophet of God.—2 *Mach.* xv. 13, 14.

II. On Earth

So we being many, are one body in Christ, and every one members one of another.—*Rom.* xii. 5.

And he hath subjected all things under his feet, and hath made him head over all the church,

Which is his body, and the fulness of him who is filled all in all.—*Eph.* i. 22, 23.

III. In Purgatory

And making a gathering, he (Judas) sent twelve thousand drachms of silver to Jerusalem for sacrifice to be offered for the sins of the dead, thinking well and religiously concerning the resurrection,

(For if he had not hoped that they that were slain should rise again, it would have seemed superfluous and vain to pray for the dead,)

And because he considered that they who had fallen asleep with godliness, had great grace laid up for them.

It is therefore a holy and wholesome thought to pray for the dead, that they may be loosed from sins.—2 Mach. xii. 43-46.

SCRIPTURES, THE HOLY

1st. Our Guide

We, though we needed none of these things, having for our comfort the holy books that are in our hands.—1 Mach. xii. 9.

For what things soever were written, were written for our learning: that through patience and the comfort of the scriptures, we might have hope.—Rom. xv. 4.

Now all these things happened to them (the Israelites) in figure: and they are written for our correction, upon whom the ends of the world are come.—1 Cor. x. 11.

And because from thy infancy thou hast known the holy scriptures, which can instruct thee to salvation, by the faith which is in Christ Jesus.

All scripture, inspired of God, is profitable to teach, to reprove, to correct, to instruct in justice,

That the man of God may be perfect, furnished to every good work.—2 Tim. iii. 15-17.

And we have the more firm prophetical word: whereunto you do well to attend, as to a light that shineth in a dark place, until the day dawn, and the day star arise in your hearts:

Understanding this first, that no prophecy of scripture is made by private interpretation.—2 Peter i. 19, 20.

Blessed is he, that readeth and heareth the words of this prophecy; and keepeth those things which are written in it; for the time is at hand.—Apoc. i. 3.

2d. Not the Sole Rule of Faith

See also: Tradition—page 736.

How then shall they call on him, in whom they have not believed? Or how shall they believe him, of whom they have not heard? And how shall they hear, without a preacher?

. . . . Faith then cometh by hearing; and hearing by the word of Christ.—Rom. x. 14, 17.

Now I make known unto you, brethren, the gospel which I preached to you, which also you have received, and wherein you stand;

By which also you are saved, if you hold fast after what manner I preached unto you, unless you have believed in vain.—1 Cor. xv. 1, 2.

Therefore, brethren, stand fast; and hold the traditions which you have learned, whether by word, or by our epistle.—2 Thess. ii. 14.

3d. Inspired by God

All scripture, inspired of God, is profitable to teach, to reprove, to correct, to instruct in justice.—2 Tim. iii. 16.

Understanding this first, that no prophecy of scripture is made by private interpretation.

For prophecy came not by the will of man at any time: but the holy men of God spoke, inspired by the Holy Ghost.—2 Peter i. 20, 21.

4th. Hard to Understand

And behold a man of Ethiopia, an eunuch, of great authority under Candace the queen of the Ethiopians, who had charge over all her treasures, had come to Jerusalem to adore.

And he was returning, sitting in his chariot, and reading Isaias the prophet.

And the Spirit said to Philip: Go near, and join thyself to this chariot.

And Philip running thither, heard him reading the prophet Isaias. And he said: Thinkest thou that thou understandest what thou readest?

Who said: And how can I, unless some man show me?—Acts viii. 27-31.

And whereas indeed he was the Son of God, he learned obedience by the things which he suffered. . . .

Of whom we have much to say, and hard to be intelligibly uttered: because you are become weak to hear.—*Heb.* v. 8, 11.

And account the longsuffering of our Lord, salvation; as also our most dear brother Paul, according to the wisdom given him, hath written to you:

As also in all his epistles, speaking in them of these things; in which are certain things hard to be understood, which the unlearned and unstable wrest, as they do also the other scriptures, to their own destruction.—2 *Peter* iii. 15, 16.

5th. Not of Private Interpretation

Understanding this first, that no prophecy of scripture is made by private interpretation.

For prophecy came not by the will of man at any time: but the holy men of God spoke, inspired by the Holy Ghost. —2 *Peter* i. 20, 21.

6th. Not to be Corrupted

You shall not add to the word that I speak to you, neither shall you take away from it: keep the commandments of the Lord your God which I command you.—*Deut.* iv. 2.

What I command thee, that only do thou to the Lord: neither add any thing, nor diminish.—*Deut.* xii. 32.

Every word of God is fire tried: he is a buckler to them that hope in him.

Add not any thing to his words, lest thou be reproved, and found a liar.— *Prov.* xxx. 5, 6.

For I testify to every one that heareth the words of the prophecy of this book: If any man shall add to these things, God shall add unto him the plagues written in this book.

And if any man shall take away from the words of the book of this prophecy, God shall take away his part out of the book of life and out of the holy city, and from these things that are written in this book.—*Apoc.* xxii. 18, 19.

SIN, GOD IS NOT THE AUTHOR OF

In the morning I will stand before thee, and will see: because thou art not a God that willest iniquity.—*Ps.* v. 5.

But to God the wicked and his wickedness are hateful alike.—*Wis.* xiv. 9.

Say not: He hath caused me to err: for he hath no need of wicked men.

The Lord hateth all abomination of error, and they that fear him shall not love it.—*Ecclus.* xv. 12, 13.

He hath commanded no man to do wickedly, and he hath given no man license to sin:

For he desireth not a multitude of faithless and unprofitable children.— *Ecclus.* xv. 21, 22.

The just Lord is in the midst thereof, he will not do iniquity: in the morning, in the morning he will bring his judgment to light, and it shall not be hid. —*Soph.* iii. 5.

SIN, ORIGINAL

1st. Probably Referred to

Who can make him clean that is conceived of unclean seed? is it not thou who only art?—*Job* xiv. 4.

For behold I was conceived in iniquities; and in sins did my mother conceive me.—*Ps.* l. 7.

2d. Declared

Wherefore as by one man sin entered into this world, and by sin death; and so death passed upon all men, in whom all have sinned. . . .

But death reigned from Adam unto Moses, even over them also who have not sinned after the similitude of the transgression of Adam, who is a figure of him who was to come.

But not as the offence, so also the gift. For if by the offence of one, many died; much more the grace of God, and the gift, by the grace of one man, Jesus Christ, hath abounded unto many.

And not as it was by one sin, so also is the gift. For judgment indeed was by one unto condemnation; but grace is of many offences, unto justification.

For if by one man's offence death reigned through one; much more they who receive abundance of grace, and of the gift, and of justice, shall reign in life through one, Jesus Christ.

Therefore, as by the offence of one, unto all men to condemnation; so also by the justice of one, unto all men to justification of life.

For as by the disobedience of one man, many were made sinners; so also by the obedience of one, many shall be made just.—*Rom.* v. 12, 14-19.

For by a man came death, and by a man the resurrection of the dead.

And as in Adam all die, so also in Christ all shall be made alive.—*1 Cor.* xv. 21, 22.

In which also we all conversed in time past, in the desires of our flesh, fulfilling the will of the flesh and of our thoughts, and were by nature children of wrath, even as the rest.—*Eph.* ii. 3.

3d. The Effects of Original Sin

I. Proneness to Evil

And the Lord smelled a sweet savor, and said: I will no more curse the earth for the sake of man: for the imagination and thought of man's heart are prone to evil from his youth: therefore I will no more destroy every living soul as I have done.—*Gen.* viii. 21.

II. Loss of Heaven

Jesus answered: Amen, amen I say to thee, unless a man be born again of water and the Holy Ghost, he cannot enter into the kingdom of God.—*John* iii. 5.

SIN, MORTAL

Being filled with all iniquity, malice, fornication, avarice, wickedness, full of envy, murder, contention, deceit, malignity, whisperers,

Detractors, hateful to God, contumelious, proud, haughty, inventors of evil things, disobedient to parents,

Foolish, dissolute, without affection, without fidelity, without mercy.

Who, having known the justice of God, did not understand that they who do such things, are worthy of death; and not only they that do them, but they also that consent to them that do them.—*Rom.* i. 29-32.

Know you not that the unjust shall not possess the kingdom of God? Do not err: neither fornicators, nor idolaters, nor adulterers,

Nor the effeminate, nor liers with mankind, nor thieves, nor covetous, nor drunkards, nor railers, nor extortioners, shall possess the kingdom of God.— *1 Cor.* vi. 9, 10.

Now the works of the flesh are manifest, which are fornication, uncleanness, immodesty, luxury,

Idolatry, witchcrafts, enmities, contentions, emulations, wraths, quarrels, dissensions, sects,

Envies, murders, drunkenness, revellings, and such like. Of the which I foretell you, as I have foretold to you, that they who do such things shall not obtain the kingdom of God.—*Gal.* v. 19-21.

For know you this and understand, that no fornicator, or unclean, or covetous person (which is a serving of idols), hath inheritance in the kingdom of Christ and of God.—*Eph.* v. 5.

Mortify therefore your members which are upon the earth; fornication, uncleanness, lust, evil concupiscence, and covetousness, which is the service of idols.

For which things the wrath of God cometh upon the children of unbelief.— *Col.* iii. 5, 6.

But the fearful, and unbelieving, and the abominable, and murderers, and whoremongers, and sorcerers, and idolaters, and all liars, they shall have their portion in the pool burning with fire and brimstone, which is the second death.—*Apoc.* xxi. 8.

SIN, VENIAL

For a just man shall fall seven times and shall rise again: but the wicked shall fall down into evil.—*Prov.* xxiv. 16.

For there is no just man upon earth, that doth good, and sinneth not.— *Eccles.* vii. 21.

But I say unto you, that every idle word that men shall speak, they shall render an account for it in the day of judgment.—*Matt.* xii. 36.

For in many things we all offend. If any man offend not in word, the same is a perfect man.—*James* iii. 2.

If we say that we have no sin, we deceive ourselves, and the truth is not in us.—*1 John* i. 8.

Probably Alluded to

For other foundation no man can lay, but that which is laid; which is Christ Jesus.

Now if any man build upon this foundation, gold, silver, precious stones, wood, hay, stubble:

Every man's work shall be manifest; for the day of the Lord shall declare it, because it shall be revealed in fire; and the fire shall try every man's work, of what sort it is.

If any man's work abide, which he hath built thereupon, he shall receive a reward.

If any man's work burn, he shall suffer loss; but he himself shall be saved, yet so as by fire.—1 *Cor.* iii. 11-15.

SUNDAY

1st. Called the Lord's Day

I was in the spirit on the Lord's day, and heard behind me a great voice, as of a trumpet.—*Apoc.* i. 10.

2d. The First Day of the Week Especially Mentioned

And on the first day of the week, when we were assembled to break bread, Paul discoursed with them, being to depart on the morrow: and he continued his speech until midnight.—*Acts* xx. 7.

Now concerning the collections that are made for the saints, as I have given order to the churches of Galatia, so do ye also.

On the first day of the week let every one of you put apart with himself, laying up what it shall well please him; that when I come, the collections be not then to be made.—1 *Cor.* xvi. 1, 2.

TEMPORAL PUNISHMENT

See: Punishment—page 723.

TRADITION

Many other signs also did Jesus in the sight of his disciples, which are not written in this book.—*John* xx. 30.

But there are also many other things which Jesus did; which, if they were written every one, the world itself, I think, would not be able to contain the books that should be written.—*John* xxi. 25.

Now I praise you, brethren, that in all things you are mindful of me: and keep my ordinances as I have delivered them to you.—1 *Cor.* xi. 2.

Therefore, brethren, stand fast; and hold the traditions which you have learned, whether by word, or by our epistle.—2 *Thess.* ii. 14.

And we charge you, brethren, in the name of our Lord Jesus Christ, that you withdraw yourselves from every brother walking disorderly, and not according to the tradition which they have received of us.—2 *Thess.* iii. 6.

Hold the form of sound words, which thou hast heard of me in faith, and in the love which is in Christ Jesus.

Keep the good thing committed to thy trust by the Holy Ghost, who dwelleth in us.—2 *Tim.* i. 13, 14.

And the things which thou hast heard of me by many witnesses, the same commend to faithful men, who shall be fit to teach others also.—2 *Tim.* ii. 2.

But continue thou in those things which thou hast learned, and which have been committed to thee: knowing of whom thou hast learned them.—2 *Tim.* iii. 14.

As for you, let that which you have heard from the beginning, abide in you. If that abide in you, which you have heard from the beginning, you also shall abide in the Son, and in the Father.—1 *John* ii. 24.

But you, my dearly beloved, be mindful of the words which have been spoken before by the apostles of our Lord Jesus Christ.—*Jude* i. 17.

TRINITY, THE HOLY

1st. Obscurely Implied in the Old Testament

And he said: Let us make man to our image and likeness.—*Gen.* i. 26.

And he said: Behold Adam is become as one of us, knowing good and evil: now, therefore, lest perhaps he put forth his hand, and take also of the tree of life, and eat, and live for ever.—*Gen.* iii. 22.

And the Lord came down to see the

city and the tower, which the children of Adam were building.

And he said: Behold, it is one people, and all have one tongue: and they have begun to do this, neither will they leave off from their designs, till they accomplish them in deed.

Come ye, therefore, let us go down, and there confound their tongue, that they may not understand one another's speech.—*Gen.* xi. 5-7.

2d. Less Obscurely as to Two Divine Persons

The Lord hath said to me: Thou art my son, this day have I begotten thee.—*Ps.* ii. 7.

The Lord said to my Lord: Sit thou at my right hand:

Until I make thy enemies thy footstool.

The Lord will send forth the sceptre of thy power out of Sion: rule thou in the midst of thy enemies.

With thee is the principality in the day of thy strength: in the brightness of the saints: from the womb before the day star I begot thee.—*Ps.* cix. 1-3.

3d. Clearly Revealed in the New Testament

And Jesus being baptized, forthwith came out of the water: and lo, the heavens were opened to him: and he saw the Spirit of God descending as a dove, and coming upon him.

And behold a voice from heaven, saying: This is my beloved Son, in whom I am well pleased.—*Matt.* iii. 16, 17.

Going therefore, teach ye all nations; baptizing them in the name of the Father, and of the Son, and of the Holy Ghost.—*Matt.* xxviii. 19.

And the angel said to her: Fear not, Mary, for thou hast found grace with God.

Behold thou shalt conceive in thy womb, and shalt bring forth a son; and thou shalt call his name Jesus.

He shall be great, and shall be called the Son of the most High; and the Lord God shall give unto him the throne of David his father; and he shall reign in the house of Jacob for ever.

And of his kingdom there shall be no end.

And Mary said to the angel: How shall this be done, because I know not man?

And the angel answering, said to her: The Holy Ghost shall come upon thee, and the power of the most High shall overshadow thee. And therefore also the Holy which shall be born of thee shall be called the Son of God.—*Luke* i. 30-35.

And I will ask the Father, and he shall give you another Paraclete, that he may abide with you for ever.—*John* xiv. 16.

But the Paraclete, the Holy Ghost, whom the Father will send in my name, he will teach you all things, and bring all things to your mind, whatsoever I shall have said to you.—*John* xiv. 26.

This Jesus hath God raised again, whereof all we are witnesses.

Being exalted therefore by the right hand of God, and having received of the Father the promise of the Holy Ghost, he hath poured forth this which you see and hear.—*Acts* ii. 32, 33.

Now he that confirmeth us with you in Christ, and hath anointed us, is God:

Who also hath sealed us, and given the pledge of the Spirit in our hearts.—*2 Cor.* i. 21, 22.

The grace of our Lord Jesus Christ, and the charity of God, and the communication of the Holy Ghost be with you all. Amen.—*2 Cor.* xiii. 13.

For by him (Christ) we have access both in one Spirit to the Father.—*Eph.* ii. 18.

For this cause I bow my knees to the Father of our Lord Jesus Christ, . . .

That he would grant you, according to the riches of his glory, to be strengthened by his Spirit with might unto the inward man.—*Eph.* iii. 14, 16.

Peter, an apostle of Jesus Christ, to the strangers dispersed through Pontus, Galatia, Cappadocia, Asia, and Bithynia, elect,

According to the foreknowledge of God the Father, unto the sanctification of the Spirit, unto obedience and sprinkling of the blood of Jesus Christ: Grace unto you and peace be multiplied.—*1 Peter* i. 1, 2.

¹And there are three who give testi-

¹This text is here used, as the arguments in

mony in heaven, the Father, the Word, and the Holy Ghost. And these three are one.—1 *John* v. 7.

VIRGINITY

1st. Its Observance Possible

His disciples say unto him: If the case of a man with his wife be so, it is not expedient to marry.

Who said to them: All men take not this word, but they to whom it is given.

For there are eunuchs, who were born so from their mother's womb: and there are eunuchs, who were made so by men: and there are eunuchs, who have made themselves eunuchs for the kingdom of heaven. He that can take, let him take it.—*Matt.* xix. 10-12.

2d. When Vowed, to be Kept

But the younger widows avoid. For when they have grown wanton in Christ, they will marry:

Having damnation, because they have made void their first faith.—1 *Tim.* v. 11, 12.

3d. Its Excellence

For I would that all men were even as myself: but every one hath his proper gift from God; one after this manner, and another after that.

But I say to the unmarried, and to the widows: It is good for them if they so continue, even as I. . . .

But as the Lord hath distributed to every one, as God hath called every one, so let him walk: and so in all churches I teach. . . .

Now concerning virgins, I have no commandment of the Lord; but I give counsel, as having obtained mercy of the Lord, to be faithful.

I think therefore that this is good for the present necessity, that it is good for a man so to be.

Art thou bound to a wife? seek not to be loosed. Art thou loosed from a wife? seek not a wife. . . .

But I would have you to be without solicitude. He that is without a wife,

favor of its authenticity are at least, probable. Consult: Manuel Biblique, by Bacuez et Vigouroux, vol. 4, p. 624; Tanquerey's Synopsis Theologiæ Dogmaticæ, vol. 1, foot-note, pp. 189-190.

is solicitous for the things that belong to the Lord, how he may please God.

But he that is with a wife, is solicitous for the things of the world, how he may please his wife: and he is divided.

And the unmarried woman and the virgin thinketh on the things of the Lord, that she may be holy both in body and in spirit. But she that is married thinketh on the things of the world, how she may please her husband. . . .

For he that hath determined, being steadfast in his heart, having no necessity, but having power of his own will; and hath judged this in his heart, to keep his virgin, doth well.

Therefore, both he that giveth his virgin in marriage, doth well; and he that giveth her not, doth better.

A woman is bound by the law as long as her husband liveth; but if her husband die, she is at liberty: let her marry to whom she will; only in the Lord.

But more blessed shall she be, if she so remain, according to my counsel; and I think that I also have the spirit of God.—1 *Cor.* vii. 7, 8, 17, 25-27, 32-34, 37-40.

And they sung as it were a new canticle, before the throne, and before the four living creatures, and the ancients; and no man could say the canticle, but those hundred forty-four thousand, who were purchased from the earth.

These are they who were not defiled with women: for they are virgins. These follow the Lamb whithersoever he goeth. These were purchased from among men, the first-fruits to God and to the Lamb:

And in their mouth there was found no lie; for they are without spot before the throne of God.—*Apoc.* xiv. 3-5.

WILL, THE

See: Free will—page 698.

WORKS ARE MERITORIOUS, GOOD

If thou do well, shalt thou not receive? but if ill, shall not sin forthwith be present at the door? but the lust thereof shall be under thee, and thou shalt have dominion over it.—*Gen.* iv. 7.

By my own self have I sworn, saith the Lord: because thou hast done this thing, and hast not spared thy only begotten son for my sake:

I will bless thee, and I will multiply thy seed as the stars of heaven, and as the sand that is by the seashore: thy seed shall possess the gates of their enemies.

And in thy seed shall all the nations of the earth be blessed, because thou hast obeyed my voice.—*Gen.* xxii. 16-18.

And the Lord will reward me according to my justice; and will repay me according to the cleanness of my hands:

Because I have kept the ways of the Lord; and have not done wickedly against my God.

For all his judgments are in my sight: and his justices I have not put away from me.

And I shall be spotless with him: and shall keep myself from my iniquity.

And the Lord will reward me according to my justice; and according to the cleanness of my hands before his eyes.—*Ps.* xvii. 21-25.

The fear of the Lord is holy, enduring for ever and ever: the judgments of the Lord are true, justified in themselves. . . .

For thy servant keepeth them, and in keeping them there is a great reward.—*Ps.* xviii. 10, 12.

God hath spoken once, these two things have I heard, that power belongeth to God,

And mercy to thee, O Lord; for thou wilt render to every man according to his works.—*Ps.* lxi. 12, 13.

All mercy shall make a place for every man according to the merit of his works, and according to the wisdom of his sojournment.—*Ecclus.* xvi. 15.

Blessed are ye when they shall revile you, and persecute you, and speak all that is evil against you, untruly, for my sake:

Be glad and rejoice, for your reward is very great in heaven.—*Matt.* v. 11, 12.

He that receiveth a prophet in the name of a prophet, shall receive the reward of a prophet: and he that receiveth a just man in the name of a just man, shall receive the reward of a just man.

And whosoever shall give to drink to one of these little ones a cup of cold water only in the name of a disciple, amen I say to you, he shall not lose his reward.—*Matt.* x. 41, 42.

For the Son of man shall come in the glory of his Father with his angels: and then will he render to every man according to his works.—*Matt.* xvi. 27.

Then shall the king say to them that shall be on his right hand: Come, ye blessed of my Father, possess you the kingdom prepared for you from the foundation of the world.

For I was hungry, and you gave me to eat; I was thirsty, and you gave me to drink; I was a stranger, and you took me in:

Naked, and you covered me: sick, and you visited me: I was in prison, and you came to me.

Then shall the just answer him, saying: Lord, when did we see thee hungry, and fed thee; thirsty, and gave thee drink?

And when did we see thee a stranger, and took thee in? or naked, and covered thee?

Or when did we see thee sick or in prison, and came to thee?

And the king answering, shall say to them: Amen I say to you, as long as you did it to one of these my least brethren, you did it to me.—*Matt.* xxv. 34-40.

For whosoever shall give you to drink a cup of water in my name, because you belong to Christ: amen I say to you, he shall not lose his reward.—*Mark* ix. 40.

Who will render to every man according to his works.

To them indeed, who according to patience in good work, seek glory and honor and incorruption, eternal life.—*Rom.* ii. 6, 7.

But glory, and honor, and peace to every one that worketh good, to the Jew first, and also to the Greek.—*Rom.* ii. 10.

For not the hearers of the law are just before God, but the doers of the law shall be justified.—*Rom.* ii. 13.

And every man shall receive his own

reward, according to his own labor.—1 *Cor.* iii. 8.

Every man's work shall be manifest; for the day of the Lord shall declare it, because it shall be revealed in fire; and the fire shall try every man's work, of what sort it is.

If any man's work abide, which he hath built thereupon, he shall receive a reward.—1 *Cor.* iii. 13, 14.

Know you not that they that run in the race, all run indeed, but one receiveth the prize? So run that you may obtain.

And every one that striveth for the mastery, refraineth himself from all things: and they indeed that they may receive a corruptible crown; but we an incorruptible one.—1 *Cor.* ix. 24, 25.

For what things a man shall sow, those also shall he reap. For he that soweth in his flesh, of the flesh also shall reap corruption. But he that soweth in the spirit, of the spirit shall reap life everlasting.

And in doing good, let us not fail. For in due time we shall reap, not failing.—*Gal.* vi. 8, 9.

I have fought a good fight, I have finished my course, I have kept the faith. As to the rest, there is laid up for me a crown of justice, which the Lord the just judge will render to me in that day: and not only to me, but to them also that love his coming.—2 *Tim.* iv. 7, 8.

For God is not unjust, that he should forget your work, and the love which you have shown in his name, you who have ministered, and do minister to the saints.—*Heb.* vi. 10.

WORKS ARE NECESSARY FOR SALVATION, GOOD

Bring forth therefore fruit worthy of penance. . . .

For now the axe is laid to the root of the trees. Every tree therefore that doth not yield good fruit, shall be cut down, and cast into the fire.—*Matt.* iii. 8, 10.

Not every one that saith to me, Lord, Lord, shall enter into the kingdom of heaven: but he that doth the will of my Father who is in heaven, he shall enter into the kingdom of heaven.—*Matt.* vii. 21.

Then shall he say to them also that shall be on his left hand: Depart from me, you cursed, into everlasting fire which was prepared for the devil and his angels.

For I was hungry, and you gave me not to eat: I was thirsty, and you gave me not to drink.

I was a stranger, and you took me not in: naked, and you covered me not: sick and in prison, and you did not visit me.

Then they also shall answer him, saying: Lord, when did we see thee hungry, or thirsty, or a stranger, or naked, or sick, or in prison, and did not minister to thee?

Then he shall answer them, saying: Amen I say to you, as long as you did it not to one of these least, neither did you do it to me.

And these shall go into everlasting punishment: but the just, into life everlasting.—*Matt.* xxv. 41-46.

I am the true vine; and my Father is the husbandman.

Every branch in me, that beareth not fruit, he will take away: and every one that beareth fruit, he will purge it, that it may bring forth more fruit.—*John* xv. 1, 2.

For not the hearers of the law are just before God, but the doers of the law shall be justified.—*Rom.* ii. 13.

What shall it profit, my brethren, if a man say he hath faith, but hath not works? Shall faith be able to save him?

And if a brother or sister be naked, and want daily food:

And one of you say to them: Go in peace, be ye warmed and filled; yet give them not those things that are necessary for the body, what shall it profit?

So faith also, if it have not works, is dead in itself. . . .

Thou believest that there is one God. Thou dost well: the devils also believe and tremble.

But wilt thou know, O vain man, that faith without works is dead?

. . . Do you see that by works a man is justified; and not by faith only? . . .

For even as the body without the spirit is dead; so also faith without works is dead.—*James* ii. 14-17, 19, 20, 24, 26.

To him therefore who knoweth to do good, and doth it not, to him it is sin. —*James* iv. 17.

And you, employing all care, minister in your faith, virtue; and in virtue, knowledge;

And in knowledge, abstinence; and in abstinence, patience; and in patience, godliness;

And in godliness, love of brotherhood; and in love of brotherhood, charity.

For if these things be with you and abound, they will make you to be neither empty nor unfruitful in the knowledge of our Lord Jesus Christ.

For he that hath not these things with him, is blind, and groping, having forgotten that he was purged from his old sins.

Wherefore, brethren, labor the more, that by good works you may make sure your calling and election. For doing these things, you shall not sin at any time.

For so an entrance shall be ministered to you abundantly into the everlasting kingdom of our Lord and Saviour Jesus Christ.—2 *Peter* i. 5-11.

WORKS, GOD WILL RENDER TO EVERY MAN ACCORDING TO HIS

See: Predestination—page 722.

APPENDIX

APPENDIX

BOOKS MENTIONED IN THE SCRIPTURES THAT HAVE SINCE BEEN LOST

1st. The Book of the Wars of the Lord

Wherefore it is said in the book of the wars of the Lord: As he did in the Red Sea, so will he do in the streams of Arnon.

The rocks of the torrents were bowed down that they might rest in Ar, and lie down in the borders of the Moabites.—*Num.* xxi. 14, 15.

2d. The Book of the Just

Then Josue spoke to the Lord, in the day that he delivered the Amorrhite in the sight of the children of Israel, and he said before them: Move not, O sun, toward Gabaon, nor thou, O moon, toward the valley of Ajalon.

And the sun and the moon stood still, till the people revenged themselves of their enemies. Is not this written in the book of the just? So the sun stood still in the midst of heaven, and hasted not to go down the space of one day.—*Jos.* x. 12, 13.

(Also he (David) commanded that they should teach the children of Juda the use of the bow, as it is written in the book of the just.)—2 *Kings* i. 18.

3d. The Parables and Poems of Solomon

Solomon also spoke three thousand parables: and his poems were a thousand and five.

And he treated about trees from the cedar that is in Libanus, unto the hyssop that cometh out of the wall: and he discoursed of beasts, and of fowls, and of creeping things, and of fishes.—3 *Kings* iv. 32, 33.

4th. The Book of the Words of the Days of Solomon

And the rest of the words of Solomon, and all that he did, and his wisdom: behold they are all written in the book of the words of the days of Solomon.—3 *Kings* xi. 41.

5th. The Book of the Words of the Days of the Kings of Israel

[1]And the rest of the acts of Jeroboam, how he fought, and how he reigned, behold they are written in the book of the words of the days of the kings of Israel.—3 *Kings* xiv. 19.

6th. The Book of the Words of the Days of the Kings of Juda

[2]Now the rest of the acts of Roboam, and all that he did, behold they are written in the book of the words of the days of the kings of Juda.—3 *Kings* xiv. 29.

7th. The Book of Nathan the Prophet

Now the acts of king David first and last are written in the book of Samuel the seer, and in the book of Nathan the prophet, and in the book of Gad the seer.—1 *Paral.* xxix. 29.

Now the rest of the acts of Solomon first and last are written in the words of Nathan the prophet, and in the books of Ahias the Silonite, and in the vision of Addo the seer, against Jeroboam the son of Nabat.—2 *Paral.* ix. 29.

8th. The Book of Gad the Seer

Now the acts of king David first and last are written in the book of Samuel the seer, and in the book of Nathan the prophet, and in the book of Gad the seer.—1 *Paral.* xxix. 29.

9th. The Books of Ahias the Silonite

Now the rest of the acts of Solomon first and last are written in the words of Nathan the prophet, and in the books of Ahias the Silonite, and in the vision

[1]Also 3 *Kings* xv. 31; xvi. 5, 14, 20, 27; xxii. 39; and 4 *Kings* i. 18; x. 34; xiii. 8, 12; xiv. 28; xv. 11, 15, 21, 26, 31.
[2]Also 3 *Kings* xv. 7, 23; xxii. 46; 4 *Kings* viii. 23; xii. 19; xiv. 18; xv. 6, 36; xvi. 19; xx. 20; xxi. 17, 25; xxiii. 28; xxiv. 5.

of Addo the seer, against Jeroboam the son of Nabat.—2 *Paral.* ix. 29.

10th. The Book of Addo the Seer

Now the rest of the acts of Solomon first and last are written in the words of Nathan the prophet, and in the books of Ahias the Silonite, and in the vision of Addo the seer, against Jeroboam the son of Nabat.—2 *Paral.* ix. 29.

Now the acts of Roboam first and last are written in the books of Semeias the prophet, and of Addo the seer, and diligently recorded.—2 *Paral.* xii. 15.

And the rest of the acts of Abia, and of his ways and works, are written diligently in the book of Addo the prophet. —2 *Paral.* xiii. 22.

11th. The Book of Semeias the Prophet

Now the acts of Roboam first and last are written in the books of Semeias the prophet, and of Addo the seer, and diligently recorded.—2 *Paral.* xii. 15.

12th. The Book of the Kings of Juda and Israel

But the works of Asa the first and last are written in the book of the kings of Juda and Israel.—2 '*Paral.* xvi. 11.

13th. The Book of the Kings of Israel and Juda

Now the rest of the acts of Joatham, and all his wars, and his works, are written in the book of the kings of Israel and Juda.—2 *Paral.* xxvii. 7.

14th. The Book of Kings

(*Possibly identical with the book of the kings of Juda and Israel.*)
And concerning his (Joas') sons, and the sum of money which was gathered under him, and the repairing the house of God, they are written more diligently in the book of kings.—2 *Paral.* xxiv. 27.

15th. The Words of the Kings of Israel

But the rest of the acts of Manasses, and his prayer to his God, and the words of the seers that spoke to him in the name of the Lord the God of Israel, are contained in the words of the kings of Israel.—2 *Paral.* xxxiii. 18.

¹Also in 2 *Paral.* xxv. 26 ; xxviii. 26 ; xxxii. 32 ; xxxv. 26, 27 ; xxxvi. 8.

16th. The Words of Jehu, the Son of Hanani

But the rest of the acts of Josaphat, first and last, are written in the words of Jehu the son of Hanani, which he digested into the books of the kings of Israel.—2 *Paral.* xx. 34.

17th. The History of Ozias, by Isaias, the Son of Amos, the Prophet

But the rest of the acts of Ozias first and last were written by Isaias the son of Amos, the prophet.—2 *Paral.* xxvi. 22.

18th. The Words of Hozai

His (Manasses') prayer also, and his being heard, and all his sins, and contempt, and places wherein he built high places, and set up groves, and statues before he did penance, are written in the words of Hozai.—2 *Paral.* xxxiii. 19.

19th. The Books of the Medes and of the Persians

And king Assuerus made all the land, and all the islands of the sea tributary.

And his strength and his empire, and the dignity and greatness wherewith he exalted Mardochai, are written in the books of the Medes, and of the Persians. —*Esther* x. 1, 2.

20th. The Book of the Days of the Priesthood of John

And as concerning the rest of the acts of John, and his wars, and the worthy deeds, which he bravely achieved, and the building of the walls, which he made, and the things that he did:

Behold these are written in the book of the days of his priesthood, from the time that he was made high priest after his father.—1 *Mach.* xvi. 23, 24.

21st. The Descriptions of Jeremias, the Prophet

Now it is found in the descriptions of Jeremias the prophet, that he commanded them that went into captivity, to take the fire, as it hath been signified, and how he gave charge to them that were carried away into captivity. . . .

It was also contained in the same writing, how the prophet, being warned by God, commanded that the tabernacle and the ark should accompany him, till he came forth to the mountain where Moses went up, and saw the inheritance of God.

And when Jeremias came thither he found a hollow cave: and he carried in thither the tabernacle, and the ark, and the altar of incense, and so stopped the door.

Then some of them that followed him, came up to mark the place: but they could not find it.—2 *Mach.* ii. 1, 4-6.

22d. The Memoirs and Commentaries of Nehemias

And these same things were set down in the memoirs and commentaries of Nehemias: and how he made a library, and gathered together out of the countries, the books both of the prophets, and of David, and the epistles of the kings, and concerning the holy gifts.— 2 *Mach.* ii. 13.

23d. The Five Books by Jason of Cyrene

Now as concerning Judas Machabeus, and his brethren, and the purification of the great temple, and the dedication of the altar:

As also the wars against Antiochus the Illustrious, and his son Eupator:

And the manifestations that came from heaven to them, that behaved themselves manfully on the behalf of the Jews, so that, being but a few, they made themselves masters of the whole country, and put to flight the barbarous multitude:

And recovered again the most renowned temple in all the world, and delivered the city, and restored the laws that were abolished, the Lord with all clemency showing mercy to them.

And all such things as have been comprised in five books by Jason of Cyrene, we have attempted to abridge in one book.—2 *Mach.* ii. 20-24.

24th. A Former Epistle of Paul to the Corinthians

I wrote to you in an epistle, not to keep company with fornicators.

I mean not with the fornicators of this world, or with the covetous, or the extortioners, or the servers of idols; otherwise you must needs go out of this world.—1 *Cor.* v. 9, 10.

25th. The Epistle of Paul to the Laodiceans

Salute the brethren who are at Laodicea, and Nymphas, and the church that is in his house.

And when this epistle shall have been read with you, cause that it be read also in the church of the Laodiceans: and that you read that which is of the Laodiceans.—*Col.* iv. 15, 16.

26th. The Prophecy of Enoch

Now of these Enoch also, the seventh from Adam, prophesied, saying: Behold, the Lord cometh with thousands of his saints,

To execute judgment upon all, and to reprove all the ungodly for all the works of their ungodliness, whereby they have done ungodly, and of all the hard things which ungodly sinners have spoken against God.—*Jude* i. 14, 15.

EXAMPLES OF GOD'S SEVERITY IN PUNISHING SIN AND REBELLION

For thus saith the Lord of hosts: As I purposed to afflict you, when your fathers had provoked me to wrath, saith the Lord,

And I had no mercy: so turning again I have thought in these days to do good to the house of Juda, and Jerusalem: fear not.—*Za^h.* viii. 14, 15.

1st. The Rebel Angels

For if God spared not the angels that sinned, but delivered them, drawn down by infernal ropes to the lower hell, unto torments, to be reserved unto judgment. —2 *Peter* ii. 4.

And the angels who kept not their principality, but forsook their own habitation, he hath reserved under darkness in everlasting chains, unto the judgment of the great day.—*Jude* i. 6.

And he (the Lord) said to them: I saw Satan like lightning falling from heaven.—*Luke* x. 18.

And there was a great battle in

heaven, Michael and his angels fought with the dragon, and the dragon fought and his angels:

And they prevailed not, neither was their place found any more in heaven.

And that great dragon was cast out, that old serpent, who is called the devil and Satan, who seduceth the whole world; and he was cast unto the earth, and his angels were thrown down with him.—*Apoc.* xii. 7-9.

2d. Adam and Eve

To the woman also he said: I will multiply thy sorrows, and thy conceptions: in sorrow shalt thou bring forth children, and thou shalt be under thy husband's power, and he shall have dominion over thee.

And to Adam he said: Because thou hast hearkened to the voice of thy wife, and hast eaten of the tree, whereof I commanded thee that thou shouldst not eat, cursed is the earth in thy work; with labor and toil shalt thou eat thereof all the days of thy life.

Thorns and thistles shall it bring forth to thee; and thou shalt eat the herbs of the earth.

In the sweat of thy face shalt thou eat bread till thou return to the earth, out of which thou wast taken: for dust thou art, and into dust thou shalt return.—*Gen.* iii. 16-19.

3d. The Flood

And God seeing that the wickedness of men was great on the earth, and that all the thought of their heart was bent upon evil at all times,

It repented him that he had made man on the earth. And being touched inwardly with sorrow of heart,

He said: I will destroy man, whom I have created, from the face of the earth, from man even to beasts, from the creeping thing even to the fowls of the air, for it repenteth me that I have made them.

. . . Behold I will bring the waters of a great flood upon the earth, to destroy all flesh, wherein is the breath of life, under heaven. All things that are in the earth shall be consumed. . . .

In the six hundredth year of the life of Noe, in the second month, in the seventeenth day of the month, all the fountains of the great deep were broken up, and the flood gates of heaven were opened:

And the rain fell upon the earth forty days and forty nights. . . .

And the waters prevailed beyond measure upon the earth: and all the high mountains under the whole heaven were covered. . . .

And all flesh was destroyed that moved upon the earth, both of fowl, and of cattle, and of beasts, and of all creeping things that creep upon the earth: and all men.

And all things wherein there is the breath of life on the earth, died. . . .

And Noe only remained, and they that were with him in the ark.—*Gen.* vi. 5-7, 17; vii. 11, 12, 19, 21-23.

4th. Sodom and Gomorrha

And the Lord said: The cry of Sodom and Gomorrha is multiplied, and their sin is become exceedingly grievous.

I will go down and see whether they have done according to the cry that is come to me: or whether it be not so, that I may know. . . .

And the Lord rained upon Sodom and Gomorrha brimstone and fire from the Lord out of heaven.

And he destroyed these cities, and all the country about, all the inhabitants of the cities, and all things that spring from the earth. . . .

And Abraham got up early in the morning, and in the place where he had stood before with the Lord,

He looked towards Sodom and Gomorrha, and the whole land of that country: and he saw the ashes rise up from the earth as the smoke of a furnace.—*Gen.* xviii. 20, 21; xix. 24, 25, 27, 28.

She (wisdom) delivered the just man who fled from the wicked that were perishing, when the fire came down upon [1]Pentapolis:

Whose land for a testimony of their wickedness is desolate, and smoketh to this day, and the trees bear fruits that ripen not, and a standing pillar of salt

[1]Pentapolis: that is, the land of the five cities, Sodom, Gomorrha, etc.

is a monument of an incredulous soul. —*Wis.* x. 6, 7.

And reducing the cities of the Sodomites, and of the Gomorrhites, into ashes, condemned them to be overthrown, making them an example to those that should after act wickedly.—*2 Peter* ii. 6.

As Sodom and Gomorrha, and the neighboring cities, in like manner, having given themselves to fornication, and going after other flesh, were made an example, suffering the punishment of eternal fire.—*Jude* i. 7.

5th. Lot's Wife

And they (the angels) brought him forth, and set him without the city: and there they spoke to him, saying: Save thy life: look not back, neither stay thou in all the country about: but save thyself in the mountain, lest thou be also consumed. . . .

And his wife looking behind her, was turned into a statue of salt.—*Gen.* xix. 17, 26.

6th. Onan

Juda therefore said to Onan his son: Go in to thy brother's wife and marry her, that thou mayst raise seed to thy brother.

He knowing that the children should not be his, when he went in to his brother's wife, spilled his seed upon the ground, lest children should be born in his brother's name.

And therefore the Lord slew him, because he did a detestable thing.—*Gen.* xxxviii. 8-10.

7th. Pharao and the Egyptians

After these things Moses and Aaron went in, and said to Pharao: Thus saith the Lord God of Israel: Let my people go that they may sacrifice to me in the desert.

But he answered: Who is the Lord, that I should hear his voice, and let Israel go? I know not the Lord, neither will I let Israel go. . . .

And the children of Israel went in through the midst of the sea dried up; for the water was as a wall on their right hand and on their left.

And the Egyptians pursuing went in after them, and all Pharao's horses, his chariots and horsemen through the midst of the sea.

And now the morning watch was come, and behold the Lord looking upon the Egyptian army through the pillar of fire and of the cloud, slew their host.

And overthrew the wheels of the chariots, and they were carried into the deep. And the Egyptians said: Let us flee from Israel: for the Lord fighteth for them against us.

And the Lord said to Moses: Stretch forth thy hand over the sea, that the waters may come again upon the Egyptians, upon their chariots and horsemen.

And when Moses had stretched forth his hand towards the sea, it returned at the first break of day to the former place: and as the Egyptians were fleeing away, the waters came upon them, and the Lord shut them up in the middle of the waves.

And the waters returned, and covered the chariots and the horsemen of all the army of Pharao, who had come into the sea after them, neither did there so much as one of them remain.—*Ex.* v. 1, 2; xiv. 22-28.

8th. The Idolatrous Jews

And the people seeing that Moses delayed to come down from the mount, gathering together against Aaron, said: Arise, make us gods, that may go before us: for as to this Moses, the man that brought us out of the land of Egypt, we know not what has befallen him.

And Aaron said to them: Take the golden earrings from the ears of your wives, and your sons and daughters, and bring them to me.

And the people did what he had commanded, bringing the earrings to Aaron.

And when he had received them, he fashioned them by founders' work, and made of them a molten calf. And they said: These are thy gods, O Israel, that have brought thee out of the land of Egypt. . . .

And rising in the morning, they offered holocausts, and peace victims, and the people sat down to eat, and drink, and they rose up to play.

And the Lord spoke to Moses, saying: Go, get thee down: thy people, which thou hast brought out of the land of Egypt, hath sinned. . . .

Then standing in the gate of the camp, he (Moses) said: If any man be on the Lord's side, let him join with me. And all the sons of Levi gathered themselves together unto him.

And he said to them: Thus saith the Lord God of Israel: Put every man his sword upon his thigh: go, and return from gate to gate through the midst of the camp, and let every man kill his brother, and friend, and neighbor.

And the sons of Levi did according to the words of Moses, and there were slain that day about three and twenty thousand men.—*Ex.* xxxii. 1-4, 6, 7, 26-28.

9th. Nadab and Abiu

And Nadab and Abiu, the sons of Aaron, taking their censers, put fire therein, and incense on it, offering before the Lord strange fire: which was not commanded them.

And fire coming out from the Lord destroyed them, and they died before the Lord.—*Lev.* x. 1, 2.

10th. The Murmuring of the Jews

A. In the meantime there arose a murmuring of the people against the Lord, as it were repining at their fatigue. And when the Lord heard it he was angry. And the fire of the Lord being kindled against them, devoured them that were at the uttermost part of the camp.—*Num.* xi. 1.

B. For a mixed multitude of people, that came up with them, burned with desire, sitting and weeping, the children of Israel also being joined with them, and said: Who shall give us flesh to eat?

We remember the fish that we ate in Egypt free cost: the cucumbers come into our mind, and the melons, and the leeks, and the onions, and the garlic.

Our soul is dry, our eyes behold nothing else but manna. . . .

Now Moses heard the people weeping by their families, every one at the door of his tent. And the wrath of the Lord was exceedingly enkindled: to Moses also the thing seemed insupportable. . . .

The people therefore rising up all that day, and night, and the next day, gathered together of quails, he that did least, ten cores: and they dried them round about the camp.

As yet the flesh was between their teeth, neither had that kind of meat failed: when behold the wrath of the Lord being provoked against the people, struck them with an exceeding great plague.—*Num.* xi. 4-6, 10, 32, 33.

C. And there the Lord spoke to Moses, saying:

Send men to view the land of Chanaan, which I will give to the children of Israel, one of every tribe, of the rulers. . . .

And they spoke ill of the land, which they had viewed, before the children of Israel, saying: The land which we have viewed, devoureth its inhabitants: the people, that we beheld, are of a tall stature. . . .

Therefore the whole multitude crying wept that night.

And all the children of Israel murmured against Moses and Aaron. . . .

And the Lord spoke to Moses and Aaron, saying:

How long doth this wicked multitude murmur against me? I have heard the murmurings of the children of Israel.

Say therefore to them: As I live, saith the Lord: According as you have spoken in my hearing, so will I do to you.

In the wilderness shall your carcasses lie. All you that were numbered from twenty years old and upward, and have murmured against me,

Shall not enter into the land, over which I lifted up my hand to make you dwell therein, except Caleb the son of Jephone, and Josue the son of Nun.

. . . Therefore all the men, whom Moses had sent to view the land, and who at their return had made the whole multitude to murmur against him, speaking ill of the land that it was naught,

Died, and were struck in the sight of the Lord.—*Num.* xiii. 2, 3, 33; xiv. 1, 2, 26-30, 36, 37.

D. The following day all the multitude of the children of Israel murmured against Moses and Aaron, saying: You have killed the people of the Lord.

And when there arose a sedition, and the tumult increased, Moses and Aaron fled to the tabernacle of the covenant. And when they were gone into it, the cloud covered it, and the glory of the Lord appeared.

And the Lord said to Moses: Get you out from the midst of this multitude, this moment will I destroy them. . . .

And the number of them that were slain was fourteen thousand and seven hundred men, besides them that had perished in the sedition of Core.—*Num.* xvi. 41-45, 49.

E. And they marched from mount Hor, by the way that leadeth to the Red Sea, to compass the land of Edom. And the people began to be weary of their journey and labor:

And speaking against God and Moses, they said: Why didst thou bring us out of Egypt, to die in the wilderness? There is no bread, nor have we any waters: our soul now loatheth this very light food.

Wherefore the Lord sent among the people fiery serpents, which bit them and killed many of them.—*Num.* xxi. 4-6.

11th. The Rebellion of Core

And behold Core the son of Isaar, the son of Caath, the son of Levi, and Dathan and Abiron the sons of Eliab, and Hon the son of Pheleth of the children of Ruben,

Rose up against Moses, and with them two hundred and fifty others of the children of Israel, leading men of the synagogue, and who in the time of assembly were called by name. . . .

And the Lord said to Moses:

Command the whole people to separate themselves from the tents of Core and Dathan and Abiron.

And Moses arose, and went to Dathan and Abiron: and the ancients of Israel following him,

He said to the multitude: Depart from the tents of these wicked men, and touch nothing of theirs, lest you be involved in their sins.

And when they were departed from their tents round about, Dathan and Abiron coming out stood in the entry of their pavilions with their wives and children, and all the people.

And Moses said: By this you shall know that the Lord hath sent me to do all things that you see, and that I have not forged them of my own head:

If these men die the common death of men, and if they be visited with a plague, wherewith others also are wont to be visited, the Lord did not send me.

But if the Lord do a new thing, and the earth opening her mouth swallow them down, and all things that belong to them, and they go down alive into hell, you shall know that they have blasphemed the Lord.

And immediately as he had made an end of speaking, the earth broke asunder under their feet:

And opening her mouth, devoured them with their tents and all their substance.

And they went down alive into hell, the ground closing upon them, and they perished from among the people.

But all Israel, that was standing round about, fled at the cry of them that were perishing: saying: Lest perhaps the earth swallow us up alive.

And a fire coming out from the Lord, destroyed the two hundred and fifty men that offered the incense.—*Num.* xvi. 1, 2, 23-35.

And strangers stood up against him (Moses), and through envy the men that were with Dathan and Abiron, compassed him about in the wilderness, and the congregation of Core in their wrath.

The Lord saw and it pleased him not, and they were consumed in his wrathful indignation.

He wrought wonders upon them, and consumed them with a flame of fire.—*Ecclus.* xlv. 22-24.

12th. The Disobedience of Achan

And let this city (Jericho) be an anathema, and all things that are in it, to the Lord. . . .

But beware ye lest you touch ought of those things that are forbidden, and you be guilty of transgression, and all the camp of Israel be under sin, and be troubled. . . .

But the children of Israel transgressed the commandment, and took to their own use of the anathema. For Achan the son of Charmi, the son of Zabdi, the son of Zare of the tribe of Juda, took something of the anathema: and the Lord was angry against the children of Israel. . . .

And the Lord said to Josue: Arise, why liest thou flat on the ground?

Israel hath sinned, and transgressed my covenant: and they have taken of the anathema, and have stolen and lied, and have hidden it among their goods.

Neither can Israel stand before his enemies, but he shall flee from them: because he is defiled with the anathema. I will be no more with you, till you destroy him that is guilty of this wickedness.

. . . And whosoever he be that shall be found guilty of this fact, he shall be burnt with fire with all his substance, because he hath transgressed the covenant of the Lord, and hath done wickedness in Israel.

. . . Then Josue and all Israel with him took Achan the son of Zare, and the silver and the garments, and the golden rule, his sons also and his daughters, his oxen and asses and sheep, the tent also, and all the goods: and brought them to the valley of Achor:

Where Josue said: Because thou hast troubled us, the Lord trouble thee this day. And all Israel stoned him: and all things that were his, were consumed with fire.—*Jos.* vi. 17, 18; vii. 1, 10-12, 15, 24, 25.

13th Heli

And the Lord said to Samuel: Behold I do a thing in Israel: and whosoever shall hear it, both his ears shall tingle.

In that day I will raise up against Heli all the things I have spoken concerning his house: I will begin, and I will make an end.

For I have foretold unto him, that I will judge his house for ever, for iniquity, because he knew that his sons

did wickedly, and did not chastise them. . . .

So the Philistines fought, and Israel was overthrown, and every man fled to his own dwelling: and there was an exceeding great slaughter; for there fell of Israel thirty thousand footmen.

And the ark of God was taken: and the two sons of Heli, Ophni and Phinees, were slain. . . .

Now Heli was ninety and eight years old, and his eyes were dim, and he could not see. . . .

And he that brought the news answered, and said: Israel has fled before the Philistines, and there has been a great slaughter of the people: moreover thy two sons, Ophni and Phinees, are dead: and the ark of God is taken.

And when he had named the ark of God, he fell from his stool backwards by the door, and broke his neck, and died. For he was an old man, far advanced in years: and he judged Israel forty years.—1 *Kings* iii. 11-13; iv. 10, 11, 15, 17, 18.

14th. Saul

And Samuel said: Why askest thou me, seeing the Lord has departed from thee, and is gone over to thy rival:

For the Lord will do to thee as he spoke by me, and he will rend thy kingdom out of thy hand, and will give it to thy neighbor David:

Because thou didst not obey the voice of the Lord, neither didst thou execute the wrath of his indignation upon Amalec. Therefore hath the Lord done to thee what thou sufferest this day. And the Lord also will deliver Israel with thee into the hands of the Philistines: and to-morrow thou and thy sons shall be with me: and the Lord will also deliver the army of Israel into the hands of the Philistines.

. . . And the Philistines fought against Israel, and the men of Israel fled from before the Philistines, and fell down slain in mount Gelboe.

And the Philistines fell upon Saul, and upon his sons, and they slew Jonathan, and Abinadab and Melchisua the sons of Saul. . . .

Then Saul took his sword, and fell upon it. . . .

So Saul died, and his three sons, and his armor bearer, and all his men that same day together.—1 *Kings* xxviii. 16-19; xxxi. 1, 2, 4, 6.

15th. Oza

And when they came to the floor of Nachon, Oza put forth his hand to the ark of God, and took hold of it: because the oxen kicked, and made it lean aside.

And the indignation of the Lord was enkindled against Oza, and he struck him for his rashness: and he died there before the ark of God.—2 *Kings* vi. 6, 7.

16th. David

A. Why therefore hast thou despised the word of the Lord, to do evil in my sight? Thou hast killed Urias the Hethite with the sword, and hast taken his wife to be thy wife, and hast slain him with the sword of the children of Ammon.

Therefore the sword shall never depart from thy house, because thou hast despised me, and hast taken the wife of Urias the Hethite to be thy wife. . . .

And David said to Nathan: I have sinned against the Lord. And Nathan said to David: The Lord also hath taken away thy sin: thou shalt not die.

Nevertheless, because thou hast given occasion to the enemies of the Lord to blaspheme, for this thing, the child that is born to thee, shall surely die.— 2 *Kings* xii. 9, 10, 13, 14.

B. And Satan rose up against Israel: and moved David to number Israel.

And David said to Joab, and to the rulers of the people: Go, and number Israel from Bersabee even to Dan, and bring me the number of them that I may know it. . . .

And God was displeased with this thing that was commanded: and he struck Israel. . . .

So the Lord sent a pestilence upon Israel. And there fell of Israel seventy thousand men.—1 *Paral.* xxi. 1, 2, 7, 14.

17th. Jerusalem and Juda

For Jerusalem is ruined, and Juda is fallen: because their tongue, and their devices are against the Lord, to provoke the eyes of his majesty.—*Is.* iii. 8.

18th. Nabuchodonosor

At the end of twelve months he was walking in the palace of Babylon.

And the king answered, and said: Is not this the great Babylon, which I have built to be the seat of the kingdom, by the strength of my power, and in the glory of my excellence?

And while the word was yet in the king's mouth, a voice came down from heaven: To thee, O king Nabuchodonosor, it is said: Thy kingdom shall pass from thee,

And they shall cast thee out from among men, and thy dwelling shall be with cattle and wild beasts: thou shalt eat grass like an ox, and seven times shall pass over thee, till thou know that the most High ruleth in the kingdom of men, and giveth it to whomsoever he will.

The same hour the word was fulfilled upon Nabuchodonosor, and he was driven away from among men, and did eat grass like an ox, and his body was wet with the dew of heaven: till his hairs grew like the feathers of eagles, and his nails like bird's claws.—*Dan.* iv. 26-30.

19th. Antiochus

At that time Antiochus returned with dishonor out of Persia. . . .

And swelling with anger he thought to revenge upon the Jews the injury done by them that had put him to flight. And therefore he commanded his chariot to be driven, without stopping in his journey, the judgment of heaven urging him forward, because he had spoken so proudly, that he would come to Jerusalem, and make it a common burying place of the Jews.

But the Lord the God of Israel, that seeth all things, struck him with an incurable and an invisible plague. For as soon as he had ended these words, a dreadful pain in his bowels came upon him, and bitter torments of the inner parts.

And indeed very justly, seeing he had tormented the bowels of others with many and new torments, albeit he by no means ceased from his malice.

Moreover being filled with pride, breathing out fire in his rage against the Jews, and commanding the matter to be hastened, it happened as he was going with violence that he fell from the chariot, so that his limbs were much pained by a grievous bruising of the body.

Thus he that seemed to himself to command even the waves of the sea, being proud above the condition of man, and to weigh the heights of the mountains in a balance, now being cast down to the ground, was carried in a litter, bearing witness to the manifest power of God in himself:

So that worms swarmed out of the body of this man, and whilst he lived in sorrow and pain, his flesh fell off, and the filthiness of his smell was noisome to the army.

And the man that thought a little before he could reach to the stars of heaven, no man could endure to carry, for the intolerable stench. . . .

Thus the murderer and blasphemer, being grievously struck, as himself had treated others, died a miserable death in a strange country among the mountains.—2 *Mach.* ix. 1, 4-10, 28.

20th. Judas

Then went one of the twelve, who was called Judas Iscariot, to the chief priests,

And said to them: What will you give me, and I will deliver him unto you? But they appointed him thirty pieces of silver.

And from thenceforth he sought opportunity to betray him. . . .

And whilst they were eating, he (Jesus) said: Amen I say to you, that one of you is about to betray me.

And they being very much troubled, began every one to say: Is it I, Lord?

But he answering, said: He that dippeth his hand with me in the dish, he shall betray me.

The Son of man indeed goeth, as it is written of him: but woe to that man by whom the Son of man shall be betrayed: it were better for him, if that man had not been born. . . .

Then Judas who betrayed him, seeing that he was condemned, repenting himself, brought back the thirty pieces of silver to the chief priests and ancients,

Saying: I have sinned in betraying innocent blood. But they said: What is that to us? look thou to it.

And casting down the pieces of silver in the temple, he departed: and went and hanged himself with an halter.— *Matt.* xxvi. 14-16, 21-24, xxvii. 3-5.

21st. Ananias and Saphira

But a certain man named Ananias, with Saphira his wife, sold a piece of land,

And by fraud kept back part of the price of the land, his wife being privy thereunto: and bringing a certain part of it, laid it at the feet of the apostles.

But Peter said: Ananias, why hath Satan tempted thy heart, that thou shouldst lie to the Holy Ghost, and by fraud keep part of the price of the land?

Whilst it remained, did it not remain to thee? and after it was sold, was it not in thy power? Why hast thou conceived this thing in thy heart? Thou hast not lied to men, but to God.

And Ananias hearing these words, fell down, and gave up the ghost. And there came great fear upon all that heard it.

And the young men rising up, removed him, and carrying him out, buried him.

And it was about the space of three hours after, when his wife, not knowing what had happened, came in.

And Peter said to her: Tell me, woman, whether you sold the land for so much? And she said: Yea, for so much.

And Peter said unto her: Why have you agreed together to tempt the Spirit of the Lord? Behold the feet of them who have buried thy husband are at the door, and they shall carry thee out.

Immediately she fell down before his feet, and gave up the ghost. And the young men coming in, found her dead: and carried her out, and buried her by her husband.—*Acts* v. 1-10.

22d. Herod Agrippa

And upon a day appointed, Herod being arrayed in kingly apparel, sat in the judgment seat, and made an oration to them.

And the people made acclamation, saying: It is the voice of a god, and not of a man.

And forthwith an angel of the Lord struck him, because he had not given the honor to God: and being eaten up by worms, he gave up the ghost.—*Acts* xii. 21-23.

EXAMPLES OF JUST MEN

Let us now praise men of renown, and our fathers in their generation.... But these were men of mercy, whose godly deeds have not failed.—*Ecclus.* xliv. 1, 10.

Henoch

And Henoch walked with God.... And all the days of Henoch were three hundred and sixty-five years.

And he walked with God, and was seen no more: because God took him.— *Gen.* v. 22-24.

Henoch pleased God, and was translated into paradise, that he may give repentance to the nations.—*Ecclus.* xliv. 16.

No man was born upon earth like Henoch: for he also was taken up from the earth.—*Ecclus.* xlix. 16.

By faith Henoch was translated, that he should not see death; and he was not found, because God had translated him: for before his translation he had testimony that he pleased God.—*Heb.* xi. 5.

Noe

But Noe found grace before the Lord.

These are the generations of Noe: Noe was a just and perfect man in his generations, he walked with God. —*Gen.* vi. 8, 9.

And the Lord said to him (Noe): Go in thou and all thy house into the ark: for thee I have seen just before me in this generation.—*Gen.* vii. 1.

Noe was found perfect, just, and in the time of wrath he was made a reconciliation.—*Ecclus.* xliv. 17.

Son of man, when a land shall sin against me, so as to transgress grievously, I will stretch forth my hand upon it, and will break the staff of the bread thereof: and I will send famine upon it, and will destroy man and beast out of it.

And if these three men, Noe, Daniel, and Job, shall be in it: they shall deliver their own souls by their justice, saith the Lord of hosts.—*Ezech.* xiv. 13, 14.

By faith Noe, having received an answer concerning those things which as yet were not seen, moved with fear, framed the ark for the saving of his house, by the which he condemned the world; and was instituted heir of the justice which is by faith.—*Heb.* xi. 7.

For if God spared not the angels that sinned: ...

And spared not the original world, but preserved Noe, the eighth person, the preacher of justice, bringing in the flood upon the world of the ungodly.— *2 Peter* ii. 4, 5.

Abraham

And the Lord said to Abram: Go forth out of thy country, and from thy kindred, and out of thy father's house, and come into the land which I shall show thee.

And I will make of thee a great nation, and I will bless thee, and magnify thy name, and thou shalt be blessed.

I will bless them that bless thee, and curse them that curse thee, and in thee shall all the kindred of the earth be blessed:

So Abram went out as the Lord had commanded him, and Lot went with him: Abram was seventy-five years old when he went forth from Haran.— *Gen.* xii. 1-4.

Thou, O Lord God, art he who chosest Abram, and broughtest him forth out of the fire of the Chaldeans, and gavest him the name of Abraham.

And thou didst find his heart faithful before thee.—*2 Esd.* ix. 7, 8.

They must remember how our father Abraham was tempted, and being proved by many tribulations, was made the friend of God.—*Judith* viii. 22.

Abraham was the great father of a multitude of nations, and there was not found the like to him in glory, who kept the law of the most High, and was in covenant with him.

In his flesh he established the covenant, and in temptation he was found faithful.—*Ecclus.* xliv. 20, 21.

Was not Abraham found faithful in temptation, and it was reputed to him unto justice?—1 *Mach.* ii. 52.

By faith he that is called Abraham, obeyed to go out into a place which he was to receive for an inheritance; and he went out, not knowing whither he went.

By faith he abode in the land, dwelling in cottages, with Isaac and Jacob, the co-heirs of the same promise.

For he looked for a city that hath foundations; whose builder and maker is God. . . .

For which cause there sprung even from one (and him as good as dead) as the stars of heaven in multitude, and as the sand which is by the sea shore innumerable. . . .

By faith Abraham, when he was tried, offered Isaac: and he that had received the promises, offered up his only begotten son;

(To whom it was said: In Isaac shall thy seed be called.)

Accounting that God is able to raise up even from the dead. Whereupon also he received him for a parable.—*Heb.* xi. 8-10, 12, 17-19.

Isaac

And the Lord appeared to him (Isaac) and said: Go not down into Egypt, but stay in the land that I shall tell thee.

And sojourn in it, and I will be with thee, and will bless thee: for to thee and to thy seed I will give all these countries, to fulfil the oath which I swore to Abraham thy father.

And I will multiply thy seed like the stars of heaven: and I will give to thy posterity all these countries: and in thy seed shall all the nations of the earth be blessed.—*Gen.* xxvi. 2-4.

And he (God) did in like manner with Isaac for the sake of Abraham his father.

The Lord gave him the blessing of all nations, and confirmed his covenant upon the head of Jacob.—*Ecclus.* xliv. 24, 25.

By faith also of things to come, Isaac blessed Jacob and Esau.—*Heb.* xi. 20.

Jacob

And he (Jacob) saw in his sleep a ladder standing upon the earth, and the top thereof touching heaven: the angels also of God ascending and descending by it;

And the Lord leaning upon the ladder, saying to him: I am the Lord God of Abraham thy father, and the God of Isaac; the land, wherein thou sleepest, I will give to thee and to thy seed.

And thy seed shall be as the dust of the earth: thou shalt spread abroad to the west, and to the east, and to the north, and to the south: and in thee and thy seed all the tribes of the earth shall be blessed.

And I will be thy keeper whithersoever thou goest, and will bring thee back into this land: neither will I leave thee, till I shall have accomplished all that I have said.—*Gen.* xxviii. 12-15.

And he (the angel) said: What is thy name? He answered: Jacob.

But he said: Thy name shall not be called Jacob, but Israel: for if thou hast been strong against God, how much more shalt thou prevail against men?—*Gen.* xxxii. 27, 28.

She (wisdom) conducted the just, when he fled from his brother's wrath, through the right ways, and showed him the kingdom of God, and gave him the knowledge of the holy things, made him honorable in his labors, and accomplished his labors.—*Wis.* x. 10.

The Lord gave him (Isaac) the blessing of all nations, and confirmed his covenant upon the head of Jacob.

He acknowledged him in his blessings, and gave him an inheritance, and divided him his portion in twelve tribes.—*Ecclus.* xliv. 25, 26.

By faith Jacob dying, blessed each of

the sons of Joseph, and [1]adored the top of his rod.—*Heb.* xi. 21.

Joseph

And Joseph was brought into Egypt, and Putiphar an eunuch of Pharao, chief captain of the army, an Egyptian, bought him of the Ismaelites, by whom he was brought.

And the Lord was with him, and he was a prosperous man in all things: and he dwelt in his master's house,

Who knew very well that the Lord was with him, and made all that he did to prosper in his hand. . . .

But the Lord was with Joseph, and having mercy upon him gave him favor in the sight of the chief keeper of the prison. . . .

Neither did he himself know any thing, having committed all things to him: for the Lord was with him, and made all that he did to prosper.—*Gen.* xxxix. 1-3, 21, 23.

And he said to his brethren: I am Joseph: is my father yet living? His brethren could not answer him, being struck with exceeding great fear.

And he said mildly to them: Come nearer to me. And when they were come near him, he said: I am Joseph, your brother, whom you sold into Egypt.

Be not afraid, and let it not seem to you a hard case, that you sold me into these countries: for God sent me before you into Egypt, for your preservation.

For it is two years since the famine began to be upon the land, and five years more remain, wherein there can be neither plowing nor reaping.

And God sent me before, that you may be preserved upon the earth, and may have food to live.

Not by your counsel was I sent hither, but by the will of God: who hath made me as it were a father to Pharao, and lord of his whole house, and governor in all the land of Egypt. —*Gen.* xlv. 3-8.

Joseph is a growing son, a growing

[1]In *Gen.* xlvii. 31. And as he (Joseph) was swearing, Israel adored God, turning to the bed's head.

son and comely to behold; the daughters run to and fro upon the wall. . . .

His bow rested upon the strong, and the bands of his arms and his hands were loosed, by the hands of the mighty one of Jacob: thence he came forth a pastor, the stone of Israel.

The God of thy father shall be thy helper, and the Almighty shall bless thee with the blessings of heaven above, with the blessings of the deep that lieth beneath, with the blessings of the breasts and of the womb.

The blessings of thy father are strengthened with the blessings of his fathers: until the desire of the everlasting hills should come; may they be upon the head of Joseph, and upon the crown of the Nazarite among his brethren.—*Gen.* xlix. 22, 24-26.

No man was born upon earth like Henoch.

. . . Nor as Joseph, who was a man born prince of his brethren, the support of his family, the ruler of his brethren, the stay of the people.—*Ecclus.* xlix. 16, 17.

Joseph in the time of his distress kept the commandment, and he was made lord of Egypt.—1 *Mach.* ii. 53.

And the patriarchs, through envy, sold Joseph into Egypt; and God was with him,

And delivered him out of all his tribulations: and he gave him favor and wisdom in the sight of Pharao, the king of Egypt; and he appointed him governor over Egypt, and over all his house.—*Acts* vii. 9, 10.

By faith Joseph, when he was dying, made mention of the going out of the children of Israel; and gave commandment concerning his bones.—*Heb.* xi. 22.

Moses

For Moses was a man exceeding meek above all men that dwelt upon earth.— *Num.* xii. 3.

The Lord came down in a pillar of the cloud, and stood in the entry of the tabernacle calling to Aaron and Mary. And when they were come,

He said to them: Hear my words: if there be among you a prophet of the

Lord, I will appear to him in a vision, or I will speak to him in a dream.

But it is not so with my servant Moses, who is most faithful in all my house:

For I speak to him mouth to mouth: and plainly, and not by riddles and figures doth he see the Lord. Why then were you not afraid to speak ill of my servant Moses?—*Num.* xii. 5-8.

And Moses called all Israel, and said to them. . . .

The Lord our God made a covenant with us in Horeb. . . .

I was the mediator and stood between the Lord and you at that time, to show you his words, for you feared the fire, and went not up into the mountain.—*Deut.* v. 1, 2, 5.

And there arose no more a prophet in Israel like unto Moses, whom the Lord knew face to face.—*Deut.* xxxiv. 10.

Moses and Aaron among his priests: and Samuel among them that call upon his name.

They called upon the Lord, and he heard them: he spoke to them in the pillar of the cloud.

They kept his testimonies, and the commandment which he gave them.

Thou didst hear them, O Lord our God: thou wast a merciful God to them.—*Ps.* xcviii. 6-8.

Moses was beloved of God, and men: whose memory is in benediction.

He made him like the saints in glory, and magnified him in the fear of his enemies, and with his words he made prodigies to cease.

He glorified him in the sight of kings, and gave him commandments in the sight of his people, and showed him his glory.

He sanctified him in his faith, and meekness, and chose him out of all flesh.—*Ecclus.* xlv. 1-4.

At the same time was Moses born, and he was acceptable to God. . . .

And Moses was instructed in all the wisdom of the Egyptians: and he was mighty in his words and in his deeds.—*Acts* vii. 20, 22.

And Moses indeed was faithful in all his house as a servant, for a testimony of those things which were to be said.—*Heb.* iii. 5.

By faith Moses, when he was grown up, denied himself to be the son of Pharao's daughter;

Rather choosing to be afflicted with the people of God, than to have the pleasure of sin for a time,

Esteeming the reproach of Christ greater riches than the treasure of the Egyptians. For he looked unto the reward.

By faith he left Egypt, not fearing the fierceness of the king: for he endured as seeing him that is invisible.

By faith he celebrated the pasch, and the shedding of the blood; that he, who destroyed the first born, might not touch them.—*Heb.* xi. 24-28.

Aaron

The Lord being angry at Moses, said: Aaron the Levite is thy brother, I know that he is eloquent: behold he cometh forth to meet thee, and seeing thee shall be glad at heart.

Speak to him, and put my words in his mouth: and I will be in thy mouth, and in his mouth, and will show you what you must do.

He shall speak in thy stead to the people, and shall be thy mouth: but thou shalt be to him in those things that pertain to God.—*Ex.* iv. 14-16.

Moses said to Aaron: Take the censer, and putting fire in it from the altar, put incense upon it, and go quickly to the people to pray for them: for already wrath is gone out from the Lord, and the plague rageth.

When Aaron had done this, and had run to the midst of the multitude which the burning fire was now destroying, he offered the incense:

And standing between the dead and the living, he prayed for the people, and the plague ceased.—*Num.* xvi. 46-48.

And the Lord spoke to Moses, saying:

Speak to the children of Israel, and take of every one of them a rod by their kindreds, of all the princes of the tribes, twelve rods, and write the name of every man upon his rod. . . .

Whomsoever of these I shall choose, his rod shall blossom: and I will make to cease from me the murmurings of the children of Israel, wherewith they murmur against you. . . .

He (Moses) returned on the following day, and found that the rod of Aaron for the house of Levi, was budded: and that the buds swelling it had bloomed blossoms, which spreading the leaves, were formed into almonds.—*Num.* xvii. 1, 2, 5, 8.

And the Lord said to Aaron: You shall possess nothing in their land, neither shall you have a portion among them: I am thy portion and inheritance in the midst of the children of Israel. —*Num.* xviii. 20.

Moses and Aaron among his priests: and Samuel among them that call upon his name.

They called upon the Lord, and he heard them: he spoke to them in the pillar of the cloud.

They kept his testimonies, and the commandment which he gave them. Thou didst hear them, O Lord our God: thou wast merciful to them.—*Ps.* xcviii. 6-8.

But the just also were afterwards touched by an assault of death, and there was a disturbance of the multitude in the wilderness: but thy wrath did not long continue.

For a blameless man made haste to pray for the people, bringing forth the shield of his ministry, prayer, and by incense making supplication, withstood the wrath, and put an end to the calamity, showing that he was thy servant.—*Wis.* xviii. 20, 21.

He (God) exalted Aaron his brother, and like to himself of the tribe of Levi:

He made an everlasting covenant with him, and gave him the priesthood of the nation, and made him blessed in glory. . . .

He chose him out of all men living, to offer sacrifice to God, incense, and a good savor, for a memorial to make reconciliation for his people.—*Ecclus.* xlv. 7, 8, 20.

Phinees

And the Lord said to Moses:

Phinees the son of Eleazar the son of Aaron the priest, hath turned away my wrath from the children of Israel: because he was moved with my zeal against them, that I myself might not destroy the children of Israel in my zeal.

Therefore say to him: Behold I give him the peace of my covenant,

And the covenant of the priesthood for ever shall be both to him and his seed, because he hath been zealous for his God, and hath made atonement for the wickedness of the children of Israel. —*Num.* xxv. 10-13.

And they provoked him with their inventions: and destruction was multiplied among them.

Then Phinees stood up, and pacified him: and the slaughter ceased.

And it was reputed to him unto justice, to generation and generation for evermore.—*Ps.* cv. 29-31.

Phinees the son of Eleazar is the third in glory, by imitating him in the fear of the Lord:

And he stood up in the shameful fall of the people: in the goodness and readiness of his soul he appeased God for Israel.

Therefore he made to him a covenant of peace, to be the prince of the sanctuary, and of his people, that the dignity of priesthood should be to him and to his seed for ever.—*Ecclus.* xlv. 28-30.

Phinees our father, by being fervent in the zeal of God, received the covenant of an everlasting priesthood.— 1 *Mach.* ii. 54.

Josue

And Moses answered him:

May the Lord the God of the spirits of all flesh provide a man that may be over this multitude. . . .

And the Lord said to him: Take Josue the son of Nun, a man in whom is the Spirit, and put thy hand upon him.

. . . And thou shalt give him precepts in the sight of all, and part of thy glory, that all the congregation of the children of Israel may hear him.— *Num.* xxvii. 15, 16, 18, 20.

Valiant in war was Jesus the son of Nave, who was successor of Moses among the prophets, who was great according to his name,

Very great for the saving the elect of God, to overthrow the enemies that rose up against them, that he might get the inheritance for Israel. . . .

And in the days of Moses he did a work of mercy, he and Caleb the son of Jephone, in standing against the enemy, and withholding the people from sins, and appeasing the wicked murmuring.—*Ecclus.* xlvi. 1, 2, 9.

Jesus, whilst he fulfilled the word, was made ruler in Israel.—1 *Mach.* ii. 55.

Caleb

In the meantime Caleb, to still the murmuring of the people that rose against Moses, said: Let us go up and possess the land, for we shall be able to conquer it.

But the others, that had been with him, said: No, we are not able to go up to this people, because they are stronger than we.—*Num.* xiii. 31, 32.

But Josue the son of Nun, and Caleb the son of Jephone, who themselves also had viewed the land, rent their garments,

And said to all the multitude of the children of Israel: The land which we have gone round is very good:

If the Lord be favorable, he will bring us into it, and give us a land flowing with milk and honey.

Be not rebellious against the Lord: and fear ye not the people of this land, for we are able to eat them up as bread. All aid is gone from them: the Lord is with us, fear ye not.—*Num.* xiv. 6-9.

But yet all the men that have seen my majesty, and the signs that I have done in Egypt, and in the wilderness, and have tempted me now ten times, and have not obeyed my voice,

Shall not see the land for which I swore to their fathers, neither shall any one of them that hath detracted me behold it.

My servant Caleb, who being full of another spirit hath followed me, I will bring into this land which he hath gone round: and his seed shall possess it.—*Num.* xiv. 22-24.

And in the days of Moses he (Josue) did a work of mercy, he and Caleb the son of Jephone, in standing against the enemy, and withholding the people from sins, and appeasing the wicked murmuring. . . .

And the Lord gave strength also to Caleb, and his strength continued even to his old age, so that he went up to the high places of the land, and his seed obtained it for an inheritance:

That all the children of Israel might see, that it is good to obey the holy God.—*Ecclus.* xlvi. 9, 11, 12.

Caleb, for bearing witness before the congregation, received an inheritance. —1 *Mach.* ii. 56.

Samuel

And the child Samuel became great before the Lord. . . .

But the child Samuel advanced, and grew on, and pleased both the Lord and men.—1 *Kings* ii. 21, 26.

And Samuel grew, and the Lord was with him, and not one of his words fell to the ground.

And all Israel from Dan to Bersabee, knew that Samuel was a faithful prophet of the Lord.—1 *Kings* iii. 19, 20.

And Samuel said to all Israel: . . .

Speak of me before the Lord, and before his anointed, whether I have taken any man's ox, or ass: If I have wronged any man, if I have oppressed any man, if I have taken a bribe at any man's hand: and I will despise it this day, and will restore it to you.

And they said: Thou hast not wronged us, nor oppressed us, nor taken ought at any man's hand.—1 *Kings* xii. 1, 3, 4.

And far from me be this sin against the Lord, that I should cease to pray for you, and I will teach you the good and right way.—1 *Kings* xii. 23.

Moses and Aaron among his priests: and Samuel among them that call upon his name.

They called upon the Lord, and he heard them: he spoke to them in the pillar of the cloud.

They kept his testimonies, and the

commandment which he gave them.—*Ps. xcviii.* 6, 7.

Samuel the prophet of the Lord, the beloved of the Lord his God, established a new government, and anointed princes over his people.

By the law of the Lord he judged the congregation, and the God of Jacob beheld, and by his fidelity he was proved a prophet.

And he was known to be faithful in his words, because he saw the God of light. . . .

And before the time of the end of his life in the world, he protested before the Lord, and his annointed: money, or any thing else, even to a shoe, he had not taken of any man, and no man did accuse him.—*Ecclus.* xlvi. 16-18, 22.

David

And David behaved wisely in all his ways, and the Lord was with him.—1 *Kings* xviii. 14.

Now these are David's last words. David the son of Isai said: The man to whom it was appointed concerning the Christ of the God of Jacob, the excellent psalmist of Israel said:

The spirit of the Lord hath spoken by me and his word by my tongue.—2 *Kings* xxiii. 1, 2.

And as the fat taken away from the flesh, so was David chosen from among the children of Israel. . . .

In all his works he gave thanks to the holy one, and to the most High, with words of glory.

With his whole heart he praised the Lord, and loved God that made him: and he gave him power against his enemies:

And he set singers before the altar, and by their voices he made sweet melody.

And to the festivals he added beauty, and set in order the solemn times even to the end of his life, that they should praise the holy name of the Lord, and magnify the holiness of God in the morning.

The Lord took away his sins, and exalted his horn for ever: and he gave him a covenant of the kingdom, and a throne of glory in Israel.—*Ecclus.* xlvii. 2, 9-13.

David by his mercy obtained the throne of an everlasting kingdom.—1 *Mach.* ii. 57.

And when he had removed him (Saul), he raised them up David to be king: to whom giving testimony, he said: I have found David, the son of Jesse, a man according to my own heart, who shall do all my wills.—*Acts* xiii. 22.

Elias

And Elias the prophet stood up, as a fire, and his word burnt like a torch.

. . . By the word of the Lord he shut up the heaven, and he brought down fire from heaven thrice.

Thus was Elias magnified in his wondrous works. And who can glory like to thee?

Who raisedst up a dead man from below, from the lot of death, by the word of the Lord God. . . .

Who wast taken up in a whirlwind of fire, in a chariot of fiery horses.

Who art registered in the judgments of times to appease the wrath of the Lord, to reconcile the heart of the father to the son, and to restore the tribes of Jacob.

Blessed are they that saw thee, and were honored with thy friendship.—*Ecclus.* xlviii. 1, 3-5, 9-11.

Behold I will send you Elias the prophet, before the coming of the great and dreadful day of the Lord.

And he shall turn the heart of the fathers to the children, and the heart of the children to their fathers: lest I come, and strike the earth with anathema.—*Malach.* iv. 5, 6.

Elias, while he was full of zeal for the law, was taken up into heaven.—1 *Mach.* ii. 58.

Elias was a man passible like unto us: and with prayer he prayed that it might not rain upon the earth, and it rained not for three years and six months.

And he prayed again: and the heaven gave rain, and the earth brought forth her fruit.—*James* v. 17, 18.

Eliseus

And when they were gone over, Elias said to Eliseus: Ask what thou wilt have me to do for thee, before I be taken away from thee. And Eliseus said: I beseech thee that in me may be thy double spirit.

And he answered: Thou hast asked a hard thing: nevertheless if thou see me when I am taken from thee, thou shalt have what thou hast asked: but if thou see me not, thou shalt not have it.—4 *Kings* ii. 9, 10.

Now Eliseus was sick of the illness whereof he died: and Joas king of Israel went down to him, and wept before him, and said: O my father, my father, the chariot of Israel and the guider thereof.—4 *Kings* xiii. 14.

Elias was indeed covered with the whirlwind, and his spirit was filled up in Eliseus: in his days he feared not the prince, and no man was more powerful than he.

No word could overcome him, and after death his body prophesied.

In his life he did great wonders, and in death he wrought miracles.—*Ecclus.* xlviii. 13-15.

Josias

Josias was eight years old when he began to reign: he reigned one and thirty years in Jerusalem. . . .

And he did that which was right in the sight of the Lord, and walked in all the ways of David his father: he turned not aside to the right hand, or to the left.—4 *Kings* xxii. 1, 2.

There was no king before him like unto him, that returned to the Lord with all his heart, and with all his soul, and with all his strength, according to all the law of Moses: neither after him did there arise any like him.— 4 *Kings* xxiii. 25.

The memory of Josias is like the composition of a sweet smell made by the art of a perfumer:

His remembrance shall be sweet as honey in every mouth, and as music at a banquet of wine.

He was directed by God unto the repentance of the nation, and he took away the abominations of wickedness.

And he directed his heart towards the Lord, and in the days of sinners he strengthened godliness.

Except David, and Ezechias, and Josias, all committed sin.—*Ecclus.* xlix. 1-5.

Isaias

He (God) was not mindful of their sins, neither did he deliver them up to their enemies, but he purified them by the hand of Isaias, the holy prophet. . . .

For Ezechias did that which pleased God, and walked valiantly in the way of David his father, which Isaias, the great prophet, and faithful in the sight of God, had commanded him.

In his days the sun went backward, and he lengthened the king's life.

With a great spirit he saw the things that are to come to pass at last, and comforted the mourners in Sion.

He showed what should come to pass for ever, and secret things before they came.—*Ecclus.* xlviii. 23, 25-28.

Jeremias

And the word of the Lord came to me, saying:

Before I formed thee in the bowels of thy mother, I knew thee: and before thou camest forth out of the womb, I sanctified thee, and made thee a prophet unto the nations.—*Jer.* i. 4, 5.

[1]After this there appeared also another man, admirable for age, and glory, and environed with great beauty and majesty:

Then Onias answering, said: This is a lover of his brethren, and of the people of Israel: this is he that prayeth much for the people, and for all the holy city, Jeremias the prophet of God. —2 *Mach.* xv. 13, 14.

Daniel

Son of man, when a land shall sin against me, so as to transgress grievously, I will stretch forth my hand upon it, and will break the staff of the bread thereof: and I will send famine upon it, and will destroy man and beast out of it.

And if these three men, Noe, Daniel,

[1]The vision of Judas Machabeus.

and Job, shall be in it: they shall deliver their own souls by their justice, saith the Lord of hosts.—*Ezech.* xiv. 13, 14.

Behold, thou art wiser than Daniel: no secret is hid from thee.—*Ezech.* xxviii. 3.

All the princes of the kingdom, the magistrates, and governors, the senators, and judges have consulted together, that an imperial decree, and an edict be published: That whosoever shall ask any petition of any god, or man, for thirty days, but of thee, O king, shall be cast into the den of lions. . . .

Now when Daniel knew this, that is to say, that the law was made, he went into his house: and opening the windows in his upper chamber towards Jerusalem, he knelt down three times a day, and adored, and gave thanks before his God, as he had been accustomed to do before.—*Dan.* vi. 7, 10.

And Daniel answering the king, said: O king, live for ever:

My God hath sent his angel, and hath shut up the mouths of the lions, and they have not hurt me: forasmuch as before him justice hath been found in me: yea and before thee, O king, I have done no offence.—*Dan.* vi. 21, 22.

Now whilst I was yet speaking, and praying, and confessing my sins, and the sins of my people of Israel, and presenting my supplications in the sight of my God, for the holy mountain of my God:

As I was yet speaking in prayer, behold the man Gabriel, whom I had seen in the vision at the beginning, flying swiftly touched me at the time of the evening sacrifice.

And he instructed me, and spoke to me, and said: O Daniel, I am now come forth to teach thee, and that thou mightest understand.

From the beginning of thy prayers the word came forth: and I am come to show it to thee, because thou art a man of desires: therefore do thou mark the word, and understand the vision.—*Dan.* ix. 20-23.

And he (the angel) said to me: Daniel, thou man of desires, understand the words that I speak to thee,

and stand upright: for I am sent now to thee. . . .

And he said to me: Fear not, Daniel: for from the first day that thou didst set thy heart to understand, to afflict thyself in the sight of thy God, thy words have been heard: and I am come for thy words.—*Dan.* x. 11, 12.

Daniel in his innocency was delivered out of the mouth of the lions. —1 *Mach.* ii. 60.

Tobias

Tobias of the tribe and city of Nephtali,

. . . When he was made captive in the days of Salmanasar king of the Assyrians, even in his captivity, forsook not the way of truth,

But every day gave all he could get to his brethren his fellow-captives, that were of his kindred.

And when he was yet younger than any of the tribe of Nephtali, yet did he no childish thing in his work.

Moreover when all went to the golden calves which Jeroboam king of Israel had made, he alone fled the company of all,

And went to Jerusalem to the temple of the Lord, and there adored the Lord God of Israel, offering faithfully all his first-fruits, and his tithes. . . .

Tobias daily went among all his kindred, and comforted them, and distributed to every one as he was able, out of his goods:

He fed the hungry, and gave clothes to the naked, and was careful to bury the dead, and they that were slain.— *Tob.* i. 1-6, 19, 20.

But Tobias fearing God more than the king, carried off the bodies of them that were slain, and hid them in his house, and at midnight buried them.

Now it happened one day, that being wearied with burying, he came to his house, and cast himself down by the wall and slept,

And as he was sleeping, hot dung out of a swallow's nest fell upon his eyes, and he was made blind.

Now this trial the Lord therefore permitted to happen to him, that an example might be given to posterity of his patience, as also of holy Job.

For whereas he had always feared God from his infancy, and kept his commandments, he repined not against God because the evil of blindness had be: allen him,

But continued immovable in the fear of God, giving thanks to God all the days of his life.—*Tob.* ii. 9-14.

When thou didst pray with tears, and didst bury the dead, and didst leave thy dinner, and hide the dead by day in thy house, and bury them by night, I offered thy prayer to the Lord.

And because thou wast acceptable to God, it was necessary that temptation should prove thee.—*Tob.* xii. 12, 13.

And the rest of his life was in joy, and with great increase of the fear of God he departed in peace.—*Tob.* xiv. 4.

Job

There was a man in the land of Hus, whose name was Job, and that man was simple and upright, and fearing God, and avoiding evil. . . .

Then Job rose up, and rent his garments, and having shaven his head fell down upon the ground and worshipped,

And said: Naked came I out of my mother's womb, and naked shall I return thither: the Lord gave, and the Lord hath taken away: as it hath pleased the Lord so is it done: blessed be the name of the Lord.

In all these things Job sinned not by his lips, nor spoke he any foolish thing against God.—*Job* i. 1, 20-22.

So Satan went forth from the presence of the Lord, and struck Job with a very grievous ulcer, from the sole of the foot even to the top of his head:

And he took a potsherd and scraped the corrupt matter, sitting on a dunghill.

And his wife said to him: Dost thou still continue in thy simplicity? bless God, and die.

And he said to her: Thou hast spoken like one of the foolish women: if we have received good things at the hand of God, why should we not receive evil? In all these things Job did not sin with his lips.—*Job* ii. 7-10.

And after the Lord had spoken these words to Job, he said to Elipha the Themanite. . . .

Take unto you therefore seven oxen, and seven rams, and go to my servant Job, and offer for yourselves a holocaust: and my servant Job shall pray for you: his face I will accept, that folly be not imputed to you: for you have not spoken right things before me, as my servant Job hath.—*Job* xlii. 7, 8.

Son of man, when a land shall sin against me, so as to transgress grievously, I will stretch forth my hand upon it, and will break the staff of the bread thereof: and I will send famine upon it, and will destroy man and beast out of it.

And if these three men, Noe, Daniel, and Job, shall be in it: they shall deliver their own souls by their justice, saith the Lord of hosts.—*Ezech.* xiv. 13, 14.

John the Baptist

And in those days cometh John the Baptist preaching in the desert of Judea.

And saying: Do penance: for the kingdom of heaven is at hand.

For this is he that was spoken of by Isaias the prophet, saying: A voice of one crying in the desert, Prepare ye the way of the Lord, make straight his paths.

And the same John had his garment of camel's hair, and a leathern girdle about his loins: and his meat was locusts and wild honey.

Then went out to him Jerusalem and all Judea, and all the country about Jordan:

And were baptized by him in the Jordan, confessing their sins.—*Matt.* iii. 1-6.

And when they went their way, Jesus began to say to the multitudes concerning John: What went you out in the desert to see? a reed shaken with the wind?

But what went you out to see? a man clothed in soft garments? Behold they that are clothed in soft garments, are in the houses of kings.

But what went you out to see? a

prophet? yea I tell you, and more than a prophet.

For this is he of whom it is written: Behold I send my angel before thy face, who shall prepare thy way before thee.

Amen I say to you, there hath not risen among them that are born of women a greater than John the Baptist: yet he that is the lesser in the kingdom of heaven is greater than he.

And from the days of John the Baptist until now, the kingdom of heaven suffereth violence, and the violent bear it away.

For all the prophets and the law prophesied until John:

And if you will receive it, he is Elias that is to come.—*Matt.* xi. 7-14.

And his disciples asked him (Jesus), saying: Why then do the scribes say that Elias must come first?

But he answering, said to them: Elias indeed shall come, and restore all things.

But I say to you, that Elias is already come, and they knew him not, but have done unto him whatsoever they had a mind. So also the Son of man shall suffer from them.

Then the disciples understood, that he had spoken to them of John the Baptist.—*Matt.* xvii. 10-13.

But the angel said to him: Fear not, Zachary, for thy prayer is heard; and thy wife Elisabeth shall bear thee a son, and thou shalt call his name John:

And thou shalt have joy and gladness, and many shall rejoice in his nativity.

For he shall be great before the Lord; and shall drink no wine nor strong drink: and he shall be filled with the Holy Ghost, even from his mother's womb.

And he shall convert many of the children of Israel to the Lord their God.

And he shall go before him in the spirit and power of Elias; that he may turn the hearts of the fathers unto the children, and the incredulous to the wisdom of the just, to prepare unto the Lord a perfect people. . . .

And all they that had heard them laid them up in their heart, saying: What an one, think ye, shall this child be? For the hand of the Lord was with him.

And Zachary his father was filled with the Holy Ghost; and he prophesied, saying: . . .

And thou, child, shalt be called the prophet of the Highest: for thou shalt go before the face of the Lord to prepare his ways:

To give knowledge of salvation to his people, unto the remission of their sins.

. . . And the child grew, and was strengthened in spirit; and was in the deserts until the day of his manifestation to Israel.—*Luke* i. 13-17, 66, 67, 76, 77, 80.

There was a man sent from God, whose name was John.

This man came for a witness, to give testimony of the light, that all men might believe through him.

He was not the light, but was to give testimony of the light.—*John* i. 6-8.

John answered them, saying: I baptize with water; but there hath stood one in the midst of you, whom you know not.

The same is he that shall come after me, who is preferred before me: the latchet of whose shoe I am not worthy to loose.

. . . The next day, John saw Jesus coming to him, and he saith: Behold the Lamb of God, behold him who taketh away the sin of the world.

This is he, of whom I said: After me there cometh a man, who is preferred before me: because he was before me. . . .

He must increase, but I must decrease.—*John* i. 26, 27, 29, 30; iii. 30.

MIRACLES OF CHRIST, THE

But of the people many believed in him, and said: When the Christ cometh, shall he do more miracles, than these which this man doth?—*John* vii. 31.

Jesus answered them: I speak to you, and you believe not: the works that I do in the name of my Father, they give testimony of me. . . .

If I do not the works of my Father, believe me not,

But if I do, though you will not believe me, believe the works: that you may know and believe that the Father is in me, and I in the Father.—*John* x. 25, 37, 38.

Arrest of Christ, the Miracle at the

Judas therefore having received a band of soldiers and servants from the chief priests and the Pharisees, cometh thither with lanterns and torches and weapons.

Jesus therefore, knowing all things that should come upon him, went forth, and said to them: Whom seek ye?

They answered him: Jesus of Nazareth. Jesus saith to them: I am he. And Judas also, who betrayed him, stood with them.

As soon therefore as he had said to them: I am he; they went backward, and fell to the ground.—*John* xviii. 3-6.

Ascension of Christ into Heaven, the

And the Lord Jesus, after he had spoken to them, was taken up into heaven, and sitteth on the right hand of God.—*Mark* xvi. 19.

And he led them out as far as Bethania: and lifting up his hands, he blessed them.

And it came to pass, whilst he blessed them, he departed from them, and was carried up to heaven. —*Luke* xxiv. 50, 51.

And when he had said these things, while they looked on, he was raised up: and a cloud received him out of their sight.

And while they were beholding him going up to heaven, behold two men stood by them in white garments.

Who also said: Ye men of Galilee, why stand you looking up to heaven? This Jesus who is taken up from you into heaven, shall so come, as you have seen him going into heaven.—*Acts* i. 9-11.

Blind Men, the Two

And as Jesus passed from thence, there followed him two blind men crying out and saying, Have mercy on us, O son of David.

And when he was come to the house, the blind men came to him. And Jesus saith to them, Do you believe that I can do this unto you? They say to him, Yea, Lord.

Then he touched their eyes, saying, According to your faith, be it done unto you.

And their eyes were opened, and Jesus strictly charged them, saying, See that no man know this.

But they going out, spread his fame abroad in all that country.—*Matt.* ix. 27-31.

¹Blind Men of Jericho, the Two

And when they went out from Jericho, a great multitude followed him.

And they came to Jericho: and as he went out of Jericho, with his disciples, and a very great multitude, Bartimeus the blind man, the son of

Now it came to pass, when he drew nigh to Jericho, that a certain blind man sat by the way side, begging.

And when he heard the

¹See: Fouard's Life of Christ, vol. ii., page 152, footnote. He concludes that the synoptists refer to the same miracle.

And behold two blind men sitting by the way side, heard that Jesus passed by, and they cried out, saying: O Lord, thou son of David, have mercy on us.

And the multitude rebuked them that they should hold their peace.

But they cried out the more, saying: O Lord, thou son of David, have mercy on us.

And Jesus stood, and called them, and said: What will ye that I do to you?

They say to him: Lord, that our eyes be opened.

And Jesus having compassion on them, touched their eyes.

And immediately they saw, and followed him.—*Matt.* xx. 29-34.

Timeus, sat by the way side begging.

Who when he had heard, that it was Jesus of Nazareth, began to cry out, and to say: Jesus Son of David, have mercy on me.

And many rebuked him, that he might hold his peace; but he cried a great deal the more: Son of David, have mercy on me.

And Jesus, standing still, commanded him to be called. And they call the blind man, saying to him: Be of better comfort: arise, he calleth thee.

Who casting off his garment leaped up, and came to him.

And Jesus answering, said to him: What wilt thou that I should do to thee? And the blind man said to him: Rabboni, that I may see.

And Jesus saith to him: Go thy way, thy faith hath made thee whole.

And immediately he saw, and followed him in the way.—*Mark* x. 46-52.

multitude passing by, he asked what this meant.

And they told him, that Jesus of Nazareth was passing by.

And he cried out, saying: Jesus, son of David, have mercy on me.

And they that went before, rebuked him, that he should hold his peace: but he cried out much more: Son of David, have mercy on me.

And Jesus standing, commanded him to be brought unto him. And when he was come near, he asked him,

Saying: What wilt thou that I do to thee?

But he said: Lord, that I may see.

And Jesus said to him: Receive thy sight: thy faith hath made thee whole.

And immediately he saw, and followed him, glorifying God. And all the people, when they saw it, gave praise to God.—*Luke* xviii. 35-43.

Blind Man of Bethsaida, the

And they came to Bethsaida; and they bring to him a blind man, and they besought him that he would touch him.

And taking the blind man by the hand, he led him out of the town; and spitting upon his eyes, laying his hands on him, he asked him if he saw any thing.

And looking up he said: I see men as it were trees, walking.

After that again he laid his hands upon his eyes, and he began to see, and was restored, so that he saw all things clearly.

And he sent him into his house, saying: Go into thy house, and if thou enter into the town, tell nobody.—*Mark* viii. 22-26.

Blind, the Man Born

And Jesus passing by, saw a man, who was blind from his birth:

And his disciples asked him: Rabbi, who hath sinned, this man, or his parents, that he should be born blind?

Jesus answered: Neither hath this man sinned, nor his parents; but that the works of God should be made manifest in him.

I must work the works of him that sent me, whilst it is day: the night cometh, when no man can work.

As long as I am in the world, I am the light of the world.

When he had said these things, he spat on the ground, and made clay of the spittle, and spread the clay upon his eyes,

And said to him: Go, wash in the pool of Siloe, which is interpreted, Sent. He went therefore, and washed, and he came seeing.—*John* ix. 1-7.

Centurion's Servant, the Cure of the

And when he had finished all his words in the hearing of the people, he entered into Capharnaum.

And the servant of a certain centurion, who was dear to him, being sick, was ready to die.

And when he had heard of Jesus, he sent unto him the ancients of the Jews, desiring him to come and heal his servant.

And when they came to Jesus, they besought him earnestly, saying to him: He is worthy that thou shouldst do this for him.

And when he had entered into Capharnaum, there came to him a centurion, beseeching him,

And saying, Lord, my servant lieth at home sick of the palsy, and is grievously tormented.

And Jesus saith to him: I will come and heal him.

And the centurion making answer, said: Lord, I am not worthy that thou shouldst enter under my roof: but only say the word, and my servant shall be healed. . . .

And Jesus said to the centurion: Go, and as thou hast believed, so be it done to thee. And the servant was healed at the same hour.—*Matt.* viii. 5-8, 13.

For he loveth our nation; and he hath built us a synagogue. And Jesus went with them. And when he was now not far from the house, the centurion sent his friends to him, saying: Lord, trouble not thyself; for I am not worthy that thou shouldst enter under my roof.

For which cause neither did I think myself worthy to come to thee; but say the word, and my servant shall be healed.

For I also am a man subject to authority, having under me soldiers: and I say to one, Go, and he goeth; and to another, Come, and he cometh; and to my servant, Do this, and he doth it.

Which Jesus hearing, marvelled: and turning about to the multitude that followed him, he said: Amen I say to you, I have not found so great faith, not even in Israel.

And they who were sent, being returned to the house, found the servant whole who had been sick.—*Luke* vii. 1-10.

Daughter of the Woman of Canaan, the Cure of the

And Jesus went from thence, and retired into the coasts of Tyre and Sidon.

And behold a woman of Canaan who came out of those coasts, crying out, said to him: Have mercy on me, O Lord, thou son of David: my daughter is grievously troubled by a devil.

And rising from thence he went into the coasts of Tyre and Sidon: and entering into a house, he would that no man should know it, and he could not be hid.

For a woman as soon as she heard of him, whose daughter had an unclean

Who answered her not a word. And his disciples came and besought him, saying: Send her away, for she crieth after us:

And he answering, said: I was not sent but to the sheep that are lost of the house of Israel.

But she came and adored him, saying: Lord, help me.

Who answering, said: It is not good to take the bread of the children, and to cast it to the dogs.

But she said: Yea, Lord; for the whelps also eat of the crumbs that fall from the table of their masters.

Then Jesus answering, said to her: O woman, great is thy faith: be it done to thee as thou wilt: and her daughter was cured from that hour.—*Matt.* xv. 21-28.

spirit, came in and fell down at his feet.

For the woman was a Gentile, a Syro-phenician born. And she besought him that he would cast forth the devil out of her daughter.

Who said to her: Suffer first the children to be filled: for it is not good to take the bread of the children, and cast it to the dogs.

But she answered and said to him: Yea, Lord; for the whelps also eat under the table of the crumbs of the children.

And he said to her: For this saying go thy way, the devil is gone out of thy daughter.

And when she was come into her house, she found the girl lying upon the bed, and that the devil was gone out.—*Mark* vii. 24-30.

Deaf and Dumb Man, the Cure of the

And again going out of the coasts of Tyre, he came by Sidon to the sea of Galilee, through the midst of the coasts of Decapolis.

And they bring to him one deaf and dumb; and they besought him that he would lay his hand upon him.

And taking him from the multitude apart, he put his fingers into his ears, and spitting, he touched his tongue:

And looking up to heaven, he groaned, and said to him: Ephpheta, which is, Be thou opened.

And immediately his ears were opened, and the string of his tongue was loosed, and he spoke right.

And he charged them that they should tell no man. But the more he charged them, so much the more a great deal did they publish it.

And so much the more did they wonder, saying: He hath done all things well; he hath made both the deaf to hear, and the dumb to speak.—*Mark* vii. 31-37.

Death of Christ, Miracles at the

Now from the sixth hour there was darkness over the whole earth, until the ninth hour. . . .

And Jesus again crying with a loud voice, yielded up the ghost.

And behold the veil of the temple was rent in two from the top even to the bottom, and the earth quaked, and the rocks were rent.

And the graves were opened: and many bodies

And when the sixth hour was come, there was darkness over the whole earth until the ninth hour.

And at the ninth hour, Jesus cried out with a loud voice, saying: Eloi, Eloi, lamma sabacthani? Which is, being interpreted, My God, my God, why hast thou forsaken me?

. . . And Jesus having cried out with a loud voice, gave up the ghost.

And it was almost the sixth hour; and there was darkness over all the earth until the ninth hour.

And the sun was darkened, and the veil of the temple was rent in the midst.

And Jesus, crying with a loud voice, said: Father, into thy hands I commend my spirit. And saying this, he gave up the ghost.

Now the centurion, seeing what was done, glori-

of the saints that had slept arose,

And coming out of the tombs after his resurrection, came into the holy city, and appeared to many.

Now the centurion and they that were with him watching Jesus, having seen the earthquake, and the things that were done, were sore afraid, saying: Indeed this was the Son of God.—*Matt.* xxvii. 45, 50-54.

And the veil of the temple was rent in two, from the top to the bottom.

And the centurion who stood over against him, seeing that crying out in this manner he had given up the ghost, said: Indeed this man was the Son of God.—*Mark* xv. 33, 34, 37-39.

fied God, saying: Indeed this was a just man.

And all the multitude of them that were come together to that sight, and saw the things that were done, returned striking their breasts.—*Luke* xxiii. 44-48.

Demoniacs of Gerasa, the

And they came over the strait of the sea into the country of the Gerasens. And as he went out of the ship, immediately there met him out of the monuments a man with an unclean spirit,

Who had his dwelling in the tombs, and no man now could bind him, not even with chains.

For having been often bound with fetters and chains, he had burst the chains, and broken the fetters in pieces, and no one could tame him.

And he was always day and night in the monuments and in the mountains, crying and cutting himself with stones.

And seeing Jesus afar off, he ran and adored him.

And crying with a loud voice, he said: What have I to do with thee, Jesus the Son of the most high God? I adjure thee by God that thou torment me not.

For he said unto him: Go out of the man, thou unclean spirit.

And he asked him: What is thy name? And

And they sailed to the country of the Gerasens, which is over against Galilee.

And when he was come forth to the land, there met him a certain man who had a devil now a very long time, and he wore no clothes, neither did he abide in a house, but in the sepulchres.

And when he saw Jesus, he fell down before him; and crying out with a loud voice, he said: What have I to do with thee, Jesus, Son of the most high God? I beseech thee, do not torment me.

For he commanded the unclean spirit to go out of the man. For many times it seized him, and he was bound with chains, and kept in fetters; and breaking the bonds, he was driven by the devil into the deserts.

And Jesus asked him, saying: What i s t h y name? But he s a i d : Legion; because m a n y devils were entered into him.

And they besought him that he would not com-

And when he was come on the other side of the water, into the country of the Gerasens, there met him two that were possessed with devils, coming out of the sepulchres, exceeding fierce, so that none could pass by that way.

And behold they cried out, saying: What have we to do with thee, Jesus Son of God? art thou come hither to torment us before the time?

And there was, not far from them, an herd of many swine feeding.

And the devils besought him, saying: If thou cast us out hence, send us into the herd of swine.

And he said to them: Go. But they going out went into the swine, and behold the whole herd ran violently down a steep place into the sea: and they perished in the waters.

And they that kept them fled: and coming into the city, told every thing, and concerning them that had been possessed by the devils.—*Matt.* viii. 28-33.

he saith to him: My name is Legion, for we are many.

And he besought him much, that he would not drive him away out of the country.

And there was there near the mountain a great herd of swine, feeding.

And the spirits besought him, saying: Send us into the swine, that we may enter into them.

And Jesus immediately gave them leave. And the unclean spirits going out, entered into the swine: and the herd with great violence was carried headlong into the sea, being about two thousand, and were stifled in the sea.

And they that fed them fled, and told it in the city and in the fields. And they went out to see what was done:

And they came to Jesus, and they see him that was troubled with the devil, sitting, clothed, and well in his wits, and they were afraid.—*Mark* v. 1-15.

mand them to go into the abyss.

And there was there a herd of many swine feeding on the mountain; and they besought him that he would suffer them to enter into them. And he suffered them.

The devils therefore went out of the man, and entered into the swine; and the herd ran violently down a steep place into the lake, and were stifled.

Which when they that fed them saw done, they fled away, and told it in the city and in the villages.

And they went out to see what was done; and they came to Jesus, and found the man out of whom the devils were departed, sitting at his feet, clothed, and in his right mind; and they were afraid.—*Luke* viii. 26-35.

Demoniac, the Dumb

And when they were gone out, behold they brought him a dumb man, possessed with a devil.

And after the devil was cast out, the dumb man spoke, and the multitudes wondered, saying, Never was the like seen in Israel.

But the Pharisees said, By the prince of devils he casteth out devils.—*Matt.* ix. 32-34.

And he was casting out a devil, and the same was dumb: and when he had cast out the devil, the dumb spoke: and the multitudes were in admiration at it:

But some of them said: He casteth out devils by Beelzebub, the prince of devils.—*Luke* xi. 14, 15.

Demoniac, the Blind and Dumb

Then was offered to him one possessed with a devil, blind and dumb: and he healed him, so that he spoke and saw.

And all the multitudes were amazed, and said: Is not this the son of David? But the Pharisees hearing it, said: This man casteth not out devils but by Beelzebub the prince of the devils.—*Matt.* xii. 22-24.

Demoniac Child, the

And one of the multitude, answering, said: Master, I have brought my son to thee, having a dumb spirit,

Who, wheresoever he taketh him, dasheth him, and he foameth, a n d gnasheth with the teeth, and pineth away; and I spoke to thy disciples to cast him out, and they could not.

And when he was come to the multitude, there came to him a man falling down on his knees before him, saying: Lord, have pity on my son, for he is a lunatic, and suffereth much: for he falleth often into the fire, and often into the water.

Who answering them, said: O incredulous generation, how long shall I be with you? how long shall I suffer you? bring him unto me.

And they brought him. And when he had seen him, immediately the spirit troubled him; and being thrown down upon t h e ground, he rolled about foaming.

And it came to pass the day following, when they came down from t h e mountain, there met him a great multitude.

And behold a m a n among the crowd cried out, saying: Master, I beseech thee, look upon my son, because he is my only one.

And I brought him to thy disciples, and they could not cure him.

Then Jesus answered and said: O unbelieving and perverse generation, how long shall I be with you? How long shall I suffer you? bring him hither to me.

And Jesus rebuked him, and the devil went out of him, and the child was cured from that hour.— *Matt.* xvii. 14-17.

And he asked h i s father: How long time is it since this hath happened unto him? But he said: From his infancy:

And oftentimes hath he cast him into the fire and into waters to destroy him. But if thou canst do any thing, help us, having compassion on us.

And Jesus saith to him: If thou canst believe, all things are possible to him that believeth.

And immediately the father of the boy crying out, with tears said: I do believe, Lord: help my unbelief.

And when Jesus saw the multitude running t o gether, he threatened the unclean spirit, saying to him: Deaf and dumb spirit, I command thee, go out of him; and enter not any more into him.

And lo, a spirit seizeth him, and he suddenly crieth out, and he throweth him down and teareth him, so that he foameth; and bruising him, he hardly departeth from him.

And I desired thy disciples to cast him out, and they could not.

And Jesus answering, said: O faithless and perverse generation, h o w long shall I be with you, and suffer you? Bring hither thy son.

And as he was coming to him, the devil threw him down, and tore him.

And Jesus rebuked the unclean spirit, and cured the boy, and restored him to his father.

And all were astonished at the mighty power of God.—*Luke* ix. 37-44.

And crying out, and greatly tearing him, he went out of him, and he became as dead, so that many said: He is dead.

But Jesus taking him by the hand, lifted him up; and he arose.—*Mark* ix. 16-26.

Demoniac of Capharnaum, the

And there was in their synagogue a man with an unclean spirit; and he cried out,

Saying: What have we to do with thee, Jesus of Nazareth? art thou come to destroy us? I know who thou art, the Holy One of God.

And Jesus threatened him, saying: Speak no more, and go out of the man.

And the unclean spirit tearing him, and crying out with a loud voice, went out of him.

And they were all amazed, insomuch that they questioned among themselves, saying: What thing is this? what is this new doctrine? for with power he commandeth even the unclean spirits, and they obey him.

And the fame of him was spread forthwith into all the country of Galilee.—*Mark* i. 23-28.

And in the synagogue there was a man who had an unclean devil, and he cried out with a loud voice,

Saying: Let us alone, what have we to do with thee, Jesus of Nazareth? art thou come to destroy us? I know thee, who thou art, the holy one of God.

And Jesus rebuked him, saying: Hold thy peace, and go out of him.

And when the devil had thrown him into the midst, he went out of him, and hurt him not at all.

And there came fear upon all, and they talked among themselves, saying: What word is this, for with authority and power he commandeth the unclean spirits, and they go out?

And the fame of him was published into every place of the country.—*Luke* iv. 33-37.

Dropsy, the Man Sick of the

And it came to pass, when Jesus went into the house of one of the chief of the Pharisees, on the sabbath day, to eat bread, that they watched him.

And behold, there was a certain man before him that had the dropsy.

And Jesus answering, spoke to the lawyers and Pharisees, saying: Is it lawful to heal on the sabbath day?

But they held their peace. But he taking him, healed him, and sent him away.—*Luke* xiv. 1-4.

Fig-Tree, the Withered

And leaving them, he went out of the city into Bethania, and remained there.

And in the morning, returning into the city, he was hungry.

And seeing a certain fig-tree by the way side, he came to it, and found noth-

And the next day when they came out from Bethania, he was hungry.

And when he had seen afar off a fig-tree having leaves, he came if perhaps he might find any thing on it.

And when he was come to it, he found nothing but leaves. For it was not the time for figs.

And answering he said to it: May no

ing on it but leaves only, and he saith to it: May no fruit grow on thee henceforward for ever. And immediately the fig-tree withered away.

And the disciples seeing it wondered, saying: How is it presently withered away?—*Matt.* xxi. 17-20.

man hereafter eat fruit of thee any more for ever. And his disciples heard it. . . .

And when they passed by in the morning they saw the fig-tree dried up from the roots.

And Peter remembering, said to him: Rabbi, behold the fig-tree, which thou didst curse, is withered away.—*Mark* xi. 12-14, 20, 21.

Fish, the First Miraculous Draught of

And it came to pass, that when the multitudes pressed upon him to hear the word of God, he stood by the lake of Genesareth,

And saw two ships standing by the lake; but the fishermen were gone out of them, and were washing their nets.

And going into one of the ships that was Simon's, he desired him to draw back a little from the land. And sitting he taught the multitudes out of the ship.

Now when he had ceased to speak, he said to Simon: Launch out into the deep, and let down your nets for a draught.

And Simon answering, said to him: Master, we have labored all the night, and have taken nothing: but at thy word I will let down the net.

And when they had done this, they enclosed a very great multitude of fishes, and their net broke.

And they beckoned to their partners that were in the other ship, that they should come and help them. And they came, and filled both the ships, so that they were almost sinking.

Which when Simon Peter saw, he fell down at Jesus' knees, saying: Depart from me, for I am a sinful man, O Lord.

For he was wholly astonished, and all that were with him, at the draught of the fishes which they had taken.—*Luke* v. 1-9.

Fish, the Second Miraculous Draught of

After this, Jesus showed himself again to the disciples at the sea of Tiberias. And he showed himself after this manner.

There were together Simon Peter, and Thomas, who is called Didymus, and Nathanael, who was of Cana of Galilee, and the sons of Zebedee, and two others of his disciples.

Simon Peter saith to them: I go a fishing. They say to him: We also come with thee. And they went forth, and entered into the ship: and that night they caught nothing,

But when the morning was come, Jesus stood on the shore: yet the disciples knew not that it was Jesus.

Jesus therefore said to them: Children, have you any meat? They answered him: No.

He saith to them: Cast the net on the right side of the ship, and you shall find. They cast therefore; and now they were not able to draw it, for the multitude of fishes. . . .

Jesus saith to them: Bring hither of the fishes which you have now caught.

Simon Peter went up, and drew the net to land, full of great fishes, one hundred and fifty-three. And although there were so many, the net was not broken.—*John* xxi. 1-6, 10, 11.

Jairus, Raised to Life, The Daughter of

As he was yet speaking these things unto them, behold a certain ruler

And when Jesus had passed again in the ship over the strait, a great

And it came to pass, that when Jesus was returned, the multitude recame, and adored him, saying: Lord, my daughter is even now dead; but come, lay thy hand upon her, and she shall live.

And Jesus rising up followed him, with his disciples. . . .

And when Jesus was come into the house of the ruler, and saw the minstrels and the multitude making a rout,

He said: Give place, for the girl is not dead, but sleepeth. And they laughed him to scorn.

And when the multitude was put forth, he went in, and took her by the hand. And the maid arose.

And the fame hereof went abroad into all that country.—*Matt.* ix. 18, 19, 23-26.

multitude assembled together unto him, and he was nigh unto the sea.

And there cometh one of the rulers of the synagogue named Jairus: and seeing him, falleth down at his feet.

And he besought him much, saying: My daughter is at the point of death, lay thy hand upon her, that she may be safe, and may live.

And he went with him, and a great multitude followed him, and they thronged him. . . .

While he was yet speaking, some come from the ruler of the synagogue's house, saying: Thy daughter is dead: why dost thou trouble the Master any further?

But Jesus having heard the word that was spoken, saith to the ruler of the synagogue: Fear not, only believe.

And he admitted not any man to follow him, but Peter, and James, and John the brother of James.

And they come to the house of the ruler of the synagogue; and he seeth a tumult, and people weeping and wailing much.

And going in, he saith to them: Why make you this ado, and weep? the damsel is not dead, but sleepeth.

And they laughed him to scorn. But he having put them all out, taketh the father and the mother of the damsel, and them that were with him, and entereth in where the damsel was lying.

And taking the damsel by the hand, he saith to

ceived him: for they were all waiting for him.

And behold there came a man whose name was Jairus, and he was a ruler of the synagogue: and he fell down at the feet of Jesus, beseeching him that he would come into his house:

For he had an only daughter, almost twelve years old, and she was dying. And it happened as he went, that he was thronged by the multitudes. . . .

And as he was yet speaking, there cometh one to the ruler of the synagogue, saying to him: Thy daughter is dead, trouble him not.

And Jesus hearing this word, answered the father of the maid: Fear not: believe only, and she shall be safe.

And when he was come to the house, he suffered not any man to go in with him, but Peter and James and John, and the father and mother of the maiden.

And all wept and mourned for her. But he said: Weep not; the maid is not dead, but sleepeth.

And they laughed him to scorn, knowing that she was dead.

But he taking her by the hand, cried out, saying: Maid, arise.

And her spirit returned, and she arose immediately. And he bid them give her to eat.

And her parents were astonished, whom he charged to tell no man what was done.—*Luke* viii. 40-42, 49-56.

her: Talitha cumi, which is, being interpreted: Damsel (I say to thee) arise.

And immediately the damsel rose up, and walked: and she was twelve years old: and they were astonished with a great astonishment.

And he charged them strictly that no man should know it: and commanded that something should be given her to eat. —*Mark* v. 21-24, 35-43.

Lazarus, the Raising of

These things he said; and after that he said to them: Lazarus our friend sleepeth; but I go that I may awake him out of sleep.

His disciples therefore said: Lord, if he sleep, he shall do well.

But Jesus spoke of his death; and they thought that he spoke of the repose of sleep.

Then therefore Jesus said to them plainly: Lazarus is dead.

And I am glad, for your sakes, that I was not there, that you may believe: but let us go to him. . . .

Jesus therefore again groaning in himself, cometh to the sepulchre. Now it was a cave; and a stone was laid over it.

Jesus saith: Take away the stone. Martha, the sister of him that was dead, saith to him: Lord, by this time he stinketh, for he is now of four days.

Jesus saith to her: Did not I say to thee, that if thou believe, thou shalt see the glory of God?

They took therefore the stone away. And Jesus lifting up his eyes, said: Father, I give thee thanks that thou hast heard me.

And I knew that thou hearest me always; but because of the people who stand about have I said it, that they may believe that thou hast sent me.

When he had said these things, he cried with a loud voice: Lazarus, come forth.

And presently he that had been dead came forth, bound feet and hands with winding bands; and his face was bound about with a napkin. Jesus said to them: Loose him, and let him go.

Many therefore of the Jews, who were come to Mary and Martha, and had seen the things that Jesus did, believed in him.—*John* xi. 11-15, 38-45.

Leper, Cure of the

And he was preaching in their synagogues, and in all Galilee, and casting out devils.

And there came a leper to him, beseeching him, and kneeling down said to him: If thou wilt, thou canst make me clean.

And Jesus having compassion on him, stretched

And when he was come down from the mountain, great multitudes followed him.

And behold a leper came and adored him,

And it came to pass, when he was in a certain city, behold a man full of leprosy, who seeing Jesus, and falling on his face, besought him, saying:

saying: Lord, if thou wilt, thou canst make me clean. And Jesus stretching forth his hand, touched him, saying: I will, be thou made clean. And forthwith his leprosy was cleansed.

And Jesus saith to him: See thou tell no man: but go, show thyself to the priest, and offer the gift which Moses commanded for a testimony unto them.—*Matt.* viii. 1-4.

forth his hand; and touching him, saith to him: I will. Be thou made clean. And when he had spoken, immediately the leprosy departed from him, and he was made clean.

And he strictly charged him, and forthwith sent him away.

And he saith to him: See thou tell no one; but go, show thyself to the high priest, and offer for thy cleansing the things that Moses commanded, for a testimony to them.—*Mark* i. 39-44.

Lord, if thou wilt, thou canst make me clean.

And stretching forth his hand, he touched him, saying: I will. Be thou cleansed. And immediately the leprosy departed from him.

And he charged him that he should tell no man, but, Go, show thyself to the priest, and offer for thy cleansing according as Moses commanded, for a testimony to them.—*Luke* v. 12-14.

Lepers, Cure of the Ten

And it came to pass, as he was going to Jerusalem, he passed through the midst of Samaria and Galilee.

And as he entered into a certain town, there met him ten men that were lepers, who stood afar off;

And lifted up their voice, saying: Jesus, master, have mercy on us.

Whom when he saw, he said: Go, show yourselves to the priests. And it came to pass, as they went, they were made clean.

And one of them, when he saw that he was made clean, went back, with a loud voice glorifying God.

And he fell on his face before his feet, giving thanks: and this was a Samaritan.

And Jesus answering, said, Were not ten made clean? and where are the nine?

There is no one found to return and give glory to God, but this stranger.

And he said to him: Arise, go thy way; for thy faith hath made thee whole.—*Luke* xvii. 11-19.

Magdalen, the Possessed

And it came to pass afterwards, that he travelled through the cities and towns, preaching and evangelizing the kingdom of God; and the twelve with him:

And certain women who had been healed of evil spirits and infirmities; Mary who is called Magdalen, out of whom seven devils were gone forth.—*Luke* viii. 1, 2.

Malchus' Ear, Healing of

And they that were about him, seeing what would follow, said to him: Lord, shall we strike with the sword?

And one of them struck the servant of the high priest, and cut off his right ear.

But Jesus answering, said: Suffer ye thus far. And when he had touched his ear, he healed him.—*Luke* xxii. 49-51.

Money Found in the Mouth of the Fish, the

And when they were come to Capharnaum, they that received the didrachmas, came to Peter and said to him: Doth not your master pay the didrachmas?

He said: Yes. And when he was come into the house, Jesus prevented him, saying: What is thy opinion, Simon? The kings of the earth, of whom do they receive tribute or custom? of their own children, or of strangers?

And he said: Of strangers. Jesus said to him: Then the children are free.

But that we may not scandalize them, go to the sea, and cast in a hook: and that fish which shall first come up, take: and when thou hast opened its mouth, thou shalt find a stater: take that, and give it to them for me and thee.—*Matt.* xvii. 23-26.

Multiplication of the Five Loaves and Two Fishes, the

And he coming forth saw a great multitude, and had compassion o n them, and healed their sick.

And when it was evening, his disciples came to him, saying: This is a desert place, and the hour is now past: send away the multitudes, that going into the towns, they may b u y themselves victuals.

But Jesus said to them, They have no need to go: give you them to eat.

They answered him: We have not h e r e , but five loaves, and t w o fishes.

He said to them: Bring them hither to me.

A n d when he had commanded the multitudes to sit down upon the grass, he took the five loaves and the two fishes, a n d l o o k i n g u p t o heaven, he blessed, a n d brake, and gave the loaves to his disciples, and the disciples to the multitudes.

And they did all

And Jesus going out saw a great multitude: and he had compassion on them, because they were as sheep not having a shepherd, and he began to teach them many things.

And when the day was now far spent, his disciples came to him, saying: This is a desert place, and the hour is n o w past:

Send them away, that going into the next villages and towns, they may b u y themselves meat to eat.

And he answering said to them: Give you them to eat. And t h e y said to him: Let us go and buy bread for two hundred pence, and we will give them to eat.

And he saith to them: How many loaves have you? go and see. And when they knew, they say: Five, and two fishes.

And he c o m - manded them that they should make them all sit down by companies upon the green grass.

Which when the people knew, they followed him; and he received them, and spoke to them of the kingdom of God, and healed them w h o h a d need of healing.

Now the day be-g a n to decline. A n d the twelve came and said to him: Send a w a y the multitude, that g o i n g i n t o the towns and villages round about, they may lodge and get victuals; for w e are here in a desert place.

But he said to them: Give y o u them to eat. And they said: We have no more than five loaves a n d t w o fishes; unless per- haps we should go and buy food for all this multitude.

Now there were a b o u t five thou- sand men. And he said to his disci- ples: Make them sit down by fifties in a company.

And they did so; and made them all sit down.

And taking the five loaves and the t w o fishes, he l o o k e d u p t o

Jesus therefore went up into a mountain, a n d there he sat with his disciples.

Now the pasch, the festival day of the Jews, was near at hand.

When J e s u s therefore h a d lifted up his eyes, and seen that a very great multi- t u d e cometh to him, he said to Philip: Whence shall we buy bread, t h a t these may eat?

And this he said to try him; for he himself knew what he would do.

Philip answered him: Two hundred pennyworth o f bread is not suffi- c i e n t for them, that every one may take a little.

One of his disci- ples, Andrew, the brother of Simon P e t e r , saith to him:

There is a boy here that hath five barley loaves, and two fishes; b u t what a r e t h e s e among so many?

Then Jesus said: Make the men sit down. Now there was much grass in

eat, and were filled. And they took up what remained, twelve full baskets of fragments.

And the number of them that did eat, was five thousand men, besides women and children.—*Matt.* xiv. 14-21.

And they sat down in ranks, by hundreds and by fifties.

And when he had taken the five loaves, and the two fishes: looking up to heaven, he blessed, and broke the loaves, and gave to his disciples to set before them: and the two fishes he divided among them all.

And they all did eat, and had their fill.

And they took up the leavings, twelve full baskets of fragments, and of the fishes.

And they that did eat, were five thousand men.— *Mark* vi. 34-44.

heaven, and blessed them; and he broke, and distributed to his disciples, to set before the multitude.

And they did all eat, and were filled. And there were taken up of fragments that remained to them, twelve baskets.— *Luke* ix. 11-17.

the place. The men therefore sat down, in number about five thousand.

And Jesus took the loaves: and when he had given thanks, he distributed to them that were sat down. In like manner also of the fishes, as much as they would.

And when they were filled, he said to his disciples: Gather up the fragments that remain, lest they be lost.

They gathered up therefore, and filled twelve baskets with the fragments of the five barley loaves, which remained over and above to them that had eaten.

Now those men, when they had seen what a miracle Jesus had done, said: This is of a truth the prophet, that is to come into the world.—*John* vi. 3-14.

Multiplication of Seven Loaves and Some Fish, the

And Jesus called together his disciples, and said: I have compassion on the multitude, because they continue with me now three days, and have not what to eat, and I will not send them away fasting, lest they faint in the way.

And the disciples say unto him: Whence then should we have so many loaves in the desert, as to fill so great a multitude?

In those days again, when there was a great multitude, and had nothing to eat; calling his disciples together, he saith to them:

I have compassion on the multitude, for behold they have now been with me three days, and have nothing to eat.

And if I shall send them away fasting to their home, they will faint in the way; for some of them came from afar off.

And Jesus said to them: How many loaves have you? But they said: Seven, and a few little fishes.

And he commanded the multitude to sit down upon the ground.

And taking the seven loaves and the fishes, and giving thanks, he brake, and gave to his disciples, and the disciples gave to the people.

And they did all eat, and had their fill. And they took up seven baskets full, of what remained of the fragments.

And they that did eat, were four thousand men, besides children and women.—*Matt.* xv. 32-38.

And his disciples answered him: From whence can any one fill them here with bread in the wilderness?

And he asked them: How many loaves have ye? Who said: Seven.

And taking the seven loaves, giving thanks, he broke, and gave to his disciples for to set before them; and they set them before the people.

And they had a few little fishes; and he blessed them, and commanded them to be set before them.

And they did eat and were filled; and they took up that which was left of the fragments, seven baskets.

And they that had eaten were about four thousand; and he sent them away.—*Mark* viii. 1-9.

Nazareth, Jesus Escapes from His Enemies at

And all they in the synagogue, hearing these things, were filled with anger. And they rose up and thrust him out of the city; and they brought him to the brow of the hill, whereon their city was built, that they might cast him down headlong.

But he passing through the midst of them, went his way.—*Luke* iv. 28-30.

Palsy, the Man Sick of the

And entering into a boat, he passed over the water and came into his own city.

And behold they brought to him one sick of the palsy lying in a bed. And Jesus, seeing their faith, said to the man sick of the palsy: Be of good heart, son, thy sins are forgiven thee.

And behold some of the scribes said within themselves: He blasphemeth.

And Jesus seeing their thoughts, said: Why do you think evil in your hearts?

Whether is easier, to say, Thy sins are forgiven thee: or to say, Arise, and walk?

But that you may know that the Son of man hath power on earth to forgive

And again he entered into Capharnaum after some days.

And it was heard that he was in the house, and many came together, so that there was no room; no, not even at the door; and he spoke to them the word.

And they came to him, bringing one sick of the palsy, who was carried by four.

And when they could not offer him unto him for the multitude, they uncovered the roof where he was; and opening it, they let down the bed wherein the man sick of the palsy lay.

And when Jesus had seen their faith, he saith to the sick of the palsy:

And it came to pass on a certain day, as he sat teaching, that there were also Pharisees and doctors of the law sitting by, that were come out of every town of Galilee, and Judea and Jerusalem: and the power of the Lord was to heal them.

And behold, men brought in a bed a man, who had the palsy: and they sought means to bring him in, and to lay him before him.

And when they could not find by what way they might bring him in, because of the multitude, they went up upon the roof, and let him down through the tiles with his bed into the midst before Jesus.

Whose faith when he

sins, (then said he to the man sick of the palsy,) Arise, take up thy bed, and go into thy house. And he arose, and went into his house. And the multitude seeing it, feared, and glorified God that gave such power to men.—*Matt.* ix. 1-8.

Son, thy sins are forgiven thee.

And there were some of the scribes sitting there, and thinking in their hearts: Why doth this man speak thus? he blasphemeth. Who can forgive sins, but God only? Which Jesus presently knowing in his spirit, that they so thought within themselves, saith to them: Why think you these things in your hearts? Which is easier, to say to the sick of the palsy: Thy sins are forgiven thee; or to say: Arise, take up thy bed, and walk? But that you may know that the Son of man hath power on earth to forgive sins, (he saith to the sick of the palsy,) I say to thee: Arise, take up thy bed, and go into thy house. And immediately he arose; and taking up his bed, went his way in the sight of all; so that all wondered and glorified God, saying: We never saw the like.—*Mark* ii. 1-12.

saw, he said: Man, thy sins are forgiven thee. And the scribes and Pharisees began to think, saying: Who is this who speaketh blasphemies? Who can forgive sins, but God alone? And when Jesus knew their thoughts, answering, he said to them: What is it you think in your hearts? Which is easier to say, Thy sins are forgiven thee; or to say, Arise and walk? But that you may know that the Son of man hath power on earth to forgive sins, (he saith to the sick of the palsy,) I say to thee, Arise, take up thy bed, and go into thy house. And immediately rising up before them, he took up the bed on which he lay; and he went away to his own house, glorifying God. And all were astonished; and they glorified God. And they were filled with fear, saying: We have seen wonderful things to-day.—*Luke* v. 17-26.

Peter's Mother-in-Law, Cure of

And when Jesus was come into Peter's house, he saw his wife's mother lying, and sick of a fever. And he touched her hand, and the fever left her, and she arose and ministered to them.—*Matt.* viii. 14, 15.

And immediately going out of the synagogue they came into the house of Simon and Andrew, with James and John. And Simon's wife's mother lay in a fit of a fever: and forthwith they tell him of her. And coming to her, he lifted her up, taking her by the hand; and immediately the fever left her, and she ministered unto them.—*Mark* i. 29-31.

And Jesus rising up out of the synagogue, went into Simon's house. And Simon's wife's mother was taken with a great fever, and they besought him for her. And standing over her, he commanded the fever, and it left her. And immediately rising, she ministered to them.—*Luke* iv. 38, 39.

Probatica, the Infirm Man at the Pond of

After these things was a festival day of the Jews, and Jesus went up to Jerusalem.

Now there is at Jerusalem a pond, called Probatica, which in Hebrew is named Bethsaida, having five porches.

In these lay a great multitude of sick, of blind, of lame, of withered; waiting for the moving of the water.

And an angel of the Lord descended at certain times into the pond; and the water was moved. And he that went down first into the pond after the motion of the water, was made whole, of whatsoever infirmity he lay under.

And there was a certain man there, that had been eight and thirty years under his infirmity.

Him when Jesus had seen lying, and knew that he had been now a long time, he saith to him: Wilt thou be made whole?

The infirm man answered him: Sir, I have no man, when the water is troubled, to put me into the pond. For whilst I am coming, another goeth down before me.

Jesus saith to him: Arise, take up thy bed, and walk.

And immediately the man was made whole: and he took up his bed, and walked. And it was the sabbath that day.—*John* v. 1-9.

Resurrection of Christ, the

And in the end of the sabbath, when it began to dawn towards the first day of the

And when the sabbath was past, Mary Magdalen, and Mary the

And on the first day of the week, very early in the morning, they came

And on the first day of the week, Mary Magdalen cometh early, when it was yet dark, unto the sepulchre; and she saw the stone taken away from the sepulchre.

She ran, therefore, and cometh to Simon Peter, and to the other disciple whom Jesus loved, and saith to them: They have taken away the Lord out of the sepulchre, and we know not where they have laid him.

Peter therefore went out, and that other disciple, and they came to the sepulchre.

And they both ran together, and that other disciple did outrun Peter, and came first to the sepulchre.

And when he stooped down, he

week, came Mary Magdalen and the other Mary, to see the sepulchre.

And behold there was a great earthquake. For an angel of the Lord descended from heaven, and coming, rolled back the stone, and sat upon it.

And his countenance was as lightning, and his raiment as snow.

And for fear of him, the guards were struck with terror, and became as dead men.

And the angel answering, said to the women: Fear not you; for I know that you seek Jesus who was crucified.

He is not here, for he is risen, as he said. Come, and see the place where the Lord was laid.

And going quickly, tell ye his disciples that he is risen: and behold he will go before you into Galilee; there you shall see him. Lo, I have foretold it to you.

And they went out quickly from the sepulchre with fear and great joy, running to tell his disciples.

And behold Jesus met them, saying: All hail. But they came up and took hold of mother of James, and Salome, bought sweet spices, that coming, they might anoint Jesus.

And very early in the morning, the first day of the week, they come to the sepulchre, the sun being now risen.

And they said one to another: Who shall roll us back the stone from the door of the sepulchre?

And looking, they saw the stone rolled back. For it was very great.

And entering into the sepulchre, they saw a young man sitting on the right side, clothed with a white robe: and they were astonished.

Who saith to them: Be not affrighted; you seek Jesus of Nazareth, who was crucified: he is risen, he is not here, behold the place where they laid him.

But go, tell his disciples and Peter that he goeth before you into Galilee; there you shall see him, as he told you.

But they going out, fled from the sepulchre. For a trembling and fear had seized them: and they said nothing to any man; for they were afraid.

But he rising to the sepulchre, bringing the spices which they had prepared.

And they found the stone rolled back from the sepulchre.

And going in, they found not the body of the Lord Jesus.

And it came to pass, as they were astonished in their mind at this, behold, two men stood by them, in shining apparel.

And as they were afraid, and bowed down their countenance towards the ground, they said unto them: Why seek you the living with the dead?

He is not here, but is risen. Remember how he spoke unto you, when he was yet in Galilee,

Saying: The Son of man must be delivered into the hands of sinful men, and be crucified, and the third day rise again.

And they remembered his words.—*Luke* xxiv. 1-8.

saw the linen cloths lying; but yet he went not in.

Then cometh Simon Peter, following him, and went into the sepulchre, and saw the linen cloths lying,

And the napkin that had been about his head, not lying with the linen cloths, but apart, wrapped up into one place.

Then that other disciple also went in, who came first to the sepulchre: and he saw, and believed.

For as yet they knew not the scripture, that he must rise again from the dead. The disciples therefore departed again to their home.

But Mary stood at the sepulchre without, weeping. Now as she was weeping, she stooped down, and looked into the sepulchre,

And she saw two angels in white, sitting, one at the head, and one at the feet, where the body of Jesus had been laid.

They say to her: Woman, why weepest thou? She saith to them: Because they have taken away my Lord; and I know not where they have laid him.

his feet, and adored him.

Then Jesus said to them: Fear not. Go, tell my brethren that they go into Galilee, there they shall see me. —*Matt.* x x v i i i. 1-10.

early the first day o f t h e week, appeared first to M a r y Magdalen, o u t o f whom he h a d c a s t seven devils.—*Mark* xvi. 1-9.

When she had t h u s said, she turned herself back, a n d saw J e s u s standing; and she knew not that it was Jesus.

J e s u s saith to her: Woman, why weepest t h o u ? whom s e e k e s t thou ? She, think-i n g that it was the g a r d e n e r, saith to him: Sir, if thou hast taken him hence, tell me where thou h a s t laid him, and I w i l l t a k e h i m away.

Jesus saith to her: Mary. She turning, saith to him: R a b b o n i (which is to say, Master).

J e s u s saith to her: Do not touch me, for I am not yet ascended to my Father. But go to my brethren, and say to them: I as-cend to my Father a n d t o y o u r Father, to my God and your God.— *John* xx. 1-17.

Ruler at Capharnaum, Cure of the Son of the

He came again therefore into Cana of Galilee, where he made the water wine. And there was a certain ruler, whose son was sick at Capharnaum.

He having heard that Jesus was come from Judea into Galilee, went to him, and prayed him to come down, and heal his son: for he was at the point of death.

Jesus therefore said to him: Unless you see signs and wonders, you believe not.

The ruler saith to him: Lord, come down before that my son die.

Jesus saith to him: Go thy way: thy son liveth. The man believed the word which Jesus said to him, and went his way.

And as he was going down, his servants met him; and they brought word, saying, that his son lived.

He asked therefore of them the hour wherein he grew better. And they said to him: Yesterday, at the seventh hour, the fever left him.

The father therefore knew, that it

was at the same hour that Jesus said to him, Thy son liveth; and himself believed, and his whole house.

This is again the second miracle that Jesus did, when he was come out of Judea into Galilee.—*John iv. 46-54.*

Tempest, the First Stilling of the

And when he entered into the boat, his disciples followed him:

And behold a great tempest arose in the sea, so that the boat was covered with waves, but he was asleep.

And they came to him, and awaked him, saying: Lord, save us, we perish.

And Jesus saith to them: Why are you fearful, O ye of little faith? Then rising up, he commanded the winds, and the sea, and there came a great calm.

But the men wondered, saying: What manner of man is this, for the winds and the sea obey him?— *Matt. viii. 23-27.*

And he saith to them that day, when evening was come: Let us pass over to the other side.

And sending away the multitude, they take him even as he was in the ship: and there were other ships with him.

And there arose a great storm of wind, and the waves beat into the ship, so that the ship was filled.

And he was in the hinder part of the ship, sleeping upon a pillow; and they awake him, and say to him: Master; doth it not concern thee that we perish?

And rising up, he rebuked the wind, and said to the sea: Peace, be still. And the wind ceased: and there was made a great calm.

And he said to them: Why are you fearful? have you not faith yet? And they feared exceedingly: and they said one to another: Who is this (thinkest thou) that both wind and sea obey him?— *Mark iv. 35-40.*

And it came to pass on a certain day that he went into a little ship with his disciples, and he said to them: Let us go over to the other side of the lake. And they launched forth.

And when they were sailing, he slept; and there came down a storm of wind upon the lake, and they were filled, and were in danger.

And they came and awaked him, saying: Master, we perish. But he arising, rebuked the wind and the rage of the water; and it ceased, and there was a great calm.

And he said to them: Where is your faith? Who being afraid, wondered, saying one to another: Who is this (think you), that he commandeth both the winds and the sea, and they obey him?— *Luke viii. 22-25.*

Tempest, the Second Stilling of the

And forthwith Jesus obliged his disciples to go up into the boat, and go before him over the water, till he dismissed the people.

And having dismissed the multitude, he went into a mountain alone to pray. And when it was

And immediately he obliged his disciples to go up into the ship, that they might go before him over the water to Bethsaida, whilst he dismissed the people.

And when he had dismissed them, he went up to the mountain to pray.

Jesus therefore, when he knew that they would come to take him by force, and make him king, fled again into the mountain himself alone.

And when evening was come, his disciples went down to the sea.

And when they had

evening, he was there alone.

But the boat in the midst of the sea was tossed with the waves: for the wind was contrary.

And in the fourth watch of the night, he came to them walking upon the sea.

And they seeing him walking upon the sea, were troubled, saying: It is an apparition. And they cried out for fear.

And immediately Jesus spoke to them, saying: Be of good heart: it is I, fear ye not.

And Peter making answer, said: Lord, if it be thou, bid me come to thee upon the waters.

And he said: Come. And Peter going down out of the boat, walked upon the water to come to Jesus.

But seeing the wind strong, he was afraid: and when he began to sink, he cried out, saying: Lord, save me.

And immediately Jesus stretching forth his hand took hold of him, and said to him: O thou of little faith, why didst thou doubt?

And when they were come up into the boat, the wind ceased.

And they that were in the boat came and adored him, saying: Indeed thou art the Son of God.— *Matt.* xiv. 22-33.

And when it was late, the ship was in the midst of the sea, and himself alone on the land.

And seeing them laboring in rowing, (for the wind was against them,) and about the fourth watch of the night, h e cometh to them walking upon the sea, and he w o u l d have passed by them.

But they seeing him walking upon t h e s e a, thought it was an apparition, and they cried out.

For they all saw him, and were troubled. And immediately he spoke with them, and said to them: Have a good heart, it is I, fear ye not.

And he went up to them into the ship, and the wind ceased: a n d t h e y were far more astonished within themselves.—*Mark* vi. 45-51.

gone up into a ship, they went over the sea to Capharnaum; and it was now dark, and Jesus was not come unto them.

And the sea arose, by reason of a great wind that blew.

When they had rowed therefore about five and twenty or thirty furlongs, they see Jesus walking upon the sea, and drawing nigh to the ship, and they were afraid.

But he saith to them: It is I; be not afraid.

They were w i l l i n g therefore to take him into the ship; and presently the ship was at the land to which they were going.— *John* vi. 15-21.

Transfiguration of Christ, the

And after six days Jesus taketh unto him Peter and James, and John his brother, and bringeth them up into a high mountain apart:

And after s i x d a y s Jesus taketh with him Peter and James a n d John, and leadeth them up into a high mountain apart by themselves, and

And it came to pass about eight days a f t e r these words, that he took Peter, and James, a n d John, and went up into a mountain to pray.

And he was transfigured before them. And his face did shine as the sun: and his garments became white as snow.

And behold there appeared to them Moses and Elias talking with him.

And Peter answering, said to Jesus: Lord, it is good for us to be here: if thou wilt, let us make here three tabernacles, one for thee, and one for Moses, and one for Elias.

And as he was yet speaking, behold a bright cloud overshadowed them. And lo, a voice out of the cloud, saying: This is my beloved Son, in whom I am well pleased: hear ye him.

And the disciples hearing, fell upon their face, and were very much afraid.

And Jesus came and touched them: and said to them, Arise, and fear not.

And they lifting up their eyes saw no one but only Jesus.

And as they came down from the mountain, Jesus charged them, saying: Tell the vision to no man, till the Son of man be risen from the dead. — *Matt.* xvii. 1-9.

was transfigured before them.

And his garments became shining and exceeding white as snow, so as no fuller upon earth can make white.

And there appeared to them Elias with Moses; and they were talking with Jesus.

And Peter answering, said to Jesus: Rabbi, it is good for us to be here: and let us make three tabernacles, one for thee, and one for Moses, and one for Elias.

For he knew not what he said: for they were struck with fear.

And there was a cloud overshadowing them: and a voice came out of the cloud, saying: This is my most beloved son; hear ye him.

And immediately looking about, they saw no man any more, but Jesus only with them.

And as they came down from the mountain, he charged them not to tell any man what things they had seen, till the Son of man shall be risen again from the dead. — *Mark* ix. 1-8.

And whilst he prayed, the shape of his countenance was altered, and his raiment became white and glittering.

And behold two men were talking with him. And they were Moses and Elias,

Appearing in majesty. And they spoke of his decease that he should accomplish in Jerusalem.

But Peter and they that were with him, were heavy with sleep. And waking, they saw his glory, and the two men that stood with him.

And it came to pass, that as they were departing from him, Peter saith to Jesus: Master, it is good for us to be here: and let us make three tabernacles, one for thee, and one for Moses, and one for Elias; not knowing what he said.

And as he spoke these things, there came a cloud, and overshadowed them; and they were afraid, when they entered into the cloud.

And a voice came out of the cloud, saying: This is my beloved Son; hear him.

And whilst the voice was uttered, Jesus was found alone. And they held their peace, and told no man in those days any of these things which they had seen. — *Luke* ix. 28-36.

Water Changed into Wine at Cana, the

And the third day, there was a marriage in Cana of Galilee: and the mother of Jesus was there.

And Jesus also was invited, and his disciples, to the marriage.

And the wine failing, the mother of Jesus saith to him: They have no wine.

And Jesus saith to her: Woman, what is that to me and to thee? my hour is not yet come.

His mother saith to the waiters: Whatsoever he shall say to you, do ye.

Now there were set there six water pots of stone, according to the manner of the purifying of the Jews, containing two or three measures apiece.

Jesus saith to them: Fill the water pots with water. And they filled them up to the brim.

And Jesus saith to them: Draw out now, and carry to the chief steward of the feast. And they carried it.

And when the chief steward had tasted the water made wine, and knew not whence it was, but the waiters knew who had drawn the water; the chief steward calleth the bridegroom,

And saith to him: Every man at first setteth forth good wine, and when men have well drunk, then that which is worse. But thou hast kept the good wine until now.

This beginning of miracles did Jesus in Cana of Galilee; and manifested his glory, and his disciples believed in him. —*John* ii. 1-11.

Widow of Naim's Son Raised to Life

And it came to pass afterwards, that he went into a city that is called Naim; and there went with him his disciples, and a great multitude.

And when he came nigh to the gate of the city, behold a dead man was carried out, the only son of his mother; and she was a widow: and a great multitude of the city was with her.

Whom when the Lord had seen, being moved with mercy towards her, he said to her: Weep not.

And he came near and touched the bier. And they that carried it, stood still. And he said: Young man, I say to thee, arise.

And he that was dead, sat up, and began to speak. And he gave him to his mother.

And there came a fear on them all: and they glorified God, saying: A great prophet is risen up among us: and, God hath visited his people.—*Luke* vii. 11-16.

Withered Hand, the Man with the

And when he had passed from thence, he came into their synagogues.

And behold there was a man who had a withered hand, and they asked him, saying: Is it lawful to heal on the sabbath days? that they might accuse him.

But he said to them: What man shall there be among you, that hath one sheep: and if the same fall into a pit on the sabbath day, will he not take hold on it and lift it up?

How much better is a man than a sheep? Therefore it is lawful to do a good deed on the sabbath days.

Then he saith to the man: Stretch forth thy hand; and he stretched it

And he entered again into the synagogue, and there was a man there who had a withered hand.

And they watched him whether he would heal on the sabbath days; that they might accuse him.

And he said to the man who had the withered hand: Stand up in the midst.

And he saith to them: Is it lawful to do good on the sabbath days, or to do evil? to save life, or to destroy? But they held their peace.

And looking round about on them with anger, being grieved for the blindness of their hearts, he saith to the man: Stretch forth thy hand. And he stretched it forth:

And it came to pass also on another sabbath, that he entered into the synagogue, and taught. And there was a man, whose right hand was withered.

And the scribes and Pharisees watched if he would heal on the sabbath; that they might find an accusation against him.

But he knew their thoughts; and said to the man who had the withered hand: Arise, and stand forth in the midst. And rising he stood forth.

Then Jesus said to them: I ask you, if it be lawful on the sabbath days to do good, or to do evil; to save life, or to destroy?

And looking round about on them all, he said

forth, and it was restored to health even as the other.—*Matt.* xii. 9-13.

and his hand was restored unto him.—*Mark* iii. 1-5.

to the man: Stretch forth thy hand. And he stretched it forth: and his hand was restored.—*Luke* vi. 6-10.

Woman, the Infirm

And he was teaching in their synagogue on their sabbath. And behold there was a woman, who had a spirit of infirmity eighteen years: and she was bowed together, neither could she look upwards at all.

Whom when Jesus saw, he called her unto him, and said to her: Woman, thou art delivered from thy infirmity.

And he laid his hands upon her, and immediately she was made straight, and glorified God.—*Luke* xiii. 10-13.

Woman with the Bloody Flux, the

And behold a woman who was troubled with an issue of blood twelve years, came behind him, and touched the hem of his garment. For she said within herself: If I shall touch only his garment, I shall be healed.

But Jesus turning and seeing her, said: Be of good heart, daughter, thy faith hath made thee whole. And the woman was made whole from that hour.—*Matt.* ix. 20-22.

And a woman who was under an issue of blood twelve years, And had suffered many things from many physicians; and had spent all that she had, and was nothing the better, but rather worse, When she had heard of Jesus, came in the crowd behind him, and touched his garment. For she said: If I shall touch but his garment, I shall be whole. And forthwith the fountain of her blood was dried up, and she felt in her body that she was healed of the evil. And immediately Jesus knowing in himself the virtue that had proceeded from him, turning to the multitude, said: Who hath touched my garments? And his disciples said to him: Thou seest the multitude thronging thee, and sayest thou, Who hath touched me? And he looked about to see her who had done this. But the woman fearing and trembling, knowing what was done in her,

And there was a certain woman having an issue of blood twelve years, who had bestowed all her substance on physicians, and could not be healed by any. She came behind him, and touched the hem of his garment; and immediately the issue of her blood stopped. And Jesus said: Who is it that touched me? And all denying, Peter and they that were with him said: Master, the multitudes throng and press thee, and dost thou say, Who touched me? And Jesus said: Somebody hath touched me; for I know that virtue is gone out from me. And the woman seeing that she was not hid, came trembling, and fell down before his feet, and declared before all the people for what cause she had touched him, and how she was immediately healed. But he said to her: Daughter, thy faith hath made thee whole; go thy way in peace.—*Luke* viii. 43-48.

came and fell down before him, and told him all the truth.

And he said to h e r : Daughter, thy faith hath made thee whole: go in peace, and be thou whole of thy disease.—*Mark* v. 25-34.

MANY MIRACLES RECORDED ONLY IN GENERAL

1st. The Miracles in Galilee

And Jesus went about all Galilee, teaching in their synagogues, and preaching the gospel of the kingdom: and healing all manner of sickness and every infirmity, among the people.

And his fame went throughout all Syria, and they presented to him all sick people that were taken with divers diseases and torments, and such as were possessed by devils, and lunatics, and those that had the palsy, and he cured them.—*Matt.* iv. 23, 24.

And he saith to them: Let us go into the neighboring towns and cities, that I may preach there also; for to this purpose am I come.

And he was preaching in their synagogues, and in all Galilee, and casting out devils.—*Mark* i. 38, 39.

2d. The Evening at Capharnaum

And when evening was come, they brought to him many that were possessed with devils: and he cast out the spirits with his word: and all that were sick he healed:

That it might be fulfilled, which was spoken by the prophet Isaias, saying: He took our infirmities, and bore our diseases. —*Matt.* viii. 16, 17.

And when it was evening, after sunset, they brought to him all that were ill and that were possessed with devils.

And all the city was gathered together at the door.

And he healed many that were troubled with divers diseases; and he cast out many devils, and he suffered them not to speak, because they knew him.—*Mark* i. 32-34.

And when the sun was down, all they that had any sick with divers diseases, brought them to him. But he laying his hands on every one of them, healed them.

And devils went out from many, crying out and saying: Thou art the Son of God. And rebuking them he suffered them not to speak, for they knew that he was Christ. —*Luke* iv. 40, 41.

3d. In the Towns and Cities of Galilee

And Jesus went about all the cities, and towns, teaching in their synagogues, and preaching the gospel of the kingdom, and healing every disease, and every infirmity.—*Matt.* ix. 35.

4th. In the Place of Retirement

And the Pharisees going out made a consultation against him, how they might destroy him.

And the Pharisees going out, immediately made a consultation w i t h t h e Herodians against him,

And coming down with them, he stood in a plain place, and the company of his disciples, and a very

But Jesus knowing it, retired from thence: and many followed him, and he healed them all.

And he charged them that they should not make him known. — *Matt.* xii. 14-16.

how they might destroy him.

But Jesus retired with his disciples to the sea; and a great multitude followed him from Galilee and Judea,

And from Jerusalem, and from Idumea, and from beyond the Jordan. And they about Tyre and Sidon, a great multitude, hearing the things which he did, came to him.

And he spoke to his disciples that a small ship should wait on him because of the multitude, lest they should throng him.

For he healed many, so that they pressed upon him for to touch him, as many as had evils.

And the unclean spirits, when they saw him, fell down before him: and they cried out, saying: Thou art the Son of God. And he strictly charged them that they should not make him known.—*Mark* iii. 6-12.

great multitude of people from all Judea and Jerusalem, and the sea coast both of Tyre and Sidon,

Who were come to hear him, and to be healed of their diseases. And they that were troubled with unclean spirits, were cured.

And all the multitude sought to touch him, for virtue went out from him, and healed all.—*Luke* vi. 17-19.

5th. The Miracles in Nazareth

And they were scandalized in his regard. But Jesus said to them: A prophet is not without honor, save in his own country, and in his own house.

And he wrought not many miracles there, because of their unbelief.—*Matt.* xiii. 57, 58.

And Jesus said to them: A prophet is not without honor, but in his own country, and in his own house, and among his own kindred.

And he could not do any miracles there, only that he cured a few that were sick, laying his hands upon them.—*Mark* vi. 4, 5.

6th. In the Desert Near the Lake

Which when Jesus had heard (viz. the death of John the Baptist), he retired from thence by a boat, into a desert place apart, and the multitudes having heard of it, fol-

And the apostles, when they were returned, told him all they had done. And taking them, he went aside into a desert place, apart, which belongeth to Bethsaida.

After these things Jesus went over the sea of Galilee, which is that of Tiberias.

And a great multitude followed him, because they saw the miracles which he

lowed him on foot out of the cities.

And he coming forth saw a great multitude, and had compassion on them, and healed their sick.—*Matt.* xiv. 13, 14.

Which when the people knew, they followed him; and he received them, and spoke to them of the kingdom of God, and healed them who had need of healing.—*Luke* ix. 10, 11.

did on them that were diseased.—*John* vi. 1, 2.

7th.　In the Country of Genesareth

And having passed the water, they came into the country of Genesar.

And when the men of that place had knowledge of him, they sent into all that country, and brought to him all that were diseased.

And they besought him that they might touch but the hem of his garment. And as many as touched, were made whole.—*Matt.* xiv. 34-36.

And when they had passed over, they came into the land of Genesareth, and set to the shore.

And when they were gone out of the ship, immediately they knew him:

And running through that whole country, they began to carry about in beds those that were sick, where they heard he was.

And whithersoever he entered, into towns or into villages or cities, they laid the sick in the streets, and besought him that they might touch but the hem of his garment: and as many as touched him were made whole.—*Mark* vi. 53-56.

8th.　In the Mountain Near the Sea of Tiberias

And when Jesus had passed away from thence, he came nigh the sea of Galilee. And going up into a mountain, he sat there.

And there came to him great multitudes, having with them the dumb, the blind, the lame, the maimed, and many others: and they cast them down at his feet, and he healed them:

So that the multitudes marvelled seeing the dumb speak, the lame walk, the blind see: and they glorified the God of Israel.—*Matt.* xv. 29-31.

9th.　In the Temple

And there came to him the blind and the lame in the temple; and he healed them.

And the chief priests and scribes, seeing the wonderful things that he did, and the children crying in the temple, and saying: Hosanna to the son of David; were moved with indignation.—*Matt.* xxi. 14, 15.

10th.　The Miracles Related to John the Baptist

And John called to him two of his disciples, and sent them to Jesus, saying: Art thou he that art' to come; or look we for another?

And when the men were come unto him, they said: John the Baptist hath sent us to thee, saying: Art thou he that art to come; or look we for another?

(And in that same hour, he cured many of their diseases, and hurts, and evil spirits: and to many that were blind he gave sight.)

And answering, he said to them: Go and relate to John what you have heard and seen: the blind see, the lame walk, the lepers are made clean, the deaf hear, the dead rise again, to the poor the gospel is preached.—*Luke* vii. 19-22.

11th.　Not Recorded

Many other signs also did Jesus in the sight of his disciples, which are not written in this book.

But these are written, that you may

believe that Jesus is the Christ, the Son of God: and that believing, you may have life in his name.—*John* xx. 30, 31.

But there are also many other things which Jesus did; which, if they were written every one, the world itself, I think, would not be able to contain the books that should be written.—*John* xxi. 25.

MIRACLES OF CHRIST

Recorded in the Order of Time in which They Were Performed

The water changed into wine at Cana.
Jesus escapes from his enemies at Nazareth.
Son of the ruler at Capharnaum cured.
The demoniac at Capharnaum.
Peter's mother-in-law cured.
The miracles in Capharnaum on the sabbath evening.
The first miraculous draught of fish.
The many miracles performed in Galilee.
Cure of the leper.
Cure of the man sick of the palsy.
The infirm man at the pond of Probatica.
The man with the withered hand.
The miracles in the place of retirement.
Cure of the centurion's servant.
The son of the widow of Naim raised to life.
The miracles related to John the Baptist.
The blind and dumb demoniac cured.
The first stilling of the tempest.
The demoniacs of Gergesa.
Cure of the woman with the bloody flux.
The daughter of Jairus raised to life.
The miracles in Nazareth.
The miracles performed during his third mission through the towns and villages of Galilee.
The miracles in the desert near the lake of Genesareth.
The first multiplication of the loaves and fishes.
The second stilling of the tempest.
The miracles performed in the country of Genesareth.

The daughter of the woman of Canaan cured.
The deaf and dumb man cured.
The miracles performed in the mountain near the sea of Tiberias.
The second multiplication of the loaves and fishes.
The blind man of Bethsaida.
The transfiguration of Christ.
Cure of the demoniac child.
The money found in the mouth of the fish.
Cure of the man born blind.
The two blind men.
Cure of the dumb demoniac.
The infirm woman.
Cure of the man sick of the dropsy.
The raising of Lazarus to life.
Cure of the ten lepers.
The two blind men of Jericho.
The withered fig-tree.
The miracles performed in the temple.
The miracle at the arrest of Christ.
Healing of Malchus' ear.
The miracles at the death of Christ.
The resurrection of Christ.
The second miraculous draught of fish.
The ascension of Christ into heaven.

Time Unknown

The cure of Magdalen and the holy women.

PROPHECIES OF CHRIST, THE

And when he was come into Jerusalem, the whole city was moved, saying: Who is this?

And the people said: This is Jesus the prophet, from Nazareth of Galilee. —*Matt.* xxi. 10, 11.

And seeking to lay hands on him, they feared the multitudes: because they held him as a prophet.—*Matt.* xxi. 46.

And he that was dead, sat up, and began to speak. And he gave him to his mother.

And there came a fear on them all: and they glorified God, saying: A great prophet is risen up among us: and God hath visited his people.—*Luke* vii. 15, 16.

And the one of them, whose name was Cleophas, answering, said to him: Art thou only a stranger in Jerusalem, and hast not known the things that have been done there in these days? . To whom he said: What things? And they said: Concerning Jesus of Nazareth, who was a prophet, mighty in work and word before God and all the people.—*Luke* xxiv. 18, 19.

The woman saith to him: Sir, I perceive that thou art a prophet.—*John* iv. 19.

Apostles, in Reference to the

And Jesus walking by the sea of Galilee, saw two brethren, Simon who is called Peter, and Andrew his brother, casting a net into the sea (for they were fishers).

And he saith to them: Come ye after me, and I will make you to be fishers of men.—*Matt.* iv. 18, 19.

And passing by the sea of Galilee, he saw Simon and Andrew his brother, casting nets into the sea (for they were fishermen).

And Jesus said to them: Come after me, and I will make you to become fishers of men.—*Mark* i. 16, 17.

Which when Simon Peter saw, he fell down at Jesus' knees, saying: Depart from me, for I am a sinful man, O Lord.

For he was wholly astonished, and all that were with him, at the draught of the fishes which they had taken. . . .

And Jesus saith to Simon: Fear not: from henceforth thou shalt catch men.—*Luke* v. 8-10.

Then Peter answering, said to him: Behold we have left all things, and have followed thee: what therefore shall we have?

And Jesus said to them: Amen, I say to you, that you, who have followed me, in the regeneration, when the Son of man shall sit on the seat of his majesty, you also shall sit on twelve seats judging the twelve tribes of Israel. —*Matt.* xix. 27, 28.

Then came to him the mother of the sons of Zebedee with her sons, adoring and asking something of him.

Who said to her: What wilt thou? She saith to him: Say that these my two sons may sit, the one on thy right hand, and the other on thy left, in thy kingdom.

And Jesus answering, said: You know not what you ask. Can you drink the chalice that I shall drink? They say to him: We can.

He saith to them: My chalice indeed you shall drink; but to sit on my right or left hand, is not mine to give to you, but to them for whom it is prepared by my Father.—*Matt.* xx. 20-23.

And James and John the sons of Zebedee, come to him, saying: Master, we desire that whatsoever we shall ask, thou wouldst do it for us:

But he said to them: What would you that I should do for you?

And they said: Grant to us, that we may sit, one on thy right hand, and the other on thy left hand, in thy glory.

And Jesus said to them: You know not what you ask. Can you drink of the chalice that I drink of: or be baptized with the baptism wherewith I am baptized?

But they said to him: We can. And Jesus saith to them: You shall indeed drink of the chalice that I drink of: and with the baptism wherewith I am baptized, you shall be baptized.

But to sit on my right hand, or on my left, is not mine to give to you, but to them for whom it is prepared.— *Mark* x. 35-40.

Lay it up therefore in your hearts, not to meditate before how you shall answer:

For I will give you a mouth and wisdom, which all your adversaries shall not be able to resist and gainsay. —*Luke* xxi. 14, 15.

Christ, the Ministry of

The same day, there came some of the Pharisees, saying to him: Depart, and get thee hence, for Herod hath a mind to kill thee.

And he said to them: Go and tell that fox, Behold, I cast out devils, and do cures to-day and to-morrow, and the third day I am consummated.

Nevertheless I must walk to-day and to-morrow, and the day following, because it cannot be that a prophet perish, out of Jerusalem.—*Luke* xiii. 31-33.

Christ's Entry into Jerusalem, the Preparation for

And when they drew nigh to Jerusalem, and were come to Bethphage, unto mount Olivet, then Jesus sent two disciples,

Saying to them: Go ye into the village that is over against you, and immediately you shall find an ass tied, and a colt with her: loose them and bring them to me.

And if any man shall say any thing to you, say ye, that the Lord hath need of them: and forthwith he will let them go.

Now all this was done that it might be fulfilled which was spoken by the prophet, saying:

Tell ye the daughter of Sion: Behold thy king cometh to thee, meek, and sitting upon an ass, and a colt the foal of her that is used to the yoke.—*Matt.* xxi. 1-5.

And when they were drawing near to Jerusalem and to Bethania at the mount of Olives, he sendeth two of his disciples,

And saith to them: Go ye into the village that is over against you, and immediately at your coming in thither, you shall find a colt tied, upon which no man yet hath sat: loose him, and bring him.

And if any man shall say to you, What are you doing? say ye that the Lord hath need of him: and immediately he will let him come hither.

And going their way, they found the colt tied before the gate without, in the meeting of two ways: and they loose him.

And some of them that stood there, said to them: What do you loosing the colt?

Who said to them as Jesus had commanded them; and they let him go with them.—*Mark* xi. 1-6.

And it came to pass, when he was come nigh to Bethphage and Bethania, unto the mount called Olivet, he sent two of his disciples,

Saying: Go into the town which is over against you, at your entering into which you shall find the colt of an ass tied, on which no man ever hath sitten: loose him, and bring him hither.

And if any man shall ask you: Why do you loose him? you shall say thus unto him: Because the Lord hath need of his service.

And they that were sent, went their way, and found the colt standing, as he had said unto them.

And as they were loosing the colt, the owners thereof said to them: Why loose you the colt?

But they said: Because the Lord hath need of him. And they brought him to Jesus.—*Luke* xix. 29-35.

Christ's Last Supper, the Preparation for

And he sendeth two of his disciples, and saith to them: Go ye into the city; and there shall meet you a man carrying a pitcher of water, follow him;

And whithersoever he shall go in, say to the master of the house,

And he sent Peter and John, saying: Go, and prepare for us the pasch, that we may eat.

But they said: Where wilt thou that we prepare?

And he said to them: Behold, as you

The master saith, Where is my refectory, where I may eat the pasch with my disciples?

And he will show you a large dining room furnished; and there prepare ye for us.

And his disciples went their way, and came into the city; and they found as he had told them, and they prepared the pasch.—*Mark* xiv. 13-16.

go into the city, there shall meet you a man carrying a pitcher of water: follow him into the house where he entereth in.

And you shall say to the goodman of the house: The master saith to thee, Where is the guest chamber, where I may eat the pasch with my disciples?

And he will show you a large dining room, furnished; and there prepare.

And they going, found as he had said to them, and made ready the pasch.—*Luke* xxii. 8-13.

Christ, the Passion of

From that time Jesus began to show to his disciples, that he must go to Jerusalem, and suffer many things from the ancients and scribes and chief priests, and be put to death, and the third day rise again.—*Matt.* xvi. 21.

And he began to teach them, that the Son of man must suffer many things, and be rejected by the ancients and by the high priests, and the scribes, and be killed: and after three days rise again.

And he spoke the word openly.—*Mark* viii. 31, 32.

And he said to them: But whom do you say that I am? Simon Peter answering, said: The Christ of God.

But he strictly charging them, commanded t h e y should tell this to no man. Saying: The Son of man must suffer many things, and be rejected by t h e ancients and chief priests and scribes, and be killed, and the third day rise again. — *Luke* i x . 20-22.

And as they came down from the mountain, Jesus charged them, saying: Tell the vision to no man, till the Son of man be risen from the dead.

And his disciples asked him, saying: Why then do the scribes say that Elias must come first?

But he answering, said to them: Elias indeed shall come, and restore all things.

But I say to you, that Elias is already come, and they knew him not, but have done unto him whatsoever they had a mind. So also the Son of man shall suffer from them.—*Matt.* xvii. 9-12.

And as they came down from the mountain, he charged them not to tell any man what things they had seen, till the Son of man shall be risen again from the dead. . . .

And they asked him, saying: Why then do the Pharisees and scribes say that Elias must come first?

Who answering, said to them: Elias, when he shall come first, shall restore all things; and as it is written of the Son of man, that he must suffer many things and be despised.

But I say to you, that Elias also is come, (and they have done to him whatsoever they would,) as it is written of him.—*Mark* ix. 8, 10-12.

And Jesus going up to Jerusalem, took the twelve disciples apart, and said to them:

And they were in the way going up to Jerusalem: and Jesus went before them, and they were

Then Jesus took unto him the twelve, and said to them: Behold, we go up to Jerusalem, and all

Behold we go up to Jerusalem, and the Son of man shall be betrayed to the chief priests and the scribes, and they shall condemn him to death.

And shall deliver him to the Gentiles to be mocked, and scourged, and crucified, and the third day he shall rise again.—*Matt.* xx. 17-19.

astonished; and following were afraid. And taking again the twelve, he began to tell them the things that should befall him.

Saying: Behold we go up to Jerusalem, and the Son of man shall be betrayed to the chief priests, and to the scribes and ancients, and they shall condemn him to death, and shall deliver him to the Gentiles.

And they shall mock him, and spit on him, and scourge him, and kill him: and the third day he shall rise again.—*Mark* x. 32-34.

things shall be accomplished which were written by the prophets concerning the Son of man.

For he shall be delivered to the Gentiles, and shall be mocked, and scourged, and spit upon:

And after they have scourged him, they will put him to death, and the third day he shall rise again.—*Luke* xviii. 31-33.

Hear ye another parable. There was a man a householder, who planted a vineyard, and made a hedge round about it, and dug in it a press, and built a tower, and let it out to husbandmen; and went into a strange country.

And when the time of the fruits drew nigh, he sent his servants to the husbandmen t h a t t h e y might receive the fruits thereof.

And the husbandmen laying hands on his servants, beat one, and killed another, and stoned another.

Again he sent other servants more than the former; and they did to them in like manner.

And last of all he sent to them his son, saying: They will reverence my son.

But the husbandmen seeing the son, said among themselves: This is the heir: come, let us kill him, and we shall have his inheritance.

And taking him, they

And he began to speak to them in parables: A certain man planted a vineyard and made a hedge about it, and dug a place for the wine vat, and built a tower, and let it to husbandmen; and went into a far country.

A n d a t the season he sent to the husbandmen a servant to receive of the husbandmen of the fruit of the vineyard.

Who having laid hands on him, beat him, and sent him away empty.

And again he sent to them another servant; and him they wounded in the head, and used him reproachfully.

And again he sent another, and him they killed: and many others, of whom some they beat, and others they killed.

Therefore having yet one son, most dear to him; he also sent him unto them last of all, saying: They will reverence my son.

B u t the husbandmen said one to another: This

And he began to speak to the people this parable: A certain man planted a vineyard, and let it out to husbandmen: and he was abroad for a long time.

And at the season he sent a servant to the husbandmen, that they should give him of the fruit of the vineyard. Who, beating him, sent him away empty.

And again he sent another servant. But they beat him also, and treating him reproachfully, sent him away empty.

And again he sent the third: and they wounded him also, and cast him out.

Then the lord of the vineyard said: What shall I do? I will send my beloved son: it may be, when they see him, they will reverence him.

Whom when the husbandmen s a w, t h e y thought within themselves, saying: This is the heir, let us kill him, that the inheritance may be ours.

So casting him out of

cast him forth out of the vineyard, a n d k i l l e d him. . . .

And when the chief priests and Pharisees had heard his parables, they knew that he spoke of them.—*Matt.* xxi.33-39,45.

is the heir; come let us kill him; and the inheritance shall be ours.

And laying hold on him, they killed him, and cast him out of the vineyard.

. . . And they sought to lay hands on him, but they feared the people. For they knew that he spoke this parable to them. —*Mark* xii. 1-8, 12.

the vineyard, they killed him. . . .

And the chief priests and the scribes sought to lay hands on him the same hour: b u t t h e y feared the people, for they knew that he spoke this parable to them.—*Luke* xx. 9-15, 19.

And it came to pass, when Jesus had ended all these words, he said to his disciples:

You know that after two days shall be the pasch, and the Son of man shall be delivered up to be crucified.—*Matt.* xxvi. 1, 2.

And he said to them. This is my blood of the new testament, which shall be shed for many.—*Mark* xiv. 24.

And all were astonished at the mighty power of God. But while all wondered at all the things he did, he said to his disciples: Lay you up in your hearts these words, for it shall come to pass, that the Son of man shall be delivered into the hands of men.

But they understood not this word; and it was hid from them, so that they perceived it not. And they were afraid to ask him concerning this word.—*Luke* ix. 44, 45.

For as the lightning that lighteneth from under heaven, shineth unto the parts that are under heaven, so shall the Son of man be in his day.

But first he must suffer many things, and be rejected by this generation.— *Luke* xvii. 24, 25.

And he said to them: With desire I

have desired to eat this pasch with you, before I suffer.—*Luke* xxii. 15.

For I say to you, that this that is written must yet be fulfilled in me: And with the wicked was he reckoned. For the things concerning me have an end.—*Luke* xxii. 37.

And as Moses lifted up the serpent in the desert, so must the Son of man be lifted up:

That whosoever believeth in him, may not perish; but may have life everlasting.—*John* iii. 14, 15.

Jesus therefore said to them: When you shall have lifted up the Son of man, then shall you know, that I am he, and that I do nothing of myself, but as the Father hath taught me, these things I speak.—*John* viii. 28.

And I, if I be lifted up from the earth, will draw all things to myself. (Now this he said, signifying what death he should die.)—*John* xii. 32, 33.

Pilate therefore said to them: Take him you, and judge him according to your law. The Jews therefore said to him: It is not lawful for us to put any man to death;

That the word of Jesus might be fulfilled, which he said, signifying what death he should die.—*John* xviii. 31, 32.

Christ Abandoned by the Apostles

Then Jesus saith to them: All you shall be scandalized in me this night. For it is written: I will strike the shepherd, and the sheep of the flock shall be dispersed.—*Matt.* xxvi. 31.

And Jesus saith to them: You will all be scandalized in my regard this night; for it is written, I will strike the shepherd, and the sheep shall be dispersed.—*Mark* xiv. 27.

Behold, the hour cometh, and it is now come, that you shall be scattered every man to his own, and shall leave me alone; and yet I am not alone, because the Father is with me.—*John* xvi. 32.

Christ Betrayed by Judas

And when they abode together in Galilee, Jesus said to them: The Son of man shall be betrayed into the hands of men.—*Matt.* xvii. 21.

And departing from thence, they passed through Galilee, and he would not that any man should know it.

And he taught his disciples, and said to them: The Son of man shall be betrayed into the hands of men.—*Mark* ix. 29, 30.

And Jesus going up to Jerusalem, took the twelve disciples apart, and said to them:

Behold we go up to Jerusalem, and the Son of man shall be betrayed to the chief priests and the scribes, and they shall condemn him to death.—*Matt.* xx. 17, 18.

And they were in the way going up to Jerusalem. . . . And taking again the twelve, he began to tell them the things that should befall him.

Saying: Behold we go up to Jerusalem, and the Son of man shall be betrayed to the chief priests, and to the scribes and ancients, and they shall condemn him to death, and shall deliver him to the Gentiles.—*Mark* x. 32, 33.

And whilst they were eating, he said: Amen I say to you, that one of you is about to betray me.

And they being very much troubled, began every one to say: Is it I, Lord?

But he answering, said: He that dippeth his hand with me in the dish, he shall betray me.

And when they were at table and eating, Jesus saith: Amen I say to you, one of you that eateth with me shall betray me.

But they began to be sorrowful, and to say to him one by one: Is it I?

Who saith to them: One of the

But yet behold, the hand of him that betrayeth me is with me on the table.

And the Son of man indeed goeth, according to that which is determined: but yet,

When Jesus had said these things, he was troubled in spirit; and he testified, and said: Amen, amen I say to you, one of you shall betray me.

The disciples therefore looked one upon another, doubting of whom he spoke.

Now there was leaning on Jesus' bosom one of his disciples, whom Jesus loved.

Simon Peter therefore beckoned to him, and said to him: Who is it

The Son of man indeed goeth, as it is written of him: but woe to that man by whom the Son of man shall be betrayed: it were better for him, if that man had not been born.

And Judas that betrayed him, answering, said: Is it I, Rabbi? He saith to him: Thou hast said it.—*Matt.* xxvi. 21-25.

twelve, who dippeth with me his hand in the dish.

And the Son of man indeed goeth, as it is written of him: but woe to that man by whom the Son of man shall be betrayed. It were better for him, if that man had not been born. —*Mark* xiv. 18-21.

woe to that man by whom he shall be betrayed.

And they began to inquire among themselves, which of them it was that should do this thing.—*Luke* xxii. 21-23.

of whom he speaketh?

He therefore, leaning on the breast of Jesus, saith to him: Lord, who is it?

Jesus answered: He it is to whom I shall reach bread dipped. And when he had dipped the bread, he gave it to Judas Iscariot, the son of Simon.

And after the morsel, Satan entered into him. And Jesus said to him: That which thou dost, do quickly.—*John* xiii. 21-27.

Then he cometh to his disciples, and saith to them: Sleep ye now and take your rest; behold the hour is at hand, and the Son of man shall be betrayed into the hands of sinners.

Rise, let us go: behold he is at hand that will betray me.—*Matt.* xxvi. 45, 46.

And he cometh the third time, and saith to them: Sleep ye now, and take your rest. It is enough: the hour is come: behold the Son of man shall be betrayed into the hands of sinners.

Rise up, let us go. Behold, he that will betray me is at hand.—*Mark* xiv. 41, 42.

Jesus answered them: Have not I chosen you twelve; and one of you is a devil?

Now he meant Judas Iscariot, the son of Simon: for this same was about to betray him, whereas he was one of the twelve.—*John* vi. 71, 72.

Jesus saith to him (Peter): He that is washed, needeth not but to wash his feet, but is clean wholly. And you are clean, but not all.

For he knew who he was that would betray him; therefore he said: You are not all clean.—*John* xiii. 10, 11.

Christ Denied by Peter

And Peter answering, said to him: Although all

But Peter saith to him: Although all shall be scan-

And the Lord said: Simon, Simon, behold Satan hath desired to have you, that

Simon Peter saith to him: Lord, whither goest thou? Jesus answered: Whither I

shall be scandalized in thee, I will never be scandalized. Jesus said to him: Amen I say to thee, that in this night before the cock crow, thou wilt deny me thrice.—*Matt.* xxvi. 33, 34.

dalized in thee, yet not I. And Jesus saith to him: Amen I say to thee, to-day, even in this night, before the cock crow twice, thou shalt deny me thrice.—*Mark* xiv. 29, 30.

he may sift you as wheat: But I have prayed for thee, that thy faith fail not: and thou, being once converted, confirm thy brethren. Who said to him: Lord, I am ready to go with thee, both into prison, and to death. And he said: I say to thee, Peter, the cock shall not crow this day, till thou thrice deniest that thou knowest me.—*Luke* xxii. 31-34.

go, thou canst not follow me now; but thou shalt follow hereafter. Peter saith to him: Why cannot I follow thee now? I will lay down my life for thee. Jesus answered him: Wilt thou lay down thy life for me? Amen, amen I say to thee, the cock shall not crow, till thou deny me thrice.—*John* xiii. 36-38.

Christ, the Death and Burial of

Then some of the scribes and Pharisees answered him, saying: Master, we would see a sign from thee.

Who answering said to them: An evil and adulterous generation seeketh a sign: and a sign shall not be given it, but the sign of Jonas the prophet.

For as Jonas was in the whale's belly three days and three nights: so shall the Son of man be in the heart of the earth three days and three nights.—*Matt.* xii. 38-40.

And the multitudes running together, he began to say: This generation is a wicked generation: it asketh a sign, and a sign shall not be given it, but the sign of Jonas the prophet.

For as Jonas was a sign to the Ninivites; so shall the Son of man also be to this generation.—*Luke* xi. 29, 30.

A wicked and adulterous generation seeketh after a sign: and a sign shall not be given it, but the sign of Jonas the prophet.—*Matt.* xvi. 4.

And when they abode together in Galilee, Jesus said to them: The Son of man shall be betrayed into the hands of men:

And they shall kill him, and the third day he shall rise again.—*Matt.* xvii. 21, 22.

And departing from thence, they passed through Galilee, and he would not that any man should know it.

And he taught his disciples, and said to them: The Son of man shall be betrayed into the hands of men, and they shall kill him; and after that he is killed, he shall rise again the third day.—*Mark* ix. 29, 30.

Even as the Son of man is not come to be ministered unto, but to minister, and to give his life a redemption for many.—*Matt.* xx. 28.

There came to him a woman having an alabaster box of precious ointment, and poured it on his head as he was at table.

And the disciples seeing it, had indignation, saying: To what purpose is this waste?

For this might have been sold for much, and given to the poor.

And Jesus knowing it, said to them: Why do you trouble this woman? for she hath wrought a good work upon me.

For the poor you have always with you: but me you have not always.

For she in pouring this ointment upon my body, hath done it for my burial.—*Matt.* xxvi. 7-12.

And when he was in Bethania, in the house of Simon the leper, and was at meat, there came a woman having an alabaster box of ointment of precious spikenard: and breaking the alabaster box, she poured it out upon his head.

Now there were some that had indignation within themselves, and said: Why was this waste of the ointment made?

For this ointment might have been sold for more than three hundred pence, and given to the poor. And they murmured against her.

But Jesus said: Let her alone, why do you molest her? She hath wrought a good work upon me.

For the poor you have always with you: and whensoever you will, you may do them good: but me you have not always.

She hath done what she could: she is come beforehand to anoint my body for the burial.—*Mark* xiv. 3-8.

Therefore doth the Father love me: because I lay down my life, that I may take it again.

No man taketh it away from me: but I lay it down of myself, and I have power to lay it down: and I have power to take it up again. This commandment have I received of my Father.—*John* x. 17, 18.

You have heard that said to you: I go away, and I come unto you. If you loved me, you would indeed be glad, because I go to the Father: for the Father is greater than I.

And now I have told you before it come to pass: that when it shall come to pass, you may believe.—*John* xiv. 28, 29.

Christ, the Resurrection of

Then some of the scribes and Pharisees answered him, saying: Master, we would see a sign from thee.

Who answering said to them: An evil and adulterous generation seeketh a sign: and a sign shall not be given it, but the sign of Jonas the prophet.

For as Jonas was in the whale's belly three days and three nights: so shall the Son of man be in the heart of the earth three days and three nights.—*Matt.* xii. 38-40.

And the multitudes running together, he began to say: This generation is a wicked generation: it asketh a sign, and a sign shall not be given it, but the sign of Jonas the prophet.

For as Jonas was a sign to the Ninivites; so shall the Son of man also be to this generation.—*Luke* xi. 29, 30.

A wicked and adulterous generation seeketh after a sign: and a sign shall | not be given it, but the sign of Jonas the prophet.—*Matt.* xvi. 4.

From that time Jesus began to show to his disciples, that he must go to Jerusalem, and suffer many things from the ancients and scribes and chief priests, and be put to death, and the third day rise again.—*Matt.* xvi. 21.

And he began to teach them; that the Son of man must suffer many things, and be rejected by the ancients, and by the high priests, and the scribes, and be killed: and after three days rise again.— *Mark* viii. 31.

And he said to them: But whom do you say that I am? Simon Peter answering, said: The Christ of God.

But he strictly charging them, commanded they should tell this to no man. Saying: The Son of man must suffer many things, and be rejected by the ancients and chief priests and scribes, and be killed, and the third day rise again.—*Luke* ix. 20-22.

And as they came down from the mountain, Jesus charged them, saying: Tell the vision to no man, till the Son of man be risen from the dead.—*Matt.* xvii. 9.

And as they came down from the mountain, he charged them not to tell any man what things they had seen, till the Son of man shall be risen again from the dead.

And they kept the word to themselves; questioning together what that should mean, when he shall be risen from the dead.—*Mark* ix. 8, 9.

And when they abode together in Galilee, Jesus said to them: The Son of man shall be betrayed into the hands of men:

And they shall kill him, and the third day he shall rise again.—*Matt.* xvii. 21, 22.

And departing from thence, they passed through Galilee, and he would not that any man should know it.

And he taught his disciples, and said to them: The Son of man shall be betrayed into the hands of men, and they shall kill him; and after that he is killed, he shall rise again the third day. —*Mark* ix. 29, 30.

And Jesus going up to Jerusalem took the twelve disciples apart, and said to them:

Behold we go up to Jerusalem, and the Son of man shall be betrayed to the chief priests and the scribes, and they shall condemn him to death.

And shall deliver him to the Gentiles to be mocked, and scourged, and cruci-

And they were in the way going up to Jerusalem: and Jesus went before them, and they were astonished; and following were afraid. And taking again the twelve, he began to tell them the things that should befall him.

Saying: Behold we go up to Jerusalem, and the Son of man shall be betrayed to the chief priests, and to the scribes and an-

Then Jesus took unto him the twelve, and said to them: Behold, we go up to Jerusalem, and all things shall be accomplished which were written by the prophets concerning the Son of man.

For he shall be delivered to the Gentiles, and shall be mocked, and scourged, and spit upon:

And after they have scourged him, they will

fied, and the third day he shall rise again.—*Matt.* xx. 17-19.

cients, and they shall condemn him to death, and shall deliver him to the Gentiles.

And they shall mock him, and spit on him, and scourge him, and kill him: and the third day he shall rise again.—*Mark* x. 32-34.

put him to death; and the third day he shall rise again.—*Luke* xviii. 31-33.

But after I shall be risen again, I will go before you into Galilee.—*Matt.* xxvi. 32.

But after I shall be risen again, I will go before you into Galilee.—*Mark* xiv. 28.

And the next day, which followed the day of preparation, the chief priests and the Pharisees came together to Pilate,

Saying: Sir, we have remembered, that that seducer said, while he was yet alive: After three days I will rise again. —*Matt.* xxvii. 62, 63.

The Jews, therefore, answered, and said to him: What sign dost thou show unto us, seeing thou dost these things?

Jesus answered, and said to them: Destroy this temple, and in three days I will raise it up.

The Jews then said: Six and forty years was this temple in building; and wilt thou raise it up in three days?

But he spoke of the temple of his body.

When therefore he was risen again from the dead, his disciples remembered, that he had said this, and they believed the scripture, and the word that Jesus had said.—*John* ii. 18-22.

Christ, the Ascension of

And no man hath ascended into heaven, but he that descended from heaven, the Son of man, who is in heaven.—*John* iii. 13.

If then you shall see the Son of man ascend up where he was before?—*John* vi. 63.

Jesus saith to her (Mary Magdalen): Do not touch me, for I am not yet ascended to my Father. But go to my brethren, and say to them: I ascend to my Father and to your Father, to my God and your God.—*John* xx. 17.

Church, the Holy Ghost Promised to the

And I send the promise of my Father upon you: but stay you in the city, till you be endued with power from on high.—*Luke* xxiv. 49.

And I will ask the Father, and he shall give you another Paraclete, that he may abide with you for ever.

The spirit of truth, whom the world cannot receive, because it seeth him not, nor knoweth him: but you shall know him; because he shall abide with you, and shall be in you.—*John* xiv. 16, 17.

But the Paraclete, the Holy Ghost, whom the Father will send in my name, he will teach you all things, and bring all things to your mind, whatsoever I shall have said to you.—*John* xiv. 26.

But when the Paraclete cometh, whom I will send you from the Father, the Spirit of truth, who proceedeth from the Father, he shall give testimony of me.—*John* xv. 26.

But I tell you the truth: it is expedient to you that I go: for if I go not, the Paraclete will not come to you; but if I go, I will send him to you.

And when he is come, he will convince the world of sin, and of justice, and of judgment.

Of sin: because they believed not in me.

And of justice: because I go to the Father; and you shall see me no longer.

And of judgment: because the prince of this world is already judged. . . . .

But when he, the Spirit of truth, is come, he will teach you all truth. For he shall not speak of himself; but what things soever he shall hear, he shall speak; and the things that are to come, he shall show you.

He shall glorify me; because he shall receive of mine, and shall show it to you.—*John* xvi. 7-11, 13, 14.

They therefore who were come together, asked him, saying: Lord, wilt thou at this time restore again the kingdom to Israel?

But he said to them: It is not for you to know the times or moments, which the Father hath put in his own power:

But you shall receive the power of the Holy Ghost coming upon you, and you shall be witnesses unto me in Jerusalem, and in all Judea, and Samaria, and even to the uttermost part of the earth.—*Acts* i. 6-8.

Church, the Propagation of the

Another parable he proposed unto them, saying: The kingdom of heaven is like to a grain of mustard seed, which a man took and sowed in his field.

Which is the least indeed of all seeds; but when it is grown up, it is greater than all herbs, and becometh a tree, so that the birds of the air come, and dwell in the branches thereof.—*Matt.* xiii. 31,32.

And he said: To what shall we liken the kingdom of God? or to what parable shall we compare it?

It is as a grain of mustard seed: which when it is sown in the earth, is less than all the seeds that are in the earth:

And when it is sown, it groweth up, and becometh greater than all herbs, and shooteth out great branches, so that the birds of the air may dwell under the shadow thereof.—*Mark* iv. 30-32.

He said therefore: To what is the kingdom of God like, and whereunto shall I resemble it?

It is like to a grain of mustard seed, which a man took and cast into his garden, and it grew and became a great tree, and the birds of the air lodged in the branches thereof.—*Luke* xiii. 18, 19.

Another parable he spoke to them: The kingdom of heaven is like to leaven, which a woman took and hid in three measures of meal, until the whole was leavened.—*Matt.* xiii. 33.

And again he said: Whereunto shall I esteem the kingdom of God to be like?

It is like to leaven, which a woman took and hid in three measures of meal, till the whole was leavened.—*Luke* xiii. 20, 21.

And this gospel of the kingdom, shall be preacher in the whole world, for a testimony to all nations, and then shall the consummation come.—*Matt.* xxiv. 14.

And unto all nations the gospel must first be preached.—*Mark* xiii. 10.

Then he opened their understanding, that they might understand the scriptures.

And he said to them: Thus it is written, and thus it behoved Christ to suffer, and to rise again from the dead, the third day:

And that penance and remission of sins should be preached in his name,

unto all nations, beginning at Jerusalem.—*Luke* xxiv. 45-47.

The woman saith to him: Sir, I perceive that thou art a prophet.

Our fathers adored on this mountain, and you say, that at Jerusalem is the place where men must adore.

Jesus saith to her: Woman, believe me, that the hour cometh, when you shall neither on this mountain, nor in Jerusalem, adore the Father.

You adore that which you know not: we adore that which we know; for salvation is of the Jews.

But the hour cometh, and now is, when the true adorers shall adore the Father in spirit and in truth. For the Father also seeketh such to adore him. God is a spirit; and they that adore him, must adore him in spirit and in truth.—*John* iv. 19-24.

But you shall receive the power of the Holy Ghost coming upon you, and you shall be witnesses unto me in Jerusalem, and in all Judea, and Samaria, and even to the uttermost part of the earth.—*Acts* i. 8.

Church, the Persecution of the

Behold I send you as sheep in the midst of wolves. Be ye therefore wise as serpents and simple as doves.

But beware of men. For they will deliver you up in councils, and they will scourge you in their synagogues.

And you shall be brought before governors, and before kings for my sake, for a testimony to them and to the Gentiles:

But when they shall deliver you up, take no thought how or what to speak: for it shall be given you in that hour what to speak.

For it is not you that speak, but the Spirit of your Father that speaketh in you.

The brother also shall deliver up the brother to death, and the father the son: and the children shall rise up against their parents, and shall put them to death.

And you shall be hated by all men for my name's sake: but he that shall persevere unto the end, he shall be saved.

And when they shall persecute you in this city, flee into another. Amen I say to you, you shall not finish all the cities of Israel, till the Son of man come.—*Matt.* x. 16-23.

Therefore behold I send to you prophets, and wise men, and scribes: and some of them you will put to death and crucify, and some you will scourge in your synagogues, and persecute from city to city:

That upon you may come all the just blood that hath been shed upon the earth, from the blood of Abel the just, even unto the blood of Zacharias the son of Barachias, whom you killed between the temple and the altar.— *Matt.* xxiii. 34, 35.

For this cause also the wisdom of God said: I will send to them prophets and apostles; and some of them they will kill and persecute.

That the blood of all the prophets which was shed from the foundation of the world, may be required of this generation,

From the blood of Abel unto the blood of Zacharias, who was slain between the altar and the temple: Yea I say to you, It shall be required of this generation.—*Luke* xi. 49-51.

Then shall they deliver you up to be afflicted, and shall put you to death: and you shall be hated by all nations for my name's sake.

But look to yourselves. For they shall deliver you up to councils, and in the synagogues you shall be beaten, and you shall stand before governors and kings for my sake, for a testimony unto them. And unto all nations the gospel must first be preached.

And when they shall lead you and deliver you

But before all these things, they will lay their hands on you, and persecute you, delivering you up to the synagogues and into prisons, dragging you before kings and governors, for my name's sake. . . .

And then shall many be scandalized: and shall betray one another: and shall hate one another.—*Matt.* xxiv. 9, 10.

up, be not thoughtful beforehand what you shall s p e a k ; but whatsoever shall be given you in that hour, that speak ye. For it is not you that speak, but the Holy Ghost.

And the brother shall betray his brother unto death, and the father his son; and children shall rise u p a g a i n s t t h e parents, and shall work their death.

And you shall be hated by all men for my name's sake. But he that shall endure unto the end, he shall be saved.—*Mark* xiii. 9-13.

And you shall be betrayed by your parents and brethren, and kinsmen and friends; and some of you they will put to death.

And you shall be hated by all men for my name's sake.—*Luke* xxi. 12, 16, 17.

Remember my word that I said to you: The servant is not greater than his master. If they have persecuted me, they will also persecute you: if they have kept my word, they will keep yours also.

But all these things they will do to you for my name's sake: because they know not him that sent me.—*John* xv. 20, 21.

These things have I spoken to you, that you may not be scandalized.

They will put you out of the synagogues: Yea, the hour cometh, that whosoever killeth you, will think that he doth a service to God.

And these things will they do to you; because they have not known the Father, nor me.

But these things I have told you, that when the hour shall come, you may remember that I told you of them.—*John* xvi. 1-4.

End of the World, the

Even as cockle therefore is gathered up, and burnt with fire: so shall it be at the end of the world.

The Son of man shall send his angels, and they shall gather out of his kingdom all scandals, and them that work iniquity.

And shall cast them into the furnace of fire: there shall be weeping and gnashing of teeth.

Then shall the just shine as the sun, in the kingdom of their Father.—*Matt.* xiii. 40-43.

Again the kingdom of heaven is like to a net cast into the sea, and gathering together of all kind of fishes.

Which, when it was filled, they drew out, and sitting by the shore, they chose out the good into vessels, but the bad they cast forth.

So shall it be at the end of the world. The angels shall go out, and shall separate the wicked from among the just.

And shall cast them into the furnace of fire: there shall be weeping and gnashing of teeth.—*Matt.* xiii. 47-50.

And immediately after the tribulation of those days, the sun shall be darkened and the moon shall not give her light, and the stars shall f a l l f r o m

But in those days, after that tribulation, the sun shall be darkened, and the moon shall not give her light.

And the stars of heaven

And there shall be signs in the sun, and in the moon, and in the stars; and upon the earth distress of nations, by reason of the confusion of the roar-

heaven, and the powers of heaven shall be moved: And then shall appear the sign of the Son of man in heaven: and then shall all tribes of the earth mourn: and they shall see the Son of man coming in the clouds of heaven with much power and majesty.

And he shall send his angels with a trumpet, and a great voice: and they shall gather together his elect from the four winds, from the farthest parts of the heavens to the utmost bounds of them. — *Matt.* **xxiv.** 29-31.

shall be falling down, and the powers that are in heaven, shall be moved. And then shall they see the Son of man coming in the clouds, with great power and glory.

And then shall he send his angels, and shall gather together his elect from the four winds, from the uttermost part of the earth to the uttermost part of heaven.—*Mark* **x i i i.** 24-27.

ing of the sea and of the waves;

Men withering away for fear, and expectation of what shall come upon the whole world. For the powers of heaven shall be moved;

And then they shall see the Son of man coming in a cloud, with great power and majesty.

But when these things begin to come to pass, look up, and lift up your heads, because your redemption is at hand.—*Luke* xxi. 25-28.

Gentiles, the Conversion of the

And Jesus hearing this, marvelled; and said to them that followed him: Amen I say to you, I have not found so great faith in Israel.

And I say to you that many shall come from the east and the west, and shall sit down with Abraham, and Isaac, and Jacob in the kingdom of heaven:

But the children of the kingdom shall be cast out into the exterior darkness: there shall be weeping and gnashing of teeth.—*Matt.* viii. 10-12.

When therefore the lord of the vineyard shall come, what will he do to those husbandmen?

They say to him: He will bring those evil men to an evil end; and will let out his vineyard to other husbandmen, that shall render him the fruit in due season.

Jesus saith to them: Have you never read in the Scriptures: T h e   s t o n e which the builders r e - jected, the same is become the head of the corner? By the Lord this has been done; and it is wonderful in our eyes.

Therefore I say to you, that the kingdom of God shall be taken from you, and shall be given to a nation yielding the fruits thereof.—*Matt.* xxi. 40-43.

What therefore will the lord of the vineyard do? He will come and destroy those husbandmen; and will give the vineyard to others.

And have you not read this scripture, The stone which the builders re- jected, the same is made the head of the corner: By the Lord has this been done, and it is won- derful in our eyes.—*Mark* xii. 9-11.

What therefore will the lord of the vineyard do to them?

He will come, and will destroy these husbandmen, and will give the vineyard to others. Which they hearing, said to him: God forbid.

But he looking on them, said: What is this then that is written, The stone which the builders re- jected, the same is become the head of the corner?— *Luke* xx. 15-17.

There shall be weeping and gnashing of teeth, when you shall see Abraham and Isaac and Jacob, and all the prophets, in the kingdom of God, and you yourselves thrust out.

And there shall come from the east and the west, and the north and the south; and shall sit down in the kingdom of God.—*Luke* xiii. 28, 29.

And I, if I be lifted up from the earth, will draw all things to myself.

(Now this he said, signifying what death he should die.)—*John* xii. 32, 33.

Jerusalem and the Temple, the Destruction of

Jerusalem, Jerusalem, thou that killest the prophets, and stonest them that are sent unto thee, how often would I have gathered together thy children, as the hen doth gather her chickens under her wings, and thou wouldest not?

Behold, your house shall be left to you, desolate.—*Matt.* xxiii. 37, 38.

Jerusalem, Jerusalem, that killest the prophets, and stonest them that are sent to thee, how often would I have gathered thy children as the bird doth her brood under her wings, and thou wouldest not?

Behold your house shall be left to you desolate.—*Luke* xiii. 34, 35.

And Jesus being come out of the temple, went away. And his disciples came to show him the buildings of the temple.

And he answering, said to them: Do you see all these things? Amen I say to you there shall not be left here a stone upon a stone that shall not be destroyed.—*Matt.* xxiv. 1, 2.

And as he was going out of the temple, one of his disciples said to him: Master, behold what manner of stones, and what buildings are here.

And Jesus answering, said to him: Seest thou all these great buildings? There shall not be left a stone upon a stone, that shall not be thrown down. —*Mark* xiii. 1, 2.

And some saying of the temple, that it was adorned with goodly stones and gifts, he said: These things which you see, the days will come in which there shall not be left a stone upon a stone that shall not be thrown down.

. . . And when you shall see Jerusalem compassed about with an army; then know that the desolation thereof is at hand.

Then let those who are in Judea, flee to the mountains; and those who are in the midst thereof, depart out: and those who are in the countries, not enter into it.

For these are the days of vengeance, that all things may be fulfilled, that are written.

But woe to them that are with child, and give suck in those days; for there shall be great distress in the land, and wrath upon this people.

And they shall fall by the edge of the sword; and

shall be led away captives into all nations; and Jerusalem shall be trodden down by the Gentiles; till the times of the nations be fulfilled.—*Luke* xxi. 5, 6, 20-24.

And when he drew near, seeing the city, he wept over it, saying:

If thou also hadst known, and that in this thy day, the things that are to thy peace; but now they are hidden from thy eyes.

For the days shall come upon thee: and thy enemies shall cast a trench about thee, and compass thee round, and straiten thee on every side,

And beat thee flat to the ground, and thy children who are in thee: and they shall not leave in thee a stone upon a stone: because thou hast not known the time of thy visitation.—*Luke* xix. 41-44.

Jews, the Rejection of the

And I say to you that many shall come from the east and the west, and shall sit down with Abraham, and Isaac, and Jacob in the kingdom of heaven:

But the children of the kingdom shall be cast out into the exterior darkness: there shall be weeping and gnashing of teeth.—*Matt.* viii. 11, 12.

But the husbandmen seeing the son, said among themselves: This is the heir: come, let us kill him, and we shall have his inheritance.

And taking him, they cast him forth out of the vineyard, and killed him.

When therefore the lord of the vineyard shall come, what will he do to those husbandmen?

They say to him: He will bring those evil men to an evil end; and will let out his vineyard to other husbandmen, that shall render him the fruit in due season.

Jesus saith to them: Have you never read in the Scriptures: The stone which the builders rejected, the same is become the head of the corner? By the Lord this has been done; and it is wonderful in our eyes.

Therefore I say to you, that the kingdom of God

Therefore having yet one son, most dear to him; he also sent him unto them last of all, saying: They will reverence my son.

But the husbandmen said one to another: This is the heir; come let us kill him; and the inheritance shall be ours.

And laying hold on him, they killed him, and cast him out of the vineyard.

What therefore will the lord of the vineyard do? He will come and destroy those husbandmen; and will give the vineyard to others.

And have you not read this scripture, The stone which the builders rejected, the same is made the head of the corner:

By the Lord has this been done, and it is wonderful in our eyes.—*Mark* xii. 6-11.

Then the Lord of the vineyard said: What shall I do? I will send my beloved son: it may be, when they see him, they will reverence him.

Whom when the husbandmen saw, they thought within themselves, saying: This is the heir, let us kill him, that the inheritance may be ours.

So casting him out of the vineyard, they killed him. What therefore will the lord of the vineyard do to them?

He will come, and will destroy these husbandmen, and will give the vineyard to others. Which they hearing, said to him: God forbid.

But he looking on them, said: What is this then that is written, The stone, which the builders rejected, the same is become the head of the corner?—*Luke* xx. 13-17.

shall be taken from you, and shall be given to a nation yielding the fruits thereof.—*Matt.* xxi. 38-43.

There shall be weeping and gnashing of teeth, when you shall see Abraham and Isaac and Jacob, and all the prophets, in the kingdom of God, and you yourselves thrust out.

And there shall come from the east and the west, and the north and the south; and shall sit down in the kingdom of God.—*Luke* xiii. 28, 29.

Jews, the Punishment of the

But Jesus turning to them, said: Daughters of Jerusalem, weep not over me; but weep for yourselves, and for your children.

For behold, the days shall come, wherein they will say: Blessed are the barren, and the wombs that have not borne, and the paps that have not given suck.

Then shall they begin to say to the mountains: Fall upon us; and to the hills: Cover us.

For if in the green wood they do these things, what shall be done in the dry?—*Luke* xxiii. 28-31.

Then began he to upbraid the cities wherein were done the most of his miracles, for that they had not done penance.

Woe to thee, Corozain, woe to thee, Bethsaida: for if in Tyre and Sidon had been wrought the miracles that have been wrought in you, they had long ago done penance in sackcloth and ashes.

But I say unto you, it shall be more tolerable for Tyre and Sidon in the day of judgment, than for you.

And thou, Capharnaum, shalt thou be exalted up to heaven? thou shalt go down even unto hell. For if in Sodom had been wrought the miracles that have been wrought in thee, perhaps it had remained unto this day.

But I say unto you, that it shall be more tolerable for the land of Sodom in the day of judgment, than for thee.—*Matt.* xi. 20-24.

Woe to thee, Corozain, woe to thee, Bethsaida. For if in Tyre and Sidon had been wrought the mighty works that have been wrought in you, they would have done penance long ago, sitting in sackcloth and ashes.

But it shall be more tolerable for Tyre and Sidon at the judgment, than for you.

And thou, Capharnaum, which art exalted unto heaven, thou shalt be thrust down to hell.—*Luke* x. 13-15.

Judgment, the Day of

For the Son of man shall come in the glory of his Father with his angels: and then will he render to every man according to his works.—*Matt.* xvi. 27.

And when the Son of man shall come in his majesty, and all the angels with him, then shall he sit upon the seat of his majesty.

And all nations shall be gathered together before him, and he shall separate them one from another, as the shepherd separateth the sheep from the goats:

And he shall set the sheep on his right hand, but the goats on his left.

Then shall the king say to them that shall be on his right hand: Come, ye blessed of my Father, possess you the kingdom prepared for you from the foundation of the world.

For I was hungry, and you gave me to eat; I was thirsty, and you gave me to drink; I was a stranger, and you took me in:

Naked, and you covered me: sick, and you visited me: I was in prison, and you came to me.

Then shall the just answer him, saying: Lord, when did we see thee hungry, and fed thee; thirsty, and gave thee drink?

And when did we see thee a stranger, and took thee in? or naked, and covered thee?

Or when did we see thee sick or in prison, and came to thee?

And the king answering, shall say to them: Amen I say to you, as long as you did it to one of these my least brethren, you did it to me.

Then he shall say to them also that shall be on his left hand: Depart from me, you cursed, into everlasting fire which was prepared for the devil and his angels.

For I was hungry, and you gave me not to eat: I was thirsty, and you gave me not to drink.

I was a stranger, and you took me not in: naked, and you covered me not: sick and in prison, and you did not visit me.

Then they also shall answer him, saying: Lord, when did we see thee hungry, or thirsty, or a stranger, or naked, or sick, or in prison, and did not minister to thee?

Then he shall answer them, saying: Amen I say to you, as long as you did it not to one of these least, neither did you do it to me.

And these shall go into everlasting punishment: but the just, into life everlasting.—*Matt.* xxv. 31-46.

Wonder not at this; for the hour cometh, wherein all that are in the graves shall hear the voice of the Son of God.

And they that have done good things, shall come forth unto the resurrection of life; but they that have done evil, unto the resurrection of judgment.—*John* v. 28, 29.

Magdalen, the

There came to him a woman having an alabaster box of precious ointment, and poured it on his head as he was at table.

And the disciples seeing it, had indignation, saying: To what purpose is this waste?

For this might have been sold for much, and given to the poor.

And Jesus knowing it, said to them: Why do you trouble this woman? for she hath wrought a good work upon me.

For the poor you have always with you: but me you have not always.

For she in pouring this ointment upon my body, hath done it for my burial.

Amen I say to you, wheresoever this gospel shall be preached in the whole world, that also which she hath done, shall be told for a memory of her.— *Matt.* xxvi. 7-13.

And when he was in Bethania, in the house of Simon the leper, and was at meat, there came a woman having an alabaster box of ointment of precious spikenard: and breaking the alabaster box, she poured it out upon his head.

Now there were some that had indignation within themselves, and said: Why was this waste of the ointment made?

For this ointment might have been sold for more than three hundred pence, and given to the poor. And they murmured against her.

But Jesus said: Let her alone, why do you molest her? She hath wrought a good work upon me.

For the poor you have always with you: and whensoever you will, you may do them good: but me you have not always.

She hath done what she could: she is come beforehand to anoint my body for the burial.

Amen, I say to you, wheresoever this

gospel shall be preached in the whole world, that also which she hath done, shall be told for a memorial of her.—*Mark* xiv. 3-9.

Miracles in the Church, Prophecy of

And he said to them: Go ye into the whole world, and preach the gospel to every creature.

He that believeth and is baptized, shall be saved: but he that believeth not shall be condemned.

And these signs shall follow them that believe: In my name they shall cast out devils: they shall speak with new tongues.

They shall take up serpents: and if they shall drink any deadly thing, it shall not hurt them: they shall lay their hands upon the sick, and they shall recover.—*Mark* xvi. 15-18.

Behold, I have given you power to tread upon serpents and scorpions, and upon all the power of the enemy: and nothing shall hurt you.—*Luke* x. 19.

Amen, amen I say to you, he that believeth in me, the works that I do, he also shall do; and greater than these shall he do.—*John* xiv. 12.

St. Peter

And I say to thee: That thou art Peter; and upon this rock I will build my church, and the gates of hell shall not prevail against it.

And I will give to thee the keys of the kingdom of heaven. And whatsoever thou shalt bind upon earth, it shall be bound also in heaven: and whatsoever thou shalt loose on earth, it shall be loosed also in heaven.—*Matt.* xvi. 18, 19.

Simon Peter saith to him: Lord, whither goest thou? Jesus answered: Whither I go, thou canst not follow me now; but thou shalt follow hereafter.—*John* xiii. 36.

Amen, amen I say to thee, when thou wast younger, thou didst gird thyself, and didst walk where thou wouldst. But when thou shalt be old, thou shalt stretch forth thy hands, and another shall gird thee, and lead thee whither thou wouldst not.

And this he said, signifying by what death he (Peter) should glorify God.—*John* xxi. 18, 19.

PARABLES OF CHRIST, THE

And he spoke to them many things in parables.—*Matt.* xiii. 3.

All these things Jesus spoke in parables to the multitudes: and without parables he did not speak to them.

That it might be fulfilled which was spoken by the prophet, saying: I will open my mouth in parables, I will utter things hidden from the foundation of the world.—*Matt.* xiii. 34, 35.

And with many such parables, he spoke to them the word, according as they were able to hear.

And without parable he did not speak unto them; but apart, he explained all things to his disciples.—*Mark* iv. 33, 34.

Cockle and the Good Seed, the

Another parable he proposed to them, saying: The kingdom of heaven is likened to a man that sowed good seed in his field.

But while men were asleep, his enemy came and oversowed cockle among the wheat, and went his way.

And when the blade was sprung up, and had brought forth fruit, then appeared also the cockle.

And the servants of the goodman of the house coming, said to him: Sir, didst thou not sow good seed in thy field? whence then hath it cockle?

And he said to them: An enemy hath done this. And the servants said to him: Wilt thou that we go and gather it up?

And he said: No, lest perhaps gathering up the cockle, you root up the wheat also together with it.

Suffer both to grow until the harvest, and in the time of the harvest I will say to the reapers: Gather up first the cockle, and bind it into bundles to burn, but the wheat gather ye into my barn. . . .

Then having sent away the multitudes, he came into the house, and his disciples came to him, saying: Expound to us the parable of the cockle of the field.

Who made answer and said to them: He that soweth the good seed, is the Son of man.

And the field, is the world. And the good seed are the children of the kingdom. And the cockle, are the children of the wicked one.

And the enemy that sowed them, is the devil. But the harvest is the end of the world. And the reapers are the angels.

Even as cockle therefore is gathered up, and burnt with fire: so shall it be at the end of the world.

The Son of man shall send his angels, and they shall gather out of his kingdom all scandals, and them that work iniquity.

And shall cast them into the furnace of fire: there shall be weeping and gnashing of teeth.

Then shall the just shine as the sun, in the kingdom of their Father.—*Matt.* xiii. 24-30, 36-43.

Debtor, the Ungrateful

Therefore is the kingdom of heaven likened to a king, who would take an account of his servants.

And when he had begun to take the account, one was brought to him, that owed him ten thousand talents.

And as he had not wherewith to pay it, his lord commanded that he should be sold, and his wife and children, and all that he had, and payment to be made.

But that servant falling down, besought him, saying: Have patience with me, and I will pay thee all.

And the lord of that servant being moved with pity, let him go and forgave him the debt.

But when that servant was gone out, he found one of his fellow servants that owed him an hundred pence: and laying hold of him, he throttled him, saying: Pay what thou owest.

And his fellow servant falling down, besought him, saying: Have patience with me, and I will pay thee all.

And he would not: but went and cast him into prison, till he paid the debt.

Now his fellow servants seeing what was done, were very much grieved, and they came and told their lord all that was done.

Then his lord called him; and said to him: Thou wicked servant, I forgave thee all the debt, because thou besoughtest me:

Shouldst not thou then have had compassion also on thy fellow servant, even as I had compassion on thee?

And his lord being angry, delivered him to the torturers until he paid all the debt.

So also shall my heavenly Father do to you, if you forgive not every one his brother from your hearts.—*Matt.* xviii. 23-35.

Debtors, the Forgiven

And Jesus answering, said to him: Simon, I have somewhat to say to thee. But he said: Master, say it.

A certain creditor had two debtors, the one owed five hundred pence, and the other fifty.

And whereas they had not wherewith to pay, he forgave them both. Which therefore of the two loveth him most?

Simon answering, said: I suppose that he to whom he forgave most. And he said to him: Thou hast judged rightly.—*Luke* vii. 40-43.

Fig-Tree, the Barren

He spoke also this parable: A certain man had a fig-tree planted in his vineyard, and he came seeking fruit on it, and found none.

And he said to the dresser of the vineyard: Behold, for these three years I come seeking fruit on this fig-tree, and I find none. Cut it down therefore: why cumbereth it the ground?

But he answering, said to him: Lord, let it alone this year also, until I dig about it, and dung it.

And if happily it bear fruit: but if

ot, then after that thou shalt cut it down.—*Luke* xiii. 6-9.

Groat, the Lost

Or what woman having ten groats; f she lose one groat, doth not light a candle, and sweep the house, and seek diligently until she find it?

And when she hath found it, call together her friends and neighbors, saying: Rejoice with me, because I have found the groat which I had lost.

So I say to you, there shall be joy before the angels of God upon one sinner doing penance.—*Luke* xv. 8-10.

Husbandmen, the Ungrateful

Hear ye another parable. There was a man, an householder, who planted a vineyard, and made a hedge round about it, and dug in it a press, and built a tower, and let it out to husbandmen; and went into a strange country.

And when the time of the fruits drew nigh, he sent his servants to the husbandmen, that they might receive the fruits thereof.

And the husbandmen laying hands on his servants, beat one, and killed another, and stoned another.

Again he sent other servants more than the former; and they did to them in like manner

And last of all he sent to them his son, saying: They will reverence my son.

But the husbandmen seeing the son, said among themselves: This is the heir: come, let us kill him, and we shall have his inheritance.

And taking him, they cast him forth out of the vineyard, and killed him.

When therefore the lord of the vineyard shall come, what will he do to those husbandmen?

They say to him: He will bring those evil men to an evil end; and will let

And he began to speak to them in parables: A certain man planted a vineyard and made a hedge about it, and dug a place for the wine vat, and built a tower, and let it to husbandmen; and went into a far country.

And at the season he sent to the husbandmen a servant to receive of the husbandmen of the fruit of the vineyard.

Who having laid hands on him, beat him, and sent him away empty.

And again he sent to them another servant; and him they wounded in the head, and used him reproachfully.

And again he sent another, and him they killed: and many others; of whom some they beat, and others they killed.

Therefore having yet one son, most dear to him; he also sent him unto them last of all, saying: They will reverence my son.

But the husbandmen said one to another: This is the heir: come let us kill him; and the inheritance shall be ours.

And laying hold on him, they killed him, and cast him out of the vineyard.

What therefore will the lord of the vineyard do? He will come and destroy

And he began to speak to the people this parable: A certain man planted a vineyard, and let it out to husbandmen: and he was abroad for a long time.

And at the season he sent a servant to the husbandmen, that they should give him of the fruit of the vineyard. Who, beating him, sent him away empty.

And again he sent another servant. But they beat him also, and treating him reproachfully, sent him away empty.

And again he sent the third: and they wounded him also, and cast him out.

Then the lord of the vineyard said: What shall I do? I will send my beloved son: it may be, when they see him, they will reverence him.

Whom when the husbandmen saw, they thought within themselves, saying: This is the heir, let us kill him, that the inheritance may be ours.

So casting him out of the vineyard, they killed him. What therefore will the lord of the vineyard do to them?

He will come, and will destroy these husbandmen, and will give the vineyard to others. Which they

out his vineyard to other husbandmen, that s h a l l render him the fruit in due season.

Jesus saith to them: Have you never read in the Scriptures: The stone which the builders rejected, the same is become the head of the corner? By the Lord this has been done; and it is wonderful in our eyes.

Therefore I say to you, that the kingdom of God shall be taken from you, and shall be given to a nation yielding the fruits thereof.

And whosoever shall fall on this stone, shall be broken: but on whomsoever it shall fall, it shall grind him to powder.

And when the chief priests and Pharisees had heard his parables, they knew that he spoke of them.—*Matt.* xxi. 33-45.

those husbandmen; a n d will give the vineyard to others.

And have you not read this scripture, The stone which the builders rejected, the same is made the head of the corner:

By the Lord has this been done, and it is wonderful in our eyes.

And they sought to lay hands on him, but they feared the people. For they knew that he spoke this parable to them.— *Mark* xii. 1-12.

hearing, said to him: God forbid.

But he looking on them, said: What is this then that is written, The stone, w h i c h the builders rejected, the same is become the head of the corner?

Whosoever shall f a l l upon that stone, shall be bruised: and upon whomsoever it shall fall, it will grind him to powder.

And the chief priests and the scribes sought to lay hands on him the same hour: but they feared the people, for they knew that he spoke this parable to them.—*Luke* xx. 9-19.

Judge and the Widow, the

And he spoke also a parable to them, that we ought always to pray, and not to faint,

Saying: There was a judge in a certain city, who feared not God, nor regarded man.

And there was a certain widow in that city, and she came to him, saying: Avenge me of my adversary.

And he would not for a long time. But afterwards he said within himself: Although I fear not God, nor regard man,

Yet because this widow is troublesome to me, I will avenge her, lest continually coming she weary me.

And the Lord said: Hear what the unjust judge saith.

And will not God revenge his elect who cry to him day and night: and will he have patience in their regard?

I say to you, that he will quickly revenge them.—*Luke* xviii. 1-8.

Laborers in the Vineyard, the

The kingdom of heaven is like to a householder, who went out early in the morning to hire laborers into his vineyard.

And having agreed with the laborers for a penny a day, he sent them into his vineyard.

And going out about the third hour, he saw others standing in the market place idle.

And he said to them: Go you also into my vineyard, and I will give you what shall be just.

And they went their way. And again he went out about the sixth and the ninth hour, and did in like manner.

But about the eleventh hour he went out and found others standing, and he saith to them: Why stand you here all the day idle?

They say to him.: Because no man hath hired us. He saith to them: Go you also into my vineyard.

And when evening was come, the lord of the vineyard saith to his steward: Call the laborers and pay them their hire, beginning from the last even to the first.

When therefore they were come, that came about the eleventh hour, they received every man a penny.

But when the first also came, they thought that they should receive more: and they also received every man a penny.

And receiving it they murmured against the master of the house,

Saying: These last have worked but one hour, and thou hast made them equal to us, that have borne the burden of the day and the heats.

But he answering said to one of them: Friend, I do thee no wrong: didst thou not agree with me for a penny?

Take what is thine, and go thy way: I will also give to this last even as to thee.

Or, is it not lawful for me to do what I will? is thy eye evil because I am good?

So shall the last be first, and the first last. For many are called, but few are chosen.—*Matt.* xx. 1-16.

Leaven, the

Another parable he spoke to them: The kingdom of heaven is like to leaven, which a woman took and hid in three measures of meal, until the whole was leavened.—*Matt.* xiii. 33.

And again he said: Whereunto shall I esteem the kingdom of God to be like?

It is like to leaven, which a woman took and hid in three measures of meal, till the whole was leavened.—*Luke* xiii. 20, 21.

Marriage Feast, the

And Jesus answering, spoke again in parables to them, saying:

The kingdom of heaven is likened to a king, who made a marriage for his son.

And he sent his servants, to call them that were invited to the marriage; and they would not come.

Again he sent other servants, saying: Tell them that were invited, Behold, I have prepared my dinner; my beeves and fatlings are killed, and all things are ready: come ye to the marriage.

But they neglected, and went their ways, one to his farm, and another to his merchandise.

And the rest laid hands on his servants, and having treated them contumeliously, put them to death.

But when the king had heard of it, he was angry, and sending his armies, he destroyed those murderers, and burnt their city.

Then he saith to his servants: The marriage indeed is ready; but they that were invited were not worthy.

Go ye therefore into the highways; and as many as you shall find, call to the marriage.

And his servants going forth into the ways, gathered together all that they found, both bad and good: and the marriage was filled with guests.

And the king went in to see the guests: and he saw there a man who had not on a wedding garment.

And he saith to him: Friend, how camest thou in hither not having on a wedding garment? But he was silent.

Then the king said to the waiters: Bind his hands and feet, and cast him into the exterior darkness: there shall be weeping and gnashing of teeth.

For many are called, but few are chosen.—*Matt.* xxii. 1-14.

Mustard Seed, the

Another parable he proposed unto them, saying: And he said: To what shall we liken the kingdom He said therefore: To what is the kingdom of

The kingdom of heaven is like to a grain of mustard seed, which a man took and sowed in his field.

Which is the least indeed of all seeds; but when it is grown up, it is greater than all herbs, and becometh a tree, so that the birds of the air come, and dwell in the branches thereof.—*Matt.* xiii. 31,32.

of God? or to what parable shall we compare it?

It is as a grain of mustard seed: which when it is sown in the earth, is less than all the seeds that are in the earth:

And when it is sown, it groweth up, and becometh greater than all herbs, and shooteth out great branches, so that the birds of the air may dwell under the shadow thereof.—*Mark* iv. 30-32.

God like, and whereunto shall I resemble it?

It is like to a grain of mustard seed, which a man took and cast into his garden, and it grew and became a great tree, and the birds of the air lodged in the branches thereof.—*Luke* xiii. 18,19.

Net Cast into the Sea, the

Again the kingdom of heaven is like to a net cast into the sea, and gathering together of all kind of fishes.

Which, when it was filled, they drew out, and sitting by the shore, they chose out the good into vessels, but the bad they cast forth.

So shall it be at the end of the world. The angels shall go out, and shall separate the wicked from among the just.

And shall cast them into the furnace of fire: there shall be weeping and gnashing of teeth.—*Matt.* xiii. 47-50.

Pearl of Great Price, the

Again the kingdom of heaven is like to a merchant seeking good pearls.

Who when he had found one pearl of great price, went his way, and sold all that he had, and bought it.—*Matt.* xiii. 45, 46.

Pharisee and the Publican, the

And to some who trusted in themselves as just, and despised others, he spoke also this parable:

Two men went up into the temple to pray: the one a Pharisee, and the other a publican.

The Pharisee standing, prayed thus with himself: O God, I give thee thanks that I am not as the rest of men, extortioners, unjust, adulterers, as also is this publican.

I fast twice in a week: I give tithes of all that I possess.

And the publican, **standing afar off,**

would not so much as lift up his eyes towards heaven: but struck his breast, saying: O God, be merciful to me a sinner.

I say to you, this man went down into his house justified rather than the other: because every one that exalteth himself, shall be humbled: and he that humbleth himself, shall be exalted.— *Luke* xviii. 9-14.

Pounds, the

As they were hearing these things, he added and spoke a parable, because he was nigh to Jerusalem, and because they thought that the kingdom of God should immediately be manifested.

He said therefore: A certain nobleman went into a far country, to receive for himself a kingdom, and to return.

And calling his ten servants, he gave them ten pounds, and said to them: Trade till I come.

But his citizens hated him: and they sent an embassage after him, saying: We will not have this man to reign over us.

And it came to pass, that he returned, having received the kingdom: and he commanded his servants to be called, to whom he had given the money, that he might know how much every man had gained by trading.

And the first came, saying: Lord, thy pound hath gained ten pounds.

And he said to him: Well done, thou good servant, because thou hast been faithful in a little, thou shalt have power over ten cities.

And the second came, saying: Lord, hy pound hath gained five pounds.
And he said to him: Be thou also)ver five cities.

And another came, saying: Lord, be-1old here is thy pound, which I have ;ept laid up in a napkin;

For I feared thee, because thou art an ιustere man: thou takest up what thou lidst not lay down, and thou reapest ;hat which thou didst not sow.

He saith to him: Out of thy own nouth I judge thee, thou wicked ser-ʋant.

Thou knewest that I was an aus-;ere man, taking up what I laid not lown, and reaping that which I did not sow:

And why then didst thou not give my money into the bank, that at my com-ng, I might have exacted it with usury?

And he said to them that stood by: Take the pound away from him, and ʒive it to him that hath ten pounds.

And they said to him: Lord, he hath ten pounds.

But I say to you, that to every one that hath shall be given, and he shall ιbound: and from him that hath not, ɛven that which he hath, shall be taken from him.

But as for those my enemies, who would not have me reign over them, bring them hither, and kill them before me.—*Luke* xix. 11-27.

Prodigal Son, the

And he said: A certain man had two sons:

And the younger of them said to his father: Father, give me the portion of substance that falleth to me. And he divided unto them his substance.

And not many days after, the younger son, gathering all together, went abroad into a far country: and there wasted his substance, living riotously.

And after he had spent all, there came a mighty famine in that country; and he began to be in want.

And he went and cleaved to one of the citizens of that country. And he sent him into his farm to feed swine.

And he would fain have filled his belly with the husks the swine did eat; and no man gave unto him.

And returning to himself, he said: How many hired servants in my father's house abound with bread, and I here perish with hunger?

I will arise, and will go to my father, and say to him: Father, I have sinned against heaven, and before thee:

I am not worthy to be called thy son: make me as one of thy hired servants.

And rising up he came to his father. And when he was yet a great way off, his father saw him, and was moved with compassion, and running to him, fell upon his neck, and kissed him.

And the son said to him: Father, I have sinned against heaven, and before thee, I am not now worthy to be called thy son.

And the father said to his servants: Bring forth quickly the first robe, and put it on him, and put a ring on his hand, and shoes on his feet:

And bring hither the fatted calf, and kill it, and let us eat and make merry:

Because this my son was dead, and is come to life again: was lost, and is found. And they began to be merry.

Now his elder son was in the field, and when he came and drew nigh to the house, he heard music and dancing:

And he called one of the servants, and asked what these things meant.

And he said to him: Thy brother is come, and thy father hath killed the fatted calf, because he hath received him safe.

And he was angry, and would not go in. His father therefore coming out began to entreat him.

And he answering, said to his father: Behold, for so many years do I serve thee, and I have never transgressed thy commandment, and yet thou hast never given me a kid to make merry with my friends:

But as soon as this thy son is come, who hath devoured his substance with harlots, thou hast killed for him the fatted calf.

But he said to him: Son, thou art always with me, and all I have is thine.

But it was fit that we should make merry and be glad, for this thy brother was dead and is come to life again; he was lost, and is found.—*Luke* xv. 11-32.

Rich Man and Lazarus, the

There was a certain rich man, who was clothed in purple and fine linen; and feasted sumptuously every day.

And there was a certain beggar, named Lazarus, who lay at his gate, full of sores,

Desiring to be filled with the crumbs that fell from the rich man's table, and no one did give him; moreover the dogs came, and licked his sores.

And it came to pass that the beggar died, and was carried by the angels into Abraham's bosom. And the rich man also died: and he was buried in hell.

And lifting up his eyes when he was in torments, he saw Abraham afar off, and Lazarus in his bosom:

And he cried, and said: Father Abraham, have mercy on me, and send Lazarus, that he may dip the tip of his finger in water, to cool my tongue: for I am tormented in this flame.

And Abraham said to him: Son, remember that thou didst receive good things in thy lifetime, and likewise Lazarus evil things, but now he is comforted; and thou art tormented.

And besides all this, between us and you, there is fixed a great chaos: so that they who would pass from hence to you, cannot, nor from thence come hither.

And he said: Then, father, I beseech thee, that thou wouldst send him to my father's house, for I have five brethren.

That he may testify unto them, lest they also come into this place of torments.

And Abraham said to him: They have Moses and the prophets; let them hear them.

But he said: No, father Abraham: but if one went to them from the dead, they will do penance.

And he said to him: If they hear not Moses and the prophets, neither will they believe, if one rise again from the dead.—*Luke* xvi. 19-31.

Rich Man, the Foolish

And he spoke a similitude to them, saying: The land of a certain rich man brought forth plenty of fruits.

And he thought within himself, saying: What shall I do, because I have no room where to bestow my fruits?

And he said: This will I do: I will pull down my barns, and will build greater; and into them will I gather all things that are grown to me, and my goods.

And I will say to my soul: Soul, thou hast much goods laid up for many years, take thy rest; eat, drink, make good cheer.

But God said to him: Thou fool, this night do they require thy soul of thee: and whose shall those things be which thou hast provided?

So is he that layeth up treasure for himself, and is not rich towards God.—*Luke* xii. 16-21.

Samaritan, the Good

But he (the lawyer) willing to justify himself, said to Jesus: And who is my neighbor?

And Jesus answering, said: A certain man went down from Jerusalem to Jericho, and fell among robbers, who also stripped him, and having wounded him, went away, leaving him half dead.

And it chanced, that a certain priest went down the same way: and seeing him, passed by.

In like manner also a Levite, when he was near the place and saw him, passed by.

But a certain Samaritan being on his journey, came near him; and seeing him, was moved with compassion.

And going up to him, bound up his wounds, pouring in oil and wine: and setting him upon his own beast brought him to an inn, and took care of him.

And the next day he took out two pence, and gave to the host, and said: Take care of him; and whatsoever thou shalt spend over and above, I, at my return, will repay thee.

Which of these three, in thy opinion, was neighbor to him that fell among the robbers?

But he said: He that showed mercy to him: And Jesus said to him: Go, and do thou in like manner.—*Luke* x. 29-37.

Seed Cast into the Earth, the

And he said: So is the kingdom of God, as if a man should cast seed into the earth,

And should sleep, and rise, night and day, and the seed should spring, and grow up whilst he knoweth not.

For the earth of itself bringeth forth fruit, first the blade, then the ear, afterwards the full corn in the ear.

And when the fruit is brought forth, immediately he putteth in the sickle, because the harvest is come.—*Mark* iv. 26-29.

Servants, the Good and the Bad

Wherefore be you also ready, because at what hour you know not the Son of man will come.

Who, thinkest thou, is a faithful and wise servant, whom his lord hath appointed over his family, to give them meat in season.

Blessed is that servant, whom when his lord shall come he shall find so doing.

Amen I say to you, he shall place him over all his goods.

But if that evil servant shall say in his heart: My lord is long a coming:

And shall begin to strike his fellow servants, and shall eat and drink with drunkards:

The lord of that servant shall come in a day that he hopeth not, and at an hour that he knoweth not:

And shall separate him, and appoint his portion with the hypocrites. There shall be weeping and gnashing of teeth.—*Matt.* xxiv. 44-51.

Take ye heed, watch and pray. For ye know not when the time is.

Even as a man who going into a far country, left his house; and gave authority to his servants over every work, and commanded the porter to watch.

Watch ye therefore, (for you know not when the lord of the house cometh: at even, or at midnight, or at the cock crowing, or in the morning,)

Lest coming on a sudden, he find you sleeping.

And what I say to you, I say to all: Watch.—*Mark* xiii. 33-37.

Let your loins be girt, and lamps burning in your hands.

And you yourselves like to men who wait for their lord, when he shall return from the wedding; that when he cometh and knocketh, they may open to him immediately.

Blessed are those servants, whom the Lord when he cometh, shall find watching. Amen I say to you, that he will gird himself, and make them sit down to meat, and passing will minister unto them.

And if he shall come in the second watch, or come in the third watch, and find them so, blessed are those servants. . . .

And Peter said to him: Lord, dost thou speak this parable to us, or likewise to all?

And the Lord said: Who (thinkest thou) is the faithful and wise steward, whom his lord setteth over his family, to give them their measure of wheat in due season?

Blessed is that servant, whom when his lord shall come, he shall find so doing.

Verily I say to you, he will set him over all that he possesseth.

But if that servant shall say in his heart: My lord

is long a coming; and shall begin to strike the men-servants and maid-servants, and to eat and to drink and be drunk:

The lord of that servant will come in the day that he hopeth not, and at the hour that he knoweth not, and shall separate him, and shall appoint him his portion with unbelievers. —*Luke* xii. 35-38, 41-46.

Sheep, the Lost

Now the publicans and sinners drew near unto him to hear him.

And the Pharisees and the scribes murmured, saying: This man receiveth sinners, and eateth with them.

What think you? If a man have an hundred sheep, and one of them should go astray: doth he not leave the ninety-nine in the mountains, and go to seek that which is gone astray?

And if so be that he find it: Amen I say to you, he rejoiceth more for that, than for the ninety-nine that went not astray.

Even so it is not the will of your Father, who is in heaven, that one of these little ones should perish.—*Matt.* xviii. 12-14.

And he spoke to them this parable, saying:

What man of you that hath an hundred sheep: and if he shall lose one of them, doth he not leave the ninety-nine in the desert, and go after that which was lost, until he find it?

And when he hath found it, lay it upon his shoulders, rejoicing:

And coming home, call together his friends and neighbors, saying to them: Rejoice with me, because I have found my sheep that was lost?

I say to you, that even so there shall be joy in heaven upon one sinner that doth penance, more than upon ninety-nine just who need not penance.—*Luke* xv. 1-7.

Shepherd, the True

Amen, amen I say to you: He that entereth not by the door into the sheep-fold, but climbeth up another way, the same is a thief and a robber.

But he that entereth in by the door is the shepherd of the sheep.

To him the porter openeth; and the sheep hear his voice: and he calleth his own sheep by name, and leadeth them out.

And when he hath let out his own sheep, he goeth before them: and the sheep follow him, because they know his voice.

But a stranger they followed not, but fly from him, because they know not the voice of strangers.

This proverb Jesus spoke to them. But they understood not what he spoke to them.—*John* x. 1-6.

Shepherd, the Good

I am the good shepherd. The good shepherd giveth his life for his sheep.

But the hireling, and he that is not the shepherd, whose own the sheep are not, seeth the wolf coming, and leaveth the sheep, and flieth: and the wolf catcheth, and scattereth the sheep:

And the hireling flieth, because he is a hireling: and he hath no care for the sheep.

I am the good shepherd; and I know mine, and mine know me.

As the Father knoweth me, and I know the Father: and I lay down my life for my sheep.—*John* x. 11-15.

Sons, the Two

But what think you? A certain man had two sons; and coming to the first, he said: Son, go work to-day in my vineyard.

And he answering, said: I will not. But afterwards, being moved with repentance, he went.

And coming to the other, he said in like manner. And he answering, said: I go, Sir; and he went not.

Which of the two did the father's will? They say to him: The first. Jesus saith to them: Amen I say to you, that the publicans and the harlots shall go into the kingdom of God before you.—*Matt.* xxi. 28-31.

Sower and the Seed, the

And he spoke to them many things in parables, saying: Behold the sower went forth to sow.

And whilst he sowed some fell by the way side, and the birds of the air came and ate them up.

And other some fell upon stony ground, where they had not much earth: and they sprung up immediately, because they had no deepness of earth.

And when the sun was up they were scorched: and because they had not root, they withered away.

And others fell among thorns: and the thorns grew up and choked them.

And others fell upon good ground: and they brought forth fruit, some an hundredfold, some sixtyfold, and some thirtyfold. . . .

Hear you therefore the parable of the sower.

When any one heareth the word of the kingdom, and understandeth it not, there cometh the wicked one, and catcheth away that which was sown in his heart: this is he that received the seed by the way side.

And he taught them many things in parables, and said unto them in his doctrine:

Hear ye, Behold, the sower went out to sow.

And whilst he sowed, some fell by the way side, and the birds of the air came and ate it up.

And other some fell upon stony ground, where it had not much earth; and it shot up immediately, because it had no depth of earth.

And when the sun was risen, it was scorched; and because it had no root, it withered away.

And some fell among thorns; and the thorns grew up, and choked it, and it yielded no fruit.

And some fell upon good ground; and brought forth fruit that grew up, and increased and yielded, one thirty, another sixty, and another a hundred. . . .

And he saith to them: Are you ignorant of this parable? and how shall you know all parables?

He that soweth, soweth the word.

And these are they by

And when a very great multitude was gathered together, and hastened out of the cities unto him, he spoke by a similitude.

The sower went out to sow his seed. And as he sowed, some fell by the way side, and it was trodden down, and the fowls of the air devoured it.

And other some fell upon a rock: and as soon as it was sprung up, it withered away, because it had no moisture.

And other some fell among thorns, and the thorns growing up with it, choked it.

And other some fell upon good ground; and being sprung up, yielded fruit a hundredfold. Saying these things, he cried out: He that hath ears to hear, let him hear.

And his disciples asked him what this parable might be.

To whom he said: To you it is given to know the mystery of the kingdom of God; but to the rest in parables, that seeing they may not see, and

And he that received the seed upon stony ground, is he that heareth the word, and immediately receiveth it with joy.

Yet hath he not root in himself, but is only for a time: and when there ariseth tribulation and persecution because of the word, he is presently scandalized.

And he that received the seed among thorns, is he that heareth the word, and the care of this world and the deceitfulness of riches choketh up the word, and he becometh fruitless.

But he that received the seed upon good ground, is he that heareth the word, and understandeth, and beareth fruit, and yieldeth the one an hundredfold, and another sixty, and another thirty.—*Matt.* xiii. 3-8, 18-23.

the way side, where the word is sown, and as soon as they have heard, immediately Satan cometh, and taketh away the word that was sown in their hearts.

And these likewise are they that are sown on the stony ground: who when they have heard the word, immediately receive it with joy.

And they have no root in themselves, but are only for a time: and then when tribulation and persecution ariseth for the word, they are presently scandalized.

And others there are who are sown among thorns: these are they that hear the word,

And the cares of the world, and the deceitfulness of riches, and the lusts after other things entering in choke the word, and it is made fruitless.

And these are they who are sown upon the good ground, who hear the word, and receive it, and yield fruit, the one thirty, another sixty, and another a hundred.—*Mark* iv. 2-8, 13-20.

hearing may not understand.

Now the parable is this: The seed is the word of God.

And they by the way side are they that hear then the devil cometh, and taketh the word out of their heart, lest believing they should be saved.

Now they upon the rock, are they who when they hear, receive the word with joy: and these have no roots; for they believe for a while, and in time of temptation, they fall away.

And that which fell among thorns, are they who have heard, and going their way, are choked with the cares and riches and pleasures of this life, and yield no fruit.

But that on the good ground, are they who in a good and perfect heart hearing the word, keep it and bring forth fruit in patience.—*Luke* viii. 4-15.

Steward, the Unjust

And he said also to his disciples: There was a certain rich man who had a steward: and the same was accused unto him, that he had wasted his goods.

And he called him, and said to him: How is it that I hear this of thee? give an account of thy stewardship: for now thou canst be steward no longer.

And the steward said within himself: What shall I do, because my lord taketh away from me the stewardship? To dig I am not able; to beg I am ashamed.

I know what I will do, that when I shall be removed from the stewardship, they may receive me into their houses.

Therefore calling together every one of his lord's debtors, he said to the first: How much dost thou owe my lord?

But he said: An hundred barrels of oil. And he said to him: Take thy bill, and sit down quickly, and write fifty.

Then he said to another: And how much dost thou owe? Who said: A hundred quarters of wheat. He said to him: Take thy bill, and write eighty.

And the lord commended the unjust steward, forasmuch as he had done wisely: for the children of this world are wiser in their generation than the children of light.—*Luke* xvi. 1-8.

Supper, the Great

But he (Jesus) said to him: A certain man made a great supper, and invited many.

And he sent his servant at the hour of supper to say to them that were invited, that they should come, for now all things are ready.

And they began all at once to make excuse. The first said to him: I have bought a farm, and I must needs go out and see it: I pray thee, hold me excused.

And another said: I have bought five yoke of oxen, and I go to try them: I pray thee, hold me excused.

And another said: I have married a wife, and therefore I cannot come.

And the servant returning, told these things to his lord. Then the master of the house, being angry, said to his servant: Go out quickly into the streets and lanes of the city, and bring in hither the poor, and the feeble, and the blind, and the lame.

And the servant said: Lord, it is done as thou hast commanded, and yet there is room.

And the Lord said to the servant: Go out into the highways and hedges, and compel them to come in, that my house may be filled.

But I say unto you, that none of those men that were invited, shall taste of my supper.—*Luke* xiv. 16-24.

Talents, the

For even as a man going into a far country, called his servants, and delivered to them his goods;

And to one he gave five talents, and to another two, and to another one, to every one according to his proper ability: and immediately he took his journey.

And he that had received the five talents, went his way, and traded with the same, and gained other five.

And in like manner he that had received the two, gained other two.

But he that had received the one, going his way digged into the earth, and hid his lord's money.

But after a long time the lord of those servants came, and reckoned with them.

And he that had received the five talents coming, brought other five talents, saying: Lord, thou didst deliver to me five talents, behold I have gained other five over and above.

His lord said to him: Well done, good and faithful servant, because thou hast been faithful over a few things, I will place thee over many things: enter thou into the joy of thy lord.

And he also that had received the two talents came and said: Lord, thou deliveredst two talents to me: behold I have gained other two.

His lord said to him: Well done, good and faithful servant: because thou hast been faithful over a few things, I will place thee over many things: enter thou into the joy of thy lord.

But he that had received the one talent, came and said: Lord, I know that thou art a hard man; thou reapest where thou hast not sown, and gatherest where thou hast not strewed.

And being afraid I went and hid thy talent in the earth: behold here thou hast that which is thine.

And his lord answering, said to him: Wicked and slothful servant, thou knewest that I reap where I sow not, and gather where I have not strewed:

Thou oughtest therefore to have committed my money to the bankers, and at my coming I should have received my own with usury.

Take ye away therefore the talent from him, and give it him that hath ten talents.

For to every one that hath shall be given, and he shall abound: but from him that hath not, that also which he seemeth to have shall be taken away.

And the unprofitable servant cast ye out into the exterior darkness. There shall be weeping and gnashing of teeth. —*Matt.* xxv. 14-30.

Treasure Hidden in a Field, the

The kingdom of heaven is like unto a treasure hidden in a field. Which a man having found, hid it, and for joy thereof goeth, and selleth all that he hath, and buyeth that field.—*Matt.* xiii. 44.

Virgins, the Wise and the Foolish

Then shall the kingdom of heaven be like to ten virgins, who taking their lamps went out to meet the bridegroom and the bride.

And five of them were foolish, and five wise.

But the five foolish, having taken their lamps, did not take oil with them:

But the wise took oil in their vessels with the lamps.

And the bridegroom tarrying, they all slumbered and slept.

And at midnight there was a cry made: Behold the bridegroom cometh, go ye forth to meet him.

Then all those virgins arose and trimmed their lamps.

And the foolish said to the wise: Give us of your oil, for our lamps are gone out.

The wise answered, saying: Lest perhaps there be not enough for us and for you, go ye rather to them that sell, and buy for yourselves.

Now whilst they went to buy, the bridegroom came: and they that were ready, went in with him to the marriage, and the door was shut.

But at last came also the other virgins, saying: Lord, Lord, open to us.

But he answering said: Amen I say to you, I know you not.

Watch ye therefore, because you know not the day nor the hour.—*Matt.* xxv. 1-13.

SHORT SIMILITUDES

Blind Leading the Blind, the

And he spoke also to them a similitude: Can the blind lead the blind? do they not both fall into the ditch?—*Luke* vi. 39.

Children of the Bridegroom, the

And Jesus said to them: Can the children of the bridegroom mourn, as long as the bridegroom is with them? But the days will come, when the bridegroom shall be taken away from them, and then they shall fast.—*Matt.* ix. 15.

And Jesus saith to them: Can the children of the marriage fast, as long as the bridegroom is with them? As long as they have the bridegroom with them, they cannot fast.

But the days will come when the bridegroom shall be taken away from them; and then they shall fast in those days.—*Mark* ii. 19, 20.

To whom he said: Can you make the children of the bridegroom fast, when the bridegroom is with them?

But the days will come, when the bridegroom shall be taken away from them, then shall they fast in those days.—*Luke* v. 34, 35.

Children in the Market Place, the

But whereunto shall I esteem this generation to be like? It is like to children sitting in the market place.

Who crying to their companions say: We have piped to you, and you have not danced: we have lamented, and you have not mourned.

For John came neither eating nor drinking; and they say: He hath a devil.

The Son of man came eating and

And the Lord said: Whereunto then shall I liken the men of this generation? and to what are they like?

They are like to children sitting in the market place, and speaking one to another, and saying: We have piped to you, and you have not danced: we have mourned, and you have not wept.

For John the Baptist came neither eating bread nor drinking wine; and you say: He hath a devil.

drinking, and they say: Behold a man that is a glutton and a wine drinker, a friend of publicans and sinners. And wisdom is justified by her children.— *Matt.* xi. 16-19.

The Son of man is come eating and drinking: and you say: Behold a man that is a glutton and a drinker of wine, a friend of publicans and sinners. And wisdom is justified by all her children.—*Luke* vii. 31-35.

Divided Kingdom, the

And Jesus knowing their thoughts, said to them: Every kingdom divided against itself shall be made desolate: and every city or house divided against itself shall not stand.

And if Satan cast out Satan, he is divided against himself: how then shall his kingdom stand? —*Matt.* xii. 25, 26.

And after he had called them together, he said to them in parables: How can Satan cast out Satan? And if a kingdom be divided against itself, that kingdom cannot stand.

And if a house be divided against itself, that house cannot stand. And if Satan be risen up against himself, he is divided, and cannot stand, but hath an end.—*Mark* iii. 23-26.

But he seeing their thoughts, said to them: Every kingdom divided against itself, shall be brought to desolation, and house upon house shall fall.

And if Satan also be divided against himself, how shall his kingdom stand? because you say, that through Beelzebub I cast out devils.—*Luke* xi. 17, 18.

Fig-tree Blossoming, the

And from the fig-tree learn a parable: When the branch thereof is now tender, and the leaves come forth, you know that summer is nigh.

So you also, when you shall see all these things, know ye that it is nigh, even at the doors.—*Matt.* xxiv. 32, 33.

Now of the fig-tree learn ye a parable. When the branch thereof is now tender, and the leaves are come forth, you know that summer is very near.

So you also when you shall see these things come to pass, know ye that it is very nigh, even at the doors.—*Mark* xiii. 28, 29.

And he spoke to them a similitude. See the fig-tree, and all the trees: When they now shoot forth their fruit, you know that summer is nigh;

So you also, when you shall see these things come to pass, know that the kingdom of God is at hand.—*Luke* xxi. 29-31.

Friend Begging at Night, the

And he said to them: Which of you shall have a friend, and shall go to him at midnight, and shall say to him: Friend, lend me three loaves,

Because a friend of mine is come off his journey to me, and I have not what to set before him.

And he from within should answer, and say: Trouble me not, the door is now shut, and my children are with me in bed; I cannot rise and give thee.

Yet if he shall continue knocking, I say to you, although he will not rise and give him, because he is his friend; yet, because of his importunity, he will rise, and give him as many as he needeth.—*Luke* xi. 5-8.

Gate, the Broad and the Narrow

Enter ye in at the narrow gate: for wide is the gate, and broad is the way that leadeth to destruction, and many there are who go in thereat.

And a certain man said to him: Lord, are they few that are saved? But he said to them:

Strive to enter by the narrow gate;

How narrow is the gate, and strait is the way that leadeth to life: and few there are that find it!—*Matt.* vii. 13, 14.

for many, I say to you, shall seek to enter, and shall not be able.—*Luke* xiii. 23, 24.

House Built on a Rock, the

Every one therefore that heareth these my words, and doth them, shall be likened to a wise man that built his house upon a rock,

And the rain fell, and the floods came, and the winds blew, and they beat upon that house, and it fell not, for it was founded on a rock.

And every one that heareth these my words, and doth them not, shall be like a foolish man that built his house upon the sand,

And the rain fell, and the floods came, and the winds blew, and they beat upon that house, and it fell, and great was the fall thereof.—*Matt.* vii. 24-27.

Every one that cometh to me, and heareth my words, and doth them, I will show you to whom he is like.

He is like to a man building a house, who digged deep, and laid the foundation upon a rock. And when a flood came, the stream beat vehemently upon that house, and it could not shake it; for it was founded on a rock.

But he that heareth, and doth not, is like to a man building his house upon the earth without a foundation: against which the stream beat vehemently, and immediately it fell, and the ruin of that house was great.—*Luke* vi. 47-49.

Householder, the

He said unto them: Therefore every scribe instructed in the kingdom of heaven, is like to a man that is a householder, who bringeth forth out of his treasure new things and old.—*Matt.* xiii. 52.

King About to Make War, the

Or what king, about to go to make war against another king, doth not first sit down, and think whether he be able, with ten thousand, to meet him that, with twenty thousand, cometh against him?

Or else, whilst the other is yet afar off, sending an embassy, he desireth conditions of peace.—*Luke* xiv. 31, 32.

Mote and the Beam, the

And why seest thou the mote that is in thy brother's eye; and seest not the beam that is in thy own eye?

Or how sayest thou to thy brother: Let me cast the mote out of thy eye; and behold a beam is in thy own eye?

Thou hypocrite, cast out first the beam out of thy own eye, and then shalt thou see to cast out the mote out of thy brother's eye.—*Matt.* vii. 3-5.

And why seest thou the mote in thy brother's eye: but the beam that is in thy own eye thou considerest not?

Or how canst thou say to thy brother: Brother, let me pull the mote out of thy eye, when thou thyself seest not the beam in thy own eye? Hypocrite, cast first the beam out of thy own eye; and then shalt thou see clearly to take out the mote from thy brother's eye.—*Luke* vi. 41, 42.

New Wine in Old Bottles, the

Neither do they put new wine into old bottles. Otherwise the bottles break, and the wine runneth out, and the bottles perish. But new wine

And no man putteth new wine into old bottles: otherwise the wine will burst the bottles, and both the wine will be spilled, and the bottles will be

And no man putteth new wine into old bottles: otherwise the new wine will break the bottles, and it will be spilled, and the bottles will be lost.

they put into new bottles: and both are preserved.—*Matt.* ix. 17.

lost. But new wine must be put into new bottles.—*Mark* ii. 22.

But new wine must be put into new bottles; and both are preserved.
And no man drinking old, hath presently a mind to new: for he saith, The old is better.—*Luke* v. 37-39.

Raw Cloth on the Old Garment, the

And nobody putteth a piece of raw cloth unto an old garment. For it taketh away the fulness thereof from the garment, and there is made a greater rent.—*Matt.* ix. 16.

No man seweth a piece of raw cloth to an old garment: otherwise the new piecing taketh away from the old, and there is made a greater rent.—*Mark* ii. 21.

And he spoke also a similitude to them: That no man putteth a piece from a new garment upon an old garment; otherwise he both rendeth the new, and the piece taken from the new agreeth not with the old.—*Luke* v. 36.

Tower, Building the

For which of you having a mind to build a tower, doth not first sit down, and reckon the charges that are necessary, whether he have wherewithal to finish it:

Lest, after he hath laid the foundation, and is not able to finish it, all that see it begin to mock him,

Saying: This man began to build, and was not able to finish.—*Luke* xiv. 28-30.

Vine, the True

I am the true vine; and my Father is the husbandman.

Every branch in me, that beareth not fruit, he will take away: and every one that beareth fruit, he will purge it, that it may bring forth more fruit.—*John* xv. 1, 2.

Woman in Labor, the

A woman, when she is in labor, hath sorrow, because her hour is come; but when she hath brought forth the child, she remembereth no more the anguish, for joy that a man is born into the world.

So also you now indeed have sorrow; but I will see you again, and your heart shall rejoice; and your joy no man shall take from you.—*John* xvi. 21, 22.

LESSONS OF THE PARABLES

Forgiving Injuries
The ungrateful Debtor.

Forgiveness of Sins
The Prodigal son.

Forgiveness of Sins, Gratitude for the
The forgiven Debtors.

Grace, Abuse of God's
The Marriage feast.
The great Supper.

Humility and Pride
The Pharisee and the publican.

Judgment, We Must Watch and be Prepared for the
The good and the bad Servants.
The wise and the foolish Virgins.
The foolish Rich man.

Kingdom of God on Earth, the
The Mustard seed.
The Leaven.
The Treasure hidden in a field.
The Pearl of great price.
The Net cast into the sea.
The Seed cast into the earth.

Love for Us, Christ's

The true Shepherd.
The good Shepherd.

Love for Sinners, Christ's

The lost Sheep.
The lost Groat.

Love of Our Neighbor

The good Samaritan.

Patience of God in His Dealings with Sinners, the

The Cockle and the good seed.
The barren Fig-tree.

Prayer, the Efficacy of

The Judge and the widow.

Rejection of Christ by the Jews, the

The ungrateful Husbandmen.

Reward of Working for God, the

The Laborers in the vineyard.

Riches, We Must Make Good Use of

The unjust Steward.

Riches, Punishment of the Bad Use of

The Rich man and Lazarus.

Will of God, Doing the

The two Sons.

Word of God, Receiving the

The Sower and the Seed.

Working for God and for Heaven

The Talents.
The Pounds.

INDEX

TO PARTS I AND II

INDEX

To Appendix

If you have enjoyed this book, consider making your next selection from among the following . . .

Prices subject to change.

Prices subject to change.

At your Bookdealer or direct from the Publisher.
Call Toll-Free 1-800-437-5876.

Prices subject to change.

NOTES

NOTES

NOTES

NOTES